DEFINING INTERNATIONAL AGGRESSION

Volume 2

Members of the United Nations Special Committee Which Defined Aggression by Consensus (12 April 1974)
(A complete list and Governments represented is shown in Doc.A/9619 p. 41-42.)

1-Mr. P.C. Reid
2-Mr. A. Parry
3-Mr. M.A. Rakotosihanaka
4-Mr. H. Steel
5-Mr. M. Malla
6-Mr. R.B. Rosenstock
7-Mr. H. Abduljalil
8-Mr. J. Azud

9-Mr. V. Bojilov
10-Mr. G. Migliuolo
11-Mr. D. Moushoutas
12-Mr. B.H.G.A. Broms
13-Mr. Y.M. Rybakov*
14-Mr. M. Güney
15-Mrs. M. Peterman*
16-Mr. C. Malek*

17-Mr. J. Sanders
18-Mr. T. Iguchi
19-Mr. M. Iijima
20-Mr. B.B. Ferencz**
21-Mr. P. Mohajer
22-Mr. K. Suziki
23-Mr. G. Menegatti
24-Mr. M. Alemán

25-Mr. H.A.K. Hassouna
26-Mr. S.E. Charles
27-M.I.M. Bessou
28-Mr. C. Job
29-Mr. M.P. Makarevich (Ukraine)
30-Mr. I.O. La
31-Mr. al-Qaysi

32-Mr. H. Mesloub
33-Mr. F. Starčević
34-Mr. V.N. Fedorov
35-Mr. G.K. Efimov
36-J. Dauchy*
37-Mr. J. Kobialka*
38-Mr. W.G. Naggaga

39-Mr. H. Shigeta
40-Mr. O.Y. Birido
41-Mr. A. Elías
42-Mr. M.J. Matheson

*Members of the Secretariat
**Non-Governmental Observer
Photo credit: United Nations/H. Grant

DEFINING INTERNATIONAL AGGRESSION

THE SEARCH FOR WORLD PEACE
A Documentary History and Analysis

by
BENJAMIN B. FERENCZ

With An Introduction By
LOUIS B. SOHN

Volume 2

1975
OCEANA PUBLICATIONS, INC.
DOBBS FERRY, NEW YORK

Library of Congress Cataloging in Publication Data
    Main entry under title:

    Defining international aggression, the search for world
        peace.

        1. Aggression (International law) I. Ferencz,
    Benjamin B., 1920-
    JX4471.D43   341.5'8   75-16473
    ISBN 0-379-00271-X (v.1)
    ISBN 0-379-00272-8 (v.2)

Manufactured in the United States of America

CONTENTS

VOLUME 1

DOCUMENTS

PART ONE: THE TRADITION OF WAR AND THE
                    ASPIRATION FOR PEACE

VOLUME 2

PART FOUR   AGGRESSION DEFINED BY CONSENSUS

PART THREE

THE UNITED NATIONS MOVES TO DEFINE AGGRESSION

PART THREE:

THE UNITED NATIONS MOVES TO DEFINE AGGRESSION

(1) The Opening Wedge   (1946-1951)

"In faith and trust we hand our Charter down to the future."
So said the old veteran of two wars, Jan Christian Smuts, when the
United Nations was formed. "We expect that those who come after
us will also show no less goodwill and good faith on their part in the
great job of peace." [1] Now began the task of trying to translate the
high hopes into reality. The Charter, like the Covenant before it,
was only a tool, to be used or allowed to rust, by the people it was
designed to serve. If it was to achieve its potential for peace,
cooperation among the powerful nations was indispensible, but the
alliances formed out of the necessities of war were already feeling
the strain of conflicting interests arising from competing social
systems.

At its first session the General Assembly, by unanimous
resolution, affirmed "the principles of international law recognized
by the Charter of the Nuernberg Tribunal and the judgment of the
Tribunal." [2] It also directed the newly created Committee on the
Codification of International Law to formulate the Nuernberg
principles in the context of a codification of offences against the
peace and security of mankind, or of an International Criminal Code.
The Committee in turn recommended the establishment of an
International Law Commission, consisting of 15 members, to deal
with the problem. [3]

During the next few years, as tensions between the Soviet
Union and its war time allies began to mount, very little progress
could be recorded in the movement toward the formulation of law
as a weapon of peace. In 1948 the Czech government appealed to
the Security Council for help on the grounds that it was being
threatened by subversion. A veto by the Soviet Union prevented any
action by the United Nations. The Soviet blockade of Berlin met a
similar fate. In June 1950 hostilities erupted in Korea when Northern
forces invaded the South over the post-war partition line which had
been established at the 38th Parallel. The Security Council, with
the USSR absent, determined that the armed attack was a breach
of the peace, and called for a withdrawal of the North Korean troops.
The USSR declared that it was South Korea which had launched an
unprovoked attack, and accused the United States of aggression. The

1

question of determining the aggressor was once more before the Council of Nations.[4]

Yugoslavia requested that "Duties of States in the event of Outbreak of Hostilities" be considered by the General Assembly. The Assembly referred the question to the First (Political and Security) Committee,[5] where Yugoslavia proposed that within 24 hours of the outbreak of hostilities every state so engaged must either declare a cease-fire and readiness to withdraw, or be considered an aggressor, and held responsible for the breach of the peace.[6] The United States, the United Kingdom and France were among those in opposition, arguing that such automatic criteria would not be realistic or effective.[7]

The USSR proposed instead that there be an agreement on a definition of aggression in order to eliminate any pretext which might be used to justify it. (DOCUMENT 1) The definition submitted by the USSR was based on their 1933 text, which had been accepted by the Committee on Security Questions of the Disarmament Conference after World War I.[8] The United States, France, and Canada led the protest against any fixed definition, maintaining that the determination of the aggressor should be left to the discretion of the Security Council. The United States also noted the absence in the proposed definition of any reference to indirect aggression, such as subversion or fomenting of civil strife. The Canadian delegate, recalling the economic blocade of Berlin by Soviet troops in 1948, objected that the Soviet definition failed to designate land blockade as an act of aggression.[9]

Syria proposed that the draft definition of aggression could better be examined in conjunction with matters being considered by the International Law Commission. It was accordingly decided to water down the Yugoslavian resolution so that the entire conduct of the States concerned would have to be taken into account before deciding whether there was an act of aggression. (DOCUMENT 2) The Soviet resolution was referred to the International Law Commission for further consideration.[10]

The International Law Commission already had its hands full. It was formulating the Nuernberg principles, including those dealing with aggressive war, and it was trying to reconcile many conflicting views on the possibility or desirability of an international criminal jurisdiction, as well as the nature and content of a draft code of offences against the peace and security of mankind.[11] On the day that the subject was shunted to the International Law Commission, the General Assembly solemnly reaffirmed that:

"Whatever the weapons used, any aggression, whether committed openly, or by fomenting civil strife in the interest of a foreign Power, or otherwise, is the gravest of all crimes against peace and security throughout the world."[12]

By 1951 the International Law Commission had stimulated a wide variety of views on the question of defining aggression. (DOCUMENT 3) The Committee took as the basis for discussion a proposed definition submitted by Mr. Alfaro of Panama, It stated:

> Aggression is the threat or use of force by one State or group of States, or by any government or group of governments, against the territory and people of other States or governments, in any manner, by any methods, for any reasons and for any purposes, except individual or collective self-defence against armed attack or coercive action by the United Nations.

The Proposal was defeated.

The Special Rapporteur of the Draft Code of Offences, Mr. J. Spiropoulos, concluded in his report that the concept of aggression was a natural one, which was not susceptible of definition. After exploring many alternatives the Commission recommended that the draft code provide:

> The following acts are offences against the peace and security of mankind:
>
> (1) Any act of aggression, including the employment by the authorities of a State of armed force against another State for any purpose other than national or collective self-defence or in pursuance of a decision or recommendation by a competent organ of the United Nations.
>
> (2) Any threat by the authorities of a State to resort to an act of aggression against any other State.

The commentary to the draft code made it clear that acts other than those described could also constitute aggression, and nine additional offences other than aggression, were also listed as violations against the peace and security of mankind.

The International Law Commission's Report was referred to the Sixth (Legal) Committee, which debated a number of alternative resolutions. The Greek representative, supported by the United States, the United Kingdom and others, proposed that aggression should not be defined, but should be left to the complete discretion of the Security Council. The Soviets put forth their own draft definition. Some sought to postpone the debate, but many of the smaller States, felt that it was important to press forward for a definition. The conclusion reached by the Sixth Committee, and approved by the Assembly, was to consider the entire subject, including the draft code, in further detail the next year, since it was considered "possible and desirable" to define aggression "by reference to the elements which constitute it." (DOCUMENT 4).

(2) The Fifteen-Member First Special Committee on the
     Question of Defining Aggression   1952-1954

When the Assembly met in 1952 it had before it the comments received from governments on the draft code of offences and the definition of aggression, (DOCUMENT 5) a very comprehensive and excellent historical and analytical report prepared by Mr. Chafic Malek and Emile Giraud, of the Secretariat,[13] various draft resolutions,[14] and the Report of the Sixth Committee.[15] All of the many complexities and differences of view concerning the definition of aggression which had been debated were spread on the record. It was enough to overwhelm the most courageous heart. The only decision which could be reached was to establish a Special Committee, of 15 members, to study the problems the following year and submit a draft definition, or statements of the notion of aggression, two years later.[16]

When the Special Committee of 15 submitted its Report in September 1953, it was able to summarize many of the problems, even if it was unable to reconcile many of the differences. (DOCUMENT 6)[17] The advisability of various types of definitions were considered - whether general, enumerative or mixed. The United States suggestion that the Security Council be given a list of factors to be taken into account when deciding a given case was also considered.[18] The Committee explored the various forms of aggression, and the effect which a definition might have on the maintenance of peace. The impact of the Code of Offences Against Peace and an International Criminal Court were also discussed. The arguments came to focus on specific resolutions submitted by the USSR, China, Mexico and Bolivia.[19]

The new Soviet definition included a reference to acts of "indirect aggression", by which was meant subversive activity. It covered "economic aggression", such as threatening another State's economic life, exploiting its natural riches, or imposing an economic blockade. "Ideological aggression", such as war propaganda or promoting hatred for other peoples, was also condemned. A long list of possible excuses were specifically excluded as justification for any form of aggression.[20]

The Chinese proposal permitted the use of force in defense against an armed attack, pending action by the U.N., or in accordance with a decision or recommendation of a competent U.N. organization. "Unarmed force" could be met by comparable reprisals.[21] Mexico wanted the notion of aggression restricted to cases involving the use of force,[22] whereas Bolivia would include as aggression "unilateral action whereby a State is deprived of economic resources . . . or its basic economy is endangered so that its security is affected . . . "[23] The Special Committee Report merely transmitted the various texts and comments to the Assembly without any proposed resolution.

While the diplomats at the U.N. were busy talking, a brutal colonial war, which had been going on in South East Asia, seemed to be coming to an end.[24] The Geneva Accords of 1954 brought a cessation of hostilities in Vietnam, a temporary partition between North and South, and the expectation of free elections. It was not then anticipated that the area would become the scene of even greater devastation and the source of violent accusations of aggression.[25]

The Sixth Committee meeting at the close of 1954, considered the comments received from various governments regarding the Report of the Special Committee, discussed various new resolutions, and issued its Report. (DOCUMENT 7) Once more there was a wide divergence of opinion on whether it was possible or desirable to define aggression, and what the form and content of any such definition might be. Argentina and Denmark expressed their opposition.[26] The United Kingdom expressed its doubts.[27] The French conveyed their general support,[28] and the Soviet bloc maintained its position in favor of the detailed exposé set forth in various USSR proposals.[29]

Some States favored a brief general definition, but the majority seemed to support a mixture of a description in general terms coupled with a list of definite acts of aggression which would illustrate, but not restrict, the general description. In the absence of any possibility of reaching agreement it was decided by the Assembly, on the recommendation of the Sixth Committee, that an enlarged Special Committee should be created, consisting of 19 rather than 15 members, to meet and report back in two years.

In the meanwhile, the committee which had been appointed in 1952 to consider the question of International Criminal Jurisdiction was also encountering difficulties. Canada, France and the Netherlands favored the establishment of an international criminal court, the Soviet Union and other socialist States were opposed, and the United Kingdom saw no use for it.[30] The International Law Commission was continuing to refine the Draft Code of Offences against the Peace and Security of Mankind.[31] The Assembly, considering the connection between the Draft Code and the question of an international criminal jurisdiction and the question of defining aggression, which had just been postponed, decided to defer any further consideration of either the international criminal court or the draft code of offences until the new Special Committee to define aggression had submitted its report.[32]

(3) The Nineteen-Member Second Special Committee (1954-1957)

Two years later the Special Committee of 19 submitted its report. (DOCUMENT 8) It was a comprehensive document which reviewed the background of the question and surveyed the ideas expressed in previous sessions regarding the possibility and desirability of a definition, its functions, the kinds of activity covered by a definition, the various types of definitions, and the views expressed regarding the many drafts before the committee. Some considered a definition essential to prevent atomic war,[33] and others, such as the Netherlands, considered a definition, if intended as a guide for United Nations organs, to be "useless, dangerous and impossible."[34]

The debate on aggression appeared rather academic in 1956 when Soviet tanks, joined by the armed forces of other satellite states, invaded Hungary for the stated purpose of suppressing a revolt against the Hungarian Communist government. The invasion, justified as aid to a threatened ally, became a fait accompli before the U.N. could take any effective action. War erupted in the Middle East with Israel and Egypt accusing each other of aggression. France and the U.K. intervened to protect their interests in the Suez canal. The U.S. and the USSR joined in demanding a cease-fire and the dispatch of U.N. Emergency Forces to police the armistice.[35] At the other side of the globe the United States was getting increasingly involved in trying to prevent a take-over of all of Vietnam by the Communist forces of North Vietnam. Under the circumstances, the Assembly decided to defer consideration of the definition of aggression, as well as the question of an international criminal court and a code of offences against the peace and security of mankind for yet another year.[36]

By the end of 1957 very little progress had been made. The Sixth Committee debated the report which had been prepared by the Special Committee,[37] and the divisions of opinion previously expressed were only reaffirmed. (DOCUMENT 9) To some members it appeared that the growing international tensions and the increasing armaments race required a clear definition of aggression more than ever before. Others, such as the United States, the United Kingdom, Japan, China and Canada argued that a definition might make peace more difficult by providing a false sense of security and restricting the flexibility of the United Nations.[38]

Most members favored postponing the question, and the United States proposed that it be postponed indefinitely.[39] As a compromise, the Sixth Committee recommended that the question be referred to the Assembly's General Committee which would be asked to report back to the Secretary General when it considered that the time was appropriate to take up the subject again. The

Assembly did not wish to hear of it for at least two years, but appointed the recommended committee under General Assembly Res. 1181 (XII) of 29 Nov. 1957.[40] In the meanwhile, the views of the 22 new States which had recently joined the U.N. would be solicited. Having again postponed the question of defining aggression, the Assembly decided to also postpone the related questions of the draft Code of Offences Against the Peace and Security of Mankind, and the establishment of an International Criminal Court, until the definition of aggression might once more be considered.[41]

(4) The Twenty-One-Member Third Special Committee (1959-1967)

The prescribed two year waiting period passed before the new Committee, enlarged to 21 members, could meet again. Its study of the 14 comments received from governments convinced it that there had been no change in attitude, and there was no reason to think that the appropriate time had come for the Assembly to again consider the question of defining aggression. The Committee, therefore, resolved, over Soviet protest, to adjourn any further consideration until April 1962, unless an absolute majority requested the Secretary General to have the members convene sooner. (DOCUMENT 10).

Tensions throughout the world were mounting and not easing. Cuba complained to the Security Council in 1960 and 1961 that the United States was committing aggression against it. The Council, recognizing the power of the United States veto, made no attempt at effective action. In 1962 the "Cuban Missile crisis" evoked a major confrontation between the United States and the USSR. The Council was doubly paralyzed.[42]

When April 1962 came around, there had still been no visible inclination to define aggression, and the committee of 21 once more resolved to adjourn, this time to April 1965, unless the majority called for an earlier session. (DOCUMENT 11).

In the meanwhile a Special Committee on Principles of International Law governing Friendly Relations and Cooperation Among States in accordance with the Charter of the United Nations began to wrestle with some of the problems which were also vexing the Aggression Committee. Relations among States were far from friendly or cooperative.

In 1963 violence erupted in Cyprus, and the dispute between the Turkish minority and the Greek majority was to occupy the U.N. agenda for many years.[43] The Soviets brought the U.N. to a stand-

7

still by refusing to contribute to the support of U.N. peacekeeping operations in Cyprus, or the Congo, where another battle was raging.[44] In 1964 Cambodia complained of aggression by the United States. The United States, escalating its military involvement, was also accused of aggression in Vietnam, while the United States in turn accused Hanoi of aggression against the Republic of Vietnam.[45]

In April 1965, the United Kingdom urged that the Special Committee on Aggression adjourn indefinitely, unless the majority called for them to reconvene. Chile would have adjourned to 1968, and five Powers preferred 1966. The compromise was an agreement to adjourn until April 1967. In the interim, further views of governments would be solicited. (DOCUMENT 12).

During the first half of 1965, India and Pakistan accused each other of aggression. The USSR accused the United States of aggression in the Dominican Republic, and in Vietnam.[46] By 1967, the situation in the middle east was nearing explosion as Egypt threatened the annihilation of Israel, ordered the eviction of U.N. Peacekeeping forces, and blockaded vital Israeli ports. In June hostilities erupted in what Israel called a defensive strike against those poised for her destruction. Egypt argued that it was not legitimate defense since there had been no armed attack on Israel territory. The USSR and allied states lined up to support the Arab bloc, as the United States and the United Kingdom voiced their support for the Israel position. Within a few days Israel succeeded in occupying large areas of the United Arab Republic, Syria and Jordan, and captured substantial amounts of Soviet-made heavy weapons. In the United Nations it became a war of competing resolutions.[47] With the Soviets threatening intervention against Israel, the Security Council finally arranged a cease-fire. The word "aggression" was on everyone's lips, but there was no agreement on what it meant.

When the Special Committee met again to define aggression in 1967, ten years had passed since it had first been designated, and it was still debating whether the time was appropriate for further Assembly action. Finding itself stalled in Committee, the USSR called for the Assembly to act to define aggression. (DOCUMENT 13) Some suspected that it was simply a propaganda move to divert attention from the debacle in the Middle East. In plenary debates, 17 states took the floor to support the new Soviet initiative.[48] In the Sixth Committee, to which the question was referred, most of those who spoke agreed that a definition of aggression was both possible and desirable. An intense debate developed and various draft resolutions were put forth by various combinations of states.[49]

The conclusion finally reached was to establish still another Special Committee, this one consisting of 35 members, "taking into consideration the principle of equitable geographical representation and the necessity that the principal legal systems of the world should be represented." The Committee was to consider all aspects of the question so that an adequate definition of aggression might be prepared, and to report all the views to the Assembly.[50]

At a time when there would have been good reason to conclude that they were chasing rainbows, the members of the United Nations were not ready to surrender. It was once more a manifestation of that indomitable determination to go on in the face of all adversity, in the continuing hope and belief that one day, if one tried hard enough and long enough, the doorway to peace would finally be found. Faced with the choice of hope or despair, there was really no choice.

(5) The Thirty-Five-Member Fourth Special Committee   (1967-1974)

In the summer of 1968 the new Special Committee began what was to become a series of annual five-week sessions alternating between New York and Geneva. Its first session was full of political recrimination, particularly between the Soviet Union and the United States and their respective allies. (DOCUMENT 14) The general debate challenged the utility of a definition in the light of all of the aggressions which had occurred while the nations were debating the definition.[51] The form and content of any definition, its relationship to other U.N. instruments and agencies, and its impact on the notion of self-defense were all explored. Four distinct draft proposals were put forward by various combinations of states.[52] After more than a month of debate there was agreement on practically nothing.

The Soviet proposal that the Committee try again the next year met with a mixed reception.[53] Among the 8 nations abstaining were Australia, France, Italy, Japan, the United Kingdom and the United States, all of which were later to join in a definitional alliance of their own.

During the summer of 1968, Czechoslovakia was suddenly invaded by Soviet tanks and troops, and encircled by the massed armed forces of its other Socialist neighbors. When the matter was brought before the Security Council the USSR maintained that what had occurred was not an act of aggression but an act of collective self-defense to aid the Czechoslovak government to maintain internal peace and security. It was argued that it was an internal affair of the Socialist bloc. It was a sad reminder of the 1956 action in Hungary, and brought forth a verbal confrontation between the North Atlantic Treaty nations of the West on the one hand, and the Warsaw Pact states of the East on the other. The Security Council resolution condemning the intervention was vetoed by the USSR.[54]

As might have been expected, when the Special Committee's report on the definition of aggression came up for debate at the Sixth Committee there were many who argued that the effort to define aggression should be abandoned. (DOCUMENT 15) What was needed was not a definition, but the political will and the power to enforce decisions. Despite the pessimistic outlook, the Sixth Committee accepted the recommendation that the Special Committee should continue its work, and the Assembly agreed.[55]

The next year the four drafts before the Special Committee were merged into three. The Soviet Union maintained its own definition, another draft was put forth by thirteen Powers (Columbia, Cyprus, Ecuador, Ghana, Guyana, Haiti, Iran, Madagascar, Mexico, Spain, Uganda, Uruguay and Yugoslavia), and for the first time, the six states which had abstained from voting for continuance of the Committee's work, and which were exceedingly skeptical about the whole thing, submitted a draft of their own. (DOCUMENT 16).

As the drafts were compared and debated, the major areas of difference began to emerge. Some of the principle problems were: Whether the definition applied to political entities which were not recognized as states; what acts should be listed as aggressive; the role of aggressive intent, what actions could not be considered aggressive, and what would be the legal consequences of aggression. Not being able to conclude their work, all of the members agreed to recommend that they be allowed to continue in 1970.[56] The Sixth Committee reconsidered the problems raised and agreed with the recommendation. (DOCUMENT 17).

When the Special Committee reconvened in Geneva in the summer of 1970 the efficient Secretariat staff had prepared a comparative chart setting forth in visual detail all of the differences and similarities of the three drafts under consideration.[57] It was clear that the thirteen-Power draft had much in common with the Soviet proposal. In contrast, the six-Power draft contained some new and thorny problems of its own.

A Working Group, composed of representatives supporting each of the different drafts, began to move toward agreement on some of the points of difference. (DOCUMENT 18) At the close of the session it was unanimously concluded that some progress had been made and that the work should be continued.[58] Once again the Sixth Committee debated the Special Committee Report, (DOCUMENT 19) and the Assembly accepted its recommendation that the Special Committee resume its work in 1971.[59]

In the meanwhile, there was growing disenchantment among the American public, and particularly its youth, about the U.S. role in Southeast Asia. Protests became widespread and were soon to have a major impact on America's political leaders.

The 1971 session of the Special Committee produced a number

of alternative texts on about half-a-dozen of the principal points of disagreement. (DOCUMENT 20) The United States, which had appeared to be the principal opponent to the Soviet proposals, came forth with new suggestions which seemed to be leaning toward an accomodation. The U.S. was trying to balance the weight to be given to the intent of the parties as compared with the significance of the fact that one party had been the first to use armed force.[60]

By the time the session ended it had generally been accepted that there should be a definition of aggression, and there was no visible disagreement about the format. All concurred that there should be a preamble, restating certain basic principles, a generic definition of aggression, an enumeration of specific acts which clearly indicated aggression, a reaffirmation that the Security Council could determine that other acts were also aggressive, and an explanation of when the use of force would be permissible.

The general content of the preamble was also clear, but there was some quibbling about the formulation of the general definition, and some disagreement about what should be included in the list of aggressive acts. It was recognized that whether or not there was a declaration of war was no longer significant. Invasion, attack, bombardment and blockade were acknowledged indicators of aggression, but the more subtle breaches of the peace, such as subversion and fomenting civil strife, continued to present difficulties.

The thirteen-Power group still insisted that nothing short of an armed attack could lawfully evoke a legitimate response of self-defense. The six Powers wanted greater flexibility and looked to the purposes of the action, while the Soviets still concentrated on which party was the first to use armed might. The Arab states, seeing parts of their land under Israel occupation, were determined to condemn any military occupation or annexation as acts of continuing aggression. Arab and African states argued that any means could lawfully be used in pursuit of the right to self-determination. Once more the conclusion was unanimously reached that the Special Committee should keep trying.[61] The Sixth Committee encouraged the Special Committee to go forward. (DOCUMENT 21).

In terms of additional accomplishment, 1972 was a relatively lean year for the Special Committee. Five separate proposals, largely restating previous positions, were made by various delegations. The Working Group had no time to consider the report of its Negotiating Group, and the Special Committee had no time to consider the report of its Working Group. All the alternatives were simply noted in the draft report, which concluded that the work should be resumed in 1973. (DOCUMENT 22) The Sixth Committee Report contained a concise summary showing the debate on eight distinct parts of the proposed definition. (DOCUMENT 23) With the picture now coming so clearly into focus the Committee joined in the recommendation that the work be resumed.[62] Despite all the differences, and the fact that progress had slowed to a snail's pace, the outlines of compromise were unmistakable, and the hope began to be expressed that a definition by consensus would soon be possible.[63] The Assembly, considering the "desirability of achieving the definition of aggression as soon as possible" resolved that the Special Committee should take up its task again in Geneva the following year.[64]

The United States was now embarked on a program of de-escalating the war in Vietnam, and moved toward possible new accommodations not only with the Soviet Union, but also with the Chinese Peoples Republic which had been admitted to the UN in 1971, and which was visited by President Nixon in 1972. The word "detente" began to be heard as often as one had previously heard the word "aggression".

As the committee met in the calm atmosphere of Geneva in 1973, there were times when the delegates expressed confidence that they were finally on the verge of reaching an agreement which had eluded statesmen and scholars for over half a century.[65] For the first time the plethora of drafts had been consolidated into a single document which allowed the few major points of difference to be isolated and exposed. The consensus definition was in sight.

The doubts about the usefulness of a definition were no longer expressed. There was recognition that it was most desirable that the definition be accepted by consensus. There was considerable harmony regarding the principles to be contained in a definition, but some differences about wording and sequence still remained. Agreement had already been reached that only the Security Council should have authority and discretion to decide about aggression. The list of enumerated acts was almost closed, and there was an understanding that minor incidents would be excluded. It was accepted that both the first use of armed force and the intent of the parties would have to be taken into account, and that certain forms of indirect aggression would have to be included in a list of aggressive acts.

The principle that defensive response would have to be proportionate to the aggressive attack, was no longer being discussed. It had been dropped in deference to the strong Soviet opposition. The circumstances under which force could lawfully be employed in self-defense was also eliminated as a problem by relying on a general reference to the Charter.

Although there were some reservations regarding some words in the preamble and the generic definition, the major disagreement hinged around less than half a dozen points. How to allocate the relative weight to be given to the fact that one party had struck the first blow, or that another had lawful intentions, still presented a problem. Some expressed doubts about whether attacks on marine and air fleets should be enumerated among the aggressive acts, and there was some uncertainty about how to deal with armed forces overstaying their welcome in another state, or using foreign territory for unlawful activities. There was strong disagreement about whether armed force could lawfully be used as part of a struggle for self-determination, and even the description of the legal consequences of aggression was not free from dispute.[66]

When the Special Committee concluded its work in May 1973 it was able to submit for further deliberation a single consolidated draft defining aggression. It consisted of a preamble and seven articles. Relatively few counter-proposals were submitted for consideration by only 10 of the 35 members of the committee. (DOCUMENT 24) The Committee noted with satisfaction that the progress had been such that it might be possible to prepare a generally acceptable draft definition at its next session.[67] The Sixth Committee commented on each article of the draft and unanimously concluded that the Special Committee should meet early in 1974 "with a view to completing its task" for the next session of the Assembly. (DOCUMENT 25) The Assembly agreed.[68] If what was conceived in Geneva in 1973 could be carried forward to New York in 1974, a consensus definition of aggression was about to be born.

PART FOUR

AGGRESSION DEFINED BY CONSENSUS

PART FOUR:

AGGRESSION DEFINED BY CONSENSUS

(1) <u>Aggression</u> <u>Defined</u>   (<u>1974</u>)

When the session of the Special Committee opened in New York
in March 1974 there was a mixture of optimism and some apprehension among the delegates. Some members of the "old crew" who had
worked so well together in Geneva the year before were still on hand.
Professor Bengt H.G.A. Broms, of Finland, who had effectively
served as Chairman of the Working Group in Geneva, and who had
published a book on the definition of aggression,[69] was quickly
elected Chairman of the Special Committee. Dinos Moushoutas of
Cyprus, who had followed in the tradition of his Ambassador, Zenon
Rossides, as an ardent champion of a definition, was one of the vice-
chairmen. Joseph Sanders of Guyana, who had shown great skill and
imagination in finding accomodations in 1973 was elected Rapporteur. George O. Lamptey of Ghana, who had earned great respect as
a persuasive spokesman for some of the non-aligned states, was
also present. The United States delegation was now headed by Robert
B. Rosenstock, who had established a good working relationship with
the veteran Soviet representative, D.N. Kolesnik. They were to form
the nucleus of an effective team which would drive the consensus
definition home. Perhaps, most important, the spirit of detente was
in the air.[70]
        The new General Counsel of the U.N., Prof. Erik Suy, opened
the session by declaring that a generally acceptable definition, even
if it failed to be perfectly clear on all points, would be of great
importance. He reminded the delegates that the General Assembly
had suspended consideration of the draft code of offences against the
peace and security of mankind and the problem of an international
criminal jurisdiction until aggression was defined.[71]
        Apprehensions arose from the fact that the progress achieved
represented a very delicate balance of interests which could easily
be upset. There was no way of knowing whether the new representatives would want to start again close to the beginning, and whether
they would have sufficient flexibility and authority to move the definition across the finish line. If the job was to be done in the few
weeks allocated to the Committee it would be necessary to have a

division of labor which would make it possible to proceed simultaneously on all fronts. The Working Group was split into Contact Groups and negotiating teams, which could meet informally and in private to try to hammer out compromises on the text of the various articles still in dispute. By frequently working late into the night, and on week-ends, it was finally possible the night before the scheduled close of the Special Committee meetings on Good Friday, April 1974, to put together a definition of aggression which could be endorsed by the consensus of the 35 nations in the group. It would still have to convince the 138 nations in the Legal Committee, but by any standard it was a historic achievement. (DOCUMENT 26).

The Special Committee recommended that the General Assembly adopt the following draft definition of aggression:

The General Assembly,

Basing itself on the fact that one of the fundamental purposes of the United Nations is to maintain international peace and security and to take effective collective measures for the prevention and removal of threats to the peace, and for the suppression of acts of aggression or other breaches of the peace,

Recalling that the Security Council, in accordance with Article 39 of the Charter of the United Nations, shall determine the existence of any threat to the peace, breach of the peace or act of aggression and shall make recommendations, or decide what measures shall be taken in accordance with Articles 41 and 42, to maintain or restore international peace and security,

Recalling also the duty of States under the Charter to settle their international disputes by peaceful means in order not to endanger international peace, security and justice,

Bearing in mind that nothing in this definition shall be interpreted as in any way affecting the scope of the provisions of the Charter with respect to the functions and powers of the organs of the United Nations,

Considering also that, since aggression is the most serious and dangerous form of the illegal use of force, being fraught, in the conditions created by the existence of all types of weapons of mass destruction, with the possible threat of a world conflict and all its catastrophic consequences, aggression should be defined at the present stage,

Reaffirming the duty of States not to use armed force to deprive peoples of their right to self-determina-

15

tion, freedom and independence, or to disrupt territorial integrity,

Reaffirming also that the territory of a State shall not be violated by being the object, even temporarily, of military occupation or of other measures of force taken by another State in contravention of the Charter, and that it shall not be the object of acquisition by another State resulting from such measures or the threat thereof,

Reaffirming also the provisions of the Declaration on Principles of International Law concerning Friendly Relations and Co-operation among States in accordance with the Charter of the United Nations,

Convinced that the adoption of a definition of aggression ought to have the effect of deterring a potential aggressor, would simplify the determination of acts of aggression and the implementation of measures to suppress them and would also facilitate the protection of the rights and lawful interests of, and the rendering of assistance to, the victim,

Believing that, although the question whether an act of aggression has been committed must be considered in the light of all the circumstances of each particular case, it is nevertheless desirable to formulate basic principles as guidance for such determination.

Adopts the following definition of aggression:*

Article 1

Aggression is the use of armed force by a State against the sovereignty, territorial integrity or political independence of another State, or in any other manner inconsistent with the Charter of the United Nations, as set out in this definition.

Explanatory note: In this definition the term "State":
  (a) Is used without prejudice to questions of recognition or to whether a State is a Member of the United Nations;
  (b) Includes the concept of a "group of States" where appropriate.

*Explanatory notes on articles 3 and 5 are to be found in the report of the Special Committee (A/9619, para. 20) (The Sixth Committee added: "The Report of the Sixth Committee contains statements on the definition in paragraphs 9 and 10 (A/9890).")

16

Article 2

The first use of armed force by a State in contravention of the Charter shall constitute prima facie evidence of an act of aggression although the Security Council may, in conformity with the Charter, conclude that a determination that an act of aggression has been committed would not be justified in the light of other relevant circumstances including the fact that the acts concerned or their consequences are not of sufficient gravity.

Article 3

Any of the following acts, regardless of a declaration of war, shall, subject to and in accordance with the provisions of article 2, qualify as an act of aggression:

(a) The invasion or attack by the armed forces of a State of the territory of another State, or any military occupation, however temporary, resulting from such invasion or attack, or any annexation by the use of force of the territory of another State or part thereof;

(b) Bombardment by the armed forces of a State against the territory of another State or the use of any weapons by a State against the territory of another State;

(c) The blockade of the ports or coasts of a State by the armed forces of another State;

(d) An attack by the armed forces of a State on the land, sea or air forces, or marine and air fleets of another State;

(e) The use of armed forces of one State, which are within the territory of another State with the agreement of the receiving State, in contravention of the conditions provided for in the agreement or any extension of their presence in such territory beyond the termination of the agreement;

(f) The action of a State in allowing its territory, which it has placed at the disposal of another State, to be used by that other State for perpetrating an act of aggression against a third State;

(g) The sending by or on behalf of a State of armed bands, groups, irregulars or mercenaries, which carry out acts of armed force against another State of such gravity as to amount to the acts listed above, or its substantial involvement therein.

Article 4

The acts enumerated above are not exhaustive and the Security Council may determine that other acts constitute aggression under the provisions of the Charter.

Article 5

No consideration of whatever nature, whether political, economic, military or otherwise, may serve as justification for aggression.

A war of aggression is a crime against international peace. Aggression gives rise to international responsibility.

No territorial acquisition or special advantage resulting from aggression are or shall be recognized as lawful.

Article 6

Nothing in this definition shall be construed as in any way enlarging or diminishing the scope of the Charter, including its provisions concerning cases in which the use of force is lawful.

Article 7

Nothing in this definition, and in particular article 3, could in any way prejudice the right to self-determination, freedom and independence, as derived from the Charter, of peoples forcibly deprived of that right and referred to in the Declaration on Principles of International Law concerning Friendly Relations and Co-operation among States in accordance with the Charter of the United Nations, particularly peoples under colonial and racist regimes or other forms of alien domination; nor the right of these peoples to struggle to that end and to seek and receive support, in accordance with the principles of the Charter and in conformity with the above-mentioned Declaration.

Article 8

In their interpretation and application the above provisions are interrelated and each provision should be construed in the context of the other provisions.

When, in October 1974, the Sixth Committee met to consider the draft of the consensus definition the world situation was once again tense. During the summer, war had erupted in Cyprus when Greek troops staged a coup d'état only to be ousted by invading Turkish troops which seized control and demanded partition. A world-wide Conference on the Law of the Sea had left unresolved some delicate questions concerning the rights of states with reference to their adjacent waters. The situation in the Middle East remained highly explosive. While the Sixth Committee was discussing aggression the General Assembly invited the Palestine Liberation Organization to participate in its deliberations on Palestine. The Israel government, citing the murder of Jewish athletes at the Olympics, and other atrocities, denounced the invitation as an encouragement of terrorism. All of these events were to have an impact on the definitional debate as the consensus threatened to come apart at the seams. The reaction of the Sixth Committee members is reflected in the following analysis of each provision of the proposed definition.

(2) Analysis of the Draft Definition

A reading of the text of the definition without knowing the background and the thinking of some of the parties might prove deceptive. The following analysis seeks to sketch some of the problems faced in the process of reaching agreement. Paragraph numbers and explanatory captions have been added, in parentheses, for easier identification and clarification of the overall pattern.

THE PREAMBLE

(First Preambular Paragraph - Refers to Fundamental U.N. Purposes)

> The General Assembly,
>
> Basing itself on the fact that one of the fundamental purposes of the United Nations is to maintain international peace and security and to take effective collective measures for the prevention and removal of threats to the peace, and for the suppression of acts of aggression or other breaches of the peace,

The text finally adopted was identical with the one earlier proposed by the USSR, and the Thirteen Powers.[72] It is an extract from Art. 1 of the Charter, except that it has omitted the phrase "to the end" before "to take collective measures . . ." It also failed to mention the settlement of disputes "by peaceful means and in conformity with the principles of justice and international law" as set out in the Charter. In the previous meeting of the Sixth Committee the Israel representative, Shabtai Rosenne, had cautioned against needlessly straying from the specific text of the Charter.[73] This variation from the Charter language intended no substantive alteration.

(Second Preambular Paragraph - Recalls
Security Council's Responsibility)

> Recalling that the Security Council, in accordance with Article 39 of the Charter of the United Nations, shall determine the existence of any threat to the peace, breach of the peace or act of aggression and shall make recommendations, or decide what measures shall be taken in accordance with Articles 41 and 42, to maintain or restore international peace and security,

The wording is identical with Article 39 of the Charter, and required only a slight restructuring of the draft submitted by the Six Powers.[74] The earlier USSR draft and Thirteen-Power draft had omitted the charter words "make recommendations, or", which would seem to be logical, since the power to decide obviously includes the power to decide to make a recommendation. The French delegate had objected to a reference to Article 39 without some reference to Article 51 dealing with self-defense,[75] but in this paragraph, in contrast with the preceding one, the precise language of the Charter prevailed. The power of the Security Council was to be further reinforced by Preambular Paragraph Four and the texts which followed in substantive Articles Two, Four, and Six.

(Third Preambular Paragraph - Recalls
Duty to Settle Disputes Peacefully)

> Recalling also the duty of States under the Charter to settle their international disputes by peaceful means in order not to endanger international peace, security and justice,

The Six-Power draft and the Thirteen-Power draft had included such language in their preambles.[76] The Charter itself used a slightly restructured text to convey the same idea.[77] The Charter language had been taken over verbatim in the Declaration on Principles of International Law concerning Friendly Relations and Cooperation Among States, which had finally emerged after seven years of drafting effort.[78] The Declaration on the Strengthening of International Security also followed the Charter text,[79] but the Special Committee did not consider itself glued to the Charter wording.

(Fourth <u>Preambular Paragraph</u> - Reserves
Powers of U.N. Organs)

> <u>Bearing in mind</u> that nothing in this definition shall be interpreted as in any way affecting the scope of the provisions of the Charter with respect to the functions and powers of the organs of the United Nations,

The gist of the above provision was proposed for the first time in 1973.[80] The final text of 1974 varied the wording a bit by accepting the Japanese suggestion to substitute the Charter words "functions and powers" for the previous "rights and duties". Iraq picked up another Japanese point by proposing "affecting the scope of" rather than "extending or diminishing".

Madagascar suggested that the phrase after the word "Charter" be deleted as redundant, but the U.K. and France insisted upon the specific reference to the "powers of the organs of the U.N." For some, like the British, the paragraph meant that the existing powers were not to be limited, while to others it meant that the powers were not to be expanded. The Spanish Delegate, Mr. A. Elias, mindful of the very broad discretion granted to the Council under the wording of substantive Article 2, feared that the Council might decide to exculpate those responsible for clear acts of aggression by declaring that it was not aggression. He did not think that the Council should be granted new powers to pardon international crimes. Preambular paragraph four helped to calm some of his apprehensions.

The scope of the Charter provisions can only be based on the Charter itself, and amendments are only possible pursuant to Chap. XVIII. The reassertion therefore that certain Charter provisions could not be modified by the definition of aggression might seem to be restating the obvious, but this was only the first of several safeguarding clauses designed to restrain the definition from going further than some of the parties intended.

(Fifth <u>Preambular Paragraph</u> - Stresses
Urgency of Defining Aggression)

> <u>Considering also</u> that, since aggression is the most serious and dangerous form of the illegal use of force, being fraught, in the conditions created by the existence of all types of weapons of mass destruction, with the possible threat of a world conflict and all its catastrophic conse-

> quences, aggression should be defined at the present
> stage,

The suggestion that such a provision be written into the preamble also appeared only in 1973,[81] and was adopted in 1974 practically without alteration.[82] Many of the smaller states had expressed concern about the use of bacteriological, chemical and
nuclear weapons, which they would have like to outlaw completely.
The reference to "all types of weapons" was designed to allay their
fears. The Soviet Union would have preferred a reference to the
Assembly Resolution prohibiting the use of muclear weapons,[83] and
Romania suggested that reference be made to the "permanent prohibition of the use of nuclear weapons".[84] Since none of the treaties
on the limitation of nuclear weapons had in fact been universally
accepted, the Romanian proposal was an overstatement.

The United Kingdom noted that "all weapons" encompassed
nuclear weapons, and France added that by referring only to nuclear
weapons it would water-down the attempt to emphasize the need to
define aggression "at the present stage" when there were so many
types of weapons of mass destruction. This was probably a rationali-
zation since the phrase "at the present stage" seemed to be a
carry-over from an earlier Soviet draft which dealt only with
"armed aggression", and sought to defer consideration of the more
contentious "indirect aggression" to a later stage, after an agreement on armed aggression had been reached.[85]

(Sixth Preambular Paragraph - Rejects Use of Force for Prohibited Purposes)

> Reaffirming the duty of States not to use armed force to
> deprive peoples of their right to self-determination, free-
> dom and independence, or to disrupt territorial integrity,

The 1969 Soviet proposal had contained a preambular paragraph that using force to deprive dependent people of their right to
self-determination was a denial of human rights and contrary to the
Charter.[86] By referring to General Assembly Res. 1415 (XV), and
repeating it in the substantive definition, it was clear that it was
intended to benefit only those who were struggling against colonialism. The Thirteen Powers had been content to rely on a general
reference to the provisions in the Charter concerning self-determination, sovereignty and territorial integrity.[87] The Syrian delegation had been particularly interested in preserving the specific
right to use armed force by those seeking self-determination.[88]
Consideration was also being given to a reaffirmation of the principle
as stated in the "Friendly Relations" Declaration to the effect that:

22

Every state has the duty to refrain from any forcible action which deprives people . . . of their right to self-determination and freedom and independence. [89]

It was the Spanish delegate who insisted in 1974, upon the addition of the final balancing clause protecting territorial integrity, and it was the American Mr. Rosenstock who reminded his colleagues of the corollary from the "Friendly Relations" Declaration that self-determination does not legitimize the dismemberment of law-abiding States.

The problem of how to reaffirm the right to self-determination and still restrain the use of force was to become one of the most vexing dilemmas facing the Special Committee. The issue came into sharper focus later in substantive article seven dealing with the same subject.

(Seventh Preambular Paragraph - Reaffirms
Inviolability of Territory)

> Reaffirming also that the territory of a State shall not be violated by being the object, even temporarily, of military occupation or of other measures of force taken by another State in contravention of the Charter, and that it shall not be the object of acquisition by another State resulting from such measures or the threat thereof,

The text was a slight variation of the wording contained in the "Friendly Relations" Declaration on the Strengthening of International Security, which had provided that:

> The territory of a State shall not be the object of military occupation resulting from the use of force in contravention of the provisions of the Charter. [90]

The new wording, as in the last clause added to Preambular Paragraph Sixth, placed added emphasis on respect for territory, by prohibiting "even temporary" occupation, and using the pejorative "violated". Even the attempt to restrict the protection by inserting the word "armed" before "force" was defeated. [91]

Several States, led by Romania, wanted to delete "in contravention of the Charter", [92] but it was just that saving clause which made the rest of the provision acceptable to others. The United States noted, for example, that it was in military occupation of West Berlin, but it was not in contravention of the Charter which specifically authorized such action under Article 107 dealing with transitional arrangements arising out of World War II. Egypt would have accepted the point by referring to Article 107 in a footnote. It was noted in opposition to the deletion that occupation might also be required under Article 42, if authorized by the Council, or under

Article 51 in self-defense. The Soviets, the United Kingdom, Japan, Columbia and Ghana expressed agreement with the United States view.[93] Romania continued to insist that the burden of proving contravention should not be placed on the victim, and proposed that the Article begin with "Reaffirming also that, in accordance with the provisions of the Charter . . ." an idea which found some support from Guyana and Iraq. The price for agreement was the addition of the final phrase, which was added only in 1974, "and that it shall not be the object of acquisition by another State resulting from such measures or the threat thereof."

(Eighth Preambular Paragraph - Reaffirms
"Friendly Relations" Declaration)

> Reaffirming also the provisions of the Declaration on Principles of International Law concerning Friendly Relations and Cooperation Among States in accordance with the Charter of the United Nations,

The Contact Group decided to insert this additional paragraph as a compromise which arose when they were debating the provision in Article 5 of the substantive text relating to the legal consequences of territorial acquisition resulting from aggression.[94] The "Friendly Relations" Declaration stated that "No territorial acquisition resulting from the threat or use of force shall be recognized as legal".[95] Incorporating the "Friendly Relations" Declaration by reference in the preamble served to reinforce the same principle, which was to be restated later in less precise and ungrammatical language.[96] An explanatory note was also to be added driving the last nail into the coffin by once more drawing attention to "the inadmissibility of territorial acquisition resulting from the threat or use of force."[97] The interplay between preamble and substantive text was to appear repeatedly and their interdependence was explicitly confirmed in the final substantive article.[98]

(Ninth Preambular Paragraph - Outlines
Usefulness of a Definition)

> Convinced that the adoption of a definition of aggression ought to have the effect of deterring a potential aggressor, would simplify the determination of acts of aggression and the implementation of measures to suppress them and would also facilitate the protection of the rights and lawful interests of, and the rendering of assistance to, the victim,

A similar provision had appeared in the original Soviet draft of 1970,[99] and had encountered no serious opposition, although France thought it rather weak.[100] The following had proved unobjectionable in 1972 and 1973:

> Convinced that the adoption of a definition of aggression would have a restraining influence on a potential aggressor, would simplify the determination of acts of aggression and the implementation of measures to stop them and would also facilitate the protection of the lawful rights and interests of the victim and the rendering of assistance to the victim.[101]

The Romanian delegate, who had not been present at Geneva the year before, came forward with suggested changes.[102] He proposed to tack on a phrase saying "in conformity with the provisions of the Charter," reasoning that since aid to the victim should be regulated by the Charter there should be a reference to it. He also preferred "the effect of deterring" rather than "have a restraining influence on." His first proposal found no support, but once having reopened the debate it was not long before other delegates came forward with other suggested improvements.

Italy proposed, and there were no objections, that "lawful rights and interests" be replaced by "the rights and lawful interests". The United States thought that "should" would be more precise than "would." The British thought it naive to assume that a definition would really have a material impact on aggression and suggested that the preamble merely "express the hope that . . .", which Canada thought would be a neat balance between realism and idealism. Various formulations combining "hope," "should," "would," "will," "convinced," "believing," "deterring," "discouraging," "dissuading" were tried, including the appropriate translations in English, French and Spanish. The formulation which fit the foot of all the delegates, without too many cries of pain, was the stilted compromise which emerged as the final text.

(Tenth Preambular Paragraph - Notes Need
to Consider All Circumstances)

> Believing that, although the question whether an act of aggression has been committed must be considered in the light of all the circumstances of each particular case, it is nevertheless desirable to formulate basic principles as guidance for such determination.
> Adopts the following definition of aggression:

Only one word was altered in the text which had appeared and had been accepted in 1973, and that was to substitute the word "desirable" for the word "appropriate", as suggested by Guyana. The provision itself was designed to reaffirm the flexibility which existed in determining whether aggression had been committed, and at the same time to give support to the view of many smaller states that the exercise of the Council's discretion could not be completely arbitrary since the definition would have to serve as a guide.

Viewed in its totality the long preamble presents some puzzling features. The primary purpose of a preamble should be to indicate, in clear and unambiguous terms, the motivation and basis for the declaration which follows. If measured by that yardstick the preamble to the definition of aggression could have met the objective by restricting itself to the first three paragraphs together with paragraph nine. Following the precise terminology of the Charter, as was done in only the second preambular paragraph, might have avoided a search for hidden meanings in the minor variations which were written into the first and third paragraphs. In fact the variations had no specific justification or purpose other than freedom from restraint.

To someone not familiar with the background bargaining, several of the preambular provisions must appear to be either redundant, irrelevant or unnecessary. Paragraph four would seem to be stating the obvious. The Fifth Paragraph is inartistically drawn, and carries with it a no-longer-applicable vestige of an earlier draft. Paragraphs Sixth, Seventh and Eighth are not essential in a definition of aggression, and, to a large extent, are repetitive of what appears elsewhere. The feeling cannot be avoided that they were inserted largely to influence political problems of the day rather than long range peace-keeping efforts.

Even the joining clause: "Adopts the following definition of aggression", was accepted with little thought and no discussion, as an improvisation of the last moment when it was detected that the phrase was lacking in the draft. It fails to meet an objection which had been made years ago that the definition should not be made to appear like an exercise in grammar.[103] The usual joining phrase: "Declares that", would have given greater strength to the definition, by implying that it was declaratory of existing law, but for lack of time it was not even discussed.

The recital of a few shortcomings should not diminish the appreciation of the great difficulties inherent in trying, under great stress and pressure, to obtain a consensus for a complicated agreement. The reader should be aware that some of the peculiarities which appear were not the product of a careful and deliberate design with profound and subtle significance. The preamble was both a product and a vehicle of compromise, and should be read, understood, and accepted in that light.

THE SUBSTANTIVE DEFINITION

Article 1

(The General Definition of Aggression)

> Aggression is the use of armed force by a State against the sovereignty, territorial integrity or political independence of another State, or in any other manner inconsistent with the Charter of the United Nations, as set out in this definition.
>
> Explanatory note: In this definition the term "State":
>
> (a) Is used without prejudice to questions of recognition or to whether a State is a Member of the United Nations;
>
> (b) Includes the concept of a "group of States" where appropriate.

By 1972 the members of the Special Committee had reached essential agreement on the text of the general definition. There were then only three points of difference. Some states insisted that there be reference to "sovereignty",[104] the inclusion of which was finally accepted. Some states wanted it spelled out that "territorial integrity" encompassed protection for territorial waters and air space, but the point was not accepted. Indonesia, in the Sixth Committee, simply added it by interpretation.[105] The most time consuming difficulty related to the insertion of the phrase "however exerted" after the word "force", but this point too was finally dropped. An examination of some of the points raised in the debate may help clarify the thinking of the parties.

The Soviet Union had objected to the inclusion of the word "sovereignty", which had first appeared in the Thirteen-Power draft,[106] on the grounds that it was superfluous, since force used against "political independence" was practically the same thing as force used against "sovereignty". The Soviets solved the difficulty by stating in the Sixth Committee that the inclusion was accepted on the understanding that violation of "sovereignty" meant "armed encroachment on the territorial integrity or political independence of a State".[107] As far as the USSR was concerned the word "sovereignty" was simply erased by interpretation.

The phrase requiring that the force be "in any other manner inconsistent with the Charter" was denounced as a loophole by Kenya and found objectionable and ambiguous by Paraguay.[108] It seemed to allow some room for aggressor states to argue that their action was not aggression since they did not consider it to be inconsistent with the Charter. These doubts were overcome in the

27

Committee by the reaffirmation in various subsequent articles that the determining body would only be the Security Council.

The six Powers had originally sought to prohibit force "overt or covert, direct or indirect",[109] and this was eventually modified by suggesting that the reference be to force "however exerted".[110] Many States also opposed a reference to force "however exerted" since they shared the Soviet fear that the broader language might increase the risk that a mere breach of the peace might be treated as an act of aggression.[111] The need for the broader terminology was diminished and the phrase was dropped once the deal had been made to list various forms of indirect aggression among the aggressive acts.[112] The Americans noted the inter-relationship between the different articles and that not every illegal use of force could be denominated as aggression, but only those "as set out in this definition."[113]

The "Explanatory Note" arose as a consequence of a protracted debate, extending over a period of years, regarding the political entities to which the definition should apply. All drafts other than the one submitted by the six-Powers referred to actions by "States". The six-Powers also spoke of "political entities" delimited by international boundaries.[114] Once it became apparent that the six-Powers were merely trying to cover clearly defined territories whose statehood was disputed, such as existed in Germany, Vietnam, Israel, China, Korea and Rhodesia, the compromise began to emerge.[115] The reference to a "group of States" brought objections in the Sixth Committee from the newly admitted German Democratic Republic. The GDR was opposed to any notion of collective responsibility.[116] Hungary expressed similar concerns,[117] as did Japan,[118] and these views were calmed by adding the concluding clause: "where appropriate."

The indomitable Romanian delegate, Mr. D. Ceausu, proposed that the words "provisions and principles of" be inserted between the words "the" and "Charter", and also that a paragraph be added to Article 1 in order specifically to preclude certain acts as possible justification for aggression. The first proposal was rejected, and the second was eventually accepted as part of Article 5.[119]

A bird's-eye view of Article 1 reveals several points which could give rise to questions. At the outset, it may be noted that Article 1 is obviously based on the prohibitions contained in the Charter's Article 2 (4):

All members shall refrain in their international relations
from the threat or use of force against the territorial
integrity or political independence of any state, or in any
other manner inconsistent with the Purposes of the United
Nations.

Yet, there are several important variations from the language and content of the Charter restrictions.

Article 1 of the consensus definition makes no reference to the threat of force, which some of the Nuernberg tribunals held to be an act of aggression even though the victim state, in the face of overwhelming power, surrendered without engaging in war.[120] At least some of the Members intended that threats in themselves would not constitute aggression which would give rise to criminal responsibility. This was made clear in the discussions of substantive Article 5, which follows.

The explicit protection of "sovereignty" in the draft definition, even though it is not mentioned in the Charter, seems to strengthen a concept which runs counter to the reaffirmation of the interdependence of all states, and the notion that nation states must, as an independent perception of their common interest, surrender some of their sovereignty if there is to be effective control over the use of armed violence.[121] Article 2 (4) of the Charter speaks of "any" state rather than "another" state, and it refers to "Purposes", whereas Article 1 of the definition refers to the "Charter" itself, which covers both the purposes and the procedures.[122] These variations of the Charter language, without any record justifying or explaining the change, only serve to further enfeeble a provision which some scholars are already inclined to consider dead.[123]

The concluding phrase "as set out in this definition", following immediately after the reference to the Charter, might seem to modify the Charter rather than the word "aggression", which appears at the start of the article. There is no indication that such an interpretation was intended by the strained construction of the sentence, but the phrase itself might be seen as an additional loophole.

The awkward placement of the "Explanatory Note", the first part of which Greece wanted included in the body of the text,[124] and its relative insignificance, also raise the question whether the Committee could not have simply relied on the travaux préparatoires to cover the points made in the note.

Admittedly it is not easy to capture in one declaratory sentence the essence of the meaning of aggression, and there must be reliance on broad generalizations. Uruguay had proposed:

> Internationally, aggression is the use of armed force by a
> State against another State in a manner inconsistent with
> the terms of the Charter of the United Nations.[125]

The Uruguayan suggestion, which was not seriously debated, was simpler than the final text, which had to be stretched to include other thoughts which seemed important to delegates whose consent was required in order to reach consensus.

That not all the delegates on the Sixth Committee would be satisfied with the general declaration was clear. The Israel representative, Mr. S. Rosenne, who considered the entire definition to be an unreasoned text which was "unsatisfactory, inadequate, incomplete and deceptive", felt that as a definition of <u>armed</u> aggression nothing more was required than was contained in Article 1.[126] Other states felt that the Special Committee had restricted itself too much by limiting its definition to armed aggression only. It was noted by Peru and Afghanistan that Resolution 2330 (XXIII) had charged the Committee to examine "all aspects" of the question, and the limitation to armed aggression was unjustified since many forms of economic and political coercion had not been adequately covered.[127] Very many states were to speak up and express their concern about the omission of any reference to economic aggression,[128] China referred to annexation, expansion, political interference, subversion and economic plunder as other forms of aggression.[129] Bolivia referred to blackmail by powerful countries in possession of vital natural resources.[130] Racist propaganda and apartheid were mentioned as acts of aggression.[131]

The Chairman of the Special Committee, Mr. Broms, in making his opening report anticipated these objections, and explained that the Committee had not been unmindful of the considerations raised, but had proceeded with the definition of armed aggression as the only practical possibility.[132] He noted that under Article 2 and Article 4 of the definition there was wide latitude on the part of the Security Council to consider acts other than the use of armed force if it chose to do so. Anyone familiar with the difficulties encountered in defining armed aggression would be inclined to agree that dealing with the other forms of coercion would have made consensus in the forseeable future impossible. Several states expressed the hope that the definition of armed aggression would be only the beginning of a more detailed elucidation of aggressive acts.[133] The next step up the legal codification ladder would, however, have to wait for another day. Article 2 of the draft definition was to reiterate that it was only concerned with the use of armed force.

Article 2

(Evidentiary Value of the First Strike
and Other Circumstances)

> The first use of armed force by a State in contravention of the Charter shall constitute <u>prima facie</u> evidence of an act of aggression although the Security Council may, in conformity with the Charter, conclude that a determination that an act of aggression has been committed would not be justified in the light of other relevant circumstances including the fact that the acts concerned or their consequences are not of sufficient gravity.

Article 2, which dealt with priority of action and aggressive intent, represented an attempt to reconcile two basically inconsistent views. The Soviet position, going back to 1933, was that the state which was the first to commit a specified unlawful act would automatically be identified as the aggressor. That view found a great deal of support as can be seen from the historical record. The six-Power position, put forth in 1964, was that before an act could be condemned as aggressive it would be essential to prove that it had been done in order to achieve one of five specifically prohibited objectives.[134] In the course of the debate over the years it had been conceded by the Western States that only "due regard" had to be given to the question of intent or the animus aggressionis, but they did not feel that the purposes of the action should be given any lesser consideration than the chronological fact of who had struck the first blow.[135] They argued that it was often impossible to determine who had acted first, that a minor first use of armed force might have been provoked or falsified as a pretext for massive retaliation, and that it was unreasonable in the atomic age to expect any nation to wait to be destroyed before taking defensive measures. The Soviets replied that it would be impossible to prove intent, that it would cast an unreasonable burden on the victim, and that objective criteria were essential.

The imaginative representative of Guyana, Joseph Sanders, proposed a compromise text which treated the first use of armed force "in contravention of the Charter" as prima facie evidence of aggression, and also gave the Security Council authority to take "other relevant circumstances" into account. In 1973 the United States was still insisting, despite strong Arab opposition,[136] that the Council would specifically have to consider the purposes of the act. This, too, was finally dropped. The shift in position was made possible by the recognition that "other relevant circumstances" was sufficiently broad, and vague, so that it could be construed to include the purposes and intent of the parties. There was also the new additional requirement that the action had to violate the Charter to be considered aggression. These new elements made the text tolerable even if not completely satisfactory to all.

Regarding the first use of force Syria still felt that it would always be aggression, and if it was also "in contravention of the Charter" Syria could not understand how it could fail to be aggression.[137] Algeria and Burundi expressed similar sentiments but were also prepared to accept the revised wording as a compromise.[138] Both Romania and Egypt noted that the first user of force would justify the victim's taking defensive action without waiting for any other determination.[139]

The requirement that the first use of force also had to be "in contravention of the Charter" seemed to imply that there could be a legitimate first use of force which was not in contravention of the Charter. Several States considered the clause to be an objectionable loophole which might also encourage a first strike as a purported preventive action.[140] Compromise was reached when France declared that she would construe the clause so that it was a matter for the Council to determine, and not the state engaged in the use of force, whether or not the action was in contravention of the Charter.[141] The inclusion in the definition of Article 5, Paragraph 1, eliminating various possible justifications for aggression, encouraged the French to be flexible.

The meaning of prima facie also gave rise to problems and conflicting interpretations. Did it mean that aggression existed until the presumption was rebutted, or did it simply mean that it gave rise to a suspicion that there might be aggression? France took the view that once armed force was used the presumption that the first user was the aggressor would prevail until the Security Council would find to the contrary.[142] Several other states felt the same way.[143] Those trained in the common law felt that the more mechanical approach went too far. The United States delegate, Mr. Rosenstock, remained convinced that prima facie evidence, like an American Grand Jury indictment, was not the same as conviction. A decision that aggression existed was dependent and conditional upon a prior finding to that effect by the Council.[144] The British had the same view.[145] The Soviets were not about to rock the boat and remained silent on the point.

In making reference to ''other relevant circumstances'' Article 2 sought to avoid a direct confrontation with the issue of whether intent and purposes could be considered. Those who favored the inclusion of the latter continued to insist that they were covered by the general language, while some of those who had been opposed to a consideration of intent still insisted that it was not relevant.[146] The Soviet Union however, now close to its goal, made full circle and now declared that the Council would have to study the intentions carefully in order to identify the true aggressor.[147]

It had earlier been agreed that there should be a de minimus clause, which was designed to prevent minor incidents from being treated as aggression.[148] The objective was achieved by adding the sentence at the end of Article 2 that the Council could conclude that an act was not aggression if it, or its consequences was not of sufficient gravity to justify a finding of aggression.[149]

Article 2 was properly regarded as a key provision of the consensus definition. Obviously there had been a trade to reach an acceptable conclusion. References to ''purposes'' had been dropped. In exchange ''other relevant circumstances'' could be considered, and there was a requirement that the act to be offensive, had to be ''in contravention of the Charter''. Who decided whether an act was "in contravention" and what was included among the "other relevant circumstances" to be considered, and exactly what was the significance of considering the first strike to have prima facie evidentiary value, were all subject to different interpretations. The delegates were eager to reach a consensus regarding the phrases in the text, but the debate, published and unpublished, made it clear that they were far from agreed regarding the meaning of the words accepted.

Article 3

(Acts Qualifying as Aggression)

> Any of the following acts, regardless of a declaration of war, shall, subject to and in accordance with the provisions of article 2, qualify as an act of aggression:

It had been recognized at an early stage that the classical illustration of aggression - a declaration of war, having gone out of style, was no longer a pre-requisite for a determination that aggression had taken place.[150] This point had been particularly welcomed by Israel in the Sixth Committee.[151] The Charter makes no reference to "war", which has been recognized as a relative and ambiguous term.[152]

Italy had noted the year before that listing acts which constitute aggression was inconsistent with provisions giving the Security Council discretion to determine aggression. It had, therefore, been suggested that a clause be inserted linking Article 2 to Article 3, and the clause above was accepted.[153] The previous text, which said that a listed act "shall constitute" an act of aggression was also modified. The Western Powers felt that it was too strong and should read "would qualify as".[154] Algeria, Mexico and Egypt felt that the proposed alteration was too weak. In a Solomon-like compromise the final text read: "shall . . . qualify".

> (a) The invasion or attack by the armed forces of a State of the territory of another State, or any military occupation, however temporary, resulting from such invasion or attack, or any annexation by the use of force of the territory of another State or part thereof;

It had been accepted by the Committee that the traditional benchmark of aggression - invasion or attack - would head the list of clearly aggressive acts.[155] There had been minor differences of wording but these had all been resolved by 1973. "Military occupation" and "annexation" were also added, in language based on the thirteen-Power draft.[156] In 1974 the clause was no longer being discussed.

It would appear that the language used reflects the intensity of the feeling which existed among various members of the Committee, and particularly those whose countries were partly under military occupation. Invasion is invariably an antecedent to "military occupation, however temporary". Invasion and temporary occupation are the unavoidable antecedents to "annexation by the use of force". Since both the invasion and the attack have already been condemned in the opening words of the article as clear acts of aggression, it may be questioned whether the addition of "occupation however temporary" or "annexation" really adds much to an offense which has already been characterized as "the gravest of all crimes against peace and security throughout the world." The U.K. was explicit in stating that it referred only to occupation resulting from such invasions or attacks as themselves constituted aggression. [157]

Military occupation and acquisition of territory resulting from the use of force, although a traditional and continuing practice among belligerent states, are surely prohibited under international law. [158] The same principle was reaffirmed in the Seventh Paragraph of the preamble. The redundant condemnation of occupation and annexation, as if they were new acts of daily aggression, while understandable from an emotional point of view, can only tend to detract from a precise juridical formulation. Complex political, ethnic and military problems do not lend themselves to solutions by special terminology being artificially injected into a definition. The final text is a further indication of the political nature of the consensus definition.

> (b) Bombardment by the armed forces of a State against the territory of another State or the use of any weapons by a State against the territory of another State;

The text finally adopted was the one basically accepted in 1972. [159] The only difference was that Syria, Iraq and Romania had reiterated a previous Soviet argument that the use of nuclear, bacteriological and chemical weapons, or weapons of mass destruction, should also be specifically listed, in order to demonstrate the particular abhorrence for such weapons, and to further restrict the permissible instruments of attack. [160] The Western Powers rejected the amendment on the grounds that it was not the weapon which determined the legality of the attack, and the reference to "any weapons" was all inclusive so that a further itemization was redundant. France and Ghana agreed, and the USSR, having obtained the reference to "weapons of mass destruction" in the Fifth Preambular Paragraph, was also prepared to accept the Western view. [161] Romania, which had led the opposition, had to settle for the confirming explanatory note which it insisted had to be included in the Report. [162]

> (c) The blockade of the ports or coasts of a State by the armed forces of another State;

The earliest definitions had listed blockade as a classical illustration of an aggressive act. The accepted formulation was originally proposed by the Thirteen Powers, and almost identical language appeared in the Soviet proposal. The Six Powers had made no mention of blockade in their draft, but were quite prepared to include it. No one on the Special Committee felt the need to debate the subject, although the meaning of "blockade" was certainly contentious,[163] and would give rise to serious problems in the Sixth Committee.

There were 30 land-locked countries in the United Nations which were without "ports or coasts", and none of them had been directly represented on the Special Committee to Define Aggression. Many of them noted correctly that cutting off access to the sea might be just as detrimental to a land-locked state as a blockade of the ports of a coastal state. Listing the one and failing to list the other was seen as an unjustified discrimination, violating the sovereign equality of states.[164] Although none of the land-locked states seemed desirous of upsetting the delicately balanced consensus definition, Afghanistan, after some hesitation, finally took the lead on behalf of many other sponsors in presenting a "Working Paper" in which it was suggested that a clause be added to the end of Article 3 (c) stating:

> as well as the blockade of the routes of free access to and from the sea of land-locked countries;[165]

It took weeks of behind-the-scenes wrangling before an acceptable compromise could be reached. In announcing the compromise Mr. Broms said it would save the definition from amendments that would have destroyed the consensus. What was finally agreed was that the footnote which had appeared in the report of the Special Committee,[166] would be augmented by an additional observation that the Report of the Sixth Committee contained statements on the definition, and the paragraphs in which those statements would be made would also be designated in the footnote. The statement itself, which was to appear in the Sixth Committee's report, was:

> The Sixth Committee agreed that nothing in the definition, and in particular article 3 (c), shall be construed as a justification for a State to block, contrary to international law, the routes of free access of a landlocked country to and from the sea. [167]

It was a savings clause for the land-locked states, which had within it another savings clause, "contrary to international law", to satisfy those who wanted the subject kept open for further clarification.

A very similar problem, and a similar technique for solution was to appear in connection with the next article as well.

> (d) An attack by the armed forces of a State on the land, sea or air forces, or marine and air fleets of another State;

The Politis definition of 1933 had listed among its acts of aggression an attack on the "vessels" or "aircraft" of another State. The effect would have been the same whether the vessel was military or civilian.[168] The Special Committee, facing the problem in 1972, agreed upon a text which characterized as aggression "An attack by the armed forces of a State on the land, sea, or air forces of another State."[169] During 1973, as a result of various disputes which had arisen regarding fishing rights in coastal waters off Iceland and other countries, the Special Committee added to its text the additional reference to an attack on "marine and air fleets" as an indicator of aggression.[170]

Japan, noting that its marine transport was vital to its existence, argued, in favor of the addition, that an attack against their maritime fleet would be just as devastating and therefore just as much an act of aggression as an invasion or blockade.[171] The Soviet Union, with its own trawlers spread throughout the world, shared the Japanese view, which was supported by the United States. On the other hand Indonesia and Ecuador, supported by Syria, argued that the reference to "marine" should be deleted since it suggested that a state might be accused of aggression, and subjected to retaliatory action in the name of self-defense, if it simply took action against fishing vessels illegally within its territorial waters.[172] They, and many other coastal states, felt that there should be no restraint on their legal right to use force if necessary to preserve their coastal resources from illegal invasion, pollution or exploitation by foreign predators.

The consensus definition had been obtained in the Special Committee on the assurance given by Ghana, that attacks on individual fishing vessels illegally in foreign waters was not intended to be regarded as aggression, and that all that was contemplated was massive attacks on fleets.[173] The reference in Article 2 to the exclusion of minor incidents as possible acts of aggression helped the Special Committee to get over the hurdle, but the objections were only temporarily suppressed and not eliminated.

In the Sixth Committee the doubts again surfaced. A Law of the Sea Conference in Caracas had not settled the question. Now it was argued that if it went without saying that coastal states could enforce their own laws within their maritime zones then it should be confirmed in writing. "Si ca va sans dire, ca va mieux en le disant". Many rose to the defense of the rights of the coastal states.[174] Finally Peru took the lead in submitting a "working Paper" proposing an additional article saying:

> Nothing in this definition, and in particular article 3 (d), shall be construed as in any way prejudicing or diminishing the authority of a coastal State to enforce its national legislation in maritime zones within the limits of its national jurisdiction. [175]

An earlier Australian suggestion that a small working group try to reconcile the differences was accepted. [176] Mr. R.Q. Quentin-Baxter of New Zealand was to receive praise for his skill as Chairman of the working group.

Just as in the case of Article 3 (c) the compromise solution which was accepted to save the consensus provided for a signalling footnote to be added to the Special Committee's report and an explanation in the Sixth Committee confirming that

> . . . nothing in the definition, and in particular article 3 (d), shall be construed as in any way prejudicing the authority of a State to exercise its rights within its national jurisdiction, provided such exercise is not inconsistent with the Charter of the United Nations. [177]

The "provided" clause was the safeguard, together with some softening of the language, which made the explanation tolerable to those who were reluctant to spell out the permissible uses of force against commercial fishing vessels. [178]

(e) The use of armed forces of one State, which are within the territory of another State with the agreement of the receiving State, in contravention of the conditions provided for in the agreement or any extension of their presence in such territory beyond the termination of the agreement;

This provision had its origins in the Six Power proposal that the use of armed forces lawfully within another state "in violation of the fundamental conditions of permission for their presence, or maintaining them there beyond the termination of permission" be listed as aggression if the force was used "to achieve a prohibited purpose". [179] France and the Soviet Union expressed misgivings about both the concept and the wording. [180] Uruguay proposed language which was more precise. [181] The present text was accepted in a spirit of compromise in 1973.

We see here a rather extreme application of the concept of territorial sanctity. A fair reading of the article would indicate that any nation retaining its troops in an area where they had been lawfully stationed might be guilty of aggression if they did not evacuate those troops on the schedule set by the host state. Perhaps the consequences of such action might not be of sufficient gravity, so that an exemption from the charge would be permissible under the last clause of Article 2, but under the strict wording of the article a violation would be included among the limited list of aggressive acts, even though the offense might have resulted in no harm done to either person or property. It is doubtful whether the offense, as formulated, (particularly after the reference to "prohibited purposes" has been deleted), is deserving of inclusion among a restricted list of the most serious of all crimes.[182]

> (f) The action of a State in allowing its territory, which it has placed at the disposal of another State, to be used by that other State for perpetrating an act of aggression against a third State;

During 1973 the world was much disturbed by guerrilla attacks being launched from the territory of one State against a neighboring State. The Working Group of the Special Committee proposed to describe as aggression:

> The action of a State placing its territory at the disposal of another State when the latter uses this territory for perpetrating an act of aggression against the third State with the acquiesence and agreement of the former.[183]

The 1933 Politis report had listed as aggression the provision of support for armed bands which invaded another territory or refusal to take whatever measures were possible to deprive such bands of assistance.[184] The original Litvinoff draft had contained no such article, but it had been picked up in the 1933 treaty definitions, and now the Soviet delegate made the same argument which had been considered four decades before. He noted that the wording proposed by the Special Committee implied unlawful acts by two parties - the one sending troops and the other making its territory available, yet only the latter was being condemned.[185] The proposed text also gave rise to the difficulty of proving "acquiesence and agreement". The Italian delegate argued that there could be no wrongdoing by the territorial state for acts carried out without its consent,[186] and Kenya shared that view.[187]

The United Kingdom and the United States thought the idea in 3 (f) should be preserved and so did Romania and Spain. Madagascar recognized that the essential delict was the complicity and felt that perhaps there should be a separate reference to complicity as an offense. The conclusion finally reached was that the wording would be improved as shown in the final 1974 text.

What the text could not resolve was the actual difficulty which might arise in cases where the local government simply did not have sufficient knowledge or effective control to curb guerrilla activities.[188] Libya wanted liberation movements to be exempt from Art. 3 (f),[189] and that complex problem was to be dealt with in the next paragraph and the Articles which followed.

(g) The sending by or on behalf of a State of armed bands, groups, irregulars or mercenaries, which carry out acts of armed force against another State of such gravity as to amount to the acts listed above, or its substantial involvement therein.

One of the major stumbling blocks to a consensus definition had, for many years, been the question whether acts of indirect aggression should be included in the definition. It had been the unalterable position of the Six Powers that indirect acts of aggression, such as support for armed bands, was the most frequent and insidious form of aggression currently being employed, and that no definition could be realistic or acceptable if it did not incorporate that fact. The Soviets, following their own 1933 aggression treaties, had included a similar provision in their initial draft. [190] The smaller States, however, feared that it might take years to reach agreement on direct aggression, and the inclusion of indirect aggression might make it possible for the more powerful States to seek out some act of support for a subversive group and use that as a justification for launching a massive counter-assault disguised as self-defense. There was great difficulty in reconciling the conflicting views.

Syria argued that actions by armed bands might be mere breaches of the peace and would not justify triggering the entire collective defense mechanism. There seemed to be some willingness to include indirect aggression but only if it was of such magnitude as to amount to an armed attack. [191] By 1973 there was agreement on the important point that indirect aggression should also be listed among the illustrative aggressive acts, but there was strong disagreement about the text.

Some insisted that it was not aggression unless the armed bands carried out "invasion or attack" or that the use of armed force had to be of such gravity as to amount to aggression as defined elsewhere on the list. The United States began making concessions by dropping its condemnation of "organizing" "encouraging" "assistance to" "knowing acquiesence in" or "lending support to" armed bands, [192] and was prepared to settle for the more objective criterion of the actual "sending" of armed bands against another State. [193] In 1973 the United States was, however, also insisting that "open and active participation" in any of the proscribed activities would also have to be condemned as aggression.

Syria, Iraq and Egypt, and the German Democratic Republic, were adamant in opposing the United States formulation, which they felt opened the door to all sorts of abuses since "participation" was an imprecise term and might really involve something which could be no more than a minor breach of the peace. [194] The USSR argued that broad language might serve to inhibit liberation movements and was, therefore, objectionable.[195] India wanted to prohibit "organizing or encouraging acts of civil strife",[196] but France felt that went too far unless there also was "participation in sending".[197] Indonesia wanted "support" included, as well as "sending".[198] Israel was primarily concerned with effective deterrence of terrorism, of which she had been the recent victim.[199] Greece felt the whole subject of indirect aggression deserved a separate article.[200]

When the debate was resumed in 1974 the Arab, African and some Socialist states, seeking to maintain a free hand for support of liberation movements, lined up against restraints, while the Western States sought to obtain as restrictive a formulation as possible. The compromise which evolved required that the previous reference to "invasion or attack" be deleted, and that the phrase "or its open and active participation therein" also be dropped. In its stead was substituted "or its substantial involvement therein", with the explanation offered by its sponsor, Joseph Sanders of Guyana, that what was substantial would have to be decided on the basis of all the circumstances.[201] The Arab states went along with the compromise in exchange for a major concession which was made to their view when it came to Article 7, dealing with the use of force and self-determination.

It is unfortunate that the process of bargaining and compromise under the pressure of time does not always allow for adequate consideration of all the facets of a problem.[202] Both the "Friendly Relations" Declaration and the Declaration on Strengthening of International Security dealt with the question of support for armed bands. By the terms of those instruments States are enjoined from "organizing or encouraging the organization of irregular forces... for incursion into the territory of another state" and from "organizing, instigating, assisting or participating in acts of civil strife or terrorist acts in another state or acquiescing in organized activities within its territory . . . (which) involve a threat or use of force." The different language used in the definition of aggression can only lead to confusion.

The nature of the permissible response to various forms of coercion which do not involve the direct use of armed force will continue to present difficulties. Perhaps the Security Council can deal with it under the general catch-all of taking "all of the circumstances" into account.

In listing only seven categories of offences which would qualify for consideration as an act of aggression the Special Committee omitted several areas which had previously been talked about as possible signposts of aggression. The de Brouckère report of 1926 had warned about the failure to observe the principle of proportionality as an indicator of aggression.[203] Since the Soviet Union had been strongly opposed to any reference to proportionality this important concept disappeared from the definition.[204] The 1924 Draft Protocol for the Pacific Settlement of Disputes would have taken as proof of aggression the failure of a state to submit a dispute to the agreed procedures for pacific settlement.[205] Failure to abide by the decisions of the Security Council or the Assembly had also been suggested as worthy of listing among acts of aggression, but all such transgressions went the way of economic and ideological aggression and were not listed as aggressive acts since they lacked the qualifying ingredient - as laid down in Articles 1 and 2 - the use of armed force. An effort was made to diminish the impact of such omissions by the general authorization which followed in Article 4.

Article 4

(Non-Exhaustive Character of the List)

> The acts enumerated above are not exhaustive and the Security Council may determine that other acts constitute aggression under the provisions of the Charter.

One point on which all members of the Special Committee had agreed for years was that the determination of the aggressor would rest with the Security Council. When the Charter was being drafted it was conceived that the Council alone was to be the enforcement agency, while the Assembly was to be the forum for discussion and debate.[206] By virtue of the "Uniting for Peace Resolution" some of the power of the Council was slipping away to the Assembly, where the smaller states had a larger role to play.[207] If the Assembly could succeed in laying down guide-lines which would bind the Council, the power of the Assembly would be further increased.

The Soviet Union, as well as the other members having veto powers on the Council, obviously would benefit if they could retain complete control in the Council, and it is not too surprising, therefore, that there were several places in the definition where the wide discretion of the Council was directly and indirectly reconfirmed.[208] The British maintained that not only could the General Assembly not make the definition binding on the Council, but even the Council itself could not do so.[209] Only China expressed doubts about the wisdom of having the Council decide on aggression. She argued that the large Powers would never condemn themselves and the decision on aggression should be shared by all States.[210] Ecuador made the very important, and largely ignored point, that a logical addition to Article 4 "would be a provision establishing an international penal tribunal having the powers currently attributed to the Security Council in the matter."[211]

The determination of what constitutes aggression is not likely to remain indefinitely within the completely unfettered discretion of a small political body in which absolute veto powers may be exercised by those who, because of their power, may be the most tempted to become offenders.[212] The Council must be guided by the existing declarations of international law and the agreed standards of international conduct. The definition of aggression, despite its many ambiguities, provides some guide to the permissible limits of the use of armed force. It is "the firm conceptual core" around which the Council's decision must focus.[213]

The consensus definition acknowledged in effect that the causes of international violence were so complex, the coercive techniques so dynamic and diverse, and the competing value systems so disparate, that no rigid rule or list of inculpating acts could possibly itemize the actions which would mark the culpability of nations and individuals. Article 4 provided the necessary flexibility, and at the same time reconfirmed that it was the Security Council, the only agency currently acceptable, which would make the final decision. Further guidelines to help differentiate between lawful and unlawful use of force, as well as an indication of some of the consequences which an act of aggression might entail were to be dealt with in the subsequent articles of the definition.

Article 5

(Considerations Not Justifying Aggression and
Legal Consequences of Aggression)

> No consideration of whatever nature, whether political, economic, military or otherwise, may serve as a justification for aggression.

This provision did not appear in any of the original three drafts. The sentence had its origins in the 1933 USSR definition. It was accepted in the Politis Report, was relied on by the United States Prosecutor at the Nuernberg Trials, and had been considered by the International Law Commission in 1951.[214] It was submitted by Romania in 1972,[215] and was accepted in principle in 1973. At that time the only doubt was where to put it. Guinea wanted the sentence to be added to Article 2.[216] Greece and Ecuador wanted it included somewhere.[217] Yugoslavia thought it might best be handled as a separate article.[218] In 1974 Romania became its most insistent champion.[219]

The United Kingdom thought the sentence was a truism which might find a suitable place in the preamble. The United States agreed. The Soviets wanted to be sure that the Council's discretion to consider everything would not be hampered and was, therefore, inclined to exclude it if possible, or at best to push it into the preamble. To satisfy the Soviet hesitation, the sentence was watered down by a tie-in to the "Friendly Relations" Declaration in the explanatory note in the Committee's Report, and particular reference was made to the admonition that no state has the right to intervene "directly or indirectly, for any reason whatever, in the internal or external affairs of any other State."[220] What had been offered as an apparent attempt to exclude <u>motive</u> as a justification for the use of armed force was dipped into the vat of compromise. What came out was a slightly different color. It now appeared as the traditional prohibition against unlawful intervention, and thereby pleased the South American states which were particularly sensitive on that point.[221] Without much public discussion of what was intended, the paragraph was placed under the same umbrella as the next two unrelated paragraphs dealing with certain consequences of aggression.

> A war of aggression is a crime against international peace. Aggression gives rise to international responsibility.

Much to the surprise of many of the delegates, the sentence dealing with the criminal nature of aggression generated a great deal of contention as the consensus was about to be reached. By 1973 there seemed to have been general agreement that "Aggression constitutes (   ) against international peace, giving rise to responsibility under international law". The main problem was to agree on the descriptive adjective to be inserted in the open bracket.[222] The only alternatives then suggested for inclusion in the open bracket were "a grave violation", "a crime", "criminal violation", or, as proposed by the Six Powers, that the subject be omitted completely.[223] In 1974, however, the United Kingdom drew attention to the fact that a reference merely to "aggression" without restricting it to "aggressive <u>war</u>" was objectionable. The International Military Tribunal had condemned aggressive <u>war</u>, and not simply aggression. The "Friendly Relations" Declaration had stated: "A war of aggression is a crime against the peace for which there is responsibility under international law." The United Kingdom representative was not willing to go any further than international law had already gone.[224] He would accept individual criminal responsibility for aggressive war, but only state responsibility, i.e., compensation, for aggression.[225] The United States and Japan supported the United Kingdom position. Australia's Sir Laurence McIntyre went even further and declared that criminal responsibility should not be construed as implying individual responsibility.[226]

To many the distinction between aggression and aggressive war was seen as an attempt to turn back the clock and reverse not merely the trend of the Nuernberg trials but also the thinking of the

International Law Commission and the General Assembly.[227] It was true that the major Nuernberg trial against Goring et al. had dealt only with aggressive <u>war</u>, but some of the subsequent trials, based on Control Council Law No. 10, had held that the invasion of Austria and Czechoslovakia, even though those countries capitulated without resistance, - and therefore there was no war, were nevertheless acts of aggression for which there was personal criminal liability. [228]

The International Law Commission had made no distinction between aggression and aggressive war. In 1951, the Commission, acting pursuant to General Assembly direction, had listed as its first offence Against the Peace and Security of Mankind: "Any act of aggression". Article 1 of the draft code had prescribed that for such crimes under international law "the responsible individuals shall be punishable".[229] Even a threat of aggression would be treated as a criminal offense against the peace. In 1952 the Assembly had referred to the "crime of aggression", without any reference to "war".[230]

The greatest objection to the British position was its insertion of the ambiguous term "War", which even the Charter had avoided. A distinguished British jurist had maintained that "when Great Britain is one of the combatant parties, it is for the Government to say whether we are at war or not." [231] Combining that reasoning with the new British requirement that there be a war before there could be personal criminal responsibility might lead to the conclusion that any government leader could engage his country in any hostilities but would be immune from criminal prosecution by simply declaring that a state of war did not exist. Although the British and the Americans were correct in pointing out that peace-keeping was more important than punishment,[232] they may have minimized the value of deterence. It was perhaps to be expected that the Japanese, some of whose leaders had suffered the consequences of a broad interpretation of personal responsibility for crimes against peace,[233] would favor a restrictive view of criminal liability. Whether they had any such purpose in mind in supporting the British proposal was not articulated. Questions were also raised about the American position.

Suspicions were voiced that the United States' view was prompted by fears that the North Vietnamese might carry out their threat to put on trial as war criminals some captured American airmen who had participated in the bombing of North Vietnam and Cambodia, countries with which the United States was not officially at war. By requiring the existence of war to be a pre-requisite for personal criminal responsibility the United States, it was surmised, hoped to avoid any possible political or legal embarrassment.[234] There was no evidence to justify such a conclusion.

The only way to break the impasse which arose over the distinction between aggression and aggressive war, was for the Soviets and the non-aligned states to accept the restrictive United Kingdom

elsewhere, was another demonstration that agreement could be reached in wording even where there was really no agreement in principle. The technique employed was one, which had almost become customary, of leaving the text so vague that the opposing parties might each interpret it to their own advantage should the need arise. In the words of one of the delegates: "The definition had reached a sufficient level of abstraction to be acceptable."

Article 8

(Interrelationship of all Provisions)

> In their interpretation and application the above provisions are interrelated and each provision should be construed in the context of the other provisions.

This article appeared only at the close of the session in 1974, and represented another compromise. Algeria insisted that the last word should go to Article 7 on self-determination which had previously appeared as Article 5.[261] The United Kingdom insisted that the definition should close as previously agreed on an article reaffirming the inviolability of the Charter. The Solomonic Chairman, Mr. Broms, persuaded them to agree to shift the self-determination article behind the inviolability article and to add the new stipulation in Article 8, which confirmed that the position didn't really mean anything.

The text of Article 8 was borrowed from the "Friendly Relations" Declaration, substituting only the word "provisions" for principles". Those who had their eye on the inferences, implications, and interrelationships tucked away in the dark shadows of the various ambiguous clauses of the definition were pleased with the new article.

Not everyone was pleased with the consensus definition finally presented by the Special Committee. Everyone knew that it had been a very long time being born, and although it wasn't a very pretty baby, no one was really ready to tell the parents to try again. When Mr. Broms presented the resolution by which the Legal Committee was to transmit their work for acceptance by the General Assembly, it was apparent that of the 35 nations on the Special Committee only 22 joined as sponsors of the resolution. The absence of the Arab states and some African states was particularly striking. The resolution itself was brief and weak. It called upon states to refrain from aggression and other uses of force contrary to the Charter and recommended that the Council take account of the definition as guidance, "as appropriate".[262] The text of the Special Committee's consensus definition had remained unaltered although the additional sentence had been added to the explanatory footnote in an effort to placate the land-locked states on Art. 3 (c) and the coastal states on Article 3 (d). When the Chairman of the Sixth Committee, Mr. Sahović of Yugoslavia, announced after a brief pause that the resolution was adopted without a vote,[263] there were several delegates clamoring to be heard.

China criticized the super-powers for deceiving the public with a definition which would not impede aggression.[264] Dahomey said the definition was far from satisfactory.[265] Paraguay protested the high-handed method in which the proposal of the land-locked states had been disposed of.[266] Tanzania criticized various articles, and El Salvador, Ecuador and Bolivia stated that if the definition had been put to a vote they would have abstained.[267] Israel referred to its previous objections. A highly charged procedural debate erupted when Chile's announcement that she would join as a co-sponsor encountered Soviet and other opposition.[268] When that too was resolved, by simply having the report of the Sixth Committee list all states which wished to become co-sponsors, everyone was relieved that the item of the definition of aggression could finally be concluded in the Sixth Committee and passed on to the General Assembly.

It was a Saturday morning when the General Assembly met in plenary session to consider the report on the definition of aggression.[269] The Rapporteur of the Sixth Committee, Mr. Sanders, said that by the adoption of the definition "history will be made", and he expressed the hope that thereby "mankind will have taken another step forward towards peace". Paraguay continued its opposition to Art. 3 (c), and China stated that if the definition had been put to a vote she would have abstained. A few states repeated positions on particular articles as expressed in the Sixth Committee, and France, straddling the Soviet and Chinese views, said the definition was "nothing but a recommendation and is therefore not binding". It was only the silver-haired Ambassador of Cyprus, Zenon Rossides, who traced the history of the definition and noted its significance in the development of international law. He now called upon the Assembly to go forward during its next session so that a draft code of offences against the peace and security of mankind and an international criminal jurisdiction could become a reality.[270]

Without a vote being taken the draft resolution recommended by the Sixth Committee was adopted by the General Assembly on 14 Dec. 1974 as Resolution 3314 (XXIX).[271] "Aggression" had been defined.

(3) The Significance of the Definition

There are those who will continue to hold that defining aggression is a meaningless and useless exercise. Surely they will be right that no definition by itself can cause all acts of future aggression to cease. It will be said that consensus does not signify universal agreement but merely that the states involved have refrained from voicing their doubts and their objections. The ambiguities, and inconsistencies within the definition, and its susceptibility to conflicting interpretations, can be exposed as evidence of its deficiencies. Its omissions will be cited as further shortcomings. It will be proclaimed that the definition has no binding effect for even by its terms it is merely a guide which the Security Council may, out of wisdom or expedience, choose to disregard. A declaration which is not enforceable will be ridiculed as no legal code at all, and those who worked so hard to bring it about will be characterized as Utopian dreamers who fail to recognize the realities of the world in which they live. All of these points must be treated with respect. They do not, however, in the opinion of this writer, tell the full story.

The fact that the General Assembly of the United Nations has given its approval to a resolution clearly implies that its terms merit universal consideration. Despite its vagaries the general thrust of the definition is clear. The Security Council cannot disregard its strictures, and acts which fall within the scrutiny of its frame now run a greater risk of condemnation than before. What is laid down as a guide is apt to rise up as a binding norm of international behavior. Those who have the destiny of others in their power become more responsible to the people as the definition of aggression enables the public better to understand, judge and influence the action of states taken in the name of self-defense and the maintenance of peace. No national leader can afford to ignore the world's opinion. The possibility that decision-makers may personally be held to culpable account cannot fail to have some impact on their thinking and their conduct.

The definition of aggression mirrors the political maturity of states as they are today. Old nations adhere to their traditional concepts and values while new nations brandish their fledgling sovereignty. Rich and powerful states brace to maintain their position and prominence while the poor and the weak cry out for equality and justice. Those united by an ethnic or spiritual bond demand the unrestrained right to determine their own destiny. Faithful government servants see as their primary duty the protection of the interests of their own homeland. The definition reflects the fears and doubts of a world community still in diverse stages of evolution and growth, in which short-term gain is often viewed as more important than long-term survival.

Two decades ago the United Nations put aside its work on a Draft Code of Offenses Against the Peace and Security of Mankind, and an International Criminal Court, until the question of defining aggression could be resolved. After much effort that missing piece has now been produced. Defining the limits of permissible coercion can only have enduring value if it becomes part of a broader pattern of emerging social justice. A definition which seeks only to preserve the status quo is a very fragile shield, but as a stepping-stone it can be of great value in helping to curb the violent outbursts of racial and religious intolerance, of economic rivalries and clashes of political ideology which today divide mankind. Now nations can resume the slow movement toward the peace and security without which the quality of all human life must remain forever tarnished. In a turbulent society, unless change by non-violent means is made possible, change by violent means will be made inevitable.[272]

Doubts may be expressed about the prospects of any attempt to codify the permissible limits of violent behavior while the states whose conduct it is designed to control are at vastly different levels of social, economic or political evolution. Terrorism, the killing of diplomats and the use of armed force which would ordinarily be characterized as aggression are, in some parts of the world, defended as legitimate means for attaining legitimate goals, while elsewhere they are condemned as the most atrocious of crimes. Independent and sovereign states, no matter what their political persuasion, must be able to recognize that it is in their own enlightened self-interest, and the interest of their people, if violence against the human body and against the human spirit can be diminished. Drafting a code involves a process of deliberation and mutual consultation. It may prove difficult and frustrating, - particularly if the parties do not share the same value systems, but it is an effective method for identifying differences and trying to reconcile them by peaceful means.

Definition, codification, adjudication and enforcement are all essential steps toward a rule of law, the effectiveness of which ultimately depends upon acceptance of its terms by those whom it seeks to restrain. The fear of failure is no excuse for inaction.[273]

Our survey of the past half-century has shown the repeated cycle of the rise and fall of man's hopes. World War I brought close to 15 million dead. There arose a strong popular movement for the creation of a more secure society, but states were still not ready to surrender the traditional prerogatives of power. It was not the League that failed; - the Nations failed the League. World War II saw 35 million dead. When the U.N. Charter was born a new promise was again held forth, but it was chained to the anchor of past practices and the cherished values of a by-gone age. Violence and the preparation for even greater violence drained the resources needed for the fulfillment of human life.

Today there is a growing awareness of man's interdependence. New international obligations, goals and opportunities are increasingly being recognized and slowly implemented. The definition of aggression by world consensus, despite all of its imperfections,

52

is once more a visible re-affirmation of the indominable hope and determination that there must be legal limits to the use of armed force, and that the existing international anarchy must be brought to an end.

In our chronicle we have noted some of the philosophers and statesmen, scholars and teachers, who have seen the vision of a rational world order in which aggression was contained and a new system for the peaceful settlement of disputes was created. Many great men have looked beyond the distant horizon into a more tranquil world of the future. Whether governments and peoples will be wise enough to make of the definition a useful tool with which to build a better world only time and experience will tell. In the last analysis the significance of the definition of aggression depends on us.

Notes

Abbreviations Used

AJIL - American Journal of International Law

GAOR - General Assembly, Official Records

   Reports to the Assembly begin with the symbol
   A/

Res. - General Assembly Resolutions

SR - Summary Record

   Those with 3 digits refer to meetings of the Special
   Committee and should be preceded by the symbol
   A/AC.134/

   Those with 4 digits refer to meetings of the Sixth
   Committee and should be preceded by the symbol
   A/C.6/

UNCIO - The United Nations Conference on International
   Organization

Notes

PART THREE:

THE UNITED NATIONS MOVES TO DEFINE AGGRESSION

1. 1 UNCIO 711, 26 June 1945.

2. Res. 95(I), GAOR, First Sess., Plenary 55, at 1144, Dec. 11, 1946.

3. Doc. A/504, GAOR, 2nd Sess., Item No. 117, Nov. 21, 1947.

4. See GAOR, Fifth Sess., Supp. 1 (A/1287), Annual Report of the Sec. Gen., 1 July 1949 - 30 June 1950, at 21-23.

5. GAOR, Fifth Sess. Meetings of the First Comm., (A/1501), 4 Nov.- 9 Nov. 1950.

6. Doc. A/C.1/604.

7. See note 5 supra.

8. Vol. I, DOCUMENT 9 at 237-238.

9. See note 5 supra.

10. DOCUMENT 2, Res. 378(V)B., 17 Nov. 1950.

11. GAOR, Fifth Sess., Supp. 12 (A/1316), Report of the ILC, 5 June- 29 June 1950, at 11-17. The Chairman of the ILC, Prof. Georges Scelle of France, had for many years been convinced that every use of armed force, even for a just cause, would constitute the crime of aggression. His views were shared by Prof. V.V. Pella of Bucharest, and Mr. Ricardo J. Alfaro of Panama, all of whom were to become outstanding champions of the idea of an international criminal court and a definition of aggression. For a contrary view and citations to some of their writings see Stone, J., Aggression and World Order (1958); see also Vol. I herein, Note 1 supra.

12. DOCUMENT 2, Res. 380 (V), 17 Nov. 1950.

13. DOCUMENT 5, (A/2211) at 17-81.

14. See Id. at 81-86. See also Johnson, ''The Draft Code of Offenses Against the Peace and Security of Mankind'', 4 Int. and Comp. Law Qtrly 445 (1955).

15. DOCUMENT 5 at 86-91.

16. Res. 688 (VII) DOCUMENT 5 at 91, 20 Dec. 1952.

17. See also Memo of the Secretariat, Some Aspects of the Definition of Aggression, A/AC.66/1, 5 Aug. 1953.

18. DOCUMENT 6 at 5.

19. See DOCUMENT 6, Annex, for texts submitted to the Committee.

20. DOCUMENT 6 at 13-14.

21. Id. at 14.

22. Id.

23. Id. at 15.

24. See Fall, B.B., Hell in a Very Small Place (1966).

25. See Falk, R.A., Ed. The Vietnam War and International Law, 3 Vols. (1968-1972): Ferencz, B.B. ''War Crimes Law and the Vietnam War,'' 17 American Univ. Law Rev. 403 (1968).

26. DOCUMENT 7 at 2.

27. Id. at 6.

28. Id. at 2.

29. Id. at 2, 3, 5.

30. GAOR, Ninth Sess., Supp. 12, (A/2645), Committee on Intern. Criminal Jurisdiction. 27 July - 20 Aug. 1953.

31. GAOR, Ninth Sess., Supp. No. 9 (A/2693), 3 June - 28 July 1954.

32. Res. 898(IX), as recommended by the Sixth Committee in its Report A/2827 and Corr. 1, and adopted by the General Assembly on 14 Dec. 1954.

33. DOCUMENT 8 at 6.

34. Id. at 6, 24.

35. See GAOR, Twelfth Sess., Supp. 1, (A/3594), Annual Report of the Sec. Gen., 16 June 1956 - 15 June 1957, at 1-25.

36. DOCUMENT 8 at iii.

37. A/3574, DOCUMENT 8 supra.

38. A/3576, DOCUMENT 9 at 2-5. At the end of 1957 Prof. Stone was completing his very critical book "Aggression and World Order" (1958) His pessimism was not universally shared. See Sohn, L.B., "The Definition of Aggression" 45 Virg. Law Rev. 697 (1959): Wright, Q., "The Prevention of Aggression", 50 AJIL 514 (1956), Brownlie, I., International Law and the Use of Force by States (1963).

39. Doc. A/C.6/L 402, DOCUMENT 9 supra at 1.

40. The text of the resolution appears in DOCUMENT 10 infra. at 1.

41. Resolutions 1186, 1187 (XII) 11 Dec. 1957. Prof. Quincy Wright considered a definition of aggression to be vital to the objective of eliminating war. See The Role of International Law in the Elimination of War (1961) at 59.

42. The Council met from Oct. 23 to 25 on request of the U.S., Cuba and the USSR. The U.S. considered the emplacement of Soviet-made long-range missiles in Cuba to be a threat to the peace. Cuba accused the U.S. of aggression when it placed a naval blockade around Cuba. The U.S. called it a "quarantine". The USSR argued that its missiles were for defense only.

43. See GAOR, Seventeenth Sess. Supp. 1, (A/5201), Ann. Report of the Sec. Gen. June 1961 - June 1962.

44. See GAOR, Eighteenth Sess., Suppl 1 (A/5501/Add. 1), Ann. Report of the Sec. Gen., June 1962 - June 1963.

45. See GAOR, Nineteenth Sess. Supp. 1, (A/5801/Add. 1), Ann. Report of the Sec. Gen., June 1963 - June 1964; and GAOR Twentieth Sess., Supp. 1A (A/600 1/Add. 1), June 1964 - June 1965.

46. See GAOR, Twenty-first Sess. Supp. 1 (A/6301), Ann. Report of the Sec. Gen., June 1965 - June 1966.

47. See GAOR, Twenty-second Sess., Supp. 1 (A/6701) Ann. Report of the Sec. Gen., June 1966 - June 1967.

48. GAOR, Twenty-second, Plenary Meetings at 1572, 1611-1618, 1637-1638. (1967).

49. A/6988, DOCUMENT 13 at 4-8.

50. Res. 2330 (XXII), 18 Dec. 1967, Text in A/7185, DOCUMENT 14 infra. at 1-2. See Hazard, J.N., Ed. Comment "Why Try Again to Define Aggression?" 62 AJIL 701 (1968).

51. A/7185, DOCUMENT 14 at 13-19.

52. Id. at 25-32.

53. Id. at 34.

54. See GAOR, Twenty-fourth Sess. Supp. 1 (A/7601) Ann. Report of the Sec. Gen., at 54-56, 23 Aug. 1968.

55. Res. 2420 (XXIII) text reproduced in A/7620, DOCUMENT 16 infra at 1. A U.S. Adviser described the search for a definition as "absolute nonsense" and explained that "you can't beat something with nothing" so a U.S. draft was prepared, and then the U.S. was committed to going along with the exercise. See N.Y. Times, Dec. 9, 1971 at 14. The Soviet representative co-authored an article sharply critical of the U.S. position. See Chkhikvadzé and Bogdanov, "Who is Hindering Progress in the Definition of Aggression?", 10 Int'l Affairs 22 (1971).

56. DOCUMENT 16 at 32.

57. Doc. A/AC.134/L.22, 24 July 1970.

58. A/8019, DOCUMENT 18 at 53.

59. Res. 2644 (XXV); text reproduced in A/8419, DOCUMENT 20 infra at 1.

60. A/8419, DOCUMENT 20 at 29.

61. A/8419, DOCUMENT 20 at 21. Prof. Schwarzenberger described the work of the Special Committee as "a comic-opera seeking to create the illusion that a solution is round the corner - never to be turned". See International Law and Order (1971) at 21.

62. A/8719, DOCUMENT 22 at 6.

63. See Ferencz, B.B. "Defining Aggression: Where it Stands and Where It's Going", 66 A.J.I.L. 491-508, July 1972; Ferencz, B.B., "A Proposed Definition of Aggression: By Compromise and Consensus", 22 Int'l and Comp. Law Qtrly, 407-433, July 1973, issued as a pre-print with an introduction by Prof. Erik Suy, by the International Commission of Jurists, Geneva, Mar. 1973.

64. Res. 2967 (XXVII) text reproduced in A/9019, DOCUMENT 24 infra at 1.

65. See U.N. Doc. A/AC.134/SR. 108,109 (1973). In Philadelphia the Bar Association proposed the enactment of a Uniform Reciprocal Peace Act making aggressive war a crime under domestic law; See remarks of Senator Hugh Scott, Cong. Rec. July 12, 1973.

66. For an analysis of the points of agreement and disagreement at the close of the 1973 session see Ferencz, B.B. "Defining Aggression, The Last Mile", 12 Columbia Jour. of Transnational Law 430-463 (1973).

67. A/9019, DOCUMENT 24 at 5.

68. Res. 3105 (XXVIII) text reproduced in A/9619, DOCUMENT 26 infra at 1.

PART FOUR:

AGGRESSION DEFINED BY CONSENSUS

69. The Definition of Aggression in the United Nations (1968).

70. Henry A. Kissinger, commenting on visits taking place between President Nixon and Secretary General Brezhnev, explained: "This change of course reflected the realities that in the nuclear age there is no alternative to peace between the great nuclear countries." N.Y. Times, June 15, 1973. When war had erupted again in the Middle East in Oct. 1973, the USA and the USSR had played a major role in obtaining compliance with the U.N.'s call for a cease-fire and bringing the parties to the Conference table. For the first time the Security Council approved a multi-national U.N. Emergency Force and a U.N. Disengagement Force to serve in the area. See GAOR 29th Sess. Supp. No. 1 (A/9601) Rept. of the Sec. Gen. June 1973 - June 1974 at 3-14.

71. SR. 110 at 2, 3.

72. A/8019, DOCUMENT 18, at 55, 56.

73. SR 1443 at 17.

74. A/8019, DOCUMENT 18, at 58.

75. SR. 108 at 7.

76. See A/8019, DOCUMENT 18, at 59.

77. Charter Art. 2 Para. 3.

78. GAOR, Twenty-Fifth Sess. Supp. 18, (A/8018); Res. 2625 (XXV), 24 Oct. 1970; reproduced in 65 AJIL 243 (1971).

79. GAOR, Twenty-Fifth Sess. Supp. 28, (A/8028) at 22; Res. 2734 (XXV), 16 Dec. 1970.

80. A/9019, DOCUMENT 24 at 15.

81. Id.

82. The word "and", in the last line, was substituted for the word "with".

83. See GAOR, Twenty-Seventh Sess. Supp. 30 (A/8730) at 5, 6; Res. 2936 (XXVII) (1972).

84. Doc. A/AC.134/WG.5/R.1, 13 Mar. 1974.

85. See A/8019, DOCUMENT 18, at 55.

86. Id.

87. Id. at 58.

88. A/8719, DOCUMENT 22, at 17.

89. See Note 78 supra, Declaration as reproduced in 65 AJIL at 246 (1971).

90. Id.

91. See A/9019, DOCUMENT 24, at 18. Egypt and Romania joined in insisting upon the last phrase to support the first, and also to strengthen the third sentence in substantive Art. 5 infra.

92. Doc. A/AC.134/WG 5/R.1; (WG 5/R.2, Madagascar); SR. 1444 at 6 (Senegal).

93. The observations are based on the author's personal notes. There are no published minutes or summary records.

94. Doc. A/AC.134/WG 5/R.4 at 4.

95. For a survey of the "Friendly Relations" Declaration see Rosenstock, R., The Declaration of Principles of International Law Concerning Friendly Relations, 65 AJIL 713 (1971).

96. See Article 5 Paragraph 3 of the consensus definition proposed by the Special Committee, A/9619, DOCUMENT 26, at 8.

97. A/9619, DOCUMENT 26, at 9.

98. Id. The U.S. was eager to see all aspects of the "Friendly Relations" Declaration reaffirmed by being thus incorporated by reference.

99. A/8019, DOCUMENT 18, at 5.

100. SR. 108 at 7.

101. A/9019, DOCUMENT 24, at 15.

102. See Doc. A/AC.134/WG 5/R.1.

103. See SR. 57 at 2, and SR. 60 at 7.

104. SR. 1442 at 13 (Yugoslavia); SR. 1442 at 15 (Indonesia).

105. See Id.; SR. 1444 at 3 (Greece); SR. 1482 at 12 (Indonesia).

106. A/8019, DOCUMENT 18 at 57.

107. SR. 1443 at 9-10; SR. 1472 at 3.

108. SR. 1474 at 8 (Kenya); SR. 1483 at 3 (Paraguay); See also SR. 1482 at 8 (Tunisia). The reference to "in any other manner." was welcomed by Zambia as permitting closure of access to the sea to be considered an act of aggression. SR. 1482 at 20.

109. A/8019, DOCUMENT 18 at 59.

110. The inclusion of "however exerted" was favored by Indonesia, SR. 1442 at 16. See also SR. 1443 at 6 (Haiti); SR. 1441 at 19 (Ecuador); SR. 1444 at 6 (Senegal). Romania, which wanted "in any form" substituted for "however exerted", SR. 1441 at 13; Turkey would have preferred retention of "however exerted". A/9619, DOCUMENT 26 at 30.

111. The inclusion of "however exerted" was opposed by India, SR. 1441 at 5. See also SR. 1443 at 6 (USSR); SR. 1443 at 20 (Hungary); SR. 1442 at 18 (Ghana); SR. 1442 at 8 (Kenya); SR. 1440 at 7 (Czechoslovakia).

112. See Doc. A/AC.134/WG.5/R.4 at 1.

113. A/9619, DOCUMENT 26 at 23, also SR. 1480 at 23. This was intended to provide an additional element of flexibility so that even a wrongful use of force, such as a first strike, did not necessarily compel a determination of aggression if there were mitigating circumstances.

114. A/8019, DOCUMENT 18 at 59.

115. See A/8419, DOCUMENT 20 at 31.

116. SR. 1441 at 5.

117. SR. 1443 at 20.

118. Op. Cit. supra note 112.

119. Id.

120. See Vol. I, Document 22.

121. See Jenks, C.W., A New World of Law (1969); See also various "world Order Models Projects" such as those advocated by Prof. Mendlovitz of Rutgers, and Prof. Sohn of Harvard.

122. The Charter "purposes" are listed in 4 paragraphs of Article 1. The broader reference to the entire Charter encompasses such additional elements as the procedures for the pacific settlement of disputes as laid down in Chapter VI.

123. See Franck, T.M. "Who Killed Art. 2(4)?" 64 AJIL 809 (1970); Giraud E., "L'Interdiction du Recours à la Force", 67 Rev. Gen. Droit Int'l Pub. 501 (1963); contra, Henkin L., "The Reports of the Death of Art. 2(4) are Greatly Exaggerated" 65 AJIL 544 (1971).

124. See SR. 1444 at 3. Greece also objected to the imprecision of the phrase "as set out in this definition" SR. 1482 at 18.

125. A/9019, DOCUMENT 24 at 26. This was a reminder of the very general Harvard Law School faculty definition: "Aggression is a resort to armed force by a state when such resort has been duly determined, by a means which the state is bound to accept, to constitute a violation of an obligation". See Harvard Research in Int'l Law, Draft Convention on Rights and Duties of States in Case of Aggression, 33 AJIL Supp. 821, at 847 (1939).

126. SR. 1480 at 18, 20.

127. SR. 1473 at 3 (Peru); SR. 1479 at 18 (Afghanistan). See also SR. 1503 at 8 (Tanzania).

128. SR. 1471 at 4 (Kenya); (Kenya would have made it clearer that the Committee was limiting its scope by beginning Art. 1 with the words: "Armed aggression is. . ." SR. 1474 at 8); SR.1474 at 6 (Chile); SR. 1477 at 3 (Pakistan); SR. 1477 at 12 (Argentina); SR. 1480

at 12 (Ruwanda); SR. 1482, (Burundi, Uruguay, Dahomey, Zambia); SR. 1483, (El Salvador, Cameroon, Sierra Leone, Nepal); SR. 1478 at 16 (India).

129. SR. 1475 at 6. Congo referred to the violation of the sovereignty of states over their own natural resources as a form of aggression. SR. 1478 at 11-12. Egypt shared that view regarding territory under occupation. SR. 1483 at 10.

130. SR. 1473 at 13. Bolivia also referred to political assasination, SR. 1473 at 14. Bolivia had advanced the idea of economic aggression as early as 1953, See A/2638, DOCUMENT 6 supra at 15. For an analysis of the "oil weapon" as a form of economic aggression see Paust, J.J., and Blaustein, A.P., "The Arab Oil Weapon - A Threat to International Peace" 68 AJIL 410 (1974).

131. SR. 1474 at 12 (Madagascar); SR. 1477 at 5 (Libya); Apartheid at SR. 1476 at 7 (German Dem. Rep.); "Colonialism and racism" at SR. 1503 at 9 (Tanzania).

132. SR. 1471 at 4. The 1953 Soviet draft had included economic and ideological aggression, but no agreement on those provisions could be reached. See A/2638, DOCUMENT 6 supra at 13. The Swedish delegate expressed the fear that the inclusion of such illegal acts as ideological or economic aggression might tend to provoke extreme interpretations of the right of self-defense. SR. 1472 at 5. For illustrations of actions which might be characterized as ideological and economic aggression, and reference to the practice in South America, see Thomas, A.V.W. and Thomas, A.J.Jr., The Concept of Aggression in International Law (1972) at 83-92. That "aggression" is wider than offensive war has been noted by de Vischer in "Theory and Reality in Public International Law" (1968) at 303-306.

133. SR. 1479 at 5 (Yugoslavia); SR. 1479 at 13 (Algeria).

134. A/8019, DOCUMENT 18 at 59.

135. A/8719, DOCUMENT 22 at 18. The USSR was prepared to consider a Czech proposal that the first use of force gave rise to a presumption of aggression. See id. at 16, 21, 22.

136. See SR. 107 at 5, SR. 108 at 4.

137. See A/9619, DOCUMENT 26 at 19; SR. 1459 at 9.

138. SR. 1479 at 12 (Algeria); SR. 1482 at 4 (Burundi).

139. SR. 1475 at 3 (Romania); SR. 1483 at 11 (Egypt). Brownlie, I., International Law and the Use of Force by States (1963) notes that intent is only relevant in determining the criminal responsibility of individuals for crimes against peace. at 377.

140. See A/9619, DOCUMENT 26 at 21 (France); at 15 (Madagascar); at 17 (Romania); SR. 1479 at 11 (Algeria); SR. 1480 at 4 (Mali); SR. 1482 at 8 (Tunisia). Bulgaria noted that the Charter authorized the first use of force in certain circumstances. SR. 1472 at 16. Yugoslavia rejected any interpretation that states or regional organizations could use force without U.N. authorization. A/9619 at 26, SR. 1479 at 4.

141. A/9619, DOCUMENT 26 at 21, SR. 1474 at 10. Concern about abuse of the veto power was expressed by Cameroon. SR. 1483 at 5.

142. SR. 1441 at 15, A/9619 at 21. The implication was strengthened by using the word "although" in Art. 2 to replace the earlier proposed words, "provided however".

143. A/9619 at 17 (Romania); at 20 (Cyprus); also SR. 1479 at 6; SR. 1482 at 17 (Greece); A/9619 at 38 (Mexico); SR. 1482 at 8 (Tunisia); SR. 1483 at 10 (Egypt); SR. 1472 at 5 (Sudan); SR. 1474 at 8 (Kenya); Kenya also noted that if action by the Council were stymied by a veto the existence of a conclusion that aggression existed would justify the defensive action by the one responding to the first attack. Prof. R.R. Baxter has correctly observed that Art. 39 of the Charter does not compel the Council to determine the aggressor and that the Council is often guided by political considerations. See The Law of Armed Conflicts (1970) at 95. New Zealand expressed similar concern SR. 1475 at 10.

144. A/9619 at 23. The Dutch shared the same view. SR. 1473 at 4; Also Paraguay; SR. 1483 at 3.

145. A/9619 at 31. Iran had a similar view. SR. 1480 at 5.

146. See A/9619 at 26, SR. 1479 at 4 (Yugoslavia); SR. 1479 at 21 (Cyprus); SR. 1475 at 4 (Romania); SR. 1479 at 12 (Algeria); SR. 1479 at 15 (Cuba).

147. SR. 1472 at 3; A/9619 at 36.

148. A/9019, DOCUMENT 24 at 17.

149. Algeria complained that the phrase "sufficient gravity" was too vague. SR. 1479 at 12.

150. See Ballis, W. The Legal Position of War: Changes in Its Practice and Theory from Plato to Vattel (1937).

151. SR. 1443 at 16. By 1974 Israel criticised the whole article as unnecessary and unsatisfactory, and particularly weak with reference to terrorism. SR. 1480 at 18.

152. See Grob, F. The Relativity of War and Peace (1949); Stone, J., Legal Controls of International Conflict (1954).

153. A/9019, DOCUMENT 24 at 24. The linkage with Article 2 was considered useless by Greece. SR. 1482 at 16.

154. The Netherlands welcomed wording which served to reinforce the discretion of the Security Council. SR. 1473 at 2. Greece wished to restrict that discretion and proposed "shall constitute" rather than "shall qualify". SR. 1482 at 16.

155. A/8419, DOCUMENT 20 at 42.

156. A/8719, DOCUMENT 22 at 14.

157. A/9619, DOCUMENT 26 at 32.

158. See the citations in connection with Seventh Preambular Paragraph, supra.

159. A/8719, DOCUMENT 22 at 14.

160. A/9019, DOCUMENT 24 at 14.

161. SR. 1443 at 9.

162. A/9619, DOCUMENT 26 at 9.

163. Recent instances of contention regarding the legality of acts similar to blockade include the U.S. mining of Haiphong Harbor, the U.S. "quarantine" of Cuba during the "Soviet Missile Crisis", and the closing of various access waterways to the State of Israel.

164. See SR. 1445 at 7 (Afghanistan); SR. 1477 at 14 (Bolivia); SR. 1478 at 5 (Iraq); SR. 1478 at 16 (India); SR. 1479 at 18 (Afghanistan); SR. 1480 at 11 (Upper Volta); SR. 1480 at 12 (Ruwanda); SR. 1480 at 4 (Mali); SR. 1482 at 4 (Burundi); SR. 1482 at 19-20 (Zambia); SR. 1483 at 4 (Paraguay); SR. 1483 at 7 (Nepal). Israel had earlier expressed the view that Art. 3 (c) should also embrace economic

warfare and boycott. SR. 1443 at 16. In 1948 the Western occupation powers had condemned the blockade by the Soviet Union and the East German republic of the land access to occupied west Berlin.

165. Doc. A/C.6/L.990, 25 Oct. 1974. See SR. 1488 at 8; Supported by Paraguay, SR. 1488 at 9, Mali, SR. 1488 at 10, Botswana, SR. 1488 at 10, and Nepal, SR. 1488 at 11.

166. A/9619, Para. 22, DOCUMENT 26 at 11.

167. SR. 1502 at 4. See A/9890, DOCUMENT 27 at 2. Paraguay protested sharply against the procedure. SR. 1503 at 5 ; Gen. Ass. Plenary Meeting 2319 at 31. India, saying she had not been consulted on Art. 3(c) insisted that other international instruments would be decisive. SR. 1504 at 3. Pakistan noted that granting rights to land-locked countries might encroach on the sovereignty of transit states, and the subject had best be left to bilateral or multi-lateral agreements as heretofor. SR. 1504 at 3.

168. See League of Nations Doc. D./C.G.108, Vol. 1 supra, DOCUMENT 11 at 8. The Litvinoff definition seemed to be limited to military vessels only since it referred to "the naval or air forces of another state" Vol. I, DOCUMENT 9 at 238.

169. A/8719, DOCUMENT 22 at 14.

170. A/9019, DOCUMENT 24 at 16. Although the English text, by using the word "marine" might have been construed as referring only to military units, the Spanish and French texts made it clear that it also applied to civilian vessels. In Spanish it was "flota mercante" and in French it was even clearer - "la marine et l'aviation civiles".

171. SR. 1443 at 7, 8; A/9619, DOCUMENT 26 at 16.

172. SR. 106 at 8, 12 (Fr.); SR. 108 at 5 (Syria); SR. 1442 at 16 (Indonesia).

173. SR. 1442 at 19.

174. See A/9619, DOCUMENT 26 at 15 (Ecuador); at 19 (Indonesia); SR. 1473 at 8 (Canada); SR. 1474 at 7 (Chile); at 12 (Madagascar); at 16 (Brazil); at 18-19 (Colombia); SR. 1475 at 7 (China); at 9 (Syrian Arab Rep.); at 11 (New Zealand); SR. 1477 at 2 (Pakistan); at 5-6 (Libya); at 12 (Argentina); SR. 1478 at 3 (Bangladesh); at 5 (Iraq); at 18 (Sri Lanka); SR. 1479 at 9 (Guatemala); at 10 (Dem. Yemen);

at 15 (Cuba); SR. 1480 at 6 (Iran); at 7 (Senegal); at 21 (Norway); SR. 1481 at 19 (Ivory Coast); SR. 1482 at 2 (Panama); at 6 (Uruguay); SR. 1481 at 19 (Ivory Coast); SR. 1482 at 2 (Panama); at 6 (Uruguay and Phillipines); at 10 (Costa Rica); at 12 (Indonesia); at 14 (Dahomey); SR. 1483 at 2 (El Salvador); at 6 (Cameroon); at 7 (Sierra Leone); at 8 (Guinea); at 11 (Egypt); at 13 (Peru). Other states which spoke in favor of the text as proposed by the Special Committee included: SR. 1476 at 5 (Belgium); SR. 1477 at 8, 9 (U.K.); SR. 1480 at 23 (USA); SR. 1482 at 13 (Yemen); SR. 1483 at 4 (Paraguay) which argued that Art. 3 (d) related only to an "unprovoked attack", hence the concern expressed by the coastal states was unjustified. Ghana cautioned against any attempt to prejudice the issues before the Law of the Sea Conference. SR. 1480 at 9.

175. Doc. A/C.6/L.988, 22 Oct. 1974. Peru was careful to note that it was not submitted as an amendment but as an attempt to find appropriate language for insertion. SR. 1483 at 14. Kenya had suggested that any formal statement should also incorporate the right of hot pursuit. SR. 1474 at 9.

176. SR. 1478 at 9.

177. SR. 1502 at 4. Peru insisted that the inclusion in the report gave it the same effect as if it had been in the text of the definition. SR. 1503 at 5, Gen. Ass. Plenary Meeting 2319 at 32. Also Mali, at 47, and Nepal, at 58-60, and Afghanistan, at 61.

178. Paraguay insisted that references in footnotes had the same legal value as inclusion in the text of the definition. SR. 1503 at Ecuador insisted on its previous interpretation of its rights, See SR. 1504 at 2. Japan considered the explanation of 3 (d) to be superfluous. Gen. Ass. Plenary Meeting 2319 at 36. Also the US, at 37; UK, at 38-40; and USSR, at 57.

179. A/8019, DOCUMENT 18 at 59, 60.

180. SR. 108 at 8; SR. 1443 at 10; A/8719, DOCUMENT 22 at 20.

181. A/9019, DOCUMENT 24 at 26. In 1974 a comma was added, after the word "state".

182. The USSR representative considered that Par. (e) was fully covered by paragraph (a). SR. 1443 at 10. The 1933 Soviet definition was very similar to the present Par. (e) in that it listed infringement of permission, particularly regarding duration or extension of the area as an act of aggression. Vol. I DOCUMENT 9 at 238.

183. A/9019, <u>DOCUMENT</u> 24 at 17. This was based on a proposal by Romania. Doc. A/AC.134/WG.4/R.6.

184. Vol. I <u>DOCUMENT</u> 11 at 8, 16. Compare Vol. I <u>DOCUMENT</u> 14.

185. SR. 1443 at 10; A/9019, <u>DOCUMENT</u> 24 at 19.

186. SR. 1472 at 10.

187. SR. 1474 at 9.

188. Professor Bowett has correctly noted that retaliation against the government of the territory may actually aid the guerrillas, who may be receiving aid from third states or even private individuals outside the country. "<u>Reprisals Involving Recourse to Armed Force</u>", 66 AJIL 1 (1972). See also Falk, R. "<u>The Beirut Raid and the Inter-national Law of Retaliation</u>" 63 AJIL 415 (1969); contra, Blum, Y.Z., "<u>The Beirut Raid and the International Double Standard</u>" 64 AJIL 73 (1970).

189. SR. 1477 at 6.

190. A/8019, <u>DOCUMENT</u> 18 at 56.

191. A/8719, <u>DOCUMENT</u> 22 at 15. This suggestion was originally made by Ambassador Rossides of Cyprus in 1971. SR. 81 at 3.

192. A/9019, <u>DOCUMENT</u> 24 at 23.

193. To France this meant that there could be no aggression until there was the crossing of a frontier. SR. 1474 at 10.

194. SR. 108 at 5 (Syria); SR. 108 at 9 (Iraq); SR. 107 at 5 (Egypt); SR. 1441 at 6 (GDR).

195. SR. 1443 at 10.

196. SR. 1442 at 4.

197. SR. 1441 at 16.

198. SR. 1442 at 16.

199. SR. 1443 at 16.

200. SR. 1444 at 4.

201. Indonesia considered the word "substantial" to be superfluous and ambiguous, since if the action were not substantial it would not be qualified as aggression. SR. 1482 at 12-13.

202. For an analysis of some of the problems relating to intervention, civil strife, and minor coercion, see Falk, R.A., Legal Order in a Violent World (1968).

203. Docs. of the Prep. Comm. for the Disarm. Conf., League of Nations, Series III at 101.

204. The final Netherlands statement expressed the hope that proportionality would continue to be considered, together with the question of shared culpability. See SR. 1473 at 3, Text of Statement of Mr. George Wehry at 5.

205. See Vol. I, DOCUMENT 3 (d), and Vol. I, DOCUMENT 6 at 25. In his closing address to the Special Committee the Japanese representative, Mr. Iguchi regretted the omission of the failure to rely on the pacific settlement of disputes and the massing of combat troops of a border as indications of aggression. A/9619, DOCUMENT 26 at 16. Guatemala referred to Res. 378 (V) on Duties of States in the Event of the Outbreak of Hostilities, according to which refusal to cease fire and withdraw would determine the aggressor. SR. 1479 at 8. See also, Wright, Q. "The Concept of Aggression in International Law" 29 AJIL 373 (1935) at 395.

206. See Goodrich and Hambro, Charter of the United Nations: Commentary and Documents (1949); Report to the President on the Results of the San Francisco Conference, Dept. of State Publ. 2349.

207. See Esfandiary M., "The Role of The General Assembly in Dealing with Threats to the Peace, Breaches of the Peace, and Acts of Aggression." (Unpublished Dissertation, Columbia Univ. 1970). See also Ed. Comment "The 'Uniting for Peace' Resolution of the U.N.", 45 AJIL 130 (1951).

208. See Preamble Paragraphs 2, 4, and 10, and substantive Articles 2, 3, 4, and 6.

209. SR. 1477 at 6, Gen. Ass. Plenary Meeting 2319 at 41. See contra. Gen. Ass. Plenary Meeting 2319 at 57 (USSR) and 42 (GDR).

210. SR. 1442 at 23, SR. 1475 at 8.

211. SR. 1441 at 20.

212. Ivory Coast drew attention to the Charter Art. 27 Para. 3, which requires Council members to abstain from voting when they are parties to the dispute. SR. 1481 at 19. Dahomey raised the question whether the prerogatives of the powerful states on the Security Council should be confirmed when Charter revision was being considered. SR. 1482 at 14. New Zealand's Mr. Quentin-Baxter noted that the Council might reach a valid or invalid decision for non-legal reasons, but the facts did not depend upon a determination by the Council. See SR. 1475 at 10.

213. See Derpa, R., Das Gewaltverbot der Satzung der Vereinten Nationen und die Anwendung nichtmilitärischer Gewalt (1970) at 84.

214. See Vol. I, DOCUMENT 11 at 16 (Politis Report); Vol. I, DOCUMENT 19 at 166 (Nuernberg); Vol. II, DOCUMENT 3 at 9 (ILC).

215. A/8719, DOCUMENT 22 at 23.

216. SR. 1444 at 3.

217. SR. 1444 at 4; SR. 1441 at 20.

218. SR. 1442 at 15.

219. See Doc. A/AC.134/WG.5/R.4.

220. A/9619, DOCUMENT 26 at 9.

221. At San Francisco Bolivia had proposed that intervention be listed as an act of aggression. Vol. I, DOCUMENT 17 (c) at 579; Prohibitions against intervention appeared in the Charter of the Organization of American States signed at Bogota on 30 April 1948. The definition of aggression did not seek to define the limits of permissible intervention.

222. See A/9019, DOCUMENT 24 at 17.

223. Id. at 20.

224. A/9619, DOCUMENT 26 at 32.

225. See Freeman, A. V. Responsibility of States for Unlawful Acts of Their Armed Forces (1957), Ferencz, B.B. "Compensating Victims of the Crimes of War", 12 Virginia Jour. of Int'l Law 343 (1972). The criminal liability of states is considered in Triffterer, O., "Jurisdiction over States for Crimes of State", Vol. II Bassiouni and Nanda, Eds. A Treatise on International Criminal Law (1973) at 86.

226. A/9619, DOCUMENT 26 at 33.

227. Yugoslavia argued that the present wording might give rise to the absurd interpretation that aggression was not a crime against peace and that a war of aggression might not give rise to international responsibility. A/9619, DOCUMENT 26 at 26, SR. 1479 at 4. Other states saw no valid basis for the distinction. A/9619 at 37 (USSR); at 39 (Mexico); SR. 1472 at 15 (Spain); SR. 1477 at 5 (Ukraine); SR. 1474 at 5 (Mongolia); SR. 1474 at 10 (Kenya); SR. 1478 at 17 (Sri Lanka); SR. 1479 at 7 (Guatemala); SR. 1479 at 13 (Algeria); SR. 1480 at 13 (Czech.); SR. 1481 at 19 (Ivory Coast); SR. 1482 at 9 (Tunisia); SR. 1482 at 18 (Greece); SR. 1483 at 4 (Paraguay); SR. 1483 at 5 (Cameroon).

228. Vol. I, DOCUMENT 22 supra.

229. A/1858, DOCUMENT 3 at 11.

230. Res. 599 (VI), DOCUMENT 4 at 17. This was referred to by Sri Lanka. SR. 1478 at 17.

231. McNair, A.D., Legal Effects of War (1944) at 1. Mr. Verosta of Austria suggested that the magnitude of the aggressive acts and/or the damage caused should determine whether or not there was a "war". SR. 1472 at 13. See Briggs, H.W. The Law of Nations (1942) 718-725.

232. See SR. 1477 at 7-8 (U.K.) SR. 1480 at 24 (USA).

233. See Minear, R.H., Victor's Justice - The Tokyo War Crimes Trials (1971).

234. See Baxter, R.R., "The Law of War", International Law Association 1873-1973, - The Present State of International Law 107 at 114. (1973).

235. Mr. Broms, Chairman of the Special Committee, pointed out in the Sixth Committee that the paragraph should not be interpreted to imply that aggression without war would not in the future lead to any criminal responsibility. The question had not been adequately debated, and its precise meaning would have to be clarified as the U.N. resumed its work on a draft code of offences against the peace and security of mankind. SR. 1471 at 4 - Mr. Robinson of Jamaica noted that legal responsibility could only be determined after tribunals had been set up to deal with the matter. SR. 1480 at 2.

236. A/9619, DOCUMENT 26 at 9.

237. A/9019, DOCUMENT 24 at 20.

238. Id. at 23; This was supported by Syria. A/9619, DOCUMENT 26 at 20. See also SR. 1479 at 10 (Dem. Yemen).

239. A/9019, DOCUMENT 24 at 20.

240. SR. 1444 at 7.

241. See Waldock, C.H., The Regulation of the Use of Force, 81 Receuil des Cours, 455, 481 (1952). Paraguay preferred "the use of armed force", instead of "aggression", to avoid an implication that territorial acquisition not resulting from aggression was lawful. SR. 1483 at 4.

242. Pakistan felt that the acquisition of territory by the use of force in any form, not merely by aggression, should also be covered by the article. SR. 1477 at 2.

243. The Spanish text used the singular "es", and the French text used the plural "sont". In the official Annexes "are" was corrected to "is".

244. For an outline of the debate on self-defense see Ferencz, B.B., "Defining Aggression: Where It Stands and Where It's Going" 66 AJIL 491 at 500-502 (1972). Cuba, in the final debate in the Sixth Committee, noted that only the Security Council, and not regional organizations, could authorize the use of force. SR. 1479 at 16.

245. See A/9019, DOCUMENT 24 at 28.

246. A/8719, DOCUMENT 22 at 23.

247. See SR. 63 at 5 (Mr. Schwebel for USA); SR. 74 at 8 (Mr. Steel for U.K.). See also SR. 72 at 7 (Mr. Mutuale of Congo); SR. 74 at 4 (Mr. Ofstad of Norway); Bowett. D.W. Self-Defense in International Law, at 269 (1958).

248. An analysis of self-defense, necessity and proportionality is contained in Mc Dougal and Feliciano, Law and Minimum World Public Order, at 217-260 (1967).

249. M. Bessou of France noted that the Article was alien to the definition since it dealt with the right of peoples whereas the definition was concerned with sovereign states. A/9619, DOCUMENT 26 at 22.

250. Yugoslavia felt that the reference to forcible deprivation was inappropriate since people could effectively be deprived of their rights by non-forcible means. SR. 1479 at 4-5. The British saw the word "forcibly" as a key term since those not "forcibly deprived" would not be justified in resisting. A/9619, DOCUMENT 26 at 32.

251. A/8019, DOCUMENT 18 at 58. At the last debate in the Sixth Committee Jamaica thought the word "shall" instead of "could" in the first line would be an improvement. SR. 1480 at 3.

252. A/8719, DOCUMENT 22 at 19.

253. Mr. Rosenstock, who represented the USA on both the "Friendly Relations" Committee and the Aggression Committee noted that the question whether force might be used was left sufficiently vague to permit acceptance by both those who believed states had a duty to send arms to support self-determination and those who felt that only moral and political support was permissible. "The Declaration on Principles of International Law Concerning Friendly Relations - a Survey, 65 AJIL 713 at 732 (1971). See also "Principles of International Law Concerning Friendly Relations and Cooperation: Essays." M. Sahović, Ed. (1973); Reviewed by Mr. Rosenstock in 68 AJIL 750 (1974).

254. A/8719, DOCUMENT 22 at 19.

255. A/9019, DOCUMENT 24 at 17.

256. SR. 108 at 12.

257. SR. 108 at 8 (France). Both Spain and Italy expressed their concern about the need to avoid territorial disruption, and Spain wanted "Territorial integrity" added as one of the rights listed in Article 7, but dropped it in exchange for the reference to territorial integrity tacked on to preambular paragraph six. See SR. 1472 at 11 (Italy), SR. 1472 at 15 (Spain). See also SR. 1477 at 3 (Pakistan).

258. Those favoring a broad interpretation and the right to use "any means at their disposal" included: SR. 113 at 11 (Yugoslavia); SR. 1472 at 18 (Jordan - but only after peaceful means had failed); SR. 1475 at 6 (China); SR. 1476 at 7 (GDR); SR. 1478 at 12 (Congo); SR. 1479 at 10 (Dem. Yemen); SR. 1479 at 13 (Algeria); SR. 1479 at 4 (Yugo.); SR. 1480 at 9 (Ghana); SR. 1481 at 19 (Ivory Coast); SR. 1482 at 9 (Tunisia); SR. 1482 at 4 (Burundi); SR. 1483 at 6 (Cameroon); SR. 1483 at 11 (Egypt); Also A/9619, DOCUMENT 26 at 15 (Madagascar); at 20 (Syria); at 40 (Egypt). Attention was also drawn to Res.

3070 (XXVIII) in which the Assembly reaffirmed "the legitimacy of the peoples struggle for liberation from colonial and foreign domination and alien subjugation by all means available including "armed struggle", and Res. 3103 (XXVIII) giving such persons legal status as combattants. Kenya, considering itself bound by the OAU Charter, would have specifically included racist oppression and apartheid against which any means might lawfully be used. SR. 1442 at 9, SR. 1474 at 9. Also SR. 1480 at 8 (Uganda).

259. See Res. 3166 (XXVIII), 14 Dec. 1973, Convention on the Prevention and Punishment of Crimes against Internationally Protected Persons, including Diplomatic Agents. Preambular Paragraph 4 recognizes that the convention does not prejudice the exercise of the right of self-determination and independence in accordance with the Charter and the "Friendly Relations" Declaration by "peoples struggling against colonialism, alien domination, foreign occupation, racial discrimination and apartheid." The attempt to formulate measures to prevent international terrorism encountered the same problem. See GAOR, 28th Sess. Annexes, Agenda Item 94, A/9410 (Dec. 1973).

260. Those states which spoke out against an authorization to use force included: The USA, whose Mr. Rosenstock noted that, when read in conjunction with Article 6, Article 7 could not legitimize acts of force which would otherwise be illegal. SR. 1480 at 24, also A/96-19, DOCUMENT 26 at 24. The Netherlands cautioned that the right to receive support did not mean "armed support". SR. 1473 at 5. See also SR. 1476 at 6 (Belgium); SR. 1477 at 3 (Pakistan); SR. 1478 at 8 (FRG and Portugal); 1473 at 9 and A/9619 at 35 (Canada). See Emerson, R., "Self-Determination" 65 AJIL 459 (1971); Nanda, V.P., "Self-Determination in International Law" 66 AJIL 321 (1972); Stevenson, J.R., "International Law and the Export of Terrorism" Record of the Ass. of the Bar of the City of New York 716 (1972). On the relativity of political crimes see Shafer, S. The Political Criminal (1974).

261. A/9019, DOCUMENT 24 at 17.

262. Doc. A.C.6/L.993 submitted on 22 Nov. 1974, SR. 1502 at 5. Mr. H. Hassouna of Egypt objected to the weakness and would have preferred a Declaration rather than a Resolution, in order to give the definition greater strength. SR. 1504 at 8.

263. SR. 1503 at 3, 26 Nov. 1974.

264. SR. 1503 at 3.

265. SR. 1503 at 4.

266. SR. 1503 at 5.

267. See SR. 1503 at 8-9 (Tanzania), SR. 1503 at 4 (El Salvador), SR. 1504 at 2 (Ecuador), SR. 1504 at 6 (Bolivia).

268. See SR. 1503 at 6-8, SR. 1505 at 15-18.

269. A/9890, DOCUMENT 27, 6 Dec. 1974.

270. See Gen. Ass. Plenary Meeting 2319 at 26, 31, 42, 51.

271. Id. at 32.

272. For a few of the writings noting the need for change see Clark, G., and Sohn, L.B. World Peace Through World Law, Haas, E., Beyond the Nation State (1964), Yost, C. The Insecurity of Nations (1968), Jessup, P., The Price of International Justice (1971), McWhinney, E., International Law and World Revolution (1967), Green, A., Political Integration by Jurisprudence (1969), Roling, B.V.A., "International Law and the Maintenance of Peace" IV Netherlands Yearbook of Int'l Law (1973), Bowett, D.W. The Law of International Institutions (1970), and many studies by the Center for the Study of Democratic Institutions, Santa Barbara, California.

273. For a survey of present thinking on the problem of an international criminal court see Stone, J., and Woetzel, R.K., Eds. Toward a Feasible International Court (1970), reviewed by Ferencz, B. 66 AJIL 213 (1972). Prof. Woetzel is President of the Foundation for the Establishment of an International Criminal Court, which has, with the support of many scholars, been drafting a code and statutes for such a court. Comments by Gross, L., 67 AJIL 508 (1973); 68 AJIL 306, 717 (1974). See also "The Court of Man", Center for the Study of Democratic Institutions (1969), N.Y. Times Apr. 24, 1973, in which Gottlieb, G.H., urges the establishment of an extra-national court of experts to cope with conflict situations.

DOCUMENTS

PART THREE

THE UNITED NATIONS MOVES TO DEFINE AGGRESSION

DOCUMENT 1

DOCUMENT A/C.1/608

Union of Soviet Socialist Republics : draft resolution on the definition of aggression

[*Original text : Russian*]
[*4 November 1950*]

The General Assembly,

Considering it necessary, in the interests of general security and to facilitate agreement on the maximum reductions of armaments, to define the concept of aggression as accurately as possible, so as to forestall any pretext which might be used to justify it,

Recognizing that all States have equal rights to independence, security and the defence of their territory,

Inspired by the desire, in the interests of general peace, to guarantee all nations the right freely to develop by such means as are appropriate to them and at the rate which they consider to be necessary, and for that purpose to provide the fullest possible protection for their security, their independence and the integrity of their territory, and also for their right to defend themselves against aggression or invasion from without, but only within the limits of their own countries, and

Considering it necessary to formulate essential directives for such international organs as may be called upon to determine which party is guilty of attack,

Declares :

1. That in an international conflict that State shall be declared the attacker which first commits one of the following acts :

(*a*) Declaration of war against another State;

(*b*) Invasion by its armed forces, even without a declaration of war, of the territory of another State;

(*c*) Bombardment by its land, sea or air forces of the territory of another State or the carrying out of a deliberate attack on the ships or aircraft of the latter;

(*d*) The landing or leading of its land, sea or air forces inside the boundaries of another State without the permission of the government of the latter, or the violation of the conditions of such permission, particularly as regards the length of their stay or the extent of the area in which they may stay;

(*e*) Naval blockade of the coasts or ports of another State;

2. Attacks such as those referred to in paragraph 1 may not be justified by any arguments of a political, strategic or economic nature, or by the desire to exploit natural riches in the territory of the State attacked or to derive any other kind of advantages or privileges, or by reference to the amount of capital invested in the State attacked or to any other particular interests in its territory, or by the affirmation that the State attacked lacks the distinguishing marks of statehood;

In particular, the following may not be used as justifications for attack :

A. The internal position of any State, as, for example :

(*a*) The backwardness of any nation politically, economically or culturally;

(*b*) Alleged shortcomings of its administration;

(*c*) Any danger which may threaten the life or property of aliens;

(*d*) Any revolutionary or counter-revolutionary movement, civil war, disorders or strikes;

(*e*) The establishment or maintenance in any State of any political, economic or social system;

B. Any acts, legislation or orders of any State, as for example :

(*a*) The violation of international treaties;

(*b*) The violation of rights and interests in the sphere of trade, concessions or any other kind of economic activity acquired by another State or its citizens;

(*c*) The rupture of diplomatic or economic relations;

(*d*) Measures in connexion with an economic or financial boycott;

(*e*) Repudiation of debts;

(*f*) Prohibition or restriction of immigration or modification of the status of foreigners;

(*g*) The violation of privileges granted to the official representatives of another State;

(*h*) Refusal to allow the passage of armed forces proceeding to the territory of a third State;

(*i*) Measures of a religious or anti-religious nature;

(*j*) Frontier incidents.

3. In the event of the mobilization or concentration by another State of considerable armed forces near its frontier, the State which is threatened by such action shall have the right of recourse to diplomatic or other means of securing a peaceful settlement of international disputes. It may also in the meantime adopt requisite measures of a military nature similar to those described above, without, however, crossing the frontier.

DOCUMENT 2

378 (V). Duties of States in the event of the outbreak of hostilities

A

The General Assembly,

Reaffirming the Principles embodied in the Charter, which require that the force of arms shall not be resorted to except in the common interest, and shall not be used against the territorial integrity or political independence of any State,

Desiring to create a further obstacle to the outbreak of war, even after hostilities have started, and to facilitate the cessation of the hostilities by the action of the parties themselves, thus contributing to the peaceful settlement of disputes,

1. *Recommends:*

(*a*) That if a State becomes engaged in armed conflict with another State or States, it take all steps practicable in the circumstances and compatible with the right of self-defence to bring the armed conflict to an end at the earliest possible moment;

(*b*) In particular, that such State shall immediately, and in any case not later than twenty-four hours after the outbreak of the hostilities, make a public statement wherein it will proclaim its readiness, provided that the States with which it is in conflict will do the same, to discontinue all military operations and withdraw all its military forces which have invaded the territory or territorial water of another State or crossed a demarcation line, either on terms agreed by the parties to the conflict or under conditions to be indicated to the parties by the appropriate organs of the United Nations;

(*c*) That such State immediately notify the Secretary-General, for communication to the Security Council and to the Members of the United Nations, of the statement made in accordance with the preceding subparagraph and of the circumstances in which the conflict has arisen;

(*d*) That such State, in its notification to the Secretary-General, invite the appropriate organs of the United Nations to dispatch the Peace Observation Commission[4] to the area in which the conflict has arisen, if the Commission is not already functioning there;

(*e*) That the conduct of the States concerned in relation to the matters covered by the foregoing recommendations be taken into account in any determination of responsibility for the breach of the peace or act of aggression in the case under consideration and in all other relevant proceedings before the appropriate organs of the United Nations;

---

[4] See resolution 377 A (V), section B.

2. *Determines* that the provisions of the present resolution in no way impair the rights and obligations of States under the Charter of the United Nations nor the decisions or recommendations of the Security Council, the General Assembly or any other competent organ of the United Nations.

308th plenary meeting,
17 November 1950.

B

The General Assembly,

Considering that the question raised by the proposal[5] of the Union of Soviet Socialist Republics can better be examined in conjunction with matters under consideration by the International Law Commission, a subsidiary organ of the United Nations,

Decides to refer the proposal of the Union of Soviet Socialist Republics and all the records[6] of the First Committee dealing with this question to the International Law Commission, so that the latter may take them into consideration and formulate its conclusions as soon as possible.

308th plenary meeting,
17 November 1950.

380 (V). Peace through deeds

The General Assembly,

Recognizing the profound desire of all mankind to live in enduring peace and security, and in freedom from fear and want,

Confident that, if all governments faithfully reflect this desire and observe their obligations under the Charter, lasting peace and security can be established,

Condemning the intervention of a State in the internal affairs of another State for the purpose of changing its legally established government by the threat or use of force,

1. *Solemnly* reaffirms that, whatever the weapons used, any aggression, whether committed openly, or by fomenting civil strife in the interest of a foreign Power, or otherwise, is the gravest of all crimes against peace and security throughout the world;

---

[5] See document A/C.1/608.
[6] See *Official Records of the General Assembly, Fifth Session, First Committee,* 384th to 390th meetings inclusive.

2. *Determines* that for the realization of lasting peace and security it is indispensable:

(1) That prompt united action be taken to meet aggression wherever it arises;

(2) That every nation agree:

(*a*) To accept effective international control of atomic energy, under the United Nations, on the basis already approved[8] by the General Assembly in order to make effective the prohibition of atomic weapons;

(*b*) To strive for the control and elimination, under the United Nations, of all other weapons of mass destruction;

(*c*) To regulate all armaments and armed forces under a United Nations system of control and inspection, with a view to their gradual reduction;

(*d*) To reduce to a minimum the diversion for armaments of its human and economic resources and to strive towards the development of such resources for the general welfare, with due regard to the needs of the under-developed areas of the world;

3. *Declares* that these goals can be attained if all the Members of the United Nations demonstrate by their deeds their will to achieve peace.

308th plenary meeting,
17 November 1950.

---

[8] See resolutions 1 (I), 41 (I), 191 (III), 192 (III), 290 (IV) and 299 (IV).

DOCUMENT 3

Chapter III

QUESTION OF DEFINING AGGRESSION[18]

35. The General Assembly, on 17 November 1950, adopted resolution 378 B (V) which reads as follows:

"*The General Assembly,*

"*Considering* that the question raised by the proposal of the Union of Soviet Socialist Republics can better be examined in conjunction with matters under consideration by the International Law Commission, a subsidiary organ of the United Nations,

"*Decides* to refer the proposal of the Union of Soviet Socialist Republics and all the records of the First Committee dealing with this question to the International Law Commission, so that the latter may take them into consideration and formulate its conclusions as soon as possible".

36. The foregoing resolution was adopted in connexion with the agenda item "Duties of States in the event of the outbreak of hostilities". The proposal of the Union of Soviet Socialist Republics,[19] referred to in this resolution, was originally submitted to the First Committee of the General Assembly. It provided that the General Assembly "considering it necessary . . . to define the concept of aggression as accurately as possible", declares, *inter alia,* that "in an international conflict that State shall be declared the attacker which first commits" one of the acts enumerated in the proposal.

37. In pursuance of the resolution of the General Assembly, the International Law Commission, at its 92nd to 96th, 108th, 109th, 127th to 129th, and 133rd meetings, considered the question raised by the aforementioned proposal of the USSR and, in that connexion, studied the records of the First Committee relating thereto.

38. The Commission first considered its terms of reference under the resolution in the light of the relevant discussions in the First Committee. Some members of the Commission were of the opinion that this resolution merely meant that the Commission should take the Soviet proposal and the discussions thereon in the First Committee into consideration when preparing the draft code of offences against the peace and security of mankind. The majority of the Commission, however, held the view that the Commission had been requested by the General Assembly to make an attempt to define aggression and to submit a report on the result of its efforts.

39. The Commission had before it a report entitled "The Possibility and Desirability of a Definition of Aggression", presented by Mr. Spiropoulos, special rapporteur on the draft code of offences against the peace and security of mankind (A/CN.4/44, chapter II). After a survey of previous attempts to define aggression, the special rapporteur stated that "whenever governments are called upon to decide on the existence or non-existence of 'aggression under international law', they base their judgment on criteria derived from the 'natural', so to speak, notion of aggression . . . and not on legal constructions". Analysing this notion of aggression, he stated that it was composed of both objective and subjective elements, namely, the fact that a State had committed an act of violence and was the first to do so and the fact that this violence was committed with an aggressive intention (*animus aggressionis*). But what kind of violence, direct or indirect, or what degree of violence constituted aggression could not be determined *a priori.* It depended on the circumstances in the particular case. He came to the conclusion that this "natural notion" of aggression is a "concept *per se*", which "is not susceptible of definition". "A 'legal' definition of aggression would be an artificial construction", which could never be comprehensive enough to comprise all imaginable cases of aggression, since the methods of aggression are in a constant process of evolution.

40. Two other members of the Commission, Mr. Amado and Mr. Alfaro, submitted memoranda on the question. Mr. Amado stated in his memorandum (A/CN.4/L.6 and Corr.1) that a definition of aggression based on an enumeration of aggressive acts could not be satisfactory, as such an enumeration could not be complete and any omission would be dangerous. He suggested that the Commission might adopt a general and flexible formula laying down that:

"Any war not waged in exercise of the right of self-defence or in application of the provisions of Article 42 of the Charter of the United Nations [is] an aggressive war".

Such a formula could, in his opinion, be applied to any factual situation and might be used by the competent organs of the United Nations without restricting their necessary freedom of action.

41. Mr. Alfaro, in his memorandum (A/CN.4/L.8), also advocated an abstract definition of aggression. On the basis of an examination of previous attempts to define aggression he expressed the view that the failure to find a satisfactory formula was due to the fact that these definitions had been based on the idea of an enumeration of various acts constituting aggression.

---

[18] Mr. Hudson voted against this chapter of the report on the ground that in resolution 378 B (V), the General Assembly did not request the Commission to formulate a definition of aggression.
[19] A/C.1/108.

In his opinion, a satisfactory result could be achieved only if the enumerative method which had proved unsuccessful were abandoned in favour of an effort to establish an abstract definition. He presented, in conclusion, a formula for such a definition (quoted in paragraph 46 below).

42. On the other hand, Mr. Yepes submitted a proposal (A/CN.4/L.7) for the determination of the aggressor based on the enumerative method. This proposal, however, was subsequently superseded by another (A/CN.4/L.12) by the same author which defined aggression in general terms as follows:

"For the purposes of Article 39 of the United Nations Charter an act of aggression shall be understood to mean any direct or indirect use of violence (force) by a State or group of States against the territorial integrity or political independence of another State or group of States.

"Violence (force) exercised by irregular bands organized within the territory of a State or outside its territory with the active or passive complicity of that State shall be considered as aggression within the meaning of the preceding paragraph.

"The use of violence (force) in the exercise of the right of individual or collective self-defence recognized by Article 51 of the Charter or in the execution of a decision duly adopted by a competent organ of the United Nations shall not be held to constitute an act of aggression.

"No political, economic, military or other consideration may serve as an excuse or justification for an act of aggression".

43. Another proposal (A/CN.4/L.11 and Corr.1) was submitted by Mr. Hsu in which particular stress was laid on indirect aggression. This draft was worded as follows:

"Aggression, which is a crime under international law, is the hostile act of a State against another State, committed by (a) the employment of armed force other than in self-defence or the implementation of United Nations enforcement action; or (b) the arming of organized bands or of third States, hostile to the victim State, for offensive purposes; or (c) the fomenting of civil strife in the victim State in the interest of some foreign State; or (d) any other illegal resort to force, openly or otherwise".

44. Finally, Mr. Córdova, with a view to including in the draft code of offences against the peace and security of mankind a provision which would make aggression and the threat of aggression offences under the code, submitted the following draft (A/CN.4/L.10):

"Aggression is the direct or indirect employment by the authorities of a State of armed force against another State for any purpose other than national or collective self-defence or execution of a decision by a competent organ of the United Nations.

"The threat of aggression should also be deemed to be a crime under this article".

45. The Commission considered the question whether it should follow the enumerative method or try to draft a definition of aggression in general terms. The sense of the Commission was that it was undesirable to define aggression by a detailed enumeration of aggressive acts, since no enumeration could be exhaustive. Furthermore, it was thought inadvisable unduly to limit the freedom of judgment of the competent organs of the United Nations by a rigid and necessarily incomplete list of acts constituting aggression. It was therefore decided that the only practical course was to aim at a general and abstract definition.

46. Undertaking to define aggression in general terms, the Commission took as a basis of discussion the text submitted by Mr. Alfaro in his memorandum (A/CN.4/L.8) as it was the broadest general definition before the Commission. Mr. Alfaro's draft read as follows:

"Aggression is the use of force by one State or group of States, or by any government or group of governments, against the territory and people of other States or governments, in any manner, by any methods, for any reasons and for any purposes, except individual or collective self-defence against armed attack or coercive action by the United Nations".

47. The Commission gave consideration to the question whether indirect aggression should be comprehended in the definition. It was felt that a definition of aggression should cover not only force used openly by one State against another, but also indirect forms of aggression such as the fomenting of civil strife by one State in another, the arming by a State of organized bands for offensive purposes directed against another State, and the sending of "volunteers" to engage in hostilities against another State. In this connexion account was taken of resolution 380 (V), adopted by the General Assembly on 17 November 1950, which states, *inter alia,* that the General Assembly

"*Solemnly* reaffirms that, whatever the weapons used, any aggression, whether committed openly, or by fomenting civil strife in the interest of a foreign Power, or otherwise, is the gravest of all crimes against peace and security throughout the world".

48. Opinion was divided on the question whether, in addition to the employment of force, the threat to use force should also constitute aggression. Some members of the Commission considered that threat of force amounted only to a threat of aggression, while others contended that it should be covered by the definition in view of the fact that threat of force had been used for aggressive purposes. The Commission finally decided to amend the definition proposed by Mr. Alfaro by including threat of force in the definition.

49. The Commission also adopted other drafting changes in the draft definition of Mr. Alfaro. This definition, as finally amended, read as follows:

"Aggression is the threat or use of force by a State or government against another State, in any manner, whatever the weapons employed and whether openly or otherwise, for any reason or for any purpose other than individual or collective self-defence or in pursuance of a decision or recommendation by a competent organ of the United Nations".

50. Some members of the Commission, however, considered this definition unsatisfactory on the ground that, in their opinion, it did not comprehend all conceivable acts of aggression and that it might prove

to be dangerously restrictive of the necessary freedom of action of the organs of the United Nations, if they were called upon in the future to apply the definition to specific cases. Some other members maintained that it did not include one or another element which they deemed essential.

51. When submitted to the final vote, the definition was rejected by 7 votes to 3, with one abstention, the vote being taken by roll-call at the request of one member, as follows:

In favour: Messrs. Alfaro, Córdova and François

Against: Messrs. Amado, Brierly, Hsu, el-Khouri, Sandström, Spiropoulos and Yepes

Abstaining: Mr. Hudson

Absent: Mr. Scelle.

52. Mr. Alfaro thereupon proposed that the Commission should not abandon its efforts to define aggression but should make further attempts on the basis of each of the texts submitted by other members. This proposal was rejected by a roll-call of 6 to 4, with one abstention, as follows:

In favour: Messrs. Alfaro, Córdova, Hsu and Yepes

Against: Messrs. Amado, Brierly, François, Hudson, el-Khouri and Sandström

Abstaining: Mr. Spiropoulos

Absent: Mr. Scelle.

53. The matter was later reconsidered at the request of Mr. Scelle who in a memorandum (A/CN.4/L.19

and Corr.1) submitted a general definition of aggression and proposed that aggression should be explicitly declared to be an offence against the peace and security of mankind. Mr. Scelle's definition read as follows:

"Aggression is an offence against the peace and security of mankind. This offence consists in any resort to force contrary to the provisions of the Charter of the United Nations, for the purpose of modifying the state of positive international law in force or resulting in the disturbance of public order"

This proposal was discussed in connexion with the preparation of the draft code of offences against the peace and security of mankind. Proposals were made by other members to a similar effect. The Commission decided to include among the offences defined in the draft code any act of aggression and any threat of aggression.

The following paragraphs were therefore inserted in article 2 of the draft code:

"The following acts are offences against the peace and security of mankind:

"(1) Any act of aggression, including the employment by the authorities of a State of armed force against another State for any purpose other than national or collective self-defence or in pursuance of a decision or recommendation by a competent organ of the United Nations.

"(2) Any threat by the authorities of a State to resort to an act of aggression against another State".

Chapter IV

DRAFT CODE OF OFFENCES AGAINST THE PEACE AND SECURITY OF MANKIND

Introduction

54. By resolution 177 (II) of 21 November 1947, the General Assembly decided:

"To entrust the formulation of the principles of international law recognized in the Charter of the Nürnberg Tribunal and in the judgment of the Tribunal to the International Law Commission, the members of which will, in accordance with resolution 174 (II), be elected at the next session of the General Assembly,"

and directed the Commission to

"(a) Formulate the principles of international law recognized in the Charter of the Nürnberg Tribunal and in the judgment of the Tribunal, and

"(b) Prepare a draft code of offences against the peace and security of mankind, indicating clearly the place to be accorded to the principles mentioned in sub-paragraph (a) above".

In 1950, the International Law Commission reported to the General Assembly its formulation under sub-paragraph (a) of resolution 177 (II). By resolution 488 (V) of 12 December 1950, the General Assembly invited the governments of Member States to express

their observations on the formulation, and requested the Commission:

"In preparing the draft code of offences against the peace and security of mankind, to take account of the observations made on this formulation by delegations during the fifth session of the General Assembly and of any observations which may be made by governments."

55. The preparation of a draft code of offences against the peace and security of mankind was given preliminary consideration by the Commission at its first session, in 1949, when the Commission appointed Mr. Spiropoulos special rapporteur on the subject, and invited him to prepare a working paper for submission to the Commission at its second session. The Commission also decided that a questionnaire should be circulated to governments inquiring what offences, apart from those recognized in the Charter and judgment of the Nürnberg Tribunal, should be included in the draft code.

56. At its second session, in 1950, Mr. Spiropoulos presented his report (A/CN.4/25) to the Commission, which took it as a basis of discussion. The subject was considered by the Commission at its 54th to 62nd and 72nd meetings. The Commission also took into con-

11

sideration the replies received from governments (A/CN.4/19, part II, A/CN.4/19/Add.1 and Add.2) to its questionnaire. In the light of the deliberations of the Commission, a drafting committee, composed of Messrs. Alfaro, Hudson and Spiropoulos, prepared a provisional text (A/CN.4/R.6) which was referred by the Commission without discussion to Mr. Spiropoulos, who was requested to continue the work on the subject and to submit a new report to the Commission at its third session.

57. At the third session, in 1951, Mr. Spiropoulos submitted a second report (A/CN.4/44) containing a new draft of a code and also a digest of the observations on the Commission's formulation of the Nürnberg principles made by delegations during the fifth session of the General Assembly. The Commission also had before it the observations received from governments (A/CN.4/45 and Corr.1, A/CN.4/45/Add.1 and Add.2) on this formulation. Taking into account the observations referred to above, the Commission considered the subject at its 89th to 92nd, 106th to 111th, 129th and 133rd meetings, and adopted a draft Code of Offences against the Peace and Security of Mankind as set forth herein below.

58. In submitting this draft code to the General Assembly, the Commission wishes to present the following observations as to some general questions which arose in the course of the preparation of the text:

(a) The Commission first considered the meaning of the term "offences against the peace and security of mankind", contained in resolution 177 (II). The view of the Commission was that the meaning of this term should be limited to offences which contain a political element and which endanger or disturb the maintenance of international peace and security. For these reasons, the draft code does not deal with questions concerning conflicts of legislation and jurisdiction in international criminal matters; nor does it include such matters as piracy, traffic in dangerous drugs, traffic in women and children, slavery, counterfeiting currency, damage to submarine cables, etc.

(b) The Commission thereafter discussed the meaning of the phrase "indicating clearly the place to be accorded to" the Nürnberg principles. The sense of the Commission was that this phrase should not be interpreted as meaning that the Nürnberg principles would have to be inserted in their entirety in the draft code. The Commission felt that the phrase did not preclude it from suggesting modification or development of these principles for the purpose of their incorporation in the draft code. It was not thought necessary to indicate the exact extent to which the various Nürnberg principles had been incorporated in the draft code. Only a general reference to the corresponding Nürnberg principles was deemed practicable.

(c) The Commission decided to deal with the criminal responsibility of individuals only. It may be recalled in this connexion that the Nürnberg Tribunal stated in its judgment: "Crimes against international law are committed by men, not by abstract entities, and only by punishing individuals who commit such crimes can the provisions of international law be enforced."

(d) The Commission has not considered itself called upon to propose methods by which a code may be given

binding force. It has therefore refrained from drafting an instrument for implementing the code. The offences set forth are characterized in article 1 as international crimes. Hence, the Commission has envisaged the possibility of an international tribunal for the trial and punishment of persons committing such offences. The Commission has taken note of the action of the General Assembly in setting up a special committee to prepare draft conventions and proposals relating to the establishment of an international criminal court. Pending the establishment of a competent international criminal court, a transitional measure might be adopted providing for the application of the code by national courts. Such a measure would doubtless be considered in drafting the instrument by which the code would be put into force.

TEXT OF THE DRAFT CODE

59. The draft Code of Offences against the Peace and Security of Mankind, as adopted by the Commission, reads as follows:

Article 1

Offences against the peace and security of mankind, as defined in this Code, are crimes under international law, for which the responsible individuals shall be punishable.

This article is based upon the principle of individual responsibility for crimes under international law. This principle is recognized by the Charter and judgment of the Nürnberg Tribunal, and in the Commission's formulation of the Nürnberg principles it is stated as follows: "Any person who commits an act which constitutes a crime under international law is responsible therefor and liable to punishment."

Article 2

The following acts are offences against the peace and security of mankind:

(1) Any act of aggression, including the employment by the authorities of a State of armed force against another State for any purpose other than national or collective self-defence or in pursuance of a decision or recommendation by a competent organ of the United Nations.

In laying down that any act of aggression is an offence against the peace and security of mankind, this paragraph is in consonance with resolution 380 (V), adopted by the General Assembly on 17 November 1950, in which the General Assembly solemnly reaffirms that any aggression "is the gravest of all crimes against peace and security throughout the world".

The paragraph also incorporates, in substance, that part of article 6, paragraph (a), of the Charter of the Nürnberg Tribunal, which defines as "crimes against peace", inter alia, the "initiation or waging of a war of aggression".

While every act of aggression constitutes a crime under paragraph (1), no attempt is made to enumerate such acts exhaustively. It is expressly provided that the employment of armed force in the circumstances specified in the paragraph is an act of aggression. It is, however, possible that aggression can be committed also by other acts, including some of those referred to in other paragraphs of article 2.

Provisions against the use of force have been included in many international instruments, such as the Covenant of the League of Nations, the Treaty for the Renunciation of War of 27 August 1928, the Anti-War Treaty of Non-Aggression and Conciliation, signed at Rio de Janeiro, 10 October 1933, the Act of Chapultepec of 8 March 1945, the Pact of the Arab League of 22 March 1945, the Inter-American Treaty of Reciprocal Assistance of 2 September 1947, and the Charter of the Organization of American States, signed at Bogotá, 30 April 1948.

85

The use of force is prohibited by Article 2, paragraph 4, of the Charter of the United Nations, which binds all Members to "refrain in their international relations from the . . . use of force against the territorial integrity or political independence of any State, or in any other manner inconsistent with the Purposes of the United Nations". The same prohibition is contained in the draft Declaration on Rights and Duties of States, prepared by the International Law Commission, which, in article 9, provides that "every State has the duty to refrain from resorting to war as an instrument of national policy, and to refrain from . . . the use of force against the territorial integrity or political independence of another State, or in any other manner inconsistent with international law and order". ·

The offence defined in this paragraph can be committed only by the authorities of a State. A criminal responsibility of private individuals under international law may, however, arise under the provisions of paragraph (12) of the present article.

(2) Any threat by the authorities of a State to resort to an act of aggression against another State.

This paragraph is based upon the consideration that not only acts of aggression but also the threat of aggression presents a grave danger to the peace and security of mankind and should be regarded as an international crime.

Article 2, paragraph 4, of the Charter of the United Nations prescribes that all Members shall "refrain in their international relations from the threat . . . of force against the territorial integrity or political independence of any State, or in any other manner inconsistent with the Purposes of the United Nations". Similarly, the draft Declaration on Rights and Duties of States, prepared by the International Law Commission, provides, in article 9, that "every State has the duty . . . to refrain from the threat . . . of force against the territorial integrity or political independence of another State, or in any other manner inconsistent with international law and order".

The offence defined in this paragraph can be committed only by the authorities of a State. A criminal responsibility of private individuals under international law may, however, arise under the provisions of paragraph (12) of the present article.

(3) The preparation by the authorities of a State for the employment of armed force against another State for any purpose other than national or collective self-defence or in pursuance of a decision or recommendation by a competent organ of the United Nations.

In prohibiting the preparation for the employment of armed force (except under certain specified conditions) this paragraph incorporates in substance that part of article 6, paragraph (a), of the Charter of the Nürnberg Tribunal which defines as "crimes against peace", inter alia, "planning" and "preparation" of "a war of aggression . . .". As used in this paragraph the term "preparation" includes "planning". It is considered that "planning" is punishable only if it results in preparatory acts and thus becomes an element in the preparation for the employment of armed force.

The offence defined in this paragraph can be committed only by the authorities of a State. A criminal responsibility of private individuals under international law may, however, arise under the provisions of paragraph (12) of the present article.

(4) The incursion into the territory of a State from the territory of another State by armed bands acting for a political purpose.

The offence defined in this paragraph can be committed only by the members of the armed bands, and they are individually responsible. A criminal responsibility of the authorities of a State under international law may, however, arise under the provisions of paragraph (12) of the present article.

(5) The undertaking or encouragement by the authorities of a State of activities calculated to foment civil strife in another State, or the toleration by the authorities of a State of organized activities calculated to foment civil strife in another State.

In its resolution 380 (V) of 17 November 1950 the General Assembly declared that "fomenting civil strife in the interest of a foreign Power" was aggression.

The draft Declaration on Rights and Duties of States prepared by the International Law Commission provides, in article 4: "Every State has the duty to refrain from fomenting civil strife in the territory of another State, and to prevent the organization within its territory of activities calculated to foment such civil strife".

The offence defined in this paragraph can be committed only by the authorities of a State. A criminal responsibility of private individuals under international law may, however, arise under the provisions of paragraph (12) of the present article.

(6) The undertaking or encouragement by the authorities of a State of terrorist activities in another State, or the toleration by the authorities of a State of organized activities calculated to carry out terrorist acts in another State.

Article 1 of the Convention for the Prevention and Punishment of Terrorism of 16 November 1937 contained a prohibition of the encouragement by a State of terrorist activities directed against another State.

The offence defined in this paragraph can be committed only by the authorities of a State. A criminal responsibility of private individuals under international law may, however, arise under the provisions of paragraph (12) of the present article.

(7) Acts by the authorities of a State in violation of its obligations under a treaty which is designed to ensure international peace and security by means of restrictions or limitations on armaments, or on military training, or on fortifications, or of other restrictions of the same character.

It may be recalled that the League of Nations' Committee on Arbitration and Security considered the failure to observe conventional restrictions such as those mentioned in this paragraph as raising, under many circumstances, a presumption of aggression. (Memorandum on articles 10, 11 and 16 of the Covenant, submitted by Mr. Rutgers. League of Nations document C.A.S. 10, 6 February 1928.)

The offence defined in this paragraph can be committed only by the authorities of a State. A criminal responsibility of private individuals under international law may, however, arise under the provisions of paragraph (12) of the present article.

(8) Acts by the authorities of a State resulting in the annexation, contrary to international law, of territory belonging to another State or of territory under an international régime.

Annexation of territory in violation of international law constitutes a distinct offence, because it presents a particularly lasting danger to the peace and security of mankind. The Covenant of the League of Nations, in article 10, provided that "the Members of the League undertake to respect and preserve as against external aggression the territorial integrity and existing political independence of all Members of the League". The Charter of the United Nations, in Article 2, paragraph 4, stipulates that "all Members shall refrain in their international relations from the threat or use of force against the territorial integrity or political independence of any State . . .". Illegal annexation may also be achieved without overt threat or use of force, or by one or more of the acts defined in the other paragraphs of the present article. For this reason the paragraph is not limited to annexation of territory achieved by the threat or use of force.

The term "territory under an international régime" envisages territories under the International Trusteeship System of the United Nations as well as those under any other form of international régime.

The offence defined in this paragraph can be committed only by the authorities of a State. A criminal responsibility of private individuals under international law may, however, arise under the provisions of paragraph (12) of the present article.

(9) Acts by the authorities of a State or by private individuals, committed with intent to destroy, in whole or in part, a national, ethnical, racial or religious group as such, including:

(i) Killing members of the group;

(ii) Causing serious bodily or mental harm to members of the group;

(iii) Deliberately inflicting on the group conditions of life calculated to bring about its physical destruction in whole or in part;

(iv) Imposing measures intended to prevent births within the group;

(v) Forcibly transferring children of the group to another group.

The text of this paragraph follows the definition of the crime of genocide contained in article II of the Convention on the Prevention and Punishment of the Crime of Genocide.

The offence defined in this paragraph can be committed both by authorities of a State and by private individuals.

(10) Inhuman acts by the authorities of a State or by private individuals against any civilian population, such as murder, or extermination, or enslavement, or deportation, or persecutions on political, racial, religious or cultural grounds, when such acts are committed in execution of or in connexion with other offences defined in this article.

This paragraph corresponds substantially to article 6, paragraph (c), of the Charter of the Nürnberg Tribunal, which defines "crimes against humanity". It has, however, been deemed necessary to prohibit also inhuman acts on cultural grounds, since such acts are no less detrimental to the peace and security of mankind than those provided for in the said Charter. There is another variation from the Nürnberg provision. While, according to the Charter of the Nürnberg Tribunal, any of the inhuman acts constitutes a crime under international law only if it is committed in execution of or in connexion with any crime against peace or war crime as defined in that Charter, this paragraph characterizes as crimes under international law inhuman acts when these acts are committed in execution of or in connexion with other offences defined in the present article.

The offence defined in this paragraph can be committed both by authorities of a State and by private individuals.

(11) Acts in violation of the laws or customs of war.

This paragraph corresponds to article 6, paragraph (b), of the Charter of the Nürnberg Tribunal. Unlike the latter, it does not include an enumeration of acts which are in violation of the laws or customs of war, since no exhaustive enumeration has been deemed practicable.

The question was considered whether every violation of the laws or customs of war should be regarded as a crime under the code or whether only acts of a certain gravity should be characterized as such crimes. The first alternative was adopted.

This paragraph applies to all cases of declared war or of any other armed conflict which may arise between two or more States, even if the existence of a state of war is recognized by none of them.

The United Nations Educational, Scientific and Cultural Organization has urged that wanton destruction, during an armed conflict, of historical monuments, historical documents, works of art or any other cultural objects should be punishable under international law (letter of 17 March 1950 from the Director-General of UNESCO to the International Law Commission transmitting a "Report on the International Protection of Cultural Property, by Penal Measures, in the Event of Armed Conflict", document 5C/PRG/6 Annex I/UNESCO/MUS/Conf.1/20 (rev.), 8 March 1950). It is understood that such destruction comes within the purview of the present paragraph. Indeed, to some extent, it is forbidden by article 56 of the regulations annexed to the Fourth Hague Convention of 1907 respecting the laws and customs of war on land, and by article 5 of the Ninth Hague Convention of 1907 respecting bombardment by naval forces in time of war.

The offence defined in this paragraph can be committed both by authorities of a State and by private individuals.

(12) Acts which constitute:
(i) Conspiracy to commit any of the offences defined in the preceding paragraphs of this article; or

(ii) Direct incitement to commit any of the offences defined in the preceding paragraphs of this article; or

(iii) Attempts to commit any of the offences defined in the preceding paragraphs of this article; or

(iv) Complicity in the commission of any of the offences defined in the preceding paragraphs of this article.

The notion of conspiracy is found in article 6, paragraph (a), of the Charter of the Nürnberg Tribunal and the notion of complicity in the last paragraph of the same article. The notion of conspiracy in the said Charter is limited to the "planning, preparation, initiation or waging of a war of aggression, or a war in violation of international treaties, agreements or assurances", while the present paragraph provides for the application of the notion to all offences against the peace and security of mankind.

The notions of incitement and of attempt are found in the Convention on Genocide as well as in certain national enactments on war crimes.

In including "complicity in the commission of any of the offences defined in the preceding paragraphs" among the acts which are offences against the peace and security of mankind, it is not intended to stipulate that all those contributing, in the normal exercise of their duties, to the perpetration of offences against the peace and security of mankind could, on that ground alone, be considered as accomplices in such crimes. There can be no question of punishing as accomplices in such an offence all the members of the armed forces of a State or the workers in war industries.

Article 3

The fact that a person acted as Head of State or as responsible government official does not relieve him from responsibility for committing any of the offences defined in this Code.

This article incorporates, with modifications, article 7 of the Charter of the Nürnberg Tribunal, which article provides: "The official position of defendants, whether as Heads of State or responsible officials in government departments, shall not be considered as freeing them from responsibility or mitigating punishment."

Principle III of the Commission's formulation of the Nürnberg principles reads: "The fact that a person who committed an act which constitutes a crime under international law acted as Head of State or responsible government official does not relieve him from responsibility under international law."

The last phrase of article 7 of the Nürnberg Charter "or mitigating punishment" was not retained in the above-quoted principle as the question of mitigating punishment was deemed to be a matter for the competent court to decide.

Article 4

The fact that a person charged with an offence defined in this Code acted pursuant to order of his government or of a superior does not relieve him from responsibility, provided a moral choice was in fact possible to him.

Principle IV of the Commission's formulation of the Nürnberg principles, on the basis of the interpretation given by the Nürnberg Tribunal to article 8 of its Charter, states: "The fact that a person acted pursuant to order of his Government or of a superior does not relieve him from responsibility under international law, provided a moral choice was in fact possible to him".

The observations on principle IV, made in the General Assembly during its fifth session, have been carefully studied; no substantial modification, however, has been made in the drafting of this article, which is based on a clear enunciation by the Nürnberg Tribunal. The article lays down the principle that the accused is responsible only if, in the circumstances, it was possible for him to act contrary to superior orders.

Article 5

The penalty for any offence defined in this Code shall be determined by the tribunal exercising jurisdiction over the individual accused, taking into account the gravity of the offence.

This article provides for the punishment of the offenses defined in the Code. Such a provision is considered desirable in view of the generally accepted principle *nulla poena sine lege*. However, as it is not deemed practicable to perscribe a definite penalty for each offence, it is left to the competent tribunal to determine the penalty, taking into consideration the gravity of the offence committed.

United Nations

GENERAL ASSEMBLY

Official Records

Agenda item 49

ANNEXES
SIXTH SESSION

7 3 |

PALAIS DE CHAILLOT, PARIS, 1951-1952

Agenda item 49 : Report of the International Law Commission covering the work of its third session, including :
(*a*) Reservations to multilateral conventions ; (*b*) Question of defining aggression ; (*c*) Review of
the Statute of the International Law Commission with the object of recommending revisions thereof to
the General Assembly

CONTENTS

---

* Since this question was discussed together with item 50, the present fascicule also contains documents relating to that item.

1

(b) Question of defining aggression

DOCUMENT A/C.6/L.206

Greece : draft resolution

[*Original text : French*]
[*4 January 1952*]

The General Assembly,

Considering resolution 378 B (V) in which it referred the proposal of the Union of Soviet Socialist Republics concerning the definition of aggression to the International Law Commission so that the question raised by the proposal might be examined in conjunction with other matters under consideration by the Commission, and requested the Commission to formulate its conclusions thereon,

Having examined the report submitted by the Commission,

Considering the apparent impossibility of defining aggression in a formula covering all possible cases of aggression,

Considering that the formulation of a definition of aggression which did not attempt to cover all possible cases of aggression, although theoretically possible, might encourage a possible aggressor to evade such a definition, and that, if the General Assembly or the Security Council were called upon in the future to determine an aggressor, the existence of such a definition might easily create doubt and confusion and delay the taking of a decision by those organs, to the advantage of any such aggressor,

Considering that it was because of these dangers that the San Francisco Conference decided not to include in the Charter a clause defining aggression, giving the Security Council full discretion to decide what constitutes an act of aggression,

Considering further that a definition of aggression drafted by the Assembly would not be binding on the Security Council and therefore cannot restrict the Council's freedom to decide at its discretion what constitutes aggression,

Considering that for all these reasons it appears to be inappropriate to attempt to define aggression,

Decides to take no action on the proposal of the Union of Soviet Socialist Republics concerning the definition of aggression and to leave it to the competent organs of the United Nations to determine at their discretion what constitutes aggression.

DOCUMENT A/C.6/L.208
Union of Soviet Socialist Republics: draft resolution

[Original text : Russian]
[5 January 1952]

The General Assembly,

Considering it necessary to formulate directives for such international organs as may be called upon to determine which party is guilty of aggression,

Declares :

1. That in an international conflict that State shall be declared the attacker which first commits one of the following acts :

(*a*) Declaration of war against another State ;

(*b*) Invasion by its armed forces, even without a declaration of war, of the territory of another State ;

(*c*) Bombardment by its land, sea or air forces of the territory of another State or the carrying out of a deliberate attack on the ships or aircraft of the latter ;

(*d*) The landing or leading of its land, sea or air forces inside the boundaries of another State without the permission of the government of the latter, or the violation of the conditions of such permission, particularly as regards the length of their stay or the extent of the area in which they may stay ;

(*e*) Naval blockade of the coasts or ports of another State ;

(*f*) Support of armed bands organized in its own territory which invade the territory of another State, or refusal, on being requested by the invaded State, to take in its own territory any action within its power to deny such bands any aid or protection ;

2. Attacks such as those referred to in paragraph 1 may not be justified by any arguments of a political, strategic or economic nature, or by the desire to exploit natural riches in the territory of the State attacked or to derive any other kind of advantages or privileges, or by reference to the amount of capital invested in the State attacked or to any other particular interests in its territory, or by the affirmation that the State attacked lacks the distinguishing marks of statehood :

In particular, the following may not be used as justifications for attack :

A. The internal position of any State, as, for example :

(*a*) The backwardness of any nation politically, economically or culturally ;

(*b*) Alleged shortcomings of its administration ;

(*c*) Any danger which may threaten the life or property of aliens ;

(*d*) Any revolutionary or counter-revolutionary movement, civil war, disorders or strikes ;

(*e*) The establishment or maintenance in any State of any political, economic or social system ;

B. Any acts, legislation or orders of any State, as for example :

(*a*) The violation of international treaties ;

(*b*) The violation of rights and interests in the sphere of trade, concessions or any other kind of economic activity acquired by another State or its citizens ;

(*c*) The rupture of diplomatic or economic relations ;

(*d*) Measures in connexion with an economic or financial boycott ;

(*e*) Repudiation of debts ;

(*f*) Prohibition or restriction of immigration or modification of the status of foreigners ;

(*g*) The violation of privileges granted to the official representatives of another State ;

(*h*) Refusal to allow the passage of armed forces proceeding to the territory of a third State ;

(*i*) Measures of a religious or anti-religious nature ;

(*j*) Frontier incidents.

3. In the event of the mobilization or concentration by another State of considerable armed forces near its frontier, the State which is threatened by such action shall have the right of recourse to diplomatic or other means of securing a peaceful settlement of international disputes. It may also in the meantime adopt requisite measures of a military nature similar to those described above, without, however, crossing the frontier.

DOCUMENT A/C.6/L.209
France, Iran and Venezuela : joint draft resolution

[Original text : French-Spanish]
[10 January 1952]

The General Assembly,

Considering that under resolution 378 B (V) of 17 November 1950 it referred the question of defining aggression, raised in the draft resolution of the Union of Soviet Socialist Republics (A/C.1/608), to the International Law Commission for examination in conjunction with matters under consideration by that Commission ;

Considering that the International Law Commission did not in its report furnish an express definition of aggression but merely included aggression among the offences defined in its draft Code of Offences against the Peace and Security of Mankind ;

Considering the importance of the problem of defining aggression to the development of international criminal law ;

Considering that the General Assembly has decided not to examine the draft Code at its sixth session and has included it in the provisional agenda of its seventh session ;

Considering that the problem of defining aggression has important political aspects ;

1. *Decides* to study the question of defining aggression when it examines the draft Code ;

2. *Requests* States Members, when transmitting their observations on the draft Code to the Secretary-General, to give in particular their views on the problem of defining aggression.

DOCUMENT A/C.6/L.210

Colombia : amendment to the draft resolution submitted by the Union of Soviet Socialist Republics (A/C.6/L.208)

[Original text : Spanish]
[11 January 1952]

1. Insert the following text after the word " *Declares* " :

" That aggression is an offence against the peace and security of mankind. This offence consists in any resort to force contrary to the provisions of the Charter of the United Nations for the purpose of modifying the state of positive international law in force or resulting in the disturbance of public order ; "

2. Replace the first sentence of operative paragraph 1 of the resolution by the following text :

" 1. That accordingly, apart from action which may be defined as aggression by the competent organs of the United Nations, in an international conflict that State shall be declared the attacker which, if not acting in pursuance of instructions by the United Nations, first commits one of the following acts : "

3. Replace the last sentence of operative paragraph 3 by the following text :

" It may also in the meantime adopt requisite measures of a military nature similar to those described above, without, however, crossing the frontier unless it is acting in self-defence or on the authority of the United Nations."

DOCUMENT A/C.6/L.211

Bolivia : draft resolution

[Original text : Spanish]
[11 January 1952]

The General Assembly,

Considering that it is necessary to describe a number of acts of aggression in order duly to preserve international peace and security in accordance with the Purposes and Principles of the Charter of the United Nations ;

Resolves

1. Apart from the determination of acts of aggression by the competent international organs of the United Nations, an act of aggression shall in all cases be considered to have been committed when any State invades the territory of another State, crossing the frontiers established by treaty or by judicial or arbitral decisions and demarcated in accordance therewith, or when, in the absence of frontiers thus demarcated, the invasion affects the territories under the effective jurisdiction of a State.

2. Also to be described as acts of aggression shall be declarations of war, armed attacks by land, sea or air forces against the territory, ships or aircraft of other States and support given to armed bands for the purposes of invasion, as well as action taken by a State, overtly or covertly, to incite the people of another State to rebellion with the object of changing the political structure for the benefit of a foreign Power.

3. Also to be considered as an act of aggression shall be any threat or use of force against the territorial integrity or political independence of any State, or any threat or use of force which is in any other way incompatible with the purposes of the United Nations, including unilateral action to deprive a State of the economic resources derived from the fair practice of international trade, or to endanger its basic economy, thus jeopardizing the security of that State or rendering it incapable of acting in its own defence and co-operating in the collective defence of peace.

4. Apart from the cases described in paragraphs 1 and 2 above, which shall justify the automatic exercise of the right of collective self-defence, other acts of aggression shall be described as they occur by the competent organs established under the Charter of the United Nations in accordance with its provisions.

DOCUMENT A/C.6/L.213
(incorporating A/C.6/L.213/Corr.1)

Egypt : amendment to the draft resolution submitted by the Union of Soviet Socialist Republics (A/C.6/L.208)

[Original text : French]
[17 January 1952]

I. Replace the preamble by the following :
" *The General Assembly,*
" *Recalling* its resolution 378 B (V), and having considered the report of the International Law Commission on the question of defining aggression,
" *Considering* that aggression is a crime against the peace and security of mankind,
" *Considering* that, although the notion of aggression may be inferred from the circumstances peculiar to each particular case, it is nevertheless desirable to define aggression by reference to the elements which constitute it,
" *Considering* that it would be of definite advantage if directives were formulated for the future guidance of such international bodies as may be called upon to determine which party is guilty of aggression,

" *Declares :*
" That any act whereby a State infringes the territorial integrity or political independence of another State constitutes aggression."

II. Replace the first two lines of paragraph 1 of the operative part by the following :
" That in any international dispute, situation or conflict that State shall be declared the attacker which first commits, *inter alia,* one of the following acts : "

III. At the end of the operative part add a paragraph 4 reading as follows :
" 4. The exercise of the right of self-defence referred to in Article 51 of the Charter shall not be deemed to be an act of aggression."

DOCUMENT A/C.6/L.214/Rev.1

Colombia : revised amendment to the joint draft resolution submitted by France, Iran and Venezuela (A/C.6/L.209)

[Original text : Spanish]
[21 January 1952]

I.   Substitute the following paragraph for operative paragraph 1 :
" 1.   *Decides* to include in the agenda of its seventh session the question of defining aggression ; "

II.   At the end, add the following two new paragraphs :
" 3.   *Appoints* a Special Committee of fifteen members, consisting of ...., to meet at the Headquarters of the United Nations ;

" 4.   Requests the said Special Committee to consider the records of the debates in the First and Sixth Committees on the question of defining aggression and the draft resolutions, amendments and other documents relating to this question, to study the problem further, and to submit a draft definition of aggression together with a report to the seventh session of the General Assembly."

DOCUMENT A/C.6/L.215

Syria : amendment to the joint draft resolution submitted by France, Iran and Venezuela (A/C.6/L.209)

[Original text : French]
[18 January 1952]

I.   Replace the third paragraph of the preamble by the following :
" *Considering* that, although the notion of aggression may be inferred from the circumstances peculiar to each particular case, it is nevertheless desirable, for the development of international criminal law, to define aggression by reference to the elements which constitute it ; ".

II.   Delete the fourth paragraph of the preamble.

III.   Replace the fifth paragraph of the preamble by the following :
" *Considering* that it would be of definite advantage if directives were formulated for the future guidance of such international bodies as may be called upon to determine the aggressor ; ".

IV.   Add the following to paragraph 1 of the operative part :
" ... and instructs the Secretary-General to submit to the General Assembly at its seventh session a report in which the question of defining 'aggression shall be thoroughly discussed in the light of the views expressed in the Sixth Committee at the sixth session of the General Assembly and which shall duly take into account the draft resolutions and amendments submitted concerning this question ; ".

V.   Amend paragraph 2 of the operative part as follows :
" 2.   *Requests* States Members to communicate to the Secretary-General, if they consider it advisable, their observations or views on the question of defining aggression."

DOCUMENT A/2087

Report of the Sixth Committee

[Original text : English]
[29 January 1952]

1.   The General Assembly, on 17 November 1950, adopted resolution 378 B (V), by which it decided to refer a proposal of the Union of Soviet Socialist Republics concerning the definition of " the concept of aggression " (A/C.1/608), and all the records of the First Committee dealing with this question, to the International Law Commission, so that the latter might take them into consideration and formulate its conclusions as soon as possible.

2.   The International Law Commission studied the matter during its third session, and devoted chapter III of its report covering the work of that session to the question of defining aggression.

3.   On 13 November 1951, the General Assembly, at its 341st plenary meeting, decided to include the International Law Commission's report in the agenda of its sixth session. At its 342nd plenary meeting on the same date, the item was referred to the Sixth Committee for consideration and report.

4.   The Committee discussed the question of defining aggression at its 278th to 295th meetings from 5 to 22 January 1952.

5.   During the discussion the Committee had before it a draft resolution submitted by Greece (A/C.6/L.206) ; a draft resolution submitted by the Union of Soviet Socialist Republics (A/C.6/L.208), with amendments thereto by Colombia (A/C.6/L.210) and by Egypt (A/C.6/L.213 and Corr.1) ; a joint draft resolution submitted by France, Iran and Venezuela (A/C.6/L.209), with amendments thereto by India (A/C.6/L.212), Colombia (A/C.6/L.214/Rev.1) and Syria (A/C.6/L.215) ; and a draft resolution submitted by Bolivia (A/C.6/L.211). At a later stage in the discussion Mexico submitted a sub-amendment (A/C.6/L.216) to the Syrian amendment to the joint draft resolution, and oral amendments to this sub-amendment were proposed by Belgium and Lebanon jointly and by Egypt.

[Note : Paragraphs 6 through 14 and paragraph 18 of this document as originally issued summarized the substance

of the draft resolutions and amendments mentioned above, the text of which appears elsewhere in this fascicule or in the summary records of Sixth Committee meetings.[4]

Consequently for each original paragraph there is here substituted a reference to the document discussed therein and, in parentheses, the number of the page of the appropriate Sixth Committee meeting.]

6. [See document A/C.6/L.206.]

7. [See document A/C.6/L.208.]

8. [See document A/C.6/L.210.]

9. [See document A/C.6/L.213 and Corr.1.]

10. [See document A/C.6/L.209.]

11. [See document A/C.6/L.212 (294th meeting).]

12. [See document A/C.6/L.214/Rev.1.]

13. [See document A/C.6/L.215.]

14. [See document A/C.6/L.216 (294th meeting).]

15. The representatives of Belgium and Lebanon orally proposed to substitute the word " crime " for the word " offence " in the Mexican sub-amendment.

16. The representative of Egypt orally proposed to insert the words " with a view to ensuring international peace and security and " after the words " possible and desirable " in the Mexican sub-amendment.

17. Mexico accepted the oral amendments of Belgium and Lebanon and of Egypt, and the Mexican amendment as thus modified was accepted by Syria.

18. [See document A/C.6/L.211.]

19. The debates of the Committee were largely devoted to the preliminary questions of the possibility and desirability of a definition of aggression.

20. Some delegations were of the opinion that the General Assembly should abandon the attempt to formulate a definition of aggression, as no satisfactory one could be found. A definition attempting to enumerate all possible acts of aggression, they argued, would necessarily leave out some acts which ought to be included and would thus be positively dangerous ; an abstract and general formula, on the other hand, would use terms which themselves required definition and would be too wide and vague to be useful. To combine both the enumerative and abstract methods would only cumulate their disadvantages. In their view, it was desirable and in accordance with the Charter that the United Nations organs called on to determine the aggressor in case of international conflict should have full discretion to consider all the circumstances of each case. The political situation of the world, some added, made it at any rate inopportune to undertake the task of defining aggression at the present time.

21. Others, while not opposing the continuance of efforts to draft a definition, nevertheless were sceptical about its value.

22. On the other hand, a number of delegations strongly supported the view that a definition was possible, and was necessary or highly desirable from the legal and political standpoints. In their opinion, a definition would be a

great step forward in international law, would assist in the avoidance of arbitrary decisions on the part of organs called upon to determine whether aggression had been committed, and, even more important, would have a deterrent effect upon potential aggressors. They considered that it would be a useful supplement to the system of collective security established by the Charter and would be a logical completion of the Charter's provisions. Even an imperfect definition, it was argued, was better than none, and any imperfections would be remedied as they were discovered ; proper drafting would avoid the dangers feared by the opponents of a definition.

23. Some were of the opinion that a definition should be formulated with a view to furnishing guidance to the Security Council and the General Assembly in their task of maintaining international peace and security ; others thought that the primary purpose to be envisaged was inclusion in a code of offences against the peace and security of mankind, which would be applied by an international criminal tribunal if one were created in the future. Many delegations desired that neither purpose should be emphasized at the expense of the other.

24. As to the kind of definition to be sought for, some thought it desirable to enumerate all the objective acts which constituted aggression, to specify the circumstances which could not be used to justify attacks, and to list the measures which might be taken by a State threatened with an attack. A satisfactory definition of this kind, they contended, could be worked out by the combined efforts of the Committee, and would have great advantages of clarity and ease of application.

25. Some delegations approved especially the proposal that a list of circumstances not justifying attacks should be included. Varying views were expressed, however, on whether particular circumstances gave rise to a right to use force in self-defence.

26. Another group of delegations feared that some objective acts constituting aggression might be overlooked in an attempt at exhaustive enumeration, and wished to include a provision either that additional acts might be qualified as aggressive by the competent organs of the United Nations or that acts of a similar nature to those enumerated would be considered aggressive.

27. In the opinion of a number of delegations the danger of omissions could best be remedied by the inclusion in the definition of a general formula in addition to a list of examples of acts of aggression. The general formula, it was argued, would serve as a safeguard, as new cases falling within the general principles enunciated could always be determined by the organs called upon to apply the definition. Some thought that any act included in the list of examples should always be deemed aggressive, while others thought the list should be merely indicative, and preferred to reserve for the organ applying the definition the discretion to decide that a particular case covered by an example did not constitute aggression.

28. Other delegations thought it impossible to define aggression solely by describing objective acts, and favoured the inclusion of a provision concerning the intent with which the acts were committed.

29. It was further suggested that the rejection by one of the parties to a conflict of measures recommended by an international organ to put an end to hostilities was an important circumstance which that organ should consider in determining the aggressor.

---

[4] See *Official Records of the General Assembly, Sixth Session, Sixth Committee.*

30. Some delegations thought that a definition should include indirect aggression by such means as subversion and economic pressure, as well as the illegal use of armed force. Others, however, opposed this view as, in their opinion, indirect aggression was a fictitious concept which found no support in the letter or the spirit of the Charter.

31. As to the practical course by which a definition could be formulated, some delegations preferred that the General Assembly should adopt one at its current session. Towards the end of the debate, however, most delegations wished the attempt to formulate a definition to be continued. There was, however, a general feeling that so much time had been devoted to preliminary questions that it had been impossible to devote sufficient study to the various draft definitions presented. A few favoured referring the question back to the International Law Commission ; others advocated the appointment of a special committee to study the problem carefully and report to the General Assembly at its next session. Many preferred to obtain the considered opinions in writing of the governments of Member States, and to take the question up again at the next session. They thought that a report by the Secretary-General, in which the question would be discussed in the light of the Sixth Committee's debates and the drafts submitted, would be useful in the Assembly's future work.

32. The Committee decided to vote first on the joint draft resolution of France, Iran and Venezuela (A/C.6/L.209), with the amendments thereto. The first amendment to be voted on was that of Colombia (A/C.6/L.214/Rev.1).

The first paragraph of the Colombian amendment was adopted by 28 votes to 14, with 6 abstentions.

The second paragraph, proposing to add two new paragraphs to the operative part, was rejected by 33 votes to 5, with 10 abstentions.

33. The Committee then voted on the amendment of Syria (A/C.6/L.215), as modified by the acceptance of the amendment of Mexico (A/C.6/L.216), which in turn was modified by the oral amendments of Belgium and Lebanon and of Egypt, which were accepted by Mexico and Syria.

The first paragraph of the Syrian amendment, as modified, was adopted by 25 votes to 24, with one abstention.

The second paragraph was rejected by 22 votes to 20, with 8 abstentions..

The third paragraph was adopted by 25 votes to 23, with 3 abstentions.

The fourth paragraph was adopted by 25 votes to 21, with 4 abstentions.

The fifth paragraph was rejected by 22 votes to 20, with 8 abstentions.

34. In view of the adoption of the first paragraph of the Syrian amendment, the amendment of India A/C.6/L.212) was not put to the vote.

35. The amended joint draft resolution of France, Iran and Venezuela as a whole was adopted by 28 votes to 12, with 7 abstentions.

36. The Committee then decided, under rule 130 of the rules of procedure, not to vote on the remaining draft resolutions and amendments.

37. The Sixth Committee therefore recommends to the General Assembly the adoption of the following resolution :

Question of defining aggression

The General Assembly,

Considering that, under resolution 378 B (V) of 17 November 1950, it referred the question of defining aggression, raised in the draft resolution of the Union of Soviet Socialist Republics (A/C.1/608), to the International Law Commission for examination in conjunction with matters which were under consideration by that Commission,

Considering that the International Law Commission did not in its report furnish an express definition of aggression but merely included aggression among the offences defined in its draft Code of Offences against the Peace and Security of Mankind,

Considering that the General Assembly on 13 November 1951 decided not to examine the draft Code at its sixth session and to include it in the provisional agenda of its seventh session,

Considering that although the existence of the crime of aggression may be inferred from the circumstances peculiar to each particular case, it is nevertheless possible and desirable, with a view to ensuring international peace and security and for the development of international criminal law, to define aggression by reference to the elements which constitute it,

Considering further that it would be of definite advantage if directives were formulated for the future guidance of such international bodies as may be called upon to determine the aggressor,

1. *Decides* to include in the agenda of its seventh session the question of defining aggression ;

2. *Instructs* the Secretary-General to submit to the General Assembly at its seventh session a report in which the question of defining aggression shall be thoroughly discussed in the light of the views expressed in the Sixth Committee at the sixth session of the General Assembly and which shall duly take into account the draft resolutions and amendments submitted concerning this question ;

3. *Requests* States Members, when transmitting their observations on the draft Code to the Secretary-General, to give in particular their views on the problem of defining aggression.

ACTION TAKEN BY THE GENERAL ASSEMBLY

At its 368th plenary meeting, on 31 January 1952, the General Assembly adopted the above draft resolution submitted by the Sixth Committee. For the final text, see resolution 599 (VI).

United Nations

DOCUMENT 5

Agenda item 54

GENERAL ASSEMBLY

Official Records

ANNEXES

SEVENTH SESSION

HEADQUARTERS, NEW YORK, 1952-1953

Agenda item 54: Question of defining aggression: report of the Secretary-General

---

CONTENTS

1

Annexes (VII) 54

DOCUMENT A/2162 and Add.1[1]

Comments received from governments regarding the draft code of offences against the peace and security of mankind and the question of defining aggression

[Original text: English, French, Spanish and Russian]

[27 August 1952]

NOTE BY THE SECRETARY-GENERAL

1. The General Assembly, on 13 November 1951, decided to delete item 50 (c) of the provisional agenda of its sixth session relating to the draft code of offences against the peace and security of mankind prepared by the International Law Commission at its third session (A/1858, chap. IV) and to include the item in the provisional agenda of its seventh session (A/1950, para. 4). The Secretary-General, by a letter of 17 December 1951, invited the attention of the governments of States Members to the draft code, and invited them to communicate to him before 1 June 1952 any comments or observations thereon which they might wish to make, for such use as the General Assembly might find desirable.

2. On 31 January 1952, the General Assembly adopted resolution 599 (VI) on the question of defining aggression. By that resolution, the Assembly, *inter alia*, requested Member States, when transmitting to the Secretary-General their observations on the draft code of offences against the peace and security of mankind, to give in particular their views on the problem of defining aggression. The Secretary-General invited the attention of Member States to the resolution by a letter of 6 February 1952.

3. By 25 August 1952, replies had been received from the Governments of Bolivia, Chile, Costa Rica,

Denmark, Egypt, France, India, Indonesia, Iraq, the Netherlands, Nicaragua, the Union of Soviet Socialist Republics and Yugoslavia. These replies are reproduced below. Any additional replies that may be received will be reproduced as addenda to the present document.[1]

1. BOLIVIA

Communication from the permanent delegation of Bolivia to the United Nations

New York, 11 July 1952

The permanent delegation of .Bolivia . . . has the honour to send herewith, for such action as may be deemed appropriate, the study prepared by Dr. Manuel Duran P., Professor of Criminal Law and Dean of the Faculty of Law of the University of San Francisco Xavier, at Sucre, Bolivia, on the draft code of offences against the peace and security of mankind.

SOME COMMENTS ON THE DRAFT CODE OF OFFENCES AGAINST THE PEACE AND SECURITY OF MANKIND

Since the principle *nullum crimen sine lege* is the guarantee *par excellence* of the rights of the individual, I consider that the drafting of an international penal code defining the offences should be the first step towards bringing to trial persons liable for violations of international law.

No comment is offered on the meaning of the expression "offences against the peace and security of mankind" as interpreted in paragraph 58 (a) of the

---

[1] Addendum 1, dated 16 September 1952, contained the comments of the United Kingdom of Great Britain and Northern Ireland.

Introduction, but the writer would like to comment on the content: whereas, in accordance with article 2 (9) of the draft code, acts by the authorities of a State or by private individuals, committed with intent to destroy, in whole or in part, a national, ethnical, racial or religious group as such, are treated as offences, such acts constitute first and foremost attacks on the *integrity* of mankind, so that the expression should be expanded to read: "offences against the peace, security and integrity of mankind", though the comments below on the acts covered by article 2 (9) should be taken into consideration.

In order better to define the nature of the offences referred to in article 1, it would not be superfluous to stress that they are "ordinary offences in international law" for which the privileged treatment reserved for political offences cannot be claimed.

Article 2 (1), which proceeds to specify offences against the peace and security of mankind, says: "Any act of aggression, including the employment by the authorities of a State of armed force against another State . . ." etc. However, if *any* act of aggression constitutes an offence against the peace and security of mankind and "no attempt [was] made to enumerate such acts exhaustively", the adverb "including" is redundant, because of all the acts of aggression the most serious is characterized precisely by the employment of armed force against another State. Accordingly, if that was the Commission's intention, the word "principally" or some other equivalent expression should have been used, instead of "including", to show that the employment of force constitutes an aggravating circumstance and hence adds to the liability of the agent.

I also believe it is worthwhile to define and clarify the concept of "national or collective self-defence" and the conditions which must be fulfilled before it can be regarded as a justification, lest the authorities of a State be able to claim the protection of supposed self-defence.

Article 2 (5) should, in addition, contain a reference to action by the authorities of a State to foment or encourage "fifth columns" or unlawful penetration, for experience has shown that "fifth-column activity" is one of the most effective ways of weakening a country's defensive capacity in the interests of another and so of compromising international peace.

With reference to article 2 (8), it should be pointed out that many historical examples show that international law does not always reflect the desires and aspirations of certain peoples concerning the nationality of their preference: either frontiers are fixed arbitrarily by treaties signed as the result of a war, or else situations continue to exist which are incompatible with the fundamental rights of States and to which a solution must be found. In such cases, annexation proper would not be involved, but rather the assertion of a claim (*rei vindicatio*) to a territory inhabited by persons whose wishes would have to be consulted and respected. Accordingly, not only annexation "contrary to international law" but also annexation contrary to the will of the inhabitants of a territory ought to be defined as an offence.

Article 2 (9), whereby the crime of genocide is defined as a punishable offence, speaks of acts by the authorities of a State or by private individuals, committed with "intent to destroy, in whole or in part, a national, ethnical, racial or religious group . . . including . . ." the acts referred to in its five sub-paragraphs. I consider that, in addition to the intent to destroy, killing and causing serious bodily or mental harm to members of the group, the article should mention the case where a group is subjected to living conditions which render its normal life within the national community impossible and which are incompatible with the free development of its activities and personality. This paragraph also suggests a question: Do the offences mentioned in it really endanger or disturb the maintenance of the peace and security of mankind? If the answer is not conclusively affirmative, the possibility would have to be considered of adding in the general title—"Offences against the peace and security of mankind"—the word "integrity" as proposed in the comments on paragraph 58 (*a*).

It would be desirable to add expressly in article 4 that, in the case of an offence ordered by the law or imposed by authority, the legality of the act does not constitute a sufficient defence.

Finally, with regard to the provision (article 5) that the penalty "shall be determined by the tribunal exercising jurisdiction over the individual accused, taking into account the gravity of the offence", while it was not thought possible to prescribe a specific penalty for each offence, in deference to the generally accepted principle *nulla poena sine lege* it will be necessary to lay down in the code, in a separate article, that the competent tribunal will be authorized to impose the most adequate penalty, taking into consideration not only the gravity of the offence but also the personality of the offender.

(Signed) Manuel DURAN P.
Professor of Criminal Law

2. CHILE

Letter from the permanent delegation of Chile to the United Nations

New York, 17 March 1952

. . . I have the honour to inform you that the Government of my country feels that the draft code submitted by the International Law Commission covers all the cases necessary for the effective judgment of offences against the peace and security of mankind and that consequently it may be approved without the introduction of any amendments or additions to the text.

(Signed) Carlos VALENZUELA
Counsellor,
Permanent delegation of Chile
to the United Nations

3. COSTA RICA

(a) *Letter from the Minister for External Relations concerning the draft code of offences against the peace and security of mankind*

San José, 10 June 1952

. . .

The Government of Costa Rica ventures to make the following observations on the said draft:

1. The Government of Costa Rica realizes that, in view of the limitations imposed by the present state of

international affairs, the code, on becoming operative, will have to pass through a transitional stage, in which it will have to follow the prudent if somewhat untechnical course of compromise. This is the reason for the provision that the code is to be applied by national tribunals. However, the Government of Costa Rica wishes to place on record its view that, preferably, the offences covered by the code should be tried by an international criminal court rather than by national tribunals, as soon as the difficulties which now prevent the organization of such a court are overcome. The competence of the international court would be beyond challenge, whereas that of a national tribunal would be open to criticism in many respects, in particular on the grounds that it would never try a case with sufficient impartiality. Internationally, it would be more feasible to set up a court in each case, with independent ideas and capable of proceeding with unimpeachable fairness. The very existence of international law demands as a logical consequence that its rules should be interpreted and applied in the light of supra-national considerations.

However, since the drafting of a statute of an international criminal court is only in its preparatory stage, and as quite possibly years may elapse before such a body can be set up, the Government of Costa Rica considers that the idea of temporarily delegating jurisdiction in respect of crimes against humanity to national tribunals is the only way in which the draft code can be made viable.

2. I should like now to refer to article 5 of the draft. This is open to serious criticism on technical grounds, for even though the Commission says that it has taken into account the generally accepted principle *nulla poena sine lege,* the truth is that this maxim of criminal law presupposes a clear determination beforehand of the penalty applicable to each category of offence, and the fact that the article in question states that there shall be penalties and that these penalties shall be determined by the tribunal concerned, does not accord with this principle. A penalty determined by a tribunal, at its discretion, after an offence has been committed, and to be applied to persons whose identity is known, does not answer the requirement of uniform and general punishment which the theory of criminal law demands.

Although the Government of Costa Rica realizes that in the present international situation it is difficult to reach agreement on so delicate a point, for it would require a genuine effort at international understanding, there are many uncontestable scientific arguments which militate against the unsatisfactory application of the principle *nullum crimen, nulla poena sine lege* in this code. If this article is allowed to stand as drafted, the code will be open to the same criticisms as were levelled against the Nürnberg Tribunal, which had to institute and apply penalties that had not been previously determined by any rule of positive law. It is my Government's view that the code should be drafted in the light of the principles which have evolved in criminal law over the centuries, and that there must be no inconsistency in applying these principles, for they reflect a technical requirement which involves the validity of the code as positive law on the one hand, and a safeguard against arbitrary action on the other.

With regard to the remaining articles, my Government has no further comment to make. It finds them perfectly satisfactory as regards both form and content.

(*Signed*) Fernando LARA

(*b*) *Letter from the Minister for External Relations concerning the definition of aggression*

San José, 3 July 1952

...

I have the pleasure to transmit to you a supplement to our note of 10 June 1952 concerning the question of defining aggression pursuant to the resolution [599 (VI)] adopted by the General Assembly on 31 January 1952.

The concept of "aggression", which is defined in Spanish as the act of killing, maiming or inflicting some injury on persons, may be an act of physical or moral violence. The term has the same meaning in the other languages of civilized peoples.

The Ministry feels that aggression so defined is in perfect accordance with the meaning which the United Nations Charter gives to that concept and that to seek new definitions may lead to confusion about the value of that term, since there would be, on the one hand, the plain and simple acceptation which derives from all modern languages and the new term devised specially for use in international law, between which there would necessarily be differences of opinion concerning the meaning of each or the situations to which each applied.

Moreover, if the meaning of the word has to be restricted in order to provide this special acceptation of the term "aggression", this Ministry thinks that the result would be contrary to the desired intention, because it would be tantamount to restricting the discretionary powers of judges with respect to it. This is proved by the variety of opinions, expressed by the jurists requested to study the expediency of a new definition pursuant to resolution 378 B (V) of the United Nations General Assembly, on the meaning of the concept, and by the tendency of some of them to indicate or point out, to a limited extent, the various acts which constitute aggression.

To keep the concept of aggression within a closely defined and precise margin, as was advocated in one of the proposals, or to determine, by reference to cases in point, the situations in which it occurs, may lead to authorizing by implication countries prone to aggression to seek means of violating international peace and security by methods not covered by the limited definition or in the list of specific cases.

This Ministry therefore feels that it would be preferable not to seek new definitions and to accept the word "aggression" in its simple and current meaning. But if, for juridical reasons, it is considered really expedient to have a definition of the said term for the exclusive use of public international law, this Ministry would favour an abstract formula which would allow judges who have to deal with each case of international violence sufficient scope in determining whether that crime against mankind, as it is understood today by all civilized, law-abiding men, has or has not been perpetrated. With regard to the last point, the Costa Rican Government considers the most satisfactory of the proposals to be that of Mr. Georges Scelle, which states: "Aggression is an offence against the peace and security of mankind. This offence consists in any resort to force contrary to the provisions of the Charter of the United Nations, for the purpose of modifying the state of positive international law in force or resulting in the disturbance of public order".

(*Signed*) Fernando LARA

4. DENMARK

Communication from the permanent delegation of Denmark to the United Nations

New York, 10 July 1952

. . .

The draft code of offences against the peace and security of mankind has been carefully examined by the competent authorities, which have stated that in their opinion the proposals of a definition of aggression hitherto submitted cannot be considered satisfactory and also that they doubt whether it would be possible or desirable, for the time being at least, to formulate such a definition.

5. EGYPT

Letter from the Minister for Foreign Affairs of Egypt

Cairo, 12 June 1952

. . .

I have the honour to communicate to you the following:

I

1. The General Assembly of the United Nations having decided, on 13 November 1951, in the course of its sixth session, to withdraw from its provisional agenda item 50 (*c*) ("Draft code of offences against the peace and security of mankind"), and to place the item on the provisional agenda of its seventh session, the Egyptian Government was requested to communicate to the Secretary-General of the United Nations, before 1 June 1952, any comments or observations which it would like to offer on the draft. Subsequently, the General Assembly, under resolution 599 (VI), adopted on 31 January 1952 at its 368th plenary meeting, requested the governments of Member States, when transmitting their observations on the draft code of offences against the peace and security of mankind to the Secretary-General, to give, in particular, their views on the problem of defining aggression.

2. So far as the definition of aggression is concerned, the Egyptian Government cannot share the point of view expressed by Mr. Spiropoulos in the section of his report (A/CN.4/44) entitled "The Possibility and Desirability of a Definition of Aggression" submitted to the International Law Commission at its third session. According to this view, a legal definition of aggression would be an artificial construction, which could never be comprehensive enough to comprise all imaginable cases of aggression, since the methods of aggression are in a constant process of evolution.

3. In criminal law—whether international or municipal—it is always desirable to define concepts and their constituent elements, for certainty is the *sine qua non* of any penal system for the prevention and punishment of crime.

4. Furthermore, the Egyptian Government is of the opinion that, while as a rule the fact of aggression may be inferred from the circumstances peculiar to each individual case, it is nevertheless possible to define the idea of aggression by reference to its constituent elements. Moreover, simultaneously with the definition of aggression in general terms, it is possible to draw up a precise list of the acts treated as "acts of aggression", though the enumeration should not be exhaustive but should be so drafted as to allow for the addition of other acts which may appear with the evolution of the methods of aggression.

5. A definition of aggression expressed in general terms as suggested would then comprise the three constituent elements of aggression, namely:

(1) *The legal element*, which is the incompatibility of the act of aggression with the rules of the positive and customary international law in force.

(2) *The material element*, which would deal with questions of attempted and indirect aggression.

(3) *The moral element*, which is represented by the existence of a premeditated intention to commit aggression and the absence of legal justification.

II

6. With reference to the code of offences against the peace and security of mankind, the Egyptian Government is of the opinion that the draft prepared by the International Law Commission at its third session is acceptable as a basis for discussion at the next session of the General Assembly.

However, even at this stage, the following observations might be made:

(1) Article 3 of the draft code provides that "The fact that a person acted as Head of State or as responsible government official does not relieve him from responsibility . . ."

This article seems to be in flat contradiction with the recognized principles of constitutional law, and hence unlikely to be acceptable to a good many of the Member States, particularly the monarchical countries.

It is, indeed, a principle of the monarchical system that the monarch is not liable and that, furthermore, his person is inviolable. This non-liability is the corollary of the legal fact that, in democratic constitutional monarchies, power is in effect exercised by the cabinet and parliament and not by the sovereign in person. And it is a well-known axiom that liability follows power.

(2) Article 4 of the draft code provides that "The fact that a person charged with an offence defined in this code acted pursuant to order of his government or of a superior does not relieve him from responsibility, provided a moral choice was in fact possible to him". The Egyptian Government is of the opinion that this article is not so clearly drafted as it should be. The expression "moral" is rather vague and therefore open to controversy and varying interpretations. It would be better to adopt another, less ambiguous, wording such as the following:

"The fact that a person acted pursuant to order of his government or of a superior does not relieve him from responsibility in international law, provided that, in the existing circumstances, the possibility of acting contrary to such order was open to him."

(3) Article 5 of the draft code provides that "The penalty for any offence defined in this code shall be determined by the tribunal exercising jurisdiction over the individual accused, taking into account the gravity of the offence". ,

The International Law Commission took the view that a provision of this kind would be desirable in view of the generally accepted principle *nulla poena sine lege.*

It seems to the Egyptian Government that by this article, in the wording proposed, the power to determine the penalty for each offence is delegated to the competent court. This delegation of power is not only a departure from the principle *nulla poena sine lege,* but would also represent a real danger, since the discretion of the judges on the competent court might be influenced by various considerations, not necessarily of a legal nature.

Accordingly, it would be preferable to try to determine an adequate penalty for each offence, with minimum and maximum penalties where necessary.

For the time being, the Egyptian Government wishes to confine itself to these brief and preliminary observations, while reserving the right to revert to the subject on the occasion of the general debate at the next Assembly.

(*Signed*) A. HASSONA

6. FRANCE

*Letter from the Ministry for
Foreign Affairs of France*

Paris, 25 June 1952

In your letter of 6 February 1952...you were good enough to draw my attention to the resolution (599 (VI)) of 31 January 1952 in which the General Assembly recommended that the Member States, when submitting their observations to you on the draft code, should "give in particular their views on the problem of defining aggression".

I have the honour to inform you herewith of my Government's views on this last point, thus completing the preliminary indications given you on this matter in my letter of 28 February 1950 (A/CN.4/19, pages 117-118).

1. As stated in that letter, the French Government has constantly favoured the establishment of an international penal jurisdiction and the definition of offences which might be brought before that jurisdiction. It still takes this position and hopes that agreement will be reached on what elements constitute aggression (as well as other international crimes) for the purposes of its prevention and punishment. Such an agreement, even though of no immediate practical consequence, would nevertheless represent an important step towards achieving more satisfactory results.

2. That being the case, the French Government's view of how the drafting of such a definition would affect the competence of the United Nations organs and the operation of certain provisions of the Charter should be noted.

The idea of aggression appears in two places in the Charter, in Chapter VII and in Article 51. Whereas Article 51, authorizes self-defence only if an armed attack occurs against a Member of the United Nations, the Security Council may take action in situations (threats to the peace, breaches of the peace) other than cases of aggression. The same comment applies in respect of action by the Assembly under resolution 377 (V).

In view of the provision in Chapter VII, a definition of aggression would allow for the right to act in situations not covered by the definition. Moreover, it was recognized at San Francisco that no organ was competent to impose an interpretation of the Charter on another organ. A General Assembly resolution on aggression could not therefore be binding on the Security Council. Lastly, while a definition expressing the common view of a large majority could provide useful guidance to political organs, every such organ would necessarily retain its inherent competence to judge for itself, so that such a definition could serve only as a directive which was in no way exclusive.

As regards the operation of Article 51, each State concerned which has been the victim of an act of force or which is party to a mutual assistance agreement must decide whether self-defence is legitimate in the case in point. Such decisions should obviously be made in good faith, but no authority has the right to substitute itself for the State until the Security Council has taken the necessary action to maintain international peace and security. A definition of aggression adopted by the General Assembly may serve to guide the State but does not affect its fundamental prerogative to judge the situation.

Thus a definition of aggression does not mean that political bodies are bound to operate automatically as a result, though such a definition can lighten their task by enabling them to base their decision on a more precise concept.

3. It may be added that a definition formulated in advance and having the advantage, therefore, of being considered impartial and objective would enable public opinion at the same time to understand and appreciate more clearly the action of organs of the United Nations or of States exercising their right of self-defence.

4. The above comments show that, in the French Government's opinion, a definition of aggression being admittedly both possible and desirable, the General Assembly should, despite the obvious difficulties, attempt to draft such a definition.

The history of this problem, dating from the time of the League of Nations, and the guidance to be drawn from the debates in the First Committee of the General Assembly in 1950 and of the Sixth Committee in 1952, together with the valuable information supplied in the report (A/1858) of the International Law Commission, show that the choice can be narrowed down to two types of formulae, those which may be described as analytical or enumerative and those which may be called synthetic or abstract. The International Law Commission decided in favour of the latter solution without, however, being able to reach any real definition, as is evident from paragraph 53 of its report.

The French Government reserves the right to give a full explanation of its views on this fundamental choice when the question comes before the General Assembly and to have an exhaustive debate on the various concrete proposals for definitions which may be submitted at that time.

It seems essential, however, to affirm the following principles here and now:

(a) The French Government does not have in mind an ideal, optimum formula which it thinks likely to give full satisfaction and to cover all forms of aggression, but it believes that, by discussions undertaken in a spirit of goodwill, co-operation and juridical understanding, it should be possible to find a formula that was adequate for the purposes which a definition of aggression may be expected to serve.

(b) The French Government rejects any enumerative definition claiming to be complete and limitative. Such a definition, far from being of real use, might paralyse action by the competent bodies, fail to allow for possible unforeseen forms of aggression and thereby play into the hands of the aggressors.

(c) The French Government likewise considers that a synthetic definition which was too broad and too abstract and which would merely repeat the provisions already contained in other terms in documents such as the United Nations Charter would not be of any real help in deciding whether aggression had occurred, and would consequently be useless.

(d) The French Government feels that the work of the General Assembly should aim at combining if possible the analytical and the synthetic approach. An enumerative list would be included only by way of illustration to emphasize the most characteristic cases of aggressive circumstances and would not be exhaustive, while the abstract portion would enable the competent body to preserve its freedom of judgment and of initiative, for such freedom is indispensable if it is to be able to cope with any type of situation that may arise.

Thus, as the General Assembly is not in a position to arrive at any enumerative definition which would be binding on political bodies, any resolution, if it is to be politically effective, will have to be based, as far as possible, on a synthetic definition with examples. The States, the Council and the Assembly itself will have to take it into account as the expression of a common or very broadly shared conviction, without thereby excluding *a priori* the possibility of classifying undefined situations as aggression.

(Signed) A. PARODI

7. INDIA

Letter from the Ministry of External Affairs of India

New Delhi, 7 May 1952

I have the honour to refer to your letters dated 17 December 1951 and 6 February 1952, in which... the comments of governments of Member States were called for on: (a) the draft code of offences against the peace and security of mankind, and (b) the question of defining aggression.

As regards (a), the Government of India is considering the matter and has no comments to offer at this stage. With regard to (b), the Government of India does not desire to make any comments at present beyond what has already been stated by its representa-

tive during the discussion of this question in the sixth session of the General Assembly.[2]

(Signed) R. K. NEHRU
Commonwealth Secretary

8. INDONESIA

Letter from the permanent representative of Indonesia to the United Nations

New York, 4 June 1952

In accordance with the instructions of my Government, I have the honour to transmit the following message for your consideration:

"The Government of Indonesia, having carefully studied the records of the proceedings of the General Assembly during its sixth session regarding the question of defining aggression, and complying with the request mentioned in the resolution (599 (VI)) adopted by the General Assembly at its 368th plenary meeting, has the honour to draw the attention of the Secretary-General to the following:

"The Indonesian Government is happy to note that a great number of States have expressed their desire to establish a definition of aggression. The Indonesian Government has also noted the general genuine desire of almost all members, originating from a feeling of insecurity, to fill this gap in the present Charter. In view of this, the Indonesian Government has no doubt that renewed efforts will be made toward this end during the next session of the General Assembly which will bring about satisfactory results concerning this most important question.

"The Government of Indonesia wishes to convey the idea to those members who have assumed a skeptical attitude in this matter that the building and rebuilding of a system which could ensure or give more guarantees for security and world peace should go on, despite the international tensions and even despite wars, since law is still intended to outlast war. It must be remembered that the League of Nations had its origin in war and that the present United Nations Charter was also born of war. Why should we not, therefore, work toward the perfection of the Charter, despite the international tensions which exist?

"While, in principle, the Government of Indonesia prefers a general definition of aggression, it is not wholly averse to the insertion of an article within this definition which would enumerate some acts of aggression. In this connexion, however, the Government of Indonesia wishes to state that, in determining what would constitute an act of aggression, the utmost attention should be given to the real proportions of such alleged acts in relation to their importance *vis-à-vis* the geographical location and potentialities of the States concerned.

"The Government of Indonesia intends to dwell in detail on this point, which has been only roughly mentioned herein, at the forthcoming seventh session of the General Assembly."

(Signed) L. N. PALAR
Ambassador,
Permanent Representative to the
United Nations for the Republic of Indonesia

---

[2] See *Official Records of the General Assembly, Sixth Session, Sixth Committee*, 295th meeting, para. 2.

9. IRAQ

*Communication from the Ministry for
Foreign Affairs of Iraq*

Baghdad, 26 July 1952

The Ministry of Foreign Affairs...has the honour to submit herewith the observations of the Iraqi Government on the draft code of offences against the peace and security of mankind with particular reference to the question of defining aggression.

The Iraqi Government is of the opinion that the draft code should contain a definition of aggression. It is clear that acts of aggression constitute the greatest danger to the peace and security of mankind. Two world wars have taught humanity the unforgettable lesson that the surest way to disaster is the appeasement of aggression. The Charter of the United Nations has clearly recognized this fact in the Preamble and Articles 1 and 2 and Chapter VII. The General Assembly, in its resolution 380 (V) of 17 November 1950, held the view that aggression "is the greatest of all crimes against peace and security throughout the world". Furthermore, the Assembly in its fifth session adopted various resolutions to strengthen the collective security system under the Charter, and in all those resolutions aggression and the threat of aggression were recognized as the deadliest enemies of peace and security. The Security Council, in its prompt and effective action in June and July, 1950, fully realized the grave dangers to the peace that were inherent in the aggression committed against the Republic of Korea and immediately determined the aggressor and devised means to resist his aggression. In view of these facts, it seems logical that a draft code of offences against the peace and security of mankind should contain a definition of the greatest and most dangerous offence, aggression.

From the discussions that were held in the General Assembly and the International Law Commission it was evident that the problem of definition resolved itself to two questions. The first relates to the possibility of providing an exhaustive enumeration of acts of aggression. The Iraqi Government is of the opinion that such an enumeration is neither possible nor desirable in view of the diversity of the means that are employed by the aggressors. The second question is whether it is possible or desirable to provide an enumerative list which would contain the obvious and universally recognized acts of aggression. Such an enumeration would not be exhaustive but indicative and would be useful for the purpose of guidance. Subsequent additions or alterations to the draft could be made by the General Assembly or the Security Council whenever a need arises. There is nothing to preclude the General Assembly or the Security Council from determining acts of aggression even if such acts were not listed in the draft.

For this reason the Iraqi Government proposes that article 2, paragraph 1 [of the draft code] should read as follows:

A. Any of the acts listed below except the use of armed force for the purpose of national or collective self-defence or in pursuance of a decision by a competent organ of the United Nations: (The list of acts should be a matter for the consideration of the General Assembly at its forthcoming session).

B. The enumeration of the acts listed in paragraph 1 will not prejudice the right of the General Assembly and the Security Council to determine acts of aggression other than those listed in the above paragraph.

Such an amendment would combine the analytic and pragmatic methods of defining aggression. The danger of an exhaustive list would thus be eliminated and the competent organs of the United Nations would have useful guiding principles for the future determination of aggression.

The Iraqi Government proposes the following paragraph (13) to be added to article 2 of the draft code:

"Failure of a State to observe and implement resolutions of the General Assembly and the Security Council that are designed for the preservation of peace and the prevention of international tension".

This paragraph, in the view of the Iraqi Government, is essential as an adequate safeguard against future violations of the decisions of the United Nations. It is the belief of the Iraqi Government that this would enhance the respect for the United Nations and strengthen its authority as the organ entrusted with the preservation of the peace and security of mankind.

10. NETHERLANDS

*Letter from the permanent representative
of the Netherlands to the United Nations*

New York, 11 July 1952

...I have the honour, upon instructions received, to enclose herewith two copies of the observations by the Netherlands Government on the draft code of offences against the peace and security of mankind.

These observations are based on the report of the commission of experts which was appointed by the Netherlands Government to study both the draft statute for an international criminal court (A/2136) and the subject mentioned above.

The observations constitute the preliminary opinion of the Netherlands Government. The Netherlands Government reserves its right further to define its opinion at a later stage.

(*Signed*) D. J. VON BALLUSECK

OBSERVATIONS BY THE NETHERLANDS GOVERNMENT ON THE DRAFT CODE OF OFFENCES AGAINST THE PEACE AND SECURITY OF MANKIND

General

The Netherlands Government is of the opinion that, simultaneously with the study which is being made of the establishment of an international criminal court, the study of the codification of international criminal law should be pursued, so that a code may be drawn up which will be acceptable to the greatest possible number of States and which may serve as a basis for the law to be applied by an international criminal court.

The Government welcomes the efforts which have been made so far to draw up such a code, and believes that the draft prepared by the International Law Commission is, in principle, acceptable. However, the Government would like to make some observations on this draft.

The title of the code might give rise to misunderstandings as the "offences against the security of mankind" should be taken to include the crimes against humanity and the conventional war crimes. As, however, the title of the code is a term of current use, the Government does not suggest an alteration of this title.

Article 1

No observations.

Article 2, paragraph (1)

Article 2, paragraph 1, is the proper place for inserting a definition of the notion of "aggression".

When considering the notion of "aggression", one should realize that aggression may have political results, whereas at the same time individuals may be held responsible according to criminal law. Seen from a political point of view aggression may afford a ground for self-defence. The individuals responsible for this aggression may be punished. Apart from this criminal (penal) liability for aggression the possibility exists that individuals may be held responsible for the preparation of aggression and other offences against peace.

First of all the question rises whether it is possible and desirable to define aggression. The Government answers both questions in the affirmative. The opinion expressed by a number of representatives during the third session of the International Law Commission and in the Sixth Committee at the sixth session of the General Assembly, to the effect that aggression is a conception which does not lend itself to further definition, is rejected by the Government.

The Government is of the opinion that the amended version of Mr. Alfaro's definition which was put to the vote by the International Law Commission (A/1858, paras. 49-51) is a good starting point. However, it seems advisable to supplement the definition on three points.

In the first place the use of force must be aimed at the territorial integrity or political independence of a State. Aggression only occurs if this integrity or independence is impaired or immediately threatened. Moreover, this criterion corresponds to the provision contained in paragraph 4 of Article 2 of the Charter of the United Nations.

In the second place it seems desirable to mention a "territory under international régime" as another object of aggression, together with political independence and territorial integrity. In this way the use of force against territories which are not sovereign States (e.g., Trust Territories) or whose status has not yet been decided upon is also denounced as aggression.

Finally, it seems desirable to specify the notion of self-defence by adding that self-defence must be used against the condemned acts, i.e., the threat or use of force, under the conditions referred to above. The difficulty of defining aggression results from the vagueness of the term "self-defence", because this notion is always used to define aggression. Therefore, it seems desirable to stipulate explicitly that self-defence can only be spoken of if the action is directed against such threat or use of force.

After ample consideration, the Government has come to the conclusion that, next to the use of force, the threat of such use should also be designated as aggression, but only in the sense of immediate threat of armed force.

The Government believes that armed violence is the chief element of the notion of aggression and that the so-called economic and ideological aggression can never constitute a reason for armed self-defence.

In the opinion of the Government, the definition of aggression in a political sense might read as follows:

"Aggression is the threat or use of force by a State or government against the territorial integrity or political independence of another State or against a territory under international régime in any manner, whatever the weapons employed and whether openly or otherwise, for any reason or for any purpose other than individual or collective self-defence against such a threat or use of force or in pursuance of a decision or recommendation by a competent organ of the United Nations".

Article 2, paragraph (2)

As the definition of aggression as proposed by the Government already contains the threat of armed force, this paragraph can be deleted.

Article 2, paragraph (3)

In connexion with the proposal to insert in paragraph (1) of article 2 a definition of aggression, paragraph (3) of article 2 may be formulated more concisely and read as follows:

"The preparation of aggression by the authorities of a State".

Article 2, paragraphs (4), (5), (6), (7) and (8)

No observations.

Article 2, paragraphs (9) and (10)

Paragraphs (9) and (10) of article 2 refer to analogous crimes. There are, however, some differences between the notion of genocide laid down in paragraph (9) and the notion of crimes against humanity laid down in paragraph (10). Unlike the crimes against humanity, there need not necessarily be a relation between genocide, and aggression or war. Another difference is that genocide is characterized by the intention to destroy a national, ethnical, racial or religious group as such. In the case of crimes against humanity, only the persecutions are linked with special motives, including political motives. For the rest, the crimes against humanity consist of acts which are in themselves inhuman acts against any civilian population. Whereas, on the one hand, the crimes against humanity have become a well-established notion in international criminal law as a result of the sentences pronounced by post-war tribunals, and, on the other hand, the notion of genocide has been laid down in a Convention already accepted by a number of States, the Government is of the opinion that, at the present stage of development of international criminal law, the distinction between the two provisions could be maintained.

When formulating paragraph (10), there are no sufficient grounds for deviating from the wording of the Charter of Nürnberg by adding the words "cultural grounds". By inserting these words no new element is added to the Nürnberg provision, which became less clear by this addition.

The Government would like to point out that the "crime against humanity" would only come under international jurisdiction if the national authorities did not deal with such crime.

As regards paragraph (10), the Government would like to remark that in view of the history of the matter the required connexion with other offences should be limited to the crimes against peace, mentioned in paragraphs (1) to (8), inclusive, of article 2.

Article 2, paragraph (11)

No comments.

Article 2, paragraph (12)

As regards the inchoate crimes enumerated in paragraph (12), the Government feel that some distinction should be made.

In connexion with the history of the matter, three categories of offences may be distinguished, viz.:

A. Crimes against peace (article 2, paragraphs (1) to (8), inclusive);

B. Genocide and crimes against humanity (article 2, paragraphs (9) and (10));

C. Crimes in violation of the laws or customs of war (article 2, paragraph (11)).

As regards group A, the Government wants to make the following observations. Conspiracy should be taken in the limited sense of the Nürnberg sentences, where conspiracy was limited to cases in which the accused had a function on policy-making level.

Direct incitement should be limited to direct incitement to aggression as defined in paragraph (1) of article 2.

There is no ground for penalizing attempts, because attempts at these offences are inherent in the definition of these offences, or in other cases attempts are incompatible with the very definition of the offences. This does not apply to paragraph (4) of article 2, but it is not desirable to declare attempts at crossing the frontier by armed bands punishable as well.

As regards complicity, this form should be excluded as it does not occur in the Nürnberg sentences. The acts of those who should be deemed to be criminally responsible for crimes against peace should fall under the definition of the offences; consequently, there is no need here for separate penalization of complicity.

As regards groups B and C, the Government is of the opinion that the four forms enumerated in paragraph (12) of article 2 should all be maintained.

Article 3

The Government does not quite understand what is meant by the words "responsible government officials" and why these officials are mentioned in article 3. It seems that the adjective "responsible" was used to qualify officials who are ultimately responsible for the government policy. This was obviously meant to express, in other words, the idea that even the highest government officials do not enjoy immunity. The Government, however, wonders whether such a provision is really necessary.

Article 4

The Government suggests the insertion after the word "responsibility" of the words "in case he could be aware of the criminal character of the act". Article 4 can only apply in case the accused knew or could have known that the order was given in violation of international law.

Article 5

No observations.

Final remark

No provision has been inserted to the effect that, in case of the accused's being exempt from criminal responsibility, no punishment will be inflicted. However, the Government thinks it may take it for granted that the drafters of the code have proceeded on the presumption that this is considered to be a rule of unwritten law.

11. NICARAGUA

Letter from the Ministry for Foreign Affairs of Nicaragua

Managua, D.N., 26 May 1952

...I have the honour to inform you that the Government of Nicaragua accepts the definition of aggression laid down in the Act of Chapultepec of 1945, part I, third section, later confirmed by the Treaty of Rio de Janeiro of 1947, to the following effect:

"Every attack of a State against the integrity or the inviolability of the territory, or against the sovereignty or political independence of a State".

(Signed) Alejandro MONTIEL ARGUELLO

12. UNION OF SOVIET SOCIALIST REPUBLICS

Communication from the permanent delegation of the Union of Soviet Socialist Republics to the United Nations

New York, 8 April 1952

The delegation of the Union of Soviet Socialist Republics to the United Nations...has the honour to state that the views of the Government of the USSR on the question of defining aggression were expressed by the delegation of the USSR to the sixth session of the General Assembly, which delegation submitted concrete proposals on the subject.

13. YUGOSLAVIA

(a) *Letter from the permanent representative of Yugoslavia to the United Nations concerning the draft code of offences against the peace and security of mankind*

New York, 18 June 1952

With reference to the decision of the General Assembly of 13 November 1951 not to examine the draft code of offences against the peace and security of mankind but to include it in the provisional agenda of the seventh session (A/1950, para. 4), I have the honour to communicate the following observations of the Government of the Federal People's Republic of Yugoslavia.

The Government of the Federal People's Republic of Yugoslavia considers that the adoption of the code of offences against the peace and security of mankind would provide the United Nations with a new and important weapon in the struggle for the maintenance of international peace and security, and would mean a significant contribution to the further development and codification of international law.

While the Government of the Federal People's Republic of Yugoslavia considers that the draft code prepared by the International Law Commission is generally satisfactory and can serve as a basis for the elaboration of a final text, it feels that certain modifications along the following lines would be desirable:

1. The wording of paragraph (4) of article 2 lacks clarity and precision as regards the determining of responsibilities for the incursion into the territory of a State by armed bands. This offence should be so defined as to provide clearly for the responsibility both of the individual members of the bands and of the authorities of a State who tolerate or organize them.

2. In paragraph (10) of article 2, crimes against humanity are qualified as offences against the peace and security of mankind only when "such acts are committed in execution of or in connexion with other offences defined in this article". Crimes against humanity, when committed in an organized manner, are in themselves offences against the peace and security of mankind, regardless of whether they have or not been committed in connexion with other offences against the peace and security of mankind. The definition of this offence would greatly gain in precision if due consideration were given to the fact whether it had been committed in an organized manner, because only organized acts of this kind may be considered offences against the peace and security of mankind, regardless of whether the offences (or the offenders) are mass or individual offences (or offenders). Paragraph (10) of article 2 should, therefore, be amended by the insertion of the word "organized" after the words "such as" and by the deletion of the part of the sentence which reads "when such acts are committed in execution of or in connexion with other offences defined in this article".

3. In paragraph (11) of article 2, it should be explicitly stated that acts in violation of the laws or customs of war are considered offences against the peace and security of mankind, regardless of the nature of the armed conflict. This paragraph should, therefore, be amended by the addition of the words "in the course of an armed conflict of any kind".

4. The definition contained in article 3 is unsatisfactory, because it merely provides that the fact that a person acted as Head of a State or as responsible government official does not relieve him of responsibility, while this fact should actually constitute an aggravating circumstance. This article should therefore be modified to read: "The fact that a person acted as Head of State or as responsible government official constitutes an aggravating circumstance with regard to responsibility for committing any of the offences defined in the present code, provided that such offences may also be committed by other persons".

5. In article 4 there is the provision that a person who acted pursuant to order of his government or of his superior may be considered responsible for committing any of the offences defined in the code only if "a moral choice was in fact possible to him". The inclusion of a provision on the possibility of a moral choice as a condition for responsibility for the commission of these offences would have an adverse effect

both as regards prevention and as regards an effective application of the code by the courts. The last sentence of this article should therefore be amended, in conformity with article 8 of the Charter of the Nürnberg Tribunal, to read "but may be taken into consideration in mitigation of punishment, when the court deems fit".

6. The Government of the Federal People's Republic of Yugoslavia is further of the opinion that consideration should be given to other acts which may be defined as offences against the peace and security of mankind, and should therefore be included in the code, such as, for instance, an economic blockade and other similar forms of economic pressure, war-mongering propaganda, membership in criminal organizations, and crimes of omission, i.e., the responsibility of persons who fail to prevent, or do not take the necessary measures to prevent, the commission of any of the crimes defined in the code, provided they were in a position to do so.

7. In addition to these more general observations, the Government of the Federal People's Republic of Yugoslavia considers that, for the sake of greater precision, the following ideas should be more clearly stated:

(a) With reference to article 1 of the draft code, it should be made clear that responsibility under international law is not precluded by the fact that an offence is not punishable under the municipal law of the country of the person who has committed it.

(b) The word "planning" should be retained in the English text of paragraph (3) of article 2, in order to lay more emphasis on combating the preparation of aggression.

(c) Article 5 should be reworded in order to make it clear that the court may pass any sentence, including sentence of death. This should be done in order to avoid any possible discussion on the powers of the court in the event municipal law does not provide for the nature of the punishment for certain offences, and also in order to ensure that the code would be observed even by States which did not accede to the international criminal court, as well as pending the establishment of such a court.

In submitting these general observations, the Government of the Federal People's Republic of Yugoslavia would like to express its appreciation to those who have taken part in the drafting of the code for the successful manner in which they have accomplished their task. It also believes that these observations will mean a contribution to the discussion of the questions to which they refer.

(*Signed*) Ales BEBLER
*Permanent representative of the
Federal People's Republic of
Yugoslavia to the United Nations*

(b) *Letter from the permanent representative of Yugoslavia to the United Nations concerning the definition of aggression*

New York, 18 June 1952

I have the honour to refer to resolution 599 (VI) adopted by the General Assembly of the United Nations on 31 January 1952, and in particular to paragraph 3 of its operative part.

With regard to the problem of defining aggression, the Government of the Federal People's Republic of Yugoslavia does not feel it has anything to add to the views set forth by the Yugoslav delegation at the sixth session of the General Assembly. The Government of the Federal People's Republic of Yugoslavia still considers that it is both legally possible and politically opportune to define aggression and to adopt such a definition as would provide a guiding principle to the competent United Nations organs in the performance of their functions with regard to the maintenance of international peace and security.

While the existence of a definition of aggression cannot, of course, in itself prevent acts of aggression, it would, none the less, in addition to its considerable moral and political effect, make it more difficult for an aggressor to seek to justify his aggressive intentions, both in the eyes of his own people and of those of other peoples and of the world community at large, by means of hypocritical propaganda. The existence of a definition of aggression would make it possible both for States and for the competent United Nations bodies to ascertain, clearly and without hesitation, the occurrence of acts of pressure, and, especially, of acts of aggression.

As regards the principles of such a definition, the Government of the Federal People's Republic of Yugoslavia considers, as was stated by the Yugoslav delegation at the sixth session of the General Assembly, that the present conditions of constant flux and development require a definition which would be enumerative without, however, being exhaustive, i.e., a definition which, while enumerating the "traditional" types of acts of aggression, would still leave the competent United Nations organs the possibility of qualifying as aggressive certain other acts which have not been included in the definition.

Although certain elements of a definition of aggression are contained in the draft code of offences against the peace and security of mankind, the Government of the Federal People's Republic of Yugoslavia is of the opinion that the adoption of a specific definition of aggression would, nevertheless, be desirable. It may well be that such a definition would provide the basis for either a general treaty on the definition of aggression or for regional or bilateral treaties among both Member and non-member States of the United Nations.

The Government of the Federal People's Republic of Yugoslavia maintains its point of view as expressed at the sixth session of the General Assembly, which may be summarized as follows:

1. It is both legally possible and politically expedient to define aggression. Such a definition would contribute to the progressive development of international law, it being obvious that such a development does not preclude the elaboration of concepts contained in the Charter of the United Nations.

2. A definition of aggression should enumerate the various acts which have so far constituted the "traditional" types of aggression, because where such acts are concerned there can be no question of invoking the political expediency of resorting to the use of force.

3. Such a definition should be flexible and provide explicitly for the possibility that the competent United Nations body, i.e., the Security Council as a rule and

the General Assembly exceptionally, may define as aggression other forms of use of force or pressure which may appear in the future.

(*Signed*) Ales BEBLER
*Permanent representative of the
Federal People's Republic of
Yugoslavia to the United Nations*

14. UNITED KINGDOM OF GREAT BRITAIN AND NORTHERN IRELAND

Letter from the permanent delegation of the United Kingdom to the United Nations

New York, 3 September 1952

...The United Kingdom Government offers the following comments of a legal and procedural nature on the draft code of offences against the peace and security of mankind as drawn up by the International Law Commission at its third (1951) session. These comments are offered without prejudice to any attitude which Her Majesty's Government may adopt generally towards the code when it is debated in the General Assembly.

I

2. There is one preliminary observation of a procedural character to be made. The draft code figured originally as item 49(*c*) on the provisional agenda (A/BUR/126 and Corr.1) of the last (sixth) session of the General Assembly, but was deleted on the recommendation of the General Committee.[3] This recommendation was based on the view expressed by Mr. Bebler (Yugoslavia) to the effect that "the draft code had only recently been communicated to governments and, in accordance with article 16 of the Statute of the International Law Commission, a one-year period of study should be allowed".[4]

It was, however, further recommended that this item be included in the provisional agenda of the seventh session of the Assembly. In so doing, it was apparently overlooked that this same article 16 of the Commission's Statute[5] also requires (see its sub-paragraphs (*i*) and (*j*)) that, when the comments of governments are furnished, they shall be considered by the Commission's rapporteur on the subject, who is to prepare, in the light of the comments, a final project for consideration and adoption by the Commission. The Commission is then (sub-paragraph (*j*) of article 16) to submit this final draft to the General Assembly *"with its recommendations"*. It is thus clear (*a*) that the comments of governments do not themselves go to the Assembly as such; and (*b*) that what goes to the Assembly is a revised draft drawn up by the Commission after considering the comments of governments, and that the Assembly is entitled to have, with this revised draft, the final recommendations of the Commission.

3. It would therefore, in the opinion of the United Kingdom Government, be premature and indeed irregular for the question of the draft code to be included in the provisional agenda of the seventh session of the

---

[3] See *Official Records of the General Assembly, Sixth Session, General Committee*, 75th meeting, para. 24.
[4] *Ibid.*, para. 23.
[5] See *Statute of the International Law Commission (A/CN.4/4) and other resolutions of the General Assembly relating to the International Law Commission.*

Assembly. According to article 16, the Assembly can only discuss the final draft as elaborated by the Commission after the latter has considered the comments of governments. The present draft of the code is not such a draft, nor are the ultimate recommendations of the Commission available. Moreover, it is the Commission, not the Assembly, which has the task of studying the comments of governments. It is only after the Commission has carried out this study and done any further necessary work on the draft that the matter can properly come before the Assembly. This could not therefore occur prior to the eighth session.

4. Should this item nevertheless figure in the provisional agenda of the seventh session, the United Kingdom Government must reserve the right to raise the question on the above grounds.

5. The same point was apparently also overlooked in drafting the General Assembly's resolution (599 (VI)) of 31 January 1952, on the question of defining aggression, where reference was made to the fact that the draft code would be considered at the seventh session. However, as paragraph 1 of the operative part of that resolution directed that the question of defining aggression be placed on the agenda of the seventh session in any event, as a separate item, this question would not be affected by the postponement of the consideration of the draft code, nor would such postponement prevent governments from acceding to the request made in paragraph 3 of the resolution, asking them, when commenting on the draft code, to furnish their views in particular on the question of defining aggression.

6. It appears indeed that there would be some advantage in separating the two matters. If the Assembly adopts a definition of aggression at its next session, it would be desirable and sufficient (if a definition of aggression were considered necessary in the code) to reproduce this same definition, or refer to it. If on the other hand, the Assembly does not adopt a definition of aggression, it would clearly be inappropriate for one to figure in the code.

II

7. On the substance of the draft code, there is one general observation to be made. Although called draft code of "offences" against the peace and security of mankind, the code is in fact, as its article 1 says, concerned with international "crimes". It deals, therefore, and can only deal, with acts that are not merely illegal or contrary to international law, but are also criminal, that is to say, have an inherent element of criminality. By no means every illegal act has this character. While it may be that most of those enumerated in paragraphs (1) to (12) inclusive, of article 2 of the draft code have or can have it, the matter needs scrutiny, for most of these paragraphs are framed in such wide and general terms that they could be held to cover acts not illegal at all in certain circumstances, or which, even if technically illegal, would be wanting in any real element of criminality. The conception of an international crime is of so serious a character as to forbid its use for the purpose of covering any but acts of a manifestly criminal nature.

III

8. The following comments are offered on the individual articles of the draft code:

Article 1

Purely as a matter of drafting, this article seems to be defective since it merely lays down the general principle that offences against the peace and security of mankind are crimes under international law. This is no doubt true, but it is in a sense self-evident for it constitutes the very basis on which the preparation of the draft code was called for. A better form of words for article 1 would seem to be something on the following lines:

"The offences specified in article 2 of the present code shall be regarded as offences against the peace and security of mankind and as crimes under international law".

This would entail a consequential alteration of the opening part of article 2 (see below). As regards the remaining words of article 1 "for which the responsible individuals shall be punishable", while there is no actual objection to this phrase, it is not clear what its exact effect is in the context, or whether it is really necessary. The term "punishable" is ambiguous. An individual may be *actually* punishable in the sense that there is an existing law in one or more countries to whose jurisdiction he is or might be amenable which makes him liable to punishment in respect of certain offences; or it may mean that he is *potentially* punishable in the sense that it is open to governments at any time to make provision under their laws for punishing him for certain offences, or by concerted action to make him punishable by an international court. These further steps would all have to be worked out. They are not part of the draft code itself, and they would depend very largely on what steps were taken or could be taken to give the code executive force, a matter to which the Commission draws attention in sub-paragraph (*d*) of paragraph 58 of its report (A/1858). It really goes without saying, as a matter of general principle, that if a certain act is an offence and a crime he who commits it must be actually or potentially "punishable", but the statement has little practical significance if not related to the arrangements to be made for enforcing such liability.

Article 2

If article 1 is amended as above suggested, the preambular phrase of article 2 might read:

"The offences against the peace and security of mankind referred to in article 1 of the present code are as follows".

Paragraph (1)

In the opinion of the United Kingdom Government, this paragraph should simply read: "Any act of aggression", omitting all the words which at present follow the word "aggression". The reasons for this view were fully explained in the statements made on behalf of the United Kingdom in the Sixth Committee during the last session of the General Assembly. Briefly, it has all along been the view of the United Kingdom Government that a satisfactory definition of aggression, covering all those cases that are truly in the nature of aggression but without prejudicing the measures of defence which it may be necessary to take or to prepare in order to resist aggression, is extremely difficult to find, and that some which have been suggested are dangerous. The definition, if such it be, included in the present text of article 2 has the further objection that it is incomplete and singles out for mention only some aspects of aggression. This is indeed expressly recognized by the Commission in the third paragraph of its commentary on this article. There is a further objection to the partial definition contained in paragraph (1), that it employs terms which themselves require definition.

All these considerations suggest that it would be preferable to omit the entire phrase coming after the words "Any act of aggression". In practice it will never be possible to establish aggression except in the light of the particular circumstances in which the act concerned takes place. No municipal system of law attempts to specify or define what particular acts constitute the crime of murder, since one and the same act may be murder, or may be excusable or even justifiable homicide, according to the circumstances in which it is committed. Precisely the same principle applies to aggression. In the opinion of the United Kingdom Government it is sufficient, for the purpose of the draft code, to specify that aggression is an offence against the peace and security of mankind and an international crime, without attempting to define it.

Paragraph (2)

There is no objection of principle to this paragraph, but taken in combination with the existing wording of paragraph (1), it illustrates very well the dangers attendant upon attempts to define aggression, particularly if these are of a partial or incomplete character. Paragraph (2), taken in conjunction with the present wording of paragraph (1), would enable a would-be aggressor State to represent that preparatory measures of a defensive character taken by other States constituted a threat to employ "armed force against another State", consequently a threat of aggression, and consequently an offence under paragraph (2). The answer that the measures were defensive would be met by the rejoinder that they were regarded by the would-be aggressor as constituting a threat, and the would-be aggressor might well be able to represent himself as having a good theoretical case on the basis of the actual language of the draft code. While the specious character of this argument might be evident, it is nevertheless undesirable that the language of the draft code should be such as could be used to support such contentions or enable an intending aggressor to employ them for propaganda purposes.

Paragraph (3)

These considerations apply with even greater force to this paragraph, and in particular the use of the term "armed force" in the second line is dangerous. This paragraph, as it now reads, would afford an excellent basis on which an intending aggressor State could challenge the defensive measures, preparations or arrangements of another State or group of States, on the ground that they were not defensive but were directed against itself. The paragraph refers specifically to preparation, and would tend to hamper in an important degree the necessary preparatory measures of States arming for resistance to aggression.

A further danger of this paragraph is revealed by the Commission's commentary on it. "Planning" is only to be punishable if it results in actual preparatory

acts, but at what precise point does planning become preparation? It would be perfectly possible for an ill-disposed State to allege that mere consultations about possible joint defensive measures to be undertaken by a group of States constituted not merely planning but actual preparation.

The paragraph would be much less objectionable if the word "aggression" were substituted for "armed force" in the second line. But in that case it would be necessary to omit the rest of the paragraph. The paragraph would then read:

"The preparation by the authorities of a State for the employment of aggression",

or simply

"The preparation of aggression by the authorities of a State".

Nothing more than this is necessary.

Paragraph (4)

Although the commentary on this paragraph makes clear what is intended, the drafting of the paragraph itself is such that if it stood alone (as it would do in the eventual code) it would be difficult to be sure exactly what it meant, and in particular by whom the offence was being committed. On its language, and in view of the phrase "incursion into the territory of a State", it might almost suggest that the offence was being committed by the State into whose territory the incursion was taking place. It should be made clearer than is at present the case that an offence is committed by the members of any armed bands that effect such incursions. Another weakness of the paragraph is the very fact that it relates directly only to the members of the armed bands themselves, and not to the authorities of the State from which the incursion comes, although, as explained in the commentary, such authorities may be liable under paragraph (12) of article 2 by reason of their complicity. There is a certain lack of realism in this system, since under modern conditions it is an extremely difficult and unlikely thing for organized incursions of armed bands to take place from the territory of one State into that of another State without the complicity, active or tacit, of the authorities of the State. While to a certain extent the question of State activity can be regarded as covered by paragraphs (5) and (6) of article 2, it would seem preferable to have a provision which would, in terms, state that it is an offence for the authorities of a State to allow their territory to be used as a base of operations or as a point of departure for the incursion of armed bands into the territory of another State.

Such action on the part of the authorities of a State ought also to be brought under the head of aggression, if that term is defined at all (see above).

Paragraphs (5) and (6)

These contain further examples of indirect aggression which should certainly be included under aggression, if that term is to be defined.

The phrases "terrorist activities" and "terrorist acts" in paragraph (6) are not defined, and there is a danger that this paragraph, and also paragraph (5), may afford a basis on which States acting in bad faith can attack the actions and policies of neighbouring countries. It would be easy to contend, for instance, that propaganda directed against totalitarian systems of government was an activity "calculated to foment civil strife in another State" within the meaning of paragraph (5). It would be easy to represent that certain activities directed to encouraging the resistance of populations to totalitarian excesses constituted the encouragement of "terrorist" activities in another State.

While no objection of principle is seen to these two paragraphs, and they are indeed a necessary part of any enumeration of offences against the peace and security of mankind, it is desirable that their drafting should be very carefully considered in order that they may not lend themselves to possible abuse.

Paragraph (7)

This paragraph is of a very wide and sweeping character. While it may be desirable in practice to impose sanctions against breaches of treaties providing for the limitation of armaments and other kindred matters, it would seem that this is rather something which should be done by the treaties themselves, and it is questionable how far it is desirable to try to do it by declaring all such breaches to be automatically offences against peace and security, and to be international crimes. In this connexion the observations made in part II above are relevant. While it may be that deliberate and major breaches of such treaties could properly be regarded as having a criminal character, it is the fact that many breaches of this kind are of a minor, unintentional or technical character. Since it is very difficult to see exactly where the line should be drawn, it might be preferable to omit this provision altogether, and to rely on the terms of any future conventions on the limitation of armaments for the sanctions to be imposed in the event of breaches.

Paragraph (8)

While there is no objection of principle to this provision, there is some doubt from the technical point of view whether it is actually necessary in the context. Illegal annexation of territory results either from direct aggression or from some means of indirect aggression. This is recognized by the commentary which says that "Illegal annexation may also be achieved without overt threat or use of force, or by one or more of the acts defined in the other paragraphs of the present article". It would seem probable that illegal annexation, though it might be effected in various ways, would in fact normally involve one or more of the acts already specified in the previous paragraphs (1) to (6). If this is so, then an offence constituting an international crime will already have been committed by virtue of one of these paragraphs, and nothing will be added by specifying the annexation as a separate offence. The annexation would indeed merely be the outcome or result of the previous act which would constitute the offence.

The paragraph is also open to criticism in that the phrase "Acts by the authorities of a State *resulting* in the annexation, etc.", while it may be necessary in order to cover annexation effected by indirect means, is of a very vague and general character. There may be endless controversy as to whether a given act has or has not actually resulted in annexation, in the sense of being one of the causes of it. The truth is that where an act clearly has this result, and the annexation is manifestly illegal, the act itself will be an offence under

one of the previous paragraphs. If it is not already an offence of itself under one of those paragraphs, it will usually be difficult, if not impossible, to show that the annexation was a resultant of that act. In other words, it will be very difficult to bring the case under paragraph (8) at all. This is an additional factor suggesting that paragraph (8) may add little or nothing to what has gone before.

It is not proposed that the idea contained in paragraph (8) should be entirely omitted from the code, but merely that its placing and wording may require further consideration.

Paragraph (9)

No special comment. This paragraph merely follows the wording of the Convention on Genocide.

Paragraph (10)

In this paragraph it seems necessary to examine the effect of the final phrase "when such acts are committed in execution of or in connexion with other offences defined in this article". This phrase makes it clear that the limitation to connexion with acts of war contained in the Nürnberg Charter is not to apply; but it has itself a limiting effect and would enable the authorities of a State to behave in the most inhuman way against sections of their own population so long as they could show (which in many cases they probably could) that this behaviour had no direct connexion with any act of the kind specified in the previous paragraphs of article 2. More accurately, it would prevent such behaviour from constituting an offence against peace and humanity or an international crime unless occurring in connexion with one of the specified acts. Possibly it is precisely one of the intentions of this phrase to make it clear that inhuman treatment by a government of its own population, however reprehensible, is a domestic matter and only comes within the class of offences against peace and humanity if occurring in connexion with one of the specified acts. The reasons for this view are not altogether evident. A government's own population may not be "humanity" at large, but it is a section of humanity. Nor can it be assumed that peace will not be disturbed merely because the action takes place within a country's own borders. The phrase could almost be read as a licence to a government to behave inhumanly so long as it avoids doing so in connexion with one of the specified acts.

Another effect of the inclusion of this phrase is to render the whole paragraph in a sense superfluous since an offence will already have been committed in any event by reason of the accompanying specified act.

A point of quite a different character is that this paragraph may well prove susceptible of grave abuse for propaganda or political purposes, by encouraging accusations to be made in respect of necessary or justifiable measures taken by the authorities of a State for the enforcement of law and order within their territory or for reasons of security. In no circumstances, of course, is an "inhuman" act justifiable, but there may be room for argument as to what is inhuman, and nothing is easier than to make accusations of inhuman conduct in order to serve an ulterior or political end. From this point of view, the limiting phrase "when such acts are committed in execution of or in connexion with other offences defined in this article" would afford a necessary safeguard.

While the idea underlying this paragraph is therefore unquestionably right, it would seem that its implications have not been fully thought out and require further consideration.

Paragraph (11)

No special comment.

Paragraph (12)

While this paragraph is right in principle, its application, when it is related to some of the previous paragraphs, may give rise to grave difficulties. It is possible, for instance, to understand a threat of aggression under paragraph (2), but what exactly is an "attempt" to threaten aggression? It is also possible to understand the preparation of aggression or the preparation of the employment of armed force under paragraph (3), but what is an "attempt to prepare"? Examples of this difficulty could be multiplied and they also arise on the other parts of the paragraph. There is, for instance, the ambiguity about the term "complicity", to which attention is drawn in the commentary. It would indeed seem that, by reason of the general language of its subhead (iv), this paragraph includes precisely those cases which the commentary says should not be regarded as involving "complicity". This term therefore requires specific definition or limitation.

There is also much in this paragraph which can lend itself to abuse. The reference to incitement, for instance, could be made the basis of accusations directed against perfectly legitimate comments in the Press of other countries, and of allegations that these comments constituted incitement to commit aggression or to interfere with the internal affairs of another State.

Article 3

It will be recollected that the reference to Heads of States in its relation to constitutional monarchies gave rise to considerable difficulties during the drafting of the Convention on Genocide. It might be well to give this point further consideration in the light of the discussions which took place at that time, to which no reference is made in the commentary on this article.

Article 4

Since everything here turns on the exact meaning of the phrase "provided a moral choice was in fact possible to him", it is for consideration whether the article should not include some of the phraseology at present contained in the commentary, for instance, the very last sentence of the commentary (though that, too, contains terms such as the word "possible", the effect of which in the context is open to a number of different interpretations).

Article 5

This article seems quite out of place in the context of the draft code. In so far as the various offences specified in the code are, or are made, offences under the municipal laws of different countries, it will be for the laws of those countries to specify the nature of the penalties for any offence, and for the judge in any given case to impose the actual penalty. In so far as the question of punishment, and of the penalties to be imposed, is regulated by an international convention, it will be for that convention to prescribe the penalties and for the parties to the convention to make these penalties applicable under their municipal laws, and for competent international courts to apply them in any case to which the convention is applicable. The draft code does not require any of this to be done, nor does this provision in the draft code have of itself any direct effect. It would seem, therefore, better to omit it. An additional reason is that its inclusion may actually suggest something which is extremely undesirable, namely, that the same offence may be susceptible of several sorts of punishment of differing degrees of gravity, according to the ideas of the particular tribunal before which it happens to come. This may be inevitable, in so far as offences are in fact tried and punished before municipal courts, but there seems to be no reason for giving some sort of apparent consecration to this position in one of the articles of the code.

DOCUMENT A/2211

Report by the Secretary-General

[*Original text: French*]

[*3 October 1952*]

CONTENTS

INTRODUCTION

PART I

HISTORICAL AND DOCUMENTARY

Title I

THE PERIOD OF THE LEAGUE OF NATIONS 22

CHAPTER I. THE COVENANT OF THE LEAGUE OF NATIONS, SUPPLEMENTARY TREATIES, STUDIES, DRAFTS

INTRODUCTION

I. TERMS OF REFERENCE OF THE SECRETARY-GENERAL

1. On 31 January 1952, at the conclusion of the discussion of the question of defining aggression at its sixth session, the General Assembly of the United Nations adopted resolution 599 (VI), whereby it

> "*Instructs* the Secretary-General to submit to the General Assembly at its seventh session a report in which the question of defining aggression shall be thoroughly discussed in the light of the views expressed in the Sixth Committee at the sixth session of the General Assembly and which shall duly take into account the draft resolutions and amendments submitted concerning this question."[1]

2. The Secretary-General considered that, as the General Assembly had instructed him to submit "a report in which the question of defining aggression shall be thoroughly discussed", it was his duty to study all aspects of the question and that accordingly the study should not be confined to examination of the views expressed in the Sixth Committee at the sixth session of the General Assembly. Since the General Assembly instructs the Secretary-General to discuss the question "in the light of" those views, it follows that while their examination must constitute an important element in the study, none of the other elements must be neglected.

II. DIVISIONS OF THE STUDY

3. The first part will be historical and documentary and will examine how the question of defining aggression was treated by the League of Nations and how it is being dealt with by the United Nations. The second part of the study will discuss the general question of defining aggression and describe the opposing schools of thought and the arguments used. It will be found that despite the changes in the international situation and the replacement of the League of Nations by the United Nations, the problem of defining aggression has remained fundamentally unchanged, at least in its theoretical aspect. The terms of the definitions of aggression now proposed are largely the same as those proposed in the past and there has been relatively little change in the arguments advanced in support of one or other school of thought. It would, however, be wrong to believe that one need do no more than repeat what has already been said. International developments since the establishment of the United Nations have given new importance to and increased the complexity of the problem of aggression.

[1] The complete text of the resolution is as follows:
"*The General Assembly*,
"*Considering* that, under resolution 378 B (V) of 17 November 1950, it referred the question of defining aggression, raised in the draft resolution of the Union of Soviet Socialist Republics to the International Law Commission for examination in conjunction with matters which were under consideration by that Commission,
"*Considering* that the International Law Commission did not in its report furnish an express definition of aggression but merely included aggression among the offences defined in its draft Code of Offences against the Peace and Security of Mankind,
"*Considering* that the General Assembly, on 13 November 1951, decided not to examine the draft Code at its sixth session but to include it in the provisional agenda of its seventh session,
"*Considering* that, although the existence of the crime of aggression may be inferred from the circumstances peculiar to each particular case, it is nevertheless possible and desirable, with a view to ensuring international peace and security and to developing international criminal law, to define aggression by reference to the elements which constitute it,
"*Considering further* that it would be of definite advantage if directives were formulated for the future guidance of such international bodies as may be called upon to determine the aggressor,
"1. *Decides* to include in the agenda of its seventh session the question of defining aggression;
"2. *Instructs* the Secretary-General to submit to the General Assembly at its seventh session a report in which the question of defining aggression shall be thoroughly discussed in the light of the views expressed in the Sixth Committee at the sixth session of the General Assembly and which shall duly take into account the draft resolutions and amendments submitted concerning this question;
"3. *Requests* States Members, when transmitting their observations on the draft Code to the Secretary-General, to give in particular their views on the problem of defining aggression."
Official Records of the General Assembly, Sixth Session Supplement No. 20, Resolutions, A/2119, pages 84-85.

PART I

HISTORICAL AND DOCUMENTARY

Title I

THE PERIOD OF THE LEAGUE OF NATIONS

4. The concept of aggression, which is closely bound up with the system of collective security, was introduced into positive law by the League of Nations. In the period between the two wars, the concept of aggressive war was a constant subject of discussion both in the League of Nations and elsewhere.

5. Attempts were made on the one hand to facilitate the application of the Covenant of the League of Nations by defining the conditions governing its application, and on the other to develop the system of the Covenant which was considered by certain Powers to be incomplete and inadequate.

Chapter I

THE COVENANT OF THE LEAGUE OF NATIONS, SUPPLEMENTARY TREATIES, STUDIES, DRAFTS

SECTION I. THE COVENANT OF THE LEAGUE OF NATIONS

6. A system of collective security comprising limited guarantees and obligations was established under the Covenant of the League of Nations. The system was designed to avoid war or to bring hostilities to an end by means of concerted action by the Members of the League.

1. THE ARTICLES OF THE COVENANT RELATING TO COLLECTIVE SECURITY

7. The system of collective security was based principally on Articles 10, 11, 12 and 16 of the Covenant.[1] Articles 10 and 12 indicated what States were prohibited from doing. Articles 11 and 16 established procedures designed either to prevent or to ensure the cessation of violations of the provisions of Articles 10 and 12 of the Covenant.

(a) *Articles concerning limitations of the right to resort to war*

8. *Article 10* provided:

"The Members of the League undertake to respect and preserve as against *external aggression* the territorial integrity and existing political independence of all Members of the League. In case of any such aggression or in case of any threat or danger of such aggression the Council shall advise upon the means by which this obligation shall be fulfilled."

9. *Article 12* provided:

"1. The Members of the League agree that if there should arise between them any dispute likely to lead to a rupture, they will submit the matter either to arbitration or judicial settlement or to inquiry by the Council, and they agree in no case to resort to war until three months after the award by the arbitrators or the judicial decision or the report by the Council.

"2. In any case under this Article the award of the arbitrators or the judicial decision shall be made within a reasonable time, and the report of the Council shall be made within six months after the submission of the dispute."

10. It will be noted that Article 10 formally embodies the concept of aggression without defining the acts constituting aggression. The concept of aggression is given the value of a juridical concept. It will also be noted that Article 12, which deals with resort to war (without using the term "aggression"), does not pro-

hibit resort to war absolutely. Its effect is to establish two types of war: unlawful wars, namely wars begun less than three months "after the award by the arbitrators or the judicial decision or the report by the Council", and lawful wars, namely wars which may occur in certain conditions after recourse has been had to the procedures laid down in the Covenant and after the expiry of the prescribed time-limit.[2]

(b) *Articles organizing procedures for the maintenance of collective security*

11. These articles are Articles 11 and 16.[3] *Article 11* provided:

"1. Any war or threat of war, whether immediately affecting any of the Members of the League or not, is hereby declared a matter of concern to the whole League, and the League shall take any action that may be deemed wise and effectual to safeguard the peace of nations. . ."

12. Article 11 was regarded as being designed essentially to avoid armed conflicts or to bring them to an end by means of negotiations and political and moral pressure exerted by the Council of the League, without any need to determine that a State was guilty of a breach of the Covenant. Great use was made of this article and it was the one first invoked whenever a State began hostilities on any considerable scale.

13. *Article 16* dealt with the sanctions of various kinds to be taken against a State which resorted to war in violation of the Covenant. Article 16, paragraph 1, made it the duty of the Members of the League themselves, i.e., of each individual Member, to apply sanctions. In principle, therefore, their decision was not conditional upon any prior decision of the Council of the League. Article 16, paragraph 2, provided, however, that it was the duty of the Council to "recommend to the several Governments concerned what effective military, naval or air force" should be used against Covenant-breaking States.

2. DEVELOPMENT OF THE COLLECTIVE SECURITY SYSTEM AND THE CONCEPT OF AGGRESSION

(a) *Diversity of policies*

14. Collective security inspired many proposals and was a constant subject of discussion. There were two opposing schools of thought on the question. One school, originally represented by France and a number of continental European States, wished to develop the system of collective security by ensuring strict application of the relevant Articles of the Covenant and by supplementing the latter by means of new international instruments. The second school, originally represented by the United Kingdom and the members of the British Commonwealth, was more reserved in its attitude. It considered that owing to the absence of the United

---

[1] Article 15 provided that international disputes were to be submitted to the Council or the Assembly of the League of Nations, and did not directly relate to collective security. In practice, however, it was invoked on several occasions in cases of armed conflict. (See below, paragraphs 89 *et seq.*)

[2] The attempt to reconcile the provisions of Article 10 and Article 12, paragraph 1, of the Covenant gave rise to a difficult problem of interpretation.

It was pointed out that while under Article 12 States were entitled in certain conditions to resort to war, resort to war that was lawful under Article 12 could not be deemed to constitute the aggression referred to in and prohibited by Article 10.

Despite differences of opinion and changing views on the

question, the tendency was to interpret Articles 10 and 12 as meaning that while Article 12 permitted resort to war in certain cases, it was necessary, if such resort to war was not to constitute an act of aggression within the meaning of Article 10, that the purpose of the State resorting to war should not be to violate the territorial integrity and political independence of the State against which it was opening hostilities.

[3] This is not a hard-and-fast classification. Article 10 could be regarded as introducing a procedure as well as establishing a principle, since it provided that: "In case of any such aggression or in case of any threat or danger of such aggression the Council shall advise upon the means by which this obligation shall be fulfilled". In practice, however, Article 10 was invoked chiefly as an article which established a principle.

States—one of the chief reasons for which was in fact Article 10 under which the Members of the League undertook "to preserve as against external aggression the territorial integrity and existing political independence of all Members of the League"—the obligations of the Covenant with respect to collective security represented too heavy a burden which exceeded what could reasonably be expected when the Covenant of the League was adopted.

15. The positions taken by States with regard to the question of collective security varied. Some States modified their attitude as the international situation changed. From 1931 on, a trend in favour of collective security became apparent, while an opposite trend developed after the failure of sanctions against Italy in 1936. In practice, the followers of the opposing schools of thought compromised on a number of points. The organs of the League of Nations drafted new international instruments to supplement the Covenant and submitted them for accession by States wishing to become parties thereto. They prepared model treaties concerning non-aggression and the settlement of international disputes. It is to be noted that the positions taken by Powers in the general discussions on collective security and their attitudes in specific cases, when they were called upon to determine an aggressor or to take collective action to put an end to an act of aggression which had been committed, were not always identical.

(b) *Influence of the work of the League of Nations on the concept of aggression*

16. As already stated, the Covenant of the League did not absolutely prohibit resort to war. In some quarters it was thought necessary to fill the gaps in the Covenant which made it possible for a State to resort to war without committing a violation of international law. For this purpose, a draft treaty of mutual assistance was drawn up (1923), followed by the Geneva Protocol (1924). After the conclusion of the Paris Pact in 1928, it was proposed to amend the Covenant of the League of Nations to bring it into harmony with the Paris Pact, which contained a general prohibition of recourse to war.

17. Article 10 of the Covenant of the League, which imposed the obligation to "preserve as against external aggression the territorial integrity and political independence" of the Members of the League, was the subject of study and discussion in the early days of the League of Nations, but the discussions and studies showed that many States were strongly opposed to or had serious reservations with regard to this Article and that in consequence the policy of the League could not be based on it. In these circumstances, attention was turned to Article 11 which, without imposing obligations on anyone, would enable the Council to intervene in the event of a threat of war, using a flexible procedure combining persuasion with political and moral pressure, to induce the parties to the dispute to agree to the action the Council deemed necessary to remove the threat of war or ensure the cessation of hostilities which had already begun. In these circumstances, it was considered that, even if the Council's action to safeguard peace failed, it might have the effect of making it easier to determine the aggressor: the aggressor would be the State

which had rejected the Council's proposals for the prevention or cessation of hostilities, had violated the decisions taken or had refused to accept the control measures which the Council deemed necessary to supervise compliance with those decisions.

18. Finally, in the course of the Disarmament Conference held under the auspices of the League of Nations, definitions were drafted enumerating the various acts to be regarded as constituting aggression. It will be noted that originally the question of defining aggression was in most cases touched upon indirectly or incidentally.

19. It may be said that until 1933 there was general acceptance of the concept of flexible criteria of aggression to be evaluated by the body qualified to determine the aggressor; it was in 1933, at the Disarmament Conference, that the concept of a precise definition of aggression excluding the use of force and rejecting the idea of provocation took shape and was put forward. Then, and in subsequent years, it was seen that there was a sharp division of opinion with regard to the two opposing concepts.

SECTION II. REPORT OF THE INTERNATIONAL BLOCKADE COMMITTEE (28 AUGUST 1921)[4]

20. This report concerning the application of Article 16 of the Covenant of the League of Nations does not deal with the question of criteria of aggression. However, the first part of the report, entitled "Under what conditions should sanctions be applied?", contains the following passage:

"By the terms of the Covenant, a State which resorts to war against a State Member of the League, in violation of the provisions of Articles 12, 13 and 15—i.e., *which undertakes armed action* against that State—is regarded as having committed an act of war against all the Members of the League."

Thus, the use by a State of its armed forces against another State constitutes aggression.

SECTION III. THE DRAFT TREATY OF MUTUAL ASSISTANCE (1923)

21. A Draft Treaty of Mutual Assistance was adopted in 1923 by the Third Committee[5] of the Assembly of the League of Nations. It was communicated to Governments for their opinions under an Assembly resolution dated 29 September 1923. A number of governments submitted observations. The draft was abandoned in 1924.

1. PREPARATION OF THE DRAFT TREATY OF MUTUAL ASSISTANCE

22. The question of the criteria of aggression was discussed on several occasions during the preparation of the Draft Treaty. Arguments on the subject of "defining aggression" are to be found in an opinion submitted jointly by the Belgian, Brazilian, French and Swedish delegations in the Permanent Advisory Commission. The opinion states that:

"Hitherto, aggression could be defined as mobilization or the violation of a frontier. This double test has lost its value."

---

[4]League of Nations, *Reports and resolutions on the subject of Article 16 of the Covenant* (League of Nations document A.14.1927.V, pages 15 *et seq*).

[5]League of Nations, *Records of the Fourth Assembly, Minutes of the Third Committee (Official Journal*, Special Supplement No. 16), page 203.

The authors of the opinion doubt "the possibility of accurately defining *a priori* in a treaty" the expression "cases of aggression". Nevertheless, they enumerate the following list of "signs which betoken an impending aggression":

"1. Organization on paper of industrial mobilization.

"2. Actual organization of industrial mobilization.

"3. Collection of stocks of raw materials.

"4. Setting-on-foot of war industries.

"5. Preparation for military mobilization.

"6. Actual military mobilization.

"7. Hostilities."[6]

23. A Special Committee of the Temporary Mixed Commission drew up a "Commentary on the definition of a case of aggression". Reproducing the words of the Permanent Advisory Commission, the Special Committee said that ". . . under the conditions of modern warfare, it would seem impossible to decide even in theory what constitutes an act of aggression." The commentary states that "the test of the violation of a frontier has also lost its value".[7]

24. The Committee accordingly rejected the idea of any definition of aggression and said:

"In the absence of any indisputable test, Governments can only judge by an *impression* based upon the most various factors, such as:

"The political attitude of the possible aggressor;

"His propaganda;

"The attitude of his press and population;

"His policy on the international market, etc."[8]

The factors mentioned by the Committee are given merely for purposes of illustration. It will also be noted that the general concept of aggression adopted by the Committee is very wide, including many other things besides armed action.

2. PROVISIONS OF THE DRAFT TREATY OF MUTUAL ASSISTANCE

25. Article 1 of the Draft Treaty provides as follows:

"The High Contracting Parties solemnly declare that *aggressive war is an international crime* and severally undertake that no one of them will be guilty of its commission.

"A war shall not be considered as an act of aggression if waged by a State which is party to a dispute and has accepted the unanimous recommendation of the Council, the verdict of the Permanent Court of International Justice, or an arbitral award against a High Contracting Party which has not accepted it, provided, however, that the first State does not intend to violate the political independence or the territorial integrity of the High Contracting Party."[9]

It can be seen that "war of aggression" is not defined, but that it is indicated that certain wars are not wars of aggression, namely wars begun by a State which

has obtained a decision in its favour from an international organ against another State which does not comply with that decision.

3. OBSERVATIONS OF GOVERNMENTS ON THE DRAFT TREATY OF MUTUAL ASSISTANCE

26. Twenty-eight governments submitted observations[10] and several governments made more or less brief statements of their views on the concept of aggression. The *German Government* stated:

"The question who is the aggressor in a war—just like the question who is responsible for a war—cannot, as a rule, be answered according to the immediate and superficial features of the case; it is a problem which can be solved only after careful recognition and appreciation of all the many intrinsic and extrinsic factors which have contributed to originate it. Its solution involves a task of historic research and the application of international law, and this, in its turn, implies the reference to all sources, the disclosure of all records, the examination of witnesses and experts, as well as the taking of all sorts of other evidence".[11]

The *Spanish Government* stated:

"The Spanish Government. . .quickly realized that it was difficult, if not impossible, to define an 'act of aggression', although it is upon this definition that all subsequent action depends".[12]

The *French Government* stated:

"Though it is difficult to define specifically all cases of aggression, it is undoubtedly possible to specify the most flagrant cases, which would in themselves furnish a solid foundation for the provisions of the draft Treaty".[13]

The *Italian Government* stated:

". . .in most cases it will be extremely difficult, if not impossible, for the Council to decide, within the brief period allowed, which party is the aggressor and which the victim; for it is not easy to define what either in law or in fact constitutes aggression".[14]

The *Polish Government* stated:

"The work of the Temporary Mixed Commission and the Commentary drawn up by the Special Committee in co-operation with certain members of the Permanent Advisory Commission show that, failing an exact definition of the word 'aggression', the chief difficulty which the Council would encounter in the matter would be the impossibility of establishing the fact that an act of aggression had really been committed, of deciding which was the aggressor State and, consequently, of putting the different clauses of the Treaty into effect".[15]

The *Romanian Government* stated:

"Unfortunately, the draft does not seem to us to provide the requisite guarantees even from this point of view.

"1. It does not define the facts which constitute aggression. It leaves the decision of this vital point to the Council".[16]

[6]*Ibid.*, pages 116-117.
[7]*Ibid.*, page 183.
[8]*Ibid.*, page 184.
[9]*Ibid.*, page 203.
[10]League of Nations, *Records of the Fifth Assembly, Minutes of the Third Committee (Official Journal*, Special Supplement No. 26), pages 129-168.

[11]*Ibid.*, page 147.
[12]*Ibid.*, page 151.
[13]*Ibid.*, page 160.
[14]*Ibid.*, page 162.
[15]*Ibid.*, page 153.
[16]*Ibid.*, page 163.

The *United Kingdom Government* stated:

"...the 'commentary on the definition of a case of aggression', drawn up by a Special Committee of the Temporary Mixed Commission, in collaboration with certain technical members of the Permanent Advisory Commission, is of great interest...It is stated therein more than once that no satisfactory definition of what constitutes an 'act of aggression' could be drawn up. Consequently, the report does not provide that element of certainty and reliability which is essential if the League of Nations is to recommend the adoption of the treaty by its Members as a basis for reduction in armaments".[17]

The *USSR Government* stated:

"The Soviet Government denies the possibility of determining in the case of every international conflict which State is the aggressor and which is the victim. There are, of course, cases in which a State attacks another without provocation, and the Soviet Government is prepared, in its conventions with other Governments, to undertake, in particular cases, to oppose attacks of this kind undertaken without due cause. But in the present international situation, it is impossible in most cases to say which party is the aggressor. Neither the entry into foreign territory nor the scale of war preparations can be regarded as satisfactory criteria. Hostilities generally break out after a series of mutual aggressive acts of the most varied character. For example, when the Japanese torpedo-boats attacked the Russian Fleet at Port Arthur in 1904, it was clearly an act of aggression from a technical point of view, but, politically speaking, it was an act caused by the aggressive policy of the Czarist Government towards Japan, who, in order to forestall the danger, struck the first blow at her adversary. Nevertheless, Japan cannot be regarded as the victim, as the collision between the two States was not merely the result of the aggressive acts of the Czarist Government but also of the imperialist policy of the Japanese Government towards the peoples of China and Korea".[18]

SECTION IV. REPLIES OF THE COMMITTEE OF JURISTS TO THE QUESTIONS SUBMITTED BY THE COUNCIL OF THE LEAGUE OF NATIONS PURSUANT TO THE CORFU INCIDENT (24 JANUARY 1924)[19]

1. THE QUESTION AND THE REPLY

27. After the Corfu incident, which was an armed action of limited scope undertaken by Italy against Greece and which was not meant to create a state of war, the Council of the League of Nations submitted a series of questions to a Committee of Jurists.[20] The fourth of these questions was as follows:

"Are measures of coercion which are not meant to constitute acts of war consistent with the terms of Articles 12 to 15 of the Covenant when they are

taken by one Member of the League of Nations against another Member of the League without prior recourse to the procedure laid down in those Articles?"

The Committee gave the following reply:

"Coercive measures which are not intended to constitute acts of war may or may not be consistent with the provisions of Articles 12 to 15 of the Covenant, and it is for the Council, when the dispute has been submitted to it, to decide immediately, having due regard to all the circumstances of the case and to the nature of the measures adopted, whether it should recommend the maintenance or the withdrawal of such measures."

2. OBSERVATIONS OF GOVERNMENTS ON THE REPLY OF THE COMMITTEE OF JURISTS

28. On 21 September 1925, the Assembly of the League of Nations adopted a resolution requesting the Council of the League to invite States Members of the League "which find, in the report of the Special Committee of Jurists, doubtful points which require elucidation, or which may have other comments to make on this report" to forward their observations to the Secretariat.

29. Eight Governments indicated that they had no observations to present or that they approved the replies of the Committee of Jurists.[21] Eleven Governments formulated criticisms of or reservations to the reply of the Committee of Jurists to the fourth question.

The *Danish Government* indicated that it

"wishes to reserve its opinion regarding Point IV..."

The *Finnish Government* stated that

"...one of the first missions of the League is to safeguard a Member against acts of violence on the part of a non-member, not only in the case of violence in the form of war properly so called, but also in the case of any measure of coercion covered by the term 'external aggression' in the sense of Article 10 of the Covenant".

The *Greek Government* stated that

"the absence of a definite criterion for distinguishing between measures of coercion which are justifiable as being compatible with the Covenant and measures which are inadmissible is liable to give rise to misunderstandings which it is important to avoid".

The *Hungarian Government* said that

"As regards No. 4, the reply is open to very serious question...Measures of coercion and acts of war are closely related, since they have the same purpose —to enable a State to impose its will upon another State by force".

---

[17]*Ibid.*, pages 143-144.
[18]*Ibid.*, page 138.
[19]See League of Nations document C.212.M.72.1926.V. This document contains the report to the Council of Viscount Ishii of 17 March 1926, the reply of the Special Committee of Jurists of 24 January 1924 and the observations of Governments.
[20]The Committee of Jurists consisted of Mr. Adatci (Japanese), Chairman, Lord Buckmaster (British), Mr. E. Buero (Uruguayan), Mr. de Castello-Branco Clark (Brazilian), Mr. Fromageot (French), Mr. van Hamel (Dutch), Mr. Rolando

Ricci (Italian), Mr. Undén (Swedish), the Marquis of Villa Urrutia (Spanish) and Mr. de Visscher (Belgian).
[21]These eight States were: Australia, Brazil, the British Empire, Estonia, France, Italy, Japan and South Africa.
The Polish Government submitted a report by the Polish Section of the International Law Society on the replies of the Special Committee of Jurists on the interpretation of Article 15 of the Covenant (League of Nations, *Official Journal*, April 1926, page 604), which contains arguments in support of the opinion formulated by the Committee of Jurists.

The *Netherlands Government* said that

"This provides no criterion by which to judge. How are permissible measures of coercion to be distinguished from those which are not permissible?"

The *Norwegian Government* said that

"in its view, the Covenant absolutely prohibits the use of armed force as a measure of coercion before a dispute has been submitted to the procedure laid down in Articles 12 to 15 of the Covenant".

The *Government of El Salvador* considered that

"acts of violence undertaken with a view to coercion for any purpose clearly contain an element of aggression".

The *Siamese Government* felt that

"a clearer answer to the fourth question is essential. Any attack, however violent, however destructive and however unjustified, may be claimed by the nation making it to be merely 'a measure of coercion not intended to constitute an act of war'...Certain so-called 'coercive measures' can be, and clearly ought to be, branded in advance as inconsistent with the terms of the Covenant".

The *Swedish Government* said that

"the use of armed forces must be considered incompatible with the provisions of the Covenant in the circumstances indicated in the fourth question".

The *Swiss Government* said that

"It must be considered incompatible with Articles 12 to 15 of the Covenant for a State to violate the territory of another State during the course of peaceful proceedings and before the expiry of the time-limit laid down in Article 12".

The *Government of Uruguay* considered that

"no measures of coercion can be consistent with the letter and the spirit of the Covenant, since the adoption of the Covenant marks the advent of an international order which precludes the employment of violence until all appropriate measures to dispense States from the necessity of taking the law into their own hands have been exhausted".

SECTION V. THE GENEVA PROTOCOL
(2 OCTOBER 1924)

30. The Geneva Protocol[22] is a draft treaty which was adopted by the Assembly of the League of Nations

on 2 October 1924 and was abandoned the following year. It contained a general prohibition against recourse to war. The relevant provisions are worded as follows:

"Article 2. The signatory States agree in no case to resort to war either with one another or against a State which, if the occasion arises, accepts all the obligations hereinafter set out, except in case of resistance to acts of aggression or when acting in agreement with the Council or the Assembly of the League of Nations in accordance with the provisions of the Covenant and of the present Protocol."

31. The Geneva Protocol introduces an original method for defining aggression and determining the aggressor.

(a) *Definition of Aggression*

32. The first paragraph of Article 10 reads as follows:

"Every State which resorts to war in violation of the undertakings contained in the Covenant or in the present Protocol is an aggressor."

(b) *Determination of the Aggressor*

33. In his report analysing the Protocol, Mr. Politis said:

"The definition of aggression is a relatively easy matter, for it is sufficient to say that any State is the aggressor *which resorts in any shape or form to force* in violation of the engagements contracted by it..."

However, he added:

"On the contrary, to ascertain the existence of aggression is a very difficult matter, for although the first of the two elements which together constitute aggression, namely, the violation of an engagement, is easy to verify, the second, namely, resort to force, is not an easy matter to ascertain. When one country attacks another, the latter necessarily defends itself, and when hostilities are in progress on both sides, the question arises which party began them.

"This is a question of fact concerning which opinions may differ."[23]

34. The Rapporteur states that to escape from the dilemma it was decided to adopt an "automatic procedure". Article 10 establishes a series of presumptions to determine the aggressor "in the event of hostilities having broken out".[24] A unanimous decision of the

---

[22]League of Nations, *Records of the Fifth Assembly, Minutes of the First Committee (Official Journal*, Special Supplement No. 24), pages 136-140.

[23]*Ibid.*, page 127.

[24]Article 10 is worded as follows:

"Every State which resorts to war in violation of the undertakings contained in the Covenant or in the present Protocol is an aggressor. Violation of the rules laid down for a demilitarised zone shall be held equivalent to resort to war.

"In the event of hostilities having broken out, any State shall be presumed to be an aggressor, unless a decision of the Council, which must be taken unanimously, shall otherwise declare.

"1. If it has refused to submit the dispute to the procedure of pacific settlement provided by Articles 13 and 15 of the Covenant as amplified by the present Protocol, or to comply with a judicial sentence or arbitral award or with a unanimous recommendation of the Council, or has disregarded a unanimous report of the Council, a judicial sentence or an arbitral award recognising that the dispute between it and

the other belligerent State arises out of a matter which by international law is solely within the domestic jurisdiction of the latter State; nevertheless, in the last case the State shall only be presumed to be an aggressor if it has not previously submitted the question to the Council or the Assembly, in accordance with Article 11 of the Covenant.

"2. If it has violated provisional measures enjoined by the Council for the period while the proceedings are in progress as contemplated by Article 7 of the present Protocol.

"Apart from the cases dealt with in paragraphs 1 and 2 of the present Article, if the Council does not at once succeed in determining the aggressor, it shall be bound to enjoin upon the belligerents an armistice, and shall fix the terms, acting, if need be, by a two-thirds majority and shall supervise its execution.

"Any belligerent which has refused to accept the armistice or has violated its terms shall be deemed an aggressor.

"The Council shall call upon the signatory States to apply forthwith against the aggressor the sanctions provided by Article 11 of the present Protocol and any signatory State thus called upon shall thereupon be entitled to exercise the rights of a belligerent."

Council is needed to reject these presumptions. Where there is no presumption, the Council has to determine, as quickly as possible, who is the aggressor. If it fails to do so, the Council must enjoin an armistice, the terms of which it will fix by a two-thirds majority. The belligerent which rejects the armistice or violates it is held to be an aggressor.

35. On close examination, the system of determining the aggressor in some respects gives the same results as a system of defining aggression. In the event of hostilities having broken out, any State is deemed to be the aggressor, unless a decision of the Council, taken unanimously, otherwise declares, if it has refused to submit the dispute to the procedure of pacific settlement or if it has violated provisional measures enjoined by the Council or does not comply with the armistice terms fixed by the Council.

36. It will be seen that this is a most unusual system. On the one hand, it is connected with the system for the peaceful settlement of disputes (first hypothesis). On the other hand, by placing the parties under the obligation to comply either with the provisional preventive measures enjoined by the Council or with the armistice terms fixed by the Council (second and third hypotheses) it is based on a practical political concept.

SECTION VI. THE LOCARNO TREATY OF MUTUAL GUARANTEE (16 OCTOBER 1925)[25]

37. The Treaty of Mutual Guarantee between Germany, Belgium, France, Great Britain and Italy, dated 16 October 1925, is of special interest from the point of view of the concept of aggression. Concluded under the auspices of the League of Nations, the Treaty placed special responsibilities on the Council of the League. Article 2 of the Treaty provides as follows:

"Germany and Belgium, and also Germany and France, mutually undertake *that they will in no case attack or invade each other or resort to war against each other.*

"This stipulation shall not, however, apply in the case of:

"(1) *The exercise of the right of legitimate defence,* that is to say, resistance to a violation of the undertaking contained in the previous paragraph or to a flagrant breach of Articles 42 or 43 of the said Treaty of Versailles if such breach constitutes an unprovoked act of aggression and by reason of the assembly of armed forces in the demilitarized zone, immediate action is necessary;

"(2) Action in pursuance of Article 16 of the Covenant of the League of Nations;

"(3) Action as the result of a decision taken by the Assembly or by the Council of the League of Nations or in pursuance of Article 15, paragraph 7, of the Covenant of the League of Nations, provided that in this last event the action is directed against a State which was the first to attack."

38. The first paragraph states in general terms what is prohibited—*attack* or *invasion,* on the one hand, and *resort to war,* on the other. The second paragraph specifies the cases in which the prohibition contained in the first paragraph does not apply. The first case is that of legitimate defence, which is defined.[26] The second case is that of collective sanctions taken by the League of Nations in pursuance of Article 16. The third case is similar to the second and is that of action as the result of a decision taken by the Assembly or by the Council of the League of Nations.

39. In a resolution of 25 September 1926, the Assembly of the League of Nations approved the treaties concluded at Locarno[27] and declared that "agreements of this kind need not necessarily be restricted to a limited area but may be applied to different parts of the world".[28] The Locarno Treaties were destined to inspire a movement to strengthen security by means of non-aggression treaties.

SECTION VII. REPORT BY MR. DE BROUCKÈRE (1 DECEMBER 1926)[29]

40. This report was made at the request of the Committee of the Council of the League of Nations. Although it was not adopted by the Committee after consideration, it has nevertheless enjoyed great authority and has often been cited. It raises the question of "the conditions which must be fulfilled before a country can be regarded as having resorted to war". The general idea expressed in the report is that every act of violence does not constitute resort to war and does not justify its victim in resorting to war.

41. The report states the following in this connexion:

"There is no need to dwell upon the case in which the aggressor State formally declares war. Apart from this eventuality, two conditions are necessary, as we said:

"(1) One country must have committed an act of war against another;

"(2) The latter country must have admitted the existence of a state of war.

"Further, the second country must have justification for taking up this attitude.

"*Every act of violence does not necessarily justify its victim in resorting to war.* If a detachment of soldiers goes a few yards over the frontier in a colony remote from any vital centre; if the circumstances show quite clearly that the aggression was due to an error on the part of some subaltern officer; if the central authorities of the 'aggressor State' reprimand the subordinate concerned as soon as they are apprised of the facts; if they cause the invasion to cease, offer apologies and compensation and take steps to prevent any recurrence of such incidents—then it cannot be maintained that there has been an act of war and that the invaded country has reasonable

[25] See League of Nations, *Treaty Series,* Vol. LIV, page 289.
[26] Legitimate defence is strictly defined. It is resistance to attack or invasion or to hostilities.
Reference is also made to certain special obligations imposed on Germany under articles 42 and 43 of the Treaty of Versailles (demilitarization of the left bank of the Rhine) a flagrant breach of which, under the terms of the Treaty, confers the right of legitimate defence.

[27] A number of other agreements, besides the Treaty of Mutual Guarantee, were concluded at Locarno. Some laid down procedures for the peaceful settlement of disputes, while others provided for mutual assistance between France and Poland, and France and Czechoslovakia.
[28] League of Nations, *Resolutions and Recommendations adopted by the Assembly during its Seventh Ordinary Session* (*Official Journal,* Special Supplement No. 43) page 16.
[29] See League of Nations document A.14.1927.V, page 60.

grounds for mobilizing its army and marching upon the enemy capital. The accident which has occurred has in no way released that country from the specific obligations laid down in Articles 12 and following. It could not be so released unless it were the victim of a flagrant aggression of such a serious character that it would obviously be dangerous not to retaliate at once. In short, to borrow the felicitous phrase used in the Treaty of Locarno, 'the country in question must be exercising the right of legitimate defence'.

"Legitimate defence implies the adoption of measures proportionate to the seriousness of the attack and justified by the imminence of the danger. If a country flagrantly exceeded these limits, even if it were affronted by some incident of little intrinsic importance, it would become in actual fact the real aggressor and it would be only fair that that country should be made the object of the sanctions provided for in Article 16.

"Accordingly, it is not so easy as it may seem at first sight to determine when a country 'resorts to war', and a decision may be a very difficult matter."[30]

SECTION VIII. PROHIBITION OF WARS OF AGGRESSION BY THE ASSEMBLY OF THE LEAGUE OF NATIONS UNDER THE RESOLUTION DATED 24 SEPTEMBER 1927

42. On 24 September 1927, the Assembly of the League of Nations, in pursuance of a Polish proposal, adopted a declaration condemning wars of aggression. The text of this declaration is as follows:

"The Assembly,

"Recognizing the solidarity which unites the community of nations;

"Being inspired by a firm desire for the maintenance of general peace;

"Being convinced that a war of aggression can never serve as a means of settling international disputes and is, in consequence, an international crime;

"Considering that a solemn renunciation of all wars of aggression would tend to create an atmosphere of general confidence calculated to facilitate the progress of the work undertaken with a view to disarmament;

"Declares:

"(1) That all wars of aggression are, and shall always be, prohibited;

"(2) That every pacific means must be employed to settle disputes, of every description, which may arise between States.

"The Assembly declares that the States Members of the League are under an obligation to conform to these principles."[31]

SECTION IX. PROHIBITION OF WARS OF AGGRESSION BY THE PAN-AMERICAN CONFERENCE (1928)

43. The Sixth Pan-American Conference which met at Havana in 1928 adopted the following resolution:

"*Considering:*

"That the American nations should always be in-

spired in solid co-operation for justice and the general good;

"That nothing is so opposed to this co-operation as the use of violence;

"That there is no international controversy, however serious it may be, which can not be peacefully arranged if the parties desire in reality to arrive at a pacific settlement;

"That war of aggression constitutes an international crime against the human species;

"*Resolves:*

"(1) All aggression is considered illicit and as such is declared prohibited;

"(2) The American States will employ all pacific means to settle conflicts which may arise between them."[32]

SECTION X. THE COMMITTEE ON ARBITRATION AND SECURITY (1928)

44. A Committee on Arbitration and Security was established on 30 November 1927 by the Preparatory Commission for the Disarmament Conference, with a view to increasing the guarantees of security and, thereby, facilitating disarmament. The work accomplished by the Committee was two-fold. In the first place, the Committee carried out studies of Articles 10, 11 and 16 of the Covenant of the League of Nations, of which the Assembly of the League expressed its appreciation in its resolution of 26 September 1928. Secondly, the Assembly prepared a number of model treaties concerning mutual assistance and non-aggression.

1. STUDIES RELATING TO SECURITY

(a) *Report by Mr. Rutgers*

45. The studies relating to security centred on the report by Mr. Rutgers (Netherlands).[33] Mr. Rutgers deals with the question of criteria for determining aggression in connexion with Articles 10 and 16, and opposes a rigid definition of aggression. His conclusions contain the following paragraph on this question:

"211. A hard-and-fast definition of the expressions 'aggression' (Article 10) and 'resort to war' (Article 16) would not be free from danger, since it might oblige the Council and the Members of the League to pronounce on a breach of the Covenant and apply sanctions at a time when it would still be preferable to refrain for the moment from measures of coercion There would also be the risk that criteria might be taken which, in unforeseen circumstances, might lead to a State which was not in reality responsible for hostilities being described as an aggressor."

46. He does not, however, confine himself to rejecting the principle of defining aggression. He considers that "it would be. . .practical to enumerate some of the facts which, according to circumstances, may serve as evidence that aggression has taken place". Adopting the argument advanced by the Temporary Mixed Commission when drawing up the Draft Treaty of Mutual

---

[30] *Ibid.*, page 69.

[31] See League of Nations, *Resolutions and Recommendations adopted by the Assembly during its Eighth Ordinary Session* (*Official Journal*, Special Supplement No. 53), page 22.

[32] See *Proceedings of the American Society of International Law at its Twenty-Second Annual Meeting*, 1928, pages 14-15

[33] See League of Nations, *Minutes of the Second Session of the Committee on Arbitration and Security* (League of Nations document C.165.M.50.1928.IX), pages 142 *et seq*

Assistance, he enumerates a series of acts, some of which constitute acts of force, and others acts preparatory to the use of force.[34]

47. He also introduces another concept: "the list of factors furnished by the Special Committee of the Temporary Mixed Commission might be supplemented by including the violation of certain undertakings; for instance, refusal to submit a dispute for pacific settlement by the methods agreed upon..."[35]

48. Lastly, he points out that the question of the measures to be taken against an aggressor (Article 16) will not arise without the Council having first to deal with the conflict to prevent its aggravation (Article 11). That being so, "the application of the procedure of Article 11 will be for the Council the best preparation for the performance of its duties under Article 16. This procedure will enlighten it as to the attitude of the two parties, and supply it with valuable information..."[36]

49. A number of critical observations were made on Mr. Rutgers' report. The French delegation in the Preparatory Commission, for example, regretted the complete abandonment of the criterion of aggression adopted in the Geneva Protocol, which, as indicated earlier in this text, established a series of presumptions for the determination of the aggressor.[37]

(b) *Resolution of the Assembly of 20 September 1928 and the report by Mr. Politis*

50. The Assembly did not come to a decision on the question of defining aggression. The resolution of 20 September 1928 merely states the following:

"The Assembly,

"......

"Considers that the *information concerning the question of the criteria of aggression contained in the Committee's documents usefully summarizes the studies made by the Assembly and the Council* and the provisions of certain treaties......"[38]

51. In his report, Mr. Politis has the following to say in this connexion:

"Mr. Rutgers and certain members of the Committee on Arbitration and Security were of the opinion that a hard-and-fast definition of these terms would be very difficult and, even if possible, would be very dangerous, for the very rigidity of such a definition *might conceivably lead the Council into a premature application of the sanctions prescribed by Article 16.*

"This opinion, however, was not general. The Committee on Arbitration and Security, in the resolution which has been adopted by the Third Committee and is now submitted for your approval, merely noted the difficulties......"[39]

(c) *Recommendation of the Assembly of 20 September 1928*

52. The Assembly also adopted the following recommendation:

"The Assembly,

"......

"Considers that the study of Article 11 of the Covenant, which stipulates that the League 'shall take any action that may be deemed wise and effectual to safeguard the peace of nations', forms the natural counterpart of the study undertaken by the Committee of the Council and approved by the Council on December 6th, 1927, on the Assembly's recommendation, and, without detracting from the value of the other articles of the Covenant, brings into prominence the fact that the League's first task is to forestall war, and that in all cases of armed conflict or of threats of armed conflict, of whatever nature, it must take action to prevent hostilities or to stop hostilities which have already begun;"[40]

53. This recommendation is based on the principle that prevention is better than punishment and that the first duty of an international body is to take the most effective action to prevent the outbreak of hostilities or to bring about the cessation of hostilities which have already begun.[41]

---

[34]Mr. Rutgers states in this connexion:
"117. First among these sources of information are the results of the investigation carried out by the Permanent Advisory Commission and the Special Committee of the Temporary Mixed Commission when drawing up the Treaty of Mutual Assistance. The reports of these bodies show that *certain acts would in many cases constitute acts of aggression;* for instance:
"(1) The invasion of the territory of one State by the troops of another State;
"(2) An attack on a considerable scale launched by one State on the frontiers of another State;
"(3) A surprise attack by aircraft carried out by one State over the territory of another State, with the aid of poisonous gases. The reports in question add that other cases may arise in which the problem would be simplified owing to some act committed by one of the parties to the dispute affording unmistakable proof that the party in question was the real aggressor.
"There are also certain factors which may serve as a basis for determining the aggressor:
"(a) Actual industrial and economic mobilization carried out by a State either in its own territory or by persons or societies on foreign territory.
"(b) Secret military mobilization by the formation and employment of irregular troops or by a declaration of a state of danger of war which would serve as a pretext for commencing hostilities.

"(c) Air, chemical or naval attack carried out by one party against another.
"(d) The presence of the armed forces of one party in the territory of another.
"(e) Refusal of either of the parties to withdraw its armed forces behind a line or lines indicated by the Council.
"(f) A definitely aggressive policy by one of the parties towards the other, and the consequent refusal of that party to submit the subject in dispute to the recommendation of the Council or to the decision of the Permanent Court of International Justice and to accept the recommendation or decision when given." (*Ibid.*, pages 143-144).
[35]*Ibid*, page 144.
[36]*Ibid*, page 152.
[37]*Ibid*, page 184 *bis*.
[38]See League of Nations, *Resolutions and Recommendations adopted by the Assembly during its Ninth Ordinary Session* (*Official Journal*, Special Supplement No. 63), page 16.
[39]League of Nations, *Records of the Ninth Ordinary Session of the Assembly, Plenary Meetings, Text of the Debates* (*Official Journal*, Special Supplement No. 64), page 114.
[40]League of Nations, *Resolutions and Recommendations adopted by the Assembly during its Ninth Ordinary Session*, (*Official Journal*, Special Supplement No. 63), page 16.
[41]Mr. Barandon indicates the support enjoyed by this idea. (Barandon, *Le système juridique pour la prévention de la guerre*, 1933, pages 8, *et seq.*, 305 *et seq.*)

2. THE MODEL TREATIES RECOMMENDED BY THE ASSEMBLY

54. Model treaties of non-aggression and mutual assistance had been prepared by the Committee on Arbitration and Security and amended as a result of the work of the First and Third Committees. Under its resolution of 26 September 1928, the Assembly recommended the treaties "for consideration by States", expressing the hope that "they may serve as a basis for States desiring to conclude treaties of this sort".[42]

55. The formula concerning non-aggression contained in the various model treaties reproduces that contained in the Locarno Treaty of Mutual Guarantee of 16 October 1925.[43] The introductory note to the model collective treaties of mutual assistance and the model collective and bilateral treaties of non-aggression contains the following comment on article 1:

"The formula by which 'each of the high contracting parties undertakes not to... resort to war against another 'contracting party' must, in the opinion of the Committee, be understood to mean that the parties, which undertake by the treaty of mutual assistance to settle all their disputes by forms of pacific procedure, *in every case exclude recourse to force in any form whatever, apart from the exceptions formally reserved in the text.*"[44]

SECTION XI. THE PACT OF PARIS (BRIAND-KELLOGG PACT) (27 AUGUST 1928)

56. The Pact of Paris is of special interest from the point of view of the definition of aggression, even though it does not contain the term "aggression". In the diplomatic correspondence exchanged on its conclusion and in the debates in national parliaments held at the time of its ratification, the Pact gave rise to discussions concerning the concepts of legitimate defence and aggression which are, of course, closely interconnected.

57. At the time of its conclusion, the Pact of Paris had a two-fold purpose, to lay down a general prohibition against recourse to war, which was not contained in the Covenant of the League of Nations, and to establish a rule of law which would be binding not only on the Members of the League of Nations but on all States throughout the world, in particular the United States of America and the Union of Soviet Socialist Republics which were not Members of the League.[45]

58. The following is the text of the Pact of Paris:[46]

(List of signatories)

"....

"Persuaded that the time has come when a frank renunciation of war as an instrument of national policy should be made to the end that the peaceful and friendly relations now existing between their peoples may be perpetuated;

"Convinced that all changes in their relations with one another should be sought only by pacific means and be the result of a peaceful and orderly process, and that any signatory Power which shall hereafter seek to promote its national interests by resort to war should be denied the benefits furnished by this Treaty.

".......

"Article I

"The High Contracting Parties solemnly declare in the names of their respective peoples that they condemn recourse to war for the solution of international controversies, and renounce it as an instrument of national policy in their relations with one another.

"Article II

"The High Contracting Parties agree that the settlement or solution of all disputes or conflicts of whatever nature or of whatever origin they may be, which may arise among them, shall never be sought except by pacific means.

"Article III

"....... "

59. Article I contains a prohibition of recourse to war to which no reservation or limitation is attached. Article II, which states that the settlement "of all disputes or conflicts of whatever nature or of whatever origin they may be...shall never be sought except by pacific means", confirms Article I.

1. EXCHANGE OF DIPLOMATIC CORRESPONDENCE ON THE CONCLUSION OF THE PACT OF PARIS

60. The conclusion of the Pact of Paris gave rise to lengthy negotiations in the course of which the scope of the prohibition established by the Pact was defined. The signatories of the Pact were generally agreed that, on the one hand, the Pact did not preclude the exercise of the right of legitimate defence and that, on the other hand, a State which violated the treaty would be denied its benefits.

---

[42] League of Nations, *Resolutions and Recommendations adopted by the Assembly during its Ninth Ordinary Session*, (*Official Journal*, Special Supplement No. 63), page 18.
There are three model treaties concerning security (*ibid*, pages 40-57):
(i) Collective Treaty of Mutual Assistance (Treaty D).
(ii) Collective Treaty of Non-Aggression (Treaty E).
(iii) Bilateral Treaty of Non-Aggression (Treaty F).
[43] Article 1 of the Collective Treaty of Mutual Assistance reads as follows:
"Each of the high contracting parties undertakes, in regard to each of the other parties, not to attack or invade the territory of another contracting party, and in no case to resort to war against another contracting party.
"This stipulation shall not, however, apply in the case of:
"(1) The exercise of the right of legitimate defence—that is to say, resistance to a violation of the undertaking contained in the first paragraph;

"(2) Action in pursuance of Article 16 of the Covenant of the League of Nations;
"(3) Action as the result of a decision taken by the Assembly or by the Council of the League of Nations or in pursuance of Article 15, paragraph 7, of the Covenant of the League of Nations, provided that in this last event the action is directed against a State which was the first to attack."
[44] See League of Nations, *Minutes of the Second Session of the Committee on Arbitration and Security* (League of Nations document C.165.M.50.1928.IX), page 207.
[45] Moreover, when the Pact was concluded, it was hoped that it might serve as a bridge between the League of Nations and the States which had not become Members of the League, and that in the event of an international crisis it would facilitate co-operation between Members of the League of Nations and non-member States with a view to the maintenance or restoration of peace.
[46] See League of Nations, *Treaty Series*, Vol. XCIV, page 57.

61. At the outset of the negotiations, the French Government proposed a formula providing for the prohibition of *wars of aggression* and expressly reserving the right of legitimate self-defence.[47]

62. In reply to this proposal, the United States Government said that the wording of the Pact must be simple if it was to have the desired effect.[48]

63. The wording proposed by the French Government was not adopted. On 23 June 1928, however, the Government of the United States communicated to each of the Governments invited to sign the Pact an identical note clarifying the scope of the Pact. The note dealt, *inter alia*, with the questions of self-defence and of relations with a treaty-breaking State.

64. With regard to *self-defence,* the note states the following:

"There is nothing in the American draft of an anti-war treaty which restricts or impairs in any way the right of self-defence. That right is inherent in every sovereign State and is implicit in every treaty. Every nation is free at all times and regardless of treaty provisions to defend its territory from attack or invasion and it alone is competent to decide whether circumstances require recourse to war in self-defence. If it has a good case, the world will applaud and not condemn its action. Express recognition by treaty of this inalienable right, however, gives rise to the same difficulty encountered in any effort to define aggression. It is the identical question approached from the other side. Inasmuch as no treaty provision can add to the natural right of self-defence, it is not in the interest of peace that a treaty should stipulate a juristic conception of self-defence since it is far too easy for the unscrupulous to mould events to accord with an agreed definition."[49]

65. In regard to *relations with a treaty-breaking State,* the note states that:

"...there can be no question as a matter of law that violation of a multilateral anti-war treaty through resort to war by one party thereto would automatically release the other parties from their obligations to the treaty-breaking State. Any express recognition of this principle of law is wholly unnecessary."[50]

66. The Governments of the States to which this note was addressed confirmed their agreement,[51] so that the note may be regarded as an authorized interpretation of the Pact.

67. On 27 August 1928, an invitation to accede to the Pact of Paris was addressed to forty-nine States, the majority of which notified their accession. Some of the accessions were accompanied by declarations, a number of which expressly noted the interpretation contained in the United States note of 23 June 1928. Other declarations specified that only the text of the Pact was acceded to or rejected some principle established in the exchange of correspondence.

68. In a note communicated on 31 August 1928, the Government of the Union of Soviet Socialist Republics stated that it could not accept the limitations on the Pact referred to in the diplomatic correspondence of the original signatories. The Soviet Government also made the following critical observations on the actual text of the Pact:

"6. With regard to the text of the pact, the Soviet Government deems it necessary to point out that there is a lack of precision and clarity in Article 1 dealing with the formula prohibiting war; this formula allows various and arbitrary interpretations. For its part, the Soviet Government believes that every international war must be prohibited whether as an instrument of what is called 'national policy', or as a method serving other purposes (for instance the suppression of national movements of liberation, etc.). In the opinion of the Soviet Government, there must be a ban on war, not only in the strict juridical meaning of the word (that is, presupposing a declaration of war, etc.), but also on such military actions as, for example, intervention, blockade, military occupation of foreign territories, of foreign ports, etc.

"The history of recent years has provided instances of military activities which have inflicted terrible hardships on the peoples. The Soviet Republics were themselves the object of such attacks, and at the

---

[47] The United States Department of State, the *General Pact for the Renunciation of War,* 1928. See page 14, the letter from Mr. Paul Claudel to Mr. Frank B. Kellogg dated 5 January 1928.
The French Government subsequently proposed, on 20 April 1928, a preliminary draft treaty reserving the right of legitimate defence and clarifying the nature of prohibited acts. This draft contained the following provisions:
"Article I
"The high contracting parties without any intention to infringe upon the exercise of their rights of legitimate self-defence within the framework of existing treaties, particularly when the violation of certain of the provisions of such treaties constitutes a hostile act, solemnly declare that they condemn recourse to war and renounce it as an instrument of national policy; that is to say, as an instrument of individual, spontaneous and independent political action taken on their own initiative and not action in respect of which they might become involved through the obligation of a treaty such as the Covenant of the League of Nations or any other treaty registered with the League of Nations. They undertake on these conditions not to attack or invade one another.
"
"Article III
"In case one of the high contracting parties should contravene this treaty, the other contracting Powers would *ipso facto* be released with respect to that party from their obligations under this treaty".
See, *ibid.,* page 22.

[48] In a letter to Mr. Paul Claudel of 27 February 1928, Mr. Frank P. Kellogg stated the following:
"If, however, such a declaration were accompanied by definitions of the word 'aggressor' and by exceptions and qualifications stipulating when nations would be justified in going to war, its effect would be very greatly weakened and its positive value as a guaranty of peace virtually destroyed. The ideal which inspires the effort so sincerely and so hopefully put forward by your Government and mine is arresting and appealing just because of its purity and simplicity; and I cannot avoid the feeling that if governments should publicly acknowledge that they can only deal with this ideal in a technical spirit and must insist upon the adoption of reservations impairing, if not utterly destroying the true significance of their common endeavours, they would be in effect only recording their impotence, to the keen disappointment of mankind in general."
See, *ibid,* page 14.
[49] *Ibid.,* pages 36-37.
[50] *Ibid.,* page 37.
[51] See, *ibid.:* Germany (page 43), France (pages 43-45), Italy (page 46), Belgium (pages 46-47), Poland (pages 42-43), United Kingdom (pages 47-48), Czechoslovakia (pages 51-53), Japan (pages 53-54).
See Myers, *Origin and Conclusion of the Paris Pact,* World Peace Foundation Pamphlets, Vol. XII, No. 2, 1929.
Union of South Africa (page 150), Australia (page 149), Canada (page 145), Irish Free State (page 144), India (page 149), New Zealand (page 150).

present time the great Chinese people are the victims of similar aggressions. Further, such military actions often develop into big wars which it is then completely impossible to stop, and yet the pact does not say a word about these questions, which are most important from the point of view of peace. Again, the same first article of the pact mentions the necessity of settling all disputes and all international conflicts exclusively by peaceful means. In this connexion, the Soviet Government considers that in the number of non-pacific means forbidden by the pact should also be included such means as the refusal to re-establish normal pacific relations between nations or the rupture of these relations, for such acts, by eliminating the pacific means which might settle differences, embitter relations and contribute to the creation of an atmosphere favourable to the outbreak of war."[52]

2. PARLIAMENTARY DEBATES ON THE PACT OF PARIS

69. Debates on the Pact of Paris were held in various parliaments (Australia, Belgium, Canada, Czechoslovakia, France, Germany, Ireland, Italy, Japan, Poland, Union of South Africa, United Kingdom and United States of America). Generally speaking, these debates confirmed the interpretations of the Pact given in the diplomatic notes exchanged prior to its conclusion.[53] The concept of self-defence figures prominently in the discussions. In some cases it was widely interpreted, while in others it was asserted that it was dangerous to have too broad a definition of self-defence which, interpreted individually by each State, would enable it to use force to protect, for example, the life and property of its nations abroad. In France, it was argued that a war waged against a State refusing to have recourse to peaceful procedures would be a defensive war.

SECTION XII. AMENDMENT OF THE COVENANT OF THE LEAGUE OF NATIONS TO BRING IT INTO HARMONY WITH THE PACT OF PARIS (1929 - 1931)

70. After the entry into force of the Pact of Paris, it was proposed that the Covenant of the League of Nations should be amended to include a general prohibition of recourse to war.[54] The Governments concerned were consulted and a committee of jurists made a study of the question.[55] A number of Governments and certain members of the Committee of Jurists argued that the balance of the system of the Covenant would be destroyed if the principle of the general prohibition of recourse to war were established without drawing the necessary conclusions from that principle, namely, the obligation of States to submit all international disputes to an international body for settlement by a bind-

ing decision and the obligation to comply with that decision. A State which resorted to war to enforce a decision in its favour would not commit an act of aggression. As an extension of this argument, a State which refuses to submit a dispute to a procedure of arbitration or judicial settlement is an aggressor.[56]

71. In the report submitted in 1931 on behalf of the First Committee,[57] Mr. Henri Rolin (Belgium) made the following statement concerning self-defence and aggression:

"5. One point appears beyond dispute—namely, that neither...in the Pact of Paris nor in the Covenant of the League in its present form does the prohibition of recourse to war exclude the right of legitimate self-defence...

"6. On the other hand, in the present state of the law, the satisfactory enumeration of the distinctive characteristics either of aggression or of legitimate self-defence appears difficult and even impossible."

SECTION XIII. THE GENERAL CONVENTION OF 26 SEPTEMBER 1931 TO IMPROVE THE MEANS OF PREVENTING WAR

72. This convention, prepared by tne Committee on Arbitration and Security, was approved by the Assembly of the League of Nations on 26 September 1931 and opened for signature by States.[58] The Convention, to the underlying conception of which a number of States were opposed, did not come into force as it failed to receive the required number of ratifications and accessions. It envisages the case of armed forces entering the territory of another State and seeks to provide a settlement without determining the aggressor and applying sanctions.[59] According to this conception, the main object is to secure the cessation of hostilities and to safeguard the peace. Only when this has been found to be impossible will an attempt be made to assign responsibility by determining the aggressor.

SECTION XIV. THE DISARMAMENT CONFERENCE (1932 - 1933)

73. The question of defining aggression was discussed at length at the Disarmament Conference. Three proposals were submitted, based on the principle that resort to force should be prohibited and that the aggressor is the State violating that prohibition.

1. DECLARATION OF NON-RESORT TO FORCE IN EUROPE

74. On 15 February 1933, Mr. Eden (United Kingdom) submitted to the Political Commission of the Disarmament Conference a draft declaration prohibiting resort to force which concerned only European states in their mutual relations.[60] The meetings held

---

[52]See Myers, *Origin and Conclusion of the Paris Pact*, World Peace Foundation Pamphlets, Vol. XII, No. 2, 1929, pages 170-171.

[53]See André Mandelstam, *L'interprétation du Pacte Briand-Kellogg par les gouvernements et les parlements des Etats signataires*, Paris, 1938.

[54]See League of Nations, *Resolutions and Recommendations adopted by the Assembly during its Tenth Ordinary Session* (*Official Journal*, Special Supplement No. 74), page 18: resolution adopted on 24 September 1929.

[55]See the report of the Committee of Jurists, followed by the observations of Governments, League of Nations document A.8.1930.V. The question came before the Assembly again in 1930 (resolution of 4 October 1930) and in 1931 (resolution of 25 September 1931); see League of Nations, Official Journal, Special Supplement No. 83, page 16, and Special Supplement No. 92, page 9.

[56]See below, paragraphs 449-453.

[57]League of Nations, *Records of the Twelfth Ordinary Session of the Assembly, Minutes of the First Committee* (*Official Journal*, Special Supplement No. 94), page 146.

[58]See League of Nations, *Resolutions and Recommendations adopted by the Assembly during its Twelfth Ordinary Session* (*Official Journal*, Special Supplement No. 92), page 24.

[59]Article 2 of this Convention reads as follows:

"If, in circumstances which, in the Council's opinion, do not create a state of war between the Powers at issue which are parties to the present Convention, the forces of one of those Powers enter the territory or territorial waters of the other or a zone demilitarized in virtue of international agreements, or fly over them, the Council may prescribe measures to ensure their evacuation by those forces."

on 15 February and 2 March were devoted to the discussion of this proposal. On 2 March, the Commission adopted the following text by 27 votes:

"The Governments of...

"Anxious to further the cause of disarmament by increasing the spirit of mutual confidence between the nations of Europe by means of a declaration expressly forbidding resort to force in the circumstances in which the Pact of Paris forbids resort to war:

"Hereby solemnly reaffirm that they will not in any event resort, as between themselves, to force as an instrument of national policy."[61]

2. PROPOSAL BY PRESIDENT ROOSEVELT

75. On 30 May 1933, Mr. Norman Davies (United States of America) submitted to the General Commission of the Conference the following proposal contained in a message from President Roosevelt:

"That all the nations of the world should enter into a solemn and definite pact of non-aggression;...and ...individually agree that they will send no armed force of whatsoever nature across their frontiers."[62]

3. THE DEFINITION OF AGGRESSION DRAFTED BY THE COMMITTEE ON SECURITY QUESTIONS[63]

76. On 6 February 1933, the USSR delegation submitted to the General Commission a proposal for the definition of aggression.[64] The text of the proposal was as follows:

"The General Commission,

"Considering that, in the interests of general security and in order to facilitate the attainment of an agreement for the maximum reduction of armaments, it is necessary, with the utmost precision, to define aggression, in order to remove any possibility of its justification;

"Recognizing the principle of equal right of all States to independence, security and self-defence;

"Animated by the desire of ensuring to each nation, in the interests of general peace, the right of free development according to its own choice and at the rate that suits it best, and of safeguarding the security, independence and complete territorial inviolability of each State and its right to self-defence against attack or invasion from outside, but only within its own frontiers; and

"Anxious to provide the necessary guidance to the international organs which may be called upon to define the aggressor:

"Declares:

"1. The aggressor in an international conflict shall be considered that State which is the first to take any of the following actions:

"(a) Declaration of war against another State;

"(b) The invasion by its armed forces of the territory of another State without declaration of war;

"(c) Bombarding the territory of another State by its land, naval or air forces or knowingly attacking the naval or air forces of another State;

"(d) The landing in, or introduction within the frontiers of, another State of land, naval or air forces without the permission of the Government of such a State, or the infringement of the conditions of such permission, particularly as regards the duration of sojourn or extension of area;

"(e) The establishment of a naval blockade of the coast or ports of another State.

"2. No considerations whatsoever of a political, strategical, or economic nature, including the desire to exploit natural riches or to obtain any sort of advantages or privileges on the territory of another State, no references to considerable capital investments or other special interests in a given State, or to the alleged absence of certain attributes of State organization in the case of a given country, shall be accepted as justification of aggression as defined in Clause 1.

"In particular, justification for attack cannot be based upon:

"A. *The internal situation in a given State,* as, for instance:

"(a) Political, economic or cultural backwardness of a given country;

"(b) Alleged mal-administration;

"(c) Possible danger to life or property of foreign residents;

"(d) Revolutionary or counter-revolutionary movements, civil war, disorders or strikes;

"(e) The establishment or maintenance in any State of any political, economic or social order.

"B. *Any acts, laws or regulations of a given State,* as, for instance:

"(a) The infringement of international agreements;

"(b) The infringement of the commercial, concessional or other economic rights or interests of a given State or its citizens;

"(c) The rupture of diplomatic or economic relations;

"(d) Economic or financial boycott;

"(e) Repudiation of debts;

"(f) Non-admission or limitation of immigration, or restriction of rights or privileges of foreign residents;

---

[60]This proposal was worded as follows:
"The Governments . . .
"Acting respectively through their undersigned representatives, duly authorized to that effect;
"Anxious to further the cause of disarmament by increasing the spirit of mutual confidence between the nations of Europe;
"Determined to fulfil, not only in the letter but also in the spirit, the obligations which they have accepted under the Pact of Paris, signed on August 27th, 1928:
"Hereby solemnly undertake that they will not in any circumstances resort to force for the purpose of resolving any

present or future differences between them".
See League of Nations, *Records of the Conference for the Reduction and Limitation of Armaments,* Series D, Vol. 5 (minutes of the Political Commission), page 11.
[61]*Ibid.,* pages 23 and 30.
[62]*Ibid.,* Series B (Minutes of the General Commission), Vol. 2, page 565.
[63]The proposal actually speaks of a "definition of 'aggressor'" and not of a "definition of aggression", but this difference of terminology is unimportant.
[64]*Ibid.,* page 237.

"(g) The infringement of the privileges of official representatives of other States;

"(h) The refusal to allow armed forces transit to the territory of a third State;

"(i) Religious or anti-religious measures;

"(j) Frontier incidents.

"3. In the case of the mobilization or concentration of armed forces to a considerable extent in the vicinity of its frontiers, the State which such activities threaten may have recourse to diplomatic or other means for the peaceful solution of international controversies. It may at the same time take steps of a military nature, analogous to those described above, without, however, crossing the frontier."

77. The USSR proposal was the subject of a general discussion in the Political Commission on 10 March 1933.[65] Following the discussion, the Commission instructed a Committee on Security Questions, under the chairmanship of Mr. Nicolas Politis,[66] to consider the question. The Committee drew up an Act relating to the Definition of the Aggressor, which provides five criteria of aggression. The report submitted by Mr. Politis on behalf of the Committee is of great interest.[67] The general idea of the Act relating to the Definition of the Aggressor is that the aggressor is the State which first employs force outside its territory,

78. The text of the Act relating to the Definition of the Aggressor is as follows:

" ...

"*Article 1*

"The aggressor in an international conflict shall, subject to the agreements in force between the parties to the dispute, be considered to be that State which is the first to commit any of the following actions:

"(1) Declaration of war upon another State;

"(2) Invasion by its armed forces, with or without a declaration of war, of the territory of another State;

"(3) Attack by its land, naval or air forces, with or without a declaration of war, on the territory, vessels or aircraft of another State;

"(4) Naval blockade of the coasts or ports of another State;

"(5) Provision of support to armed bands formed in its territory which have invaded the territory of another State, or refusal, notwithstanding the request of the invaded State, to take in its own territory all the measures in its power to deprive those bands of all assistance or protection.

"*Article 2*

"No political, military, economic or other considerations may serve as an excuse or justification for the aggression referred to in Article 1.

"*Article 3*

"The present Act shall form an integral part of the General Convention for the Reduction and Limitation of Armaments.

" ......

"*Protocol annexed to Article 22 of the Act relating to the Definition of the Aggressor*

"The High Contracting Parties signatories of the Act relating to the Definition of the Aggressor,

"Desiring, subject to the express reservation that the absolute validity of the rule laid down in Article 2 of that Act shall be in no way restricted, to furnish certain indications for the guidance of the international bodies that may be called upon to determine the aggressor:

"Declare that no act of aggression within the meaning of Article 1 of that Act can be justified on either of the following grounds, among others:

"A. The Internal Condition of a State:

"E.g., its political, economic or social structure; alleged defects in its administration; disturbances due to strikes, revolutions, counter-revolutions or civil war.

"B. The International Conduct of a State:

"E.g., the violation or threatened violation of the material or moral rights or interests of a foreign State or its nationals; the rupture of diplomatic or economic relations; economic or financial boycotts; disputes relating to economic, financial or other obligations towards foreign States; frontier incidents not forming any of the cases of aggression specified in Article 1.

"The High Contracting Parties further agree to recognize that the present Protocol can never legitimate any violations of international law that may be implied in the circumstances comprised in the above list."[68]

79. It will be seen that, in general, the Act relating to the Definition of the Aggressor reproduces the substance of the USSR proposal, but in somewhat different form. The Act, however, refers to the provision of support to armed bands (5), which is not mentioned in the USSR proposal of 6 February 1933.

80. The Act was considered by the General Commission on 25 and 29 May 1933.[69] There were differences of opinion and the Commission reserved its decision. The definition of the aggressor drafted by the Committee on Security Questions of the Disarmament Conference was adopted in a number of treaties.[70]

SECTION XV. CONSULTATION WITH GOVERNMENTS CONCERNING THE APPLICATION OF THE PRINCIPLES OF THE COVENANT (1936)

81. After the failure of sanctions against Italy, the Assembly of the League of Nations adopted a recom-

[65] *Ibid.*, Series D, Vol. 5 (Minutes of the Political Commission), page 47.

[66] The Committee consisted of the representatives of the following countries: Belgium, Cuba, Denmark, Esthonia, Finland, France, Germany, Hungary, Italy, Poland, Spain, Switzerland, Turkey, Union of Soviet Socialist Republics, United Kingdom, United States of America and Yugoslavia.

[67] See League of Nations, Conference for the Reduction and Limitation of Armaments, Conference Documents, Vol. II, page 679 (document Conf.D/C.G.108).
[68] *Ibid.*, pages 683-684.
[69] See League of Nations, *Records of the Conference for the Reduction and Limitation of Armaments*, Series B (Minutes of the General Commission), Vol. 2, pages 510-517, 547-559.
[70] See below, paragraphs 205-208.

mendation on 4 July 1936, to the effect that the Council should invite governments to formulate proposals "in order to improve the application of the principles of the Covenant".[71] In this connexion, the Governments of China, Esthonia,, Iraq, Latvia, Panama and the Union of Soviet Socialist Republics expressed their support for a definition of aggression.[72] The Argentine Government expressed what would appear to be a different point of view.[73]

Chapter II

CRITERIA APPLIED WHEN A CONFLICT HAS BEEN ACCOMPANIED BY THE USE OF FORCE

82. Article 16 of the Covenant of the League of Nations, concerning the application of sanctions against a State resorting to war in violation of the Covenant, is known to have been applied twice only: in the Italo-Ethiopian dispute (1935) and the Soviet-Finnish dispute (1939). Apart from these cases, however, the organs of the League of Nations, founding themselves on Article 11 or Article 15 of the Covenant, gave more or less explicit rulings on responsibility for armed conflicts. Of course, where a conflict was accompanied by hostilities, the organs of the League sought primarily to put an end to it by persuading the parties to cease the use of force and to accept the measures proposed to prevent a resumption of hostilities. To this end the organs of the League appealed to the good-will of the parties, refrained from condemnatory judgments which might have caused offence, and generally exercised great restraint in pronouncing on the misdeeds of parties, using great tact so that the violators of the Covenant could give way without losing face.

SECTION I. DISPUTE BETWEEN PERSIA AND THE UNION OF SOVIET SOCIALIST REPUBLICS (ENZELI INCIDENT) (1920)

83. In May 1920, USSR vessels shelled the port of Enzeli and disembarked troops to take possession of the fleet of Admiral Denikin, who had taken refuge in the port. The Persian Government appealed to the Council of the League of Nations, invoking Article 11[74] and subsequently Article 10 of the Covenant.[75]

84. On 16 June 1920 the Council of the League of Nations adopted the following resolution:

"The Council considers that the Persian Government has acted in the best interests of peace, and that it has rightly appealed to the fundamental principle of co-operation laid down in the Covenant, in asking the League of Nations to declare its willingness to maintain the territorial integrity of Persia in accordance with Article X of the Covenant.

"The Council decides that before advising upon the means by which the obligations prescribed by the Covenant shall be fulfilled, it is desirable, in order to give every opportunity for the success of the conversations now in progress, to await the result of the promises made by the Soviet authorities. In the meantime the Council requests the Persian representative to keep it informed of the march of events through the Secretary-General of the League of Nations."[76]

SECTION II. INCURSIONS OF ARMED BANDS INTO THE STATES BORDERING ON BULGARIA (INVOLVING BULGARIA, ROMANIA, YUGOSLAVIA AND GREECE) (1922)

85. As a result of a collective note addressed to it on 14 June 1922 by the Governments of Greece, Romania and Yugoslavia, the Bulgarian Government submitted the matter to the Council of the League of Nations on 17 June 1922[77] under Article 11 of the Covenant. The Bulgarian Government was accused of encouraging the formation in its territory of armed bands and their incursions over the frontiers of the neighbouring States.

86. In a resolution of 19 July 1922 the Council:

"Expresses its hope for a satisfactory conclusion to the efforts made by the interested Governments to put an end, by a direct agreement, to a situation which may become dangerous to peace;

"And requests the Governments to inform the Council at its next session of the result of the negotiations in progress, and places itself at their disposal should its intervention be again required to avoid all possibility of a conflict."[78]

SECTION III. GRECO-BULGARIAN DISPUTE (DEMIR KAPOU) (1925)

87. The report of the Commission of Enquiry into the incidents on the frontier between Bulgaria and Greece, the conclusions of which were adopted by the Council on 14 December 1925, stated the following:

"...the Commission must nevertheless record that, by occupying a part of Bulgarian territory with its military forces, Greece violated the Covenant of the League of Nations."[79]

SECTION IV. SINO-JAPANESE DISPUTE (MANCHURIA) (1931)

88. The report adopted by the Assembly on 24 February 1933 in virtue of Article 15, paragraph 4, states:

[71]See League of Nations, *Records of the Sixteenth Ordinary Session of the Assembly, Plenary Meetings, Text of the Debates, Part 2* (*Official Journal*, Special Supplement No. 151), pages 65, 66 and 68.
[72]See League of Nations, *Documents relating to the Question of the Application of the Principles of the Covenant,* (*Official Journal*, Special Supplement No. 154), pages 87 and 88.
[73]*Ibid,* page 13. The Argentine Government asked that "the previous determination of the aggressor in each case and according to circumstances should be laid down as a condition of all sanctions".
[74]Letter dated 19 May 1920 from the Ministry of Foreign Affairs of Persia to the Secretary-General of the League of Nations. See League of Nations, *Procès-Verbal of the Sixth*

Session of the Council, page 25. See also the letter of 29 May 1920, *ibid,* page 27.
[75]Memorandum of the Persian Government; dated 14 June 1920, *ibid,* page 31.
[76]*Ibid,* page 41.
[77]See League of Nations, *Official Journal,* 3rd Year, No. 8, Part II: *Nineteenth Session of the Council,* page 795.
[78]*Ibid,* page 804.
[79]See League of Nations document C.727.M.270.1925.VII, page 8. The Commission, however, recognizes various extenuating circumstances of great importance, such as the absence of premeditation. For the Council's decision of 14 December 1925 see League of Nations, *Official Journal,* 7th Year, No. 2: *Thirty-Seventh Session of the Council,* pages 172-177.

"Without excluding the possibility that, on the night of 18-19 September 1931, the Japanese officers on the spot may have believed that they were acting in self-defence, the Assembly cannot regard as measures of self-defence the military operations carried out on that night by the Japanese troops at Mukden and other places in Manchuria. *Nor can the military measures of Japan as a whole,* developed in the course of the dispute, *be regarded as measures of self-defence".*[80]

Section V. Dispute between Colombia and Peru (Leticia) (1933)

89. The report adopted by the Council on 18 March 1933[81] under Article 15, paragraph 4, contains the following passage:

"The Council reaches the following conclusions:

"1. That both parties agree:

"(*a*) That the Treaty of March 24th, 1922, between Colombia and Peru is in force;

"(*b*) That, in virtue of that Treaty, the territory known as the 'Leticia Trapezium' forms part of the territory of the Republic of Colombia;

"2. That that territory has been invaded by Peruvians, who ejected the Colombian authorities from their posts;

"3. That those Peruvians have been supported by the military authorities of the Department of Loreto (Peru);

"4. That a Peruvian post had been established at Tarapaca on Colombian territory; that this post was later captured by Colombian forces."[82]

90. Later in the report the Council recommends "the complete evacuation by the Peruvian forces of the territory contained in the *Leticia Trapezium,* and the withdrawal of all support from the Peruvians who have occupied that area".[83]

Section VI. Dispute between Bolivia and Paraguay (1934-1935)

91. The report of the Chaco Commission of 9 May 1934 states:

"In this dispute each party claims ownership of the Chaco, and therefore maintains that it is waging defensive war in its own territory. *How is the aggressor to be determined in such a conflict? No international*

frontier has been crossed by foreign troops, since the Chaco question will only be settled by a delimitation of this disputed frontier."[84]

92. The report adopted by the Assembly on 24 November 1934, in virtue of Article 15, paragraph 4, contains the following passage:

"2. The dispute which has arisen between the two countries is the consequence of the fact that their common frontier has never been fixed by any final treaty and that hostilities were brought about by the inevitable impact of the two movements of occupation of which the Chaco has been the scene: that of Paraguay to the north and west and that of Bolivia to the south and east.

"3. For several months hostilities continued without either of the Parties appealing to the League of Nations either under Article 11 or under Article 15. The Assembly is therefore bound to record that neither of the Parties has fulfilled its undertakings under Article 12 of the Covenant."[85]

Section VII. Italo-Ethiopian dispute (1935)

93. At its meeting on 5 October 1935, the Council appointed a committee of six members[86] to study the situation in the light of its latest developments. The Committee's report, which was submitted to the Council on 7 October 1935, noted certain events and found that "these events occurred before the draft report in pursuance of Article 15, paragraph 4 of the Covenant had been submitted to the Council".[87] After referring to Articles 12, 13 and 15 of the Covenant, the report came to the conclusion that "the Italian Government *has resorted to war in disregard of its covenants under Article 12 of the Covenant* of the League of Nations".[88] At the meeting on 7 October 1936 the Members of the Council declared themselves in agreement with the conclusions of the report.

Section VIII. Soviet-Finnish dispute (1939)

94. In its report[89] adopted on 14 December 1939 in pursuance of Article 15, paragraphs 4 and 10, of the Covenant of the League of Nations, the Assembly stated, first, that "in the course of the various stages of the dispute the Finnish Government has not rejected any peaceful procedure",[90] and, secondly, that "the attitude and acts of the Government of the Union of Soviet Socialist Republics, on the other hand, have been incompatible with the commitments entered into

---

[80]The statement of the recommendations contained in the report includes the following passage:
"1. Whereas the sovereignty over Manchuria belongs to China, A. Considering that the presence of Japanese troops outside the zone of the South Manchuria Railway and their operations outside this zone are incompatible with the legal principles which should govern the settlement of the dispute, and that it is necessary to establish as soon as possible a situation consistent with these principles,
"The Assembly recommends the evacuation of these troops . . ." League of Nations, *Records of the Special Session of the Assembly,* Vol. IV (*Official Journal,* Special Supplement No. 112) pages 22, 72, 75.
[81]League of Nations, *Official Journal,* 14th Year, No. 4: *Seventy-First Session of the Council,* pages 516-523.

[82]*Ibid,* page 608.
[83]*Ibid,* page 609.
[84]League of Nations document C.154.M.64.1934.VII, page 52.
[85]*Dispute between Bolivia and Paraguay, Records of the Special Session of the Assembly* (League of Nations, *Official Journal,* Special Supplement No. 132), page 48.
[86]Chile, Denmark, France, Portugal, Romania, United Kingdom. See League of Nations, *Official Journal,* 16th Year, No. 11: *Eighty-eighth Session of the Council,* page 1213.
[87]*Ibid.,* page 1224.
[88]*Ibid.,* page 1225.
[89]League of Nations, *Official Journal,* 20th ear, No. 11-12 (Part II); *One Hundred and Seventh Session of the Council,* pages 531-540 (document A.46.1939.VII).
[90]*Ibid.,* page 538.

by that country".[91] The report concludes that "the Soviet Government has violated, not only its special political agreements with Finland, but also Article 12 of the Covenant of the League of Nations and the Pact of Paris".[92]

95. The following resolution was adopted by the Assembly on 14 December 1949:

"The Assembly:

"Whereas, by the aggression which it has committed against Finland, the Union of Soviet Socialist Republics has failed to observe not only its special political agreements with Finland but also Article 12 of the Covenant of the League of Nations and the Pact of Paris;

". . . . .

"Solemnly condemns the action taken by the Union of Soviet Socialist Republics against the State of Finland;

". . . . . "[93]

96. The following resolution was adopted by the Council of the League of Nations on 14 December 1939:

"The Council,

"Having taken cognizance of the resolution adopted by the Assembly on 14 December 1939, regarding the appeal of the Finnish Government;

"1. Associates itself with the condemnation by the Assembly of the action of the Union of Soviet Socialist Republics against the Finnish State; and

"2. For the reasons set forth in the resolution of the Assembly,

"In virtue of Article 16, paragraph 4, of the Covenant;

"Finds that, by its act, the Union of Soviet Socialist Republics has placed itself outside the League of Nations. It follows that the Union of Soviet Socialist Republics is no longer a Member of the League."[94]

---

[91] *Ibid.*, page 539. The Assembly refers in this connexion to Article III of the Convention for the Definition of Aggression signed in London on 3 July 1933. The report states that:
"The order to enter Finland was given to the Soviet troops on the ground of 'further armed provocation'. The reference was to frontier incidents or alleged frontier incidents. In the Annex, however, to Article III of the Convention it is declared that no act of aggression within the meaning of Article II of the Convention can be justified by frontier incidents not forming any of the cases of aggression specified in Article II".
The report (*ibid.*, page 540) also notes a violation of Article III of the Convention by the refusal of the Soviet Government to treat with the present Government of Fin-

land, which it called the "former Finnish Government". The report states:
"The Annex to Article III specifies that aggression cannot be justified either by the international conduct of a State, for example: the violation or threatened violation of the material or moral rights or interests of a foreign State; or by the internal condition of a State, for example; its political, economic or social structure; alleged defects in its administration; disturbances due to strikes, revolutions, counter-revolutions or civil war".

[92] *Ibid.*, page 540.
[93] *Ibid.*, pages 506 and 508.
[94] *Ibid.*, pages 506 and 508.

Title II

THE ERA OF THE UNITED NATIONS

97. Attention will be directed first to the Charter of the United Nations and the expressions it uses in connexion with the prohibition of war and the use of force, and then to the question of aggression. It will, however, be noted that the latter question was approached from two different points of view.

98. In the first place, there was a discussion to determine which acts the organs and Members of the United Nations should regard as constituting aggression for the purpose of applying the collective security system.

99. Secondly, a study was made of the question of offences against peace, chief of which is the crime of aggression.

100. Though closely related, these two questions are distinct and were considered separately by the General Assembly and the International Law Commission.

101. The question of defining aggression concerns the political organs of the United Nations, since it is

their duty to organize collective action to check aggression, and to do so they might have to determine the aggressor.

102. The question of the crime of aggression also concerns international penal law, since persons who commit acts deemed to constitute the crime of aggression must be punished. In normal circumstances, the crime of aggression will be tried some time after its commission. According to some authorities, it can in practice be tried only when its authors have been apprehended after the aggressor country has been defeated.

103. At its third session, the International Law Commission considered aggression from these two different points of view, dealing separately with the "question of defining aggression" and the question of the "draft code of offences against the peace and security of mankind".[1]

104. It is to be observed that in its draft code the International Law Commission defines the crime of aggression in general terms[2] and treats as separate

---

[1] See the report of the Commission, A/1858, *Official Records of the General Assembly, Sixth Session, Supplement No. 9,* chapter III: Question of defining aggression, and chapter IV: Draft code of offences against the peace and security of mankind.
[2] "Article 2. The following acts are offences against the

peace and security of mankind:
"(1) Any act of aggression, including the employment by the authorities of a State of armed force against another State for any purpose other than national or collective self-defence or in pursuance of a decision or recommendation by a competent organ of the United Nations".

offences, that is to say, as offences other than the crime of aggression, certain acts covered by the definition of aggression prepared in 1933 by the Committee on Security Questions of the Disarmament Conference and by the definition adopted in the treaties concluded in London at that time.[3]

Chapter I

THE CHARTER OF THE UNITED NATIONS

Section I. The rules established by the Charter

105. The Charter of the United Nations introduced important innovations. It limits much more strictly than did the Covenant of the League of Nations the right of States to resort to war and to use force in international relations.

106. The system of the Charter is based on the following principles: (1) resort to war, or to the threat or use of force, is generally prohibited; (2) the cases in which the use of force is permitted are specified by the Charter.

1. Resort to war or to the threat or use of force is generally prohibited

107. Two provisions of the Charter; paragraphs 3 and 4 of Article 2, are pertinent in this connexion. Article 2, paragraph 3, provides as follows:

"All Members shall settle their international disputes *by peaceful means* in such a manner that international peace and security, and justice, are not endangered."

Once it is postulated that States must settle their disputes "by peaceful means", war is unconditionally prohibited as a means of exercising a right, opposing violation of a right or redressing a wrong of which a State may have been the victim.

108. Article 2, paragraph 4, provides as follows:

"All Members shall refrain in their international relations from the threat or use of force against the territorial integrity or political independence of any State, or in any other manner inconsistent with the Purposes of the United Nations."

This paragraph confirms and supplements the preceding paragraph. It prohibits recourse to "the threat or use of force". It is not only war properly so-called which is prohibited, but also the use of force, though it might be claimed that a limited use of force does not constitute resort to war and is not intended to do so.[4] It is not only the use of force which is prohibited, but also the threat of its use.

[3]Thus, in the above-mentioned draft code, "The incursion into the territory of a State from the territory of another State by armed bands acting for a political purpose" constitutes an offence distinct from aggression and is included as No. (4) in the list of offences against the peace and security of mankind.
[4]In view of the wording of the Article, a restrictive interpretation might suggest itself.
It is stated that "All Members shall refrain in their international relations from the threat or use of force *against the territorial integrity or political independence of any State . . .* " On the basis of the words italicized, could it not be said *a contrario* that the threat or use of force is permitted if it is not intended to infringe the territorial integrity or political independence of a State? Reference to the preparatory work shows that such an interpretation would not accord with the

2. The use of force is lawful only when prescribed by the organs of the United Nations or in application of the right of self-defence

109. In neither of these cases does the State resorting to the use of force take the initiative in doing so. In the first case, the State participates in collective action directed by the United Nations. In the second case, it exercises the right of self-defence against a State which was the first to resort to the use of force.

(a) *Action with respect to threats to the peace, breaches of the peace, and acts of aggression*

110. Such action is provided for under Chapter VII of the Charter, which determines the powers of the Security Council and the obligations of the members of the United Nations. General Assembly Resolution 377(V), entitled "Uniting for Peace", provides that if the Security Council fails to act the General Assembly may intervene.

(b) *Self-defence*

111. The right of self-defence exercised individually or collectively is explicitly recognized by Article 51 of the Charter in cases where an "armed attack" has taken place. In this connexion, Article 51 provides as follows:

"Nothing in the present Charter shall impair *the inherent right of individual or collective self-defence* if *an armed attack* occurs against a Member of the United Nations, until the Security Council has taken the measures necessary to maintain international peace and security. Measures taken by Members in the exercise of this right of self-defence shall be immediately reported to the Security Council and shall not in any way affect the authority and responsibility of the Security Council under the present Charter to take at any time such action as it deems necessary in order to maintain or restore international peace and security."

Section II. The Charter of the United Nations and the Definition of Aggression (*preparatory work*)

1. Proposals for the definition of aggression

112. Proposals were submitted by Bolivia and the Philippines to Committee 3 of the Third Commission of the San Francisco Conference.

113. The Bolivian proposal was worded as follows:

"A State shall be designated an aggressor if it has committed any of the following acts to the detriment of another State.

"(a) Invasion of another State's territory by armed forces.

intention of the authors of the Charter. The words "territorial integrity or political independence of any State" did not appear in the Dumbarton Oaks draft. When they were introduced pursuant to an amendment proposed by the Australian Government and to other draft amendments submitted by various Governments, it was done with the strongly expressed desire to ensure respect for the territorial integrity and political independence of States and not with a view to permitting resort to the threat or use of force in certain cases. The text of the Australian amendment was adopted unchanged (see discussion in Committee I/1 of the Conference of San Francisco, 7th meeting, 16 May 1945; 11th meeting, 4 June 1945. *United Nations Conference on International Organization, Documents*, Vol. 6, pages 304 and 334-335).

"(b) Declaration of war.

"(c) Attack by land, sea, or air forces with or without declaration of war, on another State's territory, shipping, or aircraft.

"(d) Support given to armed bands for the purpose of invasion.

"(e) Intervention in another State's internal or foreign affairs.

"(f) Refusal to submit the matter which has caused a dispute to the peaceful means provided for its settlement.

"(g) Refusal to comply with a judicial decision lawfully pronounced by an International Court."[5]

114. This proposal was accompanied by the following observation:

"In general the Security Council shall determine the existence of any threat to the peace, breach of the peace, or act of aggression and should make recommendations or decide on the measures to be taken to maintain or restore peace and security. If the nature of the acts investigated entails designating a State as an aggressor as indicated in the following paragraph, these measures should be applied immediately by collective action."[6]

115. The Philippine proposal was worded as follows:

"Any nation should be considered as threatening the peace or as an aggressor, if it should be the first party to commit any of the following acts:

"(1) To declare war against another nation;

"(2) To invade or attack, with or without declaration of war, the territory, public vessel, or public aircraft of another nation;

"(3) To subject another nation to a naval, land or air blockade;

"(4) To interfere with the internal affairs of another nation by supplying arms, ammunition, money or other forms of aid to any armed band, faction or group, or by establishing agencies in that nation to conduct propaganda subversive of the institutions of that nation."[7]

2. REPORT BY MR. PAUL-BONCOUR

116. In his report on Chapter VIII, Section B, presented on behalf of the above-mentioned Committee 3, Mr. Paul-Boncour stated the following:

"A more protracted discussion developed in the Committee on the possible insertion in paragraph 2, Section B, Chapter VIII, of the determination of acts of aggression.

"Various amendments proposed on this subject recalled the definitions written into a number of treaties concluded before this war but did not claim to specify all cases of aggression. They proposed a list of eventualities in which intervention by the Council would be automatic. At the same time they would have left to the Council the power to determine the other cases in which it should likewise intervene.

"Although this proposition evoked considerable support, it nevertheless became clear to a majority of the Committee that a preliminary definition of aggression went beyond the possibilities of this Conference and the purpose of the Charter. The progress of the technique of modern warfare renders very difficult the definition of all cases of aggression. It may be noted that, the list of such cases being necessarily incomplete, the Council would have a tendency to consider of less importance the acts not mentioned therein; these omissions would encourage the aggressor to distort the definition or might delay action by the Council. Furthermore, in the other cases listed, automatic action by the Council might bring about a premature application of enforcement measures.

"The Committee therefore decided to adhere to the text drawn up at Dumbarton Oaks and to leave to the Council the entire decision as to what constitutes a threat to peace, a breach of the peace, or an act of aggression."[8]

Chapter II
ATTEMPTS TO DEFINE AGGRESSION

SECTION I. GENERAL ASSEMBLY RESOLUTIONS 378 B (V) AND 380 (V) OF 17 NOVEMBER 1950

117. These two resolutions deal with the question of defining aggression, but the former, whereby the General Assembly decided to refer the matter to the International Law Commission, deals with procedure, while the latter is concerned with the substance of the question.

1. GENERAL ASSEMBLY RESOLUTION 378 B (V) OF 17 NOVEMBER 1950

118. At the 385th meeting of the First Committee of the General Assembly, held on 6 November 1950 and devoted to consideration of the question "Duties of States in the event of the outbreak of hostilities", which had been placed on the agenda at the request of the Yugoslav delegation (A/1399), the representative of the Union of Soviet Socialist Republics submitted a draft resolution (A/C.1/608/Rev.1) containing an enumerative definition of acts of aggression.[9]

119. At the 387th meeting of the First Committee, held on 7 November 1950, the Syrian representative submitted a draft resolution (A/C.1/610) suggesting that the USSR proposal should be referred for study to the competent subsidiary organ of the General Assembly, that is to say, to the International Law Commission.[10] The Commission was to include the definition of aggression in its studies when preparing a criminal code for the international crimes, and submit a report to the General Assembly.

120. The Syrian proposal was subsequently replaced by a draft resolution submitted jointly by the delegations of Bolivia and Syria (A/C.1/615).[11] This draft was adopted by the First Committee at its 390th meeting held on 9 November 1950.[12]

[5] Ibid., Vol. 3, page 585.
[6] Ibid., page 584.
[7] Ibid., page 538.
[8] Ibid., Vol. 12, page 505.
[9] See Official Records of the General Assembly, Fifth Session, First Committee, 385th meeting, paragraphs 18-35, and Annexes, item 72.
[10] See Official Records of the General Assembly, Fifth Session, First Committee, 387th meeting, paragraph 42.
[11] Ibid., 390th meeting, paragraph 11.
[12] Ibid., 390th meeting, paragraph 41.

121. The General Assembly adopted the draft resolution submitted by the First Committee at its 308th plenary meeting held on 17 November 1950.[13] Under resolution 378 B (V):

"*The General Assembly*

"*Considering* that the question raisèd by the proposal of the Union of Soviet Socialist Republics can better be examined in conjunction with matters under consideration by the International Law Com.nission, a subsidiary organ of the United Nations,

"*Decides* to refer the proposal of the Union of Soviet Socialist Republics and all the records of the First Committee dealing with this question to the International Law Commission, so that the latter may take them into consideration and formulate its conclusions as soon as possible."[14]

2. GENERAL ASSEMBLY RESOLUTION 380 (v) OF 17 NOVEMBER 1950

122. The delegation of the Union of Soviet Socialist Republics requested the President of the General Assembly in a letter addressed to him on 20 September 1950 (A/1376) to include in the agenda for the fifth session of the General Assembly the item entitled: "Declaration on the removal of the threat of a new war and the strengthening of peace and security among the nations."

123. At its 285th meeting, held on 26 September 1950, the General Assembly decided, on the recommendation of the General Committee, to place this item on its agenda and to refer it to the First Committee for consideration and report.[15]

124. The First Committee considered the item at its 372nd to 383rd meetings held from 23 October to 5 November 1950. Several draft resolutions and amendments were submitted to it.[16]

125. At its 383rd meeting held on 3 November 1950,[17] it adopted a draft resolution which was approved without discussion by the General Assembly at its 308th plenary meeting on 17 November 1950.[18]

126. Resolution 380 (V) is worded as follow:

"*The General Assembly,*

"......

"*Condemning* the intervention of a State in the internal affairs of another State for the purpose of changing its legally established government by the threat or use of force,

"1. *Solemnly* reaffirms that, whatever the weapons used, any aggression, whether committed openly, or by fomenting civil strife in the interest of a foreign Power, or otherwise, is the gravest of all crimes against peace and security throughout the world;

"......"[19]

127. It will be noted that, in this resolution, aggression is interpreted broadly by the General Assembly, since it may take the form of "fomenting civil strife in the interest of a foreign Power", and may also be committed "otherwise".

SECTION II. THE INTERNATIONAL LAW COMMISSION (THIRD SESSION: 16 MAY TO 27 JULY 1951)

128. Pursuant to resolution 378 B (V) adopted by the General Assembly on 17 November 1950, the International Law Commission devoted eleven meetings[20] to a study of the proposal (A/C.1/608/Rev.1) submitted by the Union of Soviet Socialist Republics to the First Committee of the General Assembly and of the other First Committee documents dealing with the question. The results of its work are described in its report.[21]

129. The Commission had before it a report by Mr. Spiropoulos entitled "The possibility and desirability of a definition of aggression". This report was unfavourable to the idea of such a definition.[22]

130. Definitions of a general nature were proposed by the following members of the Commission:[23] Mr. Amado, Mr. Alfaro, Mr. Yepes,[24] Mr. Hsu, Mr. Córdova and Mr. Scelle.

131. The Commission was of the opinion that it should adopt a general definition of aggression and took as the basis for discussion the text submitted by Mr. Alfaro.

132. Various modifications were introduced into Mr. Alfaro's draft definition, which was thus amended to read:

"Aggression is the threat or use of force by a State or government against another State, in any manner, whatever the weapons employed and whether openly or otherwise, for any reason or for any purpose other than individual or collective self-defence or in pursuance of a decision or recommendation by a competent organ of the United Nations."[25]

133. Nevertheless, a final roll-call vote was taken, the definition was rejected by 7 votes to 3.[26] The majority voted in favour of rejecting the text for various reasons. Some members were opposed to the very principle of defining aggression, while others considered that the definition lacked elements which they thought essential.

134. Mr. Alfaro then proposed that the Commission should not give up its attempt to define aggression, but should continue its efforts, taking as the basis for its

---

[13]See *Official Records of the General Assembly, Fifth Session, Plenary Meetings,* 308th meeting, paragraph 24.

[14]*Ibid., Supplement No. 20,* A/1775, page 13.

[15]*Ibid., Plenary Meetings,* 285th meeting, paragraph 67.

[16]*Ibid., First Committee,* 372nd to 383rd meetings, and *Annexes,* item 69.

[17]*Ibid., First Committee,* 383rd meeting, paragraph 94.

[18]*Ibid., Plenary Meetings,* 308th meeting, paragraph 57.

[19]*Ibid., Supplement No. 20,* A/1775, page 13.

[20]I.e., its 92nd, 93rd, 94th, 95th, 96th, 108th, 109th, 127th, 128th, 129th, and 133rd meetings.

[21]A/1858, *Official Records of the General Assembly, Sixth Session, Supplement No. 9,* Chapter III.

[22]See document A/CN.4/44, Chapter II.

[23]See A/1858, Chapter III, and paragraphs 470–472, 475 and 476 below.

[24]Mr. Yepes presented two definitions, one enumerative (A/CN.4/L.7), the other a slightly developed definition (A/CN.4/L.12).

[25]A/1858, paragraph 49.

[26]*For:* Mr. Alfaro, Mr. Córdova and Mr. François
Against: Mr. Amado, Mr. Brierly, Mr. Hsu, Mr. El-Khouri, Mr. Sandström, Mr. Spiropoulos and Mr. Yepes.
Abstaining: Mr. Hudson.
Absent: Mr. Scelle.

work the several texts presented by others of its members. This proposal was rejected by 6 votes to 4.[27]

SECTION III. GENERAL ASSSEMBLY RESOLUTION 599 (VI) ON THE QUESTION OF DEFINING AGGRESSION (31 JANUARY 1952)

135. At its 341st plenary meeting[28] on 13 November 1951, the General Assembly decided to place on its agenda the report of the International Law Commission covering the work of its third session[29], and, at its 342nd plenary meeting held the same day, decided to refer the question of defining aggression to the Sixth Committee for consideration and report.[30]

136. The question of defining aggression was the subject of prolonged discussion in the Sixth Committee at eighteen meetings, held from 5 January to 22 January 1952.[31] During these discussions, arguments for and against a definition of aggression were advanced.

137. As the basis for its work, the Sixth Committee had the report of the International Law Commission, a draft resolution submitted by Greece (A/C.6/L.206), a draft resolution submitted by the Union of Soviet Socialist Republics (A/C.6/L.208), a draft resolution submitted jointly by France, Iran and Venezuela (A/C.6/L.209) and a Bolivian draft resolution (A/C.6/L.211).

138. Amendments to these draft resolutions were submitted by Colombia (A/C.6/L.210) and Egypt (A/C.6/L.213) (to the draft resolution submitted by the USSR), and by Colombia (A/C.6/L.214/Rev.1), India (A/C.6/L.212) and Syria (A/C.6/L.215) (to the joint draft resolution submitted by France, Iran and Venezuela). Lastly, Mexico submitted an amendment (A/C.6/L.216) to the Syrian amendment.

139. At its 294th meeting on 21 January 1952, the Sixth Committee adopted paragraph 1 of the Colombian amendment and, after modification, paragraphs 1, 3 and 4 of the Syrian amendment. The joint draft resolution thus amended was adopted by 28 votes to 12 with 7 abstentions.[32]

140. On 31 January 1952, the General Assembly adopted[33] by 30 votes to 12 with 8 abstentions the draft resolution[34] submitted by the Sixth Committee.

Chapter III
AGGRESSION CONSIDERED AS AN INTERNATIONAL CRIME

SECTION I. THE LONDON AGREEMENT OF 8 AUGUST 1945, THE CHARTER OF THE INTERNATIONAL MILITARY TRIBUNAL AND THE JUDGMENT OF THE TRIBUNAL

1. THE LONDON AGREEMENT AND THE CHARTER OF THE TRIBUNAL

141. On 8 August 1945 the Governments of France, the Union of Soviet Socialist Republics, the United Kingdom and the United States of America signed in London an Agreement[35] providing that an International Military Tribunal should be established for the trial of war criminals whose offences had no particular geographical location (article 1).

142. To this Agreement is annexed the Charter of the International Military Tribunal. Article 6 of the Charter submits to the jurisdiction of the Tribunal three categories of crimes, the first of which, crimes against the peace, is defined as follows:

"(a) Crimes against peace: namely, *planning, preparation, initiation or waging of a war of aggression*, or a war in violation of international treaties, agreements or assurances, or participation in a Common Plan or Conspiracy for the accomplishment of any of the foregoing;"[36]

143. It is to be observed that at the Conference which drafted the Charter of the Tribunal the delegation of the United States of America proposed the inclusion in the Charter of the following definition of the crime of aggression:

"An aggressor, for the purposes of this Article, is that state which is the first to commit any of the following actions:

"(1) Declaration of war upon another state;

"(2) Invasion by its own forces, with or without a declaration of war, of the territory of another state;

"(3) Attack by its land, naval, or air forces, with or without a declaration of war, on the territory, vessels or aircraft of another state;

"(4) Naval blockade of the coasts or ports of another state;

"(5) Provision of support to armed bands formed in its territory which have invaded the territory of another state, or refusal, notwithstanding the request of the invaded state, to take in its own territory all the measures in its power to deprive those bands of all assistance or protection.

"No political, military, economic or other considerations shall serve as an excuse or justification for such actions; but exercise of the right of legitimate self-defense, that is to say, resistance to an act of aggression, or action to assist a state which has been sub-

---

[27]*For*: Mr. Alfaro, Mr. Córdova, Mr. Hsu and Mr. Yepes
Against: Mr. Amado, Mr. Brierly, Mr. François, Mr. Hudson, Mr. El-Khouri and Mr. Sandström.
Abstaining: Mr. Spiropoulos.
Absent: Mr. Scelle.
The Commission did, however, include aggression among the offences covered by its draft code of offences against the peace and security of mankind. See below, paragraph 160.
[28]See *Official Records of the General Assembly, Sixth Session, Plenary Meetings*, 341st meeting, paragraph 42.
[29]See A/1853, *Official Records of the General Assembly, Sixth Session, Supplement No. 9.*
[30]See A/2119, *Resolutions adopted by the General Assembly at its Sixth Session, Official Records of the General Assembly, Sixth Session, Supplement No. 20*, page xvii.
[31]See *Official Records of the General Assembly, Sixth Session, Sixth Committee*, 278th-295th meetings, and *Annexes*, item 49.

[32]*Ibid., Sixth Committee*, 294th meeting, paragraphs 70-73.
[33]The text of resolution 599(VI) is reproduced above, in the footnote to paragraph 1.
[34]*Ibid., Annexes*, item 49, document A/2087, Report of the Sixth Committee, paragraph 37.
[35]See *Trial of the Major War Criminals before the International Military Tribunal, Nuremberg, 14 November 1945 -1 October 1946*, Vol. 1, page 8.
Article 5 provided that *any Government of the United Nations* might *adhere to* the Agreement.
Nineteen States have adhered to the Agreement under that provision. They are as follows, in chronological order of adherence: Greece, Denmark, Yugoslavia, Netherlands, Czechoslovakia, Poland, Belgium, Ethiopia, Australia, Honduras, Norway, Panama, Luxembourg, Haiti, New Zealand, India, Venezuela, Uruguay and Paraguay.
[36]*Ibid.*, page 11.

jected to aggression, shall not constitute a war of aggression."[37]

144. The five criteria of aggression described in this proposal are taken from the definition of aggression prepared in 1933 by the Committee on Security Questions of the Disarmament Conference.[38] The United States delegation subsequently amended its proposal by deleting items 4 and 5 from the list.

145. The French delegation in turn proposed a draft definition of the crimes which the Tribunal should punish.[39] The United States proposal gave rise to a discussion,[40] in which it was opposed by General Nikitchenko, the USSR representative, who said that in the circumstances such a definition was unnecessary and that the Conference was not the body competent to prepare it.[41] The proposal was finally rejected.

2. THE UNITED NATIONS INDICTMENT AGAINST THE GERMAN LEADERS

146. This indictment was presented to the International Military Tribunal by François de Menthon, R. A. Rudenko, Sir Hartley Shawcross, and Robert H. Jackson.[42] The crimes against peace referred to in the indictment are conspiracy to commit aggression and the commission of aggression. The indictment includes the following headings:

"3. Aggressive action against Austria and Czechoslovakia.[43]

"4. Formulation of the plan to attack Poland: preparation and initiation of aggressive war: March 1939 to September 1939.[44]

"5. Expansion of the war into a general war of aggression: planning and execution of attacks on Denmark, Norway, Belgium, the Netherlands, Luxembourg, Yugoslavia, and Greece: 1939 to April 1941.[45]

"6. German invasion on 22 June 1941, of the USSR territory in violation of the Non-Aggression Pact of 23 August 1939.[46]

"7. Collaboration with Italy and Japan and aggressive war against the United States: November 1936 to December 1941."[47]

3. THE JUDGMENT OF THE TRIBUNAL OF 1 OCTOBER 1946

147. The Tribunal distinguishes two counts of the indictment relating to crimes against peace. The first

is that of "conspiring or having a common plan to commit crimes against peace". The second refers to the commission of "crimes against peace by planning, preparing, initiating, and waging wars of aggression against a number of other States". Immediately afterwards, however, the Tribunal combines these two points by stating: "It will be convenient to consider the question of the existence of a common plan and the question of aggressive war together..."[48]

148. The Tribunal then distinguishes between "acts of aggression" and a "war of aggression" and declares: "The first acts of aggression referred to in the Indictment are the seizure of Austria and Czechoslovakia; and the first war of aggression charged in the Indictment is the war against Poland begun on 1 September 1939".[49]

149. A chronological list follows:

"Preparation for Aggression".[50] The Tribunal opens its case by quoting *Mein Kampf*.

"The Planning of Aggression."[51] The Tribunal gives an account of the secret meetings held by Hitler on 5 November 1937 and 23 November 1939.

"The Seizure of Austria".[52] The Tribunal describes this as "a premeditated aggressive step in furthering the plan to wage aggressive wars against other countries." It concludes by stating "that the methods employed to achieve the object were those of an aggressor. The ultimate factor was the armed might of Germany ready to be used if any resistance was encountered".[53]

"The Seizure of Czechoslovakia."[54]

"The Aggression against Poland."[55] On this subject the Tribunal says that it is "fully satisfied by the evidence that the war initiated by Germany against Poland on 1 September 1939 was most plainly an aggressive war".[56]

"The Invasion of Denmark and Norway".[57] The Tribunal states that these invasions "were acts of aggressive war".[58]

"The Invasion of Belgium, the Netherlands, and Luxembourg".[59] The Tribunal states that this invasion was "plainly an act of aggressive war".[60]

"The Aggression against Yugoslavia and Greece".[61]

"The Aggressive War against the Union of Soviet Socialist Republics".[62] The Tribunal stated that "the

[37]See *Report of Robert H. Jackson, United States Representative to the International Conference on Military Trials. London 1945, Department of State Publication 3080* (1949), page 294.
[38]See above, paragraph 78.
[39]This proposal was worded as follows: "The Tribunal will have jurisdiction to try any person who has, in any capacity whatsoever, directed the preparation and conduct of: (1) the policy of aggression against, and of domination over, other nations, carried out by the European Axis Powers in breach of treaties and in violation of international law . . . ". *Report of Robert H. Jackson*, page 293.
[40]See meeting of 19 July 1945; *ibid.*, pages 295-309.
[41]At the 293rd meeting of the Sixth Committee of the General Assembly (21 January 1952), Mr. Morozov (USSR) stated "that General Nikitchenko had not been representing the USSR on the specific question of defining aggression, but had only been considering the question whether or not such a definition should be included in the Charter of the Nürnberg Tribunal". *Official Records of the General Assembly, Sixth Session, Sixth Committee*, 293rd meeting, paragraph 3.
[42]See *Trial of the Major War Criminals before the International Military Tribunal, Nuremberg, 14 December 1945-1 October 1946*, Vol. 1, page 27.

[43]*Ibid.*, page 36.
[44]*Ibid.*, page 38.
[45]*Ibid.*, page 39.
[46]By this invasion, the Germans began "a war of aggression against the USSR". *Ibid.*, page 40.
[47]*Ibid.*, page 40.
[48]*Ibid.*, page 186.
[49]*Ibid.*, page 186.
[50]*Ibid.*, page 187.
[51]*Ibid.*, page 188.
[52]*Ibid.*, page 192.
[53]*Ibid.*, page 194.
[54]*Ibid.*, page 194.
[55]*Ibid.*, page 198.
[56]*Ibid.*, page 204.
[57]*Ibid.*, page 204.
[58]*Ibid.*, page 209.
[59]*Ibid.*, page 209.
[60]*Ibid.*, page 210.
[61]*Ibid.*, page 210.
[62]*Ibid.*, page 213.

carefully prepared scheme launched on 22 June... was plain aggression".[63]

"War against the United States".[64] The Tribunal observes that the attack by Japan on the American fleet in Pearl Harbor was an "aggressive war" which Germany encouraged and approved by immediately declaring war on the United States.[65]

150. With regard to the judgment, two observations may be made:

(a) The Tribunal did not define either acts of aggression or wars of aggression. It merely recognized their existence in a number of specific cases.

(b) The Tribunal was careful to establish the fact that in several of the cases mentioned—the invasion of Norway,[66] the invasion of Belgium, the Netherlands and Luxembourg,[67] and the aggression against the USSR[68]—the right of self-defence could not be invoked. The Tribunal declared that Germany could not claim that it was taking the initiative either to prevent an invasion by the Allies or to prevent an attack by the countries which it was invading. Attention may be drawn to the following observation on the subject of Norway:

"...But whether action taken under the claim of self-defence was in fact aggressive or defensive must ultimately be subject to investigation and adjudication if international law is ever to be enforced."[69]

SECTION II. GENERAL ASSEMBLY RESOLUTIONS 95(I) OF 11 DECEMBER 1946 AND 177(II) OF 21 NOVEMBER 1947

151. On 11 December 1946, the General Assembly adopted resolution 95(I) whereby, after affirming "the principles of international law recognized by the Charter of the Nürnberg Tribunal and the judgment of the Tribunal", it directed the Committee on the Progressive Development of International Law and its Codification (the so-called "Committee on Methods" established under another resolution adopted on the same day)

"to treat as a matter of primary importance plans for the formulation, in the context of a general codification of offences against the peace and security of mankind, or of an International Criminal Code, of the principles recognized in the Charter of the Nürnberg Tribunal and in the judgment of the Tribunal."[70]

152. At its single session (1947), the Committee on the Progressive Development of International Law and its Codification prepared a report[71] containing a number of recommendations as to the methods by which the future International Law Commission should take action under resolution 95(I).

153. The General Assembly, to which the above-mentioned report was submitted, adopted on 21 Novem-

ber 1947 resolution 177(II) directing the International Law Commission which it had resolved to establish to:

"(a) Formulate the principles of international law recognized in the Charter of the Nürnberg Tribunal and in the judgment of the Tribunal, and

"(b) Prepare a draft code of offences against the peace and security of mankind, indicating clearly the place to be accorded to the principles mentioned in sub-paragraph (a) above."[72]

SECTION III. ACTION UNDER GENERAL ASSEMBLY RESOLUTION 177 (II)

1. THE FIRST SESSION OF THE INTERNATIONAL LAW COMMISSION (1949)

154. The International Law Commission was of the opinion that its task "was not to express any appreciation of these principles [the principles recognized in the Charter of the Nürnberg Tribunal and in the judgment of the Tribunal] as principles of international law but merely to formulate them".[73]

155. The Commission instructed a Sub-Committee to prepare a working paper containing a formulation of the Nürnberg principles.[74] When this document was submitted to it, the Commission expressed the view that the task of formulating the Nürnberg principles appeared "to be so closely connected with that of preparing a draft code of offences against the peace and security of mankind that it would be premature for the Commission to give a final formulation to these principles before the work of preparing the draft code was further advanced".[75] It therefore referred the text prepared by the Sub-Committee to a rapporteur, Mr. J. Spiropoulos, requesting him to report to the Commission at its second session.

2. THE SECOND SESSION OF THE INTERNATIONAL LAW COMMISSION (5 JUNE—29 JULY 1950)

156. Mr. Spiropoulos submitted a report[76] on the basis of which the Commission adopted a formulation[77] of the principles of international law recognized in the Charter of the Nürnberg Tribunal and in the judgment of the Tribunal. Among the seven principles formulated by the Commission, one, Principle VI, relates to crimes against peace, war crimes and crimes against humanity.

157. Principle VI refers to crimes against peace in the following terms:

"(a) Crimes against peace:

(i) Planning, preparation, initiation or waging of a war of aggression or a war in violation of international treaties, agreements or assurances;

(ii) Participation in a common plan or conspiracy for the accomplishment of any of the acts mentioned under (i)."

---

[63]Ibid., page 215.
[64]Ibid., page 215.
[65]Ibid., page 216.
[66]Ibid., pages 207 and 209.
[67]Ibid., page 210.
[68]Ibid., page 215.
[69]Ibid., page 208.
[70]See Resolutions adopted by the General Assembly during the Second Part of its First Session from 23 October to 15 December 1946, page 188.
[71]A/332, Official Records of the General Assembly, Second Session, Sixth Committee, page 211.

[72]See Official Records of the Second Session of the General Assembly, Resolutions, 16 September–29 November 1947, page 112.
[73]See the report of the International Law Commission covering its first session, A/925, Official Records of the General Assembly, Fourth Session, Supplement No. 10, paragraph 26.
[74]Document A/CN.4/W.12.
[75]A/925, paragraph 29.
[76]A/CN.4/22.
[77]See the report of the International Law Commission covering its second session, 5 June–29 July 1950, A/1316, Official Records of the General Assembly, Fifth Session, Supplement No. 12, Part III.

The International Law Commission makes the following observation:

"The Charter of the Nürnberg Tribunal did not contain any definition of 'war of aggression', nor was there any such definition in the judgment of the Tribunal. It was by reviewing the historical events before and during the war that it found that certain of the defendants planned and waged aggressive wars against twelve nations and were therefore guilty of a series of crimes."[78]

3. GENERAL ASSEMBLY RESOLUTION 488 (V) OF 12 DECEMBER 1950

158. By its resolution 488 (V) of 12 December 1950[79], the General Assembly invited the governments of Member States to furnish their observations on the principles as formulated by the International Law Commission. By the same resolution, the Assembly requested the International Law Commission, in preparing the draft code of offences against the peace and security of mankind to take account of those observations, and also of the observations made by delegations during the fifth session of the General Assembly.

4. THE THIRD SESSION OF THE INTERNATIONAL LAW COMMISSION (1951)

159. Mr. Spiropoulos submitted a report[80] which included a draft code of offences against the peace and security of mankind and a summary of the observations made by delegations at the fifth session of the General Assembly on the subject of the formulation of the Nürnberg principles as established by the Commission. The Commission also had before it the observations of a number of Governments on that formulation.[81]

160. The Commission adopted a draft code of offences against the peace and security of mankind.[82] The list of offences against the peace and security of mankind includes twelve items.[83] No. (1) is worded as follows:

"(1) Any act of aggression, including the employment by the authorities of a State of armed force against another State for any purpose other than national or collective self-defence or in pursuance of a decision or recommendation by a competent organ of the United Nations."

161. It is to be observed that while paragraph (1) refers to aggression ("Any act of aggression"), certain acts falling within the same category as those characterized by the Committee on Security Questions of the Disarmament Conference in 1933 as constituting aggression are treated as separate offences in the draft code. This applies to No. (4), which is worded as follows:

"(4) The incursion into the territory of a State from the territory of another State by armed bands acting for a political purpose."

162. Nevertheless, the commentary on offence No. (1) (aggression) contains the following statement:

"While every act of aggression constitutes a crime under paragraph (1), no attempt is made to enumerate such acts exhaustively. It is expressly provided that the employment of armed force in the circumstances specified in the paragraph is an act of aggression. It is, however, possible that aggression can be committed also by other acts, including some of those referred to in other paragraphs of article 2."

Hence it appears that paragraph (1), dealing with aggression, does not exhaust the possibilities of aggression, since the acts referred to in other paragraphs may also constitute the crime of aggression.

Chapter IV

THE CRITERIA APPLIED IN THE CASE OF CONFLICTS ACCOMPANIED BY THE USE OF FORCE. THE CASE OF KOREA

163. Several armed conflicts have occurred since the United Nations was established including that involving the new State of Israel and the neighbouring Arab States. Only once, however—in the case of the Korean war—has the Security Council pronounced on the question of aggression.

164. At its 473rd meeting on 25 June 1950, the Security Council, to which the question of the outbreak of war in Korea had been referred, adopted after amendment a draft resolution submitted by the representative of the United States of America. The following is the text of the resolution as adopted:[84]

"*The Security Council.*

"......

"*Noting* with grave concern the armed attack on the Republic of Korea by forces from North Korea,

"*Determines* that this action constitutes a breach of the peace,

"*Calls for* the immediate cessation of hostilities; and

"*Calls upon* the authorities in North Korea to withdraw forthwith their armed forces to the 38th parallel;

"......"

165. On 27 June 1950, at the 474th meeting of the Security Council, the representative of the United States of America submitted another draft resolution worded as follows:

"*The Security Council,*

"*Having determined* that the armed attack upon the Republic of Korea by forces from North Korea constitutes a breach of the peace;

"*Having called* for an immediate cessation of hostilities; and

---

[78]*Ibid.*, paragraph 113.
[79]See A/1775, *Official Records of the General Assembly, Fifth Session, Supplement No. 20, Resolutions*, page 77.
[80]Document A/CN.4/44.
[81]See documents A/CN.4/45 and A/CN.4/45/Corr.1, A/CN.4/45/Add.1 and A/CN.4/45/Add.1/Corr.1 and A/CN.4/45/Add.2
[82]The Commission devoted twelve meetings to the question, the 89th to 92nd, the 106th to 111th, and the 129th and 133rd meetings. See the report of the Commission, A/1858, Official

Records of the General Assembly, Sixth Session, Supplement No. 9, chapter IV.
[83]For the complete list of offences against the peace and security of mankind as formulated by the Commission, see document A/1858, paragraph 59.
[84]See S/1497 and *Official Records of the Security Council, Fifth Year, No. 15.* The voting was as follows:
For: China, Cuba, Ecuador, Egypt, France, India, Norway United Kingdom and United States of America;
Abstained: Yugoslavia;
Absent: Union of Soviet Socialist Republics.

"*Having called* upon the authorities of North Korea to withdraw forthwith their armed forces to the 38th parallel; and

"*Having noted* from the report of the United Nations Commission for Korea that the authorities in North Korea have neither ceased hostilities nor withdrawn their armed forces to the 38th parallel, and that urgent military measures are required to restore international peace and security; and

" ...

"*Recommends* that the Members of the United Nations furnish such assistance to the Republic of Korea as may be necessary to repel the armed attack and to restore international peace and security in the area."

This resolution was adopted without change at the same meeting.[85]

166. On 1 February 1951, at its fifth session, the

General Assembly adopted resolution 498 (V), which reads as follows:

"*The General Assembly,*

" ...

"*Noting* that the Central People's Government of the People's Republic of China has not accepted United Nations proposals to bring about a cessation of hostilities in Korea with a view to peaceful settlement, anu that its armed forces continue their invasion of Korea and their large-scale attacks upon United Nations forces there,

"1. *Finds* that the Central People's Government of the People's Republic of China, by giving direct aid and assistance to those who were already committing aggression in Korea and by engaging in hostilities against United Nations forces there, has itself engaged in aggression in Korea;

" ..."[86]

---

[85]See S/1508/Rev.1, and *Official Records of the Security Council, Fifth Year, No. 16.* The voting was as follows:
For: China, Cuba, Ecuador, France, Norway, United Kingdom, United States of America;
Against: Yugoslavia;

Abstained: Egypt, India;
Absent: Union of Soviet Socialist Republics.
[86]A/1175/Add.1, *Official Records of the General Assembly, Fifth Session, Supplement No. 20A,* page 1.

Title III

THE TERMINOLOGY USED IN REGIONAL OR INDIVIDUAL SECURITY TREATIES

Chapter I

THE HISTORICAL DEVELOPMENT

167. Regional and individual security treaties have been concluded in the course of three periods: the period prior to the First World War, the period of the League of Nations, and the United Nations period.

SECTION I. TREATIES CONCLUDED IN THE PERIOD PRIOR TO THE FIRST WORLD WAR

168. Treaties of alliance were concluded in this period. These bilateral (Franco-Russian Alliance) or multilateral (Austria-Hungary, Germany, Italy) treaties take the form of treaties of defensive alliance. The allies are therefore under obligation to render assistance to each other only if one of them is attacked. While the term "aggression" is not (generally) employed, the idea of aggression is implicit in reference to attack or invasion. There is no international organization responsible for ensuring the maintenance of peace; the parties adopt such forms of words as they find suitable, which have not been drafted or recommended by any international authority. The parties themselves are the sole judges of whether the *casus foederis* has occurred or not.

SECTION II. TREATIES CONCLUDED IN THE PERIOD OF THE LEAGUE OF NATIONS

1. REASON FOR THE SECURITY TREATIES

169. During the League of Nations period, the Covenant of the League of Nations was supposed to ensure the security of States, and, according to an opinion expressed on several occasions by a number of governments, individual treaties providing for the assistance of one State by another did not meet a need and presented dangers.

170. This opinion, however, did not gain acceptance. Some governments thought that the general engagements under the Covenant of the League of Nations were insufficient and, to be fully effective, had to be supplemented by individual engagements concluded between States which considered themselves exposed to a common danger. Furthermore, the members of the international community which did not belong to the League of Nations sought to obtain the guarantees of security they thought they needed by means of individual engagements.

2. CHARACTERISTICS OF THE SECURITY TREATIES

(a) *Purpose of the treaties*

171. Two types of treaties are to be found. There are treaties of mutual assistance, which provide that a State will be assisted by one or more others should it be the victim of aggression. These treaties have the same purpose as the treaties of alliance of the period prior to the League of Nations. There are also treaties of neutrality or non-aggression, which merely contain an undertaking by the contracting States not to commit aggression against each other and do not provide for any undertaking to render assistance should one of the contracting States become the victim of aggression.

(b) *Most of these treaties are conceived within the framework of the Covenant of the League of Nations*

172. It follows that the terminology used in these treaties is based in varying degree on that recommended or prepared by the organs of the League of

Nations. Moreover, these treaties often stipulate that their effects will not be contrary to the application of the Covenant of the League of Nations or that they will be applied with the assistance of the organs of the League.

(c) States parties to the treaties

173. Generally speaking, the treaties are bilateral, although they include a number of regional treaties which are in some cases open to accession by States which did not take part in their conclusion. These treaties are much more numerous than the treaties of alliance in force during the period prior to the League of Nations.

SECTION III. TREATIES CONCLUDED IN THE PERIOD OF THE UNITED NATIONS

174. The treaties concluded during this period do not differ materially from those concluded during the preceding period. It may be noted, incidentally, that a number of the latter are still in force.

1. STATES PARTIES TO THE TREATIES

175. A larger proportion of regional and multilateral treaties is to be observed.

2. THE TREATIES ARE CONCEIVED WITHIN THE FRAMEWORK OF THE CHARTER OF THE UNITED NATIONS

176. The terms used in the Charter of the United Nations with regard to security differ from those used in the Covenant of the League of Nations. Many of the new treaties, therefore, take into account Article 2, paragraph 4 of the Charter, which prohibits resort to "the threat or use of force".

Chapter II

THE TERMINOLOGY USED IN THE TREATIES

177. The regional or individual security treaties—non-aggression treaties, neutrality treaties, treaties of alliance, treaties of guarantee, treaties of mutual assistance, and the like—all revolve around the idea of aggression but vary in the terminology they employ. Some make use of very precise terms, such as "war", "attack", "invasion", "aggression", or "resort to arms", while others use more complex expressions and include definitions or lists. It is to be observed that some of the expressions employed are qualified by a reference to non-provocation.

178. The treaties have been classified into the following six categories according to the form of words used:

1. Attack or invasion;
2. Aggression;
3. Use of force;
4. Enumeration of prohibited actions;
5. General definitions of aggression;
6. Enumerative definitions of aggression.

179. Treaties which merely use the word "war" without further qualification have been omitted because this word does nothing to clarify the idea of aggression. In a final category, category 7, are mentioned the treaties which incorporate the idea of provocation.

SECTION I. ATTACK OR INVASION

180. The following treaties use the terms "attack" or "attacked" exclusively:

Franco-Russian Treaty of Alliance, 15-27 December 1893.

Triple Alliance between Austria-Hungary, Germany and Italy, 22 May 1882 (article 2).

Treaty of Alliance between Austria-Hungary and Romania, 20 October 1883 (article 2).

Treaty of Alliance between Great Britain and Japan, 12 August 1905 (article II).

Convention of Alliance, Kingdom of the Serbs, Croats and Slovenes and the Czechoslovak Republic, 14 August 1920 (article 1). Registered with the League of Nations under No. 154.

Political Agreement, France and Poland, 19 February 1921 (article 3). Registered with the League of Nations under No. 449.

Convention of Alliance, Romania and Czechoslovakia, 23 April 1921 (article I). Registered with the League of Nations under No. 155.

Political Agreement, Finland, Romania and Esthonia, 17 March 1922 (article 7). Registered with the League of Nations under No. 296.

Treaty of Defensive Alliance, Esthonia and Lithuania, 1 November 1923 (article 3). Registered with the League of Nations under No. 578.

Treaty of Guarantee, Poland and Romania, 26 March 1926 (article 2). Registered with the League of Nations under No. 1411.

Treaty of Friendship, France and Romania, 10 June 1926 (article 4). Registered with the League of Nations under No. 1373.

Treaty of Non-Aggression, Lithuania and Union of Soviet Socialist Republics, 28 September 1926 (article 3). Registered with the League of Nations under No. 1410.

Treaty of Friendly Understanding, Kingdom of the Serbs, Croats and Slovenes and France, 11 November 1927 (article 4). Registered with the League of Nations under No 1592.

Treaty of Neutrality and Conciliation, Bulgaria and Turkey, 6 March 1929 (article 2). Registered with the League of Nations under No. 2668.

Treaty of Guarantee, Poland and Romania, 15 January 1931 (article 2). Registered with the League of Nations under No. 2685.

Treaty of Friendship and Alliance, Union of Soviet Socialist Republics and China, 14 August 1945 (article 3). Filed and recorded by the United Nations under No. 68.

North Atlantic Treaty, Belgium, Canada, Denmark, France, Iceland, Italy, Luxembourg, Netherlands, Norway, Portugal, United Kingdom, United States of America (since 18 February 1952, Greece and Turkey), 4 April 1949 (article 5). Registered with the United Nations under No. 541.

181. The following treaties use the word "attack" in conjunction with a qualifying word or phrase:

(i) "military attack".'

Treaty of Friendship and Mutual Assistance, Union of Soviet Socialist Republics and Mongolia, 27 February 1946 (article 2). Registered with the United Nations under No. 744.

(ii) "attacked . . . with a view to threatening its independence, subjugating it or seizing certain parts of its territory":

Treaty of Friendship and Mutual Assistance, Yugoslavia and Albania, 9 July 1946 (article III). Registered with the United Nations under No. 15.

182. The following treaties use both "attack" and "invade":

Locarno Treaty of Mutual Guarantee, Germany, Belgium, France, Great Britain, Italy, 16 October 1925 (article 2). Registered with the League of Nations under No. 1292.

Treaty of Friendship, France and Romania, 10 June 1926. Registered with the League of Nations under No. 1373.

Treaty of Non-Aggression and Arbitration, Greece and Romania, 21 March 1928 (article 1). Registered with the League of Nations under No. 2508.

Section II. Aggression

183. Numerous treaties use the word "aggression" to state that the parties will abstain from committing an aggression or that they will assist the party which becomes the victim of an aggression.

184. The following treaties use the expressions "aggression", "acts of aggression", "aggressive acts", "offensive action", "war of aggression":

Treaty of Friendship and Neutrality, Turkey, Union of Soviet Socialist Republics, 17 December 1925 (article 2). Registered with the League of Nations under No. 3610.

Treaty of Non-Aggression, Lithuania and the Union of Soviet Socialist Republics, 28 September 1926 (article 3). Registered with the League of Nations under No. 1410.

Treaty of Guarantee and Neutrality, Persia and the Union of Soviet Socialist Republics, 1 October 1927 (article 2). Registered with the League of Nations under No. 2620.

Treaty of Conciliation, Judicial Settlement and Arbitration, Spain and Turkey, 28 April 1930 (article 1).

Treaty of Non-Aggression, Afghanistan and the Union of Soviet Socialist Republics, 24 June 1931 (article 2). Registered with the League of Nations under No. 3611.

Treaty of Non-Aggression and Conciliation, known as the Saavedra Lamas Pact, Rio de Janeiro, 10 October 1933 (article 1). Registered with the League of Nations under No. 3781.

Treaty of Non-Aggression, Turkey and Yugoslavia, 27 November 1933 (article 1). Registered with the League of Nations under No. 3715.

Non-Aggression Pact, China and the Union of Soviet Socialist Republics, 21 August 1937 (article 1). Registered with the League of Nations under No. 4180.

Treaty for the Peaceful Settlement of Disputes, Brazil and Venezuela, 30 March 1940 (article 1).

Treaty of Friendship and Mutual Assistance, Poland and Yugoslavia, 18 March 1946 (article 3). Registered with the United Nations under No. 13.

Charter of the Organization of American States, Bogotá, 30 April 1948 (article 5). Registered with the United Nations under No. 1609.

Treaty of Friendship, Co-operation and Mutual Assistance, Poland and Bulgaria, 28 May 1948 (article 2). Registered with the United Nations under No. 389.

General Armistice Agreement between Egypt and Israel, 24 February 1949 (article 1, paragraph 2). Registered with the United Nations under No. 654.

General Armistice Agreement between Lebanon and Israel, 23 March 1949 (article 1, paragraph 2). Registered with the United Nations under No. 655.

General Armistice Agreement between the Hashemite Kingdom of Jordan and Israel, 3 April 1949 (article 1). Registered with the United Nations under No. 656.

General Armistice Agreement between Syria and Israel, 20 July 1949 (article 1, paragraph 2). Registered with the United Nations under No. 657.

185. The following treaties use the word "aggression" or "attack" in conjunction with a qualifying word or phrase:

(i) "aggression by land, sea or air":

Pact of Non-aggression, France and the Union of Soviet Socialist Republics, 29 November 1932 (article 1). Registered with the League of Nations under No. 3615.

Pact of Friendship, Non-aggression and Neutrality, Italy and the Union of Soviet Socialist Republics (article 1). Registered with the League of Nations under No. 3418.

(ii) "armed attack":

Treaty of Alliance and Mutual Assistance, United Kingdom and France, 4 March 1947 (article 2). Registered with the United Nations under No. 132.

Brussels Treaty, Belgium, France, Luxembourg, the Netherlands and the United Kingdom, 17 March 1948 (article IV). Registered with the United Nations under No. 304.

(iii) "external aggression":

Treaty of Guarantee, Poland and Romania, 15 January 1931 (article 1). Registered with the League of Nations under No. 2685.

Treaty of Alliance, United Kingdom and Trans-Jordan, 22 March 1946 (article 3). Registered with the United Nations under No. 74.

186. One treaty uses the expression "aggressive action."

Treaty between the United States of America, the British Empire, France and Japan, 13 December 1921 (article II). Registered with the League of Nations under No. 607.

187. Several treaties use the expression "policy of aggression".

(i) Two treaties, when referring to Germany, say merely: "which had resumed her policy of aggression"

Treaty of Friendship, Mutual Aid and Peaceful Co-operation, Czechoslovakia and Yugoslavia. 9 May 1946 (article 3). Registered with the United Nations under No. 14.

Treaty of Friendship and Mutual Aid, Poland and Czechoslovakia, 10 March 1947 (article 3). Registered with the United Nations under No. 365.

(ii) Four treaties, referring to Germany, use some such phrase as the following: "which might seek to renew its policy of aggression".

Treaty of Friendship, Co-operation and Mutual Assistance, Union of Soviet Socialist Republics and Romania, 4 February 1948 (article 2). Registered with the United Nations under No. 745.

Treaty of Friendship, Co-operation and Mutual Assistance, Union of Soviet Socialist Republics and Hungary, 18 February 1948 (article 1). Registered with the United Nations under No. 743.

Treaty of Friendship, Co-operation and Mutual Assistance, Union of Soviet Socialist Republics and Bulgaria, 18 March 1948 (article 2). Registered with the United Nations under No. 741.

Treaty of Friendship, Co-operation and Mutual Aid, Poland and Hungary, 18 June 1948 (article 2). Registered with the United Nations under No. 370.

188. One treaty uses the terms "attack" and "aggression":

Treaty of Friendship and Security, Afghanistan and Persia, 27 November 1927 (article 2). Registered with the League of Nations under No. 2500.

Section III. The use of force

189. The following treaties contain an undertaking not to resort to the use of force. This undertaking is accompanied by certain particular conditions which vary from one treaty to another:

Protocol of Friendship and Co-operation, Colombia and Peru, 24 May 1934 (article 7). Registered with the League of Nations under No. 3786.

Protocol of Friendship, Rio de Janeiro, 24 May 1936 (article 5).

Germano-Soviet Treaty, 23 August 1939 (article 1).

Pact of the League of Arab States, Saudi Arabia, Egypt, Iraq, Transjordan, Lebanon, Syria, Yemen, 22 March 1945 (article 5). Filed and recorded by the United Nations under No. 241.

Charter of the Organization of American States, Bogotá, 30 April 1948 (article 18). Registered with the United Nations under No. 1609.

North Atlantic Treaty, Belgium, Canada, Denmark, France, Iceland, Italy, Luxembourg, Netherlands, Nor-way, Portugal, United Kingdom, United States of America (since 18 February 1952, Greece and Turkey), 4 April 1949 (article 1). Registered with the United Nations under No. 541.

Section IV. Enumeration of prohibited acts

190. Article I of the so-called "Gondra" Treaty between the American States, concluded on 3 May 1923, provides for an undertaking by the parties "in case of disputes, not to begin mobilization or concentration of troops on the frontier of the other Party, nor to engage in any hostile acts or preparations for hostilities".[1]

Section V. General definitions of aggression

191. Four treaties of non-aggression, concluded by the Union of Soviet Socialist Republics before 1933, give a general definition of aggression.

192. Article 1 of the treaty between Finland and the Union of Soviet Socialist Republics of 21 January 1932 provides as follows:

"Any act of violence attacking the integrity and inviolability of the territory or the political independence of the other High Contracting Party shall be regarded as an act of aggression, even if it is committed without declaration of war and avoids warlike manifestations".[2]

193. A similar wording is to be found in the treaties of non-aggression concluded between the Union of Soviet Socialist Republics and Lithuania on 5 February 1932,[3] the Union of Soviet Socialist Republics and Esthonia on 4 May 1932[4] and the Union of Soviet Socialist Republics and Poland on 25 July 1932.[5]

Section VI. Enumerative definitions of aggression

194. The instruments concerned are firstly, the treaties which follow the model definition of the aggressor prepared by the Committee on Security Questions of the Disarmament Conference,[6] and secondly, two treaties which are shorter but which nevertheless approximate more closely to the enumerative, than to the general type of definition, without falling within any clearly defined category.

1. TREATIES BASED ON THE MODEL PREPARED BY THE COMMITTEE ON SECURITY QUESTIONS OF THE DISARMAMENT CONFERENCE

195. The following four treaties reproduce almost word for word the definition of aggression prepared by

---

[1] See League of Nations, *Treaty series*, Vol. 33, treaty registered under No. 831.
[2] See League of Nations, *Treaty series*, Vol. 157, treaty registered under No. 3613.
[3] See League of Nations, *Treaty series*, Vol. 148, treaty registered under No. 3408. Article 1 of this treaty provides as follows:
"Each of the High Contracting Parties undertakes to refrain from any act of aggression directed against the other, and also from any acts of violence directed against the territorial integrity and inviolability or the political independence of the other Contracting Party, regardless of whether such aggression or such acts are committed separately or together with other Powers, with or without a declaration of war".
[4] See League of Nations, *Treaty series*, Vol. 131, treaty registered under No. 3020. Article 1 of this treaty provides as follows:
"Each of the High Contracting Parties guarantees to the other Party the inviolability of the existing frontiers be-tween them, as defined by the Peace Treaty signed on February 2, 1920, and undertakes to refrain from any act of aggression or any violent measures directed against the integrity and inviolability of the territory or against the political independence of the other Contracting Party, whether such acts of aggression or such violent measures are undertaken separately or in conjunction with other Powers, with or without a declaration of war".

[5] See League of Nations, *Treaty series*, Vol. 136, treaty registered under No. 3124. Article 1 of this treaty provides as follows:
"Any act of violence attacking the integrity and inviolability of the territory or the political independence of the other Contracting Party shall be regarded as contrary to the undertakings contained in the present Article, even if such acts are committed without declaration of war and avoid all warlike manifestations as far as possible".

[6] See above, paragraph 78.

the Security Committee of the Disarmament Conference:[7]

(1) Convention for the Definition of Aggression, with Annex and Protocol—open to all States bordering on the Union of Soviet Socialist Republics—London, 3 July 1933.[8] (Registered with the League of Nations under No. 3391).

(2) Convention for the Definition of Aggression, with Annexes—London, 4 July 1933.[9]

(3) Convention for the Definition of Aggression; Lithuania and the Union of Soviet Socialist Republics—London, 5 July 1933. Registered with the League of Nations under No. 3405.

(4) Pact of Balkan Entente, Greece, Romania, Turkey and Yugoslavia—Athens, 9 February 1934. Registered with the League of Nations under No. 3514.

196. One treaty which generally follows the same model enumerates four acts of aggression:

Treaty of Brotherhood and Alliance, Iraq and Transjordan, 14 April 1947 (article 5). Registered with the United Nations under No. 345.

197. One treaty is drawn up on the general lines of the definition prepared by the Committee on Security Questions of the Disarmament Conference, without, however, following it in all respects:

Treaty of Non-Aggression, Iran, Afghanistan, Iraq and Turkey, 8 July 1937.[10]

198. On signing the Buenos Aires Convention of 23 December 1936 for the co-ordination and extension of the treaties between the American States, Colombia submitted in the form of a reservation a definition of aggression which to some extent is based on the formula prepared by the Committee on Security Questions

of the Disarmament Conference but which adds elements not included therein.[11]

2. OTHER TREATIES

199. Two other treaties contain definitions of aggression less detailed than those prepared by the Committee on Security Questions of the Disarmament Conference.

200. The Act of Chapultepec signed by all the American Republics[12] on 8 March 1945 provides as follows:

"Whereas...

"(j)...any attempt on the part of a non-American State against the integrity or inviolability of the territory, the sovereignty or the political independence of an American State shall be considered as an act of aggression against all the American States.

"...

"Part I

"Declare:

"...

"3. That every attack of a State against the integrity or the inviolability of the territory, or against the sovereignty or the political independence of an American State, shall, conformably to Part III hereof, be considered as an act of aggression against the other States which sign this Act. In any case, invasion by armed forces of one State into the territory of another trespassing boundaries established by treaty and demarcated in accordance therewith shall constitute an act of aggression."[13]

201. The Inter-American Treaty of Reciprocal Assistance signed at Rio de Janeiro on 2 September 1947[14] provides as follows:

"Article 1. The High Contracting Parties formally condemn war and undertake in their international

---

[7]The text prepared by the Committee reads in part as follows:
"Desiring, subject to the express reservation that the absolute validity of the rule laid down in Article 2 of that Act shall be in no way restricted, to furnish certain indications *for the guidance of the international bodies that may be called upon to determine the aggressor*";
While the London treaties contain the following paragraph:
"Desiring, subject to the express reservation that the absolute validity of the rule laid down in Article III of that Convention shall in no way be restricted, to furnish certain indications for *determining the aggressor*".
[8]The following States ratified or acceded to the convention: Afghanistan, Esthonia, Finland, Iran, Latvia, Poland, Romania, Turkey, Union of Soviet Socialist Republics.
[9]The following States ratified the convention: Czechoslovakia, Romania, Turkey, Union of Soviet Socialist Republics, Yugoslavia.
[10]The provisions relating to the definition of aggression are as follows:
"The following shall be deemed acts of aggression:
"1. Declaration of war;
"2. Invasion by the armed forces of one State, with or without a declaration of war, of the territory of another State;
"3. An attack by land, naval or air forces of one State, with or without a declaration of war, on the territory, vessels or aircraft of another State;
"4. Directly or indirectly aiding or assisting an aggressor.
"The following shall not constitute acts of aggression:
"1. The exercise of the right of legitimate self-defence, that is to say, resistance to an act of aggression as defined above;
"2. Action under Article 16 of the Covenant of the League of Nations;
"3. Action in pursuance of a decision of the Assembly or Council of the League of Nations, or under Article 15, paragraph 7, of the Covenant of the League of Nations, provided

always that in the latter case such action is directed against the State which was the first to attack;
"4. Action to assist a State subjected to attack, invasion or recourse to war by another of the High Contracting Parties, in violation of the Treaty for Renunciation of War signed in Paris on August 27th, 1928" League of Nations, *Treaty series*, volume 190. treaty registered under number 4402, article 4.
[11]This definition reads as follows:
"That State shall be considered as an aggressor which becomes responsible for one or several of the following acts:
"(a) That its armed forces, to whatever branch they may belong, illegally cross the land, sea or air frontiers of other States. When the violation of the territory of a State has been effected by irresponsible bands organized within or outside of its territory and which have received direct or indirect help from another State, such violation shall be considered equivalent, for the purposes of the present Article, to that effected by the regular forces of the State responsible for the aggression;
"(b) That it has intervened in a unilateral or illegal way in the internal or external affairs of another State;
"(c) That it has refused to fulfil a legally given arbitral decision or sentence of international justice.
"No consideration of any kind, whether political, military, economic or of any other kind, may serve as an excuse or justification for the aggression here anticipated." *United States Treaty Series, No. 926*, pages 7 and 8.
[12]The Act is not subject to ratification.
[13]See Hudson, *International Legislation*, Vol. IX, pages 286, 287, 288.
[14]United Nations, *Treaty Series*, Vol. 21, Treaty No. 324. Signatories: Argentina, Bolivia, Brazil, Chile, Colombia, Costa Rica, Cuba, Dominican Republic, El Salvador, Guatemala, Haiti, Honduras, Mexico, Panama, Paraguay, Peru, United States of America, Uruguay, Venezuela.

relations not to resort to the threat or the use of force in any manner inconsistent with the provisions of the Charter of the United Nations.

"...

"Article 3. The High Contracting Parties agree that an armed attack by any State against an American State shall be considered as an attack against all the American States and, consequently, each one of the said Contracting Parties undertakes to assist in meeting the attack in the exercise of the inherent right of individual or collective self-defense recognized by Article 51 of the Charter of the United Nations.

"...

"Article 9. In addition to other acts which the Organ of Consultation may characterize as aggression, the following shall be considered as such:

(a) Unprovoked armed attack by a State against the territory, the people, or the land, sea or air forces of another State;

(b) Invasion, by the armed forces of a State, of the territory of an American State, through the trespassing of boundaries demarcated in accordance with a treaty, judicial decision, or arbitral award, or, in the absence of frontiers thus demarcated, invasion affecting a region which is under the effective jurisdiction of another State.

"..."

Section VII. The idea of provocation

202. Numerous treaties contain a form of words which, explicitly or implicitly, embodies the idea of provocation, though its exact scope is not indicated.[15]

203. Some such expression as "attacked without giving provocation" is found in the following treaties:

Political Agreement, France and Poland, 19 February 1921 (article 3). Registered with the League of Nations under No. 449.

Convention for a Defensive Alliance, Poland and Romania, 3 March 1921 (article 1). Registered with the League of Nations under No. 175.

Political Agreement, Esthonia, Finland, Lithuania and Poland, 17 March 1922 (article 7). Registered with the League of Nations under No. 296.

Treaty of Defensive Alliance, Esthonia and Lithuania, 1 November 1923 (article 3). Registered with the League of Nations under No. 578.

Treaty of Guarantee, Poland and Romania, 26 March 1926 (article 2). Registered with the League of Nations under No. 1411.

Treaty of Friendship, France and Romania, 10 June 1926 (article 4). Registered with the League of Nations under No. 1373.

Treaty of Friendship, France and Kingdom of the Serbs, Croats and Slovenes, 11 November 1927 (article 4). Registered with the League of Nations under No. 1592.

204. The expressions "in case of an unprovoked attack", "in case of an unprovoked war", or "in case of

---
[15]The idea of provocation will be dealt with in the second part of this study. See paragraphs 336 *et seq.*

an unprovoked aggression" are to be found in the following treaties:

Treaty between Great Britain and Japan, 2 August 1905 (article II).

Convention of Defensive Alliance, Kingdom of the Serbs, Croats and Slovenes and Czechoslovakia, 14 August 1920 (article 1). Registered with the League of Nations under No. 154.

Convention of Defensive Alliance, Romania and Kingdom of the Serbs, Croats and Slovenes, 7 June 1921 (article 1). Registered with the League of Nations under No. 1289.

Convention of Defensive Alliance, Romania and Czechoslovakia, 23 August 1921 (article 1). Registered with the League of Nations under No. 155.

Agreement between Italy and the Kingdom of the Serbs, Croats and Slovenes, 27 January 1924 (article 2). Registered with the League of Nations under No. 596.

Locarno Treaty of Mutual Guarantee, France and Poland, 16 October 1925 (article 1). Registered with the League of Nations under No. 1297.

Locarno Treaty of Mutual Guarantee, France and Czechoslovakia, 16 October 1925 (article 1). Registered with the League of Nations under No. 1298.

Treaty of Defensive Alliance, Albania and Italy, 22 November 1927 (article 3). Registered with the League of Nations under No. 1616.

Treaty of Friendship, Greece and Italy, 23 September 1930 (article 2). Registered with the League of Nations under No. 2510.

Treaty of Guarantee, Poland and Romania, 15 January 1931 (article 2). Registered with the League of Nations under No. 2685.

Treaty of Mutual Assistance, France and the Union of Soviet Socialist Republics, 2 May 1935 (article 2). Registered with the League of Nations under No. 3881.

Treaty of Mutual Assistance, Czechoslovakia and the Union of Soviet Socialist Republics, 16 May 1935 (article 2). Registered with the League of Nations under No. 3677.

205. The expression "attacked without direct provocation on its part" is employed in the Triple Alliance between Austria-Hungary, Germany and Italy, 22 May 1882 (article 2).

206. The phrase "despite its peaceful attitude . . . attacked", is found in the following treaties:

Treaty between Germany and the Union of Soviet Socialist Republics, 24 April 1926 (article 2). Registered with the League of Nations under No. 1268.

Treaty of Non-Aggression, Lithuania and the Union of Soviet Socialist Republics, 28 September 1926 (article 3). Registered with the League of Nations under No. 1410.

Treaty of Neutrality and Conciliation, Bulgaria and Turkey, 6 March 1929 (article 2). Registered with the League of Nations under No. 2668.

Treaty of Neutrality, Greece and Turkey, 30 October 1930 (article 2). Registered with the League of Nations under No. 2841.

PART II

GENERAL

SHOULD AGGRESSION BE DEFINED?
PROPOSED DEFINITIONS

207. The discussion on whether aggression should or should not be defined has been going on for many years. The two conflicting points of view advanced in the League of Nations still exist today, and a systematic survey of the arguments for and against definition will be given in title I of this part.

208. Various formulae have been proposed by those in favour of defining aggression: enumerative definitions, general definitions and combined definitions. They will be considered in title II of this part.

209. The effects of the adoption of a definition of aggression, i.e., the extent to which such a definition will be binding on the bodies responsible for determining the aggressor or punishing persons guilty of aggression, will be examined in title III of this part.

Title I

THE TWO POINTS OF VIEW

210. Both those in favour of and those opposed to defining aggression have advanced general arguments in support of their points of view. This title will be entirely devoted to a brief summary of these general arguments. A practical study of the problem of aggression in its many aspects has been carried out in connexion with the various proposed types of definition. All the arguments invoked will therefore be found in title II of this part.

Chapter I

IN FAVOUR OF DEFINING AGGRESSION

211. Those in favour of defining aggression point out that such a definition is not only possible but desirable.

SECTION I. POSSIBILITY OF DEFINING AGGRESSION

212. It is legally and technically possible to define aggression.

(a) THE LEGAL POSSIBILITY OF DEFINING AGGRESSION

213. Provided that the definition is not contrary to the provisions of the Charter and falls within the scope of those provisions, there are no legal, that is to say constitutional, objections to defining aggression. On the many occasions on which the question has been discussed, no one has denied that it is constitutionally possible to define aggression. The contested issue is whether, once a definition had been adopted, it would be binding on the organs of the United Nations called upon to consider cases of aggression. This question will be considered in title III of this part.

(b) THE TECHNICAL POSSIBILITY OF DEFINING AGGRESSION

214. That it is technically possible to define aggression is proved by the fact that numerous definitions have been proposed, that the Committee on Security Questions of the Disarmament Conférence drew up a definition, and that a certain number of treaties containing a definition of aggression have been concluded. Those opposed to defining aggression do not deny that it is possible, from a purely technical point of view, to define aggression,. but they maintain that such a definition would be useless or dangerous.[1]

SECTION II. THE NEED FOR DEFINING AGGRESSION

215. Aggression is the greatest crime against peace. It paves the way for war and is thus the worst threat to international public order that can arise. It sanctions recourse to legitimate individual and collective self-defence under Article 51 of the Charter and obliges the Security Council to adopt the measures of collective security for which provision is made in Chapter VII of the Charter. It also justifies the trial and punishment of those presumed responsible for the aggression.

216. That being so, the partisans of defining aggression argue, it is essential to know in advance what constitutes aggression, particularly since aggression is a legal concept, whether considered from the point of view of general international law or from the point of view of international penal law, and every legal concept must be more or less precisely defined.

(a) UNCERTAINTIES REGARDING THE CONCEPT OF AGGRESSION

217. There is no single, universally recognized concept of aggression, but, rather, several concepts which, according to their advocates, can either be combined or are mutually exclusive. Those in favour of a general definition hope thereby to determine which concept shall be applied to the exclusion of all others. Those in favour of an enumerative definition do not consider a general definition sufficient; once the principle has been adopted, rules for its application should be laid down by enumerating the cases in which it will apply.

218. In any event, those in favour of defining aggression hope to eliminate or reduce the area of uncertainty and the ambiguities and controversies concerning aggression which they regard as serious drawbacks.

---

[1] Mr. Fitzmaurice (United Kingdom) stated:
"No one had claimed that it was impossible to define aggression; what could be said was that it was impossible to reach a *satisfactory* definition which would not give rise to unforeseen results or place difficulties in the way of the defence of the victims of the aggression." *Official Records of the General Assembly, Sixth Session, Sixth Committee,* 292nd meeting, paragraph 49.

(b) DESIRABILITY OF A DEFINITION

219. Those in favour of a definition contend that it would have many advantages. Politis, introducing the Act relating to the definition of the aggressor stated:

"Its effect and its practical advantage would be that it warned States of the acts they must not commit if they did not wish to run the risk of being declared aggressors. Thanks to it, public opinion would be able, when a grave incident occurred in international relations, to form a judgment as to which State was responsible. Lastly, and above all, it would facilitate the work of the international organ called upon to determine the aggressor. Furthermore, when that organ had before it sufficiently definite proof to facilitate its task, it would be less tempted to incur the danger of excusing, on political grounds, the act of aggression which it was called upon to judge."[2]

220. A definition of aggression would be useful, first, to governments which must know what constitutes aggression if they are not to run the risk, as a result of the uncertainty surrounding the concept of aggression, of being named the aggressors without knowing that they have committed an act of aggression. Secondly it would be helpful to the organs of the international body responsible, in cases of aggression, for determining the aggressor.

221. Thirdly, it would guide the Governments of States Members of the United Nations which were called upon to decide whether they were justified, pending a decision by the Security Council, in exercising their right of individual or collective self-defence under Article 51 of the Charter, or which wished to know what attitude to adopt, should the organs of the United Nations be unable to reach a decision and leave them the responsibility of deciding. Fourthly, it would guide public opinion which must serve as a controlling factor and would find it difficult to do so in an atmosphere of doubt and confusion.[3] Lastly, the definition would help the Courts which might have to judge the alleged aggressors.

222. The definition would make it much easier to reach a decision in each individual case. There would no longer be any need to be guided by impressions or to decide a complex question on the basis of an individual appraisal of all the factors involved. After verifying whether certain acts had occurred the Court would merely have to ascertain whether they fell within the scope of the definition. Little or no room would remain for a subjective decision which might not be impartial or equitable.[4]

In submitting the report of the Committee on Security Questions of the Conference for the Reduction and Limitation of Armaments, Politis said:

". . . there would be less risk of an attempt to shield or excuse the aggressor for various political reasons without appearing to break the rule to be applied".[5]

223. The governments which had to pass judgment either within the organs of the International Organization or on their individual responsibility, would to some extent be protected against their own prejudices and likes and dislikes, on the one hand, and against their timidity and fear of assuming responsibility, on the other. In that connexion, Mr. Salvador de Madariaga (Spain) stated:

"The automatic method had the very considerable advantage of eliminating the individual responsibility of States in naming the aggressor. Everyone knew from experience how difficult it was for one State to judge the conduct of another. Consequently, it was in every way desirable that the decisions to be taken in the matter should be based on facts and not taken by persons who, as far as they could, would always avoid the necessity of giving a decision in this matter."[6]

224. Finally, the difference between various legal systems might lead governments to interpret the concept of aggression in different ways. A definition of aggression would eliminate such differences. Mr. Röling (Netherlands) stated in that connexion in the Sixth Committee of the General Assembly:

". . . a definition of aggression would give countries with different legal systems and general backgrounds a clearer understanding of the prevailing policies of States which concluded treaties excluding aggression or adopted resolutions condemning it, and of what they meant by the term".[7]

225. Those in favour of defining aggression argue that it would exclude arbitrary action. The application of a rule which was not sufficiently flexible to cover every possible contingency might undoubtedly result in injustice in certain cases. On the other hand, the absence of any rule whatever also made it possible for injustices to occur and generally speaking opened the door to arbitrary action.[8]

---

[2]League of Nations, *Conference for the Reduction and Limitation of Armaments*, Series B (Minutes of the General Commission). Vol. II, page 500.

[3]In this connexion, the representative of the French Government stated:
". . . a definition formulated in advance and having the advantage therefore, of being considered impartial and objective would enable public opinion at the same time to understand and appreciate more clearly the action of organs of the United Nations or of States exercising their right of self-defence". (Letter from the representative of the French Government to the Secretary-General of the United Nations, dated 25 June 1952; see document A/2162).

[4]Mr. Dovgalevsky (USSR representative) stated in this connexion:
"The definition and establishment of an act of aggression must leave as little opening as possible for subjective feelings and judgments. Still more, the complete definition must, as far as possible, exclude any possibility of subjective interpretation, and the more automatic the establishment of the aggressor, the better for the work of peace". (League of Nations, *Records of the Conference for the Reduction and Limitation of Armaments*, Series D, Vol. V (Minutes of the Political Commission)), page 49.

[5]League of Nations, Conference for the Reduction and Limitation of Armaments, *Documents of the Conference*, Vol. II, page 679.

[6]League of Nations, *Records of the Conference for the Reduction and Limitation of Armaments*, Series B (Minutes of the General Commission), Vol. II, page 547.

[7]*Official Records of the General Assembly, Sixth Session, Sixth Committee*, 289th meeting, paragraph 33.

[8]This point was stressed by Mr. Castañeda (Mexico) in the Sixth Committee:
"The contention that an enumerative definition would tie the hands of the United Nations and make cases not covered by it punishable was tantamount to saying that injustices could occur by virtue of such a definition. But the same criticism could be made of the description of any offence. Every rule of law involved restrictions and made it possible for injustices to occur in isolated cases. The purpose of law was not to achieve justice directly in each individual case but to create a general security. The object of rules of law was to enable every person to foresee the consequences of his acts. The opposite notion to the legal was not invariably the unjust; it was arbitrary action." *Ibid.*, 285th meeting, paragraph 13.

226. In answer to the argument that aggression will be prevented and suppressed not by the existence of a definition but rather by the courage and determination shown by the United Nations and its Members in defending peace and international order, those who advocate a definition agree that it is not a universal remedy but they maintain that it will nevertheless serve a useful purpose by making aggression harder to commit and easier to punish.[9]

Chapter II

AGAINST DEFINING AGGRESSION

227. Those opposed to defining aggression maintain that aggression, by its very nature, is incapable of definition. They also invoke practical considerations. Not only would defining aggression serve no useful purpose, but it would above all be dangerous. In addition, certain delegations maintain that in view of the current world situation it would not now be advisable to define aggression.

SECTION I. AGGRESSION IS A CONCEPT WHICH IS IN-CAPABLE OF DEFINITION

1. AGGRESSION IS NOT ESSENTIALLY A LEGAL CONCEPT

228. Even if aggression is to some extent a legal concept, it also has other characteristics, political and military,[10] and, some people add, economic and social.[11] Whereas a legal concept can generally be more or less precisely defined the same is not true of a political or military concept. It should be possible to take into consideration the special circumstances in each case and to determine the importance and significance of each.

229. Mr. Van Glabbeke (Belgium) stated in the Sixth Committee of the General Assembly:

"... the problem was predominantly political and, as such, was totally unsuited to rigid definition. To seek to circumscribe within a rigid formula the innumerable political situations to which such a definition should be applicable would be to sacrifice truth and originality to a purely artificial simplicity. It would be preferable in so complex and delicate a field to have a formula allowing all the relevant facts to be taken into consideration at their true value, if it was desired to obtain a correct view of reality

which might bring about a just determination of responsibilities in case of conflict between States."[12]

230. Mr. Fitzmaurice (United Kingdom) said:

"Real safety for the potential victim lay in the fact that the existence of aggression is not referable to or to be determined by rigid rules or definitions, but was a matter for the judgment of the whole world on the basis of facts."[13]

231. Mr. Scialoza (Italy) had previously expressed the same opinion in his own vivid and emphatic manner:

"... when we speak of aggression, we are perfectly aware of what it means. We know that it means nothing at all. We realize the difficulty of formulating a definition of aggression ... a State which is resolved to coerce its neighbours by armed force will never be the apparent aggressor, for, however unskilled its diplomacy, it will always manage to make its neighbour begin the attack. Therefore, in our attempt to fix the responsibility for the aggression we must not dwell too much on appearances. We must subject to a close scrutiny all those relations between the states concerned which have in the past given rise to differences. That is far from easy."[14]

232. Mr. Unden (Sweden) proved that the concept of aggression did not have the rigidity of a legal concept when he said:

"It has been contended that the relationship between the attacking country and the defending country is similar to the relationship between a murderer or bandit on the one hand and his victim on the other. Such a concept, however, has nothing in common with the type of situation that most frequently arises. In reality there are numerous degrees of responsibility in the case of aggression."[15]

233. A single concept can have political and legal characteristics at the same time. The more pronounced the legal characteristics, the more rigid and precise is the concept. That is why Mr. Maktos (United States of America) considers it preferable

"not to define aggression but to leave the organs of the United Nations to pass on the aggressive nature of each case submitted to them. Aggression was a legal problem still at a stage at which it should not be crystallized".[16]

---

[9]Mr. Casteneda (Mexico) said in this connexion:
"A definition might not deter an aggressor nor would it have any magical, automatic effect; nevertheless, it would serve a useful purpose. As lawyers, members of the Committee must have faith in the law as the most effective instrument for guiding the conscience of the peoples along the paths of peace and international understanding." *Ibid.*, 285th meeting, paragraph 21.
Speaking along the same lines, the Yugoslav representative said:
"While the existence of a definition of aggression cannot, of course, in itself prevent acts of aggression, it would, none the less, in addition to its considerable moral and political effect, make it more difficult for an aggressor to seek to justify his aggressive intentions, both in the eyes of his own people and of those of other peoples and of the world community at large, by means of a hypocritical propaganda." (Letter from the representative of Yugoslavia to the Secretary-General dated 18 June 1952, document A/2162).
[10]The Belgian, Brazilian, French and Swedish delegations submitted a joint opinion to the Permanent Advisory Commission of the League of Nations in which they doubted "the possi-

bility of accurately defining this expression (cases of aggression) *a priori* in a treaty, *from the military point of view,* especially as the question is often invested with a political character". League of Nations, *Records of the Fourth Assembly, Minutes of the Third Committee (Official Journal,* Special Supplement No. 16), page 117.
[11]Mr. Maktos (United States of America):
"... juridical considerations could not be divorced from political, economic and social factors". *Official Records of the General Assembly, Sixth Session, Sixth Committee,* 280th meeting, paragraph 17.
[12]*Ibid.*, 287th meeting, paragraph 8.
[13]*Ibid.*, 281st meeting, paragraph 20.
[14]League of Nations, *Records of the Eighth Ordinary Session of the Assembly, Plenary Meetings, Text of the Debates (Official Journal,* Special Supplement No. 54), page 85.
[15]Unden, *"La guerre d'agression comme problème de droit international",* Publications de la conciliation internationale, 1930, page 25.
[16]*Official Records of the General Assembly, Sixth Session, Sixth Committee,* 282nd meeting, paragraph 10.

2. THE "NATURAL" CONCEPT OF AGGRESSION

234. Mr. Spiropoulos (Greece), the exponent of this theory, says:

"If we study the international practice . . ., we are led to the conclusion that whenever governments are called upon to decide on the existence or non-existence of 'aggression under international law' they base their judgment on criteria derived from the 'natural', so to speak, notion of aggression. . ."[17]

He adds:

"The (natural) notion of aggression, as applied by governments in international practice, is composed of *objective* and *subjective* criteria."[18]

235. Mr. Spiropoulos considers that there are two "objective criteria": first, "aggression presupposes some kind of violence—even if this violence be an 'indirect' act".[19] The second objective criterion is the time element: "the State to be considered as responsible must be the first to act".[20]

236. The subjective criterion is "aggressive intention".[21] "The mere fact that a State acted as first does not, *per se*, constitute 'aggression' as long as its behaviour was not due to: *aggressive intention* . . . That the *animus aggressionis* is a constitutive element of the concept of aggression needs no demonstration. It follows from the very essence of the notion of aggression as such."[22]

237. Mr. Spiropoulos adds:

"The (natural) notion of aggression is a concept *per se*, which is inherent to any human mind and which, as a *primary notion*, is *not susceptible of definition*. Consequently, whether the behaviour of a State is to be considered as an 'aggression under international law' has to be decided not on the basis of specific criteria adopted *a priori* but on the basis of the above notion which, to sum it up, is rooted in the 'feeling' of the Governments concerned.

"It may be added that, since this general feeling of what constitutes aggression is not invariable, the 'natural' notion of aggression is not invariable either. Not all the periods of the international relations must necessarily have the same notion of aggression.

"Finally, it is to be said that the (natural) notion of aggression, as a concept having its roots in the 'feeling' of governments, will not always be interpreted by these latter in the same way, which amounts to saying that the *objective* criterion of the 'notion of aggression' will, in the last analysis, depend on the *individual* opinion of each Government concerned."[23]

238. In support of his thesis, Mr. Spiropoulos could have cited the opinion of the Special Committee of the Temporary Mixed Commission of the League of Nations, which stated in a "Commentary on the definition of a case of aggression" (1923):

"In the absence of any indisputable test, Governments can only judge by an *impression* based upon the most various factors. . ."[24]

239. Mr. Spiropoulos's theory has, however, been criticized.[25] Doubts have been cast on the value of the "natural" notion of aggression on the grounds that no such notion is universally recognized. In that connexion Mr. Castaneda (Mexico) stated:

". . . it had been said that actually they were not setting out from a preconceived rational notion but from a 'natural' notion, the vague notion of aggression that was in everybody's mind. If unfortunately not everybody had the same intuitive idea of what constituted aggression, the resulting anarchy would hardly offer a guide in international relations".[26]

240. It has also been said that it is not necessary "for Governments or for organs of the United Nations to take into consideration any element of 'feeling' or 'impression' ",[27] from which biased or ill-founded conclusions may be drawn.

SECTION II. DEFINING AGGRESSION WOULD SERVE NO USEFUL PURPOSE

241. Those opposed to defining aggression claim that neither a general definition nor an enumerative definition would serve any really useful purpose.

1. CONCERNING GENERAL DEFINITIONS

242. A general definition states briefly those concepts which are more or less unchallenged. The opponents of defining aggression maintain that such a statement would do little to advance matters. According to Mr. Spiropoulos (Greece), a general definition would add nothing to the existing texts. In that connexion, he said:

"The idea underlying the drafts most discussed by the International Law Commission had been that aggression consisted of any use of armed force by one State against another for purposes other than self defence or the execution of a decision by a competent organ of the United Nations—an idea that occurred in Article 16 of the much earlier League of Nations Covenant and was also fully covered by the United Nations Charter. Consequently, it added nothing to the existing provisions. . ."[28]

243. Mr. Fitzmaurice (United Kingdom) made the same point in speaking of the method "of defining aggression by a general formula covering all cases" He said:

". . . the difficulty was that such formulae necessarily employed terms which themselves required definition. Mr. Amado's definition in the report of the International Law Commission (A/1858), for instance, spoke of 'any war not waged in exercise of the right of self defence'. The question was, however,

[17] A/CN.4/44, page 63.
[18] *Ibid.*, page 64.
[19] *Ibid.*, page 64.
[20] *Ibid.*, page 65.
[21] *Ibid.*, page 64.
[22] *Ibid.*, page 65.
[23] *Ibid.*, pages 65 and 66.
[24] League of Nations, *Records of the Fourth Assembly, Minutes of the Third Committee* (*Official Journal*, Special Supplement No. 16), page 184.
[25] The objective criteria mentioned by Mr. Spiropoulos (use of violence by a State and the fact that the State acted first)

are not peculiar to his concept. This will be discussed in title II below, paragraphs 279 and following. The subjective criterion of aggressive intention will also be dealt with in title II, paragraphs 355 and following.
[26] *Official Records of the General Assembly, Sixth Session, Sixth Committee*, 285th meeting, paragraph 9.
[27] Mr. Alfaro, in a memorandum submitted to the International Law Commission at its third session in 1951; see document A/CN.4/L.8, page 19.
[28] *Official Records of the General Assembly, Sixth Session, Sixth Committee*, 279th meeting, paragraph 12.

when a war was being waged in self defence and when as a matter of aggression. . .

". . . such general definitions could not achieve the main object of indicating precisely in what cases aggression could be said to have occurred, and it would be impossible to say in advance whether a given act was an aggressive act or not. Although they looked well on paper, such general definitions did little to advance matters".[29]

244. Mr. Chaudhuri (India) said:

"It appeared, in fact, futile to define one concept by the use of other equally vague concepts."[30]

2. CONCERNING ENUMERATIVE DEFINITIONS

245. Enumerative definitions begin by indicating the most flagrant forms of aggression such as the declaration of war or the invasion of the territory of another State. In that connexion, Mr. Anthony Eden (United Kingdom) said at the Disarmament Conference:

". . . the actions in question were, generally speaking matters which any international body or any individual State, called upon to form an opinion as to which party to a dispute was to be considered the aggressor in any particular case, would certainly take into account. No formal instrument signed by the nations of the world was necessary to ensure that result. They were the ordinary criteria which everyone would adopt".[31]

246. He was, in fact, referring to what Mr. Fitzmaurice (United Kingdom) calls the "major aggressors", of whom he says:

"Major aggressors acted from military and political motives and would not be discouraged by a definition of aggression. The Egyptian representative thought that such a definition would make them reflect by showing them the consequences of their acts. Mr. Fitzmaurice did not think that a possible aggressor would have scruples of that kind; his main concern would be to know whether he had any chance of succeeding, for in case of victory, he would have nothing to fear from the consequences of his acts. The most a definition could do would be to induce him to modify the technique of his aggression so as to appear in the right in public opinion in his country."[32]

247. The other types of aggression involving the accidental or restricted use of force, which would necessarily be considered aggression and treated as such if aggression was defined, were minor aggressions. Mr. Fitzmaurice said of them:

"With regard to minor aggressions, which were illegalities rather than aggressions properly speaking, it did not seem desirable to run the risk of the dangers involved in the definition in order to prevent them. Even if a definition was drawn up with the greatest care, it could not provide that a specific act was always an act of aggression, because that in fact depended on the circumstances in which the act had been committed."[33]

248. Has the lack of a definition of aggression ever been felt, in practice, when the League of Nations Covenant, the United Nations Charter or other international instruments had to be applied? Mr. Spiropoulos replies to this question by stating that "lack of a definition of aggression has never been felt in the history of either the League of Nations or the United Nations".[34]

249. It has been claimed that the lack of a definition of aggression proved no deterrent to the Military Tribunal at Nürnberg which had to judge the German leaders guilty of acts of aggression.[35] The acts of aggression in question were flagrant aggressions which the German Government did not seek to conceal or justify by legal arguments.

250. With regard to the practice followed by the League of Nations, the lack of a definition did not prevent the Assembly from condemning unlawful recourse to war in violation of Article 12 of the Covenant in two cases where it felt it was its duty to do so (the Italo-Ethiopian war and the Soviet-Finnish war).

251. In a certain number of cases of the use of force, when the Council or the Assembly of the League of Nations did not wish explicitly or implictly to determine the aggressor because they felt that by refraining from so doing they would more easily achieve the desired result, namely the cessation of hostilities, the existence of a definition of aggression might have complicated what they understood to be their task. It is worth considering what the outcome would have been, particularly in the case of the Sino-Japanese conflict, had there been a rigid definition of aggression and had they taken a more severe and energetic stand.

SECTION III. DEFINING AGGRESSION IS DANGEROUS

252. Those opposed to the enumerative or analytical method of defining aggression contend that it would have three dangers: The enumeration would necessarily be incomplete; it might encourage a government to commit aggression by evading the definition; lastly, it would render the decisions of international organs more or less automatic and thus make it harder to re-establish peace.

---

[29]*Ibid.*, 281st meeting, paragraphs 16 and 17.
[30]*Ibid.*, 282nd meeting, paragraph 47.
[31]League of Nations, *Records of the Conference for the Reduction and Limitation of Armaments,* Series B (Minutes of the General Commission), Vol. II, page 513.
[32]*Official Records of the General Assembly, Sixth Session, Sixth Committee,* 292nd meeting, paragraph 45.
[33]*Ibid.*, 292nd meeting, paragraph 46.
[34]*Ibid.*, 292nd meeting, paragraph 13.
[35]Neverthless Judge Jackson's comment should be noted:
"It is perhaps a weakness in this Charter that it failed itself to define a war of aggression . . . One of the most authoritative sources of international law on this subject is the Convention for the Definition of Aggression signed at London on July 3, 1933 by Romania, Estonia, Latvia, Poland, Turkey, the Soviet Union, Persia and Afghanistan . . . In the light of these materials of international law, and so far as relevant to the evidence in this case, I suggest that 'aggressor' is generally held to be that state which is the first to commit any of the following actions: . . . (Nos. 1 to 4 of the Litvinov-Politis definition follow)."
International Military Tribunal, Trial of the Major War Criminals, Nürnberg, 14 November 1945 to 1 October 1946, page 148.
Mr. Chaumont (France) made the following comment on the Nürnberg Judgment:
"If there were no description of aggression, the legislative power would necessarily have to be vested in the judge or the executive authority. The same difficulties would then be encountered as had arisen at the time of the Judgment of Nürnberg, when improvization had been rendered necessary by the inadequacy of international penal law." *Official Records of the General Assembly, Sixth Session, Sixth Committee,* 280th meeting, paragraph 5.

1. IT IS NOT POSSIBLE TO DRAW UP A COMPLETE LIST OF THE CASES OF AGGRESSION

253. The draft resolution submitted by Greece on 4 January 1952[36] refers to "the apparent impossibility of defining aggression in a formula covering all possible cases of aggression". Mr. Spiropoulos (Greece) adds: "It is impossible to forecast what further classes of acts will be recognized in the future by the international community as constituting aggression."[37] According to the same speaker such a definition "could not but be artificial!"[38]

254 According to Mr. Fitzmaurice (United Kingdom):

". . . an incomplete list would be extremely dangerous because it would almost inevitably imply that other acts not listed did not constitute aggression. States would thus be encouraged to commit the acts not listed, because, *prima facie* at any rate, they would not be regarded as acts of aggression. In addition, the existence of an incomplete list would show potential aggressors how to accomplish their aims without actually being branded as aggressors, for they would keep their acts within the precise letter of the definition and then claim that they were technically justified".[39]

255. Those who favoured an enumerative definition had invited their opponents to complete the proposed definition. Mr. Kustov (Byelorussian Soviet Socialist Republic) said in that connexion:

"If they thought a particular definition was incomplete they had merely to complete it by adding further cases."[40]

256. The opponents of the enumerative definition, however, consider that it would be incomplete not because of certain gaps that should be filled, but because it would be practically impossible to cover all possible contingencies.

257. In answer to this objection, some of those who favour an enumerative definition have proposed that the enumeration should be merely an indication, and should not be an exhaustive list.[41] The idea of a non-exhaustive list, however, did not meet with the approval of certain representatives. Mr. Robinson (Israel) stated in that connexion:

"The fourth and last method was that of exemplification. That method was dangerous, both psycho-

logically and logically, since it directed attention to certain acts which influenced man's thinking, and divided acts of aggression into two categories, those which were explicitly listed and those which were not, thus creating a certain hierarchy of acts of aggression. . ."[42]

2. THE RISK THAT A STATE MIGHT COMMIT AGGRESSION BY EVADING THE DEFINITION

258. Sir Austen Chamberlain stated on 24 November 1927 in the House of Commons:

". . . I therefore remain opposed to this attempt to define the aggressor, because I believe that it will be a trap for the innocent and a sign-post for the guilty."[43]

259. The draft resolution submitted to the Sixth Committee of the General Assembly by Greece on 4 January 1952 considers:

"that the formulation of a definition of aggression . . . might encourage a possible aggressor to evade such a definition".[44]

3. THE DANGER OF AUTOMATISM IN THE DECISIONS OF INTERNATIONAL BODIES

260. The existence of a definition of aggression binding on international bodies would obviously oblige such bodies to apply it and declare any State which had committed an act falling within the scope of the definition to be the aggressor.

261. Those opposed to defining aggression have two comments in this connexion. First, they state that it is wrong to consider a minor act as an act of aggression because it merely falls within the scope of the Politis definition. Secondly, they contend that the obligation to name as the aggressor any State which had committed an act falling within the scope of the definition might, in certain cases, worsen an already critical international situation and prove an obstacle to the re-establishment of peace.

(a) *Secondary acts which might fall within the scope of the definition*

262. Various cases have been cited in which acts necessarily characterized as aggression under the definition were not really of very great importance and were much less serious than other acts not covered by the definition. Mr. Di Soragna (Italy) said of the Politis definition:

---

[36]See document A/C.6.L.206.
[37]*Official Records of the General Assembly, Sixth Session, Sixth Committee*, 279th meeting, paragraph 9.
[38]*Ibid.*, 292nd meeting, paragraph 2.
[39]*Ibid.*, 281st meeting, paragraph 8.
[40]*Ibid.*, 281st meeting, paragraph 39.
[41]Mr. Bernstein (Chile):
"He preferred an enumerative definition listing certain acts of aggression, but without prejudice to other acts which the General Assembly or the Security Council might subsequently characterize as aggression." *Ibid.*, 281st meeting, paragraph 32.
Mr. Urrutia Holguin (Colombia). *Ibid.*, 281st meeting, paragraph 51 U Zaw Win (Burma) proposed that the following clause should be added to the text submitted by the delegation of the Union of Soviet Socialist Republics:
"Any other act declared by the competent organ of the United Nations to be aggression." *Ibid.*, 284th meeting, paragraph 37. In his letter to the Secretary-General, dated 18 June 1952, the Representative of Yugoslavia says:
"Such a definition should be flexible and provide explicitly for the possibility that the competent United Nations body, i.e.,

the Security Council as a rule and the General Assembly exceptionally, may define as aggression other forms of use of force or pressure, which may appear in the future." See document A/2162.
[42]*Official Records of the General Assembly, Sixth Session, Sixth Committee*, 282nd meeting, paragraph 33.
Mr. Ammoun (Lebanon) expressed a similar opinion:
". . . if the list of cases of aggression was merely enumerative and not exhaustive, there would be as it were a presumption of innocence in the cases not enumerated; it was possible that new, subtle and unforeseeable forms of aggression would make their appearance, in the face of which the organ responsible for defining the aggressor, would be hesitant or powerless if an analytic definition was adopted". *Ibid.*, 286th meeting, paragraph 23.
[43]Observations of His Majesty's Government in Great Britain on the programme of work of the Committee on Arbitration and Security, *Minutes of the Second Session of the Committee on Arbitration and Security*, League of Nations document C.165.M.50.1928.IX, page 176.
[44]See document A/C.6/L.206.

"The judges were bound hand and foot. On the one hand, five quite specific cases were laid down. If any one of them occurred, even on a very small scale, full international ·action would immediately come into operation. On the other hand, no provision was made for a large number of other cases. They might be extremely serious cases. The injured party would be powerless and would have to rely on pacific procedure, which was not always very speedy. There was no need to quote examples. On the one hand, international action might be taken because a cottage had been burnt down; on the other hand, one State might massacre the nationals of another for several days without the latter being able to do anything other than to resort to pacific procedure."[45]

(b) *The compulsion of designating as the aggressor any State which committed any act falling within the scope of the definition*

263. In the opinion of those opposed to defining aggression this compulsion might have unfortunate consequences in some cases and be contrary to the interests of peace.[46] In this connexion, Mr. Fitzmaurice (United Kingdom) says:

". . . in cases where it was perfectly clear that aggression had occurred, it might be politic to refrain from actually naming the State concerned an aggressor if there seems to be any prospect of a settlement and the aggressor State seemed willing to desist·from its action. That, however, would be very difficult if certain acts were listed in advance as definitely constituting aggression".[47]

264. The idea that the organs of the international organization should sometimes relegate the question of responsibility to the background and attempt to maintain and re-establish peace by inducing the States concerned to adopt measures of conservation always had a certain following in the League of Nations[48] and still has in the United Nations.[49]

265. There are, in fact, two ways of mitigating the severity of automatic action. First, the determination of the aggressor may, if it is deemed advisable, be postponed while the parties involved in the conflict are enjoined to cease hostilities and to conform to certain measures of conservation (withdrawal of troops beyond a certain line, acceptance of an investigation on the spot by United Nations officials, etc.).

266. Secondly, the link between the determination of the aggressor and the application of sanctions may be relaxed. In this connexion, Mr. Politis stated in his report to the General Commission of the Disarmament Conference on behalf of the Committee on Security Questions:

"6. It should . . . be noted that the question of the definition of the aggressor and that of the sanctions to be taken against the aggressor while, of course, closely connected, are nevertheless separate questions. The strictness of the definition of the aggressor does not necessarily lead to the automatic application of sanctions."[50]

267. Some of those in favour of defining aggression, however, have contended that whenever a case of aggression occurs the aggressor must be named as such and sanctions applied. In that connexion, Mr. Moussa (Egypt) says:

". . . in the current debate it had been suggested that it might sometimes not be expedient to declare that an aggressor was an aggressor. Whatever the circumstances or the political situation, an aggressor ought to be condemned. The automatic application of collective sanctions in cases of aggression was essential for determining a potential aggressor".[51]

268. Mr. Abdoh (Iran) concurs:

"No less fraught with significance was the statement that in cases where it was perfectly clear that aggression had occurred, it might be politic to refrain from actually naming the State concerned an aggressor. When it was remembered that the United Nations had the task of maintaining peace in keeping with justice and not in defiance of it, such an attitude was clearly indefensible."[52]

269. In reply to these criticisms, Mr. Fitzmaurice (United Kingdom) also explained the reasons for his point of view:

"He had been criticized for saying that too rigid a definition would have the disadvantage of compelling the competent organs openly to declare a State an aggressor, whereas in some cases it might be possible, by exercising greater diplomacy, to get the guilty State to mend its ways and renounce its aggressive designs. . . What he had meant to say—and he still though it would be advisable to ponder that aspect of the problem—was that resistance to aggression implied not merely a denunciation and written decisions, but also military action imperilling human lives. The General Assembly could not therefore reasonably bring about such a catastrophe unless it was absolutely essential: in other words, unless there was a case of flagrant aggression."[53]

---

[45]League of Nations, *Records of the Conference for the Reduction and Limitation of Armaments*, Series B (Minutes of the General Commission), Vol. II, page 550.

[46]At the Disarmament Conference, Mr. Nadolny (Germany) said:

"Moreover, if no strict or rigid criteria were set up, the Council, or the international organ dealing with the question, would not be under the necessity of proceeding to establish the facts of an aggression, even in cases where it might be preferable to apply means of conciliation, which might prove ineffective from the moment when one of the parties to the conflict had been stigmatized as the aggressor." *Ibid.*, page 549. At the San Francisco Conference when a Bolivian proposal to define aggression was discussed, one argument advanced against that proposal was that it would lead to automatic sanctions and might force premature application of such sanctions. *Documents of the United Nations Conference on International Organizations, San Francisco, 1945.* Vol. 12, page 342.

[47]*Official Records of the General Assembly, Sixth Session, Sixth Committee*, 281st meeting, paragraph 12.

[48]See the recommendation of the Assembly of the League of Nations, 20 September 1928 (paragraph 52 above) and the Convention of 26 September 1931 on the means of preventing war (paragraph 72 above).

[49]See the resolution 378 A (V) of the General Assembly of the United Nations of 17 November 1950 on the "duties of States in the event of the outbreak of hostilities". A/1775, *Official Records of the General Assembly, Fifth Session, Supplement No. 20*, page 14.

[50]League of Nations, *Conference for the Reduction and Limitation of Armaments, Documents of the Conference*, Vol. II, page 679.

[51]*Official Records of the General Assembly, Sixth Session, Sixth Committee*, 291st meeting, paragraph 6.

[52]*Ibid.*, 290th meeting, paragraph 39.

[53]*Ibid.*, 292nd meeting, paragraph 28.

SECTION IV. ARGUMENT THAT IN EXISTING CIRCUM-
STANCES A DEFINITION OF AGGRESSION WOULD BE
UNTIMELY

270. Some delegations, while not opposed to defining aggression on grounds of principle, have stated
that, given the present political situation, such a definition would be untimely.

271. Mr. Amado (Brazil) referring to the Inter-
American Treaty of Reciprocal Assistance signed at
Rio de Janeiro on 2 September 1947 [54] said:

" He thought it would not be impossible to adapt
the provisions of the Treaty of Rio de Janeiro to the
international community, but he continued to believe
that any effort to do so would be vain until the
prevailing atmosphere of mistrust in the international
community was replaced by harmony which existed
between the American States. When the Great
Powers—and, to be quite frank, the USSR and
United States—had knocked down the walls which
separated them, confidence would return and the
aggression that was no longer feared could be
defined."[55]

---

[54] See paragraph 201 above.
[55] *Official Records of the General Assembly, Sixth Session,*

272. The same idea was expressed by Mr. Maktos
(United States of America).

In explaining his country's past and present position
with regard to the question of defining aggression, he
says:

"A number of delegations had said the United
States had in 1945 argued the view which was now
that of the Soviet Union. That was quite true, and
the United States did not in any way pretend that it
was not. In 1945, the United States had been in
favour of a definition of aggression because at that
time there had been every reason to believe that the
term 'international co-operation' would have a real
connotation. Unfortunately, the state of international
relations had become such as to convince the United
States that a definition of aggression had become not
only undesirable but even dangerous. The United
States delegation had not obeyed a whim; it had
adopted a position which was diametrically opposed
to the stand it had taken in 1945 and had done so in
view of international developments."[56]

Sixth Committee, 284th meeting, paragraph 26.
[56] *Ibid.,* 286th meeting, paragraph 36.

Title II
STUDY OF THE DEFINITIONS OF AGGRESSION

273. From the point of view of form, three categories of definitions may be distinguished: enumerative,
general and combined.

274. The *enumerative definitions* give a list of the
acts regarded as acts of aggression. In most cases, the
authors of these definitions have regarded it as essential
that the enumeration should be exhaustive, which
means that only the acts enumerated constitute acts of
aggression. Some authors, however, have proposed that
the international organs should be empowered to treat
as acts of aggression acts other than those enumerated
in the definition.

275. The *general definitions,* instead of listing the
acts of aggression, are couched in general terms which
cover the entire class of cases to be included. It is left
to the international organs to determine the scope of the
terms when specific cases are brought before them.

276. The *combined definitions* are a combination of
the two preceding types. They contain, first, general

terms and, second, a list, but a list which is not
exhaustive. Their object is merely to describe the
principal forms of aggression.

Chapter I
THE ENUMERATIVE DEFINITIONS
SECTION I. THE PROBLEMS STATED

1. THE de facto POSITION OF THE POLITIS DEFINITION

277. One single enumerative definition has held the
constant attention of the organs of the League of
Nations and the United Nations during discussions of
the question of aggression. This is the Politis definition
prepared in 1933 by the Committee on Security Questions of the Disarmament Conference.[1] The other—and,
incidentally, not numerous—enumerative definitions are
based on the Politis definition.

278. Some authorities regard the Politis definition
as typical of the enumerative kind and, after comment-

---

[1](a) The origin of this definition was a Soviet proposal to
the Disarmament Conference dated 6 February 1933. The Committee on Security Questions prepared an Act relating to the
Definition of the Aggressor which follows the general lines of
the Soviet proposal and which was considered by the General
Commission on 25 and 29 May 1933. See above, paragraphs
76-80.

A number of individual treaties modelled on this Act were
concluded in 1933, 1934 and 1935 and after the Second World
War. See above, paragraphs 194-201.

In 1945, at the London Conference on the establishment of
an international military tribunal, the United States of America
submitted a proposal which reproduced this Act. See above,
paragraphs 143 and 144.

In 1945, at the San Francisco Conference, Bolivia and the
Philippines proposed definitions of aggression which reproduced the Act, with some additions. See above, paragraphs
113-115.

In the First Committee of the General Assembly of the
United Nations, the Union of Soviet Socialist Republics submitted, on 6 November 1950, draft definitions similar to the
terms of its 1933 proposal to the Disarmament Conference. See
above, paragraph 118. On 5 January 1952, the Union of Soviet
Socialist Republics submitted a draft definition which reproduced the earlier proposal, with some amendments. See above,
paragraph 137.

(b) The Inter-American Treaty of Reciprocal Assistance
signed at Rio de Janeiro on 2 September 1947 reproduces in
article 9 certain elements of the Politis definition. See above,
paragraph 201.

(c) The definitions presented by Mr. Yepes and Mr. Hsu at
the third session of the International Law Commission in 1951
reproduced some of the elements of the Politis definition. See
documents A/CN.4/L.7, A/CN.4/L.11 and A/CN.4L.11/Corr. 1.

(d) On 11 January 1952, Bolivia submitted a draft definition
of aggression which reproduces the terms of the Politis definition with some fresh elements. See above, paragraph 137.

ing on it critically, conclude that all enumerative definitions must be rejected. Others, while accepting the principles and forms of this definition, propose that, though its general scheme should be left intact, a number of corrections or additions should be made. Yet others, while taking the Politis definition as a basis, propose the addition of new elements (certain cases of indirect aggression, economic aggression) which correspond to principles different from those underlying the Politis definition.

2. THE PRINCIPLES OF THE POLITIS DEFINITION

279. The Politis definition is based on the following principles strictly applied.

280. *Only acts involving the use of force constitute aggression.* This is the fundamental principle of the definition.

281. *The definition enumerates the acts involving the use of force which constitute aggression.* This enumeration is exhaustive. Any act not covered by the definition cannot be regarded as an act of aggression.

282. *The State which is the first to resort to the use of force is regarded as the aggressor.* The chronological factor is decisive. In this connexion, Politis said in his report:

"It is clearly specified that the State which will be recognized as the aggressor is the first State which commits one of the acts of aggression. Thus, if the armed forces of one State invade the territory of another State, the latter State may declare war on the invading State or invade its territory in turn, without itself being regarded as an aggressor. The chronological order of the facts is decisive here."[2]

The use of force in reply to the use of force constitutes, not aggression, but the exercise of the right of self-defence.

283. *It is specified that resort to force cannot be justified by any violation of international law which does not constitute an act of aggression under the terms of the definition.*[3] Hence, if a State regards itself as the victim of a serious violation of international law which does injury to what it considers to be its vital interests but which does not fall within the definition of aggression, it may not, of its own accord, resort to the use of force to redress the wrong of which it complains; if it does so it will itself be committing an act of aggression.

3. COMMENTS ON AND CRITICISM OF THE POLITIS DEFINITION

284. The elements of the Politis definition have been the object of much comment and criticism. Some comments relate to the forms of the definition, the principles of which are not contested. For example it has been proposed that the definition should include other acts which might be regarded as direct or indirect participation in acts of force.

285. Other comments and criticisms concern actual principles of the definition, although in some cases the authors wish to create the impression that they are not taking issue with these principles. Thus, for example, one of the fundamental principles of the definition is repudiated when it is proposed that acts which do not constitute acts of force, such as acts of economic aggression, should be added to the enumeration.

286. Eight questions will be considered:
1. The enumeration of acts of force;
2. Provocation;
3. The aggressive intention;
4. The threat of the use of force;
5. Action to prevent aggression;
6. The inclusion in the definition of acts not involving the use of force;
7. Individual or collective self-defence;
8. The collective action of the United Nations.

SECTION II. THE ENUMERATION OF THE ACTS OF FORCE COVERED BY THE POLITIS DEFINITION

287. Some authorities have criticized the five tests applied by the definition, and have occasionally proposed changes in them. Others have proposed the addition of new tests.

A. THE FIVE ACTS ENUMERATED IN THE DEFINITION

288. The five criteria applied by the Act relating to the Definition of the Aggressor prepared by the Committee on Security Questions of the Disarmament Conference are:

"(1) Declaration of war upon another State;

"(2) Invasion by its [the aggressor State's] armed forces, with or without a declaration of war, of the territory of another State;

"(3) Attack by its land, naval or air forces, with or without a declaration of war, on the territory, vessels or aircraft of another State;

"(4) Naval blockade of the coasts or ports of another State;

"(5) Provision of support to armed bands formed in its territory which have invaded the territory of another State, or refusal, notwithstanding the request of the invaded State, to take in its own territory all the measures in its power to deprive those bands of all assistance or protection."[4]

(a) *Declaration of war upon another State*

289. The USSR proposal submitted to the Sixth Committee of the General Assembly on 5 January 1952 uses the same formula: "Declaration of war against another State."[5]

290. · This criterion did not give rise to discussion. A declaration of war is a legal step. It can happen that a State which declares war on another State actually has no intention of starting hostilities against the State on which it declared war. Still, the declaration of war produces a breach of the peace and creates a state of

---

[2]League of Nations, *Conference for the Reduction and Limitation of Armaments, Conference Documents,* Vol. II, page 680.

[3]This is the purpose of the protocol annexed to article 2 of the Act relating to the Definition of the Aggressor. See above, paragraph 78.

[4]See above, paragraph 78.

[5]A/C.6/L.208.

war. Accordingly the declaration authorizes the State to which it is addressed to resort to force.[6]

(b) *Invasion by its armed forces, with or without a declaration of war, of the territory of another State*

291. The USSR proposal submitted to the Sixth Session of the General Assembly on 5 January 1952 used the following wording:

"Invasion by its armed forces, even without a declaration of war, of the territory of another State."[7]

292. There is no difference of substance between the two versions. Invasion of a territory constitutes the most obvious act of aggression.[8] Hence it was invasion that President F. D. Roosevelt was speaking of in the proposal which he transmitted on 30 May 1933 to the General Commission of the Disarmament Conference.

"That all the nations of the world should enter into a solemn and definite pact of non-aggression; that they should ... individually agree that they will send no armed force of whatsoever nature across their frontiers."[9]

293. It is immaterial what form the invasion takes whether it involves crossing the land frontier, disembarking on a coast or landing troops by parachute from aircraft. In connexion with invasion, two questions have arisen: the question of territories of uncertain or contested status, and the question of frontier incidents.

(1) *Territories of uncertain or contested status*

294. It can happen that territories are in dispute and that several States claim sovereignty over them.

295. In his report, Politis stated:

"By territory is here meant territory over which a State actually exercises authority."[10]

When Mr. Salvador de Madariaga (Spain) stated that he entertained "serious doubts as regards that last sentence, which, according to the interpretation given to it, might be harmless but might also be extremely dangerous",[11]

Politis replied that

"The idea of that sentence was not to justify unlawful occupation, but solely to protect peaceful possession against any act of force, even when the legal titles on which possession was founded might accidentally be open to dispute."[12]

296. The Inter-American Treaty of Reciprocal Assistance signed at Rio de Janeiro on 2 September 1947 adopted this idea of the *de facto* exercise of authority,[13] as did also the draft resolution submitted to the Sixth Committee by Bolivia on 11 January 1952.[14]

297. It may, however, be doubtful which State in fact exercises sovereignty over a territory. Referring to the course of lectures given by Mr. W. Komarnicki at the *Académie de droit international* at The Hague on the subject of the definition of the aggressor in modern international law,[15] Mr. Amado says that

"the territorial criterion may give rise to serious difficulties in the case of a dispute concerning a territory over which the States parties to the dispute all claim to have *de facto* power, as in the Chaco, Leticia and Vilna affairs".[16]

298. A somewhat analogous case is that in which foreign troops are authorized under an international agreement to be stationed in a certain area which has not been precisely delimited, as was the case with Japanese troops in Manchuria.[17]

(2) *Frontier incidents*

299. Invasion does not necessarily presuppose a crossing of the frontier by large armies. The size of the forces involved in an invasion is not in itself decisive.

300. Nevertheless, the definition of aggression prepared by the Committee on Security Questions of the Disarmament Conference specifies that "frontier incidents" do not constitute aggression.[18] It will be observed that such frontier incidents may take the form of an irregular crossing of the frontier in a manner resembling that of invasion (second criterion) or of a shot fired at targets beyond the frontier in a manner similar to attack (third criterion). The frontier incident was not defined either in the report by Politis or in his

---

[6]In the report of the Committee on Security Questions, Politis stated:
"The Committee considered the question whether it was advisable to take the declaration of war as a criterion of aggression, or whether the acts of aggression enumerated below would not be sufficient to define it.
"It appeared to it that the declaration of war should not be eliminated from the list of criteria of aggression. On the one hand, it is true, a declaration of war can occur before any act of hostility, and in this case it is the prelude to the hostilities which the declaring State will initiate or which the State on whom war is declared will be authorized to initiate. On the other hand, the Pact of Paris condemns resorts to war, and, as has been said, the Act defining the aggressor is regarded as an extension of the Pact of Paris." League of Nations, *Conference for the Reduction and Limitation of Armaments, Conference Documents*, Vol. II, pages 680 and 681.
[7]A/C.6/L.208.
[8]Invasion is mentioned in treaties other than those concluded on the model of the Politis definition. See above, paragraphs 180 and 182. It is also mentioned in the proposed definitions submitted by Bolivia and the Philippines to the San Francisco Conference. See above, paragraphs 113-115.
[9]League of Nations, *Records of the Conference for the Reduction and Limitation of Armaments*, Series B (Minutes of the General Commission), Vol. II, page 565.
[10]League of Nations, *Conference for the Reduction and Limitation of Armaments, Conference Documents*, Vol. II, page 681.

[11]League of Nations, *Records of the Conference for the Reduction and Limitation of Armaments*, Series B (Minutes of the General Commission), Vol. II, page 548.
[12]*Ibid:*, page 554.
[13]See article 9 of the Treaty, paragraph 201 above. It will be observed that the Act of Chapultepec of 8 March 1945 contains a different formula. It recognizes only legal sovereignty. See article 3 of the Act, paragraph 200 above.
[14]A/C.6/L.211. The draft provides:
"1. ... an act of aggression shall in all cases be considered to have been committed when any State invades the territory of another State, crossing the frontiers established by treaty or by judicial or arbitral decisions and demarcated in accordance therewith, or when, in the absence of frontiers thus demarcated, the invasion affects the territories under the effective jurisdiction of a State."
[15]*Académie de droit international, Recueil des Cours,* 1949, Vol. II, page 59.
[16]Memorandum submitted by Mr. Amado to the International Law Commission, A/CN.4/L.6, page 4. See also *Official Records of the General Assembly, Sixth Session, Sixth Committee,* 284th meeting, paragraph 13.
[17]Case quoted by Mr. Amado in the above-mentioned memorandum with reference to the course of lectures given by Mr. Komarnicki (Mr. Amado, *loc. cit.*; course of lectures by Mr. Komarnicki, page 60).
[18]See the Protocol annexed to article 2 of the Act relating to the Definition of the Aggressor, paragraph 78 above.

comments to the General Commission of the Disarmament Conference.

301. The de Brouckère report to the Preparatory Commission for the Disarmament Conference dated 1 December 1926 contains a description of the frontier incident:

"Every act of violence does not necessarily justify its victim in resorting to war. If a detachment of soldiers goes a few yards over the frontier in a colony remote from any vital centre; if the circumstances show quite clearly that the aggression was due to an error on the part of some subaltern officer; if the central authorities of the 'aggressor State' reprimand the subordinate concerned as soon as they are apprised of the facts; if they cause the invasion to cease, offer apologies and compensation and take steps to prevent any recurrence of such incidents — then it cannot be maintained that there has been an act of war and that the invaded country has reasonable grounds for mobilizing its army and marching upon the enemy capital. The incident which has occurred has in no way released that country from the specific obligations laid down in Article 12 and following."[19]

302. For the purpose of a description of what constitutes a frontier incident, the first salient feature to note is that it is on a small physical scale, the forces involved being too slight to enable an invasion or attack to be carried out. This criterion, however, would not be a very strict one: What amount of force would have to be used to constitute something which was no longer an incident but an aggression?

303. The second distinctive feature of frontier incidents is that they do not result from an aggressive intention on the part of the State responsible for them. They might be caused in certain cases by errors (involuntary crossing of the frontier) in other cases by action taken by subordinate chiefs acting without orders or misinterpreting the orders they have received.[20]

304. Mr. Spiropoulos (Greece), speaking on the subject of what acts should be held to be frontier incidents as distinct from acts of aggression, said:

"It depended on the circumstances of each act whether or not it really constituted aggression. For example, no one would ever dream of denying that the incident at Pearl Harbor had constituted aggression, but, on the other hand, if a small group of soldiers fired across a frontier and wounded some soldiers on the other side, that could hardly be termed aggression even if the soldiers had been acting on the instructions of their Government. Both cases, would, however, be regarded as aggression under sub-paragraph 1(b) of the USSR draft resolution (A/C.6/L.208)."[21]

305. Mr. Fitzmaurice (United Kingdom) criticized the inclusion of frontier incidents among the acts which

could not serve as a justification of resort to force of arms by another State. He said:

"Besides encouraging States to provoke frontier incidents and to violate their treaties, the inclusion of those two items would place the innocent States in a very difficult position. In the first place, a potential aggressor would be able to provoke even the most serious frontier incidents with impunity, because any military reaction on the part of the other State would automatically constitute aggression."[22]

306. Mr. Ogrodzinski (Poland) replied to the United Kingdom representative as follows:

"As to the question of frontier incidents, the United Kingdom representative had pushed his argument ad absurdum. The expression 'frontier incident' could mean nothing more than frontier incident, and any situation that went beyond mere incident would fall within a different category: for example, military invasion. The dividing line between certain situations and possible acts of aggression must be established in accordance with certain notions and those notions had to be defined in words."[23]

(c) Attack by its land, naval or air forces, with or without a declaration of war, on the territory, vessels or aircraft of another State

307. The USSR proposal submitted to the Sixth Committee of the General Assembly referred to:

"Bombardment by its land, sea, or air forces of the territory of another State or the carrying out of a deliberate attack on the ships or aircraft of the latter."[24]

308. The word "bombardment" is employed instead of "attack" to emphasize that in such a case there would be no penetration into the territory of the foreign State. Furthermore, the use of the word "deliberate" as applied to attacks on ships or aircraft makes it clear that in such cases there must be aggressive intention.

309. Politis states in his report:

"This hypothesis is distinct from the previous one. The territory of the State attacked is not entered by armed forces but is subject to artillery or rifle fire, air bombardment, etc."[25]

310. A large number of individual treaties, treaties of alliance or mutual assistance, refer to attack as the element which constitutes aggression.[26] This criterion of the Politis definition recurs in a number of proposals[27] and in the Inter-American Treaty of Reciprocal Assistance signed at Rio de Janeiro on 2 September 1947 (article 9a).[28]

311. Does this criterion refer only to attack directed against the vessels or aircraft forming part of the armed forces of the State, or does it also refer to attack directed against merchant vessels or civilian aircraft? Mr. Alfaro was inclined to adopt the former interpretation.[29]

---

[19]See League of Nations, document A.14.1927.V, page 69.
[20]See below, paragraphs 355 and following: the aggressive intention.
[21]Official Records of the General Assembly, Sixth Session, Sixth Committee, 279th meeting, paragraph 13.
[22]Ibid., 281st meeting, paragraph 10.
[23]Ibid., 283rd meeting, paragraph 9.
[24]A/C.6/L.208.
[25]League of Nations, Conference on the Reduction and Limitation of Armaments, Conference Documents, Vol. II, page 681.
[26]See above, paragraphs 180-182.

[27]See the proposals presented by Bolivia and the Philippines at the San Francisco Conference in 1945. See above, paragraphs 113-115. See also the proposal presented by Bolivia to the Sixth Committee of the General Assembly on 11 January 1952 (A/C. 6/L.211).
[28]See above, paragraph 201.
[29]In his memorandum to the International Law Commission, Mr. Alfaro made the following observation:
"...attack on the sea and air forces of a State is specifically mentioned as aggression, wherefore attack on merchant vessels and civil aircraft would seem to be permissible". A/CN.4/L.8, page 11.

Politis, however, interpreted it otherwise in his report:

"As regards the vessels or aircraft of another State, no distinction has been made according to whether these vessels or aircraft belong to the armed forces of the State or are of a non-military character belonging either to the State or its nationals."[80]

(d) *Naval blockade of the coast or ports of another State*

312. The USSR proposal submitted to the Sixth Committee of the General Assembly employs an equivalent formula.[81] The blockade in question is the so-called "pacific blockade" as opposed to the blockade ordered in the course of a war. The "pacific" blockade was used on several occasions in the 19th century.[82]

313. Politis says in his report:

"In spite of the objections raised by certain members at the mention of this case, the Committee considered that, while a naval blockade did not necessarily lead to war, it was nevertheless an act applying material force in a limited but real manner against another State. Only the weakness of the State against which a naval blockade is established can deter it from retaliating by acts of war. In certain cases, this weakness might also induce it to submit to a military invasion (see previous heading), which undoubtedly constitutes the most definite act of aggression."[83]

314. It has been proposed to extend the formula. In the definition offered by the Philippines at the San Francisco Conference, the formula was:

"To subject another nation to a naval, land or air blockade."[84]

315. In the International Law Commission Mr. Alfaro commented:

"Naval blockade is branded as aggression, but nothing is said about a land blockade, which produces equal effects."[85]

316. With regard to "land" blockade, the following observation might be made: A land blockade presupposes a decision on the part of a contiguous State to close the frontier separating it from the State to be blockaded. Such a step would be taken by the contiguous State on its own territory, in the exercise of its sovereignty and without resort to force. That being so, a "land" blockade would be fundamentally different from a naval blockade. It would not come within the meaning of "use of force," though possibly within that of "economic aggression," which will be spoken of below.

(e) *Provision of support to armed bands formed in its territory which have invaded the territory of another State, or refusal, notwithstanding the request of the invaded State, to take in its own territory all the measures in its power to deprive those bands of all assistance or protection*

317. The USSR proposal presented to the Sixth Committee of the General Assembly employs an equivalent formula.[86] The Bolivian proposal submitted to the San Francisco Conference in 1945 included among the acts of aggression "support given to armed bands for the purpose of invasion."[87]

318. It will be observed that article 2(4) of the draft code of offences against peace prepared by the International Law Commission at its third session speaks of an offence described as follows:

"The incursion into the territory of a State from the territory of another State by armed bands acting for a political purpose."[88]

319. However, the commentary on this clause reads:

"The offence defined in this paragraph can be committed only by the members of the armed bands, and they are individually responsible. A criminal responsibility of the authorities of a State under international law may, however, arise under the provisions of paragraph (12) of the present article."[89]

320. On the subject of armed bands, the Politis report makes the following observation:

"The Committee, of course, did not wish to regard as an act of aggression any incursion into the territory of a State by armed bands setting out from the territory of another country. In such a case, aggression could only be the outcome of complicity by the State in furnishing its support to the armed bands or in failing to take the measures in its power to deprive them of help and protection. In certain cases (character of frontier districts, scarcity of population, etc.) the State may not be in a position to prevent or put a stop to the activities of these bands. In such a case, it would not be regarded as responsible, provided it had taken the measures which were in its power to put down the activities of the armed bands. In each particular case, it will be necessary to determine in practice what these measures are."[40]

321. In the International Law Commission Mr. Alfaro commented:

"The clause relative to irregular bands fails to foresee the possibility that they be not only assisted but actually organized by the aggressor State."[41]

---

[80]League of Nations, *Conference for the Reduction and Limitation of Armaments, Conference Documents*, Vol. II, page 681.

[81]A/C.6/L.208.

[82]See *Memorandum on Pacific Blockade up to the time of the founding of the League of Nations*, League of Nations document A.14.1927.V, page 89.

[83]League of Nations, *Conference for the Reduction and Limitation of Armaments, Conference Documents*, Vol. II, page 681.

[84]See above, paragraph 115.

[85]A/CN.4/L.8, page 10.

[86]A/C.6/L.208.

[87]See above, paragraph 113. The same formula will be found in the Bolivian proposal submitted to the Sixth Committee on 11 January 1952 (A/C.6/L.211).

[88]See the report of the International Law Commission covering the work of its third session, 16 May - 27 July 1951, *Official Records of the General Assembly, Sixth Session, Supplement No. 9*, (A/1858), paragraph 59.

[89]Paragraph (12) provides:

"(The following acts are against the peace and security of mankind)"

"Acts which constitute . . .

". . .

"(iv) Complicity in the commission of any of the offences defined in the preceding paragraphs of this article."

[40]League of Nations, *Conference for the Reduction and Limitation of Armaments, Conference Documents*, Vol. II, page 681.

[41]A/CN.4/L.8, page 10.

322. It would appear that if assistance to armed bands constitutes an act of aggression, then, *a fortiori*, the direct organization of such bands would also constitute such an' act. Mr. Spiropoulos (Greece) said that in the case of the disturbances which had recently occurred in Greece, the General Assembly, although it had admitted that the Greek partisans were assisted by the neighbouring countries, had not expressly stated that Greece was the victim of an aggression.[42]

323. The situation may occur where a State maintains armed bands in a foreign country but these bands were not formed in the territory of the State which maintains them. Mr. Spiropoulos (Greece) said:

"The definition proposed by the USSR (A/C.6/ L.208) covered only the classic cases of aggression, that is, those which were indisputable. One case of aggression, however, was the complicity of a State which maintained armed bands on the territory of another State."[43]

324. Mr. Hsu (China) included in his proposed definition of aggression:

"Arming of organized bands or of third States for offence against a State marked out as victim."[44]

B. ANOTHER ACT INCLUDED IN THE DEFINITION PROPOSED BY THE UNION OF SOVIET SOCIALIST REPUBLICS

325. In addition to the acts enumerated in the Politis definition, the USSR, in the proposal which it submitted to the Sixth Committee of the General Assembly on 5 January 1952, added another act of aggression, defined as follows (paragraph *b*):

"The landing or leading of its land, sea or air forces inside the boundaries of another State without the permission of the Government of the latter, or the violation of the conditions of such permission, particularly as regards the length of their stay or the extent of the area in which they may stay;"[45]

326. The first hypothesis visualized in this definition would seem to be close akin to invasion (second act referred to in the Politis formula and in the USSR formula). The second, that of violation of the conditions under which the presence of armed forces has been authorized (case of Japanese troops in Manchuria) is admittedly not covered by the earlier definitions.

327. In the International Law Commission, Mr. François criticized the definition in these terms:

"It must...be realized that such definitions would enable the aggressors to evade responsibility for their acts by taking refuge behind legal texts. Such texts provided no real safeguard. For example, in the case

referred to in paragraph 1(*b*), of the Soviet Union draft resolution..., where one State landed or led its land, naval or air forces inside the boundaries of another State without the prior permission of the latter, it would be perfectly easy to disguise the aggression either on the grounds that permission had been given by a government that had seized power in the invaded country at the eleventh hour and was in sympathy with the invader, or by denouncing the government of the country invaded as a "Puppet Government" and refusing to recognize it as the legitimate representative of the people."[46]

C. OMISSIONS IN THE USSR DEFINITION IN THE OPINION OF CERTAIN REPRESENTATIVES

328. The representatives to the General Assembly have criticized the USSR definition and quoted cases which they claimed it did not cover in drawing attention to such gaps; some representatives did not suggest that they should be filled in, but merely cited them as examples to prove that a comprehensive definition was impossible.

(a) *Destruction of the population of another State by technical methods*

329. The acts envisaged are bacterial warfare, the poisoning of streams, and death rays. Mr. Ammoun (Lebanon) states:

"Nor did the draft mention such concrete cases as bacteriological warfare, or the possibility that a State might poison a stream rising in its territory and flowing through a neighbouring country or might alter its course so that the neighbouring country suffered thirst."[47]

Mr. Spiropoulos (Greece) says:

"If however, rays capable of destroying a whole population were invented and a State constructed installations for the purpose of using such rays against the people of a neighbouring country, that case would not be covered by the USSR definition."[48]

Would these measures be covered by the criterion of attack stated in the definition?

(b) *Participation in a war of nationals of a neutral country*

330. Mr. van Glabbeke (Belgium) says:

"...tens or hundreds of thousands of 'volunteers,' armed and equipped, had moved into Korea from China. Would the USSR representative regard communist China as an aggressor under sub-paragraph (*b*)?"[49]

---

[42]*Official Records of the General Assembly, Sixth Session. Sixth Committee*, 279th meeting, paragraphs 16 and 17:
"He cited various passages from the reports of the United Nations Special Committee on the Balkans and from General Assembly resolutions where it was fully recognized that the Governments of Albania and Bulgaria were giving aid to the Greek guerrillas, that the guerrillas depended largely on the food and supplies they received from abroad and that they often returned into Albania and Bulgaria where they could rest, reform their units and obtain new supplies in safety.
"The General Assembly had recognized that such a situation constituted a threat to the political independence and territorial integrity of Greece. In its most recent' report (A/1857) the Special Committee described a change in tactics on the part of the Greek guerrillas but emphasized that their dominant aim was still to overthrow the Greek Government by force. In General Assembly resolution 380 (V), fomenting civil strife in the interests of a foreign Power was

recognized as an act of aggression, but in spite of that and in spite of article 1, paragraph (5) of the Politis definition, the General Assembly had never stated in express terms that the activities of Albania and Bulgaria constituted aggression against Greece."
[43]*Ibid.*, 292nd meeting, paragraph 5.
[44]*Ibid.*, 278th meeting, paragraph 50.
[45]A/C.6/L.208.
[46]A/CN.4/SR.93, paragraph 19. Mr. François was referring to the 'USSR proposal submitted on 6 November 1950 to the First Committee of the General Assembly (A/C.1/608/Rev.1). The USSR proposal submitted to the Sixth Committee of the General Assembly on 5 January 1952 merely reproduced the earlier proposal.
[47]*Official Records of the General Assembly, Sixth Session, Sixth Committee*, 286th meeting, paragraph 27.
[48]*Ibid.*, 292nd meeting, paragraph 3.
[49]*Ibid.*, 287th meeting, paragraph 38.

331. Mr. Spiropoulos (Greece) states:

"Similarly, if 'volunteers' left their country of origin to go to a foreign country in order to enroll in the armed forces without any attempt on the part of their country of origin to prevent their doing so, that country would become guilty of aggression even though it had not committed any positive act."[50]

332. In accordance with traditional international law, the fact that aliens enrol in time of war in the armed forces of a belligerent Power does not, in principle, render responsible the State of which they are nationals. This is not so, however, if the recruiting of such "volunteers" is encouraged or decreed by the authorities of a neutral State. Furthermore, if the volunteers who have enrolled without any encouragement from their government are so numerous as to change the nature of the army involved, would that not give rise to a new situation?

(c) *Terrorist activities*

333. In the draft code of offences against the peace and security of mankind, the International Law Commission included the following offence as number 6 on the list:

"The undertaking or encouragement by the authorities of a State of terrorist activities in another State, or the toleration by the authorities of a State of organized activities calculated to carry out terrorist acts in another State."[51]

334. One purpose of terrorism is to kill politicians or persons holding high office (e.g., the assassination of King Alexander of Yugoslavia and of Louis Barthou, Minister of Foreign Affairs of the French Republic) whose death would seriously injure their country. Should terrorism organized or encouraged by a foreign State be considered as one form of aggression?

(d) *Refusal to put an end to hostilities which have broken out*

335. Mr. Amado (Brazil) states:

"The USSR draft resolution showed an important omission. In view of paragraph 1(b) of General Assembly resolution 378 A (V), which was a decision of that Assembly, the USSR draft resolution ought to contain a provision that any State should be declared an aggressor which, having become engaged in armed conflict with another State or States, did not immediately, and in any case not later than twenty-four hours after the outbreak of hostilities, make a public statement wherein it would proclaim its readiness, provided that the State with which it was in conflict would do the same, to discontinue military operations."[52]

SECTION III. DO PROVOCATION AND VIOLATIONS OF INTERNATIONAL LAW JUSTIFY THE USE OF FORCE?

1. STATUS OF THE QUESTION

336. A certain number of treaties of alliance and security contain a formula explicitly or implicitly covering the notion of provocation[53] but the term itself has not been defined in any international instrument.[54] An analysis of the notion of provocation shows that it can cover a number of very different acts.

337. In this connexion, Politis said:

" 'Provocation' is either one of the acts of aggression defined in Article 1—in such case the State which has been the victim of such an act can obviously retaliate by acts of a similar nature and no difficulty arises—or 'provocation' consists in a breach of international law or in the unfriendly attitude of Governments or public opinion without the commission of an act of aggression."[55]

338. The acts which might constitute provocation can be divided into four categories:

(a) Acts constituting aggression. In this case the State which meets force with force is obviously not, in view of the right of legitimate self-defence, an aggressor.

(b) Provocation may consist in preparations for aggression at some time in the near or distant future. This extremely important contingency has been the subject of controversy. It will be discussed further on.[56]

(c) Provocation may take the form of some breach of international law, involving another State or its nationals.

(d) Provocation may, as Politis said consist of "the unfriendly attitude of Governments or public opinion" without being a breach of international law, e.g., the Press in a certain country may criticize the policy of a foreign government or a certain member of that government, or crowds may demonstrate against a foreign government; in neither need there be any excesses or violence which would render the government of the country where such events occurred internationally responsible. It may be said that in this case there is no problem.

339. The case to be considered therefore is that of a breach of international law by one country in respect of another.

2. ARGUMENT THAT THOSE WHO RESORT TO FORCE TO ASSERT A RIGHT ARE COMMITTING AGGRESSION

340. The authors of the enumerative definition adopted a very adamant stand. They not only listed

[50]*Ibid.*, 292nd meeting, paragraph 5.
[51]A/1858, paragraph 59.
[52]*Official Records of the General Assembly, Sixth Session, Sixth Committee,* 284th meeting, paragraph 21.
[53]See paragraphs 202-206 above.
[54]Mr. Robinson (Israel) states:
"There was a tendency to get rid of the epithet 'unprovoked' and with that object, it was claimed that provocation could always be 'fixed'. A definition of aggression, however, could not ignore the question of provocation, which would then also need defining." *Official Records of the General Assembly, Sixth Session, Sixth Committee,* 282nd meeting, para-

graph 30. Mr. Alfaro stated in the International Law Commission:
"The Inter-American Treaty of Mutual Assistance, in classifying as aggression an 'unprovoked attack', seems to justify attack when it has been 'provoked'. Introducing the vague, imprecise and uncertain element of 'provocation' in the determination of the aggressor, may lead to most disturbing and dangerous consequences." A/CN.4/L.8, pages 10 to 11.
[55]League of Nations, *Conference for the Reduction and Limitation of Armaments, Documents of the Conference,* Vol. II, page 682.
[56]See paragraphs 380 and following below.

the acts involving the use of force which constitute aggression but took care to add that no other act may serve to justify the aggressor.

341. Article 2 of the definition prepared by the Committee on Questions of Security states:

"No political, military, economic or other considerations may serve as an excuse or justification for the aggression referred to in Article 1."[57]

342. A protocol expanding the principle laid down in Article 2 is annexed to that article and reads:

"The High Contracting Parties signatories of the Act relating to the Definition of the Aggressor . . . declare that no act of aggression in the meaning of Article 1 of that Act can be justified on either of the following grounds, among others:

"A. The Internal Condition of a State:

"E.g., its political, economic or social structure; alleged defects in its administration; disturbances due to strikes, revolutions, counter-revolutions or civil war.

"B. The International Conduct of a State:

"E.g., the violation or threatened violation of the material or moral rights or interests of a foreign State or its nationals; the rupture of diplomatic or economic relations; economic or financial boycotts; disputes relating to economic, financial or other obligations towards foreign States; frontier incidents not forming any of the cases of aggression specified in Article 1."[58]

343. It will be noted that the definition of aggression submitted to the General Commission of the Disarmaments Conference by the USSR delegation on 6 February 1933 contained a still more detailed list of the circumstances which could not be accepted as justification of aggression.[59] In this connexion, Politis stated in the General Commission:

"The Committee had felt that to insert so long a list in the body of the clause itself would make the text too heavy. In a spirit of conciliation, however, it had agreed that there should be a special Protocol annexed to Article 2 giving a certain number of illustrations."[60]

344. The proposal which the Union of Soviet Socialist Republics submitted first on 6 November 1950 to the First Committee of the General Assembly (A/C.1/608/Rev.1) and later to the Sixth Committee on 5 January 1952 (A/C.6/L.208) reproduces the list contained in the USSR proposal of 6 February 1933.

345. Replying to a comment by Mr. di Soragna (Italy), who mentioned the possibility that a State might have to witness the massacre of its nationals abroad without being entitled to assist them,[61] Mr. Politis made this statement:

"In this case, it was no longer a question of different conceptions of the nature of law, but of a sharp, a radical disagreement as to the conception of the organisation of international relations, and more especially the organisation of peace. . .

". . . provocation constituted an act which placed the victim in a position of legitimate defence, in which case the act with which the victim was charged was condoned, by reason, however, not of the act of provocation itself, but of the situation which it had brought about—that was to say, the special situation known as legitimate defence . . . or else provocation was not one of the prohibited acts, in which case aggression could not take place on any ground whatsoever and, against such an act of provocation there remained no other remedy than the application of a pacific procedure to secure the vindication of the right infringed. . .

"What was the meaning of the expressions 'prohibit recourse to force' and 'prohibit recourse to war'? They meant, as Article II of the Pact of Paris indicated, that the States undertook that in no circumstance would they employ other means than pacific forms of procedure for settling their disputes, so that, if provocation were to play any part, it could only be the part which it played in private law. If, however, it was desired to extend this idea of provocation in order to justify the use of force in international relations, that meant a very profound difference of opinion as regards the manner in which international relations were conceived. The arguments just put forward belonged, in Mr. Politis' opinion, to the past. He claimed that the conception which he was maintaining existed already in the texts adopted, and was in harmony with the object at which the civilized world was aiming in organising peace."[62]

346. Mr. Litvinov (USSR) made a statement to the same effect. After recalling the various reasons adduced to justify the use of force (defence of nationals, violations of treaties, maintenance of order and peace) he stated:

"If such theories are widely spread and are taken into account . . . it may confidently be prophesied that an aggressor will never be found in any armed conflict, and that only mutually aggressive defensive parties will be established, or, worse still, the defensive party will be considered the aggressor, and *vice versa*."[63]

347. It will be recalled that in the Corfu Incident a committee of jurists considering the case expressed the opinion that "coercive measures which are not intended to constitute acts of war may or may not be consistent with the provisions of Articles 12 to 15 of the Covenant.[64] Eleven Governments formulated criticisms or reservations in this connexion in their observations."[65]

---

[57]See paragraph 78 above.
[58]See paragraph 78 above.
[59]See paragraph 76 above.
[60]League of Nations, *Records for the Conference for the Reduction and Limitation of Armaments*, Series B (Minutes of the General Commission), Vol. II, page 501.
[61]Mr. di Soragna stated:
"On the other hand, one State might massacre the nationals of another for several days without the latter being able to do anything other than to resort to pacific procedure. Those

were, doubtless, exceptional cases, but the Commission would agree that a State might well ask with some anxiety whether it should subscribe to such onerous and rigorous undertakings, whether it could take the risk, by simply appending its signature to a document, of compromising so gravely what might be the primary interests of its nationals." *Ibid.*, page 550.
[62]*Ibid.*, pages 555–556.
[63]*Ibid.*, page 237.
[64]See paragraph 27 above.
[65]See paragraphs 28 and 29 above.

348. Several members of the International Law Commission expanded this idea that war was no longer legitimate even as a means of righting an injustice or introducing justifiable changes in the *status quo*.

349. Mr. Alfaro says:

"...war, i.e., the use of force in interstate relations, is illegal. It has been renounced too, pronounced an international crime, and is expressly prohibited. There is no distinction between *just* and *unjust* wars. Save two exceptions, all war is aggression, even if started on account of a wrong suffered by a State. Violations of rights under international law give rise to controversies which can only be decided by pacific methods and not by States taking the law into their own hands, assuming the role of party, accuser and judge, and deciding the issue by force of arms."[66]

350. Mr. Scelle says:

"... aggression [consists] of 'any resort to force contrary to the provisions of the Charter of the United Nations, the purpose or effect of which is to modify the state of positive international law in force and to disturb public peace...'"

"He wondered how a meeting of jurists could overlook the opportunity to emphasize the enormous progress represented by the absolute prohibition of resort to force in order to change a legal situation, even if the change were legitimate."[67]

351. Referring to genocide, the most serious possible violation of law, Mr. Spiropoulos (Greece) made a statement to the same effect in the Sixth Committee:

"If a State committed the crime of genocide against a large minority resident on its territory and belonging to a neighbouring State, could that be called aggression? Certainly not under Article 51 of the Charter."[68]

3. CRITICISM OF THIS OPINION

352. At the time of the Corfu Incident (1923) the Italian Government maintained that its armed intervention had been justified. Mr. Salandra (Italy) stated:

"... It (Italy's action) was merely designed to assure obligations arising out of responsibility for a terrible crime ... The creation of the League of Nations does not constitute a renunciation by States of all right to act for the defence and safety of their rights and of their dignity. If this were so, no State would desire to belong to the League."[69]

353. Mr. Fitzmaurice (United Kingdom) stated in the Sixth Committee of the General Assembly:

"Another characteristic of the USSR definition was that it listed a number of cases which would not constitute justification for armed action by other States. There were great objections of principle to the establishment of such a list, for its existence

would almost amount to an invitation to countries to embark on certain types of illegal action in the knowledge that any armed retaliation would at once be stigmatized as aggression. The list proposed in the USSR draft included 'frontier incidents' and 'the violation of international treaties. (The inclusion of those two items would encourage) . . . States to provoke frontier incidents and to violate their treaties...'."[70]

354. In 1929-1931 when an unsuccessful attempt was made to bring the Covenant of the League of Nations into line with the Pact of Paris, that is to say to revise the Covenant to include a general prohibition of recourse to war, certain governments insisted on the need for giving States some assurance that their rights would be recognized and protected by means of pacific procedures culminating in mandatory decisions the execution of which could be enforced under the control of the League of Nations.[71]

SECTION IV. AGGRESSIVE INTENTION

355. Frequent reference was made in the International Law Commission and in the Sixth Committee of the General Assembly to the subjective factor as it applies to the State committing aggression. This subjective factor is called "aggressive intention" (*animus aggressionis*).

356. Mr. Morosov (USSR) regarded the idea of aggressive intention with some suspicion. This formulation, he said,

"... would give a State which had committed one of the acts enumerated in the USSR proposal the opportunity of escaping the legal consequences of its action by claiming the absence of *animus aggressionis*."[72]

357. The meaning of "aggressive intention", a concept which has sometimes given rise to confusion, requires clarification.

1. THE CLAIM BY A STATE THAT IT WAS UNAWARE THAT ITS ACTION CONSTITUTED AGGRESSION CANNOT RELIEVE IT OF RESPONSIBILITY

358. Mr. Alfaro, after stating that there can be no aggression unless there was intent to commit aggression, added:

"But the point is that the act of using force reveals the intention by itself. If a town is unexpectedly bombarded or a port is blockaded, there can be no doubt as to the intention accompanying the bombardment or blockade, because force has been used in a manner and for purposes contrary to the present international order."[73]

359. In municipal law there is a maxim that ignorance of the law is no excuse. A person who has committed murder or fraud cannot relieve himself of responsibility by claiming that he did not know that murder was a crime, or that the act he committed

[66] A/CN.4/L.8, page 13.
[67] A/CN.4/SR.109, paragraphs 22 and 30.
[68] *Official Records of the General Assembly, Sixth Session, Sixth Committee* 292nd meeting, paragraph 7.
[69] See League of Nations, *Twenty-Sixth Session of the Council, Official Journal*, November 1923, page 1288.

It will be noted that the Polish delegate accredited to the League of Nations transmitted the observations of the Polish Branch of the International Law Association in regard to the

report of the Special Committee of Jurists. (See League of Nations, *Thirty-Ninth Session of the Council* (*Official Journal*, April 1926, page 604)). These observations contain arguments in favour of the Italian delegate's contention.
[70] *Official Records of the General Assembly, Sixth Session, Sixth Committee* 281st meeting, paragraph 10.
[71] See League of Nations document A.8.1930 V, Annex IV.
[72] *Official Records of the General Assembly, Sixth Session, Sixth Committee*, 278th meeting, paragraph 40.
[73] A/CN.4/L.8, page 20.

constituted fraud. *A fortiori,* States cannot plead ignorance of international law, which they are required to know. As Mr. François said:

"Even where an aggressor was personally convinced that he had acted within his rights, he might be guilty of aggression."[74]

360. There remain cases where doubt may exist concerning the exact requirements of international law. In such a case, if the doubt was justified, a State whose interpretation of international law had been rejected would not be relieved of responsibility; but its good faith might be taken into consideration. International organs, instead of pressing for the determination of responsibility and issuing a condemnation, might request the State which had been in error to put itself right and so end the hostilities.

2. THE EXISTENCE OR NON-EXISTENCE OF AGGRESSIVE INTENTION

361. As Mr. Spiropoulos (Greece) said: "Intention must not be confused with motive."[75] Motive is essentially different from intention; it is the reason for which an act of aggression is committed. The motives for aggression are very varied: e.g., the destruction of a State, the annexation of a territory, the establishment of a protectorate, the securing of economic advantages, the protection of the persons and property of nationals abroad, the changing of a political and social system, redress for an insult, etc.

362. Intention exists only when the State committing the act has acted deliberately. There is no aggressive intention in the two following cases (*a*) when the State committing the act has acted in genuine error; (*b*) when hostilities have broken out by accident.

First case: genuine error

363. Mr. Ammoun (Lebanon) referred to the possibility that "during a war, an air squadron might by mistake bomb a frontier town."[76] Thus, during the Second World War, Allied squadrons dropped on Swiss towns bombs meant for French or Italian towns.

364. One well-known example of error is the Dogger Bank incident. On 9 October 1904, the Russian Fleet under Admiral Rozhdestvensky opened fire in the North Sea on a fleet of British trawlers, mistaking them for Japanese torpedo boats.

Second case: accidental outbreak of hostilities

365. An outbreak of hostilities may be in the nature of a spontaneous and unpremeditated accident. On 25 May 1933, Mr. Eden said in the General Commission of the Disarmament Conference:

"It was surely the fact, for instance, in a time of tension, when troops were facing each other across a frontier and incidents were possible at any moment, the question of which force had been the first to cross the frontier might well have a comparatively slight bearing, in the light of previous history, on the question of which State was in fact the aggressor."[77]

366. In such a case the government may not have actually wished to enter into hostilities. The hostilities

may have been initiated by subordinate officers who have misunderstood their orders; or the government's orders may have been given in a state of confusion and haste on the basis of incorrect or incomplete information.

SECTION V. THREAT OF THE USE OF FORCE

1. WHAT CONSTITUTES A THREAT TO USE FORCE?

367. This occurs where a State, in order to force its will on another State, threatens to use force against it. The most typical form of this threat is the ultimatum in which the State to which it is addressed is given a time-limit in which to accept the demands made upon it, and told that if it rejects these demands war will be declared on it or certain coercive measures such as a naval blockade, bombardment, or occupation of a given territory, will be taken. However, the threat to use force is not always made in so crude and open a form. There are sometimes veiled threats which may be very effective, but are difficult to detect.

368. Again, the threat of force differs from the employment of force in the same way as the threat to kill differs from murder. The person who utters the threat may not intend to carry it out, and the threat is then only a form of intimidation and "blackmail". He may also change his mind and not resort to action.

369. De Brouckère, in his report of 1 December 1926 to the Committee of the Council of the League of Nations, stated:

"We find in history many instances of violence and aggression which have not led to war, either because the victim was too weak or too faint-hearted to offer any resistance, or because the matter was settled, by negotiation or through the mediation of a third party, before the state of war was established. The fact is that a state of war does not really exist until the country attacked takes up the challenge and thus admits the existence of a state of war."[78]

370. Similarly, a country's weakness may lead it to yield to a threat of aggression before the potential aggressor needs to take action to achieve the desired result.

2. THE INTERNATIONAL LAW COMMISSION CONSIDERS THE QUESTION FROM THE PENAL STANDPOINT

371. At its third session (1951), the International Law Commission, in preparing a draft Code of Offences against the Peace and Security of Mankind, considered the question whether the threat to resort to an act of aggression ought to be considered as actual aggression.

372. After deciding, by ten votes to one, that the threat of employment of force was an offence, it decided, by six votes to four, that such a threat did not constitute aggression.[79]

373. In the list of offences against peace drawn up by the International Law Commission, the threat to resort to an act of aggression occupies the second place,[80] the first in the list being aggression itself. In

---

[74]A/CN.4/SR.93, paragraph 18.

[75]*Official Records of the General Assembly, Sixth Session, Sixth Committee,* 292nd meeting, paragraph 9.

[76]*Ibid.* 286th meeting, paragraph 27.

[77]League of Nations, *Records of the Conference for the Reduction and Limitation of Armaments,* Series B (Minutes of

the General Commission), Vol. II, page 514.

[78]See League of Nations document A.14.1927.V, p.68.

[79]A/CN.4/SR.109, paragraph 106.

[80]This offence is defined thus:

"(2) Any threat by the authorities of a State to resort to an act of aggression against another State." A/1858, paragraph 59.

the comments accompanying the text of the draft code, the Commission points out that Article 2, paragraph 4, of the United Nations Charter prescribes that all Members shall "refrain in their international relations from the threat or use of force".

374. It must be borne in mind that in drafting its draft Code of Offences against the Peace and Security of Mankind, the International Law Commission was thinking in terms of the punishment of individuals called to personal account for their crimes. The problem confronting organs of an international institution and governments at the moment when the act is committed is somewhat different, namely, what action to take in respect of a State which resorts to aggression or the threat of aggression.

3. DISCUSSIONS ON THE THREAT OF THE EMPLOYMENT OF FORCE IN THE SIXTH COMMITTEE OF THE GENERAL ASSEMBLY

375. Mr. Robinson (Israel) said:

"...an aggressor need not use force but merely threats, explicit or implicit. The element of threat... was, moreover, contained, without being defined, in the draft Code of Offences against the Peace and Security of Mankind and in the Charter. Any definition of aggression must therefore take it into account."[81]

376. It will be noted that both the Politis definition and that proposed in the Sixth Committee on 5 January 1952 by the Union of Soviet Socialist Republics do not mention the threat of employment of force.

377. There was some discussion in the Sixth Committee on the subject of the annexation of Austria in March 1938, the annexation of the Sudetenland pursuant to the Munich agreements of September 1938 and the placing of Bohemia-Moravia under German protectorate in March 1939.

378. According to Mr. Morozov (USSR), the occupation of Czechoslovakia and Austria following a threat to employ force constituted aggression within the meaning of sub-paragraph (6) of the definition proposed by the USSR Government.[82]

379. Mr. Fitzmaurice (United Kingdom), citing the cases of Austria and Czechoslovakia, said that the aggressor might achieve his purpose just as certainly by subverting from within the will to resist of the country attacked as by the use of physical force outside. In some cases subversion was the most effective weapon. That had been clearly demonstrated by Hitler in his conquest of Austria and Czechoslovakia.[83]

SECTION VI. ACTION TO PREVENT AGGRESSION

380. The question whether a State may anticipate events and resort to force in order to prevent an expected aggression has been the subject of extensive discussion since the establishment of the League of Nations.

1. OPINION THAT A STATE WHICH, BY ATTACKING, FORESTALLS AN ACT OF AGGRESSION WHICH IS BEING PREPARED AGAINST IT DOES NOT ITSELF COMMIT AN ACT OF AGGRESSION

381. It has been asserted that the most effective way for a State—particularly a small Power—to prevent conquest by an aggressor might be to forestall the attack by itself attacking.

(a) League of Nations period

382. The Permanent Advisory Committee on armament questions formulated a theory that, in certain cases, a State which began hostilities against another State should not necessarily be considered as the aggressor.

383. The Permanent Advisory Committee stated: "...the passage of the frontier by the troops of another country does not always mean that the latter country is the aggressor. Particularly in the case of small States, the object of such action may be to establish an initial position which shall be as advantageous as possible for the defending country, and to do so before the adversary has had time to mass his superior forces. A military offensive of as rapid a character as possible may therefore be a means, and perhaps the only means, whereby the weaker party can defend himself against the stronger. It is also conceivable that a small nation might be compelled to make use of its air forces in order to forestall the superior forces of the enemy and take what advantage was possible from such action."[84]

384. The same Committee listed the "signs which betoken an impending aggression".[85] Again, it expressed this important opinion:

"It will be seen, in short, that the first act of war will precede the outbreak of military hostilities by several months or even more..."[86]

385. In its observations on the draft Treaty of Mutual Assistance (1923), the Government of the Union of Soviet Socialist Republics stated:

"Neither the entry into foreign territory nor the scale of war preparations can be regarded as satisfactory criteria. Hostilities generally break out after a series of mutual aggressive acts of the most varied character. For example, when the Japanese torpedo-boats attacked the Russian fleet at Port Arthur in 1904, it was clearly an act of aggression from a technical point of view, but, politically speaking, it was an act caused by the aggressive policy of the Czarist Government towards Japan, who, in order to forestall the danger, struck the first blow at her adversary. Nevertheless, Japan cannot be regarded as the victim, as the collision between the two States was not merely the result of the aggressive policy of the Czarist Government but also of the imperialist policy of the Japanese Government towards the peoples of China and Korea."[87]

[81] Official Records of the General Assembly, Sixth Session, Sixth Committee, 282nd meeting, paragraph 31.
[82] Ibid., 288th meeting, paragraph 19.
[83] Ibid., 281st meeting, paragraph 9.
[84] League of Nations, Records of the Fourth Assembly, Minutes of the Third Committee (Official Journal, Special Supplement No. 16) p.117.
[85] Ibid., p.117. See paragraph 22 above.
[86] Ibid., p.117.
[87] League of Nations, Records of the Fifth Assembly, Minutes of the Third Committee (Official Journal, Special Supplement No. 26), p.138.

(b) *The International Law Commission*

386.   Several members of the Commission expressed the opinion that preventive action against aggression might, in certain cases, be justified.

387.   Mr. François stated:

"The acts listed, for example, in the Soviet Union draft resolution, acts which it was proposed to prohibit altogether, might in certain circumstances be justified under international law as a defence against a premeditated and disguised act."[88]

388.   Mr. Hsu stated:

"...if Panama for example were threatened with aggression, was she to wait for the armed attack to take place? If she forestalled it, no one would denounce her as an aggressor."[89]

389.   Mr. Córdova stated:

"One further instance should be added, one which as a matter of fact could be brought under the heading of self-defence...where a State did not wait until the first shot had been fired before defending itself."[90]

(c) *Sixth Committee of the General Assembly*

390.   Mr. Spiropoulos (Greece) stated:

"There must also be aggressive intention....The right to shoot first in self-defence was recognized in all criminal codes. When there was impending aggression a State had the right to attack first in self-defence, although no actual act of aggression had taken place, to counter the aggressive intention of the other State. The League of Nations Permanent Advisory Commission (opinion of the Belgian, Brazilian, French and Swedish delegations) had expressed a similar idea."[91]

391.   Mr. Fitzmaurice (United Kingdom) stated:

"From the military point of view, there were few definitions of the enumerative type which might not have a most serious effect on the defensive prospects of a victim of aggression. On the basis of such a list of facts as was contained in the USSR draft resolution, an intending aggressor could easily make it impossible for the intended victim to protect itself adequately without committing or appearing to commit one of such acts, or could seriously prejudice its means of defence."[92]

392.   Mr. Maktos (United States of America) stated:

"The USSR draft resolution (A/C.6/L.208) provided that 'that State shall be declared the attacker which first commits' certain acts, one of which was 'the carrying out of a deliberate attack on the ships or aircraft' of another State. He wondered whether under that wording the United States of America would have been considered an aggressor if it had received prior notice of the attack on Pearl Harbour and had destroyed the enemy forces entrusted with that operation. Such a definition might require a State to let itself be attacked before it could defend itself.

"The USSR draft resolution (A/C.6/L.208) defined the aggressor as the one who was the 'first' to commit such actions. In his view that definition was illusory, for the word 'first' was not defined, nor were the expressions which followed it. To ask a State to wait so as not to be the 'first' to attack might give the enemy a great tactical advantage."[93]

393.   Mr. van Glabbeke (Belgium) said:

"...the United States would have been regarded as an aggressor if it had attacked the Japanese, even on the high seas, to prevent the bombing of Pearl Harbor; and Argentina or Brazil would be an aggressor if it destroyed aircraft-carriers, close to those States' territorial waters, which were about to bomb them with atom bombs."[94]

394.   Mr. van Glabbeke (Belgium) further stated:

"The Polish representative had taken the Belgian delegation to task for having defended an argument which might permit a 'preventive' war. But the representative of Poland had actually contended that, when his country was invaded from the east and the west in 1939, it had been the victim of aggression only on the part of Germany; the entry of the Russian armies into Poland had been a 'preventive' measure which had saved Poland from being completely occupied by the Nazi troops. There was an obvious contradiction in that argument."[95]

2.   OPINION THAT A STATE WHICH ATTACKS IN ORDER TO FORESTALL AGGRESSION IS AN AGGRESSOR

(a)   *To attack the aggressor before he commits his act of aggression is to launch a preventive war.*

395.   It was replied that, in the past, States that have started a war have usually claimed that that war was in fact a defensive one, having been intended to forestall an attack which was being prepared against them.

396.   Mr. Morozov (USSR) said:

"The United States representative's claim that the country which attacked first was not necessarily the aggressor proved that the only argument brought against the USSR's constructive proposal was a theory justifying preventive war."[96]

397.   It was pointed out that the fact that a country increases its armaments so as to achieve military superiority over another does not necessarily imply that it intends to commit an act of aggression.

398.   Mr. Alfaro said in the International Law Commission:

"...industrial mobilization, stocking of strategic materials, full-fledged functioning of war industries, scientific research in connexion with warfare, propaganda, an attitude of ill will in the press and the population of a State towards another State, espionage on the armaments and activities of other countries, even military mobilization, do not by themselves alone constitute aggression. They are preparatory acts which may lead to aggression as well as to self-defence."[97]

399.   Similarly, Mr. Robinson (Israel) said:

"...certain acts regarded by the League of Nations as constituting signs of an intention of aggression

---

[88]A/CN.4/SR.93, paragraph 19.
[89]*Ibid.*, paragraph 30.
[90]*Ibid.*, paragraph 40.
[91]*Official records of the General Assembly, Sixth Session, Sixth Committee,* 279th meeting, paragraph 10.
[92]*Ibid.*, 281st meeting, paragraph 13.

[93]*Ibid.*, 282nd meeting, paragraphs 6 and 20.
[94]*Ibid.*, 287th meeting, paragraph 39.
[95]*Ibid.*, 292nd meeting, paragraph 56.
[96]*Ibid.*, 288th meeting, paragraph 34.
[97]A/CN.4/L.8, pages 19–20.

—for example the theoretical or actual preparation of industrial mobilization or the establishment of war industries—were now no longer regarded as such."[98]

400. As was pointed out, for example, at the Disarmament Conference, it is not so much the volume of a country's armaments which creates the danger of war as the mentality of the rulers who have possession of those armaments. Hence, the Permanent Advisory Committee of the League of Nations stated that governments can only judge

"...by an *impression* based upon the most various factors, such as:

The political attitude of the possible aggressor;

His propaganda;

The attitude of his Press and population;

His policy on the international market, etc."[99]

(b) *The responsibility for taking the necessary action to prevent aggression rests with international organs, not with States acting on their sole initiative.*

401. Mr. Ogrodzinski (Poland) expressed regret, in the Sixth Committee,

"that some representatives had advocated preventive war, despite the existence of an international organization, of a system of collective security and of a body such as the Security Council whose task it was to safeguard international peace and security."[100]

402. In his report, Mr. de Brouckère stressed the importance of the role of the Council of the League of Nations in the prevention of aggression.[101]

403. It will be noted that, during its third session, the International Law Commission, in its draft Code of Offences Against the Peace and Security of Mankind, listed as two separate offences (offences 3 and 7) certain acts consisting in the preparation of aggression.[102]

404. The first of these offences is the following:

"(3) The preparation by the authorities of a State for the employment of armed force against another State for any purpose other than national or collective self-defence or in pursuance of a decision or recommendation by a competent organ of the United Nations."

405. The second offence is the following:

"(7) Acts by the authorities of a State in violation of its obligations under a treaty which is designed to

ensure international peace and security by means of restrictions or limitations on armaments, or on military training, or on fortifications, or on other restrictions of the same character."

406. But these provisions relate to penal measures applied after the event against persons responsible for acts of aggression already committed. What mainly concerns States is the prevention of aggression, an obligation which falls not on a criminal court but on the political organs of the international institution.

Section VII. Acts not involving the actual use of force which should be considered as acts of aggression

407. Reference has been made to indirect aggression, economic aggression and to the refusal to accept procedure for the peaceful settlement of disputes.

1. INDIRECT AGGRESSION

408. The concept of indirect aggression is comparatively recent, having been discussed and introduced into international law during the life of the United Nations.

(i) *Texts*

(a) *The Charter*

409. The Charter does not speak of indirect aggression. Mr. Spiropoulos (Greece) said in this connexion:

"The difficulty of defining aggression was apparent from a consideration of the case of indirect aggression. Article 51 of the Charter covered only armed attack. It was obvious, however, that a definition of aggression must fall within the framework of the Charter. Could the right of self-defence be exercised only in application of Article 51? He put the question without any attempt to answer it..."[103]

410. Mr. Röling (Netherlands) said:

"Article 51 of the charter referred only to the inherent right of self-defence in the event of 'armed attack'. But if the right of self-defence was based on the right of self-preservation, a State must surely have the right to defend itself against both types of aggression."[104]

(b) *General Assembly resolution 380 (V)*

411. In its resolution 380 (V) of 17 November 1950, the General Assembly, although it does not use the expression 'indirect aggression', seems, by the terms which it uses, to endorse the concept.[105]

---

[98] *Official records of the General Assembly, Sixth Session, Sixth Committee*, 282nd meeting, paragraph 32.
[99] League of Nations, *Records of the Fourth Assembly, Minutes of the Third Committee* (*Official Journal*, special supplement number 16, page 117.)
[100] *Official records of the General Assembly, Sixth Session, Sixth Committee* 292nd meeting, paragraph 24.
[101] Mr. de Brouckère stated:
"It cannot be repeated too often that it is not to place on record a breach of the Covenant that the Council should be convened in the ordinary course of things but to prevent it. It was in Article 11 that, with great wisdom, the authors of the Covenant prescribed the convening of the Council and not in Article 16. The declaration that Article 16 take effect may, in the worst case, be the final act of the Council, but it is unthinkable, unless the League has failed in its task, that this should be its first act and that the purpose for which it is convened should be merely to accept the irremediable.
"Between the first hostile act and a definite resort to war, a certain period of time, of varying length, will always inter-

vene. Cases can be imagined in which that period would extend over several months, others are conceivable in which it would last but a few hours. The constant purpose of the League's endeavour should be to organize in such a way that, however short a time available, it may always be in time to make a final attempt at maintaining peace.
"If the Council only met after war has been declared, if it thus neglected or lost the opportunity of doing anything more than intervening in war instead of preserving peace, its wartime task would thereby become much more difficult, for it would lack the most valuable information necessary to decide with a full knowledge of the facts, which State had really broken Article 16 and against which State the coalition of all peaceful nations should direct its action." See League of Nations document A.14.1927.V, page 70.
[102] A/1858, paragraph 59.
[103] *Official Records of the General Assembly, Sixth Session, Sixth Committee*, 292nd meeting, paragraph 6.
[104] *Ibid.*, 289th meeting, paragraph 38.
[105] See above, paragraph 126.

(c) *Report of the International Law Commission*

412. The International Law Commission declared itself in favour of including indirect aggression in the definition of aggression. In this connexion, the report of the Commission on its third session states:

"The Commission gave consideration to the question whether indirect aggression should be comprehended in the definition. It was felt that a definition of aggression should cover not only force used openly by one State against another, but also indirect forms of aggression such as the fomenting of civil strife by one State in another, the arming by a State of organized bands for offensive purposes directed against another State, and the sending of 'volunteers' to engage in hostilities against another State. In this connexion account was taken of resolution 380 (V), adopted by the General Assembly on 17 November 1950..."[106]

It will be noticed that the examples quoted refer to cases involving the complicity of a State in violent activities directed against another State.

(d) *The Charter of the Organization of American States—Bogotá, 30 April 1948*

413. Article 15 of this Charter includes the following provision:

"No State or group of States has the right to intervene, directly or indirectly, for any reason whatever, in the internal or external affairs of any other State. The foregoing principle prohibits not only armed force but also any other form of interference or attempted threat against the personality of the State or against its political, economic and cultural elements."[107]

(ii) *What constitutes indirect aggression?*

414. The characteristic of indirect aggression appears to be that the aggressor State, without itself committing hostile acts as a State, operates through third parties who are either foreigners or nationals seemingly acting on their own initiative. Representatives who have referred to indirect aggression have sometimes mentioned it in general terms, and at other times have pointed to certain facts which, in their view, constitute indirect aggression.

415. Indirect aggression is a general expression of recent use (although the practice itself is ancient), and has not been defined. The concept of indirect aggression has been construed to include certain hostile acts or certain forms of complicity in hostilities in progress. This form of indirect aggression was mentioned above[108] with reference to the discussion of possible omissions in the list of acts constituting aggression contained in the enumerative definition.

416. What will be considered here are cases of indirect aggression which do not constitute acts of participation in hostilities in progress, but which are designed to prepare such acts, to undermine a country's power of resistance, or to bring about a change in its political or social system.

(a) *Intervention in another State's internal or foreign affairs*

417. The definition of aggression submitted by Bolivia at the San Francisco Conference (1945) included among acts of aggression:

"(e) Intervention in another State's internal or foreign affairs."[109]

418. Article 15 of the Charter of the Organization of American States signed at Bogotá on 30 April 1948 provides that:

"No State or group of States has the right to intervene, directly or indirectly, for any reason whatever, in the internal or external affairs of any other State..."[110]

419. Article 3 of the draft declaration of the Rights and Duties of States prepared by the International Law Commission in 1949 states:

"Every State has the duty to refrain from intervention in the internal or external affairs of any other State."[111]

(b) *Intervention or interference in the affairs of another State*

420. This may assume the most varied forms: e.g. encouraging a party, paying it funds, sending weapons etc.

421. The definition of aggression submitted by the Philippines at the San Francisco Conference in 1945 contained this clause:

"(4) To interfere with the internal affairs of another nation by supplying arms, ammunition, money or other forms of aid to any armed band, faction or group, or by establishing agencies in that nation to conduct propaganda subversive of the institutions of that nation."[112]

(c) *Violation of the political integrity of a country by subversive action*

422. Mr. Fitzmaurice (United Kingdom) said, with regard to the USSR draft resolution:

"... it was completely silent about what had come to be generally recognized as one of the major causes of aggression, namely, the indirect aggression involved in an attempt to attack the political integrity of a country by subversive action against its government."[113]

423. Mr. Fitzmaurice referred, on another occasion, to the dispatch of nationals to a foreign country for subversive purposes:

"If a State were to send several million unarmed men into a small neighbouring State, it would give the small State a reason for exercising its right of self-defence, for several millions of even unarmed men were capable of taking over the nerve centres of a State and thus weakening it. It could be seen once more that the concepts of aggression and of self-defence were complementary and that it was impossible to define one without the other."[114]

---

[106] A/1858, paragraph 47.
[107] See Pan American Union, *Law and Treaty Series No. 23*, (Washington 1948), page 26.
[108] See above, paragraphs 328 *et. seq.*
[109] See paragraph 113 above.
[110] See Pan American Union, *Law and Treaties Series No. 23* (Washington 1948), page 26.

[111] See the report of the Commission on its first session, A/925, *Official Records of the General Assembly, Fourth Session, Supplement No. 10*, page 8.
[112] See paragraph 115 above.
[113] *Official Records of the General Assembly, Sixth Session, Sixth Committee*, 281st meeting, paragraph 9.
[114] *Ibid.*, 292nd meeting, paragraph 40.

424.   Mr. van Glabbeke (Belgium) quoted a similar case:

"The second act, given in sub-paragraph (*b*), was invasion by armed forces even without a declaration of war. But that failed to cover new refined forms of aggression, such as that employed by Hitler in sending technicians from the German army into Austria disguised as "tourists" to capture the country's means of communication and support a political party bent on seizing power with German assistance."[115]

(d) *Incitement to civil war*

425.   As indicated above, General Assembly resolution 380(V) of 17 November 1950 states that:

"...any aggression, whether committed openly, or by fomenting civil strife in the interest of a foreign Power . . . is the gravest of all crimes against peace and security throughout the world. . ."[116]

426.   On the basis of this General Assembly resolution, the International Law Commission included the following offences (No. 5) in the draft Code of Offences against the Peace and Security of Mankind:

"The undertaking or encouragement by the authorities of a State of activities calculated to foment civil strife in another State, or the toleration by the authorities of a State of organized activities calculated to foment civil strife in another State."[117]

427.   Mr. Crépault (Canada) said that it was "more important still" that the USSR proposal:

"...did not mention indirect aggression consisting of an attempt to attack the political integrity of a country . . . by fomenting civil strife."[118]

428.   On 11 January 1952 Bolivia submitted a draft resolution to the Sixth Committee to the effect that:

". . . action taken by a State, overtly or covertly, to incite the people of another State to rebellion with the object of changing the political structure for the benefit of a foreign Power"[119]

should be considered as an act of aggression.

(a) *Maintenance of a fifth column*

429.   Mr. Hsu (China) included in his definition of aggression:

"Planting of fifth columnists in a victim State. . ."[120]

(f) *"Ideological" aggression and propaganda*

430.   Mr. Röling (Netherlands) stated:

". . . nations were prepared to fight to protect their own way of life. Their way of life could be destroyed by other means than war, namely by indirect aggression, economic and ideological, which had now come to be feared even more than war itself . . ."[121]

431.   Mr. Sastroamidjojo (Indonesia), similiarly said:

". . . a country could conquer another by a 'military' aggression, 'economic' aggression or 'ideological' aggression. History was full of instances of economic and ideological aggression, which were just as dangerous as military aggression."[122]

432.   Ideological aggression is characterized by the dissemination of political ideas. Propaganda addressed by a country to its own nationals does not enter into consideration here; what is referred to is appeals directed at the inhabitants of other countries.

433.   Mr. Chaudhuri (India) said:

"Everybody was aware that aggression did not necessarily imply resort to armed force; for propaganda and aid to rebel organizations . . . were means of undermining the government of the victim State, and hence of achieving the purposes of aggression."[123]

434.   Mr. Ammoun (Lebanon) said, with reference to the USSR draft resolution:

". . . it did not mention, among what might be described as intellectual and moral cases, propaganda intended to overthrow economic, social or political systems. . ."[124]

435.   Ideological aggression might consist of propaganda in various forms directed at foreigners; e.g., radio broadcasts, dispatch of pamphlets, proclamations, etc. The object of such propaganda may simply be to disseminate a doctrine, or to discredit a government or a régime. But it may go further and constitute incitement to civil strife. The distinction between the first and second types of propaganda is sometimes difficult to make.

436.   Mr. Spiropoulos (Greece) expressed concern in this connexion:

"Resolution 380(V) of the General Assembly spoke of fomenting civil strife in the interest of a foreign Power. He was afraid that that expression could not be applied, for example, to speeches made or articles published in another State."[125]

437.   Article 19 of the Universal Declaration of Human Rights of 10 December 1948 provides that:

"Everyone has the right to freedom of opinion and expression; this right includes freedom to hold opinions without interference and to seek, receive and impart information and ideas through any media and regardless of frontiers."[126]

(iii) *Position taken by States of indirect aggression*

438.   A fairly large number of representatives supported the concept of indirect aggression; i.e., the representatives of Canada, China, Colombia, Dominican

---

[115]*Ibid.*, 287th meeting, paragraph 38.
[116]See paragraph 126 above.
[117]A/1858, paragraph 59.
[118]*Official Records of the General Assembly, Sixth Session, Sixth Committee*, 282nd meeting, paragraph 42.
[119]A/C.6/L.211.
[120]*Official Records of the General Assembly, Sixth Session, Sixth Committee*, 278th meeting, paragraph 50.

[121]*Ibid.*, 289th meeting, paragraph 37.
[122]*Ibid.*, 290th meeting, paragraph 49.
[123]*Ibid.*, 282nd meeting, paragraph 46.
[124]*Ibid.*, 286th meeting, paragraph 27.
[125]*Ibid.*, 292nd meeting, paragraph 7.
[126]*Official Records of the Third Session of the General Assembly, Part I, Resolutions*, page 74.

Republic, India, Indonesia, Iran, Lebanon, United Kingdom, Uruguay.[127]

439. Mr. Morozov (USSR) said that indirect aggression was covered by the USSR draft.

"Paragraph 1'(f) of the USSR draft resolution amply showed that the draft resolution did cover indirect aggression."[128]

440. Mr. Moussa (Egypt) expressed certain objections to the proposal to include the concept of indirect aggression. He said in that connexion:

"The problem of indirect aggression had not been considered at the San Francisco Conference. For the Charter, aggression consisted solely in armed attack. As any attempt to expand the concept of aggression beyond armed attack would be a departure from the Charter, the Committee should confine itself to that one aspect."[129]

2. ECONOMIC AGGRESSION

(a) *Emergence of the concept of economic aggression*

441. The concept of economic aggression is new. Economic aggression was covered in the draft definition submitted to the Sixth Committee by Bolivia on 11 January 1952,[130] which states:

"Also to be considered as an act of aggression shall be . . . unilateral action to deprive a State of the economic resources derived from the fair practice of international trade, or to endanger its basic economy, thus jeopardizing the security of that State or rendering it incapable of acting in its own defence and co-operating in the collective defence of peace."

442. Mr. Iturralde (Bolivia) said in support of the Bolivian proposal:

"In that connexion, however, it would be noted that, although there was legal equality as between States, there was no economic equality, and the economically powerful were in a position to exercise pressure on economically weaker States, with the result that such treaties might not always be fair to all parties. When because of such pressure, a treaty was not just, it constituted aggression."[131]

443. Mr. Röling (Netherlands) spoke of

". . . indirect aggression, economic and ideological, which had now come to be feared even more than war itself."[132]

444. Mr. Sastroamidjojo (Indonesia) said with reference to Mr. Röling's statement:

"History was full of instances of economic and ideological aggression, which were just as dangerous as military aggression."[133]

445. It will be noted that article 16 of the Charter of the Organization of American States signed at Bogotá on 30 April 1948 states that:

"No State may use or encourage the use of coercive measures of an economic or political character in order to force the sovereign will of another State and obtain from it advantages of any kind."[134]

(b) *Criticism of the concept of economic aggression*

446. The concept of economic aggression appears particularly liable to extend the concept of aggression almost indefinitely. The acts in question not only do not involve the use of force,[135] but are usually carried out by a State by virtue of its sovereignty or discretionary power. Where there are no commitments a State is free to fix its customs tariffs and to limit or prohibit exports and imports. If it concludes a commercial treaty with another State, superior political, economic and financial strength may of course give it an advantage over the weaker party; but that applies to every treaty, and it is difficult to see how such inequalities, which arise from differences in situation, can be evened out short of changing the entire structure of international society and transferring powers inherent in States to international organs.

447. Mr. Fitzmaurice (United Kingdom) said in this connexion:

". . . if all aggression was in fact illegal, every illegality was not aggression. It was not desirable to brand certain minor illegalities as acts of aggression. Such definitions might even mention as "aggression" some acts which were not illegal. There was a danger of that kind in the Bolivian draft resolution (A/C.6/L.211), which dealt with economic aggression in vague terms. He fully understood the concern of those who put forward such a theory; the fact nevertheless remained that no country could be compelled to sell its products to another country if it was not so bound by an agreement. Under too broad a definition, such an attitude, which was perfectly legal, as well as certain measures relating to customs tariffs or trade quotas, might be considered as constituting aggression. . .

"By extending the notion of aggression, the Security Council's field of action would be extended. Without supporting or opposing such a possibility, Mr. Fitzmaurice considered it an important point. Under Article 39 of the Charter, the inclusion of the idea of economic or ideological aggression would give the Security Council power to take action in cases of that nature. Yet, as the Egyptian representative had pointed out, aggression had been understood solely as armed aggression when the Charter was drafted."[136]

448. Mr. Moussa (Egypt) said:

". . . any attempt to expand the concept of aggression beyond armed attack would be a departure from the Charter. . . It was true that the Charter demanded co-operation among Member States in solving economic problems, but a breach of that pro-

[127]*Ibid.*, Canada, 282nd meeting, paragraph 42; China, 278th meeting, paragraph 50; Colombia, 281st meeting, paragraph 53; Dominican Republic, 283rd meeting, paragraph 58; India, 282nd meeting, paragraph 46; Indonesia, 290th meeting, paragraph 49; Iran, 290th meeting, paragraph 40; Lebanon, 286th meeting, paragraph 27; United Kingdom, 281st meeting, paragraph 9; Uruguay, 288th meeting, paragraph 9; Bolivia, proposal made at the San Francisco Conference (paragraph 113 above); Philippines, *idem* (paragraph 115 above).
[128]*Ibid.*, 288th meeting, paragraph 18.
[129]*Ibid.*, 291st meeting, paragraph 9.

[130]A/C.6/L.211.
[131]*Official Records of the General Assembly, Sixth Session, Sixth Committee*, 293rd meeting, paragraph 30.
[132]*Ibid.*, 289th meeting, paragraph 37.
[133]*Ibid.*, 290th meeting, paragraph 49.
[134]See Pan American Union, *Law and Treaty Series, No. 23* (Washington 1948), page 27.
[135]The naval blockade, which has far-reaching economic effects, is a military measure and must be considered as such.
[136]*Official Records of the General Assembly, Sixth Session, Sixth Committee*, 292nd meeting, paragraphs 47 and 48.

vision would not automatically lead to the application of collective security measures. If the breach became very serious and developed into a threat to the peace, any State could always complain to the Security Council."[137]

3. REJECTION OF PEACEFUL PROCEDURES

449. The idea of considering as an aggressor a State which refuses to submit an international dispute to procedure for peaceful settlement or to abide by the decision resulting from that procedure is an old one which has always been favoured in certain circles.[138]

450. It may be noted that whenever the attempt has been made to enact a general prohibition of war or the use of force through a new international instrument, the proposal has been to make peaceful settlement procedure obligatory and implementation of the decision resulting from that procedure binding. The reason given has been that if States are no longer free to take the law into their own hands by resorting to force, they must be assured of obtaining recognition and respect of their rights by some other means.

451. This idea found practical expression in the Draft Treaty of Mutual Assistance of 1933 (article 1)[139] and also in the Geneva Protocol of 1924 (article 10).[140]

452. When in 1931 it was attempted *to amend the Covenant of the League of Nations in order to bring it into harmony with the Pact of Paris*, it was very emphatically maintained by some delegates that if the "gaps" in the Covenant which allowed for the possibility of war were closed, States would in every case have to be given some means other than war to secure recognition and respect of their rights.[141]

453. At San Francisco, Bolivia submitted a draft definition of aggression under which the following were to be considered as acts of aggression:

" . . . . .

"(f) Refusal to submit the matter which has caused a dispute to the peaceful means provided for its settlement;

"(g) Refusal to comply with a judicial decision lawfully pronounced by an International Court."[142]

SECTION VIII. SELF-DEFENCE

1. THE ENUMERATIVE DEFINITION DOES NOT MENTION SELF-DEFENCE

454. The definition was criticized on that ground.[143] U Zaw Win (Burma) therefore proposed the addition of an appropriate provision to cover cases in which States acted

"in virtue of the right of self-defence, individual or collective, in the circumstances laid down in Article 51 of the Charter."[144]

455. It may be noted that the definition contained in the Inter-American Treaty of Reciprocal Assistance signed at Rio de Janeiro on 2 September 1947,[145] the definitions proposed in the International Law Commission and the first offence against the peace and security of mankind defined by the Commission[146] mention the right of self-defence.

456. It appears certain that in the minds of its sponsors the enumerative definition in no way omits or limits the right of self-defence, although the definition itself does not mention that right. Mr. Politis, in submitting to the General Commission of the Conference for the Reduction and Limitation of Armaments the definition formulated by the Committee on Security Questions, said:

" . . . in the enumeration of the acts of aggression which M. Politis would describe later, the State which first committed one of the acts mentioned was declared the aggressor. Emphasis should be laid on the word 'first'. It might very well be that, in the complicated circumstances of an international dispute, there might at one time' or another have been committed by either party certain acts coming within the scope of the definition in the Act. The only way of having a clear view in so complicated a situation and so being able to apportion the responsibilities and finally to determine the aggressor was to observe the chronological order of events—namely, to ascertain who had been the first to begin to commit one of the forbidden acts—since, once it was proved that one of the parties had been the first to commit one of those acts, the attitude of the other party would immediately be seen to be that of legitimate defence and, by that fact alone, should be excluded from the conception of aggression."[147]

---

[137] *Ibid.*, 291st meeting, paragraph 9.

[138] In May 1910, Mr. G. Moch stated at the XVIIIth Universal Peace Congress:
"As a general principle, there exists self-defence either against a State which unexpectedly attacks another State, or against a State which was offered a fair means of having a given dispute settled juridically and which declines this offer or which in practice nullifies its effect." (*XVIIIth Universal Peace Congress, Stockholm*, 1910-1911), page 219.
More recently, the group set up by the Royal Institute of International Affairs (Chatham House) to study the problem of sanctions stated:
"One definition of aggression by a state might run something on these lines: 'Aggression is the act of a state which after refusing ₊o submit a dispute to a process of peaceful settlement, or to abide by the result of such a submission, resorts to the use of armed force against the other state or states concerned." (*International Sanctions* (1938), page 185).

[139] See paragraph 25 above.

[140] See paragraphs 34 - 36 above.

[141] See, e.g., League of Nations document C.160.M.69.1930.V, pages 44 and 45.

Mr. Cassin said in the First Committee of the Assembly:
" . . . it was plain that if the total prohibition of war were incorporated in the Covenant, and if the countries were deprived of their traditional right to exercise their own discretion in carrying out an award, that would be conferring a very grave responsibility and a particularly heavy duty on the Council, since any failure on the part of the League in this matter would have incalculable consequences and might even cause a reaction."
See League of Nations, *Records of the Twelfth Ordinary Session of the Assembly, Minutes of the First Committee (Official Journal, Special Supplement No. 94, page 36).*

[142] See paragraph 113 above.

[143] See, e.g., Mr. Herrera Baez (Dominican Republic), *Official Records of the General Assembly, Sixth Session, Sixth Committee*, 283rd meeting, paragraph 39.

[144] *Ibid.*, 284th Meeting, paragraph 38.

[145] See paragraph 201 above.

[146] See A/1858, chapters III and IV.

[147] League of Nations, *Records of the Conference for the Reduction and Limitation of Armaments*, Series B (Minutes of the General Commission), Vol. II, page 500.

457. Neither the Covenant of the League of Nations nor the Pact of Paris, of that period, mentioned self-defence, whereas the United Nations Charter refers to it explicitly in Article 51.

2. SELF-DEFENCE AND THE CHRONOLOGICAL ORDER OF EVENTS

458. Self-defence is a response to an act of aggression. This is true both in municipal criminal law and in international law. In the passage just quoted, Mr. Politis said:

"... the State which first committed one of the acts mentioned was declared the aggressor. Emphasis should be laid on the word 'first'."

459. In the same connexion Mr. Spiropoulos said:

"... the State to be considered as responsible must be *the first* to act. This element, which one encounters in all the definitions of aggression, is logically inherent in any notion of aggression. Aggression is presumably: *acting as first.*"[148]

460. In the International Law Commission, Mr. Alfaro quoted the case of the United States declaration of war against Japan after the attack on Pearl Harbor.[149] Similarly, Mr. Fitzmaurice (United Kingdom) said:

"On the international plane, it was clear that an invasion, for instance, did not constitute an aggression in a case where the invader sought to gain control of bases from which aeroplanes were bombing his own territory."[150]

461. In the two cases quoted, there seems to be no possible doubt. States which react to an attack against them by declaring war, or which attempt to gain control of bases from which aeroplanes have been bombing their territory, are not committing an act of aggression because they are merely taking action against aggression directed against them.

462. In reality, the opponents of an enumerative definition do not object to the principle of the chronological sequence of events. They advance two arguments of a different kind. The first is that the acts which the definition makes it obligatory to consider as acts of aggression may not be of decisive effect. The second is that in certain cases when hostilities have broken out, the chronological order of events cannot be established.[151]

3. INDIVIDUAL AND COLLECTIVE SELF-DEFENCE

463. If the definition of aggression is to be interpreted as allowing the right of self-defence, this covers both collective and individual self-defence. Article 51 of the Charter is quite explicit on this point. Thus, if

State A commits aggression against State B, the latter, exercising its right of individual self-defence, is authorized to employ force against State A. But State C, which is a third party, is also authorized to employ force against State A by coming to the assistance of State B. It then exercises the right of collective self-defence.

464. Thus, in 1914, the United Kingdom, when it declared war on Germany, which had previously violated the neutrality of Belgium, did not commit aggression within the meaning of the definition. Nor did it commit aggression in 1939 in declaring war on Germany, which had previously attacked Poland.[152]

SECTION IX. COLLECTIVE ACTION BY THE UNITED NATIONS

465. The enumerative definition of aggression proposed by the Soviet Union was criticized for not providing for collective action by the United Nations.[153] Such collective action may be undertaken in a number of cases. The first and most important case is the restoration of peace when it has been broken as a result of aggression. Individual or collective self-defence in accordance with Article 51 of the Charter is then followed by organized action by the Security Council or, failing that, by the Assembly under resolution 377 (V) of 3 November 1950.

466. Secondly, there are the cases in which force may be used in the absence of an act of aggression or breach of the peace, pursuant to a resolution by a United Nations organ. Thus, under Article 39, the Security Council may act in cases where it merely determines "the existence of any threat to the peace" and where, under Article 96, paragraph 2, it "may ... make recommendations or decide upon measures to be taken to give effect" to a judgment of the International Court of Justice.

467. Of course, general definitions of aggression mention collective action by the United Nations as well as individual or collective self-defence. But it can apparently be said that any definition of aggression conceived within the framework of the Charter, even if it does not mention collective action, must be interpreted as in no way cancelling or limiting the powers vested in United Nations organs by the United Nations Charter.

Chapter II
GENERAL DEFINITIONS

468. As indicated above, general definitions of aggression, instead of enumerating the forms of aggression, offer a formula expressing a concept of aggression, that formula being required to cover every possible case.[154] Some treaties contain general definitions.

---

[148] A/CN.4/44, page 65.

[149] A/CN.4/L.8, page 10.

[150] *Official Records of the General Assembly, Sixth Session, Sixth Committee,* 292nd meeting, paragraph 37.

[151] See the observations on these arguments by Mr. Eden (United Kingdom) in the General Commission of the Disarmament Conference on 25 May 1933, League of Nations, *Records of the Conference for the Reduction and Limitation of Armaments,* Series B (Minutes of the General Commission), Vol. II, pages 513-514, and the reply of Mr. Politis (*Ibid.,* page 515).

[152] These cases were quoted by Mr. Alfaro (A/CN.4/L.8, page 10), by Mr. Fitzmaurice (United Kingdom) (*Official Records of the General Assembly, Sixth Session, Sixth Committee,* 281st meeting, paragraph 11), and by Mr. van Glabbeke (Belgium) (*Ibid.,* 287th meeting, paragraph 37).

[153] Mr. Maktos (United States of America) said in this connexion:

"The USSR draft resolution did not take account of the legality of the use of armed force at the request of the United Nations. Resort to force was one of the international community's means of re-establishing peace and security." (*Ibid.,* 282nd meeting, paragraph 13).

Mr. Bernstein (Chile), also, said:

"The USSR draft resolution ... omitted to state that the acts enumerated would not be regarded as acts of aggression if they were committed in consequence of a decision or recommendation of the United Nations." (*Ibid.,* 281st meeting, paragraph 29).

[154] To quote the words of Mr. Scelle, the definition must be "essential, general and abstract" (E/CN.4/SR.93, paragraph 92.)

469. When at its third session the International Law Commission took up the question of defining aggression, it set aside the method of enumerative definition and studied various drafts of a general definition, without finally adopting any.[155]

SECTION I. THE SUBSTANCE OF THE GENERAL DEFINITIONS

1. DEFINITIONS EMBODYING THE PRINCIPLE OF PROHIBITION OF THE USE OF FORCE, SUBJECT TO TWO STATED EXCEPTIONS

470. In the International Law Commission, Mr. Córdova submitted the following definition:

"Aggression is the direct or indirect employment by the authorities of a State of armed force against another State for any purpose other than national or collective self-defence or execution of a decision by a competent organ of the United Nations."[156]

471. Mr. Alfaro proposed the following definition:

"Aggression is the use of force by one State or group of States, or by any government or group of governments, against the territory and people of other States or governments, in any manner, by any methods, for any reasons and for any purposes, except individual or collective self-defence against armed attack or coercive action by the United Nations."[157]

472. The definition proposed by Mr. Amado is on the same lines as the two previous ones:

"Any war not waged in exercise of the right of self-defence or in application of the provisions of Article 42 of the Charter of the United Nations (is) an aggressive war."[158]

473. The definition drafted by the Commission, which was rejected in the final vote, is of the same type, reading as follows:

"Aggression is the threat or use of force by a State or government against another State, in any manner, whatever the weapons employed and whether openly or otherwise, for any reason or for any purpose other than individual or collective self-defence or in pursuance of a decision or recommendation by a competent organ of the United Nations."[159]

2. DEFINITIONS SPECIFYING THE AGGRESSOR'S OBJECTIVE

474. The treaty of 21 January 1939 between Finland and the Union of Soviet Socialist Republics provides that:

"Any act of violence attacking the integrity and inviolability of the territory or the political independence of the other High Contracting Party shall be regarded as an act of aggression, even if it is committed without declaration of war and avoids warlike manifestations."[160]

475. Mr. Scelle proposed the following definition:

"Aggression is an offence against the peace and security of mankind. This offence consists in any resort to force contrary to the provisions of the Charter of the United Nations, for the purpose of modifying the state of positive international law in force or resulting in the disturbance of public order."[161]

476. Mr. Yepes submitted the following definition:

"For the purposes of Article 39 of the United Nations Charter an act of aggression shall be understood to mean any direct or indirect use of violence (force) by a State or group of States..."[162]

477. The Act of Chapultepec of 8 March 1945 provides that:

"(j)...any attempt on the part of a non-American state against the integrity or inviolability of the territory, the sovereignty or the political independence of an American State shall be considered an act of aggression against all the American States."[163]

SECTION II. CRITICISM OF THE GENERAL APPROACH

478. As already stated,[164] general definitions have been criticized as useless because they would add nothing to the legal provisions—in this instance, of the United Nations Charter—already in force, and because the difficulty is to determine the scope of the general terms used in the definition.[165]

Chapter III

COMBINED DEFINITIONS

479. Supporters of the combined definition assert that it unites the advantages and avoids the disadvantages of the general definition and the enumerative definition.

480. Such a definition begins with a general statement of principles. This is followed by a list of a number of cases in which the general principles are applied. But this list is not restrictive, and the competent international organs may, in pursuance of the general principles, designate as the aggressor a State which has committed an act other than those contained in the list.

481. Mr. Bartos (Yugoslavia) said in this connexion:

"He fully recognized the defects of both the general and the enumerative methods and did not believe that either method on its own would be satisfactory. That, however, did not mean that it was impossible to define aggression. In his opinion, the two methods should be combined, with the enumeration serving as a set of examples but not as an exhaustive list. At the same time, the competent organs of the United Nations would use their own discretion in the case of acts of aggression which were not

---

[155]See paragraphs 128–134 above.
[156]A/1858, paragraph 44. The proposal includes this additional provision:
"The threat of aggression should also be deemed to be a crime under this article."
[157]Ibid., paragraph 46.
[158]Ibid., paragraph 40.
[159]Ibid., paragraph 49.
[160]See League of Nations, *Treaty Series*, Vol. 157, page 397.

[161]A/1858, paragraph 53.
[162]Ibid., paragraph 42.
[163]See paragraph 200 above.
[164]See paragraphs 242–244 above.
[165]Mr. el Khoury said in the International Law Commission: ". . . the Commission must either draw up a concrete definition or no definition at all. In any case, if an abstract definition were adopted, it must be accompanied by concrete examples . . ." (A/CN.4/SR.109, paragraph 56).

covered by the list. That method had already been used before, for example in the definition of the crime of genocide."[166]

482. In the Sixth Committee, the representatives of France,[167] Cuba,[168] Lebanon[169] and Ecuador[170] expressed some support for the idea of a combined definition.

483. On 17 January 1952 the Egyptian delegation submitted an amendment to the USSR proposal, requiring the insertion of a general formula at the beginning of the definition, and the elimination of the list's restrictive character.[171]

484. The Inter-American Treaty of Reciprocal Assistance adopted at Rio de Janeiro on 2 September

1947 was quoted[172] as a practical example of the combined definition. Article 1 of the Treaty lays down a general principle, and article 9 gives a number of practical applications.[173]

485. Some representatives questioned the advantages of the combined definition. Mr. van Glabbeke (Belgium) said in this connexion:

"The third method, combining the other two, had the disadvantages of both."[174]

486. The objections, having particular reference to the idea of a non-restrictive list, which is one of the elements of a combined definition, have been dealt with above.[175]

---

[166]*Official Records of the General Assembly, Sixth Session, Sixth Committee*, 2b9th meeting, paragraph 55.
[167]Mr. Chaumont said: "The analytic and synthetic methods could, perhaps, be combined . . ." (*Ibid.*, 280th meeting, paragraph 9).
[168]Mr. Cortina said: "There would then be a list of the main acts which might constitute aggression and, in addition, a general formula to cover any other acts which were not listed. That was no new idea. Such a solution was often used in penal codes to cover offences which would otherwise be very difficult to define." (*Ibid.*, 285th meeting, paragraph 27).
[169]Mr. Ammoun said: ". . . it would be possible to combine the advantages of the analytical and synthetic systems." (*Ibid.*, 286th meeting, paragraph 28).
[170]See Mr. Bustamante, *Ibid.*, 290th meeting, paragraph 28.
[171]A/C.6/L.213. The formula is worded thus: "That any act whereby a State infringes the territorial integrity or political independence of another State constitutes aggression."
[172]Mr. Cortina (Cuba) said: ". . . that particular method had in fact been used to define aggression in article 9 of the In-

ter-American Treaty of Reciprocal Assistance adopted at Rio de Janeiro in 1947, which, being not a mere declaration but a legally binding treaty, was an important precedent to which the Committee had not yet paid sufficient attention." (*Official Records of the General Assembly, Sixth Session, Sixth Committee*, 285th meeting, paragraph 27).
In the International Law Commission, Mr. Alfaro said: "Should it be found desirable to enumerate acts of aggression, it would be necessary to use a language similar to that of the Rio de Janeiro Treaty of 1947, and adopt a clause drafted more or less as follows: *In addition to other acts which the competent organs of the United Nations may characterize as aggression* by application of the rule contained in the preceding definition, the following shall be considered as such . . ." (A/CN. 4/L.8, pages 20-21).
[173]See paragraph 201 above.
[174]*Official Records of the General Assembly, Sixth Session, Sixth Committee*, 287th meeting, paragraph 34.
[175]See paragraphs 253 *et seq.* above.

Title III

EXTENT TO WHICH A DEFINITION OF AGGRESSION WOULD BE BINDING ON THE ORGANS RESPONSIBLE FOR DETERMINING OR PUNISHING AN AGGRESSOR

487. The definition of aggression might be applied either by a United Nations organ charged with determining the aggressor, or by an international criminal tribunal responsible for sentencing persons accused of having committed aggression.[1] In order to decide whether and to what extent the definition of aggression would be binding on United Nations organs and individual States, it must be ascertained in what form and by whom the definition would be adopted.

Chapter I

VARIOUS FORMS IN WHICH A DEFINITION OF AGGRESSION MIGHT BE ADOPTED

(a) *The amendment of the Charter*

488. This procedure was mentioned by Mr. Robinson (Israel).[2] In practice the amendment of the Char-

ter is a difficult matter. It would be particularly difficult if the point at issue was to introduce a definition of aggression into the Charter.

(b) *A convention*

489. This might be a universal convention[3] designed to regulate the operation of the international political organs (Security Council, General Assembly). Such a convention would be adopted by the General Assembly and opened for signature or accession by States.

490. It might be a regional or multilateral or bilateral convention to define the conduct and opinion of the States parties with respect to aggression.[4]

491. It might be a convention relating to international criminal law. The definition might, for example, be included in a code of offences against the

---

[1]A person accused of having committed a crime of aggression might conceivably be judged by a national tribunal; but this study is not concerned with that possibility.
[2]*Official Records of the General Assembly, Sixth Session, Sixth Committee*, 282nd meeting, paragraph 35.
[3]Mr. Robinson (Israel) suggested a universal convention as one possible method (*Ibid.*, 282nd meeting, paragraph 35).
Mr. Majid Abbas (Iraq) voiced the idea of a code of the rights and duties of States (*Ibid.*, 289th meeting, paragraph 7). Such a code could very likely be adopted in the form of a convention. In 1933, when a definition of the aggressor was

drafted by the Committee on Security Questions of the Disarmament Conference, it was contemplated that the definition might be embodied either in the convention for the regulation of armaments or in a separate declaration.
[4]The Yugoslav representative stated, in his letter of 18 June 1952 to the Secretary-General: "It may well be that such a definition would provide the basis for either a general treaty on the definition of aggression, or for regional or bilateral treaties among both Member States of the United Nations and non-member States." See document A/2162.

peace and security of mankind[5] or in a separate convention (such as the Convention on Genocide of 9 December 1948).

(c) *Adoption of a resolution by the competent organs of the United Nations*

492. The proposal to define aggression was brought before the General Assembly, which discussed the matter. The General Assembly might adopt a definition by adopting a resolution. Mr. Robertson (Israel) also mentioned the possibility of the Security Council adopting a definition. He said:

"Another possible solution might be a resolution of the General Assembly and a parallel resolution of the Security Council; there was, however, no guarantee that those two organs would adopt identical texts . . ."[6]

Chapter II

LEGAL VALUE AND AUTHORITY OF THE DEFINITION, ONCE ADOPTED

SECTION I. THE DEFINITION IS ADOPTED BY RESOLUTION OF THE GENERAL ASSEMBLY OR THE SECURITY COUNCIL

1. A RESOLUTION ADOPTED BY THE GENERAL ASSEMBLY

493. What would be the legal value and authority of such a resolution with respect to the General Assembly, the Security Council or an international criminal tribunal?

(a) *Legal value and authority of the definition with respect to the General Assembly*

494. The General Assembly might itself have occasion to apply the definition it had adopted, in the circumstances provided for in General Assembly resolution 377 (V) of 3 November 1950. The General Assembly would take action if:

"the Security Council, because of the lack of unanimity of the permanent members, fails to exercise its primary responsibility for the maintenance of international peace and security."[7]

495. It is a general principle of law that an organ is bound by statutory provisions which it has itself adopted, provided that it has not rescinded them.

(b) *Legal value and authority of the definition with respect to the Security Council*

496. It was said in the Sixth Committee that a definition adopted by the General Assembly would not be binding on the Security Council. However, a definition which expressed the opinion of the majority of the General Assembly would have undoubted moral authority. When the Council had occasion to make a

ruling it would bear the definition in mind, and would conform to it to the extent which it deemed expedient.

497. Mr. Chaumont (France) said:

"Now, should a definition of aggression be adopted by a General Assembly resolution, it will be useful as a guide to the Security Council, but would not be binding on the Council."[8]

498. Mr. Lerena Acevedo (Uruguay) said:

"Such a definition would not . . . be binding on the Security Council, since Articles 24 and 39 of the Charter conferred broad powers on the Security Council to determine the existence of threats to the peace and the spirit in which the decision had been taken showed clearly that it had not been intended to limit the powers of the Security Council in the matter."[9]

499. It is true that the Security Council bears sole responsibility for exercising the powers vested in it under Chapter VII, and cannot be bound by the Assembly to exercise them. But under Article 11, paragraph 2, the General Assembly may make "recommendations" to the Security Council with regard to "any questions relating to the maintenance of international peace and security."

500. Mr. Casteñeda (Mexico) expressed a somewhat different view. He felt that:

"Its (*sc.* the Security Council's) task was to verify the existence of a fact, and it could only describe that fact as aggression if a pre-determined criterion so allowed. The criterion was to be found in international law, which was binding on the Security Council. . ."[10]

501. In the opinion of some representatives, the resolutions of the General Assembly, particularly those of a statutory nature, might be part of international customary law.

502. Mr. Casteñeda (Mexico) said:

"A definition adopted by the General Assembly would constitute a useful guide to the Security Council, and if it became a part of international law by a convention or by any of the other means by which international law was made, the Security Council would be bound by it without any violation of Article 39 of the Charter . . ."[11]

(c) *Legal value and authority of the definition with respect to an international tribunal*

503. In the Sixth Committee the international court visualized as the organ responsible for applying the definition was a criminal court; but it is conceivable that the International Court of Justice or an *ad hoc* tribunal might have occasion to deal with a matter relating to a case of aggression.

---

[5]Mr. Chaumont (France) said: "The problem was that of the definition of an international crime for inclusion in the draft Code of Offences Against the Peace and Security of Mankind." (*Official Records of the General Assembly, Sixth Session, Sixth Committee,* 280th Meeting, paragraph 5.)

[6]*Ibid.,* 282nd meeting, paragraph 35.

[7]A/1775, *Official Records of the General Assembly, Fifth Session, Supplement No. 20, Resolutions,* page 10.

Mr. Lerena Acevedo (Uruguay) said:

"A definition of aggression might, however, be of some value in regard to the powers of the General Assembly in the cases covered by General Assembly resolution 377 (V)."

Official Records of the General Assembly, Sixth Session, Sixth Committee, 288th meeting, paragraph 6.

[8]*Official Records of the General Assembly, Sixth Session, Sixth Committee,* 283rd meeting, paragraph 33.

Mr. Chaumont said at a later meeting: ". . . the Security Council would not be bound by a definition, but might use it as it thought fit, whereas an international judicial body would be bound." *Ibid.,* 293rd meeting, paragraph 41.

[9]*Ibid.,* 288th meeting, paragraph 5.

[10]*Ibid.,* 285th meeting, paragraph 19.

[11]*Ibid.,* 285th meeting, paragraph 20.

504. Mr. Abdoh (Iran) said:

". . . that definition could serve as a guide to United Nations bodies and at the same time have mandatory force for a judicial body to be established in the future."[12]

2. A RESOLUTION ADOPTED BY THE SECURITY COUNCIL

505. If the Security Council adopted a definition of aggression, it may be assumed that what had been said above regarding the resolutions of the General Assembly would apply in principle. A definition adopted by the Security Council would not be binding on the General Assembly, just as a definition adopted by the General Assembly would not be binding on the Security Council.

506. Another possibility which has been considered is the adoption of the same definition by the General Assembly and the Security Council in concordant resolutions.

SECTION II. THE DEFINITION IS ADOPTED IN A CONVENTION

507. In this case the convention might expressly specify that it related only to the criminal liability of States committing aggression. Failing such a clause the convention would be considered as being of general application.

508. In the case of a convention the effects of the instrument with respect to individual States and international organs must be considered.

1. EFFECTS OF THE CONVENTION WITH RESPECT TO INDIVIDUAL STATES

509. So far as the States Parties to the convention were concerned, the definition of aggression would be binding in every respect. These States would have recognized in advance that they would be guilty of aggression if they committed any of the acts covered by the definition.

510. So far as States not parties to the convention were concerned, it would be a case of *res inter alios acta*. They could legitimately consider that an act did not constitute aggression even if it came within the scope of the definition adopted in the convention.

2. THE EFFECTS OF THE CONVENTION WITH RESPECT TO INTERNATIONAL ORGANS

511. This problem was the subject of a discussion of principle in the Disarmament Conference, in connexion with one of the possibilities contemplated, namely, that the definition of aggression should be embodied in a separate international instrument.

512. Mr. Politis, speaking of the Act relating to the definition of the aggressor drafted by the Conference's Committee on Security Questions, said:

". . . the Act was conceived as of universal application. It was designed to become a general law for all States. Nevertheless, it went without saying that

should it fail to command the acceptance of all States, it would only be compulsory and its rules would only apply in relations between the States which had accepted it."[13]

513. Mr. Eden (United Kingdom) voiced the following objections:

"But even on the assumption that the States represented at the Conference were free to adopt the definition or not as they might see fit, the matter still had a bearing on the position of all countries, for the object of the draft Act, according to its preamble, was to establish the rules to be followed by the international bodies responsible for determining the aggressor, and it followed therefore that either the States which had not accepted the definition would, when acting as members of any such body which was dealing with a dispute, be compelled to apply it, or the international body concerned would find itself in the very difficult position where some of its members were bound to apply the definition while others were not."[14]

514. Mr. di Soragna (Italy) similarly said:

"Nor did he see how it could be said that this Act would not bind States which did not sign it. They would even be bound to a very large extent. That was, in fact, the difficulty.

"Of course, it might be said that States which did not sign bore no responsibility, either for the verdict or for the action to be taken. But that was absolutely impossible, since there would be an advisory body consisting of two kinds of members— those who proposed to apply the principle of the free hand, who would consider things as they were, take all details and circumstances into account in determining the consequences of the acts committed, and those who, on the contrary, had in their pockets the definition of the aggressor and had a ready-made decision in their minds. How could two such opposing conceptions be reconciled?"[15]

515. Of course organs of an international institution frequently have occasion to apply a treaty to which sometimes only a small number of the members of the institution are parties. Mr. Politis drew attention to this point and quoted the example of the Pact of Locarno.[16]

516. However Mr. di Soragna remarked in this connexion:

". . . but the case before the Commission was quite a different one. The Act submitted to it contained no rules on special questions affecting only certain specific States. It contained rules relating to a problem of quite general character: the determination of the aggressor. A State could hardly risk having to accept a system under which it might, as a member of an international organization, have to help in determining the party responsible for a dispute and to determine that responsibility, not on the basis of special rules, but on the basis of a general rule which it had not accepted."[17]

---

[12]*Ibid.*, 290th meeting, paragraph 41.

Mr. Abdoh did not say whether he contemplated the adoption of the definition by an ordinary resolution of the General Assembly or by a convention. As, however, the definition of aggression has been presented in the form of a proposal to be voted on by the General Assembly, speakers are assumed to be referring to this procedure unless they state otherwise.

[13]League of Nations, *Records of the Conference for the Reduction and Limitation of Armaments*, Series B, (Minutes of the General Commission), Vol. II, page 500.

[14]*Ibid.*, page 513.

[15]*Ibid.*, page 551.

[16]*Ibid.*, page 516.

[17]*Ibid.*, page 551.

517. Mr. Politis replied:

"He now received the answer: 'Yes, but the Pact of Locarno[18] lays down special rules, whereas the rules under discussion are of a general character . . .'

". . . In what sense? In character they were general rules, but they remained special rules in so far as they were only accepted by certain parties . . .

"If, therefore, two countries had concluded, within the limits authorized by general law, special Conventions which, though binding upon themselves, did not bind third parties, and if the application of the rules thus established gave rise to a discussion before the international organ, it appeared to Mr. Politis an anachronism to say: 'How do you expect the members of the international organism, who are not contracting parties, to be able to apply these rules?' . . . the international organ and the members of which it consisted . . . had to apply rules accepted by certain parties and to apply them solely in the relations between those parties."[19]

---

[18]It will be recalled that the Pact of Locarno, to which a small number of Powers were parties, invested certain powers in the Council of the League of Nations.

[19]Ibid., page 556.

518. A definition of aggression enacted in a convention would be binding on international organs only in cases where States Parties to the convention were involved; but even then there is some doubt whether States not parties to the Convention would have to apply the definition to States Parties to the Convention.

519. Mr. Chaumont (France) said in this connexion:

". . . the Security Council would only be bound by the definition in so far as its members were bound by the convention."[20]

520. However, the situation would be different, Mr. Chaumont (France) believed, in the case of an international criminal tribunal. He stated:

"But if an international criminal code, defining aggression among other crimes, were to form part of an international convention laying legal obligations upon individual States or upon some special organ . . . the organ appointed to apply the definition under the convention would be bound absolutely to apply it."[21]

---

[20]Official Records of the General Assembly, Sixth Session, Sixth Committee, 283rd meeting, paragraph 33.

[21]Ibid., 283rd meeting, paragraph 33.

DOCUMENT A/C.6/L.264

Union of Soviet Socialist Republics: draft resolution

[Original text: Russian]

[14 November 1952]

The General Assembly,

Considering it necessary to formulate directives for such international organs as may be called upon to determine which party is guilty of aggression,

Declares:

1. That in an international conflict that State shall be declared the attacker which first commits one of the following acts:

(*a*) Declaration of war against another State;

(*b*) Invasion by its armed forces, even without a declaration of war, of the territory of another State;

(*c*) Bombardment by its land, sea or air forces of the territory of another State or the carrying out of a deliberate attack on the ships or aircraft of the latter;

(*d*) The landing or leading of its land, sea or air forces inside the boundaries of another State without the permission of the government of the latter, or the violation of the conditions of such permission, particularly as regards the length of their stay or the extent of the area in which they may stay;

(*e*) Naval blockade of the coasts or ports of another State;

(*f*) Support of armed bands organized in its own territory which invade the territory of another State, or refusal, on being requested by the invaded State, to take in its own territory any action within its power to deny such bands any aid or protection;

2. Attacks such as those referred to in paragraph 1 may not be justified by any arguments of a political, strategic or economic nature, or by the desire to exploit natural riches in the territory of the State attacked or to derive any other kind of advantages or privileges, or by reference to the amount of capital invested in the State attacked or to any other particular interests in its territory, or by the affirmation that the State attacked lacks the distinguishing marks of statehood.

In particular, the following may not be used as justifications for attack:

A. The internal position of any State, as for example:

(*a*) The backwardness of any nation politically, economically or culturally;

(*b*) Alleged shortcomings of its administration;

(*c*) Any danger which may threaten the life or property of aliens;

(*d*) Any revolutionary or counter-revolutionary movement, civil war, disorders or strikes;

(*e*) The establishment or maintenance in any State of any political, economic or social system;

B. Any acts, legislation or orders of any State, as for example:

(*a*) The violation of international treaties;

(*b*) The violation of rights and interests in the

sphere of trade, concessions or any other kind of economic activity acquired by another State or its citizens;

(c) The rupture of diplomatic or economic relations;

(d) Measures in connexion with an economic or financial boycott;

(e) Repudiation of debts;

(f) Prohibition or restriction of immigration or modification of the status of foreigners;

(g) The violation of privileges granted to the official representatives of another State;

(h) Refusal to allow the passage of armed forces proceeding to the territory of a third State;

(i) Measures of a religious or anti-religious nature;

(j) Frontier incidents.

3. In the event of the mobilization or concentration by another State of considerable armed forces near its frontier, the State which is threatened by such action shall have the right of recourse to diplomatic or other means of securing a peaceful settlement of international disputes. It may also in the meantime adopt requisite measures of a military nature similar to those described above, without, however, crossing the frontier.

DOCUMENT A/C.6/L.265

Afghanistan, Bolivia, Chile, Cuba, Dominican Republic, El Salvador, Iran, Netherlands, Peru and Yugoslavia: draft resolution

[Original text: French]

[26 November 1952]

The General Assembly,

Having regard to resolution 599 (VI),

Considering that the discussion has revealed the complexity of the question of defining aggression and the need for a detailed study of:

(a) The connexion between a definition of aggression and the maintenance of international peace and security and the development of international criminal law,

(b) The effect of a definition of aggression on the exercise of tne constitutional jurisdiction of the organs of the United Nations,

(c) The various aspects ot aggression,

1. *Decides* to establish a special committee composed of fifteen members representing each of the following

Member States: . . . to meet at the Headquarters of the United Nations in 1953,

2. *Requests* the said special committee:

(a) To study and report on all the questions raised by the adoption of a definition of aggression by resolution of the General Assembly;

(b) To submit to the General Assembly at its ninth session a draft definition of aggression or concept of aggression capable of providing guidance to the competent organs of the United Nations;

3. *Requests* the Secretary-General to communicate the special committee's report to Member States for their comments and to include the question in the agenda of the ninth session of the General Assembly.

DOCUMENT A/C.6/L.265/Rev.1

Afghanistan, Bolivia, Chile, Cuba, Dominican Republic, El Salvador, Iran, Netherlands, Peru and Yugoslavia: revised draft resolution

[Original text: French]

[2 December 1952]

The General Assembly,

Having regard to its resolution 599 (VI) of 31 January 1952,

Considering that the discussion of the question of defining aggression at the sixth and seventh sessions of the General Assembly and in the International Law Commission (A/1858, para. 35 and *ff.*) has revealed the complexity of this question and the need for a detailed study of:

(a) The various forms of aggression,

(b) The connexion between a definition of aggression and, on the one hand, the maintenance of international peace and security and, on the other, the development of international criminal law,

(c) The effect of a definition of aggression on the exercise of the jurisdiction of the various organs of the United Nations,

(d) Any other problem which might be raised by a definition of aggression;

1. *Decides* to establish a special committee of fifteen members, each representing one of the following Member States: . . . to meet at the Headquarters of the United Nations in 1953;

2. *Requests* the said special committee:

(a) To submit to the General Assembly at its ninth session draft definitions of aggression or draft statements of the notion of aggression;

(b) To study all the problems referred to above on the assumption of a definition being adopted by a resolution of the General Assembly;

3. *Requests* the Secretary-General to communicate the special committee's report to Member States for their comments and to place the question on the provisional agenda of the ninth session of the General Assembly.

DOCUMENT A/C.6/L.266

United States of America: motion

[Original text: English]
[26 November 1952]

Under rules 115 and 118 (*c*) of the General Assembly's rules of procedure, the United States of America moves that the Sixth Committee adjourn the debate, on the ground that it is not desirable to prepare and recommend a definition of aggression at the present time.

DOCUMENT A/C.6/L.266/Rev.1

United States of America: revised motion

[Original text: English]
[28 November 1952]

Pursuant to the statement made by the Chairman on 26 November 1952 the United States of America herewith submits in writing, for distribution and for voting at the end of the general debate on the subject, the following motion:

"Under rules 115 and 118 (*c*) of the General Assembly's rules of procedure, the United States of America moves that the Sixth Committee adjourn the debate on this item: the question of defining aggression."

DOCUMENT A/C.6/L.267

Turkey: amendment to the revised draft resolution (A/C.6/L.265/Rev.1) submitted by Afghanistan, Bolivia, Chile, Cuba, Dominican Republic, El Salvador, Iran, Netherlands, Peru and Yugoslavia

[Original text: English]
[3 December 1952]

Substitute the following for paragraph 1 of the operative part:

"1. *Decides* to establish a special committee composed of one representative each of fifteen Member States to be designated by the President of the General Assembly in consultation with the Chairman of the Sixth Committee, the special committee to meet at the Headquarters of the United Nations in 1953;".

DOCUMENT A/C.6/L.268 (incorporating A/C.6/L.268/Corr.1)

France: amendments to the revised draft resolution (A/C.6/L.265/Rev.1) submitted by Afghanistan, Bolivia, Chile, Cuba, Dominican Republic, El Salvador, Iran, Netherlands, Peru and Yugoslavia

[Original text: French]
[3 December 1952]

Preamble

1. Delete in sub-paragraph (*b*) of the second paragraph the words "on the one hand" and the words "and, on the other, the development of international criminal law".

2. Insert the following new sub-paragraph (*c*):

"(*c*) The problems raised by the inclusion of a definition of aggression in the code of offences against the peace and security of mankind and by its application within the framework of international criminal jurisdiction,".

The existing sub-paragraphs (*c*) *and* (*d*) will then become sub-paragraphs (*d*) and (*e*).

Operative part

3. Replace paragraph 2 of the operative part by the following:

"2. *Requests* the said special committee to study and report on all the problems raised by the adoption of a definition of aggression under a resolution of the General Assembly."

DOCUMENT A/C.6/L.269

Colombia, Egypt, Mexico and Syria: amendments to the revised draft resolution (A/C.6/L.265/Rev.1) submitted by Afghanistan, Bolivia, Chile, Cuba, Dominican Republic, El Salvador, Iran, Netherlands, Peru and Yugoslavia

[Original text: French]
[3 December 1952]

I. Delete the second paragraph of the preamble.

II. Replace paragraph 2 (*a*) of the operative part by the following text:

"(*a*) To submit to the General Assembly at its eighth session a draft definition of aggression which shall include:

"(i) A general definition of aggression by reference to the elements which constitute it;

"(ii) A non-exhaustive enumeration of cases of aggression;

"(iii) An enumeration of the reasons which may not be invoked as justification for aggression;".

III. Insert the following passage between paragraphs 2 (*a*) and 2 (*b*) of the operative part:

"*Instructs* the committee to study the following two questions in the light of the definitions it has drafted:

"(i) The connexion between a definition of aggression and, on the one hand, the maintenance of international peace and security and, on the other, the development of international criminal law;

"(ii) The effect of a definition of aggression on the exercise of the jurisdiction of the various organs of the United Nations."

IV. In paragraph 3 of the operative part, replace the word "ninth" by the word "eighth".

DOCUMENT A/C.6/L.269/Rev.1 (incorporating A/C.6/L.269/Rev.1/Corr.1)

Colombia, Egypt, Mexico and Syria: revised amendments to the revised draft resolution (A/C.6/L.265/Rev.1) submitted by Afghanistan, Bolivia, Chile, Cuba, Dominican Republic, El Salvador, Iran, Netherlands, Peru and Yugoslavia

[Original texts: French and Spanish]
[6 December 1952]

I. Delete the second paragraph of the preamble.

II. Replace paragraph 2 of the operative part by the following text:

"*Instructs* the special committee:

"(*a*) To submit to the General Assembly at its eighth session a number of draft definitions of aggression by reference to its constituent elements, one of which shall include:

"(i) A synthetic definition of aggression;
"(ii) A statement of the cases of aggression;
"(iii) An enumeration of the circumstances which may not be invoked as justification for aggression;

"(*b*) To study, in the light of the definitions it has drafted, the following two questions:

"(i) The connexion between a definition of aggression and, on the one hand, the maintenance of international peace and security and, on the other, the development of international criminal law;

"(ii) The effect of a definition of aggression on the exercise of the jurisdiction of the various organs of the United Nations;

"(*c*) To consider the above-mentioned problems as a whole on the assumption that a definition of aggression is adopted by a resolution of the General Assembly;"

III. In paragraph 3 of the operative part, replace the word "ninth" by the word "eighth".

DOCUMENT A/C.6/L.270

Indonesia: amendment to the revised draft resolution (A/C.6/L.265/Rev.1) submitted by Afghanistan, Bolivia, Chile, Cuba, Dominican Republic, El Salvador, Iran, Netherlands, Peru and Yugoslavia

[Original text: English]
[4 December 1952]

Add to the preamble a third paragraph reading as follows:

"*Considering* that continued and joint efforts shall be made to formulate a generally acceptable definition of aggression, with a view to promoting international peace and security and to developing international law;"

DOCUMENT A/C.6/L.272

Poland: amendments to the revised draft resolution (A/C.6/L.265/Rev.1) submitted by Afghanistan, Bolivia, Chile, Cuba, Dominican Republic, El Salvador, Iran, Netherlands, Peru and Yugoslavia

[*Original text: English*]
[*8 December 1952*]

Paragraph 2 (a)

1. Replace the word "ninth" by the word "eighth".
2. Replace the words "draft definitions" by the words "draft definition".

3. Delete the words "or draft statements of the notion of aggression".

Paragraph 3

4. Replace the word "ninth" by the word "eighth".

DOCUMENT A/C.6/L.273

Poland: amendments to the revised amendments (A/C.6/L.269/Rev.1) submitted by Colombia, Egypt, Mexico and Syria to the revised draft resolution (A/C.6/L.265/Rev.1) submitted by Afghanistan, Bolivia, Chile, Cuba, Dominican Republic, El Salvador, Iran, Netherlands, Peru and Yugoslavia

[*Original text: English*]
[*8 December 1952*]

Point II (a)

1. Replace the words "a number of draft definitions" by the words "a draft definition".
2. Delete sub-paragraph (i).
3. In sub-paragraph (ii) replace the words "a statement" by the words "an enumeration".
4. In sub-paragraph (iii) replace the word "aggression" by the words "an attack (aggression) of one State against another".

DOCUMENT A/C.6/L.274

Yugoslavia: amendment to the revised amendments (A/C.6/L.269/Rev.1) submitted by Colombia, Egypt, Mexico and Syria to the revised draft resolution (A/C.6/L.265/Rev.1) submitted by Afghanistan, Bolivia, Chile, Cuba, Dominican Republic, El Salvador, Iran, Netherlands, Peru and Yugoslavia

[*Original text: French*]
[*8 December 1952*]

Point II (a)

Replace sub-paragraph (ii) by the following:

"(ii) a non-exhaustive enumeration of cases of aggression;".

DOCUMENT A/C.6/L.275

Czechoslovakia: amendment to the revised draft resolution (A/C.6/L.265/Rev.1) submitted by Afghanistan, Bolivia, Chile, Cuba, Dominican Republic, El Salvador, Iran, Netherlands, Peru and Yugoslavia

[*Original text: French*]
[*8 December 1952*]

Replace paragraph 1 of the operative part by the following:

"1. *Decides* to establish a special committee of fifteen members, each representing one of the following Member States: Argentina, Bolivia, Colombia, Czechoslovakia, Egypt, France, Indonesia, Iran, Mexico, Norway, Poland, Syria, Union of Soviet Socialist Republics, United Kingdom of Great Britain and Northern Ireland and United States of America, to meet at the Headquarters of the United Nations in 1953;".

DOCUMENT A/C.6/L.275/Rev.1

Czechoslovakia: revised amendments to the revised draft resolution (A/C.6/L.265/Rev.1) submitted by Afghanistan, Bolivia, Chile, Cuba, Dominican Republic, El Salvador, Iran, Netherlands, Peru and Yugoslavia

[*Original text: French*]
[*9 December 1952*]

Paragraph 1 of the operative part:

1. Replace the word "fifteen" by the word "eighteen".

2. After the words "the following Member States:" insert the following: "Argentina, Bolivia, Colombia,

Czechoslovakia, Egypt, France, India, Indonesia, Iran, Mexico, Netherlands, Norway, Pakistan, Poland, Syria, Union of Soviet Socialist Republics, United Kingdom of Great Britain and Northern Ireland and United States of America".

DOCUMENT A/2322 (incorporating A/2322/Corr.1)

Report of the Sixth Committee

[*Original text: English*]
[*17 December 1952*]

1. The General Assembly, by resolution 599 (VI) of 31 January 1952, *inter alia,* instructed the Secretary-General to submit to it, at its seventh session, a report in which the question of defining aggression would be thoroughly discussed in the light of the views expressed in the Sixth Committee at the sixth session of the General Assembly and which would duly take into account the draft resolutions and amendments submitted concerning that question.

2. In compliance with the resolution the Secretary-General submitted a report (A/2211) to the General Assembly. The first part of that report contained a history of the question of defining aggression; the second part consisted of a study of the general question of defining aggression and described the various schools of thought and the arguments used.

3. At its 380th plenary meeting on 16 October 1952, the General Assembly decided to include in the agenda of its seventh session the item "Question of defining aggression: report of the Secretary-General". At its 382nd meeting, on 17 October, the General Assembly decided to allocate the item to the Sixth Committee for consideration.

4. The Sixth Committee considered the item at its 329th to 345th meetings inclusive, from 19 November to 9 December 1952.

5. The following draft resolutions and amendments were submitted:

(*a*) A draft resolution (A/C.6/L.264) by the Union of Soviet Socialist Republics;

(*b*) A joint draft resolution (A/C.6/L.265) by Afghanistan, Bolivia, Chile, China, Dominican Republic, El Salvador, Iran, Netherlands, Peru and Yugoslavia, which was superseded by a revised draft resolution (A/C.6/L.265/Rev.1) submitted by the same delegations;

(*c*) Amendments to the joint draft resolution by Turkey (A/C.6/L.267), by France (A/C.6/L.268 and Corr.1), by Colombia, Egypt, Mexico and Syria (A/C.6/L.269/Rev.1 and Rev.1/Corr.1), by Indonesia

(A/C.6/L.270), by Poland (A/C.6/L.272) and by Czechoslovakia (A/C.6/L.275/Rev.1);

(*d*) Sub-amendments by Poland (A/C.6/L.273) and Yugoslavia (A/C.6/L.274) to the revised joint amendments by Colombia, Egypt, Mexico and Syria.

In addition, a draft motion (A/C.6/L.266/Rev.1) was circulated by the United States of America.

6. The draft resolution (A/C.6/L.264) of the Union of Soviet Socialist Republics provided, in operative paragraph 1, that the General Assembly should declare that in an international conflict that State should be declared the attacker which first committed one of a list of enumerated acts. Operative paragraph 2 listed arguments and circumstances which could not be used as justifications for attack. Operative paragraph 3 described the rights of a State which was threatened by the mobilization or concentration by another State of considerable armed forces near its frontier.

7. The revised joint draft resolution (A/C.6/L.265/Rev.1) submitted by Afghanistan, Bolivia, Chile, Cuba, Dominican Republic, El Salvador, Iran, Netherlands, Peru and Yugoslavia stated in its preamble that the discussions of the General Assembly and the International Law Commission had revealed, *inter alia,* the need for a detailed study of various problems concerning the question of defining aggression, including the connexion between a definition of aggression and, on the one hand, the maintenance of international peace and security, and, on the other, the development of international criminal law. The operative part provided for the establishment of a special committee of fifteen members to meet at Headquarters in 1953, to submit to the General Assembly at its ninth session draft definitions of aggression or draft statements of the notion of aggression, and to study all the problems referred to in the preamble on the assumption of a definition's being adopted by a resolution of the General Assembly.

8. The amendment (A/C.6/L.267) of Turkey to the revised joint draft resolution proposed altering operative paragraph 1 so that the members of the special

committee would be designated by the President of the General Assembly, in consultation with the Chairman of the Sixth Committee.

9. The amendment (A/C.6/L.268 and Corr.1) of France to the revised joint draft resolution proposed (1) to delete in sub-paragraph (*b*) of the second paragraph of the preamble the words "on the one hand" and the words "and on the other, the development of international criminal law"; (2) to insert a new sub-paragraph (*c*) in the preamble referring to the problems raised by the inclusion of a definition of aggression in the code of offences against the peace and security of mankind and by its application within the framework of international criminal jurisdiction; and (3) to replace operative paragraph 2 by a request to the special committee to study and report on all the problems raised by the adoption of a definition of aggression under a resolution of the General Assembly.

10. The revised joint amendments (A/C.6/L.269/ Rev.1 and Rev.1/Corr.1) of Colombia, Egypt, Mexico and Syria to the joint draft resolution proposed, *inter alia,* (1) to delete the part of the preamble relating to the problems to be studied; and (2) to amend operative paragraph 2 to instruct the special committee to submit to the General Assembly at its eighth session a number of draft definitions of aggression, one of which should include a synthetic definition, a statement of cases of aggression and an enumeration of the circumstances which might not be invoked as justification for aggression; and to instruct the special committee to study two specified questions in the light of the definitions it had drafted.

Drafting amendments were proposed orally by the representatives of Syria and Mexico to the joint amendments and those oral amendments were accepted by the co-sponsors.

11. The amendment (A/C.6/L.270) of Indonesia to the revised joint draft resolution proposed to add to the preamble a paragraph stating that continued and joint efforts should be made to formulate a generally acceptable definition of aggression with a view to promoting international peace and security and to developing international law.

12. The amendments (A/C.6/L.272) of Poland to the revised joint draft resolution proposed, *inter alia,* to amend the operative part so that the special committee would be requested to submit a single draft definition to the General Assembly at its eighth session.

13. The amendments (A/C.6/L.275/Rev.1) of Czechoslovakia to the revised joint draft resolution proposed to increase the membership of the special committee to eighteen and to list the States which should be members.

14. The sub-amendments (A/C.6/L.273) of Poland to the revised joint amendments (A/C.6/L.269/Rev.1 and Rev.1/Corr.1) proposed instructing the special committee to submit to the General Assembly at its eighth session a draft definition of aggression which should include an enumeration of cases of aggression and an enumeration of the circumstances which might not be invoked as justification for "an attack (aggression) of one State against another".

15. The sub-amendment (A/C.6/L.274) of Yugoslavia to the revised joint amendments (A/C.6/L.269/ Rev.1 and Rev.1/Corr.1) proposed to request "a non-exhaustive enumeration of cases of aggression" instead of a statement of cases of aggression.

16. At the 336th meeting, the representative of the United States of America stated that he intended to submit at the end of the general debate a motion (A/C.6/L.266/Rev.1) to adjourn the debate on the item under discussion. Later, however, at the 342nd meeting, the Chairman stated his understanding that the United States delegation had decided not to submit the motion.

17. The main discussion took place between the delegations which expressed themselves in favour of defining aggression (paragraphs 18 to 22) and those which thought that it was better, at least at the present time, not to do so (paragraphs 23 to 26). Some delegations favoured a definition provided that certain conditions were fulfilled (paragraphs 27 to 30) while others stressed the difficulties to be solved before adopting a definition (paragraphs 31 to 33). The form a definition should take was discussed (paragraphs 34 and 35) and also the procedure to be followed for its adoption (paragraphs 36 to 38). Various delegations supported the idea of creating a special committee to study the question further and to present one or more draft definitions to the General Assembly (paragraphs 39 to 41).

18. A number of delegations thought it of great importance and value to have a definition of aggression. In their opinion such a definition was possible and desirable, as the General Assembly had recognized in resolution 599 (VI). A definition was already included in some treaties, as for instance in eleven treaties concluded between the Union of Soviet Socialist Republics and various other States.

19. The adoption of a definition would constitute a declaration to the world of what was meant by aggression, and the very existence of such a definition would be useful. It was essential that crimes condemned by the law should be defined. A definition would further help all governments, in particular those which might be called upon to decide whether they were justified in exercising the right of individual or collective self-defence. It would also be of considerable assistance to the organs of the United Nations responsible for the maintenance of peace and the application of collective security. In their view, it was necessary to formulate directives for such international organs as might be called upon to determine which party was guilty of aggression.

20. Although an analytical definition, it was remarked, could not list all cases of direct or indirect aggression, it was better to have a definition than to have none, as it would certainly be a factor in discouraging potential aggressors.

21. A definition, some delegations added, was particularly needed in the present tense situation of the world. It would serve as a guide to public opinion and would also constitute a step forward in the development of international law. The fact that a definition had not yet been agreed upon was not a reason sufficient in itself to discourage further efforts.

22. Some delegations, on the other hand, favoured the adoption of a common concept of aggression.

23. Other delegations emphasized that, in view of the present political situation of the world, it would be

wiser not to attempt to formulate any definition of aggression at that time. There was not enough experience in applying rules concerning aggression to proceed with a codification of the law on the subject. A definition could be interpreted differently by Member States and therefore would not be effective, while at the same time it could be used in such a way as to defeat its purpose.

24. In any analytical definition, those delegations stated, there was always a danger of omitting some type of action which ought to be considered as aggression and, if a definition did not cover all possible acts of aggression, it would in fact constitute a declaration of impunity for the acts not included. A synthetic definition, on the other hand, could only be vague and imprecise or would merely reproduce what was already contained in the Charter.

25. In any case it was very doubtful that a definition, if adopted, would prevent aggression. An aggressor could only be determined by the general impression created by its behaviour and policies. Some thought that the "animus aggressionis" was a subjective element, and therefore the determination that an act of aggression had been committed would have to be made primarily by the State victim of the aggression. That element, it was added, would not be taken into consideration if a definition was to be applied automatically.

26. It was also contended that the concept of aggression changed with time; therefore, no rigid definition could serve a useful purpose and it would not facilitate the task of the organs which had the responsibility under the Charter for determining the existence of acts of aggression and for taking measures against them. On the contrary, a definition of aggression would delay the action of such organs. Furthermore, the Charter provided adequate procedures for the determination of the aggressor by the Security Council and by the General Assembly. The adoption of a pre-established definition could not limit the action of such organs.

27. Other delegations, while in principle favouring the adoption of a definition, stressed the necessity of ensuring that a victim should never be prevented from exercising the right of self-defence in cases of direct aggression, or "reprisal" in cases of indirect aggression.

28. Some delegations declared that they would favour the adoption of a definition only if it included cases of indirect aggression, and they mentioned the possibility of economic, cultural or ideological aggression.

29. During the debate it was pointed out that a definition should be linked with the development of international criminal law, in particular with the draft code of offences against the peace and security of mankind and the creation of an international criminal jurisdiction.

30. The political aspects of the question were underlined by many delegations which therefore insisted that flexibility was necessary in any definition.

31. Some delegations stressed the difficulties which had to be solved before a definition of aggression could be adopted. It would first be necessary, in their opinion, to ascertain whether a definition could be included within the framework of the Organization and to determine the effect which a definition of aggression might have on the application of Articles 39 and 51 of the Charter.

32. The new notion of indirect aggression, according to certain delegations, also raised a difficult problem as, although it could readily be contrasted with armed aggression, there was no common agreement on what it meant. Economic aggression was a vague idea which was difficult to apply owing to the fact that there was no economic equality between States.

33. The relationship between aggression and intervention in the domestic affairs of other States was emphasized by some, while others stressed the relationship between aggression, self-defence and collective action by the United Nations.

34. As to the kind of definition to be adopted, an *a priori* definition would, in the opinion of some delegations, be less precise and valuable than a definition based on experience. An analytical definition containing a list of cases could easily be amended in keeping with the development of international law. It was sufficient to indicate the most widespread, typical and important cases of aggression.

35. A number of delegations declared themselves in favour of a combined method which would consist of a general formula followed by a list of the principal acts of aggression. It was suggested that such a list should not be restrictive, and that it should be stated that the Security Council and the General Assembly could determine the existence of aggression in cases other than those listed.

36. Various views were expressed during the debate concerning the procedure to be followed in adopting a definition. Some delegations believed that neither the Assembly nor the Security Council had the power to adopt a definition of aggression binding either upon itself or upon the other, or upon Member States; such a binding effect could be obtained only by resorting to the procedure for the amendment of the Charter. In the opinion of others, however, an amendment to the Charter would be necessary only if a new principle were introduced or if a change were made in the powers of the organs of the United Nations, which was not the case.

37. It was also contended that if a definition was to be adopted in a resolution of the General Assembly it would require a two-thirds majority vote.

38. The opinion was expressed that a definition, in order to be authoritative, should be approved by all Member States, while others insisted that in any case the permanent members of the Security Council should approve it.

39. A number of delegations concluded that it was necessary to proceed with further studies on the question and not to show undue haste.

40. Some delegations insisted, however, that it would be appropriate for the General Assembly, in view of the terms of resolution 599 (VI), to consider a concrete definition at the earliest possible date.

41. During the debate, it was suggested that a special committee should be created to study further the problems which had been raised and to present draft definitions to the General Assembly at a future session. It was stressed that that approach to the question of defining aggression constituted a compromise

solution between the conflicting points of view which had been presented by some delegations during the discussions. Various delegations expressed different opinions regarding the procedure to be followed for the designation of the members of a special committee, and regarding its terms of reference.

42. At the Committee's 345th meeting, the representative of the Union of Soviet Socialist Republics stated that his delegation considered that it was necessary and possible at that stage to adopt a definition of aggression based on the generally accepted principles of international law. Nevertheless, the USSR delegation was prepared to support the proposal to establish a special committee in order to meet the wishes of those delegations which, while agreeing that it was desirable to define aggression, thought it advisable that a special committee should be established to work on that matter. For that reason, the USSR delegation did not wish to press for a vote on its draft resolution (A/C.6/L.264), bearing also in mind that the special committee would consider the definition of aggression contained in its draft resolution. The Chairman declared that, in his opinion, that was tantamount to a withdrawal of the draft resolution, in conformity with the established procedure, and that he would treat it as such.

43. The Committee decided then to vote first on the amendments to the preamble of the revised joint draft resolution (A/C.6/L.265/Rev.1) submitted by Afghanistan, Bolivia, Chile, Cuba, Dominican Republic, El Salvador, Iran, Netherlands, Peru and Yugoslavia. The results were as follows:

44. The first amendment (A/C.6/L.269/Rev.1 and Rev.1/Corr.1) of Colombia, Egypt, Mexico and Syria to delete the second paragraph of the preamble was rejected by 30 votes to 16, with 8 abstentions.

45. The first French amendment (A/C.6/L.268 and Corr.1), to delete in sub-paragraph (b) of the second paragraph of the preamble the words "on the one hand" and the words "and, on the other, the development of international criminal law", was adopted by 20 votes to 15, with 19 abstentions.

46. The second French amendment (A/C.6/L.268 and Corr.1), to insert a new sub-paragraph (c) in the preamble, was adopted by 23 votes to 16, with 15 abstentions.

47. The Indonesian amendment (A/C.6/L.270) was then put to the vote. The word "generally", which was separately voted upon, was adopted by 24 votes to 16, with 14 abstentions.

48. The Indonesian amendment (A/C.6/L.270) as a whole, proposing the addition of a third paragraph to the preamble, was adopted by 22 votes to 15, with 18 abstentions.

49. The Committee then voted on the amendments to operative paragraph 1 of the revised joint draft resolution (A/C.6/L.265/Rev.1).

50. The first Czechoslovak amendment (A/C.6/L.275/Rev.1), to replace the word "fifteen" by the word "eighteen", which was voted upon separately, was rejected by 29 votes to 19, with 7 abstentions. As a result of that vote, no further vote was taken on the revised Czechoslovak amendments.

51. A separate vote was taken on the following words in the Turkish amendment (A/C.6/L.267):

"by the President of the General Assembly in consultation with". These words were rejected by a roll-call vote of 21 to 19, with 16 abstentions. The voting was as follows:

In favour: Australia, Belgium, Canada, Denmark, El Salvador, France, Greece, Luxembourg, Netherlands, New Zealand, Norway, Philippines, Sweden, Turkey, Union of South Africa, United Kingdom of Great Britain and Northern Ireland, United States of America, Uruguay, Venezuela.

Against: Bolivia, Brazil, Byelorussian Soviet Socialist Republic, Chile, Cuba, Czechoslovakia, Ecuador, Egypt, Haiti, Honduras, Indonesia, Mexico, Panama, Peru, Poland, Saudi Arabia, Syria, Thailand, Ukrainian Soviet Socialist Republic, Union of Soviet Socialist Republics, Yemen.

Abstaining: Afghanistan, Argentina, Burma, China, Colombia, Dominican Republic, Guatemala, India, Iran, Iraq, Israel, Lebanon, Liberia, Nicaragua, Pakistan, Yugoslavia.

As a result of that vote, no further vote was taken on the Turkish amendment.

52. The Committee then voted on the amendment to the operative paragraph 2 of the revised joint draft resolution (A/C.6/L.265/Rev.1).

53. The third French amendment (A/C.6/L.268 and Corr.1), to replace the second paragraph by the following: "*Requests* the said special committee to study and report on all the problems raised by the adoption of a definition of aggression under a resolution of the General Assembly", was rejected by a roll-call vote of 24 to 23, with 9 abstentions. The voting was as follows:

In favour: Argentina, Australia, Belgium, Brazil, Canada, Denmark, France, Greece, Honduras, Liberia, Luxembourg, New Zealand, Nicaragua, Norway, Panama, Philippines, Sweden, Thailand, Turkey, Union of South Africa, United Kingdom of Great Britain and Northern Ireland. United States of America, Venezuela.

Against: Bolivia, Byelorussian Soviet Socialist Republic, Chile, Cuba, Czechoslovakia, Dominican Republic, Ecuador, Egypt, El Salvador, Guatemala, Haiti, Indonesia, Iran, Lebanon, Mexico, Peru, Poland, Saudi Arabia, Syria, Ukrainian Soviet Socialist Republic, Union of Soviet Socialist Republics, Uruguay, Yemen, Yugoslavia.

Abstaining: Afghanistan, Burma, China, Colombia, India, Iraq, Israel, Netherlands, Pakistan.

54. The Committee voted next on the sub-amendments to the revised amendments (A/C.6/L.269/Rev.1 and Rev.1/Corr.1) of Colombia, Egypt, Mexico and Syria to the revised joint draft resolution (A/C.6/L.265/Rev.1).

55. The Polish sub-amendment (A/C.6/L.273) to point II (a), to replace the words "a number of draft definitions" by "a draft definition", was rejected by 35 votes to 5, with 11 abstentions.

The Polish sub-amendment (A/C.6/L.273) proposing the deletion of point II (a) (i) was rejected by 35 votes to 6, with 13 abstentions.

56. The Yugoslav sub-amendment (A/C.6/L.274) to replace point II (a) (ii) by the words "a non-exhaustive enumeration of cases of aggression" was adopted by 33 votes to 11, with 9 abstentions.

Consequently the Polish sub-amendment (A/C.6/L.273) to that point was not voted upon.

57. The Polish sub-amendment (A/C.6/L.273) to .eplace in point II (a) (iii) the word "aggression" by the words "an attack' (aggression) of one State against another" was rejected by 32 votes to 6, with 15 abstentions.

58. The Committee next voted on the revised amendments (A/C.6/L.269/Rev.1 and Rev.1/Corr.1) submitted by Colombia, Egypt, Mexico and Syria to operative paragraph 2 of the revised joint draft resolution (A/C.6/L.265/Rev.1).

The word "eighth", contained in point II (a) of the joint amendments, was voted upon separately and was rejected by 30 votes to 16, with 5 abstentions.

Point II (a) of the revised joint amendments was adopted, as far as the words ". . . its constituent elements", by 26 votes to 21, with 7 abstentions.

Point II (a) (i) was rejected by 25 votes to 20, with 8 abstentions.

Point II (a) (iii), as amended orally by the sponsors, was rejected by 30 votes to 15, with 10 abstentions.

Point II (a), as amended by the adoption of the Yugoslav sub-amendment (A/C.6/L.274), was rejected by 26 votes to 23, with 5 abstentions.

59. A proposal to take a new vote by roll-call on point II (a) of the revised joint amendments (A/C.6/L.269/Rev.1 and Rev.1/Corr.1) was rejected by 26 votes to 22, with 6 abstentions.

60. The Committee then decided by 30 votes to 10, with 10 abstentions, not to take any further votes on the revised joint amendments and passed to the Polish amendments (A/C.6/L.272) to operative paragraph 2 (a) of the revised joint draft resolution (A/C.6/L.265/Rev.1).

61. The Polish amendment (A/C.6/L.272) proposing in paragraph 2 (a):

(1) To replace the word "ninth" by the. word "eighth" was rejected by 31 votes to 13, with .7 abstentions.

(2) To replace the words "draft definitions" by the words "draft definition" was rejected by 32 votes to 7, with 12 abstentions.

(3) To delete the words "or draft statements of the notion of aggression" was rejected by 23 votes to 13, with 14 abstentions.

62. The Committee then voted on the revised joint draft resolution (A/C.6/L.265/Rev.1), as amended.

The second paragraph of the preamble, as amended, was adopted by a roll-call vote of 35 to 8, with 12 abstentions. The voting was as follows:

In favour: Afghanistan, Bolivia, Brazil, Burma, Canada, Chile, China, Colombia, Cuba, Denmark, Dominican Republic, Ecuador, El Salvador, France, Greece, Haiti, Indonesia, Iran, Israel, Lebanon, Liberia, Mexico, Netherlands, Nicaragua, Norway, Panama, Peru, Philippines, Sweden, Thailand, Turkey, United States of America, Uruguay, Yemen, Yugoslavia.

Against: Belgium, Byelorussian Soviet Socialist Republic, Czechoslovakia, Luxembourg, Poland, Ukrainian Soviet Socialist Republic, Union of South Africa, Union of Soviet Socialist Republics.

Abstaining: Argentina, Australia, Egypt, Guatemala, Honduras, India, Iraq, New Zealand, Saudi Arabia, Syria, United Kingdom of Great Britain and Northern Ireland, Venezuela.

The phrase "on the assumption of a definition being adopted by a resolution of the General Assembly" at the end of paragraph 2 (b) of the operative part, was voted upon separately and was adopted by a roll-call vote of 20 to 15, with 19 abstentions. The voting was as follows:

In favour: Afghanistan, Bolivia, Burma, Chile, China, Cuba, Dominican Republic, Ecuador, Egypt, El Salvador, Guatemala, Indonesia, Iran, Iraq, Mexico, Netherlands, Peru, Syria, Yemen, Yugoslavia.

Against: Australia, Belgium, Brazil, Denmark, Israel, Liberia, Luxembourg, New Zealand, Norway, Panama, Philippines, Sweden, Thailand, Turkey, United Kingdom of Great Britain and Northern Ireland.

Abstaining: Argentina, Byelorussian Soviet Socialist Republic, Canada, Colombia, Czechoslovakia, France, Greece, Haiti, Honduras, India, Nicaragua, Poland, Saudi Arabia, Ukrainian Soviet Socialist Republic, Union of South Africa, Union of Soviet Socialist Republics, United States of America, Uruguay, Venezuela.

Paragraph 2 (b) of the operative part as a whole was adopted by a roll-call vote of 26 to 6, with 22 abstentions. The voting was as follows:

In favour: Afghanistan, Bolivia, Burma, Chile, China, Colombia, Cuba, Dominican Republic, Ecuador, Egypt, El Salvador, Greece, Guatemala, Indonesia, Iran, Iraq, Mexico, Netherlands, Nicaragua, Peru, Philippines, Saudi Arabia, Syria, Uruguay, Yemen, Yugoslavia.

Against: Belgium, Byelorussian Soviet Socialist Republic, Poland, Ukrainian Soviet Socialist Republic, Union of Soviet Socialist Republics, United States of America.

Abstaining: Argentina, Australia, Brazil, Canada, Czechoslovakia, Denmark, France, Haiti, Honduras, India, Israel, Liberia, Luxembourg, New Zealand, Norway, Panama, Sweden, Thailand, Turkey, Union of South Africa, United Kingdom of Great Britain and Northern Ireland, Venezuela.

Paragraph 3 of the operative part was adopted by 40 votes to none, with 13 abstentions.

63. The revised joint draft resolution (A/C.6/L.265/Rev.1) as a whole, as amended, was adopted by a roll-call vote of 36 to 9, with 9 abstentions. The voting was as follows:

In favour: Afghanistan, Bolivia, Burma, Byelorussian Soviet Socialist Republic, Chile, China, Cuba, Czechoslovakia, Dominican Republic, Ecuador, Egypt, El Salvador, Greece, Guatemala, Haiti, Indonesia, Iran, Iraq, Israel, Liberia, Mexico, Netherlands, Nicaragua, Norway, Panama, Peru, Philippines, Poland, Saudi Arabia, Syria, Ukrainian Soviet Socialist Republic, Union of South Africa, Union of Soviet Socialist Republics, Uruguay, Yemen, Yugoslavia.

Against: Australia, Belgium, Brazil, Luxembourg, New Zealand, Sweden, Thailand, United Kingdom of Great Britain 'and Northern Ireland, United States of America.

Abstaining: Argentina, Canada, Colombia, Denmark, France, Honduras, India, Turkey, Venezuela.

64. At the 347th meeting, the Chairman announced the proposed composition of the special committee.

65. The Sixth Committee therefore recommends to the General Assembly the adoption of the following resolution:

Question of defining aggression

The General Assembly,

Having regard to its resolution 599 (VI) of 31 January 1952,

Considering that the discussion of the question of defining aggression at the sixth and seventh sessions of the General Assembly and in the International Law Commission (A/1858, para. 35 and *ff.*) has revealed the complexity of this question and the need for a detailed study of:

(*a*) The various forms of aggression,

(*b*) The connexion between a definition of aggression and the maintenance of international peace and security,

(*c*) The problems raised by the inclusion of a definition of aggression in the code of offences against the peace and security of mankind and by its application within the framework of international criminal jurisdiction,

(*d*) The effect of a definition of aggression on the exercise of the jurisdiction of the various organs of the United Nations,

(*e*) Any other problem which might be raised by a definition of aggression,

Considering that continued and joint efforts shall be made to formulate a generally acceptable definition of aggression, with a view to promoting international peace and security and to developing international law,

1. *Decides* to establish a Special Committee of fifteen members, each representing one of the following Member States: Bolivia, Brazil, China, Dominican Republic, France, India,[1] Iran, Mexico, Netherlands, Norway, Poland, Syria, Union of Soviet Socialist Republics, United Kingdom of Great Britain and Northern Ireland, United States of America, to meet at the Headquarters of the United Nations in 1953;

2. *Requests* the said Special Committee:

(*a*) To submit to the General Assembly at its ninth session draft definitions of aggression or draft statements of the notion of aggression:

(*b*) To study all the problems referred to above on the assumption of a definition being adopted by a resolution of the General Assembly;

3. *Requests* the Secretary-General to communicate the Special Committee's report to Member States for their comments and to place the question on the provisional agenda of the ninth session of the General Assembly.

---

[1] At the Committee's 357th meeting, the Chairman announced that Pakistan would replace India in the Special Committee.

DOCUMENT A/L.136

Poland: amendment to the draft resolution proposed by the Sixth Committee (A/2322)

[Original text: English]
[19 December 1952]

Operative paragraphs 2 (a) and 3:
Replace the words "ninth session" by the words "eighth session".

ACTION TAKEN BY THE GENERAL ASSEMBLY

At its 408th plenary meeting, on 20 December 1952, the General Assembly adopted the draft resolution submitted by the Sixth Committee (p.   of this fascicule). For the final text, see resolution 688 (VII)

REPORT OF THE SPECIAL COMMITTEE ON THE QUESTION OF DEFINING AGGRESSION[1]

Introduction

I. BACKGROUND OF THE QUESTION OF DEFINING AGGRESSION

1. Under resolution 378 B (V) of 17 November 1950 the General Assembly decided to refer a proposal of the Union of Soviet Socialist Republics concerning the definition of the notion of aggression (A/C.1/608) and all the records of the First Committee dealing with that question to the International Law Commission, so that the latter might take them into consideration and formulate its conclusions as soon as possible.

2. The International Law Commission studied the question at its third session and dealt with it in Chapter III of its report on the work of that session.[2]

3. At its 341st plenary meeting on 13 November 1951, the General Assembly decided to include the report of the International Law Commission in the agenda of its sixth session. At its 342nd plenary meeting on the same date, the General Assembly referred the item to the Sixth Committee for study and report.

4. The Sixth Committee examined the question of defining aggression at its 278th to 295th meetings held from 5 January to 22 January 1952.

5. At its 368th plenary meeting on 31 January 1952 the General Assembly adopted resolution 599 (VI) the text of which is as follows:

"*The General Assembly,*

"*Considering* that, under resolution 378 B (V) of 17 November 1950, it referred the question of defining aggression, raised in the draft resolution of the Union of Soviet Socialist Republics to the International Law Commission for examination in conjunction with matters which were under consideration by that Commission,

"*Considering* that the International Law Commission did not in its report furnish an express definition of aggression but merely included aggression among the offences defined in its draft Code of Offences against the Peace and Security of Mankind,

"*Considering* that the General Assembly, on 13 November 1951, decided not to examine the draft Code at its sixth session but to include it in the provisional agenda of its seventh session,

"*Considering* that, although the existence of the crime of aggression may be inferred from the circumstances peculiar to each particular case, it is nevertheless possible and desirable, with a view to ensuring international peace and security and to de-

veloping international criminal law, to define aggression by reference to the elements which constitute it,

"*Considering further* that it would be of definite advantage if directives were formulated for the future guidance of such international bodies as may be called upon to determine the aggressor,

"1. *Decides* to include in the agenda of its seventh session the question of defining aggression;

"2. *Instructs* the Secretary-General to submit to the General Assembly at its seventh session a report in which the question of defining aggression shall be thoroughly discussed in the light of the views expressed in the Sixth Committee at the sixth session of the General Assembly and which shall duly take into account the draft resolutions and amendments submitted concerning this question;

"3. *Requests* States Members, when transmitting their observations on the draft Code to the Secretary-General, to give in particular their views on the problem of defining aggression."

6. In conformity with that resolution the Secretary-General submitted a report (A/2211) to the General Assembly which decided, at its 380th plenary meeting on 16 October 1952, to include in the agenda of its seventh session the following item: "Question of defining aggression: report by the Secretary-General". The question was referred to the Sixth Committee which dealt with it at its 329th to 347th meetings held between 19 November and 11 December 1952.

7. At its 408th plenary meeting on 20 December 1952 the General Assembly adopted resolution 688 (VII) which reads as follows:

"*The General Assembly,*

"*Having regard to* its resolution 599 (VI) of 31 January 1952,

"*Considering* that the discussion of the question defining aggression at the sixth and seventh sessions of the General Assembly and in the International Law Commission has revealed the complexity of this question and the need for a detailed study of:

"(*a*) The various forms of aggression,

"(*b*) The connexion between a definition of aggression and the maintenance of international peace and security,

"(*c*) The problems raised by the inclusion of a definition of aggression in the Code of Offences against the Peace and Security of Mankind and by its application within the framework of international criminal jurisdiction,

"(*d*) The effect of a definition of aggression on the exercise of the jurisdiction of the various organs of the United Nations,

---

[1] Previously distributed as document A/AC.66/L.11.
[2] *Official Records of the General Assembly, Sixth Session, Supplement No. 9*, document A/1858.

2

"(e) Any other problem which might be raised by a definition of aggression,

"*Considering* that continued and joint efforts shall be made to formulate a generally acceptable definition of aggression, with a view to promoting international peace and security and to developing international law,

"1. *Decides* to establish a Special Committee of fifteen members, each representing one of the following Member States: Bolivia, Brazil, China, Dominican Republic, France, Iran, Mexico, Netherlands, Norway, Pakistan, Poland, Syria, Union of Soviet Socialist Republics, United Kingdom of Great Britain and Northern Ireland, United States of America, to meet at the Headquarters of the United Nations in 1953;

"2. *Requests* the said Special Committee

"(a) To submit to the General Assembly at its ninth session draft definitions of aggression or draft statements of the notion of aggression;

"(b) To study all the problems referred to above on the assumption of a definition being adopted by a resolution of the General Assembly;

"3. *Requests* the Secretary-General to communicate the Special Committee's report to Member States for their comments and to place the question on the provisional agenda of the ninth session of the General Assembly."

8. In conformity with this resolution the Special Committee on the question of defining aggression met at United Nations Headquarters, New York, from 24 August to 21 September 1953.

9. All the States designated under the above-mentioned resolution were represented in the Committee. The following is a list of the representatives and alternate representatives of those States:

Bolivia: Mr. Gaston Araoz;

Brazil: Mr. Gilberto Amado;

China: Mr. Shushi Hsu;

Dominican Republic: Mr. Tulio Franco y Franco, Mr. Enrique de Marchena;

France: Mr. Charles Chaumont;

Iran: Mr Fereydoun Adamiyat;

Mexico: Mr. Jorge Castañeda;

Netherlands: Mr. B. V. A. Röling;

Norway: Mr. Hans Engen, Mr. Erik Dons, Mr. Rasmus S. Gundersen;

Pakistan: Mr. A. H. B. Tyabji;

Poland: Mr. Josef Winiewicz;

Syria: Mr. Salaheddine Tarazi;

Union of Soviet Socialist Republics: Mr. P. D. Morozov;

United Kingdom of Great Britain and Northern Ireland: Mr. Francis A. Vallat;

United States of America: Mr. John Maktos.

10. At the Committee's first meeting, Mr. Morozov (Union of Soviet Socialist Republics) moved that a representative of the Central People's Government of the People's Republic of China should be invited to participate in the Committee's work. The Acting Chairman ruled that the Committee was not competent to

deal with the question of the representation of China. The Acting Chairman's ruling was challenged by the representative of Poland. The Committee upheld that ruling by 7 votes to 2, with 3 abstentions.

11. The Committee elected the following officers: *Chairman*: Mr. de Marchena (Dominican Republic); *Vice-Chairman*: Mr. B. V. A. Röling (Netherlands); *Rapporteur*: Mr. S. Tarazi (Syria).

II. ORGANIZATION OF THE WORK OF THE COMMITTEE

12. Opinion was divided at the outset as to whether the Committee should proceed by following the order in which sub-paragraphs (a) and (b) of paragraph 2 of the operative part of General Assembly resolution 688 (VII) were set out.

13. Some representatives argued that since the two sub-paragraphs were in logical order the Committee should immediately take up consideration of the specific draft definitions of aggression or of the draft statements of the notion of aggression. During that study the various problems referred to in the preamble to the above-mentioned resolution could be taken up and examined. Any problem not dealt with in the course of that study could be taken up at the end of the Committee's work. It would be better to proceed in that manner than to examine those various problems in the abstract.

14. Other representatives held that the Committee should rather begin by examining the various problems referred to in the preamble to General Assembly resolution 688 (VII) and then proceed to select the draft definitions of aggression or the draft statements of the notion of aggression. Mr. Röling (Netherlands) considered that paragraphs 2 (a) and 2 (b) of the operative part of the resolution in question were not in logical order. He thought that their order should have been reversed, since a study of each of the problems referred to in the five sub-paragraphs of the preamble should precede the elaboration of any definition or statement of the notion of aggression. Mr. Maktos (United States) pointed out that after a detailed study of those problems, and especially those enumerated in sub-paragraphs (a) and (b) of the preamble, it would be easier to determine what type of definition should be formulated, if a definition was to be prepared.

15. The Committee finally decided to begin its work with a general discussion of the question of defining aggression.

16. Opinion was also divided on the scope of the Committee's terms of reference.

17. Some representatives submitted that General Assembly resolution 688 (VII) did not compel the Committee necessarily to adopt one or more specific draft definitions of aggression or one or more draft statements of the notion of aggression, but left it entirely free to choose between several courses. Mr. Vallat (United Kingdom) considered that the Committee could confine itself to studying the various problems raised by the question of defining aggression and submit the results of its deliberations to the General Assembly. Mr. Maktos (United States) thought that the Committee might adopt a definite text of a definition or it might not; it might submit several draft

definitions with comments; it might submit a collective estimate of the useful elements in the various draft resolutions, explaining why they had been considered useful and which ones had been accepted by some and rejected by others. Mr. Hsu (China) argued that the Committee should first consider whether in view of the changed world situation it was possible and desirable to define aggression; if that study led it to a negative conclusion, the Committee would be freed to decide not to submit any definition to the General Assembly.

18. Other representatives held that the question whether it was possible and desirable to define aggression had already been settled affirmatively by General Assembly resolutions 599 (VI) and 688 (VII); there was no need to reopen the question. Mr. Tarazi (Syria) even argued that the Committee could not deal with the matter without exceeding its terms of reference. In the view of those representatives, the essential task entrusted to the Committee under General Assembly resolution 688 (VII) was not merely to define aggression but also to study the various problems referred to in the preamble to that resolution in relation to specific draft definitions.

19. Three plans of work were submitted in turn to the Committee: one by the representative of the Netherlands (A/AC.66/L.3), and the other two by the representatives of France, Mexico and the Netherlands (A/AC.66/L.5 and A/AC.66/L.5/Rev.1).

20. The object of the first working plan (A/AC.66/L.3), according to its sponsor, was to enable the Committee to consider first the questions listed in paragraphs (a) to (c) of the preamble to General Assembly resolution 688 (VII) and then the draft definitions of aggression submitted to it. That plan was withdrawn and replaced by another submitted jointly by France, Mexico and the Netherlands (A/AC.66/L.5). That text was in turn changed (A/AC.66/L.5/Rev.1) at the suggestion of Mr. Morozov (Union of Soviet Socialist Republics) who felt that the questions listed in General Assembly resolution 688 (VII) could be examined at the same time as the specific proposals for the definition of aggression.

21. Section I (a) 1 of the joint draft working plan (A/AC.66/L.5/Rev.1) provided that the Committee would consider "aggression in the sense of the draft Code of Offences". Some representatives felt that the provision was unnecessary and overlapped with section I (c). It was put to a vote separately and failed to obtain the necessary majority, being rejected by 6 votes to 6.

22. On the proposal of Mr. Morozov (Union of Soviet Socialist Republics), section I (a) 2 of that plan was amended to make it more clear that the Committee's basic task was to consider the notion of armed aggression.

23. Lastly, the word "final" which appeared before the words "draft definitions" in section II were deleted on the suggestion of Mr. Vallat (United Kingdom) who thought that it might introduce a concept of finality with respect to the Committee's decisions as far as the General Assembly was concerned.

24. The draft working plan (A/AC.66/L.5/Rev.1), as amended, was adopted unanimously by the Committee. Its text (A/AC.66/L.6) is as follows:

"I. Discussion of the specific draft definitions of aggression and draft statements of the notion of aggression, submitted to the Committee, with reference to the following questions, in the order as indicated:

"(a) The various forms of aggression:

"1. Aggression in the sense of the Charter,

"2. The question of the activities to be dealt with in the definition: the notion of armed aggression; the question of indirect aggression; economic measures; ideological measures, etc.,

"3. The various types of definitions of aggression (general definition, enumerative definition, mixed definition);

"(b) The connexion between a definition of aggression and the maintenance of international peace and security;

"(c) The problems raised by the inclusion of a definition of aggression in the Code of Offences against the Peace and Security of Mankind and by its application within the framework of international criminal jurisdiction;

"(d) The effect of a definition of aggression on the exercise of the jurisdiction of the various organs of the United Nations;

"(e) Any other problem which might be raised by a definition of aggression.

"II. Adoption of draft definitions of aggression or draft statements of the notion of aggression."

III. Texts submitted to the Committee

25. The following texts were submitted in turn to the Committee:

(1) A draft defintion of aggression submitted by the Union of Soviet Socialist Republics (A/AC.66/L.2/Rev.1);

(2) Two working papers submitted by China (A/AC.66/L.4/Rev.3; A/AC.66/L.7/Rev.2);

(3) A working paper submitted by Mexico (A/AC.66/L.8);

(4) A working paper submitted by Bolivia (A/AC.66/L.9).

26. The Committee decided unanimously not to put the above-mentioned texts to a vote but to transmit them as they stood to Member States and to the General Assembly. The texts in question have therefore been annexed to this report.

27. The Committee also decided that the report should mention the principal ideas put forward during the discussions of the concrete drafts of definition of aggression submitted in the Committee, bearing in mind the problems listed in the working plan (A/AC.66/L.6). For a more detailed study of the observations of the members of the Committee, the summary records of the meetings (A/AC.66/SR.1 to A/AC.66/SR.22 inclusive) should be consulted.

4

Chapter I

The various types of definitions of aggression

I. GENERAL DEFINITION

28. Some representatives favoured a general definition, that is, a definition which instead of listing acts of aggression would contain general formulæ applicable to all the cases contemplated. Responsibility for determining the scope of a formula would rest with international organs when a specific case was brought before them. It was pointed out that such a definition, which should synthesize and clarify the notion of aggression as developed in the Charter, would contribute to the evolution of international law. It would also help to avoid the risk either of amending the Charter by an interpretation or of undue rigidity of the Charter terms, which was more serious than vagueness.

29. This type of definition, however, was criticized by other members of the Committee. Mr. Winiewicz (Poland) maintained that such a definition would serve no purpose as it would not refer to the elements constituting the crime. Its vagueness would open the way for dangerous polemics on the nature of a given act; the aggressor could challenge the description given of his act and take advantage of the necessarily lengthy discussions arising out of a definition which was lacking in clarity and precision to continue his aggressive activity. Moreover, that type of definition could not help effectively to combat the many types of aggression.

30. Mr. Morozov (Union of Soviet Socialist Republics) stated that a so-called general definition of aggression was inadequate, as could be seen from the specific proposals for such a definition. For example, aggression had been defined as an international crime, which, in effect, was rather like saying that aggression was aggression. Naturally, such an approach would not help that Committee to carry out the task before it.

II. ENUMERATIVE DEFINITION

31. This type of definition was the subject of various opinions. According to Mr. Winiewicz (Poland), an enumerative definition had the advantages of setting forth the elements which constituted the crime, indicating unequivocally the type of acts to be condemned, and placing the burden of proof upon the aggressor instead of requiring the victim to prove that the action complained of was aggression. In his opinion, the Soviet draft, from this point of view, was a perfect solution of the problem.

32. In the opinion of other representatives, such a definition would be dangerous. It would necessarily be incomplete and would thereby inevitably imply that acts not enumerated did not constitute aggression. That in turn would enable a State to commit aggression by circumventing the definition. The decisions of international organs would be rendered automatic and the re-establishment of peace would thus be made more difficult.

33. Mr. Hsu (China) expressed the opinion that an enumeration could not be regarded as a true definition. It would not be sufficiently scientific and could not serve as guidance either for the organs of the United Nations responsible for the maintenance of peace and security, nor for the courts which might be set up to judge the perpetrators of crimes against humanity. The generally accepted sense of the word "define" showed that enumeration could not achieve the purpose sought which was to make clear the essential nature of a concept. From a purely practical standpoint, an enumeration of crimes could only cause criminals to change their methods. Moreover, on the one hand, the competent political or legal organs would tend to study the methods of aggression rather than the act itself, and on the other, they would not have the proper perspective for judging each individual case, and that was absolutely necessary to prevent the act or to punish the author.

34. Mr. Vallat (United Kingdom) stated that the so-called analytical definitions were the most deceiving. They were not so much definitions as incomplete catalogues of acts constituting aggression. Thus paragraphs 2, 3 and 4 not to mention the all-embracing provision of paragraph 5 had had to be added to the original text of the USSR proposal (A/AC.66/L.2/Rev.1). He questioned the value of a definition which, after listing various acts constituting aggression, stated that any other act declared to be aggression by the Security Council would also come into that category. Either the matter should be left to the Council, in which case there was no need for a catalogue, or the catalogue was effective in itself, in which case a list such as that proposed by the USSR delegation (A/AC.66/L.2/Rev.1) went too far. If applied literally, it would result in acts being wrongly declared as constituting aggression, and governments might argue that any act not covered in the text did not constitute aggression notwithstanding any decision to the contrary by the Security Council.

35. Speaking on the draft resolution he had submitted to the Committee, Mr. Morozov (Union of Soviet Socialist Republics) considered invalid the argument to the effect that the USSR proposal merely listed some acts of aggression and consequently did not give a general definition of that concept. The USSR definition was both synthetic and analytical, as had been recognized by well-known experts on international law. The definition was based on the principle that the definition of the concept of armed attack was of primary importance in defining aggression. The proposal was to confirm the recognized principle of international law that the State which under any pretext or for any reason took the initiative in starting a war, that is to say, was the first in an international conflict to take any of the actions listed in paragraph 1 of the USSR draft definition would be declared to be the attacker. The statement that aggression could not be justified by political, strategic or economic considerations was an essential element in the definition of armed attack as in the definition of aggression as a whole. The ruses commonly used by aggressors to justify their acts must not be resorted to. Another important element in the definition was the statement that in the event of the mobilization or concentration by another State of considerable armed forces near its frontier, the State which was threatened by such action should have the right of recourse to diplomatic or other means of securing a peaceful settlement of international disputes. It could also in the meantime adopt requisite measures of a military nature similar to those described above without, however, crossing the frontier. The afore-

mentioned considerations as a whole gave a general indication of the concept of armed attack. At the same time, it was stated in advance which actions, if committed in the circumstances referred to in the definition, would be regarded as aggression. There was consequently no contradiction in the provision of paragraph 5 of the USSR proposal which stated that, in addition to those acts already declared to constitute aggression, the Security Council, as the only organ competent to determine the aggression, could in specific cases declare other acts to constitute aggression. The main purpose of the United Kingdom representative's objections to the USSR proposal for a definition of aggression was, in Mr. Morozov's opinion, to avoid a clear formulation of the concept of aggression, which could only be to the advantage of aggressors.

36. Certain members of the Committee explained, with reference to examples, that they considered the test, based on the chronological order of events, of first commission of an act was unworkable. In particular, it did not take adequate account of action by the Security Council or measures taken on the recommendation of the Security Council or the General Assembly.

III. Mixed definition

37. Some members of the Committee had been in favour of a mixed definition that would start with a text in very general terms describing the characteristics of aggressive activity. This general text would be followed by an enumeration of specific acts, but the enumeration would be neither limitative nor exhaustive. It would not be obligatory but would simply be a series of examples. The advantage of a mixed definition was that it combined the merits and the positive aspects of the general and enumerative definitions. A mixed definition should therefore start with a generic concept including elements specific in their significance and be followed by an enumeration of the types of acts of aggression. The texts submitted by the delegations of Bolivia and Mexico were based on that method of definition.

38. This type of definition had been criticized by other members of the Committee as embodying the defects of the two other types.

IV. List of factors for the competent organs of the United Nations

39. Mr. Maktos (United States) said that instead of trying to establish a general formula which would probably be incomplete, it would be better to offer the competent organs of the United Nations, and in the first place the Security Council, a list of factors to be taken into account in deciding a given case. Some other members of the Committee thought this idea constructive and worth examining.

40. Mr. Winiewicz (Poland) on the other hand contended that such a list of factors could only circumvent the important problem of clearly defining aggression and would serve no useful purpose.

Chapter II

The various forms of aggression

I. Aggression in the sense of the Charter

41. The majority of the Committee agreed that it was the duty of the Committee to define aggression in the sense of the Charter. However, the relevant Articles of the Charter were interpreted differently by them. Some members were of the opinion that the notion of aggression in the sense of the Charter could be limited solely to armed aggression, whereas the representatives of Bolivia, China, Iran, Mexico, Poland, Syria and the Union of Soviet Socialist Republics maintained that, in the sense of the Charter, the notion of aggression could include other forms of aggression not necessarily consisting in the actual use of armed force. Other members maintained theses that were not strictly identified with either of these views.

42. Some members argued that a comparison of Article I, paragraph 1, and Article 39 of the Charter indicated that aggression constituted a kind of breach of the peace. In referring specifically to aggression, the drafters of the Charter had had in mind the most serious instance of a breach of the peace, namely, the unlawful use of armed force. They had intentionally avoided using the term "war", because that term did not apply to all the cases they wished to take into account.

43. Mr. Chaumont (France), interpreting Article 39 of the Charter, noted that that article made use of three concepts: threats to peace, breaches of the peace and aggression, the last being in fact a case of breach of the peace. The threat to the peace or the breach of the peace did not necessarily imply any judgment, whereas the concept of aggression was of a punitive nature. Article 40 of the Charter, for example, in dealing with measures to be taken to prevent an aggravation of the situation, provided that "the measures . . . shall be without prejudice to the rights, claims or position of the parties"; obviously such terms could not apply to an acknowledged aggressor. The actions described as "economic aggression" or "ideological aggression", although they could form part of aggressive activity, really came under the concept of threat to the peace and not under that of aggression. In any case, it would be for the Security Council to decide what use it wished to make of the concept in Article 39.

44. Mr. Vallat (United Kingdom) pointed out that according to Article 2, paragraph 4, of the Charter, Member States had to "refrain . . . from the threat or use of force against the territorial integrity or political independence of any State, or in any other manner inconsistent with the purposes of the United Nations", but that there was no reference to economic, ideological or other measures. It was therefore justifiable to conclude that the use of force was one important element in the concept of aggression in the sense of the Charter. He said further that Article 51 of the Charter provided further evidence in that regard, for it sanctioned the inherent right of individual or collective self-defence if an armed attack occurred against a Member State.

Those considerations should suffice to exclude economic and ideological aggression from the definition of aggression in the sense of the Charter.

45. Mr. Röling (Netherlands) observed that, in the interest of peace, the Charter prohibited aggression and sanctioned the adoption of the necessary countermeasures, which might go so far as to include the use of armed force and were themselves liable to disturb the peace. Hence it was important, in defining aggression, to resist the temptation of including in the definition acts susceptible of increasing the possibilities of lawfully resorting to armed force.

46. In the light of these various arguments, the draft resolution submitted by the Union of Soviet Socialist Republics (A/AC.66/L.2/Rev.1) had been criticized by some members of the Committee because it involved a definition which, on the whole, did not relate to the notion of aggression in the sense of the Charter. It was said that although the acts of aggression listed in paragraph 1 of the draft were consistent with the notion of aggression in the sense of the Charter, the same could not be said of the acts of indirect, economic and ideological aggression enumerated in other paragraphs of the draft.

47. Some members of the Committee expressed different views. Mr. Winiewicz (Poland) affirmed that in studying aggression within the meaning of the Charter, the purposes of the United Nations must never be forgotten. The relevant provisions were Article 1, paragraph 2, Article 2, paragraphs 1, 4 and 7 and Article 55. Each of the Principles mentioned in those Articles was considered essential for the maintenance of peace. Any action conflicting with any of those Principles consequently represented a threat to international peace and security, an aggression in the broad sense of the word. While the Charter laid particular stress on armed aggression, it nevertheless recognized the existence of several other forms of aggression. The definition of aggression proposed by the USSR fully met those requirements of the Charter, at the same time stressing the importance of armed aggression.

48. Mr. Morozov (Union of Soviet Socialist Republics) maintained that the USSR proposal for a definition of aggression was in conformity with the Charter. Taken together, Articles 39 and 51 of the Charter made it clear that the concept of aggression as contained in Article 39 was a much wider concept than that of armed attack mentioned in Article 51. Yet the recognition of that fact could not mean that the grounds on which States could use armed force in self-defence would be extended, since Article 51 made it clear beyond doubt that armed attack was the sole justification in such cases.

49. Mr. Castañeda (Mexico) maintained that, in principle, the Charter could not be legally interpreted as prohibiting the inclusion of elements other than armed force in the concept of aggression. In fact, Article 41 of the Charter authorized the adoption, in the cases provided for in Article 39, of measures of prevention and punishment not involving the use of armed force, which meant that if aggression took a form other than armed attack, measures other than resort to armed force could be taken. It was thus incorrect to say that in the sense of the Charter only armed attack justified the use of force.

50. In reply to the argument that Article 2, paragraph 4, of the Charter would exclude any form of aggression other than the use of armed force, the representative of Mexico recalled that paragraph 3 of the same article imposed on the Member States the obligation to settle their international disputes by peaceful means. Just as a State refusing to settle its disputes by peaceful means could not necessarily be regarded as an aggressor, so it could not be concluded from Article 2, paragraph 4, that only resort to armed force constituted aggression. He expressed doubt, however, not so much as to the possibility of extending the concept of aggression, as to the desirability of doing so, for the reason given in the working paper submitted by Mexico (A/AC.66/L.8).

51. Speaking on similar lines, Mr. Araoz (Bolivia) urged that, to obtain a satisfactory understanding of aggression within the meaning of the Charter, the Charter should not be examined Article by Article, but as a whole. Thus, a literal interpretation of Article 2, paragraph 4, might lead to the assumption that, as conceived by the Charter, aggression had a limited meaning, whereas, in the light of the other provisions of the Charter, that particular text assumed a quite different significance and provided a sound basis for defining the various forms of aggression. And those acts of aggression, as distinct from the use of armed force, were in contravention of Article 2, paragraph 4, Article 39 and Chapter IX, particularly Article 55.

52. Mr. Adamiyat (Iran) said that, within the meaning of the Charter, there were other forms of aggression apart from armed aggression. Any act which served the same ultimate purpose as armed attack or involved the use of coercion to endanger the independence of a State should be considered as aggressive. That interpretation was supported by an eminent jurist, Sir Robert Phillimore, who had said:

"Where the sufficient and only reason of a provision is undisputed and certain, such provision may be extended to cases to which the *same* reason applied, although the provision be not comprised within the significance of the terms employed. . . It was a provision in a treaty that a certain city should not be enclosed within walls; at the time when the treaty was made, walls were the only species of fortifications in use. It would not be lawful to fortify that city by means of fosses and earthworks, because the spirit and intention of the treaty was to prevent the fortification of the town."[3]

In the same way, economic aggression, although not specifically named in the Charter, was included in the Charter's general condemnation of all acts of aggression.

53. Referring to the judgments rendered by the Tribunals of Nürnberg and Tokyo and more particularly to the case of the Anschluss, Mr. Röling (Netherlands) said they distinguished between aggressive war and aggressive action. Only aggressive wars were declared criminal. Hence, the drafters of the Charter had understood by "aggression" only something that was very close to war and confined to the use of force. Consequently, the notion could not be made to include measures which related rather to the concepts of threats to the peace and breaches of the peace.

54. Mr. Hsu (China), on the other hand, pointed out that while the Nürnberg Tribunal had distinguished between "aggressive action" and "aggressive war",

[3] *Commentaries upon international law*, Sir Robert Phillimore vol. II, 3rd edition, Butterworth, London, 1882.

had not actually stated that only the latter constituted criminal acts of aggression. While in its judgment the Tribunal had kept strictly to the terms of its Statute, it had nevertheless been aware of the important problems of international law which arose and had in fact considered all forms of aggression as crimes. It should also be remembered in what circumstances the Statute of Nürnberg and the Charter of the United Nations had been drafted. Today those circumstances had changed and the time had come for a clear and precise definition of the various forms of aggression, taking into account not the letter but the spirit of the Nürnberg Statute and of the Charter of the United Nations.

II. Acts to be included in the definition

A. *The notion of armed aggression*

1. *The scope of the notion of armed aggression*

55. Certain members referred to Article 2, paragraph 4, of the Charter, and expressed the view that there could be no question of aggression within the meaning of the Charter except in the case of the use of armed force against the territorial integrity or political independence of another State. It was asserted that aggression could also be deemed to mean the use of force directed not only against the political independence or territorial integrity of the sovereign State, but against a territory placed under an international régime.

56. Mr. Hsu (China) expressed the opinion that aggression consisted in the illegal use of force, not only with a view to violating the territorial integrity or political independence of another State, but also to establishing hegemony over other States. He recalled, on the basis of historical examples, that aggression had not always been aimed at the territorial integrity or political independence of another State, but that its purpose had often been to establish some form of hegemony.

57. With regard to the concept of armed aggression in the light of the elements of force which constituted it, Mr. Röling (Netherlands) expressed the opinion that the use of force should not always and systematically be regarded as aggression within the meaning of the Charter. In that connexion, he referred to subparagraph 6 B (*j*) of the draft resolution submitted by the Union of Soviet Socialist Republics (A/AC.66/L.2/Rev.1), which provided that frontier incidents might not be used as justification for war. Nevertheless, he did not see why the draft took a much more serious view of an attack on aircraft (paragraph 1 (*c*)); such an attack might result from factors very similar to those which gave rise to frontier incidents. He pointed out that not every act of violence necessarily gave the victim the right of self-defence. In order to go to war in application of that right, a country must be the victim of obvious aggression so serious as to leave it no recourse but to take up arms in order to safeguard its territorial integrity or political independence.

58. Replying to Mr. Röling's remarks concerning point 1 (*c*) of the USSR draft definition of aggression, Mr. Morozov (Union of Soviet Socialist Republics) maintained that a frontier incident remained a frontier incident, whether it occurred on land, at sea or in the air, and could not therefore be regarded as a justification for armed attack in accordance with the provision of paragraph 1 of the USSR proposal. Paragraph 1 (*c*) of the Soviet Union draft definition of aggression did not speak of frontier incidents; it provided rather that in an international conflict the action taken by a State which first deliberately attacked the aircraft of another State should be characterized as an act of aggression.

59. Mr. Vallat (United Kingdom) did not limit the term "force" to armed force in the traditional sense. He thought that the objects towards which acts were directed might be a better criterion for a definition of aggression than the character of the acts themselves. Article 2, paragraph 4 of the Charter indicated that basically acts of aggression were those directed against the territorial integrity or political independence of any State.

2. *The threat of the use of force*

60. The members of the Committee expressed different opinions on the question whether the definition should include the threat of force, or whether the threat of use of armed force may give the right for individual or collective self-defence and whether it is necessary to include anything connected with it into the definition of aggression.

61. Certain members of the Committee interpreted Article 2, paragraph 4, of the Charter as authorizing the threat of the use of force to be considered equivalent to aggression. Nevertheless, Mr. Röling (Netherlands) stated that, for threat of the use of force to be regarded as aggression, thereby authorizing the exercise of the right of self-defence, it was necessary, firstly, that the threat should be imminent, that is, that it should be on the point of being carried out and, secondly, that it should be directed against the political independence or territorial integrity of a State. He made a distinction, however, between two notions, that of the threat of resort to force, provided in Article 2, paragraph 4 of the Charter, and that of threats to the peace provided for in Article 39 of the Charter; the first corresponded to a situation in which it was probable that a State would use force against the territorial integrity or political independence of another State and the second corresponded to a position where it was probable that peace would be violated. The second notion, which was not identical with the first, affected the functions of the Security Council, which bore responsibility for ensuring the maintenance of international peace and security.

62. Mr. Hsu (China) maintained that a threat to peace included the threat to use force. According to Article 1 of the Charter, a threat to peace was different from a dispute; whereas a dispute was essentially capable of being settled by peaceful means, a threat to the peace implied the possibility of aggression or a threat to use force. A threat to use force should therefore be regarded as indirect aggression. If indirect aggression was to be condemned, a threat to the peace, insofar as it involved recourse to force, should also be condemned.

63. Mr. Castañeda (Mexico) expressed the view that in conformity with the verbatim text of Article 51 of the Charter, only armed attack could justify recourse to self-defence. A solution contrary to that principle would be dangerous because it would authorize preventive war. In any case, if an analogy could be used, while it was true that the legal codes and jurisprudence of the various countries differed in defining the circumstances and events justifying recourse to self-defence, one common element could be said to exist in the various national legislations, namely, that the threat must be acompanied by an effort to carry it out before recourse to self-defence could be justified. The same principle

might perhaps be followed on the international level, but in reality the problem was related to that of the application of the definition by the competent organs of the United Nations. But, as regards the definition itself, nothing should be understood as suggesting justification of recourse to self-defence if no armed attack had taken place.

64. Mr. Chaumont (France) stated that if a general definition were adopted, the threat of aggression might be added to the definition, as in that case the competent organ would not be strictly bound. The circumstances in which a threat of attack might be considered equivalent to the attack itself must be closely defined in order to leave no justification whatever for a so-called preventive war.

65. Certain members of the Committee objected to any attempt to introduce the concept of threat of aggression into the definition. They stated that the Charter made no such allowances. Mr. Morozov (Union of Soviet Socialist Republics) considered that the inclusion in the definition of aggression of any provisions justifying the right of a State to be the first to attack another State on the grounds of self-defence against the threat of aggression woud radically undermine the significance of the definition of aggression. It would provide the aggressor with a loophole, for he would justify his aggressive activities by reference to self-defence. That would be contrary to the Purposes and Principles of the Charter. In that connexion Mr. Morozov also recalled the terms of Article 51 of the Charter which referred to the "inherent" right of individual or collective self-defence if an armed attack occurs against a Member of the United Nations. . . .

3. *Aggressive intent*

66. Certain members of the Committee considered that *animus aggressionis* constituted a characteristic element of the use of force. They pointed out that the draft resolution submitted by the Union of Soviet Socialist Republics (A/AC.66/L.2/Rev.1) provided for no special conditions in which the acts referred to in its paragraph 1 might be committed without aggressive intent. Mr. Chaumont (France) observed that that draft resolution defined the aggressor rather than the aggression itself and that it was not consistent in defining the operation of the factor of intention. For example, in paragraph 1 (*c*), bombardment was stated to be aggressive *per se,* with no proviso that intent must be proved, whereas the same paragraph also contained the expression "deliberate attack on . . . ships or aircraft". The same applied to paragraph 1 (*a*), which named as the aggressor the State which first declared war against another State. That excluded any examination of intention. The danger of an automatic application of the definition must be guarded against and scope must be left for interpretation in the light of circumstances.

67. In opposing those arguments, Mr. Morozov (Union of Soviet Socialist Republics) pointed out that it followed from the very nature of the activities enumerated in the Soviet definition of aggression (declaration of war, invasion, etc.) that they could only be committed intentionally.

68. It was pointed out, moreover, that even if the list of acts contained no allusion to intention, nothing could prevent a competent international organ from proving it. It was also pointed out that it might be advisable to take intention into consideration when the aggressor

would be called upon to account for his actions; at the time when force was used, the criterion should be the scope of the action undertaken and not the purposes of its author: the question was whether the territorial integrity or political independence of the victim was at stake. It was then and only then that the use of force could be qualified as aggression. The view was also expressed that the criterion for the definition of an aggressor, which was generally recognized in international law, was the principle upon which the Soviet Union's definition of the concept of aggression was based. According to that principle, the commission by a State of the acts enumerated in the definition automatically constituted conclusive evidence of aggressive intentions, provided that they were committed in an international conflict and were committed first in relation to the other State. Mr. Morozov (USSR) considered that a different presentation of the matter might result in attempts to justify an attack made upon a State on the ground that the attacker allegedly had no aggressive intentions, a plea to which, as history showed, aggressors had frequently resorted.

B. *The notion of indirect aggression*

69. In the opinion of certain members of the Committee, the notion of indirect aggression should not be introduced into the definition of aggression. They maintained that, within the meaning of the Charter, indirect aggression might be regarded not as aggression, but as a threat to peace or a breach of the peace. Other members of the Committee considered that, within the meaning of the Charter, indirect aggression was one of the forms of aggression; it should be included in any definition which was drawn up. Some members maintained that indirect aggression might come within the meaning of aggression in the sense of the Charter in case the use of force or the threat of the use of force was involved. Other members of the Committee felt that that formula expressed the notion of indirect aggression inaccurately and erroneously.

C. *The notion of economic aggression*

70. Mr. Araoz (Bolivia) maintained that economic aggression violated fundamentally three basic principles of the United Nations: the principle of the political independence of States, that of their sovereign equality and that of non-interference in their domestic affairs. An act of aggression was one which threatened the sovereignty of a State, that is to say, its political dependence or its territorial integrity. Political independence was closely linked with economic independence; thus anything which threatened economic independence was as much an act of aggression as was armed aggression. Aggression was not merely the use of armed force. Economic pressure often produced the same effects as did military aggression. Such pressures were in direct contradiction of Article 2, paragraph 4, and Article 55 of the Charter. Article 39 could not serve as a basis for rules to combat economic aggression, but it enabled any use of force against international co-operation and the right of peoples to self-determination to be so described. There were several reasons why economic aggression might be described as aggression. Firstly, the characteristics of armed aggression were the same as those of economic aggression, the latter differing from the former only in the use of force in an indirect or disguised form. Moreover, the constituent elements of the two ideas were the same: they both came from the same generic concept of aggression. Armed ag-

ression was a recourse to force, economic aggression as a recourse only to pressure, but it could lead a country not only to civil war and loss of independence, but also reduce it to poverty and famine.

71. Mr. Tarazi (Syria) pointed out that under-developed countries suffered from economic aggression. The Charter proclaimed the principle of the sovereign equality of States. If a great Power made exorbitant demands in return for the assistance it gave to a weak nation, it was acting contrary to the spirit of the Charter. When those demands threatened the independence of the country concerned, they amounted to aggression.

72. Mr. de Marchena (Dominican Republic) observed that account should be taken of indirect forms of aggression, among which it seemed to be agreed to include "economic aggression". Although it was true that in many cases it was a matter of discriminatory practices by certain countries in world trade and economic affairs, there was no doubt that those practices should place acts giving rise to "economic aggression" among forms or means of indirect aggression. The Dominican Republic had called for an analysis of the various aspects of indirect aggression, and, since it had suffered the effects of commercial and economic discriminatory practices, it trusted that the Committee would not shrink from studying the question closely, particularly in the light of the opinions expressed during the debate. Only through an exchange of ideas would it be possible to determine whether it was feasible to formulate useful definitions within the scope of resolution 688 (VII) of the General Assembly.

73. Mr. Adamiyat (Iran) pointed out that economic aggression was one of the most significant forms of indirect aggression. It was made possible by the differentiation in the economic potentialities of various States. That inequality enabled the highly industrialized nations to take advantage of the less developed countries and to cause an economic paralysis directly endangering the economic stability, and thereby the political independence of the under-developed countries. Coercive economic and political measures taken against a State directly or indirectly and designed to impede the exercise of its sovereignty over its natural resources or its efforts towards economic development constituted the most important factor in economic aggression. Although economic aggression was not expressly mentioned in the Charter, it was nevertheless true that it was included among the acts condemned by the Charter as acts of aggression.

74. Mr. Morozov (Union of Soviet Socialist Republics) pointed out that the definition of the concept of aggression he had submitted had been prepared with due regard for the statements made by the delegations of a number of States, particularly of Asia and Latin America, which had declared themselves in favour in principle of the Soviet proposal regarding the need to define aggression in the interests of maintaining peace and security and which had expressed a desire that the list of acts of aggression should also include acts of economic, ideological and indirect aggression. There was an act of economic aggression wherever a State, taking the initiative, adopted measures of economic pressure infringing the sovereignty of another State and its economic independence, and threatening the foundations of the economic life of that State; adopted measures in regard to another State impeding the exploitation by that State of its own natural resources or the nationalization of those resources; imposed on another State an economic blockade.

75. Certain members of the Committee declared that it would be contrary to the letter and spirit of the Charter to expand the notion of aggression to include anything other than armed attack. The definition of aggression in the sense of the Charter merely constituted an interpretation of the Charter. According to Mr. Vallat (United Kingdom), any attempt to ascribe to the concept of aggression a scope exceeding that attributed to it by the Charter would amount to an attempt to amend the Charter. Mr. Amado (Brazil) pointed out that, although it was true that the concept of economic aggression was becoming more and more important, that concept had not been raised at San Francisco. The idea of indirect aggression in all its forms was not contemporary with the Charter, but subsequent to it. If those new concepts of aggression were recognized, a State which considered its liberty attacked by economic pressure would be able to protect itself against that attack only by lodging a complaint with the Security Council. Yet the complaint could not be heard unless a dispute existed which could be regarded as a threat to the peace. If economic pressure were brought to bear without constituting a threat to the peace, it would not exist in the sense of the Charter. If action against economic aggression were to be taken under the system of collective security set up by the Charter, such aggression would have to be equated with an act falling within the provisions of Article 39.

76. Mr. Maktos (United States) said that serious consequences might result from extending the idea of aggression. Although it was true that a State's political independence depended on its economic independence, they could not both be placed on the same level. If such a mistake were made, it would weaken the whole concept of aggression. The definition proposed would be ineffective in the very case in which it should in principle be of the maximum use, that of armed aggression. The prestige of the United Nations could only suffer as a result.

77. The concept of economic aggression had been criticized especially in connexion with the right of self-defence provided for in Article 51 of the Charter. Those who argued against it said that economic aggression could not justify the exercise of the right of self-defence, since Article 51 was to apply only in the case of armed attack. Moreover, if it was introduced into the definition, it might automatically increase the possibilities of legitimate recourse to armed force, which could constitute a factor liable to disturb the peace rather than maintain it. Against that argument it was pointed out that, owing to the existence of the United Nations, a victim of aggression was not absolutely free to defend itself by all possible means. In the event of direct aggression, it might exercise its right of self-defence until the competent organs of the United Nations took the necessary steps, but in the case of indirect aggression it could not take such action, in view of the absence of the element of urgency which alone justified the exercise of that right. It was essential, however, to recognize the victim's right to take retaliatory measures and it was obvious that it could never use force to uphold that right.

78. Mr. Castañeda (Mexico) considered that acts constituting what was known as economic aggression might, if they constituted a threat to the peace, give rise

to equally effective action by the competent organs of the United Nations, under Article 39 of the Charter, even if such acts were not held to be aggression. But, even on the supposition that they did not constitute a threat to the peace, there was no doubt that measures of economic pressure (like subversive activities and some forms of propaganda) were illicit activities, contrary to the principle of non-intervention which played such an important part in the inter-American juridical system; there was no question that they were expressly prohibited by article 15 of the Charter of the Organization of American States.

D. *The notion of ideological aggression*

79. Some members of the Committee felt that it would be dangerous to include any reference to ideological aggression or propaganda in a definition. Mr. Maktos (United States of America) was of opinion that a pretext for attacking the freedom of the press might thereby be afforded. Aggressors undoubtedly used psychological methods. It could even be said that there was a psychological or ideological element in every aggression. The acknowledgment of such a fact did not, however, authorize anyone to state that any activity that might affect the views of men was aggression. It would be going too far to speak of ideological aggression. It would also distort the idea of aggression properly so-called by weakening the scope of the term and diminish its usefulness.

80. Commenting on the draft resolution submitted by the Union of Soviet Socialist Republics (A/AC.66/L.2/Rev.1), Mr. Vallat (United Kingdom) thought that whilst certain elements of the indirect, economic and ideological measures outlined in paragraphs 2, 3 and 4 of that draft might fit into the concept of aggression, in the aggregate they would be alien to the concept of direct or indirect use of armed force referred to in Article 2, paragraph 4, of the Charter.

81. Similarly, sub-paragraph (*b*) of paragraph 4 of the draft resolution in question was criticized by the United States representative as tending to induce the Committee to concern itself with a problem, that of atomic weapons, which in fact came within the purview of other United Nations organs. If that proposal, and that involving consideration by the Committee of the question of economic aggression, a question which concerned the Economic and Social Council rather than the Security Council, were retained, the United Nations would forfeit the respect and sympathy of public opinion. The prestige of the United Nations demanded the avoidance of all haste and of any unwarranted extension of the principles of the Charter.

82. Other members of the Committee declared themselves in favour of the notion of ideological aggression and argued that it should be introduced into the definition of aggression. Mr. Morozov (Union of Soviet Socialist Republics) considered that ideological aggression constituted one of the forms of aggression. He pointed out how exceptionally dangerous for international peace and security were the encouragement of war propaganda, the encouragement of propaganda for the use of atomic, bacterial, chemical and other types of weapons of mass destruction and also the promotion of the propaganda of fascist-nazi views, racial and national exclusiveness, hatred and contempt for other peoples. In opposing the arguments of the United States representative, Mr. Morozov pointed out that, if the

General Assembly adopted the USSR proposal, peace would be consolidated and the authority and role of the United Nations in maintaining international security would be enhanced. In Mr. Morozov's opinion, the Committee was competent to examine all matters relating to the definition of aggression. The principle of freedom of the press must not be used as a pretext to justify war propaganda and the other acts of ideological aggression specified in the USSR proposal.

E. *Other forms of indirect aggression*

83. Mr. Adamiyat (Iran) expressed the wish that the definition should include, under the heading of indirect aggression, intervention in another State's internal or foreign affairs. From the standpoint of international law, such interference would constitute a threat to peace and to national independence. To that form of indirect aggression it would also be necessary to add, as a corollary, direct or indirect incitement to civil war, threats to internal security, and incitement to revolt by the supply of arms or by other means. All those acts should appear in the wording of the contemplated definition. Mr. Araoz (Bolivia) said that he unreservedly supported the Iranian representative's view.

84. According to the draft resolution submitted by the Union of Soviet Socialist Republics (A/AC.66/L.2/Rev.1) any State which encouraged subversive activity against another State (acts of terrorism, diversion, etc.), promoted the outbreak of civil war within another State, or promoted an internal upheaval in another State or a reversal of policy in favour of the aggressor should be declared to have committed an act of indirect aggression.

85. According to the working paper submitted by China (A/AC.66/L.4/Rev.3) the arming of organized bands or third States in order to launch them against a State marked out as victim, the planting of fifth columnists in a victim State or sending subversive agents there, and inciting the citizens of the State to civil war, by means of propaganda, should be considered acts of aggression.

86. Mr. de Marchena (Dominican Republic) said that paragraph 2 (*a*) of the USSR draft resolution (A/AC.66/L.2/Rev.1) referred to encouraging "subversive activity against another State (acts of terrorism, diversion, etc.)" as an act of "indirect aggression". However, paragraph 1 (*f*) of the resolution including among acts of direct aggression "support of armed bands organized in its own territory which invade the territory of another State. . . " There seemed to be a certain relationship of cause and effect between the two cases, and they should be studied with special care before classifying them under two specific concepts. The Dominican Republic considered that subversive activity of either type—for example, the organization of armed bands to invade the territory of another State or to stir up civil war in that State—were forms of aggression which the Committee ought to define. He recalled that at the sixth Inter-American Conference in Havana, a convention had been signed and ratified by a large majority of American States laying down the rights and duties of the contracting parties in case of civil wars. The provisions of the convention covered cases of activities of armed bands, traffic in arms, incitement to civil war and a whole series of acts aimed at disturbing regional peace and harmony in the Americas. There would be nothing to prevent the extension of those rules

the international level. Article 15 of the Bogotá Char-r explicitly condemned any interference, direct or in-rect, by one State in the internal affairs of another. Subversive activities, when they included *inter alia* the arming of certain groups, training them by permitting them to use the facilities provided by the country maintaining them against another State, and by receiving subsidies and other assistance in preparation for an at-

tack on another State, were the most reprehensible and insidious forms of indirect aggression. Since such acts tended to destroy the structure of the State and its public institutions by disrupting the normal life of its inhabitants and jeopardizing peace, they were positive forms of aggression. As such, they justified relatiatory measures and the exercise of the right of self-defence by the State thus endangered.

Chapter III

The connexion between a definition of aggression and the maintenance of international peace and security

87. The representatives of Bolivia, France, Iran, Mexico, Poland, the Dominican Republic, Syria and the USSR pointed out that a definition of aggression was possible and desirable for the maintenance of international peace and security. Others took the view that such a definition would not only not be useful, but would in fact be dangerous to the maintenance of international peace and security.

88. According to the members of the Committee who declared themselves in favour of defining aggression, such a definition would contribute to the development of international law and to the principles embodied in the Charter. If the definition was not in itself sufficient to prevent aggression, it would nevertheless provide an effective instrument for preventing that crime; it would discourage a possible aggressor and would constitute a serious warning to him. Moreover, it would serve as a guide to international organs and would enable them to avoid arbitrary decisions in the event of their being called upon to determine the aggressor. It would also have the further advantage of enlightening the public.

89. In the opinion of those members of the Committee who expressed themselves against defining aggression, such a definition would, firstly, be useless; aggressors would not be discouraged by a definition; experience had shown the uselessness of such a definition just as it had shown that its absence had never yet made itself felt, whether in the operation of the system of collective security established by the Covenant of the League of Nations and the United Nations Charter, or in the judgments of the tribunals set up after the Second World War to punish war criminals.

90. Mr. Dons (Norway) recalled in that connexion that the main difficulties met with in practice had nothing to do with the definition of aggression as such, but were frequently due to ignorance of the facts of a given situation. It was hard to determine who was the aggressor because some of the States concerned deliberately concealed the facts, or presented them in a false light. A definition, however framed, would be of no use unless the facts were first agreed upon; in United Nations bodies views had been divided not on the aggressive nature of some particular act, but on whether that act had really been committed.

91. Some members asserted that to define aggression would even be dangerous, especially in the present state of international relations. It would assist the aggressor by affording him a valuable means of circumventing it and interfering with his victim's measures of self-defence. It would hinder the action of the international organs called upon to designate the aggressor and would lead them to adopt decisions which in certain cases might aggravate international tension instead of allaying it.

92. Some members of the Committee expressed the view that it was practically impossible to draft a satisfactory definition of aggression. Moreover, a defective definition would be dangerous. It might trap the innocent while allowing the aggressor to escape.

93. Mr. Morozov (Union of Soviet Socialist Republics) stated that such assertions were without foundation and that a correct solution of the question of defining the concept of aggression and the adoption by the General Assembly of a clear-cut definition would be of great importance for the maintenance of international peace and security and, in particular, for the elimination of the possibility of justifying aggression. The Security Council which, according to Chapter VII of the Charter, was the only organ competent to designate the aggressor must be guided by that definition in determining the State guilty of aggression.

94. Mr. Winiewicz (Poland) stressed that the previous discussions of the General Assembly and resolutions 599 (VI) and 688 (VII) made it sufficiently clear that a definition of aggression was not only possible, but advisable and useful. Those discussions and documents established already the connexion between the definition of aggression and the maintenance of international peace and security. Definition of crime was an essential part of national law and should be an essential part of international law. A definition of aggression, like every other act of condemnation would—among its many advantages—constitute a preventive obstacle, a serious warning to those who might be tempted to commit aggression. Thus, a definition would strengthen peace and help to maintain international security. The Soviet proposal (A/AC.66/L.2/Rev.1) served those purposes.

The problems raised by the inclusion of a definition of aggression in the code of offences against the peace and security of mankind and by its application within the framework of international criminal jurisdiction

95. Mr. Chaumont (France) recalled that his delegation had always favoured the inclusion of a definition of aggression in a code of offences against the peace and security of mankind, along with the establishment of an international criminal court. However, pending final decisions on those questions, his delegation believing that a definition of aggression would serve a useful purpose in United Nations activities, was prepared to collaborate in the Committee's work to that end.

96. Mr. Röling (Netherlands), after stating that a definition of aggression to be applied by the political organs of the United Nations could play only a negligible part in the maintenance of international peace and security, since it would bind neither the Security Council nor the General Assembly of the United Nations, expressed the view that such a definition would have a great chance of succeeding in the domain of international criminal jurisdiction. The objections that could be raised to a definition of aggression intended to be applied under the system of collective security would not all apply to a definition to be used in the more restricted field of international criminal jurisdiction. Mr. Röling stressed, however, that two problems might arise from the application by an international criminal court of a definition of aggression: firstly, a decision by such a court bearing on a case of aggression might hamper the Security Council in its essential function, which was to maintain international peace and security; it might hinder its action in the peaceful settlement of the dispute. Secondly, the Security Council and the international criminal court might pronounce two contradictory decisions on a case of aggression brought simultaneously before both of them. To obviate that difficulty, the text of the definition of aggression should include a provision under which the international criminal court would be bound by the Security Council's decisions, which would be taken on the basis of that definition. It might, however, well be that the crime of aggression would be considered, for the time being, as less comprehensive than the concept of aggression in the sense of Article 39 of the Charter. If that was the case, an international criminal court might find an act, considered as aggression by the Security Council, not criminal in the sense of a code of international criminal law.

97. In its observations on the draft Code of offences against the peace and security of mankind and on the question of defining aggression,[4] the Netherlands Government proposed that the concept of aggression should be defined as follows:

"Aggression is the threat or use of force by a State or government against the territorial integrity or political independence of another State or against a territory under international régime in any manner, whatever the weapons employed and whether openly or otherwise, for any reason or for any purpose other than individual or collective self-defence against such a threat or use of force or in pursuance of a decision or recommendation by a competent organ of the United Nations."

[4] *Official Records of the General Assembly, Seventh Session, Annexes*, agenda item 54, documents A/2162 and Add.1.

Chapter V

The effect of a definition of aggression on the exercise of the jurisdiction of the various organs of the United Nations

98. The members of the Committee were agreed that any definition of aggression included in a General Assembly resolution would merely have the status of a recommendation. It would not have a binding character. However, some members of the Committee stressed that such a definition would exercise great moral authority over the international organs called upon to pronounce on a case of aggression.

99. Mr. de Marchena (Dominican Republic) pointed out that, even though the General Assembly's resolutions had no binding force, it was nevertheless true that the rules or criteria contained in them might acquire the value of general principles of international law analogous to those consecrated by many treaties and conventions. Every General Assembly resolution added new elements to the application of the Charter and the definition of its purposes. The influence of a definition of aggression would therefore be questionable.

100. Some members of the Committee expressed the view that a definition accepted by a large majority of the Member States could not fail to exert a great influence on the exercise of their jurisdiction by the various organs of the United Nations. Mr. Röling (Netherlands) stated that a definition adopted unanimously, or at least by all the permanent members of the Security Council, would influence that Council's decisions. Consequently, if the Committee succeeded in framing such a definition, that definition would exert a profound influence on international relations. Conversely, a decision taken by a narrow majority and not adopted by the permanent members of the Security Council would scarcely have any value. In this relation, he pointed out that a definition adopted by the General Assembly would have less chance to be followed by the Security Council if it contained strictly binding provisions, as was the case with the Soviet draft.

ANNEX

Texts submitted to the Committee

I. Draft resolution submitted by the Union of Soviet Socialist Republics (A/AC.66/L.2/Rev.1)

The Special Committee on the Question of Defining Aggression recommends to the General Assembly the adoption of the following resolution:

Resolution

The General Assembly,

Considering it necessary to formulate directives with a view to determining which party is guilty of aggression,

Declares that:

1. In an international conflict that State shall be declared the attacker which first commits one of the following acts:

(*a*) Declaration of war against another State;

(*b*) Invasion by its armed forces, even without a declaration of war, of the territory of another State;

(*c*) Bombardment by its land, sea or air forces of the territory of another State or the carrying out of a deliberate attack on the ships or aircraft of the latter;

(*d*) The landing or leading of its land, sea or air forces inside the boundaries of another State without the permission of the government of the latter, or the violation of the conditions of such permission, particularly as regards the length of their stay or the extent of the area in which they may stay;

(*e*) Naval blockade of the coasts or ports of another State;

(*f*) Support of armed bands organized in its own territory which invade the territory of another State, or refusal, on being requested by the invaded State, to take in its own territory any action within its power to deny such bands any aid or protection.

2. That State shall be declared to have committed an act of indirect aggression which:

(*a*) Encourages subversive activity against another State (acts of terrorism, diversion, etc.);

(*b*) Promotes the outbreak of civil war within another State;

(*c*) Promotes an internal upheaval in another State or a reversal of policy in favour of the aggressor.

3. That State shall be declared to have committed an act of economic aggression which first commits one of the following acts:

(*a*) Takes against another State measures of economic pressure violating its sovereignty and economic independence and threatening the bases of its economic life;

(*b*) Takes against another State measures preventing it from exploiting or nationalizing its own natural riches;

(*c*) Subjects another State to an economic blockade.

4. That State shall be declared to have committed an act of ideological aggression which:

(*a*) Encourages war propaganda;

(*b*) Encourages propaganda in favour of using atomic, bacterial, chemical and other weapons of mass destruction;

(*c*) Promotes the propagation of fascist-nazi views, of racial and national exclusiveness, and of hatred and contempt for other peoples.

5. An act other than those listed in the preceding paragraphs may when committed by a State be deemed to constitute aggression if declared by resolution of the Security Council in a particular case to be an attack or an act of economic, ideological or indirect aggression.

6. Attacks such as those referred to in paragraph 1 and acts of economic, ideological and indirect aggression such as those referred to in paragraphs 2, 3 and 4 may not be justified by any arguments of a political, strategic or economic nature, or by the desire to exploit natural riches in the territory of the State attacked or to derive any other kind of advantages or privileges, or by reference to the amount of capital invested in the State attacked or to any other particular interests in its territory, or by the affirmation that the State attacked lacks the distinguishing marks of statehood.

In particular, the following may not be used as justifications:

A. The internal position of any State, as for example:

(*a*) The backwardness of any nation politically, economically or culturally;

(*b*) Alleged shortcomings of its administration;

(*c*) Any danger which may threaten the life or property of aliens;

(*d*) Any revolutionary or counter-revolutionary movement, civil war, disorders or strikes;

(*e*) The establishment or maintenance in any State of any political, economic or social system.

B. Any acts, legislation or orders of any State, as for example:

(*a*) The violation of international treaties;

(*b*) The violation of rights and interests in the sphere of trade, concessions or any other kind of economic activity acquired by another State or its citizens;

(*c*) The rupture of diplomatic or economic relations;

(*d*) Measures in connexion with an economic or financial boycott;

(*e*) Repudiation of debts;

(*f*) Prohibition or restriction or immigration or modification of the status of foreigners;

(*g*) The violation of privileges granted to the official representatives of another State;

(*h*) Refusal to allow the passage of armed forces proceeding to the territory of a third State;

(*i*) Measures of a religious or anti-religious nature;

(*j*) Frontier incidents.

7. In the event of the mobilization or concentration by another State of considerable armed forces near its frontier, the State which is threatened by such action shall have the right of recourse to diplomatic or other means of securing a peaceful settlement of international disputes. It may also in the meantime adopt requisite measures of a military nature similar to those described above, without, however, crossing the frontier.

II. Working Paper No. 1 submitted by China (A/AC.66/L.4/Rev.3)

Aggression is a crime against the peace and security of mankind. It consists of the employment of force, open or under cover, armed or unarmed, by a State for the violation, impairment or destruction of the territorial integrity or political independence of another State, or for the subversion of its political and social order, or, in a case of dispute with another State, for the coercion of that State in place of pacific settlement. Among other acts, it includes:

(*a*) Waging war, declared or undeclared, general or limited;

(*b*) Arming organized bands or third States for offence against a State marked out as victim;

(*c*) Planting fifth columnists or subversive agents in a victim State;

(*d*) Inciting civil strife in a victim State by propaganda;

(*e*) Imposing blockades, naval or economic.

Employment of force in self-defence or in reprisal, subject to the conditions laid down in international law for the exercise of these rights, and in carrying out a decision or recommendation of a competent organ of the United Nations is legitimate.

III. Working Papfr No. 2 submitted by China (A/AC.66/L.7/Rev.2)

The General Assembly,

Recalling its resolutions 599 (VI) and 688 (VII),

Mindful of the responsibilities of the Security Council concerning aggression under Article 1, paragraph 1, and Chapter VII of the Charter, and of the function of the General Assembly envisaged in Assembly resolution 377 A (V),

Considering that, although the question whether aggression has occurred must be determined in the circumstances of each particular case, it would nevertheless be advisable to formulate certain principles as guidance,

Recommends that the Security Council in the discharge of its responsibilities under Article 1, paragraph 1, and Chapter VII of the Charter, and the Members of the United Nations, when the Assembly is called upon to consider an item pursuant to resolution 377 A (V), take account *inter alia* of the following principles:

(1) That aggression is a crime against the peace and security of mankind;

(2) That it consists of the unlawful use of force by a State against another State;

(3) That the unlawful use of force may be open or under cover, and the force unlawfully used may be armed or unarmed;

(4) That the purpose of the unlawful use of force may be the violation, impairment or destruction of the territorial integrity or political independence, or the subversion of political and social order, or, in a case of dispute, the coercion of an opponent in place of pacfic settlement;

(5) That the use of force is lawful when it is resorted to in accordance with a decision or recommendation of a competent organ of the United Nations, or in self-defence against an armed attack pending the taking of measures by the competent organs of the United Nations necessary for the maintenance of peace;

(6) That the employment of comparable methods in reprisal against an attack of unarmed force, open or under cover, is likewise lawful when the competent organs of the United Nations neglect to take effective collective measures for the prevention or removal of the attack, or for its suppression, as the nature of the case may demand.

IV. Working paper submitted by Mexico (A/AC.66/L.8)

The proposed definition of the Soviet Union (A/AC.66/L.2/Rev.1) could be considerably improved and would be acceptable to the Mexican delegation with the following changes:

1. The insertion after the preamble of the following paragraph:

"Declares that:

"In an international conflict aggression shall be regarded as the direct or indirect use of force by the authorities of one State against the territorial integrity or political independence of another State or for any purpose other than legitimate individual or collective defence or compliance with a decision or recommendation of a competent organ of the United Nations. In particular, the commission of any of the following acts shall be regarded as aggression:

"(*a*) . . .

"(*b*), etc."

(There would then be inserted paragraphs (*a*) to (*f*) of paragraph 1 of the Soviet draft.)

Paragraph 5 of the Soviet draft definition would be deleted.

2. In view of the influence which the definition of aggression may have on the application and interpretation of Article 51 of the United Nations Charter, it seems, in the opinion of the Mexican delegation, hazardous to extend the concept of aggression to include separate elements of the use of force. Thus, acts constituting so-called indirect, economic or ideological aggression should be regarded as aggression only if they involve or are accompanied by the use of force. Consequently, for the purposes of the definition:

(*a*) Such acts when actually constituting aggression are already covered by the general definition proposed in paragraph (1).

(*b*) Even though such acts did not constitute aggression, they might justify enforcement measures by the Security Council as provided in Article 39 of the Charter in the same manner as though aggression had been committed if by their effect on the victim State or for any other reason they constituted a threat to the peace. This circumstance should be particularly emphasized in our Committee's report to the Assembly.

The deletion of paragraphs 2, 3 and 4 of the Soviet draft is accordingly proposed.

3. Paragraph 6, first part. Amend the wording to conform with the suggested deletion of paragraphs 3, 4 and 5. Add the words "or social" after the words "strategic or economic". Delete that part of the paragraph beginning with the words: "or by the desire to exploit . . ." up to the words: "its territory".

Amend the wording of paragraph 6, sub-paragraph B, item (a), so as to include those treaties which by their very nature justify the use of force if they are violated.

V. Working paper submitted by Bolivia (A/AC.66/L.9)

The General Assembly,

Considering it necessary to define some acts of aggression in order to maintain international peace and security, in accordance with the Purposes and Principles of the United Nations Charter,

Hereby resolves as follows:

1. Independently of acts of aggression designated as such by the competent international organs of the United Nations, the invasion by one State of the territory of another State across the frontiers established by treaties or judicial or arbitral decisions and demarcated in accordance therewith, or, in the absence of marked frontiers, an invasion affecting territories under the effective jurisdiction of a State shall in all cases be deemed to constitute an act of aggression.

2. A declaration of war, an armed attack with land, sea or air forces against the territory, ships or aircraft of another State, support given to armed bands for purposes of invasion, and the overt or covert inciting of the people of one State by another State to rebellion for the purpose of disturbing law and order in the interests of a foreign Power shall also be defined as acts of aggression.

3. Any threat or use of force against the territorial integrity or political independence of any State or in any other manner incompatible with the purposes of the United Nations, including unilateral action whereby a State is deprived of economic resources derived from the proper conduct of international trade or its basic economy is endangered so that its security is affected and it is rendered unable to act in its own defence or to co-operate in the collective defence of peace shall likewise be deemed to constitute an act of aggression.

4. Apart from the cases provided for in paragraphs 1 and 2, which shall constitute sufficient grounds for the automatic exercise of the right of collective self-defence, other acts of aggression shall be defined as such, when they take place, by the competent organs established by the United Nations Charter and in conformity with its provisions.

United Nations

GENERAL ASSEMBLY

Official Records

DOCUMENT 7

Agenda item 51

ANNEXES

NINTH SESSION

NEW YORK, 1954

Agenda item 51: Question of defining aggression: report of the Special Committee on the Question of Defining Aggression

CONTENTS

DOCUMENT A/2689 and Corr.1 and Add.1 [1]

Comments received from Governments regarding the report of the Special Committee on the Question of Defining Aggression (A/2638)

[Original text: English, French, Russian and Spanish]
[6 August and 18 October 1954]

---

[1] A/2689/Add.1, dated 18 October 1954, contained the reply of the Government of Argentina and the text that comprises paragraph 4 below.

Annexes (IX) 51

NOTE BY THE SECRETARY-GENERAL

1. The General Assembly, by resolution 688 (VII) of 20 December 1952, on the question of defining aggression, established a Special Committee composed of representatives of fifteen Member States and requested it (a) to submit to the General Assembly at its ninth session draft definitions of aggression or draft statements of the notion of aggression ; and (b) to study certain problems, referred to in the preamble of the resolution, relating to the question of defining aggression. By the same resolution, the Secretary-General was requested to communicate the Special Committee's report to Member States for their comments and to place the question on the provisional agenda of the ninth session of the General Assembly.

2. The Special Committee on the Question of Defining Aggression met at United Nations Headquarters in New York from 24 August to 21 September 1953 and drew up a report for submission to the General Assembly (A/2638). In pursuance of the aforesaid resolution of the General Assembly, the Secretary-General circulated the report of the Special Committee to the Governments of all Member States of the United Nations and, by a letter of 2 December 1953, requested those Governments to communicate to him any comments they might wish to make on the report of the Special Committee.

3. By 30 July 1954, replies containing or referring to comments relating to the report of the Special Committee had been received from the Governments of the Byelorussian Soviet Socialist Republic, Denmark, France, Greece, India, Poland, Sweden, the Ukrainian Soviet Socialist Republic, the Union of Soviet Socialist Republics and the United Kingdom of Great Britain and Northern Ireland. The Government of Argentina sent its reply on 26 August 1954.

4. The Secretary-General has also received a communication from the Government of Burma, dated 4 September 1954, stating that it had no comments to offer on the aforesaid report.

5. Comments received are reproduced below. Additional comments received from Governments subsequent to the compilation of the present document, if any, will be reproduced as addenda.

COMMENTS BY GOVERNMENTS

1. ARGENTINA

Note verbale *dated 26 August 1954 from the permanent delegation of Argentina*

[*Original text : Spanish*]

The permanent delegation of the Argentine Republic to the United Nations presents its compliments to the Secretariat of the United Nations and has the honour to refer to letter No. LEG 460/3/02(1) of 2 December 1953 on the question of defining aggression.

The Argentine Government has studied the Special Committee's report and the draft definitions submitted by various delegations. Although it regards these as a praiseworthy effort to solve a very difficult problem, it does not believe that they will lead to a satisfactory solution.

Therefore, consistently with the stand it has taken on previous occasions and, more particularly, with the position adopted by its delegation in the Sixth Committee during the seventh session of the General Assembly, the Argentine Republic still considers it inadvisable to attempt to encompass within a definition a legal situation that is in the process of development. Any definition adopted should be sufficiently broad to include not only the classical concept of armed aggression but other forms also, and particularly indirect forms, such as economic and ideological aggression, in which arms are not employed.

2. BYELORUSSIAN SOVIET SOCIALIST REPUBLIC

Cablegram *dated 29 June 1954 from the Ministry for Foreign Affairs of the Byelorussian Soviet Socialist Republic*

[*Original text : Russian*]

In reply to letter LEG.460/3/02(1) of 2 December 1953..., I have the honour to state hereby that the Government of the Byelorussian Soviet Socialist Republic supports the points contained in the draft resolution on the definition of aggression submitted by the representative of the Soviet Union in August 1953 at the session of the United Nations Special Committee on the Question of Defining Aggression.

(*Signed*) K. KISELEV
Minister for Foreign Affairs

3. DENMARK

Letter *dated 9 April 1954 from the Ministry for Foreign Affairs of Denmark*

[*Original text : English*]

With reference to your letter of 2 December 1953— LEG.460/3/02(1)—regarding the Special Committee's report on the question of defining aggression, I have the honour to inform you that the report has received the careful attention of the Danish Government who, considering, *inter alia*, the diversity of opinions set forth in the course of the Committee's meetings, still holds the view expressed by Danish delegates in earlier United Nations debates on this matter, that it seems doubtful whether, for the time being, it can be considered possible or even desirable to formulate a definition of aggression.

(*Signed*) Georg COHN

4. FRANCE

Letter *dated 16 June 1954 from the Ministry for Foreign Affairs of France*

[*Original text : French*]

By your letter No. LEG. 460/3/02(1) of 2 December 1953 you were good enough to transmit to me the report of the Special Committee on the Question of Defining Aggression and to invite me to communicate to you the French Government's comments thereon.

I have the honour to inform you herewith of my Government's views on the subject :

1. As is evident from the discussions in the General Assembly of the United Nations in 1952 and 1953, from the letter I addressed to you on 25 June 1952, and from the position taken by the representative of France in the Special Committee on the Question of Defining Aggression, the French Government has consistently taken the view that a definition of aggression is feasible and desirable for the maintenance of international peace and security. That view, to which the French Government still adheres, was endorsed by the General Assembly resolution of 20 December 1952.

2. As the representative of France pointed out during the debate in the Special Committee, the French Government favours the inclusion of a definition of aggression in the code of offences against the peace and security of mankind, along with the establishment of an international criminal court. That inclusion would not be a duplication nor would it be inconsistent with the adoption, in the form of a General Assembly resolution, of a definition of aggression capable of serving as a guide to States and to the political organs of the United Nations. Whereas the former type of definition would have the force of a provision of criminal law and, as such, would have to be applied by the competent jurisdictional body, the latter type of definition would merely serve as a point of reference for Member States, the Security Council and the General Assembly, which would retain the freedom of judgment granted to them by the Charter.

3. The French Government considers that the General Assembly should, as an act of co-operation, attempt to evolve "a mixed definition". While it is not in a position at the present stage to take a final stand on the proposals submitted to the Special Committee and annexed to its report, the French Government is prepared to co-operate in the search for a text that can command authority only if it gains a sufficiently wide measure of acceptance.

(Signed) A. PARODI

5. GREECE

Letter dated 26 April 1954 from the permanent delegation of Greece to the United Nations

[Original text: French]

In reply to your letter LEG.460/3/02(1) of 2 December 1953 concerning the observations that the Greek Government might wish to make upon the report of the Special Committee on the Question of Defining Aggression, I have the honour to inform you that my Government has studied that report with close attention.

Although the Greek delegation to the General Assembly took a sceptical view of the feasibility and desirability of defining aggression, my Government will certainly instruct its delegation to the forthcoming session of the General Assembly to co-operate with other delegations, should the General Assembly decide, after considering the valuable report of the Special Committee, to continue its efforts to evolve a definition of aggression acceptable to the great majority of States Members of the United Nations.

(Signed) Stavros G. ROUSSOS
Chargé d'Affaires ad interim

6. INDIA

Letter dated 6 July 1954 from the Ministry of External Affairs of India

[Original text: English]

I am directed to refer to your letter No. LEG.460/3/02 (1), dated 2 December 1953, and to say that the Government of India have no comments to offer at present on the report of the Special Committee on the question of defining aggression. I am to add that their representative on the Sixth Committee of the General Assembly will, however, be authorized to make a statement on the subject during the ninth session, if that is considered necessary.

(Signed) T. J. NATARAJAN
Deputy Secretary

7. POLAND

Letter dated 10 June 1954 from the permanent delegation of Poland

[Original text: French]

In reply to your letter No. LEG.460/3/02(1) of 2 December 1953, I have the honour to inform you that the Government of the People's Republic of Poland continues to adhere to the point of view expressed by its representatives at the seventh session of the General Assembly and at the meetings of the Special Committee on the Question of Defining Aggression.

(Signed) H. BIRECKI
Permanent Representative of Poland to the United Nations

8. SWEDEN

Letter dated 21 July 1954 from the Ministry of Foreign Affairs of Sweden

[Original text: English]

In reply to your letter of 2 December 1953/LEG.460/3/02(1), inviting the Swedish Government to present their comments on the report of the Special Committee on the Question of Defining Aggression, I have the honour to transmit the following observations:

The need for a definition of aggression may arise in relation to:

(a) General principles laid down in international treaties or conventions condemning war of aggression;

(b) Rules conferring on an international body, e.g., the Security Council of the United Nations, the authority or the duty to take steps for the stopping of aggressive war;

(c) Provisions in an international convention on the outlawing of war, whereby aggressive war is made a criminal offence and the authors of the war are made liable to punishment, to be imposed by tribunal, in the first place an international criminal court.

It is far from certain, however, that the same definition can be applied in these different connexions, or even that the needs for a definition makes itself as strongly felt in the various cases. These will now be examined in the order as set forth above.

(a) *The banning, per se, of aggressive war*, i.e., without sanctions against the violating of the ban.

As an example of such a "platonic" prohibition may be cited the resolution of the League of Nations Assembly of 24 September 1927, by which it was declared that wars of aggression should be prohibited, that international disputes should always be settled by pacific means, and that the Members of the League of Nations were under an obligation to conform to these principles.

The need for a definition in such cases mainly arises from the interest of the States concerned to know the delimitation between the unlawful war of aggression and the lawful war of defence. A definition of aggression provides, by implication, an answer to the question of what should be recognized as defensive war. The use of armed force in order to resist unlawful aggression should be regarded as a war of defence. Hence, the more extensive is the concept of aggression, the more extensive becomes the concept of legitimate defence.

In the category of prohibitions *per se* should also be listed the Briand-Kellogg Pact, concluded in 1928, by which the Contracting Parties declared that they refrained from war as an instrument of national policy and would employ only pacific means for the settling of international disputes.

In the Charter of the United Nations a ban is proclaimed by Article 2, paragraph 4, according to which "All Members shall refrain in their international relations from the threat or use of force against the territorial integrity or political independence of any state, or in any other manner inconsistent with the Purposes of the United Nations".

This provision does not carry any definition of aggression. Since in Article 1, paragraph 1, and in Article 39, there is a distinction between "acts of aggression" and other breaches of the peace, it is evident that the Charter takes into account the existence of other forms of breaches of the peace than aggression.

In certain respects the ban of the United Nations Charter resembles that of the Kellogg Pact. A violation of the ban is not to be followed unconditionally by sanctions, whether as applied by the Security Council or by individual Member States. Any coercive measure is subject to a decision by the Security Council, acting on the merits of free inquiry into the facts. There is consequently no obligation for the Security Council to institute coercive measures in the event of a breach of the peace or act of aggression. The Council may forgo any decision on the taking of coercive action, even though there has been a breach of the peace or act of aggression. On the other hand, such action may already be taken in the presence of a threat to the peace.

The similarity of the ban under the Charter to that of the Kellogg Pact also extends to the rules governing the action to be taken against an aggressor. According to Article 51, no provision of the Charter (thus not even Article 2, paragraph 4) shall impair the inherent right of individual or collective self-defence in the event of an armed attack. This implies, just as does the Kellogg Pact, that the aggressor not only may be faced with the self-defence of the aggrieved party but also lays himself open to armed intervention by other States. Considering the interdependence betwen unlawful aggression and legitimate self-defence, the provision in Article 51 may serve to clarify the concept of aggression in the sense of the Charter: only armed attack (*agression armée*) is deemed to constitute aggression.

No disadvantage of a practical nature is likely to arise from such a limitation of the concept of aggression. It should be remembered that the prohibition of resort to force as set out by Article 2, paragraph 4, has a meaning considerably wider than armed attack. Thus, there should be no practical need for defining exactly, in spite of Article 2, paragraph 4, the concept of aggression as against other modes of action.

(b) In a *system of collective security*, where, in the event of war, joint measures are to be taken against the aggressor, the concept of aggression is evidently of importance.

This was the case under the régime of the League of Nations. By the Covenant, Members of the League had assumed certain obligations not to resort to war. Every war was not, therefore, an unlawful war; but should an unlawful war take place—that is, should a State resort to war contrary to its obligations under the Covenant—sanctions were to be applied against the aggressor by the Members of the League. Such action should be taken on their own initiative, regardless of any decision by a body of the League. It was therefore important that a clear distinction should be drawn between "unlawful" and "lawful" wars, so that the "unlawful" wars were easily recognizable. According to the Covenant, the criterion to be applied was, *inter alia*, the attitude taken by the aggressor towards the provisions of the Covenant for the pacific settlement of international disputes. If a State went to war without previous resort to one of the methods for pacific settlement afforded by the Covenant, or if it did not conform with the anti-

cipatory settlement resulting from the use of one of these methods but instead went to war, such a State would then have acted contrary to its obligations under the Covenant and was to be subjected, unconditionally, to sanctions. "Unlawful war" had thus been defined in one particular respect, but no exhaustive definition had been provided. The idea behind the Covenant provisions was, however, that a spontaneous resort to armed force, without regard to existing procedures for peaceful settlement, constituted unlawful aggression. There remained the question as to how it should be determined who was the aggressor. The sanctions were to be directed against the aggressor, but the Covenant offered no method for establishing who he was. This limitation was looked upon as a serious disadvantage, particularly by those who advocated the widest measure of automatic application for sanctions. Numerous proposals for solving this problem were put forward in the course of a discussion that lasted almost throughout the lifetime of the League.

Several of the proposals put forward during this discussion were aimed less at a definition of the act of aggression than at establishing who was the aggressor. An example is afforded by the Geneva Protocol, voted by the League Assembly in 1924 but never ratified. In this it was declared, first, that every State that resorts to war in violation of the undertakings contained in the Covenant or the Protocol is an aggressor. Furthermore, a number of presumptions for aggression were put forward that could be reversed only by a unanimous decision of the Council. Under these presumptions any State was deemed to be an aggressor that had, in the event of hostilities, refused to submit the dispute to arbitration or other pacific procedure. In the absence of such presumptions the Council should directly determine who was the aggressor. For this purpose it could enjoin an armistice upon the belligerents, in which case a belligerent refusing to accept the armistice or violating its terms should be deemed an aggressor. The proposals that were subsequently put forward, in connexion with the treatment of the problem of security by the League, revolved to a great extent round the idea that the action of the League, in the first place that of the Council, should be directed towards forestalling and stopping hostilities. The attitude taken by the parties to the dispute towards recommendations by the Council to this end was to form a criterion as to who was the aggressor.

At the Disarmament Conference, opened in 1932, the question of a definition of the aggressor was brought to the fore in connexion with the question of security. In the early part of 1933 the Soviet delegation to the Conference put forward certain proposals which have since reappeared, with some variation.

The Soviet proposals were referred to the Security Committee and formed the basis for a definition evolved by the Committee, which was presented to the Conference with a report by M. Politis. The main idea behind this formula was that any State that first employs armed force outside its territory is an aggressor.

A definition of this kind, which might serve the Security Council of the United Nations as a guide without impairing its discretion in regard to sanctions, would, in the opinion of the Swedish Government, be well worth considering. It should be remembered, however, that the proposal under review does not settle the question of how to determine who is the aggressor when opinions are at variance as to the actual course of events. Theoretically speaking, this question could be solved either by a special rule of voting or by a system of presumptions combined with authority for the international body concerned to enjoin an armistice, i.e., the system of the Geneva Protocol.

The United Nations system for the maintenance of peace and security differs from that of the League of Nations as regards the prerequisites for the imposing of coercive measures (sanctions). It rests with the discretion of the United Nations Security Council whether such measures shall be taken, the Council having previously determined the existence of a "threat to the peace, breach of the peace, or act of aggression". An act of aggression may, of course, provide grounds for a decision that coercive measures should be taken. Such measures may also be decided upon in the event of a "threat to the peace" or "breach of the peace". Even though, on the other hand, there has been an "act of aggression", the Security Council, as has already been pointed out, is under no obligation to decide that coercive measures should be applied.

The purpose of any action taken by the Security Council is exclusively that of safeguarding peace if it is threatened, or restoring peace if it has been broken, and thus not to punish an act of aggression by reason of its being a breach of international law. Hence, the Security Council has no reason to concern itself with such matters as the responsibility for the war, the motives underlying the aggression, or which of the parties can claim historical justice for its cause.

(c) *Aggression regarded as a crime against international law*

A definition of aggression naturally becomes of importance when aggression is to constitute a crime against international law for which punishment is to be imposed by an international court of justice. The principle of legality underlying the penal law of civilized States (*nullum crimen sine lege*) manifestly presupposes that the aggression to be punished as an unlawful act should be clearly defined.

The importance of a legal definition will nevertheless diminish if other acts calculated to endanger peace are being declared illegal.

In their draft Code of Offences against the Peace and Security of Mankind, put forward in 1951 (A/1858, paragraph 59), the International Law Commission defined as such an offence, in the first place, "Any act of aggression" (article 2, paragraph 1); but furthermore "Any threat by the authorities of a State to resort to an act of aggression against another State" (paragraph 2); "The preparation by the authorities of a State for the employment of armed force against another State" (paragraph 3); "The incursion into the territory of a State by armed bands acting for a political purpose" (paragraph 4); "The undertaking or encouragement by the authorities of a State of activities calculated to foment civil strife in another State, or the toleration by the authorities of a State of organized acivities" for such purposes (paragraph 5).

Here it should again be recalled that the interdependence between aggression and self-defence makes the latter concept a wider one, in as far as a wider significance is given to the former. If, as is the case in the most recent Soviet draft definition, "aggression" is to include "indirect aggression", "economic aggression" and "ideological aggression", it obviously follows that a right to self-defence by armed force is enjoyed, for example, when a State prevents another State from exploiting its natural resources or promotes propaganda of fascist views, etc. Such an extension of the concepts of aggression and self-defence would, in the Government's opinion, be undesirable.

To sum up, the Government's views may be stated as follows:

The question as to what benefit might be drawn from a definition of the concept of aggression, and what the contents of such a definition would be, should be answered with due regard to the circumstances to which the definition is to apply.

(a) As regards the need for a definition referring to a ban on aggressive war, couched in general terms, a detailed and precise description of the elements constituting such a war would hardly seem to be required. It is sufficient to describe as an aggressor any State that first resorts to armed force against another State, provided the armed force has not been expressly declared as legal (e.g., assistance rendered to a third State that is being attacked).

(b) The need for a definition is more clearly felt in a system of collective security, with an international body authorized to impose sanctions on the aggressor. Since, however, the United Nations Charter confers upon the Security Council discretionary powers to act, or not to act, in the event of an aggression on the one hand or in the presence of a threat to the peace without aggression on the other hand, a comprehensive and precise definition would even in that case be unnecessary.

The Government is however, prepared to recognize the advantages to be gained from certain indications in this respect to the Security Council. These might be afforded by stating a number of examples of modes of aggression, to serve the Council as a guide without prejudice to its discretion. A suitable description might be obtained from the draft project adopted by the Disarmament Conference in 1933.

(c) Should aggression be constituted a crime under international law and referred to the jurisdiction of a court of law, a precise definition would naturally be required.

It should be recalled, however, that the Swedish Government has previously expressed strong doubts as to the expediency of setting up a criminal court entrusted with cases of this nature.

(*Signed*) For the Minister
Sture PETRÉN
Chief of Legal Department

9. UKRAINIAN SOVIET SOCIALIST REPUBLIC

Note verbale *dated 29 June 1954 from the Ministry for Foreign Affairs of the Ukrainian Soviet Socialist Republic*

[*Original text: Russian*]

The Ministry for Foreign Affairs of the Ukrainian Soviet Socialist Republic presents its respects to the Secretary-General of the United Nations and, in reply to letter No. LEG.460/3/02(1) of 2 December 1953 from the Principal Director of the Legal Department of the United Nations Secretariat, has the honour to state that the point of view of the Government of the Ukrainian Soviet Socialist Republic on the question of defining aggression was expressed during the discussion of that question in the United Nations, and that, moreover, the Government of the Ukrainian Soviet Socialist Republic supports the USSR draft resolution annexed to the report of the United Nations Special Committee on the Question of Defining Aggression (A/1638).

10. UNION OF SOVIET SOCIALIST REPUBLICS

Letter *dated 12 July 1954 from the Permanent Delegation of the Union of Soviet Socialist Republics*

[*Original text: Russian*]

With reference to your letter No. LEG.460/3/02(1) of 2 December 1953, I would inform you that the position of the Government of the Union of Soviet Socialist

Republics on the question of defining aggression has been exhaustively expounded in the United Nations, notably in the Special Committee on the Question of Defining Aggression. There is therefore no need to restate it now in connexion with the Special Committee's report.

(Signed) S. TSARAPKIN
Acting Permanent Representative of the USSR to the United Nations

11. UNITED KINGDOM OF GREAT BRITAIN AND NORTHERN IRELAND

Comments transmitted by a letter dated 12 May 1954 from the Permanent Delegation of the United Kingdom to the United Nations

[*Original text : English*]

Her Majesty's Government in the United Kingdom have studied the report of the Special Committee on the Question of Defining Aggression and wish to offer the following comments.

Her Majesty's Government note that the report reveals that there was a wide divergence of opinion between members of the Committee concerning the desirability and the feasibility of attempting to define aggression, and that in spite of a number of meetings there appeared to be no substantial advance towards agreement on the question at issue. While in principle they would not be averse to a definition of aggression, Her Majesty's Government have always doubted whether it is possible to evolve an entirely satisfactory definition which would not over-simplify the issue or leave loop-holes which would by implication exonerate acts not expressly included in the definition. Those doubts have been expressed by the representatives of the United Kingdom in the General Assembly and in the Special Committee, and the report of the Special Committee has done nothing to remove the doubts of Her Majesty's Government on this subject.

The views of Her Majesty's Government having been made clear on so many occasions in United Nations meetings, it would not seem that any useful purpose would be served by commenting at any greater length on the report of the Special Committee. Her Majesty's Government naturally reserve, however, the right to comment further if an item on this subject is eventually accepted for inclusion in the agenda of the ninth session of the General Assembly.

DOCUMENT A/C.6/L.332/Rev.1

Union of Soviet Socialist Republics : draft resolution

[*Original text : Russian*]
[*18 October 1954*]

The General Assembly,

Considering it necessary to establish guiding principles with a view to determining which party is guilty of aggression,

Declares that :

1. In an international conflict that State shall be declared the attacker which first commits one of the following acts :

(a) Declaration of war against another State ;

(b) Invasion by its armed forces, even without a declaration of war, of the territory of another State ;

(c) Bombardment by its land, sea or air forces of the territory of another State or the carrying out of a deliberate attack on the ships or aircraft of the latter ;

(d) The landing or leading of its land, sea or air forces inside the boundaries of another State without the permission of the Government of the latter, or the violation of the conditions of such permission, particularly as regards the length of their stay or the extent of the area in which they may stay ;

(e) Naval blockade of the coasts or ports of another State ;

(f) Support of armed bands organized in its own territory which invade the territory of another State, or refusal, on being requested by the invaded State, to take in its own territory any action within its power to deny such bands any aid or protection.

2. That State shall be declared to have committed an act of indirect aggression which :

(a) Encourages subversive activity against another State (acts of terrorism, diversionary acts, etc.) ;

(b) Promotes the fomenting of civil war within another State ;

(c) Promotes an internal upheaval in another State or a change of policy in favour of the aggressor.

3. That State shall be declared to have committed an act of economic aggression which first commits one of the following acts :

(a) Takes against another State measures of economic pressure violating its sovereignty and economic independence and threatening the bases of its economic life ;

(b) Takes against another State measures preventing it from exploiting or nationalizing its own natural riches ;

(c) Subjects another State to an economic blockade.

4. That State shall be declared to have committed an act of ideological aggression which :

(a) Encourages war propaganda ;

(b) Encourages propaganda in favour of using atomic, bacterial, chemical and other weapons of mass destruction ;

(c) Promotes the propagation of fascist-nazi views, of racial and national exclusiveness, and of hatred and contempt for other peoples.

5. Acts committed by a State other than those listed in the preceding paragraphs may be deemed to constitute aggression if declared by decision of the Security Council in a particular case to be an attack or an act of economic, ideological or indirect aggression.

6. The attacks referred to in paragraph 1 and the acts of economic, ideological and indirect aggression referred to in paragraphs 2, 3 and 4 may not be justified by any considerations of a political, strategic or economic nature, or by the desire to exploit natural riches in the territory of the State attacked or to derive any other kind of advantages or privileges, or by reference to the amount of capital invested in that territory or to any other particular interests in that territory, or by the refusal to recognize that it possesses the distinguishing marks of statehood.

In particular, the following may not be used as justification :

A. The internal situation of any State, as for example :

(a) Backwardness of any people politically, economically or culturally ;

(b) Alleged shortcomings of its administration ;

(c) Any danger which may threaten the life or property of aliens ;

(d) Any revolutionary or counter-revolutionary movement, civil war, disorders or strikes ;

(e) Establishment or maintenance in any State of any political, economic or social system.

B. Any acts, legislation or orders of any State, as for example :

(a) Violation of international treaties ;

(b) Violation of rights and interests in the sphere of trade, concessions or any kind of economic activity acquired by another State or its citizens ;

(c) Rupture of diplomatic or economic relations ;

(d) Measures constituting an economic or financial boycott ;

(e) Repudiation of debts ;

(f) Prohibition or restriction of immigration or modification of the status of foreigners ;

(g) Violation of privileges recognized to the official representatives of another State ;

(h) Refusal to allow the passage of armed forces proceeding to the territory of a third State ;

(i) Measures of a religious or anti-religious nature ;

(j) Frontier incidents.

7. In the event of the mobilization or concentration by another State of considerable armed forces near its frontier, the State which is threatened by such action shall have the right of recourse to diplomatic or other means of securing a peaceful settlement of international disputes. It may also in the meantime take countermeasures of a military nature similar to those described above, without, however, crossing the frontier.

DOCUMENT A/C.6/L.334/Rev.1

Paraguay : draft resolution

[Original text : Spanish]
[28 October 1954]

The General Assembly,

Considering that at its 368th plenary meeting it resolved "that, although the existence of the crime of aggression may be inferred from the circumstances peculiar to each particuliar case, it is nevertheless possible and desirable, with a view to ensuring international peace and security and to developing international criminal law, to define aggression by reference to the elements which constitute it " (resolution 599 (VI)),

Declares :

1. A State (or States) commits (or commit) armed aggression if it (or they) provokes (or provoke) a breach or disturbance of international peace and security through the employment of armed force against the territory, population, armed forces or the sovereignty and political independence of another State (or other States), or against the people, the territory or the armed forces of a Non-Self-Governing Territory ;

2. Without prejudice to the provisions of Article 39 of the Charter, the General Assembly recommends that in addition to other acts of aggression the following acts shall be deemed to constitute armed aggression :

(a) A declaration of war by one State against another (or others) in contravention of Articles 1 and 2 of the Charter ;

(b) The organization by a State within its territory of armed bands intended to take action against other States, either within or outside the territory of such States ; or the encouragement, support or the mere toleration of the formation or action of such armed bands in its territory.

Nevertheless, a State shall not be considered to be an aggressor if, being unable to suppress the activities of such bands in its territory or having justifiable reasons for not undertaking their suppression, it reports the matter to the competent organ of the United Nations and offers its co-operation.

DOCUMENT A/C.6/L.335 [2] and DOCUMENT A/C.6/L.335/Rev.1

Iran and Panama : revised draft resolution

[Original text : Spanish]
[6 November 1954]

The General Assembly,

Considering that, although the existence of aggression may be inferred from the circumstances peculiar to each particular case, it is nevertheless possible and desirable, with a view to ensuring international peace and security

and to developing international criminal law, to define aggression by reference to the elements which constitute it,

Considering further that it would be of definite advantage if directives were formulated for the future guidance of such international bodies as may be called upon to determine the aggressor,

Declares that :

1. Aggression is the use of armed force by a State against another State for any purpose other than the exercise of the inherent right of individual or collective self-defence or in pursuance of a decision or recommendation of a competent organ of the United Nations.

---

[2] The text of A/C.6/L.335, of 3 November 1954, not reproduced in this fascicule, is identical in substance to this text, except for the following differences : in A/C.6/L.335, operative paragraphs 1 an 2 (d) were worded as follows : "1. Aggression means any use of armed force by a State against another State for any purpose other than the exercise of the inherent right of individual or collective self-defence..." and "(d) The organization, or the encouragement of the organization, by the authorities or a State..."

2. In accordance with the foregoing definition, in addition to any other acts which such international bodies as may be called upon to determine the aggressor may declare to constitute aggression, the following are acts of aggression in all cases:

(a) Invasion by the armed forces of a State of territory belonging to another State or under the effective jurisdiction of another State;

(b) Armed attack against the territory, population or land, sea or air forces of a State by the land, sea or air forces of another State;

(c) Blockade of the coast or ports or any other part of the territory of a State by the land, sea or air forces of another State;

(d) The organization, or the encouragement of the organization, by a State, of armed bands within its territory or any other territory for incursions into the territory of another State, or the toleration of the organization of such bands in its own territory, or the toleration of the use by such armed bands of its territory as a base of operations or as a point of departure for incursions into the territory of another State, as well as direct participation in or support of such incursions.

DOCUMENT A/C.6/L.336/Rev.1 [3] and DOCUMENT A/C.6/L.336/Rev.2

China: revised draft resolution

[Original text: English]
[10 November 1954]

The General Assembly,

Recalling its resolutions 599 (VI) and 688 (VII),

Having considered the report of the Special Committee on the Question of Defining Aggression,

Mindful of the responsibilities of the Security Council concerning aggression under Article 1, paragraph 1, and Chapter VII of the Charter, and of the function of the General Assembly envisaged in Assembly resolution 377 A (V),

Considering that, although the question whether aggression has occurred must be determined in the circumstances of each particular case, it would nevertheless be advisable to formulate certain principles as guidance,

Recommends that the Security Council in the discharge of its responsibilities under Article 1, paragraph 1, and Chapter VII of the Charter, and the Members of the United Nations, when the Assembly is called upon to consider an item pursuant to resolution 377 A (V), take account, *inter alia*, of the following principles:

1. That aggression is the unlawful use of force by a State against another State, whether directly or indirectly, such as:

(a) Attack or invasion by armed force;

(b) Organization or support of incursion of armed bands;

(c) Promotion or support of organized activities in another State aiming at the overthrow by violence of its political or social institutions;

2. That the use of force is lawful when it is in pursuance of a decision or recommendation by a competent organ of the United Nations, or is in self-defence against armed attack until a competent organ of the United Nations has taken the measures necessary to maintain international peace and security;

3. That the employment of measures, other than armed attack, necessary to remove the danger arising from an indirect use of force is likewise lawful until a competent organ of the United Nations has taken steps to remove such danger.

DOCUMENT A/C.6/L.337 [4] and DOCUMENT A/C.6/L.337/Rev.1

Lebanon, Syria, and Yemen: revised draft resolution

[Original text: French]
[9 November 1954]

The General Assembly,

Recalling its resolutions 599 (VI) and 688 (VII),

Considering that the discussions to which the question of defining aggression gave rise at the ninth session of

the General Assembly have revealed the need to co-ordinate the views expressed by the State Members,

1. *Decides* to establish a Special Committee comprising one representative of each of the following State Members: ...

2. *Requests* the said Special Committee to submit to the General Assembly at its eleventh session a detailed report followed by a draft definition of aggression, having regard to the ideas expressed at the ninth session of the General Assembly and to the draft resolutions and amendments submitted;

3. *Decides* to place the question on the agenda of the eleventh session of the General Assembly.

---

[3] The text of document A/C.6/L.336/Rev.1, of 4 November 1954, not reproduced in this fascicule, is identical with this text, except for the following difference: in document A/C.6/L.336/Rev.1, point 1 included a sub-paragraph (c) worded as follows: "fomenting civil strife"; and sub-paragraph (c) of the present text was sub-paragraph (d).

[4] The text of A/C.6/L.337, of 5 November 1954, not reproduced in this fascicule, is identical in substance to this document, except for the following difference: in operative paragraphs 2 and 3 the text specified "tenth session" instead of "eleventh session".

DOCUMENT A/C.6/L.337/Add.1 [5]

Financial implications of draft resolution submitted by Lebanon, Syria and Yemen (A/C.6/L.337/Rev.1) [5]

Estimate submitted by the Secretary-General

[Original text: English]
[9 November 1954]

1. The draft resolution contained in A/C.6/L.337/Rev.1 [5] proposes the establishment of a Special Committee consisting of representatives of Member States to prepare a detailed report followed by a draft definition of aggression, for submission to the eleventh session of the General Assembly.

2. It is assumed that the Special Committee would meet at Headquarters and would be suitably scheduled within the 1956 conference programme.

3. It is also assumed that the proposed meeting would be of three to four weeks' duration; that the amount of documentation would be similar to the workload of the

Special Committee established under General Assembly resolution 688 (VII) which met in 1953; and that the expenses of representatives would be borne by their Governments.

4. Under the above assumptions, financial implications in the amount of $1,500 would arise in connexion with the printing (in five languages) of the report requested in paragraph 2 of the draft resolution.

5. Should the proposal be approved by the General Assembly, the Secretary-General would request an additional appropriation of $1,500 under Section 24 of his Budget Estimates for 1956.

DOCUMENT A/2806

Report of the Sixth Committee

[Original text: French]
[2 December 1954]

1. At its 477th plenary meeting, held on 24 September 1954, the General Assembly decided, in accordance with its resolution 688 (VII) of 20 December 1952, to place the following item on the agenda of its ninth regular session: "Question of defining aggression: report of the Special Committee on the Question of Defining Aggression" At its 478th plenary meeting, on 25 September, the General Assembly decided to refer that item to the Sixth Committee for study and report.

2. The Sixth Committee studied the item from its 403rd to 420th meetings, held between 14 October and 10 November 1954. It had before it the report of the Special Committee on the Question of Defining Aggression (A/2638), together with the text of the comments received from Governments regarding that report (A/2689 and Corr.1, A/2689/Add.1).

3. The following draft resolutions, each containing a definition of aggression, were successively submitted to the Committee:

(a) A draft resolution proposed by the Union of Soviet Socialist Republics (A/C.6/L.332/Rev.1).

(b) A draft resolution proposed by Paraguay (A/C.6/L.334/Rev.1).

(c) A draft resolution proposed jointly by Iran and Panama (A/C.6/L.335) which was later superseded by a revised draft resolution proposed by the same countries (A/C.6/L.335/Rev.1).

(d) A draft resolution proposed by China (A/C.6/L.336) which was replaced successively by two revised draft resolutions proposed by the same country (A/C.6/L.336/Rev.1 and 2).

4. The Committee also had before it two proposals relating to a procedural question.

5. The first, put forward orally by Iran, proposed the establishment of a working group to draw up a single text of a definition that would be acceptable to the great majority of Member States.

6. The second proposal formed the subject of the draft resolution proposed jointly by Lebanon, Syria and Yemen (A/C.6/L.337). Under the terms of that draft resolution, the General Assembly was to decide to establish a special committee that would be requested to submit to the General Assembly at its tenth session a detailed report followed by a draft definition of aggression, having regard to the ideas expressed at the ninth session and to the draft resolutions and amendments submitted. That draft resolution was subsequently replaced by a revised text (A/C.6/L.337/Rev.1), which provided that the special committee would submit its report to the General Assembly at the eleventh (instead of the tenth) session.

7. The sponsors of the joint draft resolution (A/C.6/L.337/Rev.1) amended their text orally at the 419th meeting, proposing that the special committee referred to in the text should meet at United Nations Headquarters in 1956.

8. The Sixth Committee opened the debate with a general discussion of the various problems raised by the question of defining aggression.

9. With regard to the preliminary question of whether it was possible and desirable to define aggression, many delegations considered that the matter had been decided affirmatively by the General Assembly in its resolutions 599 (VI) and 688 (VII), adopted on 31 January and 20 December 1952 respectively.

10. Some delegations pointed out, however, that that affirmative decision of the General Assembly had been adopted by a small majority. Others stated that it would have been more prudent to determine first of all whether

a satisfactory definition of aggression was possible ; if no satisfactory definition of aggression was possible, any definition of that concept would be not only undesirable but dangerous. It was also said that while the General Assembly had decided that it was juridically possible to define aggression, the proceedings of the present session of the General Assembly alone would show whether it was practically and politically feasible to draft such a definition.

11. Certain delegations contended that aggression was undefinable. They argued that the failure of past attempts made to define aggression proved that it was impossible to reach agreement on an *a priori* definition. Moreover, such a definition could not inspire confidence. It would be much better to allow the law to evolve empirically from specific cases.

12. A number of delegations held that even if a definition of aggression were worked out, it would be not only useless but actually dangerous. Far from discouraging a would-be aggressor, it would merely work to his victim's disadvantage. Only the risks involved, the chances of success or the possibilities of failure, would determine the conduct of aggressors. Moreover, a definition of aggression adopted under a General Assembly resolution—and hence binding neither on the Security Council nor on Member States—would have no effect of itself. In an actual case of aggression it would do little good and might even be harmful, since it would lead to long theoretical discussions that would delay a solution. A definition, even if accepted and solemnly embodied in a treaty, would be of little practical value as an effective means of preventing aggression. A definition of aggression, however worded, would be easily evaded and would carry with it grave threats that might well assume as yet unforeseeable forms. Everyone could recognize aggression when it occurred and, apart perhaps from definitions applicable regionally, it would be better not to have a definition. As far as the United Nations was concerned, however, the competent organs should be allowed to determine in each specific case whether or not aggression had occurred. Furthermore, it would be appropriate to defer any action in the matter until the new disarmament proposals had been studied at greater length and a decision taken on them.

13. Many delegations, on the other hand, considered that a definition of aggression was necessary and would be useful for the maintenance of international peace and security and that an attempt should therefore be made to formulate a definition that would be generally acceptable. Those delegations argued that a definition of aggression would consolidate the system of collective security established by the United Nations Charter and would promote the development of international law. Even if it would not *per se* prevent aggression it would be an important factor in the resistance against possible aggressors. In a world that lived in fear of aggression, the existence of a definition would do something to ease men's minds. A definition of aggression would enlighten public opinion and would ensure that any decisions made by the international organs called upon to designate the aggressor in a given dispute would be equitable. It was argued that while a definition of aggression adopted by the General Assembly would admittedly have merely the value of a recommendation and hence would not bind the Security Council, which would retain its complete freedom of action under Article 39 of the Charter, the General Assembly's recommendations yet had a certain legal value. A definition solemnly adopted by the General Assembly might become a general principle of law recognized by the civilized world and so might in future become an integral part of international law, which the Security Council could not violate.

14. Many delegations stated that no definition of aggression would be really useful unless it was accepted by a large majority of Member States. Some expressed the opinion that the majority should include the permanent members of the Security Council. Others suggested that the definition should be approved by at least a two-thirds majority, but not necessarily including all the permanent members of the Security Council.

15. With regard to the type of definition to be adopted, most delegations that favoured a definition of aggression recommended a mixed definition, that is, one in which a flexible description, couched in general terms, would precede and govern a list of definite acts of aggression, which would be included merely to illustrate and not to restrict the general description. It was said that a definition of that type would combine the advantages and avoid the defects of the two others types of definition, the general and the enumerative. It would accord with the opinion that a definition should be neither limitative nor rigid. It should not be limitative, not only for the practical reason that all possibilities in such a complex matter could not be foreseen, but also because any limitation would be contrary to the wide powers of judgment conferred upon the Security Council by Articles 24 and 39 of the Charter. It should not be rigid in the sense that it must not take the form of an order binding on States and on the competent organs of the United Nations.

16. Some delegations criticized a definition of that type as combining the defects of the other two types. In fact, it was suggested that a mixed definition would be in itself contradictory, because, if it started with the statement, for example, that aggression was the use of armed force for purposes other than self-defence or action undertaken in conformity with the Charter, it would not be possible to proceed further by giving examples in illustration of that concept. The act given as an example either would, or would not, according to the circumstances of the case, be covered by the general formula stated at the beginning. The opinion was also expressed that there would be no point in attaching a list of examples to the general statement. Thus the most familiar types of military aggression would be too standard to need enumeration, and a list might give the impression on the one hand that they could be isolated from the peculiar circumstances in which they occurred, and on the other hand that all other forms of armed aggression were of only secondary importance.

17. Other delegations declared themselves in favour of a general definition, that is, one that, instead of giving a list of acts of aggression, would contain a general formula covering all the cases to be designated. International organs would be left with the responsibility of establishing the scope of the formula in specific cases brought before them. Some of these delegations pointed out that a definition of that kind, covering in general terms all the elements that constituted aggression, would render any enumeration of definite acts of aggression superfluous. Others suggested that the general definition should be based on the Charter, which was said to contain all the elements of a definition of aggression. It should incorporate the principles of Article 2 (4) and Article 51 of the Charter. Such a definition would have the double advantage of covering all cases conceivable by the most fertile imagination and allowing the competent organ or organs of the United Nations full freedom of judgment.

18. That type of definition was, however, criticized by some delegations as being a mere repetition, in one form or another, of elementary truths ; it could therefore be of no value. It was also said that a general definition would be less dangerous than an enumerative definition,

but would be of little value because it would inevitably be drafted in terms that would themselves call for definition. Furthermore, a general definition whose basic elements could be found in the Charter would not be enough ; it was just because the Charter confined itself to dealing with the question in general terms that the General Assembly had thought it necessary to define aggression by reference to the elements that constituted it.

19. Some delegations criticized purely enumerative definitions. That kind of definition, which would be limitative and rigid and would deprive States and the organs of the United Nations of freedom of judgment, would in their opinion not be in conformity with the Charter. It would be incompatible with Articles 2 (1), 24 and 39 of the Charter and with the sovereignty of States and the principle of unanimity in the Security Council. Furthermore, such a definition would necessarily be incomplete and would leave loopholes for possible aggressors. It would also have the disadvantage that the acts listed might, in specific cases, not constitute acts of aggression.

20. With regard to content, in the view of certain delegations the definition should be confined to the notion of armed attack. It was said that, if the definition were extended to include the notion of indirect, economic, and ideological aggression, it would be a departure from the Charter, and neither the letter nor the spirit of the Charter would justify a broad interpretation of the word "aggression". Article 39 listed reprehensible acts in order of gravity, and to suggest that indirect, economic and ideological aggression constituted acts of aggression would be tantamount to considering them as more serious than threats to or breaches of the peace. Those concepts came under the heading of threats to the peace rather than under that of aggression, and it was the latter concept that the Sixth Committee was supposed to be defining. The definition of the other concepts might be considered after the preparation of a definition of armed aggression, or at least separately from it. It was also maintained that aggression as envisaged in Article 39 of the Charter and the armed attack mentioned in Article 51 were one and the same and would entail the same legal consequences. If the definition included forms of aggression not accompanied by the use of armed force, there would be a considerable increase in the number of cases in which the use of force would be justified by the right of self-defence. It was also said that by extending the definition of aggression to cases of indirect, economic and ideological aggression, the gravity of armed attack might be reduced and the term "aggression" would lose its force and acquire simply the meaning of "offence".

21. Other delegations pointed out that under the Charter aggression was not confined to the use of armed force. It was maintained that under Article 2 (4) of the Charter the term "aggression" would include not only armed attack but also indirect aggression, economic aggression, and ideological aggression. The principle of prohibiting economic aggression might also be inferred from other provisions of the Charter, such as the fourth paragraph of the Preamble and Article 55.

22. Some delegations, however, which thought that under the Charter indirect aggression, economic aggression, and ideological aggression might be included in the definition, pointed out that it would be better for the time being to confine the definition to armed attack, without prejudice to recognition of other forms of aggression.

23. Some delegations stressed the fact that, if the definition did not cover economic aggression or ideological aggression, it should at least include subversion, which

was the most typical form of indirect aggression. While subversion was a form of aggression less alarming than war, it was much more insidious and fully as dangerous. War was armed attack from outside, subversion armed attack from inside and accordingly should be outlawed equally with war. Any State that encouraged and assisted the people of another State to take up arms against its own Government was not less guilty than if it had itself taken part in an armed attack. The principle that the instigator of a crime is as guilty as the person committing it should apply both in international law and in domestic criminal law.

24. The opinion was expressed that the threat of force should be included in the definition. It was maintained that Article 2 (4) of the Charter would make it possible to put the threat of force on the same footing as aggression. The terms "the threat or use of force." mentioned in that paragraph corresponded to the term "aggression" in Article 39 and hardly had the same meaning as "threat to the peace" in the same article. But the threat of force must have a certain degree of gravity before it could constitute aggression. In determining that degree of gravity, it would be advisable to remember that in the Charter the word "aggression" had been used instead of the word "war". The decisive factor would not be the intention of the aggressor but the effect of the act. It was also stated, in relation to the question of whether self-defence was justified in face of the threat of force, that under Article 51 of the Charter the notion of armed attack would include immediate threats that left a State no other recourse than immediate exercise of its right of self-defence.

25. Many delegations maintained that the threat of force could not be considered as an element in the notion of aggression and that it would be dangerous to introduce it into a definition. Although under the terms of Article 39 of the Charter, there might be a difference between the threat of force and a threat to the peace, the threat of force in most cases constituted a threat to the peace and could therefore lead to action by the Security Council. Also, while Article 2 (4) of the Charter prohibited the threat of force, there was not in law sufficient reason to include the threat of force on an equal footing with the use of force in a definition of aggression. Furthermore, there was nothing that made it permissible to interpret Article 51 of the Charter in such a way as to conclude that the concept of armed attack set forth in that Article included the threat of force. The right of self-defence could not be exercised until an armed attack had occurred. Thus, threats of force should be excluded from the definition, so that they could not serve as a pretext for preventive war, which was not authorized under Article 51 of the Charter.

26. Some representatives held the view that the definition of aggression should take into account the aggressive intention that would be a characteristic of aggression. Others held the contrary view. They pointed out that no subjective elements could be taken into account in determining whether or not any given act could be considered as an act of aggression. Any provision that might give the impression that the absence of aggressive intention would abolish guilt would constitute an invitation to the use of subjective argument by possible aggressors.

27. In the opinion of some delegations, the chronological order of events would be an important criterion and might even be decisive in determining who was responsible for aggression. It was maintained that it would be necessary, when preparing a definition of aggression, to explain that the aggressor State would be that which first committed any of the acts enumerated in the

definition. A definition which neglected that principle of priority would not only be ambiguous, but might also be used as a justification for preventive war. In the opinion of other delegations, the chronological order of events could not stand because it would lead to dangerous consequences. An aggressor would not necessarily be the first to commit a given act considered as an act of aggression. Essentially, everything would depend on the circumstances peculiar to each particular case.

28. It was also proposed to include in the definition a certain number of circumstances which should in no case serve as a justification for aggression. That proposal was criticized by some delegations as likely to give the impression that other circumstances, not included in the definition, might justify aggression. Furthermore, it would be illogical to give various pretexts which could not serve as a justification for aggression when the basic principle was that nothing justified it.

29. At its 419th meeting, held on 10 November 1954, the Committee decided to vote first on two procedural proposals, one, an oral proposal for a working group, submitted by Iran, the other, appearing in a revised draft resolution proposed jointly by Lebanon, Syria and Yemen (A/C.6/L.337/Rev.1), for the establishment of a special committee.

30. When a vote was taken at that meeting, the first proposal was rejected by 22 votes to 17, with 9 abstentions.

31. At the 420th meeting, held on 10 November 1954, the Committee voted on the joint draft resolution proposed by Lebanon, Syria and Yemen (A/C.3/L.337/Rev.1), as amended orally by the sponsors (see paragraph 7 above). The draft resolution was adopted by 33 votes to 3, with 14 abstentions.

32. As that draft resolution had been adopted, the draft resolutions relating to the substance of the question were not put to the vote.

33. At its 424th meeting, held on 17 November 1954, the Committee decided, on the proposal of the Syrian representative, that the special committee whose establishment was proposed in the adopted draft resolution should consist of 19 member States.

34. At the 433rd meeting, held on 1 December 1954, the Chairman announced the membership that he suggested for the Special Committee. The Sixth Committee approved that proposal at its 434th meeting, held on the same day.

Recommendation of the Sixth Committee

35. The Sixth Committee therefore recommends to the General Assembly the adoption of the following draft resolution :

[*Text adopted without change by the General Assembly. See document A/RESOLUTION/243, below.*]

DOCUMENT A/RESOLUTION/243

[*Resolution 895 (IX)*]

Resolution adopted by the General Assembly at its 504th plenary meeting on 4 December 1954

QUESTION OF DEFINING AGGRESSION

The General Assembly,

Recalling its resolutions 599 (VI) of 31 January 1952 and 688 (VII) of 20 December 1952,

Considering that the discussions to which the question of defining aggression gave rise at the ninth session of the General Assembly have revealed the need to co-ordinate the views expressed by the States Members,

1. *Decides* to establish a Special Committee comprising one representative of each of the following States Members : China, Czechoslovakia, Dominican Republic, France, Iraq, Israel, Mexico, Netherlands, Norway, Panama, Paraguay, Peru, Philippines, Poland, Syria, Union of Soviet Socialist Republics, United Kingdom of Great Britain and Northern Ireland, United States of America and Yugoslavia, which will meet at United Nations Headquarters in 1956 ;

2. *Requests* the Special Committee to submit to the General Assembly at its eleventh session a detailed report followed by a draft definition of aggression, having regard to the ideas expressed at the ninth session of the General Assembly and to the draft resolutions and amendments submitted ;

3. *Decides* to place the question on the provisional agenda of the eleventh session of the General Assembly.

ACTION TAKEN BY THE GENERAL ASSEMBLY

At its 504th plenary meeting, on 4 December 1954, the General Assembly adopted the draft resolution submitted by the Sixth Committee. For the final text, see document A/RESOLUTION/243, above.

DOCUMENT 8

I. INTRODUCTION

1. Background of the question of defining aggression

1. Under resolution 378 B (V) of 17 November 1950, the General Assembly decided to refer a proposal of the Union of Soviet Socialist Republics concerning the definition of the notion of aggression (A/C.1/608)[1] and all the records of the First Committee dealing with that question to the International Law Commission, so that the latter might take them into consideration and formulate its conclusions as soon as possible.

2. The International Law Commission studied the question at its third session and dealt with it in chapter III of its report on the work of that session.[2]

3. At its 341st plenary meeting on 13 November 1951, the General Assembly decided to include the report of the International Law Commission in the agenda of its sixth session. At its 342nd plenary meeting on the same date, the Assembly referred the item to the Sixth Committee for study and report.

4. The Sixth Committee examined the question of defining aggression at its 278th to 295th meetings held from 5 January to 22 January 1952.[3]

5. At its 368th plenary meeting on 31 January 1952, the General Assembly adopted resolution 599 (VI), the text of which is as follows:

"The General Assembly,

"Considering that, under resolution 378 B (V) of 17 November 1950, it referred the question of defining aggression, raised in the draft resolution of the Union of Soviet Socialist Republics to the International Law Commission for examination in conjunction with matters which were under consideration by that Commission,

"Considering that the International Law Commission did not in its report furnish an express definition of aggression but merely included aggression among the offences defined in its draft Code of Offences against the Peace and Security of Mankind,

"Considering that the General Assembly, on 13 November 1951, decided not to examine the draft Code at its sixth session but to include it in the provisional agenda of its seventh session,

"Considering that, although the existence of the crime of aggression may be inferred from the circumstances peculiar to each particular case, it is nevertheless possible and desirable, with a view to ensuring international peace and security and to developing international criminal law, to define aggression by reference to the elements which constitute it,

"Considering further that it would be of definite advantage if directives were formulated for the future guidance of such international bodies as may be called upon to determine the aggressor,

"1. Decides to include in the agenda of its seventh session the question of defining aggression;

"2. Instructs the Secretary General to submit to the General Assembly at its seventh session a report in which the question of defining aggression shall be thoroughly discussed in the light of the views expressed in the Sixth Committee at the sixth session of the General Assembly and which shall duly take into account the draft resolutions and amendments submitted concerning this question;

"3. Requests States Members, when transmitting their observations on the draft Code to the Secretary-General, to give in particular their views on the problem of defining aggression."

6. In conformity with that resolution, the Secretary-General submitted a report (A/2211) to the General Assembly which decided, at its 380th plenary meeting on 16 October 1952, to include in the agenda of its seventh session the following item: "Question of defining aggression: report by the Secretary-General". The question was referred to the Sixth Committee which dealt with it at its 329th to 347th meetings held between 19 November and 11 December 1952.[4]

7. At its 408th plenary meeting on 20 December 1952, the General Assembly adopted resolution 688 (VII) reading as follows:

"The General Assembly,

"Having regard to its resolution 599 (VI) of 31 January 1952,

"Considering that the discussion of the question of defining aggression at the sixth and seventh sessions of the General Assembly and in the International Law Commission has revealed the complexity of this question and the need for a detailed study of:

"(a) The various forms of aggression,

"(b) The connexion between a definition of aggression and the maintenance of international peace and security,

"(c) The problems raised by the inclusion of a definition of aggression in the Code of Offences against the Peace and Security of Mankind and

---

[1] Official Records of the General Assembly, Fifth Session, Annexes, agenda item 72, p.4.

[2] Ibid., Sixth Session, Supplement No.9 (A/1858).

[3] For the report of the Sixth Committee, see Ibid., Annexes, agenda item 49, pp. 15-17, document A/2087.

[4] The report of the Secretary-General (A/2211) as well as the comments received from Governments (A/2162 and Add.1) and the report of the Sixth Committee (A/2322) may be found in Official Records of the General Assembly, Seventh Session, Annexes, agenda item 54.

by its application within the framework of international criminal jurisdiction,

"(d) The effect of a definition of aggression on the exercise of the jurisdiction of the various organs of the United Nations,

"(e) Any other problem which might be raised by a definition of aggression,

"Considering that continued and joint efforts shall be made to formulate a generally acceptable definition of aggression, with a view to promoting international peace and security and to developing international law,

"1. Decides to establish a Special Committee of fifteen members, each representing one of the following Member States: Bolivia, Brazil, China, Dominican Republic, France, Iran, Mexico, Netherlands, Norway, Pakistan, Poland, Syria, Union of Soviet Socialist Republics, United Kingdom of Great Britain and Northern Ireland, United States of America, to meet at the Headquarters of the United Nations in 1953;

"2. Requests the said Special Committee:

"(a) To submit to the General Assembly at its ninth session draft definitions of aggression or draft statements of the notion of aggression;

"(b) To study all the problems referred to above on the assumption of a definition being adopted by a resolution of the General Assembly;

"3. Requests the Secretary-General to communicate the Special Committee's report to Member States for their comments and to place the question on the provisional agenda of the ninth session of the General Assembly."

8. In conformity with that resolution, the 1953 Special Committee on the Question of Defining Aggression met at United Nations Headquarters, New York, from 24 August to 21 September 1953.

9. The Committee prepared a detailed report[5] in which were discussed the following questions: (a) the various types of definitions of aggression; (b) the various forms of aggression; (c) the connexion between a definition of aggression and the maintenance of international peace and security; (d) the problems raised by the inclusion of a definition of aggression in the Code of Offences against the Peace and Security of Mankind and by its application within the framework of international criminal jurisdiction; and (e) the effect of a definition of aggression on the exercise of the jurisdiction of the various organs of the United Nations. Several texts of definitions of aggression were submitted to the Committee, which decided, however, unanimously not to put these texts to a vote but to transmit them as they stood to Member

States and to the General Assembly. The texts were therefore annexed to the Committee's report.

10. The report of the 1953 Special Committee was circulated by the Secretary-General to the Member States for their comments; such comments were received from eleven Governments.[6]

11. The question was included in the provisional agenda of the ninth session of the General Assembly, and, at its 477th plenary meeting, on 24 September 1954, the Assembly decided to place the following items on the agenda of the session: "Question of defining aggression: report of the Special Committee on the Question of Defining Agression". At its 478th plenary meeting on 25 September, the Assembly referred the item to the Sixth Committee.

12. The Sixth Committee studied the item from its 403rd to 420th meetings held between 14 October and 10 November 1954.[7]

13. On the proposal of the Sixth Committee, the General Assembly, at its 504th plenary meeting on 4 December 1954, adopted resolution 895 (IX) which reads as follows:

"The General Assembly,

"Recalling its resolutions 599 (VI) of 31 January 1952 and 688(VII) of 20 December 1952,

"Considering that the discussions to which the question of defining aggression gave rise at the ninth session of the General Assembly have revealed the need to co-ordinate the views expressed by the States Members,

"1. Decides to establish a Special Committee comprising one representative of each of the following States Members: China, Czechoslovakia, Dominican Republic, France, Iraq, Israel, Mexico, Netherlands, Norway, Panama, Paraguay, Peru, Philippines, Poland, Syria, Union of Soviet Socialist Republics, United Kingdom of Great Britain and Northern Ireland, United States of America and Yugoslavia, which will meet at United Nations Headquarters in 1956;

"2. Requests the Special Committee to submit to the General Assembly at its eleventh session a detailed report followed by a draft definition of aggression, having regard to the ideas expressed at the ninth session of the General Assembly and to the draft resolutions and amendments submitted;

"3. Decides to place the question on the provisional agenda of the eleventh session of the General Assembly."

---

[6] Ibid., Annexes, agenda item 51, document A/2689 and Corr.1 and Add. 1.

[7] For the report of the Sixth Committee (A/2806) and the draft resolutions submitted to that Committee, see Ibid.

---

[5] Official Records of the General Assembly, Ninth Session, Supplement No. 11 (A/2638).

2. Organization of the work of the Committee

14. In pursuance of resolution 895 (IX) the 1956 Special Committee on the Question of Defining Aggression met at United Nations Headquarters, New York, and held nineteen meetings between 8 October and 9 November 1956.

15. All the States designated under the said resolution, except Panama, were represented on the Committee. The following is a list of the representatives and alternate representatives of the attending States:
China: Mr. Yu-Chi Hsueh;
Czechoslovakia: Mr. Karel Petrželka, Mr. Dusan Spáčil;
Dominican Republic: Mr. Enrique de Marchena, Mr. Ambrosio Alvarez Aybar;
France: Mr. Charles Chaumont;
Iraq: Mr. Hassen al Chalabi;
Israel: Mr. Jacob Robinson, Mr. Arthur C. Liveran;
Mexico: Mr. Rafael de la Colina, Mr. Enrique Bravo Caro;
Netherlands: Mr. Bernard V. A. Röling;
Norway: Mr. Per Vennemoe;
Paraguay: Mr. Pacífico Montero de Vargas;
Peru: Mr. Manuel F. Maúrtua;
Philippines: Mr. Felixberto M. Serrano;
Poland: Mr. Jerzy Michalowski;
Syria: Mr. Rafik Asha, Mr. Jawdat Mufti;
Union of Soviet Socialist Republics: Mr. Platon Dmitrievich Morozov;
United Kingdom of Great Britain and Northern Ireland: Mr. Patrick L. Bushe-Fox;
United States of America: Mr. William Sanders;
Yugoslavia: Mr. Djura Nincic, Mr. Aleksandar Bozovic.

16. The Committee elected the following officers:
Chairman: Mr. Enrique de Marchena (Dominican Republic);
Vice-Chairman: Mr. Karel Petrželka (Czechoslovakia);
Rapporteur: Mr. Bernard V. A. Röling (Netherlands).

17. Three proposals for a working plan were submitted to the Committee. The proposal introduced by the Philippines read as follows:

"The Special Committee;

"Considering that resolution 895 (IX) of the General Assembly has established this Special Committee 'to co-ordinate the views expressed by States Members' and to submit to the eleventh session of the General Assembly: (1) a detailed report; and (2) a draft definition of aggression,

"Considering that, in complying with the aforementioned terms of reference, this Special Committee is enjoined to take regard of 'the views expressed at the ninth session of the General Assembly and the draft resolutions and amendments submitted',

"Decides:

"A. In compliance with the first term of reference,

"1. To request the Rapporteur to prepare the detailed report, bearing in mind the need for co-ordination of:

"(a) The views expressed by States Members at the ninth session of the General Assembly. To this end, and to the extent that they may have any bearing thereto, he may examine: (1) the views expressed in, and the action taken by, the International Law Commission during its third session (A/1858, pp.8-10); (2) the report of the Secretary-General to the seventh session of the General Assembly (A/2211); and (3) the comments of States Members on the report of the fifteen-nation Special Committee (A/2689 and Corr.1 and Add.1);

"(b) The views expressed during the meetings of this Special Committee;

"2. To request the Secretariat to lend its assistance to the Rapporteur; and

"3. To request the Rapporteur to submit to this Special Committee, for its consideration and approval, the draft of the report not later than one week before the closing of the session of the Special Committee;

"B. In compliance with the second term of reference,

"1. To consider a draft definition of aggression taking into account the draft resolutions and amendments submitted and, in particular:

"(a) The views expressed by States Members and views subsequently expressed in elaboration, modification, or revision thereof;

"(b) The point or points of consensus or near consensus of views;

"(c) The point or points of divergence;

"2. To draft a definition of aggression on the basis of the consensus or near consensus of views;

"3. To deal with the controversial points along the following alternatives:

"(a) Exclude from the definition the controversial points for future determination by the General Assembly; or

"(b) Without expressly excluding or including them, formulate a general statement whereby the Security Council or any other competent international body shall decide, in appropriate cases, whether any particular act or acts not falling within the definition, constitute aggression or not; and/or

"(c) Insert a proviso affirming the authority of the Security Council, the definition of aggression notwithstanding, to deal with the cases provided for in Article 39 and other relevant provisions of the Charter".

18. The Netherlands submitted the following proposal:

"The Special Committee,

"Considering that resolution 895 (IX), after having stated that the discussions to which the question of defining aggression gave rise at the ninth session of the General Assembly have revealed the need to co-ordinate the views expressed by the States Members, established this Special Committee to submit a detailed report followed by a draft definition of aggression having regard to the ideas expressed at the ninth session and to the draft resolutions and amendments submitted,

"Considering that from this resolution it follows that to solve the question of defining aggression the different views of the States Members need to be co-ordinated, and that it is the task of this Committee to explore the possibility of such co-ordination,

"Decides:

"1. To request the Rapporteur to prepare a detailed report about the ideas expressed at the ninth session of the General Assembly, this detailed report to be submitted to this Committee for its convenience as soon as possible;

"2. To discuss the possibility of co-ordinating the views of the States Members as expressed in the discussions at the ninth session, in the draft definitions submitted to the Sixth Committee at that session, and in the discussions of this Special Committee;

"3. To determine whether or not the outcome of these discussions warrants the drafting of a definition of aggression and, in case the answer is in the affirmative, to draft a definition of aggression;

"4. To approve a detailed report about the work of this Committee."

19. The following proposal was submitted by Iraq:

"The Special Committee,

"Considering that, by its resolution 895 (IX), the General Assembly requested the Special Committee to submit a detailed report followed by a draft definition of aggression at its eleventh session,

"Considering that the Special Committee has not yet adopted a final working plan,

"Decides:

"1. To adopt as a working plan for the first part of its task the proposals contained in part A of the working plan proposed by the Philippine delegation;

"2. To perform the second part of its task in two stages:

"(a) Special discussion of the various draft definitions of aggression submitted to the Committee;

"(b) Co-ordination of the different views expressed during the general debate and the special discussion. For this purpose the Committee decides to establish a sub-committee to co-ordinate the views of the various delegations and, if possible, to draft one or more definitions of aggression within a specified period."

20. The proposals for a working plan were representative of two different trends in the Committee with respect to the interpretation of its terms of reference. One point of view, which found expression in the working plans of the Philippines and Iraq, was that, as the Committee had been requested by the General Assembly to draft a definition of aggression, its primary task was, by co-ordination of

views and elimination of controversial points, to arrive at a definition which, as a common denominator, would be acceptable to a substantial majority of Member States. According to another opinion, which formed the basis of the Netherlands plan of work, the Committee should first examine the possibilities of co-ordinating the views expressed by Member States and thereafter proceed to the drafting of a definition of aggression if this preliminary study indicated that a useful and widely acceptable definition could be achieved.

21. The Committee decided not to vote on the three working plans, but to adopt a proposal submitted by the representative of Poland, to the effect that the Committee, after a general exchange of views, should embark upon a study and discussion of the various draft definitions before it, and thereafter decide on its further procedure.

22. The Committee had at its disposal an extensive documentation on the question of defining aggression, in particular the report of the International Law Commission on its discussion of the problem [8]; the report of the Secretary-General and the views of Governments on the question [9]; the report of the 1953 Special Committee [10]; the observations of Governments on that report [11]; the relevant reports of the Sixth Committee at the sixth, [12] seventh [13] and ninth [14] sessions of the General Assembly; and the draft definitions submitted by delegations at the ninth session. [15] At the request of the Special Committee, the Secretariat prepared a working paper (A/AC.77/L.6) reproducing a number of draft definitions selected from those contained in this documentation. Since these draft definitions were referred to during the discussions, the working paper is reproduced as annex I to the present report.

23. The USSR and Paraguay reintroduced in the Committee (A/AC.77/L.4 and A/AC.77/L.7 respectively) the draft definitions which they had submitted at the ninth session of the General Assembly (A/C.6/L.332/Rev.1 and A/C.6/L.334/Rev.1 respectively). At the request of the representative of Peru, the draft definition submitted by Iran and Panama at the ninth session (A/C.6/L.335/Rev.1) was also circulated as document A/AC.77/L.9. Mexico presented a working paper (A/AC.77/L.10) which incorporated the Mexican proposal made before the 1953 Special Committee (A/AC.66/L.8). Written drafts were further submitted by Iraq (A/AC.77/L.8/Rev.1) [16] and jointly by the Dominican Republic, Mexico, Paraguay and Peru

---

[8] Official Records of the General Assembly, Sixth Session, Supplement No. 9 (A/1858).

[9] Ibid., Seventh Session, Annexes, agenda item 54, documents A/2211 and A/2162 and Add.1.

[10] Ibid., Ninth Session, Supplement No. 11 (A/2638).

[11] Ibid., Annexes, agenda item 51, document A/2689 and Corr.1 and Add.1.

[12] Ibid., Sixth Session, Annexes, agenda item 49, document A/2087.

[13] Ibid., Seventh Session, Annexes, agenda item 54, document A/2322.

[14] Ibid., Ninth Session, Annexes, agenda item 51, document A/2806.

[15] Ibid.

[16] The revised text, which incorporates changes of form only, was submitted after the discussion of the original draft (A/AC.77/L.8) had been completed.

(A/AC.77/L.11). The texts of these drafts are reproduced in annex II to the present report. In the course of the debate, the representative of the Netherlands also suggested for discussion a tentative formulation which is reproduced below in paragraph 208. It was the understanding of the Committee that besides these documents other draft definitions included in the documentation before the Committee could be taken into consideration.

24. The Committee decided not to vote on the draft definitions before it, but to transmit them with the present report to the General Assembly.

25. The Committee trusts that its work will constitute a useful contribution towards the solution of the problem of defining aggression. Many representatives expressed the hope that the development of friendly international relations would make possible in the future the formulation of a generally acceptable definition. At the last meeting the representative of the

Philippines suggested that, should the General Assembly meet the same difficulties as the Committee in co-ordinating views regarding the definition of aggression, the Assembly might concentrate on drawing up a declaration on aggression.

26. In accordance with its terms of reference, the Committee in the course of its work took into consideration primarily the ideas expressed at the ninth session of the General Assembly. A survey of these ideas is made in section II of the present report.

27. The views expressed during the discussions in the present Special Committee are set forth in section III below. In the first part of the section are summarized the opinions expressed in the Committee regarding some of the general problems connected with the formulation of a definition of aggression, while the second part contains the observations made by the representatives concerning the various draft definitions before the Committee.

II. SURVEY OF IDEAS EXPRESSED AT THE NINTH SESSION OF THE GENERAL ASSEMBLY

A. Points of view: possibility and desirability of a definition

28. In the course of the meetings of the Sixth Committee during the ninth session of the General Assembly, some eight representatives expressed the opinion that a definition of aggression was impossible and/or undesirable. Other representatives, numbering about six, doubted the possibility and/or desirability of a definition, while a third group, about twenty-six in number, considered a definition both possible and desirable. Classification of the several standpoints taken during the discussions is not easy, for reservations were often made and specific conditions presupposed. Some representatives classified in this third group declared that they supported the adoption of a generally acceptable definition ("generally acceptable" meaning acceptable to all Members, to most Members, or to a two-thirds majority including all or most of the permanent members of the Security Council); others, classified in the first or second group, declared that they opposed the adoption of a definition for the very reason that, in their opinion, a generally acceptable definition could not be found at the present time.

29. The third group of delegations which were in favour of a definition was not a homogeneous group. The delegations constituting the group differed in opinion as to the function, the content and the form of a definition, as will appear in the following sections.

30. Representatives of Member States in the first group presented the following general arguments in

favour of their negative opinion: the international situation was not sufficiently propitious to reach a generally acceptable formula; acceptance by the permanent members of the Security Council was essential, but not assured; a definition might be misused against a State entitled to use force in self-defense; a would-be aggressor could distort a definition and take advantage of loopholes; discussion of a definition in the Security Council or the General Assembly on critical occasions might cause delay; no definition would be binding on the Security Council or Member States; a definition might be applied in an automatic fashion without due regard to circumstances; a general definition would leave important concepts like self-defense unelaborated; a list of examples, on the other hand, would single out certain kinds of aggression for special emphasis.

31. Some representatives who took a positive stand as to the possibility and desirability of a definition founded their opinion on General Assembly resolution 599 (VI)[17] by which, in their view, the question had already been settled. A distinction was made by some delegations between the legal and the political possibility of a definition: the legal possibility had been decided upon by the Assembly, whereas the political possibility still had to be demonstrated.

32. Other arguments presented in favour of a definition will be found in the following sections.

[17] See para 5, above.

B. Functions of a definition

(a) Guidance for United Nations organs

33. One of the benefits to be derived from a definition of aggression was, in the opinion of a number of representatives, the guidance it would provide to United Nations organs in the interpretation and application of the Charter. That guidance, in their view, would, in

particular, consist in facilitating the identification of an aggressor and in avoiding arbitrariness in decisions designed to carry out the Organization's task of safeguarding international peace.

34. Some representatives emphasized that a definition would give mere guidance and lack any binding

force; others stressed, however, the great persuasive authority of a definition adopted by a large majority of the General Assembly.

35. Some representatives dismissed the idea of actual guidance of United Nations organs by a definition of aggression. They considered a definition useless to that end and recalled the Security Council's freedom of decision, which a recommendation of the Assembly could not impair.

36. The question of determining which organs were to be guided by a definition gave rise to some observations. Some criticized a USSR proposal (A/C.6/L.332/Rev.1)[18] to recognize only the Security Council as the competent organ to deal with aggression, whereas under resolutions 377 A (V) the Assembly was also competent in cases where the Council was unable to act. Others thought that, under the Charter, the Council was the only organ whose right and duty it was to determine the aggressor, and that to attribute to any other organ the power to determine the aggressor was to violate the Charter.

37. Many representatives held the opinion that a definition of aggression would facilitate the tasks of the United Nations of maintaining international peace and security and of preventing or deterring aggression.

38. It was emphasized that a definition of aggression would contribute to the consolidation of the United Nations security system, even if the definition should contain a special provision recognizing the freedom of the competent United Nations organs to determine that acts not mentioned in the definition constituted aggression. Some representatives maintained that the need for such a provision showed the small significance which a definition of aggression would have as a guide for United Nations organs.

(b) Function of the definition in relation with Article 51 of the Charter

39. Some delegations held that a definition of armed attack, as the term is used in Article 51 of the Charter, would contribute to the maintenance of peace and security. They considered that such a definition was essential for the proper regulation of the use of force permitted under the Charter. Different opinions existed as to the scope of the right of self-defence, and a definition should make it clear in what cases a State had the right to go to war in self-defence. Moreover, in view of the fact that the usual pretext of an aggressor was a claim to act in self-defence, a definition of "armed attack", as the term is used in Article 51, might clarify the issue and make it more difficult to pursue an aggressive policy on such a pretext.

(c) Relation with the regulation of the use of atomic weapons

40. During the discussion of the definition of aggression, attention was drawn to the proposal made on 11 June 1954 by France and the United Kingdom at the session in London of the Sub-Committee of the United Nations Disarmament Commission.[19] According to this proposal the States concerned would undertake to renounce the use of nuclear weapons except in self-defence against aggression.

41. Some delegations, in view of this proposal, considered it wise at least to postpone deliberations on a definition of aggression until the results of the disarmament discussions were known. A definition might have unforeseen and unfortunate repercussions on the disarmament negotiations. Others held the view that a definition was all the more needed since the concept of aggression appeared to be connected with the prevention of atomic warfare. Some considered that the disarmament proposal in question had no relation with the concept of armed attack as this term is used in Article 51, for the Charter forbade any use of force except in self-defence against armed attack. Consequently, the use of a specific kind of force (atomic weapons) could only be justified in defence against a specific kind of armed attack.

(d) Relation with the draft Code of Offences against the Peace and Security of Mankind

42. Part of the discussions in the Sixth Committee centred on the relation of a definition of aggression with the draft Code of Offences against the Peace and Security of Mankind prepared by the International Law Commission.[20] Some representatives were convinced that the adoption by the General Assembly of a definition of aggression would be of great use for the development of international criminal law. They particularly referred to the principle nullum crimen sine lege. Moreover, in the absence of a definition, it would be State practice and the decision of the Security Council, a political organ, which would decide whether or not a certain act constituted the criminal offence of aggression; this was a bad procedure in their view.

43. Some representatives discussed the similarity and differences between a formula defining the word "aggression" in the Charter on the one hand, and a provision for insertion in the draft Code on the other. According to one group, the two definitions served different purposes, but a contradiction between them would be unthinkable. Some representatives, following the same line of thought, pointed out that no individual should under the Code be held responsible for acts which States under the Charter would be allowed to perform unpunished.

44. Others emphasized the differences between the two kinds of definition. They stressed that the definition to be drafted by the Committee related to States, whereas a rule of international criminal law would apply to individuals. The sanctions in the two cases would be very different, and the subjects, although closely related, did not really belong in the same province. In their opinion, a definition for the purposes

---

[18] See below annex I,15; annex II,1.

[19] See annex 9 to the report of the Sub-Committee (DC/53) in the Official Records of the Disarmament Commission, Supplement for April, May and June 1954.

[20] See the report of the International Law Commission on its sixth session, Official Record of the General Assembly, Ninth Session, Supplement No.9, A/2693, chapter III.

of the Code would be much simpler to arrive at, because national interests would not conflict to the same degree.

45. Other representatives apparently saw a possibility of drafting a single definition susceptible of subsequent incorporation in the Code.

46. It was also contended that, although a definition of aggression would promote the development of international criminal law, such a definition would not be a conditio sine qua non for the adoption of a code of offences against the peace and security of mankind or for the creation of an international criminal jurisdiction.

C. Kinds of activity covered by a definition

(a) Use of military force

47. Throughout the discussions there was considerable disagreement concerning the kinds of activity to be covered by a definition of aggression. Some wanted to limit its scope to the use of force only; others wished to include the threat, or certain threats, of force; while still others thought of extending the concept of aggression to indirect, economic and ideological aggression.

48. Many representatives held that the word "aggression" in the Charter exclusively referred to armed aggression. Article 39, in their opinion, listed, in order of seriousness, threats to the peace, breaches of the peace, and acts of aggression, so that the incorporation into the concept of aggression of such activities as economic or ideological aggression would render them more serious than even breaches of the peace. They therefore favoured a limitation of the definition of aggression to the use of force.

49. Others, though in favour of a provisional limitation of a definition to armed aggression, thought that other forms of aggression might be defined later.

50. A limitation to armed aggression "or any analogous act" was advocated by some delegations, who argued that other forms of aggression should be defined in the draft Code of Offences against the Peace and Security of Mankind.

51. Since certain degrees could be said to exist in the use of force and not all of them were serious enough to be described as aggression, it was argued by some that the use of force had to be sufficiently serious to constitute aggression. In particular, frontier incidents would have to be ruled out as possible forms of aggression. In their view, when the Charter mentioned the use of force against the political independence or territorial integrity of any State, it meant warlike action.

52. In this connexion, it was observed that support of invading armed bands, though not included in the concept of aggression, was serious enough to be placed on the same footing as armed aggression.

53. The inclusion of a threat of the use of force in the definition of aggression was opposed by many. They expressed the fear that a would-be aggressor would seize a threat of the use of force as a pretext to commit an aggressive act himself under the cloak of self-defence. A threat of the use of force would in most cases constitute a threat to the peace with which the Security Council would be able to deal under Article 39 of the Charter. Whether a threat of the use of force might exceptionally be equivalent to the use of force was, in the opinion of some delegations, a matter for the competent organs of the United Nations to decide.

54. Some delegations found themselves unable to agree with the complete exclusion of the idea of a threat of the use of force from the definition of aggression. In their opinion, though not all such threats could be called acts of aggression, this certainly was so when the survival of the threatened State was at stake. Threats of the use of force could be termed aggression only if the requirement of a certain magnitude was met. The threat had in particular to be directed against the territorial integrity or political independence of another State or against the territorial integrity or political status of a territory under an international régime.

55. In this connexion, the example was quoted of the entry of the troops of one State into another "on request" of the latter, after the former State had threatened to attack. This would be aggression.

56. Reference was made also to the first report of the Atomic Energy Commission [21] dealing with the regulation of atomic weapons by means of a treaty; that report stated "that a violation [of the proposed treaty] might be of so grave a character as to give rise to the inherent right of self-defence recognized in Article 51 of the Charter of the United Nations". This recommendation, adopted by General Assembly resolution 191 (III) of 4 November 1948, presupposed that a threat might in exceptional circumstances be included in the concept of "armed attack" as the term was used in Article 51.

57. Some representatives were of the view that a definition of aggression should take into account the aggressive intent that they believed to be a characteristic of aggression. Others held a contrary view. They pointed out that no subjective elements could be taken into account in determining whether or not any given act could be considered as an act of aggression. Some considered that acts enumerated in the USSR draft could not be committed except with aggressive intent where they were first committed by a State against another State. In the opinion of some members, any provision that might give the impression that the absence of aggressive intent would exclude the existence of aggression would constitute an invitation to the use of subjective arguments by possible aggressors.

58. Finally, some delegations considered that the best course was to leave the question of aggressive intent entirely to the competent organs of the United Nations.

---

[21] Official Records of the Atomic Energy Commission, 1946, Special Supplement, Report to the Security Council, part III, Recommendations, pp. 17-19.

(b) Indirect aggression

59. Some delegations maintained that a definition of agression should include indirect aggression. The concept of indirect aggression gave rise to a good deal of discussion in the Sixth Committee. Sabotage and terrorism were mentioned as examples, as was the support of armed bands of one State against another. Certain delegations were of the opinion that a definition of aggression, which did not take into account the idea of subversion would not be complete. They considered subversion, the most typical form of indirect aggression, as dangerous as war. Any State that encouraged and assisted groups of the people of another State to take up arms against its own Government was no less guilty than if it had itself taken part in an armed attack.

60. Indirect aggression, in its form of fomenting civil strife in foreign countries through assistance to armed bands, was mentioned in the draft definitions of Paraguay (A/C.6/L.334/Rev.1) and of Iran and Panama (A/C.6/L.335/Rev.1). Indirect aggression in its form of subversion was mentioned in the draft definition submitted by China (A/C.6/L.336/Rev.2). The most elaborate references were those given in the USSR draft (A/C.6/L.332/Rev.1), where the support of invading armed bands was listed as direct aggression, and three types of subversive activity were listed under indirect aggression. 22/

61. Many representatives spoke against the specific inclusion of indirect aggression in the definition. According to some, the concept of aggression would be unduly stretched by such inclusion; others thought more especially that a reference in the definition to subversion would harm its practical applicability. Again others, referring to General Assembly resolution 380 (V) on "Peace through deeds", took the view that the use of force mentioned in the definition would include

22/ For the texts of the draft definitions mentioned in this paragraph, see annexes I and II the present report.

the hidden use of force and, consequently, would cover the cases of indirect aggression and subversive activity as far as force had been used by the foreign Power. To give special mention to subversive activity in its different aspects would, in their view, have the danger of including in the definition subversive activity without the use of force. Consequently, they held that specifically to mention subversive activity would be dangerous and not in conformity with the Charter provisions.

(c) Economic and ideological aggression

62. Some delegations wished to include in the definition specific economic or ideological activities under the description of economic or ideological aggression. They maintained that by such means the same ends might be achieved as by armed force, and that at the present time the economic and ideological means of aggression were especially important.

63. Many delegations, however, were against the inclusion of any form of economic or ideological aggression. Though some acknowledged the danger of economic or ideological measures taken for aggressive purposes, they were of the opinion that in special cases the United Nations organs could deal with such events under the concept of threat to the peace. Some maintained that in the Charter "acts of aggression" were mentioned as more dangerous events than "threats to the peace" and "breaches of the peace". Many delegations agreed that inclusion in the definition of aggression might suggest the right to go to war in self-defence against acts of economic or ideological aggression, and the inclusion of such acts would thus endanger rather than promote the peace.

64. Economic and ideological aggression were specifically mentioned in the USSR draft definition (A/C.6/L.332/Rev.1). But, in the view of many, including the sponsor, it appeared from the text that economic or ideological aggression did not entitle individual States to the same defensive action as did armed attack.

D. Various types of definition

65. With regard to the type of definition to be adopted, most delegations favouring a definition of aggression recommended a mixed definition, that is, one in which a flexible description, couched in general terms, would precede and govern a list of definite acts of aggression, which would be included merely to illustrate and not to restrict the general description. It was said that a definition of that type would combine the advantages and avoid the defects of the two other types of definition, the general and the enumerative. It would accord with the opinion that a definition should be neither limitative nor rigid. The definition should not be limitative, not only for the practical reason that all possibilities in such a complex matter could not be foreseen, but also because any limitation would be contrary to the wide powers of judgement conferred upon the Security Council by Articles 24 and 39 of the Charter. It should not be rigid, in the sense that it must

not take the form of an order binding on States and on the competent organs of the United Nations.

66. Some delegations criticized a definition of that type as combining the defects of the other two types. In fact, it was suggested that a mixed definition would be in itself contradictory because, if it started with the statement, for example, that aggression was the use of armed force for purposes other than self-defence or action undertaken in conformity with the Charter, it would not be possible to proceed further by giving examples in illustration of that concept. The act given as an example either would, or would not, according to the circumstances of the case, be covered by the general formula stated at the beginning. The opinion was also expressed that there would be no point in attaching a list of examples to the general statement. Thus, the most familiar types of military aggression

would be too standard to need enumeration, and a list might give the impression, on the one hand, that they could be isolated from the peculiar circumstances in which they occurred, and, on the other hand, that all other forms of armed aggression were of only secondary importance.

67. Other delegations declared themselves in favour of a general definition, namely one that, instead of giving a list of acts of aggression, would contain a general formula covering all the cases to be designated. International organs would be left with the responsibility of establishing the scope of the formula in specific cases brought before them. Some of these delegations pointed out that a definition of that kind, covering in general terms all the elements that constituted aggression, would render any enumeration of definite acts of aggression superfluous. Others suggested that the general definition should be based on the Charter, which was said to contain all the elements of a definition of aggression. It should incorporate the principles of Article 2, paragraph 4, and Article 51 of the Charter. Such a definition would have the double advantage of covering all cases conceivable by the most fertile imagination and allowing the competent organ or organs of the United Nations full freedom of judgement.

68. That type of definition was, however, criticized by some delegations as being a mere repetition, in one form or another, of elementary truths; it could therefore be of no value. A general definition would be less dangerous than an enumerative definition, but would be

of little value because it would inevitably be drafted in terms that would themselves call for definition. Furthermore, a general definition the basic elements of which could be found in the Charter would not be enough; it was just because the Charter confined itself to dealing with the question in general terms that the General Assembly had thought it necessary to define aggression by reference to the elements that constituted it. Emphasis was laid upon the inevitable vagueness of a general definition, which would render it rather impractical. Furthermore, it was held that many exceptions to the general formula would have to be provided for. Another objection was that the burden of proof, in case such a definition were adopted, would rest on the victim.

69. Some delegations criticized purely enumerative definitions. That kind of definition, which would be limitative and rigid and would deprive States and the organs of the United Nations of freedom of judgement would, in their opinion, not be in conformity with the Charter. The inflexibility of a merely enumerative definition was contrary to the Charter system and was dangerous. Furthermore, such a definition would necessarily be incomplete and would leave loopholes for possible aggressors. Enumeration of the acts of aggression could, moreover, lessen the importance of acts not mentioned. Furthermore, it was held that the acts specifically mentioned would themselves need definition. Also, it might well be that the acts listed would, in specific cases, not constitute acts of aggression.

E. Essential elements in the proposed definition

(a) The principle of priority

70. The draft resolution submitted by the USSR (A/C.6/L.332/Rev.1) contained a proposal to the effect that, in an international conflict, that State should be declared the attacker "which first commits" one of a series of acts subsequently enumerated. In the opinion of some delegations, the chronological order of events would be an important criterion and might even be decisive in determining who was responsible for aggression. It was maintained that it would be necessary, when preparing a definition of aggression, to explain that the aggressor State would be that State which first committed any of the acts enumerated in the definition. The priority principle was mentioned as a most important criterion for aggression and a long-recognized principle of international law, which was embodied in Article 51 of the Charter. A definition which neglected this principle of priority would not only be ambiguous, but might also be used as a justification for preventive war. Such a definition would lose most of its value.

71. Other delegations, although recognizing the significance of the priority principle, emphasized the necessity of a logical and reasonable interpretation of that principle. It was said, furthermore, that an exception to the priority principle was the case of collective measures ordered or recommended by the competent United Nations organs. In that case, the State first having recourse to armed force, and com-

mitting one of the acts enumerated in the USSR draft, should not be condemned as aggressor.

72. In the opinion of other delegations, the chronological order of events as enumerated in the USSR draft could not stand, because it would lead to dangerous consequences. They denied the existence of the priority principle, as embodied in the USSR draft, as a principle recognized in international law. Furthermore, it was often difficult to decide who acted first, especially when many States were involved in a conflict in which they were not all fighting for the same reason or object. According to that view, a country that initiated a process was not necessarily responsible for all the acts committed subsequently. The question of which State was "first" to commit a certain act was therefore basically irrelevant, and everything depended essentially upon the circumstances.

73. Other delegations maintained that, although the chronological order had significance, the decisive factor in the definition of aggression could not consist in the priority principle, but in the character of the acts forbidden to be committed first. In their opinion, the main weakness of the emphasis on the priority principle in the USSR draft was demonstrated by the fact that, on the one hand, it provided that a border-incident (which might consist of shooting, bombing or trespassing across the border) did not warrant self-defence under Article 51 and, on the other hand, that it provided that shooting, bombing, and violation of the

border were aggression if committed first; thus, the draft contained a contradiction which would make its application difficult. Others maintained that an aggressor would not necessarily be the first to commit a given act classified beforehand as an act of aggression. In their view, the circumstances peculiar to each particular case would determine whether or not aggression had been committed.

(b) The indication of cases never justifying armed attack in self-defence

74. It was proposed by some members to include in the definition of aggression a certain number of circumstances which should in no case serve as justification of aggression. In their view, such a provision formed an essential element in the definition. Accordingly, paragraph 6 of the USSR draft (A/C.6/L.332/Rev.1) mentioned circumstances which would never justify armed attacks, first in a general way, and then giving two more specific situations, under each of which were listed special cases. Preventive war, it was explained, would then be deprived of any basis or justification.

75. Other delegations, sharing this view, pointed out that the essence of this paragraph was identical with the principle of non-intervention as recognized by the States of the American hemisphere.

76. Although an enumeration of circumstances not justifying armed attack was not included in the joint draft of Iran and Panama (A/C.6/L.335/Rev.1), the representative of Iran declared himself prepared to supplement the draft resolution to the effect that aggression could not be justified by political, strategic, economic or social considerations.

77. Other delegations disputed the wisdom of paragraph 6 of the USSR draft and similar proposals. They opposed the idea of such a provision on the ground that an enumeration of considerations not justifying acts of an aggressive nature was likely to give the impression, and might easily lead to the conclusion, that other considerations than those mentioned could justify such acts. Furthermore, it would be illogical to give various circumstances which could not serve as justification for armed attack when the basic principle was that nothing justified it, except armed attack.

(c) The principle that the use of force should have a specific quality to constitute aggression

78. Some delegations maintained that the distinction made in the USSR draft (A/C.6/L.332/Rev.1) between the enumerated acts of armed force constituting aggression, on the one hand, and the frontier incidents which were apparently not considered to constitute aggression, on the other, showed the need to indicate in a definition the difference between the two kinds of armed action. This distinction, they argued, showed the need to indicate, by naming quality or quantity, the very features of aggression. Not every use of armed force, but only a specific use of armed force, may be considered as an act of aggression.

79. Some of the proposed draft definitions mentioned specific kinds of the use of armed force. The revised draft resolution submitted by Iran and Panama (A/C.6/L.335/Rev.1), after having first generally referred to the use of armed force, proposed to consider as aggression in all cases: (1) invasion; (2) armed attack against territory, population or military forces; (3) blockade; and (4) specific activities in relation with armed bands.

80. It was pointed out by some delegations that the words used would need further clarification and definition. Furthermore, attention was drawn to the fact that the activities mentioned included the organization, the toleration of the organization, or the encouragement of the organization, of armed bands for incursions into the territory of another State. It was felt that to consider these actions as aggression would promote rather than discourage preventive war, for it followed that acts could be considered as aggression without any actual fighting having taken place.

81. In the Paraguayan draft definition (A/C.6/L.334/Rev.1) only those cases of the employment of armed force were described as armed aggression (1) which are directed against the territory, population, armed forces, or the sovereignty and political independence of another State (or other States), or against the people, territory or armed forces of a non-self-governing territory; (2) by which the State provokes a breach or disturbance of international peace and security. Moreover, the Paraguayan draft specifically mentioned declaration of war, and the organization, encouragement, toleration or support of armed bands.

82. Here again the objection was made that several concepts used in the draft needed definitions. Many delegations considered "to provoke" and "disturbance of international peace and security" as vague terms, not used in the Charter, needing to be made more specific.

83. The Chinese draft definition (A/C.6/L.336/Rev.2) gave as a general description "the unlawful use of force, by a State against another State, whether directly or indirectly", followed by examples including particular forms of subversive activity.

84. In the view of several delegations, however, the definition of aggression by the formula "unlawful use of force" was useless because it gave no clarification of the concept of aggression.

85. Draft definitions were given by the Netherlands delegation as suggestions to contribute to the discussion. [23] In these drafts, the distinctive criterion to indicate the threat or use of force which would constitute aggression consisted of the circumstance that the threat or the use of force was directed "against the territorial integrity or political independence of another State or against the territorial integrity or political status of a territory under an international régime, whatever the weapons employed and whether openly or otherwise". In these drafts, exception was made for the cases of individual or collective self-defence, and for acts in pursuance of a decision or recommendation by a competent organ of the United Nations.

86. This formula, again, was critioized for its vagueness. According to many delegations it partly repeated

23/ Official Records of the General Assembly, Ninth Session, Sixth Committee, Summary Records, pp. 73 and 109.

the Charter, and partly introduced concepts which needed defining. Although it was stated by the Netherlands representative that it was not the purpose of the actor, but the purport of the act which was decisive, some delegations felt that a subjective element - a

specific kind of aggressive intent - was introduced. They considered subjective elements useless and dangerous. Furthermore, it was held that the definition lost sight of the fact that circumstances might justify acts described in the definition.

F. Legal and moral value of a General Assembly resolution defining aggression

87. Opinion differed about what legal or other value a definition adopted by a resolution of the General Assembly might have. It was generally recognized that recommendations based on a majority decision were legally not binding upon Members or organs of the United Nations. The General Assembly was not a world legislator. A majority could not impose its will on the minority. That followed, it was argued, from the principle of sovereign equality of the Member States (Article 2, paragraph 1, of the Charter).

88. Moreover, it was maintained, the Security Council had the primary responsibility for the maintenance of peace, and it would be contrary to the system adopted in the Charter to consider the Council in any way bound by a recommendation of the Assembly. In particular, it was pointed out that the Assembly could not impose on the Council any definition it adopted, when action by the Council depended upon the agreement of the five permanent members.

89. It was remarked that a definition would be generally binding only if it were inserted in the Charter or if a convention embodying the definition were signed and ratified by all Member States.

90. In the opinion of several representatives, however, a General Assembly resolution defining aggression would at any rate provide guidance for Member

States and United Nations organs. The moral authority of such a definition was recognized and highly estimated by several representatives. Such moral authority would be all the more weighty if the definition had been supported by an overwhelming majority.

91. Some delegations, recognizing the moral and political value of a definition and its influence upon United Nations organs and Member States, maintained that a definition would also have a juridical significance.

92. The view was held that a definition, based on the Charter provisions and not deviating from these provisions, would constitute a more or less authoritative interpretation of the Charter. Although such an interpretation by the General Assembly would not be strictly binding upon the Security Council or Member States, it would clarify the Charter provisions and contribute in this way to a generally accepted interpretation of the Charter.

93. On the other hand, it was stated that a definition adopted by the Assembly would constitute a general principle of law recognized by civilized nations and might in that way become part of international law. The Council would not lightly disregard such a new principle of international law embodied in an Assembly resolution. Consequently, a definition would contribute to the progressive development of international law.

III. VIEWS EXPRESSED IN THE 1956 SPECIAL COMMITTEE ON THE QUESTION OF DEFINING AGGRESSION

1. Views expressed in the general debate

A. Views about the possibility and desirability of a definition

94. General Assembly resolution 599 (VI) declared that it was possible and desirable, with a view to ensuring international peace and security and to developing international criminal law, to define aggression. In view of that resolution, some delegations thought it unnecessary and improper to consider those questions again. Others maintained that it was the function of the Special Committee to explore the possibilities of co-ordinating the views of the Member States, and that, therefore, a discussion about the possibility and desirability of defining aggression could not be avoided.

95. The overwhelming majority of the Committee considered it possible to define aggression. This was the position, in particular, of China, Czechoslovakia, the Dominican Republic, France, Iraq, Mexico, the Netherlands, Paraguay, Peru, the Philippines, Poland, Syria, the Union of Soviet Socialist Republics and Yugoslavia, which held that a definition of aggression was possible and desirable in the interests of maintaining international peace and security. It appeared,

however, that substantial differences of opinion did exist as to the question how aggression should be defined. The representative of the United States referred to the artificial and insubstantial character of the impression that a large measure of agreement existed in the United Nations on the possibility of drafting an acceptable definition of aggression. He found fundamental and irreconcilable differences among those who strongly advocated a definition and who considered that one could and should be approved (A/AC.77/SR.13, p. 3). [24]

96. General Assembly resolution 688 (VII) stated that continued efforts should be made to formulate a generally acceptable definition. What did the words "generally acceptable" mean? According to the representative of France, the definition should be acceptable to all the great Powers primarily responsible for the maintenance of international peace and security as well as to the great majority of Member States

---

[24] The references in brackets which follow are to the summary records (SR/...) of the meetings of the 1956 Special Committee.

(SR.2, p. 3). The delegate of Norway shared this view, and added that he strongly doubted the possibility of finding such a generally acceptable definition (SR.6 pp. 9 and 10). The Netherlands representative understood "generally acceptable" as acceptable to the great majority of the Member States and to all, or nearly all, the permanent members of the Security Council, and he reminded the Committee that only such a generally acceptable definition would be supported by his Government (SR.13, p. 15). The representative of the Philippines gave a statistical survey of the views expressed in the Sixth Committee, in which he noted that the mixed type of definition appeared to be favoured by the majority, although within that category there existed divergencies of views both on the character of the general formula and on the extent of the illustrative acts of aggression (SR.1, pp. 9 and 10; SR.19, pp. 4 and 5). The representative of China, however, noted that none of the views expressed in the Sixth Committee commanded the support of a majority, the advocates of defining aggression being divided as to the function, type and content of a definition (SR.3, p. 3). The Netherlands representative expressed the opinion that the discussions in 1954, as well as the discussions in the present Special Committee, had shown that it was not likely to succeed in effectively co-ordinating the views on the concept of aggression as this term was used in Article 39 of the Charter. He suggested, therefore, that efforts should be concentrated on the concept of "armed attack" in Article 51; in that way, a generally acceptable formula might perhaps be found (SR.3, p. 6; SR.8, p. 6; SR.13, p. 15). This appraisal was shared by the representative of Norway (SR.6, p. 9).

97. During the discussions, seven different draft definitions were introduced (see annex II and para. 208 below), showing the difficulty of arriving at a generally acceptable definition. In this connexion, the representative of the United Kingdom remarked that whether, considered as an abstract proposition, a definition was desirable depended on whether any satisfactory definition was possible. The desirability of adopting a particular definition depended on whether it was a satisfactory one or not (SR.6, p. 7).

98. At the end of the Committee's discussions, the representative of China stated that the present time did not seem the best to come to a generally acceptable definition of aggression. The present international community might be compared with a community where every one freely carried arms, every one freely produced arms, where no police force or courts with compulsory powers existed. In view of this the definition, which would always be imperfect, would not be very helpful. It was better, instead of attempting to define aggression, to search for means to enforce respect for the Charter provisions (SR.18, p. 6).

99. A unanimous opinion about the desirability of a definition did not exist. A large majority of the Committee considered it desirable, in principle, to define aggression. Some delegations, however, pointed to the dangers inherent in defining aggression. The problem was, as the representative of China stated, whether it was safe for States to accept a definition as a safeguard against aggression (SR.3, p. 4). The case for or against a definition of aggression, said the United

States representative, did not rest solely on its specific provisions but on its capacity, as a whole, to meet the requirements of its intended or claimed purpose. He pointed out the difficulty of putting into words something that was so dependent on circumstances, on the context as a whole, of a given situation as was the case with an act of aggression. It would be no remedy to say that any definition must, of course, be interpreted and applied in the light of circumstances. That would, in his opinion, be another way of saying that it was impossible to avoid appraising a threat or act of aggression in the light of the circumstances as a whole. Since each threat of aggression varied in its history and its facts in an infinite number of ways, it taxed human ingenuity and wisdom beyond reasonable limits to evolve a formula which would anticipate events and provide useful guidance (SR.13, p. 3).

100. The representative of the United Kingdom shared this opinion about the difficulty of covering all cases in the definition. The terms of the definition might be pleaded in justification of an act of aggression that was not explicitly covered by the definition, and in that sense the existence of a definition might have the effect of encouraging the aggressor. There was also the danger that, whatever proviso might be inserted in a definition as to the Security Council's freedom of action, that body might tend to attach less importance to acts not expressly mentioned in the definition. That had been the view taken by the Committee of the 1945 San Francisco Conference of which M. Paul-Boncour had been the rapporteur (see also para. 149 below). The Committee should not, in this respect, consider only the utility of the definitions put forward and the desirability of their adoption, but also whether in some circumstances they might be positively dangerous (SR.6, p. 8).

101. The United States representative held that any definition would create further definitional problems. He emphasized the mischief and confusion which a definition could introduce into the work for peace of the United Nations. A wrong definition might do great harm. He wondered whether the Committee had adequately considered the relationship between what was desirable and possible and what was practical, helpful and acceptable. The question was: how would it influence the decisions of States, acting collectively or individually? He pointed to the danger of hindering the Security Council in its work by defining aggression and not defining the threats to the peace and the breaches of the peace also mentioned in Article 39. A definition might have the effect of impairing the right of self-defence and, by curtailing the freedom of action of the State attacked, might even be an incentive to aggression. On the other hand, a party might be tempted, in case events occurred constituting acts of aggression under the terms of the definition, to take up arms without waiting for a decision by the Security Council. Consequently, a definition might rather be harmful than helpful (SR.5, pp. 3 et seq.; SR.13, pp. 3 et seq.).

102. It was not right, in the opinion of the United States representative, to cite in support of a general definition the precedents of the Act of Chapultepec of 8 March 1945 and the Inter-American Treaty of Reciprocal Assistance signed at Rio de Janeiro on

2 September 1947, which contained enumerations of particular acts of aggression. The signatories of those instruments belonged to the same geographical area and were united by many bonds, including a feeling of solidarity, which were not present to the same degree among the Members of the United Nations (SR.5, p. 7). This opinion, however, was not shared by the representative of the USSR. In his view, a definition of aggression would be even more useful if it were accepted by States with widely divergent opinions (SR.5, p. 10).

103. Against these considerations was emphasized the danger of not arriving at a generally acceptable definition. The representative of Yugoslavia stressed the point that, by its very adoption, a definition would indicate the determination to stop aggression. If the Committee failed, it would disappoint world hopes for peace and justice. It was better to adopt an imperfect definition, representing the highest common factor of agreement, than to adopt no definition at all (SR.7, p. 8). In this opinion the representative of Peru concurred, on the basis of what he considered a pragmatic approach; in his view, a legislator should not insist on formulating only perfect rules (SR.18, p. 9). The representative of China took exception to this point of view. A defective definition would only have a confusing effect and would therefore be harmful and dangerous. The adoption of such a definition by the Committee could only be detrimental to the prestige of the United Nations (SR.14, p. 5). Other delegations shared the latter view.

104. Many arguments were advanced in favour of defining aggression, and are more fully mentioned in the following chapters. A definition would be a factor in the promotion of peace and security, of justice and international law. A clear definition of aggression would contribute substantially to the maintenance of international peace and security. A General Assembly resolution containing such a definition was one of the measures whereby the United Nations could effectively help States to maintain and strengthen friendly relations based on the principle of coexistence regardless of differences in political and economic structure. Moreover, a definition would be a contribution to peace by preventing an aggressor from using the pretext of acting in self-defence (USSR, SR.3, pp. 9 and 11; Netherlands, SR.3, pp. 6 to 8; Czechoslovakia, SR.6, p. 4; Norway, SR.6, p. 10). A definition might not only substantially hamper a potential future aggressor, but it would also help the other Powers to recognize the nature of his acts (Czechoslovakia, SR.6, p. 4). The Mexican representative emphasized that a definition would be a safeguard for pacific settlement of disputes and would influence public opinion and understanding of the actions of United Nations organs, as well as those of States acting in self-defence. A definition would dispel many of the doubts and uncertainties which beclouded the legal concept of aggression, would have considerable persuasive force, and would contribute to the progressive development of international law (SR.7, pp. 4 and 5).

105. Some delegations agreed with the arguments against defining the "act of aggression" mentioned in Article 39 of the Charter. For that and other reasons, the Netherlands delegate suggested not defining the "act of aggression" mentioned in Article 39 but rather defining "armed attack" as that term is used in Article 51 (SR.3, pp. 6 to 8).

106. Against the thesis that a definition would be a "signpost for the guilty" and as such might encourage the aggressor, the representative of Yugoslavia remarked that such a statement would be tantamount to asserting that the existence of detailed criminal legislation encouraged criminals to commit crimes (SR.7, p. 7). The Netherlands representative called attention to the shift of emphasis in the work of the United Nations from collective security to collective conciliation. In this connexion, qualified scholars had spoken of "a new United Nations". The introduction of the Secretary-General to his latest annual report on the work of the Organization[25] reaffirmed this appraisal. Moreover, in the opinion of many Member States, the United Nations not only failed in its function to guarantee the peace through collective action, but also did not succeed in the maintenance of law and justice. It seemed that, with regard to this development, the opinion prevailed in many circles that the significance of Article 2, paragraph 4, and of Article 51, especially the prohibition of the use of force, had diminished accordingly. By defining armed attack and, by so doing, indicating the limits of self-defence, the United Nations would clarify and fortify the Charter provisions. This seemed to be more needed than ever before (SR.3, pp. 7 and 8).

B. Views about the function and scope of the definition

107. General Assembly resolution 599 (VI) considered that it was desirable to define aggression with a view to ensuring international peace and security and to developing international criminal law. General Assembly resolution 688 (VII) stated that continued efforts should be made to formulate a generally acceptable definition of aggression, with a view to promoting international peace and security and to developing international law. The question as to the respects in which the definition of aggression might promote peace and justice was discussed in the Committee.

108. In the opinion of the Netherlands representative, former discussions had shown that a definition of aggression might be relevant and significant in four respects. Firstly, a definition would serve as a guiding principle for United Nations organs in their task of maintaining peace and security. This would mean the definition of the "acts of aggression" mentioned in Article 39 of the Charter. Secondly, a definition would help to determine in what cases a State or States might act in individual or collective self-defence. This would mean the definition of "armed attack", as that term was used in Article 51 of the Charter. Thirdly, the concept of aggression might have significance in disarmament arrangements, as had been evidenced at the session held in London in 1954 of the Sub-Committee of the United Nations Disarmament Commission.[26]

---

[25] Official Records of the General Assembly, Eleventh Session, Supplement No. 1A (A/3137/Add.1).

[26] Cf. paras. 40-41 above.

Fourthly, a definition of aggression might be significant in relation with the draft Code of Offences against the Peace and Security of Mankind [27]/ (SR.8, pp. 5 and 6).

109. During the discussions, the relation of the definition of aggression to disarmament treaties concerning nuclear weapons was not elaborated, nor did an exhaustive debate develop concerning the concept of aggression in a criminal code.

110. The representative of Iraq remarked that it was an established rule of criminal law in all States that offences had to be expressly defined, and the same rule applied to international law (SR.4, p. 3). The representative of the United States of America stated in this connexion that it had been argued that legislation against an offence should not wait until the offence had been committed. That was a very creditable aim, but sufficient attention had perhaps not been given to the fact that such a code already existed in the form of the Charter of the United Nations. If an international criminal jurisdiction was ever successfully established, the law it applied would obviously be the Charter (SR.5, p. 7).

111. The Netherlands representative concurred in this opinion. The post-war trials had shown that a judge did not need a definition. A definition of aggression might be a contribution to the development of international criminal law, as General Assembly resolution 599 (VI) declared, but such a definition was not a conditio sine qua non for the preparation of a code of offences against the peace and security of mankind, or for the establishment of an international criminal jurisdiction (SR.8, p. 6).

112. General Assembly resolution 599 (VI) considered that it would be of definite advantage if directives were formulated for the future guidance of such international bodies as might be called upon to determine the aggressor. This function was referred to by many delegations during the discussion in the 1956 Special Committee, and was especially mentioned in the draft resolution submitted at the ninth session of the General Assembly by Iran and Panama, and reintroduced by Peru in the Special Committee (A/AC.77/L.9).[28]/

113. Against the misgivings expressed by the representatives of the United Kingdom (SR.6, p. 6) and of the United States (SR.13, p. 3, who elaborated on the mischief and confusion a definition could introduce into the work for peace of the United Nations), the representative of the USSR maintained that a definition would facilitate the task of the Security Council (SR.5, p. 9), and that the United States representative showed an unjustified pessimism with regard to the efficacy of United Nations organs (SR.14, p. 8). A definition would help to recognize the nature of the aggressor's acts, according to the representative of Czechoslovakia (SR.6, p. 4). The Mexican representative stressed the point that a definition would dispel many of the doubts and uncertainties which beclouded the legal concept of aggression, and would have considerable persuasive force. It would be a guide for

United Nations organs as well as for countries forced to act in self-defence (SR.7, p. 5).

114. It was pointed out, however, that the Security Council was entitled to act in case of a threat to the peace, breach of the peace and act of aggression. It might seem of little use to define aggression when the Security Council could order the same action in cases of threats to the peace and breaches of the peace (Norway, SR.6, p. 9). Moreover, almost all members of the Committee agreed that the Security Council should not be restricted in its freedom to brand as acts of aggression what it thought proper to consider as such, as had been suggested from the start by the representative of the Philippines (SR.1, p. 10). Other representatives, and in particular the USSR representative, considered that it should be the sense of the definition of aggression that, if the acts enumerated in the USSR draft were first committed by a State against another State, the Security Council should declare them to be acts of aggression. Otherwise the General Assembly's recommendation would be meaningless. It stood to reason, however, that, as provided by paragraph 5 of the USSR draft, the Council should have the right to treat as acts of aggression such acts, other than those enumerated in the definition, as might be declared to constitute acts of aggression by decision of the Council in each specific case (SR.3, p. 9; SR.5, p. 9).

115. Some delegations wondered what was left of the definition's function of guidance if such a provision was inserted (Netherlands, SR.3, p. 8; Norway, SR.6, p.9). There was also the danger, according to the United Kingdom representative, that whatever proviso might be inserted in a definition as to the Security Council's freedom of action, that body might tend to attach less importance to acts not expressly mentioned in the definition (SR.6, p.8; see also paras. 100 and 149 of the present report).

116. The freedom necessary for the Security Council or any other United Nations organ with responsibility for the maintenance of peace had, in the views of some delegations, still another aspect. The joint draft proposed by the Dominican Republic, Mexico, Paraguay and Peru (A/AC.77/L.11) [29]/ provided not only the freedom to name as acts of aggression events not mentioned in the definition, but also the freedom to determine the existence of, or take a decision upon, an act of aggression in case events before United Nations organs came under the acts mentioned in the definition. The representative of Yugoslavia expressed the view that the adoption of a definition of aggression would not make for the automatic application of the sanctions provided for in the Charter. Naming the aggressor must not necessarily be followed by measures to stop the aggression; the latter question was one within the jurisdiction of the competent United Nations organs (SR.7, p. 8).

117. This thought was embodied in the provision suggested by the representative of the Philippines: "Nothing in the definition would prevent the Security Council from dealing with the cases enumerated in the relevant provisions of the Charter in the manner it deemed proper in the circumstances" (SR.1, p.10; SR.2, p. 4). The USSR representative, however, took

27/ Cf. paras. 42-46 above.

28/ See annex II,3, below.

29/ See annex II, 6, below.

exception to such a provision. It would in fact authorize the Security Council to hold that an act did not constitute aggression even though it was an act enumerated in the definition. There would be no point in working out a definition if its efficacy was to be destroyed by such a reservation (SR.3, p. 9).

118. The representative of Syria, though advocating freedom for the Security Council, maintained that there should be provisions which would limit to a certain extent the discretionary powers of the competent organs of the United Nations, with a view to creating the feeling that they were at least morally bound to designate as an aggressor any State which had committed acts covered by the definition (SR.4, p. 6; SR.13, p. 13).

119. Different views also existed as to whether a definition serving as a guide to the Security Council, and consequently being a definition of "aggression" as used in Article 39, would also be valid for the term "armed attack" mentioned in Article 51 of the Charter. Delegations which agreed that "aggression" in Article 39 covered not only armed aggression but also indirect, economic or ideological aggression (USSR draft definition (A/AC.77/L.4) France, SR.2, p. 3; China, SR.3, p. 5; Czechoslovakia, SR.6, p. 5; Poland, SR.7, p. 3; Mexico, SR.7, pp. 5-6; Dominican Republic, SR.7, p. 9; Peru, SR.12, p. 4; Syria, SR.13, p. 10), held different views on the question of what place within this definition should be given to "armed aggression".

120. In the USSR draft, a clear distinction was made between "armed aggression" and the other forms of aggression, it being emphasized by the USSR representative that armed aggression constituted the most dangerous aspect, and was the only form of aggression entitling a State to the use of force in self-defence (SR.10, pp. 5-6). The Yugoslav representative stressed the point that any provision for aggression of the economic or ideological type could open the door to preventive war. That did not mean that such acts were not serious or that they could not represent a threat to the peace, but any reference to them in the definition of aggression would make it possible to justify so-called liberation crusades (SR.7, p. 7).

121. On the other hand, the representative of Peru maintained that self-defence was justified not only against armed attack but against all acts of aggression (SR.12, p.4). The representative of Syria emphasized the need for avoiding any abuse of the right of armed self-defence. Self-defence presupposed the use of means proportionate to the seriousness of the attack. States had to protect themselves with means other than the use of force in order to counter those types of aggression which might be called "secondary aggressions". It was therefore quite possible to draw up a definition covering both armed aggression and other forms, it being understood that only armed attack authorized states to exercise their natural right to armed self-defence under Article 51. It was of vital importance to avoid over-defining the concept of self-defence, for it was a natural right of self-preservation based on the duty of each State to ensure its own protection (SR.13, pp. 9 and 10).

122. Still another difference of view should be mentioned concerning the concept of armed aggression. Could it be said that "armed aggression" in the sense of Article 39 had the same meaning as "armed attack" in Article 51? In the view of the Netherlands representative, armed attack was a special case of armed aggression (SR.13, p. 15), and this view was shared by the representatives of Norway (SR.6, p. 9), Iraq (SR.4, p. 3) and Syria (SR.15, p. 7).

123. The representative of the USSR, however, considered it inconsistent with the Charter provisions to argue that the notion of armed aggression in Article 39 was different in principle from the notion of armed attack in Article 51. The provision of Article 39 relating to armed aggression (Article 39 was also concerned with other forms of aggression but they would have to be dealt with separately) and the provision of Article 51, in conjunction with Article 2, formed a single concept of armed aggression. Therefore, it was wrong to suggest that to define the notion of armed attack in Article 51 would not be so broad a task as to define the notion of armed aggression in Article 39. The task in either case would be one and the same (SR.10, p. 5).

124. In this respect, the representative of Czechoslovakia stated that Article 39 was the introductory article in the Chapter dealing with action against threats to the peace, breaches of the peace and acts of aggression. Consequently, it had to speak of aggression in its widest sense in order to give the Security Council due authority to intervene in every case that might arise. Article 51, on the other hand, was a specific provision regarding cases in which the State attacked was entitled to exercise its right of self-defence. By stating that the right of self-defence could be exercised only in cases of armed attack, the Charter merely singled out that form of aggression as the most flagrant and dangerous. The basic concept of aggression was nonetheless indivisible (SR.10, p.7).

125. For the reasons that a definition of the term "aggression" used in Article 39 for the guidance of United Nations organs seemed to be useless (since the United Nations organs did not need a definition, and hardly anyone wished to restrict their freedom of decision); that it was regarded as dangerous; and that in view of the divergence of opinions - it seemed to be impossible to achieve, the Netherlands representative suggested concentrating on the definition of "armed attack" as this expression is used in Article 51 of the Charter. He emphasized that such a definition would be useful, for confusion on this point did exist. States needed guidance in this regard, and the need to restrict their freedom of decision was clearly felt. A definition of "armed attack" on the basis of the Charter provisions would enlighten and contribute to the forming of public opinion. The possibility of arriving at a generally acceptable definition seemed not at all excluded (SR.3, pp. 6 et seq.; SR.8, pp. 5 et seq.; SR.13, pp. 14 et seq.).

126. The representative of Norway endorsed this suggestion; defining "armed attack" as referred to in Article 51 would mean, in effect, describing the circumstances justifying the use of force in self-defence (SR.6, p. 9). So did the representatives of

Iraq (SR.4, p. 3) and Syria, who urged the Committee to concentrate on defining "armed attack" within the meaning of Article 51 (SR.15, p. 7). He suggested, however, that a definition should have two parts, the first dealing with armed attack within the meaning of Article 51, the second with other forms of aggression (SR.13, pp. 9 et seq.).

127. The definition of "armed attack" in Article 51 aimed at the clarification and - within the lines drawn by the Charter - the limitation of self-defence. The importance of this purpose was realized by many delegations. The USSR representative stated that the primary object was to define aggression in such a way that the aggressor could not follow the familiar pattern and invoke the right of self-defence (SR.3, p.11). On the other hand, the singling out of the concept of armed attack as used in Article 51 was criticized. In the opinion of the Czechoslovak representative, the Netherlands representative had not proposed a definition of aggression but had only given an explanatory comment to aid in the interpretation and practical application of Article 51 (SR.10, p. 7).

128. Defining armed attack would, in the opinion of the Netherlands representative, mean dealing only with the use of armed force, armed attack being a specific case of armed aggression (SR.13, p. 15). The crucial point was to determine the cases of the use of armed force in which a State might go to war in self-defence. In this regard, the representatives of the United Kingdom and of the Netherlands agreed that, as a matter of course in case of border incidents, a State might take limited action in self-defence (SR.12, pp. 4 and 5). In the view of the Netherlands representative such protective action was not based on the provision of Article 51 of the Charter, but followed from the function of the State to maintain law and order in its territory (SR.13, p. 14). The representative of Iraq pointed out that the place of Article 51 - in Chapter VII dealing with "action with respect to threats to the peace, breaches of the peace and acts of aggression" - indicated that the self-defence referred to in that Article was defence against armed attacks of a specific quality constituting a breach of the peace (SR.18, pp. 7-8).

129. The representative of China stated that, although armed attack was the most obvious form of aggression, it was the one which stood least in need of definition (SR.3, p. 5), and it was not the most dangerous. Particularly since the end of the Second World War, aggressors had been resorting to more subtle forms of aggression. The most dangerous of them was subversion; it could not be left out of any definition of aggression. Subversion might well be said to be gradually taking the place of armed aggression as the method by which one State attacked the political independence of another. It was, therefore, not a commendable step to adopt a definition limited to armed attack; its effect would only be to create an illusion that aggression had been defined (SR.14, p. 4).

C. Views about the various types of definition

130. It has become usual in the discussions about defining aggression to list three types of definition: the general, the enumerative and the mixed definition. These three types were also referred to in the 1956 Special Committee. Not everyone, however, held the same opinion about the distinction between the types. The representative of the Philippines, surveying at the beginning of the Committee's work the attitudes of the Member States during the ninth session of the General Assembly, listed the USSR draft under the enumerative definitions. To this classification the representative of the USSR took exception, stating that in his view the USSR draft was at once analytical and synthetic; it did not, therefore, amount to a mere enumeration of acts of aggression, and for that reason it could be placed in the category of mixed definitions. It contained more than an enumeration, it also proposed a basic rule, including as it did the priority principle and the principle of the non-justification of the use of armed force in specific circumstances, as well as the principle that a State might never use armed force in response to a threat of force (SR.3, p. 11). The Yugoslav representative observed that a purely enumerative definition was now rejected by all the Member States (SR.7, p. 6).

131. Some delegations considered the question of form of secondary importance (China, SR.3, p. 4; Dominican Republic, SR.7, p. 10); others favoured in principle one of the three types. The representatives of France (SR.2, p. 3), Iraq (SR.4, p. 3) and the Netherlands (SR.8, pp. 5 et seq.) stated their position in favour of a general definition which indicated the basic elements of aggression. The representative of Iraq explained his preference for a general formula. He considered the Special Committee as a legislative rather than a judicial body, the idea being that the Committee should lay down the general rule of law, leaving it to the competent organ to adapt the rule to the specific cases referred to it. Another reason for favouring a general definition was that an enumerative definition, however meticulous, was bound to be incomplete and hence imperfect (SR.4, p. 5).

132. A general definition was criticized as too vague, and as being only a paraphrase of the Charter. According to the representative of Czechoslovakia, the Charter did not list the basic elements constituting aggression. General Assembly resolution 599 (VI) referred to the elements constituting aggression; they were nothing else than the acts or series of acts of aggression which constituted aggression itself (SR.6, p. 4).

133. The mixed definition, favoured by most of the members, was criticized in relation to the specific draft proposals. The United States representative associated himself with a statement made in the Sixth Committee by the representative of India: "A general definition would be of little value because it would be too vague, an enumerative definition would be dangerous because it might contain too much or too little, and a mixed definition was apt to combine the disadvantages of the other two types" (SR.13, pp. 3 and 4).

2. Views with regard to specific draft definitions

A. The USSR draft (A/AC.77/L.4)[30]

134. The USSR draft definition dealt with several forms of aggression: armed aggression, indirect, economic and ideological aggression. It was made clear that the right of individual and collective self-defence as recognized in Article 51 had to do only with defence against armed attack, the most dangerous type of breach of the peace. The representative of the USSR pointed out that the definition of armed attack was the principal task. The divergencies of views which might again become apparent regarding the definition of indirect, economic and ideological forms of aggression should not hinder an agreement on a definition of armed attack. The primary object of a definition was to define in such a way that the aggressor could not follow the familiar pattern and invoke the right of self-defence. Therefore it was necessary to concentrate on that fundamental question (SR.3, pp. 10 and 11).

135. The representative of the USSR observed that the USSR draft was at once analytical and synthetic in type. Paragraph 1 contained more than a simple enumeration, it also proposed a basic rule. It contained the principle that any State which first committed an act enumerated in that paragraph, on any pretext, should be declared an attacker. Paragraphs 6 and 7 emphasized the same point and specified that aggression could not be justified by any considerations of a political, strategic or economic nature, or by the desire to derive any kind of advantage or privilege, and that the threat of aggression could not be used as a pretext for armed attack (SR.3, p. 11). On later occasions he emphasized the significance of the essential principle of the first commission of an act (SR.14, p. 9), which constituted the basic principle (SR.15, p. 4). In particular, he pointed out that the principle that the State which first used armed force against another State should be declared the attacker was likewise derived from Article 51 of the Charter, since that Article regarded armed attack as an act antecedent to self-defence. He considered that that principle was widely recognized in international law (SR.14, p. 9).

136. The representative of Czechoslovakia concurred in attaching great importance to the priority principle, linked as it was with a list of actions which States were forbidden to commit first (SR.6, p. 5). So did the representative of Poland, who emphasized the idea that responsibility should invariably lie with the State guilty of the first attack (SR.7, P. 3).

137. The USSR draft was considered by the delegate of Syria as the most complete and specific of all those submitted. He thought that the examples given as illustrations of the various forms of aggression should be retained. But he considered that a general formula should be given to define "armed attack" as the term was used in Article 51. Other remedies than those provided in that Article were open to States in other cases of aggression. Consequently, the definition of aggression should consist of two parts, the first

dealing with armed attack within the meaning of Article 51, and the second dealing with the other (unarmed) forms of aggression. The first part would contain a general formula describing armed attack and an illustrative list of the most characteristic examples of armed attack; there should be a clause specifying the cases in which the use of individual or collective force was permitted in self-defence. Another clause would enable the competent organs of the United Nations to preserve the freedom of judgement and action necessary to deal with any situation. The second part of the definition should contain a general formula describing the secondary forms of aggression likely to endanger the maintenance of international peace and security within the meaning of the provisions of Chapter VI or the Charter. It would also contain a list - again not an exhaustive list - of the most characteristic cases of unarmed aggression, a clause which would allow the competent organs of the United Nations to designate as unarmed aggression any additional cases which might arise in the future. Such a system would be harmonious and all-inclusive; it would condemn all acts of aggression, and armed attack in particular; it would not prevent a state from claiming the right of self-defence in the case of armed attack; and, finally, it would make provision for other remedies in the case of unarmed aggression.

138. The USSR draft failed, in the opinion of the representative of Syria, to deal with two important problems: it did not specify the cases in which a victim of armed attack could resort to arms immediately in self-defence, or the remedies open to a victim of indirect aggression. The word "aggression", wherever used in the USSR text, should be qualified by whatever terms corresponded to the particular type of aggression dealt with.

139. Following these general observations, the Syrian representative suggested some particular alterations in the USSR draft. The word "social" should be inserted in paragraph 6, in conformity with the Mexican amendment. The second sub-paragraph 6 should read: "In particular, the following may not be used as justification for armed attack" (SR.13, pp. 8 et seq.). To this list of events not justifying the use of armed force should be added the nationalization by a State of foreign companies, or of companies comprising foreign elements which exploited the natural resources of a State (SR.4, p. 6). Finally, paragraph 5 should be amended so as to allow the Security Council greater freedom of action; at the same time, there should be provisions which would limit to a certain extent the discretionary powers of the Council or any other competent organ of the United Nations with a view to creating the feeling that it was at least morally bound to designate as an aggressor any State which had committed acts covered by the definition (SR.13, p. 13).

140. It will not be necessary in the present report to elaborate the differences between the USSR and the Mexican draft definitions, which follow more or less the same pattern. Those differences may be seen from a comparison of the texts.[31]

30/ See annex II, 1, below.

31/ See annex II, 1 and 5, below.

141. The same applies to the joint draft of the Dominican Republic, Mexico, Paraguay and Peru.[32/] This draft, although in important aspects different from the USSR draft, has in common with the latter the enumeration of specific acts which shall be considered as acts of aggression in all cases, and a paragraph indicating circumstances which never justify aggression. The observations of the USSR representative about the differences between the USSR draft and the joint proposal will be found in paragraph 200 below.

142. The USSR draft met with criticism from some delegations. According to the representative of the United States, the USSR definition created hazards by its omissions. It had been said that enumeration did not produce a definition at all, but rather an incomplete catalogue of methods. While considerable effort had obviously been made toward completeness, it would be unrealistic to assume that it was possible to foresee all the forms which the ingenuity of aggressors would contrive, especially if such a blueprint were given them in advance. There was a real danger, which must not be ignored, of creating a hierarchy of offences, in which the listed offences assumed, in the eyes of the State against which the act was directed as well as the eyes of the international organization responsible for dealing with it, a greater significance and seriousness than the omitted offences. Nor was the problem met by the inclusions of a provision authorizing the organs of the United Nations to find other acts to be acts of aggression. The danger was not that an organ would be precluded from making such a finding, but that the effect would be to discourage such a determination.

143. The United States representative asked how the proposed definition would affect the work of the United Nations organs responsible for the maintenance of peace. In his view the USSR draft, like any definition of its kind, created psychological hazards which would hinder the effective operation of the peace-maintaining machinery.

144. As to the question of the effect of the definition on the decisions of States, the United States representative believed that other problems were created. A look at the USSR draft suggested that it enumerated two broad categories of offences as instances of aggression. In the first category were the major and flagrant acts of aggression, such as armed attack, declaration of war, bombardment and so forth. No one could deny that those constituted acts of aggression. They also sometimes constituted acts of self-defence. What, then, he asked, was the use of that part of a definition? It did not simplify the functions of either the international organs or the State attacked to be told that major military acts of this nature were aggressive, when they might also be self-defence. It was the consideration of those acts in the context in which they were committed that constituted the problem before the United Nations and, in this respect, the question of "first act" was as deceptively simple in appearance as it was unworkable in practice.

145. The United States representative further observed that certain characteristics of the USSR draft

definition created other problems. The most conspicuous omission in the USSR draft definition was its failure to make an exception for collective security measures, whether at the behest of the Security Counsil or pursuant to Article 51. By that token, military action against a State would be aggression even though it had been called for by the Council under Article 42, and was made mandatory under Article 25.

146. It was further characteristic of the draft, he observed, that it created more definitional problems than it solved.

147. Furthermore, he did not believe that the wording of the provisions of paragraph 1 was free from danger. For instance, how would the provisions of paragraph 1 (b), (c), (d), (e) and (f) apply when the territory involved was of disputed ownership (SR.13, p. 7)?

148. In the opinion of the United States representative, a definition adopted by the General Assembly would and should weigh heavily on any debates within the Security Council concerning particular cases. To the extent that it carried such weight, the definition would tend to focus attention on the listed or enumerated acts. Such a definition would not facilitate but rather hinder expeditious action by organs of the United Nations by transferring the focus of attention from the real problem of ascertaining the facts to the artificial and formal one of determining whether the facts fitted the definition (SR.13, p. 7; SR.17, p. 4).

149. The representative of the United Kingdom associated himself with this point of view. He maintained that a definition containing a list of acts of aggression did not, as had been suggested, become free of all disadvantages by the inclusion of a provision authorizing the organs of the United Nations to find acts, other than those listed as such in the definition, to be acts of aggression. Such a provision would give rise to a tendency to regard as less important those acts not mentioned in the definition. This was not unwarranted pessimism as to the good sense of the organs of the United Nations, as the USSR representative (SR.14, p. 8) had suggested. It was of course a matter of opinion, but it was the opinion of at least the majority of the Committee whose report M. Paul-Boncour had presented at San Francisco in 1945, and which had agreed "to leave to the Council the entire decision as to what constitutes a threat to peace, a breach of the peace or an act of aggression"[33/] That Committee's decision appeared to show a greater confidence in the Council's good sense than did those who thought that the Council needed a definition in order to function efficiently. Moreover, even with such a provision it would be open to an aggressor to argue that acts not specified in the definition prima facie did not constitute aggression (SR.16, p. 3).

150. The United Kingdom representative stressed his misgivings with regard to the priority principle, the criterion of the "first act". According to the USSR representative, this principle was embodied in Article 51 of the Charter (SR.14, p. 9). But that reference did

32/ Annex II, 6, below.

33/ United Nations Conference on International Organization, vol.12, p.505, quoted in A/2211, para 116.

not justify making the priority principle the basic element in the definition of aggression. It was self-evident that for a legitimate exercise of the right of self-defence something must first have happened to call it into play. It was, however, no denial of that to say that a definition which made the first of certain specified acts the decisive criterion did not afford a simple and infallible guide to determining who was the aggressor. That question was to be determined in the light of all the facts and circumstances (SR.16, pp. 3 et seq.).

151. The Netherlands representative emphasized that the priority principle was inherent in every definition dealing with armed attack and self-defence. The only problem was to what kinds of acts the priority principle was related. In regard to the problem of the quality of acts which made them "armed attack" in the sense of Article 51, the priority principle did not contribute anything, unless it were regarded as sufficient that the act was any act of force, which apparently the USSR draft did not. For that draft mentioned frontier incidents as acts which might not be used as justification of an attack. Thus, the question arose what use of force constituted a frontier incident, and what use of force constituted attack. The practice in the time of the League of Nations showed that in the cases when both parties had used force the priority principle was not decisive. Recent history showed that opinions differed about what was a border incident. The Noman Han and Lake Kassan hostilities in the late 1930's had at that time been considered as border incidents, but had been branded as aggressive wars by the Tokyo Tribunal in 1948. The USSR representative explained this difference in evaluation by the fact that, in 1948, new light was thrown upon the actual events, wich appeared to be part of a general aggressive plan, and he recognized that it might not always be easy to establish whether a particular military action was a frontier incident or a form of aggression (SR.10, p. 4). In the opinion of the Netherlands representative, this demonstrated that the need did exist for a criterion to distinguish between frontier incidents and armed attacks. The priority principle did not give any assistance on this point. A definition designed to clarify Article 51 would necessarily indicate in what cases the use of force (amounting, as the context of Article 51 showed, to a breach of the peace) could be answered by a State by the use of its own armed forces (SR.13, p.14).

152. The representative of the Netherlands also found difficulty with the priority principle in another respect. The USSR draft recognized that other cases of armed attack than those listed did exist. Paragraph 5 of the draft definition granted the Security Council the freedom to declare other acts than those listed in paragraph 1 to be an attack. Did such freedom exist for the individual State (SR.16, p. 8)? The USSR representative answered that question in the affirmative (SR.16, p. 8). But if cases of armed attack other than those listed in paragraph 1 did exist, and a State so attacked might answer the attack with force under Article 51, what, the Netherlands representative wondered, was left of the priority principle, which declared to be the aggressor the State which first committed one of the listed acts (SR.17, p. 5).

153. The same opinion about the relation between the priority principle and the list of events enumerated in the USSR definition was held by the representative of Iraq, who considered that in that list too much emphasis was laid upon the material aspects of the events, and too little upon the legal aspects. In his view, the USSR draft lacked a distinction between acts of force which did constitute aggression and acts of force which did not. The gravity of the act and of the situation in which it was happening should be taken into account (SR.18, pp. 7 and 8).

154. In reply to the above objections, the representative of the USSR stated that in his view the United States, United Kingdom and Netherlands representatives had misinterpreted the USSR draft and, as a result, had arrived at unwarranted conclusions. In particular, it was incorrect to state that the USSR draft did not distinguish between armed aggression and self-defence. From the thecnical military standpoint, the acts enumerated in the USSR draft could be acts either of aggression or of self-defence. The USSR draft made it perfectly clear, however, that the acts it enumerated should be declared acts of aggression if they were first committed by a State against another State. That was likewise in accordance with Article 51 of the United Nations Charter, which regarded armed attack as an act antecedent to self-defence. With regard to measures of collective self-defence taken under Article 51 of the Charter and measures adopted by the Security Council, it was obvious that the USSR draft was based wholly on the provisions of the Charter, though it omitted a needless reiteration of the relevant Charter provisions. In his view, there were no grounds for the attitude that the USSR draft cast doubt on the legality of measures which might be adopted by the Security Council pursuant to Chapter VII of the Charter. In reply to the Netherlands representative, the representative of the USSR noted what he regarded as an incorrect approach to criticism of the USSR draft definition of aggression. In his opinion, it was a mistake to criticize any definition on the ground that it could not be applied without ascertaining the precise facts needed to clarify the actual situation, and that such a procedure entailed some effort, especially when a distinction had to be drawn between an act of armed aggression and a frontier incident. The USSR definition of aggression laid down the clear-cut principle that the commission of acts of aggression by a State might not be justified by a frontier incident. Again, it was incorrect to assert that the USSR draft restricted the right of self-defence where armed attack occurred in a form other than those envisaged in the draft. If there was a genuine armed attack, Article 51 of the United Nations Charter would apply even in such hypothetical cases (SR.16, p. 8; SR.17, pp. 9 and 10).

B. The Paraguayan draft (A/AC.77/L.7)[34]/

155. The representative of the United States of America considered that the Paraguayan draft definition was a mixed definition and, since it was impossible for a text to be both broad and precise, it had all the defects of both general and enumerative definitions. Coming to the specific provisions, he stated that several noticeable defects existed.

[34]/ See annex II, 2, below.

156. In particular, he asked, since according to the draft a State committed aggression when it provoked a disturbance of international peace and security by employing armed forces against the people, territory or armed forces of a non-self-governing territory, would a State putting down a revolt in its non-self-governing territory be committing aggression? Paragraph 1 appeared to envision automatic determination of aggression in that instance.

157. It was generally considered, the United States representative said, that "aggression" was the narrowest of the jurisdictional terms used in Chapter VII (i.e., breach of the peace, threat to the peace and act of aggression). Yet the definition made a "breach of international peace" a sub-heading of aggression, that is, armed aggression. This was an example of how far the attempt to define aggression broadened the concept.

158. No direct provision was made, the United States representative observed, for collective security or Chapter VII action. The effect of the phrase "provokes a breach or disturbance of international peace and security" was obscure in this connexion because of the vagueness of the phrase, especially in situations where it was clear that the victim State would bow peaceably to the threat of its larger neighbour, were it not for the reinforcement of the victim's friends or United Nations enforcement troops. The possibility of the ally of the victim State being considered the aggressor under this definition was evident.

159. In paragraph 1, he remarked, the phrase "provoke a breach or disturbance of international peace and security" was crucial, since otherwise any use of military force was prohibited, even conceivably when force was used withing the territory of the "aggressor" State. This phrase created more problems than the term aggression. For example, did "provoke" mean the first act of aggression, or would the term include hostile acts which did not constitute aggression? When had international peace and security been "breached" or "disturbed"? What actually would be required here was an ad hoc measure of the dangers of the situation, i.e., was there a dangerous "breach" or "disturbance"? This would force the Security Council back into the procedure it now followed of considering all the circumstances of the case. Thus, the definition would serve no purpose, and would merely complicate and prolong the process.

160. When were armed forces, the United States representative asked, directed "against the... sovereignty or political independence of another State"? This could only be determined, again, by an ad hoc consideration of all the facts and circumstances.

161. Paragraph 2, according to the United States representative, dealt with two rather special situations. The first was where the aggressor announced his aggression, an increasingly rare occurrence. He was compelled to ask, under paragraph 2 (a), whether the declaration of war was "in contravention of Articles 1 and 2 of the Charter". These were the Purposes and Principles of the United Nations, and they were as broad as the Charter in its entirety. The effect of this provision was to raise the question of any violation of the Charter, which was so broad, again, as to require ad hoc consideration of the whole matter. It was necessary to ask again if the only predictable consequence of this paragraph would not be to put a premium on unannounced aggression.

162. With regard to paragraph 2 (b), which concerned the organization, encouragement, support or mere toleration of armed bands intended to take action against other States, the United States representative considered that there were a number of problems. For example, when was an armed force an armed band and when was it not? Was it not necessary to qualify the "action" of the armed band with a word like "aggressive", and thereby make paragraph 2 (b) clearer (SR.13, pp. 5 and 6)?

163. The representative of the United Kingdom concurred in this appraisal, stressing the point that the Paraguayan draft was a mixed definition and, like other mixed definitions, must stand or fall by its introductory general formula. In his opinion, the draft failed in that respect. Moreover, it did not make any exception for self-defence (SR.16, p. 4).

164. The Syrian delegate considered the draft open to criticism on points of form (SR.14, p. 10).

165. The representative of the Netherlands associated himself with those who felt that words like "provoke", "breach of the peace" and "disturbance of the peace" needed definition. He considered it dangerous to introduce into the definition new general concepts not used in the Charter. He also found it dangerous to declare as aggression the organization, encouragement, support or mere toleration of the formation of armed bands intended to take action against other States (paragraph 2 (b)). In what circumstances, he asked, were bands to be considered as "intended to take action"? Was a State entitled to apply Article 51 in self-defence against such bands before they had started action against this State (SR.17, p. 5)?

166. In view of the fact that the representative of Paraguay had co-sponsored the joint Latin American draft proposal (A/AC.77/L.11, see section G below), the Paraguayan draft was not further discussed.

C. The joint draft of Iran and Panama, reintroduced by Peru (A/AC.77/L.9)[35/]

167. The representative of Peru requested that the definition proposed by Iran and Panama in the Sixth Committee at the ninth session of the General Assembly (A/C.6/L.335/Rev.1) should be circulated so that it would be taken into consideration by the present Committee (SR.14, p. 7).

168. The representative of the United States of America noted that the Iran-Panama draft like the drafts of Paraguay and China was of the mixed type, and showed the shortcomings of all mixed definitions. As was common with mixed definitions, they began with a general definition, followed by an enumeration that was generally very brief. Presumably an attempt was made to supply a broad scope by the general definition, and to supply definiteness by the enumeration. This was not possible, since the two were independent definitions loosely linked together, the latter not compensating for the former. The result

---

35/ See annex II, 3, below.

was not a broad yet precise definition. Rather, the defects and dangers of both became apparent. What were the dangers? They included an apparent hierarchy of offences and the danger of misleading the Security Council by directing attention to the wrong aspects of a situation. All of these dangers were present in mixed definitions.

169. The dangers presented by the general portions of these definitions were, in the view of the United States representative, that:

(1) A general definition might be either too narrow, so that it restricted the jurisdiction of the Security Council, or so broad that it did not help the Council in establishing whether or not an act of aggression had occurred, and created the danger of over-extension of United Nations jurisdiction;

(a) A general definition created more definitional problems than it solved. This was the inevitable effect of defining a term in other terms no more precise than itself.

170. Coming to more detailed observations, the United States representative stated that paragraph 1 defined aggression by treating it as the residue after self-defence and enforcement action had been subtracted. This created several problems: no elaboration of the limits of the right of individual or collective self-defence was offered. To state that aggression was that which was not self-defence or enforcement action, and then not to define self-defence, would not be helpful. It would be just as valid, and of just as much utility, to state that self-defence was that which was not aggression or enforcement action. That would not reduce the problem of the Security Council.

171. Paragraph 2 had, in his view, a number of defects as well. It did not effectively assimilate the exclusions of paragraph 1, although it should do so and probably was intended to do so. It stated that the listed acts constituted aggression "in all cases" yet, under paragraph 1, the acts would not be aggression if they were pursuant to a decision of the Security Council or in self-defence. That illustrated one of the dangers of any mixed definition. The problem of statutory construction, when there was a conflict between the general and the specific parts of a statute, might also occur on an international place. Confusion of that sort would impede the operation of the Security Council, or else impel it to disregard the definition altogether.

172. Paragraph 2 (a), the United States representative observed, made no provision for the determination by impartial methods of when jurisdiction over a territory was "effective". Claims that the disputed territory was in a state of chaos might be expected to precede an attempt to occupy it if such a definition was adopted.

173. Such terms as "attack" were no more meaningful than the term "aggression". Since both involved an evaluation of motive and assessment of danger, neither could be determined except on the basis of an ad hoc inquiry into all the circumstances (SR.13, p. 6).

174. The representative of the United Kingdom shared this view about the shortcomings and insuf-

ficiencies of any mixed definition. He stressed the point that the inclusion of the concept of self-defence in the definition raised the problem of the definition of self-defence (SR.16, p. 4).

175. The representative of the Netherlands considered that, by defining aggression as "the use of force against another State", the definition did not make any exception for border clashes, and would entitle a State to answer small-scale hostilities with war. He found a still greater danger in the last paragraph, which spoke of "armed bands for incursions". From that paragraph it followed that aggression already existed before any incursion had taken place and, therefore, such a provision might give a potential aggressor a very convenient pretext (SR.17, p. 6).

D. The Chinese draft (A/C.6/L.336/Rev.2)[36]

176. The representative of the United States of America considered that the Chinese definition was a variation of the other mixed definitions. The definition was a broad statement, the enumerative section apparently being purely illustrative rather than exhaustive. This raised the question whether this was properly considered an enumerative definition or a general one.

177. While it might well be, the United States representative remarked, that such loose treatment of the enumerative section of the definition reduced the dangers of over-emphasis by the Security Council of the acts of aggression mentioned therein and of under-emphasis of the omitted ones, the danger was still there, and the formula presented additional difficult definitional problems. The wording was so general that it might be doubted whether it would assist the functioning of the Council in determining whether an act of aggression had been committed. For example, when was force unlawful? What was an attack? Against whom and what must it be directed? Such questions were as difficult to define as aggression.

178. In his view, the provisions of paragraphs 2 and 3, while reasonably clear when read separately, had anomalous and contradictory implications when read together. It would appear that, although the indirect use of armed force was designated as aggression under paragraph 1, and although the right of self-defence against armed attack was recognized by paragraph 2, the use of armed force by "indirect" means would not under paragraph 3 justify the use of armed force to repel it. Under such circumstances, an elaboration of the term "direct" was essential but was not provided. This was one of the more serious definitional problems to which he had referred.

179. However the central criticism by the United States representative of the Chinese draft definition was its assumption. It was explicit in the Chinese definition, but implicit in the others. The assumption equated aggression with illegality. It was true that under the Charter aggression was unjust, i.e., illegal.

[36] Reproduced under No. 17 in working paper A/AC.77/L.6 which forms annex I to the present report. The draft definition was submitted to the Sixth Committee at the ninth session of the General Assembly and was not re-introduced in the present Special Committee.

But it was not true that everything illegal was therefore aggression. The assumption that everything illegal was aggression might be a reason for definitional difficulties. It also raised a dangerous suggestion that what was not aggression was therefore not illegal. This chain of reasoning was fallacious. It would be dangerous to seek to base Security Council action on such a fallacy.

180. The United States representative said that this was not to minimize the difficulty of ascertaining whether the nature of an act was aggressive or not. The intentions of the various persons controlling the actions of State were significant, but were only one element. An appreciation of the dangers created by the action, as well as other factors, was involved. These factors could not be reduced to a formula, and must be considered on an ad hoc basis (SR.13, p.6).

181. The representative of the United Kingdom agreed that the Chinese draft definition raised various definitional problems, including the meaning of self-defence. A specific difficulty was raised by the insertion of the concept of subversion in the definition of aggression. Although recognizing the importance of subversion, he maintained that it would be both very difficult and dangerous to insert subversive activities in the definition of aggression. Consequently, it would neither be satisfactory to include the concept, nor to exclude it. The same dilemma arose on many other points in connexion with defining aggression, which showed that it was better not to have a definition at all (SR.16, p. 4).

182. In reply to the comment of the United States representative, the representative of China observed that the words "unlawful use of force by a State against another State, whether directly or indirectly", appearing in operative paragraph 1 of the Chinese proposal, did not create further problems of definition; the terms were themselves defined in operative paragraphs 2 and 3. Moreover, the concept that unlawful use of force constitutes aggression was based on the provisions of Article 2, paragraph 4, of the Charter (SR.14, p.4).

E. The Iraq draft (A/AC.77/L.8/Rev.1)[37/]

183. The representative of Iraq, in introducing his draft definition, stated that it had been prepared after a careful comparison of the various proposals made to the organs of the United Nations, particularly the International Law Commission. He favoured a definition of the general type, giving a general rule of law, and leaving it to the competent organs to adapt the rule to the specific cases referred to them. The definition dealt with the use of force and did not cover other forms of aggression, any attempt at the moment to define indirect forms of aggression being doomed to failure. It was based on the fundamental difference between the concept of aggression under Article 39 of the Charter and that embodied in Article 51.

184. In order to distinguish between self-defence and an act of armed attack - bearing in mind that the situ-

ation in both cases was similar - the Iraqi representative had chosen a flexible criterion, taking into account both the purpose and the effect of the act in question; armed attack was an act aimed at, or resulting in, a change in the international juridical situation and a disturbance of international peace and security. The material factor was the gravity of the attack, judged by its scale and intensity.

185. The representative of Iraq emphasized that the definition took into account the fact that an international community lacking the attributes of statehood could nevertheless be a victim of aggression. Article 51 of the Charter dealt only with attacks on Member States, but it spoke of the inherent right of self-defence. Communities which were not States might also invoke that right (SR.14, pp. 5 to 7).

186. The representative of the United States considered that the Iraqi definition was open to all the objections voiced concerning definitions of the general type, which created more definitional problems than they solved (SR.17, p.3).

187. The United Kingdom representative found the Iraqi definition no more satisfactory than any other general definition. It was difficult to understand what was meant by some of the phrases employed in it: for instance, "the conditions of existence of the people and territories of a government or group of governments" and "a change in the international juridical situation" (SR.16, p.5).

188. The representative of Peru said that, in his opinion, the draft of Iraq was vague and confused in form. He considered that its most serious defect was the apparent implication that an armed attack would not necessarily constitute a breach of peace and security or a disturbance of the international juridical situation (SR.15, p.5). This view was shared by the representative of China, who feared that such a definition would impair the right of individual and collective self-defence, and might give the attacker new pretexts for his aggressive designs (SR.18, p.5).

189. The USSR representative considered the defects of the draft inherent in all definitions of a general type. The first part reproduced in essence the general formula proposed by Professor Alfaro to the International Law Commission at its third session (A/CN.4/L.8). In the light of criticism of this formula, Professor Alfaro had amended it and attached to it examples of acts of aggression. The re-appearance of the general formula was a retrograde development (SR.15, p.3). The general formula amounted, in the view of the USSR representative, to nothing more than the formula "aggression is aggression" (SR.14, p.10). The effect of the second part of the general formula used in the Iraq draft was to restrict the provisions, and even to alter the sense, of Article 51 of the United Nations Charter. Moreover, the Iraq draft contained no such over-riding criterion for the determination of the aggressor as first commission by a State of certain acts against another State. It failed to stipulate that armed aggression could not be justified on the grounds of any political, economic or strategic considerations. A definition of aggression which failed to embody those principles could not be effective.

37/ See annex II, 4, below.

190. The Netherlands representative shared the opinion of those who considered that many terms which needed definition were used in the draft. Another objection was based on the divergence of the phrasing of the definition from the wording of the Charter provisions; e.g., "independence" instead of "political independence" (SR.17, p.5).

191. On the other hand, the Netherlands representative expressed his support of two principles recognized in the Iraqi draft definition. First, a distinction was made between "aggression" in the sense of Article 39 and "armed attack" as used in Article 51. Secondly, the draft incorporated the principle that comunities not having statehood could commit, as well as be victims of, aggression (SR.13, p.15). The latter principle had also the support of the representative of China (SR.14, p.4).

192. Answering the objections, the representative of Iraq maintained that the definition was in accordance with the provisions of the Charter taken as a whole. In particular, the definition proposed by his delegation was based on Article 2, paragraphs 3 and 4, of the Charter and on the provisions of Chapter VI which prohibits any change by force in the international juridical situation and recommends the use of peaceful means for the settlement of international disputes. Not every act of violence was, in the opinion of his delegation, an aggression in the sense of Article 51 of the Charter; only an act sufficiently serious to disturb international peace and security justified the recourse to self-defence. This view was clearly reflected in the provisions of Article 51. Regarding the omission of the adjective "political" before the word "independence", referred to by the Netherlands delegate, the representative of Iraq pointed out that Article 2, paragraph 4, of the Charter prohibited the threat or use of force not only "against the territorial integrity or political independence of any State," but also "in any other manner inconsistent with the purposes of the United Nations". The formula used by the Charter in this connexion was therefore wider than political independence. (SR.18, pp.7 and 8).

F. The Mexican draft (A/AC.77/L.10)[38/]

193. In view of the fact that the representative of Mexico was a co-sponsor of the joint Latin American draft (A/AC.77/L.11) – though reserving his right to revert to his own proposal if the joint draft did not succeed in finding general support – the Mexican proposal was not thoroughly discussed. The representative of Czechoslovakia wondered why this proposal, so close in structure to the USSR draft, deviated in so many details (SR.17, p. 8). The Netherlands representative observed that sub-paragraph (d) of the Mexican proposal made a distinction between "the support to the organization of bands for incursion" and "the support for such incursions". Both events were considered as aggression, which seemed to him a too broad, and therefore dangerous, concept of aggression.

194. The Netherlands representative objected to the subjective element in the general formula "for the purpose of attacking". If the definition of "armed aggression" in the Mexican proposal constituted at the same time a definition of "armed attack" as used in Article 51, it followed that armed attack was, in the words of the Mexican draft, "the ... use of force ... for the purpose of attacking". Moreover, if the definition covered "armed attack" in Article 51, it was still more difficult to understand the enumerated events, among which one – sub-paragraph (b) – consisted of "armed attack".

195. The last paragraph was almost identical with the USSR draft. The Netherlands representative had the same misgivings as he had concerning that draft; according to Article 51, armed force could never be used except against armed force or in the service of the United Nations. To mention special circumstances not justifying the use of force would weaken the legal position (SR.17, p. 6).

G. The joint draft of the Dominican Republic, Mexico, Paraguay and Peru (A/AC.77/L.11)[39/]

196. The representative of Mexico, introducing the joint draft proposal, stated that the authors had endeavoured to produce a definition which would be acceptable, in existing circumstances, to the greatest possible number of States. To achieve a common proposal, they had made substantial sacrifices. The text could only become perfect after much time, experience, practice and adaptation (SR.16, pp. 6 and 7).

197. The representative of the Dominican Republic explained that the principal purpose of the authors of the joint draft resolution was to find an objective formula. For that reason, the draft contained no preamble; recitals could help in the interpretation of the operative part, but they might also contain features prejudicial to the objectivity of the operative clauses. In seeking to ensure that objectivity, the authors had based their proposal not only on the United Nations Charter but also on the Charter of the Organization of American States, especially articles 24 and 25 of the latter instrument, and they had also taken into consideration the 1947 Inter-American Treaty of Reciprocal Assistance as well as the various proposed definitions before the present Committee. The wording of paragraph 1 reflected the belief of the American States that provision should be made for forms of aggression other than armed attack. Paragraph 2 listed some specific cases in which the aggressor's intention was beyond dispute; that feature enhanced the proposed formula's objectivity (SR.16, p. 7).

198. It was explained by the representative of Paraguay that "declaration of war" mentioned in paragraph 2 (a) meant a declaration followed by hostilities. A more theoretical kind of declaration could not form an element of the concept of aggression (SR.18, p. 6).

199. The representative of Peru stressed the point that the draft definition dealt with any use of force. It seemed inappropriate to make in the definition a distinction between armed aggression and armed attack. In fact, Article 39 merely referred to aggression in the widest possible sense, while Article 51

38/ See annex II, 5, below.

39/ See annex II, 6, below.

dealt with one particular form which aggression might take. Armed attack had been singled out only because it was the one occurrence which justified forcible counter-measures. The four-Power draft resolution was consequently logical in stating that any use of force other than in self-defence was aggression (SR.17, pp. 8 and 9).

200. The representative of the USSR remarked that the joint draft presented by the four Latin American countries was to some extent an improvement on the drafts those countries had advocated at the ninth session of the General Assembly. It was one indication of the positive results of the present Committee's work. At the same time that draft had, he felt, the following shortcomings. Between the general formula of the draft, in which an attempt was made to express both the notion of armed aggression and other forms of aggression, and the part containing an enumeration of acts of armed aggression, there was a contradiction which, in his view, detracted from the clarity of the general definition and might give rise to a dangerous impression that force might be used in self-defence in cases other than that in which it was permissible under Article 51 of the Charter, i.e., the case of an armed attack on a State. The four-Power draft contained no such fundamental criterion for determining the attacking party as an attack first committed by a State against another State. The four-Power draft, in contrast to the USSR draft, omitted, for no good reason, the provision that the commission of acts of armed aggression could not be justified by strategic considerations, and it excluded, again for no good reason, an exhaustive enumeration of other political and economic acts which could not justify acts of aggression. Finally he felt that, in the form in which they were expressed in the draft, the provisions concerning the use of armed force upon the decision of the United Nations ran counter to Chapter VII of the Charter. While the draft contained several valid provisions, he did not feel that, as a whole, it could be considered an effective definition of aggression in accordance with the Charter (SR.18, pp. 4 and 5).

201. According to the representative of the United States, the draft demonstrated the extent to which efforts to solve the extremely difficult problems involved in the definition of aggression could fall short of producing a satisfactory formula. It revealed the effects of an eclectic approach to the problem. It also showed how a willingness to compromise on basic issues produced nothing more than a patchwork combination of so-called "common elements" which it would be highly inadvisable and unproductive for the Committee to offer to the General Assembly (SR.17, p. 3).

202. The representative of the Netherlands stated that several concepts in the definition, e.g., "territorial inviolability" and "sovereignty", would need further defining. He wondered whether, in case "any use of force" mentioned in the draft constituted "armed attack", the definition would open the door for warlike hostilities in reaction to border skirmishes. He found it difficult to grasp the meaning of the words "in all cases" in paragraph 2, in view of the opening words of this paragraph. "Armed attack" was mentioned in

paragraph 2 (c) as one of the cases of aggression. The words "armed attack" apparently had another meaning than the same words used in Article 51. Finally, he had objections to the last paragraph, for the use of force could never be justified except in self-defence against armed attack or in the service of the United Nations (SR.17, pp. 6 and 7). The representative of China shared his misgivings about the words "in all cases". He considered the last paragraph superfluous and misleading, for the reason that aggression never was justified. He missed in the definition a reference to subversive activities (SR.18, p. 6).

H. The Netherlands representative's suggestion for a definition of "armed attack"

203. The Netherlands representative considered that to define aggression as the term is used in Article 39 of the Charter, as a guide for the organs called upon to apply that Article, was useless, dangerous and impossible. It was useless, for United Nations organs did not need guidance. It was dangerous, for the definition might hinder United Nations organs in the fulfilment of their task. It was impossible, for it seemed beyond human capacity to formulate a generally acceptable definition.

204. In his opinion, former attempts to define aggression had failed for the reason that the broad definition of aggression given in Article 39 could not be reconciled with the narrow concept of armed attack presupposed in Article 51. That difficulty would no longer exist in case only "armed attack" was to be defined. Such a definition might be helpful, for different views existed as to the scope of the right of self-defence, as recognized in Article 51. A definition of "armed attack" would be a useful guide for States, and might assist in the formation of a clear public opinion.

205. Such a definition of armed attack should, in the view of the Netherlands representative, make clear in what cases a State was entitled to use armed force otherwise prohibited as constituting a breach of the peace. The place of Article 51 in Chapter VII indicated clearly that small-scale hostilities connected with border incidents fell outside the scope of that Article. The crucial problem concerning the concepts of armed attack was, in his view, to find the criterion distinguishing armed attack from any other use of force, which did not entitle the State to take the action provided for in Article 51. He found this criterion in the use of force in such circumstances that the victim State had no means other than military to preserve its territorial integrity or political independence. If the use of force was such that United Nations intervention could provide sufficient protection, an armed attack within the meaning of Article 51 did not exist.

206. Consequently, on the one hand, not every shooting, bombing or trespassing across the border constituted armed attack and, on the other hand, armed attack was possible even without a bomb having been dropped or a border having been violated. In exceptional cases the factual direction of the armed force of a State against another State might, even without actual contact, constitute such a use of armed force as would constitute an armed attack under Article 51, for example, when the Japanese battleships were approaching Pearl Harbour.

207. The Netherlands representative shared the view, expressed by the representatives of Iraq and China, that an armed attack could be launched by a group or community which was not a State, and that such a community might also be the victim of an armed attack, e.g., territories under an international régime, as Trieste was at one time. However it seemed to the Netherlands representative that, in defining "armed attack" as the expression was used in Article 51, no reference should be made to such special units or communities. Article 51 dealt only with an armed attack by a State against a State. Definition of that concept would as a matter of course have a bearing on cases in which non-States were involved.

208. On the basis of these considerations, the Netherlands representative thought that a definition of armed attack might read:

"Armed attack as this term is used in Article 51 is any use of armed force which leaves the State against which it is directed no means other than military means to preserve its territorial integrity or political independence; it being understood that the definition may never be construed to comprise acts of legitimate individual or collective self-defence or any act in pursuance of a decision or recommendation by a competent organ of the United Nations" (SR.8, pp. 5 to 10; SR.13, pp. 14 to 18).

209. Such a definition could not be automatically applied, in the view of the Netherlands representative. It presupposed the evaluation of all circumstances, and consequently differences of opinion whether or not armed attack existed in a specific case could not be excluded. But it implied clearly enough in what cases a State might not go to war in self-defence.

210. The United States representative considered the Netherlands formula a text initially as much dependent on subjective evaluation by a State considering action in self-defence as any determination that State might make under the language of Article 51 itself. It provided no additional or effective compulsion to abide by the judgements of the organs of the United Nations.

211. Article 51 did not, in his view, directly use such terms as "unprovoked" or "first". The facts of the prior history of any given situation, the intentions of the parties to it, and other factors, were made relevant by the concept of self-defence itself. It would not seem unreasonable to suggest that of equal but by no means more important weight was the factor of "room to wait for United Nations action", and that this factor was equally relevant under the self-defence concept. That it alone among all the various elements of the events leading up to a given situation should be singled out for attention raised the same sort of difficult problem that was raised by an enumerative definition.

212. There were, of course, the difficulties inherent in any elaboration of the Charter language, and the chief of those, he observed, was the introduction of new terms which themselves defied useful definition. The Netherlands formula had several of those.

213. In any event, the United States representative considered there was reason to believe that the formula might seriously prejudice resort to self-defence as recognized under Article 51. It was also possible that, by emphasizing the subjective character of the judgement to be made on timing, and providing an ambiguous new test to be applied, the "definition" could do more harm than good (SR.13, pp. 4 and 5).

214. The representative of the United Kingdom wondered whether a definition dealing solely with the concept of armed attack under Article 51 would serve a useful purpose. He doubted whether such a definition would deter any State from pursuing its aggressive designs. The term "armed attack" in Article 51 could not be satisfactorily defined without defining self-defence, and a satisfactory definition of self-defence was virtually impossible to achieve. It was, for instance, impossible, except in the light of the particular circumstances, to determine whether any particular case was a minor local attack justifying no more than the force immediately necessary to deal with it on the spot, or whether it was something more which justified more extensive measures of armed force. The ever-recurring problem was whether the reaction on the part of the victim was one which came within the scope of the concept of legitimate self-defence (SR.16, pp. 5 and 6).

215. The representative of the USSR considered it inconsistent with the Charter to argue that the notion of armed aggression in Article 39 was different in principle from the notion of armed attack in Article 51. They formed a single concept. He considered it dangerous to mention as the first element of the definition "the use of armed force", which did not in any way specify the types of acts envisaged, and lent itself to a very dangerous construction; it could be said to cover every type of military activity, including mere troop movements and routine manoeuvres which a neighbouring State regarded as menacing. The phrase thus tended to assimilate a threat of aggression to aggression proper, which would authorize a State to unleash a war on the pretext that it was only exercising its inherent right of self-defence. Furthermore, the Netherlands proposal made no mention of the role of the Security Council or of the limits on the exercise of the right of self-defence which the Council might impose in pursuance of Article 51. Again, the formula spoke of "territorial integrity and political independence", although Article 51 contained no similar phrase. The text of Article 51 was admirably clear, and elaborations of that type could be more confusing than helpful (SR.10, pp. 5 and 6).

216. The Czechoslovak representative shared this view. Moreover, in his opinion, the Netherlands representative's approach could not be reconciled with the express mandate given to the Committee. He opposed the argument that the Charter contained two different concepts of aggression (SR.10, pp. 6 and 7).

217. The representative of China was of the opinion that the idea embodied in Article 51 was made clearer by the definition. Nevertheless, the definition would not make it easier to thwart an aggressive policy. Subversion was the most dangerous form of aggression. It was not a commendable step to adopt a definition limited to armed attack. Its effects would only be to create an illusion that aggression had been defined (SR.14, p. 3).

ANNEX I

SELECTED TEXTS OF DEFINITIONS AND DRAFT DEFINITIONS OF AGGRESSION

(Working paper prepared by the Secretariat)

Note: The report on the question of defining aggression presented by the Secretary-General to the General Assembly at its seventh session (See Official Records of the General Assembly, Seventh Session, Annexes, agenda item 54, document A/2211) contains a detailed study of the problem, reproducing methodically definitions of aggression drafted up to 1952. For the convenience of the members of the 1956 Special Committee, a number of the definitions included in the said report are reproduced below. Also reproduced below are definitions submitted to the International Law Commission at its third session, to the 1953 Special Committee on the Question of Defining Aggression and at the ninth session of the General Assembly.

1. The definition of aggression drafted by the Committee on Security Questions (the Disarmament Conference, 1932-1933) (Definition reproducing the substance of the USSR proposal defining aggression submitted to the General Commission) (A/2211, paras. 76 to 80):

Act relating to the Definition of the Aggressor

Article 1

The aggressor in an international conflict shall, subject to the agreements in force between the parties to the dispute, be considered to be that State which is the first to commit any of the following actions:

(1) Declaration of war upon another State;

(2) Invasion by its armed forces, with or without a declaration of war, of the territory of another State;

(3) Attack by its land, naval or air forces, with or without a declaration of war, on the territory, vessels or aircraft of another State;

(4) Naval blockade of the coasts or ports of another State;

(5) Provision of support to armed bands formed in its territory which have invaded the territory of another State, or refusal, notwithstanding the request of the invaded State, to take in its own territory all the measures in its power to deprive those bands of all assistance or protection.

Article 2

No political, military, economic or other considerations may serve as an excuse or justification for the aggression referred to in article 1.

Article 3

The present Act shall form an integral part of the General Convention for the Reduction and Limitation of Armaments.

...

Protocol annexed to article 2

The High Contracting Parties signatories of the Act relating to the Definition of the Aggressor,

Desiring, subject to the express reservation that the absolute validity of the rule laid down in article 2 of that Act shall be in no way restricted, to furnish certain indications for the guidance of the international bodies that may be called upon to determine the aggressor:

Declare that no act of aggression within the meaning of article 1 of that Act can be justified on either of the following grounds, among others:

A. The Internal Condition of a State:

E.g., its political, economic or social structure; alleged defects in its administration; disturbances due to strikes, revolutions, counter-revolutions or civil war.

B. The International Conduct of a State:

E.g., the violation or threatened violation of the material or moral rights or interests of a foreign State or its nationals; the rupture of diplomatic or economic relations; economic or financial boycotts; disputes relating to economic, financial or other obligations towards foreign States; frontier incidents not forming any of the cases of aggression specified in article 1.

The High Contracting Parties further agree to recognize that the present Protocol can never legitimate any violations of international law that may be implied in the circumstances comprised in the above list.

2. The definition included in the Treaty between Finland and the USSR of 21 January 1932, article 1 (A/2211, para. 192):

Any act of violence attacking the integrity and inviolability of the territory or the political independence of the other High Contracting Party shall be regarded as an act of aggression, even if it is committed without declaration of war and avoids warlike manifestations.

3. The definition included in the Act of Chapultepec signed by all the American Republics on 8 March 1945 (A/2211, para. 200):

Whereas...

(j) ... any attempt on the part of a non-American State against the integrity or inviolability of the territory, the sovereignty or the political independence of an American State shall be considered as an act of aggression against all the American States.

Part I

Declare:

...

3. That every attack of a State against the integrity or the inviolability of the territory, or against the sovereignty or the political independence of an American State, shall, conformably to Part III hereof, be considered as an act of aggression against the other States which sign this Act. In any case, invasion by armed forces of one State into the territory of another trespassing boundaries established by treaty and demarcated in accordance therewith shall constitute an act of aggression.

4. The definition included in the Inter-American Treaty of Reciprocal Assistance signed at Rio de Janeiro on 2 September 1947 (A/2211, para. 201):

Article 1. The High Contracting Parties formally condemn war and undertake in their international relations not to resort to the threat or the use of force in any manner inconsistent with the provisions of the Charter of the United Nations.

...

Article 3. The High Contracting Parties agree that an armed attack by any State against an American State shall be considered as an attack against all the American States, and, consequently, each one of the said Contracting Parties undertakes to assist in meeting the attack in the exercise of the inherent right of individual or collective self-defence recognized by Article 51 of the Charter of the United Nations.

...

Article 9. In addition to other acts which the Organ of Consultation may characterize as aggression, the following shall be considered as such:

(a) Unprovoked armed attack by a State against the territory, the people, or the land, sea or air forces of another State;

(b) Invasion, by the armed forces of a State, of the territory of an American State, through the trespassing of boundaries demarcated in accordance with a treaty, judicial decision, or arbitral award, or, in the absence of frontiers thus demarcated, invasion affecting a region which is under the effective jurisdiction of another State.

5. Draft definition submitted by Bolivia to Committee 3 of the Third Commission of the San Francisco Conference (A/2211, paras. 113 and 114):

A State shall be designated an aggressor if it has committed any of the following acts to the detriment of another State:

(a) Invasion of another State's territory by armed forces.
(b) Declaration of war.
(c) Attack by land, sea, or air forces with or without declaration of war, on another State's territory, shipping, or aircraft.
(d) Support given to armed bands for the purpose of invasion.

(e) Intervention in another State's internal or foreign affairs.
(f) Refusal to submit the matter which has caused a dispute to the peaceful means provided for its settlement.
(g) Refusal to comply with a judicial decision lawfully pronounced by an International Court.

This proposal was accompanied by the following observation:

In general the Security Council shall determine the existence of any threat to the peace, breach of the peace, or act of aggression and should make recommendations or decide on the measures to be taken to maintain or restore peace and security. If the nature of the acts investigated entails designating a State as an aggressor as indicated in the following paragraph, these measures should be applied immediately by collective action.

6. Draft definition submitted by the Philippines to Committee 3 of the Third Commission of the San Francisco Conference (A/2211, para. 115):

Any nation should be considered as threatening the peace or as an aggressor, if it should be the first party to commit any of the following acts:

(1) To declare war against another nation;
(2) To invade or attack, with or without declaration of war, the territory, public vessel, or public aircraft of another nation;
(3) To subject another nation to a naval, land or air blockade;
(4) To interfere with the internal affairs of another nation by supplying arms, ammunition, money or other forms of aid to any armed band, faction or group, or by establishing agencies in that nation to conduct propaganda subversive of the institutions of that nation.

7. Resolution 380 (V) adopted by the General Assembly on 17 November 1950 (A/2211, para. 126):

The General Assembly,

...

Condemning the intervention of a State in the internal affairs of another State for the purpose of changing its legally established government by the threat or use of force,

1. Solemnly reaffirms that, whatever the weapons used, any aggression, whether committed openly, or by fomenting civil strife in the interest of a foreign Power, or otherwise, is the gravest of all crimes against peace and security throughout the world;

...

8. The Charter of the International Military Tribunal, annexed to the Agreement between France, the USSR the United Kingdom and the United States of America, signed in London on 8 August 1945, article 6 (A/2211, para. 142):

(a) Crimes against peace: namely, planning, preparation, initiation or waging a war of aggression, or a war in violation of international treaties, agreements or assurances, or participation in a Common Plan or Conspiracy for the accomplishment of any of the foregoing;

...

9. The definition drafted by Mr. Alfaro and amended by the International Law Commission (A/2211, para. 132)[1]/:

Aggression is the threat or use of force by a State or Government against another State, in any manner, whatever the weapons employed and whether openly or otherwise, for any reason or for any purpose other than individual or collective self-defence or in pursuance of a decision or recommendation by a competent organ of the United Nations.

10. The definition proposed by Mr. Amado see report of the International Law Commission covering the work of its third session (1951), Official Records of the General Assembly, Sixth Session, Supplement No. 9 (A/1858, para. 40):

Any war not waged in exercise of the right of self-defence or in application of the provisions of Article 42 of the Charter of the United Nations [is] an aggressive war.

11. The definition proposed by Mr. Yepes (A/1858, para. 42):

For the purposes of Article 39 of the United Nations Charter an act of aggression shall be understood to mean any direct or indirect use of violence (force) by a State or group of States against the territorial integrity or political independence of another State or groups of States.

Violence (force) exercised by irregular bands organized within the territory of a State or outside its territory with the active or passive complicity of that State shall be considered as aggression within the meaning of the preceding paragraph.

The use of violence (force) in the exercise of the right of individual or collective self-defence recognized by Article 51 of the Charter or in the execution of a decision duly adopted by a competent organ of the United Nations shall not be held to constitute an act of aggression.

No political, economic, military or other consideration may serve as an excuse or justification for an act of aggression.

12. The definition proposed by Mr. Hsu (A/1858, para. 43):

Aggression, which is a crime under international law, is the hostile act of a State against another State, committed by (a) the employment of armed force other than in self-defence or the implementation of United Nations enforcement action; or (b) the arming of

organized bands or of third States, hostile to the victim State, for offensive purposes; or (c) the fomenting of civil strife in the victim State in the interest of some foreign State; or (d) any other illegal resort to force, openly or otherwise.

13. The definition proposed by Mr. Córdova (A/1858, para. 44):

Aggression is the direct or indirect employment by the authorities of a State of armed force against another State for any purpose other than national or collective self-defence or execution of a decision by a competent organ of the United Nations.

The threat of aggression should also be deemed to be a crime under this article.

14. The definition proposed by Mr. Scelle (A/1858, para. 53):

Aggression is an offence against the peace and security of mankind. This offence consists in any resort to force contrary to the provisions of the Charter of the United Nations, for the purpose of modifying the state of positive international law in force or resulting in the disturbance of public order.

15. The definition proposed by the USSR (Official Records of the General Assembly, Ninth Session, Annexes, agenda item 51, document A/C.6/L.332/Rev.1)[2]/:

16. The Mexican amendment (A/AC.66/L.8) to the USSR definition (A/AC.66/L.2/Rev.1) (see report of the 1953 Special Committee on the Question of Defining Aggression, Official Records of the General Assembly, Ninth Session, Supplement No. 11 (A/2638, p. 14). The text of the USSR definition was, with the exception of drafting changes, the same as that of document A/C.6/L.332/Rev.1 mentioned under 15 above;

The proposed definition of the USSR (A/AC.66/L.2/Rev.1) could be considerably improved and would be acceptable to the Mexican delegation with the following changes:

1. The insertion after the preamble of the following paragraph:

Declares that:

In an international conflict aggression shall be regarded as the direct or indirect use of force by the authorities of one State against the territorial integrity or political independence of another State or for any purpose other than legitimate individual or collective defence or compliance with a decision or recommendation of a competent organ of the United Nations. In particular, the commission of any of the following acts shall be regarded as aggression:

(a) ...

(b), etc.

(There would then be inserted paragraphs (a) to (f) of paragraph 1 of the Soviet draft.)

Paragraph 5 of the Soviet draft definition would be deleted.

1/ This definition was not adopted by the International Law Commission. However the Commission decided to insert the following paragraphs in article 2 of its draft Code of Offences against the Peace and Security of Mankind:

"The following acts are offences against the peace and security of mankind:

"(1) Any act of aggression, including the employment by the authorities of a State of armed force against another State for any purpose other than national or collective self-defence or in pursuance of a decision or recommendation by a competent organ of the United Nations.

"(2) Any threat by the authorities of a State to resort to an act of aggression against another State" (A/1858, para. 53).

2/ For the text of the definition, see annex II, 1, below.

2. In view of the influence which the definition of aggression may have on the application and interpretation of Article 51 of the United Nations Charter, it seems, in the opinion of the Mexican delegation, hazardous to extend the concept of aggression to include separate elements of the use of force. Thus, acts constituting so-called indirect, economic or ideological aggression should be regarded as aggression only if they involve or are accompanied by the use of force. Consequently, for the purposes of the definition:

(a) Such acts when actually constituting aggression are already covered by the general definition proposed in paragraph (1).

(b) Even though such acts did not constitute aggression, they might justify enforcement measures by the Security Council as provided in Article 39 of the Charter in the same manner as though aggression had been committed if by their effect on the victim State or for any other reason they constituted a threat to the peace. This circumstance should be particularly emphasized in our Committee's report to the Assembly.

The deletion of paragraphs 2, 3 and 4 of the Soviet draft is accordingly proposed.

3. Paragraph 6, first part. Amend the wording to conform with the suggested deletion of paragraphs 3, 4 and 5. Add the words "or social" after the words "strategic or economic". Delete that part of the paragraph beginning with the words: "Or by the desire to exploit..." up to the words: "[interests in that] territory".

Amend the wording of paragraph 6, sub-paragraph B, item (a), so as to include those treaties which by their very nature justify the use of force if they are violated.

17. The definition proposed by China (Official Records of the General Assembly, Ninth Session, Annexes, agenda item 51, document A/C.6/L.336/Rev.2):

The General Assembly,

Recalling its resolutions 599 (VI) and 688 (VII),

Having considered the report of the Special Committee on the Question of Defining Aggression,

Mindful of the responsibilities of the Security Council concerning aggression under Article 1, paragraph 1, and Chapter VII of the Charter, and of the function of the General Assembly envisaged in Assembly resolution 377 A (V),

Considering that, although the question whether aggression has occurred must be determined in the circumstances of each particular case, it would nevertheless be advisable to formulate certain principles as guidance,

Recommends that the Security Council in the discharge of its responsibilities under Article I, paragraph 1, and Chapter VII of the Charter, and the Members of the United Nations, when the Assembly is called upon to consider an item pursuant to resolution 377 A (V), take account, inter alia, of the following principles:

1. That aggression is the unlawful use of force by a State against another State, whether directly or indirectly, such as:

(a) Attack or invasion by armed forces;
(b) Organization or support of incursion of armed bands;
(c) Promotion or support of organized activities in another State aiming at the overthrow by violence of its political or social institutions;

2. That the use of force is lawful when it is in pursuance of a decision or recommendation by a competent organ of the United Nations, or is in self-defence against armed attack until a competent organ of the United Nations has taken the measures necessary to maintain international peace and security;

3. That the employment of measures, other than armed attack, necessary to remove the danger arising from an indirect use of force is likewise lawful until a competent organ of the United Nations has taken steps to remove such danger.

18. The definition proposed by Bolivia (working paper A/AC.66/L.9 submitted to the 1953 Special Committee on the Question of Defining Aggression, Official Records of the General Assembly, Ninth Session, Supplement No. 11 (A/2638, p. 15):

The General Assembly,

Considering it necessary to define some acts of aggression in order to maintain international peace and security, in accordance with the Purposes and Principles of the United Nations Charter,

Hereby resolves as follows:

1. Independently of acts of aggression designated as such by the competent international organs of the United Nations, the invasion by one State of the territory of another State across the frontiers established by treaties or judicial or arbitral decisions and demarcated in accordance therewith, or, in the absence of marked frontiers, an invasion affecting territories under the effective jurisdiction of a State shall in all cases be deemed to constitute an act of aggression.

2. A declaration of war, an armed attack with land, sea or air forces against the territory, ships or aircraft of another State, support given to armed bands for purposes of invasion, and the overt or covert inciting of the people of one State by another State to rebellion for the purpose of disturbing law and order in the interests of a foreign Power shall also be defined as acts of aggression.

3. Any threat or use of force against the territorial integrity or political independence of any State or in any other manner incompatible with the purposes of the United Nations, including unilateral action whereby a State is deprived of economic resources derived from the proper conduct of international trade or its basic economy is endangered so that its security is affected and it is rendered unable to act in its own defence or to co-operate in the collective defence of peace shall likewise be deemed to constitute an act of aggression.

4. Apart from the cases provided for in paragraphs 1 and 2, which shall constitute sufficient grounds for the automatic exercise of the right of collective self-defence, other acts of aggression shall be defined as

such, when they take place, by the competent organs established by the United Nations Charter and in conformity with its provisions.

19. The definition proposed by Paraguay (Official Records of the General Assembly, Ninth Session,

, document A/C.6/L.334/Rev. 1)[3]:

20. The definition proposed by Iran and Panama (Ibid., document A/C.6/L.335/Rev. 1)[4]:

---

[3] For the text of the definition, see annex II, 2, below.
[4] See annex II, 3, below.

ANNEX II

DRAFT DEFINITIONS SUBMITTED TO THE 1956 SPECIAL COMMITTEE

1. Union of Soviet Socialist Republics: draft resolution (A/AC.77/L.4)

The 1956 Special Committee on the Question of Defining Aggression recommends to the General Assembly the adoption of the following resolution:

The General Assembly,

Considering it necessary to establish guiding principles with a view to determining which party is guilty of aggression,

Declares that:

1. In an international conflict that State shall be declared the attacker which first commits one of the following acts:

(a) Declaration of war against another State;

(b) Invasion by its armed forces, even without a declaration of war, of the territory of another State;

(c) Bombardment by its land, sea or air forces of the territory of another State or the carrying out of a deliberate attack on the ships or aircraft of the latter;

(d) The landing or leading of its land, sea or air forces inside the boundaries of another State without the permission of the Government of the latter, or the violation of the conditions of such permission, particularly as regards the length of their stay or the extent of the area in which they may stay;

(e) Naval blockade of the coasts or ports of another State;

(f) Support of armed bands organized in its own territory which invade the territory of another State, or refusal, on being requested by the invaded State, to take in its own territory any action within its power to deny such bands any aid or protection.

2. That State shall be declared to have committed an act of indirect aggression which:

(a) Encourages subversive activity against another State (acts of terrorism, diversionary acts, etc.):

(b) Promotes the fomenting of civil war within another State;

(c) Promotes an internal upheaval in another State or a change of policy in favour of the aggressor.

3. That State shall be declared to have committed an act of economic aggression which first commits one of the following acts:

(a) Takes against another State measures of economic pressure violating its sovereignty and economic independence and threatening the bases of its economic life;

(b) Takes against another State measures preventing it from exploiting or nationalizing its own natural riches;

(c) Subjects another State to an economic blockade.

4. That State shall be declared to have committed an act of ideological aggression which:

(a) Encourages war propaganda;

(b) Encourages propaganda in favour of using atomic, bacterial, chemical and other weapons of mass destruction;

(c) Promotes the propagation of fascist-nazi views, of racial and national exclusiveness, and of hatred and contempt for other peoples.

5. Acts committed by a State other than those listed in the preceding paragraphs may be deemed to constitute aggression if declared by decision of the Security Council in a particular case to be an attack or an act of economic, ideological or indirect aggression.

6. The attacks referred to in paragraph 1 and the acts of economic, ideological and indirect aggression referred to in paragraphs 2, 3 and 4 may not be justified by any considerations of a political, strategic or economic nature, or by the desire to exploit natural riches in the territory of the State attacked or to derive any other kind of advantages or privileges, or by reference to the amount of capital invested in that territory or to any other particular interests in that territory, or by the refusal to recognize that it possesses the distinguishing marks of statehood.

In particular, the following may not be used as justification:

A. The internal situation of any State, as for example:

(a) Backwardness of any people politically, economically or culturally;

(b) Alleged shortcomings of its administration;

(c) Any danger which may threaten the life or property of aliens;

(d) Any revolutionary or counter-revolutionary movement, civil war, disorders or strikes;

(e) Establishment or maintenance in any State of any political, economic or social system.

B. Any acts, legislation or orders of any State, as for example:

(a) Violation of international treaties;

(b) Violation of rights and interests in the sphere of trade, concessions or any other kind of economic activity acquired by another State or its citizens;

(c) Rupture of diplomatic or economic relations;

(d) Measures constituting an economic or financial boycott;

(e) Repudiation of debts;

(f) Prohibition or restriction of immigration or modification of the status of foreigners;

(g) Violation of privileges recognized to the official representatives of another State;

(h) Refusal to allow the passage of armed forces proceeding to the territory of a third State;

(i) Measures of a religious or anti-religious nature;

(j) Frontier incidents.

7. In the event of the mobilization or concentration by another State of considerable armed forces near its frontier, the State which is threatened by such action shall have the right of recourse to diplomatic or other means of securing a peaceful settlement of international disputes. It may also in the meantime take counter-measures of a military nature similar to those described above, without, however, crossing the frontier.

2. Paraguay: draft resolution (A/AC.77/L.7)

The 1956 Special Committee on the Question of Defining Aggression recommends to the General Assembly the adoption of the following resolution:

The General Assembly,

Considering that at its 368th plenary meeting it resolved that, although the existence of the crime of aggression may be inferred from the circumstances peculiar to each particular case, it is nevertheless possible and desirable, with a view to ensuring international peace and security and to developing international criminal law, to define aggression by reference to the elements which constitute it" (resolution 599 (VI)),

Declares:

1. A State (or States) commits (or commit) armed aggression if it (or they) provokes (or provoke) a breach or disturbance of international peace and security through the employment of armed force against the territory, population, armed forces or the sovereignty and political independence of another State (or other States), or against the people, the territory or the armed forces of a Non-Self-Governing Territory;

2. Without prejudice to the provisions of Article 39 of the Charter, the General Assembly recommends that in addition to other acts of aggression the following acts shall be deemed to constitute armed aggression:

(a) A declaration of war by one State against another (or others) in contravention of Articles 1 and 2 of the Charter;

(b) The organization by a State within its territory of armed bands intended to take action against other States, either within or outside the territory of such States; or the encouragement, support or the mere toleration of the formation or action of such armed bands in its territory.

Nevertheless, a State shall not be considered to be an aggressor if, being unable to suppress the activities of such bands in its territory or having justifiable reasons for not undertaking their suppression, it reports the matter to the competent organ of the United Nations and offers its co-operation.

3. Iran and Panama: draft resolution (A/AC.77/L.9)

The following draft resolution submitted by Iran and Panama at the ninth session of the General Assembly is circulated to the 1956 Special Committee at the request of the representative of Peru:

The General Assembly,

Considering that, although the existence of aggression may be inferred from the circumstances peculiar to each particular case, it is nevertheless possible and desirable, with a view to ensuring international peace and security and to developing international criminal law, to define aggression by reference to the elements which constitute it,

Considering further that it would be of definite advantage if directives were formulated for the future guidance of such international bodies as may be called upon to determine the aggressor,

Declares that:

1. Aggression is the use of armed force by a State against another State for any purpose other than the exercise of the inherent right of individual or collective self-defence or in pursuance of a decision or recommendation of a competent organ of the United Nations.

2. In accordance with the foregoing definition, in addition to any other acts which such international bodies as may be called upon to determine the aggressor may declare to constitute aggression, the following are acts of aggression in all cases:

(a) Invasion by the armed forces of a State of territory belonging to another State or under the effective jurisdiction of another State;

(b) Armed attack against the territory, population or land, sea or air forces of a State by the land, sea or air forces of another State;

(c) Blockade of the coast or ports or any other part of the territory of a State by the land, sea or air forces of another State;

(d) The organization, or the encouragement of the organization, by a State, of armed bands within its territory or any other territory for incursions into the territory of another State, or the toleration of the organization of such bands in its own territory, or the toleration of the use by such armed bands of its territory as a base of operations or as a point of departure for incursions into the territory of another State, as well as direct participation in or support of such incursions.

4. Iraq: revised draft resolution (A/AC.77/L,8/Rev.1)

The Special Committee on the Question of Defining Aggression,

Considering that the General Assembly, in resolution 895 (IX), requested the Special Committee to submit to the General Assembly at its eleventh session a draft definition of aggression,

Recommends to the General Assembly the adoption of the following draft definition of aggression:

The General Assembly,

Considering that a definition of aggression would contribute greatly to the maintenance of international peace and security, and to the development of international law and international justice,

Declares that aggression, within the meaning of Article 39 of the Charter of the United Nations, is the use of force in international relations, and, within the meaning of Article 51 of the Charter of the United Nations, the use of armed force in international relations.

Aggression, within the meaning of both Article 39 and Article 51, is the use of force by a State or group of States, or by a Government or group of Governments, against the territorial integrity or independence of a State or group of States, or against the conditions of existence of the people and the territories of a Government or group of Governments, in any manner, by any method and for any purpose whatever, other than that of enforcement action in pursuance of a decision or recommendation of a competent organ of the United Nations, or than that of individual or collective self-defence against an armed attack which is aimed at, or results in, a change in the international juridical situation and a disturbance of international peace and security and with respect to which the competent organ of the United Nations has not taken measures necessary to maintain international peace and security and to enable it to take the place of the party possessed of the right of individual or collective self-defence.

5. Mexico: working paper (A/AC.77/L.10)

1. Resolution 895 (IX), in accordance with which this Special Committee has met to discuss the question of defining aggression, requests this Committee, among other things, to "submit to the General Assembly at its eleventh session a detailed report followed by a draft definition of aggression, having regard to the ideas expressed at the ninth session of the General Assembly and to the draft resolutions and amendments submitted".

2. In accordance with the foregoing instructions, the Special Committee has been carefully examining various documents but has given special attention to drafts submitted or reintroduced by various representatives. We have, on the other hand, referred only incidentally to definitions contained in previous proposals made to the General Assembly at its ninth session or in various treaty provisions, such as the definitions appearing in the first few pages of document A/AC.77/L.6, which was prepared through the kindness of the Secretary-General.

3. Although the Mexican delegation to the 1953 Special Committee proposed a specific formula, which was in the form of an amendment to the USSR draft resolution, the Mexican representative to the present Special

Committee has considered it appropriate to embody that formula in a draft resolution so that, as expressed in his statement of 22 October, some of the ideas contained in the formula might be used in preparing a single draft as requested by the General Assembly.

4. Although the Mexican delegation is endeavouring, together with other Latin American delegations, to draft a joint text which it is hoped will prove acceptable to other members of this Special Committee, it is aware that, in spite of our efforts, we may be unable to attain the objective referred to in resolution 895 (IX).

5. In that event, the draft included in this working paper will once more stand in its entirety, for, as can be readily seen, it contains important distinctive elements which will probably have to be sacrificed in drafting a joint proposal that will naturally entail mutual concessions. Such a sacrifice would be justified only if we could reach an agreement that would enable us to fulfil the noble mission entrusted to us by the General Assembly.

6. The Mexican delegation considers that the definition of aggression should:

(a) Be confined to the idea of the use of force, and thus leave out of consideration the so-called indirect, ideological or economic forms of aggression and, in particular, the threat of force, except where an attempt to give effect to that threat has been initiated;

(b) Contain a general statement expressing in concise form all the basic characteristic features constituting aggression, including the principle under which, in an international conflict, the responsibility lies with the party that is the first to take the initiative in carrying out an act designated as aggression;

(c) Contain a non-exhaustive enumeration of the more usual types of aggression;

(d) Specify that the powers of deliberation and decision of the competent international organs called upon to designate an aggressor would remain unimpaired but that such organs, in applying the definition, could not at their discretion regard as aggression any other case not included in the definition;

(e) Embody the idea that no considerations of a political, economic, strategic or social nature can justify the commission of an act constituting aggression.

7. In accordance with the foregoing points, the Mexican delegation proposes the following text:

Draft resolution

The General Assembly,

Recalling its resolutions 599 (VI), 688 (VIII) and 895 (IX),

Declares that:

In an international conflict, the direct or indirect use of force by the authorities of a State taking the initiative for the purpose of attacking the territorial integrity or political independence of another State, or for any purpose other than individual or collective self-defence or compliance with a decision or recommendation of a competent organ of the United Nations, shall be regarded as aggression.

In particular, the commission of any of the following acts shall be regarded as aggression:

(a) Invasion by the armed forces of one State of territory belonging to, or under the effective jurisdiction of, another State;

(b) Armed attack against the territory or population or the land, sea or air forces of one State by the land, sea or air forces of another State;

(c) The blockading of the coast or ports or any other part of the territory of one State by the land, sea or air forces of another State;

(d) The organization, or the encouragement of the organization, by one State, of armed bands within its territory or any other territory for incursions into the territory of another State; or the toleration of the organization of such bands in its own territory, or the toleration of the use by such armed bands of its territory as a base of operations or as a point of departure for incursions into the territory of another State, as well as direct participation in or support of such incursions.

In no event may an act constituting aggression be justified by any considerations of a political, economic, strategic or social nature.

In particular, aggression may not be justified on any of the following grounds:

I. The internal situation of a State, as for example:
(a) The political, economic or cultural backwardness of a people;
(b) Administrative shortcomings;
(c) Dangers which may threaten the life or property of aliens;
(d) Revolutionary movements, civil war, disorders or strikes;
(e) The establishment or maintenance of any political, economic or social system in a State.

II. Any act, legislation or regulations of a State, as for example:
(a) Violation of rights or interests acquired by another State or its nationals with regard to trade, concessions or any other kind of economic activity;
(b) Breaking-off of diplomatic or economic relations;
(c) Measures constituting an economic or financial boycott;
(d) Repudiation of debts;
(e) Prohibition or restriction of immigration or modification of the status of aliens;

(f) Violation of privileges accorded to the official representatives of another State;
(g) Refusal to allow the passage of armed forces proceeding to the territory of a third State;
(h) Measures of a religious nature;
(i) Frontier incidents.

6. **Dominican Republic, Mexico, Paraguay and Peru: draft resolution (A/AC.77/L.11)**

The 1956 Special Committee on the Question of Defining Aggression recommends to the General Assembly the adoption of the following draft resolution:

The General Assembly,

Recalling its resolutions 599 (VI) 688 (VIII) and 895 (IX),

Declares that:

1. Any use of force by a State (or States) against the territorial integrity or inviolability or the sovereignty or political independence of another State (or States), or against a territory under the effective jurisdiction of another State, or for any purpose other than the exercise of the inherent right of individual or collective self-defence or the execution of a decision or recommendation of a competent organ of the United Nations, shall be regarded as aggression;

2. In accordance with the foregoing definition, and without prejudice to the power of the competent international organs to determine the existence of, or take a decision upon, an act of aggression, the following shall be acts of aggression in all cases:

(a) Declaration of war by one State against another State (or States) in violation of the Charter of the United Nations;
(b) The invasion by the armed forces of one State of the territory of another State or of a territory under the effective jurisdiction of another State;
(c) Armed attack against the territory or population or the land, sea or air forces of one State by the land, sea or air forces of another State;
(d) The blockading of the coast or ports or any other part of the territory of one State by the land, sea or air forces of another State; and
(e) Incursions into the territory of one State by armed bands organized by, or with the participation or direct assistance of, another State.

In no event may aggression by justified by any considerations of a political, economic or social nature.

United Nations

GENERAL ASSEMBLY

Official Records

DOCUMENT 9

Agenda item 54

ANNEXES

TWELFTH SESSION

NEW YORK, 1957

Agenda item 54: Question of defining aggression: report of the Special Committee

CONTENTS

DOCUMENT A/C.6/L.402

United States of America: draft resolution

[Original text: English]
[4 November 1957]

The General Assembly,

Having considered the report of the 1956 Special Committee on the Question of Defining Aggression (A/3574),

1. Expresses its appreciation to the Special Committee;

2. Takes note of the report and commends it to the Governments of Members of the United Nations for examination and study;

3. Decides to postpone indefinitely further consideration of the question of defining aggression.

DOCUMENT A/C.6/L.403 *

Chile, Colombia, Cuba, Ecuador, El Salvador, Philippines and Venezuela: draft resolution

[Original text: Spanish]
[4 November 1957]

The General Assembly,

Recalling its resolutions 599 (VI) of 31 January 1952, 688 (VII) of 20 December 1952 and 895 (IX) of 4 December 1954, all referring to a definition of aggression,

---

* Incorporating document A/C.6/L.403/Corr.1, dated 8 November 1957, in which it was indicated that the name of the Dominican Republic, which had appeared in the original list of sponsors of the draft resolution, should be deleted.

Considering that, in spite of the progress made in the study of the question, the discussion at the present session shows the need for the elucidation of other aspects of the definition of aggression,

Considering that the report presented by the 1956 Special Committee on the Question of Defining Aggression (A/3574) is an important study based on the views expressed by States Members of the United Nations up to the date of the preparation of the report,

Annexes (XII) 54

Considering , that twenty-two additional States have recently joined the Organization and that it would be useful to know their views on the matter,

Resolves :

1. To take note of the report of the 1956 Special Committee on the Question of Defining Aggression and to express appreciation for the valuable work done ;

2. To ask the Secretary-General to request the views of the new Member States on the question, and to renew the request to Member States which have not done so to submit comments as provided in General Assembly resolution 688 (VII) of 20 December 1952, furnishing them with the documentation produced after the adoption of that resolution ;

3. To ask the Secretary-General to report to the General Assembly at its fourteenth session on the replies received ;

4. To place the question on the provisional agenda of the fourteenth session of the General Assembly.

DOCUMENT A/3756

Report of the Sixth Committee

[Original text : English]
[27 November 1957]

1. The General Assembly, at its 682nd plenary meeting on 20 September 1957, included in the agenda of its twelfth session the item " Question of defining aggression : report of the Special Committee ", and referred it to the Sixth Committee.

2. The Sixth Committee considered the item at its 514th to 528th meetings, held between 7 October and 4 November, and its 530th to 538th meetings, held between 6 and 21 November 1957.

3. At the outset of the debate, the representative of the Netherlands, Mr. B. V. A. Röling, Rapporteur of the 1956 Special Committee on the Question of Defining Aggression, introduced the report of that Committee (A/3574). He stated that the Special Committee had not succeeded in fulfilling a part of the task entrusted to it by General Assembly resolution 895 (IX), that is, to draw up a draft definition of aggression ; however, it had fulfilled the other part, which was to study the question of aggression " having regard to the ideas expressed at the ninth session of the General Assembly and to the draft resolutions and amendments submitted ".

Proposals and amendments

4. Two draft resolutions containing a definition of aggression were submitted to the Committee :

(a) By the Union of Soviet Socialist Republics (A/C.6/L.399) ;

(b) By Iran and Panama (A/C.6/L.401).

5. In addition, a text containing a definition of aggression was proposed as a working document by the representative of Belgium at the 514th meeting.

6. The representative of Afghanistan submitted an oral amendment to the USSR draft resolution at the 520th meeting, to add to the list of acts of aggression contained in that draft resolution the closure of historical trade routes of a land-locked country or the creation of difficulty in the way of free and normal trade and commerce. He also submitted a similar amendment to the draft resolution of Iran and Panama.

7. Two draft resolutions relating to procedure were also submitted :

(a) By the United States of America (A/C.6/L.402), whereby the General Assembly would decide to postpone indefinitely further consideration of the question of defining aggression. This draft resolution was later withdrawn.

(b) By Chile, Colombia, Cuba, Ecuador, El Salvador, the Philippines and Venezuela (A/C.6/L.403). Under the terms of that draft resolution, the Assembly would : (i) take note of the report of the Special Committee on the Question of Defining Aggression and express appreciation for the valuable work done ; (ii) ask the Secretary-General to request the views of the new States Members on the question and renew the request to States Members which have not done so to submit comments as provided in General Assembly resolution 688 (VII), furnishing them with the documentation produced after the adoption of that resolution ; (iii) ask the Secretary-General to report to the Assembly at its fourteenth session on the replies received ; and (iv) place the question on the provisional agenda of the fourteenth session.

8. An amendment to the seven-Power draft resolution (A/C.6/L.403) was submitted by Afghanistan, Bolivia, Guatemala, Haiti, Mexico and Peru (A/C.6/L.404) to replace operative paragraphs 2 and 3 by the following :

"2. To re-establish the Special Committee on the Question of Defining Aggression established by resolution 895 (IX) of 4 December 1954, and to increase its membership by adding the following members . . .

"3. To request the Special Committee to convene, in accordance with its terms of reference, in 1959, and to submit its report to the fourteenth session of the General Assembly ".

9. A sub-amendment to this amendment was submitted by Ceylon, Egypt and Indonesia (A/C.6/L.406) to insert in paragraph 3 the phrase " to give priority in its work to the elaboration of the notion of armed aggression " after the words " in 1959 ".

10. Amendments to the seven-Power draft resolution (A/C.6/L.403) were also submitted by the United States of America (A/C.6/L.407) : (a) to delete the words " which have not done so " from operative paragraph 2 ; (b) to replace operative paragraphs 3 and 4 by the following :

" 3. To ask the Secretary-General to refer the replies of Member States to a committee composed of the Member States whose representatives have served on the General Committee of the most recent regular session of the General Assembly, which committee shall study the replies for the purpose of determining when it shall be appropriate for the General Assembly to consider again the question of defining aggression, and shall report to the Secretary-General when it has determined that the time is appropriate, setting forth the consideration which led to its decision ;

" 4. To request the Secretary-General to place the question of defining aggression on the provisional agenda of the General Assembly, not earlier than at its fourteenth session, when the committee has advised him that it considers the time appropriate ;

" 5. To request the Secretary-General to convene the first meeting of the committee prior to the fourteenth session of the General Assembly."

11. Further amendments to the seven-Power draft resolution (A/C.6/L.403) were submitted by Egypt (A/C.6/L.409) : (a) To replace the third and fourth paragraphs of the preamble by the following :

"*Having considered* the report of the 1956 Special Committee on the Question of Defining Aggression";

(b) To replace operative paragraphs 2, 3 and 4 by the following :

"2. To postpone further consideration of the question of defining aggression during the present session of the General Assembly;

"3. To place the question on the provisional agenda of the fourteenth session of the General Assembly."

Poland later joined Egypt as a co-sponsor of these amendments.

12. An oral amendment to the seven-Power draft resolution (A/C.6/L.403) was submitted by the representative of India at the 535th meeting, to replace in the second paragraph of the preamble the words " of the definition of aggression" by the words " of a definition of aggression ".

13. The sponsors of the draft resolution accepted the amendments of India and of the United States (A/C.6/L.407), and issued a revised text incorporating the United States amendments (A/C.6/L.403/Rev.1).

14. An oral amendment to this revised text was submitted at the 537th meeting by the representative of Ceylon (also on behalf of Egypt and Indonesia) to insert the following paragraph after the second preambular paragraph :

"*Considering* that the debate on the question of defining aggression at the twelfth session of the General Assembly has revealed the desire of a great number of delegations that priority should be given to the elaboration of the notion of armed aggression."

GENERAL DEBATE

15. Many delegations were of the opinion that the importance of a definition of aggression was becoming steadily greater. At a time when the international atmosphere remained tense and alarming and the armaments race was gathering speed, public opinion was calling for a definition of aggression. Such a definition should take its place among the measures designed to eliminate the threat of a new war, for it would serve as a warning to aggressors, and would make it harder to justify aggression. A definition of aggression would reduce international tension, serve to develop international criminal law, and provide guidance for the competent organs of the United Nations responsible for maintaining peace and security.

16. On the other hand, a number of delegations held that a definition of aggression would hardly facilitate the task of the Security Council or of the General Assembly, since it would restrict the discretion which those organs possessed under the Charter. Moreover, the practical importance of a definition was very limited, because, however worded, it would be easily evaded. In case of aggression, the main thing was not to have a definition but to ensure that the system of collective security would be applied. In the past, the achievements of the United Nations in maintaining international peace and security had been accomplished without the aid of a definition of aggression; its failures could hardly be attributed to the absence of such a definition.

17. Another argument against defining aggression was that the international situation had placed greater emphasis on the functions of conciliation and mediation of the United Nations rather than on the coercive function. Member States were reluctant to undertake collective military action for fear of provoking a third world war. Consequently, it might be a sound policy to refrain from branding as an aggressor one of the parties to a dispute which might be settled by mediation.

18. It was also felt by some delegations that any hasty attempt to define aggression would not promote international peace, but would only accentuate the existing international tension. In addition, international law at the present time could not foresee all the problems created by the possible use of nuclear and thermonuclear weapons, and by experiments made to promote their further development.

19. Many delegations stated that no definition of aggression would be really useful unless it was accepted by a large majority of Member States. Some expressed the opinion that the majority should include the permanent members of the Security Council.

20. It was said that the General Assembly should limit itself, at least for the time being, to assembling and, if possible, interpreting the most serviceable and pertinent provisions of the Charter on the matter, and only thereafter attempt to analyse what exactly constituted armed attack and the other forms of aggression which various States considered definable.

21. With regard to the type of definition to be adopted, the delegations that favoured a definition of aggression recommended a mixed definition, that is, one in which a general description would precede and govern a list of definite acts of aggression, which would be included merely to illustrate and not to restrict the general description.

22. With regard to content, several delegations stated that there was no need to define aggression within the meaning of Article 39 of the Charter, but that the definition should be confined to the notion of armed attack, in the sense of Article 51 of the Charter. It was conceivable that certain acts other than aggression might be declared illegal in an international convention, but it would only lead to confusion if they were included in the notion of aggression.

23. On the other hand, many delegations pointed out that under the Charter aggression was not confined to the use of armed force, and that the notion of " armed attack" mentioned in Article 51 of the Charter was but a special case of armed aggression in the sense of Article 39. Article 39 authorized the Security Council to take measures in the event of a threat to the peace, and in modern times it was indisputable that certain economic or ideological measures might constitute such a threat. Attempts to deprive a State of economic resources or to endanger its trade or trade routes should be considered acts of aggression.

24. Some delegations, however, which thought that under the Charter indirect aggression, economic aggression and ideological aggression might be included in the definition, pointed out that it would be better for the time being to confine the definition to armed attack, without prejudice to the recognition of other forms of aggression.

25. One delegation held the view that particular attention should be paid to the practical functions that a definition of aggression might be called upon to serve. Since the main purpose of the definition was to assist the competent organs of the United Nations in performing their functions, it was necessary to decide at what stage in a dispute — the beginning of the dispute, its development leading to intervention by United Nations organs, the decision or recommendation of those organs, the

attitude of the parties towards such a decision, and, finally, the reaction of the United Nations to that attitude — such a definition would be needed by the United Nations organs. Accordingly, the problem would only have to be faced if any of the States concerned refused to accept the decision of the United Nations, and only at that point would it be necessary to determine who was the aggressor.

26. In the opinion of some delegations, the chronological order of events was an important criterion, and would be decisive in determining who was responsible for aggression. It was maintained that it would be necessary, when preparing a definition of aggression, to explain that the aggressor State would be that which first committed any of the acts enumerated in the definition. A definition which neglected that principle of priority would not only be ambiguous, but might also be used as a justification for preventive war.

27. For other delegations, the definition could not be based on the chronological order of events, because that would lead to dangerous consequences. The aggressor would not necessarily be the State which first committed an act considered as an act of aggression. Whether or not the State was the aggressor would depend on the circumstances peculiar to each particular case.

28. It was also proposed to include in the definition a certain number of circumstances which in no case should serve as a justification for aggression. That proposal was criticized by some delegations as likely to give the impression that other circumstances, not included in the definition, might justify aggression. Furthermore, some critics contended that it would be illogical to give various pretexts which could not serve as justification for aggression when the basic principle was that nothing justified aggression.

Procedural debate

29. During the general debate, it appeared that a majority of the delegations were not in favour of defining aggression at the present session, but wanted the question to be postponed. Some delegations wished to postpone the question indefinitely; others were in favour of placing the question on the provisional agenda of the fourteenth session of the General Assembly.

30. Among the latter, many delegations suggested that the States newly admitted to the United Nations, as well as those other Members which had not submitted their comments as provided in General Assembly resolution 688 (VII) of 20 December 1952, should be given the opportunity to do so between the present and the fourteenth sessions. They also wanted the Secretary-General to report at the fourteenth session on the observations received.

31. Several other delegations considered such a procedure insufficient. They were in favour of re-establishing the Special Committee on the Question of Defining Aggression established by resolution 895 (IX) of 4 December 1954 and to increase its membership, in particular by adding some Member States newly admitted to the Organization. The Special Committee should report to the General Assembly at its fourteenth session.

32. Towards the end of the discussion, another proposal presented as a compromise solution found considerable support, namely, that the Secretary-General should refer the replies of Member States to a committee composed of the Member States where representatives have served on the General Committee of the most recent regular session of the Assembly, and that this new committee should study the replies with a view to determining when it would be appropriate for the Assembly again to consider the question of defining aggression. This proposal was incorporated in the amendments submitted by the United States of America (see para. 10 above).

33. Several delegations strongly opposed that proposal on the ground that its was not a compromise solution, but would, in fact, amount to an indefinite postponement of the question, because it would be left to a small political body to decide when the time was appropriate for reconsidering the matter. Some feared that the adoption of the United States proposal would restrict the right of Member States to propose an item for inclusion in the General Assembly's agenda and would set a dangerous precedent.

34. Many delegations which favoured the adoption of the United States proposal stated that their attitude should not be construed as meaning that they were against a definition of aggression. Indeed, they were of the opinion that a postponement of the question until circumstances were more favourable would, in fact, enhance the possibilities of achieving a definition of aggression.

Voting

35. At its 537th meeting, on 20 November 1957, the Committee decided to vote first on the revised draft resolution of Chile, Colombia, Cuba, Ecuador, El Salvador, the Philippines and Venezuela (A/C.6/L.403/Rev.1) and the amendments thereto.

Operative paragraph 1 of the draft resolution was adopted by 61 votes to none, with 9 abstentions.

Operative paragraph 2 as proposed in the amendment submitted by Afghanistan, Bolivia, Guatemala, Haiti, Mexico and Peru (A/C.6/L.404) was rejected by a roll-call vote of 34 to 28, with 11 abstentions, as follows:

In favour: Afghanistan, Albania, Bolivia, Bulgaria, Burma, Byelorussian Soviet Socialist Republic, Ceylon, Czechoslovakia, Egypt, Ethiopia, Guatemala, Haiti, Hungary, Indonesia, Iran, Iraq, Mexico, Panama, Peru, Poland, Romania, Saudi Arabia, Syria, Tunisia, Ukrainian Soviet Socialist Republic, Union of Soviet Socialist Republics, Yemen, Yugoslavia.

Against: Australia, Belgium, Brazil, Canada, China, Colombia, Cuba, Denmark, Dominican Republic, Ecuador, El Salvador, Finland, France, Honduras, Iceland, Israel, Italy, Japan, Liberia, Luxembourg, Netherlands, New Zealand, Nicaragua, Norway, Pakistan, Paraguay, Philippines, Portugal, Spain, Sweden, Turkey, United Kingdom of Great Britain and Northern Ireland, United States of America, Venezuela.

Abstaining: Argentina, Austria, Cambodia, Chile, Costa Rica, Greece, India, Malaya (Federation of), Nepal, Thailand, Uruguay.

In view of this result, operative paragraph 3, as proposed in the amendment, and the sub-amendment submitted by Ceylon, Egypt and Indonesia (A/C.6/L.406) were not voted upon.

Operative paragraphs 2 and 3 as proposed in the amendment submitted by Egypt and Poland (A/C.6/L.409) were rejected by a roll-call vote of 35 to 28, with 10 abstentions, as follows:

In favour: Afghanistan, Albania, Bulgaria, Burma, Byelorussian Soviet Socialist Republic, Ceylon, Czechoslovakia, Egypt, Ethiopia, Greece, Guatemala, Haiti, Hungary, India, Indonesia, Iran, Iraq, Mexico, Panama, Poland, Romania, Saudi Arabia, Syria, Tunisia, Ukrainian Soviet Socialist Republic, Union of Soviet Socialist Republics, Yemen, Yugoslavia.

Against: Argentina, Australia, Belgium, Brazil, Canada, China, Colombia, Costa Rica, Cuba, Denmark,

Dominican Republic, Ecuador, El Salvador, France, Honduras, Iceland, Israel, Italy, Japan, Liberia, Luxembourg, Netherlands, New Zealand, Nicaragua, Norway, Pakistan, Paraguay, Philippines, Portugal, Spain, Sweden, Turkey, United Kingdom of Great Britain and Northern Ireland, United States of America, Venezuela.

Abstaining: Austria, Bolivia, Cambodia, Chile, Finland, Malaya (Federation of), Nepal, Peru, Thailand, Uruguay.

Operative paragraphs 2 to 5 of the draft resolution (A/C.6/L.403/Rev.1) were adopted by 41 votes to 23, with 9 abstentions.

No vote was taken on the amendment to the preamble submitted by Egypt and Poland (A/C.6/L.409) or on the amendment proposed orally by Ceylon (see para. 14 above).

The second preambular paragraph of the draft resolution was adopted by 54 votes to none, with 16 abstentions.

The preamble as a whole was adopted by 43 votes to none, with 27 abstentions.

The draft resolution as a whole was adopted by a roll-call vote of 41 to 21, with 11 abstentions, as follows:

In favour: Argentina, Australia, Belgium, Brazil, Canada, Chile, China, Colombia, Costa Rica, Cuba, Denmark, Dominican Republic, Ecuador, El Salvador, Ethiopia, Finland, France, Honduras, Iceland, Israel, Italy, Japan, Liberia, Luxembourg, Nepal, Netherlands, New Zealand, Nicaragua, Norway, Pakistan, Paraguay, Philippines, Portugal, Spain, Sweden, Thailand, Turkey, United Kingdom of Great Britain and Northern Ireland, United States of America, Uruguay, Venezuela.

Against: Afghanistan, Albania, Bulgaria, Byelorussian Soviet Socialist Republic, Ceylon, Czechoslovakia, Egypt, Guatemala, Haiti, Hungary, Indonesia, Mexico, Poland, Romania, Saudi Arabia, Syria, Tunisia, Ukrainian Soviet Socialist Republic, Union of Soviet Socialist Republics, Yemen, Yugoslavia.

Abstaining: Austria, Bolivia, Burma, Cambodia, Greece, India, Iran, Iraq, Malaya (Federation of), Panama, Peru.

36. As the procedural draft resolution had been adopted, the draft resolutions relating to the substance of the question (A/C.6/L.399 and A/C.6/L.401) were not put to the vote.

Recommendation of the Sixth Committee

37. The Sixth Committee therefore recommends to the General Assembly the adoption of the following draft resolution:

[*Text adopted without change by the General Assembly. See "Action taken by the General Assembly" below.*]

DOCUMENT A/L.237 and Add.1 **

Ceylon, Egypt, Guatemala, Indonesia, Mexico, Poland and Syria: amendments to the draft resolution proposed by the Sixth Committee in document A/3756

[*Original text: English*]
[*28 November 1957*]

1. In operative paragraph 2, delete the words "and to renew the request to Member States to submit comments as provided in General Assembly resolution 688 (VII) of 20 December 1952, furnishing them with the documentation produced after the adoption of that resolution".

2. Delete operative paragraph 3.

3. Redraft operative paragraph 4 (renumbered 3) to read as follows:

"To request the Secretary-General to place the question of defining aggression on the provisional agenda of the fourteenth session of the General Assembly".

4. Delete operative paragraph 5.

** Document A/L.237/Add.1, dated 29 November 1957, indicated the addition of Guatemala to the list of sponsors of the amendments.

ACTION TAKEN BY THE GENERAL ASSEMBLY

At its 724th plenary meeting, on 29 November 1957, the General Assembly adopted the draft resolution submitted by the Sixth Committee. For the final text, see resolution 1181 (XII) below.

At the same meeting, the amendments in document A/L.237 and Add.1 to the draft resolution submitted by the Sixth Committee were rejected by the General Assembly.

Resolution adopted by the General Assembly

1181 (XII).   QUESTION OF DEFINING AGGRESSION

The General Assembly,

Recalling its resolutions 599 (VI) of 31 January 1952, 688 (VII) of 20 December 1952 and 895 (IX) of 4 December 1954, all referring to a definition of aggression,

Considering that, in spite of the progress made in the study of the question, the discussion at the present session shows the need for the elucidation of other aspects of a definition of aggression,

Considering that the report presented by the 1956 Special Committee on the Question of Defining Agression (A/3574) is an important study based on the views expressed by States Members of the United Nations up to the date of the preparation of the report,

Considering that twenty-two additional States have recently joined the Organization and that it would be useful to know their views on the matter,

Resolves:

1. To take note of the report of the 1956 Special Committee on the Question of Defining Aggression and to express appreciation for the valuable work done;

2. To ask the Secretary-General to request the views of the new Member States on the question, and to renew the request to Member States to submit comments as provided in General Assembly resolution 688 (VII) of 20 December 1952, furnishing them with the documentation produced after the adoption of that resolution;

3. To ask the Secretary-General to refer the replies of Member States to a committee composed of the Member States whose representatives have served on

the General Committee at the most recent regular session of the General Assembly, which committee shall study the replies for the purpose of determining when it shall be appropriate for the General Assembly to consider again the question of defining aggression, and shall report to the Secretary-General when it has determined that the time is appropriate, setting forth the considerations which led to its decision;

4. To request the Secretary-General to place the question of defining aggression on the provisional agenda of the General Assembly, not earlier than at its fourteenth session, when the committee has advised him that it considers the time appropriate;

5. To request the Secretary-General to convene the first meeting of the committee prior to the fourteenth session of the General Assembly.

> *724th plenary meeting,*
> *29 November 1957.*

CHECK LIST OF DOCUMENTS

NOTE. This check list includes all the documents mentioned during the consideration of agenda item 54 which are not reproduced in the present fascicle.

Document No.	Title	Observations and references
A/1399	Letter dated 26 September 1950 from the Vice-President of the Government and Minister of Foreign Affairs of the Federal People's Republic of Yugoslavia addressed to the Secretary-General	Official *Records of the General Assembly, Fifth Session. Annexes*, agenda item 72
A/2211	Report by the Secretary-General	*Ibid., Seventh Session, Annexes*, agenda item 54
A/2638	Report of the Special Committee on the Question of Defining Aggression (24 August-21 September 1953)	*Ibid., Ninth Session, Supplement No. 11*
A/2693	Report of the International Law Commission covering the work of its sixth session (3 June-28 July 1954)	*Ibid., Supplement No. 9*
A/3574	Report of the 1956 Special Committee on the Question of Defining Aggression (8 October-9 November 1956)	*Ibid., Twelfth Session, Supplement No. 16*
A/3592	Report of the Special Committee on the Problem of Hungary	*Ibid., Eleventh Session, Supplement No. 18*
A/3594/Add.1	Introduction to the annual report of the Secretary-General on the work of the Organization (16 June 1956 - 15 June 1957)	*Ibid., Twelfth Session, Supplement No. 1A*
A/AC.77/SR.7	Summary record of the seventh meeting of the 1956 Special Committee on the Question of Defining Aggression	Mimeographed
A/C.1/608	Union of Soviet Socialist Republics: draft resolution	Official *records of the General Assembly, Fifth Session, Annexes*, agenda item 72
A/C.6/L.335/Rev.1	Iran and Panama: revised draft resolution	*Ibid., Ninth Session, Annexes*, agenda item 51
A/C.6/L.399	Union of Soviet Socialist Republics: draft resolution	Same text as A/AC.77/L.4. See A/3574, annex II, section 1
A/C.6/L.401	Iran and Panama: draft resolution	Same text as A/AC.77/L.9. See A/3574, annex II, section 3
A/C.6/L.403/Rev.1	Chile, Colombia, Cuba, Ecuador, El Salvador, Philippines and Venezuela: revised draft resolution	For the text of this document, as corrected in the Sixth Committee (537th meeting, para. 36), see A/3756, para. 37
AC.6/L.404	Afghanistan, Bolivia, Guatemala, Haiti, Mexico and Peru: amendment to document A/C.6/L.403	Incorporated in A/3756, para. 8
A/C.6/L.406	Ceylon, Egypt and Indonesia: amendment to document A/C.6/L.404	Incorporated in A/3756, para. 9
A/C.6/L.407	United States of America: amendments to document A/C.6/L.403	Incorporated in A/3756, para. 10

Document No.	Title	Observations and references
A/C.6/L.409	Egypt and Poland : amendments to document A/C.6/L.403	Incorporated in A/3756, para. 11
A/CN.4/L.8	Memorandum by Ricardo J. Alfaro	Mimeographed
DC/53	Report of the Sub-Committee of the Disarmament Commission	*Official Records of the Disarmament Commission, Supplement for April, May and June 1954*

LIST OF MEETINGS AT WHICH AGENDA ITEM 54 WAS DISCUSSED

Sixth Committee : 514th to 528th meetings, 530th to 538th meetings
Plenary meetings : 724th meeting

UNITED NATIONS

GENERAL

ASSEMBLY

DOCUMENT 10

Distr.
GENERAL

A/AC.91/2
24 April 1959
ENGLISH
ORIGINAL: FRENCH

COMMITTEE ESTABLISHED UNDER GENERAL ASSEMBLY
 RESOLUTION 1181 (XII) (QUESTION OF
 DEFINING AGGRESSION)

REPORT OF THE COMMITTEE

Rapporteur: Mr. Basile VITSAXIS (Greece)

INTRODUCTION

1.   At its 724th plenary meeting, on 29 November 1957, the General Assembly
adopted resolution 1181 (XII) on the proposal of the Sixth Committee.   The
text of this resolution is as follows:

"The General Assembly,

"Recalling its resolutions 599 (VI) of 31 January 1952, 688 (VII)
of 20 December 1952 and 895 (IX) of 4 December 1954, all referring to
a definition of aggression,

"Considering that in spite of the progress made in the study of
the question, the discussion at the present session shows the need
for the elucidation of other aspects of a definition of aggression,

"Considering that the report presented by the 1956 Special Committee
on the Question of Defining Aggression (A/3574) is an important study
based on the views expressed by States Members of the United Nations
up to the date of the preparation of the report,

"Considering that twenty-two additional States have recently
joined the Organization and that it would be useful to know their
views on the matter,

59-10467

/...

255

"Resolves:

"1.   To take note of the report of the 1956 Special Committee on the Question of Defining Aggression and to express appreciation for the valuable work done;

"2.   To ask the Secretary-General to request the views of the new Member States on the question, and to renew the request to Member States to submit comments as provided in General Assembly resolution 688 (VII) of 20 December 1952, furnishing them with the documentation produced after the adoption of that resolution;

"3.   To ask the Secretary-General to refer the replies of Member States to a committee composed of the Member States whose representatives have served on the General Committee at the most recent regular session of the General Assembly, which committee shall study the replies for the purpose of determining when it shall be appropriate for the General Assembly to consider again the question of defining aggression, and shall report to the Secretary-General when it has determined that the time is appropriate, setting forth the considerations which led to its decision;

"4.   To request the Secretary-General to place the question of defining aggression on the provisional agenda of the General Assembly, not earlier than at its fourteenth session, when the committee has advised him that it considers the time appropriate;

"5.   To request the Secretary-General to convene the first meeting of the committee prior to the fourteenth session of the General Assembly."

2.   In conformity with this resolution, on 10 march 1958, the Secretary-General sent out two circular letters, one requesting the views of the new Member States on the question of defining aggression and the other renewing the request to the other Member States to submit comments on the same question.

3.   Fourteen replies were received and transmitted (document A/AC.91/1) to the Committee provided for in operative paragraph 3 of resolution 1181 (XII).

4.   In accordance with the same paragraph, the Secretary-General convened the Committee on 14 April 1959 at United Nations Headquarters.   Between that date and 24 April 1959, the Committee held seven meetings.

5.   The following is a list of the representatives and alternate representatives of the States members of the Committee:

Australia	Mr. J.D.L. Hood, Mr. R.H. Robertson;
Ceylon:	Mr. H.O. Wijegoonawardena;
China:	Mr. Yu-Chi Hsueh

/...

Czechoslovakia:	Mr. Karel Kurka, Mr. Zdenek Cernik;
Ecuador:	Mr. José A. Correa;
El Salvador:	Mr. Miguel Rafael Urquía, Mr. Francisco Antonio Carillo;
France:	Mr. Claude Chayet;
Greece:	Mr. Basile Vitsaxis;
Indonesia:	Mr. Ali Sastroamidjojo, Mr. Amin Azeharie;
Ireland:	Mr. Frederick H. Boland, Mr. Eamonn L. Kennedy;
Japan:	Mr. Koto Matsudaira;
Lebanon:	Mr. Georjes Hakim;
Mexico:	Mr. Francisco Cuevas Cancino;
Nepal:	Mr. Rishikesh Shaha;
Netherlands:	Mr. Jan Polderman;
Pakistan:	Mr. Agha Shahi, Mr. R.S. Chhatari;
Romania:	Mr. Mihai Magheru;
Union of Soviet Socialist Republics:	Mr. Arkady Aleskandrovich Sobolev, Mr. Vladimir Pavlovich Suslov;
United Kingdom of Great Britain and Northern Ireland:	Mr. W.V.J. Evans;
United States of America:	Mr. Albert Bender, Jr., Mr. Ernest L. Kerley;
Uruguay:	Mr. Enrique Rodriguez Fabregat.

6. The Committee elected the following officers:

Chairman:	Mr. Ali Sastroamidjojo (Indonesia);
Vice-Chairman:	Mr. José A. Correa (Ecuador);
Rapporteur:	Mr. Basile Vitsaxis (Greece).

7. When the Committee considered the wording of item 3 of its agenda
(A/AC.91/L.1), "Study of the replies of Member States in accordance with
paragraph 3 of General Assembly resolution 1181 (XII) of 29 November 1957", it
decided to reword the item as follows: "Study of the replies of Member States
in accordance with paragraph 3 of General Assembly resolution 1181 (XII) of
29 November 1957 and determination of the question whether the time is appropriate
for the General Assembly to consider against the question of defining aggression".

/...

DRAFT RESOLUTIONS AND AMENDMENT

8.   The Committee had before it two draft resolutions.

9.   The representative of the Union of Soviet Socialist Republics submitted the following draft resolution (A/AC.91/L.2):

"The Committee,

"Taking into account the directive in General Assembly resolution 1181 (XII) concerning the determination of the appropriate time for the United Nations to consider again the question of defining aggression,

"Taking into account that during the discussion of the question of defining aggression at the twelfth session of the General Assembly the majority of States Members of the United Nations favoured the preparation of a definition of aggression by the United Nations,

"Having also studied the replies from States Members of the United Nations submitted to the Secretary-General in accordance with paragraph 3 of General Assembly resolution 1181 (XII) of 29 November 1957,

"Recommends that the Secretary-General place on the provisional agenda of the fourteenth session of the General Assembly an item entitled 'Question of defining aggression'."

10.   The representative of El Salvador submitted a draft resolution which he revised in the course of the discussion.[1]/   In its revised form, (A/AC.91/L.3/Rev.1), this draft is identical to the resolution adopted by the Committee (see para. 14 below) with the exception of the words "April 1962" in operative paragraph 1, which the representative of Ireland proposed orally should be substituted for the words "April 1961".

---

[1]/   The revision was of the third preambular paragraph, which in its original form read as follows:

"Having regard to the fact that nine of these States still adhere to the views they expressed in the General Assembly, three have no comments to make on the question at present, another considers that it would be inappropriate to try to reach hasty conclusions on the matter and that no useful purpose would be served by discussion of the substance of the question until there has been an improvement of atmosphere in international relations and unless a good prospect is in sight for reaching an agreement on the contents of such a definition among the Member States, and yet another reiterates its opinion that it would not be appropriate to resume discussion until there had been a change in the attitudes of a substantial number of Member States towards the question of defining aggression,".

/...

VOTING

11. On the proposal of the Salvadorian representative, the Committee decided
by 12 votes to 4, with 4 abstentions, at its sixth meeting, on 16 April 1959,
to vote first on the revised draft resolution submitted by El Salvador
(A/AC.91/L.3/Rev.1).

12. The Committee then adopted:

(a) the Irish representative's oral amendment by 10 votes to 7, with
3 abstentions;

(b) the revised draft resolution submitted by El Salvador
(A/AC.91/L.3/Rev.1), as amended, by 17 notes to none, with 3 abstentions.

13. As the revised Salvadorian draft resolution had been adopted, the Committee
did not proceed to a vote on the draft resolution submitted by the Union of
Soviet Socialist Republics (A/AC.91/L.2).

DECISION

14. The Committee accordingly adopted the following resolution:

"The Committee

"Having been established by General Assembly resolution 1181 (XII) of
29 November 1957 in order to study the replies of the States Members of
the United Nations to the request made by the Secretary-General pursuant
to that resolution, for the purpose of determining when it shall be
appropriate for the General Assembly to consider again the question of
defining aggression,

"Having considered the replies submitted by fourteen Member States
(A/AC.91/1/Rev.1),

"Having regard to the fact that these replies indicate no change in
the attitudes of Member States and give no reason to think that the
appropriate time has come for the General Assembly to consider again
the question of defining aggression,

"Confident that many Member States will wish to facilitate the work
of the Committee and to submit their views and comments on the question
in conformity with paragraph 2 of General Assembly resolution 1181 (XII)
of 29 November 1957,

/...

"Decides:

"1.   To adjourn until April 1962 further consideration of the question of determining when it shall be appropriate for the General Assembly to consider again the question of defining aggression, unless an absolute majority of the members of the Committee, in the light of the views and comments received and the situation prevailing in international relations, considers it desirable for the Committee to meet at an earlier date and requests the Secretary-General to convene it;

"2.   To request the Secretary-General to transmit this resolution to all Member States and to reconvene the Committee in either of the two cases provided for in the preceding paragraph."

UNITED NATIONS

GENERAL

ASSEMBLY

DOCUMENT 11

Distr.
GENERAL

A/AC.91/3
3 April 1962

ORIGINAL: ENGLISH

COMMITTEE ESTABLISHED UNDER GENERAL ASSEMBLY
 RESOLUTION 1181 (XII) (QUESTION OF DEFINING
 AGGRESSION)
Second session

REPORT OF THE COMMITTEE

Rapporteur: Dr. Gonzalo ORTIZ (Costa Rica)

INTRODUCTION

1.   The General Assembly, by resolution 1181 (XII) of 29 November 1957, noted
inter alia that twenty-two States had recently joined the United Nations, asked
the Secretary-General to request the views of the new Member States on the
question of defining aggression, and further asked the Secretary-General

> "... to refer the replies of Member States to a committee composed of the
> Member States whose representatives have served on the General Committee
> at the most recent regular session of the General Assembly, which Committee
> shall study the replies for the purpose of determining when it shall be
> appropriate for the General Assembly to consider again the question of
> defining aggression, and shall report to the Secretary-General when it has
> determined that the time is appropriate, setting forth the considerations
> which led to its decision."

2.   The Committee held its first session in April 1959, and adopted a
resolution which is reproduced in its report (A/AC.91/2). By that resolution
the Committee decided

> "1.   To adjourn until April 1962 further consideration of the
> question of determining when it shall be appropriate for the General
> Assembly to consider again the question of defining aggression, unless
> an absolute majority of the members of the Committee, in the light of the
> views and comments received and the situation prevailing in international
> relations, considers it desirable for the Committee to meet at an earlier
> date and requests the Secretary-General to convene it;

> "2.   To request the Secretary-General to transmit this resolution
> to all Member States and to reconvene the Committee in either of the two
> cases provided for in the preceding paragraph."

62-08310

/...

3. In pursuance of this resolution the Secretary-General reconvened the Committee on 2 April 1962 at United Nations Headquarters. Between that date and 9 April 1962, the Committee held five meetings.

4. The following is a list of the representatives and alternate representatives of the States members of the Committee:

Argentina:	Mr. Enrique Ros;
Bulgaria:	Mr. Yordan Tchobanov, Mr. Decho Dincho Stamboliev;
China:	Mr. Yu-Chi Hsueh, Mr. Wang Meng-hsien;
Costa Rica:	Mr. Gonzalo Ortiz, Mr. Javier Oreamuno;
Cyprus:	Mr. Zenon Rossides;
Czechoslovakia:	Mr. Zdenek Cernik, Mr. Stanislav Myslil;
Denmark:	Mr. Aage Hessellund-Jensen,
	Mr. William F. McIlquham Schmidt;
France:	Mr. Pierre Millet, Mr. Jean-Louis Plihon;
Ghana:	Mr. Alex Quaison-Sackey, Mr. Kenneth K.S. Dadzie,
	Mr. Johnson K.D. Appiah;
Greece:	Mr. Dmitri S. Bitsios, Mr. Alexandre Demetropoulos;
Italy:	Mr. Palo Tallarigo, Mr. Marco Pisa;
Liberia:	Mr. Nathan Barnes, Mr. Nathaniel Eastman;
Mexico:	Mr. Jorge Castañeda, Mr. Joaquin Mercado;
Netherlands:	Mr. Jan Poldermann, Mr. Lodewyk H.J.B. van Gorkom;
Niger:	Mr. Illa Salifou;
Panama:	Mr. Cesar Quintero;
Philippines:	Mr. Eduardo Quintero, Mr. Zoilo M. Alberto;
Tunisia:	Mr. Chedly Ayari;

Union of Soviet Socialist Republics: Mr. Platon Dmitrievich Morozov,
Mr. Konstantin Grigoryevich Fedoseev, Mr. Igor I. Yakovlev;

United Kingdom of Great Britain and Northern Ireland: Mr. C.T. Crowe,
Miss J.A.C. Gutteridge;

United States of America: Mr. Charles Phelps Noyes, Mr. Ernest L. Kerley,
Mrs. Carmel Carrington Marr.

5. The Committee elected the following officers:

Chairman:	Mr. Nathan Barnes (Liberia);
Vice-Chairman:	Mr. Dmitri Bitsios (Greece);
Rapporteur:	Mr. Gonzalo Ortiz (Costa Rica).

/...

DRAFT RESOLUTIONS

6.   The Committee had before it a draft resolution submitted by the representative of Cyprus (A/AC.91/L.7) which was later revised by its sponsor (A/AC.91/L.7/Rev.1) by the addition in operative paragraph 2 of the words "and to renew the request to the other Member States to submit their views". In its revised form the draft is identical with the resolution adopted by the Committee.

VOTING

7.   The Committee, at its twelfth meeting on 9 April 1962, by 16 votes to none, with 4 abstentions, adopted the resolution reproduced hereunder.

RESOLUTION

The Committee,

Considering its terms of reference as laid down in General Assembly resolution 1181 (XII) of 29 November 1957,

Noting that there have not been sufficient indications of the attitudes of Member States to allow the determination of any particular time as appropriate for the General Assembly to consider again the question of defining aggression,

Further noting that many new Member States have not yet expressed their views on that question, and being confident that new Member States will wish to facilitate the work of the Committee by submitting their views and comments,

Decides:

1.   To adjourn until April 1965 further consideration of the question of determining when it shall be appropriate for the General Assembly to consider again the question of defining aggression, unless an absolute majority of the members of the Committee, in the light of the views and comments received and the situation prevailing in international relations, considers it desirable for the Committee to meet at an earlier date and requests the Secretary-General to convene it;

2.   To ask the Secretary-General to request States admitted to the United Nations since the session of the Committee in 1959 to submit, not later than

/...

1 November 1964, their views on the question in conformity with paragraph 2 of
General Assembly resolution 1181 (XII) of 29 November 1957, and to renew the
request to the other Member States to submit their views;

3.   To request the Secretary-General to transmit this resolution to all
Member States, and to reconvene the Committee in either of the two cases
provided for in paragraph 1.

UNITED NATIONS

GENERAL

ASSEMBLY

Distr.
LIMITED

A/AC.91/5
26 April 1965

ORIGINAL: ENGLISH

COMMITTEE ESTABLISHED UNDER GENERAL
 ASSEMBLY RESOLUTION 1181 (XII)
 (QUESTION OF DEFINING AGGRESSION)
Third Session

REPORT OF THE COMMITTEE

Rapporteur: Mr. Rafik ASHA (Syria)

INTRODUCTION

1.   The General Assembly, by resolution 1181 (XII) of 29 November 1957, noted
inter alia that twenty-two States had recently joined the United Nations, asked
the Secretary-General to request the views of the new Member States on the Question
of defining aggression, and further asked the Secretary-General

> "... to refer the replies of Member States to a committee composed of the
> Member States whose representatives have served on the General Committee at
> the most recent regular session of the General Assembly, which Committee
> shall study the replies for the purpose of determining when it shall be
> appropriate for the General Assembly to consider again the Question of
> defining aggression, and shall report to the Secretary-General when it has
> determined that the time is appropriate, setting forth the considerations
> which led to its decision."

2.   The Committee held its first session in April 1959, and adopted a resolution
which is reproduced in its report (A/AC.91/2). By that resolution the Committee
decided

> "1.   To adjourn until April 1962 further consideration of the question
> of determining when it shall be appropriate for the General Assembly to
> consider again the question of defining aggression, unless an absolute
> majority of the members of the Committee, in the light of the views and
> comments received and the situation prevailing in international relations,
> considers it desirable for the Committee to meet at an earlier date and
> requests the Secretary-General to convene it;
>
> "2.   To request the Secretary-General to transmit this resolution to all
> Member States and to reconvene the Committee in either of the two cases
> provided for in the preceding paragraph."

65-08926

/...

3. In pursuance of that resolution the Committee held its second session in April 1962, and adopted a further resolution, reproduced in its report (A/AC.91/3), by which it decided:

"1. To adjourn until April 1965 further consideration of the question of determining when it shall be appropriate for the General Assembly to consider again the question of defining aggression, unless an absolute majority of the members of the Committee, in the light of the views and comments received and the situation prevailing in international relations, considers it desirable for the Committee to meet at an earlier date and requests the Secretary-General to convene it;

"2. To ask the Secretary-General to request States admitted to the United Nations since the session of the Committee in 1959 to submit, not later than 1 November 1964, their views on the question in conformity with paragraph 2 of General Assembly resolution 1181 (XII) of 29 November 1957, and to renew the request to the other Member States to submit their views;

"3. To request the Secretary-General to transmit this resolution to all Member States, and to reconvene the Committee in either of the two cases provided for in paragraph 1."

4. Accordingly, the Secretary-General reconvened the Committee on 5 April 1965 at United Nations Headquarters. As the General Assembly, at its nineteenth session, elected only a President but not the other members of the General Committee, the Secretary-General extended invitations on the basis of the composition of the General Committee at the eighteenth session of the General Assembly, and also invited Ghana, whose representative had been elected President of the nineteenth session. Between 5 and 16 April 1965, the Committee held ten meetings.[1]/

5. The following is a list of representatives and alternate representatives of the States members of the Committee:

Argentina:	Mr. Carlos Alberto Goñi Demarchi;
Bulgaria:	Mr. Milko Tarabanov, Mr. Matey Karasimeonov;
Cameroon:	Mr. William F. Lima Forcho;
Canada:	Mr. Gordon E. Cox, Miss M.A. Macpherson;
Chile:	Mr. Javier Illanes, Miss Leonora Kracht, Mr. Ronald Geiger;
China:	Mr. Yu Chi Hsueh, Mr. Erh Chung Peng;
Cyprus:	Mr. Zenon Rossides

1/ See A/AC.91/SR.13-22.

El Salvador:	Mr. Antonio Alvarez Vidaurre, Mr. Carlos Alberto Lievano,
	Mr. Felipe Vega-Gomez, Mr. José Martino Seguí;
France:	Mr. Claude Arnaud, Mr. Jean-Noël de Bouillane de Lacoste;
Ghana:	Mr. N.A. Quao, Mr. W.W.K. Vanderpuije, Mr. E.Y. Agorsor;
Guinea:	Mr. Achkar Marof, Mr. M'Baye Cheik Omar;
Iceland:	Mr. Hannes Kjartansson;
Netherlands:	Mr. J. Polderman, Mr. L.H.J.B. van Gorkom;
Romania:	Mr. Mihail Haseganu, Mr. Constantin Nedelea,
	Mr. Dinu Marasescu;
Somalia:	Mr. Ahmed Mohamed Darman;
Syria:	Mr. Rafik Asha, Mr. Adnan Nachabe;
Turkey:	Mr. Muammer Tunçer, Mr. Aydin Yegen;

Union of Soviet Socialist Republics: Mr. Nikolai Trofimovich Fedorenko,
                    Mr. Platon Dmitrivich Morozov,
                    Mr. Yakov Arkadyevich Ostrovski,
                    Mr. Anatoly Vasilyevich Grodsky,
                    Mr. Leonid Ivanovich Verenikin;

United Kingdom of Great Britain and Northern Ireland: Mr. C. Peter Hope,
                    Mr. I.M. Sinclair;

United States of America: Mr. Francis T.P. Plimpton, Mr. Albert F. Bender, Jr.,
                    Mr. Seymour M. Finger, Mr. J. Lawrence Hargrove,
                    Mrs. Carmel Carrington Marr, Mr. Robert B. Rosenstock,
                    Mr. Donald R. Toussaint;

| Venezuela: | Mr. Tulio Alvarado. |

6. The Committee elected the following officers:

Chairman:	Mr. Antonio Alvarez Vidaurre;
Vice-Chairman:	Mr. Zenon Rossides;
Rapporteur:	Mr. Rafik Asha.

/...

267

DRAFT RESOLUTIONS AND AMENDMENTS

7.   Argentina and the United Kingdom submitted a draft resolution (A/AC.91/L.11) which reads as follows:

The Committee,

Considering its terms of reference as laid down in General Assembly resolution 1181 (XII) of 29 November 1957,

Noting that there have not been sufficient indications of the attitudes of Member States to allow the determination of any particular time as appropriate for the General Assembly to consider again the question of defining aggression,

Further noting that, since the Committee last met in April 1962, the General Assembly has been discussing an agenda item entitled "Consideration of principles of international law concerning friendly relations and co-operation among States in accordance with the Charter of the United Nations",

Taking into account that, among the principles of international law now under consideration in the context of this agenda item, is the principle that States shall refrain in their international relations from the threat or use of force against the territorial integrity or political independence of any State, or in any other manner inconsistent with the purposes of the United Nations,

Recognizing that the work now in progress with respect to this principle would in part be duplicated if the General Assembly were to consider again at this stage the question of defining aggression,

Decides:

"1.   To adjourn further consideration of the question of determining when it shall be appropriate for the General Assembly to consider again the question of defining aggression until such time as a majority of the members of the Committee, in the light of the views and comments received and the situation prevailing in international relations, considers it desirable for the Committee to meet and requests the Secretary-General to convene it;

"2.   To ask the Secretary-General to request States admitted to the United Nations since the session of the Committee in 1962 to submit their views on the question in conformity with paragraph 2 of General Assembly resolution 1181 (XII) of 29 November 1957;

"3.   To request the Secretary-General to transmit this resolution to all Member States, and to reconvene the Committee in the case provided for in paragraph 1."

8.   To this draft resolution Chile submitted an amendment (A/AC.91/L.14) which would replace the first operative paragraph by the following text:

"1.   To adjourn until April 1968 further consideration of the question of determining when it shall be appropriate for the General Assembly to consider again the question of defining aggression unless a majority of the members

of the Committee, in the light of the views and comments received and the
situation prevailing in international relations, considers it desirable for
the Committee to meet at an earlier date with a view to considering the
possibility of recommending to the General Assembly that it should study the
question again and requests the Secretary-General to convene it;"

9.   The Union of Soviet Socialist Republics submitted a draft resolution
(A/AC.91/L.12) reading as follows:

The Committee,

Considering that it was requested in General Assembly resolution 1181 (XII) to
determine when it should be appropriate for the General Assembly to consider again
the question of defining aggression,

Recalling that, in the discussion at the sessions of the General Assembly of
the question of defining aggression, the majority of States Members of the United
Nations supported the adoption of such a definition, based on the Charter of the
United Nations, considering that this could have great significance for the
maintenance of friendly relations between nations, the prevention of acts of
aggression and the strengthening of universal peace and security,

Having regard to the replies from Member States submitted to the Secretary-
General in accordance with paragraph 3 of General Assembly resolution 1181 (XII)
of 29 November 1957,

Noting that experience has shown that the lack of a precise definition of
aggression plays into the hands of those Powers which are pursuing a policy of
interference in the internal affairs of other States and which, for the attainment
of their purposes, even resort to the use of armed force,

Recognizing that the drafting and adoption by the United Nations of a
definition of aggression would correspond to the interests of all peace-loving
States and be in accord with the purposes and principles of the United Nations,

Decides to recommend that the General Assembly of the United Nations should
at its twentieth session resume work on the definition of the concept of aggression,
and accordingly requests the Secretary-General of the United Nations to include in
the provisional agenda of the twentieth session of the General Assembly the item:
"Question of defining aggression: Report of the Committee established pursuant to
resolution 1181 (XII) of 29 November 1957".

10.   To this draft resolution an oral amendment was submitted by Ghana which would
replace "twentieth session" in the operative paragraph by "twenty-second session".

11.   Cameroon, Ghana, Guinea, Somalia and Syria submitted a draft resolution
(A/AC.91/L.13) reading as follows:

/...

269

The Committee,

Considering that its terms of reference as laid down in General Assembly resolution 1181 (XII) of 29 November 1957 are to determine when it should be appropriate for the General Assembly to consider again the question of defining aggression,

Recalling that by its resolution 599 (VI) of 31 January 1952, the General Assembly considered that it was "possible and desirable, with a view to ensuring international peace and security and to developing international criminal law, to define aggression", and that "it would be of definite advantage if directives were formulated for the future guidance of such international bodies as may be called upon to determine the aggressor",

Having regard to the replies from Member States submitted to the Secretary-General in accordance with paragraph 3 of General Assembly resolution 1181 (XII) of 29 November 1957,

Noting that, since the Committee last met in April 1962, the General Assembly has been discussing an agenda item entitled "Consideration of principles of international law concerning friendly relations and co-operation among States in accordance with the Charter of the United Nations",

Taking into account that, among the principles of international law now under consideration in the context of this agenda item, is the principle that States shall refrain in their international relations from the threat or use of force against the territorial integrity or political independence of any State, or in any other manner inconsistent with the purpose of the United Nations,

Recognizing that a definition of aggression will be helpful in further consideration of this principle,

Further recognizing that the drafting and adoption by the United Nations of a definition of aggression would correspond to the interests of all States and be in accord with the purposes and principles of the United Nations,

Decides:

"1. To adjourn and reconvene in April 1966 with a view to recommending to the General Assembly that it should resume consideration of the question of defining aggression;

"2. To ask the Secretary-General to request States admitted to the United Nations since the session of the Committee in 1962 to submit their views on the question in conformity with paragraph 2 of General Assembly resolution 1181 (XII) of 29 November 1957."

12. At the close of the discussion, Cyprus submitted a draft resolution
(A/AC.91/L.15 and Corr.1, Spanish only) which was adopted by the Committee and is
reproduced at the end of this report.

VOTING

13. At its twenty-second meeting the Committee adopted without objection the
draft resolution submitted by Cyprus (A/AC.91/L.15 and Corr.1, Spanish only).
The representative of the USSR explained his position in regard to the resolution.

RESOLUTION

14. The Committee thus adopted the following resolution:
The Committee,

Considering its terms of reference as laid down in General Assembly
resolution 1181 (XII) of 29 November 1957,

Decides:

1. To reconvene in April 1967 with a view to consider recommending to the
General Assembly that it should study again the question of defining aggression,
unless a majority of the members of the Committee, who will be consulted in writing
in January 1966 by the Secretary-General, considers that it is desirable for the
Committee to meet in April 1966, and request the Secretary-General to convene it
at that time;

2. To ask the Secretary-General to request States admitted to the United
Nations since the session of the Committee in 1962 to submit their views on the
question in conformity with paragraph 2 of General Assembly resolution 1181 (XII)
of 29 November 1957;

3. To request the Secretary-General to transmit this resolution to all
Member States. and to reconvene the Committee as provided for in paragraph 1.

271

United Nations

GENERAL ASSEMBLY

Official Records

DOCUMENT 13

Agenda item 95

ANNEXES

TWENTY-SECOND SESSION

NEW YORK, 1967

Agenda item 95:* Need to expedite the drafting of a definition of aggression in the light of the present international situation

CONTENTS

* For the discussion of this item, see *Official Records of the General Assembly, Twenty-second Session, Sixth Committee,* 1017th to 1023rd and 1025th meetings; *ibid., Fifth Committee,* 1226th meeting; and *ibid., Plenary Meetings,* 1611th to 1618th, 1637th and 1638th meetings.

DOCUMENT A/6833**

Union of Soviet Socialist Republics: request for the inclusion of an additional item in the agenda of the twenty-second session

[Original text: Russian]
[22 September 1967]

LETTER DATED 22 SEPTEMBER 1967 FROM THE MINISTER FOR FOREIGN AFFAIRS OF THE UNION OF SOVIET SOCIALIST REPUBLICS TO THE PRESIDENT OF THE GENERAL ASSEMBLY

On instructions from the Government of the Union of Soviet Socialist Republics, I request the inclusion in the agenda of the twenty-second session of the General Assembly, as an important and urgent matter, of an item entitled "Need to expedite the drafting of a definition of aggression in the light of the present international situation".

The most important task of the United Nations is to safeguard peace and to halt and prevent aggression.

The Charter of the United Nations states that one of the main purposes of the Organization is to main-

---
** Incorporating document A/6833/Corr.1 dated 25 September 1967.

tain international peace and security and, to that end, to take effective collective measures for the prevention and removal of threats to the peace and for the suppression of acts of aggression or other breaches of the peace. In prohibiting aggression, the Charter imposes a strict obligation on States to refrain from the threat or use of force against the territorial integrity or political independence of any State, or in any other manner inconsistent with the purposes of the United Nations.

Of late, there have been increasing instances of the use of armed force to commit acts of aggression against sovereign States and to crush peoples struggling against colonialism and for freedom and independence. Acts of aggression which are undermining world peace and international security are causing grave concern among peoples. They are increasing the danger of the outbreak of a new world conflict, with all the disastrous consequences that would follow.

1

Annexes (XXII) 95

In conjunction with the vigorous condemnation of aggression and the adoption of measures for preventing it, the formulation of a definition of aggression could, particularly in the present international situation, make an important contribution to the cause of peace. It is well known that the States which are resorting to armed force in violation of the purposes and principles of the United Nations have often, taking advantage of the absence of a generally accepted concept of aggression, sought to make use of various artificial pretexts and unfounded reservations in order to cover up and justify their aggressive actions against peace-loving States. A definition of the concept of aggression would contribute greatly to the maintenance of international peace and the adoption of effective measures to prevent aggression; it would be a stern reminder to the forces of aggression and war that they bear responsibility for violating international peace.

The Soviet Union, which pursues a foreign policy based on observance of the purposes and principles of the United Nations and respect for the rights of both large and small nations, which consistently and steadfastly supports the adoption of effective measures for strengthening peace and the security of peoples and for preventing aggression, now favours, as it has in the past, the formulation of a definition of aggression. All States which hold dear the ideals of peace, freedom and independence and to which the principles of the Charter represent a firm basis for the maintenance of international peace and security are in favour of taking effective measures to combat aggression. At the ninth session of the General Assembly, it will be recalled, more than two thirds of the States Members of the United Nations voted for a resolution (895 (IX)) endorsing the preparation of a definition of aggression. Because of the stubborn opposition of certain States, however, this decision has not yet been carried out.

The Soviet Government deems it essential that the General Assembly should consider at its twenty-second session, as an important and urgent matter, an item entitled "Need to expedite the drafting of a definition of aggression in the light of the present international situation". The Government of the USSR hopes that the General Assembly will consider this matter at its twenty-second session with the utmost seriousness and with a sense of responsibility for the fate of the world.

I should be grateful if you would regard this letter as the explanatory memorandum provided for by rule 20 of the rules of procedure of the General Assembly and if you would circulate it as an official United Nations document.

(*Signed*) A. GROMYKO
*Minister for Foreign Affairs of the
Union of Soviet Socialist Republics*

[*The text of a draft resolution (subsequently issued as document A/C.6/L.636) was annexed to the above letter and is reproduced in paragraph 2 of document A/6988 below.*]

DOCUMENT A/C.6/378

Letter dated 29 September 1967 from the President of the General Assembly to the Chairman of the Sixth Committee

[*Original text: French*]
[*29 September 1967*]

I have the honour to inform you that at its 1572nd plenary meeting, held on 28 September 1967, the General Assembly decided to include the following item in the agenda of its twenty-second session:

"95. Need to expedite the drafting of a definition of aggression in the light of the present international situation."

The General Assembly also decided that the item should be allocated to plenary meetings and, in the light of the debate and the results obtained, should be examined by the Sixth Committee.

As soon as the plenary Assembly has finished its debate on this agenda item, I shall so inform you.

(*Signed*) Corneliu MANESCU

DOCUMENT A/C.6/384

Letter dated 5 December 1967 from the President of the General Assembly to the Chairman of the Sixth Committee

[*Original text: French*]
[*5 December 1967*]

I have the honour to inform you that the General Assembly, at its 1618th plenary meeting, on 4 December 1967, concluded its debate on agenda item 95 entitled "Need to expedite the drafting of a definition of aggression in the light of the present international situation".

In accordance with the decision taken by the General Assembly at its 1572nd plenary meeting, on 28 September 1967, this item is transmitted to the Sixth Committee for consideration.

I attach hereto document A/6833 on this question and the verbatim records of the plenary meetings during which it was examined (1611th to 1618th plenary meetings).

(*Signed*) Corneliu MANESCU

DOCUMENT A/C.6/L.641

Letter dated 11 December 1967 from the Chairman of the Committee on Conferences to the Chairman of the Sixth Committee

[Original text: English]
[12 December 1967]

The Committee on Conferences, established under General Assembly resolution 2239 (XXI), has examined draft resolution A/C.6/L.636, paragraph 2 of which "establishes a special committee composed of ...", and paragraph 3 of which "instructs the Special Committee, having regard to the present resolution and the international legal instruments relating to the matter in question, to draw up a draft definition of aggression and submit it to the General Assembly at its twenty-third session".

The Committee has decided to recommend, if this draft resolution is adopted, that the special committee on the question of defining aggression be convened at Geneva from 4 June to 5 July 1968.

The Committee was informed that the holding of this session at Geneva will involve additional costs, a statement of which will be submitted by the Secretary-General to the Sixth Committee under rule 154 of the rules of procedure of the General Assembly.

(*Signed*) Brian J. LYNCH

DOCUMENT A/C.6/L.643

Administrative and financial implications of the draft resolutions contained in documents A/C.6/L.636 and A/C.6/L.637 and Add.1 and 2

Note by the Secretary-General

[Original text: English]
[12 December 1967]

1. Under the terms of the draft resolutions before the Sixth Committee in documents A/C.6/L.636 and A/C.6/L.637 and Add.1 and 2, the General Assembly would establish a special committee on the question of defining aggression, which would report to the Assembly at its twenty-third session.

2. The Secretary-General has ascertained that it would only be possible to accommodate such a committee in 1968 if the committee were to meet from 4 June to 5 July at Geneva and were to hold one meeting a day, alternating with the meetings of the International Law Commission, and if no subsidiary body or working group requiring any conference servicing were established. It is assumed that the following requirements would arise for the proposed committee:

(*a*) Interpretation from and into English, French, Russian and Spanish;

(*b*) Pre-session documentation for distribution in four languages, comprising 50 pages of new text and also substantial prior documentation on this question;

(*c*) Summary records averaging 15 pages per day in English, French and Spanish;

(*d*) In-session documentation for distribution in four languages totalling approximately 50 pages, as well as a draft report of approximately 50 pages;

(*e*) Reproduction and distribution of the report of the committee as a document of the General Assembly.

3. Conference servicing of the committee would require the recruitment of temporary staff, consisting of 3 précis-writers, 7 translators, 3 revisers and 13 stenographer/typists. Interpretation could be provided by the team of interpreters who will also service the International Law Commission. The substantive secretariat of the committee would consist of part of the staff to be sent from Headquarters for the International Law Commission, as well as the Legal Counsel, 2 additional Professional staff members and 2 secretaries.

4. The additional costs involved may be estimated as follows:

United States dollars

Pre-session costs

Translation and reproduction of pre-session documentation 3,500

In-session costs

Translation and typing staff for summary records and in-session documentation (3 précis-writers, 7 translators, 3 revisers, 13 stenographer/typists) 33,000

Other staff (travel and subsistence of the Legal Counsel and 2 substantive staff from Headquarters and salaries of 2 temporary secretaries 5,000

Document reproduction and distribution 2,500

Post-session costs..

No additional costs would be involved, as the report would be reproduced as part of the documentation for the twenty-third session of the General Assembly .... —

TOTAL 44,000

5. Accordingly, the Secretary-General informs the Sixth Committee that, should the General Assembly decide to establish a special committee on the question of defining aggression, an additional appropriation of $44,000 would be required in the budget estimates for 1968.

DOCUMENT A/C.5/1158

Administrative and financial implications of the draft resolution submitted by the Sixth Committee in document A/6988

Note by the Secretary-General

[*Original text: English*]
[*14 December 1967*]

1. At its 1025th meeting, on 14 December 1967, the Sixth Committee adopted a draft resolution under the terms of which the General Assembly would establish a special committee on the question of defining aggression, composed of thirty Member States to be appointed by the President of the Assembly, and instructed to report to the Assembly at its twenty-third session.

2. The Secretary-General has ascertained that it would only be possible to accommodate such a committee in 1968 if the committee were to meet from 4 June to 5 July at Geneva and were to hold one meeting a day, alternating with the International Law Commission, and if no subsidiary body or working group requiring any conference servicing were established. It is assumed that the following requirements would arise for the proposed committee:

(*a*) Interpretation from and into English, French, Russian and Spanish;

(*b*) Pre-session documentation for distribution in four languages, comprising 50 pages of new text and also substantial prior documentation on this question;

(*c*) Summary records averaging 15 pages per day in English, French and Spanish;

(*d*) In-session documentation for distribution in four languages totalling approximately 50 pages, as well as a draft report of approximately 50 pages;

(*e*) Reproduction and distribution of the report of the committee as a document of the General Assembly.

3. Conference servicing of the committee would require the recruitment of temporary staff, consisting of 3 précis-writers, 7 translators, 3 revisers and 13 stenographer/typists. Interpretation could be provided by the team of interpreters who will also service the International Law Commission. The substantive secretariat of the committee would consist of part of the staff to be sent from Headquarters to service the International Law Commission, as well as the Legal Counsel, 2 additional Professional staff members and 2 secretaries.

4. The additional costs involved may be estimated as follows:

	United States dollars
Pre-session costs	
Translation and reproduction of pre-session documentation	3,500
In-session costs	
Translation and typing staff for summary records and in-session documentation (3 précis-writers, 7 translators, 3 revisers, 13 stenographer/typists)	33,000
Other staff (travel and subsistence of the Legal Counsel and 2 substantive staff from Headquarters and salaries of 2 temporary secretaries	5,000
Document reproduction and distribution	2,500
Post-session costs	
No additional costs would be involved, as the report would be reproduced as part of the documentation for the twenty-third session of the General Assembly	—
TOTAL	44,000

5. Accordingly, the Secretary-General informs the Fifth Committee that, should the General Assembly decide to establish a special committee on the question of defining aggression, an additional appropriation of $44,000 would be required in the budget estimates for 1968, under a new chapter in section 2 (Special meetings and conferences).

DOCUMENT A/6988

Report of the Sixth Committee

[*Original text: English and Spanish*]
[*15 December 1697*]

CONTENTS

I. INTRODUCTION

1. The Union of Soviet Socialist Republics, by a letter dated 22 September 1967 (A/6833), requested the inclusion in the agenda of the twenty-second session of the General Assembly, as an important and urgent matter, of an item entitled "Need to expedite the drafting of a definition of aggression in the light of the present international situation". The General Committee, in its second report at the twenty-second session (A/6840/Add.1), recommended that the item be included in the agenda, and that it be allocated to the Sixth Committee. The General Assembly, at its 1572nd plenary meeting on 28 September 1967, decided to place the item on the agenda, and further decided that it should be allocated to plenary meetings of the Assembly

and, in the light of the debate and the results obtained, should be examined by the Sixth Committee (A/C.6/378). The General Assembly considered the item at its 1611th to 1618th plenary meetings, from 28 November to 4 December 1967. Upon the conclusion of the debate in plenary meeting, the item was transmitted to the Sixth Committee for consideration (A/C.6/384). The Sixth Committee considered the item at its 1017th to 1023rd and 1025th meetings, from 7 to 14 December 1967.

II. Proposals and amendments

2. A draft resolution submitted by the Union of Soviet Socialist Republics at the 1017th meeting, on 7 December 1967 (A/C.6/L.636) read as follows:

"*The General Assembly,*

"*Considering* that, in conformity with the Charter of the United Nations, all Members of the United Nations must refrain in their international relations from the threat or use of force against the territorial integrity or political independence of any State, or in any other manner inconsistent with the purposes of the United Nations,

"*Considering* that one of the main purposes of the United Nations is to maintain international peace and security and, to that end, to take effective collective measures for the prevention and removal of threats to the peace and for the suppression of acts of aggression or other breaches of the peace,

"*Deeply concerned* over the acts of aggression which have recently been taking place in various regions of the world,

"*Firmly convinced* that a precise definition of aggression would have considerable importance for the maintenance of international peace and the adoption of effective measures for preventing such acts as armed attack by one State against another, invasion of the territory of one State by the armed forces of another State and the seizure or occupation of the territory of one State by the armed forces of another State,

"*Noting with regret* that there is still no generally recognized definition of aggression,

"1. *Considers* it necessary for aggression to be defined as soon as possible;

"2. *Establishes* a special committee composed of ... ;

"3. *Instructs* the Special Committee, having regard to the present resolution and the international legal instruments relating to the matter in question, to draw up a draft definition of aggression and submit it to the General Assembly at its twenty-third session;

"4. *Decides* to include in the agenda of its twenty-third session an item entitled 'Report of the Special Committee on the Question of Defining Aggression'."

3. An amendment proposed by Australia, the United Kingdom of Great Britain and Northern Ireland and the United States of America (A/C.6/L.640) to the USSR draft resolution (A/C.6/L.636) was circulated at the 1021st meeting. It sought:

(*a*) To add the following new preambular paragraph between the third and fourth preambular paragraphs:

"*Earnestly desiring* to maintain the integrity of the United Nations Charter and make more effective its collective security system,";

(*b*) To reword the fourth preambular paragraph as follows:

"*Having heard* all views on the question whether a precise definition of aggression would have considerable importance for the maintenance of international peace and the adoption of effective measures for preventing such acts as armed attack by one State against another, invasion of the territory of one State by the armed forces of another State and the seizure or occupation of the territory of one State by the armed forces of another State, in violation of the Charter, and all other forms of such use of force by one State against another, whether overt or covert or direct or indirect, as well as for the effectiveness in other respects of the United Nations collective security system,";

(*c*) To replace the final preambular paragraph by the following paragraphs:

"*Convinced* that the primary problem confronting the United Nations in the maintenance of international peace remains the strengthening of the will of States to respect Charter obligations already clearly understood,

"*Taking into account* the nature, and present stage of progress, of the work of the Special Committee on Principles of International Law concerning Friendly Relations and Co-operation among States,

"*Considering also* the large number of United Nations meetings on important legal subjects now scheduled in the near future,";

(*d*) To reword the operative part to read as follows:

"1. *Decides* to defer the question of establishing a special committee to undertake to draft a definition of aggression;

"2. *Calls upon* all States to reaffirm their commitment to respect all obligations under international law, including the United Nations Charter, in respect of threats to the peace, breaches of the peace, or acts of aggression."

4. A draft resolution circulated at the 1020th meeting and proposed by Afghanistan, Algeria, Burma, Cyprus, Ghana, Guinea, India, Indonesia, Kuwait, Mauritania, Syria, the United Arab Republic, the United Republic of Tanzania, Yugoslavia and Zambia (A/C.6/L.637 and Corr.1), later joined by Cameroon (A/C.6/L.637/Add.1) and by Liberia, Morocco, Romania and Sudan (A/C.6/L.637/Add.2) differed from the USSR draft resolution (A/C.6/L.636) as follows:

(*a*) It contained the same first two preambular paragraphs as the USSR draft, but omitted its third preambular paragraph;

(*b*) It replaced the next preambular paragraph of the USSR draft resolution by the following:

"*Firmly convinced* that a definition of aggression would have considerable importance for the maintenance of international peace and for the adoption of effective measures under the Charter of the United Nations for preventing acts of aggression,";

(*c*) It contained the same final preambular paragraph and the same first two operative paragraphs as the USSR draft resolution, but included the following two operative paragraphs, in replacement of operative paragraph 3 of that draft:

"3. *Instructs* the Special Committee, having regard to the present resolution and the international legal instruments relating to the matter, to examine all aspects of the question with a view to drawing up a draft definition of aggression and to submit a report to the General Assembly at its twenty-third session ;

"4. *Requests* the Secretary-General to provide the Special Committee with the necessary facilities and services ;",

ending with operative paragraph 5, which was identical with operative paragraph 4 of the USSR draft resolution.

5. Amendments submitted by Chile, Colombia, Uruguay and Venezuela (A/C.6/L.638) to the twenty-Power draft resolution (A/C.6/L.637 and Add.1 and 2) and circulated at the 1021st meeting proposed the replacement of operative paragraph 3 of that proposal by the following :

"3. *Instructs* the Special Committee, having regard to the present resolution, the international legal instruments relating to the matter and relevant precedents, methods, practices and criteria, to submit a complete report to the General Assembly at its twenty-third session for the purpose of assisting it in the study and preparation of an adequate legal definition of aggression"

and the replacement of the final operative paragraph by the following :

"5. *Decides* to include in the provisional agenda of its twenty-third session an item entitled 'Report of the Special Committee on the question of aggression with a view to the preparation of a legal definition thereof'."

6. Chile, Colombia, Uruguay, and Venezuela later issued a revision (A/C.6/L.638/Rev.1) of their amendments to the twenty-Power draft resolution (A/C.6/L.637 and Corr.1 and Add.1 and 2). That revision, circulated at the 1025th meeting, proposed the replacement of paragraph 3 by the following :

"3. *Instructs* the Special Committee, having regard to the present resolution, the international legal instruments relating to the matter and relevant precedents, methods, practices and criteria, to submit to the General Assembly at its twenty-third session a complete report, to include the proposals of the States which are members of the Special Committee, for the purpose of assisting the General Assembly in the study and preparation of an adequate definition of aggression ;";

It also proposed the replacement of the final operative paragraph by the following :

"5. *Decides* to include in the provisional agenda of its twenty-third session an item entitled 'Report of the Special Committee on the question of aggression with a view to the preparation of an adequate definition thereof';".

7. Algeria, Burma, Cameroon, Cyprus, Ghana, Guinea, India, Indonesia, Jordan, Kenya, Kuwait, Lebanon, Liberia, Libya, Malaysia, Mauritania, Morocco, Nigeria, Romania, Sudan, Syria, the United Arab Republic, the United Republic of Tanzania, Yemen, Yugoslavia and Zambia submitted at the 1025th meeting a draft resolution (A/C.6/L.644) which was identical with that recommended by the Sixth Committee (see paragraph 21 below).

8. The Sixth Committee also had before it a recommendation of the Committee on Conferences, transmitted in a letter of 11 December 1967 from the Chairman of that Committee to the Chairman of the Sixth Committee (A/C.6/L.641), and a statement by the Secretary-General of the administrative and financial implications of the proposal to establish a special committee on the question of defining aggression (A/C.6/L.643).

III. DEBATE

9. A number of representatives referred to the history of the efforts to define aggression which had been made since the end of the First World War, in the organs of the League of Nations and of the United Nations. In particular, several maintained the positions taken by their own delegations in the discussions in plenary meetings which had immediately preceded the beginning of work on the item by the Sixth Committee, and some referred to the positions taken by them in the United Nations debates since 1950.

10. As to the possibility and desirability of a definition of aggression, the greater number of representatives who spoke agreed that such a definition was both possible and desirable, as the General Assembly had declared in the preamble to its resolution 599 (VI) of 31 January 1952. It was an important task of the United Nations, and in particular of the General Assembly, to promote the progressive development and codification of international law, especially of those rules which would promote the cause of peace. Though previous efforts in the United Nations to define aggression had not been successful, it was remarked that in recent years there had been important progress in regard to various principles of the Charter of the United Nations and to legal rules in other fields of great difficulty. The formulation of a definition of aggression would be of assistance to the Security Council in its functions relating to the maintenance of international peace and security; the Council would retain all its powers under the Charter, including the power to decide on the facts and on the rules of law applicable to each case, but would have the advantage of a clarification of the legal rules. Moreover, it was said that a definition would have a moral and political effect in discouraging potential aggressors through mobilizing world public opinion. The task of definition was undoubtedly difficult, but the necessity of legal rules could not be denied by the claim that their formulation would raise problems of interpretation and application. Furthermore, laws were sometimes violated, but were nevertheless an essential of social order. The present political circumstances in the world, it was said, made the need to expedite the definition of aggression even more urgent; there was no use in waiting for a more propitious moment, since during the ten years since the General Assembly had last discussed the definition of aggression, and before some present tensions had arisen, the same delegations that now opposed the work had continually asserted that the time was not appropriate.

11. On the other hand, some other delegations considered that it was unwise and unnecessary to attempt to define aggression at the present time, since there was now no reason to expect greater success than in the more than thirty previous years of repeated failures, and since at best a definition would be unlikely to be sufficiently useful to justify the expenditure of time and effort involved, and at worst would hamper the maintenance of international peace and security. It was said that because of the present stage of development of international relations the Charter could not be a fully and precisely developed body of law, and that the problem was rather to ensure that all States had the

will to respect the few and simple rules which the Charter laid down. Though aggression had occupied an important place in the security system of the Covenant of the League of Nations, the San Francisco Conference had not adopted proposals to define it in the Charter, under which the Security Council was also called upon to determine the existence of any threat to the peace, breach of the peace, or act of aggression. The functions of the Security Council, it was argued, had the character of police actions rather than of those of a tribunal, and were usually exercised without any determination of the aggressor. In such a context, a definition of aggression, which could not possibly cover all the cases which could arise, would only be a source of misunderstanding and of lengthy debates. A definition, it was said, was indeed important to international criminal law, e.g. as in the Charter of the Nürnberg Tribunal, but a definition in a General Assembly resolution would hardly help settle questions of international criminal liability. For United Nations purposes, work should first be devoted to the Charter principles under study by the Special Committee on Principles of International Law concerning Friendly Relations and Co-operation among States; once they were formulated, attention might perhaps again be given to the question of defining aggression, but until then, to take that question up would only hinder the work on friendly relations.

12. A few representatives expressed views relating to the form and content of a definition of aggression, and to certain conditions it should fulfil. In particular, some stressed the need that a definition should be acceptable to a large majority of States, and to the Powers primarily responsible for the maintenance of international peace and security. Some considered that the primary task should be to deal with aggression using armed force. Others, however, wished the scope of the subject to be as broad as possible, and to include political, economic and other forms of aggression.

13. As for the procedure to be followed in formulating a definition, the greater number of speakers supported the idea of establishing a special committee composed of Member States. That, they said, was the usual procedure in complex matters where extensive preparatory work was to be done. The question could not be referred to any existing body, as all of them were already heavily burdened with work; that was particularly true of the Special Committee on Principles of International Law concerning Friendly Relations and Co-operation among States, which furthermore was called upon to consider a number of principles not related to aggression.

14. Some other representatives advocated that the question should be dealt with in some other manner. Some suggested referral to the Special Committee on Principles of International Law concerning Friendly Relations and Co-operation among States, one of them on the ground that an essential condition for a final formulation of a definition of aggression was agreement on the scope and content of Article 2, paragraph 4, of the Charter. Another preferred a body of legal experts, while others considered that the Sixth Committee should undertake the task, with the assistance of a working group. Still others thought it unnecessary and undesirable to take any further steps in the consideration of the question.

15. Some representatives inquired how a session of a new special committee could be fitted into the unprecedentedly heavy schedule of legal meetings in 1968. It was explained by the representative of the Secretary-General that a session was possible on the assumption that the special committee would meet at Geneva from 4 June to 5 July 1968, as recommended by the Committee on Conferences (A/C.6/L.641), and would hold only one meeting a day, alternating with the International Law Commission.

16. In regard to the composition of the special committee, there was no dissent from the proposal that the members should be appointed by the President of the General Assembly, taking into consideration the principles of equitable geographical representation and the necessity that the principal legal systems of the world should be represented. At the end of the debate it was proposed in the twenty-six-Power draft resolution (A/C.6/L.644) that the special committee should be composed of thirty Member States, and that proposal was adopted by the Sixth Committee. Some representatives, however, believed that a smaller committee would have been more effective in performing the task assigned to it, and regretted that there had not been more extensive consultations on the question of membership.

17. As to the terms of reference of the special committee, the USSR draft resolution (A/C.6/L.636) proposed that the special committee be instructed to draw up a draft definition of aggression and to submit it to the General Assembly at its twenty-third session. It was also pointed out that the most important thing was to take up the work, and that if a definition was not completed in time for the twenty-third session, the work could be continued at later sessions. In the twenty-Power draft resolution (A/C.6/L.637 and Corr.1 and Add.1 and 2) the special committee was asked to examine all aspects of the question with a view to drawing up a draft definition of aggression and to submit a report to the General Assembly at its twenty-third session. The amendment of Chile, Colombia, Uruguay and Venezuela (A/C.6/L.638) proposed that the special committee be instructed to submit a complete report to the General Assembly at its twenty-third session for the purpose of assisting the latter in the study and preparation of a definition; it was stated on behalf of the sponsors that it was envisaged that the special committee would not present a draft definition to the General Assembly, but would only do preparatory work which would permit the Assembly to decide on further procedure. Some representatives said that the special committee should study the different types of aggression from the technical viewpoint, the relation of a definition to the maintenance of international peace and security and the legal consequences of a definition formulated in a General Assembly resolution. The Committee finally approved the twenty-six-Power draft resolution (A/C.6/L.644), in which the Special Committee was instructed to consider all aspects of the question in order that an adequate definition of aggression might be prepared, and to submit a report reflecting all the views expressed and the proposals made.

18. One representative explained that he had abstained on operative paragraph 3 of the twenty-six-Power draft resolution (A/C.6/L.644) as he found it ambiguous, and a less objective framework for the further examination of the question than that in the twenty-Power draft resolution (A/C.6/L.637 and Corr.1 and Add.1 and 2). Other representatives explained that they had voted against that paragraph as it was less acceptable than compromise formulae which had been unofficially suggested.

IV. Voting

19. At its 1025th meeting, held on 14 December 1967, the Sixth Committee proceeded to a vote. The representative of Colombia, on behalf of the sponsors of the amendments submitted by Chile, Colombia, Uruguay and Venezuela (A/C.6/L.638/Rev.1) withdrew those amendments. The representative of India, on behalf of the sponsors of the twenty-Power draft resolution (A/C.6/L.637 and Corr.1 and Add.1 and 2), withdrew that draft in favour of the twenty-six-Power draft resolution (A/C.6/L.644). The representative of India proposed that the Sixth Committee should vote first on the twenty-six-Power draft resolution (A/C.6/L.644), and this proposal, with the agreement of the representative of the USSR, the sponsor of draft resolution A/C.6/L.636, was adopted by the Committee. The voting on the twenty-six-Power draft resolution (A/C.6/L.644) was as follows:

(a) Paragraph 1, on which a separate vote was requested by the representative of New Zealand, was adopted by 65 votes to 14, with 6 abstentions;

(b) Paragraph 2, on which a separate vote was requested by the representative of Australia, was adopted by 67 votes to 4, with 16 abstentions;

(c) Paragraph 3, on which a separate vote had been requested by the representative of New Zealand, was adopted on a roll-call vote (requested by the representative of Czechoslovakia) by 68 votes to 8, with 12 abstentions. The voting was as follows:

In favour: Algeria, Argentina, Brazil, Bulgaria, Burma, Byelorussian Soviet Socialist Republic, Cambodia, Cameroon, Chad, Chile, Colombia, Congo (Democratic Republic of), Cuba, Cyprus, Czechoslovakia, Dahomey, Dominican Republic, Ecuador, Ethiopia, Finland, France, Ghana, Guatemala, Guinea, Guyana, Haiti, Hungary, India, Indonesia, Iran, Ivory Coast, Jamaica, Jordan, Kenya, Kuwait, Lebanon, Liberia, Libya, Madagascar, Malaysia, Mauritania, Mexico, Monoglia, Morocco, Nigeria, Pakistan, Philippines Poland, Romania, Rwanda, Senegal, Sierra Leone, Spain, Sudan, Sweden, Syria, Trinidad and Tobago, Tunisia, Turkey, Ukrainian Soviet Socialist Republic, Union of Soviet Socialist Republics, United Arab Republic, United Republic of Tanzania, Uruguay, Venezuela, Yemen, Yugoslavia, Zambia.

Against: Australia, Belgium, Luxembourg, Netherlands, New Zealand, Portugal, United Kingdom of Great Britain and Northern Ireland, United States of America.

Abstaining: Afghanistan, Austria, Canada, China, Denmark, Ireland, Israel, Italy, Japan, Malta, Norway, South Africa.

(d) The twenty-six-Power draft resolution (A/C.6/L.644), as a whole, was adopted by 68 votes to none, with 19 abstentions.

The representative of the USSR stated that he did not intend to press for a vote on draft resolution A/C.6/L.636.

20. At the same meeting, the representatives of Argentina, Australia, Belgium, Canada, Ecuador, France, Ireland, Israel, Italy, Jamaica, New Zealand, Spain, Tunisia, the United Kingdom of Great Britain and Northern Ireland, the United States of America and Venezuela gave explanations of their votes.

Recommendation of the Sixth Committee

21. The Sixth Committee therefore recommends to the General Assembly the adoption of the following draft resolution:

NEED TO EXPEDITE THE DRAFTING OF A DEFINITION OF AGGRESSION IN THE LIGHT OF THE PRESENT INTERNATIONAL SITUATION

The General Assembly,

Considering that in conformity with the Charter of the United Nations all Members of the United Nations must refrain in their international relations from the threat or use of force against the territorial integrity or political independence of any State, or in any other manner inconsistent with the purposes of the United Nations,

Considering that one of the main purposes of the United Nations is to maintain international peace and security and, to that end, to take effective collective measures for the prevention and removal of threats to the peace and for the suppression of acts of aggression or other breaches of the peace,

Convinced that a primary problem confronting the United Nations in the maintenance of international peace remains the strengthening of the will of States to respect all obligations under the Charter,

Considering that there is a widespread conviction that a definition of aggression would have considerable importance for the maintenance of international peace and for the adoption of effective measures under the Charter for preventing acts of aggression;

Noting that there is still no generally recognized definition of aggression,

1. *Recognizes* that there is a widespread conviction of the need to expedite the definition of aggression;

2. *Establishes* the Special Committee on the Question of Defining Aggression, composed of thirty Member States to be appointed by the President of the General Assembly, taking into consideration the principle of equitable geographical representation and the necessity that the principal legal systems of the world should be represented;

3. *Instructs* the Special Committee, having regard to the present resolution and the international legal instruments relating to the matter and the relevant precedents, methods, practices, criteria and the debates in the Sixth Committee and in plenary meetings of the Assembly, to consider all aspects of the question so that an adequate definition of aggression may be prepared and to submit to the General Assembly at its twenty-third session a report which will reflect all the views expressed and the proposals made;

4. *Requests* the Secretary-General to provide the Special Committee with the necessary facilities and services;

5. *Decides* to include in the provisional agenda of its twenty-third session an item entitled "Report of the Special Committee on the Question of Defining Aggression".

Twenty-Third Session, Agenda Item 86 - Report of Special Committee, Question of Defining Aggression, A/7185/Rev. 1, 4 Jun. - 6 Jul.

I. INTRODUCTION

1.   On the recommendation of the Sixth Committee,[1]/ the General Assembly, at its 1638th plenary meeting held on 18 December 1967, adopted resolution 2330 (XXII) entitled "Need to expedite the drafting of a definition of aggression in the light of the present international situation", which reads as follows:

"The General Assembly,

"Considering that in conformity with the Charter of the United Nations all Members of the United Nations must refrain in their international relations from the threat or use of force against the territorial integrity or political independence of any State, or in any other manner inconsistent with the purposes of the United Nations,

"Considering that one of the main purposes of the United Nations is to maintain international peace and security and, to that end, to take effective collective measures for the prevention and removal of threats to the peace and for the suppression of acts of aggression or other breaches of the peace,

"Convinced that a primary problem confronting the United Nations in the maintenance of international peace remains the strengthening of the will of States to respect all obligations under the Charter,

"Considering that there is a widespread conviction that a definition of aggression would have considerable importance for the maintenance of international peace and for the adoption of effective measures under the Charter for preventing acts of aggression,

"Noting that there is still no generally recognized definition of aggression,

"1. Recognizes that there is a widespread conviction of the need to expedite the definition of aggression;

"2. Establishes a Special Committee on the Question of Defining Aggression, composed of thirty-five Member States to be appointed by the President of the General Assembly, taking into consideration the principle of equitable geographical representation and the necessity that the principal legal systems of the world should be represented;

"3. Instructs the Special Committee, having regard to the present resolution and the international legal instruments relating to the

---

1/ Official Records of the General Assembly, Twenty-second Session, Annexes, agenda item 95, document A/6988, para. 21.

/...

matter and the relevant precedents, methods, practices and criteria and the debates in the Sixth Committee and in plenary meetings of the Assembly, to consider all aspects of the question so that an adequate definition of aggression may be prepared and to submit to the General Assembly at its twenty-third session a report, which will reflect all the views expressed and the proposals made;

"4. Requests the Secretary-General to provide the Special Committee with the necessary facilities and services;

"5. Decides to include in the provisional agenda of its twenty-third session an item entitled 'Report of the Special Committee on the Question of Defining Aggression'."

2. Under the terms of operative paragraph 2 of the above resolution, the President of the General Assembly, after appropriate consultations, appointed the following thirty-five Member States to serve on the Special Committee on the Question of Defining Aggression (A/7061): Algeria, Australia, Bulgaria, Canada, Colombia, Congo (Democratic Republic of), Cyprus, Czechoslovakia, Ecuador, Finland, France, Ghana, Guyana, Haiti, Indonesia, Iran, Iraq, Italy, Japan, Madagascar, Mexico, Norway, Romania, Sierra Leone, Spain, Sudan, Syria, Turkey, Uganda, Union of Soviet Socialist Republics, United Arab Republic, United Kingdom of Great Britain and Northern Ireland, United States of America, Uruguay and Yugoslavia. The list of representatives to the 1968 session is annexed to the present report.

3. The Special Committee on the Question of Defining Aggression met at the United Nations Office at Geneva and held twenty-four meetings from 4 June to 6 July 1968. With the exception of Haiti and Sierra Leone, all States members of the Special Committee participated in its work. At its first and second meetings, on 4 and 5 June, the Special Committee elected the following officers:

Chairman:	Mr. Mustafa Kamil Yasseen (Iraq)
Vice-Chairmen:	Mr. Milko Harizanov (Bulgaria)
	Mr. José Martínez Cobo (Ecuador)
	Mr. Francesco Capotorti (Italy)
Rapporteur:	Mr. George O. Lamptey (Ghana)

The session was opened on behalf of the Secretary-General by Mr. Constantin A. Stavropoulos, the Legal Counsel of the United Nations. Mr. Anatoly P. Movchan, Director of the Codification Division of the Office of Legal Affairs, served as Secretary. Mr. Pierre Raton and Mr. Eduardo Valencia-Ospina served as Deputy-Secretary and Assistant Secretary, respectively.

/...

4.　At its first meeting, the Special Committee adopted the following agenda
(A/AC.134/L.1):

"1.　Opening of the session.

2.　Election of officers.

3.　Adoption of the agenda.

4.　Organization of work.

5.　Consideration of the question of defining aggression
(General Assembly resolution 2330 (XXII)).

6.　Adoption of the report."

5.　The Special Committee discussed the organization of its work at the first two
meetings of the session, on 4 and 5 June.　It was generally agreed to hold an
initial general debate, which lasted until the 11th meeting, on 18 June.　A further
debate on the draft definitions submitted to the Special Committee took place at
the 14th to 21st meetings, from 25 June to 4 July 1968.　The Special Committee
devoted the last three meetings of the session, the 22nd to 24th meetings, held on
5 and 6 July 1968, to a debate on a draft resolution submitted by the Union of
Soviet Socialist Republics concerning the resumption of the Special Committee's
work and to the consideration and adoption of the present report.

II.　PROPOSALS AND AMENDMENTS

6.　The Special Committee had before it a number of draft proposals.　They are
reproduced in paragraphs 7 to 12 below in the order in which they were submitted.

7.　At the 14th meeting, on 25 June 1968, the following draft proposal was
submitted by Algeria, the Congo (Democratic Republic of), Cyprus, Ghana, Guyana,
Indonesia, Madagascar, the Sudan, Syria, Uganda, the United Arab Republic and
Yugoslavia (A/AC.134/L.3 and Corr.1 and 2 - French only - and Add.1):

"The 1968 Special Committee on the Question of Defining Aggression,
pursuant to General Assembly resolution 2330 (XXII), recommends to the
General Assembly the adoption of the following Declaration:

/...

'Draft Declaration on Aggression

'The General Assembly,

'Believing that the maintenance of international peace and
security may be enhanced by the adoption of a definition of the term
"aggression" as employed in the Charter of the United Nations,

'Mindful of the responsibilities of the Security Council
concerning aggression under Article 1, paragraph 1, and Chapter VII
of the Charter,

'Bearing in mind also the discretionary authority of the Security
Council embodied in Article 39 of the Charter in determining the
existence of any threat to the peace, breach of the peace, or act of
aggression,

'Considering that, although the question whether aggression has
occurred must be determined in the circumstances of each particular
case, it is nevertheless appropriate to formulate certain principles
for the guidance of the competent organs of the United Nations,

'Convinced that the adoption of a definition of aggression
would serve to discourage potential aggression,

'Reaffirming that the territory of a State is inviolable and may
not be the object, even temporarily, of military occupation or of
other measures of force taken by another State on any grounds whatever,
and that such territorial acquisitions obtained by force shall not be
recognized,

'Reaffirming as a peremptory norm of international law that only
the United Nations has original competence to employ force in the
fulfilment of its functions to maintain international peace and
security and that therefore the use of force by one State or a group
of States against another State or group of States is illegal and
violates the purposes and principles of the Charter of the United
Nations and contemporary international law,

'Reaffirming also that the inherent right of individual or
collective self-defence can only be exercised in cases of armed
attack (armed aggression) in accordance with Article 51 of the
Charter,

'Declares that:

'1. Aggression is the use of force in any form by a State or
group of States against the people or the territory of another State
or group of States or in any way affecting the territorial integrity,

/...

sovereignty and political independence of such other State, other than in the exercise of the inherent right of individual or collective self-defence or when undertaken by or under the authority of a competent organ of the United Nations.

'2. In accordance with the foregoing definition, and without prejudice to the declaration of other acts as forms of aggression in the future, the following shall in particular constitute acts of aggression:

(a) A declaration of war made by one State against another in violation of the Charter of the United Nations;

(b) The invasion by the armed forces of a State of the territory of another State, or the military occupation or annexation of the territory or part of it;

(c) Armed attack against the territory, territorial waters or air space of a State by the land, sea, air or space forces of another State;

(d) The blockade of the coasts or ports of a State by the armed forces of another State;

(e) Bombardment of, or the employment of ballistic missiles or any other means of destruction against the people or the territory, territorial waters or air space of a State by the land, sea, or space forces of another State.

'3. Any use of force tending to prevent a dependent people from exercising its inherent right to self-determination in accordance with General Assembly resolution 1514 (XV), is a violation of the Charter of the United Nations.

'4. No political, economic, strategic, security, social or ideological considerations, nor any other considerations, may be invoked as excuse to justify the commission of any of the above acts, and in particular the internal situation in a State or any legislative acts by it affecting international treaties may not be so invoked.'"

8. At the 15th meeting, on 26 June, the following draft proposal was submitted by Colombia, Ecuador, Mexico and Uruguay (A/AC.134/L.4/Rev.1 and Corr.1 - Spanish only - and Add.1):

"1. The use of force by a State or group of States against another State, other States or another group of States is illegal and violates the Purposes and Principles of the Charter of the United Nations.

/...

"2. In the performance of its functions to maintain international peace and security, the United Nations alone has original competence to use force in conformity with the Charter.

"3. Consequently, the prohibition on the use of force does not affect the legitimate use of force by a competent organ of the United Nations, or under its authority, or by a regional agency, or in exercise of the inherent right of individual or collective self-defence, in accordance with the Charter of the United Nations.

"4. The exercise of the right of individual or collective self-defence recognized by Article 51 of the Charter, is justified solely in the case of an armed attack (armed aggression).

"5. A State which is the victim of subversive or terroristic acts supported by another State or other States may take reasonable and adequate steps to safeguard its existence and its institutions.

"6. The use of force by regional agencies, except in the case of self-defence, shall require the express authorization of the Security Council, in accordance with Article 53 of the Charter of the United Nations.

"7. The use of force to deprive dependent peoples of the exercise of their inherent right to self-determination, in accordance with General Assembly resolution 1514 (XV) is a violation of the Charter of the United Nations.

"8. In particular, the following shall be deemed acts of direct aggressions:

(a) A declaration of war by one State against another, in violation of the Charter of the United Nations;

(b) Invasion by the armed forces of a State of the territory of another State;

(c) Armed attack **against** the territory of a State by the land, naval or air forces of another State;

(d) The blockade of coasts, ports or any other part of the territory of a State by the land, naval or air forces of another State;

(e) Bombardment of the territory of a State by the land, naval or air forces of another State, or by means of ballistic missiles;

(f) The use of atomic, bacteriological or chemical weapons or of any other **weapon of mass destruction.**

/...

"9. No political, economic, strategical, social or ideological consideration may be invoked to justify the acts referred to in the foregoing paragraphs.

"10. This definition shall not affect the discretionary power of competent organs of the United Nations called upon to determine the aggressor."

9.   At the 20th meeting, on 3 July, the following draft proposal was submitted by Colombia, the Congo (Democratic Republic of), Cyprus, Ecuador, Ghana, Guyana, Indonesia, Iran, Mexico, Spain, Uganda, Uruguay and Yugoslavia (A/AC.134/L.6 and Add.1 and 2):

"The 1968 Special Committee on the Question of Defining Aggression, pursuant to General Assembly resolution 2330 (XXII), recommends to the General Assembly the adoption of the following Declaration:

'Draft Declaration on Aggression

'The General Assembly,

'1.   Believing that the maintenance of international peace and security may be enhanced by the adoption of a definition of the term "aggression" as employed in the Charter of the United Nations,

'2.   Convinced that armed attack (armed aggression) is the most serious and dangerous form of aggression and that it is proper at this stage to proceed to a definition of this form of aggression,

'3.   Mindful of the responsibilities of the United Nations Organization for the maintenance of peace and security under the pertinent Articles of its Charter and the duty of all States to comply in good faith with the obligations placed on them by the Charter,

'4.   Bearing in mind also the discretionary authority of the Security Council, embodied in Article 39 of the Charter, to determine the existence of any threat to the peace, breach of the peace, or act of aggression, and to decide the measures to be taken in accordance with Articles 41 and 42, to maintain or restore international peace and security,

'5.   Considering that, although the question whether aggression has occurred must be determined in the circumstances of each particular case, it is nevertheless appropriate to formulate certain principles as a guidance for such determination,

'6.   Convinced that the adoption of a definition of aggression would serve to discourage potential aggression,

'7.   Reaffirming the inviolability of the territorial integrity of a State,

/...

'Declares that:

'1. For the purposes of this definition, aggression is the use of armed force, direct or indirect, by a State against the territory, including the territorial waters or air space of another State, irrespective of the effect upon the territorial integrity, sovereignty and political independence of such State, other than when undertaken by or under the authority of the Security Council or in the exercise of the inherent right of individual or collective self-defence;

'2. In the performance of its function to maintain international peace and security, only the United Nations, and primarily the Security Council, has competence to use force in conformity with the Charter, and therefore the use of armed force by one State against another State, save under the provisions of paragraph 3 below, is illegal;

'3. The inherent right of individual or collective self-defence of a State can be exercised only in case of the occurrence of armed attack (armed aggression) in accordance with Article 51 of the Charter;

'4. Enforcement action or any use of armed force by regional agencies may only be resorted to in cases where the Security Council acting under Article 53 of the Charter decides to utilize for the purpose such regional agencies;

'5. In accordance with the foregoing, the following shall in particular constitute acts of armed aggression:

   (i) Declaration of war by one State against another State in violation of the Charter;

   (ii) Any of the following acts with or without a declaration of war:

      (a) The invasion or attack by the armed forces of a State, against the territory of another State, and any military occupation, however temporary, or any forcible annexation of the territory of another State or part thereof;

      (b) Bombardment by the armed forces of a State of the territory of another State or the carrying out of a deliberate attack on the ships or aircraft of the latter State, or the use of weapons of mass destruction by a State against the territory of another State;

      (c) The blockade of the coasts of ports of a State by the armed forces of another State;

/...

'6. By virtue of the duty imposed on States by the Charter of the United Nations to settle their disputes by pacific methods and to bring their disputes to the attention of the Security Council or the General Assembly, no considerations of whatever nature, save as stipulated in paragraph 3 above, may provide an excuse for the use of force by one State against another State;

'7. Nothing in paragraph 3 above shall be construed as entitling the State exercising a right of individual or collective self-defence, in accordance with Article 51 of the Charter, to take any measures not reasonably proportionate to the armed attack against it;

'8. When a State is a victim in its own territory of subversive and/or terrorist acts by irregular, volunteer or armed bands organized by another State, it may take all reasonable and adequate steps to safeguard its existence and its institutions, without having recourse to the right of individual or collective self-defence against the other State under Article 51 of the Charter;

'9. Armed aggression as defined herein, and the acts enumerated above, shall constitute crimes against international peace, giving rise to international liability and responsibility;

'10. An act other than those enumerated in paragraph 5 above may be deemed to constitute aggression, armed or otherwise, if declared as such by the Security Council.'"

10. At the 24th meeting, on 6 July, the Sudan and the United Arab Republic submitted the following amendment (A/AC.134/L.8) to the draft proposal contained in paragraph 9 above:

"1. In operative paragraph 1 delete the words 'direct or indirect'.

"2. After operative paragraph 7 add the following paragraph as operative paragraph 8:

'Any use of force tending to deprive any people of its inherent right to self-determination, sovereignty and territorial integrity, is a violation of the Charter of the United Nations.'

"3. Renumber paragraphs 8, 9, 10 accordingly."

11. At the 22nd meeting, on 5 July, the Union of Soviet Socialist Republics submitted the following draft resolution (A/AC.134/L.7):

/...

"The 1968 Special Committee on the Question of Defining Aggression recommends that the General Assembly adopt the following draft resolution:

'The General Assembly,

'Considering that resolution 2330 (XXII) recognized the widespread conviction of the need to expedite the definition of aggression and instructed the Special Committee to consider all aspects of the question so that an adequate definition of aggression might be prepared,

'Considering that the Committee's deliberations revealed the sincere desire of the overwhelming majority of the Committee's members to complete their work by submitting to the General Assembly a report containing a definition of armed aggression (attack) unanimously approved by the Committee,

'Noting, nevertheless, that, unfortunately, there was not enough time in which to complete this important work,

'Decides:

'1. That the Special Committee on the Question of Defining Aggression shall resume its work before the end of 1968 in New York or at Geneva, so that it can complete its formulation of a definition of armed aggression (attack) and submit its proposals to the twenty-third session of the General Assembly;

'2. To request the Secretary-General to provide the Special Committee with the necessary facilities and services.'"

12. At the 24th meeting, on 6 July, Ghana submitted an oral amendment to the foregoing draft resolution. The text of the oral amendment, accepted by the sponsor of the draft resolution, was as follows:

"1. In the second preambular paragraph:

(a) Insert the word 'draft' before the word 'definition';

(b) Delete the words 'armed', '(attack)', and 'unanimously'.

"2. In the third preambular paragraph:

(a) Delete the words ', nevertheless,', and ', unfortunately,';

(b) After the word 'Noting' insert the words: 'the progress made by the Committee and the fact';

(c) Substitute the word 'this' by the word 'its'.

"3. In the first operative paragraph:

(a) Before the words 'before the end' insert the words 'as soon as possible';

(b) Substitute the words 'formulation of a definition of armed aggression (attack) and submit its proposals' by the words 'work by submitting a report containing a generally accepted draft definition of aggression'."

III. DEBATE

A. General discussion

Introduction

13. The importance of the task entrusted to the Special Committee was stressed by most of the representatives. They pointed out that it was indeed a complex question, which had been discussed since the time of the League of Nations as early as 1923. In February 1933 the USSR submitted the first definition of aggression to the General Commission of the Disarmament Conference. This definition was later referred to as the Litvinov-Politis definition.[2/]

14. The question was considered by the San Francisco Conference in 1945. Since then, the question of defining aggression had been considered off and on by the General Assembly itself, the Sixth Committee, and the International Law Commission, as well as by two Special Committees established in 1953 and 1956 respectively and the Special Committee established under resolution 1181 (XII), but in spite of numerous efforts no definition was approved, although the General Assembly adopted several resolutions on the subject, namely, resolution 599 (VI) of 31 January 1952, resolution 688 (VII) of 20 December 1952, resolution 895 (IX) of 4 December 1954, resolution 1181 (XII) of 29 November 1957 and lastly resolution 2330 (XXII) of 18 December 1967 which set up the present Special Committee.

15. Some representatives stated that the fact that the question was not an easy one should not be used as an argument for postponing a decision. Indeed many

---

[2/] For the history of the question of defining aggression see Official Records of the General Assembly, Seventh Session, Annexes, agenda item 54, document A/2211.

/...

problems discussed by United Nations organs were just as difficult, and lengthy discussions were needed before results could be achieved. All difficulties could and must be overcome with goodwill and a real concern for the elaboration of a definition of aggression.

Mandate of the Committee

16. From the outset there was some discussion on the mandate of the Committee as set out in General Assembly resolution 2330 (XXII). For most representatives the Special Committee had a specific task, namely, according to the title of resolution 2330 (XXII), to expedite the drafting of a definition of aggression in the light of the present international situation. Moreover, operative paragraph 3 of the same resolution instructed the Committee to consider all aspects of the question, so that an adequate definition of aggression might be prepared. The question was no longer whether or not aggression should be defined, since resolution 2330 (XXII) had put an end to that discussion. The task of the Committee was to submit specific proposals for the definition of aggression. To declare that the Committee's terms of reference did not include the elaboration of a definition of aggression would not correspond to the powers entrusted to the Committee. However, some representatives pointed out that the resolution did not specify which organ was entrusted with the preparation of an adequate definition.

17. For other representatives, the only instruction contained in resolution 2330 (XXII) was that the Committee should consider all aspects of the question and submit a report to the General Assembly, the consideration of draft definitions of aggression being a possibility, the realization of which would depend on the submission of proposals to the Special Committee. It was pointed out that the text of operative paragraph 3 of the USSR draft resolution submitted to the Sixth Committee (A/C.6/L.636)[3]/ had proposed that a Special Committee be explicitly instructed to draft a definition of aggression but that the text of resolution 2330 (XXII) was worded differently. This did not mean, however, that the Committee must confine itself to an academic debate; on the contrary, the discussion could

---

3/ See Official Records of the General Assembly, Twenty-second Session, Annexes, agenda item 95, document A/6988, para. 2.

/...

lead the Committee either to include a definition of aggression in its report or do no more than submit a report to the General Assembly reflecting all the views expressed and the proposals made during the debate.

Value of a definition of aggression

18.   In the opinion of several representatives, a legal definition of aggression would provide guidance for Member States and the United Nations, especially the Security Council. It was recalled that the Security Council, which was empowered under the Charter to determine the existence of any breach of peace or act of aggression, had not hitherto been equipped with such a criterion and had been compelled to take action on specific situations as they arose.

19.   Some representatives stated that legal considerations should predominate in the elaboration of a definition of aggression. Others, while agreeing with these views, stated that that definition of aggression must be based on real events in international life, since it was only from the examination of those events that the constituent elements of the phenomenon of aggression could be determined. Apart from legal considerations some representatives agreed that a definition of aggression was necessary for political reasons, especially in the prevailing state of international tension created by the aggressive policies of imperialist and colonialist States. The absence of a definition of aggression, they asserted, had made it easier to perpetrate crimes against the peoples of dependent countries in all parts of the world, to carry out acts of military aggression against national liberation movements and to intervene forcibly in the domestic affairs of other States.

20.   Some representatives stated that at the very time the Security Council was debating the situation in the Middle East, Israel launched a war of aggression, on 5 June 1967, against three Arab States and that this aggression was continuing in the form of military occupation of parts of the territories of these States.

21.   Portugal was said to have launched a war of aggression against Mozambique, Angola and other Territories under Portuguese oppression. The illegal régime of Southern Rhodesia and the Government of South Africa were also sharply criticized for denying the right of self-determination to the peoples of Zimbabwe and Namibia.

/...

22.   The representatives of Algeria, Bulgaria, Romania and Syria were of the
opinion that the United States had committed aggression in Viet-Nam.   The
representative of Algeria mentioned also the blockading of and armed intervention
in certain States in Latin America by United States forces.

23.   The representative of the USSR also stated that the United States had committed
aggression in Viet-Nam and had launched the most barbarous and criminal war since
the aggression by Hitlerites against the peoples of Europe.   He further stated
that the United States had also committed other acts of aggression in Latin
America, in Cuba, in Panama and in the Dominican Republic.   Finally, current acts
of aggression by the imperialist countries provided the necessary data for
analysing specific forms of aggression.

24.   The representatives of Australia and the United Kingdom did not accept the
attribution of responsibility for aggression in Viet-Nam to the United States.

25.   In reply to the USSR representative, the representative of the United States
stated that it was true, as the representative of the Soviet Union had asserted,
that an act of aggression had been committed in that part of the world, but the
United States delegation categorically rejected the conclusion that the aggressor
was the United States.   The only aggressor was North Viet-Nam, and those in
complicity with it.   The United States delegation would be interested to hear the
reasoning underlying the conclusions of the Soviet representative.   He stated that
the Hanoi régime, recognized by the Government of the USSR, which maintained
diplomatic relations with it, and which had proposed it for membership in the
United Nations, was bound by the obligations of international law enunciated in
Article 2, paragraph 4, of the United Nations Charter.   He said that the Government
of North Viet-Nam was bound in the strictest terms by the Geneva Agreements of 1954
to refrain from using or even from permitting the use of force against the Republic
of North Viet-Nam.   He recalled also that North Viet-Nam had assumed obligations
when signing the Geneva Agreement of 1962 on Laos.   Those obligations, which had
been accepted voluntarily by the Government of North Viet-Nam, were the same in
essence as the principles on which the Charter was based.   It was those obligations
which the Hanoi Government had violated.   If the representative of the Soviet
Union did not deny that North Viet-Nam was bound by those obligations, perhaps he
denied that North Viet-Nam was in fact using force, in an effort to impose control

/...

of North on South Viet-Nam. He would in that case have to refute the political
murders, terrorism, massive open and clandestine military operations waged by North
Viet-Nam for years with the avowed purpose of changing the Government of the
Republic of Viet-Nam and indeed the whole social system of that country. He would
have to deny also that the territory of Laos had been turned into an open military
staging ground and conduit of supply by the Hanoi régime - as Laotian
representatives themselves had repeatedly made clear in the United Nations. He
would have to deny further the random murder of the civilian population of Saigon,
with the avowed purpose of changing the Government of the Republic of Viet-Nam.
He recalled that the Soviet Union was a major material supplier of that aggression.
He stated that the view of the Soviet Union betrayed an unwillingness to have the
situation in Viet-Nam examined in light of the provisions of the Charter, recalling
that the USSR had thwarted all efforts to have the matter considered by the Security
Council. The United States delegation agreed with the representative of the USSR
that the Committee should never lose sight of actual events. It was puzzled,
however, by his statement that aggressors had always been confident that they would
not be judged aggressors, and that indeed no such judgement had ever been made.
Members of the Committee had already corrected that historical error. The Soviet
Union occupied, in fact, the almost unique position among world Powers of having
been formally judged an aggressor by a world body. It was instructive that the
Soviet representative seemed to think that history, as well as international law,
could be switched off at will.
26. The United States representative mentioned that at the twenty-second session
of the General Assembly, the United States had felt it useful to recall some of the
definitions of aggression proposed on a number of occasions by the Government of
the Soviet Union, comparing them with the actions of a country which should have
appeared an exemplar of virtue in its own international conduct. He had recalled
in chronological order that in 1933 the Soviet Union had **incorporated its** proposed
definition of aggression into **non-aggression** treaties with Estonia and Lithuania.
A dozen years later those States had been forcibly **occupied and incorporated** into
the Soviet Union. Everyone recalled the invasion of Finland in 1939 and the
judgement by the League of Nations of aggression by the Soviet Union. A
non-aggression treaty had also been signed with Czechoslovakia but, in 1948, the

/...

freely chosen Government of that country, under the threat of force, had been
subverted with the assistance of agents of Soviet communism and a pro-Soviet
régime had been installed. Czechoslovakia had appealed to the Security Council,
but the Soviet Union had paralysed the Council by a double veto. Four years later,
the Government of the Soviet Union had had the temerity to include in its proposed
definition a paragraph calling it aggression to "promote an internal upheaval in
another State or a reversal of policy in favour of the aggressor". Another version
of the Soviet definition prohibited "invasion by its armed forces, even without a
declaration of war, of the territory of another State". When the communist régime
of North Korea had done just that in 1950, the Government of the USSR had acted as
an accomplice. Everyone was familiar with the judgement of aggression which had been
the result of consideration of the matter by the United Nations. The United States
representative also stated that in 1956 the Soviet Union had overthrown the free
Government set up by Hungarian patriots and had reimposed a communist régime by
slaughtering those opposed to it. The Hungarian people must draw cold comfort from
the pious declaration of the Government of the Soviet Union that no State could
invade another State, retain its armed forces in another State without permission,
or use any revolutionary or counter-revolutionary movement, civil war, disorders or
strikes to justify an attack upon another. Soviet proposals had also always
identified as aggression the "naval blockade of the coasts or ports of another
State". A situation had arisen barely a year before in which a State Member of the
United Nations had formally complained to the Security Council that just such an
act had been committed. The very least that the Council could have done if it
were to fulfil its responsibilities was to call on the parties to forgo those
actions which threatened peace, to enable it to examine the competing charges.
Just such proposals were made. The representative of the Soviet Union in the
Security Council, who, it had been hoped would show a greater sense of

/...

responsibility, had instead taken the position that the forces of imperialism had invented a crisis for their own purposes and that there was no need for the Council to bother doing anything about the situation. The Committee did not need to be reminded of the catastrophic consequences of the Council's inaction at that time. That sampling of the record had shown that the Soviet Union had repeatedly condemned itself by acting against its own declarations.

27. In reply the USSR representative stated that the most flagrant case of aggression since the Second World War was that of the United States in Viet-Nam, where half a million United States troops were slaughtering a patriotic people trying to defend their country. The United States Government's stock response to accusations in that regard was that it was acting in self-defence, nothwithstanding the fact that its own troops had attacked Viet-Nam and not vice versa. Even eminent United States citizens found their Government's position untenable from the standpoint of international law. It had violated the 1954 Geneva Agreements. It was now trying to take the credit for initiating the Paris talks, whereas the credit was due entirely to the efforts of peace-loving forces throughout the world. The USSR representative repudiated the United States representative's statement regarding Soviet action in the Baltic States and Hungary. The peoples of the Baltic States had themselves overthrown their bourgeois régimes, which had been prepared to support Hitler, and on the basis of a free referendum had proclaimed socialist republics and had voluntarily joined the USSR with the same rights as the other republics of the Union. The facts of the counter-revolution staged by reactionary elements in Hungary with the active participation of imperialist Powers were well known. Nevertheless, the United States representative had cited that clear case of United States-inspired indirect aggression against Hungary as Soviet interference in Hungary's internal affairs. The true position could be seen from the statements of Hungarian representatives on the subject in various United Nations bodies. He thought it injudicious of the United States representative to have mentioned the subject of naval blockades. The United States Government systematically used its fleets for intimidating small independent countries and

/...

imposing its will on them. It would have succeeded in strangling Cuba's economic
life if the USSR and other socialist countries had not come to that country's
assistance. The United States representative had also distorted the facts about
Israel's aggression in the Middle East and United States action in Korea.

28. Replying to the statement made by the United States representative, the
representative of Czechoslovakia objected to the ill-founded allusion to the events
which had taken place in Czechoslovakia in February 1948. He rejected the assertion
that those events had been produced by interference from outside. The changes made
then had been in accordance with the country's Constitution and were an expression
of the sovereign will of the Czechoslovak people. Czechoslovakia was and intended
to remain an independent sovereign State.

29. The representative of the United Arab Republic stated that the allegation made
by Israel after it had committed its war of aggression, that a naval blockade took
place prior to 5 June 1967, was merely a desperate attempt to justify its war of
aggression. The representative of the United Arab Republic asserted that neither
his country nor any other Arab country had proclaimed or resorted to a naval
blockade. He also expressed his country's opposition to the policy of naval
blockade at the Security Council meeting on 24 October 1962, when the crisis in the
Caribbean was considered. He reaffirmed his country's opposition to any use of
force on the high seas or in the territorial waters of other States.

30. In the view of most representatives a definition of aggression could
constitute a legal and political indictment of aggression in any form. It would
be of fundamental importance, not only for the development of international law,
but for the maintenance of international peace and security. It would, in
addition, have a moral authority and a political value, especially if the definition
had been supported by an overwhelming majority. Many stressed the view that the
majority should include the permanent members of the Security Council. A
definition would help to reinforce the conviction that aggression was an
international crime and avoid misunderstanding or false interpretation that might
confuse world opinion. It would also help to create a system of collective
security.

/...

31. A definition of aggression would reflect the conscience of mankind and would be a first step towards the realization of the lex perfecta. It would be neither more nor less than a formulation of the general principles of law recognized by civilized nations as envisaged in Article 38, paragraph 1 c, of the Statute of the International Court of Justice.

32. However, doubts were expressed by some representatives as to the value of a definition, especially one enumerating concrete acts of aggression, for it might cause serious danger to the security of a nation unless it were used in conjunction with an appropriate fact-finding system organized by international agreement. Aggressors might be tempted to concentrate their efforts upon evading the acts that were enumerated and the definition might result in encouraging acts of aggression not enumerated, but in fact much more serious.

33. Some delegations also expressed doubts as to the **advisability of defining** aggression at all. Some of these were of the opinion that a definition would hardly facilitate the task of the Security Council since it would restrict the discretion which the Council possessed under the Charter. The main thing needed to deter or suppress aggression was not to have a definition, but to ensure that the system of collective security would be applied and until now it was not the absence of a definition of aggression which had hampered the organs of the United Nations in their efforts to maintain peace and security. Success or failure had depended on the willingness, or lack of willingness, of States Members to respect their Charter obligations. Consequently there was the danger that a definition would create an illusion of accomplishment when none in fact had been made.

Type of definition

34. Of the three types of definition hitherto proposed, i.e., general definition, enumerative definition and mixed definition, the latter was the one preferred by most representatives. In such a definition, a flexible description, couched in general terms, would precede and govern a list of definite acts of aggression, which would be included merely to illustrate and not to restrict the general description.

35. It was pointed out that previous objections to the mixed type of definition had not been objections to the concept of a mixed definition, but only to draft proposals that had been submitted.

/...

36. However, it was held that one could doubt the wisdom of enumerating concrete acts of aggression even in a mixed formula for any non-exhaustive enumeration would be open to abuse and would omit examples that could not be predicted.

Form to be given to the instrument embodying a definition

37. The inclusion of a definition of aggression in the United Nations Charter was ruled out by some representatives in view of the difficulties of procedure which would be involved in any attempt to amend the Charter. It was also recalled that the United Nations Conference in San Francisco had decided not to include a definition of aggression in the Charter.

38. Another possibility was to draw up a multilateral convention including such a definition, but procedural difficulties in this event would also be substantial and even if it proved politically possible to draft and agree on such a convention, it would take far too long for it to come into effect. Such a procedure might however not be excluded later.

39. It was emphasized by some representatives that the only feasible approach at present appeared to be the adoption of a resolution by the General Assembly, whose competence was established by Articles 10, 11 and 13 of the Charter.

40. It was noted that the central role of the Security Council should be taken into account in deciding the appropriate manner of promulgating a definition.

Relations between the definition and the Charter

41. Several representatives considered that every part of a definition of aggression should refer specifically to appropriate Articles of the Charter. It was stated that a comparison of Article 1, paragraph 1, and Article 39 of the Charter indicated that the concept of aggression was clearly connected with the maintenance of international peace and security and, more especially, with breaches of peace. Nowhere did the Charter contain any elaboration, interpretation or definition of the word "aggression". That omission had been decided by the San Francisco Conference which had chosen to leave the matter to the absolute discretion of the Security Council. Therefore a definition of aggression based on the Charter could be used only in accordance with the procedure laid down in Article 39, which empowered the Security Council to determine the existence of an

/...

act of aggression and to decide what measures should be taken to restore peace and
security. No United Nations organ, not even the General Assembly, could compel the
Security Council to adopt a given line of conduct on the matter. The discretionary
authority of the Security Council with respect to determination of acts of
aggression, threats to peace and breaches of the peace, must be fully preserved.
A definition of aggression to be acceptable to a large majority must, therefore,
be general enough to leave untouched the powers of the Security Council under the
Charter. It was indispensable to preserve the flexibility of the discretionary
power of the Security Council and not to alter the roles of the Security Council
and the General Assembly.

42. It was stated that any definition that went beyond the Charter could have only
the force of a moral obligation, not of a contractual obligation. To convert such
a moral obligation into a contractual obligation, the Charter itself would have to
be amended in accordance with Article 108.

Meaning of the concept of aggression

43. Some representatives were of the opinion that it was necessary first to agree
on the meaning of the concept of aggression. It was stated that it was not
sufficient to know what sorts of acts a definition might properly characterize as
"aggression"; one must also know by whom and against whom a definition is to provide
that those acts may be committed and what political entities may commit or be made
the victim of aggression.

44. It was generally accepted that Article 2, paragraph 4, of the Charter whereby
all Member States "shall refrain in their international relations from the threat
or use of force against the territorial integrity or political independence of any
State, or in any other manner inconsistent with the Purposes of the United Nations"
expresses a principle of international law binding on all States. In addition, the
general authority of the United Nations with respect to the maintenance of
international peace and security is expressly extended by Article 2, paragraph 6,
to States not Members of the United Nations and to certain political entities whose
status in international law is in fact disputed. Any definition of aggression
should take account of that fact.

/...

Activities proposed for inclusion in the concept
of aggression

Direct aggression

45. A large number of the representatives were of the opinion that priority should be given in a definition to the direct use of force or what they termed "direct aggression". Other representatives said that a definition should include all methods of using force whether direct or indirect although it could not properly extend, for example, to economic or political activities. It was pointed out that aggression within the meaning of the Charter, and especially Article 2, paragraph 4, could only be a certain use of armed force and could not have an unlimited meaning covering all forms of economic, political or ideological pressure. That form of coercion was covered in particular by the principle of non-intervention in the domestic and external affairs of States. Moreover, not all uses of armed force could be considered to warrant action by the United Nations. Under the Charter, only the use or threat of force against the territorial integrity or political independence of a State, or in any other manner inconsistent with the purposes of the United Nations, could justify such action.

46. Among those in favour of giving priority to the definition of "direct armed aggression", a large group of representatives specified that their position did not prevent consideration of forms of "indirect aggression", including "economic" and "ideological aggression".

47. One representative however was of the opinion that the Committee should not start by defining armed aggression. The first priority should be a definition of aggression itself.

Indirect aggression

48. Some representatives maintained that a definition of aggression should include "indirect aggression". As examples of "indirect aggression", activities which might involve only the indirect use of force were mentioned such as the support of armed bands of one State against another, sabotage, terrorism and subversion. Some representatives considered subversion, claimed to be the most typical form of indirect aggression, as dangerous as war.

/...

49. However, according to some representatives, the concept of aggression would be unduly stretched by the inclusion of "indirect aggression" in the definition.

50. The view was expressed by some representatives that classification of acts of aggression as "direct" or "indirect" should be avoided as all representatives were not necessarily using these expressions to denote the same kinds of acts.

Economic and ideological aggression

51. Some representatives wished to include in the definition specific economic or ideological activities under the description of "economic or ideological aggression". They maintained that by such means the same ends might be achieved as by armed force, and that at the present time the economic and ideological means of aggression were especially important.

52. However, other representatives were opposed to such a solution because the concept of aggression as used in the Charter did not in their view include ideological or economic aggression, unless they involved some recourse to armed force. These activities, although they could be considered as a threat to the peace, fell into quite a different category and were not of the competence of the Special Committee.

Activities involving the use of force, direct or indirect, overt or covert

53. Some representatives rejected the distinction among various "forms" of aggression set forth in the foregoing paragraphs since they considered this foreign to the Charter. They were of the view that a definition must be concerned simply with aggression, which would extend to all methods of the use of armed or physical force, whether direct or indirect, overt or covert.

The principle of priority

54. The priority principle was mentioned by some representatives as an important criterion for aggression and a long-recognized principle of international law, embodied in Article 51 of the Charter. A definition which neglected the principle of priority would not only be ambiguous, but might also be used as a justification for preventive war which is a violation of the Charter. Since the inherent right of individual or collective self-defence was enshrined in Article 51 of the Charter,

/...

it was essential that the definition of aggression should stipulate the aggressor
was the State which first committed any of the acts listed as constituting
aggression. Some representatives, although recognizing the significance of
this principle, emphasized the necessity of a logical and reasonable interpretation
of that principle. According to them an exception to the principle was the case
of collective measures ordered or recommended by the competent United Nations
organs.

55. Some representatives denied the existence of the priority principle as a
principle recognized in international law. They stated that the aggressor would
not necessarily be the State which first committed an act considered as an act of
aggression. Whether or not the State was the aggressor would depend on the
circumstances peculiar to each particular case.

Aggression and self-defence

56. This question was considered as closely linked with the preceding one. It
was reaffirmed by most representatives that the inherent right of individual or
collective self-defence could only be exercised in cases of armed attack in
accordance with Article 51 of the Charter.

57. In particular, some representatives asserted that no political, economic,
strategic, social, ideological or security consideration could be invoked for
justifying a preventive war. However, some considered that a State which is the
victim of subversive or terroristic acts supported by another State could take
reasonable and adequate steps to safeguard its existence and its institutions.

58. Some representatives held the view that this would give rise to the
application of Article 51, while others were of a contrary opinion.

59. Some representatives stressed, however, that a definition of aggression
though it must take into account self-defence should not attempt to spell out the
limits of that concept or other lawful use of force.

Acts considered as not constituting acts of aggression

60. Several representatives were of the opinion that action taken by subject or
colonized peoples for their national liberation should be considered legitimate
in accordance with the terms of the Charter.

/...

61. These views were opposed by other representatives who considered that
provisions on this question would not be appropriate for inclusion in a definition
of aggression.

62. In the same manner, repelling an invader and resisting occupation forces
should not be considered acts of aggression.

Relationship between a definition of aggression and the question of friendly relations

63. The view was expressed by some representatives that the Special Committee
should recommend co-ordinating the results of its work with that of the Special
Committee on Principles of International Law concerning Friendly Relations and
Co-operation among States, which was studying the principle of
Article 2, paragraph 4, of the Charter dealing with the question of threat or use
of force against the territorial integrity or political independence of any State,
or in any other manner inconsistent with the Purposes of the United Nations.

64. Some representatives pointed out that a definition of aggression should not,
therefore, deal with the details of the conditions of lawful use of force. Other
representatives held the opposite view.

Connexion between a definition of aggression and the Draft Code of Offences against the Peace and Security of Mankind and the question of an international criminal jurisdiction

65. One representative recalled that the Draft Code of Offences against the Peace
and Security of Mankind[4] formulated in 1951 by the International Law Commission
had remained in abeyance pending a definition of aggression, following a decision
adopted by the General Assembly at its ninth session in 1954 (resolution 897 (IX)).
The General Assembly considered that the Draft Code of Offences raised problems
closely related to that of the definition of aggression. Likewise, the General
Assembly, by resolution 898 (IX), decided to postpone consideration of the question
of an international criminal jurisdiction until it could take up again the question
of defining aggression.

66. A number of representatives pointed out that the Special Committee was not to
be concerned with the definition of aggression within the meaning of international
criminal responsibility.

4/ Official Records of the General Assembly, Sixth Session, Supplement No. 9
(A/1858), pp. 11-14.

/...

B. Debate on draft proposals

67. Representatives expressed their appreciation to the sponsors of the draft proposals submitted respectively by twelve Powers (A/AC.134/L.3 and Add.1) and four Powers (A/AC.134/L.4/Rev.1 and Add.1), for their genuine efforts in submitting texts taking into account the different views expressed on the question of defining aggression. The texts were considered as being a real contribution towards the completion of the Committee's task.

68. Some representatives regretted, however, that both drafts did not take sufficiently into account drafts on aggression submitted previously to United Nations organs.

69. It was pointed out that in spite of similarities, there were fundamental differences between the draft submitted by the twelve Powers (A/AC.134/L.3 and Add.1) and the draft of the four Powers (A/AC.134/L.4/Rev.1 and Add.1) both as to approach and as to structure.

70. For example, the four Power draft did not contain a preamble and a reference to military occupation or annexation, as was the case in the twelve Power draft while the latter did not make reference to subversive or terroristic acts supported by another State or to the use of force by regional agencies. Consequently, most representatives commented on them separately, although cross-refernces to both texts were frequent and comments frequently applied to both texts. Several representatives expressed appreciation at the fact that both texts adopted a mixed definition and were limited to direct or armed aggression.

71. Some delegations stressed that both drafts failed in a variety of fundamental ways to satisfy the criteria of an adequate definition. It was said that both drafts went beyond the concept of aggression in attempting to define various aspects of the lawful use of force, such as the inherent right of self-defence or the use of force by regional organizations, and, in addition, deviated from the Charter in their treatment of these other concepts, although most delegations rejected this contention.

72. Both drafts were criticized for failure adequately to preserve and reflect the Charter system in which the term "aggression" was to be applied, particularly in respect of the discretionary power of the Security Council. Further it was pointed out that both drafts failed to apply to certain political entities which might not be generally recognized as States, but which were nevertheless subject to the

/...

prohibitions of international law regarding force and aggression. Some stressed, as a major fault of both drafts, their failure to apply to use of force by one State against another, directly or indirectly, through such means as infiltration of armed bands, terrorism, or subversion. In the view of these delegations, no definition would be acceptable which did not deal adequately with such cases of aggression. Other delegations held this view untenable.

73. Some noted that both drafts failed to exclude trivial or de minimis violations of the prohibition on the use of force, a failure which debased the meaning of the term "aggression" and was not appropriate to its role in the Charter system.

74. Most delegations, however, emphasized the many constructive and positive aspects of both draft proposals. They nevertheless recognized the need to modify certain points with a view to arriving at a single draft which would facilitate the Committee's task of defining aggression.

75. Sponsors of both drafts were conscious that their texts could be improved and they were prepared to accept amendments which would make the texts acceptable to more representatives. A possible combination of both texts was envisaged during the debate and sponsors set up informal working groups with a view to achieving that goal.

Twelve-Power draft proposal (A/AC.134/L.3 and Add.1)

76. Some representatives were opposed to the formulation of the proposal as a "Draft Declaration on Aggression". Other representatives expressed preference for a text of a definition cast as a resolution. They were of the opinion that the discretionary powers of the Security Council would be affected by a Declaration.

77. Some representatives questioned the usefulness and desirability of the extensive preamble, which they claimed were without parallel in the drafts relating to the definition of aggression prepared since 1951. They said it gave the definition a political rather than a legal character, because it introduced ideas not contained in the definition itself. Some representatives were of the opinion that a preamble should be confined to references to the successive General Assembly resolutions on the subject and to an affirmation of the objectives and basic principles underlying the provisions of the operative part. This view was not shared by the majority.

/...

78. Some representatives, while recognizing that preambular paragraphs 2, 3 and 4 could be considered as a genuine attempt to safeguard the role of the Security Council, thought that the whole draft was not entirely satisfactory in that respect, mainly because it made references to indirect aggression. It was also said that in paragraph 4 the "competent organs" of the United Nations should be replaced by the "Security Council".

79. Some representatives regretted the absence of a reference to Article 24 of the Charter in preambular paragraphs 2 and 3.

80. Some representatives objected to the wording of preambular paragraph 7, which contained such expressions as "original competence to employ force", "peremptory norm of international law" and "contemporary international law".

81. Some representatives pointed out that there was ambiguity between the general formula contained in operative paragraph 1, which pertained to the use of force "in any form" and the acts of aggression listed in operative paragraph 2, which were restricted to armed aggression. It was, therefore, not clear whether the word "force" in paragraph 1 was to be understood as including indirect forms of aggression. This ambiguity was strengthened by the wording of paragraphs 7 and 8 of the preamble, which made a distinction between the two notions of aggression. It was held that in operative paragraph 1 the notion of aggression should be defined by means of a criterion which took into account the nature and the gravity of the act in question. Some representatives also objected to the mention of groups of States as being unnecessary.

82. A number of representatives pointed out that the criterion that the definition should be applicable to entities not generally recognized as States was not met by the draft declaration.

83. Some representatives also pointed out that the acts listed under sub-paragraphs (a), (b), (c) and (d) of operative paragraph 2 could either be considered as acts of aggression or acts of self-defence. Some of them considered that this was because the definition did not take into account the principle of priority whereby the State should be declared the attacker "which first commits" the acts listed. They held that this principle was absolutely necessary to determine whether an act is licit or illicit.

84. Other representatives, while agreeing that it was not possible to determine whether the acts listed constituted acts of aggression or acts of self-defence, did

/...

not consider the "priority principle" as being sufficient or desirable as an essential element of aggression. A reference to that intent would, however, be necessary.

85. Some representatives stated that the list of acts of aggression was incomplete as it did not include cases of aggression perpetrated without a declaration of war. Some representatives, on the other hand, held that it was unnecessary to list declaration of war or blockade as acts of aggression since they might not involve the use of force and that annexation would constitute aggression only if force was used.

86. Some representatives were opposed to the insertion in operative paragraph 2 of the phrase "and without prejudice to the declaration of other acts as forms of aggression in the future" as being both unnecessary and potentially dangerous. If it applied to acts due to the use of armed force, the acts in question should be listed clearly. The formula should not be used if it referred to purely hypothetical acts, as it could affect the prerogative of determining the existence of acts of aggression conferred upon the Security Council by Article 39 of the Charter.

87. Operative paragraph 3, relating to the right of self-determination in accordance with General Assembly resolution 1514 (XV), was considered by some representatives as not, legally speaking, constituting a part of a definition of aggression.

88. Likewise, several representatives stated that operative paragraph 4 had no real connexion with the definition of aggression and that its inclusion was neither useful nor desirable. Since aggression was to be condemned, there was no justification for acts of aggression as such.

Four-Power draft proposal (A/AC.134/L.4/Rev.1 and Add.1)

89. Some representatives were of the opinion that the four-Power draft was not in fact a "definition" of aggression, but a mere enumeration of instances providing no criterion by which one could consider the enumerated acts "aggression" or as "aggression" acts not enumerated.

90. It was also stated by some representatives that the first seven paragraphs of the draft dealt exclusively with the scope of the principles of non-use of force rather than with the concept of aggression.

/...

91. A number of representatives were of the opinion that the same ambiguity as to the meaning of "force" which existed in the twelve-Power draft resolution also applied to the four-Power draft resolution. Attention was drawn by some representatives to the fact that while paragraph 8 concerned only direct aggression, paragraph 5 dealt with indirect aggression, although the consensus of the Committee had been to restrict the definition, for the time being at least, to direct armed aggression. Other delegations rejected the distinction between "direct" and "indirect" aggression in a definition, maintaining that both direct and indirect uses of force should be covered. The absence of a general introductory clause in paragraph 8 before the list of acts of aggression was considered as depriving the definition of any practical usefulness.

92. Some representatives were opposed to paragraph 5 whereby a State, victim of subversive or terroristic acts supported by another State, was allowed to take reasonable and adequate steps to safeguard its existence and institutions. Some were of the opinion that this was inappropriate and dangerous because it would be hard to accept the idea of punitive or preventive attack against a State which provided only material support to the subversive elements in another country. The question would be different if a State sent its own nationals to commit subversion in another State. In that case, it would be in direct aggression and as the Committee was for the time being restricting a definition to direct armed aggression, it was not proper to consider that case now.

93. Other representatives pointed out that paragraph 5 was inadequate and inappropriate since, in so far as the reasonable and necessary measures it permitted were internal, the paragraph had no bearing on international law, and since terrorism and subversion, as well as armed bands, could be uses of force by one State against another constituting acts of aggression. In any event they gave rise to a right of self-defence against that other State as recognized in Article 51, irrespective of the nationality of the agents, terrorists, or infiltrators used.

94. Some representatives objected to the reference in paragraph 6 to the legality of the use of force by regional agencies with the authorization of the Security Council in accordance with Article 53 of the Charter and of its use without the authorization of the Security Council in cases of self-defence. They were of the opinion that Article 53 referred to action by regional agencies as agents of the Security Council, whereas the draft represented the Council as a mere controlling organ, which could permit or not an action decided on by the regional agency.

/...

95. Other representatives questioned the relevance and legal accuracy of this paragraph. To them it seemed to be at variance with the Charter, since Article 53 spoke neither of "express" authorization nor of "use of force", and the paragraph failed to take into account Article 52. Some representatives, however, strongly objected to this interpretation.

96. Paragraphs 7 and 9 which corresponded to operative paragraphs 3 and 4 of the twelve-Power text were considered by some representatives as being out of place in the draft as they had no connexion with a definition of aggression, while other representatives considered them as being of supreme importance in relation to present or foreseeable situations.

97. Some representatives who objected to operative paragraph 4 of the twelve-Power draft were prepared to accept paragraph 9 of the four-Power draft.

Thirteen-Power draft proposal (A/AC.134/L.6 and Add.1-2)

98. Most of the representatives who spoke on the draft proposal submitted by the thirteen Powers stated that in view of the fact that the text had been distributed at the final stage of the session their comments would be of a preliminary nature.

99. Several representatives expressed their appreciation to the co-sponsors for their genuine efforts to concern themselves with the points of criticism made during the debate on the four-Power and the twelve-Power drafts. Some representatives regretted, however, that such a compromise text had been possible to achieve only by omitting or blurring critical points of differences. Such result was dangerous as it gave the illusion of an agreement between several schools of opinion where in fact it did not exist. Other representatives stated that a number of their basic criticisms had apparently still not been met.

100. Preambular paragraph 5 was claimed to be defective because it did not state which organ was responsible for declaring that aggression had occurred, whereas the Charter made it clear that such a right belonged to the Security Council.

101. Some representatives stated that one important defect of the draft was the mention in operative paragraph 1 of the indirect use of force, whereas the consensus of the Committee had been to restrict the definition, at least for the time being, to the direct use of force. For some representatives the inclusion of indirect force would unduly enlarge the scope of aggression by branding as aggression trivial

/...

cases of use of force, whereas it did not really permit States to use their right of self-defence. The same uncertainty was said to exist also in respect of operative paragraph 10.

102. Other representatives however, pointed out that the inclusion of "indirect" use of force was a step in the right direction, albeit one regrettably not carried out elsewhere in the draft.

103. Another important defect was said to be the absence in the text of the definition of a clear statement proclaiming the right of resistance of peoples who are forcibly prevented from exercising their inherent right to self-determination.

104. Some representatives stated that the text was unacceptable because the priority principle was not mentioned and in this respect the new text was not an improvement. Others, however, considered the priority principle as not relevant in every instance or not legally sound.

105. Some representatives stated that in operative paragraph 2 only the Security Council should be given the competence to use force in conformity with the Charter, a view challenged by others.

106. Some representatives were of the opinion that operative paragraph 8 was objectionable because it was seriously at variance with the United Nations Charter. Other representatives objected to this paragraph because it referred mainly to internal affairs of States, except in its prohibition of the recourse to self-defence (Article 51 of the Charter) in retaliation for acts of subversion.

107. It was stated that the description in operative paragraph 9 of armed aggression as a crime against international peace, giving rise to international liability and responsibility was too vague and indefinite. Other representatives, however, questioned the propriety of this paragraph.

Draft resolution submitted by the USSR (A/AC.134/L.7)

108. Several representatives expressed their appreciation to the representative of the USSR for submitting a draft resolution recommending to the General Assembly to decide that the Special Committee should resume its work before the end of 1968 in New York or Geneva so that it could complete its formulation of a draft definition of armed aggression (attack) and submit its proposals to the twenty-third session of the General Assembly.

/...

109. They expressed the majority view that significant progress had been made during the session of the Committee and if agreement could not be reached on a text of a draft definition of aggression it was not for lack of co-operation or understanding, but for lack of time and, therefore, if the Committee were reconvened there was hope that a text of a definition could meet with the approval of the Committee.

110. Other representatives stated that it was premature to settle an issue which should be decided by the General Assembly. The only procedure to follow would therefore be to refer the draft proposals of the Committee to the General Assembly without making any recommendations. They pointed out that the USSR proposal had been submitted too late for them to receive specific instructions from their Governments. Some representatives stated that before taking a decision on the USSR draft resolution a statement of financial implications ought to be prepared and submitted to the Committee in accordance with rule 154 of the rules of procedure of the General Assembly.

111. Other representatives considered that an acceptable outcome of the Committee's consideration of this aspect would be the inclusion of a paragraph in the report of the Committee recommending to the General Assembly that the Committee's mandate be extended.

112. The representative of Canada, supported by other representatives, proposed the following text:

> "It was the consensus of the Committee that the General Assembly should consider, as a matter of priority, the extension of the mandate of the Special Committee so as to enable it to actively pursue its work, before the end of 1968 or early in 1969, on the question of defining aggression."

113. At the request of the representative of the USSR, his draft resolution was put to the vote and adopted. A dispute then ensued with respect to the compatibility of the adopted resolution with the Canadian proposal. Subsequently the representative of Canada withdrew his proposal.

114. The view that the 1968 Special Committee had achieved much progress predominated the consideration of this last item.

115. Before a vote was taken the Secretary of the Committee drew attention, in accordance with rule 154 of the rules of procedure of the General Assembly, to the financial implications of the USSR draft proposal.

/...

IV. VOTING

116. At its 24th meeting, on 6 July, the Special Committee voted on the draft resolution submitted by the Union of Soviet Socialist Republics (A/AC.134/L.7) incorporating the oral amendments submitted by Ghana and accepted by the sponsor. The draft resolution, as amended, was adopted by a roll-call vote of 18 to none, with 8 abstentions. The voting was as follows:

In favour: Algeria, Bulgaria, Cyprus, Czechoslovakia, Ecuador, Finland, Ghana, Indonesia, Iran, Iraq, Mexico, Romania, Spain, Sudan, Syria, Union of Soviet Socialist Republics, United Arab Republic, Yugoslavia.

Against: None.

Abstaining: Australia, France, Italy, Japan. Norway, Turkey, United Kingdom of Great Britain and Northern Ireland, United States of America.

V. RECOMMENDATION OF THE SPECIAL COMMITTEE

117. The text of the resolution adopted by the Special Committee reads as follows:

"The 1968 Special Committee on the Question of Defining Aggression recommends that the General Assembly adopt the following draft resolution:

'The General Assembly,

'Considering that General Assembly resolution 2330 (XXII) of 18 December 1967 recognized the widespread conviction of the need to expedite the definition of aggression and instructed the Special Committee on the Question of Defining Aggression to consider all aspects of the question so that an adequate definition of aggression might be prepared,

'Considering that the Committee's deliberations revealed the sincere desire of the overwhelming majority of the Committee's members to complete their work by submitting to the General Assembly a report containing a draft definition of aggression approved by the Committee,

'Noting the progress made by the Committee and the fact that there was not enough time in which to complete its important work,

/...

'Decides:

'1. That the Special Committee on the Question of Defining Aggression shall resume its work as soon as possible before the end of 1968 in New York or at Geneva, so that it can complete its work by submitting a report containing a generally accepted draft definition of aggression to the General Assembly at its twenty-third session;

'2. To request the Secretary-General to provide the Special Committee with the necessary facilities and services.'"

ANNEX

MEMBERSHIP OF THE SPECIAL COMMITTEE

ALGERIA

Representative: Mr. Smail Hamdani

Alternate: Mr. Nadjib Boulbina

Advisers: Mr. Mohamed Khaled Khelladi
                    Mr. Mohamed Lamine Allouane
                    Mr. Mohamed Laala

AUSTRALIA

Representatives: Sir Kenneth Bailey
                    Mr. Peter J. Curtis

Alternate: Mr. David Wyke Evans

Adviser: Mr. S.B. Murphy

BULGARIA

Representative: Mr. Milko Harizanov

CANADA

Representative: Mr. John Alan Beesley

Alternate: Mr. D.M. Miller

Advisers: Mr. Richard McKinnon
                    Mr. Jacques Corbeil

COLOMBIA

Representative: Mr. Humberto Ruiz

CONGO (DEMOCRATIC REPUBLIC OF)

Representative: Mr. Vincent Mutuale

/...

CYPRUS

Representative: Mr. Zenon Rossides

Alternates: Mr. Özdemir Ösgür
Mr. Constantinos Pilavachi

CZECHOSLOVAKIA

Representatives: Mr. Stanislav Myslil
Mr. Ladislav Jahoda
Mr. Otto Jackek

ECUADOR

Representatives: Mr. José R. Martínez Cobo
Mr. Gonzalo Alcívar

Adviser: Mr. Horacio Sevilla Borja

FINLAND

Representatives: Mr. Björn-Olof Alholm
Mr. Bengt Broms
Mr. Björn Ekblom

FRANCE

Representative: Mr. François Renouard

Adviser: Mr. Pierre-André Mutter

GHANA

Representative: Mr. K.B. Asante

Alternate: Mr. Sam Quarm

Adviser: Mr. George O. Lamptey

GUYANA

Representative: Mr. Duke E.E. Pollard

INDONESIA

Representative: Colonel August Marpaung

Alternates: Mr. Mohamad Sidik
Mr. Surjo-Atmono

IRAN

Representative: Mr. Jafar Nadim

Alternate: Mr. Mehdi Ehsassi

IRAQ

Representative: Mr. Mustafa Kamil Yasseen

Advisers: Mr. Farouk El-Obaidi
Mr. Talal Pachachi

ITALY

Representatives: Mr. Francesco Capotorti
Mr. Vincenzo Starace

Adviser: Mr. Francesco Capece Galeota

JAPAN

Representative: Mr. Naomichi Tsukahara

Adviser: Mr. Takeshi Minagawa

MADAGASCAR

Representative: Mr. Alfred Ramangasoavina

Alternate: Mr. Maxime Pascal Zafera

MEXICO

Representative: Mr. Jorge Castañeda

Alternate: Mr. Sergio González Gálvez

NORWAY

Representative: Mr. Peter Motzfeldt

/...

ROMANIA

Representative: Mr. Gheorghe Badescu

Alternate: Mr. Ilie Tudor

SPAIN

Representative: Don Juan I. Tena

Alternate: Don José Cuenca

Adviser: Doña Elisa Perez-Vera

SUDAN

Representative: Mr. Seif El Din Ahmed Suliman

SYRIA

Representatives: Mr. Salah El Dine Tarazi
                      Mr. Mowaffak Allaf
                      Mr. Lotfi Al-Attrash

TURKEY

Representative: Mr. Suat Bilge

Alternate: Mr. Uner Kirdar

UGANDA

Representative: Mr. Frederick K. Isingoma

UNION OF SOVIET SOCIALIST REPUBLICS

Representatives: Mr. Victor Chkhikvadze
                      Mr. Dmitry Kolesnik

Advisers: Mr. Marklen Lazarev
                      Mr. G. Bulgakov

UNITED ARAB REPUBLIC

Representative: Mr. Hussein Khallaf

Alternates: Mr. Omar Sirry
                      Mr. El Sayed El Reedy

UNITED KINGDOM OF GREAT BRITAIN AND NORTHERN IRELAND

Representative: Mr. J.R. Freeland

Alternate: Mr. Antony Acland

UNITED STATES OF AMERICA

Representative: Mr. John Lawrence Hargrove

Adviser: Mr. David H. Small

URUGUAY

Representative: Mr. Héctor Gros Espiell

Alternate: Mrs. María Elena Bidart de López

YUGOSLAVIA

Representative: Mr. Aleksandar Jelić

Alternate: Mr. Kazimir Vidas

DOCUMENT A/7402*

Report of the Sixth Committee

[Original text: French]
[13 December 1968]

CONTENTS

I. INTRODUCTION

1. At its 1676th plenary meeting, on 27 September 1968, the General Assembly decided to include in the agenda for the twenty-third session the item entitled "Report of the Special Committee on the Question of Defining Aggression" and allocated it to the Sixth Committee for consideration and report.

2. At its 1028th meeting, on 2 October 1968, the Sixth Committee began by considering part V of the report of the Special Committee on the Question of Defining Aggression (A/7185/Rev.1). The Committee's 1073rd to 1082nd meetings, held from 18 to 27 November 1968, were devoted to consideration of parts I-IV of the report.

3. At the 1073rd meeting, on 18 November 1968, Mr. Lamptey, the representative of Ghana and Rapporteur of the Special Committee on the Question of Defining Aggression, introduced the Special Committee's report. He said that the remarkably constructive attitude of delegations had made the 1968 session one of the best held on that question since the matter had first been examined in the League of Nations in 1923. He added that a reading of the report revealed the justification for the Special Committee's optimism in recommending to the General Assembly the extension of its mandate.

4. At the 1080th meeting on 25 November 1968, Mr. Secarin, the Rapporteur of the Sixth Committee, raised the question whether the Committee intended to include in its report to the General Assembly a summary of the views expressed in the course of the discussions on the question of defining aggression. After referring to paragraph (f) of the annex to General Assembly resolution 2292 (XXII), he informed the Committee of the financial implications of such a summary. The Committee decided that its report on the important question of defining aggression should contain a summary reflecting the broad trends in legal thinking which had emerged during the debate.

---

* Incorporating document A/7402/Corr.1, dated 17 December 1968.

II. CONSIDERATION OF PART V OF THE REPORT OF THE SPECIAL COMMITTEE ON THE QUESTION OF DEFINING AGGRESSION

5. Part V of the report of the Special Committee on the Question of Defining Aggression contains the text of a draft resolution recommended by the Committee for adoption by the General Assembly; under the terms of the resolution, the Assembly would decide:

"That the Special Committee on the Question of Defining Aggression shall resume its work as soon as possible before the end of 1968 in New York or at Geneva, so that it can complete its work by submitting a report containing a generally accepted draft definition of aggression to the General Assembly at its twenty-third session."

6. In the course of a brief discussion on the draft resolution, many representatives observed that it would be difficult to schedule meetings of the Special Committee in 1968 during the annual session of the General Assembly. The Sixth Committee therefore decided, on an oral proposal by the representative of Ghana, not to recommend that the General Assembly should schedule meetings of the Special Committee in 1968.

III. CONSIDERATION OF PARTS I-IV OF THE REPORT OF THE SPECIAL COMMITTEE ON THE QUESTION OF DEFINING AGGRESSION

7. Parts I-IV of the report of the Special Committee on the Question of Defining Aggression deal with the work done by the Committee. During the discussion of those parts of the report, opinions were expressed on various aspects of the question of defining aggression and on the draft proposals submitted to the Special Committee. The Sixth Committee also had before it a draft resolution calling for the extension of the Special Committee's mandate.

A. *Draft resolution submitted to the Sixth Committee*

8. The draft resolution reproduced below was submitted by the following countries: Algeria, Congo (Democratic Republic of), Cyprus, Ecuador, El Salvador, Ethiopia, Ghana, Guatemala, Guyana, Haiti, India, Jamaica, Kenya, Liberia, Mexico, Pakistan, Panama, Peru, Romania, Sudan, Spain, Syria, Uganda, the United Arab Republic, the United Republic of Tanzania, Uruguay, Venezuela, Yugoslavia and Zambia (A/C.6/L.733/Rev.1 and Add. 1-3).

"*The General Assembly,*

"*Having considered* the Report of the Special Committee on the Question of Defining Aggression (A/7185/Rev.1),

"*Taking note* of the progress in the Special Committee in its consideration of the question of defining aggression and on the draft definition reflected in the report of the Special Committee,

"*Considering* that it was not possible for the Special Committee to complete its consideration on the question of defining aggression and of the draft definition before the end of 1968,

"Considering that in its resolution 2330 (XXII) of 18 December 1967, the General Assembly recognized the widespread conviction of the need to expedite the definition of aggression,

"1. *Decides* that the Special Committee on the Question of Defining Aggression shall resume its work, in accordance with General Assembly resolution 2330 (XXII), as early as possible in 1969;

"2. *Requests* the Secretary-General to provide the Special Committee with the necessary facilities and services;

"3. *Decides* to include in the provisional agenda of its twenty-fourth session an item entitled 'Report of the Special Committee on the Question of Defining Aggression'."

B. *General debate*

9. As to the preliminary question whether it was possible and desirable to define the notion of aggression, several representatives expressed the opinion that it was. A number of General Assembly resolutions were cited in that connexion, particularly resolution 599 (VI) of 31 January 1952 and resolution 2330 (XXII) of 18 December 1967. It was also argued that a definition of aggression, besides being of paramount importance to the maintenance of international peace and security, would facilitate the implementation of the system of collective security provided for in the Charter of the United Nations, while at the same time promoting the development of international law. Such a definition would enable the Security Council to take more vigorous and effective action, thus significantly strengthening the activities of the United Nations and the means of applying the Charter. It would have a preventive effect by deterring possible aggressors. The point was also made that it was absurd to contend that a definition of aggression would be of no value because it would not prevent all cases of aggression. Those who advanced that argument, it was asserted, had a mistaken view of the role and function of legal definitions, which were not designed to prevent or encourage a given type of behaviour but rather to demarcate the area within which States could carry on their activities. Miraculous results could not, of course, be expected from the existence of a definition; however, no reasonable man would suggest that, because murders and other crimes continued to be committed, the legal rules defining those crimes should be abolished. In point of fact, the existence or absence of aggression would depend on the effectiveness of the enforcement machinery which provided the foundation for whatever definition was adopted. It was also pointed out that, while it was true that a definition of aggression would serve primarily to guide the political organs of the United Nations, the fact remained that such a definition would be directed at world public opinion, which decisively influenced the course of international relations. To the extent that a definition created an enlightened public opinion and enabled people to form clearer judgements of the behaviour of Governments, it could serve to restrain possible aggressors. In any case, there was no question that the main purpose of the definition would be to provide legal safeguards within the framework of the Charter, since it would make it possible to break out of the indecision and subjectivism which characterized political judgements that were not limited by law. In specific cases, of course, it might be desirable, in the interest of maintaining world peace, for the competent United Nations organs

to be able to exercise their discretionary powers, even if it was done in an arbitrary manner. It must be recognized, however, that widespread and continuing recourse to arbitrary methods would ultimately produce a complete absence of security and a complete separation between United Nations political activities and international law. It was also pointed out that, at the present time at least, no one was suggesting that a definition of aggression should be incorporated into the Charter through an amendment. Hence, the definition would not apply automatically. It would not be a question of replacing one rule of the Charter by another but of giving a legal interpretation to the rule, i.e., defining its scope and content; the Security Council would remain completely free at all times to evaluate the facts of a case and decide, in discharging its responsibility for the maintenance of peace, that the most appropriate course of action might be to refrain from declaring a State an aggressor and take a different approach to the problem.

10. In the view of those representatives who were in favour of formulating a definition of aggression, the Special Committee on the Question of Defining Aggression should hold further meetings in an effort to carry out the mandate entrusted to it. They observed that it was, in their view, apparent from the Special Committee's report that it had been lack of time rather than any lack of co-operation and understanding that had prevented agreement on a draft definition. It was significant that, for the first time since consideration of the question had begun, States situated in four different continents and representing different schools of thought in the matter of international law had joined in proposing a draft definition of aggression; that was an encouraging fact which served as an argument for permitting the Special Committee to resume its work in 1969, so that it could formulate an adequate definition of aggression.

11. Some representatives, on the other hand, expressed doubts as to whether it was possible or useful to define the concept of aggression. It was argued that the concept was essentially vague and that it would not be easy to arrive at a practical definition of it in legal terms that were acceptable. In any case, however aggression was defined, the definition would be superfluous. In this connexion, it was pointed out that in the Charter of the United Nations, as opposed to the Covenant of the League of Nations, the definition of the notion of aggression was not indispensable to the security system. There were, it was said, certain general principles of international law which made it possible to identify aggression fairly easily in any particular case. Those principles were stated in the Charter of the United Nations, which every Member State had undertaken to respect. Since its foundation, the United Nations, acting through the General Assembly and the Security Council, had frequently applied those fundamental principles, sometimes calling upon Member States to respect them and sometimes taking measures to reduce the risk of violation, or even to halt aggression which had been started. On some occasions, the General Assembly or the Security Council had tried to interpret the principles in question or had cited them in connexion with particular resolutions. The view was also expressed that to think that a definition of aggression would have been enough to prevent certain disputes and violations of international law would be to delude oneself about political reality in the modern world. Reference was made to existing bilateral and multilateral

conventions including a definition, which, however, was not followed. It was not the lack of a definition as such which prevented the Security Council from acting effectively. The problem was not the lack of legal criteria on which the Security Council could base a decision on a case of aggression, but the fact that the Council had not been able at the political level to agree whether or not a particular act had constituted aggression or whether it was desirable to label it as such. In point of fact, the Security Council was not obliged to determine the existence of an act of aggression before it could exercise the powers conferred on it in Chapter VII of the Charter. When situations had been brought before it, rather than identify the guilty party and inflict the punishment that the idea of aggression called for, the Council had always sought to play the part of a mediator or conciliator in order to re-establish international peace. The point was also made that it was doubtful whether a definition of aggression could really help to improve the security machinery established by the Charter. While the development of legal rules should be continued, even if the possibility of their violation still remained, it was open to question whether a definition, which would be used principally by the Security Council, would represent, at the present stage in international relations, a means of making the Council's work more effective. It would not give the Council any more authority; only when the Council, and the United Nations, had more authority would it be possible to identify and punish cases of aggression more effectively.

12. In the opinion of some of the representatives who expressed doubts about the possibility and desirability of defining aggression, there would be no point in reconvening the Special Committee on the Question of Defining Aggression. Issue was taken with the assertion that significant progress such as to justify continuation of its work had been made by the Special Committee. Indeed, some representatives asserted that the report disclosed deep cleavages of opinion on matters of fundamental importance, making it difficult to come to optimistic conclusions regarding the possibility of arriving at a definition. They pointed in particular to the fact that the great Powers were a long way from agreement and for that reason alone it was difficult to avoid the conclusion that any further consideration of the question of defining aggression would have little value. It was pointed out that, even among those delegations which believed most firmly in the necessity and possibility of defining aggression, there were differences of opinion on several important aspects of the question. What was more, the debates on elements of a definition of aggression duplicated the work of the Special Committee on the Principles of International Law concerning Friendly Relations and Co-operation among States. In the circumstances, it was said, it would be better to refer the question to that Committee and await the results of its work before trying to put forward a definition of aggression.

13. Some representatives, while expressing reservations as to whether it was useful and desirable, at least in the present circumstances, to define the concept of aggression, stated that they would not oppose the drawing up of a definition, on condition that it was satisfactory. In their opinion, an inadequate and incomplete definition would encourage rather than discourage acts of aggression and would be far worse than no definition at all. To be satisfactory, a definition should, essentially, have the following characteristics: it should safeguard the discretionary power of the Security Council and give it a flexible rather than rigid framework to work in; it should avoid using terminology incompatible with the provisions of the Charter, but should, on the contrary, base itself on the Charter; it should recognize the primary role of the Security Council with regard to the maintenance of international peace and security; it should include the idea of felonious intent and not be either so general as to be merely a repetition of the terms of the Charter or so precise as to give the impression of being exhaustive; it should apply both to direct and to indirect aggression; it should recognize the exceptions to the prohibition of the use of force made in the Charter; and it should be acceptable to the majority of Members of the General Assembly and to all the permanent members of the Security Council.

14. Some representatives expressed their views on the form and content of a definition of aggression. The great majority of them were in favour of a mixed type of definition, which would begin with a text in general terms stating the characteristics of acts of aggression; this would be followed by a list of specific instances, which would be neither restrictive nor complete but would be designed to provide a series of examples. This type of definition, however, was criticized by one representative as having all the drawbacks of an enumerative definition.

15. Several representatives considered that the proposed definition should confine itself solely to what constituted aggression resulting from the use of armed force in its direct form. It was said in that connexion that it would be dangerous to try to make the definition cover all the forms of pressure to which a State could be subjected that would extend the scope of Article 2, paragraph 4, of the Charter; such an extension would result in legitimizing acts of individual or collective defence specifically prohibited by Article 51, which expressly stated that self-defence was only justified in the event of armed attack. Forms of coercion other than armed force, it was added, were covered by other principles of modern international law, and, in particular, the principle of non-interference in the internal or external affairs of States.

16. In the opinion of some representatives, on the other hand, the idea of the indirect form of aggression ought to be included in the definition. It was argued that no analysis of the concept of aggression would be acceptable if it did not deal with the use of force in such forms as infiltration by armed bands, terrorism and subversion. Of the two forms of aggression, direct and indirect, the definition should not stress one at the expense of the other, since international peace and security were endangered both by the various forms of direct armed aggression and by indirect aggression. It was recognized that there would be difficulty in reaching general agreement on the description of the various forms that indirect aggression could take, but the matter was one of considerable practical interest, in view of the fact that the problem of indirect aggression lay behind many serious states of tension or possible states of tension. In addition, according to some representatives, the definition should cover all methods of using force, including economic and political aggression. It was necessary, they said, to take into account such forms of aggression as *apartheid*, colonialism and racism. It was also said that any definition should recognize the principle that it was legitimate for peoples under colonial domination to use force in their struggle for liberation and independence.

17. Opinions were expressed on the question whether the definition should include the threat of the use of force and whether the threat of the use of armed force could give rise to the right of self-defence. In the view of some representatives, Article 51 of the Charter only recognized the right of self-defence in so far as the State using force was the subject of an armed attack; that meant that any other act, whether serious threats or a violation of international obligations, would not constitute the necessary condition for exercising the right of self-defence. It was said, however, that in some cases the threat of the use of force was equivalent to the use of it; any problem of that kind would have to be solved by the bodies applying the definition, which would have to interpret it in a reasonable and flexible way and take into account the conditions prevailing at the time. It was also pointed out that Article 51 of the Charter had been drawn up at a time when the situation resulting from the threat or use of nuclear weapons had not been foreseen. Since the use of such weapons would have such disastrous effects that the victim would in no case be in a position to exercise the right of self-defence, it was essential to recognize that the threat to use them would by itself entitle the intended victim to the full exercise of that right.

18. In the opinion of some representatives, measures which were not reasonably proportionate to the armed attack could not be justified on grounds of self-defence. There were customary rules which established the conditions applicable in areas where the Charter was silent, to the effect that there should be a direct link and a certain proportion between the illicit act which was the basis for acting in self-defence and the defensive reaction.

19. The principle of priority was also raised. Some representatives maintained that it should be included in the definition. That was an unavoidable necessity and to try to do otherwise would lead to other important problems. If it was necessary to determine not who had attacked first or crossed a frontier, but who had prepared for the war, the situation would be hopeless, since at the present time preparations for war were too closely identified with the arms race. In the view of some representatives, the principle of priority was altogether too simplistic; a State wishing to avoid being labelled an aggressor would engage in feinting tactics and in those circumstances the definition might prove a trap for the innocent.

20. Some representatives considered that the definition should be expressly applicable to entities which were not generally recognized as States or whose status in international law could be contested on some other grounds, but which were required to respect the fundamental obligations imposed by international law with regard to the use of force.

21. Regarding the procedure for the adoption of a definition of aggression, the opinion was expressed by some representatives favouring a definition that it should take the form of a declaration included in a General Assembly resolution, in order to show the special importance the Assembly attached to the question and to give the definition a greater influence on the progressive development of international law. While it was true, they said, that such a resolution would not be strictly binding either on States or on the Security Council, it could not be categorically stated that it would be without any legal force. Considering that the idea of the illegality of aggression

was established by many international treaties, it was not possible to rule out *a priori* the possibility that with the passage of time a definition of aggression solemnly approved by an overwhelming majority of the General Assembly would take on a binding character and become a permanent part of international law.

22. Several representatives referred to a new doctrine which, if they understood it well, seemed to assert that mutual relations of certain groups of States were regulated exclusively by their own arrangements among themselves. These representatives pointed out that such a doctrine would run directly contrary to the fundamental concepts of the Charter and could not be made consistent with any definition of the term aggression in the Charter. On the other hand, the view was expressed that all the allegations regarding some sort of doctrines had the purpose of diverting attention from the aggressive policies of certain States aimed against various countries in various parts and continents of the world. These representatives emphasized that such aggressive policies trampled on the principles and norms of international law and the Charter of the United Nations and necessitated the adoption of corresponding measures to oppose such aggressive policies.

C. *Discussion of draft proposals submitted to the Special Committee*

23. The draft proposals submitted to the Special Committee were the subject of various comments by representatives in the Sixth Committee. With regard to the twelve-Power draft proposal (A/7185/Rev.1, para. 7), one representative felt that operative paragraph 1 should not include both the definition of aggression and the right of self-defence and would have preferred the latter to be dealt with in a separate paragraph. Another representative considered that neither that draft proposal nor the thirteen-Power draft proposal (*ibid.*, para. 9) approached the question from a strictly legal standpoint. The chief defect in both was the saving clause, which introduced a subjective criterion; in addition, both contained vague and imprecise terms and phrases.

24. Various views were expressed especially on the thirteen-Power draft proposal, which was supported in principle by many representatives.

25. Some representatives observed that the draft did not mention the violation of the Charter which consisted of the use of force to prevent dependent peoples from exercising their inherent right of self-determination. According to those representatives, the Sixth Committee should approve the addition to the draft proposal of a paragraph concerning the guaranteeing of the right of self-determination.

26. One representative said it was most important that the specific acts enumerated should not in any way prejudice the general character of the definition or preclude the possibility of other acts being considered as acts of aggression by the United Nations in the future. It would therefore be appropriate to include a provision on the lines of the opening words of operative paragraph 2 of the twelve-Power draft proposal.

27. Some representatives were opposed to the words "direct or indirect" qualifying the expression "the use of force" in operative paragraph 1 of the thirteen-Power draft proposal, because they introduced the idea of indirect aggression, discussion of which had

been postponed by the Special Committee because of its special complexity.

28. According to one representative, the maintenance of operative paragraph 1 in the proposed form might result in a dangerous extension of the scope of self-defence. That danger was even greater since there was no indication in the fifth preambular paragraph of who would decide, in the circumstances of each particular case, whether armed aggression had occurred. Furthermore, operative paragraph 2 did not indicate which body would be empowered to use force in accordance with the provisions of the Charter; the paragraph seemed to reinforce the idea that other bodies than the Security Council were empowered to use force under the Charter. If operative paragraph 3 was considered in the general context of the preambular part of the draft proposal, and particularly in relation to operative paragraph 5, the concept of self-defence could be extended to other acts of aggression than those mentioned in paragraph 5, since the list in that paragraph was not exhaustive. Although operative paragraph 4 was based on the provisions of Article 53 of the Charter, it nevertheless allowed the possibility that a regional agency could invoke the right to collective self-defence without referring the matter to the Security Council. It was true that operative paragraph 10 provided that no act other than those enumerated in paragraph 5 could be deemed to constitute aggression unless the Security Council so decided, but if a group of States resorted to force under the pretext of self-defence, that use of force could remain unpunished if the Security Council failed to reach a conclusion.

29. The view was expressed that operative paragraph 8 of the thirteen-Power draft proposal was contradictory; it prohibited recourse to individual or collective self-defence while at the same time authorizing "reasonable and adequate steps". Those terms were subjective and might lead to abuse by permitting States to take disproportionate measures with regard to the States accused. It was also said that operative paragraph 8 was highly ambiguous. The theoretical effect of any definition along those lines, based upon an utterly unreal and unviable distinction between direct and indirect aggression, could be to allow the victim of aggression to defend itself against a dramatic and violent attack from the outside, while on the other hand the same victim would presumably find itself on the wrong side of the law if it took appropriate action, in exercise of its right of self-defence, to protect itself from being throttled or from succumbing to slow poisoning. It was enough to state the proposition to see how unreal it was and how far it was in contradiction to the established law of nations and the law of the Charter according to which,

when the territorial integrity or political independence of a State was endangered by threats or acts of aggression, appropriate measures of self-defence were admissible irrespective of whether a purely doctrinal classification would assign such threats or acts to the category of direct or indirect aggression. The view was expressed that operative paragraph 8 should be deleted, since it was out of place in the definition of aggression and was more relevant to the field dealt with by the Special Committee on the Principles of International Law concerning Friendly Relations and Co-operation among States.

D. *Voting*

30. At its 1081st meeting, on 26 November 1968, the Sixth Committee, at the request of the Mexican representative, took a roll-call vote on the draft resolution before it (A/C.6/L.733/Rev.1 and Add. 1-3). The draft resolution was adopted by 74 votes to none, with 16 abstentions. The voting was as follows:

In favour: Afghanistan, Algeria, Argentina, Austria, Brazil, Bulgaria, Burma, Burundi, Byelorussian Soviet Socialist Republic, Cameroon, Canada, Ceylon, Chad, Chile, Colombia, Congo (Democratic Republic of), Cuba, Cyprus, Czechoslovakia, Dahomey, Ecuador, Ethiopia, Finland, France, Gabon, Ghana, Greece, Guatemala, Guinea, Guyana, Haiti, Hungary, India, Indonesia, Iran, Iraq, Jamaica, Kenya, Kuwait, Lebanon, Lesotho, Liberia, Libya, Madagascar, Mexico, Mongolia, Niger, Nigeria, Pakistan, Panama, Peru, Philippines, Poland, Romania, Rwanda, Southern Yemen, Spain, Sudan, Sweden, Syria, Thailand, Togo, Trinidad and Tobago, Tunisia, Turkey, Uganda, Ukrainian Soviet Socialist Republic, Union of Soviet Socialist Republics, United Arab Republic, United Republic of Tanzania, Uruguay, Venezuela, Yugoslavia, Zambia.

Against: None.

Abstaining: Australia, Belgium, China, Denmark, Ireland, Israel, Italy, Japan, Netherlands, New Zealand, Norway, Portugal, Saudi Arabia, South Africa, United Kingdom of Great Britain and Northern Ireland, United States of America.

Recommendation of the Sixth Committee

31. The Sixth Committee therefore recommends that the General Assembly adopt the following draft resolution:

REPORT OF THE SPECIAL COMMITTEE ON THE QUESTION OF DEFINING AGGRESSION

[*Text adopted by the General Assembly without change. See "Action taken by the General Assembly" below.*]

DOCUMENT A/7431

Administrative and financial implications of the draft resolution submitted by the Sixth Committee in document A/7402

Report of the Fifth Committee

[*Original text: English and Spanish*]
[*17 December 1968*]

1. At its 1288th meeting, held on 16 December 1968, the Fifth Committee, in compliance with rule 154 of the rules of procedure of the General Assembly, considered a note by the Secretary-General (A/C.5/1212) on the administrative and financial implications of the draft resolution submitted by the Sixth Com-

mittee (see A/7402, para. 31). The Chairman of the Advisory Committee on Administrative and Budgetary Questions made an oral statement.

2. Under the draft resolution, the Special Committee on the Question of Defining Aggression would resume its work in 1969, in accordance with General Assembly resolution 2330 (XXII). The Secretary-General estimated at $25,600 the additional costs of a five-week session in New York during the period 24 February to 28 March 1969. The Advisory Committee agreed that an additional provision in this amount would be required.

3. Accordingly, the Fifth Committee decided to advise the General Assembly that the adoption of the draft resolution would necessitate an additional appropriation in the amount of $25,600 under section 2 (Special meetings and conferences) of the budget for the financial year 1969.

ACTION TAKEN BY THE GENERAL ASSEMBLY

At its 1746th plenary meeting, on 18 December 1968, the General Assembly adopted the draft resolution submitted by the Sixth Committee (A/7402, para. 31) by a vote of 71 to none, with 16 abstentions. For the final text, see *Official Records of the General Assembly, Twenty-third Session, Supplement No. 18,* resolution 2420 (XXIII).

CHECK LIST OF DOCUMENTS

NOTE. This check list includes the documents mentioned during the consideration of agenda item 86 which are not reproduced in the present fascicle.

Document No.	Title or description	Observations and references
A/7185	Report of the Special Committee on the Question of Defining Aggression	Replaced by A/7185/Rev.1
A/7185/Rev.1	Report of the Special Committee on the Question of Defining Aggression	See *Official Records of the General Assembly, Twenty-third Session,* agenda item 86
A/C.6/L.733/Rev.1 and Add.1-3	Algeria, Congo (Democratic Republic of), Cyprus, Ecuador, El Salvador, Ethiopia, Ghana, Guatemala, Guyana, Haiti, India, Jamaica, Kenya, Liberia, Mexico, Panama, Pakistan, Peru, Romania, Spain, Sudan, Syria, Uganda, United Arab Republic, United Republic of Tanzania, Uruguay, Venezuela, Yugoslavia and Zambia: draft resolution	Adopted without change. See A/7042, para. 8.

DOCUMENT 16

Twenty-Fourth Session, Supp. No. 20, A/7620,
Report of Special Committee, 24 Feb. - 3 Apr.

I. INTRODUCTION[1]/

1.   At its 1676th plenary meeting, on 27 September 1968, the General Assembly decided to include in the agenda of its twenty-third session the report of the Special Committee on the Question of Defining Aggression on the work of its session held at the United Nations Office at Geneva from 4 June to 6 July 1968. [2]/ In addition, it referred the report to the Sixth Committee, which considered it at its 1028th meeting, on 2 October 1968, and at its 1073rd to 1082nd meetings, held from 18 to 27 November 1968. [3]/ At its 1746th plenary meeting, on 18 December 1968, the General Assembly adopted resolution 2420 (XXIII), which reads as follows:

"The General Assembly,

"Having considered the report of the Special Committee on the Question of Defining Aggression,

"Taking note of the progress made by the Special Committee in its consideration of the question of defining aggression and on the draft definition reflected in the report of the Special Committee,

"Considering that it was not possible for the Special Committee to complete its consideration of the question of defining aggression and of the draft definition before the end of 1968,

"Considering that in its resolution 2330 (XXII) of 18 December 1967 the General Assembly recognized the widespread conviction of the need to expedite the definition of aggression,

"1. Decides that the Special Committee on the Question of Defining Aggression shall resume its work, in accordance with General Assembly resolution 2330 (XXII), as early as possible in 1969;

"2. Requests the Secretary-General to provide the Special Committee with the necessary facilities and services;

"3. Decides to include in the provisional agenda of its twenty-fourth session an item entitled 'Report of the Special Committee on the Question of Defining Aggression'."

---

[1]/ For a survey of previous United Nations action on the question of defining aggression, see document A/AC.134/1 and Add.1.

[2]/ For the report, see Official Records of the General Assembly, Twenty-third Session, agenda item 86, document A/7185/Rev.1.

[3]/ For the report of the Sixth Committee to the General Assembly, see ibid., Annexes, agenda item 86, document A/7402.

2.   In accordance with that resolution, the Special Committee on the Question of Defining Aggression, whose composition is given in paragraph 2 of its report on the work of its 1968 session, met again at United Nations Headquarters in New York and held twenty-seven meetings, from 24 February to 3 April 1969. All the States members of the Special Committee took part in its work. The list of representatives to the 1969 session is annexed to this report (annex II).

3.   At its 25th meeting, on 24 February, the Special Committee elected the following officers:

Chairman:	Mr. Fakhreddine Mohamed (Sudan)
Vice-Chairmen:	Mr. Leopoldo Benites (Ecuador)
	Mr. Roeslan Abdulgani (Indonesia)
	Mrs. Elena Gavrilova (Bulgaria)
Rapporteur:	Mr. Matti Cawén (Finland)

4.   The 1969 session was opened on behalf of the Secretary-General by Mr. Constantin A. Stavropoulos, Legal Counsel of the United Nations. Mr. Anatoly P. Movchan, Director of the Codification Division of the Office of Legal Affairs, and Mr. Chafic Malek served respectively as Secretary and Deputy Secretary of the Special Committee. Mr. Tatsuro Kunugi and Mr. Eduardo Valencia-Ospina served as assistants to the Secretary.

5.   At the same meeting, the Special Committee adopted the following agenda (A/AC.134/L.9):

   (a) Opening of the session;

   (b) Election of officers;

   (c) Adoption of the agenda;

   (d) Organization of work;

   (e) Consideration of the question of defining aggression (General Assembly resolutions 2330 (XXII) and 2420 (XXIII);

   (f) Adoption of the report.

   On the proposal of the representative of Cyprus, the Special Committee also decided to resume its work at the stage it had reached at the end of the 1968 session by continuing debate on the draft proposals before it at that time, on the understanding that representatives would still be free to express their views on the whole question of defining aggression.

6.   At its 35th meeting, on 14 March, a draft proposal on the organization of the work was submitted to the Special Committee by the following countries: Colombia, Ecuador, Haiti, Mexico and Uruguay (A/AC.134/L.14 and Corr.1 and 2 and Add.1). The Committee took no decision on the draft proposal. It read as follows:

"The Special Committee,

"Decides to establish a Working Group composed of all its members;

"Requests the Working Group, applying the rules of procedure of the General Assembly for the conduct of its work, to prepare at this first stage a draft definition of aggression bearing in mind:

"A. The various documents and specific suggestions submitted by its members or which may be submitted in the Working Group;

"B. The following points, as far as they are an expression of the general wishes of the majority of the Committee:

"1. This definition of aggression should include only the concept of the use of armed force;

"2. The definition should contain an abstract formula setting forth, in a condensed form, the essential and characteristic elements constituting aggression;

"3. The definition of aggression should contain a non-exhaustive enumeration of the most common types of aggression;

"4. The idea should be expressed that the definition cannot prejudice the powers of evaluation and decision of the competent international organs which may be called upon to determine the aggressor;

"5. The idea should be expressed that no consideration of a political, economic, strategic, social or security nature can justify the commission of the acts constituting aggression."

"The principles enumerated above will in no way prejudice the position of States either in the Working Group or in the Special Committee and the Assembly, and will not restrict their right to submit the same proposals or new proposals or to alter those already in existence or to submit amendments."

7. At its 37th meeting, on 18 March, the Special Committee, on the proposal of the representative of the United Arab Republic, decided to establish a working group of the whole, and instructed it to pursue the Special Committee's task by giving more detailed consideration to the proposals, suggestions and points of view presented. The report of the working group, which was adopted by the Special Committee, at its 48th meeting, on 27 March (A/AC.134/L.19), is annexed to the present report (annex I).

II. PROPOSALS AND AMENDMENTS

8.   The Special Committee had before it various draft proposals. The draft proposals listed below, which had been submitted during its 1968 session, are reproduced in paragraphs 7 to 10 of its report on the work of that session: 4/

(a) A draft proposal submitted by the following twelve countries: Algeria, Congo (Democratic Republic of), Cyprus, Ghana, Guyana, Indonesia, Madagascar, Sudan, Syria, Uganda, United Arab Republic and Yugoslavia.

(b) A draft proposal submitted by the following four countries: Colombia, Ecuador, Mexico and Uruguay.

(c) A draft proposal submitted by the following thirteen countries: Colombia, Congo (Democratic Republic of), Cyprus, Ecuador, Ghana, Guyana, Indonesia, Iran, Mexico, Spain, Uganda, Uruguay and Yugoslavia.

(d) A draft amendment to the draft proposal mentioned in sub-paragraph (c) above, submitted by Sudan and the United Arab Republic.

9.   During the 1969 session, at its 27th meeting, on 26 February, the Special Committee had before it the following draft proposal, submitted by the Union of Soviet Socialist Republics (A/AC.134/L.12 and Corr.1 (Spanish only)):

"The General Assembly,

"Basing itself on the fact that one of the fundamental purposes of the United Nations is to maintain international peace and security and to take effective collective measures for the prevention and removal of threats to the peace, and for the suppression of acts of aggression or other breaches of the peace,

"Noting that according to the principles of international law the planning, preparation, initiation or waging of an aggressive war is a most serious international crime,

"Bearing in mind that the use of force to deprive dependent peoples of the exercise of their inherent right to self-determination in accordance with General Assembly resolution 1514 (XV) is a denial of fundamental human rights, is contrary to the Charter of the United Nations and hinders the development of co-operation and the establishment of peace throughout the world,

"Considering that the use of force by a State to encroach upon the social and political achievements of the peoples of other States is incompatible with the principle of the peaceful coexistence of States with different social systems,

---

4/   Official Records of the General Assembly, Twenty-third Session, agenda item 86, document A/7185/Rev.1.

"Recalling also that Article 39 of the Charter states that the Security Council shall determine the existence of any threat to the peace, breach of the peace or act of aggression and shall decide what measures shall be taken in accordance with Articles 41 and 42 to maintain or restore international peace and security,

"Believing that, although the question whether an act of aggression has been committed must be considered in the light of all the circumstances in each particular case, it is nevertheless appropriate to formulate basic principles as guidance for such determination,

"Convinced that the adoption of a definition of aggression would have a restraining influence on a potential aggressor, would simplify the determination of acts of aggression and the implementation of measures to stop them and would also facilitate the rendering of assistance to the victim of aggression and the protection of his lawful rights and interests,

"Considering also that armed aggression is the most serious and dangerous form of aggression, being fraught, in the conditions created by the existence of nuclear weapons, with the threat of a new world conflict with all its catastrophic consequences and that this form of aggression should be defined at the present stage,

"Declares that:

"1. Armed aggression (direct or indirect) is the use by a State, first, of armed force against another State contrary to the purposes, principles and provisions of the Charter of the United Nations.

"2. In accordance with and without prejudice to the functions and powers of the Security Council:

"A. Declaration of war by one State, first, against another State shall be considered an act of armed aggression;

"B. Any of the following acts, if committed by a State first, even without a declaration of war, shall be considered an act of armed aggression:

"(a) The use of nuclear, bacteriological or chemical weapons or any other weapons of mass destruction;

"(b) Bombardment of or firing at the territory and population of another State or an attack on its land, sea or air forces;

"(c) Invasion or attack by the armed forces of a State against the territory of another State, military occupation or annexation of the territory of another State or part thereof, or the blockade of coasts or ports.

"C. The use by a State of armed force by sending armed bands, mercenaries, terrorists or saboteurs to the territory of another State and engagement in other forms of subversive activity involving the use of armed force with the aim of promoting an internal upheaval in another State or a reversal of policy in favour of the aggressor shall be considered an act of indirect aggression.

6

"3. In addition to the acts listed above, other acts by States may
be deemed to constitute an act of aggression if in each specific instance
they are declared to be such by a decision of the Security Council.

"4. No territorial gains or special advantages resulting from armed
aggression shall be recognized.

"5. Armed aggression shall be an international crime against peace
entailing the political and material responsibility of States and the
criminal responsibility of the persons guilty of this crime.

"6. Nothing in the foregoing shall prevent the use of armed force
in accordance with the Charter of the United Nations, including its use
by dependent peoples in order to exercise their inherent right of self-
determination in accordance with General Assembly resolution 1514 (XV)."

10. At its 42nd meeting, on 24 March, the Special Committee had before
it the following draft proposal submitted by the following thirteen countries:
Colombia, Cyprus, Ecuador, Ghana, Guyana, Haiti, Iran, Madagascar, Mexico, Spain,
Uganda, Uruguay and Yugoslavia (A/AC.134/L.16 and Corr.1 (Spanish only)
and Add.1 and 2):

"The General Assembly,

"1. Basing itself on the fact that one of the fundamental purposes
of the United Nations is to maintain international peace and security and
to take effective collective measures for the prevention and removal of
threats to the peace, and for the suppression of acts of aggression or
other breaches of the peace,

"2. Convinced that armed attack (armed aggression) is the most
serious and dangerous form of aggression and that it is proper at this
stage to proceed to a definition of this form of aggression,

"3. Further convinced that the adoption of a definition of aggression
would serve to discourage possible aggressors and would facilitate the
determination of acts of aggression,

"4. Bearing in mind also the powers and duties of the Security Council,
embodied in Article 39 of the Charter, to determine the existence of any
threat to the peace, breach of the peace, or act of aggression, and to
decide the measures to be taken in accordance with Articles 41 and 42, to
maintain or restore international peace and security,

"5. Considering that, although the question whether aggression has
occurred must be determined in the circumstances of each particular case,
it is nevertheless appropriate to facilitate that task by formulating
certain principles for such determination,

"6. Reaffirming further the duty of States under the Charter of the
United Nations to settle their international disputes by pacific methods
in order not to endanger international peace, security and justice,

"7. <u>Convinced</u> that no considerations of whatever nature, save as stipulated in operative paragraph 3 hereof, may provide an excuse for the use of force by one State against another State,

"<u>Declares</u> that:

"1. In the performance of its function to maintain international peace and security, the United Nations only has competence to use force in conformity with the Charter;

"2. For the purpose of this definition, aggression is the use of armed force by a State against another State, including its territorial waters or air space, or in any way affecting the territorial integrity, sovereignty or political independence of such State, save under the provisions of paragraph 3 hereof or when undertaken by or under the authority of the Security Council;

"3. The inherent right of individual or collective self-defence of a State can be exercised only in case of the occurrence of armed attack (armed aggression) by another State in accordance with Article 51 of the Charter;

"4. Enforcement action or any use of armed force by regional arrangements or agencies may only be resorted to if there is decision to that effect by the Security Council acting under Article 53 of the Charter;

"5. In accordance with the foregoing and without prejudice to the powers and duties of the Security Council, as provided in the Charter, any of the following acts when committed by a State first against another State in violation of the Charter shall constitute acts of aggression:

"(a) Declaration of war by one State against another State;

"(b) The invasion or attack by the armed forces of a State, against the territories of another State, or any military occupation, however temporary, or any forcible annexation of the territory of another State or part thereof;

"(c) Bombardment by the armed forces of a State against the territory of another State, or the use of any weapons, particularly weapons of mass destruction, by a State against the territory of another State;

"(d) The blackade of the coasts or ports of a State by the armed forces of another State;

"6. Nothing in paragraph 3 above shall be construed as entitling the State exercising a right of individual or collective self-defence, in accordance with Article 51 of the Charter, to take any measures not reasonably proportionate to the armed attack against it;

"7. When a State is a victim in its own territory of subversive and/or terrorist acts by irregular, volunteer or armed bands organized or supported by another State, it may take all reasonable and adequate steps to safeguard its existence and its institutions, without having recourse to the right of individual or collective self-defence against the other State under Article 51 of the Charter;

"8. The territory of a State is inviolable and may not be the object, even temporarily, of military occupation or of other measures of force taken by another State on any grounds whatever, and that such territorial acquisitions obtained by force shall not be recognized;

"9. Armed aggression, as defined herein, and the acts enumerated above, shall constitute crimes against international peace, giving rise to international responsibility;

"10. None of the preceding paragraphs may be interpreted as limiting the scope of the Charter's provisions concerning the right of peoples to self-determination, sovereignty and territorial integrity."

11. At its 44th meeting, on 25 March, the Special Committee had before it the following draft proposal submitted by the following six countries: Australia, Canada, Italy, Japan, the United States and the United Kingdom (A/AC.134/L.17 and Corr.1 (Spanish only) and Add.1):

"I. Under the Charter of the United Nations, 'aggression', is a term to be applied by the Security Council when appropriate in the exercise of its primary responsibility for the maintenance of international peace and security under Article 24 and its functions under Article 39.

"II. The term 'aggression' is applicable, without prejudice to a finding of threat to the peace or breach of the peace, to the use of force in international relations, overt or covert, direct or indirect, by a State against the territorial integrity or political independence of any other State, or in any other manner inconsistent with the Purposes of the United Nations. Any act which would constitute aggression by or against a State likewise constitutes aggression when committed by a State or other political entity delimited by international boundaries or internationally agreed lines of demarcation against any State or other political entity so delimited and not subject to its authority.

"III. The use of force in the exercise of the inherent right of individual or collective self-defence, or pursuant to decisions of or authorization by competent United Nations organs or regional organizations consistent with the Charter of the United Nations, does not constitute aggression.

"IV. The uses of force which may constitute aggression include, but are not necessarily limited to, a use of force by a State as described in paragraph II.

"A. In order to:

(1) diminish the territory or alter the boundaries of another State;

(2) alter internationally agreed lines of demarcation;

(3) disrupt or interfere with the conduct of the affairs of another State;

(4) secure changes in the Government of another State; or

(5) inflict harm or obtain concessions of any sort;

"B. By such means as:

(1) invasion by its armed forces of territory under the jurisdiction of another State;

(2) use of its armed forces in another State in violation of the fundamental conditions of permission for their presence, or maintaining them there beyond the termination of permission;

(3) bombardment by its armed forces of territory under the jurisdiction of another State;

(4) inflicting physical destruction on another State through the use of other forms of armed force;

(5) carrying out deliberate attacks on the armed forces, ships, or aircraft of another State;

(6) organizing, supporting or directing armed bands or irregular or volunteer forces that make incursions or infiltrate into another State;

(7) organizing, supporting or directing violent civil strife or acts of terrorism in another State; or

(8) organizing, supporting or directing subversive activities aimed at the violent overthrow of the Government of another State."

12. At its 49th meeting on 28 March, the Special Committee had before it the following draft resolution submitted by: Colombia, Congo (Democratic Republic of), Cyprus, Ecuador, Ghana, Guyana, Haiti, Madagascar, Mexico and Uruguay (A/AC.134/L.18):

"The Special Committee on the Question of Defining Aggression,

"Bearing in mind resolutions 2330 (XXII) and 2420 (XXIII) of the General Assembly,

"Recognizing the progress made during this session in the consideration of the question of defining aggression and on the draft definition, as reflected in the report of the Special Committee,

"<u>Noting</u> that new proposals concerning a draft definition of aggression were submitted in 1969,

"<u>Noting further</u> that there was not enough time in which to complete its important task,

"<u>Recommends</u> to the General Assembly, at its twenty-fourth session, that the Special Committee be asked to resume its work early in 1970."

III. DEBATE

13. The debate dealt essentially with the draft proposals before the Special Committee. During the consideration of those proposals, views were expressed on certain general aspects of the question of defining aggression. Part A of this section will contain an account of the views expressed on those general aspects; parts B and C will deal with the views expressed on the draft proposals submitted.

A. VIEWS EXPRESSED ON CERTAIN GENERAL ASPECTS OF THE QUESTION
OF DEFINING AGGRESSION

14. Some representatives expressed doubts regarding the possibility of agreeing on a definition of aggression and regarding the usefulness of a definition, even if it could be agreed upon. Indeed, the value of trying to define the term was questioned and it was stated that it would not be useful to continue to do so. It was emphasized that although a substantial majority of the members of the Special Committee clearly wished to submit a draft definition to the General Assembly, it would be wise to consider whether, in view of the manifest differences of opinion reflected in the texts which had been submitted, it was really necessary to adopt a definition at the present time. The fact that the Security Council's power to act under Articles 41 and 42 of the Charter in no way depended upon a determination that an act of aggression had been committed had been one of the major reasons why the San Francisco Conference had rejected proposals to include a definition of aggression in the Charter. Moreover, there was some doubt that the adoption of a definition would discourage potential aggressors; it might have the opposite effect.

15. On the other hand, several representatives expressed the view that a definition of aggression would constitute a basic element of international law and would be indispensable for purposes of ensuring order in the international community. There were constitutional, legislative and political reasons, they said, for completing the task of defining aggression by an early date. From the constitutional point of view, the General Assembly had already accomplished much substantive work in elaborating certain basic concepts of the Charter such as human rights, self-determination and the sovereign equality of States. Legislatively, the General Assembly had taken a number of important steps to develop international criminal law, but had deferred action on the draft code of offences against the peace and security of mankind and on international criminal jurisdiction, since it considered those subjects related to the question of defining aggression. It was stated that the political reasons for expediting a definition of aggression were cogently stated in the seventh preambular paragraph of the USSR draft proposal.

16. Some argued that there was no longer any question, at the present stage, of wondering whether or not a definition of aggression was necessary because the task of the Special Committee, as stated by the Committee itself in the resolution it had adopted at its first session, was to define aggression at the earliest possible

date and to submit a report to the General Assembly containing a draft definition of aggression. Others disagreed with this interpretation of the mandate of the Special Committee.

17. Some representatives, while reserving their positions regarding the utility and wisdom of defining aggression, said that they were not against working out a definition which could contribute to the maintenance of international peace and security by means of the system of collective security provided for in the Charter, and the protection of the territorial integrity and political independence of States. To achieve that objective, a definition should above all: be compatible with the Charter and be based on the Charter; not affect the discretionary power of the Security Council and, generally speaking, the division of powers and functions made by the Charter between the organs of the United Nations; fully recognize the right of self-defence; not be so restrictive in its enumeration of what constituted aggression as to exclude certain specific cases of armed attack; enjoy the support of all the permanent members of the Security Council. The section of this report which follows and which deals with the discussion of the draft definitions proposed will reflect the various views expressed concerning those conditions and others regarded by some representatives as indispensable for a satisfactory definition.

18. It should be indicated here, however, that all the members of the Special Committee agreed that the definition should be compatible with the Charter and based on the Charter. The view that the definition should have the support of all the permanent members of the Security Council was challenged by several representatives. While they recognized that the definition should be acceptable to the overwhelming majority of Member States of the United Nations, they wondered why the support of the great Powers was particularly necessary. Moreover, the Charter contained no provision justifying such a requirement. It was stated that there was no reason to think that the definition of aggression would be used only by the Security Council; to make that assumption would be to prejudge a question which was for the General Assembly to decide; it was therefore astonishing, in view of General Assembly resolution 2330 (XXII) and the fact that one permanent member of the Security Council was not a member of the Committee, to hear it asserted that the definition would have to be approved by all the permanent members of the Council. It was also said that a definition of aggression supported by the vast majority of Member States, even if it was opposed by the great Powers, would give notice to world public opinion of the restrictions placed on the use of violence in international relations; the definition would enable individual citizens to judge the foreign policy decisions of Governments and would encourage them to exert pressure for changes in policies which deviated markedly from acceptable international conduct. A definition of aggression, even if it was only adopted by majority vote, would help to bring about a better legal order. In response it was pointed out that, in order to be satisfactory, the definition would have to be useful to the Security Council and that the concurrence of its permanent members would be indispensable.

B. VIEWS EXPRESSED ON THE DRAFTS SUBMITTED AT THE 1968 SESSION
AND ON THE USSR DRAFT (A/AC.134/L.3, 4, 6, 8 and 12)

19. The discussion centred mainly on the USSR draft (A/AC.134/L.12) and the
thirteen-Power draft (A/AC.134/L.6), both of which were supported in principle by
a large number of members of the Special Committee. With respect to the USSR
proposal, submitted to the Special Committee on 26 February 1969, several
representatives stressed its constructive character and considered that it
furnished a good working basis. The views expressed on those drafts, including
their preambles, are set forth below under the appropriate headings.

1. Application of the definition

(a) The definition and the power of the Security Council

20. Most representatives felt that the definition should preserve the
discretionary power vested in the Security Council as the organ of the United
Nations with primary responsibility for the maintenance of peace; it should not
restrict the power of the Council to determine the existence of an act of
aggression in cases of threats to or breaches of the peace. It was further
argued that the definition should in no circumstances apply automatically; it
should leave the task of deciding whether or not it should be applied to the
Security Council. It was stressed that, according to the USSR draft proposal,
whereas the Security Council enjoyed a certain measure of latitude with respect
to acts other than those enumerated in the draft proposal, it did not enjoy the
same latitude with respect to the application of the definition to the acts
specifically mentioned; thus, the effect of the Soviet draft proposal might be to
force the Security Council to act in a certain way in certain circumstances, and
thereby diminish its power of discretion. It was also held that it would be
desirable for the definition to be founded entirely on respect for that
discretionary power; not only should the definition contain a specific provision
in that regard, but it should also contain nothing which would actually run counter
to that principle and destroy the freedom of action of the Security Council. The
element of automaticity in the application of the idea of priority contained in
the Soviet draft proposal might create serious difficulties. It had also been
said that any wording similar to that in operative paragraph 1 of the twelve-Power
draft proposal, for example, or operative paragraph 3 of the four-Power text or
operative paragraph 2 of the thirteen-Power draft proposal would not be acceptable
if it did not place sufficient emphasis on the exclusive power vested in the
Security Council under Article 39 of the Charter both to determine the existence
of aggression and to make recommendations or take measures accordingly. The
Council's exclusive jurisdiction in that respect was beyond question.

21. Other representatives felt that operative paragraph 10 of the thirteen-Power
draft and operative paragraph 3 of the USSR text should be reworded because they
might be construed as empowering the Security Council to add, or to classify as
aggression, acts other than those enumerated in the definition. If the present

wording was retained, those two paragraphs would not only make any definition useless, but they would also destory its raison d'être, because to lay down a legal definition implied limiting a field of competence. In working out a definition of aggression, they said, the Special Committee should choose once and for all between two alternatives: either a definition had its own intrinsic value, in which case the Security Council should respect it, or, if the Security Council was to retain its freedom of action in the matter, the conclusion should be that a definition was of no value whatsoever, for it was illogical to accept a definition and then to authorize non-compliance. It was pointed out that regardless of the value of a definition of aggression from the standpoint of international law, international law played a lesser role in the United Nations than in the League of Nations because the purpose of the United Nations was not to restore the legal order once it had been violated, but rather to maintain peace. Since that was so, a practical effort should be made to bring political action as closely as possible into line with international law. For instance, instead of insisting on the power of discretion vested in it by the Charter, which authorized it even to go against a general principle of law, the Security Council should endeavour to abide by the principles of international law and, consequently, a definition of aggression should not have regard to the power of discretion vested in the Security Council.

22. One representative expressed the view that while a reference to the powers of the Security Council could really do no harm, it was not necessary. The powers of the Council, like those of the other organs of the United Nations, he explained, derived from the Charter, and the provisions of the Charter could not be modified in any circumstances except those specified in Article 108. Consequently, the definition could not modify the powers which the Charter vested in the Security Council. Nor could it confirm the existence of those powers. In any event, far from reducing the Council's power of judgement, it would enable it to discharge its task more effectively. The same representative pointed out that the Charter conferred two distinct powers on the Security Council, namely, a sovereign power of assessment, exercised by the Council in judging the situation under consideration, and the discretionary power to take whatever measures it thought best; that distinction was clearly fundamental if it was borne in mind that the Security Council's power of assessment could not be strengthened by the existence of a definition of aggression, while, on the other hand, its discretionary power could not be lessened by such a definition. Furthermore, it was argued, the General Assembly was also legally empowered, under the Charter, to determine the existence of an act of aggression. To be strictly correct, it would perhaps be better to omit any reference to the General Assembly from the definition of aggression. Such an omission, however, would not diminish the generally recognized competence of the General Assembly to consider questions concerning the maintenance of peace.

(b) Political entities to which the definition should apply

23. Some representatives considered that any definition of aggression should be specifically applicable to political entities which were not generally recognized as States or whose status in international law could be questioned in some other way, but which were bound to respect the obligations imposed by international law as regards the use of force. It was pointed out that the Soviet draft proposal

was less flexible than the Charter, which envisaged the possibility of aggression committed by an entity which was not universally recognized as a State or of aggression committed against such an entity.

24. It was stated, on the other hand, that if the term "political entity" was interpreted in the usual way, it might encompass any opposition party in a democracy. But if it was intended to mean a "geopolitical entity" that term should be used. In any case, any definition of aggression strictly in conformity with the Charter should necessarily exclude any geopolitical entity not envisaged by the provisions of the Charter - in short, all entities which were not States - the only exception being the United Nations itself.

2. Acts proposed for inclusion in the concept of aggression

25. Most representatives expressed the view that the definition should be limited, at least for the time being, to the idea of armed aggression as envisaged in the Charter. However, different interpretations were given as regards the scope of that idea. One of the problems was to decide whether, for purposes of exercising the right of self-defence, the idea of aggression included what was generally known as indirect armed aggression. The question whether the concept of aggression extends to forms of aggression not involving the actual use of armed force was also raised.

26. With regard to that point, some representatives held that the concept of aggression applied only to the use of force in violation of Article 2 (4) of the Charter, that is, the use of armed force or physical force, direct or indirect. The Soviet draft proposal, it was said, appeared to extend the concept of aggression to acts not involving the use of force within the meaning of that provision of the Charter. While it was true that the operative provisions of that proposal were limited to acts which were regarded as constituting "armed aggression", the very use of the expression "armed aggression" seemed to imply that there were other forms of aggression within the meaning of the Charter than "armed" aggression, which was confirmed by the last preambular paragraph. It was further pointed out that the same applied to the thirteen-Power draft, which enlarged the concept of aggression in its operative paragraph 1 by extending it to all forms of the use of force in international relations, which clearly went beyond the provisions of Article 2 (4) of the Charter. It was also stated that the concept of aggression which emerged from the Charter was based on two essential factors: the use of armed force and an attack on the territorial integrity or political independence of another State. If, therefore, the definition of aggression was to conform to the Charter, it should contain no indication or qualification which might give the impression that forms of aggression other than armed aggression remained to be defined; nor should it appear to exclude certain serious, less direct, uses of force in violation of paragraph 4 of Article 2 of the Charter. It was also pointed out that the concept of aggression included only armed attack as discussed in Article 51 of the Charter. The aggression with which the Committee was concerned, they noted in that connexion, was "armed attack", the phrase used in the English text of the Article, which alone would establish the connexion between aggression and self-defence, the latter right being established under the Charter only if the attack was armed. In any other case, there might be a threat, but it was not precisely within the

purview of the Special Committee. Enumerating the essential characteristics of "armed attack", they stated that the attack should constitute a breach of the peace, in other words, it should be of sufficient seriousness, the degree of which could be gauged by the Security Council; that the connexion between the idea of aggression and a breach of the peace followed from Article 1 (1) of the Charter which, by referring to "acts of aggression or other breaches of the peace", put aggression in the category of breaches of the peace; that such a breach of the peace should be the result of action taken by the aggressor. In that connexion, it was suggested that the first sentence introducing the enumerations in all the drafts submitted to the Committee (it would be added to paragraph 2 B of the USSR text) should be reworded as follows: "Any one of the following acts, committed by a State first, as a breach of the peace and without its adversary having committed such an act, shall be considered an act of armed aggression". It was felt that the expression "contrary to the purposes, principles and provisions of the Charter" in operative paragraph 1 of the Soviet draft, would present some danger as it might induce States to invoke those purposes and principles in order to justify the use of force. It was therefore suggested that more precise and restricted wording should be used, such as the following, which would replace the end of operative paragraph 1 of the USSR draft: "... in any manner other than in application of the relevant provisions of the Charter, as essentially contained in Chapter VII".

27. Furthermore, while they recognized that the definition should be restricted to armed aggression within the meaning of Article 51 of the Charter, several representatives pointed out that there were other forms of aggression. In that connexion, it was argued that economic and political pressure should be regarded as part of the concept of force. Economic pressure, it was asserted, could mean starvation and starvation killed as surely as the atomic bomb. There could therefore be no doubt that such pressure constituted an unlawful act which violated the Charter. Even if it was accepted that the concept of force as used in the Charter was restricted to armed force, that did not necessarily lead to the conclusion that armed aggression was the only form of aggression. Aggression implied an attack, which could take many forms. By limiting the exercise of the right of self-defence solely to the cases of armed attack under Article 51, the Charter had recognized that there were other types of aggression. However, those forms of aggression could not be equated with the recognized forms of armed aggression within the meaning of Article 51 of the Charter.

28. With regard to armed aggression in its indirect form, some representatives argued that the definition should be applicable to that form of aggression, as well as to direct armed aggression. It was pointed out that the thirteen-Power draft referred to the indirect use of force in its general definition of aggression in operative paragraph 1, but did not include any such act in its enumeration in paragraph 5. Moreover, it explicitly denied the right of self-defence in most cases where the aggressor indirectly used force; that approach was, in some essential respects, inconsistent with the Charter and, in any event, mistaken. Similarly, it was stated, the Soviet draft was not true to the Charter when it drew a distinction between "direct aggression" and "indirect aggression"; if a State used force in violation of Article 2 (4) of the Charter, that act constituted aggression; to speak of "direct" or "indirect" aggression in a definition was to introduce a distinction which was both alien to the Charter and superfluous. Though an obvious improvement on the thirteen-Power draft, the Soviet proposal

still has serious shortcomings in that respect. Paragraph 2 C did treat the
indirect use of force as an act of aggression in certain circumstances, but it did
not recognize as acts of aggression the support of armed bands, the encouragement
of subversive activity against another State or the refusal to take all necessary
measures to deny armed bands aid or protection. Moreover, the intent referred to
in operative paragraph 2 C of the Soviet draft seemed too narrow to be compatible
with the Charter; the aggression described in that provision could be due to many
other reasons, such as threats to the territorial integrity or political
independence of a State or attempts totally to destroy that State. It was pointed
out that the failure to give adequate space to the question of the indirect use
of force in the text of the Soviet draft probably made it unacceptable to a number
of Member States, and in particular to some permanent members of the Security
Council. Apart from the fact that it defined the concept of indirect use of
force too narrowly, the Soviet draft placed such acts in a separate legal category.
Whether it was direct or indirect, however, aggression had precisely the same
legal consequences under the Charter and a definition of aggression should not
suggest otherwise; if the indirect use of force was included, as it should be, in
the definition of aggression within the meaning of Article 39 of the Charter, it
followed that it would naturally give rise to the right of individual or
collective self-defence provided for in Article 51 of the Charter; the validity
of operative paragraph 8 of the thirteen-Power draft was therefore questionable.

29. Some representatives expressed the view that the words "direct" and "indirect"
used in operative paragraph 1 of the thirteen-Power draft and operative paragraph 1
of the Soviet draft to qualify armed aggression should be deleted; those words
did not appear in the Charter and might cause confusion. In the view of those
representatives and of several others, the definition should relate only to
direct armed aggression, which alone, according to Article 51 of the Charter,
would justify the exercise of the right of self-defence. Nevertheless, it was
argued that the definition should mention types of action which a State should
be prohibited from taking when confronted with unfriendly measures falling short
of armed attack and of the counter-measures which are permissible. Subversion
and terrorism by another State undoubtedly threatened the territorial integrity
and independence of the victim State; acts of that kind were prohibited by the
Charter but, if they were equated with armed attack, that might jeopardize the
restriction in Article 51 placed on the right of self-defence. It was noted that,
while the wording of operative paragraph 8 of the thirteen-Power draft might be
confusing, its inclusion was based on the distinction between those measures
which could be adopted by a State, in exercising the right of sovereignty, against
subversive and terrorist acts, on the one hand, and the exercise of the right of
self-defence against armed attack, on the other. The definition should indicate
that distinction without any possible ambiguity. It was true that the Soviet
draft designated certain acts of indirect armed aggression; however, it might be
concluded, on the basis of operative paragraph 1 of that draft, that such acts
justified the exercise of the right of self-defence, and that was unacceptable.

30. One representative emphasized the difficulties inherent in defining indirect
armed aggression. The greatest uncertainty lay in the difficulty of providing
proof; yet the fact that what was involved was not merely non-intervention but
the more serious idea of aggression made the importance of proof all the more
decisive, and the sponsors of the texts which had been submitted had not tried to
solve that problem.

31.   On the question whether the concept of aggression applied only to acts of armed aggression or whether it also included preparations for aggression, it was stated that it would be more in accordance with modern legal ideas and contemporary international practice to consider aggression in its broadest sense, as a complex of interrelated acts, i.e., the planning, preparation and launching of an aggressive war.   The second preambular paragraph of the Soviet draft was clearly based on such modern principles of international law.

32.   The question of "provocation" was raised.   One representative observed that the question, whether, and how far, provocation exonerated an attacking State from the charge of aggression had been much discussed in the time of the League of Nations and since that time.   The Soviet draft took no account of the vital element of provocation in the definition of aggression.   Another representative emphasized that any use of force was prohibited, except in the case of a United Nations action in conformity with the Charter or in the case of the exercise of the right of self-defence; Article 51 of the Charter precisely defined the limits of that right, which a State could use only if an armed attack occurred, and not in the event of threats, provocations or preparations for an armed attack against it.

33.   With regard to the actual enumeration of acts of aggression in the Soviet draft, some representatives observed that declaration of war, annexation of territory and the blockade of coasts or ports were an extremely serious matter, and in most cases constituted a threat within the meaning of Article 2 (4) of the Charter, but that none of them necessarily involved the actual use of force, and they might amount to nothing more than a claim for a certain right which, being in violation of international law and the Charter, was without international legal effect.   When those acts did result in the use of force in violation of the Charter, it was the use of force itself which was to be regarded as aggression.

34.   Some representatives considered it inappropriate to mention in the definition the kind of weapons used.   It was, they said, clearly not just the use of weapons of mass destruction, referred to in operative paragraph 2 B (a) of the USSR draft, which constituted aggression, but their use by one State against another in violation of the Charter; but that was true of weapons of any kind, and it was therefore not relevant in a definition of aggression to include certain kinds of weapons to the exclusion of others.   Whether aggression had been committed was determined not by the kind of weapons used, but by the nature of the acts committed.   On the other hand, it was stated that, while aggression could be committed otherwise than by the use of nuclear weapons or other weapons of mass destruction, it was nevertheless necessary to place the emphasis in the definition on the prohibition of the use of such weapons, which were beyond any doubt by far the most horrible weapons; since there was not at the present time a special convention prohibiting the use of nuclear weapons, it would be useful to indicate in the definition of aggression that, from the legal point of view, the use of such weapons was inadmissible; that would help to prevent the outbreak of nuclear conflicts and would also pave the way for the subsequent conclusion of a special convention in that field.

35.   The opinion was expressed that if a State permitted another State to use its territory in order to attack a third State, that constituted an act of indirect aggression; it was also said that States should refrain from using force by

mobilizing or concentrating their armed forces near the border of another State, a point which should be regarded as a concrete proposal for the consideration of the Committee.

3. Aggressive intent

36. Some representatives took the view that animus aggressionis would be a characteristic element of the use of force. In addition to the unlawful act, the definition should take into account intent - two elements which, when combined, would constitute aggression. Other representatives expressed a different view, stating that a definition of aggression could not take into account the element of intent if the criterion of strict interpretation of the Charter was to be maintained. The context in which the Charter had been drafted and the wording of Article 2 (4) argued against the view that intent was a necessary component of aggression. If that element were included in the definition, it might tempt an aggressor to rely on such spurious defences as anticipatory self-defence, duress per minas or mistake. No legitimate defence of mistake could be open to a State inadvertently unleashing a nuclear attack.

37. It was also stated that the idea which was implicit in the fourth preambular paragraph of the USSR draft could be interpreted as sanctioning the doctrine of limited sovereignty; it would be better to use the broader terminology of the Charter and to refer, for instance, to acts which might encroach upon the territorial integrity or political independence of States. As worded, that paragraph of the Soviet draft, by speaking of the peaceful coexistence of States with different social systems, would imply that the use of force was permissible between States with similar social systems. Nowhere did the Charter distinguish between uses of force which encroached upon the social and political achievements of peoples and other uses of force. Any use of force in international relations, it was noted, was incompatible with the principle of peaceful coexistence of States; all States, irrespective of their political or social systems, had the right to a peaceful existence. That was a principle of jus cogens, because it was directly related to the maintenance of international public order, and hence affected all States.

38. It was stated, on the other hand, that the purpose of the fourth paragraph of the USSR draft was to highlight the necessity of preventing any attempt by one State to change the social and political system of another. That was of particular importance to countries which had recently acquired their independence; the use of force by a State to encroach upon the social and political achievements of peoples was, in all circumstances, contrary to international law, whether the States involved had different social systems or similar ones. The principle of good-neighbourliness laid down by the Charter covered the principle of peaceful coexistence, and to criticize the latter would be to criticize a principle of the Charter. The fourth preambular paragraph of the Soviet draft was designed to protect the sovereignty and independence of all countries, including those which were not yet regarded as States. In that connexion, it should be noted that the term "State" used in operative paragraph 1 of the Soviet draft should be interpreted as applying also to States in the process of formation.

4. The principle of priority

39. Several representatives argued that the principle of priority or "first use" should be included in the definition, and felt that the USSR draft was satisfactory

on that point. In the view of those representatives, that principle should be
the main criterion in determining who was the aggressor in an international
conflict; even greater problems would be created by trying not to include it in
the definition. Those who argued that the question was not who had crossed the
frontier first or who had attacked first but who had prepared for war were
overlooking the fact that, in the present age of the armaments race, with that
criterion it would be impossible to identify the aggressor unless a historical
or strategical study was made of the reasons why each side had started to add to
its arsenal. The "first use" principle must be included also because Article 51
of the Charter endorsed it as a condition for exercising the right of self-defence:
the words "if an armed attack occurs against a Member of the United Nations"
clearly meant that the right of self-defence derived exclusively from an armed
attack. Hence, while recognizing the incredible variety of strategical
implications, they concluded that the "first use" principle must be included in
the definition, as it was in the Soviet draft.

40. It was also stated that the principle of priority was not a new principle;
it was referred to in some of the deliberations of the League of Nations; it was
also affirmed in certain treaties and was recognized by renowned experts on
international law. In short, those holding these views pointed out that it was
generally recognized that a State which was the first to resort to armed force
against another State was the aggressor; and that view was confirmed by the
studies of the International Law Commission, the Special Committee and other
United Nations bodies. The omission of that principle from a definition of
aggression would have the effect of justifying the theory of preventive war, but
acceptance of that theory would render meaningless not only the definition of
aggression but also all the measures which the United Nations took under
Chapters I and VII of the Charter. Even assuming that it would be difficult to
determine who had committed armed aggression first, investigation and evidence
would be required in order to determine priority; and the Security Council, which
was responsible for that task, had several means of establishing who had
committed aggression first.

41. On the other hand, the principle of priority was disputed by some
representatives, who took the view that it was incompatible with the Charter and
might be dangerous. It was stated that the consequence of that principle was
that the right of self-defence would be arbitrarily restricted either to a
response by the same methods as those used by the aggressor or to the use of
some means of defence not covered by any of the acts enumerated in operative
paragraph 2 B of the USSR draft. Perhaps aggression should be taken to mean the
commission by a State of any one of the acts enumerated, if none of those acts
had already been committed against it; in that case, a victim of any one of
those enumerated acts could defend itself by any one or several of those acts,
since in so doing it would not be considered to be the first to commit one of
those acts. However, an even more serious difficulty would then arise: if a
State committed one relatively inconsequential act (say, an attack on a ship or
a single shot across a border), the victim could respond with the whole of his
military might, including nuclear weapons, without being held an aggressor; such
was not the rule of the Charter, under which defensive measures should be
proportionate to the attack and the use of force greatly exceeding that used by
the aggressor might constitute aggression. If the Soviet draft was not to be
interpreted as modifying or restricting the right of self-defence, which was the
express intention of the general saving clause in operative paragraph 6,
paragraphs 1 and 2 B should be regarded as ruling out first uses of force except

in self-defence. However, such an interpretation would imply that States could use force first in self-defence, in anticipation of the use of force. It was also pointed out that the principle of priority raised problems of interpretation and would not be appropriate in the case of frontier incidents. Since its application in specific cases would be very difficult, it would be desirable to leave it to the Security Council to determine whether an act of aggression had been committed.

42. One representative stated that he did not agree with the emphasis on the principle of priority in operative paragraphs 1 and 2 B of the USSR draft. Since the legitimate use of force, under Article 51 of the Charter, necessarily involved a response to an illegal military move, it was hard to conceive of a situation in which the aggressor would be any other than a State first resorting to force in contravention of the relevant Charter provisions. Moreover, operative paragraph 2 B of the Soviet draft did not appear to express the intention of its sponsor, since a State could resort first to any of the acts enumerated pursuant to a determination of the Security Council, as operative paragraph 6 appeared to recognize. Another representative observed that the principle of priority appeared valid if considered in the abstract, since the idea of armed aggression was inseparable from that of initiative in the use of armed force. As formulated in the Soviet draft, however, that principle appeared to involve dangers. The fundamental danger was that it might be taken to imply that if a State was attacked by the armed forces of another State it was entitled to counter-attack in self-defence. Although an aggressor must be censured and its victim protected, both nevertheless remained subject to the provisions of the Charter, in particular with regard to the peaceful settlement of disputes. Self-defence should only be considered to cover acts necessary to halt aggression; beyond that point it became unlawful and itself constituted aggression.

5.   Legitimate use of force

(a) Self-defence

43. Several representatives stressed the need to include in the definition of aggression a clear and precise provision recognizing the right of self-defence as provided for in Article 51 of the Charter. The absence of clear and undisputed criteria for distinguishing aggression from the legitimate use of force would not only make the definition meaningless but would also be fraught with dangerous consequences. Both types of action involved the physical use of armed force, but they were fundamentally different in their legal, moral and political nature. Under Article 51 of the Charter and in accordance with generally accepted international rules, a State had the right to use armed force in its own defence only to repeal an armed attack against it. It could not do so in order to take preventive measures or to respond to violations of its rights other than armed attack. The Soviet draft, it was stated, made a clear distinction between the legal and illegal use of force.

44. It was pointed out, on the other hand, that the USSR draft did not expressly mention individual or collective self-defence, which was referred to only indirectly in operative paragraphs 1 and 6. Express mention should be made of the provisions of the Charter that were referred to in operative paragraph 6 of the draft.

45. It was also stated that operative paragraph 6 of the USSR draft, mentioning the use of force in accordance with the Charter as an exception to the principle of the prohibition of the threat or use of force, significantly effected the legal content of the principle of the prohibition of war as an instrument for the settlement of international disputes. Only the competent organs of the United Nations had the right to use force in order to maintain international peace and security. Accordingly, the use of force by any State constituted the crime of aggression and entailed the liability deriving from the rules of law in force, just like a crime under a national system of law. The definition of aggression should begin by referring to the monopoly of force vested in the United Nations, which was the point of departure taken in the thirteen-Power draft. In that respect, the Soviet draft raised some difficulties. It was also stated that the right of self-defence was not an exception to the principle laid down in Article 2 (4) of the Charter, just as it was not an exception to the criminal code of any country with respect to the crime of homicide. Under the Charter, no State was empowered to use force; Article 51 recognized the right of self-defence only to the extent that it exempted the State using force to repel an armed attack from liability until the Security Council had determined what means were to be employed to maintain international peace and security. The thirteen-Power draft carefully placed the only two cases in which the Charter recognized the use of force as legitimate in the legal context of the system of security set up by the United Nations.

(b) Organs empowered to use force

46. Some representatives stressed the importance of the principle, originally included in the four-Power draft, that, in the performance of its functions to maintain international peace, the United Nations alone had competence to use force, except when States exercised their right of self-defence. That extremely important principle was embodied in the thirteen-Power text, although in a slightly modified form, but was missing from the Soviet draft, although it might be implicit in the fifth preambular paragraph.

47. One representative stated that operative paragraph 1 of the thirteen-Power draft appeared to exclude the General Assembly, without any valid legal reason, from United Nations organs which might authorize the use of force in accordance with the Charter, by including the words "other than when undertaken by or under the authority of the Security Council or in the exercise of the right of individual or collective self-defence".

48. Several representatives stressed that operative paragraph 4 of the thirteen-Power draft concerning regional agencies should be included in the definition of aggression. In the view of other representatives, however, that paragraph deviated from the Charter, in that it referred to "any use of armed force", whereas Article 53 of the Charter spoke only of "enforcement action". One of the consequences of that variation was to deny the possibility of collective self-defence, as recognized in Article 51 of the Charter, through regional agencies.

6. Acts considered not to constitute acts of aggression

49. Several representatives stated that the definition should include a clause providing for an exception when the use of force was necessary to ensure the

exercise of the right of peoples to self-determination. The definition should be based on the principle that the use of force against people exercising their right to self-determination was a violation of the Charter and gave those peoples the right to act in self-defence. Some delegations, however, argued that such a provision would be out of place in a definition of aggression that was limited to inter-State relations. Accordingly, one representative felt that the last part of operative paragraph 6 of the Soviet draft, beginning with the word "including", should be deleted. Another representative expressed the view that the amendment submitted by the Sudan and the United Arab Republic, and operative paragraph 6 of the Soviet draft, would be improved if they were worded as follows: "Nothing in the foregoing may be interpreted as restricting the scope of the provisions of the Chapter relating to the right of peoples to self-determination." It was also stated that repelling an invader and resisting occupation forces should not be considered acts of aggression.

7. Legal consequences of aggression

(a) The question of responsibility

50. Some representatives expressed objections to operative paragraph 5 of the USSR draft. It was stated that that paragraph raised the problem of the responsibility of individuals under international law - a very difficult and complex problem, consideration of which was outside the terms of reference of the Special Committee, whose task was to define aggression, and not to consider the various legal consequences of the commission of an act of aggression. In the view of other representatives, those objections were groundless as it was impossible, after defining a crime, to say nothing at all about its consequences. Reference was made to the principle nullum crimen nulla poena sine lege, and it was stated that, since the law could not define a crime without prescribing the punishment for it, there could not be any crime without a punishment or, conversely, any punishment without a crime. That meant that there was no crime without responsibility, and that was the principle applied in the Soviet draft. The inclusion of that principle in the draft was also based on another consideration. As it was essential to produce a definition which was clear and precise, all points relating to aggression must be included in the draft definition, and it would therefore be wrong to set aside certain elements for incorporation in other instruments.

(b) Non-recognition of territorial gains

51. The idea expressed in operative paragraph 4 of the USSR draft was considered by some delegations to be out of place in a definition of aggression. Non-recognition of advantages resulting from aggression could not form part of a definition of aggression. Other delegations, however, stated that the question of the consequences of aggression and the question of responsibility were essential elements of the definition of aggression. It was stressed that the definition would be of no value unless it indicated to the organ empowered to apply it - namely, the Security Council - what the responsibility of the aggressor was and what political and moral sanctions should be applied to it under the Charter. Without provisions of that kind, the definition would lose its preventive character and would not be the effective instrument it should be in the hands of the United Nations.

C. VIEWS EXPRESSED ON THE NEW THIRTEEN-POWER DRAFT AND THE SIX-POWER DRAFT (A/AC.134/L.16 and 17)

52. Following its consideration of the draft proposals submitted at the 1968 session and beginning of the 1969 session, summarized above in section III B, the Special Committee held a preliminary discussion on the two additional draft proposals submitted respectively by thirteen and six Powers at the concluding stage of the session (see paras. 10 and 11 above).

53. With regard to the first of the additional drafts, namely, that submitted by the thirteen Powers (A/AC.134/L.16 and Add.1 and 2 - hereinafter referred to as the "new thirteen-Power draft"), several representatives pointed out that it was in a sense a revision of the draft submitted likewise by thirteen Powers at the 1968 Geneva session (A/AC.134/L.6), while taking into account the views set forth in the USSR draft (A/AC.134/L.12) as well as those expressed during the debate on these two latter drafts. On the other hand, some representatives considered that the submission of the second additional draft, namely, that sponsored by six Powers (A/AC.134/L.17 and Add.1 - hereinafter referred to as the "six-Power draft") had been prompted by the fact that none of the other drafts before the Committee had taken account of the views expressed by the delegations of the sponsoring Powers on a number of important issues.

54. Some representatives were of the view that the new thirteen-Power draft, far from encouraging general agreement, only widened the differences of opinion between certain members of the Committee. Several other representatives regarded the six-Power proposal as one which was negative in spirit and could under no circumstances serve as a basis for the Committee's future work. A number of representatives, however, welcomed the submission of the two drafts as a positive contribution to the fulfilment of the Committee's task. In particular, the six-Power proposal was regarded by several representatives as evidence that no delegation had any longer a negative attitude to the principle that aggression should be defined. It was, however, emphasized in this respect that the sponsorship of that proposal did not mean a change in long-standing reservations regarding the usefulness of a definition of aggression.

55. Those representatives who expressed general support for either of the two drafts including the preambular part of one of them, did so mainly in so far as one or the other met the criteria which in their opinion any proposed definition should fulfil. Several representatives were of the view that the new thirteen-Power proposal was compatible with and based on the Charter of the United Nations. Some other representatives held a similar view regarding the six-Power draft. Some representatives stressed that the new thirteen-Power draft represented a considerable step forward and that there was a basis for bringing closer together the provisions of that draft and the provisions of the USSR draft during the course of the Committee's further work. Others felt that the new thirteen-Power draft represented an increasing divergence from sound and reasonable interpretations of the Charter.

56. Some representatives clarified their position on the question of the desirability that a draft definition of aggression should be acceptable to the permanent members of the Security Council emphasizing that that was not a legal requirement but a political one. The minimum constitutional requirement was that the definition should be acceptable to the General Assembly and the Security Council.

57. The lack of a preamble in the six-Power draft was regarded by some representatives as a retrograde step. For some other representatives, the absence of a preamble should not be taken to indicate a negative attitude towards having one or towards the idea of defining aggression.

58. In the opinion of some representatives, the six-Power draft treated aggression merely as a term which was "applicable" or "to be applied", thus reducing the importance of the definition and the work done by the Committee, which had been established not to deal with terminological points but with the principal crime in international law. Other representatives, however, pointed out that the Committee was dealing with the problem of defining the term aggression, that is, with the problem of its proper application, and not with the problem of aggression itself.

1. Application of the definition

(a) The definition and the power of the Security Council

59. In the opinion of a number of representatives, the provisions in the two drafts were without prejudice to the powers and duties of the Security Council as provided in the Charter. It was stated that the words "facilitate that task" had been used in the new thirteen-Power draft instead of "as a guidance" in order to indicate that there was no question of limiting the Security Council's power of determination. Some representatives expressed the view that the Charter did not grant the Security Council discretionary powers; it simply stated that the Council should determine the existence of an act of aggression; the new thirteen-Power draft referred to the "powers and duties" of the Security Council in order to remain faithful to the purposes and principles of the Charter. It was also stated that the six-Power draft preserved the discretionary power of the Security Council as the organ having primary responsibility for the maintenance of peace; this draft would not require the Council to determine the existence of aggression in every case of a breach of the peace, since it allowed for the application of the definition "when appropriate", nor would it require the Council to find that an act of aggression existed even in a case where the circumstances were clearly covered by the definition, that is, there was no element of automaticity in the definition; the non-exhaustive list of possible cases contained in paragraph IV of the proposal was meant to provide general guidance only. It was also pointed out that the six-Power draft was of a very abstract and artificial character which did not contribute towards a clearer idea of the definition of aggression and that the draft could therefore hardly serve to help the Security Council in the discharge of its functions.

(b) Political entities to which the definition should apply

60. A number of representatives drew attention to the second sentence of paragraph II of the six-Power draft, which was intended to ensure that a definition of aggression covered acts by or against those political entities whose claims to statehood might not be universally recognized but upon which the obligations of the Charter and international law as regards the use of force nevertheless fell. Regret was expressed in this connexion that the new thirteen-Power draft had failed to deal with such aspect of the definition of aggression. Other representatives, however, considered that the introduction of

new and irrelevant concepts such as "political entity" complicated instead of
facilitating the Committee's task. It was also said that that concept was
difficult to accept from the point of view of positive international law. The
term "State" should be retained, in keeping with the framework and language of
the Charter, without prejudice to the possibility of its interpretation in a
broader sense, that is, not requiring that the "State" concerned should be
totally and unanimously recognized by all Member States of the United Nations.

2. Acts proposed for inclusion in the concept of aggression

61. Some representatives considered that any definition of aggression must be
based on Article 2 (4) of the Charter and it should state clearly the unlawful
nature of any unjustified use of force. The definition, therefore, should fully
cover aggression involving indirect or covert uses of illegal force intended to
infringe the territorial integrity and the political independence of States. It
was stated that this point was amply covered, first, by the inclusion of the
phrase "overt or covert, direct or indirect" in paragraph II of the six-Power
proposal and, secondly, by the enumeration of certain typical cases of such acts
in paragraph IV; the uses of force which could not constitute aggression under
the terms of the Charter were defined in paragraph III of the proposal. Some
representatives stated that a definition which did not contain an adequate
provision regarding armed bands would make little contribution to the task of
applying the Charter to contemporary facts.

62. Several representatives were of the opinion that acts constituting what was
generally known as indirect aggression should not be placed on the same plane as
direct armed aggression, in particular with respect to the right of self-defence.
It was stated that this point was indicated by operative paragraphs 5 and 7 of
the new thirteen-Power proposal; paragraph 5 was designed to permit the exercise
of the right of self-defence in accordance with Article 51 of the Charter, and
paragraph 7 indicated that certain acts, including those of armed bands, in the
territory of a State were not sufficient cause for that State to have recourse to
the right of self-defence by military action by virtue of Article 51. It was
said in this connexion that the expression "armed attack" used in Article 51 of
the Charter referred directly to the expression "act of aggression" used in
Article 39. In support of this position, a reference was made to the draft
Code of Offences against the Peace and Security of Mankind, in which a distinction
was drawn between acts of aggression, on the one hand, and the organization of
armed bands and coercive measures of an economic or political nature, on the
other. Some representatives further emphasized the danger that indirect armed
aggression such as invasion by armed bands might be invoked not only to exercise
the right of self-defence but also, under cover of that right, to commit
interventions.

63. Other representatives were opposed to the inclusion of any provision
relating to indirect aggression for various reasons such as the following:
indirect aggression fell within the scope of another principle of international
law - namely, the duty of State to refrain from interference in the internal
affairs of other States; the circumstances could differ greatly from one case of
indirect aggression to another; State responsibility was not incurred by moral
support or even overt condonement of acts of indirect aggression; the principle
relating to indirect aggression was irrelevant at the present state of the
Committee's work. Some representatives also expressed doubt about the

advisability of including indirect use of force to the scope of a definition, in view of the difficulties in establishing proof. In this respect, it was pointed out, however, that even in cases of open conflict, it was at times difficult to establish which side had fired first.

64. According to several representatives the concept of aggression as stated in operative paragraph 2 and certain other provisions of the new thirteen-Power draft, if adopted, would amount to a revision of the relevant articles of the Charter such as Articles 2 (4), 51, 53. The approach of the draft was considered also unacceptable to some representatives as it seemed to declare that the question of whether force had been used or not and whether a State had the right to defend itself depended simply on the methods employed.

65. The principle of proportionality was raised concerning the question of subversion by armed bands organized or supported by another State. It was argued that to deny the victim of armed subversion the right to determine for itself whether it was justified to exercise its right of self-defence was fraught with danger at a time when armed subversion was increasingly becoming a substitute for the more conventional methods of armed aggression. Some representatives considered therefore that paragraph 7 of the new thirteen-Power draft should be modified to take account of the fact that, in certain circumstances, the presence of armed bands constituted an imminent danger similar to an armed attack. In this respect it was stated that a formula could be considered which would specify that in the event of a large-scale invasion by armed bands involving imminent danger comparable to that resulting from an armed attack, the victim of the invasion could react as if it were exercising its right of self-defence under Article 51, without first bringing the matter before the Security Council.

66. With regard to the enumeration of acts which constituted acts of aggression, some representatives expressed the view that a legal connexion should be established between the various elements of the enumeration in such a way that, if a State which was the victim of an act of aggression not featuring in the acts enumerated resorted to self-defence, it would not for that reason be considered an aggressor itself. As to the specific enumeration in paragraph IV of the six-Power draft, some representatives considered that insufficient account had been taken of the basic differences among the various means listed in part B, since they alone helped to clarify the very difficult question of distinguishing internal revolts or dissident movements from acts of aggression of external origin. It was also stated that some of the activities listed in paragraph IV B should not be included in the same paragraph with invasion or bombardment, for such activities would not create the same emergency as an open attack against a State.

67. The six-Power proposal was criticized for its failure to refer to the most dangerous aspects of aggression, namely the use of weapons of mass destruction as a means of committing an act of aggression.

3. Aggressive intent

68. Some representatives considered that a definition of aggression should focus on the two elements of unlawful intent and illegality of the act itself. It was stated that that point was met by the formula employed in the six-Power proposal; reference to intent was made in paragraph II, which spoke of acts of aggression

by a State against the territorial integrity or political independence of any other State; in paragraph III, which dealt with the use of force in self-defence or pursuant to decisions of the United Nations or other competent organizations; and in much greater detail in paragraph IV; part A of paragraph IV described the intended effects of a breach of the peace which justified the Security Council in concluding that an act of aggression had been committed and part B listed examples of specific means whereby the intentions described in part A were carried out.

69.   Some representatives pointed out that while paragraph IV of the six-Power draft took full account of the wide variety of the forms of illegal use of force which could constitute aggression under the Charter, the enumeration of intentions and means was illustrative and not exhaustive; there must therefore be cases in which one would have to rely on Article 2 (4) of the Charter, which was the keystone of the six-Power proposal. Some representatives emphasized that it was essential to exclude acts which were unintentional, and that that requirement was met by paragraph IV A (5) of the six-Power proposal. With regard to the view that intentions were often difficult to prove, it was stated that, if the facts of the case were really so unclear that the Security Council could not determine even that the act was intentional, i.e., calculated to inflict the harm which it in fact inflicted, then presumably no one would wish the Security Council to decide that aggression had occurred.

70.   Several representatives, however, did not agree that the approach taken in the six-Power proposal was satisfactory. It was said that, while the intentions of an accused aggressor were no doubt relevant to make a determination of aggression dependent on them would be highly dangerous in the present state of the international community. Moreover such a criterion would hardly be an effective deterrent to potential aggressors. Not only would it be impossible to list all possible intentions, but aggressors always claimed that their goal was a legitimate one. In the view of some representatives the introduction of such subjective elements in the criteria for determining aggression would serve to encourage invasions or other acts ostensibly carried out for purposes not mentioned in paragraph IV of the six-Power proposal. It was also said that the definition must be based on objective, not subjective, criteria, deriving from the nature of the act itself. In that connexion, it was observed that the USSR draft and the new thirteen-Power draft had the advantage of taking only material facts into account, basing themselves particularly on the principle of priority. It was also pointed out that only the Latin American draft (A/AC.134/L.4) and the two thirteen-Power drafts used solely objective criteria.

4.   The principle of priority

71.   Certain representatives pointed out that the principle of the first use of force had been incorporated in operative paragraph 5 of the new thirteen-Power draft but had been omitted from the six-Power proposal. In the opinion of several representatives, that was the only principle on which a definition of aggression could be based. It was further stated that the new thirteen-Power draft, basing itself particularly on the principle of priority, had taken only material facts into account, which made it possible to avoid the difficulties arising from a list of objectives such as that included in paragraph IV of the six-Power draft. Other representatives, however, recalling their previous objections on the matter (see para. 41 above), stressed that the new

thirteen-Power draft had failed to avoid the anomalies attendant upon any effort to substitute the concept of "first use" for the inherent right of self-defence as a criterion for determining the legitimacy of acts of force in international relations. The definition should focus rather than on "first use" on the two elements of unlawful intent and illegality of the act itself as had been done in the six-Power draft.

5. Legitimate uses of force

(a) Self-defence

72. Several representatives noted with satisfaction the inclusion of the inherent right of self-defence in the two additional draft proposals. In the opinion of some representatives the only legitimate exceptions to the Charter's prohibition of the use of force were the inherent right of individual or collective self-defence and participation in measures to maintain or restore international peace and security decided on by the appropriate organs of the United Nations or by other competent bodies. As regards self-defence, the view was expressed that the key questions were at what point in time the right came into being and what kind of action constituted aggression: whether it was sufficient to ask merely who fired the first shot; whether there must be an actual use of force; whether a threat of force could be so serious as to constitute a threat to the peace and, as such, aggression; whether a State which massed troops on its border in order to menace a neighbouring State was guilty of aggression; and whether a country must await the actual use of force before invoking its right of self-defence. It was further stated that the right of self-defence could be exercised, not in response to threats and provocations, but only in response to an armed attack, which must therefore precede it; those who maintained the contrary were drawing their arguments either from analogy with domestic law, where the concept of self-defence was highly developed, or from international law as it had existed prior to the Charter, when force had been accepted as a means of pursuing national policies. Some representatives considered that paragraph III of the six-Power draft had followed a wise course by indicating the general exceptions to the prohibition of force and leaving the Security Council to determine whether those exceptions were applicable in any given instance. In the view of some representatives, it would be even wiser to reproduce in its entirety, in paragraph III, the language of the first paragraph of Article 53 of the Charter.

73. Several representatives supported the inclusion of the principle of proportionality in operative paragraph 6 of the thirteen-Power draft. It was stated that the purpose of the principle was to oblige a State which was the victim of an armed attack and which was using armed force in self-defence to control its reactions and to keep them within the bounds of what was necessary and sufficient to halt the aggression. The view was further expressed that as for the scale of the attack, no one claimed that the right of self-defence was an unlimited right and that it justified an action of any scale without regard for the scale of the attack suffered. Some representatives, however, reserved their position with regard to the principle since in their opinion such a notion was difficult to handle, except if it was regarded as signifying that there was aggression only when the operations were sufficiently serious.

(b) Organs empowered to use force

74. Referring to operative paragraph 1 of the new thirteen-Power draft, some representatives emphasized that it did not prejudge the question of the respective rights and duties of the Security Council and the General Assembly with regard to the maintenance of peace; that was why the text stated that the United Nations only had competence to use force in conformity with the Charter, without specifying the competent body; similarly, the fact that the Security Council was mentioned in operative paragraph 2 of the same draft did not imply that the draft adopted any particular position on the question. In the opinion of some representatives, however, although operative paragraph 1 of the thirteen-Power draft did not prejudice the issue, it was a little too broad. It would be preferable to state unequivocally that the Security Council had competence to determine an act of aggression in accordance with Article 39 of the Charter. It was also argued that operative paragraph 2, read together with operative paragraph 1, clearly decided the issue, depriving the General Assembly of its most important responsibilities for the maintenance of international peace and security. In this connexion reference was made to Article 11 of the Charter and General Assembly resolution 377 (V) "Uniting for Peace".

75. Some representatives referred to the difference of language in paragraphs I and III of the six-Power draft, which referred respectively to the Security Council and "the competent United Nations organs". The latter provision was said to mean that United Nations bodies other than the Security Council could authorize the use of force, a view unacceptable to some representatives. In this respect some representatives pointed out that the Charter conferred "primary" but not sole responsibility on the Council; in certain cases such as those concerning colonial problems the General Assembly could play a role; paragraph III of the six-Power draft covered the cases in which a decision on the use of force had to be made by organs other than the Security Council without prejudging the various points of view regarding the competence of other United Nations organs.

76. In the view of some representatives, operative paragraph 4 of the new thirteen-Power draft, unlike paragraph III of the six-Power draft, was compatible with Article 53 of the Charter. Some representatives considered, however, that the Charter provision had been inaccurately paraphrased in the new thirteen-Power draft, particularly by the use of the terms "armed force" and "decisions" instead of "enforcement action" and "authorization" respectively. In the opinion of some representatives, paragraph III of the six-Power draft was contrary to the letter and spirit of the Charter since it placed regional organizations on the same footing as the United Nations. In their view, the Charter made it perfectly clear that the coercive measures decided upon by regional organizations could not be taken until they were authorized by the Security Council. In this respect, some representatives indicated that the six-Power text used the phrase "consistent with the Charter of the United Nations". It was further stated that a provision authorizing the use of force by regional organizations or arrangements was contained in Article 52 of the Charter, and Article 53 envisaged the granting of a similar authorization in specific circumstances.

6. <u>Acts considered not to constitute acts of aggression</u>

77. Several representatives noted with approval that the new thirteen-Power draft contained, in operative paragraph 10, the principle of the right of peoples to self-determination, sovereignty and territorial integrity. In their view, the exercise of the right of self-determination was rightly included in a draft definition of aggression since it often involved more than one State and helped make clearer that definition by stating what did not constitute aggression; in many instances, colonial situations constituted continued aggression since an external Power was maintaining its domination over the people by military force. A reservation was however made to the second part of paragraph 10 for if there was to be a mention of sovereignty and territorial integrity it should be made plain that it concerned States, and reference should also be made to Article 2 (1) and (4) of the Charter. The six-Power draft was criticized by some representatives not only for completely ignoring the struggle of peoples for their national independence, self-determination and sovereignty, but also for attempting, in their view to give legal sanction to the colonial system by using the expression "territory under the jurisdiction of another State" in paragraph IV B (1) and (3). They considered that in so doing, the six-Power draft introduced a new idea intended to claim that the territory of colonial dependencies was under the jurisdiction of metropolitan Powers, thus contributing to perpetuate the colonial system and encouraging aggression. This interpretation was however rejected by some representatives who considered that the Charter provisions were clear as regards the progress of dependent peoples towards self-government and independence, and who saw no difference between the expression in question and the expression "territory of another State".

7. <u>Legal consequences of aggression</u>

(a) <u>The question of responsibility</u>

78. Some representatives noted with satisfaction the inclusion in the new thirteen-Power draft of the concept of international responsibility for acts of aggression since, in their opinion, the Special Committee's task was to show what was the international crime of aggression and to indicate the consequences of that crime. Other representatives expressed the view that such a notion was no part of a definition of aggression and consequently did not fall within the Committee's terms of reference.

(b) <u>Non-recognition of territorial gains</u>

79. In the opinion of several representatives, the principle of non-recognition of territorial acquisitions obtained by force, contained in operative paragraph 8 of the new thirteen-Power draft and in operative paragraph 4 of the USSR draft, was an essential ingredient in a definition of aggression; it was a principle fully in accordance with the provisions of the Charter, well established by a number of basic international legal instruments and emphasized by the Security Council; further the retention by the aggressor of the fruits of his action made the aggression a continuing crime, a concept which existed in all systems of criminal law. Some representatives, however, regarded the reference to non-recognition as irrelevant or thought that the principle might be placed more appropriately in the preamble rather than in the definition itself since it concerned a legal consequence of the act of aggression.

IV. RECOMMENDATION OF THE SPECIAL COMMITTEE

80. At its 50th meeting, on 28 March, the Special Committee considered the draft resolution submitted by Colombia, Congo (Democratic Republic of), Cyprus, Ecuador, Ghana, Guyana, Haiti, Madagascar, Mexico and Uruguay (A/AC.134/L.18). At the same meeting the representative of Cyprus on behalf of the sponsors orally submitted a revised text of the above draft resolution which the Committee adopted without objection.

The text of the resolution adopted by the Special Committee reads as follows:

"The Special Committee on the Question of Defining Aggression,

"Bearing in mind resolution 2330 (XXII) and 2420 (XXIII) of the General Assembly,

"Recognizing the progress made during this session in the consideration of the question of defining aggression and on a draft definition, as reflected in the report of the Special Committee,

"Noting that new proposals concerning a draft definition of aggression were submitted in 1969,

"Noting also the common will of the members of the Special Committee to continue consideration of the question of defining aggression,

"Noting further that there was not enough time in which to complete its task,

"Recommends to the General Assembly, at its twenty-fourth session, that the Special Committee be asked to resume its work as early as possible in 1970".

ANNEX I

Report of the Working Group of the Whole

1.   The Working Group of the Whole, established by a decision of the Special Committee taken at its 37th meeting on 18 March 1969, held nine meetings from 19 to 27 March 1969.

2.   At its 4th meeting on 20 March 1969 the Working Group, on the basis of a proposal made by the representative of the USSR as amended by the representative of Canada concerning the method of work, decided as follows:

-- To concentrate first, with a view to their formulation, on those paragraphs with respect to which agreement can be reached among all members of the Working Group, not only as to their content but also as to their actual form of words;

- To take up next those paragraphs with respect to which agreement can be reached among all members of the Working Group as to their content although not as to their actual form of words and on which two or more formulations could be submitted;

-- To consider then those paragraphs with respect to which there are grave differences among members of the Working Group and on which alternative formulations could be submitted;

-- To have an initial consideration of all paragraphs to ascertain whether or not there is general agreement on the concepts reflected in each paragraph, leaving aside questions of terminology if there is some disagreement to second reading.

At its 5th meeting on 21 March 1969 the Working Group reaffirmed the foregoing procedural decision.

3.   The representative of Canada in referring to the procedural decision reflected in paragraph 2 above explained that his understanding of the amended proposal as decided on by the Committee, was that the Working Group would leave aside until second reading all disputed questions relating to the actual language of those provisions which might be included in a definition of aggression and would confine itself during first reading to an attempt to place the provisions in the appropriate categories, intended to reflect varying degrees of agreement, as set out in the amended proposal. He was prepared, however, to accept the decision as reflected in paragraph 2 above. The Committee then adopted the proposal as contained in paragraph 2 above.

4.   A number of representatives further expressed the view that the procedural decision referred to in paragraph 2 above, as well as any decisions which the Working Group might take regarding provisions of the proposals under its consideration, would be without prejudice to their positions on the question of their ultimate adoption for inclusion in a definition of aggression.

5.   The Working Group agreed to include the first preambular paragraph of the USSR proposal among those provisions in regard to which there was general agreement as to their content but not as to their particular formulation.

6.   The Working Group agreed to include the fifth preambular paragraph of the USSR proposal, as amended by the representative of France, among those provisions in regard to which there was general agreement both as to their content and to the form of words.   As amended, this preambular paragraph includes the words "make recommendations, or" before the word "decide".   Thus this paragraph, as amended, reads as follows:

    "Recalling also that Article 39 of the Charter states that the Security Council shall determine the existence of any threat to the peace, breach of the peace or act of aggression and shall make recommendations or decide what measures shall be taken in accordance with Articles 41 and 42 to maintain or restore international peace and security".

7.   The Working Group agreed to include the sixth preambular paragraph of the thirteen–Power proposal, as well as the seventh and eighth preambular paragraphs of the USSR proposal, among those provisions in regard to which there was general agreement as to their content but not as to their particular formulation.   It was generally accepted that there was a common core of agreement expressed in these paragraphs, although a number of delegations entered reservations that certain aspects of some of the particular formulations of these paragraphs considered in the Working Group would prejudice their positions of substance in a way unacceptable to them.

ANNEX II

Membership of the Special Committee

ALGERIA

Representative:	Mr. Nourredine Harbi
Alternate:	Mr. Mohamed Berrezoug

AUSTRALIA

Representative:	Sir Kenneth Bailey
Alternate:	Mr. David Wyke Evans

BULGARIA

Representative:	Mrs. Elena Gavrilova
Alternate:	Mr. D. Kostov

CANADA

Representative:	Mr. John Alan Beesley
Alternates:	Mr. D.M. Miller
	Mr. A.W.J. Robertson

COLOMBIA

Representative:	Mr. José María Morales Suárez

CONGO (DEMOCRATIC REPUBLIC OF)

Representative:	Mr. Vincent Mutuale

CYPRUS

Representative:	Mr. Zenon Rossides
Alternates:	Mr. A.J. Jacovides
	Mr. Michael El Sherifis

CZECHOSLOVAKIA

Representatives:	Mr. Ladislav Jahoda
	Mr. Jiří Mladek

ECUADOR

    Representatives: Mr. Leopoldo Benites
                            Mr. Gonzalo Alcívar
                            Mr. Hugo Játiva

FINLAND

    Representative: Mr. Matti Cawén

    Advisers: Mr. Erik Castrén
                            Mr. Tapani Brotherus

FRANCE

    Representatives: Mr. Charles Chaumont
                            Mr. Claude Chayet
                            Miss Sylvie Alvarez

GHANA

    Representative: Mr. R.M. Akwei

    Alternate: Mr. Emmanuel Sam

GUYANA

    Representative: Sir John Carter

    Alternate: Mr. Duke Pollard

HAITI

    Representative: Mr. Max Duplessy

INDONESIA

    Representative: Mr. H. Roeslan Abdulgani

    Alternates: Mr. J.B.P. Maramis
                            Mr. Partono
                            Mr. Suroso Prawirodirdjo

IRAN

    Representative: Mr. Davaud Hermidas Bavand

IRAQ

    Representative: Mr. Mustafa Kamil Yasseen

    Alternate: Mr. Adnan Raouf

    Adviser: Mr. A.A.R. Munir

ITALY

    Representatives: Mr. Francesco Capotorti
                            Mr. Vincenzo Starace

    Alternate: Mr. Joseph Nitti

JAPAN

    Representative: Mr. Hisashi Owada
    Alternate: Mr. Kojiro Takano
    Adviser: Mr. Hiromu Nitta

MADAGASCAR

    Representative: Mr. Armand Rafalihery
    Alternate: Mrs. Reine Raoelina

MEXICO

    Representative: Mr. Sergio González Gálvez
    Alternate: Mr. José Luis Vallarta Marrón

NORWAY

    Representatives: Mr. Peter M. Motzfeldt
                            Mr. Per G. Ravne
                            Mr. Per E.S. Tresselt

ROMANIA

    Representative: Mr. Gheorghe Diaconescu
    Alternate: Mr. Gheorghe Badescu
    Adviser: Mr. Vergiliu Ionescu

SIERRA LEONE

    Alternate: Miss Meliora Taylor

SPAIN

    Representative: Mr. Gabriel Cañadas
    Alternate: Mr. Fernando Arias-Salgado

SUDAN

    Representative: Mr. Fakhreddine Mohamed

    Alternate: Mr. Omer El-Sheikh

SYRIA

    Representative: Mr. M. George J. Tomeh

    Alternates: Mr. Dia-Allah El-Fattal
                                  Mr. Rafic Jouejati

TURKEY

    Representative: Mr. Ahmet Akyamac

    Alternate: Mr. Erkut Onart

UGANDA

    Representatives: Mr. A.M. Ogola
                                  Mr. S. Twine-Bigombe

UNION OF SOVIET SOCIALIST REPUBLICS

    Representative: Mr. Viktor H. Chkhikvadzé

    Alternates: Mr. E.N. Nasinovsky
                                  Mr. D.N. Kolesnik

    Advisers: Mr. V.I. Menjinsky
                                  Mr. O.V. Bodganov

UNITED ARAB REPUBLIC

    Representative: Mr. Abdullah El-Erian

    Alternate: Mr. M.M. El Baradei

UNITED KINGDOM OF GREAT BRITAIN AND NORTHERN IRELAND

    Representative: Mr. H.G. Darwin

    Alternates: Mr. P.J.S. Moon
                                Miss S.M. Harden

UNITED STATES OF AMERICA

    Representative: Mr. John Lawrence Hargrove

    Alternates: Mr. Robert B. Rosenstock
                                Mr. Everett E. Briggs

URUGUAY

    Representative: Mr. Pedro P. Berro

    Alternate: Mr. Alberto D. Fajardo

YUGOSLAVIA

    Representative: Mr. Živojin Jazič

    Adviser: Mrs. Gordana Diklić-Trajković

United Nations
GENERAL ASSEMBLY
Official Records

DOCUMENT 17

Agenda item 88

ANNEXES

TWENTY-FOURTH SESSION

NEW YORK, 1969

Agenda item 88:* Report of the Special Committee on the Question of Defining Aggression**

CONTENTS

---

* For the discussion of this item, see *Official Records of the General Assembly, Twenty-Fourth Session, Sixth Committee,* 1164th to 1170th meetings; *ibid., Fifth Committee,* 1345th meeting; and *ibid., Plenary Meetings,* 1831st meeting.

** This question has been discussed by the General Assembly at the twenty-second session under agenda item 95 and at the twenty-third session under agenda item 86.

DOCUMENT A/C.5/1278

Administrative and financial implications of the draft resolution submitted by the Sixth Committee in document A/7853

Note by the Secretary-General

[Original text: English]
[5 December 1969]

1. At its 1169th meeting, on 3 December 1969, the Sixth Committee adopted a draft resolution (A/7853, para. 25). Under the terms of the draft resolution, the General Assembly would: (*a*) decide that the Special Committee on the Question of Defining Aggression shall resume its work in accordance with General Assembly resolution 2330 (XXII), in Geneva, in the second half of 1970; (*b*) request the Secretary-General to provide the Special Committee with the necessary facilities and services; and (*c*) decide to include in the provisional agenda of its twenty-fifth session an item entitled "Report of the Special Committee on the Question of Defining Aggression".

2. In estimating the cost of this proposal, the Secretary-General has assumed that the Special Committee would meet for a period of five weeks, from 13 July to 14 August 1970, on the assumption that the meetings could be integrated into the calendar of meetings drawn up by the Committee of Conferences. On this basis, it has been estimated that an additional appropriation of $103,200 would be required in the budget estimates for the financial year 1970. This estimate is based on the assumption that the Special Committee would hold two meetings a day for which interpretation and summary records in English, French, Russian and Spanish would be provided, and that the in-session documenta-

tion other than the summary records would not exceed 120 pages. The provision of these services would make it necessary to recruit 8 interpreters, 22 translator/précis-writers, 8 revisers, 22 stenographer/typists, 1 secretary, 1 meetings-service officer and 3 technicians. In addition, 7 substantive staff members would have to be sent from New York to service the meetings. Accordingly, the total cost of convening the 1970 session of the Special Committee at Geneva would therefore be as follows:

	United States dollars
(*a*) Staff to be recruited at Geneva	90,500
(*b*) In-session documentation and provisional and final summary records	8,000
(*c*) Travel and subsistence for substantive staff to be sent from New York	4,700
TOTAL	103,200

3. Accordingly, should the General Assembly adopt the draft resolution submitted by the Sixth Committee, an additional appropriation of $103,200 would be required under section 2 (Special meetings and conferences) of the budget estimates for the financial year 1970. The final arrangements with respect to the session would be subject to the recommendations of the Committee on Conferences.

1

Annexes (XXIV) 88

DOCUMENT A/7838

Report of the Advisory Committee on Administrative and Budgetary Questions

[*Original text: English*]
[*8 December 1969*]

1. The Advisory Committee on Administrative and Budgetary Questions has considered the note by the Secretary-General (A/C.5/1278) on the administrative and financial implications of the draft resolution submitted by the Sixth Committee (A/7853, para. 25). Under the terms of this draft resolution the General Assembly would decide that the Special Committee on the Question of Defining Aggression should resume its work, in accordance with General Assembly resolution 2330 (XXII), in Geneva, in the second half of 1970, and request the Secretary-General to provide it with the necessary facilities and services. An item on the report of the Special Committee would be inscribed in the provisional agenda of the General Assembly at its twenty-fifth session.

2. In estimating the administrative and financial implications of this draft resolution, the Secretary-General has assumed that the Special Committee would meet from 13 July to 14 August 1970, a period of five weeks, provided that its meetings could be integrated into the calender of meetings drawn up by the Committee on Conferences. On this basis he estimates that an additional appropriation of $103,200 would be needed under section 2 (Special meetings and conferences) of the budget estimates for the financial year 1970, as follows:

[*Table identical with that appearing in document A/C.5/1278, paragraph 2, above.*]

3. In its consideration of the above estimate of financial implications, the Advisory Committee noted that the dates provisionally selected for the session of the Special Committee overlap to a considerable degree the period during which the Economic and Social Council is scheduled to hold its forty-ninth session in Geneva, and that this could have a significant impact on the number of staff that the Secretary-General would need to recruit locally. The Advisory Committee was informed that the proposed timing reflected a desire that the session of the Special Committee should follow the session of the International Law Commission, scheduled for the period from 4 May to 10 July 1970, also in Geneva.

4. Moreover, the Advisory Committee understands that basically the same substantive staff from Headquarters would service the meetings of the International Law Commission and of the Special Committee, as well as those of the Special Committee on Principles of International Law concerning Friendly Relations and Co-operation among States, which have been scheduled for the period from 31 March to 1 May 1970.[1] The Secretary-General's estimate of requirements referred to in item (*c*) of the table appearing in paragraph 2 above reflects these arrangements.

5. On this basis, and subject to any recommendations by the Committee on Conferences as to arrangements for the proposed session, the Advisory Committee concurs in the Secretary-General's estimate of overall financial implications of the draft resolution of the Sixth Committee. The Fifth Committee may therefore wish to inform the General Assembly, that, if it adopts the draft resolution, an additional appropriation of $103,200 will be required under section 2 of the budget estimates for 1970.

6. In connexion with the points raised in paragraph 4 above, the Advisory Committee would point out that provision for travel for substantive staff from New York to Geneva for the session of the International Law Commission has been made under section 5, chapter I (Travel of staff to meetings) of the budget estimates for 1970;[2] furthermore, provision for similar travel was included in the estimate of requirements arising from a session of the Special Committee on Principles of International Law concerning Friendly Relations and Co-operation among States.[1] Should the latter session be held at Geneva, the Advisory Committee would therefore believe that some savings could automatically be expected under section 5, chapter I, item (vi) (International Law Commission), of the budget for 1970.

---

[1] See *Official Records of the General Assembly, Twenty-fourth Session, Annexes*, agenda item 89, document A/7831.
[2] *Ibid., Twenty-fourth Session, Supplement No. 6*, vol. I, para. 5.4 (vi).

DOCUMENT A/7853

Report of the Sixth Committee

[*Original text: French*]
[*10 December 1969*]

CONTENTS

I. INTRODUCTION

1. During its twenty-second session, on 18 December 1967, the General Assembly, on the recommendation of the Sixth Committee,[3] adopted resolution 2330 (XXII), establishing a Special Committee on the Question of Defining Aggression and defining its composition and terms of reference.

2. The Special Committee established pursuant to that resolution met at the United Nations Office at

---

[3] For the report of the Sixth Committee, see *Official Records of the General Assembly, Twenty-second Session, Annexes* agenda item 95, document A/6988.

Geneva from 4 June to 6 July 1968, and prepared a report[4] which the General Assembly, on 27 September 1968, included in the agenda for the twenty-third session, allocating it to the Sixth Committee for consideration. On 18 December 1968, the Assembly, on the recommendation of the Sixth Committee,[5] adopted resolution 2420 (XXIII), in which it decided that the Special Committee on the Question of Defining Aggression should resume its work, in accordance with General Assembly resolution 2330 (XXII), as early as possible in 1969.

3. In accordance with that resolution, the Special Committee on the Question of Defining Aggression reconvened at United Nations Headquarters in New York from 24 February to 3 April 1969, and prepared a report (A/7620) containing a summary of the views expressed in the Special Committee on certain general aspects of the question of defining aggression, and on the various draft proposals submitted to it at its 1968 and 1969 sessions. The report also contained the text of a resolution adopted by the Special Committee, in which it noted that there was not enough time in which to complete its task and recommended to the General Assembly, at its twenty-fourth session, that the Special Committee be asked to resume its work as early as possible in 1970.

4. At its 1758th plenary meeting, on 20 September 1969, the General Assembly decided to include in the agenda for its twenty-fourth session the item entitled "Report of the Special Committee on the Question of Defining Aggression", and allocated it to the Sixth Committee, which considered it at its 1164th to 1170th meetings, held from 1 to 4 December 1969.

5. At its 1169th meeting, on 3 December, the Sixth Committee decided that its report on that agenda item should contain a summary of the general juridical views expressed during the debate, the financial implications of such a summary having previously been brought to its attention in accordance with General Assembly resolution 2292 (XXII).

II. Draft resolution submitted to the Sixth Committee

6. The draft resolution submitted by Algeria, Bolivia, Central African Republic, Chad, Cyprus, Dahomey, Ecuador, Ethiopia, Ghana, Greece, Guyana, Haiti, India, Jamaica, Kenya, Libya, Mali, Mexico, Mongolia, Morocco, Nicaragua, Niger, Pakistan, Paraguay, Peru, Romania, Sierra Leone, Southern Yemen, Sudan, Syria, Tunisia, Uganda, Union of Soviet Socialist Republics, United Arab Republic, United Republic of Tanzania and Yugoslavia (A/C.6/L.785) was introduced at the 1168th meeting by the representative of Ghana on behalf of the sponsors.

[*For the text of the draft resolution, see para. 25 below.*]

III. Debate

A. *Views expressed on certain general aspects of the question of defining aggression*

7. Most of the representatives who spoke said it was both possible and desirable to define the concept of

---

[4] *Ibid., Twenty-third Session,* agenda item 86, document A/7185/Rev.1.
[5] For the report of the Sixth Committee, see *Official Records of the General Assembly, Twenty-third Session, Annexes,* agenda item 86, document A/7402.

aggression, as the General Assembly had affirmed as early as its sixth session in resolution 599 (VI) of 31 January 1952. In that connexion, reference was also made to the progress achieved by the Special Committee on the Question of Defining Aggression and to the fact that one of the draft definitions submitted to that Committee had been co-sponsored by countries which had often expressed misgivings about the possibility and desirability of defining aggression. It was also observed that a definition of aggression was particularly important in view of the current international situation and the arms race, which was endangering world peace and security. The formulation of a satisfactory definition of aggression could only further the cause of peace. The Security Council would find such a definition very useful in exercising the functions assigned to it by the Charter of the United Nations. It would constitute an important step forward in the codification and progressive development of international law. It was pointed out that, until a definition of aggression was formulated, several international instruments, such as the draft Code of Offences Against the Peace and Security of Mankind and the question of international criminal jurisdiction, would remain in abeyance. Furthermore, a definition adopted by the General Assembly would facilitate international efforts to safeguard the sovereignty, independence and territorial integrity of States in the cases of threat or use of force which now occurred, particularly against small countries. Such a definition would not, of course, completely discourage a potential aggressor, but it would at least help the United Nations to expose the aggressor and establish his international responsibility. It was also observed that a definition of aggression approved by a large majority of countries would strengthen the part played by law within the United Nations and would eliminate the element of indecision and subjectivity which characterized any political judgement for which the law failed to establish guidelines.

8. On the other hand, some representatives felt that it was neither possible nor desirable to define the concept of aggression. It was observed that the submission of the six-Power draft proposal (see A/7620, para. 11) to the Special Committee on the Question of Defining Aggression did not mean that the sponsors of that proposal had abandoned their long-standing scepticism about the usefulness of the definition of aggression. They had submitted their proposal because the other drafts submitted thus far to the Special Committee not only failed to provide a satisfactory definition but had in fact helped to accentuate rather than resolve the differences of opinion in that Committee. The view was expressed that the adoption of a definition would be superfluous and might even hinder the operations of the United Nations in the field of international peace and security. It was also observed that attempts to define aggression would not promote the codification and progressive development of international law. Although it was recognized that aggression played a part in international relations, it was felt that for the time being it would not be opportune to define the concept of aggression.

9. Most of the representatives who spoke supported the proposal that the Special Committee should resume its work in 1970 in order that it might try to complete its work, if possible, before the twenty-fifth anniversary of the United Nations. Some representatives, however, considered that the problem entrusted to the Special Committee was very complex and deserved

the full attention not only of the members of the Committee itself but of the Members of the United Nations in general. The view was therefore expressed that it would be more expedient not to convene the Special Committee until 1971 or 1972, so that the Secretary-General could study any relevant proposals received from States Members of the United Nations.

10. Several representatives expressed the view that in order to be satisfactory any definition of aggression should conform to and be based on the Charter. It should also be supported by the large majority of the States Members of the United Nations, including all the permanent members of the Security Council. The latter condition was, however, contested by some representatives, who considered it incompatible with the Charter and in particular with the basic principle of the sovereign equality of States. The view was expressed that in the adoption of a definition of aggression there should be no hesitation about resorting, if necessary, to the procedures used in the General Assembly, namely, the rule of the majority.

11. Certain representatives supported the view that the definition should safeguard the discretionary power of the Security Council, the United Nations organ which bore the main responsibility for the maintenance of peace. In connexion with that view, it was explained that leaving the Security Council the discretionary power to determine the existence of a case of aggression did not mean that the Council, in exercising its functions, would not be obliged to take account of the relevant provisions of international law. Some representatives, on the other hand, considered that if the definition was to be useful it must be binding on the organ called upon to apply it. The view was also expressed that the definition, while being based on the concept of the discretionary power of the Security Council, should not make that power exclusive to the point where a deadlock in the Security Council would prevent other competent United Nations organs, particularly the General Assembly, from taking a decision concerning the existence of a case of aggression; according to the Charter, the Security Council bore the main, but not the exclusive, responsibility for the maintenance of international peace and security.

12. Some representatives considered that the definition should be expressly applicable to entities not generally recognized as States. Other representatives said that the definition should refer only to "States" and avoid any excessively general expression such as "political entities"; the Security Council should be left a measure of discretionary power in that connexion.

13. Several representatives said that the definition should be limited exclusively to aggression resulting from the direct use of armed force. It was felt that the incorporation into the definition of varied and imprecise acts to which a State might be subjected would confer upon Article 2, paragraph 4, of the Charter an exclusive meaning which it did not have; such an extension of the concept of aggression would also lead to the legitimation of acts of individual or collective self-defence which were prohibited under Article 51 of the Charter, which authorized self-defence only in the case of armed attack. On the other hand, other representatives considered that the concept of indirect or covert uses of force must be included in any definition for it to conform to the Charter. Forms of the use of force such as the infiltration of armed bands, terrorism or subversion represented just as

great a threat to international peace and security as other forms of physical force and consequently were comprised in the term "aggression" as used in the Charter. It should be possible to exercise the right of individual or collective self-defence provided for in the Charter against both direct and indirect forms of the illegal use of force. Moreover, some representatives felt that the definition should encompass all the forms of aggression which did not involve the use of armed force, such as economic, financial and political pressures, which could be just as dangerous as military aggression.

14. Some representatives considered that the inclusion in the definition of a provision condemning weapons of mass destruction would be very appropriate and useful, for it would back up United Nations efforts to prohibit such weapons. Other representatives, on the other hand, felt that it would be unnecessary to specify in the definition the nature of the weapons used.

15. According to some representatives, *animus aggressionis* should be taken into account in the formulation of a definition of aggression. They pointed out that the element of intent could be determined by examination of objective facts and that it served the purpose, *inter alia,* of excluding *de minimis* incidents which no one could claim were acts of aggression justifying the application of the provisions of Chapter VII of the Charter. In the view of several representatives, however, the definition should be based not on intent, which was a subjective element, but on the objectivity of the act. In that connexion, it was said that the element of intent would be virtually impossible to establish as far as States were concerned and that it could operate as a sanction for anticipatory attacks and enable them to be passed off as preparations justified by the exercise of the right of self-defence.

16. The principle of priority was criticized by some representatives as being incompatible with the Charter. Objections were raised to it in connexion with certain draft proposals submitted to the Special Committee and reviewed below. Several representatives, on the other hand, were in favour of including the principle of priority in the definition. The notion of first use was stated to be of fundamental importance. It was a logical and inevitable idea, and even greater problems would be created by trying to do without it, since those who argued that the question was not who had crossed the frontier first or had attacked first but who had prepared for war overlooked the fact that in reality preparation for war was inseparable from the arms race; it would be impossible to identify the aggressor unless a historical and strategical study was made, and it must be remembered that it was very difficult to distinguish between preparations connected with self-defence and preparation for a war of aggression. The point was also made that although the principle of priority was certainly very difficult to apply, that was no justification for ignoring it; the definition should take the principle into account and leave it to the Security Council to judge the issue in the light of the facts.

17. With regard to the legitimate use of force, several representatives stressed the need to include in the definition of aggression a clear and precise provision recognizing the right of individual and collective self-defence as provided for in the Charter. It was observed in that connexion that even where the righ

of self-defence represented a response to armed aggression, it was a restricted right which should not detract from the right of the Security Council to act in the interest of the maintenance of international peace and security; any definition of aggression should be based on Article 51 of the Charter as far as the right of self-defence was concerned. It was also stated that the exercise of that right should be recognized only as a means of defence to be used by a victim of an act of aggression for the sole purpose of repelling the aggressor; it would operate as a sanction against the aggressor and not as an exception to the principle of the non-use of force, which would preclude any possibility of the right being exercised for preventive purposes. With regard to the legitimate use of force by regional agencies, some representatives pointed out that under Article 53 of the Charter those agencies were prohibited from taking enforcement action without the authorization of the Security Council; that point needed to be spelt out in the definition. Other representatives stated that such a view was restrictive and was contrary to Articles 52 and 53 of the Charter.

18. Several representatives maintained that the definition should contain a clause recognizing the right of dependent peoples to use force in the exercise of their right to self-determination. It was stated in that connexion that the use of force against a people exercising its right to self-determination would constitute a flagrant violation of the Charter.

19. Some representatives referred to the question of the legal consequences of aggression. The view was expressed that the definition should contain a clause establishing the responsibility of the aggressor and laying down the principle that any gains he obtained should not be recognized.

B. *Views expressed on the drafts submitted to the Special Committee*

20. The discussion centred mainly on the USSR draft (see A/7620, para. 9), the thirteen-Power draft (*ibid.*, para. 10) and the six-Power draft (*ibid.*, para. 11) submitted to the Special Committee on 26 February and 24 and 25 March 1969 respectively.

21. Several representatives supported the USSR and thirteen-Power drafts in principle. It was observed that those texts revealed a substantial convergence of attitudes with regard to the fundamental principles on which the definition of aggression should be based. With regard to the USSR draft, it was observed that operative paragraph 1, taken in conjunction with the eighth preambular paragraph, implied the existence of forms of aggression other than armed aggression, whereas within the meaning of the Charter the concept of aggression was confined to acts involving the use of armed or physical force. Moreover, the possible consequences of the criterion of first use as embodied in the USRR draft were felt to be unacceptable. It was said that the rigid application of that criterion by the USSR draft signified disregard for Article 2, paragraph 4, of the Charter, which prohibited not only the use of force but also the threat of force. It was further stated that operative paragraph 2 C of the USSR draft excessively circumscribed those indirect forms of the use of force which could constitute acts of aggression. It was observed that the idea expressed in operative paragraph 3 of the USSR draft ought not to be included in the definition; the Security Council should not have the power to classify acts as acts of aggression

unless they were included in the definition. The fourth preambular paragraph of the USSR draft was criticized as suggesting that the use of force would be permitted among States with similar social systems.

22. The thirteen-Power draft was said to deviate from the Charter scheme by arbitrarily excluding the indirect or covert use of force from the concept of aggression as conceived in the Charter, thus, *inter alia,* denying in certain serious cases of aggression, the right of self-defence which the Charter allowed the victims. It was also said that paragraph 2 of that draft constituted a revision of Article 2, paragraph 4, of the Charter and that paragraph 4 of the draft conflicted with Article 53 of the Charter; similarly, paragraphs 1 and 2 of the draft tended to conflict with Charter law by depriving the General Assembly of its fundamental responsibilities regarding the maintenance of international peace and security. According to one representative, paragraph 2 of the thirteen-Power draft seemed to support an unacceptable view—that some United Nations organs other than the Security Council were competent to use force in conformity with the Charter.

23. In the opinion of some representatives, the six-Power draft tended to place the *onus probandi* on the victim of aggression by emphasizing the psychological aspects of aggression—the *animus aggressionis*—at the expense of the material elements. In addition, it failed to provide for some very important elements in aggression; in particular, it did not refer to the right of dependent peoples to use armed force in the exercise of their right to self-determination, and it placed regional organizations on the same footing as the United Nations, contrary to Article 53 of the Charter.

IV. VOTING

24. At its 1169th meeting, on 3 December 1969, the Sixth Committee took a vote on the draft resolution before it (A/C.6/L.785).

(*a*) At the request of the representative of the United Republic of Tanzania, a roll-call vote was taken on a proposal of the Belgian representative that the words "the urgency of defining aggression and" in the fifth preambular paragraph of the draft resolution be deleted. The Belgian proposal was rejected by 56 votes to 15, with 13 abstentions. The voting was as follows:

In favour: Australia, Belgium, Canada, Denmark, Israel, Italy, Japan, Netherlands, New Zealand, Norway, Portugal, South Africa, Sweden, United Kingdom of Great Britain and Northern Ireland, United States of America.

Against: Afghanistan, Algeria, Bulgaria, Burma, Byelorussian Soviet Socialist Republic, Central African Republic, Ceylon, Chad, Chile, Congo (Brazzaville), Congo (Democratic Republic of), Cuba, Cyprus, Ethiopia, Finland, Ghana, Greece, Guatemala, Guyana, Haiti, Hungary, India, Indonesia, Iran, Iraq, Ivory Coast, Jamaica, Lebanon, Libya, Mali, Mexico, Mongolia, Morocco, Niger, Pakistan, Peru, Philippines, Poland, Romania, Saudi Arabia, Sierra Leone, Southern Yemen, Spain, Sudan, Syria, Thailand, Togo, Trinidad and Tobago, Tunisia, Uganda, Ukrainian Soviet Socialist Republic, Union of Soviet Socialist Republics, United Arab Republic, United Republic of Tanzania, Yugoslavia, Zambia.

Abstaining: Argentina, Austria, Barbados, Brazil, Cameroon, Colombia, France, Ireland, Liberia, Mauritius, Turkey, Uruguay, Venezuela.

(*b*) The Committee then voted on a proposal of the United Kingdom representative that the words "at Geneva in the second half of" in operative paragraph 1 of the draft resolution be replaced by the word "in". The United Kingdom proposal was rejected by 46 votes to 16, with 22 abstentions.

(*c*) The draft resolution was adopted without change by 68 votes to 1, with 15 abstentions.

Recommendation of the Sixth Committee

25. The Sixth Committee therefore recommends to the General Assembly the adoption of the following draft resolution:

REPORT OF THE SPECIAL COMMITTEE ON THE QUESTION OF DEFINING AGGRESSION

The General Assembly,

Having considered the report of the Special Committee on the Question of Defining Aggression on the work of its session held in New York from 24 February to 3 April 1969,

Taking note of the progress made by the Special Committee in its consideration of the question of defining aggression and on the draft definition, as reflected in the report of the Special Committee,

Considering that it was not possible for the Special Committee to complete its task, in particular its consideration of the proposals concerning a draft definition of aggression submitted to the Special Committee during its sessions held in 1968 and 1969,

Considering that in its resolutions 2330 (XXII) of 18 December 1967 and 2420 (XXIII) of 18 December 1968 the General Assembly affirmed the widespread conviction of the need to expedite the definition of aggression,

Considering the urgency of defining aggression and the desirability of achieving this objective, if possible, by the twenty-fifth anniversary of the United Nations,

1. *Decides* that the Special Committee on the Question of Defining Aggression shall resume its work, in accordance with General Assembly resolution 2330 (XXII), at Geneva in the second half of 1970;

2. *Requests* the Secretary-General to provide the Special Committee with the necessary facilities and services;

3. *Decides* to include in the provisional agenda of its twenty-fifth session an item entitled "Report of the Special Committee on the Question of Defining Aggression".

[*Text adopted by the General Assembly without change. See "Action taken by the General Assembly" below.*]

DOCUMENT A/7861

Administrative and financial implications of the draft resolution submitted by the Sixth Committee in document A/7853

Report of the Fifth Committee

[*Original text: English*]
[*10 December 1969*]

1. At its 1345th meeting, on 9 December 1969, the Fifth Committee, in compliance with rule 154 of the rules of procedure of the General Assembly considered the note by the Secretary-General (A/C.5/1278) and the report of the Advisory Committee on Administrative and Budgetary Questions (A/7838) with respect to the administrative and financial implications of the draft resolution contained in paragraph 25 of the report of the Sixth Committee (A/7853).

2. Under the terms of the draft resolution the General Assembly would: (*a*) decide that the Special Committee on the Question of Defining Aggression shall resume its work, in accordance with General Assembly resolution 2330 (XXII), at Geneva in the second half of 1970; (*b*) request the Secretary-General to provide the Special Committee with the necessary facilities and services; and (*c*) decide to include in the provisional agenda of its twenty-fifth session an item entitled "Report of the Special Committee on the Question of Defining Aggression".

3. In his note the Secretary-General indicated that the cost of convening a meeting of the Special Committee in Geneva for approximately five weeks, from 13 July to 14 August 1970, would amount to $103,200. This estimate provides for two meetings a day with interpretation and summary records in English,

French, Russian and Spanish and in-session documentation not to exceed 120 pages. The provision of these services would make it necessary to recruit 8 interpreters, 22 translator/précis-writers, 8 revisers, 22 stenographer/typists, 1 secretary, 1 meetings-service officer and 3 technicians. In addition, 7 substantive staff members would have to be sent from New York to service the meetings. The total cost of convening the 1970 session of the Special Committee in Geneva was therefore estimated as follows:

	United States dollars
(*a*) Staff to be recruited in Geneva	90,500
(*b*) In-session documentation, provisional and final summary records	8,000
(*c*) Travel and subsistence for substantive staff to be sent from New York	4,700
TOTAL	103,200

4. In concurring with the estimates of requirements submitted by the Secretary-General above, the Advisory Committee indicated that its approval was subject to any recommendations by the Committee on Conferences as to the arrangements for the proposed session of the Special Committee. In this connexion, the Advisory Committee drew attention to the fact that

provision had already been made for the travel of substantive staff from New York to Geneva for the session of the International Law Commission[6] from 4 May to 10 July 1970 and for a session of the Special Committee on Principles of International Law concerning Friendly Relations and Co-operation among States from 31 March to 1 May 1970. Since the Advisory Committee understood that the substantive staff from Headquarters to service the meetings of the International Law Commission, the Special Committee on Principles of International Law concerning Friendly Relations and Co-operation among States and the Special Committee on the Question of Defining Aggression would be basically the same, the Advisory Committee felt that some savings could be expected under section 5, chapter I (Travel of staff to meetings),

item (vi) (International Law Commission), of the budget for 1970.

5. During the discussions on this question, one delegation indicated that it would have wished to vote against the proposal of the Sixth Committee, since it believed the proposal to be inconsistent with the pattern of conferences established by the Committee on Conferences.

6. Accordingly, the Fifth Committee wishes to inform the General Assembly that, should the Assembly adopt the draft resolution of the Sixth Committee and the recommendation of the Fifth Committee concerning the pattern of Conferences,[7] an additional appropriation of $103,200 would be required under section 2 (Special meetings and conferences) of the budget estimates for 1970.

---

[6] See *Official Records of the General Assembly, Twenty-fourth Session, Supplement No. 6*, vol. I, para. 5.4 (vi).

[7] *Ibid., Twenty-fourth Session, Annexes*, agenda item 76, document A/7914, para. 16.

ACTION TAKEN BY THE GENERAL ASSEMBLY

At its 1831st plenary meeting, on 12 December 1969, the General Assembly adopted the draft resolution submitted by the Sixth Committee (A/7853, para. 25) by a vote of 83 to 1, with 18 abstentions. For the final text, see *Official Records of the General Assembly, Twenty-fourth Session, Supplement No. 30*, resolution 2549 (XXIV).

CHECK LIST OF DOCUMENTS

NOTE. This check list includes the documents mentioned during the consideration of agenda item 88 which are not reproduced in the present fascicle.

Document No.	Title or description	Observations and references
A/7620	Report of the Special Committee on the Question of Defining Aggression (24 February-3 April 1969)	*Official Records of the General Assembly, Twenty-fourth session, Supplement No. 20*
A/C.5/L.785	Algeria, Bolivia, Central African Republic, Chad, Cyprus, Dahomey, Ecuador, Ethiopia, Ghana, Greece, Guyana, Haiti, India, Jamaica, Kenya, Libya, Mali, Mexico Mongolia, Morocco, Nicaragua, Niger, Pakistan, Paraguay, Peru, Romania, Sierra Leone, Southern Yemen, Sudan, Syria, Tunisia, Uganda, Union of Soviet Socialist Republics, United Arab Republic, United Arab of Tanzania and Yugoslavia: draft resolution	Adopted without change. See A/7853, para. 6
A/C.6/L.786	Administrative and financial implications of the draft resolution submitted by the Sixth Committee in document A/7853: note by the Secretary-General	Mimeographed

DOCUMENT 18

Twenty-Fifth Session, Report of Special Committee,
Supp. No. 19 A/8019, 13 Jul. - 14 Aug.

I.   INTRODUCTION

1.   At its twenty-second session, on 18 December 1967, the General Assembly adopted, on the recommendation of the Sixth Committee, 1/ resolution 2330 (XXII), by which it established a Special Committee on the Question of Defining Aggression, specified its composition and defined its terms of reference.

2.   The Special Committee set up under this resolution met at the United Nations Office at Geneva from 4 June to 6 July 1968 and prepared a report 2/ which, on 27 September 1968, the General Assembly included in the agenda of its twenty-third session and referred to the Sixth Committee for consideration. On 18 December 1968, the General Assembly, on the recommendation of the Sixth Committee, 3/ adopted resolution 2420 (XXIII), by which it decided that the "Special Committee on the Question of Defining Aggression shall resume its work, in accordance with General Assembly resolution 2330 (XXII), as early as possible in 1969".

3.   In accordance with this resolution, the Special Committee on the Question of Defining Aggression met at United Nations Headquarters, New York, from 24 February to 3 April 1969 and prepared a report 4/ which, on 20 September 1969, the General Assembly included in the agenda of its twenty-fourth session and referred to the Sixth Committee for consideration. On 12 December 1969, the General Assembly, on the recommendation of the Sixth Committee, 5/ adopted resolution 2549 (XXIV), which reads as follows:

"The General Assembly,

"Having considered the report of the Special Committee on the Question of Defining Aggression on the work of its session held in New York from 24 February to 3 April 1969,

"Taking note of the progress made by the Special Committee in its consideration of the question of defining aggression and on the draft definition, as reflected in the report of the Special Committee,

"Considering that it was not possible for the Special Committee to complete its task, in particular its consideration of the proposals concerning a draft definition of aggression submitted to the Special Committee during its sessions held in 1968 and 1969,

---

1/   Official Records of the General Assembly, Twenty-second Session, Annexes, agenda item 95, document A/6988, para. 21.

2/   Ibid., Twenty-third Session, agenda item 86, document A/7185/Rev.1.

3/   Ibid., Annexes, agenda item 86, document A/7402, para. 31.

4/   Ibid., Twenty-fourth Session, Supplement No. 20 (A/7620).

5/   Ibid., Twenty-fourth Session, Annexes, agenda item 88, document A/7853, para. 25.

"Considering that in its resolutions 2330 (XXII) of 18 December 1967 and 2420 (XXIII) of 18 December 1968 the General Assembly recognized the widespread conviction of the need to expedite the definition of aggression,

"Considering the urgency of defining aggression and the desirability of achieving this objective, if possible, by the twenty-fifth anniversary of the United Nations,

"1. Decides that the Special Committee on the Question of Defining Aggression shall resume its work, in accordance with General Assembly resolution 2330 (XXII), at Geneva in the second half of 1970;

"2. Requests the Secretary-General to provide the Special Committee with the necessary facilities and services;

"3. Decides to include in the provisional agenda of its twenty-fifth session an item entitled 'Report of the Special Committee on the Question of Defining Aggression'."

4. In accordance with this resolution, the Special Committee on the Question of Defining Aggression, whose composition is given in paragraph 2 of its report on the work of its 1968 session, met at the United Nations Office at Geneva from 13 July to 14 August 1970. With the exception of Czechoslovakia, Haiti and Sierra Leone, all the States members of the Special Committee took part in its work. The list of representatives attending the 1970 session is reproduced in annex III to this report.

5. At its 53rd meeting, on 14 July, the Special Committee elected the following officers:

Chairman: Mr. Fakhreddine Mohamed (Sudan)

Vice-Chairmen: Mr. Zenon Rossides (Cyprus)
                   Mr. Gonzalo Alcívar (Ecuador)
                   Mr. G. Badesco (Romania)

Rapporteur: Mr. E.F. Ofstad (Norway)

6. The session was opened on behalf of the Secretary-General by Mr. Anatoly P. Movchan, Director of the Codification Division of the Office of Legal Affairs, who also represented the Secretary-General at the session and acted as Secretary of the Special Committee. Mr. Chafic Malek served as Deputy Secretary. Mr. Tatsuro Kunugi and Mr. Eduardo Valencia-Ospina served as Assistant Secretaries.

7. At its 53rd meeting, on 14 July, the Special Committee adopted the following agenda (A/AC.134/6):

(1) Opening of the session.

(2) Election of officers.

(3) Adoption of the agenda.

(4)   Organization of work.

(5)   Consideration of the question of defining aggression
      (General Assembly resolutions 2330 (XXII), 2420 (XXIII) and
      2549 (XXIV)).

(6)   Adoption of the report.

8.   At its 54th meeting, on 15 July, the Special Committee decided to devote
five meetings to a general discussion of the three draft proposals before it
(see paragraph 10 below).   At its 61st meeting, on 23 July, it decided to
consider these draft proposals paragraph by paragraph, according to the concepts
on which the paragraphs were based.

9.   At its 74th meeting, on 7 August, the Special Committee decided to establish
a working group of eight members representing the sponsors of the three draft
proposals in proportion to their number, that is, one representative for the
USSR draft, five representatives for the thirteen-Power draft and two
representatives for the six-Power draft.   The Working Group was requested to help
the Special Committee in the fulfilment of its task by formulating an agreed or
generally accepted definition of aggression and, in case it was unable to reach
such a definition, to report to the Special Committee its assessment of the
progress made during the session, indicating both the points of agreement and
disagreement.   The Working Group held ten meetings from 10 to 14 August and brought
its report to the attention of the Special Committee at its 78th meeting, on
14 August (A/AC.134/L.25/Rev.1).   At the same meeting, the Special Committee
decided to take note of the report of the Working Group and to annex it to the
report of the Special Committee, with the understanding that, for lack of time,
the Special Committee had been unable to examine the report of the Working
Group.   The report of the Working Group is reproduced in annex II to the present
report.

II. DRAFT PROPOSALS AND DRAFT RESOLUTION
BEFORE THE SPECIAL COMMITTEE

10. The Special Committee had before it three draft proposals which had been submitted during its 1969 session, namely, the draft proposal of the USSR (A/AC.134/L.12), the new thirteen-Power draft proposal (A/AC.134/L.16 and Add.1 and 2) and the six-Power draft proposal (A/AC.134/L.17 and Add.1). The text of these three draft proposals is reproduced in annex I to this report.

11. On 16 July 1970, the sponsors of the six-Power draft proposal submitted a preamble (A/AC.134/L.17/Add.2) to their proposal. The text of this preamble is incorporated in the draft proposal.

12. At its 78th meeting, on 14 August, the Special Committee had before it the following draft resolution submitted by Bulgaria (A/AC.134/L.26):

"The Special Committee on the Question of Defining Aggression,

"Bearing in mind General Assembly resolutions 2330 (XXII) of 18 December 1967, 2420 (XXIII) of 18 December 1968 and 2549 (XXIV) of 12 December 1969, which recognized the need to expedite the definition of aggression,

"Noting the progress made by the Special Committee and the fact that it did not have sufficient time to complete its task at its current session,

"Noting also the common desire of the members of the Special Committee to continue their work on the basis of the results achieved and to arrive at a draft definition,

"Recommends that the General Assembly, at its twenty-fifth session, invite the Special Committee to resume its work as early as possible in 1971."

III. DEBATE

13. As indicated above (paragraph 8), the Special Committee undertook its work by first engaging in a general discussion on the draft proposals before it and then considering these proposals paragraph by paragraph, having regard to the underlying principles. Part A of this section contains an account of the views expressed during the general discussion of the draft proposals; part B will deal with the views expressed on the various provisions of these draft proposals in relation to the principles which they embody.

A. VIEWS EXPRESSED DURING THE GENERAL DISCUSSION OF THE DRAFT PROPOSALS

14. For the sake of convenience, these views are presented under appropriate headings. Mention should, however, be made here of the opinions expressed on certain general aspects of the question of defining aggression.

15. The preliminary question of the desirability of defining aggression was raised. Some representatives, while stating that they would welcome a definition of aggression which, in their view, was sound and generally accepted, pointed out that the doubts which their delegations had previously expressed on a number of occasions concerning the advisability of defining aggression, and particularly concerning the impact that a definition would have on the behaviour of States, had not been completely dissipated. In their view, a definition might render more difficult the task of United Nations organs concerned with international peace and security. Several representatives, however, maintained that a definition of aggression was necessary. Such a definition would provide a legal basis for establishing the existence of acts contrary to a rule of jus cogens. In addition to contributing to the progressive development of international law, and representing an important stage in its development, it would dispel much of the imprecision associated with the concept of aggression and would help to deter potential aggressors. It would also assist the competent organs of the United Nations in establishing the existence of an act of aggression and would help to promote the peaceful settlement of international conflicts. It would, in addition, enable world public opinion to understand the basis for the adoption of collective measures by the United Nations to restore peace, as well as for acts of self-defence by States. It was further pointed out that a definition of aggression was long overdue; it was needed not only as a guide to the Security Council and to States with respect to the exercise of the right of self-defence but, what was more important, it was needed to complete important legislative proposals, such as the draft Code of Offences against the Peace and Security of Mankind, the question of an international criminal jurisdiction and many international instruments concerning matters of security, including the Charter of the United Nations. The view was also expressed that efforts to define aggression were an integral part of efforts by supporters of progress to promote and strengthen the authority of justice and law in international relations and of the basic principles underlying those relations, which essentially postulated respect for every nation's right to self-determination, national sovereignty and independence, equality of rights and non-interference in the internal affairs of other countries.

16.   As regards the procedure for the adoption of the definition of aggression, some representatives expressed the view that it was necessary to draft a definition commanding a consensus in the Committee and, particularly, accepted by all the permanent members of the Security Council. However, a substantial number of representatives considered that if unanimity, although desirable, could not be reached, a definition which would command the agreement of a large majority of the Committee would serve a useful purpose. The consent of all permanent members of the Security Council was not indispensable. It was observed in that connexion that a demand for unanimity would show too little respect for the will of the majority of States and too much for the will of the minority. If unanimity proved impossible, there should be no balking at a majority decision, such as was provided for in the rules of procedure of the General Assembly. It would of course be an advantage if the definition was accepted by all the permanent members of the Security Council, but that was in no way a prerequisite for the accomplishment of the Special Committee's task, since the foundation stone of the United Nations was the principle of the sovereign equality of States; the right of veto was an exception applicable to matters of security, and there was no question of extending it to questions relating to the progressive development of international law and world order. It would be better to present the General Assembly with a draft definition accepted by a large majority of the members of the Committee than to have no definition at all; moreover, a definition supported by the majority could influence the attitude of the minority, so that sooner or later it would be possible, on the basis of such a definition, to frame one expressing a consensus.

17.   In the opinion of other representatives, however, if the definition was to be of value and not to be harmful and a source of division, it should have the support of all members of the international community. It was stated that the Special Committee's task was to draft a definition which, once adopted by the General Assembly, would be an authoritative statement of the law generally recognized and an authoritative interpretation of the Charter. However, the General Assembly did not make the law, not having the power to do so; all it could do was to declare what the law generally recognized was, such a declaration having legal weight only if accurate. In the case in point, if the General Assembly adopted a resolution purporting to be declaratory of international law and if, for example, the sponsors of the six-Power draft proposal voted against it, the resolution would be invalid in law or, at any rate, it could not be declaratory of international law. Six States, representing a significant portion of the world's power, economic vitality, political leadership, military strength and legal tradition, would be saying that the law was otherwise. The same would be true if the resolution was opposed by other consequential elements of the General Assembly's membership. The fact that the resolution would be opposed by at least two permanent members of the Security Council would make it an a fortiori case. Accordingly, the Committee must succeed in drafting a definition which reflected a consensus.

18.   It was remarked in this respect by a representative that the duty of the Committee as a legal body was to draft the legal document of a definition and send it to the General Assembly in accordance with its mandate. It was for the General Assembly, where all the membership of the United Nations is represented, to consider the expediency of the political aspect of unanimity of the membership.

1. Application of the definition

   (a) The definition and the power of the Security Council

19. All the representatives who spoke on this point agreed in recognizing that the definition should safeguard the power of the Security Council as the United Nations organ primarily responsible for the maintenance of international peace and security. But their views differed on the extent to which the Security Council should be free in the application of the definition.

20. According to some representatives, it was of fundamental importance that any definition of aggression should preserve the discretionary power of the Security Council in determining whether any specific situation involved an act of aggression within the meaning of the Charter. In that sense a definition of aggression should not be intended for automatic and categorical application, but should be understood as providing guidance for the Security Council in the exercise of its responsibilities under the relevant provisions of the Charter. Under the Charter, it was for the Security Council to determine whether or not an act of aggression had been committed. The definition could not in any way circumscribe or take away that function of the Council. It would even be dangerous to use a form of words which might suggest that such was the Committee's intention. In the view of those representatives, the six-Power draft would be satisfactory in that respect.

21. On the other hand, several representatives expressed the view that the definition should not leave the Security Council entirely free to determine whether an act of aggression had been committed. A definition which fully maintained the discretionary power of the Council would be useless. The definition could not, of course, affect the Security Council's powers under the Charter, but should be worded in such a way as to prevent the Security Council from taking arbitrary decisions. It could even be said that if the definition was based on the Charter, the Security Council would be bound to observe it in performing its functions. Regarding operative paragraph I of the six-Power draft, it was argued that the wording of that paragraph contributed nothing to a definition of aggression. It was open to different interpretations and would give the impression that the Security Council would have discretionary powers in the application of the definition. If the definition was not to be applicable in the same way in all cases, not only would it be of little use, but it might become a subject of procedural disputes in the Security Council. If, however, the intention of the paragraph was that the Security Council should determine the existence of the act of aggression, it would be better to use those words, which were those of Article 39 of the Charter. With such a wording, paragraph I of the six-Power draft would partly correspond to the fourth preambular paragraph of the thirteen-Power draft. The Security Council must, of course, act in accordance with its constitutional powers, which were not unlimited, being strictly subject to the purposes and principles of the United Nations; but the text of paragraph I of the six-Power draft gave the impression that aggression was no more than a term used in the Charter to be interpreted as the Security Council saw fit, i.e. as the permanent members of the Security Council saw fit, with all that that implied.

22. One representative, while recognizing the need to safeguard the discretionary power of the Security Council, expressed the view that the definition should not make that power exclusive to a point where a deadlock in the Security Council would prevent other competent United Nations organs, particularly the General Assembly, from deciding upon the existence of a case of aggression.

(b)   <u>Political entities to which the definition should apply</u>

23.   Some representatives considered that the definition should contain a provision which would place on the same footing States and political entities that are not universally recognized as States but which are delimited by international frontiers or internationally agreed lines of demarcation.

24.   Several representatives felt, however, that such a provision would be contrary to the Charter, would lead to confusion and would even be dangerous. The illusion that aggression could be committed by political entities other than States, it was said, introduced concepts which were not found in contemporary international law or in the Charter of the United Nations. Any definition of aggression must be based on the premise that only full subjects of international law, that was to say, States, performed acts at the international level. It was true that the possibility was not excluded of aggression by international organizations with legal status under international law and sometimes with armed contingents under their control. But there was no need to include a special provision to cover that eventuality in a definition of aggression. Any real threat would be from States, and not from international organizations or entities "delimited by internationally agreed lines of demarcation". It was also pointed out that most, if not all, of the entities which were described as political entities were genuine sovereign States. The fact that they were not recognized by some Governments did not alter their status as such. Implicitly to deny such entities the status of States by describing them as political entities, in a declaration of the General Assembly, would be to place one more obstacle in the way of the principle of universality, subscribed to by the United Nations. The view was also expressed that if the definition was to deal with direct armed aggression, it must be made clear that only States could be aggressors or victims of aggression. The reference to political entities in operative paragraph II of the six-Power draft would be meaningless in a definition confined to direct armed aggression and might be dangerous, as it could be interpreted as a means of obtaining recognition of a pre-existing situation.

25.   With regard to the various criticisms of the concept of a political entity referred to in the six-Power draft, it was pointed out in the first place that the Charter spoke of "aggression" without specifying whether it was an act committed by a State or by an entity recognized to be a State. When the Charter referred to a State in that connexion, it was to an "enemy State" in the very special clause which was Article 53. It was pointed out, in the second place, that in so far as the argument concerned Article 2, paragraph 4, of the Charter, which did not employ the word "aggression", it was true that the paragraph referred to "all Members" and "any State", and did not speak of Members or States not recognized to be such. But it would be pedantic literalism to suggest that Article 2, paragraph 4, of the Charter could not accordingly apply to an entity whose statehood was disputed. The argument that only States could be victims or authors of aggression need only be stated to be refuted. A definition of aggression which included the concept of an entity not recognized as a State would be very helpful. It would, in fact, be dangerous if a definition of aggression did not expressly refer to that concept.

2.   <u>Acts proposed for inclusion in the definition of aggression</u>

26.   The idea that the definition should be limited, for the present at least, to the concept of armed aggression as understood under the Charter, was approved by

most of the members of the Special Committee. However, different views were
expressed on the question whether, for purposes of the exercise of the right of
self-defence, this concept should cover armed aggression in its indirect form.
The question was raised whether the definition should extend to this form of
aggression.

27. Some representatives felt that the definition should be applicable to so-
called indirect armed aggression. They argued that infiltration across frontiers
or internationally agreed lines of demarcation by armed bands, external
participation in acts of terrorism and subversion, or other use of force intended
to violate the territorial integrity or independence of States were activities
which could constitute threats to the maintenance of international peace and
security that were quite as serious as acts of direct aggression. The Charter
provided that Members of the United Nations should refrain in their international
relations from the threat or use of force, not against other Members or against
other States, but against "the territorial integrity or political independence
of any State, or in any other manner inconsistent with the Purposes of the United
Nations". In view of the obvious interrelationship between the prohibition of
the threat or use of force and the Charter concept of aggression, the definition
of aggression must take account of the Charter's fundamental purpose of protecting
the territorial integrity and political independence of States. In the view of
those representatives, the six-Power proposal, which was based on the idea that
indirect aggression must be assimilated to direct aggression, would be in conformity
with the Charter. Thus the acts of indirect aggression mentioned in that proposal
would imply a use of force which was prohibited in Article 2, paragraph 4, of the
Charter; if a State used force, even through the agency of volunteers, terrorists
and the like, it would, according to the conception on which the six-Power proposal
was based, be violating that provision of the Charter. In that regard, it was
noted that the USSR draft definition was much closer to the six-Power draft than
to the thirteen-Power draft. The latter did not ignore acts of indirect
aggression, but did not treat them as acts of aggression; in particular, it
deprived States of their right under the Charter and under general international
law to have recourse to individual or collective self-defence when they were the
victims of subversive or terrorist acts by irregular bands.

28. On the other hand, several representatives were of the opinion that the
Special Committee should endeavour first to define armed direct aggression; the
definition of indirect armed aggression and other forms of aggression not involving
the direct use of armed force should be undertaken later. Furthermore, the
aggression to be defined should be armed agression within the meaning of the Charter.
The definition would essentially be linked with Articles 39 and 51 of the Charter;
Article 2, paragraph 4, of the Charter also dealt with the use of force, but went
beyond what was needed for the definition of aggression. The Committee was
concerned with the definition of an action and not of the rights and obligations
of States. The violation of lines of demarcation or of armistice lines might
constitute a violation of an international obligation and not necessarily an act
of aggression. If a link was to be established between the provisions of Article 2,
paragraph 4, concerning the use of force and those of Article 51 concerning the
right of self-defence, the concept of aggression should be limited to cases in
which it took the form of the use of direct armed force; other illegal acts of
pressure against a State were covered by the principle of international law
prohibiting intervention in the domestic affairs of other States, a principle which

the Special Committee on Principles of International Law concerning Friendly Relations and Co-operation among States had incorporated in the draft Declaration 6/ adopted at its recent session; there was no doubt that such acts violated the Charter, but they could not be termed aggression within the meaning of Article 51 of the Charter, which authorized the exercise of the right of self-defence only in the case of armed attack. It was stated that one reason why the right of self-defence under Article 51 was granted only in the case of a direct armed attack was because such an attack posed an immediate danger and there was no time for deliberation or appropriate action by the Security Council. Infiltration by armed bands or saboteurs into the territory of another State constituted a form of direct aggression whether or not a uniform was worn and regardless of the legal status of the armed forces used; however, most forms of indirect aggression were breaches of the peace and it would not only be unwise but contrary to the Charter to include in a definition of aggression breaches of the peace which fell short of aggression.

29. Some representatives challenged the view that there would be no point in defining indirect aggression immediately, since it was not the main element in the definition. In their view, it was not possible to define some forms of aggression and to postpone the definition of others. The result would be an inaccurate and misleading definition which might be harmful as well as unrealistic. Furthermore, aggression today was increasingly tending to take an indirect form, and the Committee should be careful not to give the impression of licensing that type of aggression. If aggression was to be defined in two stages, a start should be made with indirect aggression. The draft Declaration of the Special Committee on Principles of International Law concerning Friendly Relations and Co-operation among States admittedly contained provisions relating to indirect acts of aggression, but if the Committee was to exclude from the definition everything concerning aggression contained in that Declaration, it would be very difficult for it to draft a definition; aggression by indirect means might certainly constitute intervention in the affairs of a State, but it was none the less aggression. With regard to the argument that it would be difficult to prove responsibility in cases of indirect aggression, it was pointed out that questions concerning proof of the aggressor's responsibility were not an integral part of the definition. Moreover, the difficulties of proof might be even greater in the classic case of bombardment or invasion than in the case of less direct use of force.

30. One representative noted the absence from all the drafts submitted to the Committee of any reference to the case where one State put its territory at the disposal of another for use as a base in an armed attack against a third State. He nevertheless considered that that was an act of aggression which merited inclusion in the list of acts of aggression which the definition would contain.

3.   The principle of priority

31. Several representatives expressed themselves in favour of the principle of "first use" embodied in the USSR draft and in the thirteen-Power draft. It was

---

6/   Ibid., Twenty-fifth Session, Supplement No. 18 (A/8018), para. 83.

argued that the principle of "first use" was justified by the letter and spirit of the Charter, since the latter authorized the use of force only in specific cases, including that of self-defence as laid down in Article 51. That Article sanctioned the "first use" principle, since it authorized a State which was the subject of an armed attack to exercise its right of self-defence. Clearly, an armed attack must precede the exercise of the right of self-defence. It was also stated that the "first use" principle was embodied in both municipal and international law and was not therefore new. It was to be found in certain studies carried out under the League of Nations. All the countries which had proposed definitions in connexion with the discussions on disarmament had referred to this principle. In practice, world public opinion and certain major Powers had recourse to the principle in determining the existence of aggression. The point was also made that the "first use" principle had the fundamental advantage of providing an objective criterion in determining the existence of an act of aggression; it placed the burden of proof, not on the victim, but on the one who acted first. Moreover, it did not carry with it an irrefutable presumption of culpability. It was stated, in this connexion, that there was a presumption juris tantum that the first to use armed force should be considered the aggressor. Aggression was a fact and should be judged according to objective criteria. It was not a question of an intellectual exercise to ascertain what a State's intentions were, but of specific acts which resulted in one State becoming the victim of aggression by another.

32. Several representatives considered, however, that the principle of "first use" should not be automatically applied. There was not an absolute cause and effect relationship between the "first use" of force and the designation of the aggressor; although the principle of "first use" was fundamental to the determination of the aggressor, there could be exceptions. In that respect, they considered the thirteen-Power draft more satisfactory than the USSR proposal, because the latter adopted an inflexible position on this principle. One representative found the thirteen-Power draft not fully satisfactory in this respect, for by including a reference to the principle of "first use" in its operative paragraph 5 and omitting such a reference in paragraph 2, it might give the impression that different criteria for determining the aggressor were used in the two paragraphs.

33. With reference to the principle of "first use" incorporated in the thirteen-Power draft, the view was expressed that there could be no question of the automatic application of that principle for the purpose of determining whether or not an act of aggression had been committed. It was for the Security Council to determine whether an act of aggression existed, in accordance with Article 39 of the Charter. Except in the case of self-defence, no situation, even though it involved the violation of an uncontestable right, justified a war. There were procedures for determining who was right and who was wrong in a dispute. The important point was to avoid war and if it broke out, to prevent it from spreading by localizing the conflict. The concept of priority might, of course, in special circumstances or in the case of error, lead to disastrous results, but that could be overcome by using, in the operative part of the definition, the phrase "in the circumstances of each particular case", referred to in the preamble of each of the drafts submitted.

34. The "first use" principle was challenged, however, by some representatives who considered it unduly facile and even potentially dangerous. The principle of priority, as formulated in the USSR draft and in the thirteen-Power draft, could only be interpreted in one of two opposite ways, neither of which provided for proportionality of response by a victim using methods other than those employed by the aggressor. The "first use" concept could be interpreted either as compelling the victim to respond by employing the same method as that used by the aggressor, or else as placing no limitation whatsoever upon the victim's response. There were also serious practical difficulties in determining what, in fact, should be regarded as "first use". Consequently, the sponsors of the six-Power draft had felt that analysis should be left to the discretion of the Security Council, in preference to applying a blanket "first use" approach. It was stated that, in the view of the sponsors of the draft, "first use" was important and sometimes even very important, but not decisive. It was for the Security Council to decide whether or not there was aggression. The "first use" theory had its superficial attractions, but it was spurious. If the six-Power draft did not mention the "first use" of certain weapons of mass destruction as aggression, the omission was deliberate and well founded. Supposing the armed forces of a major Power attacked a neighbouring country and the latter used atomic weapons because it had no alternative, that country could not be accused of an act of aggression.

4. Aggressive intent

35. Some representatives considered that in determining aggression in a specific dispute, due consideration should be given not only to the element of illegality of the act committed, but also to the element of intent on the part of the entity committing that act. It was pointed out that the possibility could be envisaged of certain illegal acts being committed accidentally without any intention of aggression; it went without saying that such acts should not be treated as acts of aggression; it was also true that an act which on the face of it might present all the physical characteristics of use of force, might well be an act of self-defence and not an act of aggression according to the concrete circumstances of the case; in the determination of an act as aggression, the element of intent was, therefore, essential.

36. Several representatives expressed a different opinion. It was argued that the adoption of intent as a basis would tend to place the burden of proof on the victim of aggression. Furthermore, such a subjective fact as intent would often be impossible and in any event extremely hard to prove. It was also pointed out that none of the provisions of the Charter, including Articles 39 and 51, referred to animus agressionis.

37. It was noted that it was an indisputable principle of universal judicial practice that the intent was presumed when an illegal act was committed; the onus of proof rested with the accused and not with the victim, still less with the judge; it was true that what was apparently an act of aggression might have been committed by mistake, without any aggressive intent; but there was nothing to prevent evidence to that effect from being produced before the competent political or judicial body, though error was not in itself sufficient to exempt from responsibility; furthermore, the introduction of the element of intent would open the door to abuse, as the absence of aggressive intent could be invoked in all kinds of circumstances; an inexhaustible list could be prepared of the possible

motives a State could adduce in order to claim that it had not been actuated by the purposes described in paragraph IV A of the six-Power proposal; human ingenuity was far too great to allow the adoption of aggressive intent as the criterion; in fact, if such a criterion was adopted, it would have the effect of inviting war; it would put the clock back to the days of just and unjust wars and would make recourse to war a legal right.

38. In connexion with the six-Power draft, the question was raised whether the uses of force enumerated in paragraph IV B would be licit if applied for purposes other than those listed in paragraph IV A. It might be asked, for example, whether a State would be justified in using one of the means listed in paragraph IV B, not for one of the purposes provided for in paragraph IV A, but for the purpose of enforcing a favourable decision of a court of arbitration or an international tribunal; or whether a State which was the object of a threatened aggression was entitled to use any of the means listed in paragraph IV B first, in other words, to launch a preventive war; it was impossible to list all intentions; the same applied to material acts of aggression, but at least there was the possibility of listing a minimum number of acts with regard to which agreement could be reached; the difficulty could perhaps be overcome by repeating the phrase "in the circumstances of each particular case" in the operative part of the draft; in that way, the concern of the sponsors of the six-Power draft regarding the concept of intent would be met without distorting the definition of aggression. In view of the difficulties that might be raised by adoption of the criterion of intent, one representative said he preferred imputability to intent as the criterion; in his view, imputability would have the advantage of facilitating the solution of the problem of error; an act committed by mistake, he noted, could involve the responsibility of a State, but could not be imputed to it.

39. It was argued in support of the inclusion of the concept of intent in the six-Power draft that its inclusion was necessary in the first place by reason of the provisions of the Charter. Obviously, it was pointed out, there might be a threat to the peace or a breach of the peace which did not amount to aggression; clearly, therefore, it was necessary to distinguish between those three concepts, and a criterion must be found to define "act of aggression" as opposed to other illicit uses of force; the element of "intent" seemed to be the only adequate criterion found in many years of study. Moreover, if aggression was to be defined as a crime giving rise to international criminal responsibility, the element of "intent" could hardly be ignored; under the general principles of law, intent and criminal responsibility were inextricably interwoven. The argument that the introduction of the element of intent into the definition would cause the burden of proof to fall on the victim was untenable; it was clear from Article 51 of the Charter that the victim did not need to wait to defend itself until the Security Council had established an act of aggression. Contrary to what had been claimed, proof of "objective" facts was not always easy; proof of intent would, as a rule, be even more difficult, but that was no reason to deny the relevance of the criterion; when States referred their case to the Security Council, it was for the latter to establish aggression "in the light of all the circumstances of each particular case", as stated in all the drafts submitted; intent was certainly one of the circumstances to be examined by the Council, whose discretionary power was not disputed by any member of the Special Committee. Furthermore, to argue that the most benevolent intent did not justify the slightest interference with the territorial integrity or political independence of another State was to confuse intent with the wrongdoer's motive; a State resorting to force with intent to

deprive another State of its political independence was an aggressor, even if its avowed motive was to liberate the people of that State from the rule of an oppressive government; the motive would be irrelevant, but the intent would be most relevant. It was also argued that where the facts were clear, namely, where in a particular case the only reasonable conclusion that could be drawn from an examination of the facts was that an act of aggression had been committed, there might well be no need expressly to examine the question of intent; however, generally speaking, determination of acts of aggression was likely to be exceedingly difficult; for that very reason, the discretionary authority of the Security Council must be safeguarded in order to enable it to look at the intent of the alleged aggressor in the light of the circumstances of each particular case.

40. It was argued that a distinction ought to be made between acts of aggression according to their gravity; where an act by itself constituted a breach of the peace, there was no need to ascertain whether it had been carried out with or without aggressive intent; but where it was a matter of illegal acts which might cause a breach of the peace if they reached a certain magnitude, then the criterion of intent was required; there was no need to introduce the concept of intent into a general definition; it was when specific examples were given that the question of deliberate perpetration became relevant.

5. Legitimate use of force

(a) Self-defence

41. Most representatives emphasized the need to include in the definition of aggression a provision recognizing the right of self-defence as laid down in the Charter. The Charter, it was stated, safeguarded the inherent right of individual or collective self-defence (Article 51) and sanctioned regional security arrangements (Article 52); both Articles constituted exceptions to the Charter prohibition of the use of force; the exception which was implicit in Article 51 and which raised the issue of the relationship between the right of self-defence and the concept of aggression was one of the most difficult problems facing the Special Committee; there was, first and foremost, the problem of the point in time at which the right of self-defence arose; then there was the problem of whether there must have been an actual use of force or whether a threat of force could suffice to bring the right of self-defence into operation. Given the complexity of those problems, the course of wisdom would be to indicate in the definition itself, as the six-Power draft did, the general exceptions to the prohibition of the use of force and to leave it to the Security Council to determine whether, in a given instance, such exceptions were applicable. Paragraph 6 of the USSR proposal, it was noted, was based on the same idea, but its wording was inadequate; in the thirteen-Power proposal, too, there was a contradiction between operative paragraph 1, which stated that the United Nations only had competence to use force, and operative paragraphs 3 and 4, which concerned other cases where the use of force was permitted.

42. Several representatives pointed out that the right of individual or collective self-defence did not carry with it an unlimited power to use force; it was a right that could be exercised exclusively to repel an armed attack, and then only within the limits and under the conditions provided for in Article 51 of the Charter; to consider the application of enforcement measures provided for

in Chapter VII and the exercise of the right of self-defence recognized in Article 51 of the Charter as exceptions to the prohibition of the threat or use of force set forth in Article 2, paragraph 4, would be to misinterpret the principle involved, which, being a rule of jus cogens, could not be subject to any exceptions whatsoever; the confusion stemmed from the fact that the use of force was permitted in only two cases: preventive action taken or sanctions applied by the world Organization in carrying out its primary function of maintaining international peace and security, and defensive action taken by States, individually or collectively, to repel an armed attack; the possibility of the former was inherent in the authority vested in the United Nations as the government of the universal international community; the latter was an act of necessity, not a power, which exampted from responsibility only those exercising their right of self-defence in the circumstances prescribed by the rules of international public order.

43. The principle of proportionality, which was included in the thirteen-Power draft, was supported by several representatives. It was argued that it was in the interests of all that the use of force to repel armed attack should be commensurate with the armed attack itself; an unrestricted right of self-defence could not provide protection, particularly for small States. On the other hand, it was pointed out that, although the principle of proportionality was sometimes referred to in international affairs, it was not laid down in any instrument nor was it directly mentioned in the Charter; moreover, its incorporation might hinder acceptance of the definition; it would also raise the problem of determining the proportionality of measures adopted in self-defence and the action to be taken if they were deemed disproportionate.

(b) Organs empowered to use force

44. Several representatives stressed the importance of the principle set forth in operative paragraph 1 of the thirteen-Power draft, namely, that the United Nations only has competence to use force in conformity with the Charter. If the definition of aggression was to conform to the principles of the Charter and lend itself to a proper interpretation and application, it was pointed out in that connexion, the definition must include an expression of that principle, to which there could be no exceptions; the right to use force under regional arrangements or through regional agencies must be conferred solely on the legally organized international community as a whole, i.e. with the express authorization of the Security Council in accordance with Article 53 of the Charter; operative paragraph 4 of the thirteen-Power draft contained a provision to that effect; the right of individual or collective self-defence mentioned in operative paragraph 3 of that draft did not constitute an exception to the principle enunciated in paragraph 1, but was an instrument of last resort to be used in a situation where international responsibility no longer existed; the two paragraphs were therefore complementary; although paragraph III of the six-Power draft combined the substance of the provisions of operative paragraphs 3 and 4 of the thirteen-Power draft, it permitted regional organizations to use force before a decision had been taken by the Security Council, and that was inconsistent with Article 53 of the Charter. It was stated that a radical amendment to the Charter would be required, if regional organizations were to be empowered to use force in the way suggested in the six-Power draft; in matters relating to the maintenance of international peace and security, the regional organizations were, as could be seen from Chapter VIII of the Charter, strictly and absolutely

subordinate to the authority of the Security Council; under Article 53, the only enforcement action they were permitted to take without the Council's authorization was against States which, during the Second World War, had been enemies of any signatory of the Charter.

45. Some representatives, however, found operative paragraph 1 of the thirteen-Power draft not wholly satisfactory, since it might be inferred from it that not only the Security Council but other organs of the United Nations were competent in the matter of the use of force; that would be contrary to the provisions of the Charter, particularly those of Article 24 and Chapter VII, and might have unfortunate consequences. A reference to the powers and duties of the Security Council in operative paragraph 5 of the thirteen-Power draft would be quite appropriate and would, in fact, be sufficient.

46. It was pointed out, on the other hand, that the six-Power draft excluded the use of force pursuant to decisions of or authorization by competent United Nations organs or regional organizations "consistent with the Charter of the United Nations"; some Members of the United Nations believed that the General Assembly and regional organizations had a limited competence in that sphere, illustrated by Articles 52 and 53 of the Charter and by the practice of the General Assembly, the Security Council and the Organization of American States; other Members held different views about that competence and some of them even denied it altogether; the phrase "consistent with the Charter of the United Nations" in operative paragraph III of the six-Power draft had, among its other virtues, that of recognizing the position of other Members; if any Members believed that an action of a United Nations organ or regional organization was inconsistent with the Charter, the provision in question enabled them to state their point of view. Some representatives nevertheless thought that the phrase "consistent with the Charter of the United Nations" in paragraph III of the six-Power draft did not suffice to remove doubts concerning the compatibility of that paragraph with Article 53 of the Charter.

6. Acts considered not to constitute acts of aggression

47. Several representatives criticized the six-Power draft for not taking into account the struggle of nations for independence, self-determination and sovereignty; in their view, the definition of aggression should include, as did the USSR and the thirteen-Power proposals, a provision making an exception where the use of force was necessary to ensure the exercise of the right of peoples to self-determination. They stated that such a provision was essential in a period of vigorous national liberation movements; it would be a safeguard as necessary and important as the safeguard in Article 51 of the Charter concerning the right to self-defence or the safeguard concerning the use of force pursuant to a decision or authorization of a competent United Nations body. Some representatives argued, however, that the principle of self-determination would be extraneous to the definition of aggression. While recognizing the importance of the principle, they believed that it should be treated in a different context. It was stated that the six-Power draft did not contain a clause safeguarding the principle of self-determination because nothing in it impaired that principle; there was no need to make a gratuitous statement and the absence of such a statement in no way limited the application of the Charter provisions concerning the exercise of the right of peoples to self-determination.

7.   Legal consequences of aggression

48.   Several representatives said that the definition of aggression should expressly state, as did the USSR and the thirteen-Power proposals, that territorial acquisitions obtained by force would not be recognized;   they considered that a provision of that kind was quite appropriate in a definition of aggression, since occupation of the territory of another State following aggression was contrary to the principle of inviolability of the territory of a State and was tantamount to continued aggression.   It was useful, in their view,. that the principle of the aggressor's international responsibility should be stated;   that was not an element which, strictly speaking, formed part of the definition, but it was closely linked with it.   Some representatives stated that military occupation, annexation and other forms of the acquisition of territories by force constituted aggression in its most serious form;   and that the principle of non-recognition of the acquisition of territories by force, a principle based on the Charter, should properly be considered under the heading of "consequences of aggression".   It was also said that paragraph 8 of the thirteen-Power draft raised certain complex issues connected, on the one hand, with the non-recognition of territorial acquisitions obtained by force in the past and, on the other, with the competence of the Security Council;   as those matters had been carefully considered by the Special Committee on Principles of International Law concerning Friendly Relations and Co-operation among States, it would be inappropriate to draft a text dealing with such matters without taking into account that Committee's work, as reflected in the draft Declaration which was to be submitted to the General Assembly by that Committee.

49.   Some representatives, however, opposed the inclusion in the definition of a provision relating to non-recognition of territorial acquisitions obtained by force.   It was pointed out that the sponsors of the six-Power draft had not mentioned the matter in their proposal because they doubted the need to deal with it in a definition of aggression;   they also wished to remain within the framework of the Charter, which was silent on that point;   the omission was also explained by the fact that the matter had already been dealt with by the Special Committee on Principles of International Law concerning Friendly Relations and Co-operation among States;   the six Powers had therefore been anxious not to upset the very delicate balance of the formulae put forward by the Special Committee, not to impair them by reproducing them in part and not to try to amend them indirectly.   It was argued, however, that the fact that the Special Committee on Principles of International Law concerning Friendly Relations and Co-operation among States had concerned itself with the non-recognition of territorial acquisitions obtained by force did not justify the exclusion of that question from the definition of aggression;   if it was to be excluded from the definition for that reason, it would also be necessary to exclude from the definition the other topics dealt with by that Special Committee, such as the question of indirect aggression;   though the Charter did not mention such acquisitions, neither did it mention cases of aggression by subversion.   The view was expressed, on the other hand, that it was necessary to use judgement and to exclude those elements of the draft Declaration on Principles of International Law concerning Friendly Relations and Co-operation among States which were inappropriate in a definition of aggression, but that there should be no hesitation in including relevant elements.

B. VIEWS EXPRESSED ON THE VARIOUS PROVISIONS OF THE DRAFT
PROPOSALS IN RELATION TO THE CONCEPTS INVOLVED

50. The arrangement of this section is based on the order in which the Special
Committee examined the various provisions of the draft proposals. It is divided
into sub-sections, with headings indicating the relevant paragraphs and the
underlying principles. As far as possible, views already recorded in the previous
section will be omitted from this section.

1. Paragraph 1 of the USSR draft, paragraph 2 of the thirteen-Power draft and
paragraph II of the six-Power draft: Direct or indirect aggression, the
principle of priority and political entities

(a) Direct or indirect aggression

51. Some representatives stated that to define aggression meant to give fullness
of meaning to the term; at the outset, therefore, mention should be made of the
characteristics of aggression, among which was that aggression could be committed
by overt or covert and by direct or indirect means. It was said that their
viewpoint was based on the Charter, which referred to aggression, armed attack and
the use of armed force, but did not at any point confine those terms to "direct"
aggression; the Charter prohibited aggression by any means whatsoever. In this
connexion, it was also observed that all the three draft definitions under
consideration included what was generally known as indirect aggression, from which
it appeared that there was a general consensus that it was a form of aggression.
Some representatives noted further that the members of the Committee were almost
unanimous in thinking that the indirect use of force was at least as dangerous to
international peace and security as aggression committed by obvious means and that
indirect aggression was the most frequent form of aggression in the world today.
In the circumstances, they argued, any definition which concerned the direct use
of force and which left unsettled the question whether the indirect use of force
did or did not constitute aggression would not be a satisfactory definition. One
representative pointed out that treaties defining aggression that had been
concluded in the past always contained a paragraph dealing with support given to
armed bands, and he maintained that even a minimum definition must include
indirect armed aggression; economic or ideological aggression had not the same
affinity to indirect aggression as the latter had to direct aggression.

52. Several representatives felt that in order to achieve agreement, the Committee
should focus attention first of all on direct aggression, leaving aside the
question of indirect aggression to be considered at a later stage. It was said
that it should not be difficult to agree on what constituted armed aggression,
which was referred to in the Charter and against which a victim State could exercise
the right of self-defence under Article 51. To define the conditions under which
the right of self-defence could justifiably be exercised in the face of indirect
aggression was a difficult problem, which would take time to solve. In addition,
it was argued that a definition of armed aggression was what was most urgently
needed; in the case of less direct and less obvious forms of aggression there was
generally time to seek action through the Security Council, whereas armed
aggression generally required defensive action without waiting for a decision by
the Security Council. Some representatives expressed the view that all the three
drafts envisaged aggression in reference to Articles 39 and 51 of the Charter, and

that was "armed aggression"; there was no disagreement that some forms of indirect aggression were armed aggression; and once a definition of armed aggression had been drawn up, the Committee could see how such forms of indirect aggression might be included.

53. In the opinion of some representatives, a distinction drawn between "direct" and "indirect" aggression was alien to the Charter, which did not contain such terms. One representative observed that what was generally referred to as indirect aggression was a matter of particular concern to small countries, because of their vulnerability to it; but if the word "aggression" was qualified by such vague terms as "covert" or "indirect", the safeguard in Article 51 might be weakened and give States an opportunity to use force under the pretext of self-defence.

54. On the other hand, some representatives felt that the question whether direct and indirect aggression were mentioned in the Charter was of no importance; if the Committee was to be bound by the terminology used in the Charter, it would be unnecessary for it to define aggression at all. Furthermore, it was said that there was no justification in the Charter for describing aggression by certain means and excluding aggression by other means; the Charter did not stipulate that acts by armed bands, saboteurs and the like did not constitute aggression. In arguing for the retention of the terms "direct" or "indirect", some representatives maintained that the wording of the Charter might not be clear enough to embrace the essence of aggression in all its practical manifestations and unless direct and indirect aggression were mentioned expressly, the definition might not be readily understood to refer to both direct and indirect use of force. In response to the expressed concern lest the inclusion of indirect use of force might unduly dilute the concept of aggression and expand the scope of permissible self-defence, one representative considered that there was a simple answer to that point: to be legitimate, the use of force in self-defence must be proportionate; the same cardinal principle would apply whether the use of force was by direct or indirect means.

55. The representative of the USSR stated that his delegation was prepared to delete the words "direct or indirect" appearing in parenthesis in paragraph 1 of the USSR draft. In doing so, it had accepted the view that the draft definition to be prepared at the present stage should not cover indirect aggression; but that did not mean that his delegation considered that there was no need to define such form of aggression; on the contrary, it attached great importance to the task of defining indirect aggression, which the United Nations would undertake at a later date. The representative of the USSR also said that as paragraph 2 C in the USSR draft referred to indirect aggression, it would be deleted in consequence of the deletion of the words "direct or indirect" from paragraph 1.

56. Nearly all the representatives who supported the view that the Committee should first concentrate on defining direct aggression specified that it was solely for procedural reasons due to the difficulties involved in defining indirect aggression that they supported that view; they attached as much importance to indirect aggression as to direct aggression; the Committee's task would not be completed until it had dealt with defining indirect aggression. Certain representatives suggested that no matter what definition was drawn up at this stage, the preamble to it should contain a paragraph specifying that the definition did not cover the whole concept of aggression and that forms of aggression not covered would be defined later.

57. The deletion of the words "direct or indirect" from the USSR draft was welcomed by some representatives, as the deletion, in their opinion, made the USSR draft much closer to the thirteen-Power draft. One representative observed, however, that if the qualification of aggression was omitted from paragraph 1, and if paragraph 2 C was deleted from the USSR draft, that might be interpreted as giving licence to States to resort to the use of armed force through the medium of armed bands, saboteurs and the like. He would have preferred it if the USSR delegation had decided to delete only the word "indirect" before the word aggression at the end of paragraph 2 C; however, as the whole paragraph had been deleted, he wondered whether the USSR delegation would be prepared to reinsert the reference to direct aggression in paragraph 1, the beginning of which would then read: "Direct armed aggression is the use by a State ..."; it would then be clear that the definition did not cover the whole concept of aggression.

(b) The principle of priority

58. A large number of representatives expressed the view that the principle of priority should hold a very important place in the definition of aggression. It was said that the principle, enunciated for the first time twenty-five years ago, had been sanctioned by many international instruments; it was the only objective criterion which could be applied; and it was directly based on the provisions of the Charter, particularly Article 51 which described the sequence of events leading to the exercise of the right of self-defence, and according to which the use of force was authorized only in response to an armed attack; if the principle was not included, the definition would depart from the provisions of the Charter. Some representatives emphasized that under the Charter, legitimate use of force was confined to the United Nations and that this warranted the conclusion that whoever used force first automatically committed an act of aggression. In their view, objection on the score of the automatic character of the principle was groundless, because the Security Council had to determine who the aggressor was, and it was precisely for that purpose that it had to determine who had used force first; in other words, "first use" was an essential element which had to be appraised by the Security Council in determining whether the right of self-defence had been exercised in conformity with Article 51. One representative stressed that, while it was true that the Security Council had to take into account facts that took place after the launching of an attack, it was not possible to disguise the original fact as such a launching. Several representatives noted that there was general consensus among the members of the Committee that the principle of "first use" had a place in the definition; that it was an important factor which the Security Council should take into account, although the Council was not called upon to make its decision on the basis of that criterion alone.

59. On the other hand, several representatives raised questions as to the nature of the principle and the possibility of making it a criterion to be generally applied. One representative stated that if the criterion of priority was considered as a simple or rebuttable presumption, as had been suggested by some of its proponents, he would have no objection to its being given a place on that basis in the definition of aggression, due weight being given to other factors of aggression; however, neither the USSR draft nor the thirteen-Power draft presented priority as a simple presumption but rather as an automatic and determinative rule; besides, the objectivity of the principle as a criterion was only superficial and it would in practice provide no more reliable information than would purely subjective tests. Some representatives referred to various situations in which the

application of the "first use" criterion would be very difficult or would lead to surprising results. For instance, in a case where a State exercised the right of self-defence, by virtue of a mutual defence agreement with another State, without itself having been a victim of aggression, would that State be considered the aggressor? If, in reply to an armed attack of very limited scale, a State committed a disproportionately aggressive act, the application of the "first use" criterion would lead to an unjust result. It might also happen that two States attacked each other, each intending to attack the other at the same time. If there was a declaration of war followed by an act of aggression by the State against which war had been declared, the latter could not automatically be considered as the aggressor because it had been the first to use force.

60. With regard to these questions and others raised earlier, several representatives, who supported the principle of priority, stated that the principle was not the only principle to be applied to determine who was the aggressor, but it was certainly one of the most important principles to be applied for such a purpose; the principle did not limit the discretionary power of the Security Council to appraise the circumstances of each case. As to the argument that the priority principle might bring about the launching of a war by mistake, it was pointed out that acts to be considered as constituting aggression were such acts characterized by a particular intensity that they could not be committed by mistake. It was also said that some of the criticisms of the priority principle seemed to be a direct appeal in favour of preventive war, a concept likely to bring about the collapse of the system of collective security established by the United Nations. As for the question relating to a mutual defence agreement, it was said that such a case was covered by the right of individual or collective self-defence and it had no connexion with the principle of "first use"; a State could not unilaterally base its action upon the agreement in order to invoke self-defence, because that concept had an essentially subjective element. Concerning the hypothetical case of two States which attacked each other simultaneously, one representative considered that the principle of "first use" was of decisive importance, while another representative felt that the application of the principle was excluded, since there was a contradiction between the simultaneity of the attack and the concept of "first use". As regards the remark made in relation to a declaration of war, one representative wondered whether the USSR draft could be improved to take that remark into account. For that purpose, he suggested that sub-paragraph A of operative paragraph 2 of the draft might be deleted provided it had been reflected in a preambular paragraph and the words "even without a declaration of war" in sub-paragraph B of the same paragraph might be replaced by the words "with or without a declaration of war".

61. With regard to the relationship between the priority principle and the question of aggressive intent, one representative observed that several of the sponsors of the thirteen-Power draft supported the argument that the principle of priority raised a presumption of guilt; if that argument was accepted as valid, the only way of rebutting the presumption was to furnish proof of absence of animus. It was said by other representatives that the members of the Committee who supported the criterion of "first use" agreed that other criteria could be used, notably intent; the criterion of "first use" and that of intent were not irreconcilable; the priority principle should perhaps be amplified by the concept of intent. In the opinion of one representative, the six-Power draft contained positive ideas which should induce its sponsors to give the criterion of priority preference over that of intent; in cases where it was possible to determine who had first resorted to force the principle of priority was by far the more

important; when applied within the context of the idea of self-defence, the principle could render legitimate a form of resort to force which had appeared to be illegal, and vice versa.

62. Noting the views expressed by some of the sponsors of the six-Power draft, some representatives stated that neither the USSR draft nor the thirteen-Power draft allowed an automatic application of the principle of "first use" and that it would now be possible for the sponsors of those two drafts to meet the concern of the sponsors of the six-Power draft in respect of such automaticity by transferring that part of the preamble which dealt with the taking into account of all the circumstances in each case to the operative part of the drafts. One representative suggested specifically that the USSR delegation might consider inserting at the beginning of operative paragraph 1 of its text a phrase to read as follows: "Without prejudice to the conclusions the Security Council may reach in analysing the circumstances pertaining to the facts ...", and the sponsors of the thirteen-Power draft might include an identical phrase in operative paragraph 5 of their text. Some of the sponsors of the six-Power draft stated that they were prepared to agree that the factor of priority in the use of force should be given due, but not determinative, weight in a definition of aggression, together with other factors.

(c) Political entities to which the definition should apply

63. Some representatives stated that many conflicts which had arisen in the world since the adoption of the Charter, involving political entities whose statehood had been challenged, showed how important it was that the definition of aggression should cover such entities. It was said that the position of the sponsors of the six-Power draft was that entities whose statehood was challenged but which exercised governmental authority over a territory were bound by the obligations of international life, and in particular by Article 2, paragraph 4, of the Charter. Consequently, an entity not recognized as a State did not have the right to attack a recognized State; and, conversely, a recognized State did not have the right to attack an entity not so recognized. It was stated that the supporters of the USSR and thirteen-Power drafts might take up either of two alternative positions which were mutually exclusive: that entities whose statehood was challenged could not be the victims of perpetrators of aggression; or, conversely, they could be, but that was so obvious that it need not be stated in a definition of aggression, and that the case could be covered by adopting a broad enough idea of what was meant by "State". While the second position was defensible, the first position took no account of the realities of international life.

64. Some representatives who spoke on this subject held the view that entities whose statehood was challenged could nevertheless be perpetrators or victims of aggression; but it was not necessary to mention such entities in a definition of aggression; the term "State", as used in the Charter and as adopted in practice by the United Nations, was broad enough to cover entities whose recognition as sovereign States was far from general; besides, the parties to aggression were most often independent sovereign States. In the opinion of other representatives, political entities whose statehood was disputed could not be considered as States; the concept of such entities was alien to the Charter and it had no basis in other sources of international law; the definition of aggression should be based on the concept of the State in international

relations without invoking the recognition of States as a criterion. Several
representatives said that the inclusion of the concept of political entities in the
definition was not only unnecessary but also undesirable; it would have disadvantages
and would raise legal and political problems. The inclusion would constitute
departure from the Charter, which did not mention "political entities", and it
might lead to the attribution of a more restrictive meaning to the term "State" in
all other texts where the term appeared; it might also make the distinction between
international conflicts and civil wars more confusing. Paragraph II of the six-
Power draft linked the question of political entities with the delimitation of those
entities by international boundaries or internationally agreed lines of demarcation,
thus further complicating the issue, although not every violation of a demarcation
or armistice line necessarily constituted an act of aggression. Some
representatives expressed their concern that those wishing to apply the definition
of aggression to political entities whose statehood was in dispute were seeking to
prejudice the right of all peoples to self-determination; in fact, the sponsors of
the six-Power draft had not deemed it necessary to specify in their text that the
definition would not affect the right of self-determination of peoples. In the
absence of any provision relating to self-determination, paragraph II of the six-
Power draft was tantamount to sanctioning the use of force by certain metropolitan
States, as well as to an acceptance of the delimitations of colonial boundaries
which such States had made. Moreover, a provision pertaining to political entities
might be used according to the convenience of the moment, for instance, as a cloak
for acts of aggression: thus, in the case of an entity which unlawfully declared
its independence, the State which was responsible under international law for that
entity could exercise its discretion whether or not to invoke the definition if
another State sent arms or troops into that entity; and that was something which
should not be possible.

65. Some representatives felt that the term "political entities" would be
irrelevant in so far as it referred to States whose statehood was disputed, but it
might have some relevance if it referred to national liberation movements. In the
opinion of one representative, it would represent progress to understand the term
"political entities" as referring to national liberation movements as entities
capable of being the active or negative subjects of aggression.

66. With regard to the question whether the provision in the six-Power draft
relating to political entities referred to peoples trying to exercise their right of
self-determination, some of the sponsors of the draft stated that the provision
referred to entities whose status as States was disputed; consequently, it could
only relate to such peoples if they really constituted entities delimited by
international boundaries or internationally accepted lines of demarcation. Failing
that, such peoples could neither commit nor be victims of acts of aggression, which
implied the crossing of such boundaries or lines of demarcation; consequently the
provision in paragraph II of the draft did not in the ordinary course of things
concern peoples trying to exercise their right of self-determination. More
generally, they considered that the prohibition of aggression applied to all
international boundaries or internationally accepted lines of demarcation,
irrespective of the political régime of States or entities they delimited; the fact
that a social system violated certain norms of international law did not justify the
use of force to punish such violation. It was also said that the reason why the
six-Power draft contained no provision similar to that in paragraph 10 of the
thirteen-Power draft was precisely because the sponsors of the former draft
considered that their text did not contain any provision limiting the scope of the

Charter's provisions concerning the right of peoples to self-determination, sovereignty and territorial integrity. It was also stated that the term "political entity" in paragraph II of the six-Power draft was not applicable to national liberation movements; since what was prohibited was the use of force "against the territorial integrity or political independence ...", paragraph II could only apply to entities which possessed such territorial integrity or political independence; the expression "in international relations" in paragraph II generally meant relations between governments, whereas the problem of national liberation movements had a very different setting.

67. Some representatives, on behalf of the sponsors of the six-Power draft, responded favourably to a specific suggestion made by one representative – a suggestion which consisted in replacing the words "other political entity" in paragraph II of the draft by the words "a State whose statehood was disputed"; those terms, it was said, covered exactly what the sponsors of the six-Power draft had in mind. One representative expressed the view that the words "and not subject to its authority" at the end of paragraph II of the six-Power draft constituted a real danger, because that wording implied that aggression against an entity subject to an authority was admissible. Certain representatives felt that the sponsors of the six-Power draft should shelve the question of political entities for the time being, so that the Committee could elaborate a definition of aggression and, at the same time, formulate an interpretative definition of the term "State", which could be annexed to the definition of aggression. In the opinion of some representatives, the three texts under consideration all suffered from a lack of precision: every time the word "State" was used in each of the three paragraphs, it should be followed by the words "or a group of States".

2. Paragraph 6 of the USSR draft, paragraphs 1, 3 and 4 of the thirteen-Power draft and paragraph III of the six-Power draft: Legitimate use of force

68. Some representatives pointed out that the question of the legitimate use of force was dealt with in the three drafts; it was referred to in the USSR draft only indirectly, whereas the two other drafts referred to it in a more direct manner; the latter drafts differed, however, as regards substance and form. It was stated that since the Charter referred to the use of force, both legitimate and illegitimate, the definition of aggression must make a clear distinction between the legitimate and the illegitimate use of armed force; a provision should therefore be included in the definition of aggression covering cases in which the use of force was legitimate, since it would help to define more clearly the notion of armed attack; such a provision should be based on Articles 51 and 53 of the Charter.

(a) Self-defence

69. A number of representatives addressed themselves specifically to the role of self-defence in the definition of aggression. In the opinion of some of those representatives, this was a question on which the thirteen-Power and and six-Power drafts had adopted completely different approaches. In their view, the sponsors of the thirteen-Power draft, on the basis that Article 51 of the Charter authorized self-defence in cases of aggression, regarded self-defence as the obverse of aggression and as providing the criterion by which aggression could be defined; since aggression was the use of force which gave rise to the right of self-defence, self-defence would therefore have to be defined within the framework of a definition of aggression.

However, those representatives noted that it was only the French text of Article 51 of the Charter which referred to "<u>aggression armée</u>", whereas the English and Spanish texts referred to "armed attack"; moreover, assuming that Article 51 did refer to aggression, it failed to define it in any way; it simply indicated what a State might do if aggression occurred; in the present case, the rule that one variable could not be defined by reference to another variable was applicable: if the nature of self-defence was unknown or not agreed on, it was impossible to define aggression, which meant different things to different persons, in terms of self-defence. In the opinion of those representatives, aggression was a broader concept than the mere obverse of self-defence. Moreover, the Committee's real task was to define aggression, not the limits of self-defence, which was only of incidental importance in relation to aggression; it would also have to be determined whether any attempt to define self-defence might not hamper rather than help the Committee in the accomplishment of its real task. In the opinion of those representatives, the use of force in the exercise of the right of self-defence was obviously not aggression, and any definition of aggression should make that clear so as to safeguard the right of self-defence; however, as regards self-defence, the Committee's task stopped there. In this connexion, it was suggested that, as the Committee was not called upon to define self-defence as such, but to relate it to aggression, it would be enough to state in the definition that self-defence under the Charter did not constitute aggression.

70. Other representatives, however, were of a different view in regard to the above question. At the outset they stressed that although the use of force had formerly been legitimate, the international legal order had been so transformed as to rule out recourse to force, thus establishing a general principle which had been part of positive international law even before the adoption of the Charter, which in that respect was merely declaratory and simply confirmed an existing rule. It was reaffirmed in this connexion that the principle of a United Nations monopoly of the use of armed force was incontestable. According to that principle, the use of armed force by any State Member of the United Nations constituted an act of armed aggression because the international community forming the United Nations alone was authorized to use armed force. The right of self-defence was a right which the United Nations granted States as members of the international community and not an exception to the principle of the prohibition of the use of armed force. In the opinion of those representatives, the rule being, then, that the use of force was banned, any derogation was in principle condemned by the international community. The Charter itself, however, envisaged the use of force in certain cases. The Committee therefore could not define aggression, which consisted essentially in the use of force, without clarifying the uses of force provided for in the Charter. The first such use was self-defence. There were cases where an armed attack, namely, the use of force against a State, although it had all the physical characteristics of an act of aggression, was not in fact aggression since it was considered to be self-defence. Logic demanded that to ascertain the meaning of aggression, especially armed aggression, the scope of self-defence must be defined. It was also said that it was most important to define, in the context of the definition of aggression, the opportunities for action open to the victim of aggression, for, in the absence of such definition, the position of the victim would be decidedly prejudiced. There was no reason why only illegitimate activities should be examined and legitimate activities left aside. The concept of self-defence was found in practically all legal systems, and, internationally, it had been characterized in the Charter as an inherent right and should, therefore, be

clearly stated. Although neither the Security Council nor the General Assembly had
so far taken any decision involving an interpretation of Article 51 in this respect,
the principle in question was of such paramount importance that it should be
referred to in the definition of aggression.

71. In the opinion of some representatives, the inherent right of individual cr
collective self-defence referred to in Article 51 of the Charter was a right which
had existed throughout man's history, enjoyed by all States under international
law, independently of Article 51 by which it was in no way circumscribed. It was
said that under this interpretation, self-defence was legitimate not only in the
event of armed attack, but also in the event of a threat or a real danger of armed
attack, in which case it was for the State concerned to decide whether the
situation was such as to justify self-defence. It was further said that unless a
non-restrictive interpretation was given to it, Article 51 would not cover the
case where a State started a bacteriological war against another State, a
possibility which could not be ruled out in view of the advance of science and
technology since the Charter had been drafted: in such a case, as the victim
State would not be the subject of armed aggression it would not be able to exercise
its right of self-defence.

72. In the opinion of several representatives, on the other hand, the traditional
concept of the right of self-defence had been modified under the Charter, and self-
defence was truly justified only in the case of armed attack under the conditions
indicated in Article 51. It was said that the right of self-defence, which had
been borrowed from criminal law, did not constitute an authorization to use force,
but merely grounds for absolving from liability anyone who, in the circumstances
provided by law, had to face an armed attack. It was also said that the provision
in Article 51 enabled the victim to react immediately, before the Security Council
took action; but the same provision required immediate reporting to the Security
Council. In the view of some representatives, if it were to respect the Charter,
the Committee should try to limit the cases of legitimate uses of force, as was
provided for in the thirteen-Power draft, which contained a very specific provision
on the subject, whereas the six-Power draft left the way open to other uses of
force by not confining self-defence to cases of armed attack. Furthermore, it was
stated that self-defence must be subsequent to the attack. It was recalled in
this connexion that at the Nürnberg trial the idea of preventive self-defence had
been ruled out; the Charter too, left no room for doubt on the subject. It was
also stated that subversive or terrorist acts could constitute an "armed attack"
within the meaning of Article 51, however indirect such an attack might be, and
that consequently, a State which was the victim of such acts should not be
prohibited from exercising its inherent right of self-defence.

73. In the opinion of some representatives, the use of force was also legitimate
in the case of national liberation movements or oppressed peoples which had
recourse to armed force. This was an accepted principle of international law,
which found support in the Declaration on the Granting of Independence to Colonial
Countries and Peoples and in the draft Declaration on Principles of International
Law concerning Friendly Relations and Co-operation among States. References to
that question were found in operative paragraph 6 of the USSR draft and in
paragraph 10 of the thirteen-Power draft. The definition of aggression should
therefore refer to that third case of legitimate use of force deriving from the
very principle of the inherent right of individual or collective self-defence,
although it was not indispensable that such mention be made precisely in the

provision corresponding to the present paragraph III of the six-Power draft or paragraphs 3 and 4 of the thirteen-Power draft, and such mention could be included in a special safeguard paragraph as was done by the USSR draft and the thirteen-Power draft.

74. Some representatives, however, considered that a reference to the use of armed force by dependent peoples was unacceptable. It could be interpreted either as a reference to the right to revolt or as authorizing the use of force across international boundaries and the latter would be consistent with the rejected theory of just wars. Other representatives were of the view that since the prohibition of the threat or use of force obviously related only to international relations, Article 51 in principle did not apply to civil wars or to liberation movements. It was difficult to determine how far a State was compelled to refrain from the use of force against a people fighting for its right to self-determination, and it was recognized that a colonial conflict could develop into an international conflict, entailing action by the Security Council.

(b) Organs empowered to use force

75. A number of representatives made reference to the expression "competent United Nations organs" in paragraph III of the six-Power draft. In the opinion of some representatives, the definition of aggression should safeguard the discretionary power of the Security Council, the principal United Nations organ responsible for peace-keeping, abut without preventing any other United Nations organ, for example, the General Assembly, from intervening in the event of an impasse. In their view, that position found support in Articles 10, 11 and 14 of the Charter and in the consistent practice of the Organization since 1950.

76. One representative, however, considered that if the six-Power draft was meant to imply that organs other than the Security Council would be competent in the matter, its wording was ambiguous; if the six-Power draft wished to attribute limited competence to the General Assembly in respect of the use of force, it should have used the word "recommendations".

77. Still other representatives considered that the expression used in paragraph III of the six-Power draft was unacceptable, since it was intended to endow the General Assembly with the competence to use force even though under the relevant provisions of the Charter the only United Nations organ which could, in accordance with Articles 39 and 42 of the Charter, decide to engage in enforcement action entailing the use of armed force was the Security Council.

78. In the opinion of some representatives, Article 53 of the Charter referred only to enforcement action; the possibility of the use of force in the exercise of the right of collective self-defence by regional arrangements or agencies should therefore in no way be denied. In this connexion, some representatives found paragraph 4 of the thirteen-Power draft concerning the use of force by regional arrangements or agencies, unacceptable, as it departed from both the text of the Charter and United Nations practice. Article 53 of the Charter referred, not to a decision, but to an authorization by the Security Council and it did not specify whether such authorization should be anterior or posterior, expressed or implied. Nevertheless, practice had shown that it could be posterior and implied. In the opinion of those representatives, the consistent practice of the Security Council

and of the Organization of American States, as authoritative interpretations of the Charter, could not be ignored. In their view, and generally speaking, it was clearly the abuse of the right of veto in the Security Council which had prevented that body from exercising the powers conferred on it under Chapter VIII of the Charter and which had led the international community to turn to the General Assembly or to regional bodies.

79.   Several representatives, however, considered that paragraph III of the six-Power draft was unacceptable because its provisions made the United Nations and the regional agencies equally competent to have legitimate recourse to force; yet, according to the Charter, whose provisions in this respect were perfectly clear, no enforcement action could be taken by regional agencies without the authorization of the Security Council; regional agencies might play a co-operative role in the maintenance of peace and security, but their role was strictly subject to the authorization of the Security Council; furthermore, the use of force could not be justified a posteriori - the Security Council must first examine the matter and take a decision; in view of the language used by the Charter, it was clear that authorization must precede action; on this subject, however, there was no precedent since the Security Council had never authorized the use of force under a regional arrangement or by a regional agency. The Council had often been paralysed, not only by the use of the veto, but also by the abstentions of members which prevented it from taking decisions; the Council's inaction, however, could not be considered as an authorization to use force. In the view of those representatives, the word "decision" in the thirteen-Power draft was admittedly not used in the Charter; nevertheless, the Security Council gave its authorization in fact by way of a decision; moreover, in order "to utilize" the regional agencies, as provided for in Article 53 of the Charter, the Security Council must decide, in each case, whether such agencies ought to be utilized; the possibility of implied authorization was therefore excluded; the fact that action might have been taken as a result of exceptional emergency situations and that authorization might have been given only after the event must not be confused with the well-established rule.

80.   In the opinion of some representatives, it was clear that Article 53 of the Charter authorized the Security Council to utilize regional arrangements or agencies for enforcement action, but it did not indicate whether such enforcement action went as far as to cover the use of armed force. In this respect, both paragraph 4 of the thirteen-Power draft, referring to cases in which force could be used legitimately under Article 53, and paragraph III of the six-Power draft, which took that provision into account in more general terms, should be rephrased in order to bring them more into line with the provisions of Article 53.

81.   In addition to discussing the above two issues, a number of representatives addressed themselves to the approaches of the three draft proposals. In expressing support for the thirteen-Power draft, several representatives mentioned the fact that it specifically referred to Article 51 of the Charter in paragraph 3. It was also stated that paragraphs 3 and 4 of that draft contained provisions in complete harmony with the Charter, unlike paragraph III of the six-Power draft. It was said that while the six-Power draft dealt simultaneously with the use of force in the exercise of the right of self-defence or pursuant to authorization by a competent United Nations organ, the thirteen-Power draft rightly considered those two questions separately; such separate treatment was justified by the fact that, in the Charter, the right of self-defence was dealt with in Chapter VII while the

question of regional arrangements and agencies was dealt with in Chapter VIII;
moreover, in Chapter VIII, the expression "use of force" was nowhere to be
found: the expression used was "enforcement action". The opinion was also
expressed that, as regards form, the thirteen-Power draft was preferable since
its provisions dealing with the legitimate use of force were worded in a
restrictive manner, stating, and rightly so if the possibilities of legitimate
use of force were to be reduced to the minimum, that force could be used only
in specified cases; the six-Power draft, on the other hand, did not, in general,
seek to discourage the use of force and stated, in permissive terms, when the
use of force in certain circumstances did not constitute aggression. Some
representatives considered further that the detailed treatment given to the
question in the thirteen-Power draft could be acceptable if the wording of the
Charter were followed more closely, particularly in paragraphs 1 and 10, and
the relevant provisions should be grouped either at the end of the operative
part or immediately after the general definition.

82. In the opinion of other representatives, the thirteen-Power draft had
the disadvantage of including overly restrictive clauses governing self-
defence; although the draft mentioned Article 51, it limited its scope
somewhat by saying that the right of self-defence "can be exercised only in
case of the occurrence of armed attack (armed aggression)"; a fact of
international life was that the question whether resort to self-defence was
justified would invariably be determined by the State threatened with
aggression; the Committee should therefore not circumscribe or delimit the
inherent right of self-defence; it should indicate in the definition itself
the Charter's general exceptions to the prohibition of the use of force and
leave it to the Security Council to determine whether in a given instance,
such exceptions were applicable. Further, the thirteen-Power draft's detailed
treatment of the question would inevitably lead to disagreement. It was also
stated that the main vice of paragraph 3 of the thirteen-Power draft was that
it was too faithful to the language of the Charter; thus, according to
Article 51, the right of self-defence was allowed only to Members of the
United Nations; accordingly, that right would not be allowed to non-members
of the United Nations who were victims of armed attack; it was doubtful
whether the Charter should be interpreted as prohibiting non-member States having
joint security arrangements with Members of the United Nations from seeking help
from their allies in the case of armed attack; if that was acknowledged to be an
issue, it would be possible for the sponsors of the thirteen-Power draft to
consider how the Charter should be interpreted, for it had to be admitted that
so literal an interpretation of some of the Charter's provisions did not
reflect international reality.

83. In the view of some representatives, the best solution was offered by the
provision in paragraph 6 of the USSR draft; it had the advantage of being concise
and, as it was strictly in accordance with the Charter, was legally
unexceptionable; by its general wording, it covered all cases of the legitimate
use of armed force, which should be distinguished from an act of aggression, the
result of an illegitimate use of armed force; by not seeking to define the limits
of self-defence, it steered clear of any question of interpretation for which the
Committee was not competent and left it to the Security Council to decide whether
Article 51 of the Charter restricted the use of self-defence to the case of armed
attack; the problem had been dealt with in the same way in the draft Declaration
on Principles of International Law concerning Friendly Relations and Co-operation
among States. Other representatives shared the above views as regards, however,
only the first phrase of paragraph 6 of the USSR draft.

84. In expressing support for the six-Power draft, some representatives made reference to the fact that it dealt with the question of self-defence in general terms, without defining its scope, thus providing the only basis on which a consensus could be arrived at; the draft had safeguarded the use of force in exercise of the inherent right of individual or collective self-defence as stated in the Charter in a way acceptable to the two schools of thought existing on the question; the draft made no reference to Article 51 since the definition of aggression need not establish any limitation of the right to exercise self-defence; the Committee should base itself not only on Article 51 but also on the purposes and principles of the Charter.

85. In the opinion of some representatives, the provisions of paragraph 6 of the USSR draft were so similar to the corresponding paragraphs of the thirteen-Power draft that there was a basis for agreement. Other representatives thought that there was a common approach in the six-Power draft and in the first phrase of paragraph 6 of the USSR draft, that phrase being the one most in keeping with the Charter. The opinion was, however, expressed that if the Committee wished to be specific, it should seek a middle ground between the thirteen-Power and the six-Power drafts; it might refer expressly to Article 51 without describing the right of self-defence as "inherent" but also without limiting the scope of the Article; the following wording was therefore suggested: "The exercise of the right of individual or collective self-defence in accordance with Article 51 of the Charter does not constitute aggression".

3. Paragraph IV A of the six-Power draft: Aggressive intent

86. Some representatives expressed support for the inclusion of the concept of intent in the definition of aggression. It was stated that the sponsors of the six-Power draft had included that concept precisely because in the absence of aggressive intent certain acts might not constitute aggression. Such acts might nevertheless give rise to responsibility based, for instance, on negligence. While malicious intent was an essential element of a breach of the peace, which was a voluntary and intentional act, the deliberate use of force was not always unlawful; an obvious exception was its use in self-defence, as provided for in Article 51 of the Charter. The existence of unlawful acts which were not necessarily acts of aggression was recognized in the Charter, for example in Article 1, paragraph 1, which referred to "acts of aggression or other breaches of the peace"; the six-Power draft had introduced the concept of intent as a perfectly relevant criterion for determining whether a particular case of the use of force constituted an act of aggression; the draft did not require evidence of intent in order to support a finding that aggression had been committed but made it clear that in the absence of aggressive will, a State could be exonerated from a charge of aggression. Conversely, by adopting intent as a criterion, an aggressor could never be considered innocent of aggression; in international affairs there were many cases of the use of force which did not constitute aggression; there was a close relation between operative paragraph IV A of the six-Power draft and at least part of Article 2, paragraph 4, of the Charter which in a way already qualified the use of force, relating to certain intentions; to facilitate classification among the types of unlawful acts, the sponsors of the draft had, by way of example, listed typical acts which constituted aggression; such qualitative distinctions between unlawful acts were common in criminal law; also, the list was not intended to be limitative; the sponsors of the draft had adopted violation of territorial integrity and political independence as the primary criterion for distinguishing between acts of aggression and mere breaches

of the peace. In international law, the purpose of the act determined its gravity; for example, it would be extending the concept of aggression too far to regard as an act of aggression shots aimed at a fugitive which struck one or more inhabitants of another country; the crossing of a frontier by a police patrol might or might not be considered aggression according to what the purpose had been; but there was undoubtedly an act of aggression when an act manifested an intent to acquire territory or to interfere in the domestic affairs of a State; with reference to minor border incidents, it was well to bear in mind the principle of "de minimis non curat lex"; a use of force in a manner so limited in nature and in duration of time could not be described as an act of aggression; that did not, of course, mean that such an incident could not be found to be a threat to the peace or even a breach of the peace. Through its definition of aggression, the Committee would help the Security Council to determine which of the uses of armed force prohibited by Article 2, paragraph 4, were of sufficient gravity to warrant characterization as acts of aggression; that Article of the Charter provided some parameters to that effect; they were insufficient, however, to distinguish an act of aggression from lesser breaches of the peace. It was true that what was important at the present stage was to make that distinction and not to define a breach of the peace; the latter problem must not, however, be considered a secondary one, since United Nations practice often spoke of the two together; Article 51 might be invoked in any particular case of armed action, and it was, therefore, important to give attention to the boundary between the two ideas. As for the text of the definition of aggression, if the Committee were to content itself with listing obvious examples, from which intent might normally be presumed, the basic question would not be settled, and the Security Council would not be able to apply the definition to less obvious forms of aggression; that method could lead to the erroneous description as acts of aggression of certain acts in which the element of intent was lacking; it would be much better to recognize that the offence of aggression contained a mental element and that account should be taken of the purpose aimed at. Another reason for accepting the criterion of intent was that the definition of aggression should serve in establishing international penal responsibility; it would be strange if the perpetration of an act involved responsibility when the accused was unable to exonerate himself by proving that he had no culpable intent; if intent were not considered to be an element of the offence, however, the absence of intent could not lead to acquittal.

87. On the other hand, several representatives reaffirmed their views contrary to the inclusion of the element of "intent" in the definition of aggression. It was said that any aggressor, knowing that he had that means of defence at his disposal, would argue that he had no "intent" of inflicting harm through an act of aggression; it was further stated that since the general principle was the prohibition of the use of force in international relations, only in the cases and in the manner authorized by the Charter was that use justified; the Committee's task was to give meaning to those instances mentioned in the Charter in terms of specific situations and in clearly defined language; the idea could not be accepted that a laudable intention could justify the use of force; the result of including the element of intent or purpose in a definition of aggression would be to add to the very few exceptional cases where the use of force was legitimate or permissible under the Charter; the idea that the use of force might or might not constitute aggression depending upon the objective aimed at might be acceptable only if the definition included an exhaustive list of objectives for the uses of force recognized as permissible under the Charter and by the United Nations, namely, self-defence in the face of armed attack, for enforcement action by or with the authorization of the competent United Nations body, and for liberating oppressed

peoples and securing their right of self-determination; a longer, non-exhaustive
list would only extend the range of cases in which the use of force was permissible;
it would have the effect of giving a green light to aggression and could only
multiply the causes of war. It was also said that an armed attack, not by accident
or in error, by a State against another State, for any purpose other than in
self-defence, was aggression; there were no instances of the use of armed force
which did not constitute aggression other than those covered by Article 51 of the
Charter; most instances of the use of armed force not within the provisions of that
Article and most of the acts of indirect aggression were breaches of the peace,
in which cases no resort to arms was legitimate; besides, the Committee's task
was not to define breaches of the peace but aggression; there was no point in
trying to list all the possible purposes of armed attack, which were innumerable,
when all that needed to be mentioned were the exceptions; there could be any number
of "motives", good and bad; they did not fall within the definition of aggression;
the Charter merely required that in case of aggression, the countries concerned
should refer the matter to the Security Council; the Committee could not give its
assent to a definition which defeated the Charter; a proposal to include "motive"
in the definition as a necessary factor in the identification of aggression
conflicted flagrantly with Article 51, which provided that should an armed attack
be made (except in cases of accident or error), the victim could exercise the right
of self-defence, as aggression had occurred; moreover, in view of the difficulties
experienced by psychoanalysts in determining the motives of individuals, the
difficulty the Security Council would have in determining those of peoples could
well be imagined. The view was further expressed that intent could not convert
the threat or use of force referred to in Article 2, paragraph 4, of the Charter
into aggression; it was the material nature of the act that determined its gravity,
and whether an act was a simple use of force or aggression depended on the
circumstances in each particular case; thus, economic pressure might be
considered a use of force, while bombing was aggression; it was the objective
element and not the intent that determined the distinction; for example, if a
State A intended to change the Government of another State B, it might bring
economic pressure to bear on State B or it might invade State B; in either case,
the intention of State A would be the same, but, in the first case, its action would
be a threat or use of force and, in the second, aggression. As regards the case of
a State deliberately pursuing a fugitive on the territory of a neighbouring State
and opening fire on that territory without any intent to harm that other State,
that was strictly speaking an act of aggression: no State could pursue a fugitive
on the territory of another State by means of armed attack without infringing the
sovereignty of that other State; as soon as the fugitive crossed the frontier
the State which was pursuing him had to use other means, for instance request
the neighbouring State to extradite the person concerned. Also, with reference
to the characterization which had been made of limitations in time and/or in
intensity in the case of an armed attack as not being sufficient for determining
the aggressive character of the act, it was stated that the brevity of duration
of an attack might be due to factors outside the will or design of the aggressor,
for instance, to the intervention of a third party, such as the Security Council,
or to the intensity of the self-defensive action; moreover, a short attack might
be a question of tactics; it could not be taken as indicating an absence of
aggressive design; furthermore, several brief attacks could not be considered
as less harmful than a prolonged act of aggression; similar considerations were
equal applicable to the intensity of an attack.

88. In the opinion of some representatives, whereas intent was the subjective element of an offence, the objective element was the attack, invasion, bombardment or other act when first committed; an offence could not be defined in terms of one of the two elements only; in the case of aggression, the subjective element was an expression of the degree of the aggressor's culpability, for there could be no responsibility without fault committed; intent was an important factor in the offence but was not the only one; it was not possible to say which was the more important, the objective factor of "first use" or the subjective factor of intent, since they were the two constituents of the offence and were of equal importance.. As to whether or not there was a place for the subjective element in the definition of aggression, opinions might differ; the widely established legal rule could be favoured whereby in defining an offence, it was enough to define the objective element, and to leave the subjective element as being implicit; for example, when one State attacked another, the mere fact that there had been an "attack" implied that there had been no element of chance but a premeditated purpose; nevertheless, the inclusion of the subjective element of intent in the definition of aggression was not opposed because it was better to say too much than not enough; however, it would be as well if the definition of aggression did not mention that subjective element, since the very concept of aggression implied aggressive intent.

89. Referring specifically to the enumeration contained in paragraph IV A of the six-Power draft, some representatives emphasized that the cases listed in this paragraph were merely examples, perhaps the most obvious, and no more; the list was not exhaustive, as was evident from the phrase at the beginning of that paragraph: "but are not necessarily limited to"; it was perfectly conceivable that an act of the type described in paragraph IV A might prove to be an act of aggression even though it was committed with an objective different from those set out in this paragraph; thus an act intended not to "secure changes in the Government of another State" (paragraph IV A (4)) but to prevent such changes, would certainly constitute aggression in the sense of paragraph IV A; indeed, such an act would constitute aggression in the sense of paragraph IV A (3) already. In any event it was for the Security Council to decide the matter. The list was not concerned with unlawful acts of a minor character; it gave examples of those with grave consequences; the first four were indisputably major acts; the fifth might involve minor material consequences, but the use of force to obtain even relatively minor concessions still constituted aggression.

90. On the other hand, the view was expressed that it would be easy to imagine other "motives" as valid as those listed in sub-paragraphs (1) to (5) of paragraph IV A; did the absence of those further "motives" from that list mean that there was no aggression in such cases? If the objectives enumerated in paragraph IV A were to be considered as aggressive objectives, the logical implication would be that other objectives were not aggressive; inclusion of the words "but are not necessarily limited to" in the introductory part of the paragraph or even of a very clear statement that the list was not exhaustive would not suffice to remove the difficulty; the impression was given that objectives not listed were not so serious or so aggressive as those listed, and that could only work to the advantage of the aggressor; besides, a careful reading of that introductory phrase led logically to the conclusion that it did not relate to paragraph IV A but to paragraph IV B, since it concerned the uses of force and not the purposes of the use of force. Furthermore, in any list of "intentions" which provided a basis for a finding that aggression had occurred, there was a danger of seriously impeding the Security Council in the exercise of its powers of assessment, even though the

list might not be exhaustive; thus, for example, the intention not to "secure changes in the Government of another State" (paragraph IV A (4)) but to "prevent" such changes would not serve as effectively to prove aggression.

91.   The opinion was expressed that to dispel the doubts arising in connexion with "intent", the list in paragraph IV A should be made less restrictive, and then, instead of stating that with one or another "motive" the attacking State would be deemed the aggressor, it should state that when one or another "motive" was honourable, the attacking State would not be deemed the aggressor. In regard to the criticism that there was some doubt whether paragraph IV A of the six-Power draft was exhaustive, the sponsors said that they would consider redrafting that paragraph. The objection raised could be met by replacing the words "In order to" by the words "For such purposes as", showing that the list was not exhaustive; the full stop at the end of the introductory sentence would be deleted. It was, however, considered that to change the expression "In order to" to "For such purposes as" was not sufficient to alter the meaning and did not make it any clearer that the list was not exhaustive.

92.   A number of representatives considered that an element of confusion had been introduced by the use of various terms such as "intent", "motive", "objective", "purpose" and "animus aggressionis". In the opinion of some representatives, what the sponsors of the six-Power draft meant by "intent" was the "purpose" or "objective"; in any event, it was a question of the mental element, which clearly existed in every case of the use of force and which emerged from the facts, and not a question of the secret or psychological motivations of Governments. Support was expressed for the term "purpose" as being more precise than "intent" or "motive"; all legal systems distinguished between purpose and intent, the latter being a much broader concept since it could be direct or indirect: in the first case, the culprit, the aggressor in the present context, knew that he was committing an offence and was perfectly aware of the consequences that would flow from that offence; in the second case the culprit knew that he was committing a dangerous act but did not foresee the consequences of that act; it was therefore better in a definition of aggression to use the concept of purpose which was, moreover, equivalent to the notion of direct intent; motive, on the other hand, was a very different, subjective element, being that which induced a person to a course of action: in the case of aggression, the motive of the aggressor might be the desire to obtain economic advantages; accordingly, the concept of motive should be excluded from the definition of aggression.

93.   Doubts were, however, voiced whether the notion of "purpose" thus supported coincided with that of the sponsors of the six-Power draft; it appeared that the latter saw aggression as a matter of "mental elements" which would have the effect of exonerating the aggressor from guilt even when his purpose had been to commit an aggressive act against the victim; in other words, his purpose might have been aggressive, but he would be innocent of aggression unless what he had had in mind had been to diminish the territory or alter the boundaries of his victim, etc.; thus, for example, a State which attacked another with the intent of causing destruction by bombardment, etc., or of overthrowing its Government or institutions while having in mind the defence of an oppressed minority, might be declared innocent of aggression; if that was so, there was a difference between the "purpose" for which support had been expressed and the idea of "mental elements" proposed by the six Powers, which more closely resembled "motives". It was also said that

whereas the factors listed in paragraph IV A of the six-Power draft constituted nothing else but illicit motives, the sponsors of the six-Power draft used the terms "purpose" or "objective" to retain the option of considering that no crime had been committed; technically, if those factors were described as "motives", any act based on one or the other of those motives would necessarily be a crime.

94. The view was further expressed that, on close examination, the six-Power draft constantly confused the notions of "intent" and "motive"; if, according to the six Powers, the crime that aggression represented on the international plane derived from an intention, that intention could neither be anything else nor more than the intent to inflict harm contrary to the Charter; all the rest was but "motive"; the only element in the list in paragraph IV A of the six-Power draft, which could be construed as an intention, corresponded therefore to the first two words of sub-paragraph (5), "inflict harm"; all the other elements quoted in sub-paragraphs (1) to (4) and in the second part of sub-paragraph (5) were nothing more than "motives"; for the purposes of defining aggression resulting from an intent to inflict harm contrary to the Charter, it was the element "contrary to the Charter" which was of the greatest importance. In the opinion of some representatives, a general formula of the type thus suggested was an excellent way of presenting the idea which recurred throughout the six-Power draft. In this connexion reference was made to a suggestion made during the general debate, namely that a provision should be incorporated in the operative part of the draft definition, to read: "The Security Council, in qualifying the act of aggression, shall duly take into account the declared intentions and aims pursued by the States in question"; such a provision would meet the concern of the sponsors of the six-Power draft and others regarding the concept of intent and might also allay the fears of those who would like to see less danger of wars that might be considered just and of the aggressors being exonerated from guilt in practically all cases.

95. As regards the question of how to establish the existence of aggressive intent, it was noted that the criterion of intent had been described as a subjective one and, consequently, more difficult to determine than more objective criteria; however, it was just as difficult to determine objective criteria such as who had made the first use of force, yet it was possible to do so as a result of the progress made in science and technology; it was precisely by reference to objective factors that intent was proved; in the case of a large-scale attack, the facts would often - but not invariably - enable a guilty intent to be presumed; conversely, in the case of a minor incident, the facts would suggest that there was no aggressive intent; in the final analysis the finding of an act of aggression would always be made in the light of the facts by which the State manifested its intent.

96. With respect to the question as to the burden of proof, the opinion was expressed that when the element of "intent" was taken to be an integral part of an offence, the formulation itself of the offence said so in clear terms, in which case the onus of proof rested with the party that alleged that the offence in question had been committed; in cases of aggression, however, when the element of "intent" was not recognized as indispensable to a verdict of crime, the onus of proof rested with the party that sought to exonerate itself from the charge; in such cases, the principle of "first use" was of overriding importance, since it enabled the party against whom intent had been alleged to defend itself objectively. In this connexion, and with reference to the case of an accidental dropping of a bomb by an aircraft belonging to one State on the territory of another, some

representatives considered that in such case there was a legal presumption of intent to inflict harm which laid the burden of proof on the State which owned the aircraft; it would be absurd to lay the burden of proof on the victim. A further view was also expressed to the effect that the question of proof had no place in a definition of aggression. To speak of purpose or intent in that connexion would imply that the onus of proof lay with the victim of the aggression, but it was the international community, represented by the Security Council, which had the task of establishing the facts and of determining who was the aggressor in a given instance and to what extent that aggressor was responsible. On the other hand, in the opinion of some representatives, the burden of proof was neither unilateral nor determining; according to cases, the facts would be adduced by the author of the indicted act, by the victim or by a United Nations organ; depending upon the gravity or the minor character of the attack, the burden of proof would lie on the acting party or the victim of the act respectively, although it was not possible to establish a comparison with the rules applicable in domestic law systems; the burden of proof was a decisive element in courts, which were bound by certain procedures designed to safeguard the positions of the parties; the Security Council was not a court and was not even required to hear the parties in all cases; it was required to act on its own initiative to establish the facts of a case by whatever means it considered appropriate and was not tied to a specific procedure; in any event, it would appear that the Security Council had never gone into the matter, nor did the six-Power draft introduce a procedure of proof similar to that of municipal law.

97. Most representatives agreed that an act committed by accident or in error did not constitute aggression; in the opinion of some representatives, the question of accident or error need not be taken into account in the definition, first because such cases were very rare, and second because it was usually clear to all when an attack had been so made; wars did not start as a result of acts committed by accident or in error; if the effect of an act was very extensive, however, no one would expect the victim to wait for an apology or a possible second attack before taking action in self-defence; moreover, the Security Council already had the power to take the absence of deliberateness into account and to declare that a given act had been committed in error and hence did not constitute an act of aggression. The view was also expressed that, as the use of force was never authorized except in the cases covered by Articles 42, 51 and 53 of the Charter, acts committed by mistake would not be regarded as acts of aggression provided that a clause were included at the beginning of the definition to the effect that no intention or motive could authorize a State to use force first against another State. On the other hand, it was stated that if it was correct that proof of intent was to be the criterion for differentiating between certain acts involving the use of force, a solution would have been thereby provided for the problem of the use of force by accident or in error. If, as a result of an emergency situation aboard an aircraft, bombs had to be jettisoned by the aircraft over the sea and they damaged a ship on the high seas or an oil installation in a State's territorial waters, how would it be possible for the Security Council to determine, without examining the objective or purpose of the act, whether or not there had been armed attack in the sense of paragraph 5 (c) of the thirteen-Power draft? With regard to the foregoing example, it was stated that, in that case, there was no act of aggression; all that was involved was the civil liability of the pilot and of the State to which the aircraft belonged; the most probable outcome of the case would be for the State whose aircraft was involved to take the initiative in offering the victim State compensation for the material

damage caused by what in all probability was an accident; if however the victim State, in an excess of zeal, referred the incident to the Security Council, the State to which the aircraft belonged would have to prove that it was an accident.

98. Some representatives considered that the disagreements which still divided representatives on the question of "intent" might be overcome so as to find a generally acceptable text. In this respect it was noted that the co-sponsors of the six-Power draft had indicated that they maintained a flexible attitude with respect to the form of words of the six-Power draft definition of aggression when considering the various drafts before the Committee. They had also clearly stated that the list in paragraph IV A of their draft was not exhaustive; the indication had been given that it might be possible to envisage rather a general mention of intent. It was also said that the observations of a number of representatives seemed to indicate considerable interest in the approach adopted by the sponsors of the six-Power draft and even an agreement on the substance of that approach, as their reservations related only to details of formulation; moreover, it had been indicated that intent, or rather purpose, was an important while not a determinant factor, as was also the principle of "first use"; there was, in fact, no contradiction between those two elements.

99. However, the greater number of thoe who spoke objected to any specific inclusion of intent in the draft definition of aggression and insisted that the thirteen-Power draft and the USSR draft were completely right in excluding this element from their texts.

4. Paragraphs 2 A, 2 B, 2 C and 3 of the USSR draft, paragraph 5 (a), (b), (c) and (d) of the thirteen-Power draft and paragraph IV B (1) to (8) of the six-Power draft: Acts proposed for inclusion in the concept of aggression

100. The representative of the USSR, as sponsor of one of the drafts before the Committee, stated that some light might be thrown on the problem of which acts should be included in the concept of aggression by glancing again briefly at the principles underlying the definition proposed by the Soviet Union. In the approach adopted by his delegation, a scientific attitude was combined with one of compromise. The scientific approach was concerned with the proper understanding of a definition such as the one the Special Committee was called upon to prepare. First, it should be an abstract, yet substantive definition which would be helpful when applied to any situation arising in life, and not merely empty verbiage. The examples included should therefore present the most characteristic or typical symptoms of a particular phenomenon, for no definition could claim to comprehend them all. Second, the purpose of the definition of aggression was to provide a norm of international law on the basis of which, together with the United Nations Charter, the Security Council would find it possible to determine whether there had been aggression in any particular case. The Committee was thus preparing a model and a guide. It would be impossible to make a legal norm automatically applicable. Basing itself on the foregoing considerations, the Soviet Union delegation had adopted an attitude of compromise. Although it would, of course, like the Committee's definition of aggression to be based on the USSR's experience as expressed in its draft, it realized that the definition must be based on the experience of the whole world as it was intended to serve the whole world. It listed several acts which his delegation considered the most important in any consideration of whether aggression had taken place. The list was not, and could not be, exhaustive; and it did not claim to envisage every possible situation.

101. Agreement was expressed with the views of the Soviet Union representative as to the kind of definition the Committee should elaborate. It was also stated that other members of the Committee, sponsors of the two other drafts, were not lagging behind in approaching the task before the Committee in a spirit of compromise. However, the attitude to compromise could not be expected to be such that the only compromise possible was for the sponsors of one draft to abandon their own draft definition completely and accept the other drafts.

(a) Declaration of war

102. In the opinion of some representatives, as a declaration of war had many legal consequences and implications under both international and municipal law in such matters as trade with enemy countries, acts against the property of aliens, protection of the property of neutrals and the rights of combatants, the Committee would be wise to consider carefully the whole question of declarations of war in the context of the definition of aggression.

103. Several representatives favoured the inclusion of the declaration of war in the definition. In the opinion of some representatives, although declarations of war were things of the past, as wars were now not generally declared but simply started, they had not lost their legal significance, nor could the possibility of declarations of war in the future be ruled out. A declaration of war was unlikely unless there was the intention and readiness to launch an armed attack; therefore, it should be treated as an act of aggression although it did not itself constitute the use of force. It was further stated that the declaration of war should be included in the list of acts of aggression mainly to ensure the proper application of Article 51 of the Charter. A declaration of war was an act of legal significance which gave rise to the right of self-defence. Since declarations of war were generally accompanied or followed by armed attack, the victim should be permitted to take immediate, practical measures in self-defence. A country declaring war laid itself open to attack by the country against which it declared war. Moreover, the first declaration of war was a clear, unambiguous manifestation of aggressive intent; when a country declared war, aggressive intent must be presumed. If aggressive intent was a major element of aggression, it was only logical to regard a declaration of war as an act of aggression. Also, since an attempt to commit an offence was in itself an offence, a declaration of war could be equated with an act of aggression and should be included in the list of acts constituting aggression. Some representatives stated that the classification of a declaration of war as an act of aggression in both the USSR draft and the thirteen-Power draft was without prejudice to the powers of the Security Council and therefore subject to the findings of the Council. The existence or absence of aggression could not be determined solely on the basis of the scale of activities observed on the front at a given time. There might, for example, be a prolonged lull in the fighting after an initial exchange of fire. The actual use of force was therefore not always a valid criterion. Also, there were material consequences for the country against which war was declared. The declaration of war was no less important an element of aggression than the others mentioned in the three drafts as worthy of consideration in the determination of aggression. Such an important element should not be lightly discarded. The act of declaring war should not go unpunished.

104. The view was also expressed that the words "In accordance with the foregoing" at the beginning of operative paragraph 5 of the thirteen-Power draft linked the

statement that a declaration of war constituted an act of aggression with the
statement in operative paragraph 2 that "For the purpose of this definition,
aggression is the use of armed force". In that opinion, therefore, according to
the thirteen-Power draft, a declaration of war without the use of force would not
be an act of aggression but an unlawful act. Only if it was accompanied by the
use of armed force could the victim legitimately resort to the use of force in
self-defence under Article 51 of the Charter. Where a declaration of war was not
accompanied by armed attack, the victim could take any appropriate defensive
measures short of armed force.

105. The opinion was also expressed that the definition should make clear that a
declaration of war constituted the most serious form of threat of force.
However, although the threat of force was recognized as unlawful under the
Charter and the draft Declaration on Principles of International Law concerning
Friendly Relations and Co-operation among States, it did not entitle a country
to use force in self-defence. On this basis, and bearing in mind that it might
be the first step in an act of war, the declaration of war should be dealt with
in the definition either in a separate paragraph or in a provision corresponding
to paragraphs 6, 7 or 10 of the thirteen-Power draft.

106. Some representatives stated that the difficulty or inappropriateness of
referring to declarations of war in a definition of the use of armed force that
constituted aggression justified its exclusion from the six-Power draft. In
this connexion, it was stated that a declaration of war was not a clear indication
of aggressive intent. But even if it were, no one claimed that aggressive intent
could by itself constitute aggression; it was merely an aspect of a physical act,
and the combination of both elements constituted aggression. In other words, a
declaration of war, if not accompanied by materially aggressive acts, did not
constitute aggression. A declaration of war was merely a formal act expressing
the intention to start a war; it was doubtful whether such a formal act could,
in isolation, be considered as an armed attack within the meaning of Article 51
of the Charter. A declaration of war could not be considered to be sufficient
grounds for warranting the use of force in self-defence under Article 51; the
drafters of the Charter had intended that a country threatened with attack but
not yet attacked should submit the case to the Security Council before resorting
to force in self-defence. Furthermore, if to constitute aggression, a
declaration of war must be accompanied by the use of force, there was no need to
speak of a declaration of war in the draft definition as it would be the accompanying
use of force that would be the decisive act.

107. The view was also expressed that, since it was apparently agreed that when
a declaration of war was accompanied by a simultaneous or immediately subsequent
use of force it constituted aggression, what the Committee was concerned with was
therefore the case of a declaration of war which was not accompanied by an
immediate use of force. It was said that in such cases, it might be necessary to
distinguish between a "credible" declaration of war, or one in which there was
an imminent threat of the use of force, and a "non-credible" declaration of war,
or one in which the possibility of using force was left in the air. The question
so far as concerned the "credible" declaration of war was whether it should
necessarily be automatically classified as aggression without reference to other
criteria; it was considered that on that point there was a difference of opinion,
but that intent might well be the key. So far as concerned the "non-credible"
declaration of war, such delcaration by itself could not be construed as identical
with armed attack in the sense of Article 51 of the Charter. In other words,

there was not a mechanical relationship between the right of self-defence and an act of aggression; the problem, however, was worth further reflection. In this connexion, it was recalled that the need for limiting the scope of application of Article 51 of the Charter had been repeatedly stressed during the Committee's current session; on such basis, the hypothetical case where there was an interval between the declaration of war and the use of force should therefore be seen in the light of a formal interpretation of that Article, which laid down the emergency procedure to be followed in face of armed attack. If a declaration of war was not accompanied by the use of armed force, it could be interpreted as a breach of the peace. The State against which war had been declared could only appeal to the Security Council, which would certainly recommend the State that had declared war to refrain from using force. That State might accept the Security Council's recommendation and refrain from using armed force, but the "victim" might have no faith in the Security Council and might in the meantime attack the "aggressor" State. To determine then which State was the aggressor, the principle of priority was not so effective as it might appear at first sight; it left the problem of the relationship between a declaration of war and the use of force unresolved and would therefore provide no easy means of determining the aggressor in such cases. It was for the Security Council to consider the element of intent and the element of priority and to assess each particular case in the light of the circumstances. A declaration of war might perhaps be the decisive proof, but it did not itself constitute an act of aggression.

108. In the opinion of some representatives, it was impossible to ignore completely the concept of the declaration of war in the definition, but that did not mean that a declaration of war must be listed as an act of aggression. In this connexion, it was suggested that the list of material acts constituting aggression might be qualified by a statement to the effect that they constituted aggression whether or not they were accompanied by a declaration of war.

(b) Use of weapons of mass destruction

109. Some representatives objected to the inclusion of a special reference to weapons of mass destruction in the definition of aggression; there were conceptual and doctrinal objections to the inclusion of such reference. It was not the use of any specific type of weapon but the use of weapons of any kind by one State against another in violation of the Charter which constituted aggression. Since the aggressive character of an act did not depend on the weapons used, a distinction between different kinds of weapons would not help the Committee to distinguish between acts which constituted aggression and those which did not. The hope was therefore expressed that the sponsors of the thirteen-Power draft would agree to delete the phrase "particularly weapons of mass destruction" in paragraph 5 (c). Further, and with reference to paragraph 2 B (a) of the USSR draft, the fear was expressed that if that provision was intended to raise the question of the prohibition of nuclear, bacteriological and chemical weapons, the Committee's work would slow down. Moreover, unless the element of intent and the effect of the act were taken into account, the underground testing of nuclear devices, for example, would constitute an act of aggression.

110. Other representatives agreed that technically it was not the type of weapons used but the use of any weapons by one State against another in violation of the Charter which constituted aggression. Nevertheless, they considered that the

transcendent character of weapons of mass destruction, particularly as their use
was opposed by public opinion throughout the world and the consequences were of
universal concern, warranted a special reference in a definition of aggression.
Some representatives, while holding the above views, nevertheless considered
that the corresponding phrase in the thirteen-Power draft might be deleted.
Other representatives, however, indicated that they could not agree to the deletion
of the phrase in that draft. It was also stated that nuclear, bacteriological or
chemical weapons were mentioned in the USSR draft as examples of weapons of mass
destruction; although they might seem of overriding importance at the present
day, a case might occur in the near future in which weapons of a kind not yet
heard of were used. In that draft, therefore, the mention of such weapons was
qualified by the phrase "or any other". Nevertheless, and in a spirit of
compromise, the USSR was disposed to delete the corresponding sentence from its
draft.

111. The opinion was also expressed that the difficulty lay, not in the inclusion
or omission of a reference to such weapons, but in the fact that the reference
would encroach on the right of self-defence by preventing a country under attack
from using such weapons first. The inclusion of a specific reference to weapons
of mass destruction would not give rise to objections if it was made clear that
their use, in itself, would not constitute aggression.

112. It was also stated that, while there could be some degree of agreement with
the objections raised to the inclusion of the phrase, the opinion could also be
shared whereby a reference to weapons of mass destruction would reflect the
universal concern about the consequences of their use. With the constant
development of new, unconventional weapons, it was conceivable that a country
might employ, for example, a bacteriological means of warfare which would not
be recognized by some countries as a weapon. The suggestion was therefore made
to add a paragraph to the preamble stating that the use of certain weapons, for
example, nuclear, bacteriological and chemical weapons and napalm, was inhuman,
besides constituting an aggressive act. The operative paragraph might then refer
only to "the use of any weapon". While some representatives supported this
solution, doubts were, however, expressed about its usefulness.

(c) Invasion, attack, military occupation and annexation

113. Several representatives expressed support for the inclusion in the definition
of aggression of a provision such as that of paragraph 2 B (c) of the USSR
draft and paragraph 5 (b) of the thirteen-Power draft. According to those texts,
invasion, attack, military occupation and annexation all constituted acts of
aggression. In the opinion of those representatives, occupation and annexation
were not merely consequences of invasion and, therefore, of aggression, but were
in themselves acts of aggression; they could not be excluded from the definition
on semantic grounds. It was as necessary to mention occupation and annexation
as invasion, since they were the continuation of invasion. Unlike the act of
invasion, however, they were of an indefinite or permanent character. Both were
continuing acts of aggression since they relied on the use of armed forces; both
were condemned by international law and in the Charter. Their condemnation had
first been stated in the Charter of the Organization of American States, an
instrument which was not only of Latin American origin but which represented the
jurisprudence of all the Americas. In this connexion, some representatives
indicated that they preferred the thirteen-Power text to that of the Soviet Union,
firstly because it was more precise in stating military occupation "however

temporary" to be aggression and, secondly, because the use of the adjective
"forcible" to quality annexation should obviate any misgivings in connexion with a
possible annexation by means of a peace treaty. The thirteen-Power text referred
to unilateral annexation resulting from the use of force, and that was an act of
aggression.

114. Some representatives, however, took a different view in this regard. It was
thus stated that the invasion by one State of the territory of another State could
be carried out in circumstances which did not render it aggression. There were
such cases; for example, where the armed forces of one State invaded the territory
of another State in order to defend or attack a third State, as had been done by
allied forces during the Second World War. Such an invasion was not an aggressive
invasion; if it was to be considered as such, with the result that the armed forces
of the defending State would always have to stop short at the defending State's own
frontiers, the aggressor could never lose, even though he might not win. Likewise,
when the armed forces of one State invaded the territory of another State in the
exercise of the right of self-defence. The opinion was also expressed that both in
the thirteen-Power and the USSR drafts, invasion and attack were grouped together
as similar concepts, whereas they were quite different. An attack could consist of
bombardment and need not involve the entry of armed forces into the territory of
another State. It would therefore be more appropriate to add the concept of attack
to the sub-paragraph dealing with bombardment and delete it from the one dealing
with invasion. It was further stated that no military occupation, however
necessary, was _ipso facto_ aggression; there was the case of territories occupied
and sometimes annexed both before and after the Second World War; military
occupation might become aggression in certain circumstances, for example, when
occupation was no longer necessary. The view was expressed that, as the Committee
was trying to determine what forms of the use of force constituted aggression, it
would be inappropriate to introduce into the definition such matters as military
occupation and annexation which were consequences of aggression. No State's
interests, whatever its political situation, would be prejudiced by the omission
from the definition of a provision dealing with the consequences of aggression.
It was also stated that the concepts of occupation and annexation had not been
completely ignored in the six-Power draft; paragraph IV B (2) was based on the
notion of an attack by one State against the territorial integrity of another, and
that implied diminution of territory; according to paragraph IV A (1), if the
purpose of the act was to diminish the territory or alter the boundaries of
another State, it would constitute an act of aggression, and hence the act
mentioned in paragraph IV B (2), which was tantamount to annexation, would
constitute an act of aggression. Similarly, the acts mentioned in
paragraph IV B (2) were a form of occupation and if committed for any of the
purposes listed in paragraph IV A, they would not be the consequence of aggression,
but would themselves constitute aggressive acts. If the thirteen Powers
acknowledged that their draft went too far in that respect, their approach could
be reconciled with that of paragraph IV B (2) of the six-Power draft.

115. Some representatives expressed doubts in particular about the inclusion of
annexation among the acts which constituted aggression. The view was expressed
that invasion and occupation presupposed a continuing state of war whereas
annexation implied a post-war situation which had legal implications, created by
a declaration or a treaty changing the status of occupation. It was also stated

that in so far as annexation was a manifestation of the use of armed force, there was no doubt that it constituted aggression and nothing to that effect need be added to the definition. When, however, annexation took place after the use of armed force, it could not in itself be regarded as an aggressive act; annexation was different in nature from aggression and it would be doing the international community a disservice to put it on the same footing. The above views should not, however, be taken as justifying forcible annexation, which was contrary to the principles of international law. The question was rather whether or not annexation should have a place in the definition of aggression; in this respect, it was stated that although annexation should be avoided in a list of acts of · aggression, it might be included in a provision corresponding to that of paragraph 8 of the thirteen-Power draft.

116. Other representatives, however, objected to the idea that it was unnecessary to mention annexation in the definition on the grounds that it would be covered by the inclusion of invasion. In this respect it was stated that history provided irrefutable proof that wars and acts of aggression were primarily motivated by the acquisition of territory. In the view of some representatives, as far as responsibility was concerned, occupation and annexation were the same thing, although the circumstances might not coincide. From the legal point of view, the difference lay in the declaration of annexation. For other representatives, however, annexation aggravated the original act of aggression; being permanent, it was worse than occupation from the point of view of international law. The view was also expressed that the difference between invasion, occupation and annexation was mainly a matter of time. Invasion might take place in only a few hours: the troops might then be withdrawn and there would be no occupation. If they remained, that would be occupation, namely a continuing act of aggression. Annexation was not merely the result of an illegal declaration; it transformed continuing aggression into a state of permanent aggression, at least in the intention of the aggressor. Moveover, annexation was not always simply a declaration: it was sometimes accompanied by the imposition of political, social, economic and cultural changes, all of which were acts of aggression; if invasion and occupation were included, annexation must be included also; they were three stages of the same act. As regards the suggestion that a reference to annexation might be made in the provision corresponding to paragraph 8 of the thirteen-Power draft, it was pointed out that paragraph 8 also referred to occupation. If both annexation and occupation could be mentioned under paragraph 8, it was difficult to understand why they could not both be mentioned also under paragraph 5 (b) of the same draft.

117. Several representatives criticized the expression "under the jurisdiction of another State" in paragraph IV B (1) of the six-Power draft. It was said that if that expression meant the territory of another State, the question arose why the words "the territory" had not been sufficient; if it meant something else, that should be stated. It was also considered that under such provision, a State which tried to regain territory occupied by foreign troops or annexed would be considered an aggressor. It was further stated that as such expression could only refer to a colony, it had no place in a definition of aggression.

118. On the other hand, the opinion was expressed that the suspicions and doubts about the words "territory under the jurisdiction of another State" were unjustified. That expression envisaged two cases: the case of a territory concerning which there was a dispute as to whether it lawfully belonged to the

State attacked; and the rarer case of a territory of one State which had been placed under the jurisdiction of another State by virtue of a particular regulation, for example, the Panama Canal Zone. Moreover, in no way could that expression be interpreted as having anything to do with colonialism.

119. Some representatives considered the provisions of paragraph IV B (2) of the six-Power draft unacceptable. In this respect, the view was expressed that that paragraph dealt with a matter which concerned the bilateral relations between States and not the definition of aggression. The international community should not be allowed to interfere in such matters prematurely. Such cases did not constitute a serious danger to peace and therefore did not warrant a special reference in the definition. It was also considered that that paragraph tended to give a permanent character to situations which were contrary to the spirit of decolonization, i.e. the practice of establishing military bases and stationing troops in foreign territory. The reference to conditions of permission for the presence of foreign troops implied acceptance of that practice. Besides, the behaviour of troops on foreign soil was irrelevant to the definition of aggression. The opinion was also expressed that there was a contradiction in the position adopted by the six Powers; they argued that retention of armed forces on the territory of a State beyond the period to which permission for their presence applied constituted aggression, but they did not recognize that military occupation was always aggression. Occupation was, in fact, the retention of armed troops on the territory of another State without permission or beyond the period to which permission applied; it was an act of aggression.

120. On the other hand, some representatives expressed support for paragraph IV B (2) of the six-Power draft. They pointed out that that paragraph covered an unusual form of aggression where foreign armed forces invited by a State, a practice permitted under international law, had refused to withdraw when asked. A situation might arise in which those armed forces were used in a manner that went beyond the conditions attached to the permission for their presence or in which they were not withdrawn on the expiry of the period to which the permission related or at the request of the host State. In such situations, the continued retention of those armed forces on the territory of another State constituted aggression. It was also stated that there was nothing in that text about colonialism or that could be taken as justifying colonialism.

121. The view was also expressed that, as the situation provided for in paragraph IV B (2) might give rise to aggression, the idea contained in that paragraph could be retained with the proviso that it must specify that the permission was accorded by the constitutional bodies of the State concerned. That point had been made more clearly and precisely in proposals that had been advanced by the Soviet Union in 1950, 1953 and 1956; the wording of the paragraph could be improved accordingly.

(d) Bombardment, attack on land, sea or air forces, blockade and the use of other forms of armed force

122. As pointed out by some representatives, bombardment was referred to as an act of aggression in all the three drafts. In this respect, the expression "territory under the jurisdiction of another State" in paragraph IV B (3) of the six-Power draft was criticized as being both vague and ambiguous; it would be

better to keep to the simple formula, "territory of another State", used in the other two drafts. The opinion was also expressed that if the notion that bombardment was an act of aggression was retained, as it should be, and paragraph 2 B (a) of the USSR draft and the comparable part of paragraph 5 (c) of the thirteen-Power draft relating to the use of weapons of mass destruction were deleted, as had been suggested in the context of those two paragraphs, that would be tantamount to saying that the use of nuclear weapons, for example, was not an act of aggression. While it was true that the question of prohibiting the use of nuclear weapons was not within the Committee's competence, that was not what the relevant passages of the USSR and the thirteen-Power drafts were about: they dealt with the question of the first use of arms or weapons.

123. Support was expressed for the wording of paragraph IV B (4) of the six-Power draft, as it covered all possible uses of force by any means. The comparable part of paragraph 2 B (b) of the USSR draft was considered to be not so comprehensive; it would not, for example, cover the use of force in space.

124. The word "deliberate" in paragraph IV B (5) of the six-Power draft was criticized as being unclear; if what was in mind was that all the acts listed must be deliberate, the word should appear in each case. It was unnecessary, however, to use the word at all, because what was being listed were acts committed first; if an act was committed first, it was aggression, otherwise it was not.

125. Support was also expressed for the inclusion of blockade of coasts or ports as an act of aggression in the definition.

   (e)   Armed bands, volunteer forces and terrorist and subversive activities

126. Some of the sponsors of the six-Power draft emphasized that acts mentioned in sub-paragraphs (6), (7) and (8) of paragraph IV B of the draft formed an integral part of any concept of aggression, because they were inseparably tied with the use of force in international relations, namely, the use of force across boundaries; the use of force across international boundaries was only justified in exceptional cases under the Charter. It was said that any definition of aggression that did not cover unlawful uses of force by indirect means - which most of the members of the Committee agreed constituted aggression - would not be acceptable; to omit consideration, even temporarily, of unlawful uses of force such as those described in the three sub-paragraphs would be to omit consideration of the principal methods by which acts of aggression were committed in the contemporary world; the inclusion of such acts in a definition was entirely consistent with the Charter and with recent history and was essential to the attainment of the purposes which a definition of aggression was intended to serve.

127. On the other hand, several representatives argued that the indirect use of force could be sufficiently serious to be characterized as aggression but was not necessarily aggression in all cases; the right of self-defence arose at the point where such use of force was on a sufficient scale to constitute direct armed aggression; indirect aggression, not being as serious or as dangerous as direct aggression, should be left for further consideration at a later stage of the Committee's work. Some representatives stated that they were prepared to accept a

definition at the present stage which, first, recognized and affirmed that the use of force violated the United Nations Charter; second, included a paragraph similar to operative paragraph 7 of the thirteen-Power draft; and third, expressly stated that indirect aggression would be defined at a later stage. It was said that the concept of armed attack in Article 51 was more restrictive than the concept of aggression in Article 39, and that was the criterion used in paragraph 7 of the thirteen-Power draft; a victim of indirect aggression had the right to take reasonable measures to safeguard its institutions, but not to proceed so far as to use the armed force to which self-defence under Article 51 was applicable. It was also pointed out that, if the armed bands or mercenaries imperilled the national existence of a State and were considered by the Security Council to be tantamount to armed attack, the State would be authorized to resort to self-defence; such authorization in the case of incursions by armed bands as distinct from an all-out open attack therefore depended on the degree of the danger they constituted. In the opinion of one representative, acts mentioned in sub-paragraphs (6) and (7) of paragraph IV B of the six-Power draft could in certain cases constitute aggression, but it was difficult to include the acts described in sub-paragraph (8) in the cases of aggression as the latter necessarily entailed the use of armed force by an aggressor State. It was also said that the hesitation of some members of the Committee concerning sub-paragraphs (6), (7) and (8) was largely due to their fear that the inclusion of those sub-paragraphs might lead to the recognition of the concept of preventive war; in certain circumstances it might be easy for a Government with expansionist ambitions to claim that a political opposition group within the country was a subversive organization directed by another State and to launch an armed attack against that State under the pretext of legitimate self-defence. It was suggested in this connexion that the definition of aggression should perhaps include a clear statement that the Security Council could assimilate serious, flagrant cases of subversion to direct armed aggression within the meaning of Article 51; paragraph 7 of the thirteen-Power draft might be amended along those lines; in the definition, certain cases of subversion which did not give rise to the right of self-defence could also be described as constituting aggression but expressly within the meaning of Article 39 and not Article 51.

128. Some representatives rejected the argument that unlawful uses of armed force in international relations could be divided into two categories - those which permitted recourse to the inherent right of self-defence and those which did not - on the basis of the directness of the manner in which armed force was used. This argument, in their view, had no foundation in fact or in law; if the Security Council was unable to act or to act quickly, the existence of a State which was the victim of the incursion of armed bands or widespread violence directed from a neighbouring State might be jeopardized, and no State whose national existence was thus imperilled would hesitate to take whatever action was necessary to repel an aggressor where the choice was between self-defence and waiting for rescue which might not arrive. Furthermore, the argument was inconsistent with the Charter; the right to self-defence referred to in Article 51 of the Charter was an inherent right and nothing expressed or implied in the text of that Article, nothing in its drafting history and nothing in United Nations practice since its adoption suggested that self-defence was not available to repel aggression, for example, in the form of incursions by armed bands. It was also said that the argument could have serious implications for the future of world peace; if the definition stated that the procurement of mercenaries to make incursions into the

desired territory to terrorize and demoralize the population would not be an act of aggression and that the victim State would not have lawful recourse to measures of self-defence, the State with expansionist amibitions would have reason to believe that its objective could be gained without the risk of counter-attack or even of being condemned as an aggressor; if that plan was carried out, the definition would make it more difficult for the victim State to obtain assistance from the United Nations; moreover, if the victim State found that the only way to stop persistent incursions by mercenaries was to attack their base across the frontier and did so, it might itself be condemned as an aggressor.

129. In the opinion of some representatives, the proposition underlying paragraph 7 of the thirteen-Power draft was that, in cases described in sub-paragraphs (6), (7) and (8) of paragraph IV B of the six-Power draft, the right of self-defence was either not available or limited; the argument in support of that proposition was unacceptable. It was true that Article 51 spoke of the right of self-defence if an "armed attack" occurred; but it did not say direct armed attack, and the examples put forward in sub-paragraphs (6), (7) and (8) were "armed attack". In the view of another representative, the accepted terminology under international law for such acts as hot pursuit of criminals was "border incidents"; such acts were not invasions and were not armed attacks in the sense of Article 51.

130. Several representatives felt that at the current session, the Committee was unlikely to produce more than a draft on direct aggression; it would however be useful to list the points of agreement and disagreement; it did not seem essential to produce a complete, generally acceptable definition of indirect aggression at this stage; there were in fact many points of disagreement on that subject. Some representatives, on the other hand, stated that a definition which covered only part of the acts which all considered as aggression would be of no use to the Security Council and would not find sufficient support in the Committee; the definition of aggression should cover so-called direct and indirect aggression without making a distinction expressis verbis or specifying what consequences should follow in each case.

5.   Paragraph 6 of the thirteen-Power draft: Proportionality

131. In the opinion of some representatives, the intimate relationship between aggression and self-defence made it necessary to clarify the limits of self-defence in a definition of aggression; in certain situations, measures used in self-defence could be transformed into acts of aggression; proportionality, therefore, was an important principle to be included in the definition. The legal scope of the principle and its basis were explained as follows. First, the proportionality principle established a relationship between the defensive action and the attack by conferring on a victim State the right to use force when necessary to halt an attack and, at the same time, by placing on it the obligation to limit the use of force to the amount necessary to halt the attack. Secondly, the principle stemmed from the notion that the use of force in self-defence was legitimate only because the victim of an armed attack must defend itself immediately; under the Charter, once that use of force had accomplished its purpose, no further use of force was permissible. Thirdly, without the principle of proportionality a State which was the victim of an armed attack could invoke the right of self-defence for undertaking a war of revenge; without the priority principle, preventive wars would be permissible, and, without the proportionality principle, wars of revenge would be permissible. The principle would also help to ensure that the use of force was centralized in the hands of the United Nations, which delegated its prerogative in the matter of the use of force only in cases of self-defence.

132. Several representatives expressed the view that the concept of proportionality was relevant to the question of legitimate recourse to self-defence; but the concept was irrelevant to a definition of aggression, which should not attempt to define the limits of self-defence; it was therefore unnecessary for the Committee to try to solve the difficult problem of how far and in what circumstances proportionality was a relevant or determining factor. It was said that the principle of proportionality was important and had a place in international law; but it was only one of several attributes of the inherent right of self-defence, others being for example necessity and immediacy; all these principles were included in the concept of self-defence, as embodied in customary international law. Some representatives felt that the question of proportionality needed further study; it was difficult to establish at what stage the aim of self-defence was achieved: whether it was when an armed attack was repulsed or when the security of the victim had been ensured; proportionality could not be taken to mean an exact balance, and any estimate of what constituted a reasonably proportionate response would depend on the circumstances. In the opinion of some representatives, the principle of proportionality did not require that a catalogue of means to be used in self-defence must be included in the definition; evaluation of what was reasonable and proportionate should be left to the Security Council; although such evaluation might sometimes be difficult, the principle should be accepted in the cases of flagrantly disproportionate or inhuman methods of self-defence.

133. Some representatives considered that Article 51 of the Charter did not include the concept of proportionality; a time-limit was built in by the phrase "until the Security Council has taken measures ...", but proportionality in the sense of the intensity and extent of the reply and the type of weapons used did not appear. It was also pointed out that when Article 51 was drawn up, there had been proposals that it should include provision for the "necessary" self-defence, embodying the idea of proportionality; it had, however, been omitted and the words "inherent right of" had been used instead. From the viewpoint that the question of proportionality should be considered in the light of actual instances of aggression, it was stated that the inclusion of the proportionality principle would unreasonably tie the hands of the victim of aggression, who had all the disadvantages, and would give undue benefit to the aggressor, who had all the advantages, such as surprise and unrestricted choice of means of attack; it was unreasonable to try to limit the victim's choice of weapons and scale of defensive response when it was the aggressor whose hands should be tied. In the opinion of one representative, the concept of proportionality had no basis in modern jurisprudence as far as self-defence was concerned; the right to self-defence was recognized as inherent and was not limited; the introduction of the concept of proportionality would only benefit the attacker and impose on the victim the burden of proving that the action was necessary for defence and relating the quality of that action to that of the attack.

134. The view was expressed by some representatives that the usefulness of the concept of proportionality depended on the substance of the definition of aggression. If the definition was to mention acts of indirect aggression and minor means of aggression, it would perhaps be necessary to include proportionality, for otherwise a limited attack might be alleged as a pretext for aggression under the name of self-defence. If, however, it was agreed that the definition should be confined to the most serious cases of direct armed aggression, the question of proportionality could be left to the Security Council.

135. One representative raised the question of the right of a State to take similar measures, if another State mobilized or concentrated its armed forces near the common frontier, without crossing the frontier.

6.   Paragraphs 4 and 5 of the USSR draft and paragraphs 8 and 9 of the
     thirteen-Power draft: legal consequences of aggression

136. Many representatives, who held the view that it was essential to include the consequences of aggression in any definition of aggression, stated that in order to be complete, the definition must recognize the immediate legal consequences of aggression and reflect an international attitude towards it; the non-recognition of territory acquired by force was an obligation, assumed by all members of the international community under the Charter: Article 1 of the Charter placed an obligation on all Member States to participate in collective measures for the suppression of acts of aggression or other breaches of the peace, and under Article 2, paragraph 2, States undertook to fulfil in good faith the obligations assumed in accordance with the Charter and therefore not to encourage or tolerate aggression or the acquisition of territory by force. Moreover, in order that the definition should be a deterrent to a potential aggressor, it should contain elements which would show a potential aggressor that no matter how he camouflaged his acts, he would be branded as an aggressor and would not profit from his deeds; under various criminal codes, an individual was entitled to know what his punishment would be if he committed a certain act, and the same should be the case under international criminal law. It was recalled in this connexion that, on the basis of political and legal considerations, the Special Committee on Principles of International Law concerning Friendly Relations and Co-operation among States had, in its draft Declaration, introduced the legal consequences of aggression in the formulation of the principle of the non-use of force; these considerations were equally relevant to the definition of aggression.

137. Some representatives expressed doubt about the deterrent effect of the definition; it was a historical fact that some States signed non-aggression treaties, but they were not deterred thereby from subsequently committing the very acts proscribed under those treaties against the State with which the treaty had been signed. It was also said that the analogy drawn between the definition of aggression and the provisions of criminal codes was inappropriate; whereas criminal codes described offences and prescribed penalties and procedures, the Committee's task was not to draw up a criminal code, but simply to define aggression; it was more likely to accomplish that task by considering only what was essential to the definition.

138. One representative stated that, to facilitate agreement on a definition of aggression, it might be wise to exclude from the definition any disputed elements which were not indispensable; and, in his view, classification of aggression as a crime and the criminal responsibility it gave rise to were both consequences of aggression and not essential to the definition. On the other hand, the occupation and annexation of territory were closer to aggression itself than to its consequences; they had rightly been linked with paragraph IV B (2) of the six-Power draft, which recognized that the maintenance of armed forces in the territory of another State could in itself be aggression; occupation and annexation should therefore be mentioned in the definition, whereas other elements which were clearly consequences of aggression could be omitted from it.

139. In the opinion of some representatives, paragraph 8 of the thirteen-Power draft was preferable to paragraph 4 of the USSR draft; the former was more specific and exhaustive than the latter, and would thus afford more protection to small States; it was very important to such States to provide that they "may not be the object, even temporarily, of military occupation or of other measures of force..."; it was essential that the principle of the inviolability of the territory of a State should be enshrined in the definition. However, other representatives preferred the wording of paragraph 4 of the USSR draft; it was more precise and stated the principle involved, without referring to matters which had only an indirect bearing on that principle; it also referred to the non-recognition, not only of territory acquired by force, but also of other advantages resulting from armed aggression.

140. Some representatives felt that paragraph 5 of the USSR draft and paragraph 9 of the thirteen-Power draft were almost identical, the only difference being one of drafting. One representative preferred paragraph 5 of the USSR draft, which dealt with the responsibility not only of States, but also of individuals in accordance with the principle established in international law by the Charter of the Nürnberg Tribunal. Another representative preferred the wording of paragraph 9 of the thirteen-Power draft, since international responsibility was generic, and no aggressor would be able to claim, for example, that only criminal or civil responsibility attached to the act committed.

7. Paragraph 6 of the USSR draft and paragraph 10 of the thirteen-Power draft: the right of self-determination

141. The principle enunciated in paragraph 6 of the USSR draft and in paragraph 10 of the thirteen-Power draft was supported by several representatives. Some of them considered, however, that paragraph 10 of the latter draft was more satisfactory and better expressed the respect due to the Charter. Paragraph 6 of the USSR draft, it was noted, had the merit of stating very clearly that dependent peoples had the right to use armed force, but its defect was that it only referred to General Assembly resolution 1514 (XV); paragraph 10 of the thirteen-Power draft, on the other hand, placed a broader interpretation on that right, since it mentioned not only the right of self-determination, but also the right of sovereignty and territorial integrity. That was justified, since it was also necessary to take into account the case of peoples who were victims of neo-colonialism and of peoples whose territory was occupied, for they also were oppressed. Paragraph 10 of the thirteen-Power draft therefore had the merit of acknowledging the right of all oppressed peoples, and not only of dependent peoples in the sense of General Assembly resolution 1514 (XV). It had been argued consequently that the best formula would be a combination of paragraph 6 of the USSR draft and paragraph 10 of the thirteen-Power draft; thus the last part of the latter paragraph might read as follows: "... concerning the right of peoples to use force in order to achieve self-determination, sovereignty and territorial integrity".

142. Some representatives, on the other hand, considered that the definition of aggression should not include any provision concerning the right of self-determination. A common denominator of the three drafts, it was stated, was that they defined aggression as an act directed by one State against another; for that reason, the use of force by dependent peoples in the exercise of their right of self-determination did not come within the range of the definition of aggression.

In addition, the problem had been discussed at length in the past and had been given a balanced solution in the draft Declaration on Principles of International Law concerning Friendly Relations and Co-operation among States, one part of which dealt with the right of peoples to self-determination; it would therefore be inadvisable to return to the same question in an entirely different context, at the risk of introducing an element of incoherence into the global action of the United Nations. Moreover, self-determination and the administration of dependent territories had been carefully regulated by the Charter, which had instituted a system that had proved effective. That system did not envisage the use of armed force by dependent Territories. A definition of aggression in international law could not describe as aggression the use of force by a State to repress a rebellion on its own territory; that was a fact imposed on the Committee by its terms of reference. Furthermore, since the Committee was concerned with acts performed in international relations, it was impossible to accept a provision, the effect of which would be that an act that would otherwise be defined as aggression by one State against another would not be considered aggression simply because it had been accomplished in a "self-determination context"; such a provision would be unacceptable, since it would completely distort the notion of aggression. In any event, it was emphasized that nothing in the six-Power draft derogated from the right of dependent peoples to exercise their right of self-determination.

143. In support of including a provision concerning the right of self-determination in the definition of aggression, it was argued that such a provision would be in conformity with the Charter and with the purposes of the United Nations. One of those purposes, it was stated, was to develop friendly relations among nations based on respect for the principle of equal rights and self-determination of peoples. The United Nations had pursued that purpose since its establishment and had tried to give substance to the principle of self-determination. Those efforts had reached their peak with the adoption of General Assembly resolution 1514 (XV) on the granting of independence to colonial peoples, which had been the signal for bringing colonialism to an end. Dependent countries therefore had had the right to fight for their liberation, and in doing so they were fulfilling an international function. The Special Committee, it was also argued, was not dealing with the principle of self-determination per se; it was discussing cases in which the use of force was lawful and could not therefore be qualified as aggression. Among such cases, there were the exercise of the right of self-defence and the measures taken by the Security Council. The use of force by dependent peoples to liberate themselves from oppression stemmed directly from the notion of self-defence provided for in Article 51 of the Charter, as those peoples were the victims of a permanent attack on their sovereignty. They were, in fact, defending themselves against Powers that were preventing them from forming independent States. The Special Committee on Principles of International Law concerning Friendly Relations and Co-operation among States had, of course, dealt with relations between States, as its very title indicated. It had nevertheless dealt with the question of the use of force by dependent peoples. Thus, it was difficult to see why that question should not be dealt with by the Special Committee on the Question of Defining Aggression. The argument that the definition of aggression should not qualify as aggression the use of force by a State to suppress a rebellion on its own territory was irrelevant. If the territory was a colonial or occupied one, the situation was different, for the colonial or occupying Power was not acting on its own territory.

144. It was also pointed out that although the definition of aggression should, of course, apply only to States, it must not be forgotten that there were organizations recognized by the United Nations, such as the Organization of African Unity, which gave dependent peoples aiming at self-determination the right to be supported by independent African States. The relationship between such a provision and the definition of aggression was obvious, for otherwise the definition might be misinterpreted as meaning that a State which gave its support to a dependent people must be considered as indirectly supporting an aggression. In law, however, a person assisting a lawful act did not commit an offence; consequently, the definition of aggression should contain a provision which would protect those independent States which helped dependent peoples struggling for their right of self-determination.

145. The view was also expressed that the definition should cover the case where a dependent people was operating from another territory than its own and attacking the geographical region which rightly belonged to it. It was held that such a case should be regarded as an exception to the principle that any armed attack constituted aggression. It was pointed out, on the other hand, that that condition of dependence was a fact of international life which had certain consequences in international law. Perhaps such a situation should be ended, but that was a different question and one that was being dealt with by other bodies.

146. The view that the definition of aggression should be broadened to include not only dependent peoples, but also oppressed peoples, was contested by some representatives. Such a digression, it was said, well demonstrated the danger of introducing self-determination into the definition. The extension of that notion to oppressed peoples would mean that a democratic State was entitled to overthrow the government of a dictatorial State whose people seemed to it to be oppressed. In the view of those representatives, such a doctrine was false, both in law and in politics, and it had never been recognized by the United Nations.

IV.   RECOMMENDATION OF THE SPECIAL COMMITTEE

147. At its 78th meeting, on 14 August, the Special Committee considered the draft resolution submitted by Bulgaria (A/AC.134/L.26).   At the same meeting the Special Committee unanimously adopted the draft resolution.   The text of the resolution reads as follows:

"The Special Committee on the Question of Defining Aggression,

"Bearing in mind General Assembly resolutions 2330 (XXII) of 18 December 1967, 2420 (XXIII) of 18 December 1968 and 2549 (XXIV) of 12 December 1969, which recognized the need to expedite the definition of aggression,

"Noting the progress made by the Special Committee and the fact that it did not have sufficient time to complete its task at its current session,

"Noting also the common desire of the members of the Special Committee to continue their work on the basis of the results achieved and to arrive at a draft definition,

"Recommends that the General Assembly, at its twenty-fifth session, invite the Special Committee to resume its work as early as possible in 1971."

ANNEX I

Draft proposals before the Special Committee

A.   Draft proposal submitted by the Union of Soviet Socialist Republics
     (A/AC.134/L.12):

The General Assembly,

Basing itself on the fact that one of the fundamental purposes of the United
Nations is to maintain international peace and security and to take effective
collective measures for the prevention and removal of threats to the peace, and for
the suppression of acts of aggression or other breaches of the peace,

Noting that according to the principles of international law the planning,
preparation, initiation or waging of an aggressive war is a most serious
international crime,

Bearing in mind that the use of force to deprive dependent peoples of the
exercise of their inherent right to self-determination in accordance with General
Assembly resolution 1514 (XV) of 14 December 1960 is a denial of fundamental human
rights, is contrary to the Charter of the United Nations and hinders the development
of co-operation and the establishment of peace throughout the world,

Considering that the use of force by a State to encroach upon the social and
political achievements of the peoples of other States is incompatible with the
principle of the peaceful coexistence of States with different social systems,

Recalling also that Article 39 of the Charter states that the Security Council
shall determine the existence of any threat to the peace, breach of the peace or
act of aggression and shall decide what measures shall be taken in accordance with
Articles 41 and 42 to maintain or restore international peace and security,

Believing that, although the question whether an act of aggression has been
committed must be considered in the light of all the circumstances in each
particular case, it is nevertheless appropriate to formulate basic principles as
guidance for such determination,

Convinced that the adoption of a definition of aggression would have a
restraining influence on a potential aggressor, would simplify the determination of
acts of aggression and the implementation of measures to stop them and would also
facilitate the rendering of assistance to the victim of aggression and the
protection of his lawful rights and interests,

Considering also that armed aggression is the most serious and dangerous form
of aggression, being fraught, in the conditions created by the existence of nuclear
weapons, with the threat of a new world conflict with all its catastrophic
consequences and that this form of aggression should be defined at the present
stage,

Declares that:

1.   Armed aggression (direct or indirect) is the use by a State, first, of armed force against another State contrary to the purposes, principles and provisions of the Charter of the United Nations.

2.   In accordance with and without prejudice to the functions and powers of the Security Council:

A.   Declaration of war by one State, first, against another State shall be considered an act of armed aggression;

B.   Any of the following acts, if committed by a State first, even without a declaration of war, shall be considered an act of armed aggression:

(a) The use of nuclear, bacteriological or chemical weapons or any other weapons of mass destruction;

(b) Bombardment of or firing at the territory and population of another State or an attack on its land, sea or air forces;

(c) Invasion or attack by the armed forces of a State against the territory of another State, military occupation or annexation of the territory of another State or part thereof, or the blockade of coasts or ports.

C.   The use by a State of armed force by sending armed bands, mercenaries, terrorists or saboteurs to the territory of another State and engagement in other forms of subversive activity involving the use of armed force with the aim of promoting an internal upheaval in another State or a reversal of policy in favour of the aggressor shall be considered an act of indirect aggression.

3.   In addition to the acts listed above, other acts by States may be deemed to constitute an act of aggression if in each specific instance they are declared to be such by a decision of the Security Council.

4.   No territorial gains or special advantages resulting from armed aggression shall be recognized.

5.   Armed aggression shall be an international crime against peace entailing the political and material responsibility of States and the criminal responsibility of the persons guilty of this crime.

6.   Nothing in the foregoing shall prevent the use of armed force in accordance with the Charter of the United Nations, including its use by dependent peoples in order to exercise their inherent right of self-determination in accordance with General Assembly resolution 1514 (XV).

B.   Draft proposal submitted by Colombia, Cyprus, Ecuador, Ghana, Guyana, Haiti, Iran, Madagascar, Mexico, Spain, Uganda, Uruguay and Yugoslavia (A/AC.134/L.16 and Add.1 and 2):

The General Assembly,

Basing itself on the fact that one of the fundamental purposes of the United Nations is to maintain international peace and security and to take effective collective measures for the prevention and removal of threats to the peace, and for the suppression of acts of aggression or other breaches of the peace,

Convinced that armed attack (armed aggression) is the most serious and dangerous form of aggression and that it is proper at this stage to proceed to a definition of this form of aggression,

Further convinced that the adoption of a definition of aggression would serve to discourage possible aggressors and would facilitate the determination of acts of aggression,

Bearing in mind also the powers and duties of the Security Council, embodied in Article 39 of the Charter of the United Nations, to determine the existence of any threat to the peace, breach of the peace, or act of aggression, and to decide the measures to be taken in accordance with Articles 41 and 42, to maintain or restore international peace and security,

Considering that, although the question whether aggression has occurred must be determined in the circumstances of each particular case, it is nevertheless appropriate to facilitate that task by formulating certain principles for such determination,

Reaffirming further the duty of States under the Charter of the United Nations to settle their international disputes by pacific methods in order not to endanger international peace, security and justice,

Convinced that no considerations of whatever nature, save as stipulated in operative paragraph 3 hereof, may provide an excuse for the use of force by one State against another State,

Declares that:

1.   In the performance of its function to maintain international peace and security, the United Nations only has competence to use force in conformity with the Charter;

2.   For the purpose of this definition, aggression is the use of armed force by a State against another State, including its territorial waters or air space, or in any way affecting the territorial integrity, sovereignty or political independence of such State, save under the provisions of paragraph 3 hereof or when undertaken by or under the authority of the Security Council;

3.   The inherent right of individual or collective self-defence of a State can be exercised only in case of the occurrence of armed attack (armed aggression) by another State in accordance with Article 51 of the Charter;

4.   Enforcement action or any use of armed force by regional arrangements or agencies may only be resorted to if there is decision to that effect by the Security Council acting under Article 53 of the Charter;

5.   In accordance with the foregoing and without prejudice to the powers and duties of the Security Council, as provided in the Charter, any of the following acts when committed by a State first against another State in violation of the Charter shall constitute acts of aggression:

(a) Declaration of war by one State against another State;

(b) The invasion or attack by the armed forces of a State, against the territories of another State, or any military occupation, however temporary, or any forcible annexation of the territory of another State or part thereof;

(c) Bombardment by the armed forces of a State against the territory of another State, or the use of any weapons, particularly weapons of mass destruction, by a State against the territory of another State;

(d) The blockade of the coasts or ports of a State by the armed forces of another State;

6. Nothing in paragraph 3 above shall be construed as entitling the State exercising a right of individual or collective self-defence, in accordance with Article 51 of the Charter, to take any measures not reasonably proportionate to the armed attack against it;

7. When a State is a victim in its own territory of subversive and/or terrorist acts by irregular, volunteer or armed bands organized or supported by another State, it may take all reasonable and adequate steps to safeguard its existence and its institutions, without having recourse to the right of individual or collective self-defence against the other State under Article 51 of the Charter;

8. The territory of a State is inviolable and may not be the object, even temporarily, of military occupation or of other measures of force taken by another State on any grounds whatever, and that such territorial acquisitions obtained by force shall not be recognized;

9. Armed aggression, as defined herein, and the acts enumerated above, shall constitute crimes against international peace, giving rise to international responsibility;

10. None of the preceding paragraphs may be interpreted as limiting the scope of the Charter's provisions concerning the right of peoples to self-determination, sovereignty and territorial integrity.

C. Draft proposal submitted by Australia, Canada, Italy, Japan, the United Kingdom of Great Britain and Northern Ireland and the United States of America (A/AC.134/L.17 and Add.1 and 2):

The General Assembly,

Conscious that a primary purpose of the United Nations is to maintain international peace and security, and, to that end, to take effective collective measures for the prevention and removal of threats to the peace, and for the suppression of acts of aggression or other breaches of the peace,

Recalling that Article 39 of the Charter of the United Nations provides that the Security Council shall determine the existence of any threat to the peace, breach of the peace, or act of aggression and shall make recommendations, or decide what measures shall be taken in accordance with Articles 41 and 42, to maintain or restore international peace and security,

Reaffirming that all States shall settle their international disputes by peaceful means in such a manner that international peace and security, and justice, are not endangered,

Believing that, although the question of whether an act of aggression has been committed must be considered in the light of all the circumstances of each particular case, a generally accepted definiton of aggression may nevertheless provide guidance for such consideration,

Being of the view that such a definition of aggression may accordingly facilitate the processes of the United Nations and encourage States to fulfil in good faith their obligations under the Charter of the United Nations,

Adopts the following definition:

I.   Under the Charter of the United Nations, "aggression" is a term to be applied by the Security Council when appropriate in the exercise of its primary responsibility for the maintenance of international peace and security under Article 24 and its functions under Article 39.

II.   The term "aggression" is applicable, without prejudice to a finding of threat to the peace or breach of the peace, to the use of force in international relations, overt or covert, direct or indirect, by a State against the territorial integrity or political independence of any other State, or in any other manner inconsistent with the purposes of the United Nations. Any act which would constitute aggression by or against a State likewise constitutes aggression when committed by a State or other political entity delimited by international boundaries or internationally agreed lines of demarcation against any State or other political entity so delimited and not subject to its authority.

III.   The use of force in the exercise of the inherent right of individual or collective self-defence, or pursuant to decisions of or authorization by competent United Nations organs or regional organizations consistent with the Charter of the United Nations, does not constitute aggression.

IV.   The uses of force which may constitute aggression include, but are not necessarily limited to, a use of force by a State as described in paragraph II.

A.   In order to:

(1) Diminish the territory or alter the boundaries of another State;

(2) Alter internationally agreed lines of demarcation;

(3) Disrupt or interfere with the conduct of the affairs of another State;

(4) Secure changes in the Government of another State; or

(5) Inflict harm or obtain concessions of any sort;

B.   By such means as:

(1) Invasion by its armed forces of territory under the jurisdiction of another State;

(2) Use of its armed forces in another State in violation of the fundamental conditions of permission for their presence, or maintaining them there beyond the termination of permission;

(3) Bombardment by its armed forces of territory under the jurisdiction of another State;

(4) Inflicting physical destruction on another State through the use of other forms of armed force;

(5) Carrying out deliberate attacks on the armed forces, ships or aircraft of another State;

(6) Organizing, supporting or directing armed bands or irregular or volunteer forces that make incursions or infiltrate into another State;

(7) Organizing, supporting or directing violent civil strife or acts of terrorism in another State; or

(8) Organizing, supporting or directing subversive activities aimed at the violent overthrow of the Government of another State.

ANNEX II

Report of the Working Group

1.   The Working Group established pursuant to the decision taken by the Special Committee at its 74th meeting, held ten meetings from 10 to 14 August 1970. The Working Group decided to bring the present report to the attention of the Special Committee.

A general definition of aggression

2.   Independently of the question of "direct or indirect" aggression, the following alternative texts were proposed:

(a) "Aggression is the use of armed force by a State against the territorial integrity /including the territorial waters and airspace/ /or sovereignty/ or political independence of another State, or in any other manner inconsistent with the purposes of the United Nations";

(b) "Aggression is the use of armed force by a State against another State, or in any way affecting the territorial integrity /including the territorial waters and airspace/ /or sovereignty/ or political independence of such State".

3.   However, a number of delegations considered that the foregoing texts were not satisfactory and stated that they would maintain the draft definition of aggression contained in paragraph 2 of the thirteen-Power draft. The representatives of the co-sponsors of the USSR draft and the six-Power draft also maintained their respective paragraphs.

4.   On the question of "direct or indirect" aggression, the members of the Working Group were agreed that the general definition of aggression should reflect the concept of aggression as contained in the Charter. Further, the view was expressed by several members that the general definition of aggression should refer only to the use of armed force, without qualifying it as "direct" or "indirect". The point of view was otherwise expressed by some members that the general definition should, if it did not refer to the use of armed force, overt or covert, direct or indirect, at least refer to armed force "however exerted".

The principle of priority

5.   The Working Group noted that all members were in favour of introducing the principle of priority into the definition. However, several members believed that the definition should specify that the element of priority was not the determining factor by itself, and that other elements should also be taken into account by the Security Council or any other body required to determine whether or not aggression had been committed. That point of view was embodied in the following text, proposed by one member:

"In determining whether force was used by a State in order to act against the territorial integrity or political independence of another State, or in any manner inconsistent with the purposes of the United Nations, due weight shall be given to the question which of those States first used force."

However, several delegations considered that the foregoing text was not satisfactory.

Political entities other than States

6.   The Working Group noted that many members wished the definition to refer only to States, while others believed that, if the text did not expressly include States whose statehood was disputed, an explanatory note should be annexed to the definition to the effect that the term "States" included States whose statehood was disputed. Some delegations noted that they saw a connexion between the concept of political entities and national liberation movements.

Legitimate use of force

7.   The Working Group took note that the following two texts had been proposed:

(a) "The use of armed force in accordance with the Charter to maintain or restore international peace and security, or in the exercise of the inherent right of individual or collective self-defence, does not constitute aggression";

(b) "The use of armed force in accordance with the Charter to maintain or restore international peace and security, or in the exercise of the inherent right of individual or collective self-defence, does not constitute aggression.

"The inherent right of individual or collective self-defence of a State can be exercised only in case of the occurrence of armed attack (armed aggression) by another State in accordance with Article 51 of the Charter.

"Enforcement action or any use of armed force by regional arrangements or agencies may only be resorted to under Article 53 of the Charter."

8.   Neither of these two texts received enough support from the Working Group. In the light of the foregoing, the representatives of the sponsors of the three drafts maintained their original texts.

Aggressive intent

9.   The Working Group noted that there were three points of view on this subject. Some members were in favour of a general statement to the effect that the Security Council should take purposes and intentions into account in determining whether an act of aggression had been committed. Some members considered that it was acceptable to list examples of purposes which might make the use of force aggression, as is done in paragraph IV A of the six-Power draft, or in the following proposed text:

"The use of armed force shall be recognized as aggression when undertaken with the following purposes:

To eliminate another State;

To annex territory of another State or to alter the boundaries of another State;

To change the existing political or social régime in another State;

To suppress national liberation movements in colonies and dependent territories and to keep peoples in colonial dependence;

To receive economic and other advantages from another State."

10. However, there was no agreement among the adherents to this second view on the particular examples cited in the foregoing text or in paragraph IV A of the six-Power draft.

11. Some members were opposed to any reference to the concept of intent in the definition and to the elaboration of any list of purposes.

Acts proposed for inclusion

12. It was agreed that the list of acts constituting aggression should be preceded by a statement to the effect that they were listed without prejudice to the fullness of the powers of the Security Council as provided in the Charter, particularly in declaring other acts to be aggression. To the extent that agreement was reached on the basic concept of priority, this concept should be mentioned. Those who advocated the inclusion of the concept of "intent" felt that that concept should also be mentioned in this connexion.

Declaration of war

13. The Working Group noted that there were two points of view on this question. Some members considered that a declaration of war was an act of aggression and should be included in the list of acts constituting aggression. Other members did not hold that view, but were prepared to accept a statement to the effect that the acts so listed constituted aggression whether or not they were accompanied by a declaration of war.

Use of weapons of mass destruction

14. The Working Group noted that some members were in favour of omitting specific reference to weapons of mass destruction from the definition, while others thought it might be necessary to mention them specifically in a general reference to weapons because of the special consequences of their use. It was decided that the final views of other members of the Committee on that point should be ascertained.

Invasion and attack

15. The Working Group agreed that the term "invasion" should be retained and that the inclusion or omission of the words "or attack" was a matter of drafting.

Occupation and annexation

16. Several members believed that occupation and annexation were in themselves acts of aggression, while others maintained that they were consequences of aggression and should not therefore be included in the list of acts constituting aggression.

Bombardment of the territory of another State

17. The Working Group noted that there was agreement on the inclusion of bombardment in the list of acts constituting aggression.

Blockade

18. The Working Group noted a readiness to agree on the inclusion of a reference to blockade, although some members did not believe that such a reference was necessary and would agree to it only by way of compromise in the context of broader agreement on a definition.

Maintenance of armed forces in another State

19. There was no agreement on paragraph IV B (2) of the six-Power draft. Some members who had doubts about it thought it might be acceptable in the context of broader agreement. Some members expressed the view that, as they considered that the concept had not been explained, they could not commit themselves to it. Inasmuch as the concept related to illegality of military occupation, they were ready to consider this paragraph of the draft.

20. The Working Group took note of the following text proposed as a possible alternative to paragraph IV B (2) of the six-Power draft:

"Where the armed forces of one State are within the territory of another State by virtue of permission given by the receiving State, any use of such forces in contravention of the conditions provided for in the permission or any extension of their presence in such territory beyond the termination or revocation of the permission by the receiving State."

Attacks on the armed forces, ships or aircraft of another State

21. The Working Group noted that there was agreement on the substance of this concept, as embodied in paragraph 2 B (b) of the USSR draft and paragraph IV A (5) of the six-Power draft. A suitable text would be drafted.

Indirect use of force

22. Because of the lack of time the Working Group's discussion on this subject was inconclusive. The Working Group agreed that the question needed further study. The Working Group took note of the following text proposed as a possible substitute for paragraph IV B (6) to (8) of the six-Power draft:

"The sending by a State of armed bands of irregulars or mercenaries which invade the territory of another State in such force and circumstances as to amount to armed attack as envisaged in Article 51 of the Charter."

23. This proposal was made on the understanding that the sending of armed bands under the circumstances envisaged therein could amount to direct armed aggression.

24. Some members of the Working Group were of the view that the foregoing proposal's treatment of aspects of the aggressive use of force by indirect means was incomplete and inadequate.

25. Independently of their interest in the foregoing text, some other members of the Working Group expressed the view that only armed attack could give rise to the right of self-defence in accordance with Article 51 of the Charter.

26. Some delegations felt that while the proposal was worth considering as a possible solution to the problem facing the Committee, their ultimate attitude would largely depend on providing adequate safeguards for the protection of the struggle of peoples deprived of their right to self-determination.

Proportionality

27. The Working Group noted that some members supported and others disputed the principle of proportionality. A number of members took a flexible position as to its inclusion in a definition of aggression. A number of members favoured its inclusion, although they took a flexible position on the manner of treating it within the definition.

Legal consequences of aggression:
(a) Non-recognition of territorial gains
(b) The question of responsibility

28. Independently of the question whether military occupation and annexation were in themselves acts of aggression, several members considered it necessary to reflect in the definition the concept of the non-recognition of territorial gains resulting from aggression and the concept of responsibility for aggression. Some of those members believed that the definition should also make it clear that the territory of a State was inviolable and could not be the object of military occupation by another State. Other members maintained, without derogating from the views to which their Governments had subscribed on those concepts in any other contexts, that consequences of aggression should not be included in the definition.

The right of peoples to self-determination

29.   Some members believed that, since the use of force was involved, it would be appropriate to refer in the definition to the rights of peoples under the Charter and to the recognition by the United Nations of the right of colonial peoples opposing forcible efforts to deprive them of their right to self-determination to receive support in accordance with the principles of the Charter. Some of those members considered that the mention of the right of peoples to sovereignty and territorial integrity should be included together with the provision on self-determination, such as is done in the thirteen-Power draft.

30.   Other members considered it unnecessary to mention the right of peoples to self-determination in the definition of aggression, as the two matters were not related.

*

*   *

Provisional character of the positions taken

31.   It was unanimously agreed that the positions taken by any delegation on any matter were provisional and that their final positions would depend upon the definition ultimately to be agreed on.

ANNEX III

List of representatives[a]

Algeria: Mr. Khélifa Lokmane

Australia: Mr. R.J. Smith, Mr. G.J.L. Coles*

Bulgaria: Mr. Téniu Petrov, Mr. Luben Koulichev

Canada: Mr. J.A. Beesley, Mr. P.A. Lapointe,* Mr. L.S. Clark,* Mr. R. Auger**

Colombia: Mr. Antonio Bayona

Congo (Democratic Republic of): Mr. Vincent Mutuale

Cyprus: Mr. Zenon Rossides, Mr. Ozdemir Ozgur,* Mr. Alecos Siambos**

Ecuador: Mr. Gonzalo Alcívar

Finland: Mr. Holger Rotkirch, Mr. Garth Castrén*

France: Mr. Charles P. Chaumont, Mr. Philippe Petit*

Ghana: Mr. K.B. Asante, Mr. E.K. Wiredu,* Mr. E. Sam**

Guyana: Mr. Duke E. Pollard

Indonesia: Mr. Umarjadi Njotowijono, Mr. Datuk Mulia,* Mr. Mohamad Sidik*

Iran: Mr. Jafar Nadim, Mr. Mehdi Ehassi*

Iraq: Mr. Mustafa K. Yasseen

Italy: Mr. Francesco Capotorti, Mr. Vincenzo Starace, Miss G. Simbolotti,**
       Mr. Alberto Schepisi**

Japan: Mr. Hideo Kagami, Mr. Kojiro Takano*

Madagascar: Mr. Maxime Zafera

---

*   Alternate.

**   Adviser.

[a] See paragraph 4 of the report.

Mexico: Mr. Bernardo Sepulveda, Mr. Ricardo Valero*

Norway: Mr. E.F. Ofstad, Mr. J.B. Heggemsnes

Romania: Mr. Gheorghe Badesco, Mr. Costel Mitran*

Spain: Mr. Enrique Valera, Mr. José Cuenca Anaya*

Sudan: Mr. Fakhreddine Mohamed, Mr. Omer El Sheikh*

Syria: Mr. Mowaffak Allaf, Miss S. Nasser*

Turkey: Mr. A. Coskun Kirca, Mr. Suat Bilge, Mr. Nüzhet Kandemir,
         Mr. Tugay Uluçevik, Mr. Ürner Kirdar*

Uganda: Mr. Samusoni Twine Bigombe

Union of Soviet Socialist Republics: Mr. Victor Chkhikvadzé, Mr. D. Kolesnik,*
                                       Mr. Oleg Bogdanov,** Mr. G. Boulgakov**

United Arab Republic: Mr. Omar Sirry, Mr. El Sayed Abdel Raouf El Reedy

United Kingdom of Great Britain and Northern Ireland: Mr. H. Steel, Mr. P.J. Allott*,
                                                       Mr. D.J. Johnson,*
                                                       Miss Candida Wheatley*

United States of America: Mr. Stephen M. Schwebel, Mr. Michael H. Newlin,*
                           Mr. James H. Michel**

Uruguay: Mr. Hector Gros Espiell, Mr. Sergio Pittaluga-Stewart*

Yugoslavia: Mr. A. Jelić, Mr. Borut Bohte

---

*   Alternate.

**   Adviser.

United Nations

GENERAL ASSEMBLY

Official Records

DOCUMENT 19

Agenda item 87

ANNEXES

TWENTY-FIFTH SESSION

NEW YORK, 1970

Agenda item 87:* Report of the Special Committee on the Question of Defining Aggression**

CONTENTS

* For the discussion of this item, see *Official Records of the General Assembly, Twenty-fifth Session, Sixth Committee,* 1202nd to 1209th and 1211th to 1213th meetings; and *ibid.,* Plenary Meetings, 1914th meeting.

** Since 1967, this question has been discussed by the General Assembly at the following sessions: Twenty-second session (agenda item 95), twenty-third session (agenda item 86) and twenty-fourth session (agenda item 88).

DOCUMENT A/8171

Report of the Sixth Committee

[Original: English/French]
[19 November 1970]

CONTENTS

I. INTRODUCTION

1. Pursuant to General Assembly resolution 2549 (XXIV) of 12 December 1969, the Special Committee on the Question of Defining Aggression reconvened at the United Nations Office at Geneva from 13 July to 14 August 1970 in order to resume its work in accordance with General Assembly resolution 2330 (XXII) of 18 December 1967, and prepared a report covering the work of its 1970 session.[1]

[1] *Official Records of the General Assembly, Twenty-fifth Session, Supplement No. 19.*

2. At its 1843rd plenary meeting, on 18 September 1970, the General Assembly decided to include in the agenda for its twenty-fifth session the item entitled "Report of the Special Committee on the Question of Defining Aggression", and allocated it to the Sixth Committee for consideration and report.

3. The agenda item was considered by the Sixth Committee at its 1202nd to 1209th and 1211th to 1213th meetings held between 16 October and 2 November 1970. At the 1202nd meeting, on 16 October 1970, Mr. Ofstad, the representative of Norway, and Rapporteur of the Special Committee on the Question of Defining Aggression, introduced the Special Committee's report.

4. At its 1209th meeting, on 28 October 1970, the Sixth Committee decided that its report on the agenda item should contain a summary of the principal juridical views expressed during the debate, the financial implications of such a summary having previously been brought to its attention in accordance with General Assembly resolution 2292 (XXII).

II. DRAFT RESOLUTION SUBMITTED TO THE SIXTH COMMITTEE

5. At its 1211th meeting, on 29 October, the Sixth Committee had before it the following draft resolution, which was introduced by the representative of Cyprus on behalf of Algeria, Bulgaria, the Byelorussian Soviet Socialist Republic, the Central African Republic, Cyprus, Czechoslovakia, Ecuador, Ethiopia, Ghana, Guyana, Haiti, India, Iran, Kenya, Kuwait, Libya, Madagascar, Mali, Mexico, Morocco, Poland, Romania, Sierra Leone, Southern Yemen, the Sudan, Syria, Tunisia, Uganda, the Ukrainian Soviet Socialist Republic, the Union of Soviet Socialist Republics, the United Arab Republic and the United Republic of Tanzania (A/C.6/L.799), which Guinea, Hungary, Indonesia and Yugoslavia subsequently joined.

1

"The General Assembly,

"Having considered the report of the Special Committee on the Question of Defining Aggression on the work of its session held at Geneva from 13 July to 14 August 1970,

"Taking note of the progress made by the Special Committee in its consideration of the question of defining aggression and on the draft definition, as reflected in the report of the Special Committee,

"Considering that it was not possible for the Special Committee to complete its task, in particular its consideration of the proposals concerning a draft definition of aggression submitted to the Special Committee during its sessions held in 1969 and 1970,

"Considering that in its resolutions 2330 (XXII) of 18 December 1967, 2420 (XXIII) of 18 December 1968 and 2549 (XXIV) of 12 December 1969 the General Assembly recognized the widespread conviction of the need to expedite the definition of aggression,

"Considering the urgency of defining aggression and the desirability of achieving this objective as soon as possible,

"Noting also the common desire of the members of the Special Committee to continue their work on the basis of the results achieved and to arrive at a draft definition,

"1. *Decides* that the Special Committee on the Question of Defining Aggression shall resume its work, in accordance with General Assembly resolution 2330 (XXII), as early as possible in 1971;

"2. *Requests* the Secretary-General to provide the Special Committee with the necessary facilities and services;

"3. *Decides* to include in the provisional agenda of its twenty-sixth session an item entitled 'Report of the Special Committee on the Question of Defining Aggression'."

6. At the 1213th meeting, on 2 November 1970, the sponsors, which Cambodia and Yemen joined, submitted a revised draft (A/C.6/L.799/Rev.1), in which the fifth preambular paragraph had been replaced by the following:

"Considering the urgency of bringing the work of the Special Committee to a successful conclusion and the desirability of achieving the definition of aggression as soon as possible".

III. Debate

7. The trends of the opinions expressed in the Sixth Committee are summarized below under appropriate headings.

A. *Opinions expressed on certain general aspects of the question of defining aggression*

8. Most of the representatives who spoke expressed the view that the formulation of a definition of aggression would help considerably towards the maintenance of international peace and security. It was said that in addition to contributing to the progressive development of international law, especially with regard to the principle of the non-use of force in international relations, a legal definition of aggression would make it possible to consolidate the mechanism of collective security based on the Charter of the United Nations, a mechanism which turned not only on the prohibition

of the use of force but also on the right of self-defence and the power of the Security Council; a clear demarcation between aggression and the right of self-defence could assist the Security Council in determining the existence of an act of aggression and help to ensure that adequate measures were taken and international disputes were settled peacefully as a result. It was also observed that a legally precise and generally acceptable definition of aggression would not only dissuade potential aggressors but also protect States against the arbitrary characterization of the use of force automatically as aggression. In the view of some representatives a definition would also assist the international community in fixing responsibility for illegal use of force falling within its terms. Several representatives stressed the urgency of defining aggression and the desirability of achieving this objective as soon as possible. It was said that, since the General Assembly stated such urgency in resolution 2549 (XXIV) of 12 December 1969, nothing had occurred to change the situation; on the contrary, the need for the definition had become even more urgent in the light of the debates which had taken place at the present Assembly session and in order to complete such texts as the Declaration on Principles of International Law concerning Friendly Relations and Co-operation among States in accordance with the Charter of the United Nations (resolution 2625 (XXV)) and the draft Code of Offences against the Peace and Security of Mankind,[2] as well as other international legal instruments on security matters. It was also stated that the speedy formulation of a definition of aggression was of particular concern to small- and medium-sized countries and to newly-independent countries whose economic and social progress depended on the maintenance of international peace and security.

9. On the other hand, some representatives expressed doubts about the usefulness of a definition of aggression. The view was also expressed that there was no urgency for achieving a definition of aggression shortly after the adoption by the General Assembly of the Declaration on Friendly Relations, which already contained provisions relating to the prohibition of the use of force, self-determination and legal consequences of aggression. It was noted in this connexion that the Security Council could act under Chapter VII of the Charter without the finding of an act of aggression, and indeed too great an emphasis on a definition might hinder its efforts to deal with the matter. It was also said that the nature of the subject and the present political climate made it advisable to defer the question of defining aggression for a year or two.

10. A number of representatives felt that the Special Committee had made encouraging progress in the three years since its establishment, considering the vain attempts made for forty years to define aggression, and the 1967 debates in the General Assembly, when a number of delegations had seen no need for and no possibility of defining aggression. It was noted with satisfaction that all the groups of States represented in the Special Committee had submitted draft proposals and demonstrated their desire to arrive at a generally acceptable definition; the work of the Special Committee at the 1970 session had enabled the sponsors of the various draft proposals to clarify their positions and the gap between different points of view had been narrowed. Moreover, in the opinion of some repre-

---

[2] See *Official Records of the General Assembly, Sixth Session, Supplement No. 9*, para. 59.

sentatives, the area of agreement that had emerged from the Special Committee's 1970 session was much wider than was indicated in its report, which could only record official positions. All these positive results were said to give grounds for hoping that the Special Committee might be able to complete its work successfully. A large majority of the representatives who spoke therefore supported the recommendation of the Special Committee on the resumption of its work as early as possible in 1971 (A/8019, para. 147).

11. In the opinion of some representatives, however, the progress made by the Special Committee warranted neither optimism nor pessimism. It was said that a few common factors which had emerged from the Committee's 1970 session concerned only the less difficult questions, and on the whole, the results of the session were rather poor, the only encouraging factor being that the discussions had taken place in an atmosphere of co-operation and goodwill. One representative suggested that the Special Committee's work might be suspended until 1973 and the Secretary-General might be requested to seek comments and proposals from Member States. Another representative considered that the Special Committee's mandate should not be renewed unless it was assigned a specific task of submitting to the next session of the General Assembly conclusions recommending a compromise between the various tendencies which would serve as a basis for a generally acceptable definition of aggression.

12. With regard to the procedure to be followed in preparing and adopting a definition of aggression, several representatives maintained that such a definition must be capable of attracting overwhelming support among the States Members of the United Nations; in other words, it must be a consensus definition; the process of working by consensus might be slow but it could have rewarding results. The view was also expressed that unanimity of Member States, including all the permanent members of the Security Council, would be essential in order that the definition should provide a useful guidance for the Security Council in discharging its responsibility. It was argued that, since the definition of aggression was not only a juridical task but also an important political question, the Special Committee should spare no effort to reach the broadest possible agreement; the Special Committee should retain the consensus method, which would be the most suitable procedure for the adoption of the definition.

13. Other representatives were also in favour of working for unanimity and fully recognized the value of a mutually agreed text, but they nevertheless believed that, if unanimity could not be achieved, the Special Committee should vote on controversial matters, so that a draft definition that commanded a large majority of its members could be produced; a very wide majority in the Special Committee would be a sufficient basis for submitting a draft definition to the General Assembly, which could then consider whether a unanimous decision was necessary. In the opinion of some representatives, it was unrealistic to try to adopt a definition of aggression by consensus. Besides, it was not essential that the definition should be acceptable to the permanent members of the Security Council; there could be no question of accepting any veto in the progressive development of international law; a definition approved by a large majority of States would constitute a weighty legal basis which could not be ignored by the United Nations bodies responsible for maintaining international peace and security.

B. *Opinions expressed on the content of the definition*

1. *The definition and the power of the Security Council*

14. As to the question of the definition of aggression and the powers of the Security Council, many representatives observed that any definition should in no way curtail or fetter the Council's discretionary powers under Article 39 of the Charter, that is, its freedom of judgement in determining whether any specific situation involved an act of aggression. The definition would simply be used by the Security Council as one of many legal sources to draw on in its work; it was not to be automatically applied by that organ. In the opinion of some representatives since the discretionary powers of the Security Council were of a political character, it would not be logical to impose a binding definition of aggression on the Council. It was considered doubtful if the General Assembly, which was only empowered to make recommendations, could restrict the powers of the Security Council; any definition adopted by the Assembly, it was said, could never enjoy binding legal force, even though it would have a definite moral value for public opinion and for the Security Council.

15. In the opinion of several other representatives, however, the definition ought to be worded in such a way as to prevent the Security Council from taking arbitrary decisions, although the definition should in no way affect the powers conferred on the Council by the Charter. It was stated that once the General Assembly had adopted a definition, based strictly on the Charter or uncontested principles of international law, it would be binding on all bodies, including the Security Council; thus, if all the conditions set forth in the definition were fulfilled, the Council would be bound to affirm the existence of an act of aggression and take the appropriate action under Articles 41 or 42 of the Charter; on the other hand, the Security Council should not be limited to the list of acts in the definition and it should be free to determine the existence of an act of aggression in all cases not fully covered by the definition. The opinion was also expressed that the list of acts constituting aggression should be preceded by a statement to the effect that they were listed without prejudice to the full powers of the Security Council as provided in the Charter—a fact which should not be taken to mean that the Council had the right to add other acts to the list. Certain representatives felt that reference to the Security Council's powers was irrelevant to the definition; the General Assembly, as well as the Security Council, would automatically be guided by any definition that might be produced.

2. *Political entities to which the definition should apply*

16. Some representatives maintained that the definition of aggression should be applicable to any author of an aggression; for the victim of an aggression it was irrelevant whether the aggressor was a State or some other political entity. It was also said that it should not be possible to argue that, by reason of the disputed status of a particular political entity by or against which force had been used, that use of force did not constitute aggression. Certain representatives supported the suggestion that an explanatory note should be annexed to the definition to the effect that the term "State" included those whose statehood was disputed.

17. Several representatives were, however, opposed to the inclusion in a definition of aggression of the idea

of political entities, an idea which was alien to the Charter. Such inclusion, in their view, could encourage a restrictive interpretation of the term "State" and blur the distinction between international conflicts and civil wars. In that connexion, it was stressed that the definition of aggression should be based on the concept of the State in international relations, without making the existence of the State dependent on the recognition of its statehood by other States. Moreover, such inclusion would encourage certain States to prevent the exercise of the right of peoples to decide their own future by labelling national liberation movements as aggressors and invoking the self-defence argument against them. It was also pointed out that, if the term "political entities" was intended to cover States whose statehood is in dispute, then relevant rules already existed in international law and the issue had no place in a definition of aggression.

3. *Acts proposed for inclusion in the definition of aggression*

18. A number of representatives expressed the view that the practical way of achieving a definition of aggression was by dealing first with direct armed aggression, which constituted the gravest threat to international peace and security at the present time, leaving the question of other forms of aggression to a later date. It was said that while it should not be difficult to agree on what constituted the most serious and obvious cases of armed aggression against which a victim State could exercise the right of self-defence, to try to draw up a definition of aggression in the widest sense would raise many difficulties which would hold up the work too long; since many crimes had been committed in the name of self-defence, it was urgent to ascertain which acts entitled States to take defensive actions in its name. Most of those representatives also specified that they attached great importance to the question of indirect aggression. It was stated that indirect aggression was of particular interest to small countries, particularly vulnerable to that form of aggression, and to countries still under colonial domination, which were frequently the victims of it; armed aggression could assume two forms, direct or indirect, although it was difficult to find a precise criterion for affirming whether a case of indirect aggression was or was not armed aggression under the terms of Article 1 of the Charter. In this connexion, the decision of the Soviet Union to delete the words "direct or indirect"[3] from its draft proposal[4] was welcomed by some representatives, who appealed to the sponsors of the six-Power draft[5] to make a similar concession.

19. On the other hand, several representatives maintained that any definition of aggression must cover all uses of force, whether or not they were direct. It was said that the labels "indirect aggression" for covert forms and "direct aggression" for overt armed attack were at variance with the Charter and only the six-Power draft fully covered all forms of aggression; to the victim, infiltration of terrorists and armed bands and acts of sabotage were no less direct, no less illegal and no less a breach of the peace than the same acts when committed by regular military forces; the most serious threats to international peace and security at the present time stemmed from the less direct and less overt uses of force; a partial definition covering only so-called "direct" aggression would not be consistent with the Charter and would not therefore be acceptable.

20. In the opinion of some representatives, the definition of aggression should, at the present stage, cover only the use of force, without qualifying it as direct or indirect; in this respect paragraph 2 of the thirteen-Power draft[6] was satisfactory. It was stated that the proposed definition of indirect aggression could not be exhaustive; it should therefore include a minimum list of the most serious cases of aggression under Articles 39 and 51 of the Charter; it would be possible to include the sending of armed bands by one State into the territory of another, and also to consider certain cases of indirect aggression which would constitute acts of aggression as defined in Article 39 but would not give rise to the right of self-defence as defined in Article 51. Also, certain representatives said that they were willing to support a more general definition referring to armed force "however exerted".

21. Some representatives considered that the definition should cover various other forms of aggression such as economic, financial, political, cultural or ideological pressures, although the value of inclusion of such forms was contested by other representatives. It was felt that the definition should mention a form of aggression whereby a State made its territory available to another State for the purpose of an armed attack against a third State, and that it should also contain a paragraph designed to prevent a State from invoking any consideration relating to another State's internal or foreign policy to justify the use of force against the latter.

22. Some representatives were of the opinion that a declaration of war was intrinsically an act of aggression; although a declaration of war did not necessarily coincide with the commencement of hostilities, it was a patent manifestation of the existence of belligerent intent; it seemed dangerous and realistic for the State against which war had been declared to be forced to wait for an actual attack before taking defensive measures. Other representatives felt that a declaration of war did not necessarily constitute an act of aggression *per se*, but on the grounds of its formal legal consequences and its intrinsically serious nature, it should constitute an important element to be taken into account in determining the commission of an act of aggression. On the other hand, however, it was observed that a declaration of war was not necessarily relevant to the existence of aggression; it might be made long after the commencement of hostilities, for purely judicial or administrative reasons, in which case neither its existence nor its timing was indicative of aggression or aggressive intent.

23. In the opinion of some representatives, weapons of mass destruction should be expressly mentioned in a definition of aggression, since their use was not only a direct aggression but a violation of human rights. Other representatives thought that a reference to the use of weapons of mass destruction should be made only for information; they represented a way of committing aggression, not a constituent element of it. It was observed that the employment of such weapons might raise the question of the proportionality of an act and thus affect the burden of proof of justification; its mention in the definition was therefore acceptable, but the words "weapons of mass destruction" needed definition. It was also noted that the view appeared

---

[3] See A/AC.134/SR.61.
[4] See *Official Records of the General Assembly, Twenty-fifth Session, Supplement No. 19*, annex I, draft proposal A.
[5] *Ibid.*, draft proposal C.

[6] *Ibid.*, draft proposal B.

widely shared in the Special Committee that the definition should not rule out the possibility of nuclear weapons being used in self-defence against an attack by an aggressor using conventional weapons.

24. Several representatives considered that invasion, attack, military occupation and annexation of territory belonging to another State constituted flagrant acts of aggression which should be incorporated in any definition. However, the view was expressed that military occupation and annexation were essentially consequences either of the legitimate use of force or of acts of aggression and that they should not therefore be included in the definition.

25. Several representatives stressed that any definition of aggression should include a mention of infiltration into the territory of a State by irregular forces or armed bands, subversion, terrorism or other indirect uses of force intended to violate the political independence and territorial integrity of a State, while other representatives felt that such acts did not present a danger to peace so serious as direct aggression and an attempt to define such acts would run into many difficulties. In that connexion, it was noted that one of the sponsors of the thirteen-Power draft suggested the possible addition of the infiltration of armed bands to the list of acts of aggression.

4. *The principle of priority*

26. The introduction of the concept of priority into the definition of aggression did not seem to meet, in principle, with any opposition. Different views were, however, expressed regarding the degree of importance which should be accorded to that concept in the definition. On the one hand, it was observed that the principle of priority, which was sanctioned by many international instruments and was based directly on the provisions of the Charter and in particular on Article 51, constituted the only objective criterion applicable in determining the aggressor; it laid the burden of proof on the State which attacked first and raised a presumption that the State which attacked first was the aggressor; its purpose was to prevent States from committing acts of aggression in the guise of preventive wars. It was also stated that the principle of priority formed the fundamental criterion; that criterion was applied in all systems of municipal law and should take a prominent place in any objective and realistic definition of aggression. Furthermore, it was difficult to formulate a definition of aggression without referring to the principle of priority; although it was not, perhaps, the only valid principle, it was certainly the most important to be applied; since armed aggression was the most serious form of aggression, the definition should embody that principle, which should be the main criterion in determining the aggressor in an international conflict. On the other hand, the view was expressed that the principle of priority should figure in the definition only as one element among others. In many cases, an automatic application of that principle would lead to surprising results. Because of the difficulty of determining the facts, the definition should not include prior resort to force as an unqualified general criterion of automatic application, for every case should be judged on its merits and the priority of resort to force was only one of the elements of an act of aggression, although an important element; if the concept of priority were to be included in the definition, the latter would have to be drafted in such a way that the Security Council would be able to consider all the relevant aspects of a case before reaching a conclusion. Furthermore, it was pointed out that the principle of priority could not be unconditionally accepted without implying a controversial interpretation of the right of self-defence recognized in Article 51 of the Charter; moreover, it was not the task of the Special Committee to define the scope of that right; the Special Committee could not elaborate a good definition of aggression if, in the process, it sought not merely to define the right of self-defence but to do so in a way which would be interpreted by many States as circumscribing that fundamental right.

27. One representative, while stating that he favoured the principle of priority, raised the query whether or not a distinction should be made in the definition between acts of aggression proper and border incidents. In his view, a border incident should not entail the type of reaction appropriate to an armed attack. He therefore suggested that the words "in an international conflict" should be inserted before the word "first" in the relevant paragraphs of the USSR draft proposal and the thirteen-Power draft proposal.

5. *Aggressive intent*

28. A number of representatives were opposed to including the element of intent in the definition of aggression. Reference was made to the principle of priority, embodied in the USSR and the thirteen-Power drafts, and to the element of intent, embodied in the six-Power draft, and the view was expressed that no subjective element of any kind should be introduced into the definition of aggression. That did not mean that priority would be the sole determining factor in deciding whether or not aggression had been committed; the fifth preambular paragraph of the thirteen-Power draft and the sixth preambular paragraph of the USSR draft both stated that all circumstances had to be taken into account in each particular case: in other words, there was no automatic application of the principle of priority and the powers and duties of the Security Council were in no way diminished. On the other hand, it was stated that the element of priority was apparently irreconcilable with the element of intent; it was therefore unacceptable to place the two elements on the same footing in the definition, even though it was conceivable that the Security Council might take into consideration expressions of intent by the States involved; however, the lack of aggressive intent could not establish the innocence of a State that had been the first to commit an act of aggression. Furthermore, it was pointed out that the idea that an act of aggression could be unintentional was inconceivable; intent was intrinsic to aggression; motive was an altogether different concept, which should not be included in the definition sought. The view was also expressed that including the concept of intent in the definition of aggression would have the effect of placing the burden of proof on the victim; furthermore, it would enable the aggressor to take shelter behind the definition in order to deny that he had had any aggressive intent. In addition, it was observed that the concept of aggression led to the theory of just and unjust wars, which was a mediaeval theory; since the Charter referred only to acts and not to motives, the inclusion of that concept in the definition would be unacceptable, since the purpose of the definition was to restrain aggression, not to provide justification for it, and to give effect to the Charter, not to restrict its application.

29. On the other hand, some representatives maintained that the definition of aggression should take into account the element of intent, which in their view would be one of the most important elements in determining whether or not aggression had occurred. If intent were not recognized as an element of aggression, a limited, erroneous or unauthorized attack could unjustly be labelled as aggression. It was pointed out that that element, which was referred to by implication in paragraph IV A of the six-Power draft, was also implicit in the other drafts submitted to the Special Committee; furthermore, the element of intent was not necessarily subjective: it was generally inferred, especially in criminal law, from the objective circumstances of the offence.

6. Legitimate use of force

30. According to some representatives, any definition of aggression should acknowledge that the use of force in the exercise of a State's inherent right to individual or collective self-defence did not constitute aggression. It was recalled that it had been recognized at the San Francisco Conference that the use of arms in self-defence remained admitted and unimpaired and that that principle had been enshrined in Article 51 of the Charter. A literal reading of that Article showed that individual or collective self-defence was an "inherent right", which therefore did not arise from the Charter and was not limited by any provision of the Charter; that right existed until the Security Council had taken the measures necessary to maintain international peace and security. Other representatives said that efforts should be made to establish the limits of the right of self-defence vested in States by virtue of Article 51 of the Charter, in order to prevent any possible ambiguity between any kind of military action and an aggression in the proper sense of the word. It was maintained that not all breaches of the peace would give a State the right to self-defence. A State could exercise that right only if force had been used, and not merely threats.

31. It was stated that paragraph 4 of the thirteen-Power draft should be amended so as not to diminish the right of self-defence, individual or collective, embodied in Article 51 of the Charter; similarly, paragraph 7 of that draft should be reworded, since it gave the impression that the internal measures a State might take to safeguard its existence and institutions were dependent on international permission and were not within its own competence, thus contradicting Article 2 (7) of the Charter.

32. Some representatives favoured including the principle of proportionality in the definition of aggression. In that connexion, it was observed that an unconditional right of self-defence could not be protective, particularly in the case of small States; the principle of proportionality seemed to provide the only safe guarantee that a defensive action would not turn into aggression; paragraph 6 of the thirteen-Power draft, which embodied that principle, was quite reasonable and should be accepted. Other representatives said that the question of proportionality should play little part in the definition of aggression. Over-reaction by the victim did not alter the aggression itself; furthermore, Article 51 of the Charter did not mention the principle of proportionality and placed no limitations upon the means that the victim of armed aggression could use to repel the aggressor. Apart from the difficulty of establishing when the stage of successful self-defence

had been reached, the inclusion of the principle would handicap the victim State by obliging it to decide how much force to use to repel the aggressor; moreover, the principle had no basis in modern jurisprudence in the context of self-defence.

33. Some representatives, referring to paragraph III of the six-Power draft, observed that the use of armed force by regional arrangements or agencies would be legitimate only if there had been a prior decision to that effect by the Security Council under Article 53 of the Charter. That Article authorized the Security Council to use regional arrangements or agencies where necessary, but no regional enforcement action could be taken without the Security Council's prior authorization; the phrase "consistent with the Charter of the United Nations" in paragraph III of the six-Power draft did not suffice to remove the ambiguity introduced into the interpretation of Article 53 of the Charter. The view was also expressed that according to Articles 39 and 42 of the Charter, only the Security Council could decide to resort to enforcement measures involving the use of force; any formula designed to give the General Assembly or regional agencies powers which were not granted to them by the Charter would therefore be unacceptable. It was also felt that paragraph 4 of the thirteen-Power draft and paragraph III of the six-Power draft should be reworded in order to bring them into line with the provisions of Article 53 of the Charter; enforcement action did not necessarily involve the use of armed force; it consisted basically of the application of sanctions, which might be diplomatic, economic and financial or military in nature.

7. The right of self-determination

34. Many representatives were in favour of including in the definition of aggression a provision envisaging an exception when the use of force was necessary to ensure the exercise of the right of peoples to self-determination. Such a provision was of paramount importance to countries which were prepared to support national liberation movements; colonialism qualified as aggression, and the use of force by dependent peoples in the exercise of their right to self-determination should not be regarded as an act of aggression. Furthermore, the view was expressed that the use of force to prevent a people under colonial or alien rule from exercising its right to self-determination was a form of armed aggression; in the exercise of that right, the organizing of armed bands and the instigation of civil strife should be considered legitimate means. It was also stated that the definition of aggression should take into account the situation of oppressed peoples, particularly those who were the victims of apartheid and other forms of racial discrimination.

35. On the other hand, some representatives observed that the use of force by colonial peoples was not envisaged in the system established by the Charter and should be excluded from the definition of aggression. In that connexion, it was noted that the question of self-determination and administration of dependent territories had been carefully regulated by the Charter, which had instituted an effective system that did not envisage the use of armed force by dependent territories; furthermore, recognition of the legitimacy of the use of force in order to give aid to dependent and oppressed peoples might provide a pretext for manifest acts of aggression; in view of the universal scope of the right to self-determination, there were many cases in which such abuses might occur. It was also observed that the legal questions raised by the right to self-

determination had been satisfactorily solved in the drafting of the Declaration on Friendly Relations, and that it might therefore be questioned whether it was necessary to revert to those questions for the purposes of defining aggression. One representative, while acknowledging that there was no need for the right to self-determination to be mentioned in the definition of aggression, said that he would not oppose the inclusion in the definition of the formulation used in paragraph 6 of the Declaration on the Occasion of the Twenty-fifth Anniversary of the United Nations, adopted by the General Assembly on 24 October 1970 (resolution 2627 (XXV)), on the understanding that the term "appropriate means" used in that formulation meant "means in accordance with the Charter".

8. Legal consequences of aggression

36. A number of representatives considered that the definition should contain provisions concerning the legal consequences of aggression. It should state clearly that the unlawful use of force entailed responsibility and conferred no rights. The principle of the non-recognition of territorial gains or any other advantage obtained by force had already been recognized in several international instruments, and recently in the Declaration on Friendly Relations; similarly, the principle of the responsibility of the aggressor, which was also undisputed, had already been embodied in international practice, for instance, at the Nuremberg and Tokyo tribunals; the USSR draft rightly stated that armed aggression entailed the political and material responsibility of States and the criminal responsibility of the guilty persons. Paragraphs 4 and 5 of the USSR draft and paragraphs 8 and 9 of the thirteen-Power draft concurred in that respect; however, paragraph 8 of the latter text was both more profound and more precise in that it referred to the inviolability of the territory of a State, which might not be the object, even temporarily, of military occupation or other measures of force; that formula was a worthy contribution to the cause of international law, and might prove generally acceptable if it was specified that it was not only territorial gains obtained by force which should

not be recognized, but also "any other special advantage", a concept taken from paragraph 4 of the USSR draft.

37. On the other hand, other representatives felt that it would not be necessary to include the legal consequences of aggression in the definition. The view was also expressed that the question of non-recognition of territorial gains and the question of responsibility could not be included in the definition without impairing the clarity of the text and the effectiveness of the guidance it was expected to provide; besides, those questions went beyond the Special Committee's mandate and had moreover been dealt with in the Declaration on Friendly Relations; to reconsider them in the context of the definition could only lead either to repetition or to contradiction. In this connexion, it was suggested that it would be more appropriate to deal with the question of non-recognition of territorial gains obtained by force in the preamble of the definition than in its operative part, since it concerned a legal consequence of aggression and was not an element of aggression itself.

IV. Voting

38. At its 1213th meeting, on 2 November 1970, the Sixth Committee adopted without objection the revised draft resolution (A/C.6/L.799/Rev.1). Statements in explanation of vote were made by the representatives of Australia, Belgium, Canada, France, Israel, Italy, Japan, Liberia. the United Kingdom and the United States.

Recommendation of the Sixth Committee

39. The Sixth Committee recommends to the General Assembly the adoption of the following draft resolution:

REPORT OF THE SPECIAL COMMITTEE ON THE QUESTION OF DEFINING AGGRESSION

[*Text adopted by the General Assembly without change. See "Action taken by the General Assembly" below.*]

ACTION TAKEN BY THE GENERAL ASSEMBLY

At its 1914th plenary meeting, on 25 November 1970, the General Assembly adopted without objection the draft resolution submitted by the Sixth Committee (A/8171, para. 39). For the final text, see *Official Records of the General Assembly, Twenty-fifth Session, Supplement No. 28,* resolution 2644 (XXV).

CHECK LIST OF DOCUMENTS

NOTE. This check list includes the documents mentioned during the consideration of agenda item 87 which are not reproduced in the present fascicle.

Document No.	Title or description	Observations and references
A/8019	Report of the Special Committee on the Question of Defining Agression (13 July-14 August 1970)	Official Records of the General Assembly, Twenty-fifth session, Supplement No. 19
A/C.1/L.513	Draft Declaration	Ibid., Twenty-fifth session, Annexes, agenda item 32, document A/8096, para. 5(a)
A/C.1/L.518	Draft Declaration	Ibid., para. 5 (f)
A/C.6/L.799	Draft resolution	See A/8171, para. 5
A/C.6/L.799/ Rev.1	Revised draft resolution	Ibid., para. 6

DOCUMENT 20

Twenty-Sixth Session, Supp. No. 19, A/8419,
Report of Special Committee, 1 Feb. - 5 Mar.

INTRODUCTION

1. At its 1843rd plenary meeting of 18 September 1970, the General Assembly
decided to include in the agenda of its twenty-fifth session the consideration of
the report of the Special Committee on the Question of Defining Aggression on the
work of its session held at the United Nations Office at Geneva from 13 July to
14 August 1970. 1/ It also referred this report to the Sixth Committee, which
considered it at its 1202nd to 1209th and 1211th to 1213th meetings between
16 October and 2 November 1970. 2/ At its 1914th plenary meeting on
25 November 1970, the General Assembly adopted resolution 2644 (XXV), which reads
as follows:

"The General Assembly,

"Having considered the report of the Special Committee on the Question of
Defining Aggression on the work of its session held at Geneva from 13 July
to 14 August 1970,

"Taking note of the progress made by the Special Committee in its
consideration of the question of defining aggression and on the draft
definition, as reflected in the report of the Special Committee,

"Considering that it was not possible for the Special Committee to complete
its task, in particular its consideration of the proposals concerning a draft
definition of aggression submitted to the Special Committee during its sessions
held in 1969 and 1970,

"Considering that in its resolutions 2330 (XXII) of 18 December 1967,
2420 (XXIII) of 18 December 1968 and 2459 (XXIV) of 12 December 1969 the
General Assembly recognized the widespread conviction of the need to expedite
the definition of aggression,

"Considering the urgency of bringing the work of the Special Committee to
a successful conclusion and the desirability of achieving the definition of
aggression as soon as possible,

"Noting also the common desire of the members of the Special Committee to
continue their work on the basis of the results achieved and to arrive at a
draft definition,

"1. Decides that the Special Committee on the Question of Defining
Aggression shall resume its work, in accordance with General Assembly
resolution 2330 (XXII), as early as possible in 1971;

1/ See Official Records of the General Assembly, Twenty-fifth Session,
Supplement No. 19 (A/8019).

2/ Ibid., Twenty-fifth Session, Annexes, agenda item 87, document A/8171.

"2.   Requests the Secretary-General to provide the Special Committee with the necessary facilities and services;

"3.   Decides to include in the provisional agenda of its twenty-sixth session an item entitled 'Report of the Special Committee on the Question of Defining Aggression'.

2.   In accordance with this resolution, the Special Committee on the Question of Defining Aggression, whose composition is given in paragraph 2 of its report on the work of its 1968 session, 3/ met at United Nations Headquarters in New York from 1 February to 5 March 1971. All the States members of the Special Committee took part in its work. The list of representatives attending the 1971 session is reproduced in annex V to the present report.

3.   At its 79th and 80th meetings, held on 1 and 2 February respectively, the Special Committee elected the following officers:

Chairman: Mr. Augusto Legnani (Uruguay)

Vice-Chairmen: Mr. Ilja Hulinský (Czechoslovakia)
                 Mr. Vincent Mutuale (Democratic Republic of the Congo)
                 Mr. Matti Cawén (Finland)

Rapporteur: Mr. Riyadh Al-Qaysi (Iraq).

4.   The session was opened on behalf of the Secretary-General by Mr. Constantin A. Stavropoulos, Legal Counsel of the United Nations. Mr. Anatoly P. Movchan, Director of the Codification Division of the Office of Legal Affairs, and Mr. Chafic Malek served respectively as Secretary and Deputy Secretary of the Special Committee. Mr. Tatsuro Kunugi and Mr. Eduardo Valencia-Ospina served as Assistant Secretaries.

5.   At its 80th meeting on 2 February, the Special Committee adopted the following agenda:

1. Opening of the session

2. Election of officers

3. Adoption of the agenda

4. Organization of work

5. Consideration of the question of defining aggression (General Assembly resolutions 2330 (XXII), 2420 (XXIII), 2549 (XXIV) and 2644 (XXV))

6. Adoption of the report.

6.   At the same meeting, the Special Committee decided, at the Chairman's suggestion, to devote its first six meetings to the consideration of specific

---

3/ Ibid., Twenty-third Session, agenda item 86, document A/7185/Rev.1.

questions mentioned in the report of the Working Group reproduced in annex II to the Special Committee's report on the work of its 1970 session; as noted in paragraph 9 of its report for 1970, the Special Committee had been unable, for lack of time, to examine the report of the Working Group. The Special Committee also decided to re-establish the Working Group.

7.   In accordance with the decision taken by the Special Committee at its 88th meeting on 12 February, the Working Group was composed of the same eight member States as at the 1970 session, together with the Rapporteur, namely: Cyprus, Ecuador, France, Ghana, the Union of Soviet Socialist Republics, the United Arab Republic, the United Kingdom of Great Britain and Northern Ireland and the United States of America. It was understood that, at the current session only, the members of the Special Committee who were not members of the Working Group could take part in the Group's work but not in its decisions. The Group was instructed to help the Special Committee in the fulfilment of its task by formulating an agreed or generally accepted definition of aggression and, in case it was unable to reach such a definition, to report to the Special Committee its assessment of the progress made during the session, indicating both the points of agreement and disagreement. It was also invited to report periodically to the Special Committee on the progress of its work.

8.   The Working Group held twenty-three meetings from 12 February to 4 March 1971. It submitted two successive reports (A/AC.134/L.30 and Corr.1 and A/AC.134/L.35) to the Special Committee, the text of which is reproduced in a single document annexed to this report (annex III). In addition, a working paper submitted to the Special Committee by Mexico (A/AC.134/L.28), is reproduced in annex IV.

9.   The first report of the Working Group (A/AC.134/L.30 and Corr.1), covering the work done from 16 to 18 February 1971, reflected the outcome of the Working Group's discussions on the general definition of aggression and the principle of priority. The second report (A/AC.134/L.35), covering the work done from 19 February to 4 March 1971, reflected the outcome of the Working Group's discussions on the questions of political entities other than States, legitimate use of force, aggressive intent, acts proposed for inclusion in the definition of aggression, proportionality, legal consequences of aggression and the right of peoples to self-determination.

10.   The Special Committee considered the first report of the Working Group at the Committee's 89th meeting, on 22 February 1971. An account of the discussion on that report is given below (paras. 45 to 65), in particular with reference to the two questions covered therein. At the same meeting, the Special Committee decided to take note of the Working Group's first report and to annex it to the report of the Special Committee. Also at the eighty-ninth meeting and in connexion with its consideration of the Working Group's first report, the Special Committee held a short discussion on the organization of its work on the basis of a proposal made by the representative of the Soviet Union to the effect that a second working group should be established. The Special Committee deferred its decision on the foregoing proposal. At the same meeting, one representative suggested that the Special Committee should end its work one week sooner than scheduled to prevent the session frcm overlapping with that of the important Committee on the Peaceful Uses of the Sea-Bed and the Ocean Floor, scheduled to meet at Geneva on 1 March.

11. At its 90th meeting, on 5 March 1971, the Special Committee had before it the second report of the Working Group; it decided to take note of it and to annex it to its own report, indicating that for lack of time, it had been unable to examine it.

12. At the 91st meeting of the Special Committee, on 5 March 1971, some members, who were also members of the Working Group, noted that the Working Group had not had before it in writing paragraphs 21 and 24 of the report of the Working Group and that they were unable to agree that the proposals on legal consequences and self-determination referred to in paragraphs 21 and 24 could usefully serve as a basis for discussion, although they had stressed in the Working Group their willingness to have these proposals set out in full in the Working Group's report.

13. At the same meeting of the Special Committee, one representative expressed the view that the Committee should have discussed, and decided to include a reference to, the question of the purposes of the definition of aggression in the present report.

I. DRAFT PROPOSALS BEFORE THE SPECIAL COMMITTEE

14. The Special Committee had before it three draft proposals submitted to it at its 1969 session, namely, the draft of the Union of Soviet Socialist Republics (A/AC.134/L.12), the new thirteen-Power draft (A/AC.134/L.16 and Add.1 and 2) and the six-Power draft (A/AC.134/L.17 and Add.1). The text of these three draft proposals is reproduced in annex I to this report.

15. On 22 February 1971, the United States representative submitted a draft proposal (A/AC.134/L.31) concerning the principle of priority. On 23 February 1971, he submitted a draft proposal (A/AC.134/L.32) concerning aggressive intent. The text of these two drafts is reproduced in annex II to this report.

16. At its 91st meeting, on 5 March 1971, the Special Committee had before it a draft resolution (A/AC.134/L.34) submitted by Czechoslovakia and Mexico, the text of which reads as follows:

"The Special Committee on the Question of Defining Aggression,

"Bearing in mind General Assembly resolutions 2330 (XXII) of 18 December 1967, 2420 (XXIII) of 18 December 1968, 2549 (XXIV) of 12 December 1969 which recognized the need to expedite the definition of aggression,

"Bearing also in mind that in its resolution 2644 (XXV) of 25 November 1970 the General Assembly considered the urgency of bringing the work of the Special Committee to a successful conclusion and the desirability of achieving the definition of aggression as soon as possible,

"Noting the progress so far achieved and the fact that the Special Committee has been already engaged in efforts to draft generally acceptable formulations of the individual elements of a definition,

"Noting also the common desire of the members of the Special Committee to continue their work on the basis of the results attained and to arrive at a draft definition,

"Recommends that the General Assembly, at its twenty-sixth session, invite the Special Committee to resume its work in 1972."

II. DEBATE

17. As indicated above (paragraph 6), the Special Committee first undertook the consideration of the report of the Working Group reproduced in annex II to the report of the Special Committee on the work of its 1970 session. Part A of this section contains an account of the views expressed on the Working Group's report. Part B will deal with the views expressed on the first report submitted to the Special Committee by the Working Group during the 1971 session in accordance with the Committee's decision to which reference is made above (para. 7).

A. Views expressed on the report submitted by the Working Group to the Special Committee at its 1970 session

18. For the sake of convenience, these views are presented in the same order and under the same headings as in the Special Committee's earlier reports.

19. It should be noted that most representatives stressed the value of the work accomplished by the Working Group as well as the progress it had made. It was observed that the Group's report indicated clearly the areas of agreement and disagreement as well as the possibilities for compromise; it also provided clear evidence of willingness on the part of the various delegations to resolve their difficulties and reconcile differences of opinion. It was noted further that the progress made by the Working Group was encouraging; in particular, its members had agreed on two very important considerations which were referred to in paragraphs 4 and 12 of its report, namely, that the general definition of aggression should reflect the concept of aggression as contained in the Charter and that the list of acts constituting aggression should be accompanied by a statement to the effect that they were listed without prejudice to the fullness of the powers of the Security Council, as provided in the Charter, particularly in declaring other acts to be aggression.

20. With regard to the procedure to be used for adopting a definition of aggression, several representatives expressed the view that the only way of arriving at an acceptable and lasting definition of aggression was by means of consensus; to take any other course would be to deprive the definition of all meaning. It was, however, noted that it was not necessary to apply the consensus method to all aspects of the Special Committee's work, including even the least essential.

1. Application of the definition

(a) The definition and the power of the Security Council

21. There appeared to be no objection to the view that any definition of aggression should safeguard the discretionary power of the Security Council as the United Nations organ primarily responsible for the maintenance of international peace and security. Nevertheless, one representative observed that the Security Council should not be given the power to interpret the term "aggression" as it pleased. Another representative felt that even if it was acknowledged that the list of acts

of aggression to be drawn up would not be restrictive and even if the list was
introduced by a statement safeguarding the power of the Security Council, that
statement could not be interpreted as authorizing the Council to add other acts to
the list; it was simply intended to indicate that the definition did not affect the
Council's power to judge and decide who was the aggressor.

(b) Political entities to which the definition should apply

22.   Several representatives questioned the advisability of referring to political
entities other than States in the definition of aggression. In that connexion,
it was stated that reference to such entities might be construed as meaning that
the legal existence of a State could be placed in doubt simply because it was not
recognized by a majority of members of the international community; the existence
of a State did not depend on its recognition by other States. It was pointed out
that the definition should apply to all States, whether or not they were recognized
by certain States Members of the United Nations; otherwise, the Special Committee
would be compelled to establish a precise definition of the terms "State" and
"political entity", a task which would be outside its terms of reference. It was
further stated that only States were full subjects of international law and were
the only "political" entities that could commit or be the victims of an act of
aggression; the reference to political entities other than States in paragraph II
of the six-Power draft had no basis in the Charter and lent itself to differing
interpretations. Important as it might be, it was added, the question of
recognition, to which the six-Power draft seemed to refer, had nothing to do with
the definition of aggression; the term "State", as used in the Charter, was broad
enough to cover all situations to which the definition should apply. The view was
also expressed that the reference to political entities other than States would
give rise to a restrictive interpretation of the term "State" and blur the
distinction between international conflicts and civil wars; furthermore, any
extension of the political entity concept to cover territories which had not yet
achieved independence might raise extremely delicate problems; moreover, the fact
that a State had not been recognized by other States should not prevent the
application of enforcement action against that State.

23.   According to one representative, any definition of aggression formulated by
the Special Committee should apply only to States which had acceded to the Charter.
He did not deny that a State not a Member of the United Nations could commit
aggression, but a definition of aggression based on the Charter could not be
applied to such a State; acts of aggression committed by States not Members of the
United Nations had to be dealt with under general international law; the terms
"States" and "political entities" should therefore be replaced in the three draft
definitions before the Special Committee by the expression "Members of the
Organization". Some representatives, however, considered that that solution might
raise substantial difficulties in cases where the Security Council would have to
apply a definition which was so limited that it would not take into account the
situations involving non-member States.

24.   Some representatives commented favourably on the compromise solution in
paragraph 6 of the report of the Working Group and observed that if the definition
of aggression did not expressly include political entities, an explanatory note
should be annexed to the definition to the effect that the term "State" included
States whose statehood was disputed. In that connexion, it was observed that the
concept of political entities had been used for the sole purpose of ensuring that

the definition was given the broadest application in international relations in perfect accord with one of the purposes of the United Nations, namely "the suppression of acts of aggression".

25. In another connexion, one representative observed that one or several States could commit an act of aggression against another or several other States; in his view, the definition should refer not only to a State" but also to groups of States.

2.   Acts proposed for inclusion in the definition of aggression

26. There was no fundamental objection to the idea that the definition should be limited to the use of armed force; according to some representatives, the forms of aggression other than armed force should be defined at a later stage. Different opinions were, however, expressed with regard to the question whether the definition should cover, for the purposes of the exercise of the right of self-defence, the indirect use of armed force.

27. Several representatives said that the definition should cover only direct armed aggression, which they considered to be the only form of aggression justifying the exercise of the right of self-defence under Article 51 of the Charter. In that connexion, it was observed that the constituent elements of aggression could be defined only by reference to the Charter, which in Article 1 and Article 39 referred to threats to the peace, breaches of the peace and acts of aggression, and in Article 51 to armed attack; it followed that the notion of aggression embraced several types of situations, the most dangerous of which was armed attack; however, the fact that the Charter did not mention indirect aggression did not preclude the drawing of a distinction between direct and indirect aggression; both forms constituted a threat to international peace, and the difference between the two forms of aggression was the same as that existing between armed attack and a breach of the peace; under Article 51 of the Charter, only armed attack, and not other breaches of the peace, gave rise to the right of self-defence. It was also pointed out that the word "aggression" meant primarily a physical act which was objectively observable and especially serious; Article 2 (4) of the Charter did not define aggression but merely mentioned categories of prohibited behaviour, of which aggression was only one example; Article 39 enumerated such behaviour in order of seriousness, the highest level being the act of aggression, which was thus the most serious act, and entitled the victim to exercise the right of self-defence under Article 51 in the event of armed attack. It was further said that an analysis of Article 1 of the Charter showed that it drew a distinction between "threats to the peace" and "acts of aggression or other breaches of the peace", the former being governed by Chapter VI and the latter by Chapter VII; the Charter dealt equally severely with acts of aggression and other breaches of the peace; however, the latter did not justify the exercise of the right of self-defence under Article 51; the purpose of the Charter was to limit the risk of war; that was why, in the event of a breach of the peace, States did not have the right to defend their own cause but had to appeal to the Security Council to take action. Similarly, in Article 39 the Charter drew a distinction between a breach of the peace and an act of aggression; any United Nations body responsible for preparing a definition of aggression should take that distinction into account. Acts such as organizing, supporting or directing armed bands that infiltrated into another State did not entitle the State against which they were directed to exercise its right of self-defence under Article 51 of the Charter; it must, however, be admitted that there

were marginal cases in which the infiltration was so substantial and the danger so great that they were tantamount to an armed attack and justified the exercise of the right of self-defence; it might perhaps be advisable to include a provision to that effect in the definition. One representative observed that paragraph IV B of the six-Power draft enumerated acts which in fact would result only in a breach of the peace, unless they were of particularly great intensity. He added that in any case, if the expression "armed force however exerted", suggested in paragraph 4 of the Working Group's report, was used in the definition, it should be explained that that meant armed force justifying the exercise of the right of self-defence as established in Article 51 of the Charter.

28. On the other hand, other representatives maintained that the definition should apply to so-called "indirect" armed aggression and that, in their view, that form of aggression was covered by the right of self-defence mentioned in Article 51 of the Charter. According to these representatives, any definition in order to be consistent with the Charter would have to be complete, which required that it must include indirect uses of force. Indirect uses of force such as those covered by paragraph IV B of the six-Power draft could not be considered in contemporary circumstances as "mere" infiltration or subversion; nor could an armed response to them be regarded as anything other than a legitimate use of the inherent right of self-defence; such problems must be resolved in a manner properly reflecting the experiences and needs of the international community. The view was also expressed that the Special Committee should avoid engaging in an inconclusive conceptual debate on whether the term used in Article 1 and Article 39 of the Charter on the one hand, and the different term used in Article 51 on the other, were necessarily identical or equivalent; the Charter was not drafted that way and the collective security system was not intended to operate on that basis. The function of Article 39, which had to do with activating the collective security system, and the quite different function of Article 51, which was designed to exempt the inherent right of self-defence from the prescriptions of Article 2, illustrated the difficulties in adopting such an approach. The terms used were different and the context was different. Any attempt to merge those two concepts would produce a distortion of the legal régime embodied in the Charter. There might indeed be breaches of the peace where the collective security mechanism ought to be activated but which it would be neither right nor practical to designate as acts of aggression. However, in that case the criterion should not be the means employed, for it mattered little whether the act had been committed by soldiers in uniform or by a band of armed saboteurs. The notion that a State was not entitled in every case to use the whole of its military might against another State in response to an isolated act also had some merit. Once again, the criterion was not whether the isolated act had been a shell fired by the regular army of the other State on the orders of the Head of State or a bomb smuggled across the border by a terrorist. It was also said that it could not be argued that the direct or overt use of armed force to destroy the political independence or territorial integrity of another State was aggression while at the same time maintaining that the indirect or covert use of armed force for such purposes was not aggression. The clandestine infiltration of armed bands into the territory of another State could be at least as dangerous as an open invasion and was the commonest form of aggression in the present-day world. It was contended that provisions such as those in operative paragraph 7 of the thirteen-Power draft did not belong in a definition of aggression. The limits of the right of self-defence were not derived from the means employed by the aggressor, but from the basic objective of self-defence, which was to safeguard the State, the Government and its institutions; it was only where self-defence went beyond that objective that it ceased to constitute an acceptable use of force

under the norms of the international order and might become an illegal act. But it was impossible, it was added, to determine a priori in what situations a State which used force by virtue of its right of self-defence was abusing that right; under Article 51 of the Charter, the assessment of specific situations must be left either to the State or States concerned or to the Security Council, to which the State or States concerned were required to report immediately any measures taken in the exercise of the right of self-defence; it was therefore not possible to establish general rules making the exercise of that right dependent on the means of aggression used. Some representatives expressly rejected the idea that the right of self-defence derived from Article 51 of the Charter and arose only in the event of what that article described as "an armed attack". They stressed the use of the term "inherent" in Article 51 in support of this view.

29. On the subject of specific acts of aggression that might be mentioned as examples in the definition, one representative observed that a declaration of war was an element which must be taken into account in determining whether an act of aggression had been committed. Another representative wondered whether it was advisable to mention in the definition the use of weapons of mass destruction as a typical act of aggression. Consideration should be given to the possibility of reaching compromise formulas on a question which, although not of primary importance, was fundamental for certain States, in particular for the nuclear Powers; the principle to be maintained was that the legality of the use of nuclear weapons should not be recognized in all cases of self-defence. At the same time, it should be indicated whether the annexation of a territory could ipso facto be described as aggression; no one could deny that territorial acquisition resulting from the unlawful use of force was illegal; a State could not annex the territory or part of the territory of another State in the exercise of its right of self-defence, a principle which had long been recognized. The question was, of course, whether it was really desirable to include such provisions in a definition of aggression. In the opinion of other representatives, occupation and annexation of a territory should be considered as constituting aggression in themselves. While it was true that occupation and annexation were the result of an invasion or an armed attack, it was no less true that they could constitute an end in themselves; the definition of aggression could not ignore the concept of permanent aggression and the responsibilities arising therefrom. The view was also expressed that any military occupation, even if temporary, should be included among the examples of acts of aggression, since it constituted a flagrant violation of the Charter principles that States should refrain from the use of force.

30. According to one representative, the examples of acts of aggression to be enumerated in the definition should include the case in which a State made its territory available to another State so that the latter could commit aggression against a third State.

3. The principle of priority

31. No representatives appear to have objected to the inclusion of the principle of priority in the defniition of aggression. However, according to some representatives, the definition should specify that the element of priority itself was not the determining factor and that other elements should also be taken into account. It was pointed out that the automatic application of the principle might result in classifying acts committed by accident or the use of force based on the

right of self-defence as acts of aggression. It was obvious, one representative stated, that in formulating guidelines for determining the existence of an act of aggression within the meaning of Article 39 of the Charter, the Special Committee must avoid providing States with excuses for interpreting Article 51 as authorizing them to over-react to an act of violence committed against them. That was the risk incurred by a simplistic application of the principle of priority, which could not be accepted as an absolute. It was stated, however, that the principle was not determinative in every case, particularly in the case of indirect aggression; other factors must therefore be taken into account in establishing that aggression had been committed. In that connexion it was suggested that the wording proposed by a member of the Working Group, in paragraph 5 of its report, might serve as a basis for a compromise solution.

32. However, the wording proposed in paragraph 5 of the Working Group's report was considered unacceptable by several representatives. The principle of priority, it was said, was a fundamental criterion, not an incidental one which should merely be given "due weight"; it should be determinative, although it might be difficult to say whether there had been aggression when there had been a border incident first. It was suggested that it would be advisable to study whether or not a distinction should be made, in the definition of aggression, between acts of aggression and border incidents. It was also suggested that consideration should be given to the possibility of stating that armed aggression was the use by a State, first, of armed force "in an international conflict", which would make it clear that the party which committed an act of aggression was not necessarily the party committing one of the isolated acts enumerated in the definition but rather the party which took the initiative in making illegitimate use of force and thus triggered an armed conflict.

4. Aggressive intent

33. In the view of some representatives, the concept of intent should be a fundamental element in any definition of aggression. In this respect, it was said that the concept of intent was a basic principle of law, and it was difficult to conceive of a definition which did not indicate the principal illegal purposes constituting aggression; a definition must necessarily indicate the nature of the aggressive intent. It was also pointed out that the criterion of intent enabled an act of aggression to be distinguished from an unpremeditated incident; an act of aggression was the result of conscious and premeditated human activity carried out with a definite aim in view; the pursuit of an unlawful end was therefore inherent in an act of aggression, and any definition of aggression must take that fact into account. The question of intent, it was also stated, should be accorded full treatment in the definition; it was an element which invariably played a very important part in the definition of premeditated crime in all legal systems; aggression was a serious international crime, and the responsibility of the aggressor was directly related to his intention; aggression and the responsibility of the aggressor should therefore be considered simultaneously.

34. It was also said that the principle of priority led only to a rebuttable presumption of guilt, i.e., that the principle of priority necessarily involved presumed intent; no situation could be conceived in which the presumption of guilt could be rebutted except by proof of absence of intention; the enumeration in paragraph IV A of the six-Power draft appeared to confuse intent with motive; the

mens rea in an act of aggression could be construed simply as the intention to affect in any way the sovereignty, political independence or territorial integrity of a State contrary to the provisions of the Charter; as such, intent was the mens rea of an act of aggression and was undeniably an important element.

35. Several representatives made a distinction between aggressive intent and the motives of the aggression. Although in theory, it was said, intent could be different from the motives of aggression, which might be the desire to obtain revenge, to secure economic advantages, to annex the territory or to overthrow the Government of a State, etc., there was no need to refer to motives in a definition of aggression; aggressive intent would suffice. Consequently, some representatives regarded paragraph IV A of the six-Power draft as unacceptable. It was stated that the enumeration in the said paragraph confused intent with motive; the element of intent could be construed only in the sense of a deliberate act as distinct from one due to accident or mistake. It was further said that paragraph IV A of the six-Power draft definition contained an enumeration of purposes of aggression; the Charter of the United Nations did not mention intent in connexion with an act of aggression, but the element of intent was clearly implied; acts committed by mistake presented no problem and were not covered by the Charter; intent was not mentioned in the thirteen-Power draft proposal because an element of intent was implicit in any act of aggression; however, in order to accommodate certain delegations, that draft might be amended, if necessary, to include an explicit reference to the element of intent. It had also been argued that the first use of force could not be divorced from aggressive intent inasmuch as the second use of force was of necessity bound up with the concept of self-defence. Questions of intent, motivation and objectives were relevant criteria before the prohibition of wars of aggression. In the contemporary international legal system, however, the first use of force automatically created a presumption of guilt.

36. One representative, referring to the three draft definitions before the Special Committee, pointed out that they took into account the two criteria of priority and intent, which, in his view, were not incompatible. Each draft definition laid more stress on one or the other of the two principles, he noted; a formula should be found which would give equal weight to the two criteria. The problem was to determine the value to be attached to each of those criteria. It was argued that the objective criterion was simpler and more effective whereas the subjective criterion was merely an aid in the refinement and qualification of the judgement formed on the basis of the objective criterion. In defining aggression, the objective criterion should be paramount; the question of aggressive intent should not be neglected in the process, but it was no more than a secondary consideration. There was no question that the Security Council had the power to inquire into the intent of a party committing an act of aggression, but it was extremely difficult to mention that right in a general definition of aggression. It would be preferable to refer to it in a paragraph defining the Council's powers.

37. Some representatives considered that aggression should be defined without resorting to a subjective criteria. Inclusion of the element of intent in a definition, they said, might distort the legal framework for the exercise of the right of self-defence. That did not mean that aggressive intent or the aims of aggression should be overlooked; those elements should be evaluated by the Security Council. It was also said that the view that the element of intent was not necessarily subjective and that it was generally inferred from the objective

circumstances of the act was not acceptable. Moreover, the principle of priority and that of intent could not be given equal weight; the element of intent became irrelevant once the Security Council had determined that a certain State had been the first to use armed force against another State. The inclusion of that element in the definition would give the aggressor the opportunity to justify his act. The burden of proof should always be on the aggressor, not on the victim, and that principle of law could be applied in the context of aggression only by excluding the element of intent from the definition. In the opinion of one representative, aggressive intent could be a determinative factor only in some cases. Where an act of aggression in itself constituted a breach of the peace, it was argued, there was no need to establish whether it had been committed with intent. However, where it was a question of illegal acts which might cause a breach of the peace if they were generalized, the criterion of intent became relevant. The criterion of intent therefore belonged not in a general definition of aggression but in an enumeration of specific cases. According to another representative, the inclusion in the definition of aggression of the concept of intent introduced a subjective criterion which could open the way to countless abuses. As a compromise, he pointed out, it might be possible to find a solution which did not treat animus aggressionis as the decisive element in determining whether an act of aggression had been committed.

5.   Legitimate use of force

(a) Self-defence

38.   Several representatives pointed out that the definition of aggression should draw the line between aggression and the legitimate use of force. To do so, it was noted, it need only state clearly and unambiguously the circumstances in which the use of force was legitimate. The best solution would be to have a general statement which excluded from the scope of the definition all cases in which the use of force was legitimate. The wording in paragraph 6 of the draft of the Union of Soviet Socialist Republics was considered satisfactory in that respect. Other representatives felt that the Special Committee's task was to define aggression, not self-defence. The right of self-defence, they held, should be mentioned only in so far as it had a bearing on the definition of aggression. In that connexion, the formulation proposed in paragraph 7 (a) of the Working Group's report laid the groundwork for a possible compromise; on the other hand, the text of paragraph 7 (b) was not relevant to the Committee's main task. It was further pointed out that Article 51 of the Charter and the inherent right of self-defence should not be taken as a point of departure for a definition of aggression. The Special Committee would be wise to be content with a general formulation safeguarding the inherent right of self-defence, which existed independently of the Charter. Furthermore, that right was not affected by Article 2 (4) of the Charter; it was not dependent on Article 51 and was not limited by that article.

39.   One representative held the view that the definition should make clear that no political, military or other consideration could justify the use of force by a State or group of States. Such a provision, he pointed out, was contained in the preamble of the thirteen-Power draft, but in view of the importance of emphasizing the preventive nature of the definition of aggression, it should be stated in the operative part of the text.

40. Several representatives opposed the inclusion of the principle of
proportionality in the definition of aggression. Apart from the fact that it
was not universally accepted in international law, that principle hardly lent
itself to a legal definition and might even be advantageous to the aggressor.
The Charter, it was further stated, contained no reference to that principle,
which, in diplomatic practice and in international law, had been applied to
reprisals. The real limit of self-defence did not derive from the fact that the
measures taken by the victim State were proportionate to the aggression suffered,
but from the fact that they conformed to the basic purpose of self-defence, as
recognized by the international community. There was no general rule that would
make it possible to determine whether such conformity existed; that must be done,
in accordance with Article 51 of the Charter, by the State or States concerned
and the Security Council. The principle of proportionality, it was further stated,
could not by itself be used to establish whether or not an act of aggression had
been committed; a disproportionate reaction to an act of aggression did not
necessarily constitute aggression; it might be due, for example, to a mistaken
evaluation of the facts. That principle, it was also pointed out, could be
applied in the case of an indirect armed attack or breach of the peace, where
the danger was less imminent; in any case, Article 51 of the Charter recognized
the right of self-defence as an inherent right, without any restriction
whatsoever; the meaning of that article could not be stretched to include the
principle of proportionality.

41. According to other representatives, the inclusion of the principle of
proportionality in the definition of aggression would be useful. It would
dispose not only of any disagreements concerning the definition of individual
or collective self-defence but also of the difficulties which might arise
with regard to the inclusion in the definition of a provision concerning armed
bands.

(b) Organs empowered to use force

42. Several representatives stated that they could not endorse proposals which
sought to give the General Assembly and regional organizations powers that were
not granted to them by the Charter. Under Articles 39 and 42 of the Charter,
the only organ which could decide to take the coercive measures involving the
use of armed force was the Security Council. Accordingly, the use of force
under regional agreements or by regional bodies would be legitimate only after
a prior decision to that effect by the Security Council, acting under Article 53
of the Charter. Other representatives expressed opposing views. It was pointed
out that, according to certain Members of the United Nations, the use of force
could be authorized not only by the Security Council but also, in cases where
the Council was powerless to act, by the General Assembly under Articles 10, 11
and 14 of the Charter; furthermore, several Member States held that, since
Article 51 of the Charter recognized the right of collective self-defence, it
allowed organizations whose purpose was to establish a collective system of
defence to use force in carrying out that objective; moreover, while Article 53
of the Charter made enforcement action by regional agencies contingent upon the
authorization of the Security Council, it was arguable that in certain cases
that authorization for enforcement action might follow or be given implicitly.
In view of such different interpretations of the Charter by Member States, it
would be best to adopt as neutral a formula as possible, such as that contained
in paragraph III of the six-Power draft.

6. Acts considered not to constitute acts of aggression -

Right of self-determination

43. Several representatives stated that the definition of aggression should cover situations in which the use of force was legitimate, in particular, the exercise by colonial peoples of their inalienable right to oppose by force any attempt to deprive them of their right to self-determination. Such a right, which had recently been reaffirmed in the Declaration on the Principles of International Law concerning Friendly Relations and Co-operation among States, must be upheld in a. safeguard clause in the same way as the rights derived from Articles 51 and 53 of the Charter. On the other hand, some representatives felt that the definition should not refer to that right. In the three draft definitions submitted to the Special Committee aggression was defined as an act directed by one State against another State, and therefore the use of force by dependent peoples in the exercise of their right to self-determination did not come within the scope of a definition of aggression; it would not be possible to accept a provision to the effect that an act which under all other circumstances would be defined as aggression would not be considered as such if it was committed in the context of self-determination. Moreover, provisions concerning that question were already included in the Declaration on the Principles of International Law concerning Friendly Relations and Co-operation among States; there was therefore no point in repeating them in a definition of aggression.

7. Legal consequences of aggression

44. The question whether the definition should include a provision on the legal consequences of aggression, or otherwise, was taken up by some representatives, who answered it in the affirmative. The inadmissibility of the acquisition of territory by force and the principle of responsibility for aggression were two points on which a number of accepted principles of international law existed and which should be taken into account in the definition. The occupation of a territory as a result of aggression or territorial gains resulting from the use of force were no less important than aggression itself; the legal order established by the Charter was based on the inviolability of the territory of States; forcible annexation of a territory as well as other forms of territorial acquisition were not only the result of armed attack but they themselves constituted aggression; consequently, continued occupation by force of a territory by another State should be considered as continued aggression against that State. It was also stated that if the definition was to be adequate, and therefore effective, it must refer either in the preamble or in the operative part to the consequences of aggression.

B. Views expressed on the first Report submitted by the Working Group to the Special Committee at its 1971 Session.1/

45. Some representatives considered that the Working Group deserved the Special Committee's gratitude for its businesslike approach to the task entrusted to it; during its discussions, the positions of different delegations had been clarified, and some progress had been made. This was evidenced in the Working Group's report,

---

1/ See above, paras. 7 to 11.

even though its rather short length did not do full justice to the work actually accomplished in the Group. Other representatives, however, were of the opinion that the deliberations of the Working Group, as reflected in its report, indicated no change from positions previously taken.

46. In the opinion of some representatives, the Working Group had done well to use the device of putting controversial parts of the text in brackets. It was to be hoped, however, that the phrases within brackets did not reflect definitive positions since middle positions on some issues were possible; accommodations could still be made. There was no reason why the brackets should not be progressively eliminated in the course of further negotiations. On the other hand, the view was expressed that if fundamental difficulties remained, the Working Group should not attempt to solve them through the use of drafting devices; the ambiguities that would arise from such a solution might lead to serious dangers.

47. Some representatives stated that if a useful definition was to be reached, its text would have to be acceptable to a majority of the Committee and the membership of the United Nations, and to the permanent members of the Security Council; if the definition did not meet the latter requirement, it could not guide the Council in the discharge of its primary responsibility for the maintenance of international peace and security. On the other hand, the view was expressed that although ideally the definition of aggression should enjoy the largest possible support in the United Nations and the agreement of the five permanent members of the Security Council, the permanent members, which were entitled to use their veto in the Council, did not have the right to impede the development of international law, for which many small countries felt a strong responsibility.

1. General definition of aggression

48. In the opinion of one representative, the general definition of aggression could not be dissociated from the definition as a whole; only when the Committee saw the entire definition could it evaluate the relative importance of the general definition; accordingly, the text submitted by the Working Group should be left in its present form for the moment and reconsidered only after the Working Group had reported on all other elements of the definition.

49. The view was also expressed that the text on the general definition of aggression reflected three different positions, despite the praiseworthy efforts of the Working Group aimed at producing a single text. A first position was said to be that which defined aggression as "the use of armed force by a State against another State or in any way affecting the sovereignty or the territorial integrity, including the territorial waters and airspace, or political independence of another State, or in any other manner inconsistent with the purposes of the United Nations". It was stated that this formulation was acceptable because it was the closest to the original thirteen-Power draft.

50. A second position was said to be that which defined aggression as "the use of armed force by a State against the sovereignty or the territorial integrity or political independence of another State, or in any other manner inconsistent with the purposes of the United Nations". It was said in this connexion that although the wording of that text was close to that of Article 2 (4) of the Charter, it was not satisfactory, firstly because there could be cases in which the object

of armed aggression was not limited to the territorial integrity or political
independence of a State and, secondly, because it omitted the concept of
"territorial waters and airspace", which, though implicit in the concepts of
territorial integrity and sovereignty, should nevertheless be expressly stated.

51.   In relation to the foregoing two positions, the opinion was expressed that
they seemed to be easily reconcilable. Also with reference to those positions,
it was said that there seemed to be no reason to place the words "the sovereignty
or" in brackets, since it was untenable and contrary to the Charter to suggest
that an armed attack against the sovereignty of a State was not aggression. It was
stated that the phrase had been placed in brackets because it did not appear in
Article 2 (4) of the Charter, but that although paragraph (4) covered aggression,
it was concerned with the more general notion of the threat or use of force.
Accordingly, there was no need to follow the wording of the article, since the
Committee was concerned solely with aggression, which was exclusively the use of
armed force within the meaning of Articles 1 and 39 of the Charter. That point
should not therefore be a stumbling-block. On the other hand, the view was
expressed that the reference to sovereignty could be deleted from the general
definition since that notion was already contained in the terms "territorial
integrity" and "political independence".

52.   The third of the positions reflected in the general definition was said to
be implied in the bracketed phrase "however exerted". In the opinion of some
representatives, that phrase was unnecessary as it was implicit in the use of the
words "armed force" without any qualification. That phrase had been proposed in
order to cover the idea of indirect aggression, but, in the view of some
representatives, it did not in fact do so. Moreover, it introduced a highly
controversial element in the text, which only complicated the Committee's task,
since it reopened the question of direct and indirect aggression; although other
phrases in brackets in the general definition were also controversial, that
phrase was more objectionable because it departed so basically from the position
taken by the majority of members and because it prejudged the question of
proportionality. The view was therefore expressed that, despite the statement in
paragraph 3 of the Working Group's report that the phrase "however exerted" was
unacceptable to many members, the Working Group should have presented two texts
instead of one.

53.   Other representatives stated that the insertion of the phrase "however
exerted" in the general definition had been proposed by those States which felt
that a definition which did not include all possible types of aggression would
be a dangerous one. Nevertheless, it was said that while the sponsors of the
six-Power draft felt that the phrase "however exerted" was felicitous, they were
not wedded to it, although it was difficult to consider that phrase in isolation
from other parts of the definition. It was also stated that the phrase could
be safely eliminated although the idea must appear elsewhere in the definition.
In this connexion the view was expressed that the idea should appear in any list
of specific acts which was eventually agreed upon.

54.   Regarding the question of indirect aggression, the opinion was expressed that
the object of the definition of aggression should be to guide the Security Council
in determining whether or not any particular use of force constituted an act of
aggression, to limit the legitimate use of force to a minimum, and to discourage
States from using armed attack as an instrument of national policy under any pretext

whatsoever. The Charter did not ignore the idea of indirect aggression, as could be seen from its references to "breaches of the peace" and "threats to the peace", but to seek to enlarge that concept into a consideration of the circumstances of a casus belli would be to go beyond the Charter and the Committee's mandate.

55. On the other hand, it was said that although the question was a controversial one whether or not a reference to armed aggression "in any form" should be included in the general definition of aggression and whether or not such a reference should also be included in the passages of the definition listing specific acts of aggression, the attempt to include such a reference should not be abandoned. The formulation of the principle regarding the non-use of force in the Declaration on Principles of International Law concerning Friendly Relations and Co-operation among States in accordance with the Charter of the United Nations contained provisions regarding the forms of aggression other than direct armed aggression. The three draft definitions before the Committee, each contained, although in very different words, the idea of the use of force "in any form", showing that their authors understood the necessity for such a reference in the definition. Furthermore, the inclusion of such a reference would be in full conformity with the principles of international law embodied in the Charter and would serve to make the definition an effective political and legal instrument which would discourage possible aggressors.

56. Some representatives stated that the attacks or infiltration by armed bands or mercenaries were as serious as other uses of force and, whether overt or covert, were covered by Article 1 (1) of the Charter, which referred to the suppression of acts of aggression or other breaches of the peace; they were also covered by Article 39. However, the right of self-defence under Article 51 could be invoked only in the event of armed attack; infiltration by armed bands and other forms of indirect aggression should, if they did not amount to armed attack, be treated as breaches of the peace. If a State's independence was threatened by an armed attack, it was a serious situation giving rise, under Article 51, to the right of self-defence, and the State under attack was entitled to take defensive measures not only in its own territory but also beyond its frontiers. In the case of attacks or infiltration by armed bands, as a result of which a State's independence was not threatened, the State's right of self-defence should be limited to its own territory. Not all indirect uses of force were acts of aggression, although some might be, and it should be possible to reach agreement on the subject on the basis of the text set out in paragraph 22 of the Working Group's 1970 report.

57. The view was also expressed that, with regard to the question of the inclusion in the definition of indirect uses of force, there might be a middle position involving a formulation which made it clear that while not every use of force was an act of aggression, some were, depending on the circumstances and on the discretion of the Security Council. In this connexion, one representative observed that a number of States now were agreed that the extent and circumstances of indirect aggression should determine whether it was included in the definition, although some States were adamant that it should be excluded. The hope was expressed by some representatives that it would be possible to find a formula flexible enough not to exclude indirect aggression; a compromise might be reached along the lines suggested in the statements made before the Committee.

58. One representative stated that his delegation had proposed in the Working Group the insertion in the general definition of a reference to the fact that aggression could also be committed by a group of States against a State or group of States. Aggression by groups of States, usually belonging to the same military alliance, was a fact of history, and a reference to the idea in the general definition would make it conform to Article 51 of the Charter, which provided for individual or collective self-defence.

2. The principle of priority

59. One representative pointed out that all members of the Working Group had unanimously expressed their willingness to accept the principle of priority. Nevertheless, it was said that the text submitted by the Working Group raised more questions than it answered; specifically, it raised three problems: the discretionary powers of the Security Council with regard to the first use of force, whether or not priority was determinative, and animus aggressionis.

60. In the opinion of some representatives priority was of the very essence of aggression, as was shown in Article 51 of the Charter and not a mere condition; the principle of priority must be dealt with clearly and on its own merits; it should not be confused with other elements. In the context of the principle of priority, the reference made in the Working Group's text to the powers and duties of the Security Council was irrelevant because the discretion of the Security Council would apply throughout the whole of the definition rather than merely to the question of priority. It was also stated that the phrase "due weight shall be given to the question whether" an act was committed first, deprived the principle of priority of both its obligatory and its determinative nature and would mean that while the Security Council was to give due weight to that principle, it would not actually be required to take it into account; such a formulation was self-defeating and completely unacceptable. The view was further expressed that as the principle of priority had been honoured by time, it seemed likely that agreement could be reached on the principle that the first State to carry out an invasion was the aggressor. There was no reason why the Security Council could not make an alternative finding if special circumstances existed in a particular case.

61. On the other hand, it was said that although the principle of priority was of great importance, its automatic application would only detract from its essence. It had been to prevent such automatic application that the preamble of the USSR and thirteen-Power drafts both stated that the question whether an act of aggression had been committed must be considered in the light of all the circumstances in each particular case. In view of the interpretative value of a preamble, some such formula should guide the Security Council in deciding whether or not an act of aggression had been committed; thus, the Council would declare a State an aggressor only after thorough examination of all the relevant circumstances and after giving primary, but neither exclusive nor absolute, importance to the principle of priority. That was why the phrase relating to the powers and duties of the Security Council had been proposed. Support could, therefore, be given to a formula which, while not affecting the essence of the principle, would make its application contingent on the circumstances of particular cases.

62. One representative stated that the sponsors of the six-Power draft were now
prepared to accept the inclusion of the principle of priority, although there was
still concern that priority might become a de jure presumption, which might, for
example, damage the interests of an innocent State that had been involved in a
minor border incident. The other State involved could use such an incident as an
excuse to unleash an aggressive attack and invoke the right of self-defence
referred to in Article 51 of the Charter.

63. The opinion was also expressed that the principle of priority, although
important, was not the sole factor which should determine whether or not any
particular use of force constituted aggression; priority could not be separated
from other elements, particularly the question of intent. On the other hand, it
was said that paragraph 4 of the Working Group's report clearly showed that few
of its members still believed that the use of armed force could be divorced from
animus aggressionis: thus, the controversy on the question of "intent" had crept
into the question of the principle of priority, prejudging the Working Group's
future work. No other element could be regarded as being equal in importance
to the first use of force in determining whether or not an act of aggression had
been committed, and its equation with any other element would only confuse
and paralyse the Security Council.

64. It was further said that with respect to the connexion between the principle
of priority and aggressive intent, which was an essential part of the position
adopted by the sponsors of the six-Power draft, the first State to launch an
attack was showing aggressive intent. It could not be denied that actions
undertaken for the purposes set out in article IV A of the six-Power draft were
acts of aggression.

65. In reference to the text on the principle of priority, one representative said
that he favoured replacing the words "an act referred to in... constitutes
aggression" by the words "an act of aggression had occurred" in view of the fact
that the general definition would precede the text on the principle of priority.

III. RECOMMENDATION OF THE SPECIAL COMMITTEE

66. At its 91st meeting, on 5 March 1971, the Special Committee considered the draft resolution submitted by Czechoslovakia and Mexico (A/AC.134/L.34). At the same meeting the Special Committee adopted the draft resolution unanimously. The text reads as follows:

"The Special Committee on the Question of Defining Aggression,

"Bearing in mind General Assembly resolutions 2330 (XXII) of 18 December 1967, 2420 (XXIII) of 18 December 1968, 2549 (XXIV) of 12 December 1969 which recognized the need to expedite the definition of aggression,

"Bearing also in mind that in its resolution 2644 (XXV) of 25 November 1970 the General Assembly considered the urgency of bringing the work of the Special Committee to a successful conclusion and the desirability of achieving the definition of aggression as soon as possible,

"Noting the progress so far achieved and the fact that the Special Committee has been already engaged in efforts to draft generally acceptable formulations of the individual elements of a definition,

"Noting also the common desire of the members of the Special Committee to continue their work on the basis of the results attained and to arrive at a draft definition,

"Recommends that the General Assembly, at its twenty-sixth session, invite the Special Committee to resume its work in 1972."

[Editor's note: Pages 23-28 of A/8419 are omitted. They contain Draft proposals submitted by the USSR (A/AC.134/L.12), the 13-Powers (A/AC.134/L.16 and Add. 1 and 2), and the Six-Powers (A/AC.134/L.17 and Add. 1 and 2), all of which have appeared in A/8019, DOCUMENT 18 supra.]

ANNEX II

Other draft proposals submitted to the Special Committee

A.   Draft proposal concerning the principle of priority, submitted by the United States of America (A/AC.134/L.31):

In determining whether an act of aggression has taken place, due weight shall be given to the question which State first used force.

B.   Draft proposal concerning aggressive intent, submitted by the United States of America (A/AC.134/L.32):

In determining whether an act of aggression has taken place, the Security Council shall ascertain the existence of aggressive intent and determine whether a State's actions were or were not undertaken for such purposes as to:

(1)   diminish the territory or alter the boundaries of another State;

(2)   alter internationally agreed lines of demarcation;

(3)   disrupt or interfere with the conduct of the affairs of another State;

(4)   secure changes in the Government of another State;

(5)   inflict harm or obtain concessions of any sort;

or otherwise for the purpose of violating the territorial integrity or political independence of another State.

ANNEX III

Report of the Working Group a/

1.   The Working Group established pursuant to the decision taken by the Special Committee at its 88th meeting on 12 February 1971 held twenty-three meetings from 16 February to 4 March 1971.

2.   Generally speaking, the Working Group sought to combine the various positions adopted by its members in a single text by offering different versions of the text through the use of square brackets. The phrases which were not acceptable to all members appear in brackets.

General definition of aggression

3.   The following text was worked out:

"Aggression is the use of armed force /however exerted/ by a State against /another State/ /or in any way affecting/ /the sovereignty or/ the territorial integrity /including the territorial waters and airspace/ or political independence of another State, or in any other manner inconsistent with the purposes of the United Nations."

4.   It should be noted that the phrase /however exerted/ in the general definition of aggression was unacceptable to many members of the Working Group, while other members regarded it as essential. Differences were also expressed as to the other bracketed phrases in the general definition.

Principle of priority

5.   The following text was worked out:

"/Without prejudice to the powers and duties of the Security Council/ /in determining whether/ an act referred to in... constitutes aggression /due weight shall be given to the question whether/ /it shall be established/ if it was committed by a State which so acted first /against another State in violation of the Charter/."

6.   Although all members of the Group were in favour of incorporating the principle of priority into the definition of aggression, some members regarded it as a determinative factor while others felt that it should merely be taken into account together with other elements. The various positions are clearly apparent if one reads the text both with the phrases in brackets and without them. Other proposals

---

a/   The following two reports submitted by the Working Group are combined in the present single report: the first report of the Working Group on the questions covered in paragraphs 3 to 6 of the present report; and the second report of the Working Group on the questions covered in paragraphs 7 to 25 of the present report.

were submitted to the Group by some of its members or of the members of the Committee. Certain delegations expressed reservations concerning the text which was worked out.

Political entities other than States

7.   Many members of the Working Group agreed that the definition itself should refer to States only and not to political entities as referred to in the six-Power draft. Some of these members denied any notion of political entities.

8.   Some delegations noted that any extension of the so-called political entity concept to cover territories which had not yet achieved independence raised problems which have a direct bearing on national liberation movements; others denied the existence of a connexion with national liberation movements and recalled that the concept, as stated in the six-Power draft, related to political entities delimited by international boundaries or internationally agreed lines of demarcation. In the light of the wide-spread willingness in the Working Group to entertain the possibility of disposing of the question by an explanatory note annexed to the definition, a method envisaged in the report of the 1970 Working Group, further consideration was given to this idea. The Working Group was, however, unable at this stage to reach agreement on the terms in which an explanatory note might be formulated, although various possible texts were suggested. Among these texts was the following:

"The term 'State' is without prejudice to the question of the recognition of States or to whether or not a State is a Member of the United Nations."

Representatives of the co-sponsors of the six-Power draft considered, however, that the explanatory note should relate clearly, as did the corresponding part of the six-Power draft, to the case of political entities delimited by international boundaries or internationally agreed lines of demarcation.

Legitimate use of force

9.   The Working Group took note of the following three texts which were proposed to it:

(a) "In the performance of the function to maintain or restore international peace and security, the United Nations only has competence to use force in conformity with the Charter.

"The inherent right of individual or collective self-defence of a State can be exercised only in case of the occurrence of armed attack (armed aggression) by another State in accordance with Article 51 of the Charter.

"Enforcement action or any use of armed force by regional arrangements or agencies may only be resorted to under Article 53 of the Charter."

(b) "The use of armed force in accordance with the Charter to maintain or restore international peace and security, or in the exercise of the inherent right of individual or collective self-defence, does not constitute aggression.

"Only the Security Council has the right to use force on behalf of the United Nations to maintain or restore international peace and security.

"Enforcement action by regional arrangements or agencies consistent with the Purposes and Principles of the United Nations, may only be taken under Article 53 of the Charter."

(c) "The use of force in the exercise of the inherent right of individual or collective self-defence, or pursuant to decisions of or authorization by competent United Nations organs or regional organizations consistent with the Charter of the United Nations, does not constitute aggression."

10. None of the three texts received sufficient support on the part of the Working Group.

Aggressive intent

11. There was agreement in the Working Group that there was no aggression without aggressive intent. Many delegations maintained that it was not necessary to include a reference to aggressive intent or the purposes of aggression in the definition, since aggressive intent was necessarily implied in any act of aggression, and the purposes of the aggressor never justified the commission of such an act. Others considered, however, that it was necessary to include express references to purposes which might make the use of force aggression.

12. The following five texts were proposed and were examined by the Working Group:

(a) "The use of armed force shall be recognized as aggression when undertaken with the following purposes:

"To eliminate another State;

"To annex territory of another State or to alter the boundaries of another State;

"To change the existing political or social régime in another State;

"To suppress national liberation movements in colonies and dependent territories and to keep peoples in colonial dependence;

"To receive economic and other advantages from another State."

(b) "In determining whether an act of aggression has taken place, the Security Council shall ascertain the existence of aggressive intent and determine whether a State's actions were or were not undertaken for such purposes as to:

"(1)   Diminish the territory or alter the boundaries of another State;

"(2)   Alter internationally agreed lines of demarcation;

"(3)   Disrupt or interfere with the conduct of the affairs of another State;

"(4)   Secure changes in the Government of another State;

"(5)   Inflict harm or obtain concessions of any sort;

or otherwise for the purpose of violating the territorial integrity or political independence of another State."

(c)   "In determining an act of aggression, the Security Council shall duly take into account the stated intentions and the aims pursued by the States concerned."

(d)   "Intent shall be presumed to exist in the commission of any act of aggression, without such presumption detracting from the right of the accused State to prove its innocence."

(e)   "In determining whether an act of aggression has taken place, the Security Council shall presume that such an act was committed with aggressive intent unless the accused State proves otherwise."

13.   However, none of the texts received sufficient support on the part of the Working Group.

Acts proposed for inclusion

14.   The following text was worked out:

"In accordance with the foregoing and without prejudice to the powers and duties of the Security Council, as provided in the Charter, any of the following acts when committed by a State /first/ /with aggressive intent/ against another State in violation of the Charter shall constitute acts of aggression /, independently of a declaration of war/:

"/Declaration of war/

"/(a)   Declaration of war by a State first against another State /when accompanied by an armed attack/;/

"/Invasion, attack, occupation or annexation/

"(b)   The invasion or attack by the armed forces of a State of the territory /under the jurisdiction/ of another State /, or any military occupation, however temporary, or any /forcible/ annexation of the territory of another State or part thereof/;

"/̄Bombardment; use of any weapons, particularly weapons
of mass destructio̲n/

"(c̲) Bombardment by the armed force̲s of a State of the territory /̄and
the populatio̲n/ /̄under the jurisdictio̲n/ of another State, or the use of any
weapons, /̲particularly weapons of mass destruction̲,/ by a State against the
territory of another State;

"/̄Blockad̲e/

"/̲(d̲) The blockade o̲f the coasts of ports of a State by the armed
forces of another State;̲/

"/̄Attack on the forces of another Stat̲e/

"/̲(e̲) An attack by t̲he armed forces of a State on the land, sea or air
forces of another State;̲/

"/̄Other acts of armed forc̲e/

"/̲(f̲) Other acts of armed force committ̲ed by a State against a̲nother
State i̲n such a way as to cause it /̲seriou̲s/ physical destruction.̲/

"/̄Maintenance of armed forces in another Stat̲e/

"/̲(g̲) Use of the armed forces by a State in another State i̲n violation
of the fundamental conditions of permission for t̲heir presence,̲ or maintaining
them there beyond the termination of permission.̲/

"/̄Indirect use of forc̲e/

"/̲(a̲) The use by a State of armed force by sending armed bands,
mercenaries, terrorists or saboteurs to the territory of another
State and engagement in other forms of subversive activity
involving the use of armed force with the aim of promoting an
internal upheaval in another State or a reversal of policy in
favour of the aggressor shall be considered an act of indirect
aggression.

"/̲(b̲) When a State is a victim in its own territory of subversive
and/or terrorist acts by irregular, volunteer or armed bands
organized or supported by another State, it may take all reasonable
and adequate steps to safeguard its existence and its institutions,
without having recourse to the right of individual or collective
self-defence against the other State under Article 51 of the
Charter.

"/̲(c̲) The sending by a State of armed bands of irregulars or
mercenaries which invade the territory of another State in such
force and circumstances as to amount to armed attack as envisaged
in Article 51 of the Charter.

"/(h)7 /(d)7 The carrying out, directing, assisting or encouraging by a State of acts of incursion, infiltration, terrorism or violent civil strife or subversion in another State, whether by regular or irregular forces, armed bands, including mercenaries, or otherwise, or the acquiescing by a State in organized activities within its territory directed towards the commission of such acts.

"/Additional acts as declared by the Security Council7

"/In addition to the acts listed above, other acts by States may be deemed to constitute an act of aggression if in each specific instance they are declared to be such by the Security Council.7"

15. Some delegations expressed the opinion that the quantitative element implied in the word "/serious7" in paragraph (f) should not be taken into account solely in the cases covered by the paragraph; it could also be applied to other acts of aggression. Many delegations strongly objected to the inclusion of paragraph (f) which, they considered, had no place in the definition of aggression. Several delegations expressed the view that, subject to any future agreement on the acts listed in paragraph 14, those acts, in order to be aggression, should constitute the "armed attack" referred to in Article 51 of the Charter.

16. Some delegations indicated their support for the insertion of paragraph (g), while others objected to it. Other delegations felt that the text of paragraph (g), as well as the following formula appearing in paragraph 20 of the Working Group's report for 1970, merited more detailed study:

"Where the armed forces of one State are within the territory of another State by virtue of permission given by the receiving State, any use of such forces in contravention of the conditions provided for in the permission or any extension of their presence in such territory beyond the termination or revocation of the permission by the receiving State."

17. It was understood that there were differences of opinion among delegations as to the inclusion of some of the concepts listed in paragraph 14. As regards the question of indirect use of force, several delegations maintained the view that such use of force should be dealt with elsewhere in the definition by a provision such as /(a)7 or /(b)7 or /(c)7 or /(h)7 /(d)7 above under the heading /Indirect use of force/, either because in their opinion it constituted aggression of a different kind or because they considered that it did not constitute aggression at all. Therefore they objected to the inclusion of paragraph /(h)7 /(d)7 in the list of acts considered as direct aggression. Others considered it essential that any list of acts of aggression should include acts of the kind referred to in /(h)7 /(d)7.

18. Some delegations felt that, irrespective of the question of the discretion of the Security Council to find other acts to be acts of aggression, the definition should expressly state that the list of acts given above should not be regarded as exhaustive.

Proportionality

19. The Working Group was not able to study this question in detail because of the lack of time. Some delegations felt that the notion of proportionality did not apply to legitimate self-defence, and consequently had no place in the definition. Other delegations pointed out that the concept of proportionality was not to be found in the Charter, and therefore it should not be included in the definition. Other delegations, on the other hand, felt that the concept was of great importance and could be studied on the basis of paragraph 6 of the thirteen-Power draft. In the view of other delegations, the concept required a delicate assessment not only of the means of retaliation, but also of the extent of the threat as perceived by the retaliating State; such assessment was, they felt, better left to the Security Council. Some delegations pointed out that the concept of proportionality should be included in the definition, to avoid invocation of the right to self-defence being used as a pretext for reprisals.

Legal consequences of aggression:

(a) Non-recognition of territorial gains

(b) The question of responsibility

20. Independently of the question whether military occupation and annexation were in themselves acts of aggression, several members considered it necessary to reflect in the definition the concept of the non-recognition of territorial gains resulting from aggression and the concept of responsibility for aggression. Some of those members believed that the definition should also make it clear that the territory of a State was inviolable and could not be the object of military occupation by another State. Other members maintained, without derogating from the views to which their Governments had subscribed on those concepts in any other contexts, that consequences of aggression should not be included in the definition.

21. It was agreed that paragraphs 4 and 5 of the draft proposal of the Union of Soviet Socialist Republics and paragraphs 8 and 9 of the thirteen-Power draft proposal could serve as a basis of discussion.

The right of peoples to self-determination

22. Some members believed that, since the use of force was involved, it would be appropriate to refer in the definition to the rights of peoples under the Charter and to the recognition by the United Nations of the right of colonial peoples opposing forcible efforts to deprive them of their right to self-determination to receive support in accordance with the principles of the Charter. Some of those members considered that the mention of the right of peoples to sovereignty and territorial integrity should be included together with the provision on self-determination, such as is done in the thirteen-Power draft.

23. Other members considered it unnecessary to mention the right of peoples to self-determination in the definition of aggression, as the two matters were not related.

24. It was agreed that paragraph 6 of the draft proposal of the Union of Soviet Socialist Republics and paragraph 10 of the thirteen-Power draft could serve as a basis of discussion.

Purposes of the definition of aggression

25. Because of the lack of time, the Working Group was not able to discuss in detail the question of the purposes of the definition of aggression. It was agreed that the matter could usefully be discussed at a later stage, if the Working Group's terms of reference were renewed.

* * *

Provisional character of the positions taken

26. The hope was generally expressed that, while the present text admittedly contained too many bracketed passages, a generally acceptable definition would be arrived at as a result of mutual give and take. It was pointed out in this connexion that the various elements of a definition were closely related to each other, and that the final positions of delegations would depend on the over-all solution arrived at.

ANNEX IV

Working paper submitted to the Special Committee

Working paper submitted by Mexico (A/AC.134/L.28):

Note. The sole purpose pursued in submitting this working paper was to attempt a summing-up of the stage reached in the negotiations of the Special Committee since its inception. The working paper should not be seen as representing a change in the position of the submitting delegation, which is one of the sponsors of the draft proposal set out in document A/AC.134/L.16 and Add.1 and 2.

1. Preambular paragraphs on which there is general agreement, subject to drafting changes, according to the report of the Working Group of the Whole established at the 1969 session (1969 report of the Special Committee, annex I)

   The General Assembly,

   "Basing itself on the fact that one of the fundamental purposes of the United Nations is to maintain international peace and security and to take effective collective measures for the prevention and removal of threats to the peace, and for the suppression of acts of aggression or other breaches of the peace," (paragraph 5 of the report of the Working Group of the Whole)

   "Recalling also that Article 39 of the Charter states that the Security Council shall determine the existence of any threat to the peace, breach of the peace or act of aggression and shall make recommendations or decide what measures shall be taken in accordance with Articles 41 and 42 to maintain or restore international peace and security," (paragraph 6 of the report of the Working Group of the Whole)

   "Reaffirming further the duty of States under the Charter of the United Nations to settle their international disputes by pacific methods in order not to endanger international peace, security and justice,

   "Convinced that the adoption of a definition of aggression would have a restraining influence on a potential aggressor, would simplify the determination of acts of aggression and the implementation of measures to stop them and would also facilitate the rendering of assistance to the victim of aggression and the protection of his lawful rights and interests,

   "Considering also that armed aggression is the most serious and dangerous form of aggression, being fraught, in the conditions created by the existence of nuclear weapons, with the threat of a new world conflict with all its catastrophic consequences and that this form of aggression should be defined at the present stage," (paragraph 7 of the report of the Working Group of the Whole).

2. Elements in operative paragraphs on which there is general agreement, according to the report of the Working Group established at the 1970 session (1970 report of the Special Committee, annex II)

   (a) There is general agreement that this definition of aggression should be limited to the concept of the use of armed force and should include an abstract formulation expressing in a balanced way the essential elements and the characteristics of the concept.

USSR proposal

1. Armed aggression (direct or indirect) is the use by a State, first, of armed force against another State contrary to the purposes, principles and provisions of the Charter of the United Nations. (Paragraph 1)

Thirteen-Power proposal

2. For the purpose of this definition, aggression is the use of armed force by a State against another State, including its territorial waters or air space, or in any way affecting the territorial integrity, sovereignty or political independence of such State, save under the provisions of paragraph 3 hereof or when undertaken by or under the authority of the Security Council. (Paragraph 2)

Six-Power proposal

II. The term aggression is applicable, without prejudice to a finding of threat to the peace or breach of the peace, to the use of force in international relations, overt or covert, direct or indirect, by a State against the territorial integrity or political independence of any other State, or in any other manner inconsistent with the Purposes of the United Nations.... (Paragraph II)

Texts proposed in the Working Group

(i) "Aggression is the use of armed force by a State against the territorial integrity /including the territorial waters and air space/ /or sovereignty/ or political independence of another State, or in any other manner inconsistent with the purposes of the United Nations;"

(ii) "Aggression is the use of armed force by a State against another State, or in any way affecting the territorial integrity /including the territorial waters and air space/ or political independence of such State."

(b) There is general agreement that the concept of "priority" or "first use" should be introduced into the definition; however, there are two ways of doing this:

(1) specific mention, as in the USSR draft (paragraph 1) and the thirteen-Power draft (paragraph 5);

(2) reference to this factor in a formulation of the kind found in paragraph 5 of the Working Group's report, which reads:

"In determining whether force was used by a State in order to act against the territorial integrity or political independence of another State, or in any manner inconsistent with the purposes of the United Nations, due weight shall be given to the question which of those States first used force."

(c) There is general agreement that it is essential to include in the definition a reference to the legitimate uses of force in accordance with the Charter.

USSR proposal

6. Nothing in the foregoing shall prevent the use of armed force in accordance with the Charter of the United Nations, including its use by dependent peoples in order to exercise their inherent right of self-determination in accordance with General Assembly resolution 1514 (XV). (Paragraph 6)

Thirteen-Power proposal

3. The inherent right of individual or collective self-defence of a State can be exercised only in case of the occurrence of armed attack (armed aggression) by another State in accordance with Article 51 of the Charter;

4. Enforcement action or any use of armed force by regional arrangements or agencies may only be resorted to if there is decision to that effect by the Security Council acting under Article 53 of the Charter; (Paragraphs 3 and 4)

Six-Power proposal

III. The use of force in the exercise of the inherent right of individual or collective self-defence, or pursuant to decisions of or authorization by competent United Nations organs or regional organizations consistent with the Charter of the United Nations, does not constitute aggression. (Paragraph III)

Texts proposed in the Working Group

(i) "The use of armed force in accordance with the Charter to maintain or restore international peace and security, or in the exercise of the inherent right of individual or collective self-defence, does not constitute aggression;"

(ii) "The use of armed force in accordance with the Charter to maintain or restore international peace and security, or in the exercise of the inherent right of individual or collective self-defence, does not constitute aggression.

"The inherent right of individual or collective self-defence of a State can be exercised only in case of the occurrence of armed attack (armed aggression) by another State in accordance with Article 51 of the Charter.

"Enforcement action or any use of armed force by regional arrangements or agencies may only be resorted to under Article 53 of the Charter."

(d) There is general agreement that the non-exhaustive list of the most common cases of aggression should be preceded by a statement to the effect that the enumeration is made without prejudice to the authority vested in the Security Council by the Charter.

USSR proposal

"2.   In accordance with and without prejudice to the functions and powers of the Security Council:

"3.   In addition to the acts listed above, other acts by States may be deemed to constitute an act of aggression if in each specific instance they are declared to be such by a decision of the Security Council." (Paragraphs 2 and 3)

Thirteen-Power proposal

"3.   In accordance with the foregoing and without prejudice to the powers and duties of the Security Council, as provided in the Charter,...." (Paragraph 5)

Six-Power proposal

"I.   Under the Charter of the United Nations, 'aggression', is a term to be applied by the Security Council when appropriate in the exercise of its primary responsibility for the maintenance of international peace and security under Article 24 and its functions under Article 39." (Paragraph I)

(e) There are two views on the inclusion of the concept of "declaration of war" among the typical acts of aggression:

(1) "Declaration of war" should be included among typical acts of aggression.

(2) A statement should be included before the listing of typical acts indicating that the acts included in the list constitute aggression whether or not they are accompanied by a declaration of war.

(f) There is general agreement on the desirability of including in the list of typical acts of aggression the following cases:

Invasion of the territory of another State

USSR proposal

"(c) Invasion or attack by the armed forces of a State against the territory of another State, military occupation or annexation of the territory of another State or part thereof," (Paragraph 2.B.c.)

Thirteen-Power proposal

"(b) The invasion or attack by the armed forces of a State, against the territories of another State, or any military occupation, however temporary, of any forcible annexation of the territory of another State or part thereof;" (Paragraph 5.b)

Six-Power proposal

"(1) Invasion by its armed forces of territory under the jurisdiction of another State;" (Paragraph IV.B.1)

Bombardment of the territory of another State

USSR proposal

"(b) Bombardment of or firing at the territory and population of another State...." (Paragraph 2.B.b)

Thirteen-Power proposal

"(c) Bombardment by the armed forces of a State against the territory of another State,...." (Paragraph 5.c)

Six-Power proposal

"(3) Bombardment by its armed forces of territory under the jurisdiction of another State." (Paragraph IV.B.3)

Attack on the armed forces, ships or aircraft of another State

USSR proposal

"(b) ... or an attack on its land, sea or air forces;" (Paragraph 2.B.b)

Six-Power proposal

"(5) carrying out deliberate attacks on the armed forces, ships, or aircraft of another State;" (Paragraph IV.B.5)

Indirect use of force

(g) There is general agreement that reference should be made in the definition to the problem of armed bands or irregular forces; however, there is no agreement on how to do this.

USSR proposal

"C. The use by a State of armed force by sending bands, mercenaries, terrorists or saboteurs to the territory of another State and engagement in other forms of subversive activity involving the use of armed force with the aim of promoting an internal upheaval in another State or a reversal of policy in favour of the aggressor shall be considered as an act of indirect aggression." (Paragraph 2.C)

Thirteen-Power proposal

"7. When a State is a victim in its own territory of subversive and/or terrorist acts by irregular, volunteer or armed bands organized or supported by another State, it may take all reasonable and adequate steps to safeguard its existence and its institutions, without having recourse to the right of individual or collective self-defence against the other State under Article 51 of the Charter;" (Paragraph 7)

Six-Power proposal

"(6) organizing, supporting or directing armed bands or irregular or volunteer forces that make incursions or infiltrate into another State;

"(7) organizing, supporting or directing violent civil strife or acts of terrorism in another State; or

"(8) organizing, supporting or directing subversive activities aimed at the violent overthrow of the Government of another State." (Paragraph IV.B 6, 7 and 8)

Text proposed in the Working Group

The following text was proposed in the Working Group to replace paragraph IV.B, 6, 7, and 8 of the six-Power proposal:

"The sending by a State of armed bands of irregulars or mercenaries which invade the territory of another State in such force and circumstances as to amount to armed attack as envisaged in Article 51 of the Charter."

3.   Points on whose inclusion there is no agreement

(a)   Recognition of the fact that the power of decision to use force is centralized in the United Nations and consequences of the application of this principle in the activities of the regional agencies in accordance with Article 53 of the Charter.

(b)   Application of the definition to political entities other than States.

(c)   Inclusion of the use of weapons of mass destruction as a typical case of aggression.

(d)   Naval blockade as a typical case of aggression.

(e)   Question of maintaining armed forces in another State.

(f)   Principle of proportionality.

(g)   Inclusion of the concept of "aggressive intent".

(h)   Inclusion in the definition of the legal consequences of aggression, fundamentally of the following:

(i)   Aggression is a crime against peace and commission of this crime entails international responsibility;

(ii)   There exists an obligation not to recognize the occupation and acquisition of territory by force.

(i)   Inclusion in the definition of the question of the right of peoples to self-determination of.

ANNEX V

List of representatives[a]

Algeria: Mr. Noureddine Harbi, Mr. Mohamed Berrezoug

Australia: Sir Laurence McIntyre, Mr. H.C. Mott,* Mr. G.J.L. Coles*

Bulgaria: Mr. Dimitar T. Kostov

Canada: Mr. J.A. Beesley, Mr. H. Lyon Weidman,* Mr. L.S. Clark*

Colombia: Mr. Aujusto Espinosa, Mr. José María Morales-Suárez*

Congo (Democratic Republic of): Mr. Nicolas Bofunga, Mr. Vincent Mutuale

Cyprus: Mr. Z. Rossides, Mr. A.J. Jacovides, Mr. D. Moushoutas

Czechoslovakia: Mr. Ilja Hulinsky, Mr. Václav Kralik

Ecuador: Mr. Gonzalo Alcívar, Mr. Horacio Sevilla-Borja

Finland: Mr. Matti Cawén,, Mr. Holger Rotkirch

France: Mr. François de la Gorce, Mr. Alain Deschamps, Mr. Philippe Petit,
Mrs. Catherine Boivineau

Ghana: Mr. R.M. Akwei, Mr. G.C.N. Cudjoe,* Mr. Emmanuel Sam**

Guyana: Mr. P.A. Thompson, Mr. S.R. Insanally, Mr. Duke E. Pollard

Haiti: Mr. M.C. Duplessis

Indonesia: Mr. H. Roeslan Abdulgani, Mr. Datuk Mulia,* Mr. Mohamed Sidik*

Iran: Mr. Hooshang Amirmokri, Mr. Farrokh Parsi*

Iraq: Mr. Talibh El-Shibib, Mr. Adnan Raouf,* Mr. Wissam Al-Zahawie,*
Mr. Riyadh Al-Qaysi*

Italy: Mr. Francesco Capotorti, Mr. Joseph Nitti,* Mr. Vincenzo Starace*

Japan: Mr. Hideo Kagami, Mr. Takao Kawakami,* Mr. Yoji Ohta**

Madagascar: Mr. Moïse Rakotosihanaka

---

   * Alternate.

  ** Adviser.

  a/ See paragraph 2 of the report.

Mexico: Mr. Sergio González-Gálvez, Mr. José L. Vallarta*

Norway: Mr. Per E.S. Tresselt, Mr. Haakon B. Hjelde*

Romania: Mr. Gheorghe Diaconescu, Mr. Vergiliu Ionescu*

Sierra Leone: Mr. Oulu W. Harding

Spain: Mr. José Luis Messia, Mr. Amador Martinez Morcillo,* Mr. José Cuenca

Sudan: Mr. Omer El Sheikh

Syria: Mr. Dia-Allah El-Fattal

Turkey: Mehmet Güney

Uganda: Mr. S.T. Bigombe

Union of Soviet Socialist Republics: Mr. V. Chkhikvadzé, Mr. D. Kolesnik,*
Mr. O. Bogdanov,** Mr. E. Nasinovsky,
Mr. J. Rybakov**

United Arab Republic: Mr. Mohamed H. El-Zayyat, Mr. Aly Ismail Teymour,
Mr. Mohamed M. El-Baradei**

United Kingdom of Great Britain and Northern Ireland: Mr. J.R. Freeland,
Mr. N.C.R. Williams*

United States of America: Mr. Herbert K. Reis, Mr. Morris Rothenberg,*
Mr. Robert B. Rosenstock*

Uruguay: Mr. Augusto Legnani, Mrs. Ana A.Fasanello de Gamou,* Miss Graziella Dubra*

Yugoslavia: Mr. Miljan Komatina, Mr. Aleksandar Jelić, Mr. Zlatan Kikic,*
Mrs. Gordana Diklić-Trajković,** Mr. Radomir Zećević**

---

* Alternate.

** Adviser.

United Nations

GENERAL ASSEMBLY
Official Records

DOCUMENT 21

Agenda item 89

ANNEXES

TWENTY-SIXTH SESSION

NEW YORK, 1971

Agenda item 89:* Report of the Special Committee on the Question of Defining Aggression**

CONTENTS

* For the discussion of this item, see *Official Records of the General Asembly, Twenty-sixth Session, Sixth Committee,* 1268th to 1276th, 1281st and 1285th meetings; *ibid., Fifth Committee,* 1460th meeting; and *ibid., Plenary Meetings,* 1999th meeting.

** Since 1967, the reports of this Committee have been discussed by the General Assembly at the following sessions: twenty-second (agenda item 95), twenty-third (agenda item 86), twenty-fourth (agenda item 88) and twenty-fifth (agenda item 87).

DOCUMENT A/8525

Report of the Sixth Committee

[Original: French]
[19 November 1971]

CONTENTS

INTRODUCTION

1. Pursuant to General Assembly resolution 2644 (XXV) of 25 November 1970, the Special Committee on the Question of Defining Aggression reconvened at United Nations Headquarters at New York from 1 February to 5 March 1971 in order to resume its work in accordance with General Assembly resolution 2330 (XXII) of 18 December 1967, and prepared a report covering the work of its 1971 session (A/8419).

2. At its 1939th plenary meeting, on 25 September 1971, the General Assembly decided to include in the agenda for its twenty-sixth session the item entitled "Report of the Special Committee on the Question of Defining Aggression", and allocated it to the Sixth Committee for consideration and report.

3. The agenda item was considered by the Sixth Committee at its 1268th-1276th and 1281st meetings, held between 26 October and 15 November 1971. At the 1268th meeting, on 26 October 1971, Mr. Al-Qaysi, the representative of Iraq and Rapporteur of the Special Committee on the Question of Defining Aggression, introduced the Special Committee's report.

4. At its 1281st meeting, on 15 November 1971, the Sixth Committee decided that its report on the agenda item should contain a summary of the principal juridical trends which had emerged during the debate, the financial implications of such a summary having previously been brought to its attention in accordance with General Assembly resolution 2292 (XXII).

I. DRAFT RESOLUTION SUBMITTED TO THE SIXTH COMMITTEE

5. At its 1281st meeting, on 15 November 1971, the representative of Mexico submitted a draft resolution (A/C.6/L.827) sponsored by the following States: Bulgaria, Byelorussian Soviet Socialist Republic, Colombia, Cyprus, Czechoslovakia, Ecuador, Egypt, Ethiopia, Ghana, Haiti, Hungary, India, Iran, Jordan, Kenya, Libyan Arab Republic, Mali, Mexico, Mongolia, Poland, Romania, Sierra Leone, Syrian Arab Republic, Uganda, Ukrainian Soviet Socialist Republic, Union of Soviet Socialist Republics, United Republic of

1

Annexes (XXVI) 89

Tanzania, Yugoslavia and Zambia. Guinea, Guyana, Madagascar and Pakistan subsequently joined the sponsors. The draft resolution reads as follows:

[*For the text, see para. 42 below.*]

II. Debate

6. Sections A and B below contain a summary of the main trends which emerged during the debate on certain general aspects of the question of defining aggression and on the content of the definition. It is, however, appropriate to draw attention here to the views expressed on the state of advancement of the work of the Special Committee and on its mandate, working methods and composition.

7. Several representatives pointed out that the Special Committee had made encouraging progress which they felt gave grounds for hope that a generally acceptable definition of aggression could be formulated in the near future. Hence, most of the representatives who spoke supported the resolution in which the Special Committee recommended that the General Assembly invite it to continue its work in 1972 (A/8419, para. 66). One representative, however, was unable to share the optimism of those who believed that the Special Committee was on the verge of completing its work, and said he could not support the proposal that the mandate of the Special Committee should be renewed in 1972. In his opinion, it could either be dissolved temporarily or permanently or its work could be suspended for two years so as to allow States time for further reflection and, perhaps, informal consultations. Another representative also opposed extending the Special Committee's mandate, expressing the view that to do so, in addition to placing a financial burden on the Organization and creating additional work for Member States, would merely increase the ambiguity already existing, jeopardize the basic rights embodied in the Charter, and adversely affect the powers of the various organs of the United Nations, particularly the discretionary power of the Security Council.

8. With regard to the method of work, some representatives estimated that the Special Committee should establish more than one working group, arguing that the single Working Group was insufficient since it consisted of a limited number of members, some of whom did not seem to be biased in favour of expediting the conclusion of the Special Committee's work, and that several small but representative working groups should be established which would meet concurrently to consider the major differences of opinion and report to the Special Committee. One representative said that the composition of the Working Group established by the Special Committee at its 1971 session was unsatisfactory and that if other working groups were appointed in the future, provision should be made for the representation of States other than those which had sponsored the various draft proposals submitted to the Special Committee. Another representative noted that the Committee had frequently been unable, for lack of time, to consider all the topics on its agenda or those it had assigned to its Working Group, and said that there were various ways of solving that problem: (a) the Special Committee could refer certain principles, preferably those in which there was a near consensus, to its Working Group, which could make a thorough study of them with a view to reaching a definitive decision; (b) the time allotted to the Special Committee could be increased by five working days to en-

able it to make a detailed examination of the texts drawn up by its Working Group; (c) the general debate which took place at the beginning of each session of the Special Committee could be eliminated, since the positions of all delegations were currently well known. He suggested that it might be preferable to adopt solution (a), if necessary combined with solution (c).

9. Regarding the composition of the Special Committee, several representatives said that the People's Republic of China should be invited to participate in its work.

A. Opinions expressed on certain general aspects of the question of defining aggression

10. A large number of representatives drew attention to the urgent need for a definition of aggression. A number of General Assembly resolutions were cited in that connexion, including resolution 2644 (XXV) and resolution 2734 (XXV) of 16 December 1970, containing the Declaration on the Strengthening of International Security. It was further pointed out that the adoption of a definition of aggression would not only contribute to the codification of international law but would also strengthen the system of collective security established by the Charter and promote the rule of law. It was said that a definition of aggression could contribute towards the formation of an enlightened public opinion, could be a yardstick against which to measure the conduct of States in the light of their obligations under the Charter, and could serve as a warning to any potential aggressor. It was observed that world public opinion had a strong influence on the development of international affairs, and in that connexion the definition of aggression could constitute an indirect but effective deterrent to acts of aggression; in particular, it would supply a legal basis, within the framework of the United Nations, for eliminating the lack of precision and the subjective nature of political judgements. It was also pointed out that a definition of aggression would be particularly useful for protecting small countries.

11. On the other hand, some representatives expressed doubts regarding the usefulness of a definition of aggression, holding that the clarification of legal norms was a useful step in promoting the rule of law but that it must be recognized that an agreed definition of aggression was not vital to the attainment of the purposes and principles of the Charter. It was argued that even if such a definition could be established it could neither have any impact on the development of international penal law nor remove provocation and aggression; moreover, after 26 years of activity, no evidence could be found that the Security Council had difficulty in performing its task of determining the existence of aggression merely because it lacked an appropriate definition. The opinion was expressed that international peace in fact depended on the political will of States; rules of law were at best no more than guides, whether for individuals or for States. Furthermore, the various juridical instruments of general application at the disposal of the international community were quite adequate for its needs.

12. One representative said that, although his delegation still doubted the usefulness of a definition of aggression, it was prepared to support the continuance of the Special Committee's work. Yet it should b⸱ recognized, he said, that one unfortunate consequenc of the decades of failure to define aggression was t⸱·

further work had been suspended on other important legal matters: the formulation of the principles recognized in the Charter of the Nürnberg Tribunal and in the judgement of the Tribunal,[1] the draft code of offences against the peace and security of mankind,[2] and the question of an international criminal jurisdiction;[3] several developments seemed to indicate that it would be possible, at least to some extent, to resume work on those questions without awaiting a definitive definition of aggression.

13. One representative observed that the major difficulties encountered by the Special Committee in the formulation of a definition of aggression were largely due to political factors and that there was little hope that they would be quickly resolved. He therefore suggested, as an interim measure, that a provisional definition should be produced, covering those areas on which agreement already existed. In the view of another representative, that proposal seemed incompatible with the notion of a comprehensive definition, and an incomplete definition might well leave loopholes that would tempt a potential aggressor.

14. With regard to the procedure to be followed for the formulation and adoption of a definition of aggression, some representatives considered that the only way of arriving at an acceptable and lasting definition of aggression was by consensus. Other representatives, however, held that it would not be necessary to apply that method to all aspects of the Special Committee's work, particularly those which were of relatively minor importance. It was also maintained that the definition should have the widest possible support of Member States, without which it would have little political or legal value. The opinion was expressed that instead of trying to resolve difficulties by decisions taken by majority vote, the Special Committee should follow the example of the Special Committee on Principles of International Law concerning Friendly Relations and Co-operation among States, which had taken all its decisions unanimously; it was doubtful what value and use a definition of aggression would have if, for example, one or more of the permanent members of the Security Council opposed it. In the view of several representatives, where it was not possible to reach a consensus, the value of the definition adopted by a simple majority should not be disregarded; even though such a definition could not establish international legal norms, it could nevertheless exert an influence on world opinion and pave the way for the positive development of international law. It was also held that the method of seeking the consent of all the permanent members of the Security Council was obstructive and undemocratic, and should be abandoned; the fact that the Security Council had primary responsibility for the maintenance of international peace and security did not entitle it to reject rules of international law which were being elaborated by the General Assembly, in the present instance through the Special Committee set up by the Assembly to deal with the question of aggression.

15. One representative said that a definition of aggression would gain in importance if it was adopted in a General Assembly resolution similar to that by which the Assembly had adopted the Declaration on Principles of International Law concerning Friendly Relations and Co-operation among States in accordance with the Charter of the United Nations.[4] Another representative held that, though General Assembly resolutions were not mandatory either for States or for the Security Council, recommendations by the Assembly had more force than the mere exertion of moral pressure and were not devoid of all juridical value. He said that the establishment of rules of international conduct within international bodies had already had a palpable influence with regard to the scope and value of subsidiary sources of international law and the general principles of law, jurisprudence and theory; thus it was impossible to discard a priori the idea that a solemn declaration by the General Assembly embodying a definition of aggression, and approved by the majority of Member States, could serve as a basis for a general principle of law; although a General Assembly recommendation was not mandatory in itself, it could acquire juridical value by becoming incorporated into international law.

B. OPINIONS EXPRESSED ON THE CONTENT OF THE DEFINITION

1. General definition of aggression

16. In the view of some representatives, the text of a general definition of aggression formulated by the Working Group in its 1971 report (ibid., annex III, para. 3) provided a constructive basis for further work. One representative said apropos of the text that it would be advisable to avoid defining aggression by concepts which were themselves ill-defined, such as "territorial waters" and "air space". Another representative said that because of the lack of agreement among nations regarding the breadth of territorial waters, it was important for coastal States that a reference to "territorial waters" should be included in the general definition of aggression; there should be no objection to the inclusion of a reference to "air space"; and the differences of opinion regarding the inclusion of the term "sovereignty" in the general definition might be solved by finding a way to reflect the rights implicit in that principle. One representative held the view that the phrase "or in any other manner inconsistent with the purposes of the United Nations" contained in the text of a general definition might be taken to mean that force could be used in achieving the purposes of the United Nations as defined in Article 1 of the Charter, which would of course be a false interpretation. Admittedly, that phrase was included in Article 2, paragraph 4, of the Charter, but only to emphasize that force should not be used in international relations; however, to insert those words in a general definition of aggression might well blur the Charter rules regarding the non-use of force.

17. One representative expressed the view that a general definition of aggression rationally combining the agreed elements might read as follows:

> "Without prejudice to the discretion of the Security Council to make a contrary finding, that State shall be presumed to be an aggressor which resorts to the use of armed force, first, against another State, in order to affect in any manner the territorial integrity, sovereignty or political integrity of the State aggrieved, contrary to the relevant provisions of the Charter."

That definition, he argued, would appear to contain all the elements agreed by the members of the Special

---

[1] See Official Records of the General Assembly, Fifth Session, Supplement No. 12, para. 97.
[2] Ibid., Sixth Session, Supplement No. 9, para. 59.
[3] Ibid., Fifth Session, Supplement No. 12, paras. 128-145.

[4] General Assembly resolution 2625 (XXV).

Committee to constitute aggression, since it preserved the discretionary powers of the Security Council, was confined to armed attack, raised the priority principle as a presumption, rebuttable by proof of the absence of intention, was restricted to States, recognized the necessity of *animus aggressionis*, was in strict conformity with the Charter, and was not applicable to situations where armed confrontation was legally permissible under the Charter.

18. One representative remarked that if the Special Committee intended to produce a compromise between the various projects before it, several years would no doubt be necessary. But in view of the importance and urgency of the problem, the Special Committee might do well to replace the definition by a description, merely giving a general formulation of aggression by way of a recital of its constituent factors, specifying the means to be used in identifying the culprit, and fixing the responsibility of the State concerned. That procedure would bring together all the aspects of aggression. Moreover, an unduly precise definition would have the drawback of enabling a potential aggressor to distort its provisions, for example by making use of the latest scientific inventions.

19. In the opinion of one representative, the definition should refer not only to "a State", but also to groups of States. An act of aggression could be committed by one or several States against one or several other States.

20. One representative said that the definition of aggression should cover the use of force by one or more States in a manner incompatible with any régime whatsoever established by the international community in respect of areas which were outside the limits of national jurisdiction or which fell within the limits of national jurisdiction but had been expressly isolated from the arms race or any particular form of the arms race. The inclusion of that point in the definition of aggression would give additional publicity to, and strengthen, efforts at demilitarization. One representative expressed considerable reservations about that suggestion. One of the most valuable features of the progress recently made by the Special Committee, he said, was its agreement to define aggression as that term was used in the Charter. The use of force within certain specified zones could not possibly be described as falling within the ambit of the phrase "act of aggression" as used in the Charter, for example in Article 39.

2. *The definition and the power of the Security Council*

21. Some representatives referred to the idea, generally accepted in principle, that the definition of aggression should safeguard the discretionary power of the Security Council as the United Nations organ with primary responsibility for the maintenance of international peace and security. One representative said that no definition of aggression could bind the Security Council in determining a particular case of aggression. The Security Council was and remained an organ of security. Without detracting from the Council's discretionary powers of appraisal, a definition should be prepared, within the framework of the Charter, which would give it guidance. The powers of appraisal which the Council exercised in connexion with any situation representing a threat to peace would also help to guard against the possibility of a fairly flexible definition being distorted by an aggressor. Another

representative pointed out that the Security Council could not exceed the powers accorded to it under the Charter. Of course, the practice of the Council could contribute to the interpretation of the Charter, but it seemed difficult to maintain, as the Working Group had done in paragraph 12 of its 1970 report,[5] that the Security Council had fullness of power under the Charter to extend the definition of aggression while, at the same time, presenting for the guidance of the Council a definition of aggression also derived from the Charter. Another representative wondered whether the incorporation of a definition of aggression in international law would not have the effect of curtailing the powers of the Security Council. It must not be forgotten that action by the United Nations was not designed to restore legal order once it had been upset, but rather to maintain or restore peace. The aim must be to ensure that the United Nations organs as far as possible respected pre-established objectives and general legal principles rather than to place powers of absolute discretion at their disposal. There was no doubt, however, that the Security Council and the General Assembly could hardly openly defy a principle established by the General Assembly.

3. *Political entities to which the definition should apply*

22. Several representatives opposed the inclusion in the definition of aggression of a reference to political entities other than States. They argued that the definition of aggression should apply to all sovereign and independent States, whether they were Members of the United Nations or not. Otherwise the Special Committee would be obliged to find a precise definition of "State" and "political entity", and that was outside its mandate. Moreover, the notion of "political entity" was not embodied in the Charter, which had no provision for making the existence of a sovereign State dependent on its recognition by other States. They further argued that the term "political entities" had no precise meaning either in political science or in international law. Its inclusion in the definition might cause difficulties in its interpretation and application. It would imply a hierarchy among States, which would be tantamount to recognizing situations that were incompatible with the purposes of the Charter. States should be regarded in the definition as the only subjects of international law capable of committing or being the victim of an act of aggression. To ensure that the definition was given the widest possible application, some representatives suggested resorting to the compromise solution envisaged in paragraph 8 of the Working Group's 1971 report (*ibid.*, annex III), namely to annex to the definition an explanatory note to the effect that the term "State" included States whose statehood was disputed. Other representatives expressed reservations regarding that solution, arguing that if it was to be complete, the definition should include the concept of political entities. Agreement on certain aspects of that problem had been achieved in the Declaration on Friendly Relations, and it should be no more difficult in the present case. Making a distinction between the subject of aggression and its object, one representative said that with regard to the subject of aggression, the principles of the Charter were applicable only to States; in the absence of any indication in the Charter, the term "State" must be defined in the sense of general international law, i.e., as those

---

[5] See *Official Records of the General Assembly, Twenty-fifth Session, Supplement No. 19,* annex II.

political entities which met certain well-known factual criteria. When a State met those criteria no question of recognition arose. Until the explanatory note in question was produced, the relevant part of the general definition proposed by the Working Group in paragraph 3 of its 1971 report should be interpreted in that light. On the other hand, the object of aggression, i.e., its victim, might include political entities other than States.

4. Acts proposed for inclusion in the definition of aggression

23. A large number of representatives expressed the view that the definition should be limited, at least at the present stage, to the use of armed force. Different opinions were, however, expressed with regard to the question whether the definition should cover, for the purposes of the exercise of the right of self-defence, the so-called indirect use of armed force.

24. Several representatives maintained that at the current stage of its work the Special Committee should not concern itself with defining "indirect aggression" because of the extreme difficulty of finding a precise definition and because of the time-consuming process of obtaining a consensus. With reference to the text of the general definition contained in the 1971 report of the Working Group, they stressed that if the phrase "however exerted" in the text were to be retained, it should be qualified to mean armed force necessitating recourse to self-defence under Article 51 of the Charter. They said that care should be taken not to confuse the concept of "breach of the peace" with that of "armed attack" or "aggression"; the Special Committee's report had cited as examples of acts constituting aggression acts which, in fact, would only result in a breach of the peace unless they had been of such intensity as to necessitate recourse to self-defence, in which case they would pose an imminent danger to life and property as well as to the existence of a State. They also argued that the definition should make it possible to limit the legitimate use of force to a minimum and to discourage States from using armed attack as an instrument of national policy under any pretext whatsoever; the Charter did not ignore the idea of the indirect use of force, as was evident from its references to "breaches of the peace", but any attempt to enlarge the concept to include consideration of the circumstances of a *casus belli* would go beyond the Charter and the Special Committee's mandate. They also said that the definition should contain a list specifying the most serious kinds of aggression, i.e., those contemplated in Articles 39 and 51 of the Charter; the inclusion in that list of the sending of armed bands by one State into the territory of another might be justified; however, unduly vague concepts such as support for acts of subversion should be excluded, since a State might use them as a pretext for aggression under the guise of self-defence.

25. On the other hand, some representatives maintained that the definition of aggression should cover any illegal use of armed force, whether direct or indirect. They said that a definition of aggression must be exhaustive and not partial; attempts to draw a distinction between "direct" and "indirect" aggression sometimes were cited as an excuse for accepting a partial definition. Such a distinction had no basis in the Charter, which in Article 2, paragraph 4, referred to the "use of force" in international relations and did not differentiate between the various kinds of illegal resort to force. Articles 1 and 39 referred to "aggression"; they made no distinction between the various types of aggression on the basis of the means employed by the aggressor; there was no provision in the Charter which suggested that a State could in any way escape the Charter's condemnation of illegal acts of force against another State by a judicious selection of means to an illegal end. It was further contended that indirect aggression was the most serious contemporary manifestation of aggression and that any enumeration of acts of aggression which overlooked that particular form would have no great practical value; current violations of the provisions of the Charter were due as much to indirect as to direct aggression. The view was advanced that action such as infiltration of armed bands across frontiers and external participation in terrorism and subversion must be categorized as aggression in appropriate circumstances. With regard to the suggestion that that categorization could be considered liable to lead to an extension of the right of self-defence, it was stated that the concept of proportionality might find a useful application in that connexion. Referring to the general definition of aggression prepared by the Working Group and contained in its 1971 report, it was observed that the part of the text on which the Working Group had agreed: "Aggression is the use of armed force by a State against the territorial integrity or political independence of another State, or in any other manner inconsistent with the purposes of the United Nations", was to a large extent based on Article 2, paragraph 4, of the Charter; that provision necessarily covered the use of armed force in all its forms, including indirect forms; if the primary purpose of defining aggression was to deter potential aggressors, the definition should certainly not contain any loopholes, and it would be dangerous to classify indirect aggression as a less serious violation of the Charter than direct aggression.

26. According to one representative, the definition of aggression should be first and foremost comprehensive and should not be limited to armed aggression; there were a great many kinds of aggression, and any definition covering only direct forms would be incomplete and therefore dangerous. Some representatives stressed the necessity of defining economic aggression. According to one, the Special Committee should consider the inclusion in the definition of an appropriate reference to that form of aggression as one of the most serious forms of attack or challenge. Others felt that the Special Committee should recognize the need to define the concept of economic aggression at a later stage.

27. Regarding the specific acts which should be enumerated in the definition as examples of aggression, one representative maintained that a declaration of war in itself was generally considered an act of aggression. As to whether a declaration of war constituted aggression, another representative observed that the view seemed to be emerging that it was not necessarily the case but was an important element in determining an act of aggression, because of its inherent seriousness and the formal juridical consequences that flowed from it. He added that occupation which was initially legitimate, for example, under a treaty, might become illegal if continued against the will of the host State, and thus amount to aggression. One representative expressed the view that the most serious act of aggression was invasion or attack on the territory of a State by the armed forces of another State, and the occupa-

tion of that territory; the aggressor might go so far as to annex part of the territory of another State or incorporate it within its frontiers; the Special Committee should therefore include the notions of occupation or annexation of the territory of a State by force in the definition of aggression. Referring to paragraph 14 of the Working Group's 1971 report, another representative stated that he was unable to support the inclusion of the text proposed in the paragraph under the subheading "Other acts of armed force" and "Maintenance of armed forces in another State", since the former seemed unduly vague and the latter would amount to interference in the internal affairs of sovereign States in their bilateral treaty agreements.

28. According to one representative, the definition should specify that where a State placed a territory at the disposal of another to enable it to commit aggression against a third State, that likewise constituted an act of aggression.

5. *The principle of priority*

29. There seemed to be no basic objection to the inclusion of the principle of priority in the definition of aggression. According to several representatives, however, that principle must be retained as being a basic and determinative criterion. Accordingly, they argued, the principle of priority made it impossible for an aggressor State to plead innocence on the grounds that it was conducting a preventive war; the burden of proof was placed on the State which first resorted to force; hence the view that priority was a factor of secondary importance that should merely be "taken into account" was not acceptable; similarly, the clause "due weight shall be given to the question whether" in paragraph 5 of the Working Group's 1971 report was unsuitable for the purpose sought by the definition of aggression. It was observed that if the element of priority was not to have decisive weight, it would be impossible to prevent States from committing acts of aggression in the guise of "preventive" wars; furthermore, the phrase "without prejudice to the powers and duties of the Security Council", which appeared in paragraph 5 of the Working Group's report, was not acceptable. The discretion of the Security Council should apply to the whole of the definition rather than to the question of priority in particular.

30. Other representatives were of the opinion that the principle of priority could not in itself constitute a determining factor and should only figure in the definition as one element among others. It should not be applied automatically. In that regard it was stated that certain acts of aggression, such as blockade, could oblige the State against which they were directed to have recourse to its inherent right of collective or individual self-defence. It was also observed that the question of priority might be solved by postulating that the Security Council should determine, in each case, which party first used force and treat its finding as a fact of considerable significance, but without prejudice to the ultimate consequences of the finding. It was further suggested that care should be taken to ensure that the onus of proof would be on the accused and not on the victim State and that the presumption of the culpability of the aggressor should be rebuttable.

31. According to one representative, it was essential to pinpoint in the definition of aggression exactly when the illegal use of force took place. He wondered whether it was when the territorial integrity of the victim State was violated by the arms of the aggressor State, or when the victim had taken the irrevocable step of launching its weapons of destruction, even if they had not yet violated the territorial boundary of the victim State. The Special Committee would be all the more justified in studying that question in that it was intimately bound up with the principle of priority; if first use of nuclear weapons was in all instances illegal, what was the position of the victim State? Was it entitled to use nuclear devices as a means of self-defence, or would it in turn become an aggressor if it used such devices before the weapons launched by the other State violated its territory? The definition would be incomplete if it did not specify how to determine the time and place of the act of aggression.

6. *Aggressive intent*

32. In the view of some representatives, the element of intent should be a fundamental ingredient of any definition of aggression. It was observed that since aggression was a crime, that element could not be overlooked; it was the intention which determined the act, and it should be remembered that the Security Council, when determining the existence of an act of aggression, had to take into consideration the intention of the parties. The view was expressed that it was essential to include the element of intent in the definition of aggression, since it made it possible to distinguish between an act of aggression properly speaking, on the one hand, and an unpremeditated incident or an act of self-defence, on the other. However, several representatives felt that since aggressive intent was necessarily implied in any act of aggression, it would not be necessary to include the principle in the definition; the principles of priority and of aggressive intent could not be placed on the same footing; the element of intent became irrelevant when the Security Council had determined that a certain State had been the first to use armed force against another State; the inclusion of the element of intent in a definition would in fact permit an aggressor State to seek to justify its actions; the burden of proof should always be on the aggressor and not on the victim State, and that legal principle could not be applied in the context of aggression unless the element of intent was excluded from the definition. It was also stated that the question of aggressive intent should be a matter for the discretionary power of the Security Council, which should take motive and purpose into consideration in determining the existence or non-existence of aggression; inclusion of the notion of intent in the definition could only add to the complexity of the problem.

33. Several representatives drew a distinction between aggressive intent and the motive for aggression. It was stated that one of the main difficulties facing the Special Committee was the unwillingness of some members to differentiate between motive and intention; intention implied that a person committing an act not only foresaw but also desired the possible consequences of his act, whereas motive denoted a legally impermissible emotion evoked by an external objective to be achieved by the contemplated act; in other words, the motive merely explained the crime while intention was an essential ingredient of it; for the purposes of defining aggression, aggressive intent was the will to inflict harm on a State, contrary to the provisions of the Charter; motives, on the other hand, were set out in paragraph IV A of the six-Power draft (*ibid.*, annex I, draft proposal C).

7. *Legitimate use of force*

34. Some representatives pointed out that the definition of aggression should distinguish clearly between aggression and the legitimate use of force. In that connexion, it was observed that the Charter provided expressly in Article 51 that the right of self-defence could be exercised in the event of armed attack. That Article could be incorporated bodily into the definition of aggression; a definition not expressly based on that Article would run the risk of encouraging the use of force in violation of the provisions of the Charter. Other representatives maintained that the Special Committee's terms of reference did not entitle it to embark on a definition of the right of self-defence and that any attempt to do so would simply place an insurmountable obstacle in its way. All that was required, it was argued, was that the definition should contain a suitable saving provision to the effect that the definition did not apply to what was done in the exercise of the inherent right of self-defence. Reference was also made to the following provision of the Declaration on Friendly Relations: "Nothing in the foregoing paragraphs shall be construed as enlarging or diminishing in any way the scope of the provisions of the Charter concerning cases in which the use of force is lawful". It was suggested that the Special Committee might proceed on the basis of that provision, which would help it to avoid other dangerous pitfalls such as an attempt to determine the organs or institutions competent to authorize the use of force and the question of proportionality in cases of self-defence.

35. One representative considered that it should be expressly stipulated in the definition of aggression that no consideration of a political, military, economic or other character could be invoked by a State to justify the use of force against another State.

36. Some representatives were opposed to including the concept of proportionality in the definition of aggression. It was observed that no such concept appeared in the Charter and that it was by no means universally recognized in international law; its inclusion in the definition would favour the aggressor by throwing the burden of proof on the victim of aggression; furthermore, a State that had been attacked should not be required to assess the strength of the enemy forces in order to ensure that its defence was commensurate with the aggression; such a concept would encourage rather than discourage the aggressor, which was quite contrary to the purpose of the definition. That concept, it was also maintained, might be applied in the case of indirect armed attack or breaches of the peace, which were less urgent; in any case, Article 51 of the Charter recognized the right of self-defence as an inherent right without any restrictions whatsoever; the meaning of that Article could not be stretched to subject its operation to the concept of proportionality, which had now become obsolete, at least in the context of the right of self-defence. Other representatives considered that it would be useful to include the concept of proportionality in the definition. The view was expressed that the concept was not a new one in municipal law and that it would be relatively easy to transfer it to international law; the fear that incorporating the concept in the definition of aggression would only encourage aggression was not supported by the facts; proportionality should be based on the danger rationally perceived by the victim. The view was also expressed that the concept of proportionality would be an excellent criterion for determining whether an action was defensive or aggressive; the right of self-defence should be closely linked to the concept of proportionality; any definition of aggression should be so worded as to make it impossible for a State to find loopholes to provide a pretext for waging a preventive war.

37. With regard to the organs empowered to use force, some representatives maintained that the Security Council alone could decide on the use of force. Article 11 of the Charter, it was observed, left no room for doubt on that question; any attempt to grant such powers to other organs would be tantamount to a revision of the Charter. It was also observed that, under Article 53 of the Charter, the use of armed force by regional arrangements or agencies was not legitimate without prior authorization by the Security Council. Other representatives were of the opinion that the questions raised regarding regional agencies had been based on a confusion between the authorization of the use of force and the taking of enforcement action. The view was expressed that the Security Council and the General Assembly could authorize the use of force in certain circumstances; similarly, regional agencies could authorize the use of force in so far as the use involved was compatible with Article 2, paragraph 4, of the Charter.

38. One representative observed that there was some disagreement as to whether Chapter VIII of the Charter could be applied to regional agencies established for the defence of one specific region or whether such agencies were subject only to Article 51, which dealt with the question of collective security. In his view, that distinction was an important one, for States linked in collective defence covenants exercised their right without the authorization of the Security Council, to the extent of course that armed aggression had occurred, whereas in the case of regional agreements the authorization of the Security Council was required in order to apply enforcement action; there was clearly a difference between collective self-defence and enforcement action; collective self-defence was a reaction against armed aggression, whereas the purpose of enforcement action was to maintain international peace and security. He pointed out that although the definition of enforcement action was perfectly clear, the sponsors of the 13-Power draft (*ibid.*, draft proposal B) had decided to make express mention of the use of force, since some members of the Special Committee still maintained that action not involving the use of force would not be enforcement.

8. *The right of self-determination*

39. Several representatives pointed out that logically it was a duty of the Special Committee, the body responsible for defining aggression, namely, the illegal use of force, to consider situations in which the use of force was legitimate, in particular the inalienable right of colonial peoples to oppose any attempt to deprive them by force of their right to self-determination. The legitimacy of the use of force in exercising the right of self-determination, it was said, flowed from the Charter and from several General Assembly resolutions. In the opinion of some representatives, that right should not be mentioned in the definition of aggression. It was argued that the right of self-determination was dealt with in other instruments and therefore was not relevant to the definition of aggression; it could not be made part of that definition without an unacceptable distortion of the scope and function which the definition should have. It was further observed that the care-

fully prepared provisions of the Declaration on Friendly Relations should be respected; the relevant provisions could either be reproduced in the definition or expressly referred to. One representative thought that there was no need to include the right of peoples to self-determination in the definition unless it was done in the form in which that right was presented in paragraph 10 of the 13-Power draft.

9. Legal consequences of aggression

40. Several representatives said that the definition of aggression should include a provision concerning the legal consequences of aggression. It was stated, in this connexion, that the task of the Special Committee was to work on a general theory of aggression which would necessarily include both its component elements and its legal consequences; it must be stated that aggression, once established, entailed responsibility; it was also important to mention the principle of non-recognition and to declare that no territorial gain from aggression should be recognized. The principle of non-recognition of any territorial gain acquired by the threat or use of force, it was further observed, was in keeping with the collective security system established by the Charter to protect the sovereignty, territorial integrity and political independence of States; that principle must be applied from the moment when force was used against the territory of any State until the termination of aggression through the restoration of any occupied or annexed territory or piece of territory to the injured State. On the other hand, some representatives maintained that the definition should not mention the legal consequences of aggression. In their view, that was a question that went beyond the Special Committee's terms of reference and, in any case, had been adequately dealt with in the Declaration on Friendly Relations: the clear language of the Declaration made it unnecessary to try to cover that matter in a definition of aggression.

III. Voting

41. At its 1281st meeting, on 15 November 1971, the Sixth Committee adopted the 33-Power draft resolution (A/C.6/L.827) by 85 votes to none, with 3 abstentions. The representatives of Belgium, Cameroon, Liberia, the United Kingdom and the United States of America made statements in explanation of their votes.

Recommendation of the Sixth Committee

42. The Sixth Committee recommends to the General Assembly the adoption of the following draft resolution:

REPORT OF THE SPECIAL COMMITTEE ON THE QUESTION OF DEFINING AGGRESSION

The General Assembly,

Having considered the report of the Special Committee on the Question of Defining Aggression on the work of its session held in New York from 1 February to 5 March 1971,

Taking note of the progress made by the Special Committee in its consideration of the question of defining aggression and on the draft definition, as reflected in the report of the Special Committee,

Considering that it was not possible for the Special Committee to complete its task at its 1971 session,

Considering that in its resolutions 2330 (XXII) of 18 December 1967, 2420 (XXIII) of 18 December 1968, 2549 (XXIV) of 12 December 1969 and 2644 (XXV) of 25 November 1970 the General Assembly recognized the widespread conviction of the need to expedite the definition of aggression,

Considering the urgency of bringing the work of the Special Committee to a successful conclusion and the desirability of achieving the definition of aggression as soon as possible,

Noting also the common desire of the members of the Special Committee to continue their work on the basis of the results achieved and to arrive at a draft definition,

1. *Decides* that the Special Committee on the Question of Defining Aggression shall resume its work, in accordance with General Assembly resolution 2330 (XXII), as early as possible in 1972;

2. *Requests* the Secretary-General to provide the Special Committee with the necessary facilities and services;

3. *Decides* to include in the provisional agenda of its twenty-seventh session an item entitled "Report of the Special Committee on the Question of Defining Aggression".

ACTION TAKEN BY THE GENERAL ASSEMBLY

At its 1999th plenary meeting, on 3 December 1971, the General Assembly by a vote of 110 to none, with 3 abstentions, adopted the draft resolution submitted by the Sixth Committee (A/8525, para. 42). For the final text, see *Official Records of the General Assembly, Twenty-sixth Session, Supplement No. 29,* resolution 2781 (XXVI).

DOCUMENT 22

Twenty-Seventh Session, Supp. No. 19, A/8719.
Report of Special Committee, 31 Jan. - 3 Mar.

INTRODUCTION

1.   At its 1939th plenary meeting, on 25 September 1971, the General Assembly
decided to include in the agenda of its twenty-sixth session the report of the
Special Committee on the Question of Defining Aggression on the work of its
session held at United Nations Headquarters in New York from 1 February to
5 March 1971. 1/   The Assembly also referred this report to the Sixth Committee,
which considered it at the 1268th to 1276th and 1281st meetings, held between
26 October and 15 November 1971. 2/   At its 1999th plenary meeting, on
3 December 1971, the General Assembly adopted resolution 2781 (XXVI), which reads
as follows:

"The General Assembly,

"Having considered the report of the Special Committee on the
Question of Defining Aggression on the work of its session held in
New York from 1 February to 5 March 1971, 3/

"Taking note of the progress made by the Special Committee in
its consideration of the question of defining aggression and on the
draft definition, as reflected in the report of the Special Committee,

"Considering that it was not possible for the Special Committee
to complete its task at its session held in 1971,

"Considering that in its resolutions 2330 (XXII) of 18 December 1967,
2420 (XXIII) of 18 December 1968, 2549 (XXIV) of 12 December 1969 and
2644 (XXV) of 25 November 1970 the General Assembly recognized the
widespread conviction of the need to expedite the definition of aggression,

"Considering the urgency of bringing the work of the Special
Committee to a successful conclusion and the desirability of achieving
the definition of aggression as soon as possible,

"Noting also the common desire of the members of the Special
Committee to continue their work on the basis of the results achieved
and to arrive at a draft definition,

"1.   Decides that the Special Committee on the Question of Defining
Aggression shall resume its work, in accordance with General Assembly
resolution 2330 (XXII), as early as possible in 1972;

1/   Official Records of the General Assembly, Twenty-sixth Session,
Supplement No. 19   (A/8419).

2/   Ibid., Twenty-sixth Session, Annexes, agenda item 89, document A/8525.

3/   Ibid., Twenty-sixth Session, Supplement No. 19   (A/8419).

"2. Requests the Secretary-General to provide the Special Committee with the necessary facilities and services;

"3. Decides to include in the provisional agenda of its twenty-seventh session an item entitled 'Report of the Special Committee on the Question of Defining Aggression'."

2. In accordance with this resolution, the Special Committee on the Question of Defining Aggression, whose composition is given in paragraph 2 of its report on the work of its 1968 session, 4/ met at United Nations Headquarters in New York from 31 January to 3 March 1972. All of the States members of the Special Committee were represented: Algeria, Australia, Bulgaria, Canada, Colombia, Cyprus, Czechoslovakia, Ecuador, Egypt, Finland, France, Ghana, Guyana, Haiti, Indonesia, Iran, Iraq, Italy, Japan, Madagascar, Mexico, Norway, Romania, Sierra Leone, Spain, Sudan, Syrian Arab Republic, Turkey, Uganda, Union of Soviet Socialist Republics, United Kingdom of Great Britain and Northern Ireland, United States of America, Uruguay, Yugoslavia and Zaire. The list of representatives attending the 1972 session was issued under the symbol A/AC.134/INF.1.

3. At its 93rd meeting, held on 2 February, the Special Committee elected the following officers:

Chairman: Mr. Zenon Rossides (Cyprus)

Vice-Chairmen: Mr. Ion Datcu (Romania)
                   Mr. Gonzalo Alcívar (Ecuador)
                   Mr. Erik B. Wang (Canada)

Rapporteur: Mr. Aly Ismail Teymour (Egypt)

4. The session was opened on behalf of the Secretary-General by the Legal Counsel of the United Nations. The Director and other members of the Codification Division of the Office of Legal Affairs served as the secretariat of the Special Committee.

5. At the same meeting, the Special Committee adopted the following agenda:

1. Opening of the session.

2. Election of officers.

3. Adoption of the agenda.

4. Organization of work.

5. Consideration of the question of defining aggression (General Assembly resolutions 2330 (XXII), 2420 (XXIII), 2549 (XXIV), 2644 (XXV) and 2781 (XXVI)).

6. Adoption of the report.

4/ Ibid., Twenty-third Session, agenda item 86, document A/7185/Rev.1.

6.   At its 94th meeting, on 3 February, the Special Committee decided to
re-establish a Working Group composed of the following members: Cyprus,
Czechoslovakia, Ecuador, France, Ghana, Italy, Mexico, Spain, Syrian Arab
Republic, Union of Soviet Socialist Republics, United Kingdom of Great Britain
and Northern Ireland, United States of America, and the Committee's Rapporteur.
It was understood that the members of the Special Committee who were not members
of the Working Group could take part in the Group's work, but not in its decisions.
The Group was instructed to help the Special Committee in the fulfilment of its
task by formulating an agreed or generally accepted definition of aggression to
be submitted for consideration by the Special Committee and, in case it was unable
to reach such a definition, to report to the Special Committee its assessment of
the progress made during the session, indicating the points of agreement and of
disagreement.   It was also invited to report periodically to the Special
Committee on the progress of its work.

I. DRAFT PROPOSALS BEFORE THE SPECIAL COMMITTEE

7.   The Special Committee had before it the three main draft proposals submitted to it at its 1969 session, namely, the draft of the Union of Soviet Socialist Republics (A/AC.134/L.12), the new 13-Power draft (A/AC.134/L.16 and Add.1 and 2) and the six-Power draft (A/AC.134/L.17 and Add.1).   The texts of those three draft proposals are reproduced in annex I to the present report.

8.   At the 95th meeting, on 1 March 1972, the Special Committee also had before it a draft resolution (A/AC.134/L.38) submitted by Czechoslovakia, Mexico, Romania and the Syrian Arab Republic, the text of which read as follows:

"The Special Committee on the Question of Defining Aggression,

"Bearing in mind General Assembly resolutions 2330 (XXII) of 18 December 1967, 2420 (XXIII) of 18 December 1968, 2549 (XXIV) of 12 December 1969, 2644 (XXV) of 25 November 1970, which recognized the need to expedite the definition of aggression,

Bearing in mind also that in its resolution 2781 (XXVI) of 3 December 1971 the General Assembly considered the urgency of bringing the work of the Special Committee to a successful conclusion and the desirability of achieving the definition of aggression as soon as possible,

Noting with satisfaction the progress so far achieved in formulating individual elements of a definition of aggression during the session of the Special Committee held in 1972,

Noting also the common desire of the members of the Special Committee to continue their work on the basis of the results attained and to arrive at a draft definition,

Recommends that the General Assembly, at its twenty-seventh session, invite the Special Committee to resume its work in 1973."

9.   At the 98th meeting, on 2 March, the sponsors of the foregoing draft resolution orally revised their text as follows:

(a) By inserting as preambular paragraph 3 the following text:

"Expressing the view that the achievement of a generally acceptable definition of aggression depends upon the willingness of all members of the Special Committee to act in a spirit of mutual understanding and accommodation,";

(b) By deleting in former preambular paragraph 3 the words "with satisfaction".

10. At the same meeting, the representative of Australia submitted an oral amendment, accepted by the sponsors, to substitute the word "recognized" for "acceptable" in the new preambular paragraph 3.

11. At the 95th meeting, the representative of Guyana submitted the following proposal (A/AC.134/L.39), which was withdrawn at the 98th meeting:

> "Given the irreconcilable principles contained in the draft definitions of aggression before the Special Committee that the Special Committee pronounce itself, by vote if necessary, on that text, which should be used as the basis of future efforts towards arriving at a generally acceptable definition of aggression."

II. REPORT OF THE WORKING GROUP

12. The Working Group submitted a report (A/AC.34/L.37 and Addenda 1 and 2) for the consideration of the Special Committee. The report included, as annex I, a "Summary of the report of the informal negotiating group established by the Working Group" and, as annex II, draft proposals and comments concerning certain elements of a definition of aggression submitted during the current session, respectively, by: (a) Australia, Canada, Italy, Japan, the United Kingdom of Great Britain and Northern Ireland and the United States of America; (b) the Syrian Arab Republic; (c) the Union of Soviet Socialist Republics; (d) Czechoslovakia; (e) Romania; (f) Algeria, Colombia, Cyprus, Ecuador, Egypt, Ghana, Guyana, Haiti, Indonesia, Iran, Iraq, Madagascar, Mexico, Sierra Leone, Spain, the Sudan, the Syrian Arab Republic, Uganda, Uruguay and Yugoslavia. The report of the Working Group, together with its annexes, is reproduced in annex II to the present report.

13. The report of the Working Group was considered by the Special Committee at its 95th to 98th meetings, held on 1 and 2 March 1972. The views expressed at those meetings are reflected in the corresponding summary records (A/AC.134/SR.95 to 98). At its 98th meeting, the Special Committee approved the report of the Working Group.

III. RECOMMENDATIONS OF THE SPECIAL COMMITTEE

14. At its 98th meeting, on 2 March, the Special Committee adopted unanimously the draft resolution submitted by Czechoslovakia, Mexico, Romania and the Syrian Arab Republic (A/AC.134/L.38) as revised (see paragraphs 9 and 10 above), which read as follows:

> "The Special Committee on the Question of Defining Aggression,
>
> "Bearing in mind General Assembly resolutions 2330 (XXII) of 18 December 1967, 2420 (XXIII) of 18 December 1968, 2549 (XXIV) of 12 December 1969 and 2644 (XXV) of 25 November 1970, which recognized the need to expedite the definition of aggression,

"Bearing in mind also that in its resolution 2781 (XXVI) of
3 December 1971 the General Assembly considered the urgency of bringing
the work of the Special Committee to a successful conclusion and the
desirability of achieving the definition of aggression as soon as possible,

"Expressing the view that the achievement of a generally recognized
definition of aggression depends upon the willingness of all members of
the Special Committee to act in a spirit of mutual understanding and
accommodation,

"Noting the progress so far achieved in formulating individual
elements of a definition of aggression during the session of the
Special Committee held in 1972,

"Noting also the common desire of the members of the Special
Committee to continue their work on the basis of the results attained
and to arrive at a draft definition,

"Recommends that the General Assembly, at its twenty-seventh session,
invite the Special Committee to resume its work in 1973."

15. At its 99th meeting on 3 March 1972, the Special Committee recommended,
at the suggestion of the Chairman, that, in the period between now and the
twenty-seventh session of the General Assembly, the members of the Special
Committee carry on informal consultations with a view to overcoming existing
differences and difficulties, and devote their utmost efforts to ensuring
the success of their common task.

[Editor's note: Pages 7-12 of A/8719 are omitted. They contain Draft proposals
submitted by the USSR (A/AC.134/L.12), the 13-Powers (A/AC.134/L.16 and Add.
1 and 2), and the Six-Powers (A/AC.134/L.17 and Add. 1 and 2), all of which have
appeared in A/8019, DOCUMENT 18 supra.]

ANNEX II

REPORT OF THE WORKING GROUP

1.   The Working Group, which was reconstituted in accordance with the decision taken by the Special Committee at its 94th meeting, held on 3 February 1972, held 14 meetings between 4 and 29 February under the chairmanship of the representative of France.

2.   During the first phase of its work, the Group based its discussions on the report of the 1971 Working Group, reproduced in annex III of the report of the Special Committee on its last session. a/ The Working Group began its work by a brief exchange of views on the general definition of aggression and on the principle of priority dealt with in paragraphs 3 to 6 of the report of the 1971 Working Group. It then considered in greater detail the principle of proportionality, the legal consequences of aggression and the right of peoples to self-determination, which are dealt with in paragraphs 19 to 24 of the report of the 1971 Working Group.

3.   In the intervals between formal meetings of the Working Group, informal negotiations were held with a view to overcoming the difficulties which had arisen and reaching generally acceptable compromise solutions on the various elements of the definition. At its meeting on 24 February, the Working Group had before it a report submitted on behalf of an informal negotiating group by Mr. González-Gálvez, representative of Mexico, who had acted as the group's Chairman. At the same meeting, the Working Group decided to use that report as a basis for discussion. After a brief exchange of views, the Working Group, at its meeting on 25 February, decided, owing to lack of time, to take note of the report and to transmit it as it stood to the Special Committee for consideration. The Working Group took this decision because it felt that the report constituted a step forward in the process of formulating a generally acceptable definition of the concept of aggression and therefore warranted the attention of the Special Committee.

4.   The text of the report submitted on behalf of the informal negotiating group is annexed to the present report. The Working Group decided that proposals submitted to it by delegations should also be annexed to its report.

---

a/   Official Records of the General Assembly, Twenty-sixth Session, Supplement No. 19 (A/8419).

APPENDIX A

SUMMARY OF THE REPORT OF THE INFORMAL NEGOTIATING GROUP
ESTABLISHED BY THE WORKING GROUP

The informal negotiations were carried out on the understanding that the acceptance of one or several of the elements of the definition was subject to the over-all formulation of the definition of aggression in view of the interrelation which exists between the different elements. Furthermore, only some elements were discussed. Therefore, the present report does not reflect the position of the various delegations as regards other elements which an acceptable definition should contain.

I.   There was general agreement that the definition of aggression should include the following texts:

General definition of aggression

Aggression is the use of armed force /however exerted/ by a State against the territorial integrity /sovereignty/ or political independence of another State, or in any other manner inconsistent with the Charter of the United Nations.

It was proposed that the following text be added:

The term "territorial integrity" includes territorial waters and air space.

Acts proposed for inclusion

Any of the following acts, regardless of a declaration of war, shall constitute an act of aggression:

(a) The invasion or attack by the armed forces of a State of the territory of another State, or any military occupation, however temporary, resulting from such invasion or attack, or any annexation by the use of force of the territory of another State or part thereof;

(b) Bombardment by the armed forces of a State against the territory of another State or the use of any weapons /including weapons of mass destruction/ by a State against the territory of another State;

(c) The blockade of the ports or coasts of a State by the armed forces of another State;

(d) An attack by the armed forces of a State on the land, sea or air forces of another State; a/

---

a/   It was unanimously approved on the understanding that there should be a clause on minor incidents.

(e) The use of armed forces of one State which are within the territory of another State with the agreement /permission of/ the receiving State, in contravention of the conditions provided for in the agreement /permission/ or any extension of their presence in such territory beyond the termination /or revocation/ of the agreement /permission of the receiving State/.

It was proposed that in (e) the word /revocation/ be replaced by /expiring or revocation/.

General part

In this definition, the term "State" is used without prejudice to questions of recognition or to whether a State is a member of the United Nations and includes the concept of a "group of States".

<u>Questions regarding which several proposals were examined in the informal negotiations without having reached general agreement</u>

II. The following proposals were submitted:

Indirect use of force

Alternative 1

The sending by a State of armed bands, irregulars or mercenaries which invade the territory of another State in such force and circumstances as to amount to armed attack as envisaged in Article 51 of the Charter.

When a State is victim in its own territory of subversive and/or terrorist acts by armed bands, irregulars or mercenaries organized or supported by another State, it may take all reasonable and adequate steps to safeguard its existence and its institutions, without having recourse to the right of individual or collective self-defence against the other State.

Alternative 2

Every State has the duty to refrain from organizing, or encouraging the organization of irregular forces or armed bands, including mercenaries, for incursion into the territory of another State.

Every State has the duty to refrain from organizing, instigating, assisting or participating in acts of civil strife or terrorist acts in another State or acquiescing in organized activities within its territory directed towards the commission of such acts, when the acts referred to in the present paragraph involve a threat or use of force.

Indirect use of force and minor incidents

The Security Council may, however, in a particular case refrain from the determination of an act of aggression if the act concerned either in regard to intent or extent is too minimal to justify such action.

Legal uses of force, including the question of centralization

Alternative 1

Nothing in this definition shall be construed as enlarging or diminishing in any way the scope of the provisions of the Charter concerning cases in which the use of force is lawful.

No consideration of whatever nature, whether political, economic, military or otherwise, relating to the internal or foreign policy of a State, may serve as a justification for aggression as herein defined.

Alternative 2

1.   According to the Charter, only the United Nations /through the Security Council exercising its primary responsibility for the maintenance of international peace and security/ has the authority /competence/ to use force in the performance of its functions to maintain international peace and security. However, under the Charter, the use of force is also legitimate in the case referred to in paragraph 2 hereof, or when it is undertaken subject to the provisions of Article 53 of the Charter.

2.   The inherent right of individual or collective self-defence of a State can be exercised only in case of the occurrence of armed attack /armed aggresssion/ by another State in accordance with Article 51 of the Charter.

Questions of priority and aggressive intent

Alternative 1

Without prejudice to the powers and duties of the Security Council, under Chapter VII of the United Nations Charter, to determine the existence of any act of aggression, it shall be presumed that an act referred to in paragraph _____ of the definition constitutes aggression if it was committed by a State which so acted first.

It was proposed that the concept of "rebuttal" be included.

Alternative 2

Without prejudice to the power of the Security Council, under Chapter VII of the United Nations Charter, to take into account all the circumstances of each particular case in determining the existence of any act of aggression, due regard shall be given to the questions whether an act referred to in...was committed by a State which so acted first and whether it was committed with any of the following purposes:

(1) To diminish the territory or to alter the boundaries of another State;

(2) To alter internationally agreed lines of demarcation;

(3) To disrupt or to interfere with the conduct of the affairs of another State;

(4) To secure changes in the Government of another State;

(5) To inflict harm or to obtain concessions of any sort;

(6) Or otherwise to violate the territorial integrity or political independence of another State.

The right of peoples to self-determination

Alternative 1

None of the preceding paragraphs may be interpreted as limiting the scope of the Charter's provisions concerning the right of peoples to self-determination, sovereignty and territorial integrity.

Alternative 2

None of the preceding paragraphs shall be interpreted as limiting the scope of the Charter's provisions concerning the equal rights and self-determination of peoples as elaborated in the Declaration on Principles of International Law concerning Friendly Relations and Co-operation among States in accordance with the Charter of the United Nations.

Among other suggestions made, it was proposed to add at the end of alternative 1 the following:

"; or as preventing the use of armed force by dependent peoples in order to exercise their inherent right of self-determination".

Legal consequences of aggression

The following formulations were proposed:

A. 1. Aggression, as defined herein, constitutes a crime against international peace giving rise to responsibility under international law.

2. A war of aggression constitutes a crime against the peace, for which there is responsibility under international law.

3. Include in the general definition of aggression at the beginning, after the word "aggression", "which is a crime against peace".

B. The territory of a State is inviolable and shall not be the object, even temporarily, of military occupation or of other measures of force taken by another State /on any grounds whatever/ /resulting from aggression/. No territorial gains /acquisition/ or special advantages resulting from aggression shall be recognized.

It was proposed that the words "as legal" be added after the word "recognized". On the other hand, it was suggested that the last sentence be replaced by the following:

"Any territorial gains /acquisition/ or special advantages resulting from aggression shall be null and void."

APPENDIX B

PROPOSALS SUBMITTED TO THE WORKING GROUP

A. Australia, Canada, Italy, Japan, United Kingdom of
Great Britain and Northern Ireland and United
States of America; proposals

1. Acts proposed for inclusion

Include in the list of specific acts:

"1. The organization or encouragement of the organization of irregular
forces or armed bands, including mercenaries, for incursion into the
territory of another State.

"2. The organization or instigation of or assistance or participation in
acts of civil strife or terrorist acts in another State, or acquiescence in
organized activities within its territory directed towards the commission of
such acts."

2. Political entities other than States

Include in the definition the following explanatory provision:

"In this definition the term 'State' is used without prejudice to
questions of recognition or to whether a State is a member of the United
Nations."

3. The questions of priority and aggressive intent

Include in the definition the following provisions:

"Without prejudice to the power of the Security Council under Chapter VII
of the United Nations Charter to take into account all the circumstances of
each particular case in determining the existence of any act of aggression,
due regard shall be given to the questions whether an act referred to in...
was committed by a State which so acted first and whether it was committed
with any of the following purposes:

"(1) To diminish the territory or to alter the boundaries of another
State;

"(2) To alter internationally agreed lines of demarcation;

"(3) To disrupt or to interfere with the conduct of the affairs of
another State;

"(4)   To secure changes in the Government of another State;

"(5)   To inflict harm or to obtain concessions of any sort;

"(6)   Or otherwise to violate the territorial integrity or political
independence of another State."

4.   Legitimate use of force

Include in the definition the following provision:

"Nothing in this definition shall be construed as enlarging or
diminishing in any way the scope of the provisions of the Charter concerning
cases in which the use of force is lawful."

B.   Syrian Arab Republic: proposal

The right of peoples to self-determination

Proposed alternative 3

"None of the preceding paragraphs may be interpreted as limiting the
scope of the Charter's provisions concerning the right of peoples to
self-determination, sovereignty and territorial integrity; or as preventing
the use of armed force by dependent peoples in order to exercise their
inherent right of self-determination."

C.   Union of Soviet Socialist Republics: proposals and comments relating to the summary of the report of the informal negotiating group established by the Working Group

General definition of aggression

In the opinion of the Soviet delegation, the insertion of the words "however
exerted" is unacceptable, since this would unjustifiably, and contrary to the
United Nations Charter, extend the concept of aggression to acts constituting
merely "breaches of the peace".

There is also no reason to insert the word "sovereignty", since its meaning
is covered by the concept of "political independence" and, moreover, its inclusion
would lead to a distortion of the meaning of Article 2, paragraph 4, of the
United Nations Charter.

The Soviet delegation believes that, in the formulation of a general definition
of aggression, the terms used in Article 2 of the United Nations Charter should be
strictly followed, and it therefore insists on the words "inconsistent with the
purposes of the United Nations" or "inconsistent with the purposes and principles
of the Charter of the United Nations".

Acts proposed for inclusion

The Soviet delegation considers a specific reference to weapons of mass destruction in subparagraph (b) inappropriate, since this subparagraph refers to the inadmissibility of the use of "any weapons". Striving consistently for a complete ban on the use of weapons of mass destruction, and in keeping with the proposals submitted in 1969, the Soviet delegation might consider some wording such as the following: "including weapons of mass destruction not used in the exercise of the inherent right of self-defence".

With regard to subparagraph (e), the Soviet delegation sees no need to replace the word "agreement" with the word "permission", since, if the latter word were used, the rights of one of the contracting parties would be infringed.

Indirect use of force

The Soviet delegation considers alternative 1 an acceptable basis for broad agreement. On the other hand, it regards as completely unacceptable alternative 2, which is an attempt to extend the concept of aggression to cover practically all cases of interference in the internal affairs of States. While recognizing the illegality of any interference in the internal affairs of other States, the Soviet delegation nevertheless cannot agree to describe such acts, contrary to the provisions of the United Nations Charter, as acts of aggression.

Legal uses of force, including the question of centralization

In the opinion of the Soviet delegation, alternative 1 provides a basis for agreement. According to the United Nations Charter, only the Security Council has the right to use force. The Soviet delegation might, therefore, accept the text of alternative 1 with the following addition:

"Only the Security Council has the right to use force on behalf of the United Nations to maintain or restore international peace."

Alternative 2, relating to the so-called centralization of force, allows an ambiguous interpretation of the United Nations Charter and is therefore completely unacceptable.

As a possible variant of the solution to the problem of the legal uses of force, the Soviet delegation reintroduces for subsequent consideration its 1971 proposal, which reads as follows:

"Acts undertaken in accordance with the Charter of the United Nations to maintain or restore peace, or in the exercise of the inherent right of individual or collective self-defence, do not constitute aggression.

"Only the Security Council has the right to use force on behalf of the United Nations to maintain or restore international peace.

"Enforcement actions under regional arrangements or by regional agencies, consistent with the purposes and principles of the United Nations, may be taken only in accordance with Article 53 of the Charter of the United Nations."

Questions of priority and aggressive intent

The Soviet delegation supports alternative 1 as providing a basis for broad agreement.

Alternative 2 weakens the element of priority and unjustifiably emphasizes the element of so-called aggressive intent in the formulation proposed by six Western Powers. The enumeration of the purposes of aggression, in its present form, reflects the point of view of only one group of States and, moreover, essentially leaves a potential aggressor free to act. Alternative 2 is therefore completely unacceptable.

The right of peoples to self-determination

Each of the alternatives only partially reflects the concept of the self-determination of peoples, as set forth in the well-known General Assembly resolution 1514 (XV) of 14 December 1960, and fails to single out as the most important aspect of this problem in the present situation the exercise of the right of self-determination by dependent and colonial peoples.

Nevertheless, the Soviet delegation is prepared to consider the proposed formulations in the context of an agreement that may be reached with regard to the other elements in the definition of aggression.

Legal consequences of aggression

The Soviet delegation is willing to support formulation B, provided that the words "resulting from aggression" or the words "in violation of the provisions of the Charter of the United Nations" are included in the first sentence. The addition of these words appears necessary in the light of the provisions of the United Nations Charter and of the Declaration on Principles of International Law concerning Friendly Relations and Co-operation among States in accordance with the Charter of the United Nations.

In addition to the issues dealt with in the document describing the progress of the informal consultations, the Soviet delegation considers it necessary that the definition should refer to the Security Council's right to determine the existence of an act of aggression even when a State takes actions other than those explicitly enumerated in the definition.

The text of such an article might read as follows:

"In addition to the actions enumerated in the preceding paragraphs, other actions by States may be deemed to constitute acts of aggression if in each specific instance they are recognized as such by a decision of the Security Council."

The preambular part of the definition of aggression should contain the text agreed upon at the 1969 session of the Special Committee. This should be supplemented by a provision concerning the purposes served by a definition of aggression.

This provision might be formulated as follows:

"Believing that, although the question whether an act of aggression has been committed must be considered in the light of all the circumstances in each particular case, it is nevertheless appropriate to formulate basic principles as guidance for such determination."

D. Czechoslovakia: proposal

Principle of priority

"Without prejudice to the power of the Security Council under Chapter VII of the United Nations Charter to determine the existence of any act of aggression with due regard to all circumstances of each particular case, it shall be presumed that an act referred to in Article ... of this document constitutes aggression if it was committed by a State which so acted first."

E. Romania: proposals submitted to the Working Group and to the informal negotiating group established by the Working Group

1. Draft text concerning the general definition of aggression

"Aggression is the use of armed force in any form, by a State or group of States against the territorial integrity, the sovereignty or political independence of another State or group of States, or in any other manner inconsistent with the purposes of the United Nations."

2. Draft text concerning a paragraph of general scope to be included in the definition

"No considerations of whatever nature, whether political, economic, military or otherwise, relating to the internal or foreign policy of a State may serve as a justification for the use of armed force against this State, by another State or group of States."

3. Draft text concerning the right of peoples to self-determination

"Nothing in the foregoing paragraphs shall be construed as affecting the right of all peoples, in conformity with the principle of equal rights and self-determination of peoples as elaborated in the Declaration on Principles of International Law concerning Friendly Relations and Co-operation among States in accordance with the Charter of the United Nations, to react against, and resist to, any forcible action which would be taken against these peoples by any State and which deprives them of their right to self-determination and freedom and independence."

4. Draft text concerning the legal consequences of aggression

"The territory of a State is inviolable and shall not be the object, even temporarily, of military occupation or of other measures of force taken by another State on any grounds whatever and no territorial acquisitions as well as any other special advantages obtained by the use of force shall be recognized."

F. Algeria, Colombia, Cyprus, Ecuador, Egypt, Ghana, Guyana, Haiti, Indonesia, Iran, Iraq, Madagascar, Mexico, Spain, Sierra Leone, Sudan, Syrian Arab Republic, Uganda, Uruguay and Yugoslavia: comments

The above-mentioned delegations considered the report submitted on behalf of the informal negotiating group, but, owing to lack of time, it was not possible to proceed further. The said delegations believe they have shown a spirit of accommodation during the negotiations and express their willingness to do so in the future. Therefore it was decided:

(a) To take note of the report submitted on behalf of the informal negotiating group;

(b) To reiterate their position on the basis of the 13-Power draft, by whose principles they stand, in regard to the various elements that the definition of aggression should include.

United Nations

GENERAL ASSEMBLY

Official Records

DOCUMENT 23

Agenda item 88

ANNEXES

TWENTY-SEVENTH SESSION

NEW YORK, 1972

Agenda item 88:* Report of the Special Committee on the Question of Defining Aggression**

CONTENTS

---

* For the discussion of this item, see: Official Records of the General Assembly, Twenty-seventh Session, Sixth Committee, 1346th to 1352nd and 1366th, 1368th and 1371st meetings; ibid., Fifth Committee, 1542nd meeting; and ibid., Plenary Meetings, 2109th meeting.

** Since 1968, the reports of this Committee have been discussed by the General Assembly at the following sessions: twenty-third (agenda item 86), twenty-fourth (agenda item 88), twenty-fifth (agenda item 87) and twenty-sixth (agenda item 89).

DOCUMENT A/8929

Report of the Sixth Committee

Original: English
7 December 1972

CONTENTS

I. Introduction

1. Pursuant to General Assembly resolution 2781 (XXVI) of 3 December 1971, the Special Committee on the Question of Defining Aggression reconvened at United Nations Headquarters from 31 January to 3 March 1972, in order to resume its work in accordance with General Assembly resolution 2330 (XXII) of 18 December 1967, and prepared a report covering the work of its 1972 session (A/8719).

2. At its 2037th plenary meeting, on 23 September 1972, the General Assembly decided to include in the agenda of its twenty-seventh session the item entitled "Report of the Special Committee on the Question of Defining Aggression", and allocated it to the Sixth Committee for consideration and report.

3. The item was considered by the Sixth Committee at its 1346th to 1352nd and 1366th, 1368th and 1371st meetings, held between 31 October and 24 November

1

1972. At the 1346th meeting, on 31 October, Mr. A. I. Teymour, the representative of Egypt and Rapporteur of the Special Committee on the Question of Defining Aggression, introduced the Special Committee's report.

4. At its 1366th meeting, on 20 November, the Sixth Committee decided that its report on the item should contain a summary of the principal juridical trends which had emerged during the debate, the financial implications of such a summary having previously been brought to its attention in accordance with General Assembly resolution 2292 (XXII).

II. Draft resolution submitted to the Sixth Committee

5. At its 1371st meeting, on 24 November, the representative of Mexico submitted a draft resolution sponsored by the following States: Cyprus, Ecuador, Egypt, Guyana, Kenya, Madagascar, Mexico, Morocco, Spain, Sudan, Uganda, Ukrainian Soviet Socialist Republic, Uruguay and Yugoslavia (A/C.6/L.868), joined by Bulgaria, Czechoslovakia, Iran, Nicaragua, Romania, Zaire and Zambia. The draft resolution read as follows:

"*The General Assembly*,

"*Having considered* the report of the Special Committee on the Question of Defining Aggression on the work of its fifth session, held in New York from 31 January to 3 March 1972,

"*Noting* the progress so far achieved by the Special Committee in its consideration of the question of defining aggression and on the draft definition as reflected in the report of the Special Committee,

"*Considering* that there was not sufficient time for the Special Committee to complete its task at its fifth session,

"*Considering* that in its resolutions 2330 (XXII) of 18 December 1967, 2420 (XXIII) of 18 December 1968, 2549 (XXIV) of 12 December 1969, 2644 (XXV) of 25 November 1970 and 2781 (XXVI) of 3 December 1971 the General Assembly recognized the widespread conviction of the need to expedite the definition of aggression,

"*Considering* the urgency of bringing the work of the Special Committee to a successful conclusion and the desirability of achieving the definition of aggression as soon as possible,

"*Noting also* the common desire of the members of the Special Committee to continue their work on the basis of the results achieved and to arrive at a draft definition,

"1. *Decides* that the Special Committee on the Question of Defining Aggression shall resume its work, in accordance with General Assembly resolution 2330 (XXII), as early as possible after 1 April 1973;

"2. *Requests* the Secretary-General to provide the Special Committee with the necessary facilities and services;

"3. *Decides* to include in the provisional agenda of its twenty-eighth session the item entitled 'Report of the Special Committee on the Question of Defining Aggression'."

6. At the same meeting, the representative of Mexico, on behalf of the sponsors, orally revised the draft resolution as follows:

(a) The third preambular paragraph should read

"*Considering* that it was not possible for the Special Committee to complete its task at its fifth session";

(b) The sixth preambular paragraph should read

"*Noting also* the common desire of the members of the Special Committee to continue their work on the basis of the results achieved and to arrive with due speed at a draft definition in a spirit of mutual understanding and accommodation".

He further stated that the revision of the sixth preambular paragraph should not be interpreted as meaning that the Special Committee could not proceed in accordance with the rules of procedure of the General Assembly. In this connexion, some representatives stated that the draft resolution should not be interpreted as justifying any retreat from the principle of consensus which has proved to be so useful in the work of the Special Committee.

7. Also at the same meeting, the representative of Ghana orally proposed to insert "at Geneva" in operative paragraph 1, after the word "work". This proposal was adopted by 29 votes to 26, with 46 abstentions.

III. Debate

8. Section A below contains a summary of the opinions expressed on certain preliminary questions relating to the Special Committee. The principal juridical trends are summarized under sections B and C, which deal with the opinions expressed on certain general aspects of the question of defining aggression and on the content of the definition.

A. Opinions expressed on certain preliminary questions relating to the Special Committee

9. With regard to the mandate of the Special Committee, most of the representatives who spoke supported the Committee's recommendation that the General Assembly invite it to resume its work in 1973 (A/8719, para. 14). They pointed out that the Special Committee had made great progress towards reaching a generally acceptable definition of aggression. It was stated that, although no such agreement had yet been achieved, the summary of the report of the informal negotiating group (ibid., annex II, appendix A) showed

clearly that the Special Committee's task was nearer solution than ever before; it contained a list of a number of basic elements of the definition on which agreement had been reached. Still more important, perhaps, was the fact that the summary afforded a clear view of the issues which were still causing some difficulties. The Special Committee, it was observed, had been criticized for its slow rate of progress, but such criticism failed to take account of the complexity and difficulty of the task; it might be useful to recall that it had taken 10 years to produce the Declaration on Principles of International Law concerning Friendly Relations and Co-operation among States in accordance with the Charter of the United Nations. Some representatives, however, maintained that the outcome of the Special Committee's 1972 session had been disappointing. Although the informal negotiations, it was said, had made it possible to reach agreement on some elements of the definition, it should be remarked that acceptance of those elements, which were closely interrelated, was subject to an over-all solution, as noted in the introductory paragraph to the summary of the report of the informal negotiating group. It was further said that, while agreement had been reached on a few minor points, such as the question of political entities other than States and while there seemed to be a basis for agreement on the right of peoples to self-determination, the most difficult problems were still unresolved, namely, those of priority and aggressive intent, the indirect use of force and the legitimate use of force. In view of the slow progress of the Special Committee's work, it was said, the Sixth Committee might consider either renewing its mandate for 1973 or giving it time to reflect by deferring its next session until 1974. It was also said that, if no progress on the issue were achieved in 1973, the General Assembly should re-examine its priorities and consider carefully whether to allow a certain breathing space during which countries could take stock and perhaps try to bridge their differences through informal negotiations.

10. Regarding the working methods followed by the Special Committee, some representatives supported the establishment of a working group and favoured the holding of informal negotiations carried out between formal meetings of a working group. In the opinion of one representative, however, the fact that the functions of the 1972 Working Group had effectively been discharged by an informal negotiating group pointed to the advisability of dispensing with the Working Group; instead, informal consultations should be held within the broader framework of the Special Committee as a whole.

11. With regard to the composition of the Special Committee, some representatives reiterated the plea they had made the previous year for the participation of China; that participation would be a positive element in the search for a balanced and generally acceptable definition.

12. Some representatives were of the opinion that the Special Committee should not be convened early in 1973. They considered that, in the past, the Committee had been requested to resume its work too soon after the end of the session of the General Assembly, so that delegations had tended to restate their former positions because they had not had time to consult their Governments and other interested delegations. There should be, therefore, a reasonable interval between the end of the current session of the General Assembly and the beginning of the 1973 session of the Special Committee in order to permit delegations to take a fresh look at their positions and initiate informal negotiations.

13. In the opinion of some representatives, the Special Committee's next session should take place at Geneva, having regard to the principle of rotation.

B. Opinions expressed on certain general aspects of the question of defining aggression

14. Most of the representatives who spoke stressed the necessity of defining aggression. A definition of aggression, it was observed, would have a considerable impact at a time of easing of international tensions. It would enhance the effectiveness of the United Nations as an instrument for the maintenance of peace, provide the Security Council with positive guidance and make the existence of acts of aggression easier to determine. It would indicate to States how far they might properly go in the exercise of their right to self-defence. Furthermore, it would establish the rights and obligations of States and pave the way for the preparation of further instruments, such as the code of offences against the peace and security of mankind. It would also represent an important contribution to the codification and progressive development of international law. As time passed, it was also observed, the need for a definition of aggression was increasingly recognized as a more than helpful factor in eliminating the elements of indecision and subjectivity which characterized situations where the issue was, if not to discourage a potential aggressor, at least to expose it and establish its international responsibility. Moreover, apart from the fact that it would enlighten international public opinion and associate it with the work of the United Nations bodies responsible for testifying to acts of aggression, the definition would facilitate the task of those bodies and enable them to carry it out properly and impartially. It would also protect certain States against their own weaknesses by bringing out, for example, certain forms of favouritism, and it would enable them to fulfil their peace-making role more effectively. It was essential, especially for the sake of the developing countries, that a definition of aggression should be worked out as soon as possible. Such a definition was the primary basis of international law, which the small countries urgently needed for their national reconstruction, the safeguarding of their dignity and their relations with big Powers.

15. On the other hand, some representatives continued to question the necessity or desirability of a definition of aggression. In this connexion, it was held that Article 2, paragraph 4, of the Charter provided sufficient direction to the Security Council in applying Article 39 with regard to the determination of the existence of acts of aggression. Furthermore, doubts were

expressed about the feasibility of defining in a legal and abstract manner something which was constantly changing from the political viewpoint. It was observed that the task of formulating a definition of aggression was particularly difficult in that it meant working not merely on a list of specific acts which ought not to be committed, but on a term which implied judgement of the conduct of States and directly involved the operation of the collective security mechanism. The founding fathers of the United Nations had decided that a definition of aggression was not essential to the operation of the system of security established by the Charter. Indeed, a generally acceptable definition might be of some utility in helping the United Nations to deal with certain types of situations, although that did not mean that even the most perfect of definitions should be binding on the relevant organs of the United Nations. It could well be that in a particular case the most effective action on which agreement could be obtained to trigger the collective security mechanism would be to find that there had been a threat to or a breach of the peace rather than an act of aggression.

16. With regard to the procedure to be followed for the formulation and adoption of a definition of aggression, some representatives considered that, if the definition were to serve its purpose, it must be adopted by consensus. While acknowledging that consensus was the best method in the case of such an important question, other representatives felt that it was nevertheless essential to achieve results quickly; if general agreement could not be reached, the Special Committee must face up to its responsibilities and ensure that the views of the overwhelming majority prevailed. It was observed that the Special Committee had endeavoured over the last few years to reach a consensus, but it was now high time to consider the application of the majority rule; after all, that was how certain provisions of the Charter had been adopted; a definition accepted by a majority was better than no definition at all. Some representatives believed that any attempt to take decisions other than by consensus was too vulnerable both from the political and juridical points of view. They failed to see what could be the political and juridical value of a definition of aggression unless it were supported by the overwhelming majority of States, including the permanent members of the Security Council. If any other rule than that of consensus were followed, it was said, a potential aggressor could always cite the lack of unanimity as a pretext to justify its attitude. Moreover, it could not be seriously thought that an interpretation of a document to which all were parties could be imposed by a majority of States or a minority.

17. In this connexion and with special reference to the three main draft proposals before the Special Committee (ibid., annex I) some representatives expressed the opinion that the Committee should agree to work on the basis of one draft instead of three and to choose the draft favoured by the majority, if unanimity could not be reached. Other representatives felt that it was inadvisable to concentrate exclusively on one draft proposal, however widely supported, and ignore the others; a definition that was not acceptable to all States would remain a dead letter of purely academic interest.

C. Opinions expressed on the content of the definition

1. General definition of aggression

18. Some representatives referred to the general definition of aggression appearing in the summary of the report of the informal negotiating group established by the Working Group. Regarding the words "however exerted" placed in square brackets, the opinion was expressed by some representatives that these words should be omitted, since they placed aggression and any other breach of the peace on the same footing, whereas according to the Charter they differed in gravity and should be evaluated differently. The removal of the brackets, it was observed, depended on whether or not it was decided to include in the definition a provision relating to the indirect use of force; as the inclusion of such a provision appeared likely, the bracketed words should not present any real problem. It was pointed out that in order that the definition should be as precise and comprehensive as possible, it would be desirable to include wording such as "in any form whatsoever", so that the definition would cover every use of force. It was further stated that the word "armed" appearing in the general definition in question was too restrictive in scope and should be deleted.

19. With regard to the word "sovereignty", which also appears in square brackets, some representatives felt that the use of this word was unjustified and the definition should follow the terminology used in Article 2, paragraph 4, of the Charter. In the opinion of other representatives, the Special Committee's task was not to define the principle of the non-use of force, which was proclaimed in that clause of the Charter, but to set out some of the acts affecting territorial integrity, sovereignty and political independence which were contrary to international law.

20. The inclusion in the general definition of aggression of a sentence to clarify the meaning of the term "territorial integrity" was considered as superfluous by one representative, who observed that every specialist in international law knew that territory included territorial waters and air space. While agreeing with the view that territorial integrity included territorial waters and air space, another representative felt that the concept should be expanded to cover all marine areas within national jurisdiction, to conform more closely with the modern approach, which was gaining ground in the Committee on the Peaceful Uses of the Sea-Bed and the Ocean Floor beyond the Limits of National Jurisdiction in connexion with the future law of the sea. It was also suggested that the words "the purpose of" should be inserted before the words "the Charter of the United Nations" appearing in the general definition in question.

2. The definition and the power of the Security Council

21. The opinion was stressed that the definition of aggression was useful only if it respected the powers

and duties of the Security Council; those powers were political in nature and their exercise was a matter for the discretion of the Council; it was therefore debatable whether it was possible to bind the Council by a definition. It was also observed that, under Article 39 of the Charter, the Security Council was authorized to determine the existence of any threat to the peace, breach of the peace, or act of aggression; no restriction could be placed on those powers other than by a reform of the Charter. On the other hand, it was stated that the powers of the Security Council were not discretionary, because under Article 24 of the Charter the Council had only "primary", and not exclusive, responsibility for the maintenance of peace. There should not be any confusion between discretionary powers and arbitrary powers, and the Security Council, whatever its powers might be, could never exercise them without the sanction of the Charter. If the definition were to constitute a correct interpretation of the Charter, it was said, the Security Council would be under an obligation to apply it.

3. Acts proposed for inclusion in the definition of aggression

22. The question whether or not the definition should cover the so-called indirect use of armed force was raised by some representatives. In this connexion, it was said that the definition could not be exhaustive and should contain a minimum list of the most serious cases of aggression, corresponding to Articles 39 and 51 of the Charter. However, the list of acts of aggression could include the sending of armed bands by one State into the territory of another State. It could also include some acts of indirect aggression which would be considered as such under Article 39 of the Charter, but which would not confer the right of self-defence under Article 51. It was essential to ensure that notions as imprecise as "support of subversion" did not make it possible wrongly to invoke self-defence to justify a preventive war taking the form of an armed attack; it was juridically unacceptable to say that in such cases the right of self-defence under Article 51 could be invoked provided that it was proportionate to the indirect aggression. On the other hand, it was stated that there was no basis in the Charter for limiting the interpretation of the term "aggression" to direct, as distinct from indirect, uses of force. The term in its ordinary meaning and in the context in which it appeared was entirely apt to cover a use of force of either kind. Moreover, in the modern world the indirect use of force was tending to take the place of direct aggression. Consequently, any definition of aggression must include both forms of the use of force, since they were comparable in their purposes and their effects. It was further maintained that the Charter did not distinguish between different types of aggression. The use of force referred to in Article 2, paragraph 4, did not differentiate among the various kinds of illegal force, ascribing to them degrees of illegality according to the nature of the technique of force employed. Similarly, Articles 1 and 39 spoke of "aggression" without specifying the various methods a particular aggressor might favour. There was no provision in the Charter enabling a State to escape from the Charter's condemnation of illegal acts of force by a judicious selection of means to an illegal end. The temptation to settle for a partial definition of aggression was puzzling in view of the fact that the Declaration on Principles of International Law concerning Friendly Relations and Co-operation among States in accordance with the Charter of the United Nations, which had been accepted by consensus, already contained wording covering indirect uses of force. If it were the fear that a State which was the victim of aggression might overreact that troubled certain delegations, the fear could be appeased by recourse to the concept of proportionality without distorting the basic concept of the term "aggression" as used in the Charter.

23. Some representatives were of the opinion that the definition should not be limited to armed aggression, but should take into account forms of aggression involving methods other than armed force. It was stated that, if there were a grave threat to the livelihood of the population of another State, which could on occasion be more destructive and devastating than the threat caused through an open armed attack, such an act should be regarded as constituting an act of aggression as much as an armed attack. Armed aggression, it was also stated, was the most dangerous and naked form of aggression, but other forms—economic, political or cultural—were equally dangerous. In order to ensure the progressive development of international law, it was further said, the scope of the definition should subsequently be extended to cover other forms of indirect aggression, such as political and ideological warfare conducted by radio or by the distribution of subversive literature calculated to undermine a country's power of resistance or to bring about a change in its political or social system; in particular, stress should be placed on the importance of economic aggression, as in the case of a trade embargo. It was pointed out that the essential concept of aggression was not limited to a straightforward and open armed attack; it could also be extended to cover other acts. As there was agreement on some elements of the definition, it was felt that the most urgent need was to consolidate whatever agreement existed and to leave the definition open-ended so that at some future stage other elements could be included in it.

24. With regard to specific provisions under the heading "Acts proposed for inclusion" appearing in section I of the summary of the report of the informal negotiating group, it was suggested that specific reference might be made to attack by chemical and bacteriological weapons or any other weapons of mass destruction. On the other hand, such reference was considered as constituting an unjustified extension of the problems relating to aggression. It was further stated that the reference between square brackets in paragraph (b) to weapons of mass destruction was unnecessary, since the text already referred to "the use of any weapons"

25. Of the two alternative texts under the heading "Indirect use of force" appearing in section II of the summary of the report of the informal negotiating group, some representatives preferred the first. It was

said that that alternative enumerated specific, easily established acts; thus, the sending of armed bands was a manifestation of the concepts of violation of territorial integrity and of the use of armed force contained in the general definition. On the other hand, the second alternative was much less specific: for example, the terms "organizing, or encouraging the organization" and "for incursion" were imprecise and did not contain the element of violation of territorial integrity. Other representatives favoured alternative 2, which was in conformity with the language used on that subject in the Declaration on Principles of International Law concerning Friendly Relations and Co-operation among States in accordance with the Charter of the United Nations. The opinion was expressed that the section concerning "Indirect use of force and minor incidents" should be deleted, since the Security Council would clearly take into consideration whether an act of aggression was too minimal to be declared as such.

4. The principle of priority

26.   As to various elements of a definition of aggression, several representatives considered that, in the first place, the principle of priority, a fundamental criterion to be found in all systems of municipal law, was of paramount importance in any such definition. It was the basic criterion in identifying an aggressor, since it would prevent States from committing acts of aggression under the pretext of waging a so-called preventive war. It was not enough to say that it would be given "due regard"; priority was a constituent element of aggression, referred to implicitly in Article 51 of the Charter. It was said that all States had the right to respond by force of arms as soon as the act of aggression started, regardless of the intentions or motives of the aggressor, since the victim had no means of ascertaining the aggressor's intentions. The competent bodies of the United Nations could take such motives into consideration in deciding on collective measures, but establishment of the motives of the State which had first used force should not have the effect of absolving that State from responsibility or reversing the positions of the two parties. It was for that reason, it was added, that the definition should include a provision stating that no considerations relating to the internal or foreign policy of a State could serve as a justification for the use of armed force against that State by another State or group of States. It was also observed that priority was only a presumption, since the State presumed to be the aggressor must be allowed the right to adduce proof to the contrary, by showing for example that its act constituted self-defence.

27.   In view of the complexity of actual situations, other representatives expressed strong reservations about the possibility of a quasi-automatic application of the principle of priority. They continued to believe that the remaining difficulties on the questions of priority and aggressive intent could be resolved on the basis of the progress achieved at the 1971 session of the Special Committee, provided delegations resisted the temptation to return to their earlier positions. It was said that there was in fact no incompatibility between those two criteria, which would make it possible to distinguish between acts of aggression and acts of self-defence. The criterion of priority made it possible to establish a presumption of intent. It implied an objective imputation of guilt and should be given preference in cases of armed aggression: it was for the alleged originator of the aggression to prove its innocence. In the case of indirect aggression, within the meaning of Article 39 of the Charter, guilty intent was once again an essential element of the offence, but its existence was for the Security Council to determine.

5. Aggressive intent

28.   Some representatives continued to believe that the element of intent should be a fundamental ingredient of any definition of aggression. The question of aggressive intent, it was observed, gave rise to a persistent misunderstanding; there were those who persisted in equating the element of intent, as employed by the sponsors of the six-Power proposals (ibid., draft proposal C), with subjectivity. The existence of intent must be inferred on the basis of objective analysis from the surrounding circumstances, as was normally the case in municipal law. The stated intention was no doubt a factor to be taken into account, but it was not determinative, and it should be discontinued when it is inconsistent with the weight of the evidence. There was therefore no ground for saying that the inclusion of the element of aggressive intent in a definition would enable a State to escape condemnation.

29.   Several representatives were opposed to including the aggressive intent in the definition. It was said that the notion of animus aggressionis had no place in a definition, since it was a subjective element: an act of aggression came into existence per se as soon as it was committed, and the motives for such an act were totally irrelevant. Moreover, to stipulate that aggressive intent was an essential element for determining aggression was tantamount to placing the burden of proof on the victim of aggression and might conceivably result in the aggressor being found innocent. It was further said that the principle of priority was irreconcilable with the criterion of intent and that the two criteria should not be included in the definition on the same footing. The combination of priority and intent would provide a loop-hole for escaping condemnation as an aggressor which would go far beyond the current provisions of the Charter and cast doubt on the usefulness of a definition containing such elements.

6. Legitimate use of force

30.   Regarding the right of self-defence, it was stated that to define the notion of aggression was in effect also to define that right, as embodied in Article 51 of the Charter; the definition should be made an effective means of sanctioning the right of self-defence against the unlawful use of force. It was also observed that, while Article 51 of the Charter recognized that self-defence constituted an exception to the prohibition of the use of armed force, it provided that that right could be exercised only in cases in which the victim of an armed attack was a Member of the United Nations and only until the Security Council had taken the neces-

sary means to maintain international peace and security; those members of the Special Committee who disassociated the exercise of the inherent right of self-defence from the provisions of Article 51 were thus disregarding both the letter and the spirit of the Charter. It was further said that the right of self-defence under that Article existed independently of the Charter, which could not and should not be used or misused as a pretext for enlarging the scope of what was recognized as the legal use of force, especially in Chapter VII of the Charter.

31. Some representatives were of the opinion that the concept of proportionality should not be included in the definition of aggression. It was observed that that concept had been accepted by international law in connexion with the right of self-defence long before the drawing up of the Charter. Since the adoption of the Charter, the right of self-defence could, under Article 51, be exercised only in response to armed aggression. That limitation on the right of self-defence had achieved the objective previously sought by the concept of proportionality. It was easy to imagine the unfavourable consequences which the introduction of the latter concept into the definition could have for a State suffering aggression, which would be restricted even in its choice of the moment at which to retaliate. Other representatives felt that it would be useful to include the concept of proportionality in the definition. In that regard, it was stated that that concept was a safe guarantee that a defensive action would remain defensive and was not a cover for an aggressive act. It was further said that the proper application of the concept of proportionality was in distinguishing between aggression and self-defence. Even there, however, the legal maxim summum jus summa injuria should be followed, since, if the means of defence were sharply disproportionate to the means of attack, self-defence might degenerate into another form of aggression.

32. Some representatives referred to the question concerning the organs empowered to use force. It was maintained that the Security Council alone had the authority to decide on the use of force. It was also said that the most important principle of the definition was the one set out in paragraph 1 of the 13-Power draft proposal (ibid., draft proposal B), namely, that the United Nations only had competence to use force in conformity with the Charter. An argument which had proved to be a stumbling-block to agreement was that the sole authority of the Security Council to authorize the use of force should be mentioned in the definition. It was enough to state that that right was vested in the international community; it was quite unnecessary to specify in the definition what organ of the United Nations could exercise the right. Some representatives opposed the inclusion in the definition of aggression of a provision recognizing the legitimacy of the use of force by regional arrangements or agencies without the prior authorization of the Security Council, because that could only weaken the very clear provisions of Article 53 of the Charter.

7. The right of self-determination

33. In the opinion of several representatives, the definition of aggression should include a provision concerning the right of peoples to self-determination. In that regard, it was said that the use of force by peoples under colonial domination was justified in Article 51 of the Charter, since colonial domination could be assimilated to continued aggression. The same applied to military occupation, another type of continued aggression which gave its victims the right to seek to recover the territories occupied. The right of enslaved peoples to fight for their freedom and independence could in no way be considered as an act of aggression and must be stated explicitly in any definition. It was further said that States which gave material support to dependent peoples, in accordance with their obligations under the Charter and with the relevant resolutions of the United Nations, should not be unjustly accused of supporting acts of aggression. Peoples which were denied the right to self-determination were entitled to request and receive all assistance including military aid. It was also stated that the right of self-determination was not a secondary right which could receive only justification and defence; it was a fundamental right which required that any act impeding its exercise should be condemned. It was therefore suggested that the definition should include the following tentative text making the imposition of foreign rule an act of aggression:

"The use of armed forces or other instruments of control to impose or maintain colonial rule over a people or deprive them of their fundamental right to self-determination and independence."

34. On the other hand, it was observed that the definition of aggression was too complex a question to be complicated further by efforts to introduce elements which had nothing to do with the notion to be defined. There was no basis in the Charter or the works of legal writers for linking the concept of aggression to the right to self-determination, a step which merely created an extraneous issue. The question of self-determination was carefully regulated in the Charter, which contained no provisions permitting any alternative to peaceful means of settling possible disputes in that area. There could be no exception to Article 2, paragraph 4, which guaranteed respect for the principle of non-intervention in the internal affairs of States.

35. In that connexion, it was said that reference to the relevant provisions of the Charter and of the Declaration on Principles of International Law concerning Friendly Relations and Co-operation among States in accordance with the Charter of the United Nations could provide a possible solution to the conflict of views as to whether self-determination had any place at all in the definition of aggression. It was also observed that the two alternatives concerning the right of peoples to self-determination, appearing in section II of the summary of the report of the informal negotiating group, should not present any great difficulties. inasmuch as all members of the informal negotiating

group had acknowledged the need to include a special guarantee in that respect in the definition of aggression.

8. Legal consequences of aggression

36. In the opinion of the representatives who spoke on this subject, the definition should contain a provision concerning the legal consequences of aggression. In this regard, it was stated that no definition of aggression could serve the cause of peace and security if it failed to recognize the legal consequences of an aggressive action; any complete definition should therefore include a provision regarding the international responsibility of the aggressor as well as the inadmissibility of any territorial or other gain resulting from acts of aggression. It was said that the illegal occupation of territory through an act of aggression could not be recognized; that was a reaffirmation of the principle, proclaimed at the time of the League of Nations, that an act of war could not create, modify or extinguish any right. Aggression, it was further stated, should be declared a crime against international peace, a step which would discourage potential aggressors and lay the legal foundations for the criminal responsibility of the individuals who had launched the acts of aggression and the international responsibility of the guilty State. The opinion was expressed that the Special Committee should deal with the question of non-recognition of territorial gains obtained by force in the preamble of the definition and not in the operative part, because it concerned the legal consequences of aggression and was not an element of aggression itself.

IV. Voting

37. At its 1371st meeting, on 24 November, the Sixth Committee adopted draft resolution A/C.6/L.868, as revised and amended, by 101 votes to none, with 2 abstentions. The representatives of the Soviet Union and the United Kingdom made statements in explanation of their votes.

Recommendation of the Sixth Committee

38. The Sixth Committee recommends to the General Assembly the adoption of the following draft resolution:

Report of the Special Committee on the Question of Defining Aggression

The General Assembly,

Having considered the report of the Special Committee on the Question of Defining Aggression on the work of its fifth session, held in New York from 31 January to 3 March 1972,[1]

Noting the progress so far achieved by the Special Committee in its consideration of the question of defining aggression and on the draft definition, as reflected in its report,

Considering that it was not possible for the Special Committee to complete its task at its fifth session,

Considering that in its resolutions 2330 (XXII) of 18 December 1967, 2420 (XXIII) of 18 December 1968, 2549 (XXIV) of 12 December 1969, 2644 (XXV) of 25 November 1970 and 2781 (XXVI) of 3 December 1971 the General Assembly recognized the widespread conviction of the need to expedite the definition of aggression,

Considering the urgency of bringing the work of the Special Committee to a successful conclusion and the desirability of achieving the definition of aggression as soon as possible,

Noting also the common desire of the members of the Special Committee to continue their work on the basis of the results achieved and to arrive with due speed at a draft definition in a spirit of mutual understanding and accommodation,

1. Decides that the Special Committee on the Question of Defining Aggression shall resume its work at Geneva, in accordance with General Assembly resolution 2330 (XXII), as early as possible after 1 April 1973;

2. Requests the Secretary-General to provide the Special Committee with the necessary facilities and services;

3. Decides to include in the provisional agenda of its twenty-eighth session the item entitled "Report of the Special Committee on the Question of Defining Aggression".

---

[1] Official Records of the General Assembly, Twenty-seventh Session, Supplement No. 19 (A/8719).

ACTION TAKEN BY THE GENERAL ASSEMBLY

At its 2109th plenary meeting, on 14 December 1972, the General Assembly, by a vote of 57 to 32, with 31 abstentions, rejected an oral amendment proposed by the United States of America at that meeting which would eliminate the words "at Geneva" in paragraph 1 of the draft resolution submitted by the Sixth Committee (A/8929, para. 38).

At the same meeting, the General Assembly, by a vote of 121 to none, adopted the draft resolution. For the final text, see: Official Records of the General Assembly, Twenty-seventh Session, Supplement No. 30, resolution 2967 (XXVII).

CHECK LIST OF DOCUMENTS

NOTE. This check list includes the documents mentioned during the consideration of agenda item 88 which are not reproduced in the present fascicle.

Document No.	Title or description	Observations and references
A/8719	Report of the Special Committee on the Question of Defining Aggression	Official Records of the General Assembly, Twenty-seventh Session, Supplement No. 19
A/C.6/L.868	Draft resolution	For the sponsors and the text, see A/8929, para. 5
A/C.6/L.875	Administrative and financial implications of draft resolution A/C.6/L.868	Mimeographed

Administrative and financial implications of the draft resolution submitted by the Sixth Committee in document A/8929

A/C.5/1478	Note by the Secretary-General	Offset
A/8708/Add.13	Report of the Advisory Committee on Administrative and Budgetary Questions	See: Official Records of the General Assembly, Twenty-seventh Session, Supplement No. 8A
A/8946	Report of the Fifth Committee	Ibid., Twenty-seventh Session, Annexes, agenda item 73

DOCUMENT 24
Twenty-Eighth Session, Supp. No. 19, A/9019.
Report of Special Committee, 25 Apr. - 30 May.

I. INTRODUCTION

1.   At its 2037th plenary meeting, on 23 September 1972, the General Assembly decided to include in the agenda of its twenty-seventh session the item entitled "Report of the Special Committee on the Question of Defining Aggression". The report covered the work of the session of the Special Committee held at United Nations Headquarters in New York from 31 January to 3 March 1972. 1/ The Assembly also referred this report to the Sixth Committee, 2/ which considered it at the 1346th to 1352nd, 1366th, 1368th and 1371st meetings, held between 31 October and 24 November 1972. At its 2109th plenary meeting, on 14 December 1972, the General Assembly adopted resolution 2967 (XXVII), which reads as follows:

"The General Assembly,

"Having considered the report of the Special Committee on the Question of Defining Aggression on the work of its fifth session held in New York from 31 January to 3 March 1972, 1/

"Noting the progress so far achieved by the Special Committee in its consideration of the question of defining aggression and on the draft definition, as reflected in its report,

"Considering that it was not possible for the Special Committee to complete its task at its fifth session,

"Considering that in its resolutions 2330 (XXII) of 18 December 1967, 2420 (XXIII) of 18 December 1968, 2549 (XXIV) of 12 December 1969, 2644 (XXV) of 25 November 1970 and 2781 (XXVI) of 3 December 1971 the General Assembly recognized the widespread conviction of the need to expedite the definition of aggression,

"Considering the urgency of bringing the work of the Special Committee to a successful conclusion and the desirability of achieving the definition of aggression as soon as possible,

"Noting also the common desire of the members of the Special Committee to continue their work on the basis of the results achieved and to arrive with due speed at a draft definition in a spirit of mutual understanding and accommodation,

"1. Decides that the Special Committee on the Question of Defining Aggression shall resume its work at Geneva, in accordance with General Assembly resolution 2330 (XXII), as early as possible after 1 April 1973;

"2. Requests the Secretary-General to provide the Special Committee with the necessary facilities and services;

"3. Decides to include in the provisional agenda of its twenty-eighth session the item entitled 'Report of the Special Committee on the Question of Defining Aggression'."

1/ Official Records of the General Assembly, Twenty-seventh Session, Supplement No. 19 (A/8719).

2/ For the report of the Sixth Committee, see Official Records of the General Assembly, Twenty-seventh Session, Annexes, agenda item 88, document A/8929.

2.   In accordance with this resolution, the Special Committee on the Question
of Defining Aggression, whose composition is given in paragraph 2 of its report on
the work of its 1968 session, 3/ met at the United Nations Office at Geneva from
25 April to 30 May 1973. With the exception of Haiti, Madagascar, Sierra Leone
and Zaire, all of the States members of the Special Committee were represented:
Algeria, Australia, Bulgaria, Canada, Colombia, Cyprus, Czechoslovakia, Ecuador,
Egypt, Finland, France, Ghana, Guyana, Indonesia, Iran, Iraq, Italy, Japan,
Mexico, Norway, Romania, Spain, Sudan, Syrian Arab Republic, Turkey, Uganda,
Union of Soviet Socialist Republics, United Kingdom of Great Britain and
Northern Ireland, United States of America, Uruguay and Yugoslavia. The list
of representatives attending the 1973 session was issued under the symbol
A/AC.134/INF.2.

3.   At its 102nd meeting, held on 30 April 1973, the Special Committee elected
the following officers:

Chairman:	Mr. Dragutin Todorić (Yugoslavia)
Vice-Chairmen:	Mr. Luigi Ferrari-Bravo (Italy)
	Mr. Teodoro Bustamante Muñoz (Ecuador)
	Mr. Riyadh Al-Adhami (Iraq)
Rapporteur:	Mr. Matey Karassimeonov (Bulgaria)

The Special Committee also elected Mr. Bengt H. G. A. Broms (Finland) as one of the
Committee's officers and Chairman of the Working Group (see para. 6 below).

4.   The session was opened on behalf of the Secretary-General by
Mr. Yuri M. Rybakov, Director of the Codification Division of the Office of Legal
Affairs, who also represented the Secretary-General at the session and acted as
Secretary of the Special Committee. Mr. Chafic Malek served as Deputy Secretary.
Miss Jacqueline Dauchy and Mr. Joseph Kobialka served as Assistant Secretaries.

5.   At the same meeting, the Special Committee adopted the following agenda:

1.   Opening of the session.

2.   Election of officers.

3.   Adoption of the agenda.

4.   Organization of work.

5.   Consideration of the question of defining aggression (General Assembly
      resolutions 2330 (XXII), 2420 (XXIII), 2549 (XXIV), 2644 (XXV),
      2781 (XXVI) and 2967 (XXVII)).

6.   Adoption of the report.

3/   Official Records of the General Assembly, Twenty-third Session,
agenda item 86, document A/7185/Rev.1.

6.   At its 103rd meeting, also held on 30 April 1973, the Special Committee decided to establish a Working Group open to all delegations with the same rights of participation and decision. The Working Group was requested to attempt to prepare and submit to the Special Committee a draft definition of aggression, taking as the basis of its work the report of the informal negotiating group reproduced in annex II, appendix A, of the Committee's report on its 1972 session. 1/ The Chairman of the Working Group was requested to report periodically to the Special Committee, either orally or in writing. One or more groups could be established within the Working Group to consider specific questions.

II.   DRAFT PROPOSALS BEFORE THE SPECIAL COMMITTEE

7.   The Special Committee had before it the three main proposals submitted to it at its 1969 session, namely, the draft of the Union of Soviet Socialist Republics (A/AC.134/L.12), the new 13-Power draft (A/AC.134/L.16 and Add.1 and 2) and the 6-Power draft (A/AC.134/L.17 and Add.1 and 2). The texts of those three draft proposals are reproduced in annex I to the present report.

8.   At its 107th meeting, on 28 May 1973, the Special Committee also had before it a draft resolution submitted by Algeria, Czechoslovakia, Egypt, Iraq, Romania and the Syrian Arab Republic (A/AC.134/L.43), the text of which reads as follows:

"The Special Committee on the Question of Defining Aggression,

"Bearing in mind General Assembly resolutions 2330 (XXII) of 18 December 1967, 2420 (XXIII) of 18 December 1968, 2549 (XXIV) of 12 December 1969, 2644 (XXV) of 25 November 1970 and 2781 (XXVI) of 3 December 1971, which recognized the need to expedite the definition of aggression,

"Bearing in mind also that in its resolution 2967 (XXVII) of 14 December 1972 the General Assembly considered the urgency of bringing the work of the Special Committee to a successful conclusion and the desirability of achieving the definition of aggression as soon as possible,

"Noting with satisfaction the further progress so far achieved in formulating both individual elements of a definition of aggression and the definition as a whole during the session of the Special Committee held in 1973,

"Believing that such progress makes it a practical possibility for the Special Committee to elaborate a generally acceptable draft definition of aggression at its next session,

"Noting also the common desire of the members of the Special Committee to complete their work on the basis of the results attained and to arrive at a final draft definition,

"Recommends that the General Assembly, at its twenty-eighth session, invite the Special Committee to resume its work as soon as possible but not later than in 1974."

9.   At the 108th meeting, on 29 May, the representative of Uganda orally proposed to delete, in the operative paragraph of the draft resolution, the words "as soon as possible but not later than". This amendment was accepted by the co-sponsors.

III.   REPORT OF THE WORKING GROUP

10.   At its 106th meeting, on 28 May, the Special Committee had before it a report submitted by the Working Group (A/AC.134/L.42 and Corr.1 and Add.1). The report reproduced, as annex I, a consolidated text of the reports of the contact groups and of the drafting group and, as annex II, proposals and comments submitted during the current session, respectively, by Ecuador, Indonesia, the United States of America, Algeria, Egypt, Guyana, Italy, Mexico, Romania and Uruguay. The report of the Working Group, together with its annexes, is reproduced in annex II to the present report.

11.   The report of the Working Group was considered by the Special Committee at its 106th to 109th meetings, held between 28 and 30 May 1973.

12.   Most of the representatives who spoke expressed their satisfaction with the substantial progress made and the positive results achieved during the current session of the Special Committee. It was observed that constructive and progressive efforts were carried out within the framework of the Working Group, where the informal nature of discussion gave way to a broad exchange of views; progress had been made in the Working Group which permitted hopeful optimism about the completion of the further work on the definition. It was further noted that, in the course of the present session, the positions of the delegations had become clearer and many gaps were narrowed. The atmosphere was much better and much more willingness was demonstrated to find a compromise definition; this change of atmosphere would bear its fruits and it was imperative that its momentum be maintained to accomplish the task of the Committee. While recognizing that the results achieved in the course of the current session were encouraging, some representatives pointed to a lack of agreement on certain important points and stressed the urgent need to exercise the final effort of goodwill in order to reach a compromise. The views expressed on the report of the Working Group are reflected in the relevant summary records (A/AC.134/SR.106 to 109).

13.   At its 109th meeting, on 30 May, the Special Committee took note of the report of the Working Group but emphasized that, in the absence of agreement on a draft definition, each proposed article must be read together with the comments thereon.

IV. RECOMMENDATION OF THE SPECIAL COMMITTEE

14. At its 109th meeting, the Special Committee adopted without objection the draft resolution submitted by Algeria, Czechoslovakia, Egypt, Iraq, Romania and the Syrian Arab Republic (A/AC.134/L.43) as orally revised (see para. 9 above), which read as follows:

"The Special Committee on the Question of Defining Aggression,

"Bearing in mind General Assembly resolutions 2330 (XXII) of 18 December 1967, 2420 (XXIII) of 18 December 1968, 2549 (XXIV) of 12 December 1969, 2644 (XXV) of 25 November 1970 and 2781 (XXVI) of 3 December 1971, which recognized the need to expedite the definition of aggression,

"Bearing in mind also that in its resolution 2967 (XXVII) of 14 December 1972 the General Assembly considered the urgency of bringing the work of the Special Committee to a successful conclusion and the desirability of achieving the definition of aggression as soon as possible,

"Noting with satisfaction the further progress so far achieved in formulating both individual elements of a definition of aggression and the definition as a whole during the session of the Special Committee held in 1973,

"Believing that such progress makes it a practical possibility for the Special Committee to elaborate a generally acceptable draft definition of aggression at its next session,

"Noting also the common desire of the members of the Special Committee to complete their work on the basis of the results attained and to arrive at a final draft definition,

"Recommends that the General Assembly, at its twenty-eighth session, invite the Special Committee to resume its work in 1974."

[Editor's note: Pages 7-12 of A/9019 are omitted. They contain Draft proposals submitted by the USSR (A/AC.134/L.12), the 13-Powers (A/AC.134/L.16 and Add. 1 and 2), and the Six-Powers (A/AC.134/L.17 and Add. 1 and 2), all of which have appeared in A/8019, DOCUMENT 18 supra.]

ANNEX II

Report of the Working Group

1.   The Working Group, established in accordance with the decision taken by the Special Committee at its 103rd meeting on 30 April 1973, held 14 meetings, between 2 and 25 May 1973, under the chairmanship of the representative of Finland, Mr. Bengt H. G. A. Broms.

2.   At its 1st meeting, on 2 May, the Working Group decided to begin its work with the first reading of the report of the informal negotiating group, reproduced in annex II, appendix A, of the report of the Special Committee on its 1972 session. a/ It also decided to examine the various aspects of the definition of aggression in the following order: general definition of aggression and acts proposed for inclusion; indirect use of force and clause on minor incidents; legal uses of force, including the question of centralization; questions of priority and aggressive intent; the right of peoples to self-determination; legal consequences of aggression. It was understood that the following items would also be examined: use of the territory of a State as basis for attack against another State, attribution of the United Nations organs, and the principle of proportionality.

3.   At its 2nd meeting, held on the same day, the Working Group decided to establish a first contact group, to which it referred for consideration the text of the general definition of aggression, in particular the terms "sovereignty" and "territorial integrity" contained therein. The group was composed as follows: Colombia, France, Ghana, Romania, Syrian Arab Republic, Turkey, Union of Soviet Socialist Republics and United States of America. It was placed under the chairmanship of the Chairman of the Working Group. The group held four meetings.

4.   After completing its first reading of the report of the informal negotiating group of the last session, the Working Group decided at its 7th meeting, on 8 May, to establish two other contact groups - the second and third groups - which were also placed under the chairmanship of the Chairman of the Working Group. The second contact group was instructed to examine the following points: acts proposed for inclusion, indirect use of force, clause on minor incidents and the right of peoples to self-determination. It was composed as follows: Bulgaria, Cyprus, France, Ghana, Romania, Syrian Arab Republic, Union of Soviet Socialist Republics, and two member States designated among the sponsors of the six-Power draft. The third contact group was instructed to consider the questions of priority and aggressive intent. It was composed as follows: Czechoslovakia, Egypt, France, Guyana, Mexico, Spain (later replaced by Ecuador), Turkey, Union of Soviet Socialist Republics and two member States designated among the sponsors of the six-Power draft. The second group held 11 meetings and the third group held eight meetings.

5.   At its 8th meeting, on 15 May, the Working Group decided to establish a fourth contact group, which was instructed to consider the legal uses of force and the

---

a/ Official Records of the General Assembly, Twenty-seventh Session, Supplement No. 19 (A/8719).

legal consequences of aggression. This group, which was also placed under the
chairmanship of the Chairman of the Working Group, was composed as follows:
Czechoslovakia, France, Indonesia, Iraq, Romania, Spain, Turkey, Uganda, Union of
Soviet Socialist Republics and two member States designated among the sponsors of
the six-Power draft. The group held four meetings.

6.   At its 11th meeting, on 23 May, the Working Group decided to establish a
drafting group which was instructed to prepare a draft preamble and to consider
other questions of a drafting character. This group, which was also under the
chairmanship of the Chairman of the Working Group, was composed as follows:
Canada, Egypt, France, Ghana, Iran, Spain, Union of Soviet Socialist Republics and
United States of America. The group held two meetings.

7.   At its 12th meeting, on 24 May 1973, the Working Group had before it a
working paper presented by the Chairman of the Working Group. At its 13th meeting,
on 25 May, the Working Group had before it the present report which reproduces, in
appendix A, a consolidated text of the reports of the contact groups and of the
drafting group. At its 14th meeting on the same day, the Working Group decided to
take note of this report. It also decided that proposals submitted to it by
delegations would be reproduced in appendix B to the present report.

APPENDIX A

Consolidated text of the reports of the contact groups and of the drafting group

Preambular paragraphs

Basing itself on the fact that one of the fundamental purposes of the United Nations is to maintain international peace and security and to take effective collective measures for the prevention and removal of threats to the peace, and for the suppression of acts of aggression or other breaches of the peace,

Recalling that Article 39 of the Charter states that the Security Council shall determine the existence of any threat to the peace, breach of the peace or act of aggression and shall make recommendations or decide what measures shall be taken in accordance with Articles 41 and 42 to maintain or restore international peace and security,

Recalling also the duty of States under the Charter of the United Nations to settle their international disputes by peaceful means in order not to endanger international peace, security and justice,

Bearing in mind that nothing in this definition shall be interpreted as in any way extending or diminishing the provisions of the United Nations Charter with respect to rights and duties of the organs of the United Nations,

Considering also that since aggression is the most serious and dangerous form of the illegal use of force, being fraught, in the conditions created by the existence of all types of weapons of mass destruction, with the possible threat of a world conflict with all its catastrophic consequences, aggression should be defined at the present stage,

Reaffirming the duty of States not to use armed force to deprive peoples of their right to self-determination, freedom and independence,

Reaffirming also that the territory of a State shall not be violated by being the object, even temporarily, of military occupation or of other measures of force taken by another State in contravention of the Charter,

Convinced that the adoption of a definition of aggression would have a restraining influence on a potential aggressor, would simplify the determination of acts of aggression and the implementation of measures to stop them and would also facilitate the protection of the lawful rights and interests of the victim and the rendering of assistance to the victim,

Believing that, although the question whether an act of aggression has been committed must be considered in the light of all the circumstances in each particular case, it is, nevertheless, appropriate to formulate basic principles as guidance for such determination,

General definition of aggression

Article 1

Aggression is the use of armed force /however exerted/ by a State against the sovereignty, territorial integrity or political independence of another State, or in any other manner inconsistent with the Charter of the United Nations, as set out in this definition.

Explanatory note: In this definition the term "State"

(a) is used without prejudice to questions of recognition or to whether a State is a Member of the United Nations, and

(b) includes the concept of a "group of States".

Questions of priority and aggressive intent

Article 2

The first use of armed force in contravention of the Charter shall constitute **prima facie** evidence of an act of aggression provided, however, that the Security Council may in conformity with the Charter conclude that a determination to that effect would not be justified in the light of other relevant circumstances, including, as evidence, the purposes of the States involved.

Acts proposed for inclusion

Article 3

Any of the following acts, regardless of a declaration of war, shall constitute an act of aggression:

(a) The invasion or attack by the armed forces of a State of the territory of another State, or any military occupation, however temporary, resulting from such invasion or attack, or any annexation by the use of force of the territory of another State or part thereof;

(b) Bombardment by the armed forces of a State against the territory of another State or the use of any weapons by a State against the territory of another State;

(c) The blockade of the ports or coasts of a State by the armed forces of another State;

(d) An attack by the armed forces of a State on the land, sea or air forces, marine and air fleets of another State;

(e) The use of armed forces of one State which are within the territory of another State with the agreement of the receiving State, in contravention of the conditions provided for in the agreement or any extension of their presence in such territory beyond the termination of the agreement;

(f) The action of a State placing its territory at the disposal of another
State when the latter uses this territory for perpetrating an act of
aggression against a third State with the acquiescence and agreement of
the former;

(g) The sending by or on behalf of a State of armed bands, groups,
irregulars or mercenaries, which carry out invasion or attack involving
acts of armed force against another State of such gravity as to amount
to the acts listed above, or its open and active participation therein.

Provision on the non-exhaustive character of the list and the clause on minor incidents

Article 4

The acts enumerated above are neither exhaustive nor do they prevent the
Security Council from refraining from the determination of an act of aggression
if the act concerned is too minimal to justify such action.

Conversely, the Security Council may determine other acts as constituting
aggression under the provisions of the Charter.

The right of peoples to self-determination

Article 5

None of the preceding paragraphs may be interpreted as limiting the scope of
the Charter's provisions concerning the right of peoples to self-determination or
as preventing peoples under military occupation or any form of foreign domination
in their actions against and resistance to such alien domination from using force
and seeking or receiving support and assistance in order to exercise their inherent
right to self-determination in accordance with the principles of the Charter and in
conformity with the Declaration on Principles of International Law concerning
Friendly Relations and Co-operation among States in accordance with the Charter of
the United Nations.

Legal consequences of aggression

Article 6

Aggression constitutes $\boxed{}$ against international peace
giving rise to responsibility under international law.

No territorial acquisition or special advantage resulting from aggression is
lawful, nor shall it be recognized as such.

Legal uses of force, including the question of centralization

Article 7

Nothing in this definition shall be construed as in any way enlarging or diminishing the scope of the Charter including its provisions concerning cases in which the use of force is lawful.

*

*   *

The following wording has been considered, but it has not been decided where it should be inserted:

"No consideration of whatever nature, whether political, economic, military or otherwise, may serve as a justification for aggression."

Comments contained in the reports of the contact groups and of the drafting group

Preambular paragraphs

With regard to the sixth paragraph, two members of the drafting group reserved their position until related provisions of the operative text have been agreed upon. One member reserved his position as to the substance of the paragraph, asking that a reference be made to the principle of territorial integrity.

With regard to the seventh paragraph, one member proposed that the word "armed" be inserted before the word "force". One member approved the addition of the word "armed". One member objected to the words "in contravention of the Charter" at the end of the sentence.

Article on "General definition of aggression"

One member of the relevant contact group proposed that the words "/however exerted/" be replaced by "in any form" and that the text read "inconsistent with the principles and purposes of the Charter". Another member proposed that the text should read "inconsistent with the principles and provisions of the Charter". One member proposed to delete the words between brackets in view of the inclusion, in the list of acts of aggression, of subparagraph (g).

One member reserved his position as to the term "sovereignty" and as to explanatory note (b).

One member, while accepting the idea behind the words "as set out in this definition", said he would like to see these words redrafted.

It was furthermore felt that it was not necessary to specify that the territory of the State covers its territorial waters and air space, because this is a generally recognized concept in international law.

Article on "Questions of priority and aggressive intent"

There was no general agreement within the relevant contact group as to the text to be adopted.

Whereas many members expressed their willingness to consider this text as one which could be accepted, objections were expressed by some members as to the inclusion of the words "in contravention of the Charter" and the words "including, as evidence, the purposes of the States involved". Some amendments as to the drafting were also presented. One member proposed to replace the words "in contravention of the Charter" in the first line by the words "as set out in this definition".

Notwithstanding intensive negotiations, it was not possible to find at this stage a formula which would have been accepted by consensus.

Acts proposed for inclusion

As to the introductory sentence, it was suggested that this would have to be redrafted to ensure consistency with other provisions.

As to subparagraph (d), one member reserved his position on the words "marine and air fleets".

As to subparagraph (e), it was proposed that the words "beyond the termination of the agreement" be deleted and replaced by the following words: "after the agreement ceases to be in force".

One member reserved his position on the text as a whole.

As to subparagraph (f), one member reserved his position.

As to subparagraph (g), there was no general agreement but the text reproduced above was discussed during the last stages of consultations. It was proposed that the indirect use of force should rather be covered by a separate article than by inclusion as a subparagraph to the list of acts. The words "or its collaboration therein" were strongly opposed when they were first introduced at the end of the text and the objections remained as to the present wording: "or its open and active participation therein".

Other reservations were based on the view that the subparagraph was too narrow and omitted acts which should be covered.

Article on "The right of peoples to self-determination"

There was no general agreement as to the text to be adopted. The text reproduced in the present document was considered in the final stages of consultations.

The following preambular paragraph was proposed in connexion with this paragraph:

"Reaffirming the duty of States not to use armed force to deprive peoples of their right to self-determination, freedom and independence,".

Some members reserved their positions as to the above texts referring either to points of drafting or to the substance.

One member proposed that after the word "self-determination" in the second line the following words be added: ", sovereignty and territorial integrity".

Article on "Legal consequences of aggression"

With respect to the first paragraph, five various alternatives were considered as regards the brackets. These alternatives are as follows:

1. "a grave violation"

2. "a crime"

3. "criminal violation"

4. No provision on the legal consequences of aggression at all.

5. To insert, instead of the present text of the paragraph, the text:

"Aggression gives rise to responsibility under international law."

With respect to the second paragraph, one member of the relevant contact group supported the inclusion of the following text:

"The territory of a State is inviolable and shall not be the object, even temporarily, of military occupation or of other measures of force taken by another State on any grounds whatever and no territorial acquisitions as well as any other special advantages obtained by the use of force shall be recognized."

Another member reserved his position as to the words "special advantage".

It was furthermore proposed by one member that the following paragraph be included in the preamble of the definition of aggression:

"Reaffirming that the territory of a State is inviolable and that it shall not be the object, even temporarily, of military occupation or of other measures of force taken by another State in contravention of the Charter,".

Article on "Legal uses of force, including the question of centralization"

On behalf of the 13-Power group it was announced that the group had not taken a final decision on the question of the legal uses of force.

Additional text

One member reserved his position.

One member proposed the following text:

"No consideration of whatever nature, whether political, economic, military or otherwise, relating to the internal or foreign policy of a Sta may serve as a justification for aggression as herein defined.

APPENDIX B

Proposals submitted to the Working Group

A. Ecuador

Questions of priority and aggressive intent

Delete the words "including, as evidence, the purposes of the States involved".

Acts proposed for inclusion

In subparagraph (d) delete the words "marine and air fleets".

Legal consequences of aggression

Replace the second paragraph by the following:

"No territorial acquisition or other special advantage obtained by the use of force shall be recognized."

B. Indonesia

Acts proposed for inclusion

1. Subparagraph (d) should read as the original relevant text appearing in the report of the informal negotiating group annexed to the 1972 report of the Special Committee:

"(d) An attack by the armed forces of a State on the land, sea or air forces of another State."

2. The last line of subparagraph (g) should read as follows:

"... to the acts listed above, or its support or its open and active participation therein.".

C. United States of America

The following texts are proposed for inclusion in the definition:

Acts proposed for inclusion

The provisions of article ____ (article on priority and purpose) shall apply to any of the following uses of armed force, regardless of a declaration of war:

...

Indirect uses of force

The organization by a State, or encouragement of the organization of, or assistance to, irregular forces or armed bands or other groups, volunteers, or mercenaries, which participate in incursions into another State's territory or in the carrying out of acts involving the use of force in or against another State, or knowing acquiescence in organized activities within its own territory directed toward and resulting in the commission of such acts.

D. Algeria

Questions of priority and aggressive intent

Delete the words "in contravention of the Charter" and the words "including, as evidence, the purposes of the States involved".

The right of peoples to self-determination

After the words "None of the preceding paragraphs" add the words "and particularly article 3, subparagraph (g),".

E. Egypt

Seventh paragraph of the preamble

Delete the words "in contravention of the Charter".

Questions of priority and aggressive intent

Replace the text of article 2 by the following:

"The first use of armed force in contravention of the Charter shall constitute prima facie evidence of an aggression. The Security Council may, however, in conformity with the Charter, conclude that a determination to that effect would not be justified."

Legal consequences of aggression

In the text of article 6, replace the words "resulting from aggression" by the words "resulting from the threat or use of force".

F. Guyana

Questions of priority and aggressive intent

Add the following paragraph to the text of the proposed article:

"However, no consideration of whatever nature, whether political, economic, military or otherwise, may serve as a justification for aggression."

Acts proposed for inclusion

In the first line of subparagraph (g), after the word "sending", insert the words "organizing or supporting".

The right of peoples to self-determination

Replace the proposed article by the following:

"Nothing in this definition shall be construed so as to impair the inherent rights to self-determination and independence of peoples under colonial régimes and other forms of foreign domination or to invalidate the legitimacy of their struggle, in particular, the just struggle of national liberation movements in accordance with the purposes and principles of the United Nations Charter and the Declaration on Principles of International Law concerning Friendly Relations and Co-operation among States in accordance with the Charter of the United Nations."

G. Italy

Preamble

1.   The Italian delegation reserves its position on the sixth paragraph.

2.   The French version of the seventh paragraph of the preamble should be brought into line with the English version.

3.   In the English version of the eighth paragraph, the words "lawful rights and interests" should be replaced by "rights and lawful interests".

Questions of priority and aggressive intent

In the French text, replace the words "constitue la preuve suffisante à première vue" by the words "constitue la preuve prima facie".

Acts proposed for inclusion

1.   Amend the introductory paragraph to read as follows:

"Without prejudice to article 2 (Questions of priority and aggressive intent), any of the following acts, whether or not there has been a declaration of war, shall constitute prima facie evidence of an act of aggression:".

2.   Amend subparagraph (f) to read as follows:

"The action of a State in placing its territory at the disposal of another State for perpetrating an act of aggression against a third State;".

In any case, the Italian delegation reserves its position with respect to the phrase "with the acquiescence and agreement of the former", contained in subparagraph (f).

Provision on the non-exhaustive character of the list and the clause on minor incidents

1. Delete the second paragraph.

2. Amend the first paragraph to read as follows:

"The above list of acts is not exhaustive nor shall it prevent the Security Council from refraining from determining an act as an act of aggression if the behaviour concerned is too insignificant to justify such a determination."

Legal consequences of aggression

Amend the first paragraph to read as follows:

Aggression constitutes (   ) peace giving rise to international responsibility."

Order of presentation of articles

The Italian delegation proposes the following order:

Article 1:	General definition of aggression
Article 2:	Questions of priority and aggressive intent
Article 3, first paragraph:	Acts proposed for inclusion
second paragraph:	Provision on the non-exhaustive character of the list and the clause on minor incidents
Article 4:	Legal consequences of aggression
Article 5, first paragraph:	Legal uses of force
second paragraph:	The right of peoples to self-determination.

H. Mexico

Questions of priority and aggressive intent

Replace the text of article 2 by the following:

"The first use of armed force in contravention of the United Nations Charter shall constitute *prima facie* evidence of an act of aggression. This principle, however, does not in any way limit or detract from the powers of the Security Council, in accordance with the Charter, to examine all relevant circumstances, including, *inter alia*, factually supported purposes with a view to restoring peace and security."

I. Romania

Preambular part

The Romanian delegation reserves the right to express its opinion on the whole text of the preambular part at the next session.

Acts proposed for inclusion

The Romanian delegation proposes that a provision on the prohibition of the weapons of mass destruction should be included in the operative part of the definition.

J. Uruguay

General definition of aggression

The definition might be worded as follows:

"Internationally, aggression is the use of armed force by a State against another State in a manner inconsistent with the terms of the Charter of the United Nations."

Acts proposed for inclusion

The article might be worded as follows:

"Regardless of a declaration of war, acts which injure the sovereignty, political independence or territorial integrity of a State, including its territorial waters and air space, shall constitute acts of aggression, for example:

(a) The invasion or attack by the armed forces of a State of the territory of another State, or any military occupation, however temporary, resulting from such invasion or attack, or any annexation by the use of force of the territory of another State or part thereof;

(b) Bombardment by the armed forces of a State against the territory of another State or the use of any weapons by a State against the territory of another State;

(c) The blockade of the ports or coasts of a State by the armed forces of another State;

(d) An attack by the armed forces of a State on the land, sea or air forces of another State;

(e) The use of armed forces of one State which are within the territory of another State with the consent of the latter, in contravention of the conditions or the period of time for which such consent was given;

(f) The sending, organization or support by a State of armed bands,
groups of irregulars or mercenaries which invade the territory of
another State."

Circumstances which help to determine the existence or seriousness of aggression and of consequent responsibility

I.   The term "State", which is used, does not imply the expression of any
opinion concerning matters relating to its recognition or to the question whether
or not it possesses the status of a Member of the United Nations.

II.   The concept of a State as an active or passive agent of aggression
includes that of a "group of States".

III. To determine the existence and seriousness of aggression and of the
consequent responsibility, account can be taken of circumstances that make it
possible to establish unequivocally which State acted first in time, and whether
the aggression was committed with one of the following motives:

(a) To diminish the territory or alter the boundaries of another State;

(b) To alter internationally agreed lines of demarcation;

(c) To disrupt or interfere with the conduct of the affairs of
another State;

(d) To secure changes in another State;

(e) To inflict harm, or obtain concessions of any sort;

(f) To violate in any other manner the territorial integrity or the political
independence of another State.

IV.   In cases of minor significance, the Security Council may, without
expressing an opinion on the existence of acts of aggression, urge the parties to
settle the conflict by the means provided for in the Charter (Article 33 of the
Charter).

Legal uses of armed force

The article might be worded as follows:

"Apart from the use of armed force ordered by the Security Council for
the maintenance or restoration of international peace and security (Article 42
of the Charter) and the use made for the same purposes under regional
arrangements or agencies with the authorization of the Security Council
(Articles 52 and 53 of the Charter), the use of armed force by States shall
be legal only in exercise of the right of individual or collective
self-defence in case of armed attack (Article 51 of the Charter)."

Legal consequences of aggression

The article may be worded as follows:

"Aggression, being an offence against international peace and security, shall not create rights or advantages that can be recognized and shall give rise to responsibility under international law."

Additional provision

Interpretation of provisions defining aggression

"Nothing contained in the terms of the preceding norms of definition shall enlarge or diminish the scope of the Charter's provisions relating to:

(A) The functions and powers of the Security Council laid down in Article 39 of the Charter, in determining the existence of any threat to the peace, breach of the peace, or act of aggression, or in deciding what measures are to be taken in accordance with Articles 41 and 42 of the Charter to maintain or restore international peace and security;

(B) The right of peoples to self-determination, sovereignty and territorial integrity;

(C) The use of force in exercise of the inherent right of individual or collective self-defence."

UNITED NATIONS

GENERAL
ASSEMBLY

Distr.
GENERAL

A/9411
10 December 1973
ENGLISH
ORIGINAL: FRENCH

Twenty-eighth session
Agenda item 95

REPORT OF THE SPECIAL COMMITTEE ON THE
QUESTION OF DEFINING AGGRESSION

Report of the Sixth Committee

Rapporteur: Mr. Simon BOZANGA (Central African Republic)

CONTENTS

73-28593

/...

CONTENTS

/...

I. INTRODUCTION

1.   In pursuance of General Assembly resolution 2967 (XXVII) of 14 December 1972, the Special Committee on the Question of Defining Aggression met at the United Nations Office at Geneva from 25 April to 30 May 1973 to resume its work in accordance with resolution 2330 (XXII), adopted on 18 December 1967 by the General Assembly, and prepared a report on the work of its 1973 session. 1/

2.   At its 2123rd plenary meeting on 21 September 1973, the General Assembly decided to include in the agenda of its twenty-eighth session the item entitled "Report of the Special Committee on the Question of Defining Aggression", which it referred to the Sixth Committee for consideration and report.

3.   The Sixth Committee considered this agenda item at its 1439th to 1445th meetings, held between 15 and 23 November 1973. At the 1439th meeting on 15 November, Mr. Matey Karassimeonov, representative of Bulgaria and Rapporteur of the Special Committee on the Question of Defining Aggression, introduced the Committee's report.

4.   At its 1444th meeting on 21 November, the Sixth Committee decided that its report on this agenda item would contain a summary of the main legal trends reflected during the discussion, the financial implications of such a summary having been earlier brought to its attention in accordance with General Assembly resolution 2292 (XXII).

II. PROPOSAL

5.   At the 1441st meeting on 19 November, the representative of Guyana introduced a draft resolution (A/C.6/L.957) sponsored by the following States: Australia, Bulgaria, Cyprus, Czechoslovakia, Ecuador, Ghana, Guyana, Haiti, Indonesia, Jamaica, Mexico, Romania, Uruguay, Yugoslavia and Zambia, which were subsequently joined by the following States: Austria, Byelorussian Soviet Socialist Republic, Canada, Egypt, Gabon, German Democratic Republic, Guinea, India, Iran, Liberia, Madagascar, Mongolia, Nepal, Nicaragua, Panama, Senegal, Sudan, Ukrainian Soviet Socialist Republic and Union of Soviet Socialist Republics. The draft resolution read as follows:

"The General Assembly,

"Having considered the report of the Special Committee on the Question of Defining Aggression on the work of its sixth session held in Geneva from 25 April to 30 May 1973,

---

1/ Official Records of the General Assembly, Twenty-eighth Session, Supplement No. 19 (A/9019).

/...

"Noting the progress so far achieved by the Special Committee in its consideration of the question of defining aggression and on the draft definition, as reflected in its report,

"Believing that such progress makes it a practical possibility for the Special Committee to elaborate a generally acceptable draft definition of aggression at its next session,

"Considering that it was not possible for the Special Committee to complete its task at its sixth session,

"Considering that in its resolutions 2330 (XXII) of 18 December 1967, 2420 (XXIII) of 18 December 1968, 2549 (XXIV) of 12 December 1969, 2644 (XXV) of 25 November 1970, 2781 (XXVI) of 3 December 1971, and 2967 (XXVII) of 14 December 1972, the General Assembly recognized the widespread conviction of the need to expedite the definition of aggression,

"Considering the urgency of bringing the work of the Special Committee to a successful conclusion and the desirability of achieving the definition of aggression as soon as possible,

"Noting also the common desire of the members of the Special Committee to continue their work on the basis of the results achieved and to arrive with due speed at a draft definition in a spirit of mutual understanding and accommodation,

"1. Decides that the Special Committee on the Question of Defining Aggression shall resume its work, in accordance with General Assembly resolution 2330 (XXII), early in 1974 in ... with a view to completing its task and to submitting to the General Assembly at the twenty-ninth session a draft definition of aggression;

"2. Requests the Secretary-General to provide the Special Committee with the necessary facilities and services;

"3. Decides to include in the provisional agenda of its twenty-ninth session the item entitled 'Report of the Special Committee on the Question of Defining Aggression'."

6.   At the 1442nd meeting on 20 November 1973, Kenya, joined subsequently by Canada, submitted an amendment (A/C.6/L.958), which was withdrawn at the 1445th meeting on 23 November 1973, that would have substituted the following wording for paragraph 1 of draft resolution A/C.6/L.957:

"1. Decides that the Special Committee on the Question of Defining Aggression shall resume its work in accordance with resolution 2330 (XXII), early in 1974 in New York, to complete its work and to submit to the General Assembly at the twenty-ninth session a draft definition of aggression;".

/...

III. DEBATE

A. Opinions expressed on certain preliminary questions relating to the terms
of reference of the Special Committee, the status of its work and its
working methods

7.   All the representatives who spoke supported the resolution in which the
Special Committee recommended that the General Assembly should invite it to resume
its work in 1974. They pointed out that the Special Committee had made significant
progress at its last session, and they believed that it would be in a position to
prepare a generally acceptable draft definition of aggression at its next session.
In that connexion, the report of the Special Committee on the work of its
1973 session was cited, especially paragraph 12, where it was stated that the
atmosphere had been much better and that much more willingness had been demonstrated
to find a generally acceptable definition of aggression. It had been observed
that the Special Committee had succeeded for the first time at that session in
producing, on the basis of the three main draft definitions submitted to its
1969 session, 2/ a consolidated draft text consisting of an elaborate preamble and
various operative articles; it had, for the first time, been able to reach agreement
or a rapprochement of views on a number of important questions; it had never
before been so close to a broadly acceptable definition. It was stated that
although there was as yet no consensus on the draft consolidated text, it was
nevertheless a generally acceptable working document providing a basis for the
elaboration of a definition of aggression. While approving the idea generally
favoured by delegations that the Special Committee should be invited to hold
another session in 1974, one representative felt that 'that session should be
regarded as the last one and that delegations should come determined to reach a
definition.

8.   A number of representatives expressed the opinion that the working methods
adopted by the Special Committee at its last session seemed to have been the best
way to proceed in order to achieve constructive results. The fact that the
Committee had been able to produce a consolidated draft definition was largely due
to the method of unofficial consultations and negotiations that had been used,
allowing for freer and broader exchanges of views than would have been possible at
official meetings. Reference had also been made to the importance of operating
through an informal working group and contact groups.

B. Opinions expressed on certain general aspects of the question of defining
aggression

9.   The importance of defining aggression was re-emphasized by several
representatives. In that connexion, it was stated that a generally acceptable
definition of aggression was of the utmost importance to the peoples of the
world and would greatly facilitate the task of determining acts of aggression.
Such a definition would not only be useful for the maintenance of international
peace and security but would contribute to the unification and consolidation of
the system of international security and would promote the codification and

---

2/ Ibid., Twenty-fourth Session, Supplement No. 20 (A/7620).

/...

progressive development of international law. It was true that a definition would
not act like magic to prevent aggression, but it would certainly exercise a
restraining influence on possible aggressors. It was also said that the
prevention of wars of aggression and the safeguarding of world peace were matters
of great concern to all peoples and they should be the basic aim of the work of
the Special Committee on the Question of Defining Aggression. On the other hand,
one representative said that although he shared the view that the Special Committee
should continue the work of defining aggression, it was doubtful whether a
definition would have a restraining influence on a potential aggressor, would
simplify the determination of acts of aggression and the implementation of measures
to stop them and would facilitate the protection of the lawful rights of the victim
and the rendering of assistance to the victim. It was also stated that a
definition would not be useful in view of the well-known opportunism which
characterized the activities of the United Nations organs which were required to
determine concrete cases of aggression. Not for nothing had the San Francisco
Conference decided not to attempt to define the concept of aggression.

10. With regard to the procedure to be followed in adopting a definition of
aggression, a number of representatives stated that, in view of the extreme
importance of defining aggression and the great complexity of some of the points
involved, it was absolutely essential that agreement on the text should be reached
on the basis of consensus. It was stated that a generally acceptable and workable
definition of aggression could not be arrived at by voting but only by taking
decisions on the basis of consensus, with due regard for the interests of all
groups of States. A definition of aggression must receive general agreement if its
status as an authentic and authoritative expression of the view of the international
community was to be beyond doubt, and it must be consonant with the movement towards
international agreement on the principles of international law. The view was also
expressed that a modest compromise now was more important than continuous
deliberations on a more comprehensive definition; a limited consensus could clear
the way for continuing efforts to codify and progressively develop international
law in some important fields. The instrument embodying the definition of aggression
should take the form of a resolution of the General Assembly, as had been done in
the case of the Declaration on Principles of International Law concerning Friendly
Relations and Co-operation among States in accordance with the Charter of the
United Nations and the Declaration on the Strengthening of International Security.

C. Opinions expressed on the consolidated text of the draft definition contained
    in appendix A of annex II of the Report of the Special Committee on its
    1973 session 3/

1. Preamble

11. Several representatives expressed the view that the preamble of the draft
consolidated text constituted, in its broad outline, an equitable compromise,

---

3/ Ibid., Twenty-eighth Session, Supplement No. 19 (A/9019).

/...

carefully balanced and satisfactorily formulated from the political and legal viewpoints. It was stated that the preamble, which seemed to have been generally accepted by the Special Committee, required some slight revision, particularly if the Special Committee decided to solve minor differences of opinion by inserting in it provisions on the issues concerned. It was pointed out that the first and third preambular paragraphs departed somewhat from the language of the Charter; the text of the definition must not directly or indirectly imply surreptitious · amendment of the Charter brought about in a manner inconsistent with the relevant provisions of the Charter; the Special Committee should pay special attention to that aspect. With regard to the sixth preambular paragraph, the view was expressed that the duty of States not to use armed force to deprive peoples of their right to self-determination, freedom and independence should apply to all forms of the use of force and that there should be a reference to the principle of territorial integrity in that paragraph. It was therefore proposed that the paragraph should be amended to read: "Reaffirming the duty of States not to use force to deprive peoples of their right to self-determination, freedom and independence, or against the territorial integrity of any other State". It was further suggested that the Declaration on Principles of International Law concerning Friendly Relations and Co-operation among States and the Declaration on the Strengthening of International Security should be specifically recalled in a preambular paragraph.

2.   General definition of aggression (article 1)

12.   The general definition of aggression enunciated in article 1 of the draft consolidated text was considered generally acceptable by several representatives. Some representatives expressed misgivings about including the words in brackets "however exerted" and felt that they should be deleted, since certain acts which constituted breaches of international peace would not necessarily be acts of aggression. If retained, they would unduly broaden the concept of aggression in a manner inconsistent with the Charter. Since the general principle enunciated in article 1 was explained by the following articles, the words in brackets were not necessary and could lead to misinterpretation; in the interest of a clear general definition, it would be better to delete those words. On the other hand, some other representatives expressed the view that the general definition should not be limited to the use of armed force alone but should embrace all kinds of force that might be used against the sovereignty, territorial integrity or political independence of a State. The deletion in the general definition of the word "armed" before the word "force" and the retention of the words "however exerted" were accordingly suggested.

13.   Some representatives were in favour of keeping the word "sovereignty" in the text of the general definition, since that idea constituted an essential element of the concept of the State, which as such, was the subject of flagrant violations through the use of the armed forces of another State. It was of particular importance to small countries that sovereignty should be mentioned as one of the things which could be violated by an act of aggression. The theory that "territorial integrity" and "political independence", which were mentioned in Article 2, paragraph 4, of the Charter, coincided with the concept of sovereignty should be rejected; territorial integrity and political independence seemed to be limited concepts, in view of the experience gained since the adoption of the

/...

Charter; moreover, it should not be forgotten that Article 2, paragraph 1, of the Charter constituted an application of the concept of sovereignty. It was stated that the phrase "inconsistent with the Charter of the United Nations" in the text of the general definition had the merit of being concise and that the proposals to refer to the "principles and purposes" or the "principles and provisions" of the Charter did not seem to add to the clarity of the article.

14. Some representatives felt that a more explicit formulation of the notion of territory was desirable in order to cover unequivocally "territorial waters" and "airspace". Some other representatives were of the opinion that the expression "territorial integrity" embraced those two concepts and that there was therefore no need to make explicit mention of them in the text. Moreover, some representatives maintained that the concept of a "group of States" mentioned in subparagraph (b) of the explanatory note on article 1 was extraneous to the definition of aggression. It was stated that in international law, a State bore the sole responsibility for its actions and could not be made responsible for the actions of another State. The concept of collective guilt or collective responsibility of a group of States was foreign to international law and could give rise to numerous complicated questions as to who should decide, and how, whether a State belonged to a group of States. In determining aggression, the decisive factor was whether the State concerned had committed certain acts which must be characterized as aggression according to articles 2, 3 and 4 of the draft definition. Therefore, the concept of a "group of States" was not justified in a definition of aggression.

3. Questions of priority and aggressive intent (article 2)

15. A number of representatives expressed the view that the text of article 2 represented a compromise which established a judicious balance between the principle of priority and aggressive intent. In the article, it was pointed out, priority was considered as constituting only prima facie evidence of an act of aggression, while aggressive intent was considered to be an evidentiary element. It should not, however, be forgotten that in fact the Security Council would have to consider all the elements of each particular case in determining whether an act of aggression had been committed. It was felt that article 2 should win general support. It was also stated that the importance of article 2 derived primarily from the fact that it recognized the right of every State to use armed force once an act of aggression had been committed; however, while there was no intention of questioning the competence of the Security Council, the article should be clarified by the addition of a sentence reading: "No consideration concerning the domestic or foreign policy of a State may serve as justification for the use of armed force against that State by any State or group of States".

16. In the opinion of some representatives, the principle of priority alone would not suffice to establish the existence of an act of aggression and it must be combined with the criterion of aggressive intent. The Charter did lay down certain circumstances in which the use of armed force was consistent with the Charter. The definition should be so worded that it could not be used to render illegitimate that which was permitted under the Charter and under general international law. It was observed that, although significant progress had been made on the difficult questions of priority and aggressive intent, article 2 of the consolidated text

/...

placed exaggerated emphasis on the element of priority. It was true that the provision now recognized to some degree that determination of an act of aggression could only be made in the light of all the relevant circumstances, but it could be further improved if it was worded in such a way as to strike the correct balance between the first use of armed force and the many other circumstances, including intent, which must be taken into account. In that connexion, a distinction should be made between a violation of Article 2, paragraph 4, of the Charter and a determination that an act of aggression had been committed under Article 39: both gave rise to international responsibility, but the function and purpose of Article 39 differed significantly from those of Article 2, and to blur that distinction could only lead to confusion.

17.   Several representatives, on the other hand, considered that the principle of priority should be sufficient to justify the presumption that an act of aggression had occurred. In order for the formulation of the principle of priority to be acceptable, it must indicate unequivocally that any State which was the first to use armed force should be regarded as having committed an act of aggression (subject to the clause on minor incidents), and that such use of force justified the exercise of the right of self-defence provided for in Article 51 of the Charter. The formulation should also enable the Security Council to refuse to qualify such an act as an act of aggression, taking into account its powers under the Charter. But if the matter was not brought before the Security Council, or if the latter could not take a decision, then the objective existence of an act of aggression would be presumed to have resulted from the use of armed force by the State which took the initiative. With reference to article 2 of the consolidated text, it was stated that, in order to promote general agreement on the content, it was possible to accept a reference to the notion of aggressive intent, not as a constituent element of the offence but as one of the circumstances which the Security Council might use in determining whether or not an act should be qualified as an act of aggression. Therefore, while the substance of article 2 was acceptable, its wording should be reviewed and an attempt made to improve it by using two separate sentences making it possible to distinguish between the objective existence of an act of aggression as determined by applying the rule of priority and the Security Council's power of review of that a priori determination. Moreover, the expression "in contravention of the Charter" should be deleted to the extent that it implied that a use of armed force which was not contrary to the Charter would not constitute an act of aggression. The view was expressed that one of the deficiencies of the text of article 2 could be removed by replacing the words "in contravention of the Charter" by the words "as set out in this definition" or by including a reference to article 3 (Acts proposed for inclusion).

18.   Some representatives saw no relevance whatsoever in the reference to "the purposes of the States involved" as one of the factors to be considered by the Security Council in determining that a State had committed aggression. If aggressive intent was to be made a criterion for judging aggression, it was held, that would inevitably play into the hands of the aggressors; such a definition would not protect the interests of the victims of aggression. While intent was a subjective element, it was nevertheless manifested through concrete acts of aggression. Consequently, the objective acts must be taken as the basis for judging whether a certain action constituted aggression, including whether the State committing it had aggressive intent, and definitely not the other way round, i.e. the existence of an act of aggression could not be determined on the basis of

/...

whether it was committed with aggressive intent. In order to exclude the notion
of intent from the definition, it was suggested that article 2 might be worded to
read: "The first use of armed force shall constitute _prima facie_ evidence of an
act of aggression provided, however, that the Security Council may conclude that a
determination to that effect would not be justified in the light of other relevant
circumstances. No consideration of whatever nature, whether political, economic,
military or otherwise, may serve as a justification for aggression".

4. Acts proposed for inclusion (article 3)

19. The list of the acts covered by article 3 of the consolidated text was, to a
considerable extent, regarded as acceptable in principle by several representatives.
The near-consensus on the list was ascribed largely to the consensus on article 4,
concerning the non-exhaustive character of the list and the clause on minor
incidents. It was stated that the words "regardless of a declaration of war" at
the beginning of article 3 put that matter in a correct perspective, were in
conformity with the letter and the spirit of the Charter and corresponded to modern
realities, and that, in any redrafting of those introductory words, it would be
highly desirable to retain that idea in an appropriate form.

20. It was pro₊.sed that there should be an express reference to weapons of mass
destruction in article 3 (b). With regard to the reference to "blockade" in
subparagraph (c), it was argued that it could not, in that context, imply the
traditional concept of blockade; that type of blockade had virtually gone out of
use, so that the reference could only be understood as having any relevance to
present-day realities if it embraced direct and indirect blockade in whatever form
and extent, i.e., blockade not only in the traditional sense but also all forms of
economic warfare, boycott and blockade, by whatever name they were called. Doubts
were expressed as to whether to retain the words "marine and air fleets" in
subparagraph (d), which, it was argued, would allow countries possessing modern
fishing fleets to deplete at will the fishing resources of less advanced countries,
which would be deprived of the right to defend themselves. On the other hand, it
was contended that those words should be retained to take account of cases involving
a country whose economic survival depended on its foreign trade, which could be
destroyed by an attack on its merchant marine fleet. Moreover, the words "marine
and air fleets" implied a massive attack and not isolated acts.

21. It was pointed out that subparagraph (e) did not reveal any new characteristic
of an aggressive act and was fully covered by subparagraph (a) of the same article.
With regard to subparagraph (f), it was stated that, according to its literal
meaning, the responsibility for the aggression rested exlusively with the State
which placed its territory at the disposal of another State. It was argued that a
State which had agreed to the stationing in its territory of the armed forces of
another State should not be held liable for the latter's acts if it was not in a
position to do anything about them. In other words, to be classified as an
aggressor, the receiving State must be a willing accomplice, a fact which was
reflected in the text of the subparagraph in the reference to the "acquiescence and
agreement" of that State. It was further stated that subparagraph (f) should not
in any way affect the right of peoples to struggle for self-determination.

/...

22.   Some representatives pointed out with regard to subparagraph (g) that, as
currently formulated, it was open to a broad interpretation according to which not
only the sending of armed bands but also the rendering of assistance to such bands
might be regarded as an act of aggression. In practice, it was said, that might
legitimize the right to make a pre-emptive strike and would also deny the generally
recognized right to assist national liberation movements. Indirect aggression
required the presence of a direct link between the sending of the armed bands and
the State sending them and a certain degree of intensity of the actions of such
bands if it was to be comparable to the other acts of aggression listed in the
definition. In the view of other representatives, the text of subparagraph (g)
dealt with the problem of the indirect use of force in an appropriate manner, for it
specified that only the sending of armed bands by or on behalf of a State
constituted an act of aggression, provided, of course, that the gravity of the
attack was comparable to that of the acts mentioned in the preceding subparagraphs.
Furthermore, if subparagraph (g) was read carefully, in conjunction with article 5
on the right of peoples to self-determination, it was clear that it imposed no
limitation on the liberation movements and should therefore be accepted as a fair
compromise. While, in a spirit of compromise, readiness was expressed to support
the current text of the subparagraph in principle, it was found unacceptable that
the mere fact that the receiving State organized, helped to organize or encouraged
the formation of armed bands should constitute an act of aggression independently
of whether or not it also participated in sending them on the incursions. Nor was
it acceptable, a fortiori, that by making its territory available to such armed
bands a State could be considered as committing an act of aggression.

23.   While satisfaction was expressed that indirect aggression was placed on the
same level as direct aggression, attention was drawn to the all too common attitude
of passivity towards acts of indirect aggression and terrorism, an attitude which
might be found not to have been adequately treated. Indirect aggression, which was
one of the most dangerous and provocative forms that naked aggression could assume,
was still the most important part of the draft definition on which a consensus had
yet to be reached. The viability of the whole endeavour would depend on the
successful outcome of the deliberations on that point. On the other hand, it was
argued that subparagraph (g) as it stood was too narrow. It should be worded so as
to be applicable to a State which organized or encouraged acts of civil strife or
terrorist acts in the territory of another State. The Declaration on Principles of
International Law concerning Friendly Relations and Co-operation among States
provided useful formulations on that question which the Special Committee should be
able to use in drafting the text on the question of indirect aggression. In
addition, to cover cases of indirect aggression perpetrated by armed bands of
dissidents organized and supported by external Powers, it was proposed that the
words "or its support" should be inserted in subparagraph (g).

24.   While it was recognized that the list of acts in article 3 was not exhaustive,
it was stated that specific reference should be made to economic aggression, either
in the list or in a separate provision. It was further pointed out that aggression
was not necessarily territorial but could also be political, as in cases where a
State provoked a coup d'état in another country or conducted an international
propaganda campaign against another State. The Special Committee should take that
aspect of aggression into account. Reference was also made to the need to take
cultural aggression into account.

/...

5.   **Provision on the non-exhaustive character of the list and the clause on minor incidents (article 4)**

25.   Several representatives expressed support for article 4. Any rule which reaffirmed and strengthened the ample powers of the Security Council with regard to the the maintenance of international peace and security, it was said, deserved full support. It was also stated that the article was particularly necessary in view of the fact that many countries considered that there were other possible forms of expression. The comment was also made that more express emphasis on the Security Council's powers under Chapter VII of the Charter would seem to be in order. Seeking to determine the identity of the aggressor, it was pointed out, was not necessarily the best way of obtaining the required results. The real need was to implement the collective security machinery rather than to apportion blame. With any other approach, the Committee's work could hinder rather than further the cause of peace. On the other hand, some representatives expressed serious reservations as to the advisability of including in the definition a provision leaving the Security Council with the absolute power to decide whether a specific act constituted an act of aggression. Any definition containing such a provision would serve no useful purpose.

6.   **The right of peoples to self-determination (article 5)**

26.   Several representatives considered that article 5 constituted an essential element of the definition. It set forth the principle that the definition of aggression should not infringe upon the right of peoples to self-determination. The efforts of oppressed peoples to regain their independence and national territory and to struggle against foreign domination, it was pointed out, could not be considered a form of aggression. Acts committed in order to realize the right to self-determination and independence in a struggle against foreign occupation or domination were clearly legitimate exercises of the right of self-defence, as proclaimed in Article 51 of the Charter; under no circumstances could such acts be considered acts of aggression. It was also argued that the right to self-determination was an inherent right of all peoples recognized under the Charter and under international law; any form of colonialism, military occupation or any form of foreign domination constituted in itself an act of continuing aggression which gave rise to the right to self-defence by the peoples affected. Article 5 was of fundamental importance, and it was not enough simply to reflect in the preamble the principles which it proclaimed.

27.   Some representatives, although they agreed in principle that the definition should contain a reaffirmation of the provisions of the Charter concerning the right of peoples to self-determination, considered that the right should be exercised only by peaceful and non-violent means. Reference to that right should not lead to the weakening either of the prohibition of aggression in the narrower sense or of the prohibition of the use of force in the wider sense. The definition should be regarded, above all, as an instrument designed to restrain violence and not to encourage it, and wherever the language was not absolutely clear on that point, it must be modified.

28.   In order to overcome the difficulties encountered in drafting article 5, some

/...

representatives suggested that the Special Committee should try to agree on a
carefully worded and well-balanced provision based on the corresponding clause of
the Declaration on Principles of International Law concerning Friendly Relations and
Co-operation among States.

7.   Legal consequences of aggression (article 6)

29.   Several representatives supported in principle the provisions of article 6,
which they regarded as constituting an extremely important element of the definition.
They considered that the first paragraph of the article should include, in the space
left blank between the square brackets, the most appropriate expression to bring out
clearly the principle that aggression constituted a "crime" against international
peace giving rise to responsibility under international law. Contemporary
international law, it was pointed out, accepted that principle, which derived from
many international instruments, such as the Charters of the Nuremberg and Tokyo
International Military Tribunals, the basic principles of which had been widely
accepted. The blank left in the first paragraph of article 6, it was said, could be
filled by using words borrowed from the fifth preambular paragraph; a formulation on
the lines of that used in the Declaration on Principles of International Law
concerning Friendly Relations and Co-operation among States could also be used. It
was suggested that the first paragraph of article 6 might be worded to read:
"Aggression constitutes a crime against international peace giving rise to
responsibility under international law". The view was also expressed that aggression
in any form was a crime against humanity which must be punished as such. The
second paragraph of article 6 was, it was observed, a natural corollary to the
prohibition and condemnation of aggression. The comment was made that it was in
conformity with provisions of the Declaration on Principles of International Law
concerning Friendly Relations and Co-operation among States and the Declaration on
the Strengthening of International Security, both of which stipulated that the
territory of a State should not be the object of military occupation or acquisition
by another State resulting from the threat or use of force and that no such
territorial acquisitions should be recognized as legal; those fundamental principles
had also been reaffirmed in many General Assembly and Security Council resolutions.

30.   On the other hand, some representatives expressed grave doubts regarding the
necessity for an article on the legal consequences of aggression, at least in the
form envisaged. It was observed that there could be no doubt that an established
act of aggression would _ipso facto_ engage the international responsibility of the
State concerned. It was, however, extremely doubtful whether any useful purpose was
served by mere repetition of that truism. That aspect of the legal consequences of
aggression belonged in the law of State responsibility - which, the International
Law Commission was currently engaged in codifying - and not in the search for a
definition of aggression. Moreover, it was, to say the least, curious and probably
inadmissible for the article to ignore the one major consequence of aggression
specifically mentioned in Article 51 of the Charter. The view was also expressed
that the argument for including in the definition provisions relating to the legal
consequences of aggression was unconvincing. Such provisions were in fact redundant
in view of the wealth of relevant international instruments, such as the Charter of
the International Military Tribunal, Nuremberg, the Charter of the International

/...

Military Tribunal, Tokyo, the General Assembly resolutions affirming the principles recognized by the Charter of the International Military Tribunal, Nuremberg, and the judgement of that Tribunal, as well as the Declaration on Principles of International Law concerning Friendly Relations and Co-operation among States. Similarly, the inclusion of the provision on territorial acquisition was an unnecessary complication in view of the existence of a more explicit provision on the subject in that Declaration.

8. Legal uses of force, including the question of centralization (article 7)

31. Some representatives expressed the view that article 7 was satisfactory. In that connexion, it was observed that, since the Charter was one of the fundamental international legal instruments for combating threats to the peace, it would be desirable to include in the text of the definition a provision along the lines of that article, according to which all of the relevant provisions of the Charter should be taken into account in determining cases of aggression. It was further stated that it should be recalled that Article 51 of the Charter had been interpreted differently by a number of States, which had taken irreconcilable positions on the matter; in those circumstances, article 7 should be generally acceptable. While recognizing that that article logically restricted the legal uses of force to those covered by the relevant provisions of the Charter, other representatives considered that the proposed extension of the article was extremely important; it was observed that legal justification of aggression was a contradiction in terms; all forms of aggression, whether overt or covert, flagrant or concealed, must be condemned, without any possibility of a posteriori justification by fallacious and specious arguments. It was also stated that article 7 should be so worded as to limit the use of force by regional organizations, thereby putting an end to the abusive interpretation of Chapter VIII of the Charter. The definition should not include ambiguous formulas which did not dispel the doubts raised about the interpretation of the clear provisions of Article 53 of the Charter.

IV. VOTING

32. At its 1445th meeting on 23 November, the Sixth Committee decided, by 52 votes to none, with 46 abstentions, that the Special Committee's 1974 session would be held in New York. By 102 votes to none, the Sixth Committee adopted draft resolution A/C.6/L.957, with the addition of "New York" in paragraph 1 (see paragraph 33 below).

V. RECOMMENDATION OF THE SIXTH COMMITTEE

33. The Sixth Committee recommends that the General Assembly should adopt the following draft resolution:

Report of the Special Committee on the Question of Defining Aggression

The General Assembly,

Having considered the report of the Special Committee on the Question of Defining Aggression on the work of its sixth session 4/ held in Geneva from 25 April to 30 May 1973,

Noting the progress so far achieved by the Special Committee in its consideration of the question of defining aggression and on the draft definition, as reflected in its report,

Believing that such progress makes it a practical possibility for the Special Committee to elaborate a generally acceptable draft definition of aggression at its next session,

Considering that it was not possible for the Special Committee to complete its task at its sixth session,

Considering that in its resolutions 2330 (XXII) of 18 December 1967, 2420 (XXIII) of 18 December 1968, 2549 (XXIV) of 12 December 1969, 2644 (XXV) of 25 November 1970, 2781 (XXVI) of 3 December 1971, and 2967 (XXVII) of 14 December 1972, the General Assembly recognized the widespread conviction of the need to expedite the definition of aggression,

Considering the urgency of bringing the work of the Special Committee to a successful conclusion and the desirability of achieving the definition of aggression as soon as possible,

Noting also the common desire of the members of the Special Committee to continue their work on the basis of the results achieved and to arrive with due speed at a draft definition in a spirit of mutual understanding and accommodation,

1.   Decides that the Special Committee on the Question of Defining Aggression shall resume its work, in accordance with General Assembly resolution 2330 (XXII), early in 1974 in New York, with a view to completing its task and to submitting to the General Assembly at the twenty-ninth session a draft definition of aggression;

2.   Requests the Secretary-General to provide the Special Committee with the necessary facilities and services;

3.   Decides to include in the provisional agenda of its twenty-ninth session the item entitled "Report of the Special Committee on the Question of Defining Aggression".

1/ Official Records of the General Assembly, Twenty-eighth Session, Supplement No. 19 (A/9019).

UNITED NATIONS

GENERAL
ASSEMBLY

Distr.
GENERAL

A/9411/Corr.1
15 December 1973

ORIGINAL: ENGLISH

Twenty-eighth session
Agenda item 95

REPORT OF THE SPECIAL COMMITTEE ON THE QUESTION
OF DEFINING AGGRESSION

Report of the Sixth Committee

Corrigendum

Page 3, paragraph 4

At the end of paragraph 4 insert

It was also agreed that the Secretary-General would forward to the Special Committee on the Question of Defining Aggression the records of the discussions at the twenty-eighth session of the General Assembly on the Committee's report on the work of its 1973 session.

Page 10, paragraph 20, fourth line

For traditional concept of blockade read formal concept of blockade as set forth in the Declaration of Paris of 1856

73-30702

555

DOCUMENTS

PART FOUR

AGGRESSION DEFINED BY CONSENSUS

DOCUMENT 26

Twenty-Ninth Session, Supp. No. 19, A/9619,
Report of Special Committee, 11 Mar. - 12 Apr.

I. INTRODUCTION

1.   At its 2123rd plenary meeting, on 21 September 1973, the General Assembly
decided to include in the agenda of its twenty-eighth session the item entitled
"Report of the Special Committee on the Question of Defining Aggression". The
report covered the work of the session of the Special Committee held at the
United Nations Office at Geneva from 25 April to 30 May 1973. 1/ The Assembly
also referred this report to the Sixth Committee, 2/ which considered it at its
1439th to 1445th meetings, held between 15 and 23 November 1973. At its 2197th
plenary meeting, on 12 December 1973, the General Assembly adopted resolution
3105 (XXVIII), which reads as follows:

"The General Assembly,

"Having considered the report of the Special Committee on the Question
of Defining Aggression on the work of its sixth session, held at Geneva from
25 April to 30 May 1973,

"Noting the progress so far achieved by the Special Committee in its
consideration of the question of defining aggression and on the draft
definition, as reflected in its report,

"Believing that such progress makes it a practical possibility for the
Special Committee to elaborate a generally acceptable draft definition of
aggression at its next session,

"Considering that it was not possible for the Special Committee to
complete its task at its sixth session,

"Considering that, in its resolutions 2330 (XXII) of 18 December 1967,
2420 (XXIII) of 18 December 1968, 2549 (XXIV) of 12 December 1969, 2644 (XXV)
of 25 November 1970, 2781 (XXVI) of 3 December 1971 and 2967 (XXVII) of
14 December 1972, the General Assembly recognized the widespread conviction
of the need to expedite the definition of aggression,

"Considering the urgency of bringing the work of the Special Committee
to a successful conclusion and the desirability of achieving the definition
of aggression as soon as possible,

"Noting also the common desire of the members of the Special Committee
to continue their work on the basis of the results achieved and to arrive
with due speed at a draft definition in a spirit of mutual understanding and
accommodation,

_____

1/ Official Records of the General Assembly, Twenty-eighth Session,
Supplement No. 19 (A/9019).

2/ For the report of the Sixth Committee, see Official Records of the
General Assembly, Twenty-eighth Session, Annexes, agenda item 95, document A/9411.

"1.   Decides that the Special Committee on the Question of Defining Aggression shall resume its work, in accordance with General Assembly resolution 2330 (XXII), early in 1974 in New York, with a view to completing its task and to submitting to the Assembly at the twenty-ninth session a draft definition of aggression;

"2.   Requests the Secretary-General to provide the Special Committee with the necessary facilities and services;

"3.   Decides to include in the provisional agenda of its twenty-ninth session the item entitled 'Report of the Special Committee on the Question of Defining Aggression'."

2.   In accordance with this resolution, the Special Committee on the Question of Defining Aggression, whose composition is given in paragraph 2 of its report on the work of its 1968 session, 3/ met at United Nations Headquarters in New York from 11 March to 12 April 1974. All the States members of the Special Committee were represented: Algeria, Australia, Bulgaria, Canada, Colombia, Cyprus, Czechoslovakia, Ecuador, Egypt, Finland, France, Ghana, Guyana, Haiti, Indonesia, Iran, Iraq, Italy, Japan, Madagascar, Mexico, Norway, Romania, Sierra Leone, Spain, Sudan, Syrian Arab Republic, Turkey, Uganda, Union of Soviet Socialist Republics, United Kingdom of Great Britain and Northern Ireland, United States of America, Uruguay, Yugoslavia and Zaire. The list of representatives attending the 1974 session is reproduced in annex II to this report.

3.   The Special Committee elected the following officers:

Chairman: Mr. Bengt H. G. A. Broms (Finland)

Vice Chairmen: Mr. Dinos Moushoutas (Cyprus)
                 Mr. Moïse Rakotosihanaka (Madagascar)
                 Mr. Ján Azud (Czechoslovakia)

Rapporteur: Mr. Joseph Sanders (Guyana)

4.   The session was opened on behalf of the Secretary-General by Mr. Erik Suy, Legal Counsel of the United Nations.

5.   The secretariat of the Special Committee was composed as follows: Mr. Yuri M. Rybakov, Director of the Codification Division of the Office of Legal Affairs, as Secretary of the Special Committee; Mr. Chafic Malek, Deputy Director for Research and Studies, as Deputy Secretary; Miss Jacqueline Dauchy, Senior Legal Officer, and Mr. Josef Kobialka, Legal Officer, as Assistant Secretaries.

6.   At its 110th meeting, on 11 March 1974, the Special Committee adopted the following agenda:

1.   Opening of the session.

2.   Election of officers.

_____

3/ Official Records of the General Assembly, Twenty-third Session, agenda item 86, document A/7185/Rev.1.

3.   Adoption of the agenda.

4.   Organization of work.

5.   Consideration of the question of defining aggression (General Assembly resolutions 2330 (XXII), 2420 (XXIII), 2549 (XXIV), 2644 (XXV), 2781 (XXVI), 2967 (XXVII) and 3105 (XXVIII)).

6.   Adoption of the report.

7.   At the same meeting, the Special Committee also decided to establish an open-ended Working Group which would be chaired by the Chairman of the Special Committee and which would use as the basis of its work the consolidated text contained in appendix A of annex II to the report of the Special Committee on its 1973 session.

II. REPORT OF THE WORKING GROUP AND CONSIDERATION
OF THAT REPORT BY THE SPECIAL COMMITTEE

A. Report of the Working Group 4/

8. The Working Group, established in accordance with the decision referred to in paragraph 7 above, held nine meetings, between 12 March and 11 April 1974, under the chairmanship of the representative of Finland, Mr. Bengt Broms.

9. At its 2nd meeting, on 12 March, the Working Group devoted itself to a first reading of the consolidated text of the draft definition contained in appendix A of annex II to the report of the Special Committee on its 1973 session.

10. It then decided to hold a preliminary discussion of the preamble of the draft definition as contained in the consolidated text, and spent its 3rd and 4th meetings, held on 13 and 15 March respectively, on that task.

11. As regards the operative part of the definition, the Working Group decided to undertake its work through Contact Groups. At its 2nd meeting it established Contact Group I to which it referred, for consideration, articles 1 and 2 of the consolidated text, as well as the additional provision reproduced on page 18 of the report of the Special Committee on its 1973 session. This Contact Group was chaired by the representative of Ghana, Mr. George Lamptey. At its 4th meeting, on 15 March, the Working Group established Contact Group II, which was instructed to consider articles 3, 4 and 5 of the consolidated text. Contact Group II was chaired by the representative of Guyana, Mr. Joseph Sanders. At its 5th meeting, on 20 March, the Working Group established Contact Group III, to which it referred article 6 and 7 of the consolidated text. Contact Group III was chaired by the representative of Canada, Mr. Erik Wang.

12. It was agreed that participation in the work of Contact Groups I, II and III would be on the following basis: two members representing the co-sponsors of each of the three main proposals before the Special Committee, two members representing those who were not co-sponsors of any of these proposals, and any other members having expressed the desire to participate. The three Contact Groups held a number of meetings. Each set up small negotiating teams which met throughout the day and sometimes at night.

13. After it had received the reports of Contact Groups I, II and III, the Working Group established at its 6th meeting, on 1 April, an open-ended Contact Group IV, chaired by the representative of Finland, Mr. Bengt Broms, which was instructed to prepare a new consolidated text in the light of the reports of Contact Groups I, II and III. Contact Group IV also held a number of meetings and itself established a small negotiating team which also met throughout the day and sometimes at night and week-ends.

4/ Originally circulated as document A/AC.134/L.46.

14.   At its 8th meeting, on 11 April, the Working Group had before it the revised consolidated text of the draft definition prepared by Contact Group IV. Following discussion of this text, the Working Group decided to refer it for final review to a drafting group composed as follows: Algeria, Colombia, Egypt, France, Ghana, Japan, Mexico, Romania, Spain, the Union of Soviet Socialist Republics, the United Kingdom of Great Britain and Northern Ireland and the United States of America. It was agreed that the drafting group would be chaired by the representative of Finland, Mr. Bengt Broms, and that the representative of Guyana would also attend in his capacity as Rapporteur of the Special Committee.

15.   At its 9th meeting, held on the same day, the Working Group considered the text of the draft definition of aggression as finally reviewed by the drafting group. It took note of the report of the Chairman of the drafting group and decided by consensus to submit to the Special Committee, for its approval, the text of the draft definition.

16.   The Working Group also decided to recommend to the Special Committee that the following notes regarding articles 3 and 5 of the draft definition should be included in the Committee's report:

(1)   With reference to article 3, subparagraph (b), the Special Committee agreed that the expression "any weapons" is used without making a distinction between conventional weapons, weapons of mass destruction and any other kind of weapon.

(2)   With reference to the first paragraph of article 5, the Committee had in mind, in particular, the principle contained in the Declaration on Principles of International Law concerning Friendly Relations and Co-operation among States in accordance with the Charter of the United Nations according to which "No State or group of States has the right to intervene, directly or indirectly, for any reason whatever, in the internal or external affairs of any other State".

(3)   With reference to the second paragraph of article 5, the words "international responsibility" are used without prejudice to the scope of this term.

(4)   With reference to the third paragraph of article 5, the Committee states that this paragraph should not be construed so as to prejudice the established principles of international law relating to the inadmissibility of territorial acquisition resulting from the threat or use of force.

17.   It was agreed that the text of the draft definition should be accompanied by the following foot-note: "Explanatory notes on articles 3 and 5 are to be found in the report of the Special Committee".

18.   The text of the draft definition as submitted by the Working Group to the Special Committee for its approval read as follows:

"The General Assembly,

"Basing itself on the fact that one of the fundamental purposes of the United Nations is to maintain international peace and security and to take effective collective measures for the prevention and removal of threats to the peace, and for the suppression of acts of aggression or other breaches of the peace,

"Recalling that the Security Council, in accordance with Article 39 of the Charter of the United Nations, shall determine the existence of any threat to the peace, breach of the peace or act of aggression and shall make recommendations, or decide what measures shall be taken in accordance with Articles 41 and 42, to maintain or restore international peace and security,

"Recalling also the duty of States under the Charter to settle their international disputes by peaceful means in order not to endanger international peace, security and justice,

"Bearing in mind that nothing in this definition shall be interpreted as in any way affecting the scope of the provisions of the Charter with respect to the functions and powers of the organs of the United Nations,

"Considering also that, since aggression is the most serious and dangerous form of the illegal use of force, being fraught, in the conditions created by the existence of all types of weapons of mass destruction, with the possible threat of a world conflict and all its catastrophic consequences, aggression should be defined at the present stage,

"Reaffirming the duty of States not to use armed force to deprive peoples of their right to self-determination, freedom and independence, or to disrupt territorial integrity,

"Reaffirming also that the territory of a State shall not be violated by being the object, even termporarily, of military occupation or of other measures of force taken by another State in contravention of the Charter, and that it shall not be the object of acquisition by another State resulting from such measures or the threat thereof,

"Reaffirming also the provisions of the Declaration on Principles of International Law concerning Friendly Relations and Co-operation among States in accordance with the Charter of the United Nations,

"Convinced that the adoption of a definition of aggression ought to have the effect of deterring a potential aggressor, would simplify the determination of acts of aggression and the implementation of measures to suppress them and would also facilitate the protection of the rights and lawful interests of, and the rendering of assistance to, the victim,

"Believing that, although the question whether an act of aggression has been committed must be considered in the light of all the circumstances of each particular case, it is nevertheless desirable to formulate basic principles as guidance for such determination,

"Adopts the following definition:

Article 1

"Aggression is the use of armed force by a State against the sovereignty, territorial integrity or political independence of another State, or in any other manner inconsistent with the Charter of the United Nations, as set out in this definition.

Explanatory note: In this definition the term 'State':

    (a)   Is used without prejudice to questions of recognition or to whether a State is a Member of the United Nations, and

    (b)   Includes the concept of a 'group of States' where appropriate.

Article 2

"The first use of armed force by a State in contravention of the Charter shall constitute prima facie evidence of an act of aggression although the Security Council may, in conformity with the Charter, conclude that a determination that an act of aggression has been committed would not be justified in the light of other relevant circumstances including the fact that the acts concerned or their consequences are not of sufficient gravity.

Article 3

"Any of the following acts, regardless of a declaration of war, shall, subject to and in accordance with the provisions of article 2, qualify as an act of aggression:

    (a)   The invasion or attack by the armed forces of a State of the territory of another State, or any military occupation, however temporary, resulting from such invasion or attack, or any annexation by the use of force of the territory of another State or part thereof;

    (b)   Bombardment by the armed forces of a State against the territory of another State or the use of any weapons by a State against the territory of another State;

    (c)   The blockade of the ports or coasts of a State by the armed forces of another State;

    (d)   An attack by the armed forces of a State on the land, sea or air forces, or marine and air fleets of another State;

    (e)   The use of armed forces of one State which are within the territory of another State with the agreement of the receiving State, in contravention of the conditions provided for in the agreement or any extension of their presence in such territory beyond the termination of the agreement;

(f) The action of a State in allowing its territory, which it has placed at the disposal of another State, to be used by that other State for perpetrating an act of aggression against a third State;

(g) The sending by or on behalf of a State of armed bands, groups, irregulars or mercenaries, which carry out acts of armed force against another State of such gravity as to amount to the acts listed above, or its substantial involvement therein.

Article 4

"The acts enumerated above are not exhaustive and the Security Council may determine that other acts constitute aggression under the provisions of the Charter.

Article 5

"No consideration of whatever nature, whether political, economic, military or otherwise, may serve as a justification for aggression.

"A war of aggression is a crime against international peace. Aggression gives rise to international responsibility.

"No territorial acquisition or special advantage resulting from aggression are or shall be recognized as lawful.

Article 6

"Nothing in this definition shall be construed as in any way enlarging or diminishing the scope of the Charter including its provisions concerning cases in which the use of force is lawful.

Article 7

"Nothing in this definition, and in particular article 3, could in any way prejudice the right to self-determination, freedom and independence, as derived from the Charter, of peoples forcibly deprived of that right and referred to in the Declaration on Principles of International Law concerning Friendly Relations and Co-operation among States in accordance with the Charter of the United Nations, particularly peoples under colonial and racist régimes or other forms of alien domination; nor the right of these peoples to struggle to that end and to seek and receive support, in accordance with the principles of the Charter and in conformity with the above-mentioned Declaration.

Article 8

"In their interpretation and application the above provisions are interrelated and each provision should be construed in the context of the other provisions."

B. Consideration of the report of the Working Group by the Special Committee

19. At its 112th meeting, on 12 April 1974, the Special Committee had before it the report reproduced above. It adopted by consensus the text of the draft definition of aggression contained therein.

20. The Committee also adopted the notes regarding articles 3 and 5 contained in paragraph 16 above and decided that they should be included in its report, in accordance with the recommendation of the Working Group. These notes read as follows:

1. With reference to article 3, subparagraph (b), the Special Committee agreed that the expression "any weapons" is used without making a distinction between conventional weapons, weapons of mass destruction and any other kind of weapon.

2. With reference to the first paragraph of article 5, the Committee had in mind, in particular, the principle contained in the Declaration on Principles of International Law concerning Friendly Relations and Co-operation among States in accordance with the Charter of the United Nations according to which "No State or group of States has the right to intervene, directly or indirectly, for any reason whatever, in the internal or external affairs of any other State".

3. With reference to the second paragraph of article 5, the words "international responsibility" are used without prejudice to the scope of this term.

4. With reference to the third paragraph of article 5, the Committee states that this paragraph should not be construed so as to prejudice the established principles of international law relating to the inadmissibility of territorial acquisition resulting from the threat or use of force.

21. At the 112th and 113th meetings, on 12 April, members of the Special Committee expressed their views on the text of the draft definition. In accordance with a decision taken by the Special Committee at its 112th meeting, the views thus expressed are reflected in annex I to the present report.

III. RECOMMENDATION OF THE SPECIAL COMMITTEE

22. The Special Committee recommends to the General Assembly the adoption of the following draft definition:

The General Assembly,

Basing itself on the fact that one of the fundamental purposes of the United Nations is to maintain international peace and security and to take effective collective measures for the prevention and removal of threats to the peace, and for the suppression of acts of aggression or other breaches of the peace,

Recalling that the Security Council, in accordance with Article 39 of the Charter of the United Nations, shall determine the existence of any threat to the peace, breach of the peace or act of aggression and shall make recommendations, or decide what measures shall be taken in accordance with Articles 41 and 42, to maintain or restore international peace and security,

Recalling also the duty of States under the Charter to settle their international disputes by peaceful means in order not to endanger international peace, security and justice,

Bearing in mind that nothing in this definition shall be interpreted as in any way affecting the scope of the provisions of the Charter with respect to the functions and powers of the organs of the United Nations,

Considering also that, since aggression is the most serious and dangerous form of the illegal use of force, being fraught, in the conditions created by the existence of all types of weapons of mass destruction, with the possible threat of a world conflict and all its catastrophic consequences, aggresion should be defined at the present stage,

Reaffirming the duty of States not to use armed force to deprive peoples of their right to self-determination, freedom and independence, or to disrupt territorial integrity,

Reafffirming also that the territory of a State shall not be violated by being the object, even temporarily, of military occupation or of other measures of force taken by another State in contravention of the Charter, and that it shall not be the object of acquisition by another State resulting from such measures or the threat thereof,

Reaffirming also the provisions of the Declaration on Principles of International Law concerning Friendly Relations and Co-operation among States in accordance with the Charter of the United Nations,

Convinced that the adoption of a definition of aggression ought to have the effect of deterring a potential aggressor, would simplify the determination of acts of aggression and the implementation of measures to suppress them and would also facilitate the protection of the rights and lawful interests of, and the rendering of assistance to, the victim,

Believing that, although the question whether an act of aggression has been committed must be considered in the light of all the circumstances of each particular case, it is nevertheless desirable to formulate basic principles as guidance for such determination.

Adopts the following definition of aggression:*

Article 1

Aggression is the use of armed force by a State against the sovereignty, territorial integrity or political independence of another State, or in any other manner inconsistent with the Charter of the United Nations, as set out in this definition.

Explanatory note: In this definition the term "State":

   (a) Is used without prejudice to questions of recognition or to whether a State is a Member of the United Nations;

   (b) Includes the concept of a "group of States" where appropriate.

Article 2

The first use of armed force by a State in contravention of the Charter shall constitute prima facie evidence of an act of aggression although the Security Council may, in conformity with the Charter, conclude that a determination that an act of aggression has been committed would not be justified in the light of other relevant circumstances including the fact that the acts concerned or their consequences are not of sufficient gravity.

Article 3

Any of the following acts, regardless of a declaration of war, shall, subject to and in accordance with the provisions of article 2, qualify as an act of aggression:

   (a) The invasion or attack by the armed forces of a State of the territory of another State, or any military occupation, however temporary, resulting from such invasion or attack, or any annexation by the use of force of the territory of another State or part thereof;

   (b) Bombardment by the armed forces of a State against the territory of another State or the use of any weapons by a State against the territory of another State;

---

* Explanatory notes on articles 3 and 5 are to be found in the report of the Special Committee (A/9619, para. 20).

(c) The blockade of the ports or coasts of a State by the armed forces of another State;

(d) An attack by the armed forces of a State on the land, sea or air forces, or marine and air fleets of another State;

(e) The use of armed forces of one State, which are within the territory of another State with the agreement of the receiving State, in contravention of the conditions provided for in the agreement or any extension of their presence in such territory beyond the termination of the agreement;

(f) The action of a State in allowing its territory, which it has placed at the disposal of another State, to be used by that other State for perpetrating an act of aggression against a third State;

(g) The sending by or on behalf of a State of armed bands, groups, irregulars or mercenaries, which carry out acts of armed force against another State of such gravity as to amount to the acts listed above, or its substantial involvement therein.

Article 4

The acts enumerated above are not exhaustive and the Security Council may determine that other acts constitute aggression under the provisions of the Charter.

Article 5

No consideration of whatever nature, whether political, economic, military or otherwise, may serve as a justification for aggression.

A war of aggression is a crime against international peace. Aggression gives rise to international responsibility.

No territorial acquisition or special advantage resulting from aggression are or shall be recognized as lawful.

Article 6

Nothing in this definition shall be construed as in any way enlarging or diminishing the scope of the Charter, including its provisions concerning cases in which the use of force is lawful.

Article 7

Nothing in this definition, and in particular article 3, could in any way prejudice the right to self-determination, freedom and independence, as derived from the Charter, of peoples forcibly deprived of that right and referred to in the Declaration on Principles of International Law concerning Friendly Relations and Co-operation among States in accordance with the Charter of the United Nations, particularly peoples under colonial and racist régimes or other forms of alien domination; nor the right of these peoples to struggle to that end and to seek and receive support, in accordance with the principles of the Charter and in conformity with the above-mentioned Declaration.

Article 8

In their interpretation and application the above provisions are interrelated and each provision should be construed in the context of the other provisions.

ANNEX I

Views expressed by members of the Special Committee at the concluding
stage of the Special Committee's session a/

Mr. MIGLIUOLO (Italy) expressed great satisfaction at the Committee's
successful accomplishment of its task and congratulated the Chairman and the
members. The definition was the result of long and difficult efforts which had
begun nearly half a century ago under the auspices of the League of Nations. It
was to be hoped that - as indicated in the ninth preambular paragraph - the adoption
of a definition of aggression would have the effect of deterring possible future
acts of aggression. It was certain, in any event, that the definition would
represent an invaluable point of reference for the Security Council in its
deliberations; it also constituted a further step forward towards the codification
of general international law. His delegation reserved the right to comment in detail
on the specific provisions of the definition during the twenty-ninth session of the
General Assembly, by which time his Government would have had an opportunity to
scrutinize the text thoroughly from both the legal and political standpoints. That
procedure was in keeping with United Nations practice inasmuch as all the work
accomplished in the subsidiary bodies of the General Assembly was subject to the
approval of Governments and of the Assembly itself. In order to reach a consensus,
his delegation, like others, had had to move a long way from its original position.
It had done so in a spirit of compromise, believing that it was in the interests of
the international community as a whole to seek an accommodation of divergent views
and paying particular attention to the positions of Arab and African States. He
hoped that the text prepared by the Special Committee would be approved without
substantive modifications at the twenty-ninth session of the General Assembly. If,
however, amendments were introduced at that time, his delegation reserved the right
to do likewise. During the debate in the Sixth Committee his delegation intended to
give its interpretation of the nature and scope of the definition as a whole and
also comment on specific articles.

Mr. RAKOTOSIHANAKA (Madagascar) congratulated the Chairman and all
delegations on the result achieved by the Committee, which had taken an entire
generation to accomplish. By dint of hard work and patient negotiations, the
Committee had overcome many difficulties and reconciled substantial divergences
of views. The result was a text formulated with the participation of all, which
could be generally acceptable. The Secretariat was also to be commended for its
efficient and dedicated contribution to the Committee's work.

Inasmuch as the definition of aggression was subject to final adoption by the
General Assembly, his delegation would at the present stage confine itself to taking
note of the document and would transmit it to its Government for detailed
examination. On the whole, however, it was regrettable that the text had appeared in

_____

a/ Reproduced in the order in which they were expressed at the 112th and
113th meetings of the Committee.

a somewhat negative form. Of course it was not an easy matter to draft a compromise formulation fully satisfactory to all parties. His delegation was well aware of the concessions that had been made on all sides. With regard to article 1, his delegation was not completely satisfied with the present wording and would have preferred to retain the phrase "in any form"; however, it had agreed to the deletion of those words in a spirit of compromise. Article 2, as now worded, might give rise to some misunderstanding, and his delegation could not unreservedly agree to the inclusion of the phrase "in contravention of the Charter". The Charter provided no justification for a State to use force, except in a certain specific context. Moreover, it should be noted that only the Security Council was able to determine the legitimacy of such a recourse to force. With regard to article 3, it was regrettable that the Working Group had made the introductory part unduly cumbersome and thereby somewhat altered the substance of the article. His delegation was also not satisfied with the expression "qualify as an act of aggression". Article 7, too, was not entirely satisfactory; his delegation would have preferred a clear declaration that the right of oppressed peoples to struggle for their freedom was a sacred right in no way contrary to the purposes of the Charter and indeed in full accordance with article 51 thereof. In his delegation's view, the meaning of article 7 was that such peoples had the right to struggle by all means available to them.

Mr. ALEMAN (Ecuador) said that his delegation wished to reserve its position with regard to the words "marine and air fleets" in article 3 (d) of the draft definition. That expression, as his delegation had maintained on numerous occasions, should be deleted since it was unprecedented in all previous instruments of international law and could give rise to unnecessary disputes in the future. He wished also to take the present opportunity to reiterate his Government's firm position that it was a legitimate exercise of national sovereignty for a country to detain and impose penalties upon any foreign vessel or aircraft engaged in unlawful activities within its territorial waters or airspace. He hoped that the foregoing reservations would be reflected accurately in the Special Committee's report to the General Assembly.

The delegation of Ecuador, which alone was able to interpret the thinking of the Ecuadorian Government, would at the next session of the General Assembly make general observations and state the official position of Ecuador on the whole of the draft definition just adopted by the Committee.

Mr. IGUCHI (Japan) congratulated the Chairman of the Committee, the Chairman of the Contact Groups and the Drafting Group, and the Rapporteur and members of the Committee on the efforts which had finally led to an acceptable definition of aggression. If that definition was adopted at the twenty-ninth session of the General Assembly, a new chapter would be written in the annals of international law and the dream of many celebrated jurists would be realized. It was to be hoped that the success achieved by the Committee was an omen of better times ahead in the whole field of international relations.

The agreed text on the definition of aggression was the product of extremely delicate compromises, and it would therefore be unrealistic to suppose that the wording of the definition was flawless or that the meaning of each article was so lucid that a different interpretation was inconceivable. However, the definition was fairly simple and well balanced and could serve as a broad guideline for Member

States and the Security Council. In interpreting and applying the provisions of the definition, it was essential to have a comprehensive understanding of the definition as a whole, including the preamble and the explanatory notes. All the provisions were interrelated, as was stated in article 8. Furthermore, the definition should be read together with the relevant provisions of the Charter and the Declaration on Principles of International Law concerning Friendly Relations and Co-operation among States in accordance with the Charter of the United Nations. The close interrelationship between those three documents had been rightly stressed.

His delegation had expressed its views on the definition of aggression on a number of occasions. It had repeatedly emphasized the importance of striking a proper balance between the question of priority - the objective element - and the question of intent - the subjective element. However, in a last-minute compromise his delegation had not insisted on explicit reference to the question of intent, on the clear understanding that that was one of the essential factors to be considered by the Security Council in determining whether an act of aggression had been committed. Article 2 was based on a delicate compromise and must be carefully read in order to understand the complex issues involved. Referring to Ecuador's reservation regarding article 3 (d), he said that his delegation had always attached great importance to the provisions concerning an attack on marine and air fleets, since such an attack on his country's fleet would be equivalent to a blockade of Japan's coast. There was no essential difference between the Japanese and the Ecuadorian view. It was his delegation's understanding that the paragraph in question was not intended to cover isolated and minor incidents, but it could not accept a remedial measure taken by a coastal State which contravened international law. All legitimate acts must conform strictly to international law.

His delegation was pleased to note the improvement in the wording of article 3 (f) and (g) and article 4. The inclusion of indirect acts of aggression in the definition was one of the important landmarks in the Committee's work and would undoubtedly help to promote international peace and security. Appropriate reference was made to the right to self-determination in article 7, it being, of course, understood that the struggle for self-determination by peoples forcibly deprived of that right and the efforts to support their struggle must be in conformity with the principles of the Charter and the Declaration on Friendly Relations. In connexion with the legal consequences of aggression, his delegation had always maintained that an act of aggression which was not part of a war of aggression gave rise only to State responsibility and that the question of individual responsibility for an act of aggression should be left for future study. His delegation welcomed the fact that the provisions of the Charter concerning the legal use of force were not to be affected by the definition.

His delegation felt that the definition as a whole was satisfactory. Personally, he would have been in favour of including a reference to the importance of utilizing the available means of achieving pacific settlement of disputes. A relevant factor in the historical study of aggression seemed to be the full mobilization and massive concentration of combat-ready forces along the borders of a State without provocation. Furthermore, the list of acts of aggression in article 3 might not be extensive enough. All in all, however, the Committee had analysed virtually all aspects of the definition of aggression, and, in his delegation's view, the text of the draft definition deserved the unanimous approval of the Committee. He urged members to co-operate in seeking its adoption by consensus in the Sixth Committee and the plenary General Assembly at its next session.

<u>Mr. CEAUSU</u> (Romania) congratulated the members of the Committee and the Chairman on the successful outcome of the Committee's work. Those States which were concerned about maintaining peace, extending the application of law in international relations and prohibiting the use or threat of force were particularly interested in defining aggression. Once war had ceased to be regarded as a legal instrument, the need to define aggression had become evident. The anti-social and inhuman aspect of the use of force in international relations had become obvious over the years, and international relations were today acceptable only if they were based on moral and legal principles of the kind embodied in the United Nations Charter.

Like other States, Romania endorsed the total elimination of the use or threat of force and the prevention and suppression of aggression, which was the most dangerous form of the use of force in present times, when any military conflict could easily assume world-wide proportions. His country had always taken a great interest in the definition of aggression and considered it an essential element in the legal framework of system of State security. The adoption of the United Nations Charter had been an event of particularly great impcrtance, since the Charter not only prohibited aggression but also formulated the minimum international legal principles and standards which must be respected if international peace and security were to be maintained. Romania was particularly interested in the definition of aggression because its foreign policy was based on respect for the principles of national independence and sovereignty, equality before the law, non-interference in the internal affairs of other States and avoidance of the threat or use of force.

The draft definition before the Committee was the fruit of seven years' work. Although far from perfect, it represented a generally acceptable compromise. His delegation had been mainly concerned with drafting a definition that was as complete as possible and devoid of any loop-holes which might encourage the use of force or enable aggressors to justify their acts. His delegation was pleased to note that its concerns were reflected in the draft definition. The official position of Romania would be stated when the draft was discussed in the General Assembly. However, he wished to draw attention to certain points which Romania found particularly important.

Regarding article 1, his delegation had been opposed to deletion of the phrase "in any form". Article 2 embodied the principle of priority. Under that text, a State first using armed force against another State was committing an act of aggression. That constituted sufficient evidence of the existence of an act of aggression. The same article provided for the possibility that the Security Council might exculpate the State which had first used armed force. In order to do so, however, the Security Council had to reach a decision, taken in accordance with the rules established by the Charter. If the Council was unable to adopt such a decision, the presumption of aggression remained. The Romanian delegation also had reservations concerning the wording of article 2, particularly the inclusion of the words "in contravention of the Charter", and concerning the phrase "qualify as an act of aggression" in the introductory part of article 3, which had replaced the original phrase "constitute an act of aggression", favoured by his delegation.

Article 5 contained one of the essential provisions for the operation of the definition. Since article 2 provided for the possibility that the State which had first used force might be exculpated in the Security Council, it had been specified in article 5 that "No consideration of whatever nature, whether political, economic, military or otherwise, may serve as a justification for aggression".

By that provision, a possible aggressor had been forbidden to seek justification for his acts by invoking circumstances relating to the internal or external policy of the victim. Indeed, the Special Committee had specified, in the explanatory note to article 5, that in drafting the paragraph on the inadmissibility of justifications for aggression, it had had in mind the principle that "No State or group of States has the right to intervene, directly or indirectly, for any reason whatever, in the internal or external affairs of any other State".

One of the essential aims of the definition of aggression was to help the victim to defend himself against the aggressor. Any act of aggression automatically brought into play the right of self-defence. In that connexion, his delegation was glad to note that the lawful use of force had been reaffirmed in article 6 of the draft definition. Article 7 prevented any interpretation of the definition as affecting the sacred right of all peoples to resist oppression or foreign domination.

The draft definition would be considered, improved where necessary and adopted by the General Assembly and would then serve as a guide to all United Nations organs, including the Security Council, in the maintenance of international peace and security. However, it was also addressed to States, since it concerned their conduct. It was to be hoped that States would maintain friendly relations, thus obviating the need to invoke the draft definition. His delegation reiterated its belief that adoption of the definition of aggression would help to strengthen the role of the United Nations in maintaining international peace and security, since it would provide the Organization with a political and legal instrument for preventing and eliminating threats to peace and acts of aggression. At the same time, the definition would be helpful in safeguarding the fundamental rights of States, particularly the legitimate right of self-defence against any attack upon national sovereignty and independence.

Mr. ELIAS (Spain) congratulated the Chairman, the Bureau and members of the Committee on their work and on the spirit of conciliation which showed that the United Nations was on the road leading to the attainment of its three great objectives: peace, co-operation and law. The text of the draft definition just adopted by consensus was not perfect, but it marked a great step forward. If the General Assembly adopted it, particularly by consensus, the Committee would have helped considerably in developing international law on one of the most important aspects of peace and security.

His delegation was not entirely satisfied with article 7, having proposed the inclusion of territorial integrity as an inseparable element of self-determination - an idea which had finally been incorporated into the sixth preambular paragraph. His delegation was aware that article 7 was intended to place the definition of aggression in the context of rights already proclaimed. However, the discussion had shown that there was a tendency to regard territorial integrity only as the right of a State, whereas in his delegation's view, it was the right of peoples and there were documents which embodied that right in international law. Regarding the second paragraph of article 5, it was Spain's understanding that the legal

characterization of a war of aggression as a crime in no way prejudged the legal
characterization of acts of aggression. Spain also understood that the reference
to a war of aggression in article 5 could not be interpreted to mean that that
concept had been adequately defined by the definition of aggression. That was one
of the most vulnerable points in the draft, and he would like his delegation's views
on it reflected in the Committee's report. He reserved his delegation's right to
make further comments on the draft definition in the Sixth Committee at the twenty-
ninth session of the General Assembly.

Mr. ABDULDJALIL (Indonesia) said that his delegation's views on the
consolidated text of the definition were already known. However, he wished to
draw attention to its reservations with regard to article 3 (d) and (g).

His delegation maintained its position that the inclusion of paragraph (d)
in the enumeration of acts of aggression did not prevent a State from taking
measures to protect its legitimate rights against foreign air and marine forces
operating illegally in its territory, including its territorial waters. He also
felt that the word "substantial" in article 3 (g) was superfluous, since the
concept of substantiality applied to the entire draft definition.

He paid tribute to the Chairman, the Rapporteur and all those involved in the
work of the Special Committee.

Mr. SIAGE (Syrian Arab Republic) praised the Chairman and the Bureau for
their success in directing the work of the Special Committee.

His delegation had always been anxious to co-operate in the work of the
Special Committee and had followed its discussions with great interest, since
Syria had recently been the victim of repeated aggression and part of its territory
was still occupied by a foreign force as a result of aggression. Its sole aim was
to assist in arriving at a fair and judicious definition of aggression which would
serve to detect and discourage possible acts of aggression. His delegation was
pleased that a consensus had been reached, but it had certain reservations regarding
the text which had been produced.

He welcomed the fact that the words "however exerted" in the original version
of article 1 had been omitted from the text, for that expression would have been
more acceptable if applied to aggression rather than to the use of armed force,
which, in certain cases, could be legitimate under the Charter. In addition, the
expression did not conform to the distinction laid down in Article 39 of the
Charter between a threat to peace, a breach of the peace and an act of aggression.
The Charter recognized the victim's inherent right of self-defence (Article 51)
only in the case of an act of aggression.

His delegation supported the part of article 2 relating to first use but did
not understand why the first use of armed force constituted only prima facie
evidence of an act of aggression and not aggression as such. He considered that
the first use of armed force in contravention of the Charter always constituted
an act of aggression. No organ, even the Security Council, could justify the use
of armed force in violation of the Charter, although the Security Council, in
conformity with the provisions of the Charter, was fully competent to determine
whether or not an act of aggression had been committed. He therefore suggested that

the words "prima facie evidence of" should be deleted from article 2. His delegation was pleased to note the progress that had been made in the new wording of article 2 in rejecting the justification of an act of aggression on the grounds of the intentions of the aggressor.

His delegation feared that article 3 (d) could lead to the interpretation of a minor incident as an act of aggression. With regard to article 7, he was glad to note that progress had been made in linking it with article 3, although it would have been preferable for it to be linked only with paragraph (g) of the latter article. The original text had mentioned the right of people under military occupation or any other form of foreign domination to resort to the use of force, while the new text only mentioned the right to struggle. He would like to see a reference to the legitimacy of all means, including the use of force. His delegation had difficulty in accepting the text of article 7 and would prefer to see it amended along the lines of the original draft.

With regard to article 5, his delegation was pleased to note that aggression had been termed a crime against international peace. He supported the Egyptian representative's proposal that the word "aggression" in the third paragraph of article 5 should be replaced by the words "the threat or use of force". He would prefer to see the note on that paragraph appear immediately after the article.

Mr. ROSSIDES (Cyprus) said that the Committee had reason to rejoice. It was some 50 years since the first attempts had been made to find a definition of aggression; efforts made at the League of Nations, and later by the International Law Commission and by committees and commissions of the United Nations, had produced no results. He emphasized the importance of the fact that a definition of aggression had been arrived at, regardless of any imperfections it might contain. The Committee had avoided the danger of making a definition that was not a definition of aggression but a definition for aggression. He praised the Chairman and members of the Committee for their work.

In arriving at a definition of aggression, the Committee was opening the way to the adoption of a code of offences against the peace and security of mankind. The code had been prepared by the International Law Commission many years previously, but the General Assembly had been unable to adopt it because of the absence of a definition of aggression. The elaboration of international criminal jurisdiction also hinged on the existence of a definition of aggression.

He observed that the Charter, in Article 39, stated that the Security Council should determine the existence of any threat to the peace, breach of the peace, or act of aggression. In determining the degree of an offence, the Council could only be guided by Article 2, paragraph 4, of the Charter, which was a general prohibition of the threat or use of force and did not state in what circumstances the use of force constituted an act of aggression. The consolidated text enumerated in article 3 the acts which qualified as acts of aggression and thus provided guidelines for the Security Council. In that connexion, he welcomed the inclusion of the words "armed bands" in article 3 (g).

Article 2 would also provide guidance for the Security Council regarding the first use of force. From the legal standpoint, prima facie evidence of use of force would conclusively establish aggression unless more conclusive evidence to the contrary would be produced. In such circumstances, the Security Council would have to be satisfied that the additional evidence was important enough to negate the prima facie evidence of aggression. He agreed with other representatives that it was important to exclude the question of intent or purpose in article 2; that would make a mockery of the whole definition.

In other respects, the definition was perhaps a little too prolix, but it was basically sound. In defining the principle of priority (article 2), it followed more or less the lines of the definition prepared, but not finally adopted, by the League of Nations in 1924 (Geneva Protocol) and in 1933 and also the definition proposed at the United Nations by the United States delegation in 1945. The consolidated text, therefore, satisfied all the main requirements for a definition of aggression.

Mr. BESSOU (France) considered that agreement by consensus on a draft definition of aggression was a considerable achievement. His Government would formulate its comments on the text during the forthcoming General Assembly session; meanwhile, he would offer some preliminary observations ad referendum. His comments on the articles of the definition were to be understood in the light of his delegation's basic concept of the scope and purpose of the draft definition, the value of which did not reside solely in the fact that it gave guidelines to the Security Council for action under Article 39 of the Charter; the draft went further and clarified in some measure the right of self-defence against armed attack provided by Article 51 of the Charter. Thus, it was, to that extent, also an effective means of frustrating potential aggression. Consequently, he could only regret the absence of any mention of Article 51 of the Charter in the second preambular paragraph of the draft definition.

Article 1 of the text satisfactorily established the framework within which aggression was to be defined: it must entail the use of a degree of armed force.

Article 2, on the other hand, had proved most difficult to prepare. The article seemed to comprise two principles, the first of which was that "the first use of armed force ... in contravention of the Charter shall constitute prima facie evidence of an act of aggression". That gave pride of place to the concept of priority, which his delegation had always supported. The first use of force raised a presumption of aggression, which could only be rebutted through the Security Council, acting in accordance with the second principle of the article. Nevertheless, the expression "in contravention of the Charter" was infelicitous because of the uncertainty which might arise if the provision were invoked. Contravention of the Charter was, indeed, a necessary element of an act of aggression, but it was hardly fitting that the determination whether an act of aggression had been committed should be left to the discretion of the aggressor, who would thus become a judge in his own cause. An aggressor's argument that he was acting within the Charter was fallacious, and there seemed no need to provide such a loop-hole in the definition. The reference to the Charter in the article was addressed solely to the Security Council, and his delegation would interpret the article in that light.

The second principle of article 2 concerned the powers of the Security Council, and, in that it tempered the somewhat peremptory affirmation at the beginning of the article, he welcomed it.

Article 3 (g) referred to the sending of armed bands. Until they had been dispatched, no act of aggression had occurred; the mere fact of organizing or preparing armed bands did not of itself constitute an act of aggression.

He had no comments on article 4 save that it was indeed essential to state clearly that the enumeration in article 3 was not exhaustive.

The French delegation had always believed that the study of the legal consequences of aggression mentioned in article 5 was not a matter for the Committee; it involved questions of international penal law, a concept which was still evolving, and presented pitfalls - for example, the Security Council might find itself in the position of both political tribunal and arbiter. The text which the Committee had finally worked out was, however, acceptable, to the extent that it merely noted the present status of international law without prejudging its development.

Article 6 served a useful purpose in stressing that the Charter was the only legal basis for the draft definition. The latter might acquire the legal status of a General Assembly resolution, but it could not modify the Charter in any way.

Article 7 was a safeguarding clause, essentially political in nature, which was to be found in various forms in many United Nations documents. In the present instance, the clause had not been put in what seemed its most logical form, that of a guarantee that those who supported peoples struggling for their freedom would not be accused of aggression. As drafted, the safeguarding clause seemed in fact somewhat alien to the text of the definition, since it was not concerned with aggression as defined in article 1, i.e. between sovereign States.

Finally, he welcomed, the Committee's success in achieving a draft definition of aggression; he attributed it in large measure to the patience and sense of compromise of the Chairman, the chairmen and members of the subgroups, and the Committee as a whole.

Mr. ZAHAWIE (Iraq) paid a tribute to the spirit of compromise in the Committee which had made it possible to achieve a draft definition of aggression by consensus. The text might not be entirely satisfactory to all, but it represented the maximum degree to which the aggregate of delegations' interests, as expressed in the Committee, could be accommodated. The outcome of the Committee's work was to be evaluated politically and juridically by the United Nations. Consequently, although he accepted the consensus draft definition ad referendum, his Government's position would be further defined during the forthcoming session of the General Assembly.

Mr. ROSENSTOCK (United States of America) acknowledged the patience and spirit of compromise of members of the Committee which had made it possible to achieve a draft definition of aggression. He saw no objection to the draft text going forward to the General Assembly, even though it was by no means perfect. Indeed, even a legally perfect definition might do more harm than good if given too much emphasis. The text that had been produced was a recommendation of the General Assembly for use by the Security Council. The law concerning the use of force was found in the Charter and in the Declaration on Friendly Relations, as was underlined by the preambular reaffirmation. It would, however, misconstrue and frustrate the purposes of Chapter VII of the Charter if the Council were led by the

draft definition to delay urgent action under Chapter VII while it debated whether
an act of aggression had occurred, if a finding of a threat to the peace or breach
of the peace would more effectively activate the collective security mechanism of
the Charter.

The second and fourth preambular paragraphs of the draft definition recalled
that the term "act of aggression" with which the text dealt was that contained in
Article 39 of the Charter and thus reflected a primary responsibility of the
Security Council. The third preambular paragraph emphasized the importance of the
peaceful settlement of disputes, of negotiation, inquiry and conciliation to avoid
the escalation of differences between States. For such methods to be effective,
and if the principle of the sovereign equality of States was to be maintained, the
possibility of referring disputes to binding third party settlement must be an
available option for all States as against every other State.

The fifth preambular paragraph, while recognizing the dangers which would flow
from an illegal use of force amounting to aggression, correctly stated the view
that not every act of force in violation of the Charter constituted aggression.

The right of all peoples to equal rights and self-determination was stated in
the sixth preambular paragraph; the final clause of the paragraph reaffirmed the
principle that the right of self-determination did not imply the legitimation of
action which would disrupt the territorial integrity of a State which conducts
itself in compliance with the principle of equal rights and self-determination and
thus possesses a government representing the people belonging to the territory.

Article 1 contained a general statement which must be understood in the light
of the other articles. It properly made no distinction based on the means of armed
force used, and the phrase "as set out in this definition" indicated that not all
illegal uses of armed force could be denominated acts of aggression.

In article 2, the definition suggested the considerations which the Security
Council should bear in mind in determining whether an act of aggression had
occurred. The Council would be well advised to take account of which State first
used force and to give due weight to all relevant circumstances. It had been
agreed that it was unnecessary to make special reference to the intent or purpose
(including the proof of _animus_) of the States involved, that notion being covered
by the phrase "other relevant circumstances". He understood the article to mean
that the first use of armed force by a State in contravention of the Charter
was only _prima facie_ evidence of an act of aggression; the Security Council might
or might not in the particular case find that there had actually been an action of
aggression. If the Security Council did not make a finding of an act of aggression,
the Council must be presumed not to have found the _prima facie_ evidence persuasive.
That interpretation accorded with the Council's _modus operandi_, which was to
consider whether a finding under Article 39 of the Charter would be justified -
rather than determining that it would not be justified. This definition accordingly
could only be resonably interpreted in the light of the whole history of the
Council's method of operation and, of course, in any event could not alter the
intent of Article 39 of the Charter.

Article 3 of the draft definition gave certain familiar examples of the use
of force which the Security Council might reasonably consider, in the manner
set forth in article 2, as potential acts of aggression. The scope of the list

made it clear that no distinction was made as to the means employed or the directness or otherwise of their use. There was no suggestion that article 3 was intended to be an exhaustive list of all illicit uses of force which might constitute acts of aggression; indeed, article 4 expressly stipulated that article 3 was not exhaustive.

The first paragraph of article 5 said in effect that illicit activities were those for which there was no justification; that was a useful addition to the extent that it represented a further safeguard against misuse of the definition.

The second paragraph of article 5 noted the continued validity of the principles which formed the basis of the trials following the Second World War, enunciated in the Moscow Declaration of 1943, the London Agreement of 1945 and the Charter of the International Military Tribunal for the Far East. The second sentence noted that States were responsible for their wrongful acts.

The third paragraph of the article, while being a formulation of the Stimson Doctrine and of the relevant principles of the Declaration on Friendly Relations, did not alter or extend existing international law with regard to the consequences for States or individuals involved in acts of aggression.

Articles 6 and 7 were classic rulings clauses which by their very nature did not function to create rights but merely to provide express assurance with regard to rules not being dealt with. Article 6 merely recalled that the purpose of the definition was to elucidate the means by which certain types of illicit conduct on the part of States might be determined to constitute aggression, rather than to examine cases in which the use of force might be lawful. That was, indeed, already clear from the text of article 2.

Article 7 expressly affirmed that the definition defined aggression and not the right of self-determination. His Government was always ready to support any text which reasonably reaffirmed the right of all peoples to self-determination and it could therefore accept a formulation which did not speak of the use of force but of actions in accordance with the principles of the Charter and the Declaration on Friendly Relations. Thus, the article did not legitimize acts of armed force by a State, which would otherwise constitute aggression. Even if it mentioned the use of force (which it did not), the article would not constitute an assertion that such use by a State in those circumstances was legal. Rather, it might amount to a recommendation to the Security Council, in considering a particular case, to bear in mind the purposes of the States involved, when considering whether a particular illegal activity should be denominated an act of aggression under Article 39 of the Charter.

Article 8 reaffirmed the need to construe each part of the definition in the context of all other relevant parts. That was particularly true in the case of articles 1 to 4, which formed an integrated whole.

Mr. JOB (Yugoslavia) expressed gratification at the Committee's success in achieving a draft definition of aggression by consensus and paid tribute to the spirit of compromise in the Committee which had made that possible. His delegation was convinced that the legal formulation of a concept of aggression would be beneficial for the better functioning of the United Nations system of collective security since it provided a firmer basis for the work of the United

Nations organs charged with maintaining international peace and security. It also represented a further step towards the transformation of progressive political principles into legal rules, and it stressed the importance of the United Nations as a centre for the codification and progressive development of international law. The definition would furnish a precedent for other legal documents and would enhance further efforts towards the codification of international responsibility for aggression and the establishment of an international criminal jurisdiction.

Adoption of the definition would strengthen the role of the United Nations in the maintenance and consolidation of international peace and security. Acts of aggression and foreign interference still occurred in international relations, and, as long as such acts were committed, as long as foreign territories were held under occupation, the right to self-determination was denied and colonial and neo-colonial dependence was maintained, there was a need for the international organization to exert all efforts to remedy those situations and provide for the peaceful settlement of disputes. The definition of aggression was designed to promote these efforts. The Security Council as the organ primarily responsible for the maintenance of international peace and security should use the definition as a guidance to fulfil more effectively its duties. The adoption of the definition should, as its preamble stated, deter potential aggressors and facilitate the protection of the rights and lawful interests of the small and developing countries, which were the principal victims of aggression. When adopted by the General Assembly, the definition would take its place alongside the Declaration on the Strengthening of International Security and the Declaration on Principles of International Law concerning Friendly Relations and Co-operation among States in accordance with the Charter of the United Nations, as an example of the growing awareness in the international community that the use of force in international relations was to be condemned and prevented.

The text was not perfect in all its parts and contained formulations which his delegation would have preferred to see expressed differently. Nevertheless, it reflected the present stage of development of international relations. Its main significance lay in the fact that it was possible, for the first time, for a United Nations body to produce a text that might be acceptable to all Member States. That is why it had to be regarded as a success in spite of possible short-comings. His comments on individual articles were based on two premises: that his Government would be able to state its views when the draft was considered by the General Assembly and that, because of the need to achieve a definition by consensus, the wording of some articles could give rise to different interpretations. It was to those articles that his observations particularly referred.

Article 2 accorded with his delegation's view that the first use of force was the most important element in determining an act of aggression. He could nevertheless wish that the text had gone beyond the statement that the first use of armed force, even in contravention of the Charter, was only _prima facie_ evidence of an act of aggression. He failed to see why the first use of force should not be specifically designated an act of aggression, since the article expressly reserved the right of the Security Council to conclude, in the light of other relevant circumstances, that a determination that an act of aggression had been committed would not be justified. The use of the words "in contravention of the Charter" in that connexion was undesirable in view of some of the underlying concepts which those words had been inserted to safeguard. The only cases in which

26

force might be used first were those in which there was an explicit authorization by United Nations organs. He rejected any interpretation which would give States or regional organizations the right to use force without such authorization, and any such use of force was to be regarded as an act of aggression. Nor did he regard the words "other relevant circumstances" as covering the purposes which the States involved had had in mind, since no purposes could justify the commission of aggression.

He regretted that it had not been possible to state clearly in article 5 that aggression constituted a crime against international peace giving rise to responsibility under international law. Many international legal precedents - the Nuremberg principles and General Assembly resolutions among them - showed that aggression was an international crime; yet, some delegations, and particularly those whose countries had been most active in establishing the Nuremberg principles, had argued that the term "crime" should be used only in respect of wars of aggression. The latter concept had not been specifically defined; its insertion thus did not contribute to the clarity of the article. To draw a distinction between "aggression" and "war of aggression" was a theoretical exercise having possibly undesired implications, and to maintain that the use of the word "crime" in respect of aggression was not justified was unfounded and arbitrary. The provision, as now formulated, would permit the absurd interpretation that aggression might not be a crime against international peace and that a war of aggression might not give rise to international responsibility.

He welcomed the inclusion of important principles in the first and third paragraphs of article 5. He shared the view that the third paragraph could not be interpreted in a manner contrary to the established principles of international law, especially the relevant provisions of the Declaration on Principles of International Law concerning Friendly Relations.

With regard to article 6, he considered that the only cases in which use of force was not prohibited under the Charter were cases of individual or collective self-defence under Article 51 of the Charter and the cases in which it was authorized by the relevant United Nations organs. He would have been happier if that had been spelt out since less room would have been left for misconstructions. His comments on article 2 of the draft definition were equally applicable to that aspect of article 6.

Article 7 contained a principle to which his country, in common with the vast majority of countries of the world, especially those which had had to struggle for independence, attached great importance. The right of peoples under colonial and racist régimes or other forms of alien domination to fight for their self-determination, freedom and independence could never be regarded as aggression, and the formulation of the article was an explicit reaffirmation of that principle, although he would have preferred the omission of the word "forcibly" on the ground that peoples deprived of their rights by subtle rather than forcible means were equally entitled to fight for them. Finally, he regarded the word "struggle" as used in the article as implying "struggle by all means at their disposal".

Mr. CAICEDO (Colombia) said that, in his Government's view, the international community could not continue to do without a clear definition of what had always been described as the greatest violation of international law, because collective security machinery was meaningless and ineffectual without such a definition. To complement the principle of compulsory use of methods of peaceful

settlement of international disputes, there still did not yet exist a clear and
definitive prohibition of the use of force; for that reason, the provisions of the
text agreed on by the Special Committee on the Question of Defining Aggression
were of vital importance and represented a step forward towards a final definition
of the use of force.

In that context, the Colombian delegation considered that the definition
which the Special Committee would submit to the General Assembly, in accordance
with its mandate, represented a reasonable advance in international law which
confirmed the existence of a primary, but shared, responsibility of the United
Nations in that regard.

The definition of aggression formulated by the Special Committee represented
a reasonable advance in international law, firstly, because it struck the right
balance between existing theories, permitting the emergence of a universal
consensus, and, secondly, because it reflected the spirit of co-operation and
flexibility which had led participating delegations to accept that compromise.
Article 1, by defining aggression as the use of armed force, covered the most
obvious cases of aggression and filled one of the most important gaps in the
United Nations legal structure relating to the maintenance of international peace
and security. Article 2 of the definition made a start in a new process of
progressive codification of international law relating to first use of armed force
by a State. Article 3 achieved what had seemed completely impossible some years
previously, and article 4 left open the possibility that additions might
subsequently be made to the enumeration in article 3. The provisions of article 7
linked to the definition the extremely important right to self-determination,
freedom and independence of peoples, and more specifically confirmed the right of
peoples under colonial and racist régimes to struggle in order to obtain their
national independence and respect for the totality of their human rights. Those
provisions undoubtedly represented very positive progress in the codification of
international law.

His delegation considered that the definition was reasonable also because the
agreed text left aside those problems which would have delayed for several more
years the drafting of a definition of aggression: economic aggression which did
not involve the use of armed force was not covered by the text; nor did the text
deal with the question - basic to international collective security - whether the
existing provisions of the United Nations Charter were sufficiently effective
to maintain international peace and security, and whether it would not be advisable
to work more actively on a revision of those provisions, as the Colombian
delegation had advocated on several occasions. The fact that the definition of
aggression did not provide a solution to those problems, on which its effectiveness
depended, strengthened the conviction of the Colombian Government that it was
necessary and essential to raise them again in the competent organs of the United
Nations.

The definition of aggression formulated by the Special Committee confirmed
the existence of a primary, but shared, responsibility of the United Nations with
regard to the maintenance of international peace and security.

On the basis of the assumption that one of the purposes of the United
Nations was to maintain international peace and security and to take effective
collective measures for the prevention and removal of threats to the peace, and

for the suppression of acts of aggression or other breaches of the peace, the definition confirmed that the Organization had basic responsibilities and functions in that regard. That was established in the second preambular paragraph and in article 2. That affirmation was balanced by the stipulation in the fourth preambular paragraph to the effect that nothing in the definition should be interpreted as in any way affecting the scope of the provisions of the Charter with respect to the functions and powers of the organs of the United Nations. In the opinion of the Colombian delegation, that competence could not be exclusive and it should be considered that the power to determine the existence of an act of aggression was shared by the United Nations with the other international organizations competent in the matter of the maintenance of international peace and security.

His delegation considered that the cases in which the use of force was lawful, which were mentioned in article 6 of the definition, should include cases deriving from the application of Articles 51 and 53 of the United Nations Charter. In other words, the provisions of the Charter did not prevent regional collective security agencies from being competent also to determine the existence of an act of aggression. For example, in the inter-American system, according to the provisions of chapter VI of the Charter of the Organization of American States and the provisions of the Inter-American Treaty of Reciprocal Assistance, the Organ of Consultation, consisting of the Meeting of Consultation of Ministers of Foreign Affairs, could decide to characterize an act as aggression and agree on whatever measures it considered appropriate to restore peace in America. The Colombian delegation considered that the use of force by a regional collective security agency did not in that case constitute an act of aggression under the Charter of the United Nations or the definition of aggression as it appeared in the text agreed on by the Special Committee.

His delegation was grateful to the Special Committee for having taken into account its repeated observations on the procedure for the interpretation of the provisions of the definition. Since the provisions were interrelated, each provision should be construed in the context of the other provisions.

With regard to the question of the scope of the definition, once it had been adopted by the General Assembly, his delegation would consider it as a peremptory norm of general international law, in accordance with the definition given in article 53 of the Vienna Convention on the Law of Treaties.

His delegation reserved the right to make further comments during the discussion to be held in the United Nations General Assembly.

Mr. BOJILOV (Bulgaria) said that six years after the General Assembly, through the efforts of the Soviet Union, had established the Special Committee, his delegation was pleased to note that the latter had been successful in arriving at a consensus. The political significance of the definition was that the international community wished to curb aggressors by accepted legal norms and to exclude the possible use of armed force in violation of the principles of the Charter. The definition was a positive contribution to détente, international peace and security and the development of international law. It should also be realized that the Committee's success was due to the improvement in the international climate and to the fact that the third world countries also wanted a definition of aggression. While the text was not ideal, it reflected a consensus based on compromise and mutual respect.

His delegation supported the text of the preamble and believed that the Special Committee was correct in deleting the phrase "however exerted" from article 1, since it would have no meaning in the light of the other provisions.

Article 2 was the nucleus of the definition. While his delegation would have preferred some improvement in the text, it had agreed to the compromise final version, but it reserved the right to explain its interpretation of that article in the Sixth Committee of the General Assembly.

Article 3 (f) was not quite in harmony with the other provisions of that article. The Special Committee had worked out a definition of basic principles as guidance for the Security Council, which must, under the Charter, decide which State, in a given conflict, was the aggressor and should therefore bear the international legal consequences. The element of "double aggression" introduced by article 3 (f) might be used to complicate the process of identifying and condemning an aggressor.

Article 5 was the Achilles' heel of the definition. It would be difficult for members of the General Assembly to understand just what the first paragraph of that article had to do with the legal consequences of aggression. Perhaps it should have been in the preamble, since it was declaratory in nature. Besides, his delegation was not sure that the Special Committee had been correct in not stating that aggression was a crime against international peace. Having accepted the principle that a "war of aggression" was a "crime against international peace", the Special Committee should perhaps have pursued it to its logical conclusion: the findings of the Nuremberg Tribunal.

Bulgaria had always supported the right to self-determination, freedom and independence of the peoples suffering under the colonial yoke and racist régimes and from other forms of alien domination. His delegation was therefore not entirely satisfied with the text of article 7: it had never felt that the Charter and the Declaration on Principles of International Law concerning Friendly Relations and Co-operation among States were the only documents which should be quoted with respect to those rights. Since, however, that was the only generally accepted text, his delegation supported it.

Compromise was needed in order to give effect to the definition, and his delegation believed that the General Assembly should be aware of that fact and adopt the text by consensus. His delegation would do its utmost to obtain its Government's support of the text.

Mr. LAMPTEY (Ghana) said that his delegation had already expressed its views on the subject of defining aggression at the session of the Special Committee in Geneva in 1973. To a remarkable degree, the present definition maintained the integrity of the Geneva compromise proposals, and his delegation would commit itself to the maintenance of the principles of that skilfully negotiated and highly sensitive consensus during its consideration by the General Assembly. The Special Committee's success was due to the great effort made by every delegation to complete a task of historic proportions, and his delegation wished to thank all for a truly commendable achievement.

Mr. GUNEY (Turkey) said that his country, as a member of the Special Committee since its establishment, had always sought the formulation of a generally acceptable definition of aggression that would conform to the Charter and strengthen the organs responsible for the maintenance of international peace and security.

His delegation welcomed the adoption of the draft definition as a historic event in the codification and progressive development of international law. While its adoption by consensus was the outcome of mutual concessions, all delegations had demonstrated a spirit of understanding, co-operation and objectivity. His delegation, which warmly welcomed the consensus, accepted the draft definition ad referendum.

Turning to the text of the draft definition, he said he would confine himself to a few preliminary comments, while reserving his Government's right to state its final views at the twenty-ninth session of the General Assembly. While the definition was far from perfect, it was simple and well-balanced. The preamble reaffirmed the basic provisions of the Charter as well as the provisions of the Declaration on Principles of International Law concerning Friendly Relations and Co-operation among States in accordance with the Charter of the United Nations, one of the principles of which was that States should fulfil in good faith their obligations under the Charter, the generally recognized principles and rules of international law and international agreements.

With regard to article 1, his delegation would have preferred retention of the words "however exerted". A reference in those terms in that article to indirect aggression would have been desirable but, in view of the inclusion of paragraph (g) in article 3, his delegation, in a spirit of compromise, had not insisted on that point. Article 2, which was a very delicately balanced compromise between anteriority and aggressive intent, lay at the heart of the definition. With regard to article 3, it was particularly important to establish a complete definition dealing not only with direct aggression but also with indirect aggression, which was currently attaining an almost equally serious level; paragraph (g) of article 3 met that need. Article 4 established a mixed definition by stating that the acts enumerated in the preceding article were not exhaustive and preserving the power of the Security Council to determine that other acts constituted aggression under the provisions of the Charter. Article 6, which safeguarded the scope of the Charter, thus making it possible to overcome considerable difficulties, was a source of satisfaction to his delegation. In article 7, the reference to article 3 as a whole rather than to a specific paragraph of that article was, in his view, quite justified, while the text of article 7 as a whole was the result of compromise and long negotiation. His country had been one of the first to support the sacred right of self-determination. Article 8, taken from the Declaration on Friendly Relations, would facilitate future interpretation, application and comprehension of the definition.

In conclusion, he paid a warm tribute to the Chairman of the Special Committee and of the Contact Groups, as well as to the Director and staff of the Codification Division. His delegation hoped that the adoption of the definition by the General Assembly would discourage any future aggressor and would facilitate the determination of acts of aggression and the implementation of measures against them.

Mr. STEEL (United Kingdom) expressed his delegation's pleasure and relief at the successful conclusion of a task begun some 50 years earlier. While his delegation would state its considered view of the draft definition at the twenty-ninth session of the General Assembly, he wished to comment briefly on his delegation's attitude to the exercise on which the Committee had been engaged, on the function expected of the draft definition and on a few of its provisions.

To a certain extent, his delegation still entertained some scepticism and apprehension with regard to the formulation of a formal definition of aggression. If the definition was not used and interpreted in good faith, and with fairness, common sense and realism, it might do more harm than good. However, the fact that those qualities had manifested themselves more and more during the recent sessions of the Committee inspired the necessary confidence that the definition would indeed serve the international community in good stead. Yet the definition did not have the binding force of domestic law.

It was always necessary to remember just what the definition was. It was the international equivalent of a piece of domestic legislation having binding force on all competent organs. Under the Charter, the Security Council was the competent organ to determine whether a threat to the peace, a breach of the peace or an act of aggression had been committed, or to refrain from making any such determination, and its discretion in that matter remained absolutely unfettered. Nothing in the definition could, or purported to, qualify that discretion which the Charter conferred. His delegation therefore viewed the definition as constituting valuable guidance to the Security Council - no less and no more - in performing its functions under Article 39 of the Charter.

Certain paragraphs of the preamble, for example the fourth, were of importance and should especially be borne in mind when considering the substantive provisions of the definition. His delegation also welcomed the insertion of the eighth preambular paragraph relating to the Declaration on Friendly Relations. There were some areas in which the contents of the draft definition overlapped with the contents of that Declaration, and the definition quite rightly made it clear that there was no intention to detract from or qualify the carefully-formulated provisions of the Declaration. This applied to a number of provisions in the definition including, for example, the sixth and seventh paragraphs of the preamble itself.

Article 1, which required little comment, was based substantially on Article 2, paragraph 4, of the Charter. The general agreement reached with regard to the deletion of the words "however exerted" was due to the fact that, though they were not wrong, they were, in the light of other provisions on indirect aggression, no longer required.

The way in which article 2 was formulated reflected the way in which the Security Council was required to carry out - and in fact carried out - its functions under Article 39 of the Charter. In other words, the Council took into account all the factors of the situation - of which the first use of armed force was an important piece of evidence, but by no means the sole or determinative one - before determining whether an act of aggression had indeed been committed. His delegation had been able to agree to the deletion from article 2 of the specific reference to "purposes" on the understanding that the reference to "other relevant circumstances" necessarily covered a reference to "purposes".

As to article 3, his delegation interpreted the opening words of the article, the text of which was at last reasonably satisfactory, to mean that the acts enumerated were merely typical examples of ways in which aggression could be committed, and could be considered as acts of aggression only if the Security Council so determined. With regard to subparagraph (a), it should be made clear that the reference to military occupation was intended to relate to such occupation resulting from an invasion or attack which itself constituted an act of aggression. As to subparagraph (b), his delegation did not object to the inclusion of the explanation of that paragraph in the report at the request of another delegation, though it perhaps stated the obvious. Subparagraph (d) gave rise to no problems, so far as his delegation was concerned, and the same was substantially true of the remaining paragraphs of the article, although it might wish to elaborate its views on some of them at the twenty-ninth session. His delegation could state that it regarded some of them as being no more than a partial illustration of matters dealt with more fully and more precisely in the Declaration of Friendly Relations.

Article 4 was unexceptionable. So too was article 5; the fact that the first paragraph was perhaps only a truism did not make it objectionable. The first sentence of the second paragraph adequately reflected the principles embodied in the Nuremberg Charter and repeated in the Declaration on Friendly Relations. That was as far as international law had gone in dealing with criminal liability in the field of aggression, and it was therefore right not to attempt a wider formulation. The second sentence of the second paragraph stated a proposition, not in the context of criminal law, with which all members could agree. The third paragraph of article 5 embodied a well-recognized principle of international law, and his delegation fully subscribed to it, as it had always done.

Article 6 spoke for itself, but its importance in the definition in emphasizing the overriding nature of the provisions of the Charter must never be underrated. Article 7 represented a fair compromise reached after a great deal of discussion. While his delegation still had some doubts about the relevance of such a provision in a definition of aggression, which ex hypothesi dealt with acts committed by one State against another, it did not wish to resist a reaffirmation in proper terms of the right of peoples to self-determination, freedom and independence, as derived from the Charter. His delegation interpreted the article as doing no more than emphasizing the propriety of the legitimate exercise of that right and of action taken by peoples forcibly deprived of it to resist such forcible deprivation and, in so doing, to seek and receive support from others.

Article 8, based on a corresponding provision in the Declaration on Friendly Relations, was a useful and valuable addition to the draft.

In conclusion, he wished to pay a tribute to the Chairmen of the Special Committee and the Contact Groups for their patience, negotiating skill, legal acumen and, above all, their fine sense of what was both fair and possible, as well as to Ambassador Rossides of Cyprus, Ambassador Yasseen of Iraq (whose work had been so effectively carried forward by Mr. Al-Qaysi) and the late Ambassador Alcivar of Ecuador for the outstanding part they had played in the past work of the Special Committee.

Mr. LA (Sudan) said that his delegation reserved the right to state its views in the General Assembly at its twenty-ninth session, at which time it would pay a tribute to the Chairman and other members of the Committee.

Sir Laurence McINTYRE (Australia) expressed his delegation's satisfaction and relief that the Special Committee had finally been able to reach by consensus an agreed definition of aggression. Since the Committee's inception in 1967, his delegation had been guided by the need for balance and precision on the one hand - especially having in mind the paramount responsibilities and functions of the Security Council - and for reasonable flexibility on the other if the United Nations was to reach agreement on a definition that would command the acceptance and respect of all its Members.

His delegation had always attached the greatest importance to the need for adoption of any definition of aggression by consensus: anything less than consensus would undermine its value. His delegation therefore hoped that the draft definition would be accepted unanimously by the General Assembly at its twenty-ninth session. Australia regarded the adoption of the definition as an important part of the process of orderly evolution of the principles of international law. It had sought a balanced definition which would be consistent with the Charter and which would at the same time take account of political realities. His delegation had been concerned, among other things, that on the crucial question of the right of peoples to self-determination there should not emerge an unbalanced definition which could be construed as exculpating States which committed acts of aggression by fomenting armed civil strife or by organizing or supporting armed bands or other forces in the territory of other States. His delegation had also been anxious that any reference to criminal responsibility should not be construed as implying individual responsibility. While the agreed definition was not ideal in every respect, there had necessarily been compromise all round in order to achieve a solution that had eluded the efforts of the international community for many decades.

His delegation had been gratified by the conduct of the work throughout the Special Committee's final session, at which there had been continuing evidence of widespread determination to reach an agreed definition. In that respect, he wished to pay a particular tribute to the Chairman and the Rapporteur, and to acknowledge the extremely helpful role played by Mr. Lamptey of Ghana as mediator among differing approaches. His delegation was extremely gratified to have been involved in such an achievement after a history of frustration and failure extending over a pierod of some 50 years.

Mr. MORKVED (Norway), associating himself with the tributes paid to the Chairman by earlier speakers, recalled the scepticism of several delegations during earlier years as to the utility of the Committee's work. He was pleased to note that in the draft definition adopted, the basic positions of all delegations had been met. The draft definition appeared to be as balanced and complete as possible, and his delegation hoped that it would command the support of the great majority of States, including the permanent members of the Security Council.

The outcome of the session was a new manifestation of the improved relations among States. It was to be hoped that the favourable international climate would also influence efforts relating to the codification of international law in other fields. His delegation reserved the right to present further comments and interpretations of the draft definition at the twenty-ninth session of the General Assembly.

Mr. WANG (Canada), expressing his delegation's satisfaction at the
positive outcome of the Special Committee's work, said he wished to pay a
particular tribute to the Chairman and the Rapporteur for their efforts. It was
not difficult to understand why a consensus had eluded the international community
for over 50 years. The question of legal prohibitions regarding the use of force
by States had been one of the most important and at the same time most
controversial problems of international law, touching upon the vital interests of
States and the foundations of international peace and security. The achievement
of a consensus was due above all to a sense of realism in the Committee as to what
could be demanded of a definition and the purposes that it might serve. The
definition adopted, reflecting as it did compromise on all sides, inevitably opened
the door to differing interpretations.

In past years, there had been an understandable tendency for delegations to
seek formulations which would seem to place in a favourable or unfavourable light
one or other of the sides in recent or current conflicts. The underlying approach
had often been to seek a definition which was as restrictive as possible with
regard to the use of force by certain States whose cause was not favoured, and yet
as permissive as possible with regard to the use of force by other States whose
cause was favoured. In the changing pattern of international relations over the
years, there had been changes in the way in which States perceived particular
threats or acts of force which were judged condemnable or laudable. Those changes
were reflected in some of the changes of emphasis in various formulations submitted
during the past 50 years.

The ambiguities in the present definition were therefore an inevitable
reflection of the complexity of the real world of international relations and a
reflection of a realistic desire to develop guidelines which would be generally
acceptable and widely applied to future conflicts. As indicated in the preamble,
the definition should be regarded as a formulation of basic principles as
guidance for a determination as to whether an act of aggression had been committed
in the light of all the circumstances of each particular case. It was clear from
article 2 and other articles that nothing in the definition could prejudice the
Security Council's ultimate discretion in the exercise of its responsibilities
under the Charter for the maintenance of international peace and security.

The 29-year history of the United Nations had demonstrated that the Security
Council had approached the question of such a determination with great care and
great caution. In fact the Council had not hitherto arrived at a determination
of aggression, although it had in one somewhat exceptional instance determined
that an armed attack constituted a breach of the peace.

The Security Council, in the exercise of its discretion and in fulfilling
its responsibility, had in practice adopted more the role of peace-maker than
the role of judge pronouncing on guilt or innocence, legality or illegality. In
conflict situations with deep historical roots and complex interactions between
the parties, the Council had often, quite properly, avoided judgements which might
be harmful to the task of terminating hostilities, restoring peace and promoting
just and peaceful reconciliation. Nothing in the draft definition could be said
to limit that important discretionary power.

While his delegation would reserve its detailed comments for the twenty-
ninth session of the General Assembly, he wished to make a few preliminary comments

on certain provisions. His delegation noted with satisfaction that article 3 (g), relating to armed bands, reflected acceptance of the thesis that the distinction between direct and indirect aggression was artificial. The determining criterion had been and was whether or not a sufficient degree of armed force had been used to amount to an act of aggression by the State to which such acts could be attributed.

As to article 7, relating to self-determination, his delegation shared the view that nothing in the definition should result in any inference that its application could impede the right of peoples under colonial rule to self-determination in accordance with the Charter. He wished to reiterate, however, that his Government did not support the use of violence as a means of settling political conflicts or differences. His country supported the efforts of those engaged in the struggle for self-determination and human dignity. Accordingly, his Government interpreted the reference to struggle in article 7 as being struggle by peaceful means, and did not regard the formulation as condoning the use of force in situations other than in self-defence or other than in accordance with the Charter.

In general, his delegation considered that the definition was adequate, if not ideal. It safeguarded the discretionary authority of the Security Council, and provided the latter with flexibility rather than rigidity. It was in no way inconsistent with the Charter, and was in fact founded upon the Charter. It recognized the primary role of the Security Council in the maintenance of international peace and security. The definition did not prejudice the ability of the Security Council to make a finding of aggression or a threat to the peace or a breach of the peace, or to refrain from making such a finding. The definition enabled the Council to take account of all the relevant circumstances in any particular instance, including the intentions of the States concerned. The definition avoided being so general as merely to repeat the Charter, and yet avoided being so specific as to suggest that it was exhaustive. It was applicable to both direct and indirect uses of force, and embraced the prohibition under the Charter of the use of force, as well as the exceptions encompassed by the Charter. His delegation hoped that the definition would be found acceptable by the General Assembly and the permanent members of the Security Council.

Finally, his delegation attached great importance to the fact that the Committee's recommendations had been adopted by consensus. In matters of such importance, it would be meaningless to have a definition which did not reflect the consensus of the international community and which could be brushed aside because of its unacceptability to one or more of the permanent members of the Council or to a significant segment of the international community. His delegation therefore hoped that the definition would be looked upon in the same spirit in the forthcoming session of the General Assembly. If after seven years of debate and negotiation, amendments were introduced which could upset the fundamental balance of the definition, other delegations, including his own, might see no alternative but to propose other amendments, thus upsetting the carefully-devised and hard-won balance and consensus which would enable the definition to become a useful contribution to international law and to the maintenance of international peace and security.

Mr. KOLESNIK (Union of Soviet Socialist Republics) expressed satisfaction with the results of the Special Committee's work; the draft definition of aggression was generally regarded as an acceptable compromise, and its adoption by the General Assembly would represent a victory for international diplomacy and the forces of peace. The definition would help the Security Council in its difficult task of determining the existence of acts of aggression and taking appropriate action under the Charter. Like all compromises, the draft definition did not completely satisfy certain delegations. During the seven years of work by the Special Committee, the Soviet delegation, actively participating in the formulation of a definition of aggression, had consistently upheld the United Nations Charter and had constantly sought to insert wording consistent with the Charter. His delegation reserved the right to present its definitive views at the twenty-ninth session of the General Assembly; in the meantime he would offer a preliminary evaluation of the definition, basing himself on the Charter.

The preamble of the draft definition reflected a political will to see an end to wars of aggression and the illegal use of force. Without wishing to minimize the importance of the other provisions of the preamble, he stressed the paramount importance of the sixth, seventh and ninth paragraphs.

Article 1 was a concise version of the Charter provisions regarding the illegal use of armed force. In a spirit of compromise, his delegation had agreed to the use of the word "sovereignty" in the text, on the understanding that, in the context of the article, violation of the sovereignty of a State meant the use of armed force against territorial integrity and political independence.

Article 2 was a key provision which had given rise to wide disagreement. There had been much discussion whether to include the phrase "in contravention of the Charter", and his delegation had maintained that unless those words were included, State acts committed in strict conformity with the Charter of the United Nations could be regarded as acts of aggression within the meaning of the article. There must be no room for misunderstandings in such an important document as the definition of aggression, and the opposing views put forward by some delegations were unconvincing. The Charter definitely sanctioned the use of force in well-known specific cases, and any disregard of its provisions would not help the cause of peace. The Security Council was the only United Nations organ empowered to determine the existence of acts of aggression. His delegation was pleased that that fact had been brought out in the definition. It had also wanted to ensure that the wording of the definition should not leave open the possibility of branding an innocent party as an aggressor. That was the idea underlying the statement in article 2 that the Security Council might in conformity with the Charter conclude that a determination that an act of aggression had been committed would not be justified in the light of other circumstances which might be taken into account by the Security Council. Aggression was a grave international crime, and in investigating any armed conflict, the Security Council must carefully analyse all the circumstances, including their nature and the seriousness of their consequences for the course of peace. His delegation attached great importance to the intentions of the States parties to a conflict. Some delegations had not wished to see the question of intent dealt with in article 2, but his delegation felt that the Security Council, if it was to adopt correct decisions, must analyse the intentions of the States involved, since a careful study of intentions would make it easier for the Council to identify the true aggressor.

With regard to article 3, he stressed that nothing in the wording of paragraph (g) could be construed as casting doubt on the legitimacy of national liberation struggles, guerrilla warfare or resistance movements. There was a certain connexion between that paragraph and article 7. His delegation attached great weight to the fact that not a single delegation, during the drafting of the definition, had expressed opposition to the right of peoples to self-determination. But it was no longer sufficient to recognize that right without also recognizing the elements comprised in it: the right of peoples to take up arms against the colonialists. Peoples engaged in that struggle had a right to seek and receive political and material aid· not only was the armed struggle of colonial peoples and peoples under the domination of racist régimes legitimate, but the aid which they received from many States was equally so.

One of the important elements of the draft definition concerned the question of responsibility for aggression. His delegation had agreed as a compromise that article 5 should be reworded to take account of the provisions of article 6 of the consolidated text; nevertheless, he felt that there were no solid grounds for the distinction made between "a war of aggression" and "aggression" in article 5. Not only a war of aggression but any other act of aggression was a crime against international peace. Any act of aggression must engage international responsibility. His delegation's concept of responsibility for aggression was based in particular on the Charter of the Nuremberg Military Tribunal: there was no difference between "international responsibility" and "responsibility under international law", since the former presupposed the latter, i.e. responsibility for acts designated as crimes in relevant international legal instruments.

With regard to article 5, he agreed that no consideration of whatever nature could serve as a justification for aggression. The Special Committee had not intended to extend the concept of aggression, much less replace it by the concept of interference by a State in the domestic affairs of another State. Such interference was certainly prohibited under contemporary international law, but it could not be placed on the same footing as aggression.

The international legal doctrine followed by the USSR was based on the fact that the United Nations Charter was a code of conduct for sovereign States. Strict compliance with the Charter was necessary if the aims of the Organization, namely, the establishment and maintenance of international peace, were to be achieved, and it was for that reason that his Government regarded article 6 as being of such significance.

The definition of aggression was the culmination of unceasing efforts by the Government of the USSR. Lenin, the founder of the Soviet State, had proclaimed as the Soviet ideal an end to war, peace between peoples and the cessation of pillage and violence. The Soviet Government had put forward a definition of aggression in 1933, and since that time relations between peoples had become more friendly through the application of the principle of peaceful coexistence, but the structure of peace was not yet complete. In conclusion, he praised the part played by the third world countries in the preparation of the draft definition of aggression and paid a tribute to the Chairman and officers of the Special Committee.

Mr. NAGGAGA (Uganda) contratulated the Chairman and officers of the Special Committee and the Secretariat staff who had assisted its work. He accepted the definition of aggression in principle, while stating that his Government's views would be fully developed at the twenty-ninth session of the General Assembly.

Mr. AZUD (Czechoslovakia), recalling that Czechoslovakia had participated since 1953 in the task of defining aggression, welcomed the positive results which had been achieved. He thanked the Chairman of the Special Committee and its officers, the Chairmen of the Contact Groups and the Secretariat staff. His delegation would make its views known at the twenty-ninth session of the General Assembly, where he hoped that the draft definition would be adopted by consensus.

Mr. MESLOUB (Algeria) was gratified that owing to the spirit of co-operation shown by its members, the Special Committee had been able to arrive at a definition of aggression; the text represented a compromise which naturally did not fully reflect the views and hopes of all, but his delegation had accepted it while reserving the right to set forth its Government's definitive views at the twenty-ninth session of the General Assembly.

With respect to article 7 in particular, it should be noted that the exercise of the right to self-determination must be placed on the same footing as self-defence and included not only the right of peoples subject to any form of alien domination to resort to armed force, but also the right and the duty of all States Members of the United Nations to assist those peoples.

Articles 2, 5 and 7 raised some doubts, and his delegation considered that it had accepted the definition ad referendum because it had not been able to consult its Government on the matter.

However, it was to be hoped that the definition worked out by the Special Committee would be adopted by the General Assembly, for it was a worthy contribution even though it would serve only as a safeguard when used by the competent organs of the United Nations.

Mr. CORREA (Mexico) was pleased that the Special Committee had been able to carry out the difficult task which had been entrusted to it. The definition represented a delicate compromise between the three drafts which had served as the basis for the Special Committee's work. While it was too early to make an exhaustive analysis of the text, his delegation reserved the right to do so at the twenty-ninth session of the General Assembly.

Some remarks could, however, be made on the Mexican delegation's interpretation of some of the basic provisions. The difficult negotiations conducted for so many years on article 2, and particularly at the present session, had left no doubt that the words "although" in English, "aunque" in Spanish and "bien que" in French separated two quite distinct questions, one of principle and the other of procedure. The first part of article 2 established a presumption that could be overthrown only by a negative decision of the Security Council, and that presumption would prevail if the Council could not establish whether or not an act of aggression had been committed. If that presumption had been made subject to a decision of the Security Council, as would have been the case if the words "provided that" in English, "siempre y cuando" in Spanish and "étant entendu que" in French had been used, the balance between two opposing positions would have been altered and the principle of anteriority would virtually have been rendered void. In addition, he welcomed the fact that all mention of the intent of States employing armed force in

violation of the Charter had been deleted. The intentions of States had no
juridical relevance within the context of the definition, which did not authorize
the Security Council to invoke the intention of a State in order to overthrow
the presumption established by the first part of article 2. The expression "other
relevant circumstances" could not be interpreted as enlarging the competence of the
Security Council under Article 39 of the Charter, for the notion of intent was
totally foreign to the Charter and contrary to the system of collective security
which it established.

Article 3 (g) could under no circumstances be interpreted as adding to the
number of situations in which the right of self-defence in accordance with the
Charter could be invoked. It would be counterproductive if a State could use that
provision to invoke the right of self-defence if it used armed force against
another State when acts of subversion or terrorism took place in its territory.
The definition of aggression, instead of discouraging the use of armed force,
would then serve to legitimize it. The acts contemplated in article 3 (g)
could be characterized as acts of aggression only if their gravity was such as to
make them equivalent to the other acts enumerated in that article and if the
participation of another State was fully established. It was for that reason that
the words "o de su parte" in the final version of the Spanish text had been
replaced by the words "o en su nombre" so as to bring it more into line with the
English text.

In connexion with article 5, there was no legal distinction between a war of
aggression and an act of aggression. The term "war" was a military and not a
juridical term. The fact that the text did not expressly say that aggression was
a crime against peace could not be construed as authorizing a contrario
interpretation. The negotiations made it clear that, although it was not possible
to deny that the commission of an act of aggression gave rise to individual
responsibility under international law, it was not possible to establish the exact
scope of that responsibility.

His delegation was pleased that the Special Committee had accomplished the
task entrusted to it. He recognized, however, that further problems would arise
in the General Assembly, since the text represented a compromise and was therefore
completely satisfactory neither to his own nor to other delegations.

Mr. HASSOUNA (Egypt) said he wished to express his satisfaction and to
recall that his delegation had always attached great importance to the question o'
defining aggression. In 1967, when that question had once again been brought to
the forefront of international discussion, his delegation had strongly supported
the idea of formulating a definition, not only because Egypt strictly adhered to
the principles of the Charter which prohibit the use of force against the
territorial integrity or political independence of States but also because the
situation in the Middle East was a living example of the subject-matter and a
concrete application of the legal principles formulated in the definition.

While welcoming the adoption of a definition in the preparation of which his
delegation had participated, he reserved the right of his Government to state its
definitive position at the twenty-ninth session of the General Assembly and wished
now to reaffirm certain positions of principle.

United Nations

GENERAL ASSEMBLY

Official Records

DOCUMENT 27

Agenda item 86

ANNEXES

TWENTY-NINTH SESSION

NEW YORK, 1974

Agenda item 86:* Report of the Special Committee on the Question of Defining Aggression**

CONTENTS

---

* For the discussion of this item, see: Official Records of the General Assembly, Twenty-ninth Session, Sixth Committee, 1471st to 1483rd, 1488th, 1489th and 1502nd to 1504th meetings; and ibid., Plenary Meetings, 2319th meeting.

** Since 1969, the reports of this Committee have been discussed by the General Assembly at the following sessions: twenty-fourth (agenda item 88), twenty-fifth (agenda item 87), twenty-sixth (agenda item 89), twenty-seventh (agenda item 88) and twenty-eighth (agenda item 95).

DOCUMENT A/9890

Report of the Sixth Committee

Original: English
6 December 1974

1. In pursuance of General Assembly resolution 3105 (XXVIII) of 12 December 1973, the Special Committee on the Question of Defining Aggression met at the United Nations Headquarters from 11 March to 12 April 1974 to resume its work in accordance with General Assembly resolution 2330 (XXII) of 18 December 1967, and prepared a report on the work of its 1974 session (A/9619 and Corr.1).

2. At its 2236th plenary meeting, on 21 September 1974, the General Assembly decided to include in the agenda of its twenty-ninth session the item entitled "Report of the Special Committee on the Question of Defining Aggression", which was referred to the Sixth Committee with the following note:

"The General Assembly decided to take note of the observations on this item by the Secretary-General in paragraph 26 of his memorandum (A/BUR/182) and to consider whether, as envisaged in resolutions 1186 (XII) and 1187 (XII) and in the decision taken at the twenty-third session, it should take up again the question of a draft Code of Offences against the Peace and Security of Mankind and the question of an international criminal jurisdiction." (See A/C.6/427.)

3. The report of the Special Committee on the Question of Defining Aggression on the work of its 1974 session contained a draft definition of aggression adopted by consensus by the Special Committee and recommended to the General Assembly for approval. At the 1471st meeting of the Sixth Committee, on 8 October 1974, the Rapporteur of the Special Committee introduced the Committee's report.

4. The Sixth Committee considered the item at its 1471st to 1483rd, 1488th, 1489th and 1502nd to 1504th meetings, held between 8 October and 22 November 1974. The summary records of those meetings contain, inter alia, the views of Member States concerning the draft definition of aggression.

5. At the 1483rd meeting, on 23 October, the representative of Peru introduced a working paper (A/C.6/L.988) spon-

sored by Guinea, Peru and the Philippines, subsequently joined by Brazil, Ecuador, El Salvador, Iceland, the Ivory Coast, Madagascar, Morocco, Panama, Senegal and Somalia.

6. At the 1488th meeting, on 30 October, the representative of Afghanistan introduced a working paper (A/C.6/L.990) sponsored by Afghanistan, Bolivia, Botswana, Burundi, the Central African Republic, Chad, Laos, Lesotho, Mali, Nepal, the Niger, Paraguay, Rwanda, Swaziland, Uganda, the Upper Volta and Zaire, subsequently joined by Zambia.

7. At the 1502nd meeting, on 20 November, the representative of Finland introduced a draft resolution (A/C.6/L.993) sponsored by Australia, Bulgaria, Canada, Colombia, Cyprus, Czechoslovakia, Finland, France, Ghana, Guyana, Italy, Japan, Mexico, Norway, Romania, Turkey, the Union of Soviet Socialist Republics, the United Kingdom of Great Britain and Northern Ireland, the United States of America, Uruguay and Yugoslavia. At the 1502nd and 1503rd meetings, on 20 and 21 November, the representatives of the following Member States expressed the wish of their delegations to become co-sponsors of the draft resolution: the Byelorussian Soviet Socialist Republic, Chile, Liberia, Mongolia, New Zealand, Nicaragua, Poland, Uganda, the Ukrainian Soviet Socialist Republic and Zaire.

8. At the 1503rd meeting the Sixth Committee decided to include in the present report the statements which are the subject of paragraphs 9 and 10 below, read by the Chairman at the same meeting.

9. The Sixth Committee agreed that nothing in the Definition of Aggression, and in particular article 3 (c), shall be construed as a justification for a State to block, contrary to international law, the routes of free access of a land-locked country to and from the sea.

10. The Sixth Committee agreed that nothing in the Definition of Aggression, and in particular article 3 (d), shall be construed as in any way prejudicing the authority of a State to

exercise its rights within its national jurisdiction, provided such exercise is not inconsistent with the Charter of the United Nations.

11. At the same meeting, the Sixth Committee adopted the draft resolution (A/C.6/L.993) without a vote (see para. 13 below).

12. Statements were made by the representatives of China, Dahomey, El Salvador, Israel, Paraguay, Peru, Mongolia, the United Republic of Tanzania, Ecuador, India, Indonesia, Honduras, Pakistan, the Union of Soviet Socialist Republics, Botswana, the Sudan, Bolivia, Canada, the Ivory Coast, the Upper Volta, the Ukrainian Soviet Socialist Republic, Iran, Egypt and the Dominican Republic.

Recommendation of the Sixth Committee

13. The Sixth Committee recommends to the General Assembly the adoption of the following draft resolution:

Definition of Aggression

The General Assembly,

Having considered the report of the Special Committee on the Question of Defining Aggression, established pursuant to its resolution 2330 (XXII) of 18 December 1967, covering the work of its seventh session held from 11 March to 12 April 1974, including the draft Definition of Aggression adopted by the Special Committee by consensus and recommended for adoption by the General Assembly (see A/9619 and Corr.1, para. 22),

Deeply convinced that the adoption of the Definition of Aggression would contribute to the strengthening of international peace and security,

1. *Approves* the Definition of Aggression, the text of which is annexed to the present resolution;

2. *Expresses its appreciation* to the Special Committee on the Question of Defining Aggression for its work which resulted in the elaboration of the Definition of Aggression;

3. *Calls upon* all States to refrain from all acts of aggression and other uses of force contrary to the Charter of the United Nations and the Declaration on Principles of International Law concerning Friendly Relations and Co-operation among States in accordance with the Charter of the United Nations;[1]

4. *Calls the attention* of the Security Council to the Definition of Aggression, as set out below, and recommends that it should, as appropriate, take account of that Definition as guidance in determining, in accordance with the Charter, the existence of an act of aggression.

ANNEX

Definition of Aggression

The General Assembly,

Basing itself on the fact that one of the fundamental purposes of the United Nations is to maintain international peace and security and to take effective collective measures for the prevention and removal of threats to the peace, and for the suppression of acts of aggression or other breaches of the peace,

Recalling that the Security Council, in accordance with Article 39 of the Charter of the United Nations, shall determine the existence of any threat to the peace, breach of the peace or act of aggression and shall make recommendations, or decide what measures shall be taken in accordance with Articles 41 and 42, to maintain or restore international peace and security,

---

[1] General Assembly resolution 2625 (XXV), annex.

Recalling also the duty of States under the Charter to settle their international disputes by peaceful means in order not to endanger international peace, security and justice,

Bearing in mind that nothing in this Definition shall be interpreted as in any way affecting the scope of the provisions of the Charter with respect to the functions and powers of the organs of the United Nations,

Considering also that, since aggression is the most serious and dangerous form of the illegal use of force, being fraught, in the conditions created by the existence of all types of weapons of mass destruction, with the possible threat of a world conflict and all its catastrophic consequences, aggression should be defined at the present stage,

Reaffirming the duty of States not to use armed force to deprive peoples of their right to self-determination, freedom and independence, or to disrupt territorial integrity,

Reaffirming also that the territory of a State shall not be violated by being the object, even temporarily, of military occupation or of other measures of force taken by another State in contravention of the Charter, and that it shall not be the object of acquisition by another State resulting from such measures or the threat thereof,

Reaffirming also the provisions of the Declaration on Principles of International Law concerning Friendly Relations and Co-operation among States in accordance with the Charter of the United Nations,

Convinced that the adoption of a definition of aggression ought to have the effect of deterring a potential aggressor, would simplify the determination of acts of aggression and the implementation of measures to suppress them and would also facilitate the protection of the rights and lawful interests of, and the rendering of assistance to, the victim,

Believing that, although the question whether an act of aggression has been committed must be considered in the light of all the circumstances of each particular case, it is nevertheless desirable to formulate basic principles as guidance for such determination,

Adopts the following Definition of Aggression:[a]

Article 1

Aggression is the use of armed force by a State against the sovereignty, territorial integrity or political independence of another State, or in any other manner inconsistent with the Charter of the United Nations, as set out in this Definition.

Explanatory note: In this Definition the term "State"

(a) Is used without prejudice to questions of recognition or to whether a State is a Member of the United Nations;

(b) Includes the concept of a "group of States" where appropriate.

Article 2

The first use of armed force by a State in contravention of the Charter shall constitute prima facie evidence of an act of aggression although the Security Council may, in conformity with the Charter, conclude that a determination that an act of aggression has been committed would not be justified in the light of other relevant circumstances including the fact that the acts concerned or their consequences are not of sufficient gravity.

Article 3

Any of the following acts, regardless of a declaration of war, shall, subject to and in accordance with the provisions of article 2, qualify as an act of aggression:

(a) The invasion or attack by the armed forces of a State of the territory of another State, or any military occupation, however temporary, resulting from such invasion or attack, or any annexation by the use of force of the territory of another State or part thereof;

(b) Bombardment by the armed forces of a State against the territory of another State or the use of any weapons by a State against the territory of another State;

---

[a] Explanatory notes on articles 3 and 5 are to be found in paragraph 20 of the report of the Special Committee on the Question of Defining Aggression (A/9619 and Corr.1). Statements on the Definition are contained in paragraphs 9 and 10 of the report of the Sixth Committee (see above).

(c) The blockade of the ports or coasts of a State by the armed forces of another State;

(d) An attack by the armed forces of a State on the land, sea or air forces, or marine and air fleets of another State;

(e) The use of armed forces of one State which are within the territory of another State with the agreement of the receiving State, in contravention of the conditions provided for in the agreement or any extension of their presence in such territory beyond the termination of the agreement;

(f) The action of a State in allowing its territory, which it has placed at the disposal of another State, to be used by that other State for perpetrating an act of aggression against a third State;

(g) The sending by or on behalf of a State of armed bands, groups, irregulars or mercenaries, which carry out acts of armed force against another State of such gravity as to amount to the acts listed above, or its substantial involvement therein.

Article 4

The acts enumerated above are not exhaustive and the Security Council may determine that other acts constitute aggression under the provisions of the Charter.

Article 5

1. No consideration of whatever nature, whether political, economic, military or otherwise, may serve as a justification for aggression.

2. A war of aggression is a crime against international peace. Aggression gives rise to international responsibility.

3. No territorial acquisition or special advantage resulting from aggression is or shall be recognized as lawful.

Article 6

Nothing in this Definition shall be construed as in any way enlarging or diminishing the scope of the Charter, including its provisions concerning cases in which the use of force is lawful.

Article 7

Nothing in this Definition, and in particular article 3, could in any way prejudice the right to self-determination, freedom and independence, as derived from the Charter, of peoples forcibly deprived of that right and referred to in the Declaration on Principles of International Law concerning Friendly Relations and Co-operation among States in accordance with the Charter of the United Nations, particularly peoples under colonial and racist régimes or other forms of alien domination; nor the right of these peoples to struggle to that end and to seek and receive support, in accordance with the principles of the Charter and in conformity with the above-mentioned Declaration.

Article 8

In their interpretation and application the above provisions are interrelated and each provision should be construed in the context of the other provisions.

ACTION TAKEN BY THE GENERAL ASSEMBLY

At its 2319th plenary meeting, on 14 December 1974, the General Assembly adopted by consensus the draft resolution submitted by the Sixth Committee (A/9890, para. 13). For the final text, see: Official Records of the General Assembly, Twenty-ninth Session, Supplement No. 31, resolution 3314 (XXIX).

CHECK LIST OF DOCUMENTS

NOTE. This check list includes the documents mentioned during the consideration of agenda item 86 which are not reproduced in the present fascicle.

Document No.	Title or description	Observations and references
A/9619 and Corr.1	Report of the Special Committee on the Question of Defining Aggression	Official Records of the General Assembly, Twenty-ninth Session, Supplement No. 19 and corrigendum
A/C.6/427	Letter dated 21 September 1974 from the President of the General Assembly to the Chairman of the Sixth Committee	Mimeographed
A/C.6/L.988	Working paper	For the sponsors see A/9890, para. 5
A/C.6/L.990	Working paper	Idem, para. 6
A/C.6/L.993	Draft resolution	For the sponsors and the text, see A/9890, paras. 7 and 13

UNITED NATIONS

SECRETARIAT

ST/LIB/32
24 October 1973

DEFINITION OF AGGRESSION
A Select Bibliography

LA DEFINITION DE L'AGRESSION
Bibliographie sélective

73-22496

<u>INTRODUCTORY NOTE</u>

Agenda item 95 of the twenty-eighth session of the General
Assembly concerns the question of defining aggression. This list
brings together references to monographs and periodical literature,
with the exception of the League of Nations and United Nations
documentation, in an effort to assist those who are engaged in elaborating a generally acceptable draft definition of aggression.
The majority of references cited herein are available in the Dag
Hammarskjold Library.

<u>NOTE LIMINAIRE</u>

Dans l'ordre du jour de la 28ème session de l'Assemblée
générale le point 95 est consacré à la question de la définition
de l'agression. Pour aider ceux qui cherchent à établir un projet
de définition généralement acceptable, la présente bibliographie
rassemble des monographies et articles de périodique traitant de ce
sujet à l'exclusion, toutefois, des publications de la Société des
Nations et de l'Organisation des Nations Unies. La majorité des
ouvrages cités peuvent être consultes ou empruntés à la Bibliothèque Dag Hammarskjöld.

DEFINITION OF AGGRESSION

Aleksandrov, G. Protive ideologii agressii i voiny. Moskva, Gospolitizdat,
1954. 81 p.
[Opposition to the concept of aggression and war]

Alfaro, R. J. La cuestion de la definición de la agresión. Revista de derecho
internacional (Habana)59:361-380, septiembre 1951.

Angriff und verbotener Krieg. Zeitschrift für öffentliches Recht (Vienna)16:
68-78, 1936.
[Analysis of the problem of war]

Aroneanu, Eugène. La définition de l'agression; exposé objectif. Paris, Les
Editions internationales, 1958. 405 p.

Baginian, K. A. Agressiia - tiagchaishee mezhdunarodnoe prestuplenie; k voprosu ob opredelenii agressii. Moskva, Izdat. Akademii Nauk SSSR, 1955.
126 p.
[Aggression - a grave international crime; the question of definition
of aggression]

Balicki, Jan. Pojecie agresji w prawie miedzynarodowym. Warszawa, Wydawnictwo
Prawnicze, 1952. 176 p.
[Concept of aggression in international law]

Balicki, Jan. O definicji agresji. Panstwo i prawo (Warszawa)7:48-60, lipiec
1952.
[Concerning the definition of aggression]

Barajas, M. de los D. El concepto juridico de la agresion. México, 1965.
147 p. (Tesis - Universidad Nacional Autónoma de México)

Bartolomeo Carlomagno, Roberto. El conflicto de Corea y los principios jurí-
dicos acerca de la agresión. 2. e. Córdoba, Argentina, Imprenta de la
Universidad, 1952. 44 p.

Baumgarten, Arthur. Der völkerrechtliche Begriff der Aggression. Neue Justiz
(Berlin)5:442-443, 1951.

Baxter, R. R. The legal consequences of the unlawful use of force under the
Charter. In Proceedings of the American Society of International Law at
its sixty-second annual meeting, April 25-27, 1968. Washington, D.C., 1968.
p. 68-82.

Bierzanek, Remigiusz. Definicja agresji w świetle prac Komitetu Specjalnego
ONZ. Sprawy międzynarodowe (Warszawa)23:77-91, sierpień 1970.
[Definition of aggression in the Special Committee of the United Nations]

Bilfinger, C. Die russische Definition des Angreifers. Zeitschrift für aus-
ländisches öffentliches Recht und Völkerrecht (Stuttgart)7:483-496, 1937.

/...

604

Bittencourt Camara, L. de S. O agressor ante o direito internacional público moderno. Bahía, 1939.

Blix, Hans. Is there a need for a definition of "aggression"? In Dag Hammarskjöld Seminar on the Structure, Role and Functions of the UN System, Uppsala, 1968, Part I. Uppsala, Dag Hammarskjöld Foundation, 1969 (Lectures, no. 7) p. 1-14.

Boutros Samaan, S. Définition de l'agression. Revue égyptienne de droit international (Le Caire)24:187- , 1968.
    In Arabic.

Braatoy, B. The quest for treaty definitions of aggression. Nordisktidsskrift for international ret (København)5:29-40, 1934.

Bramson, A. Definicja agresji a ustawy o obronie pokoju. Sprawy międzynarodowe (Warszawa)no 3:60-68, maj-czerwiec 1952.
    [Definition of aggression and peacekeeping charters]

Braun, Elizabeth Esser. La definición de "agresión" en el seno de la Organización de las Naciones Unidas, 1950-1968. Foro internacional (México)10: 436-452, abril-junio 1970.

Broms, Bengt. The definition of aggression in the United Nations. Turku, 1968. 162 p. (Turku, Finland. Yliopisto. Julkaisuja. Sarja B: Humaniora, 108)

Brownlie, Ian. International law and the use of force by states. Oxford, Clarendon Press, 1963. xxviii, 532 p.
    Bibliography; p. 475-519.

Brownlie, I. The use of force in self-defence. In British yearbook of international law, v. 37, 1961. London, Oxford U.P., 1962. p. 183-268.

Carballa, Juan B. La legítima defensa en la jurisprudencia nacional. Montevideo, 1944. 160 p. (Montevideo. Universidad. Facultad de Derecho y Ciencias Sociales. Biblioteca de publicaciones oficiales, sección 2, 29)
    Tésis. Universidad de Montevideo.
    Facultad de Derecho y Ciencias Sociales, 1944.

Castrén, Erik. Recognition of insurgency. Indian journal of international law (New Delhi)5:443-454, October 1965.

Chacko, C. J. International law and the concept of aggression. Indian journal of international law (New Delhi)3:396-412, October 1963: 4:85-96, January 1964.

Chacko, C. J. and S. N. Sinha. Aggression and international law. In Proceedings of the Indian Society of International Law, New Delhi, 1964. p. 66-80.

Chkhikvadze, V. and O. Bogdanov. Definition of aggression - an important instrument in the struggle for peace. International affairs (Moscow)no 7: 27-32, July 1969.

/...

Chkhikvadze, V. and O. Bogdanov. Who is hindering progress in the definition of aggression. International affairs (Moscow)no 10:22-28, 1971.

Cockram, B. The United Nations and resistance to aggression. South African law journal (Cape Town)80:490-504, November 1963.

Cooper, John Sherman. U.N. legal committee discusses the question of defining aggression. Department of State [United States] bulletin (Washington, D.C.) 59:664-672, 23 December 1968.

Corning, Peter A. and Constance Hellyer Corning. Toward a general theory of violent aggression. Social science information (Paris)11:7-35, June-August 1972.

Die Definition des Angreifers auf der Abrüstungskonferenz. Friedenswarte (Zürich)33:200-204, 1933.

De la Brière, R. P. Yves. La définition de l'agresseur. L'Esprit international (Paris)7:616-625, 1933.

Delivanis, Jean. La légitime défense en droit international public moderne; le droit international face à ses limites. Paris, Librairie Générale de Droit et de Jurisprudence, 1971. xv, 201 p. (Bibliothèque de droit international, 59)
    Thèse. Caen, France. Université. Faculté de Droit et des Sciences Economiques, 1969.

Derriennic, Jean-Pierre. Theory and ideologies of violence. Journal of peace research (Oslo)9:361-374, 1972, no. 4.
    Summary in Russian.

Diamandesco, Jean. Le problème de l'agression dans le droit international public actuel. Paris, Pedone, 1936. 252 p.
    Bibliography.

Dmitriev, D. i E. Skakunov. Opredelenie agressii i ustav OON. Mezhdunarodnaia zhizn' (Moskva)no 4:73-79, 1973.
    [Definition of aggression and the Charter of the United Nations]

Eagleton, C. The attempt to define aggression. N.Y., Carnegie Endowment for International Peace, 1930. (International conciliation, 264)

Erich, R. L'interdiction de la guerre d'agression. Revue de droit international (Paris)1:755-759, 1927.

Erich, R. Les traités de non-agression entre membres et non-membres de la Societé des Nations. Revue de droit international et de législation comparée (Bruxelles)7:613-621, 1926.

Esfandiary, Mohsen Sadigh. The role of the General Assembly in dealing with threats to the peace, breaches of the peace and acts of aggression. Ann Arbor, Mich., University Microfilms [1962] 329 p. (O-P book)

Estrada y de Miguel, Emilio. Agresión y Legítima Defensa. In Estudios de derecho internacional público y privado; homenaje al profesor Luis Sela Sampil, v. 2. Oviedo, Spain, Secretariado de Publicaciones, Universidad de Oviedo, 1970. p. 769-799.

/...

Falk, R. A. Quincy Wright: on legal tests of aggressive war. American
    journal of international law (Washington, D.C.)66:560-571, July 1972.

Falk, Richard A. Legal order in a violent world. Princeton, N.J., Princeton
    U.P. for the Center of International Studies, Princeton University, 1968.
    xvi, 610 p.

Faut-il proscrire seulement la guerre d'agression ou toutes les guerres?
    Revue générale de droit international public (Paris)39:498-511, 1932.

Feinberg, N. The question of defining "armed attack". In Mélanges en
    l'honneur de Gilbert Gidel. Paris, 1961. p. 257-274.

Ferencz, Benjamin B. Defining aggression as a means to peace. [Washington,
    D.C.] B'nai B'rith International Council [1972] 32 p.

Ferencz, B. B. Defining aggression: where it stands and where it's going.
    American journal of international law (Washington, D.C.)66:491-508, July
    1972.

Finch, G. A. Development of international law [definition of aggression]
    with discussion. In Proceedings of the American Society of International
    Law at its forty-second annual meeting, April 22-24, 1948. Washington,
    D.C. 1948. p. 16-40.

France. Direction de la Documentation. L'U.R.S.S. et la définition de
    l'agression. Paris, 1959. 27 p. (Its: Travaux et recherches, 6)

Franklin, Mitchell. The formulation of the conception of aggression.
    [Brussels] International Association of Democratic Lawyers, [1952?] 30 p.

Franzke, H. G. Die militärische Abwehr von Angriffen auf Staatsangehörige
    im Ausland: insbesondere ihre Zulässigkeit nach der Satzung der Vereinten
    Nationen. Osterreichische Zeitschrift für öffentliches Recht (Wien)16:
    128-175, 1966, no. 1-2.

Freeman, Alwyn V. Why try again to define aggression? American journal of
    international law (Washington, D.C.)62:701-722, July 1968.

Friede, W. Die Ostpakte über die Definition des Angreifers. Zeitschrift für
    Ostrecht (Berlin)7:719-723, 1933.

Galtung, Johan. Fredsforskning. [Till svenska av L. Sahlin. Stockholm]
    Bokförlaget Prisma [1967] 174 p. (Verdandi debatt, 33)

Galtung, Johan. A structural theory of aggression. Journal of peace research
    (Oslo)2:95-119, 1964.

García Lupo, Rogelio. Contra la ocupación extranjera. 2. ed. [Buenos Aires]
    Editorial Sudestada, 1968. 190 p. (Colección presente político)

/...

Garnett, J. C. and M. Wright. The concept of aggression in international politics. International relations (London)3:702-716, May 1970.

Georgetown University, Washington. School of Foreign Service. Institute of World Policy. The law of limited international conflict; a study. Washington, D.C., 1965. xviii, 258 p.
    Bibliography: p. 218-255.

Gilberto, A. La question de la définition de l'agression. Revue de droit international de sciences diplomatiques et politiques (Genève)30:147-155, avril-juin 1952.

Giraud, Emile. L'interdiction du recours à la force; la théorie et la pratique des Nations Unies. A propos de l'affaire cubaine, la quarantaine. Paris, Editions A. Pedone, 1963. 43 p.
    Extract from: Revue générale de droit international public, juillet-septembre 1963, no. 3.

Glaser, S. "Agression spatiale" à la lumière du droit international pénal. Schweizerische Zeitschrift für Strafrecht (Berne)77:129-161, 1961.

Gordon, E. Evolution de la notion d'"agression" en droit international public. In Mélanges offerts à Ernest Mahaim. Paris, Sirey, 1935, v. 2, p. 134-145.

Green, R. T. and G. Santori. A cross cultural study of hostility and aggression. Journal of peace research (Oslo)no 1:13-22, 1969.

Grey, F. T. Aggression and the aggressor. Transactions of the Grotius Society (London)24:169-178, 1938.

Hambro, Edvard. The question of the definition of aggression before the 22nd session of the General Assembly. 15 p. (In: Festskrift til professor Alf Ross. København, 1969. p. 153-167)

Hazard, J. N. Why try again to define aggression? American journal of international law (Washington, D.C.)62:701-710, July 1968.

Henkin, Louis. Force, intervention, and neutrality in contemporary international law. In Proceedings of the American Society of International Law at its 57th annual meeting, April 25-27, 1963. Washington, D.C., 1963. p. 147-173.

Herezegh, Géza. The prohibition of the threat and use of force in contemporary international law. In Questions of international law, 1964. Budapest, Hungarian Branch of the International Law Association [1964] p. 70-92.

Hertz, W. G. Das Problem des völkerrechtlichen Angriffs. Leiden, A. W. Sijthoff, 1935. 183 p.

Higgins, R. Legal limits to the use of force by sovereign states - United Nations practice. In British yearbook of international law, v. 37, 1961. London, Oxford U.P., 1962. p. 269-319.

Hollitscher, W. "Instinctive aggression" in man? Man misrepresented as an animal. Peace and the sciences (Vienna)no 3:13-24, 1970.

Horsburgh, H. J. N. Non-violence and aggression: a study of Gandhi's moral equivalent of war. London, Oxford University Press, 1968. 207 p.

Hula, Erich. Fundamentals of collective security. N.Y., 1957. 36 p. Concerning methods for dealing with aggression.
    (Reprint from: Social research, vol. 24, no. 1, spring 1957)

Jazić, Z. United Nations and definition of aggression. Jugoslovenska revija za medunarodno pravo (Beograd)17:185-206, 1970, no. 2-3.

Jelf, E. A. What is war? What is aggressive war? In Transactions of the Grotius Society, 1934. London, 1934. p. 103-114.

Jones, Goronwy J. Security from aggression. Cardiff, Priory Press, 1949. 55 p.

K voprosu ob opredelenii agressii. Novoe vremia (Moskva)no 51:1-2, 17 dekabria 1952.
    [The question of definition of aggression]

Kahn, S. G. Private armed groups and world order. In Netherlands yearbook of international law, v. 1, 1970. Leiden, A. W. Sijthoff, 1971. p. 32-54.

King, James E. Jr. Aggression and collective defence [difficulties in defining aggression in order to set into motion collective defense machinery]. SAIS R (Washington, D.C.)3:23-28, spring 1959.

Klein, F. Der Begriff des "Angriffs" in der UN-Satzung. In Cologne. Universität. Rechtswissenschaftliche Fakultät. Festschrift Hermann Jahrreiss. Köln, 1964. p. 163-188.

Komarnicki, Waclaw. La définition de l'agresseur dans le droit international moderne. Paris, Sirey, 1949. 113 p.

Kopal, V. Povinnost vystřihat se hrozby silou a použití síly v mezinárodních vztazích. Casopis pro mezinárodni právo (Praha)7:185-213, 1963.
    [The obligation to refrain from the threat or use of force in international relations]
    Summary in English.

Kopelmans, L. The problem of aggression and the prevention of war. American journal of international law (Washington, D.C.)31:244-257, April 1937.

Kulakov, V. M. Ideologiia agressii. Moskva, Voennoe Izd-vo Ministerstva Oborony SSSR, 1970. 366 p.
    [Ideology of aggression]

Langer, Robert. Seizure of territory, the Stimson doctrine and related principles in legal theory and diplomatic practice. Princeton, Princeton Univ. Press, 1947. viii, 313 p.
    Bibliography: p. 291-298.

Laun, R. Angriff und Verteidigung. Zeitschrift für Völkerrecht (Breslau)10: 504-546, 1917-1918.

Lauterpacht, E. Legal irrelevance of the "state of war". In Proceedings of the American Society of international law at its sixty-second annual meeting, April 25-27, 1968. Washington, D.C., 1968. p. 58-67.

Lazarev, M. I. Ob opredelenii poniatiia agressii. In Soviet yearbook of international law, 1969. Moscow, Publishing House Nauka, 1970. p. 109-124.
   [On the definition of the notion of aggression]
   Summary in English.

Le Borgne, Claude. La violence expressive. In Annales d'études internationales, v. 3, 1972. Geneva, Association des Anciens Etudiants de l'Institut Universitaire de Hautes Etudes Internationales, 1972. p. 85-90.

Lederer, Z. J. La définition de l'agresseur. Revue de droit international (Genève)13:119-125, 1935.

LeFur, L. L'agression; travaux de Genève et Conventions de Londres. Revue de droit international (Paris)12:251-283, 1933.

LeFur, L. Les Conventions de Londres (1933) et la définition de l'agresseur. Revue de droit international (Genève)11:179-191, 1933.

Liang, Y. Notes on legal questions concerning the United Nations: the question of defining aggression. American journal of international law (Washington, D.C.)46:667-681, 1952.

Liang, Y. L. Third session of the International Law Commission: review of its work by the General Assembly: the question of defining aggression. American journal of international law (Washington, D.C.)46:671-681, October 1952.

Liang, Y. L. La question de la définition de l'agression. Revue de droit international de sciences diplomatiques et politiques (Genève)47:175-181, janvier-mars 1969.

Lumb, R. D. Individual responsibility for aggressive war; the crime against peace. University of Queensland law journal (Brisbane)3:333-   , December 1959.

McConnell, J. R. Can law impede aggressive war? American Bar Association journal (Chicago)50:131-135, February 1964.

McDougal, M. S. and F. P. Feliciano. International coercion and world public order: the general principles of the law of war. Yale law journal (New Haven, Conn.)67:771-845, April 1958.

McDougal, M. S. and F. P. Feliciano. Legal regulation of resort to international coercion: aggression and self-defense in policy perspective. Yale law journal (New Haven, Conn.)68:1057-1165, May 1959.

Mackay, C. J. Agressiviteit en oorlog. Internationale spectator ('s-
   Gravenhage)16:510-530, 8 November 1962; 569-585, 8 December 1962.
      Abstract in English.

Mandelstam, A. N. Réflexions sur la constatation de l'agression. In
   Mélanges Streit. Athens, 1939. p. 557-573.

Matei, George. Rumyniia i Londonskaia konventsiia ob opredelenii agressora
   (iiul'1933 g.). Revue roumaine d'études internationales (Bucarest)no 3:
   131-148, 1971.
      [Romania and the London Convention on the Definition of Aggression]

Megargee, Edwin I. The dynamics of aggression; individual, group, and
   international analyses. Edited by E. I. Megargee and J. E. Hokansen.
   N.Y., Harper and Row [1970] 271 p.

Morawiecki, Wojciech. Walka o definicje agresji w prawie międzynarodowym.
   Warszawa, Państwowe Wydawnictwo Naukowe, 1956. 422 p.
      Bibliography.

Murty, P. N. Aggression in international law. India quarterly (New Delhi)
   7:269-281, July-September 1951.

Myslil, Stanislav. Zákaz agrese a jiného pouzítí sily a hrozby silou v
   posledních navrzích státu. Casopis pro mezinárodní právo (Praha)13:
   168-178, 1969, no. 2.
      [The prohibition of aggression and other use of force and of threat
      or force contained in recent proposals of states]

Nicholson, M. B. Defining aggression. Twentieth century (London)175:6-10,
   August 1966.

Nogueira, Ataliba. As Naçoes-Unidas e a definiçao de agressao. Sao Paulo,
   Emprêsa Gráfica de Revista dos Tribunais, 1959. [5] p.
      Extract from: Revista da Faculdade de Direito, da Universidade de
      Sao Paulo, ano 54, 1959, fasc. 1.

Norden, Albert. Le secret des guerres; genèse et techniques de l'agression.
   [Tr. from the German] Paris, Le Pavillon [1972] 374 p.

Novogrod, J. C. Collective security under the Rio treaty; the problem of
   indirect aggression. JAG journal (Washington, D.C.)24:99-110, 1969-1970.

Odescalchi, Edmond P. The nature and control of aggression. Modern age
   (Chicago)11:374-380, fall 1967.

Orlovskii, A. V. Otvetstvennost' gosudarstva za agressiiu. Minsk, Nauka
   i tekhnika, 1969. 146 p.
      [The State's responsibility for aggression]

Osgood, Robert Endicott. Force, order, and justice, by R. E. Osgood and
   R. W. Tucker. Baltimore [Md.] Johns Hopkins Press [1967] 374 p.

/...

Pal, R. What is aggressive war? Indian law review (Calcutta)4:99-142, 1950.

Pimont, Yves. La subversion dans les relations internationales contemporaines. Revue générale de droit international public (Paris)76:768-799, juillet-septembre 1972.

Piper, Donald C. The legal control of the use of force and the definition of aggression. Georgia journal of international and comparative law (Athens, Georgia)2:1-17, 1972, supplement 1.
     Discussion by Salo Engel, James L. Tanbee, et al, p. 37-43.

Pompe, C. A. Aggressive war, an international crime. The Hague, Nijhoff, 1953. 382 p.
     Bibliography

Pordea, G. L'agression, ses critères déterminatifs et sa définition. Revue de droit international de sciences diplomatiques et politiques (Genève)30: 367-383, octobre-décembre 1952.

Quelques observations sur la notion de guerre d'agression. Revue de droit international et de législation comparée (Bruxelles)12:262-267, 1931.

Radoikovitch, M. La définition de l'agresseur. Beograd, Association Yougoslave de Droit international, 1934.

Reichhelm, Konrad. Der Angriff; eine fölkerrechtliche Untersuchung über Begriff, von dr. Konrad Reichhelm. Berlin-Grünewald, Verlag für Staatswissenschaften und Geschichte g.m.b.h., 1934. vii, 71 p. (Internationalrechtliche Abhandlungen... 27. Abhandlung)

Research in international law. I. Judicial assistance. II. Rights and duties of neutral States in naval and aerial war. III. Rights and duties of States in case of aggression. Drafts of conventions prepared for the codification of international law. [Concord, N.H., printed at the Rumford Press, 1939]

Romashkin, P. S. Agressia - tiagchaishee prestuplenie protiv mira i chelovechestva. Sovetskoe gosudarstvo i pravo (Moskva)no 1:55-67, January 1963.
     [Aggression; the gravest crime against peace and humanity]

Samsonow, Michael S. Political philosophy of aggression. Pacific Coast Publishers, Menlo Park, California, 1961. 35 p.

Schücking, W. Die Definition des Angriffs. Völkerbund (Bern)no 12, 1932.

Serra, Enrico. ... L'aggressione internazionale. Milano, U. Hoepli, 1946. 1 p. 1, 5-203 [1] p.
     Bibliographical footnotes.

Sharmazanashvili, Givi Vladimirovich. Printsip nenapadeniia v mezhdunarodnom prave (Otvet. redaktor: G. P. Zadorozhnyi) Moskva, Izdat. Akademii Nauk SSSR, 1958. 94 p.
     [Principle of non-aggression in international law]

612

Sidjanski, D. and S. Castanos. L'agression au point de vue idéologique et réel. Revue de droit international de sciences diplomatiques et politiques (Genève)30:44-55, janvier-mars 1952.

Soderlund, Walter C. An analysis of the guerilla insurgency and coup d'état as techniques of indirect aggression. International studies quarterly (Detroit)14:335-360, December 1970.

Sohn, L. B. Definition of aggression. Virginia law review (Charlottesville, Va.)45:697-701, June 1959.

Sottile, A. Agression idéologique, économique. Revue de droit international de sciences diplomatiques et politiques (Genève)38:418-421, octobre-décembre 1960.

Spiropoulos, J. La question de la définition de l'agression devant les Nations Unies. In Mélanges en l'honneur de Gilbert Gidel (Paris, 1961) p. 543-556.

Stone, Julius. Aggression and world order; a critique of United Nations theories of aggression. London, Stevens, 1958. 226 p. (The Library of world affairs, 39)
"Published under the auspices of the London Institute of World Affairs"

Sukijasović, Miodrag. Pojam agresije u medunarodnom pravu. Beograd, Institut za Medunarodnu Politiku i Privredu, 1967. 302 p.
[The concept of aggression in international law]
Summaries in English and Russian.

Sukijasović, M. Zastoj u radu ujedinjenih nacija na definisanju agresije. Archiv za pravne i drustvene nauke (Beograd)50:429-434, Juli-September 1953.
[Difficulty in the work of the United Nations concerning the definition of aggression]

Supervielle Saavedra, Bernardo. La nuevas formas de agresión; ensayo de derecho internacional público. Montevideo [Editorial Martín Bianchi Altuna] 1961. 196 p.
Bibliography.

Théry, R. La notion d'agression en droit international. Paris, Pedone. 1937. 256 p.
Bibliographie: p. 249-254.

Thirring, H. Who is an aggressor? Bulletin of atomic scientists (Chicago) 9:68-72, April 1953.

Thomas, A. J. The international law of indirect aggression and subversion [by] A. J. Thomas, A. van Wynen Thomas [and] O. A. Salas. Additional working papers presented by H. J. Taubenfeld [and others] Dallas, Tex., Southern Methodist U.P., 1966. 547 p.

Thomas, Ann van Wynen. The concept of aggression in international law [by]
A. van Wynen Thomas [and] A. J. Thomas. Dallas [Tex.] Southern Methodist
U.P. [1972] 114 p. (Dallas. Southern Methodist University. School of
Law. SMU Law School study)

Torres Bernardez, Santiago. Examen de la définition de l'agression; troisième
session du Comité créé en application de la résolution 1181 (XII) de
l'Assemblée générale (New York, 1965). In Annuaire français de droit international, v. 11, 1965. Paris, Centre National de la Recherche Scientifique,
1966. p. 528-545.

Tucker, Robert W. Reprisals and self-defense; the customary law. American
journal of international law (Washington, D.C.)66:586-596, July 1972.

Tunkin, G. Sovetskoe opredelenie agressii v Organizatsii Ob'edinennykh Natsii.
Sovetskoe gosudarstvo i pravo (Moskva)no 2-3:89-101, 1953.
[Soviet definition of aggression in the United Nations]

Undén, O. Quelques observations sur la notion de guerre d'agression. Revue
de droit international et de législation comparée (Paris)12:262-267, 1931.

Vignol, R. Définition de l'agresseur dans la guerre. (Thesis) Paris, 1933.

Wittig, P. The notion of aggression in the linguistic usage of States and
international organisations. In Deutsche Gesellschaft für Volkerrechtliches
Gewaltverbot und Friedenssicherung. p. 33-73 (Baden-Baden) 1971.
In German.

Wright, Q. The concept of aggression in international law. American journal
of international law (Washington, D.C.)29:373-395, 1935.

Wright, Q. Prevention of aggression. American journal of international law
(Washington, D.C.)50:514-532, July 1956.

Zakharova, N. V. Agressiia - naibolee gruboe narushenie prav cheloveka.
Sovetskoe gosudarstvo i pravo (Moskva)no 12:55-63, December 1968.
[Aggression - the most flagrant violation of human rights]

Zivić, J. Definition of aggression. Review of international affairs (Belgrade)
21:11-41, 20 January 1970.

Zourek, Jaroslav. La définition de l'agression et le droit international,
développements récents de la question. Leyde, A. W. Sijthoff, 1957. [10] p.
Bibliography.

INDEX

Act Defining Aggression, 1:33
Adopts
    use of, instead of "declares that", 2:26
Afghanistan
    objections to limitation to armed ag-
        gression, 2:30
    on blockade of routes used by land-
        locked states, 2:35
Aggression
    acts constituting, in Politis Report,
        1:31-32
    Article 10, League of Nations Covenant
        1:8
    as international crime, 2:43
    as international crime under League of
        Nations Assembly declaration, 1:20
    Consequences (article 5 of definition)2:43
    Defined in American plan for treaty of
        mutual guarantee, 1:14
    defined in Politis proposals, 1:21
    defined in Rutgers' proposal, 1:22
    defined under articles of Protocol for
        the Pacific Settlement of International
        Disputes, 1:15-16
    definition in Charter of International
        Military Tribunal, 1:40
    factors indicating, in Draft Treaty of
        Mutual Assistance, 1:13
    forms of, 1:28
    Grotius on assistance to aggressor, 1:4
    in Draft Treaty of Mutual Assistance,
        1:11-14
    justifications proposed, 2:4
    "large scale" attack as, 1:12
    League Covenant definition, 1:8
    no justifications for, 2:18
    presumption of
        and difficulties in decision making,
            1:16-17
        by invading party, 1:12
        under Protocol for the Pacific Settle-
            ment of International Disputes,
            1:22-23
    refusal to accept decision of Permanent
        Court as indication of, 1:14
    refusal to cooperate with decisions of
        League Council as indication of,
        1:15, 16, 22, 23
    refusal to withdraw forces as suggested
        by League Council as, 1:13
    sanctions prescribed by Protocol for

Aggression (cont'd)
    the Pacific Settlement of International
        Disputes, 1:16-17
    secret military mobilization as, 1:13
    security against without weapons, 1:28
    Soviet definition, 1:30
    subversive activities as, 1:13
    surprise attack as, 1:12
    to be defined by Disarmament Confer-
        ence, 1:27
    urgency to define, 2:21
    victims of See Victims of aggression
    violation of demilitarized zones as,
        1:22
    Who judges? 1:29
Aggressive war
    aggression differentiated, 2:43-44
Air attack
    in Rutgers' proposal, 1:22
Air space
    in Article 1, Draft definition, 2:27
Alexander, King of Yugoslavia
    murder of, 1:35
Alexander the Great, 1:4
Alfaro, Ricardo J.
    on aggression, 2:3, 55
Algeria
    on first use, 2:31
Alliances
    as means of obtaining power, 1:5
Apartheid
    as act of aggression, 2:30
Appleman, J.A., 1:60
Arab states
    on aggression, 2:11
Arbitration
    failure to compel, 1:6
    League of Nations Covenant on, 1:8-9
Argentina
    opposition to definition by First Spe-
        cial Committee, 2:5
Armed aggression, 2:22
Armed force
    allowing use of territory by third party
        as act of aggression, 2:17
    as national policy, 1:4
    efforts to restrain, 1:3-4
    lawful use, 2:46-47
Aroneanu, E., 1:48
Atlantic Charter, 1:37
Attack See also Invasion
    as indication of aggression, 2:11, 33

Attack (cont'd)
    on forces (land, sea, air) of one state
        by another, as act of aggression,
        2:36-37
Australia
    on rights of a state to protect its terri-
        torial waters, 2:37

Ballis, W., 2:66
Bassiouni, M. Cherif, 2:71
Baxter, R.R., 2:65, 72
Belgium
    proposals on fact-finding in case of
        aggression, 1:31
Benes, Edward, 1:15, 17
Bentham, Jeremy
    on court for decision of differences be-
        tween nations, 1:5
Bessou, Jean-Michel, 2:73
Blaustein, A.P., 2:64
Blockade
    as indication of aggression, 1:32, 33,
        35; 2:11, 17, 35
    land-locked states objection to limita-
        tations, 2:35
Bloodshed See Violence
Blum, Y.Z., 2:69
Bogdanov, O., 2:58
Bolivia
    on acts of aggression, 2:30
    on definition of aggression, 1:38
    on draft definition, 2:50
    on international justice, 1:38
    proposal for definition, 2:4
Bolivia-Paraguay dispute, 1:28-29
Bombardment
    as indication of aggression, 2:11, 17, 34
Boncour, Paul, 1:39
    on definition of aggression, 1:33
    on futility of League action, 1:36
    on international force to enforce deci-
        sions of Security Council, 1:39
Borchard, E.M., 1:54
Bowett, D.W., 2:69, 73, 76
Briand, Aristide, 1:24
Briggs, H.W., 2:72
Broms, B., 1:48; 2:14, 30, 35, 49, 72
Brown, B.F., 1:60
Brownlie, I., 2:57, 65
Burundi
    on first use, 2:31
Byzantium, 1:4

Cambodia
    complaint of U.S. aggression, 2:8
Canada
    on usefulness of defining aggression,
        2:25
Ceausu, D.
    proposals for Article 1, Draft definition
        2:28
Chaco See Bolivia-Paraguay dispute
Chile
    co-sponsor of definition, 2:50
China
    agreement with Soviet position, 1:31
    on economic acts of aggression, 2:30
    on ineffectiveness of definition, 2:50
    proposal on definition, 2:4
    start of "detente", 2:12
Chkhikvadze, V.M., 2:58
Christianity
    Papacy, conflicts created by, 1:4
Churchill, Winston
    Atlantic Charter issued, 1:37
Clark, G., 2:76
Collective responsibility
    German Democratic Republic objec-
        tions, 2:28
Collective security
    abandoned, 1:36
    French proposals, 1:28, 29
Colombia-Peru dispute, 1:29
Commission to Study the Responsibility
    of the Authors of the War,
        on aggressive war as crime against
        peace, 1:7
Committee of Jurists
    international criminal court recom-
        mendation, 1:10
Committee on Security Questions
    report on aggression, 1:31-34
Complicity
    as an offense, 2:38
Compulsory arbitration
    under League, 1:27
Conciliation Commission, 1:19
Conference on the Law of the Sea, 2:19
Congo, 2:8
Congress of Nations
    Ladd's idea for international relations,
        1:5
Convention for the Definition of Aggres-
        sion, 1:34

Falk, R.A., 2:56, 69, 70
Fall, B.B., 2:56
Feliciano, Florentino P., 1:48; 2:73
Ferencz, B.B., 2:56, 59, 71, 73, 76
Feudalism
  neutrality under, 1:4
Finch, G.A., 1:56
Finland
  invasion by Germany, 1:36
  plan to make funds available for pos-
    sible aggression, 1:26
First International Congress of Penal Law
  on international court for international
    crimes, 1:20
First use of armed force
  in contravention of the Charter clause,
    2:31-32
  prima facie evidence of aggression,
    2:17, 30-32
Fishing
  Rights of states to protect, by force
    if necessary, against illegal use of
    territorial waters, 2:36-37
Fomenting civil strife
  as indication of aggression, 2:11
Force however exerted
  in Article 1, Draft definition, 2:27-28
Four Freedoms declaration, 1:37
France
  on first use, 2:32
  on inclusion of self-determination in
    definition, 2:48
  on nuclear weapons, 2:22
  on participation with armed bands, 2:40
  on usefulness of definition as deterrent
    2:25
  support of definition by First Special
    Committee, 2:5
Franck, T.M., 2:63
Freeman, A.V., 2:71

General Assembly
  meeting to consider Report on defini-
    tion, 2:50
  recommendation by Special Committee
    on adoption of Draft Definition, 2:15ff
General Convention to Improve the Means
  of Preventing War, 1:26
General Treaty for the Renunciation of
  War (Kellogg-Briand Pact), 1:24-25
Geneva Accord, 2:5

Germany
  annexation of Czechoslovakia, 1:36
  invasion of Finland, 1:36
  invasion of Poland, 1:36
  on Act Defining Aggression, 1:33
  on participation with armed bands, 2:39
  opposition to collective responsibility,
    2:28
  remilitarization, 1:34-35
  withdrawal from League, 1:34
Giroud, E., 2:63
Glueck, S., 1:50
Goodrich, Leland M., 2:70
Goring, Hermann, 1:42
Gottlieb, G.H., 2:76
Great Britain
  compromise proposals for Charter of
    International Military Tribunal, 1:41
  objections to Dumbarton Oaks propos-
    als, 1:39
  on definition of aggression, 1:31, 33
  on guerrilla attacks, 2:38
  on nuclear weapons, 2:22
  on use of self-defense to repel aggres-
    sion, 2:46
  on usefulness of definition as deterrent,
    2:25
  opposition to definition by First Special
    Committee, 2:5
Greece
  on explanatory note to Article 1, 2:29
  on indirect aggression, 2:40
  on veto power, 1:38
Greece-Bulgaria dispute, settlement of,
  1:19
Green, A., 2:76
Grob, F., 2:66
Gros, Andre
  on aggressive wars, 1:41
Gross, L., 2:76
Grotius, Hugo
  on assistance to aggressor, 1:4
  on dispute settlement, 1:5
  on just war, 1:4
Guerrilla warfare
  participation as only "minor breach of
    the peace", 2:39
  participation in any way by any state as
    act of aggression, 2:39
  question of consent of state being used
    to launch attack on third state, 2:38

Guyana
    on definition of aggression, 2:26
    on first use, 2:31
    on restraints against support of armed
        bands, 2:40

Haas, E., 2:76
Hague Peace Conference, 1st, 1899
    Russia's attempts at achieving dis-
        armament, 1:5
Hague Peace Conference, 2d, 1907, 1:5
Hambro, Edvard, 2:70
Harley, J., 1:49
Harvard Law School
    Draft Convention on the Rights and
        Duties of States in Case of Aggres-
        sion, 1:36
Hassouna, H., 2:75
Hazard, J.N., 2:58
Henkin, L., 2:63
Hess, Rudolph, 1:43
Hitler, Adolf, 1:42
Holy Roman Empire
    end of, 1:5
Horwitz, S., 1:60
House, E.M., 1:50
Hudson, M., 1:55
Hungary
    objections to collective responsibility,
        2:28
    revolt, 1956, 2:6

Iguchi, Takeo, 2:70
India
    on encouraging civil strife, 2:40
India-Pakistan dispute, 2:8
Indirect aggression, 2:22. See also
    Aggression; Direct aggression; Draft
        definition of aggression
    modification, 2:28
    support for armed bands, 2:39
Indonesia
    on attack on maritime fleet, 2:36
    on participation with armed bands,
        2:40
    on territorial waters and air space,
        2:27
Intent
    as evidence of aggression, support for,
        2:31
    significance of in determination of ag-
        gressor, 2:11, 12, 13

Interference. See Intervention
International Criminal Court, 1:10
    countries favoring in 1952, 2:5
    postponement of question of establish-
        ment, 2:7
International Law Association
    on international court for international
        crimes, 1:20
    on need for international criminal court,
        1:10
International Law Commission
    on difference between aggression and
        aggressive war, 2:44
    on justification for aggression, 2:42
    Report to 6th (Legal) Committee, 2:3
International Military Tribunal
    Charter
        absence of definition in, 1:41
        definition of aggression, 1:40
        drawing up procedure, 1:40-41
    conviction of Nazi War Criminals, 1:42
    Nuernberg War Crimes Trials. See
        Nuremberg War Crimes Trials
    principles, 1:43
Inter-Parliamentary Union
    on international court for international
        crimes, 1:20
Intervention
    attitude toward aggression related to,
        1:4
    third-party, 1:6
    to help victim of flagrant aggression,
        1:26
Invasion. See also Attack
    as indication of aggression, 2:11, 17,
        33-34
    used in Rutgers' proposal, 1:22
Iran
    on definition of aggression, 1:38
Iraq
    on participation with armed bands, 2:39
Islam, 1:4
Isolationism
    U.S. policy, 1:9-10
Israel
    on act of aggression, 2:33
    on deterrence of terrorism, 2:40
    on draft definition, 2:50
    War with Egypt, 1956, 2:6
Italy
    aggression against Ethiopia, 1:34
    on definition of aggression, 1:31

Italy (cont'd)
　　on guerrilla attacks, 2:38
　　on listing acts in definition, 2:33
　　on usefulness of definition as deterrent,
　　　　2:25

Jackson, Robert H.
　　in Nuremberg War Crimes Trials, 1:42
　　plans for International Military Tri-
　　　　bunal, 1:40
Japan
　　Aggressive acts by, 1:27
　　invasion of Manchuria, 1:26-27
　　objections to collective responsibility,
　　　　2:28
　　on attack on maritime fleet, 2:36
　　on definition of aggression, 1:31
　　opposition to League of Nations, 1:27
　　Tokyo War Crimes Trial See Tokyo
　　　　War Crimes Trial
Japan-China dispute, 1:27
Jenks, C.W., 2:63
Jessup, P.C., 1:55; 2:76
Jodl, 1:43
Johnson, J.E., 2:56
Just war
　　concept, of, 1:4

Kant, Immanuel
　　Essay on Eternal Peace, 1:5
Keenan, J.B., 1:60
Keitel, General, 1:43
Kellogg-Briand Pact See General Treaty
　　for the Renunciation of War
Kenya
　　on force, 2:27
Kissinger, Henry A.
　　on aggression, 2:60
Kolesnik, D.N., 2:14
Komarnicki, W., 1:48
Koo, Wellington, 1:33

Ladd, William
　　Congress of Nations idea, 1:5
Lamptey, G.O., 2:14
Lauterpacht, Sir Hersch, 1:54
Law of the Sea Conference, Caracas, 2:36
League of Nations
　　Bolivia-Paraguay dispute, 1:29
　　Collapse, 1:34-36
　　Council
　　　　powers under Draft Treaty of Mutual
　　　　　　Assistance, 1:10-14

League of Nations (cont'd)
　　Covenant
　　　　action to safeguard peace, 1:8
　　　　adoption, 1:7
　　　　aggression considered, 1:8
　　　　article 10, on aggression, 1:8
　　　　U.S. refusal to sign, 1:9-10
　　early unsuccessful attempts, 1:6
　　Membership and organization, 1:7-8
　　Peace Conference, 1:6ff
　　purposes, 1:7-8
　　without U.S. cooperation, 1:10
Letane, J.H., 1:49
Litvinoff, Maxim
　　Delegate to Disarmament Conference,
　　　　1:29-30
Locarno, Treaties of, 1:18ff
London Conference, 1:40-41

McDougal, Myres S., 1:48; 2:73
McNair, A.D., 2:72
McWhinney, E., 2:76
Madariaga, S. de, 1:34
"Make the World Safe for Democracy",
　　1:8
Marburg, T., 1:49
Mediation
　　Convention for Pacific Settlement of In-
　　　　ternational Disputes, 1:5-6
Mendlovitz, Saul, 2:63
Mexico
　　on aggressor, 1:38
　　proposal on definition, 2:4
Middle East War, 2:6
　　pro-Arab action, 2:8
Military occupation
　　as act of aggression, 1:17; 2:33-34
　　under Draft definition, 2:23-24
Miller, D.H., 1:50, 54
Minear, R.H., 2:72
Mo Ti, 1:4
Mobilization
　　in Rutgers' proposal, 1:22
Model treaties of non-aggession
　　general act, 1:24
Monroe Doctrine
　　League of Nations Covenant on, 1:9
Moushoutas, Dinos, 2:14
Mutale, 2:73
Mutual security
　　Draft Treaty of Mutual Assistance,
　　　　1:10-14

Temperly, H.W.V., 1:50

Temporary Mixed Commission for the Reduction of Armaments
  appointment of, 1:10
  proposals, 1:10-14

Territorial integrity See also Territorial waters
  debate on use of term, 2:27
  inviolability of, 2:22, 23
  military occupation beyond limit of agreement as act of aggression, 2:37-38
  non-recognition of territorial acquisition resulting from aggression, 2:45
  violation of, as act of aggression, 2:17

Territorial waters
  in Article 1, Draft definition, 2:27
  right of coastal states to protect against illegal use or invasion, 2:36-37

Terrorism
  encouraged by U.N. action favoring PLO, 2:19
  on elimination of, 2:52

Third-party intervention See Intervention

Thirty Years War, 1:5

Thomas, A.J. Jr., 1:48; 2:64

Thomas, A.V.W., 1:48; 2:64

Threats of force
  as not constituting aggression, 2:29

Tokyo War Crimes Trial, 1:45-46

Treaties of Locarno. See Locarno, Treaties of

Treaty of Mutual Assistance
  opposition by Soviet Union, 1:30
  provisions, 1:10-11

Treaty of Mutual Assistance (Draft) 1923,
  basis for new plan for mutual security, 1:21

Treaty of Mutual Guarantee See also Treaty of Mutual Assistance
  American proposals for a treaty, 1:14
  purposes, 1:18

Treaty of non-aggression
  Afghanistan, Iraq, Iran and Turkey, 1:35

Treaty of Versailles
  inviolability, 1:18

Triffterer, O., 2:71

Truman, Harry
  on U.N. Charter, 1:39

United Nations
  action in Czechoslovakia invasion by U.S.S.R., 2:9
  actions on Israel-Arab war, 2:8
  Charter
    omission of definition of aggression in, 1:39
    differences from League, 1:37
    functions under Draft definition, 2:20-21
    need for defining aggression, 1:1
    policy on aggressors, 1:4
    San Francisco Conference, 1:37-39

United Nations Emergency Forces
  in Middle East, 2:6

United States
  domination over Latin America, 1:28
  on aggression and aggressive war, 2:44
  on definition of aggression, 1:31
  on guerrilla attacks, 2:38
  on occupation in contravention of Charter, 2:23-24
  on self-determination on definition, 2:48
  on use of self-defense to repel aggression, 2:46
  on usefulness of definition as deterrent, 2:25
  opposition to Dumbarton Oaks proposals, 1:39
  proposal to postpone question of definition, 2:6-7
  recognition of World Court, 1:20
  views on criminal responsibility for aggression, 2:44

Uniting for Peace Resolution, 2:41

Uruguay
  proposal for Article 1, 2:29

Vaughan, C.E., 1:49

Verosta, Stephan, 2:72

Victims of aggression
  aid to, 1:4-5
  Draft definition on, 2:24-25

Vietnam
  Geneva Accord See Geneva Accord
  U.S. involvement, 2:6, 8
    de-escalation, 2:12
    protests against, 2:10-11

Violence
  effect on world, 1:3

625

Violence (cont'd)
  history of mankind, 1:4
  inadequacy of preventive means, 1:5
Volkerbund
  Kant's idea for union of nations, 1:5

Waldock, C.H., 2:73
Walters, F.P., 1:50, 54, 57
War See also Violence
  as worst crime, 1:4
  early attempts at avoiding, 1:4ff
  justification under provisions of Treaty
    of Mutual Guarantee, 1:18-19
  League of Nations Covenant on, 1:8-9
  omitted from U.N. Charter, 2:33
  prohibition by League of Nations As-
    sembly, 1:20
  Prohibition in Protocol for the Pacific
    Settlement of International Disputes,
    1:15
  rules governing conduct of, 1:5-6
War of aggression See also Aggression;
  Definition of aggression, Draft definition
  as international crime, 2:18

Weapons See also Nuclear weapons
  classification, 1:27-28
  use in self-defense, 1:27-28
  use of, under Draft definition, 2:22
Wehry, George, 2:70
Westphalia, Peace of, 1:5
Wicked causes
  Grotius on, 1:4
Willoughby, W.W., 1:54
Wilson, Woodrow, 1:39
  Fourteen points for peace proposal,
    1:6
Woetzel, R.K., 1:59, 60; 2:76
Wood, B., 1:55
Woolsey, L.H., 1:55
World Court
  restricted adherence by U.S., 1:20
Wright, Q., 1:49, 54, 57; 2:57, 70

Yost, C., 2:76
Yugoslavia
  murder of King Alexander, 1:35

Zimmern, A., 1:51

DATE DUE
